Finance, Law, and the Courts

Finance, Law, and the Courts

Financial Disputes and Adjudication

MARCO LAMANDINI AND DAVID RAMOS MUÑOZ

Great Clarendon Street, Oxford, OX2 6DP,
United Kingdom

Oxford University Press is a department of the University of Oxford.
It furthers the University's objective of excellence in research, scholarship,
and education by publishing worldwide. Oxford is a registered trade mark of
Oxford University Press in the UK and in certain other countries

© Marco Lamandini and David Ramos Muñoz 2023

The moral rights of the authors have been asserted

First Edition published in 2023

All rights reserved. No part of this publication may be reproduced, stored in
a retrieval system, or transmitted, in any form or by any means, without the
prior permission in writing of Oxford University Press, or as expressly permitted
by law, by licence or under terms agreed with the appropriate reprographics
rights organization. Enquiries concerning reproduction outside the scope of the
above should be sent to the Rights Department, Oxford University Press, at the
address above

You must not circulate this work in any other form
and you must impose this same condition on any acquirer

Public sector information reproduced under Open Government Licence v3.0
(http://www.nationalarchives.gov.uk/doc/open-government-licence/open-government-licence.htm)

Published in the United States of America by Oxford University Press
198 Madison Avenue, New York, NY 10016, United States of America

British Library Cataloguing in Publication Data
Data available

Library of Congress Control Number: 2023944883

ISBN 978–0–19–289869–2

DOI: 10.1093/oso/9780192898692.001.0001

Printed and bound by
CPI Group (UK) Ltd, Croydon, CR0 4YY

Links to third party websites are provided by Oxford in good faith and
for information only. Oxford disclaims any responsibility for the materials
contained in any third party website referenced in this work.

Foreword

As a young lawyer, and just after the signature of the Maastricht Treaty, I moved from the Legal Service of the Council in Brussels—where I had worked for some years on the fundamental freedoms and fundamental rights that would later be incorporated into the EU Charter—to the European Monetary Institute in Frankfurt. I remember being struck by the fact that legal considerations had not as much of a central role in the works of the preparatory body for monetary union than in the works of the European Community legislator. Economists were not used to including legal aspects and implications in their equations, and central banking activities were conducted in a confidential manner, often on the basis of practice and in the absence of any written rules. It was thought that in such a technical field there was no really valuable input that the law could contribute. To the surprise of these economists, the European Central Bank (ECB) was nonetheless established as a creature of the law with clearly defined conferred competences[1] within a complex institutional structure that required legal interpretation and implementation and the decisions of which were subject by the Treaty to judicial control: as one of them put it to me then, 'with the Maastricht Treaty, law has lost its irrelevance in monetary policy'.

Beyond central banking law, looking at the broader financial and banking activities and at the way in which citizens manage their economic relationships, one can see that financial contracts have existed for centuries, in some form or another. Certainly, in fifteenth-century Italy, when the Medici and other families were collecting deposits on a *banco* (literally a wooden desk) close to a market place (again, in the literal sense), those were contracts which were subject to the—very limited in scope at the time—banking law; and certainly the agreements between parties gathering at Lloyd's coffee house in seventeenth-century London would qualify as financial contracts.

Even so, while 'banking law' is a term which has been in use long enough to identify the norms governing contracts in the private sphere, it has not traditionally encompassed those provisions regulating the banking business from a public interest perspective, which is mostly what comes to mind today when we speak of banking law. For this, we need to come closer to our time, starting immediately after the First World War.

At that time, a new global order had to be established, and finance was no exception. The new financial order was grounded on the gold standard and the convertibility of banknotes; in the decades after the war the function of the issuance of *banknotes* was centralized with *central banks*, and commercial banks, which had lost this function, focused on the provision of credit, ie the intermediation between those willing to deposit savings and those wanting to borrow capital. In a fractional-reserve system, experience tells us that the outcome of this intermediation is a precarious equilibrium—as the crisis of 1929 notably taught us. That was the moment banking regulation entered the scene to prevent crises that would disrupt the orderly functioning of the financial system, and thereby of financial institutions and

---

[1] Although these competences remained silent on some issues, as did all the central bank statutes at the time, for example on providing emergency liquidity assistance to banks.

financial contracts. The advent of banking regulation implied an important innovation in the landscape of the time which had been characterized by a strong belief in *laissez-faire*: with banking regulation, the administrative authority was vested with important powers to be involved with the internal management and conduct of the business of banks, as well as with the relationships between banks and their counterparties. The latter included, at least in some jurisdictions, the case of insolvency, where an administrative procedure for the dissolution of banks in crisis was introduced, which can be considered the historical antecedent of resolution. Although this approach was followed later in other fields of the economy, a speciality of the financial and banking sector was that in most cases the powers entrusted to the administrative authority were at the time not challenged by the banks that were subject to these rules. This was partly due to the fact that the rules worked well in preventing crises from breaking out, but partly also because banks preferred to accept the extent, scope, and content of the powers conferred upon the relevant administrative authorities, as interpreted and applied by the authorities themselves, which in turn was possible because the absence of crises helped avoid disputes from arising in the first place. Administrative authorities in charge of the financial sector looked favourably on the fact that the exercise of their powers would not be challenged: the absence of legal disputes could indeed be seen as a 'consensual interpretation and application' of banking regulation, which in turn could be interpreted as the banks' acknowledgement of the supervisor's powers, and thus as a source of legitimacy for the underlying rules. Certainly, as the exercise of these powers was not disputed, the courts did not have the opportunity to play their role as validators.

Half a century later, a first interruption to this 'no-challenge' situation came from the Herstatt Bank crisis. The emergence of the crisis did not jeopardize the credibility of the banking regulation and supervision system, which continued to be voluntarily accepted and observed by the market operators. The crisis however demonstrated the system's limits: although banking regulation was inevitably national in nature, finance is inherently international, and this gap needed to be filled.

In the attempt to fill this gap, recourse was made to 'soft law'. This is a form of law which is neither directly supported by administrative powers vested with an administrative authority, nor can it be directly invoked before the courts for its enforcement and application. But this form of law, owing to its high degree of technicality, is characterized by the involvement of market players from the early stages of the process leading to the adoption of the rules and by the fact that it relies on peer pressure for voluntary enforcement, having its roots in the collective agreement to go in a certain direction. The introduction of soft law in the system initiated a process which eventually delivered the outcomes explored in this book. Jurisdictions started to 'transpose' such soft law into their legal systems by means of 'hard law'. This ultimately led to a proliferation in the number of rules susceptible in their application of being the trigger to a dispute between a supervised entity and its supervisor.[2] The Great Financial Crisis was a defining moment in this process of 'transposition': on the one hand, the magnitude of the crisis called for legislative intervention of a comparable size; on the other hand,

---

[2] In Europe the implementation of the Basel Accord, itself soft law, was instrumental to an alignment of legislation which both made possible and was the catalyst for the first, and more importantly, the second banking directive (Council Directive 77/780/EEC and Council Directive 89/646/EEC of 15 December 1989 respectively), which were based on the mutual recognition of each Member State's rules (and on the home country control). The process then continued with the Capital Requirements Regulation (CRR) and Directive (CRD).

the belief that the costs of compliance with the rules were an acceptable trade-off for a protective shield from crises was shaken to its foundations.[3]

In the last forty years, the quantity and complexity of banking regulation has increased in an exponential manner. From the first banking directive in 1977,[4] which contained 15 articles, to today's CRR[5] with its 521 articles and the CRD's 165 articles,[6] the detail, the specificity, and the dynamic of the rules—amendments are adopted every few years—have become of a qualitatively different nature. Because of the perception of the importance of financial and banking activity for the well-being of society and because of the risks that it can represent for financial stability and growth, calls for higher accountability of competent authorities have been voiced and more control over various aspects of banking activities introduced.

A characteristic feature of public law in financial regulation is the close involvement of the public authority with the ongoing management of the business. One of the reasons for this close involvement of the state in finance is that, while in other economic activities the fact that less efficient firms are expelled from the market is consistent with the latter's good functioning, in the financial system the bankruptcy of a firm could be harmful also for other components of the system, potentially for all, and for financial stability more generally. Another reason is that, as already mentioned, an international element existed in finance and was inherent to it well before government started to be involved with its regulation: finance had transboundary effects from very early on. This is why agreed practices were developed by market players as soft law instruments;[7] but then, those standards and best practices used by financial players in the management of their business were transformed by the government into regulations with a binding force.[8] In other words, the soft law developed across different stages, incorporating the international practices, but then required government to transpose it into hard law.

For all these reasons the law, seen as the intervention of the legislator through its acts in order to regulate, limit, and control, has historically been to some extent almost in opposition to finance, seen as the free development of the market forces which will enable naturally the best allocation of resources for society and as the expression of the (contractual) free will of the participants in transactions. This has fuelled the long-standing debate, first, on the advantages, for society and its growth, of leaving the market to self-regulate, with some scholars asserting that the best type of regulation in the financial field is a 'principles regulation' which allows the market to develop and explore new solutions and ultimately find a proper

---

[3] The foundations for an ambitious programme at global level were laid down in the Leaders' Statement at the end of the Pittsburgh Summit of the G20 on 24–25 September 2009. See in particular the section entitled 'Strengthening the International Financial Regulatory System'.
[4] First Council Directive 77/780/EEC of 12 December 1977 on the coordination of laws, regulations and administrative provisions relating to the taking up and pursuit of the business of credit institutions [1997] OJ L 322/ 30 (17 December 1977). See also the Second Council Directive 89/646/EEC of 15 December 1989 on the coordination of laws, regulations and administrative provisions relating to the taking up and pursuit of the business of credit institutions and amending Directive 77/780/EEC ([1989] OJ L386/1 (30 December 1989), with twenty-five articles.
[5] Regulation (EU) No 575/2013 of the European Parliament and of the Council of 26 June 2013 on prudential requirements for credit institutions and amending Regulation (EU) No 648/2012 [2013] OJ L176/1 (27 June 2013).
[6] Directive 2013/36/EU of the European Parliament and of the Council of 26 June 2013 on access to the activity of credit institutions and the prudential supervision of credit institutions, amending Directive 2002/87/EC and repealing Directives 2006/48/EC and 2006/49/EC ([2013] OJ L176/338 (27 June 2013).
[7] One may see in the contractual clauses developed for merchants in the Middle Ages an antecedent to what we mean as 'soft law'. See A Cordes, *The Search for a Medieval Lex Mercatoria* (2003) Oxford U Comparative L Forum 5 ouclf.law.ox.ac.uk, text after n 35.
[8] See Günther Teuber, *Law as an Autopoietic System* (Blackwell Publishers 1993).

natural equilibrium between the various interests, leaving broad discretion to market participants on how to apply those principles to the new creative contracts that are developed; and, second, on the risk that such 'principles regulation', de facto implemented by a group of stronger parties and powerful lobbies in a self-interested way, could bring to excessive (for society) risk-taking; and finally on the possible consequences of externalizing such risks to society at large and tax-payers, even bringing about a de facto redistribution of wealth outside the realm of any democratic procedure. There are also those who contest the vision of the free and self-regulating market: an important school of thought argues that any market is based on a network of contracts which, in turn, rely on the law and the action of the courts for their enforcement, and financial markets are no exception.[9] For these scholars, it is the law that shapes the markets, not vice-versa, which means that in reality there is an important responsibility for the legislator to promote growth for society and equal opportunities and to ensure an acceptable level of risk for the collectivity.

It is no surprise that the tension, or dialectic relationship, between (i) the state involvement with the management of the banks to protect the public good through legislation, (ii) the discretion granted to the independent supervisor and the open issues of democratic accountability, (iii) the free market economy and trust in the dynamic of the market to promote the efficient allocation of resources has led the number of disputes relating to financial law to increase exponentially over the last fifteen years, in particular with regard to public law disputes. In the field of private law, disputes were frequent also in the past, so much so that many cases which are still relevant today and are examined by the authors of this book date back to the last century.[10] Nevertheless, in this domain, the increase in crises has generated more occasions for private parties to disagree on the application of the law and therefore to call on the intervention of a court to decide.

The increasing number of judicial (but one may argue, at least to some extent, also administrative) decisions which have intervened to clarify and apply the law in concrete cases has resulted in a substantive body of decisions which may in itself be considered 'law' insofar as one believes that such a body of jurisprudence should inform and guide future cases.

An important issue dealt with in the book is the need to have a systemic approach to adjudication in the financial sector, to avoid the risk that each case is disconnected from the other, and any inherent coherence is lost in the process. The fundamental principles of the legal system should always shape the judicial control of financial disputes ahead of and above the technical application of the specific norms: fundamental principles should be used as a key interpretative device to guide in the clarification and application of the law especially in *hard* cases, where different provisions are potentially applicable with diverging potential outcomes and an ensuing tension between norms, which is for the courts to resolve. The application of fundamental principles as a guide in interpretation would also allow the consistency of the law applicable in the financial sector to be re-established (sometimes ex post) with the law in general, broadly speaking, ie including also the general framework and other sectors of the law which may occasionally overlap and collide with finance. The question then is whether there are advantages that might plead in favour of courts specialized in financial cases. In my view this would risk loosening precisely the link between the concrete

---

[9] K Pistor, 'A Legal Theory of Finance' (2013) 41(2) J Comp Econ 315.
[10] By way of example, a case from 1898 (*Groves v Wimborne* [1898] 2 QB 402 (Lord Browne-Wilkinson)) is mentioned as good law in relation to the impossibility, in the UK legal framework, for private rights in statutes creating a regulatory system to apply for the benefit of the public as a whole.

cases in the financial dispute and the general framework of the law, with a retreat to sectoral specialization (and the risk of having the economic reasoning prevail on the legal statement of reasons): there is an inherent trade-off between specialization in a certain branch of law and familiarity with the general principles.

Another topic which is addressed in the book is that of the relationship between administrative authorities and courts, and between their respective decisions. In both cases an institution created by the law is entrusted with a public power to apply the law to a specific case—a power which, in turn, necessarily presupposes the power to interpret that law. A very well-known problem of a 'constitutional nature', which is discussed in the book also in the light of the different legal traditions and ways of addressing the issue on both sides of the Atlantic, is that of the source of legitimacy of the power entrusted to administrative authorities, especially insofar as they are independent (as is increasingly the case, both for central banks but also for banking supervisors, in line with the Basel Core Principles), which some would argue puts them outside the circuit of democratic legitimacy.

An even more interesting question for the purposes of this book concerns the limits which are inherent to these powers. Again, the responses to this question can differ on either side of the Atlantic depending on the specificities and traditions of each legal system, yet interestingly, but perhaps not surprisingly, the outcome is not so different in practice. Depending on what the legislator believes to be desirable, appropriate, and possible, administrative authorities are afforded different margins of discretion when applying the law to a specific case. In some cases, this discretion is narrower in nature and is limited to the understanding of complex facts from which certain legal consequences should follow which—once ascertained—should result in these consequences almost automatically ('technical discretion'). In other cases, the legislator entrusts the administrative authority with broader margins of discretion, which extends also to the choice of the most appropriate consequence which should ensue from the acknowledgement of the facts.[11]

The acknowledgement of the existence of this 'policy discretion' as being different in nature from the technical one is all but deprived of consequences for courts and their role and prerogatives in financial cases. To the extent that the law has indeed opted for this kind of discretion, the courts, in their role as *viva vox iuris*, should ensure the full application of the law by respecting the margin of discretion which is afforded to the administrative authority. The courts should therefore limit themselves to reviewing the correct appraisal of the facts and the reasonableness of the choice made by the administrative authority in the exercise of its discretion. A different outcome would not only be contrary to the spirit of the specific provision applied in the specific case, but also have implications from a systemic perspective, as it would relate to the constitutional principle of the separation of powers. A very important judgment has been issued in this respect by the Court of Justice of the European Union (CJEU), protecting the institutional balance between the ECB and the Court, and the room for discretion granted by the legislator to the ECB. The CJEU annulled the judgment of the General Court as it had 'exceeded the scope of its judicial review' by substituting its own assessment for the one of the ECB (which was granted discretion by the law) 'without establishing how the ECB's assessment set out in that decision was, in that regard, vitiated by a manifest error of assessment' and as it had wrongly concluded that 'the ECB had failed to

---

[11] Opinion of Advocate General Emiliou in Case C-389/21 P *ECB v Crédit Lyonnais* ECLI:EU:C:2022:844, paras 47–53.

fulfil its obligation ... to examine carefully and impartially all the relevant aspects of the situation in question'.[12]

This book looks into the dialectic of the close interactions and tensions between law and finance; into the relationship between judicial review and the free market; and into the complementarity of private initiative and contractual freedom on the one hand, and preservation of the public good on the other, through ensuring that the fundamental legal principles on which our democratic society is built are applied and respected even in a fast developing and highly technical area such as finance and financial relations. The comparison between the US institutional set-up and jurisprudence, and the European Union one, identifying similarities and differences, and in particular the separation in Union law between 'banking regulation' (for which the legislator is responsible) and 'banking supervision' (which relates to the provisions applied by the institutions entrusted with the administrative powers to control and regulate the banking sector, rather than the banks themselves)[13] adds another layer of complexity. The courts are the instrument for ensuring that the more stable and universal legal principles, ie the principles that are fundamental in the jurisdiction, and the rules that have been established to govern the conflicting (private, but also public) interests in the area of banking and finance continue to apply in a clear and equal manner to all participants in the financial markets, and that the holders of power, the supervisory authorities in this case, are accountable for the way in which they use the discretion granted to them by the legislator.

It is difficult to imagine a more fascinating and multi-faceted topic. Let us consider the interaction of different disciplines, the interplay of different interests, and the issues of accountability and discretion of the administrative authorities, as well as the intensity of the judicial review of their decisions, ie the relationship with the court. We continue with the different instruments of dispute resolution that are available (judicial, pre-judicial, arbitral) and the different sources of obligations, or those who set the standards of behaviour. Finally, we move on to the multi-layered exercise of powers in a transnational and supranational environment, where some aspects need to be addressed at national level; and to the speed of development and the high technicality of the legislation accompanied by the challenge of not allowing the technical complexity to become an obstacle to conscious policy and political decisions.

The two authors, with their exceptional practical expertise and sharp analytical capabilities, have succeeded in presenting all of these topics in a comprehensive yet fresh and clear way, focusing on the role of judicial review in preserving the rule of law in a technical and complex field in which the competent authority is granted a measure of discretion. Their book comprises an impressively detailed and well-structured analysis of a wealth of cases, providing a systemic explanation and categorization of the judicial activity of courts along with guidance on the interpretation of the law in other cases in the future—especially those for which there is no easy answer directly in the law or in any precedent. It is not only well-suited for judges and lawyers involved in disputes, but also for any lawyer in financial authorities

---

[12] See judgment of 4 May 2023,- C-389/21 P *ECB v Crédit Lyonnais* (n 11), paras 72, 74.
[13] MS GIannini, *Il Potere Discrezionale della Pubblica Amministrazione: Concetto e Problemi* (Giuffrè, 1939) 42, 43; MS GIannini, 'Osservazioni sulla disciplina della funzione creditizia' in *Scritti per Santi Romano II* (Cedam 1939) 707.

tasked with applying the law, as well as for financial entities or indeed anyone having an interest in financial law.

Professor Chiara Zilioli
General Counsel and Director General of the Legal Services at the European Central Bank
Johann Wolfgang Goethe Universität in Frankfurt am Main, 30 June 2023

Summary Contents

Table of Cases	xxi
Table of Legislation	xlix
List of Abbreviations	lvii
Authors' Biographies	lix

PART I: THE CONCEPTUAL FRAMEWORK

1. An Introduction to Courts' and Principles-Based Interpretivism	3
2. Finance, the Rule of Law, and the Courts	37

PART II: PUBLIC LAW DISPUTES IN THE LAW OF FINANCE

3. An Anatomy of Issues in Public Law Disputes	55
4. A Matter of principles: Justiciability and accountability in the public law of finance	65
5. Courts' review of monetary and financial stability decisions	117
6. Courts' Review of Regulatory and Supervisory Decisions	131
7. Courts' Review of Crisis Management Decisions	179

PART III: PRIVATE LAW DISPUTES IN THE LAW OF FINANCE

8. An Anatomy of Issues in Private Law Disputes	223
9. Courts and the Law of Liability for Misstatements in Securities Offerings	235
10. Courts and Financial Contract Disputes	293
11. Courts in insolvency, collateral, and creditor coordination disputes	339

PART IV: TOWARDS BETTER JUSTICE IN FINANCE: THE CASE FOR SPECIALIZED COURTS IN EUROPE

12. Dispute Resolution in Finance and Its Shortcomings: Europe as a Test Case	389
13. A Snapshot of the Current Court System's Nodes and Challenges	427
14. A way forward: Specialized courts in the law of finance in the EU	465

Bibliography	475
Index	499

Detailed Contents

Table of Cases	xxi
Table of Legislation	xlix
List of Abbreviations	lvii
Authors' Biographies	lix

PART I: THE CONCEPTUAL FRAMEWORK

1. An Introduction to Courts' and principles-Based Interpretivism

1 Disputes in the law of finance and courts' principles-based interpretivism	1.01
2 Principles, financial stability, and interpretation	1.23
3 Principles-based interpretivism, heuristics, and biases	1.29
4 Principles-based interpretivism and legitimacy	1.31
5 Critical views: Rules-based positivism and pragmatism	1.35
6 Principles-based interpretivism versus plausibly similar alternatives in the adjudication of law of finance: the case of cost-benefit analysis and the discourse theory of justice	1.47

2. Finance, the Rule of Law, and the Courts

1 Legal institutions and financial development	2.01
2 Law, finance, and crises	2.12
2.1 (Rule of) law and (financial) emergencies: expediency, stability, and legitimacy: the role of courts and legal principles	2.13
2.2 Courts, crises, and biases: reframing urgency, seeking consistency, transitioning to 'normalcy'	2.30
3 Courts and finance beyond crises: hard cases	2.39
3.1 Courts beyond financial crises: hard cases, interstitial, and pivotal role	2.40
3.2 Courts and finance: from back seat to front seat	2.43

PART II: PUBLIC LAW DISPUTES IN THE LAW OF FINANCE

3. An Anatomy of Issues in Public Law Disputes

1 Courts, horizontal separation, and vertical allocation of powers	3.02
2 Independent authorities/agencies and discretion	3.06
3 The individuals within the system: Standing to sue and fundamental rights	3.10

4. A Matter of principles: Justiciability and accountability in the public law of finance

1 Justiciability challenges of monetary and financial stability decisions	4.01
1.1 Immunity of sovereign debtors, central banks, and international organizations	4.01
1.2 Justiciability of financial stability and crisis management decisions in the EU	4.08

	1.3 Justiciability of central banks' decisions	4.11
2	Justiciability issues in regulatory, supervisory, and crisis management decisions	4.14
	2.1 Exclusions and limitations of liability	4.15
	2.2 Agency discretion, justiciability, and the legitimacy of delegation	4.18
	2.3 Soft law acts in financial regulation and supervision: justiciability, legal relevance, and control of shadow legislation	4.25
	2.4 Challengeability of acts in complex proceedings	4.38
	2.5 Standing to challenge decisions	4.49
3	Accountability beyond justiciability: access to documents, appointments, and quasi-judicial review	4.62
	3.1 Transparency and access to documents	4.62
	3.1.1 The experience in the United States	4.62
	3.1.2 The EU legal framework ... or patchwork on access to document	4.70
	3.1.3 The case law on access to documents in the SSM and SRM	4.76
	3.2 Independence and appointment of members of financial regulatory bodies	4.83
	3.3 The relationship between court review and administrative review	4.90

5. Courts' review of monetary and financial stability decisions

1	Introduction: monetary and financial stability and their legal challenges	5.01
2	Financial stability and fiscal backstops	5.06
3	Monetary policy decisions	5.08
4	Open issues: lender of last resort (LoLR) and appointment of central bank members	5.21

6. Courts' Review of Regulatory and Supervisory Decisions

1	Introduction: regulatory and supervisory frameworks and their legal challenges	6.01
2	Vertical allocation of powers and judicial review in regulatory and supervisory decisions	6.06
	2.1 The experience in the US: branching restrictions, FinTech, and administrative discretion	6.06
	2.2 EU law: constitutional frictions, composite procedures, and EU authorities' application of national laws	6.10
3	Horizontal separation of powers and judicial review in regulatory and supervisory decisions	6.22
4	Courts and the regulatory perimeter: shadow banking, parallel unregulated activities, and banking groups	6.33
	4.1 Shadow banking and parallel activities	6.34
	4.2 Financial groups	6.42
5	A comparative assessment of courts' standard of review	6.47
	5.1 US courts' 'arbitrary and capricious' standard: the 'demanding' version, and its challenge to the substantive application of the law	6.48
	5.2 EU Courts' substantive-leaning and finalistic review: Their role as ultimate authorities in defining key concepts of the law of finance	6.52
	5.3 US courts' 'arbitrary and capricious' standard and procedural safeguards	6.66
	5.4 EU Courts' process-based review and procedural safeguards	6.69
6	Enforcement measures, sanctions, and penalties: safeguards and standard of review	6.75

7. Courts' Review of Crisis Management Decisions

1	Introduction: crisis management frameworks and the courts	7.01

2. The legitimacy of crisis management frameworks	7.07
2.1 Delegation and accountability of enforcement powers and funding schemes	7.08
2.2 Crisis management funding: deposit guarantees and resolution funds	7.14
3. Substantive review: 'property' and other rights	7.23
3.1 Substantive safeguards in bank crises	7.24
3.2 Substantive safeguards in sovereign crises	7.39
3.3 Substantive review beyond 'property': conditions for intervention	7.44
3.4 Substantive review beyond 'property' (II): cases involving depositors	7.50
3.5 Substantive review beyond 'property' (III): EU state aid cases' implications for shareholders and creditors	7.59
4 Procedural safeguards: 'Arbitrary and capricious', 'good administration' and judicial protection	7.63
4.1 US safeguards under the 'arbitrary and capricious' standard	7.64
4.2 EU process review and procedural safeguards	7.73
4.3 A brief mention to investment treaties arbitration	7.83
5 Cross-border recognition and cooperation	7.87
5.1 The regional (EU) context	7.88
5.2 The international context	7.93

PART III: PRIVATE LAW DISPUTES IN THE LAW OF FINANCE

8. An Anatomy of Issues in Private Law Disputes	
1 Private disputes and vertical allocation of powers	8.01
2 Beyond verticality: private law disputes, jurisdiction, and applicable law	8.08
3 Vertical, horizontal tensions, and private plaintiffs: regulatory provisions and private law doctrines	8.16
4 Access to justice and collective redress	8.23
5 Contract interpretation: party autonomy, boilerplate, or hard cases?	8.25
9. Courts and the law of liability for misstatements in securities offerings	
1 Introduction: Liability for misstatements and pure economic loss in private law	9.01
2 The development of a statute-based liability system: the US Exchange Act and Securities Act	9.11
2.1 Implying a private right of action, and federalizing securities litigation	9.12
2.2 Determining what investors deserve protection: materiality, reliance, and class actions	9.26
2.3 Section 10b and rule 10b-5 and defendants (renvoi)	9.37
2.4 Registration statement and prospectus liability under the Securities Act 1933	9.38
2.5 Section 10b, rule 10b-5 and vertical balance: Summary and latest developments	9.44
2.6 Insider trading: a major source of criminal liability, a relatively secondary source of private law liability	9.50
3 The creeping codification of securities liability for misstatements in the EU	9.52
3.1 Prospectus liability: an EU provision with doctrinal traction	9.53
3.2 Courts' steps towards harmonizing prospectus remedies: scope, damages, and invalidity	9.58
3.3 The dawn of a doctrine of 'reliance' and 'fraud-on-the-market' in domestic and EU courts?	9.70
3.4 Liability beyond prospectus: other disclosures and failures to disclose (market abuse)	9.84

4 Specialties of 'secondary actor' and gatekeeper liability — 9.95
   4.1 Constitutional dimension: statements versus opinions and free speech in US law — 9.96
   4.2 Private law considerations — 9.106
   4.3 Regulatory dimension (I): secondary actors as 'makers' of statements? — 9.122
   4.4 Regulatory considerations (II): Liability under securities laws and gatekeeper regulation in EU countries — 9.137

10. Courts and Financial Contract Disputes

1 Introduction — 10.01
2 Validity disputes: the (un)enforceability of complex/speculative financial transactions in light of corporate 'capacity' and public policy — 10.06
3 Disputes about intermediaries' duties and representations — 10.24
   3.1 Duties of advisers and broker–dealers in the US, and their significance in private actions — 10.25
   3.2 Banks' marketing duties under private law, absent advisory relationships — 10.37
   3.3 Regulatory requirements and private law duties in the EU (I): Fashioning private remedies for breach of regulatory duties — 10.49
   3.4 Regulatory requirements and private law duties in the EU (II): causal link, reliance, and basis clauses — 10.82
4 Financial contracts' interpretation: express versus implied duties, specificity versus coherence — 10.93
   4.1 Contract interpretation: reasonableness, express, and implied terms — 10.94
   4.2 Contract interpretation: general considerations, events of default and valuation — 10.105
   4.3 Materially adverse events — 10.122

11. Courts in insolvency, collateral, and creditor coordination disputes

1 Introduction — 11.01
2 Special purpose vehicles (SPVs) insolvency and clawback risk — 11.11
   2.1 Structured transactions risks in theory: avoidance, recharacterization and substantive consolidation — 11.12
   2.2 Structured credit and claw-back risks in practice: interim asset control in insolvency, and the treatment of bespoke transactions — 11.29
3 Derivatives disputes in insolvency — 11.37
4 Disputes over financial collateral: characterization, custody, and segregation — 11.43
   4.1 Classifying complex collateral arrangements as a recognizable security — 11.44
   4.2 Custody, intermediation, and segregation risk — 11.48
5 Inter-creditor disputes ensure bankruptcy remoteness (shielding the assets from formal bankruptcy proceedings) — 11.53
   5.1 Limiting bankruptcy filing by SPV directors, and fiduciary duties — 11.54
   5.2 Limiting bankruptcy filing by creditors: non-petition and non-recourse clauses, and other mechanisms — 11.59
6 Inter-creditor coordination disputes in collective enforcement, liquidation, and restructuring — 11.71
   6.1 Collectively enforcing claims: 'insolvency events' clauses and their hybrid (contract-statutory) construction by courts — 11.72
   6.2 Restructuring claims and inter-creditor conflict: disenfranchisement and oppression — 11.77
7 Inter-creditor coordination disputes and the role of agents and trustees — 11.89
   7.1 The role of agent banks — 11.90
   7.2 Creditor coordination and the role of trustees (I): Duties and responsibilities — 11.93

7.3 Creditor coordination and the role of trustees (II): Discretion and discretion-constraining clauses	11.101
8 Inter-creditor disputes over the distribution of proceeds	11.106

PART IV: TOWARDS BETTER JUSTICE IN FINANCE: THE CASE FOR SPECIALIZED COURTS IN EUROPE

12. Dispute Resolution in Finance and Its Shortcomings: Europe as a Test Case

1 Courts' fragmentation in the law of finance	12.01
2 Courts' independence and impartiality	12.08
3 Courts' expertise and specialization	12.16
3.1 An 'external' perspective	12.17
3.2 An 'internal' perspective	12.30
4 Courts' organization and procedure	12.41
5 Courts and inter-institutional 'dialogue' (I): the exercise of discretion and the standards of review	12.44
6 Courts and inter-institutional 'dialogue' (II): inter-court coordination (or lack thereof) and its systemic effects	12.55
6.1 The 'threshold' issue	12.56
6.2 The 'linearity' issue	12.62

13. A Snapshot of the Current Court System's Nodes and Challenges

1 Introduction	13.01
2 Nodes of the courts' system in public financial law disputes	13.03
2.1 Vertical coordination of courts	13.04
2.2 Horizontal coordination (and competition) of courts	13.09
2.3 Horizontal coordination by courts and quasi-courts	13.11
3 Nodes of the courts' system for private law disputes in the law of finance	13.38
3.1 Private law disputes: precedents in domestic practice and hybrid international commercial courts	13.39
3.2 Mass, small-ticket disputes, and the role of alternative dispute resolution (ADR)	13.44
3.3 Private law disputes as a follow-up of public law disputes	13.50
4 Specialized financial courts and arbitration: friends or foes? Nuances between commercial and investment arbitration, and their relationship to private and public law disputes	13.59

14. A way forward: Specialized courts in the law of finance in the EU

1 European specialized courts for public law disputes and Article 257 TFEU	14.01
2 A European specialized court for cross-border private law disputes and Articles 81(2) and 67(4) TFEU	14.04
3 The Unified Patent Court as a controversial blueprint	14.06
4 Specialized courts, EU general principles of national procedural autonomy, equivalence and effectiveness, and national constitutional counter-limits	14.08
5 A cautious proposal for adjustments to the existing court system in the law of finance	14.10

Bibliography	475
Index	499

Table of Cases

ECTHR (EUROPEAN COURT OF HUMAN RIGHTS)

Agrotexim v Greece, App no 14807/89 (7 July 2002) 4.54
Albert and Others v Hungary, App no 5294/14 (7 July 2020) 4.54
A and B v Norway, App nos 24130/11 and 29758/11 (15 November 2016) 3.08
Anheuser-Busch Inc v Portugal, App no 73049/01 (11 January 2007) 7.28
Apostolakis v Greece, App no 39574/07 (22 October 2009) 7.39
Ásmundsson v Iceland, App no 60669/00 (12 October 2004)................. 7.28, 7.39
Ástráðsson v Iceland, App no 26374/18 (1 December 2020)...........................12.10
Bellet, Huertas and Vialatte v France, App nos 40832/98, 40833/98, and 40906/98
    (27 April 1999) 7.39
Bosphorus Airways v Ireland, App no 45036/98 (30 June 2005)........................3.13
Bramelid and Malmström v Sweden, App nos 8588/79 and 8589/79 (12 December 1983)........7.28
Capital Bank AD v Bulgaria, App no 49429/99 24 (24 November 2005)............ 4.54, 6.83, 7.74
Credit and Industrial Bank v the Czech Republic, App no 29010/95
    (21 October 2003) 4.54, 7.73, 7.74
Didier v France, App no 58188/00 (27 August 2002) 6.81
Dubus SA v France, App no 5242/04 (11 June 2009) 6.81
Engel & Others v Netherlands, App no 5100/71 (8 June 1976) 6.81
Fell v United Kingdom, App nos 7819/77 and 7878/77 (19 March 1981) 12.11
Flux (No 2) v Moldova, App no 31001/03 (3 October 2007) 12.11
Freire Lopes v Portugal, App no 58598/21 (23 February 2023)...........................7.28
Funke JB v Switzerland, App no 31827/96 (3 May 2001) 6.87
Gaygusuz v Austria, App no 39/1995/545/631 (23 May 1996) 7.39
Grainger and Others v United Kingdom, App no 34940/10 (10 July 2012)...............7.28
Korporativna Targovska Banca AD v Bulgaria, Apps nos 46564/15 and 68140/16
    (30 August 2022) 4.54
Koufaki v Greece, App nos 57665/12 and 57657/12 (7 May 2013) 7.39
Langborger v Sweden, App no 11179/84 (22 June 1989) 12.11
Lilly France SA v France, App no 53892/00 (3 December 2002)........................6.81
Lormines v France, App no 65411/01 (9 November 2006) 12.11
Majorana v Italy, App no 75117/01 (26 May 2005)..................................12.11
Mamatas and Others v Greece, App nos 63066/14, 64297/14, and 66106/14
    (21 July 2016) 7.41, 7.42
Matthews v United Kingdom, App no 24833/94 (29 October 1997) 3.13
Menarini Diagnostics v Italy, App no 43509/08 (27 September 2011)...................6.91
Olczak v Poland, App no 30417/96 (7 July 2002) 4.54
Ringeisen v Austria, App no 2614/65 (16 July 1971) 12.11
Sabeh El Leil v France, App 34869/05, ECLI:CE:ECHR:2008:1021DEC003486905 ....4.03
Saunders v United Kingdom, App no 19187/91 (17 December 1996) 6.87
Siglfirdingur Ehf v Island, App no 34142/96 (7 September 1999).....................12.11
Skórkiewicz v Poland, App no 39860/98 (1 June 1999) 7.39
Sporrong and Lönroth v Sweden, App no 7151/75, 7152/75 (23 September 1982) 7.28
Süzer and Eksen v Turkey, App no 6334/05 (23 October 2012) 4.54
Tedesco v France, App no 11950/02 (10 May 2007)..................................12.11
Traktörer Aktiebolag v Sweden, App no 10873/84 (7 July 1989) 7.28
Urban and Urban v Poland, App no 23614/08 (30 November 2010) 12.11
Xero Flor w Polsce sp Zoo v PolandApplication, App no 4907/18 (7 May 2021) 12.11
Zolotas v Greece, App no 38240/02 (2 June 2005) 12.11

EFTA COURT

Aresbank SA and Landsbankinn hf, Fjármálaeftirlitið (the Financial Supervisory
    Authority) and Iceland, Case E-17/11 (22 November 2012)............................7.53
EFTA Surveillance Authority v Iceland, Case E-16/11 (28 January 2013)...............7.52, 7.53
LBI hf v Merrill Lynch International Ltd, Case E-28/13 (17 October 2014)...................7.88
Pascal Nobile v DAS Rechtsschutz-Versicherungs AG, Case E-21/16 [2017]..................12.11

EUROPEAN UNION

A v ESMA, BoA D 2021 02 (12 March 2021)................................... 4.20, 13.17, 13.19
A v SRB Decision, Case 4/2018 (13 August 2018)...7.15
A v SRB Decision, Case 5/2018 (20 July 2018) 7.15
A v SRB Decision, Case 8/2018 (16 October 2018).......................................13.28
A v SRB Decision, Case 1/21 (28 June 2021)..12.48
A v SRB Decision, Case 1/22, decision on admissibility (29 June 2022) 13.30
A v SRB Decision, Case 1/22 (14 April 2023) 7.05
Aalborg Portland A/S, Irish Cement Ltd, Joined Cases C-204/00 P and C-205/00 P.............6.81
AB Volvo and DAF Trucks NV v RM, Case C-267/20, ECLI:EU:C:2022:494................13.55
ABLV Bank AS v SRB, Case T-280/18, ECLI:EU:T:2022:429 .... 4.23, 4.24, 4.34, 4.44, 4.45,
    4.56, 6.62, 7.48, 7.49, 7.76, 13.06, 13.31
ABLV Bank v SRB, Case C-202/21 P, ECLI:EU:C:2022:734 ....7.15
ABLV v ECB, Joined Cases C-551/19 P and C-552/19 P, ECLI:EU:C:2021:16 ....4.45
Accord ECG UE-Canada, Opinion 1/17, ECLI:EU:C:2019:341............................12.11
Accorinti v ECB, Case T-79/13, ECLI:EU:T:2015:756........................... 7.40, 7.41, 7.42
ACER v Aquind, Case C-46/21, ECLI:EU:C:2023:182............................ 3.03, 12.47
Activos e Inversiones Monterosso v SRB, Case T-16/18 (pending) 13.37
Activos y Inversiones Monterroso, Case T-16/19 (pending)................................4.82
Adikko Bank, Case C-407/18, ECLI:EU:C:2019:537......................................10.54
Aeris Invest v Commission and SRB, Case T-628/17, ECLI:EU:T:2022:315......... 4.45, 7.13, 7.45,
    7.76, 7.78, 7.77, 7.79, 7.80, 7.82, 13.07
Aeris Invest v ECB, Case T-827/17, ECLI:EU:T:2021:660.............................. 4.81, 5.21
Aeris Invest v SRB, Case T-62/18 (pending) 4.82, 13.37
Aeris Invest v SRB, Case T-599/18, ECLI:EU:T:2019:740; Case C-874/19 P,
    ECLI:EU:C:2021:1040 .... 4.56, 7.78, 13.36
AK and Others (Independence of the Disciplinary Chamber of the Supreme Court,
    Joined Cases C-585/18, C-624/18 and C-625/18 .... 12.11, 12.12
Åklagaren v Hans Åkerberg Fransson, Case C-617/10, ECLI:EU:C:2013:105 ....3.13, 6.81
Alassini v Telecom Italia, Case C-317/08, ECLI:EU:C:2010:146 ....13.47
Algebris and Ancorage Capital Group v SRB, Case C-934/19, ECLI:EU:T:2021:1042 ......7.78, 13.36
Algebris v Commission & SRB, Case T-570/17, ECLI:EU:T:2022:314...... 4.45, 7.13, 7.37, 7.45, 7.76,
    7.78, 7.79, 7.80, 7.82, 13.07, 13.36
Algebris v SRB, Case T-2/19, ECLI:EU:T:2019:741 ....4.56
Amministrazione delle Finanze v Fratelli Vasanelli, Joined Cases 67, 127 and 128/79,
    ECLI:EU:C:1980:101 ....12.64
Andechser Molkerei Scheitz v Commission, Case C-682/13 P, not published,
    ECLI:EU:C:2015:356 ....4.58
Anglo Austrian AAB v ECB, Case T-797/1, ECLI:EU:T:2022:389 .... 6.18, 6.21, 6.58, 6.59,
    6.73–6.76, 6.85, 6.94, 6.95, 12.06
Aquind v ACER, Case T-735/18, ECLI:EU:T:2020:542; Case C-46/21 P, ECLI:EU:C:2023:182.......12.47
Arkéa Direct Bank and Others v ECB, Case T-149/18, ECLI:EU:2020:393.....................7.22
Artedogan and Others v Commission, Case T-40/00, ECLI:EU:T:2002:283 ....4.43
Arysta LifeScience Netherlands v European Food Safety Authority, Case T-725/15,
    ECLI:EU:T:2018:977 ....4.43
Associação Sindical dos Juízes Portugueses, Case C-64/16, ECLI:EU:C:2018:117 ....12.12
Association de Médiation Sociale (AMS) v Union locale des Syndicats, Case C-176/12,
    ECLI:EU:C:2014:2 ....1.28

Asturcom, Case C-40/08, ECLI:EU:C:2009:615 ....10.54
Aziz, Case C-415/11, ECLI:EU:C:2013:164 ....10.54, 12.65
B v ESMA, BoA D 2018/02 (10 September 2018) 13.17
BaFin v Ewald Baumeister, Case C-15/16, ECLI:EU:C:2018:464 .... 4.76, 4.78, 4.77, 13.35
Banca Popolare di Bari SpA (formerly Banca Tercas), Fondo intercbancario di
 tutela die depositi v Commission, Joined Cases T-98/16, T-196/16 and T-198/16,
 ECLI:EU:T:2019:167 .... 7.60, 7.61
Banco Cooperativo Español v SRB, Case T-323/16, ECLI:EU:C:2013:856 ....7.18
Banco de Portugal and Novo Banco Spain v VR, Case C-504/19, ECLI:EU:C:2021:335 .....1.12, 7.91,
 7.92, 13.04
Banco di Desio e della Brianza, Case C-831/19, ECLI:EU:C:2022:395 ....12.64, 13.04
Banco Espanol de Credito v Joaquin Calderon Camino, Case C-618/10,
 ECLI:EU:C:2012:349 ....13.51
Banco Primus Sa v Jesus Gutierrez Garcia, Case C-421/14, ECLI:U:C:2017:60 ....13.51
Banco Santander SA v JAC and MPCR, Case C-410/20, ECLI:EU:C:2022:351 ....7.38, 7.39,
 9.64, 9.66, 12.69
Banesto, Case C-618/10, ECLI:EU:C:2012:349 ....10.51
Banka Slovenije and Republic Slovenije, Case C-45/21, ECLI:EU:C:2022:670 ....4.13
Bankia v Union Mutua Asistencial de Seguros (UMAS) (Bankia III), Case C-910/19,
 ECLI:EU:C:2021:433 .... 9.78, 9.80, 9.81
Banque Postale v ECB, Case T-733/16, ECLI:EU:T:2018:477 ....3.08, 4.22, 4.24, 4.23, 6.63,
 6.64, 6.66, 12.49, 13.25
BASF Grenzach v ECHA, Case T-125/17, ECLI:EU:T:2019:638 ....3.03
BASF v ECHA, Case T-125/17, ECLI:EU:T:2019:638, Case C-565/17, ECLI:EU:C:2018:340 ....12.47
Belgium v Commission, Case C-16/16 P, ECLI:EU:C:2018:79 .... 4.30, 7.58
Berlusconi and Finanziaria d'investimento Fininvest SpA (Fininvest) v Banca d'Italia and
 Istituto per la Vigilanza Sulle Assicurazioni (IVASS), Case C-219/17,
 ECLI:EU:C:2018:102 .... 4.39, 4.40, 6.16, 6.22, 13.06
Bernis and Others v ECB, Case T-283/18, ECLI:EU:T:2019:295, Joined Cases
 C-551/19 P and C-552/19 P, ECLI:EU:C:2021:369 .... 4.45, 4.56, 13.06
Bertelsmann and Sony Corporation of America v Impala, Case C-413/06,
 ECLI:EU:C:2008:392 ....12.50
Biuro Podrozy Partner v Prezes Urzedu Ochrony Konkurencji I Konsumentow,
 Case C-119/15, ECLI:EU:C:2016:987 ....12.42
BNP Paribas Personal Finance, Joined Cases C-776/19 to C-782/19, ECLI:EU:C:2021:470 ......10.54
BNP Paribas v ECB, Case T-768/16, ECLI:EU:T:2018:471 ....3.08
BNP Paribas/BCE, Joined Cases T-150/18 and T-345/18, ECLI:EU:2020:394 ....7.22
Bourdouvali and Others v Council and Others, Case T-786/14, ECLI:EU:T:2018:487 ....7.35
BPC Lux 2 and Others v Commission, Case T-812/14., ECLI:EU:T:2017:560 ....4.57
BPC Lux 2 Sàrl v European Commission, Case C-544/17 P, ECLI:EU:C:2018:880 ....4.57
BPCE and Others v ECB, Case T-146/18, ECLI:EU:2020:392 ....7.22
BPCE v ECB, Case T-745/16, ECLI:EU:T:2018:476 .... 3.08, 6.63, 12.49
Braesch and Others v European Commission, Case T-161/18, ECLI:EU:T:2021:102 ....4.58, 4.59, 4.61
Brasserie du Pêcheur, Factortame III, Joined Cases C-46/93 and C-48/93, ECLI:EU:C:1996:79 ......8.21
BT v Balgarska Narodna Banka, Case C-501/18, ECLI:EU:C:2021:249 .... 4.15, 4.16, 4.32,
 4.33, 4.57, 7.35, 7.37, 7.53, 7.54, 7.57, 7.58
Buccioni v Banca d'Italia, Case C-594/16, ECLI:EU:C:2018:717 .... 4.76–4.79, 13.35
C v EBA, BoA-D-2022-01 (7 July 2022) 4.20, 13.19
Caisse régionale de crédit agricole mutuel Alpes Provence and Others v ECB,
 Joined Cases T-133/16–T-136/16, ECLI:EU:T:2018:219 .... 4.94, 4.96, 6.19, 6.54,
 6.56, 6.58, 6.63–6.65, 12.06
Cajamadrid v Ausbanc, Case C-484/08, ECLI:EU:C:2010:309 ....10.51
Cartesio, Case C-210/06, ECLI:EU:C:2008:723 ....8.06
Carvalho and Others v European Parliament and Council, Case C-565/19 P,
 ECLI:EU:C:2021:252 ....4.52
Centros, Case C-212/97, ECLI:EU:C:1999:126 ....8.06

Chalkor AE Epexergasias Metallon v European Commission, Case C-386/10 P,
    ECLI:EU:C:2011:815 .... 12.44
Chrysostomides K & Co and Others v Council and Others, Case T-680/13,
    ECLI:EU:T:2018:486 .... 7.35
Chvatal and Others v Court of Justice of the European Communities, Case T-154/96,
    ECLI:EU:T:1998:229 .... 13.26
CIVAD, Case C-533/10, ECLI:EU:C:2012:347 .... 7.15, 13.26
Commission of the European Communities v European Central Bank, Case C-11/00,
    ECLI:EU:C:2003:395 .... 4.13
Commission v Alrosa, Case C-441/07 P, ECLI:EU:C:2010:377 .... 3.08
Commission v Council, Case C-22/70, ECLI:EU:C:1971:32 .... 4.30
Commission v Edition Odile Jacob, Case C-404/10, ECLI:EU:C:2012:393 .... 4.82, 13.34
Commission v EnBW, Case C-365/12 P, ECLI:EU:C:2014:112 .... 4.82, 13.34
Commission v Greece, Case 63/87, ECLI:EU:C:1988:285 .... 13.26
Commission v Greece, Case C-475/01, ECLI:EU:C:2004:585 .... 13.26
Commission v Greencore, Case C-123/03 P, [2004] ECR I-11647 .... 4.39
Commission v Ireland, Case C-89/08, ECLI:EU:C:2009:742 .... 12.50
Commission v Italy, Fondo Interbancario di tutela dei depositi, Banca d'Italia and
    Banca Popolare di Bari, Case C-425/19 .... 4.34, 7.60
Commission v Jégo-Quéré & Cie SA, Case C-263/02, [2004] ECR I-3425 .... 3.11
Commission v Netherlands and ING Groep, Case C-224/12 P, ECLI:EU:C:2014:213 .... 4.39
Commission v Poland, Case C-619/18, ECLI:EU:C:2019:615 .... 12.11
Commission v Poland (Independence of ordinary courts), Case C-192/18,
    ECLI:EU:C:2019:924 .... 12.12
Commission v Tetra Laval, Case C-12/03 P, ECLI:EU:C:2004:318 .... 12.50
Compagnie Interagra SA v Commission, Case C-217/81, [1982] ECR 2233 .... 3.11
Confédération national de Crédit mutuel v ECB, Case T-751/16,
    ECLI:EU:T:2018:475 .... 3.08, 4.93, 4.94, 6.63
Confédération national du Crédit mutuel v ECB, Case T-145/18, ECLI:EU:2020:391 .... 7.22
Consten and Grundig v Commission, Case C-56/64, ECLI:EU:C:1966:41 .... 12.44
Corneli v ECB, Case T-502/19, ECLI:EU:T:2022:627; Joined Cases C-777/22 P and
    C-789/22 P (pending) 3.11, 4.55, 4.81, 6.19, 13.35
Costa v ENEL, Case 6/64, [1964] ECR 585 .... 3.04
Council v Access Info Europe, Case C-280/11, ECLI:EU:C:2013:671 .... 4.82, 13.34
Courage v Bernard Crehan, Case C-453/99, ECLI:EU:C:2001:465 .... 13.54
CR v Parliament, Case F-128/12, ECLI:EU:C:2014:38 .... 7.15, 13.26
Crédit Agricole and Others v ECB, Case T-144/18, ECLI:EU:T:2020:390 .... 7.22
Crédit Agricole v ECB, Case T-758/16, ECLI:EU:T:2018:472 .... 3.08, 6.19, 6.54, 6.76, 12.49
Crédit Lyonnais v ECB, Case T-504/19, ECLI:EU:T:2021:185 .... 3.08, 4.23, 6.63–6.67, 12.49
Crédit Mutuel Arkéa v ECB, Case T-712/15, ECLI:EU:T:2017:900;, Joined Cases C-152/18
    and C-153/18, ECLI:EU:C:2019:810 .... 4.33, 4.93, 6.19, 6.46, 6.47, 12.06
Credito Fondiario v SRB, Case C-69/19 P, ECLI:EU:C:2020:178 .... 7.18
Credito Fondiario v SRB, Case T-661/16, ECLI:EU:T:2018:806, Case C-69/19 P,
    ECLI:EU:C:2020:178 .... 7.18
Creditreform Rating AG v EBA, BoA-D-2019-05 .... 4.43, 13.21
Criminal proceedings against Massimo Romanelli and Paolo Romanelli, Case C-366/97,
    [1999] ECR I-00855 .... 6.40
Cruz v Beto 405 US 319 (1972) 3.14
Dalmine SpA v Commission, Case C-407/04, ECLI:EU:C:2007:53 .... 6.87
Danfoss, Case C-109/88, ECLI:EU:C:1989:383 .... 12.56
DB v Consob, Case C-481/19, ECLI:EU:C:2021:84 .... 1.28, 6.82, 6.87, 6.88, 6.89, 12.06
Deckmyn and Vrijheidsfonds, Case C-201/13, ECLI:EU:C:2014:2132 .... 9.57, 9.144
Del Valle Ruiz and Others v Commission and SRB, Case T-510/17, ECLI:EU:T:2022:312 .... 4.45, 4.82,
                                    7.13, 7.37, 7.45–7.48, 7.76, 7.77, 7.79–7.81, 13.07, 13.37
Del Valle Ruiz and Others v SRB, Case T-512/19, ECLI:EU:T:2022:331 .... 4.56
Del Valle Ruiz and Others v SRB, Case T-514/18 (pending) 4.82

Deutsche Post AG v Commission, Joined Cases C-463/10 P and C-475/10 P,
    ECLI:EU:C:2011:656 .... 4.39, 4.43
Di Masi and Varoufakis v ECB, Case T-798/17, ECLI:EU:T:2019:154;
    Case C-342/19 (pending) 4.76, 4.79, 4.80, 13.35
di Puma v Consob, Joined Cases C-596/16 and C-597/16, ECLI:EU:C:2018:192 .... 6.99
Dillenkofer and Others v Federal Republic of Germany, Joined Cases C-178, 179,
    188, 189 and 190/94 .... 8.21
Dorsch Consult, Case C-54/96, ECLI:EU:C:1997:413 .... 12.12
Dowling and Others v Minister for Finance, Case C-41/15, ECLI:EU:C:2016:836 .... 7.29
E and F, Case C-550/09, ECLI:EU:C:2010:382 .... 12.50
ECB v Crédit Lyonnais, Case C-389/21 P, ECLI:EU:C:2023:368 .... 4.23, 6.65, 6.66, 12.50
ECB v Trasta Komercbanka, Joined Cases C-663/17 P, C-665/17 P and C-669/17 P,
    ECLI:EU:C:2019:923 .... 3.11, 4.54, 4.55
Edwin Co Ltd, Case C-263/09 P, ECLI:EU:2011:C:30 .... 12.49
Egenberger, Case C-414/16, ECLI:EU:C:2018:257 .... 12.35
Eleveté Invest Group and Others v Commission and SRB, Case T-523/17,
    ECLI:EU:T:2022:313 .... 4.45, 7.13, 7.37, 7.45, 7.46, 7.47, 7.48, 7.76, 7.77, 7.79–7.82, 13.07
EMB Consulting and Others v ECB, Case C-571/19, ECLI:EU:C:2020:208 .... 4.10
Ernests Bernis v SRB and ECB, Case C-364/20 P, ECLI:EU:C:2022:115 .... 3.11
Erste Group Bank & Others v Commission, Joined Cases C-125/07 P, C-133/07 P &
    C-137/07 P, ECLI:EU:C:2009:576 .... 6.87
Espirito Santo Financial Group v European Central Bank, Case T-730/16, ECLI:EU:T:2019:161 ...... 4.76
Espirito Santo Financial v European Central Bank, Case T-251/15, ECLI:EU:T:2018:234;
    Case C-442/18 P, ECLI:EU:C:2019:1117 .... 4.76, 5.21, 13.35
Estonia v Commission, Case C-334/17 P, ECLI:EU:C:2018:914 .... 4.39
European Central Bank v Crédit Lyonnais, Case C-389/21 P, ECLI:EU:C:2022:844 .... 12.50
European Central Bank v Republic of Latvia, Case C-238/18, ECLI:EU:C:2018:1030 .... 5.24
European Commission v CK Telecoms, Case C-376/20, ECLI:EU:C:2022:817 .... 12.50
Europese Gemeenshap v Otis, Case C-199/11, ECLI:EU:C:2012:684 .... 12.12
Fédération bancaire française (FBF) v Autorité de contrôle prudentiel et de
    résolution (ACPR), Case C-911/19, ECLI:EU:C:2021:599 .... 4.35, 4.36, 6.30, 6.33, 6.32
FinancialCraft Analytics v ESMA, BoA D 2017/01 (3 July 2017) 13.20
Finanziaria d'investimento Fininvest SpA (Fininvest)/Silvio Berlusconi v
    ECB (Berlusconi II), Case T-913/16, [2022] ECLI:EU:T:2022,
    Joined Cases C-512/22 P and C-513/22 P pending 4.40, 6.15, 6.16, 6.21, 6.22,
                                                    6.59, 6.73, 6.74, 6.85, 6.92, 6.95, 12.06, 13.06
Fish Legal and Shirley, Case C-279/12, ECLI:EU:C:2013:853 .... 8.21, 9.57, 9.144
Florescu and Others, Case C-258/14, ECLI:EU:C:2017:448 .... 4.10, 4.30, 7.39
FMC Chemical SPRL v EFSA, Case T-311/06, ECLI:EU:T:2007:67 .... 4.43
Fondazione Cassa di Risparmio di Pesaro and Others v Commission, Case T-635/19,
    ECLI:EU:T:2021:394 .... 7.61, 7.62
Foto-Frost v Hauptzollamt Lübeck-Ost, Case 314/85, [1987] ECR 4200 .... 3.05, 12.07, 13.26
France v Commission, Case C-366/88, ECLI:EU:C:1990:348 .... 4.30
France v Commission, Case C-303/90, ECLI:EU:C:1991:424 .... 4.30
France v Commission, Case C-325/91, ECLI:EU:C:1993:245 .... 4.30
France v Commission, Case C-57/95, ECLI:EU:C:1997:164 .... 4.30
France v Commission, Case C-233/02, ECLI:EU:C:2004:173 .... 4.10
France v Ladbroke Racing and Commission, Case C-83/98, ECLI:EU:C:1999:577 .... 12.50
France v SRB, Case T-540/22 (pending) 13.37
Francovich and Bonifaci v Republic of Italy, Joined Cases C-6 and 9/90, ECLI:EU:C:1991:428 ..... 8.21
French Republic v Commission of the European Communities, Case C-327/91,
    ECLI:EU:C:1994:305 .... 4.10
Fresh del Monte Produce Inc v Commission, Joined Cases C-293/13 P and C-294/13 P,
    ECLI:EU:C:2015:416 .... 6.87
Fundacion Tatiana Pérez de Guzmán el Bueno v SRB, Case T-481/17, ECLI:EU:T:2022:311 ..... 4.45, 4.46,
                                            7.13, 7.37, 7.45–7.47, 7.48, 7.76, 7.77, 7.78, 7.80, 7.81, 13.07
Garlsson Real Estate v Consob, Case C-537/16, ECLI:EU:C:2018:193 .... 3.08, 6.99

Gauweiler and Others, Case C-62/14, ECLI:EU:C:2015:400 .... 5.10, 5.12–5.15, 5.17,
  5.19, 5.20, 6.10, 6.11, 6.12, 6.76, 12.42, 12.62
Geltl v Daimler AG, Case C-19/11, ECLI:EU:C:2012:397.............................. 9.85, 9.86
Genil 48 SL and Others v Bankinter SA and Others, Case C-604/11, ECLI:EU:C:2013:344...... 9.57,
  10.55, 10.57, 10.76, 10.77, 10.80, 13.57
Georgsmarienhütte and Others v Bundesrepublik Deutschland, Case C-135/16 P,
  ECLI:EU:C:2018:582 .... .4.31
Germany v Council, Case C-359/92, [1994] ECR I-3681 .... .6.28
Global Private Rating Company 'Standard Rating' Ltd v ESMA, BoA D 2013-14
  (10 January 2014).. .13.20
Granaria, Case C-101/78, ECLI:EU:C:1979:38....................................... 7.15, 13.26
Grande Stevens v Italy, App no 18640/10, 18647/10, 18663/10, 18668/10 and 18698/10
  (4 March 2014)... 6.82, 6.83, 6.91
Grimaldi v Fonds des maladies professionnelles, Case C-322/88, ECLI:EU:C:1989:646 .... 4.10, 4.30
Groener v Minister for Education, Case C-379/87, ECLI:EU:C:1989:599.................... .1.13
Grossmania, Case C-177/20, ECLI:EU:C:2022:175 .... .13.04
Gutiérrez Naranjo, Joined Cases C-154/15, C-307/15 and C-308/15,
  ECLI:EU:C:2016:980 .... 10.53, 10.54, 12.64
Hans-Otto Wagner GmbH Agrarhandel KG v Commission of the European Communities,
  Case 12/79, [1979] ECR 3657 .... .3.11
Hirmann v Immofinanz AG, Case C-174/12, ECLI:EU:C:2013:856 .... .9.61, 9.63,
  9.75, 9.81, 9.84, 10.59
Hochtief, Case C-300/17, ECLI:EU:C:2018:635...................................... .13.58
Howerton v EBA, BoA D 2021/01 (7 January 2021)................................... .13.17
Howerton v EIOPA, BoA D 2020/02 (29 October 2020) 13.17
Howerton v ESMA, BoA D 2020/01 (9 October 2020) 13.17
Hungary v Parliament, Case C-650/18, ECLI:EU:C:2021:426 .... .4.43
IATA, Case C-344/04, ECLI:EU:C:2006:10.. .13.26
Ibercaja Banco, Case C-600/19, ECLI:EU:C:2022:394.................... 10.54, 12.64, 13.04
IBM v Commission, Case 60/81, [1981] ECR 2639 .... .4.39
Iccrea v Banca d'Italia, Case C-414/18, ECLI:EU:C:2019:1036........................ 4.40, 13.06
IMC Securities, Case C-445/09, ECLI:EU:C:2011:459 .... .9.85
Impuls Leasing Romania, Case C-725/19, ECLI:EU:C:2022:396................. 10.54, 12.64, 13.04
Inuit Tapiriit Kanatami & Others v European Parliament & Council, Case T-18/10,
  [2011] ECR 11-05599, Case C-583/11, ECLI:EU:C:2013:625............. 3.11, 4.52, 13.04, 13.26
Investor Protection Europe sprl v ESMA, BoA D 2014/05 (10 November 2014) 12.46, 13.17
Italy v Commission, Case C-47/91, ECLI:EU:C:1992:284............................... .4.43
Italy v Commission, Joined Cases T-98/16, T-196/16 and T-198/16,
  ECLI:EU:2019:T:2019:167 .... .4.34
Jakeliūnas v ESMA, Case T-760/20, ECLI:EU:T:2021:512 .... 4.20, 13.19
Jégo-Quéré & Cie SA v Commission, Case T-177/01, [2002] ECR II-2365..................... .3.11
Jonsson v Société du Journal L'Est Républicain, Case C-554/17, ECLI:EU:C:2019:124......... .13.44
Kantarev v Balgarska Narodna Banka, Case C-571/16, ECLI:EU:C:2018:807 .... 4.15–4.17, 4.33,
  7.53, 7.54, 7.58
Kásler, Case C-26/13, ECLI:EU:C:2014:282 .... 10.52, 10.53
Keeling v OHIM, Case T-148/97, [1998] ECR II-2217................................. .3.03
Kesko v Commission, Case T-22/97, ECLI:EU:T:1999:327.............................. .3.08
Kik v OHIM, Case T-120/99, ECLI:EU:T:2001:189 .... 7.15, 13.26
Kluge v EBA, BoA D 2016/001 .... .13.17
KME Germany AG, Case C-272/09 P, ECLI:EU:C:2011:810 .... .3.08
Kolassa v Barclays Bank plc, Case C-375/13, ECLI:EU:C:2015:37 .... 8.10, 8.11
Kotnik and Others, Case C-526/14, ECLI:EU:C:2016:767 .... 4.28, 4.29, 7.29, 7.30,
  7.34, 7.37, 7.86, 7.89
Laboratoires pharmaceutiques Bergaderm SA and Jean-Jacques Goupil v Commission
  of the European Communities, Case C-352/98 P, [2000] ECR I-5291.................... .3.11
Lafonta v Autorité des marchés financiers, Case C-628/13, ECLI:EU:C:2015:162............... .9.86
Landesbank Baden Württemberg v SRB, Case T-14/17, ECLI:EU:T:2018:812.................. .7.18

Landesbank Baden-Württemberg v SRB, Case T-411/17, ECLI:EU:T:2020:435;
  Joined Cases C-584/20 P and C-621/20 P, ECLI:EU:C:2021:601 .... 7.18, 7.19, 13.25
Landeskreditbank Baden-Württemberg v ECB, Case T-122/15, ECLI:EU:T:2017:337;
  Case C-450/17 P, ECLI:EU:C:2019:372 .... 4.21, 4.22, 4.24, 4.93, 6.10–6.12, 6.15, 6.76
LBI hf v Kepler Capital Markets SA and Frédéric Giraux, Case C-85/12,
  ECLI:EU:C:2013:697 .... 7.88, 7.90
Ledra Advertising and Others v Commission, Case T-289/13, ECLI:EU:T:2014:981,
  Joined Cases C-8/15 and C-10/15, ECLI:EU:C:2016:701 .... 4.09, 4.10, 7.31, 7.32,
    7.34, 7.35, 7.37, 7.86
Les Verts, Case C-294/83, [1986] ECR I-1357... 3.03, 3.06
Lexitor sp zoo v Spółdzielcza Kasa Oszczędnościowo—Kredytowa im Franciszka Stefczyka,
  Santander Consumer Bank SA, mBank SA, Case C-383/18 ....12.63
Liaño Reig v SRB, Case T-557/17, ECLI:EU:T:2019:771; Case C-947/19, ECLI:EU:C:2021:172 .... 4.56
Losch, Case T-13/97, ECLI:EU:C:T:1998:230..13.26
LPN and Finland v Commission, Joined Cases C-514/11 P and C-605/11 P,
  ECLI:EU:C:2013:738 .... 4.82, 13.34
Malacalza Investimenti v ECB, Case T-552/19, ECLI:EU:T:2020:294 ....4.80
Mallis, Case C-105/15, ECLI:EU:C:2016:702 .... 7.31, 7.32
Marcin Bonda v Commission, Case C-489/10, ECLI:EU:C:2012:319 ....6.81
MAS and MB, Case C-42/17, ECLI:EU:C:2017:936.......................................3.05
Matei, Case C-143/13, ECLI:EU:C:2015:127.. 10.52, 10.53
Melki and Abdeli, Joined Cases C-188/10 and C-189/10, ECLI:EU:C:2010:2016 ....13.26
Melloni v Ministerio Fiscal, Case C-399/11, ECLI:EU:C:2013:107 ....3.05
Menci v Procura della Repubblica, Case C-524/15, ECLI:EU:C:2018:197 .... 3.08, 6.99
Menini v Banco Popolare, Case C-75/16, ECLI:EU:C:2017:457............................13.47
Meroni v High Authority, Case 9/56, [1957–8] ECR 133................. 1.33, 3.08, 3.09, 4.43, 4.44,
    6.27–6.29, 7.13, 13.36
Microsoft, Case T-201/04, ECLI:EU:T:2007:289 ....12.50
Miles and Others v Écoles européennes, Case C-196/09, ECLI:EU:C:2011:388................12.59
Modelo Continente Hipermercados, Case C-343/13, ECLI:EU:C:2015:146 .... 8.21, 9.57, 9.144
Mory and Others v Commission, Case C-33/14 P, ECLI:EU:C:2015:609 ....4.58
Mostaza Claro, Case C-168/05, ECLI:EU:C:2006:675 ....10.54
Netherlands v Commission, Case C-308/95, ECLI:EU:C:1999:477........................4.30
Neurim Pharmaceuticals v OHIM, Case T-218/06, ECLI:EU:T:2008:379 .... 7.15, 13.26
Nordea Bank v ESMA, BoA D 2019 07 ....6.41
Nordic Banks v ESMA, BoA D in Cases 1/18, 2/18, 3/18 and 4/18,
  (27 February 2019).. 6.93, 13.20, 13.57
Nordsee v Reederei Mond, Case C-102/81, ECLI:EU:C:1982:107 ....12.56
NRW Bank v SRB, Case T-446/16, ECLI:EU:T:2019:445, Case C-662/19 P, ECLI:EU:C:2021:846 ..... 13.25
OC and Others v Banca d'Italia and Others, Case C-686/18, ECLI:EU:C:2020:567 .... 6.53, 6.54
OCU v SRB, Case T-496/18(pending) 4.82
Oleificio Borell v Commission, Case C-97/91, ECLI:EU:C:1992:491 ....4.40
Onix v EIOPA, BoA D 2015/001 (24 November 2014) 13.17
Ontier España, Case T-480/ 18, ECLI:EU:T:2018:871 ....4.82
Opinion 1/09 of the Court, ECLI:EU:C:2011:123................................. 13.64, 14.07
Opinion 1/17 of the Court, ECLI:EU:C:2019:341................................. 12.13, 13.64
Opinion 2/13 on the accession of the EU to the ECHR of 18 December 2014,
  ECLI:EU:C:2014:2454 ....13.62
Orkem v Commission, Case C-374/87, ECLI:EU:C:1989:387 .... 6.87, 6.89
Österreichischer Rundfunk, Case C-195/06, ECLI:EU:C:2007:613........................12.58
Otis and Others, Case C-199/11, ECLI:EU:C:2012:684....................................12.50
Pannon, Case C-243/08, ECLI:EU:C:2009:350...10.54
Parfums Christian Dior v Evora, Case C-337/95, ECLI:EU:C:1997:517 ....12.59
Parodi v Banque H Albert de Bary, Case C-222/95, [1997] ECR I-3899 ....6.40
Paul and Others, Case C-222/02, ECLI:EU:C:2004:606................... 4.15, 4.17, 7.52, 7.55
Pilatus Bank plc and Pilatus Holding Ltd v ECB, Case T-27/19,
  ECLI:EU:T:2022:46 .... 4.21, 4.42, 6.61, 6.84, 6.98, 13.07, 13.26

Plaumann & Co v Commission, Case 25/62, [1963] ECR 95 . . . . 3.11, 4.52, 13.04
PNB Banka v ECB, Case T-275/19, ECLI:EU:T:2022:781 . . . . .6.17
PNB Banka v ECB, Case T-301/19, ECLI:EU:T:2022:774 . . . . .6.17
PNB Banka v ECB, Case T-330/19, ECLI:EU:T:2022:775 . . . . .6.17
PNB Banka v ECB, Case T-230/20, ECLI:EU:T:2022:782 . . . . .6.17
Polbuod, Case C-106/16, ECLI:EU:C:2017:804 . . . . .8.06
Portigon v SRB, Case T-365/16, ECLI:EU:T:2019:824 . . . . 4.41, 7.18, 13.25
Pringle v Government of Ireland and Others, Case C-370/12,
    ECLI:EU:C:2012:756 . . . . 4.09, 4.10, 5.07, 5.12, 5.20
Procter & Gamble v OHIM, Case T-63/01, [2002] ECLI:EU:T:2002:317 . . . . .12.48
Puskar v Finance EU, Case C-73/16, ECLI:EU:C:2017:725 . . . . .12.61
Queen v Treasury and Commissioners of Inland Revenue ex parte Daily Mail and
    General Trust plc, General Trust plc, Case C-81/87, ECLI:EU:C:1988:456 . . . . .8.06
Réexamen Simpson v Council, Joined Cases C-542/18 RX-II and C-543/18 RX-II,
    ECLI:EU:C:2020:232 . . . . .12.11
Remia BV and Others v Commission of the European Communities, Case C-42/84,
    ECLI:EU:C:1985:327 . . . . 12.44, 12.50
Repsol Comercial de Productos Petroliferos, Case C-25/21, ECLI:EU:C:2022:659 . . . . .13.55
Rewe v Landwitschaftskammer Saarland, Case C-33/76, [1976] ECR 1989 . . . . .13.04
Reynolds Tobacco v Commission, Case C-131/03 P, ECLI:EU:C:2006:541 . . . . .4.39
Rimšēvičs v Latvia and European Central Bank v Republic of Latvia, Joined Cases
    C-202/18 and C-238/18, ECLI:EU:C:2019:139 . . . . .5.24
Romano v INAMI, Case 98/80, [1981] ECR 1259 . . . . 3.09, 6.27, 13.36
Roquette Frères v Commission, Case T-322/01, ECLI:EU:T:2006:267 . . . . .6.99
RTL Belgium, Case C-517/09, ECLI:EU:C:2010:82 . . . . .12.12
RWE, Case C-92/11, ECLI:EU:C:2013:180 . . . . .10.53
Saint-Gobain Glass Deutschland, Case C-60/15, ECLI:EU:C:2017:540 . . . . 4.82, 13.34
Sales Sinues v Caixabank SA Case C-381/14, ECLI:EU:C:2016:252 . . . . .13.51
Salgoil v Italy, Case C-13/68, [1968] ECR 453 . . . . .13.04
Satabank v ECB, Case T-494/20, ECLI:EU:T:2021:797 . . . . 4.20, 4.21
Schrems v Data Protection Commissioner, Case C-362/14, ECLI:EU:C:2015:650 . . . . 7.15, 13.26
Scope Ratings GmbH v ESMA, BoA D 2020/03 (28 December 2020) 12.48, 13.22
SEVIC, Case C-411/03, ECLI:EU:C:2005:762 . . . . .8.06
Siragusa, Case C-206/13, ECLI:EU:C:2014:126 . . . . .3.13
Skandinaviska Enskilda Banken v ESMA, BoA D 2019 05 . . . . 6.41, 13.21
Slowakische Republik v Achmea BV, Case C-284/16, ECLI:EU:C:2018:158 . . . . 12.56, 13.62–13.64
SNUPAT Snupat v High Authority, Joined Cases 32/58 and 33/58, [1959] ECR 127 . . . . .3.03
Societatea de Asigurare-Reasigurare City Insurance SA v EIOPA, BoA D 2021/03
    (14 April 2021) 13.23
Société Générale v ECB, Case T-757/16, ECLI:EU:T:2018:473 . . . . 3.08, 6.63, 7.22
Sogelma, Case T-411/06, [2008] ECR II-2771 . . . . 3.03, 3.06
Spain and Italy v Council, Joined Cases C-274/11 and C-295/11, ECLI:EU:C:2013:240 . . . . .14.07
Spain v Commission, Case C-312/90, ECLI:EU:C:1992:282 . . . . .4.43
Spain v Commission, Case C-57/95, ECLI:EU:C:1997:164 . . . . .4.30
Spain v Eurojust, Case C-160/03, [2005] ECR I-2101 . . . . 3.03, 12.43
Spain v European Parliament and Council, Case C-146/13, ECLI:EU:C:2015:298 . . . . .14.07
Spector Photo Group, Case C-45/08, ECLI:EU:C:2009:806 . . . . 6.82, 6.98
SPV Project 1503 Srl and Others v YB and Others v YX and ZW,
    Joined Cases C-693/19 . . . . 12.64, 13.04
SRB Appeal Panel Decision on Admissibility, case 1/22, June 2022 . . . . .4.47
State Street Bank International GmbH v Banca d'Italia, Case C-255/18, ECLI:EU:C:2019:967 . . . .7.15
Steinhoff and Others v ECB, Case T-107/17, ECLI:EU:T:2019:353 . . . . .4.10
Stichting Woonpunt and Others v Commission, Case C-415/15 P, ECLI:EU:C:2017:216 . . . . .4.39
SV Capital v EBA, BoA 2013-008; Ref EBA C 2013 002 (24 June 2013), Case T-660/14,
    ECLI:EU:T:2015:608 . . . . 4.20, 4.24, 4.96, 13.16, 13.17, 13.19
Svenska Handelsbanken, BoA D 2019 01 . . . . 6.41, 6.93, 13.20
Swedbank v ESMA, BoA D 2019 06 . . . . .6.41

Sweden and Others v API and Commission, Case C-514/07 P, ECLI:EU:C:2010:541......4.82, 13.34
Sweden v Commission, Case C-64/05 P, ECLI:EU:C:2007:802 ....4.40
Sweden v Commission, Case C-562/14 P, ECLI:EU:C:2017:356 .... 4.40, 4.82, 13.34
T Port GmbH & Co KG v Commission, Case T-52/99, [2001] ECR II-981...................3.11
Taricco and Others, Case C-105/14, ECLI:EU:C:2015:555......................................3.05
Technische Universität München, C-269/90, ECLI:EU:C:1991:438 ....3.08
Telefónica SA v Commission, Case C-274/12, ECLI:EU:C:2013:852........................3.11
Thomae v Commission, Case T-123/00, [2002] ECR II-05193............................3.03
ThyssenKrupp Stainless AG v Commission, Case T-24/07, ECLI:EU:T:2009:236..............6.99
T&L Sugars, Case C-456/13, ECLI:EU:C:2015:284 ....13.26
Toshiba & Others v Commission, Case C-17/10, ECLI:EU:C:2012:72 .... 6.81, 6.99
Trade Agency Ltd v Seramico Investments Ltd, Case C-619/10, ECLI:EU:C:2012:531..........13.44
TWD Textilwerke Deggendorf, Case C-188/92, ECLI:EU:C:1994:90 ....4.31
Überseering, Case C-208/00, ECLI:EU:C:2002:632....................................8.06
UBS Europe and Alain Hondequin and Others v DV and Others, Case C-358/1,
    ECLI:EU:C:2018:715 ....4.76, 4.78, 4.79, 13.35
Ukrselhosprom v ECB, Joined Cases T-351/18 and T-584/18, ECLI:EU:T:2021:669 ....6.15, 6.17,
    6.75, 6.76, 6.85, 6.92, 6.95, 13.07
Umweltanwalt von Kärnten, Case C-205/08, ECLI:EU:C:2009:767.........................12.58
Unicaja Banco, Case C-869/19, ECLI:EU:C:2022:397 .... 10.54, 12.64, 13.04
UniCredit Bank Austria v Verein für Konsumenteninformation, Case C-555/21,
    ECLI:EU:C:2023:78 ....12.63
Unifrex v Council and Commission, Case 281/82, [1984] ECR I-1969......................3.11
Union de Pequeños Agricultores v Council, Case C-50/00 P, ECLI:EU:C:2002:462...... 3.11, 4.52, 13.04
United Kingdom of Great Britain and Northern Ireland v European Parliament and
    Council, Case C-507/13, ECLI:EU:C:2014:2394 ....6.29
United Kingdom v European Central Bank, Case T-496/11, ECLI:EU:2015:133................4.31
United Kingdom v Parliament, Case C-217/04, [2006] ECR I-3771 ....6.28
United Kingdom v Parliament and Council, Case C-270/12, ECLI:EU:C:2014:18 ....3.09, 4.19,
    6.27, 6.28, 13.36
Vaassen (neé Göbbels), Case C-61/65, ECLI:EU:C:1966:39 ....12.12, 12.56
Versorgungswerk der Zahnärztekammer Schleswig-Holstein v European Central Bank,
    Case T-376/13, ECLI:EU:T:2015:361...4.82, 13.34
Vorarlberger Landes- und Hypothekenbank v SRB, Case T-414/17, ECLI:EU:T:2020:437 ....7.18
VQ v ECB, Case T-203/18, ECLI:EU:T:2018:261 .... 6.91, 6.92, 6.96, 6.98
VR-Bank Rhein-Sieg v SRB, Case T-42/17, ECLI:EU:T:2018:813 ....7.18
VTB Bank (Austria) v Finanzmarktaufsichtsbehörde, Case C-52/17, ECLI:EU:C:2018:648......6.85
Weiss and Others, Case C-493/17, ECLI:EU:C:2018:1000 .... 5.10, 5.15, 5.17, 5.19, 5.20,
    6.10–6.13, 6.76, 12.62
Wilson v Ordre des avocats du barreau du Luxembourg, Case C-506/04, ECLI:EU:C:2006:587 ......12.12
Ziegler SA v Commission, Case C-439/11 P, ECLI:EU:C:2013:513....................13.37, 14.14
ZSE Energia as v RG, Case C-627/17, ECLI:EU:C:2018:941..............................13.44
Zuckerfabrik Schoeppenstedt v Council, Case 5/71, [1971] ECR I-975 ....3.11

INTERNATIONAL ARBITRATION

BG Group plc v Republic of Argentina (2007) Final Award 7.84
CME Czech Republic BV v Czech Republic (2003) Award by Wolfgang Kühn,
    Stephen Schwebel, and Ian Brownlie under UNCITRAL Rules........................7.74
CME v Czech Republic (2001) Partial Award..7.84
GMB Global and Others v Spain, ICSID case 2018/33..................................13.62
International Thunderbird Gaming Corporation v United Mexican States (2006) Arbitral Award......7.84
Metalclad Corporation v The United Mexican States (2002) 5 ICSID Rep 209................7.84
Saluka Investments BV v Czech Republic (2006) Case No 2001-04, Partial Award,
    PCA Case Repository (Perm Ct Arb)..7.84
Tippets, Abbett, McCarthy, Stratton v TAMS-AFFA Consulting Engineers of Iran
    (1984) 6 Iran-US Cl Trib Rep 219...7.84

Valle Ruiz and Others v Spain, PCA Case 2019/17 .... 13.62
Waste Management Inc v The United Mexican States (2004) ICSID Case
    No ARB(AF)/00/3, 6 ICSID Rep 538 .... 7.84

INTERNATIONAL COURT OF JUSTICE

Case Concerning the Barcelona Traction, Light & Power Co [1970] ICJ Rep 3 .... 4.06
Jurisdictional Immunities of the State (Germany v Italy) [2012] ICJ Rep 99
    (3 February 2012) 4.03, 4.07

NATIONAL CASES

Australia

Cuthbertson & Richards Sawmills Pty Ltd v Thomas (1998) 28 ACSR 310 .... 11.74
Enron Australia Finance Pty Ltd (in liq) v TXU Electric Ltd (2003) 48 ACSR 266 (NSW) 10.114,
                                                                                10.117, 10.119
Lewis v Doran (2005) 219 ALR 555 .... 11.74
Southern Cross Interiors Pty Ltd v Deputy Commissioner of Taxation (2001) 39 ACSR 305 ..... 11.74

AUSTRIA

Constitutional Court, G-239/14, AUT-2015-1-002 (3 July 2015) 7.34
OGH judgment 6 Ob 28/12d (15 March 2012) 9.61
OGH judgment 7 Ob 77/10i (30 March 2011) 9.61

CANADA

Canadian National Railway v Norsk Pacific Steamship Co 91 DLR (4th) 289 (1992) 9.04
Metropolitan Toronto Police Widows and Orphans Fund v Telus Communications Inc
    (2005) 75 OR (3d) 784 (CA) 11.18

FRANCE

Conseil d'Etat [1989] no 108243 .... 3.05
Cour de cassation 73-13556 .... 3.05
Cour de cassation (1ère Chambre Civile) no 10-25/ 938, 11-10/450 and 11-13/323
    (28 March 2013) 4.03, 4.04
Cour de cassation (Chambre commercial, financière et économique)
    no 10-13.988/10-13.989/10-13.990 (8 March 2011) 11.71
Paris Commercial Court (3 November 2008) RG no 2008077996 and RG no 2008077997 .... 11.71
Paris Court of Appeal 25 February 2010, RG no 09/22756 .... 11.71

GERMANY

BGH (Federal Supreme Court)
    I ZR84/54 (28 February 1956) BGHZ 20, 119 .... 10.10
    BGHZ 66, 51, NJW 1976, 712 (28 January 1976) 9.08
    1979, 548, NJW 1979, 1595 (12 February 1979) 9.08
    II ZR 124/81 (24 May 1982) 9.59
    II ZR 172/81, NJW 1982, 2827 (12 July 1982) 9.73
    III ZR 201/88 (13 July 1989) 10.14
    III ZR 217/85 (15 January 1987) XI ZR 252/89 (13 March 1990) 10.14
    XI ZR 12/93 (6 July 1993) 10.71
    XI ZR 214/92 (16 November 1993) BGHZ 124 .... 10.90
    III ZR 245/96 (2 April 1998) 9.114
    III ZR 62/99 (13 January 2000) 10.75

V ZR 437/99 (19 January 2001) BGHZ 146 298 (19 January 2001) 10.14
X ZR 250/02 (20 April 2004). 9.115, 9.117
X ZR 283/02 (8 June 2004). 9.140
II ZR 393/02 (14 June 2004) 10.46
II ZR 218/03, BGHZ 160 (19 July 2004). 9.87
XI ZR 255/03 (26 October 2004) 10.46
II ZR 187/02, NZG 2005 (9 May 2005). 9.87
III ZR 413/04 (12 May 2005). 10.75
III ZR 256/04 (6 April 2006) 9.115, 9.117
XI ZR 204/04 (19 September 2006) 10.46
II ZR 80/04, NZG 2007 (guidance order of 28 November 2005) 9.87
XI ZR 56/05 (19 December 2006). 10.76
XI ZR 414/04 (20 March 2007). 10.46
III ZR 218/06 (22 March 2007). 10.75
III ZR 145/06- NJW-RR 2007 (12 July 2007). 10.75
XI ZR 322/03 (6 November 2007). 10.47
XI ZR 510/07 (20 January 2009) 10.73
III ZR 17/08 (5 March 2009) 10.75
III ZR 277/08 (7 May 2009). 9.115, 9.117
VII ZB 37/08 (1 October 2009). 4.06
XI ZR 93/09 (9 March 2010) 10.15
III ZR 249/09 (8 July 2010) 10.90
III ZR 144/10 (17 February 2011). 10.75
XI ZR 191/10, WM2011 (9 March 2011). 10.73
XI ZR 33/10 (22 March 2011) 10.72, 10.75, 10.90
XI ZR 178/10 (27 September 2011) 10.71
XI ZR 182/10 (27 September 2011) 10.71, 10.73
III ZR 103/10 (17 November 2011) 9.59
XI ZR 220/10 (29 November 2011) 10.14
NJW 2012 (13 December 2011) 9.88
XI ZR 51/10 NJW 2012 (13 December 2011) 9.91
II ZR 30/10 (23 April 2012) 9.59
II ZR 211/09 (23 April 2012). 9.59
XI ZR 262/10 (8 May 2012) 10.90
IX ZR 145/11 (14 June 2012). 9.116
XI ZR 344/11, BGHZ 195 NJW 2013, 539 (18 September 2012) 9.59, 9.73
II ZR 82/11 (23 October 2012) 9.59
II ZR 252/11 (5 March 2013). 9.59
VII ZB 63/12 (4 July 2013). 4.06
XI ZR 332/12 (19 December 2013). 10.76
IX ZR 245/12 (6 February 2014). 9.116
III ZR 156/13 (24 April 2014) 9.116, 9.140
XI ZR 147/12 (3 June 2014). 10.74
XI ZR 316/13 (20 January 2015) 10.75
XI ZR 378/ 13, BGHZ205, 117 Rn. 69 (28 April 2015). 10.10, 10.13, 10.14
IX ZR 252/15 (21 July 2016) 9.116
KZR 73/15 (15 November 2016). 9.91
III ZR 93/16 (23 March 2017). 10.90
XI ZR 152/17 (19 December 2017). 10.15
VII ZR 232/17 (21 November 2018). 9.116, 9.140
III ZR 109/17 (10 January 2019) 10.90
II ZB 18/17 (22 January 2019). 9.140
III ZR 498/16 (7 February 2019). 10.90
III ZR 176/18 (16 May 2019). 10.90
VII ZR 236/19 (12 March 2020) 9.118
VI ZR 252/19 (25 May 2020). 9.90
II ZB 10/19 (16 June 2020). 9.90

II ZB 31/14 (17 December 2020) ECLI: DE:BGH:2020:171220BIIZB31.14.0 .... 9.88
BVerfG (Federal Constitutional Court)
    2 BvL 52/71 (29 May 1974) (Solange I) 3.05
    2 BvR 2, 197/83 (22 October 1986) (Solange II) 3.05
    2 BvR 2134/92, 2 BvR 2159/92 (12 October 1993) (Maastricht)................... 3.02, 5.18
    2 BvE 2/08, 2BvE 5/08, BVerfG 2 BvR 1010/08, 2 BvR 1022/08, 2 BvR 1259/08 and
        2 BvR 182/09123 (30 June 2009) (Treaty of Lisbon)........................... 3.05, 5.18
    2 BvR 2661/06 (6 July 2010), BVerfGE 126 Case 2 BvR 2661/06 (6 July 2010) (Honeywell).....3.05
    2 BvR 2728/13 (14 January 2014) 5.10
    2 BvR 2728/13, 2 BvE 13/13, 2 BvR 2731/13, 2 BvR 2730/13, 2 BvR 2729/13 (21 June
        2016) (Gauweiler II).. 5.14
    2 BvR 1685/14, 2 BvR 2631/14 (SSM/SRM) (30 July 2019) 4.89, 5.20, 6.10, 6.12–6.14, 7.09, 7.10
    2 BvR 739/17, Order of the Second Senate (13 February 2020) 14.06
    2 BvR 859/15, 2 BvR 1651/15, 2 BvR 2006/15 and 2 BvR 980/16
        (5 May 2020) (Weiss II) 5.15–5.19
    1 BvR 2656/18, 1 BvR 288/20, 1 BvR 96/20, 1BvR 78/20 (24 March 2021) 12.39
    2 BvR 2216/20 (23 July 2021) 14.06
Higher Regional Court of Stuttgart, resolution of 27 March 2019 (Case No 20 Kap 2 – 4/17) 9.90
LG Berlin judgment – 11 o 5/19 (5 May 2020) 9.117
OLG Dresden, 5 U 1146/18 (6 March 2019) 9.117
OLG Düsseldorf, 6 U 50/17 (2 August 2018)... 9.117
OLG Munich, KAP 3/10 (15 December 2014) 9.91
OLG Stuttgart, 2 U 102/14 (26 March 2015) BeckRS 2015, 05690 .... 9.91
Regional Court, Munich I, BayernLB v Hypo Alpe Adria [2015] BeckRS 2015 .... 7.89, 7.90
Reichsgericht (Sixth Civil division) RGZ 78, 239, JW 1912, 191 (7 December 1911) 9.08

HONG KONG

Incorporated v Yun Choy Limited and the Standard Chartered Bank (Hong Kong)
    Limited [2012] 1 HKLRD 11.18

IRELAND

Quinn v Irish Bank Resolution Corp [2015] IESC 29 .... 10.22

ITALY

Consiglio di Stato, judgment no 06254/2022 (17 July 2022) 12.50
Constitutional Court
    no 29 (25 February 2002).. 12.69
    no 218 (21 July 2011) 13.49
    no 162 (27 June 2012).. 13.10
    no 94 (15 April 2014) 13.10
    no 267 (17 December 2017) 12.06
    no 84/21 (30 April 2021) 6.90, 12.06
Court of Appeal of Milan
    15 April 2009.. 10.77
    18 September 2013 .... 10.20
    15 January 2014... 9.74
    28 July 2020 .... 10.21
Supreme Court
    Cass Civ n 7776 (5 April 2004) 10.77
    Cass Civ n 17340 (25 June 2008).. 10.77
    Cass Civ n 14056 (11 June 2010).. 9.58, 9.74
    Cass Civ n 26724, 26725 (19 December 2007) 10.78
    Cass Civ n 24675 (19 October 2017) 12.69
    Cass Civ n 8770 (12 May 2020)....................................... 10.12, 10.19, 10.47

Tribunal of Milan
  1 July 2011 .... 9.120
  17 January 2014. .... 9.74
14 October 2020 .... 10.21
Tribunal of Rome, 27 March 2015 .... 9.120
Tribunal of Treviso, 5 May 2022 .... 12.69
Tribunal of Turin, 2 November 2021 .... 12.64
Tribunal of Venezia, 5 June 2019. .... 12.69

LITHUANIA

Constitutional Court, Case no 17/02-24/02-06/03-22/04 (14 March 2006) 3.05

NETHERLANDS

Hoge Raad, HR, nr 07/11104 (27 November 2009) ECLI:NL:HR:2009:BH2162
  (World Online). 9.70, 9.71, 9.75

POLAND

Constitutional Court
  K 18/04 (11 May 2005). 3.05
  SK 7/06 (24 October 2007) 12.11

PORTUGAL

Lisbon Court of Appeal, 2118-10.2TVLSB.L1.-2 (2 July 2015). 10.19
Supreme Court of Justice
  531/11.7TVLSB.L1.S1 (29 January 2015) 10.19
  309/11.8TVLSB.L1.S1 (11 February 2015) 10.19
  876/12.9TVLSB.L1 (26 January 2016). 10.19

SPAIN

Audiencia Nacional, 29 September 2020 (no 13/2020) 9.64, 9.78
Constitutional Court
  STC 64/1991 (22 March 1991) 3.05
  STC 26/2014 (13 February 2014) 3.05
Supreme Court
  27 April 1992 (RJ 1992/3414) 8.20
  2 February 2001 (RJ 2001/1685). 11.23
  11 February 2003 (RJ 2003/938). 11.23
  27 June 2003 (RJ 2003/4313). 11.23
  5 March 2004 (RJ 2004/1811) 11.23
  28 May 2004 (RJ 2004/3553) 11.23
  6 October 2004 (RJ 2004/5986). 11.23
  4 December 2007 (RJ 2007/8897). 11.23
  9 October 2008 (Roj 5445/2008). 9.119
  14 October 2008 (RJ 2008/6913) 9.119
  5 March 2009 (no 115/2009) 9.119
  27 May 2009 (no 355/2009). 9.119
  19 June 2009 (RJ 2009/4449) 10.06
  7 June 2012 (no 338/2012). 9.119
  21 November 2012 (STS 683/12, RJ 2012/11052) ES:TS:2012:7843. .... 10.79, 12.65
  3 January 2013 (RJ 2013/1628) 11.28
  9 May 2013 (STS 1916/2013) ES:TS:2013:1916. .... 10.52, 12.66
  20 January 2014 (RJ 2014/781) 10.80, 10.91, 12.66

7 July 2014 (n 384/2014) ES:TS:2014:2659 ....10.80
7 July 2014 (n 385/2014) ES:TS:2014:2660 ....10.80
15 December 2014 (RJ 56/2015) ECLI:ES:TS:2014:5411...................................12.66
12 January 2015 (RJ 608/2015) 12.66
15 September 2015 (RJ 3993/2015) ECLI:ES:TS:2015:3868 ....12.66
16 September 2015 (RoJ 4004/2015) ECLI:ES:TS:2015:4004 ....12.66
15 October 2015 (RJ 5030/2015) ECLI:ES:TS:2015:4237 ....12.66
13 November 2015 (RJ 4664/2015 ....12.66
4 December 2015 (RJ 5461/2015) ECLI:ES:TS:2015:4946..................................12.66
9 December 2015 (RJ 674/2015) ECLI:ES:TS:2015:5154....................................12.66
10 December 2015 (RJ 5777/2015) ECLI:ES:TS:2015:5156 ....12.66
3 February 2016 (nos23/2016, and 24/2016)................................... 9.64, 9.75, 9.78
25 February 2016 (RoJ 610/2016) ECLI:ES:TS:2016:610....................................12.66
8 April 2016 (RJ 1496/2016) ECLI:ES:TS:2016:1644 ....12.66
19 May 2016 (JUR 117371/2016) 12.66
3 June 2016 (RJ 3863/2016) ECLI:ES:TS:2016:2596..12.66
29 June 2016 (RoJ 3138/2016) ECLI:ES:TS:2016:3138 ....12.66
13 July 2016 (RJ 3194/2016) ECLI:ES:TS:2016:3461 ....12.66
15 July 2016 (RJ 3201/2016) ECLI:ES:TS:2016:3465 ....12.66
30 September 2016 (RJ 4581/ 2016) ECLI:ES:TS:2016:4304..............................12.66
5 October 2016 (RJ 225150/2016) 12.66
23 November 2016 (no 691/2016; JUR 261556/2016) 12.66
21 September 2018 (no 520/2018) 9.119
1 June 2021 (no 380/2021) ECLI:ES:TS:2021:2251 (Bankia II)..................... 9.78, 9.82
2 June 2022 (STS 2150/2022) ECLI:ES:TS:2022:2150 .... 9.78, 9.82

UNITED KINGDOM

ABN AMRO Bank NV v Bathurst Regional Council [2014] FCAFC 65 ....9.110
Acevedo v Imcopa Importacao [2012] EWHC 1849 (Comm) 11.78
Achilleas, The [2008] UKHL 48, [2009] 1 AC...10.65
Adams v Options Sipp UK LLP and Financial Conduct Authority [2020] EWHC 1229 (Ch) 10.67
Adams v Options UK Personal Pensions LLP [2021] EWCA Civ 474 .... 10.66, 10.67, 10.86–10.88
AG of Belize v Belize Telecom Ltd [2009] UKPC 10..11.92
Antaios Compania Naviera SA v Salen Rederierna AB [1985] AC 191 ....10.97
Anthracite Rated Investments (Jersey) Ltd v Lehman Brothers Finance SA
    [2011] EWHC 1822 (Ch).. 10.118
Armitage v Nurse [1998] Ch 241 .... 11.94, 11.102
Ashbury Railway v Riche (1875) LR 7 HL 653 ....10.06
Assénagon Asset Management SA v Irish Bank Corp Ltd [2012] EWHC 2090 (Ch)...... 11.84, 11.87
Associated Provincial Picture Houses Ltd v Wednesbury Corporation [1948] 1 KB 223 ...... 10.100
Azevedo v Imcopa Importaçao [2012] EWHC 1849 (Comm); [affd] [2013] EWCA Civ 364.....11.84
Banca Intesa Sanpaolo SPA & Anor v Comune Di Venezia [2022] EWHC 2586 (Comm) 10.12
Bank Leumi (UK) Plc v Wachner [2011] EWHC 656 (Comm) 10.39, 10.41
Bank of NY v Montana Board Investments [2008] EWHC 1594 (UK) 11.65, 11.104
Bankers Trust International v PT Dharmala Sakti Sejahter [1996] CLC 518 ....10.37
Banque Bruxelles Lambert SA v Eagle Star Insurance Co Ltd [1996] UKHL 10................9.106
Barclays Bank plc and Others v HHY Luxembourg SARL and Another
    [2010] EWCA Civ 1248..10.98
Bathurst Regional Council v Local Government Financial Services Pty Ltd (No 5)
    [2012] FCA 1200 ....9.110
BNY Corporate Trustee Services Ltd v Eurosail-UK 2007-3BL plc and Others (BNY Ltd v
    Eurosail plc (CA)) [2011] EWCA Civ 227...................................11.65, 11.70, 11.75, 11.76
BNY Corporate Trustee Services Ltd v Eurosail-UK 2007-3BL plc and Others
    [2010] EWHC 2005 (Ch)...11.70
Boyse (International) Ltd v NatWest Markets plc and Another [2021] EWHC 1387 (Ch) 9.92
BPE Solicitors v Hughes-Holland [2017] UKSC 21 ....9.108

Braganza v BP Shipping [2015] UKSC 17 .... 10.100
Britannia Bulk plc v Pioneer Navigation Ltd and Others
 [2011] EWHC 692 (Comm) 10.115, 10.117–10.119
Caparo Industries PLC v Dickman [1990] UKHL 2........................ 9.04, 9.05, 9.106, 9.107,
9.110, 9.115, 9.143, 13.58
Cassa Di Risparmio Della Repubblica Di San Marino Spa v Barclays Bank Ltd
 [2011] EWHC 484 (Comm) 10.39
Casurina Ltd Partnership v Rio Algom Ltd [2004] 40 BLR (3d) 112 ....11.78
Charnley Davies Ltd (No 2), Re [1990] BCLC 760......................................11.77
Chartbrook Ltd v Persimmon Homes Ltd [2009] 1 AC 1101 ....10.97
Charter Reinsurance Co Ltd [1997] AC 313 .... 11.110
Cheyne Finance plc (In Receivership), In re [2007] EWHC 2402 (Ch), [2008] Bus LR 1562,
 [2008] 2 All ER 987, [2008] BCC 182, [2008] 1 BCLC 741, [2008] 1 BCLC 732........... 11.65,
11.72, 11.73, 11.74, 11.76, 11.109, 11.112
Citibank NA v MBIA (CA) [2007] All ER (D) 141 ....11.101, 11.105
Citicorp Trustee Co Ltd v Barclays Bank Plc [2013] EWHC 2608 (Ch)................ 11.86, 11.87
Cornish v Midland Bank [1985] 3 All ER 513.....................................10.37, 10.43
Credit Suisse International v Stichting Vestia Groep [2014] EWHC 3103 (Comm) 10.10
Crestsign Ltd v National Westminster Bank Plc & Anor [2014] EWHC 3043 (Ch)...... 10.41–10.43,
10.65, 10.69, 10.83, 10.85
Customs and Excise Commissioners v Barclays Bank plc [2006] UKHL 28, [2007] 1 AC 181 . . . .9.106
Cutler v Wandsworth Stadium Ltd [1949] AC 398..8.18
Dadourian v Simms and Others [2009] EWCA Civ 169 ....10.39
Derry v Peek [1889] UKHL 1 ....9.106
Deutsche Bank AG London v Commune di Busto Arsizio [2021] EWHC 2706 (Comm) 10.12
Deutsche Bank AG v Comune di Savona [2017] EWHC 1013 (Comm) 12.70
Dexia Crediop SpA v Comune di Prato [2015] EWHC 1746 (Comm) 10.16
Donoghue v Stevenson [1932] All ER Rep 1, [1932] AC 562........................ 9.05, 9.106
Eckerle and Others v Wickeder Westfalenstahl GmbH & Another [2013] EWHC 68 (Ch) 11.48
Elektrim SA v Vivendi Holdings 1 Corp Law Debenture Trust Corp plc v
 Vivendi Holdings 1 Corp [2008] EWCA Civ 1178....................11.61, 11.62, 11.65, 11.78
Elliott International LP and Others v Law Debenture Trustees Limited
 [2006] EWHC 3063 (Ch)..11.63, 11.78
Enviroco Ltd v Farstad Supply A/S [2010] Bus LR 1008 ....11.76
F2G Realisations Ltd: Gray v GTP Group Limited, Re [2011] 1 BCLC 313...................11.45
Forsta AP-Fonden v Bank of New York Mellon [2013] EWHC 3127 (Comm)................10.65
Gan Insurance Co Ltd v Tai Ping Insurance Co Ltd [2001] CLC 1103;
 [2011] EWCA Civ 1047; [2001] 2 All ER (Comm) 299 ....10.97
George Inglefield Ltd, In Re [1933] Ch 1 ....11.16, 11.17
Golden Key Ltd (In Receivership), In the Matter of [2009] EWCA Civ 636 ....10.98
Golden Key Ltd (In Receivership), v In the Matter of the Insolvency Act 1986
 [2009] EWHC 148 (Ch)......................... 11.59, 11.61, 11.65, 11.112, 11.114, 11.115
Goldman Sachs v Novo Banco [2015] EWHC 2371 (Comm); [2018] UKSC 34............ 7.89, 7.90
Green and Rowley v Royal Bank of Scotland plc [2012] EWHC 3661 (QB) 10.65
Groves v Wimborne [1898] 2 QB 402 ....8.18
Grupo Hotelero Urvasco SA v Carey Value Added SL [2013] EWHC 1039 .... 10.108,
10.109, 10.123, 10.124
Guardians of New Zealand Superannuation Fund and Others v Novo Banco
 [2016] EWCA Civ 109 ....7.89
Harrison, In re [1880] 14 Ch D 19 ....11.34
Haugesund Kommune v Depfa ACS Bank [2010] EWCA Civ 579.....................10.07, 10.65
Hazell v Hammersmith and Fulham London Borough Council 1992] 2 AC 1.................10.07
Hedley Byrne & Co Ltd v Heller & Partners Ltd [1964] AC 465 .... 9.05, 9.07, 9.106,
10.37, 10.43, 10.65, 10.83, 13.58
Henderson v Merrett Syndicates Ltd [1995] 2 AC 145...................................10.85
Highberry Ltd v Colt Telecom Group Plc (No 1) [2002] EWHC 2503 (Ch) 11.61, 11.78
HIH Casualty and General Insurance Ltd [2008] UKHL 21 ....7.98

IFE Fund SA v Goldman Sachs International [2006] EWHC 2887 (Comm) 10.39
International Fina Services AG v Katrina Shipping Ltd (The Fina Samco)
    [1995] 2 Lloyd's Rep 344 . . . . .10.97
Investors Compensation Scheme Ltd v West Bromwich Building Society
    [1997] UKHL 28 . . . . 10.95, 11.110
Irvani v Irvani [2000] Lloyd's Rep 412 . . . . .10.60
Junior Books Ltd v Veitchi Co Ltd [1983] 1 AC 520 . . . . .9.07
Katz v Oak Industries Inc 508 A2d 873 (Del Ch 1986) 11.78
Kookmin Bank v Rainy Sky SA and Others [2010] 1 CLC 829, [2010] EWCA Civ 582,
    [2011] 1 All ER (Comm) 18, 130 Con LR 19 . . . . .10.97
Law Debenture Trust Corporation PLC v Ukraine [2017] EWHC 655,
    [2023] UKSC 11 . . . . 1.12, 4.04, 4.05, 12.70
LBI EHF v Raiffeisen Zentral Bank Osterreich [2017] EWHC 522) 10.100
Lehman Brothers International (Europe), In re [2009] EWHC 3228 (Ch) 11.50
Lehman Brothers International (Europe), In re [2010] EWCA Civ 917 .11.50
Lehman Brothers International (Europe) (in administration)
    [2012] EWHC 2997 (Ch) 11.44, 11.45, 11.50
Lehman Brothers International (Europe) v JFB Firth Rixson [2010] EWHC 3372 . . . . 10.100
Lehman Brothers Special Financing Inc v Carlton Communications Ltd
    [2011] EWHC 718 (Ch) 10.115
Lomas and Others v JFB Firth Rixson Inc and Others [2010] EWHC 3372 (Ch) 10.115
Lomas and Others v JFB Firth Rixson Inc and Others 2010] EWHC 3372 (Ch) 10.115
Lomas and Others v JFB Rixson [2012] EWCA 419 . . . . 10.115, 10.118, 10.119
Lomas v RAB Market Cycles (Master Fund) Limited [2009] EWHC 2545 (Ch) 11.46
Lonrho Ltd v Shell Petroleum Co Ltd (No 2) [1982] AC 173 . . . . .8.18
Mannai Investments Co Ltd v Eagle Star Life Assurance Co Ltd [1997] 2 WLR 945 . . . . .10.95
Marine Trade SA v Pioneer Freight Futures Co Ltd BVI and Another
    [2009] EWHC 2656 (Comm) 10.115, 10.119
Martin v Britannia Life Ltd [2000] Lloyds Rep 412 . . . . .10.60
Mercantile Inv & General Trust Co v International Co of Mexico [1893] 1 Ch 484 . . . . .11.84
Miramar Maritime Corp v Holborn Oil Trading Ltd [1984] 1 AC 676 . . . . 11.110
Mitsui Construction Co Ltd v A-G of Hong Kong 10.97
Money Markets International Stockbrokers Ltd v London Stock Exchange Ltd
    [2002] 1 WLR 1150 . . . . 11.34, 11.35
MTR Bailey Ltd v Barclays Bank plc [2014] EWHC 2882 QB 10.39
NML Capital Ltd v Republic of Argentina [2011] UKSC 31 . . . . 4.03, 4.06
Orion Finance Ltd v Crown Financial Management Ltd [1996] BCC 621 . . . . 11.17, 11.104
Parabola Investments Ltd & Another v Browallia CAL Ltd & Others
    [2009] EWHC 901 (Comm) 10.44
Paragon Finance plc v Nash and Others [2001] EWCA Civ 1466, [2002] 1 WLR 685 . . . . .10.99
Parmar & Another v Barclays Bank plc [2018] EWHC 1027 (Ch) 10.65, 10.69, 10.85
Peekay Intermark v Australia and New Zealand Banking Group [2006] EWCA Civ 386 . . . . 10.38,
    10.39, 10.63, 10.69, 10.83, 10.84
Peregrine Fixed Income v Robinson Department Store [2000] EWHC 99 (Comm) 10.117, 10.118
Perpetual Trustee Co Ltd v BNY Corporate Trustee Services Ltd [2009] EWCA Civ 1160,
    [2010] Bus LR 632, [2010] BCC 59, [2010] BPIR 174 . . . . 11.33–11.36, 11.38, 11.39, 11.41, 11.42
Pioneer Freight Futures Company Limited v TMT Asia Limited
    [2011] EWHC 778 (Comm) 10.117, 10.118, 10.121
Pioneer Freight Futures Company Ltd v Cosco Bulk Carrier Company Ltd
    [2011] EWHC 1692 (Comm) 10.115, 10.117, 10.119
Pioneer v TMT (No 2) [2011] EWHC 1888 (Comm) 10.119
Polly Peck International plc (In Administration), Re (No 4) [1996] 2 All ER 433,
    [1996] BCC 486 . . . . .11.28
Property Alliance Group (PAG) v Royal Bank of Scotland [2018] EWCA Civ 355 . . . . 9.92,
    9.93, 10.42–10.44
R v McQuoid [2009] EWCA Crim 1301, [2009] 4 All ER 388 . . . . .9.92
Raiffeisen Zentralbank Osterreich AG v The Royal Bank of Scotland Plc
    [2010] EWHC 1392 (Comm) 10.39, 10.63, 10.83

Rainy Sky and Others v Kookmin Bank [2011] UKSC 50 .... 11.92
Rainy Sky SA and Others v Kookmin Bank [2011] UKSC 50, 1 All ER (Comm) 1 .... 10.96–10.98
Redwood Master Fund Ltd v TD Bank Europe Ltd [2002] All ER (D) 141 .... 11.84
Roe v Sheffield City Council (No 1) [2004] QB 653 Court of Appeal (Civil Division) 8.18
Rolled Steel Products (Holdings) Ltd v British Steel Corp [1982] Ch 478 .... 10.06
Ross v Caunters (1980) Ch 297 .... 9.07
Rubenstein v HSBC Bank Plc [2011] EWHC 2304 (QB), [2012] EWCA Civ 1184 ...... 10.63, 10.64,
 10.67, 10.69, 10.83–10.85
RZB v RBS [2010] EWHC 1392 (Comm) 10.39, 10.40
Santander Totta v Companhia de Carris de Ferro de Lisboa [2016] EWHC 465 (Comm) 10.11,
 10.12, 10.17–10.19
SCM (United Kingdom) Ltd v WJ Whittall & Son Ltd [1971] 1 QB 337 .... 9.05
Sigma Finance Corporation (in administrative receivership), In Re [2009] UKSC 2;
 [2010] 1 All ER 571 .... 10.98
Sigma Sigma Corp, In Re [2009] BCC 393 .... 11.109, 11.110
Sigma Sigma Fin Corp (in administration) Re, In Re [2008] EWHC 2997 .... 11.65, 11.92, 11.109
Sinochem International Oil (London) Ltd v Mobil Sales and Supply Corp [2000] CLC 878 ..... 10.97
Socimer International Bank Ltd v Standard Bank London Ltd [2008] Bus LR 1304,
 [2008] 1 Lloyd's Rep 558, [2008] EWCA Civ 116 .... 10.99
South Australia Asset Management Corporation v York Montague Ltd (SAAMCO)
 [1996] 3 WLR 87 .... 9.106–9.108, 10.84, 10.85
Spartan Steel & Alloys Ltd v Martin & Co (Contractors) Ltd [1973] 1 QB 27 .... 9.05
Spectrum Plus Ltd, Re [2005] UKHL 41 .... 12.70
Springwell Navigation Corp v JP Morgan Bank [2008] EWHC 1186 (Comm);
 [2008] EWHC 1793 .... 10.39
Springwell Navigation Corp v JP Morgan Bank [2010] EWCA Civ 1221 .... 10.39
Standard Chartered v Ceylon Petroleum Corporation (CPC) [2011] EWHC 1785 (Comm),
 [2012] EWCA Civ 1049 .... 10.12
Stanford International Bank Ltd, ;Re [2010] EWCA Civ 137 .... 7.95
Thornbridge v Barclays [2015] EWHC 3430 (QB) 10.42, 10.69
Titan Steel Wheels Limited v Royal Bank of Scotland Plc [2010] EWHC 211 (Comm) 10.39
Torre Asset Funding v RBS [2013] EWHC 2670 .... 11.90
Torre v The Royal Bank of Scotland [2013] EWHC 2670 (Ch) [2013] WLR(D) 343 ... 10.100, 10.108,
 10.109, 11.91, 11.92
UBS AG, London Branch v Glas Trust Corporation Ltd & Fairhold Securitisation Ltd
 [2017] EWHC 1788 (Comm) 12.70
Ukraine v The Law Debenture Trust Corporation Plc (Rev 1) [2018] EWCA Civ 2026 .... 4.05
Walford v Miles [1992] 2 AC 128 .... 10.94
Walker v Inter-Alliance Group plc [2007] EWHC 1858 (Ch) 10.60, 10.67
Whistlejacket, Re [2008] EWHC 463 (Ch) 11.65, 11.93, 11.108, 11.113–11.115
Wickman Machine Tools Sales Ltd v Schuler AG [1974] AC 235 .... 10.97
X (Minors) v Bedfordshire County Council [1995] 2 AC 633 .... 8.18
Yam Seng Pte v International Trade Corp [2013] EWHC 111 (QB) 10.94

UNITED STATES

Aaron v SEC 446 US 680 (1980) 9.22, 10.34
Abbott Labs v Gardner 387 US 136 (1967) 3.02
Ables v Major Funding Corp 82 BR 443 (Bankr,SD Tex 1987) 11.20
Abrams v Dep't of Treasury 243 F App'x 4 (5th Cir 2007) 4.67
Abrams v OCC [2006] No 3:05-CV-2433-N ECF 4.66, 4.67
Abramson v Newlink Genetics Corp 965 F 3d 165 (2d Cir 2020) 9.29
Absolute Activist Value Master Fund Ltd v Ficeto 677 F 3d 60 (2d Cir 2012) 8.14, 8.15
Abu Dhabi Commercial Bank and Others v Morgan Stanley & Co Incorporated and
 Others 651 F Supp 2d 155 (SDNY 2009) 9.100, 9.103
Adams, In The Matter of Patrick OCC AA-EC-11-50 .... 6.70
ADE Systems Inc v Energy Labs Inc 183 A D 3d 791 (2d Dept 2020) 10.103
Affiliated Ute Citizens of Utah v United States 406 US 128 (1972) 9.19, 9.28

AG Capital Funding Partners LP v State Street Bank & Trust Co 896 N E 2d 61 (NY 2008) 11.95
AIG Advisor Group, In re 390 Fed Appx 495 (2d Cir 2009) 10.30
Akanthos Capital Management LLC v Compucredit Holdings Corp F 3d,
    2012 WL 1414247, 1 (11th Cir 2012)... 11.60, 11.78
Alexander v Compton (In re Bonham) 229 F 3d 750 (9th Cir 2000) 11.24
Alexander v Sandoval 532 US 275 (2001) 8.18
Alfred Dunhill of London Inc v Republic of Cuba 425 US 682 (1976).........................4.02
Allen v Wright 468 US 737 (1984) 3.10
Alliance Federal Savings and Loan Association v Federal Home Loan Bank Board
    (FHLBB) 782 F 2d 490, modified on other grounds, 790 F 2d 34 (5th Cir 1986) 7.68
Altria Group v Good 555 US 70 (2008) 3.04
Alves v United States 133 F 3d 1454 (Fed Cir 1998)..7.26
American Airlines Inc v United States 551 F 3d 1294 (Fed Cir 2008) 7.26
American Continental Corp, 22 Cl Ct (1991)...7.25
American Equity Investment Life Insurance Co v SEC 613 F 3d 166 (DC Cir 2010)........ 1.49, 6.50
American Express Co v Italian Colors Restaurant 333 S Ct 2304 (2013).....................13.61
Amgen Inc v CT Ret Plans & Trust Funds 568 US 455 (2013).........................9.33–9.36
Anderson v Abbott 321 US 349 (1944)...4.06
Anixter v Home-Stake Prod Co 77 F 3d 1215, (10th Cir 1998).............................9.125
Anschutz Corp v Merrill Lynch & Co WL 1134321 (ND Cal 2010)..........................9.100
Aon Financial Products v Société Générale 476 F 3d 90 (2d Cir 2007) 10.106
Appalachian Power Co v EPA 208 F 3d 1015 (DC Cir 2000)................................4.26
Archdiocese of Milwaukee Supporting Fund Inc v Halliburton Co 597 F 3d 330 (5th Cir 2010) 9.33
Arthur Andersen LLP v United States 544 US 696 (2005)............................. 2.43, 2.45
Assassination Archives Research Ctr Inc v Cent Intelligence Agency
    720 F Supp 217 (DDC 1989) 4.67
Associated Randall Bank v Griffin, Kubik, Stephens & Thompson Inc 3 F 3d 208
    (7th Cir 1993) 10.27
Atkinson v Inter-American Development Bank 156 F 3d 1335 (DC Cir 1998) 4.07
AT&T Mobility LLC v Conception 536 US 333 (2011) 13.61
Audax Credit Opportunities Offshore Ltd v TMK Hawk Parent Corp No 2021-50794
    (NY Sup Ct 2021) 11.60, 11.61, 11.83
Auer v Robbins 519 US 452 (1997).. 3.07, 4.27, 4.28
Ball v Board of Governors of Federal Reserve System 87 F Supp 3d 33 (DDC 2015)............4.62
Banco Espanol de Credito v Security Pacific National Bank 763 F Supp 36 (SDNY 1991),
    aff'd 973 F 2d 51 (2d Cir1992)..11.90
Banco Nacional de Cuba v Sabbatino 376 US 398 (1964) 4.01
Bank Markazi v Peterson 578 US 212, 136 S Ct 1310 (2016)..................................4.06
Bank of America v AIG Fin Prod Corp WL 5065477 (SDNY 2013) aff'd in part,
    509 F App'x 24 (2d Cir 2013).. 11.107
Bank of America v AIG Financial Products 08-Civ-6134-LAP (SDNY 2010) 11.107
Bank of New York Trust Co v Official Unsecured Creditors' Committee 584 F 3d 229 (2009)....11.31
Bank of New York v FDIC 453 F Supp 2d 82 (DDC 2006) aff'd 508 F 3d 1 (DC Cir 2007) 11.31,
                                                                                        11.32, 11.103
Bank of New York v First Millennium 607 F 3d 905 (2010)......... 11.32, 11.67, 11.88, 11.107, 11.111
Bank of NY 598 F Supp 2d... 11.111
Bank of NY Mellon Trust Co v Liberty Media Corp 29 A 3d 225 (Del 2011) 8.29
Bankers Life & Casualty Co v Crenshaw 486 US 71 (1988)...................................9.83
Banque Arabe et Intern d'inv v Maryland National Bank [1993] 819 F Supp 1282 (SDNY 1993).... 11.90
Banque Arabe et Internationale v Maryland National Bank 57 F 3d 146 (2d Cir 1995)..........11.90
Basic Inc v Levinson 485 US 224 (1988) 1.13, 1.14, 9.26, 9.27, 9.29–9.31, 9.33–9.36, 9.72, 9.83
Bates v Dow Agrosciences LLC 544 US 431 (2005) 3.04
Bear Stearns High-Grade Structured Credit Strategies Master Fund, re 374 BR 122
    (Bankr SDNY 2007) aff'd 389 BR 325 (SDNY 2008) 11.67
Bear v Coben (In re Golden Plan of Calif. Inc) 829 F 2d 705 (9th Cir 1986) 11.20
Becker v Bank of New York Mellon Trust Co NA, 172 F Supp 3d 777 (ED Pa 2016) 11.96
Bennett v Spear 520 US 154 (1997).. 3.10, 4.38

Berliner, Zisser, Walter & Gallegos v SEC 962 F Supp 1348 (D Colo 1997) 4.65, 4.66
Bily v Arthur Young & Co 3 Cal 4th 370, 834 P.2d 745, 11 Cal Rptr 2d 51 (1992) 9.111, 9.112
Birnbaum v Newport Steel Corp 193 F 2d 461 (1952) 9.19
Block v Community Nutrition Institute 467 US 340 (1984) 3.02
Bloomberg LP v Bd. of Governors of the Fed. Reserve System 649 F Supp 2d 262 (SDNY 2009) 4.64
Bloomberg v SEC 357 F Supp 2d 156 (DDC 2004) 4.68
Blue Chip Stamps v Manor Drug Stores 421 US 723 (1975) 1.13, 9.19, 12.70
BNP Paribas Mortgage Corp v Bank of America NA 778 F Supp 2d 375 (SDNY 2011) 11.98, 11.100
Board of Governors, FRS v Investment Co Inst 450 US 46 (1981) 6.23, 6.36
Board of Governors of Fed Reserve System v First Lincolnwood Corp 439 US 234, 238 (1978) 6.44
Board of Governors of FRS v Dimension Financial 474 US 361 (1986) 6.37
Board of Governors of the Federal Reserve System v MCorp Financial, Inc. aff'd in part
    and rev'd in part 112 S Ct 459 (1991) 6.44
BOKF NA v Caesars Entertainment Corp 144 F Supp 3d 459 (SDNY 2015) 11.81
Bowles v Russell 551 US 205 (2007) 3.02, 9.25
Bowles v Seminole Rock & Sand Co 325 US 410 (1945) 3.07
Bruce Energy Centre Ltd v Orfa Corp of America (In re Orfa Corp of Philadelphia)
    129 BR 404 (Bankr ED Pa 1991) 11.25
Bryan v Federal Open Market Committee 235 F Supp 877 (D Mont 1964) 4.12, 5.09
Bush v Gore 531 US 98 (2000) 12.05
Business Roundtable v SEC 647 F 3d 1144 (DC Cir 2011) 1.49, 6.50, 6.51
Butner v United States 440 US 48 (1979) 11.22
California Housing Securities, 959 F 2d 955 (Fed Cir 1992) 7.25
California Public Employees' Retirement System (Calpers) v Moody's Corp
    CGC-09-490241 (Super Ct Cal, SF County 2010) 9.102
Camp v Pitts 411 US 138 (1973) 7.66
Capital Network Systems Inc v FCC 28 F 3d 201 (DC Cir 1994) 3.07, 4.27
Carl v Galuska 785 F Supp 1283 (ND Ill 1992) 10.34
Carras v Burns 516 F 2d 251 (4th Cir 1975) 10.30
Carvelli v Ocwen Fin Corp 934 F 3d 1307 (11th Cir 2019) 9.28
Castaneda v Partida 430 US 473–77 (1977) 9.22
Central Bank Of Denver NA v First Interstate Bank Of Denver NA and Jack K Naber
    511 US 164 (1994) no 92-854 .... 9.31, 9.122, 9.123
Central European Industrial Development Company (CEIDCO) LLC d/b/a Ceidco,
    In Re 288 BR572 (Bankr ND Cal 2003) 576 .... 11.25
Chadbourne & Parke LLP v Troice 571 US 377 (2014) 9.45
Chamber of Commerce v SEC 412 F 3d 133 (DC Cir 2005) 1.49, 6.50
Charles Hughes & Co v SEC 139 F 2d 434 (2d Cir 1943) 10.28
Charter Communications Inc Securities Litigation, In re 443 F 3d 987 (2006) 9.126
Chasins v Smith, Barney & Co 438 F 2d 1167 (2d Cir 1970) 10.30
Chemical Bank; National Westminster Bank, USA v Security Pacific National Bank
    [1994] 20 F 3d 375 (9th Cir 1994) 11.90
Chesapeake Energy Corp v Bank of New York Mellon Trust Co NA No 13-1893 (2d Cir 2014) 10.102
Chesapeake Energy Corporation v Bank of New York Mellon Trust Company NA
    [2013] 57 F Supp 2d 316 (SDNY) 10.102
Chevron USA Inc v NRDC 467 US 837 (1984) 3.07, 4.27, 4.28, 6.24, 6.26, 6.70, 7.52, 12.51
Chiarella v United States 445 US 222 (1980) 9.50
Chicago & Southern Air Lines Inc v Waterman SS Corp 333 US 103 (1948) 4.38
Chrysler Corp v Brown, 441 US 281 S Ct (1979) 4.26
Chrysler Inc, Re 405 BR 79 (Bankr SDNY 2009) 4.53, 5.06
Cisneros v Alpine Ridge Group 508 US 10 (1993) 10.111
Citizens to Preserve Overton Park Inc v Volpe 401 US 402 (1971) 2.15, 3.02, 7.66, 7.70, 12.51
City of Dearborn Heights Act 345 Police & Fire Ret Sys v Align Tech Inc 856 F 3d 605
    (9th Cir 2017) 9.29
Clarke v SIA 479 US 388 (1987) 6.07
Clarkson v Greenspan No 97-2035 (DDC 1998) 4.66
Cleveland v United States 531 US 12 (2000) 2.45

Coeur Alaska Inc v Southeast Alaska Conservation Council 557 US 261 (2009) 3.07, 4.27
Cohens v Virginia 19 US 264 (1821). 3.04
Collie v FHLBB 642 F Supp 1147 (ND Ill 1986) 7.69
Collins v Yellen 141 S Ct 1761 (2021) 4.86, 4.87, 4.91, 5.23
Committee for Monetary Reform v Board of Governors No 83-1730
    (DDC 26 October 1983) aff'd, 766 F 2d 538 (DC Cir 1985) 4.12, 5.23
Commonwealth Acceptance Corp v Jordan 198 Cal 618, 246 Pac 96 (1926) 8.02
Compuware Corp v Moody's Investor Services Inc 499 F 3d 520 (6th Cir 2007) 9.99
Connick v Myers 461 US 147–48, 103 S Ct 1690 (1981) 9.97
Consumers Union of the US Inc v Heimann 589 F 2d 531 (DC Cir 1978) 4.65, 4.66
Consumers Union v Office of the Comptroller of Currency No 86-1841 (DDC 1988) 4.66
Convergent Techs Sec Litig, In re 948 F 2d 507 (9th Cir 1991) 9.27
Cort v Ash 422 US 66 (1975) 8.18
Credit Alliance Corporation v Arthur Andersen & Co (1985) 483 NE 2d 110 . . . . .9.110
Credit Lyonnais Bank Netherland NV v Pathé Communications Co
    [1991] Del Ch (Dec). 11.57, 12.70
Cromwell v Benson 285 US 22 (1932) 3.07, 12.09
Cruden v Bank of NY 957 F 2d 961 (2d Cir 1992) 11.60
CSBS v Office of the Comptroller of the Currency 313 F Supp 3d 285 (DDC 2018). 4.51, 6.10
CTS Corp v Dynamics Corp of America (1987) 481 US 69 . . . . .8.03
Cyan Inc v Beaver County Employees Retirement Fund 583 US (2018) 9.45–9.47
Dakota National Bank v First National Bank & Trust Co 414 F Supp 1161 (DND 1976),
    rev'd, 554 F 2d 345 (8th Cir 1977) cert denied, 434 US 877 (1977) 6.06
Dalton v Specter 511 US 462 (1994) 4.26
Davis v Merrill Lynch, Pierce, Fenner & Smith Inc 906 F 2d 1206 (8th Cir 1990) 10.26
Davis v Passman 442 US 228 (1979) 3.10
De Kwiatkowski v Bear, Stearns & Co Inc 306 F 3d 1293 (2d Cir 2002) 10.27, 10.30
Dean Witter Reynolds Inc v Byrd 470 US 213 (1985) 10.35
Demarest v Flack 128 NY 205, 28 NE 645 (1891) 8.02
Dennis v United States 341 US 494 (1951) 3.14
Deutsche Bank Trust Co Americas v Elliot International LP No 09 Civ 5242(WHP)
    2011 WL 2421297 (SDNY 2011); 2011 WL 10901798 (SDNY 2011). 10.107
Dietary Supplemental Coalition Inc v Kessler 978 F 2d 560 (9th Cir 1992) 4.26
Dirks v SEC 463 US 646 (1983) 9.50
Doctors Hospital of Hyde Park Inc, In re WL 5524696 (Bankr ND Ill 2013) 11.15
Doctors Hospital of Hyde Park Inc v Desnick and Others 360 BR 787
    (Bankr ND Ill 2007) 11.15, 11.21, 11.26, 11.27
Dun & Bradstreet Inc v Greenmoss Builders Inc 472 US 749, 105 S Ct 2939 (1985) 9.96–9.99, 9.101
Dura Pharmaceuticals Inc v Broudo 544 US 336 (2005) 9.31, 9.32
Edgar v MITE Corp [1982] 457 US 624 . . . . 3.04, 8.03
EEOC v Arabian American Oil Co 499 US 244 (1991) 8.12–8.14
EF Hutton Southwest Properties II Ltd v Union Planters National, Re 953 F 2d 963
    (5th Cir 1992) 11.95
Ellington Credit Fund v Selected Portfolio Serv 837 F Supp 2d 162 (SDNY 2011). 11.96
Elliot Association v J Henry Schroder Bank & Trust Co 838 F 2d 66 (2d Cir 1988) 11.95, 11.99
EM Ltd v Banco Central de la República Argentina 800 F 3d 78 (2015) .4.06
EM Ltd v Republic of Argentina 473 F 3d 463 (2d Cir 2007) 4.06
Endico Potatoes Inc v CIT Group/Factoring Inc 67 F 3d 1063 (2d Cir 1995) 11.19
Energy Future Holdings Corp, In re 842 F 3d 247 (3d Cir 2016) 10.113
English v General Electric Company 496 US 72 (1990) 12.04
Enron Corp Securities, In re, 511 F Supp 2d 742 (SD Tex 2005) Derivative &
    'ERISA' Litig 9.99, 9.125, 9.127
Enron Corporation Securities and ERISA Litigation, In re F Supp 2d) WL 744823,
    70 Fed R Serv 3d 113 (SD Tex 2008) 11.60
Envirodyne Indus Inc v Conn Mut Life Co (In re Envirodyne Indus Inc) 174 BR 986
    (Bankr ND Ill 1994) 11.60
Erica P John Fund Inc v Halliburton Co 563 US 180 (2010) 9.33

Ernst & Ernst v Hochfelder 425 US 185 (1976)..................................... 9.19, 9.20, 9.39
Eternity Global Master Fund Ltd v Morgan Guar Trust Co of NY 375 F 3d 168
 (2d Cir 2004).. 10.106
Fagot v FDIC [1984] 584 F Supp 1168 (DPR)..4.65
Fahey v Malone, 332 US 245 (1947)................................. 3.07, 3.09, 7.08, 7.24, 7.64
FCC v Fox Television Stations Inc 556 US 502 (2009).......................................4.27
FDA v Brown & Williamson Tobacco Corp 529 US 120 (2000)..............................3.07
FDIC v Bank of Coushatta 930 F 2d 1122 (5th Cir 1991)....................................6.70
FDIC v Bank of New York 479 F Supp 2d 1 (DDC 2007) (NextBank II) 11.32, 11.103
FDIC v Philadelphia Gear Corp 476 US 426 (1986)...................................7.51, 7.52
Federal Housing Finance Agency for Federal National Mortgage Association v
 Nomura Holding Am Inc 873 F 3d 85 (2d Cir 2017)....................................9.42
Federal Open Market Committee (FOMC) v Merrill Lynch [1979] 443 US 340 (1979) 4.63
Federated Strategic Income Fund v Mechala Group Jamaica Ltd No 99 CIV 10517 HB,
 1999 WL 993648 (SDNY 1999)..11.81
Feldbaum v McCrory Corp WL 119095 (Del Ch 1992)...........................11.60, 11.78
Feshbach v SEC 5 F Supp 2d 774 (ND Cal 1997)...4.65
Fesseha v TD Waterhouse Investment Services 305 A D 2d 268 (1st Dept 2003)............. 10.103
Fidelity Federal Sav & L Association v De la Cuesta [1982] 458 US 141 ....6.69
Fidelity Savings & Loan Association v Federal Home Loan Bank Bd 540 F Supp 1374
 (ND Cal 1982), rev'd on other grounds, 689 F 2d 803 (9th Cir) cert denied
 461 US 914 (1983) 7.67
Figueroa v United States 57 Fed Cl 488 (2003) 7.26
Financial Planning Association v SEC 482 F 3d 481 (DC Cir 2007)..........................10.25
FindWhat Investor Group v FindWhat.com 658 F 3d 1282 (CA11 2011).................. 9.34, 9.36
Finn v United States (1970) 192 Ct Cl 814..7.26
First Citizens Federal Savings and Loan Association v Worthen Bank and Trust Co
 919 F 2d 510 (9th Cir 1990)..11.90
First National Bank in Plant City v Dickinson 396 US 122 (1969) 6.06
First National Bank of Bellaire v Comptroller of the Currency 697 F2d 674 (5th Cir 1983).......6.69
First National Bank of Logan v Walker Bank & Trust Co 385 US 252 (1966) 6.06, 6.07
First National Bank v Missouri 263 US 640 (1924)..6.06
First National City Bank v Banco Nacional de Cuba 406 US 759 (1972) 4.01, 4.06
First National City Bank v Banco para el Comercio Exterior de Cuba 103 S Ct 2591 (1983) 4.06
Fitch, In re 330 F 3d 104 (2nd Cir 2003)... 9.99, 9.102
Fogel v Vega 759 F App 18 (2d Cir 2018) 9.29
Fox News Network LLC v Board of Governors of the Fed Reserve System 639 F Supp 2d 384
 (SDNY 2009)...4.64
Franklin Sav Association v Director 742 F Supp 1089 (D Kan 1990).........................7.69
Franklin Savings Association v OTS 934 F 2d 1127 (8th Cir 1991) 7.68, 7.70, 7.71
Free Enterprise Fund v Public Company Accounting Oversight Board
 561 US 477 (2010) 2.43, 2.45, 4.50, 4.83, 4.84, 4.91, 5.23
Freytag v Commissioner 501 US 868 (1991)....................................... 4.91, 12.09
Frontier State Bank Oklahoma v FDIC 702 F3d 588 (10th Cir 2012).........................6.70
Gabelli v SEC 568 US 442 (2013) 6.78
Galena Street Fund v Wells Fargo [2013] No 12-cv-006870-BNB-KMT,
 2013 WL 2114372 (D Colo) 11.97
Galli v Metz 973 F 2d 145 (2d Cir 1992)... 11.111
Gandy, In re 299 F 3d 489 (5th Cir 2002)...11.31
Ganino 228 F 3d 154 (2d Cir 2000)...9.28
Garrison v Louisiana 379 US 64, 85 S Ct 209, 13 L Ed 2d 125 (1964)........................9.97
Geffner v Coca-Cola Co 928 F 3d 198 (2d Cir 2019) 9.27
General Growth Properties, In re 409 BR 43 (Bankr SDNY 2009)............... 11.30, 11.54–11.57
Gertz v Robert Welch Inc (1974) 418 US 323, 94 S Ct 2997, 41 L Ed 2d 789 .... 9.96, 9.97
Gilman v Shearson/American Express Inc 577 F Supp 492 (DNH 1983) 10.34
Glickenhous & Co v Household International Inc 787 F 3d 408 (7th Cir 2015)............ 9.34, 9.36
Golden Pacific Bancorp and Miles P Jennings, Jr v United States 15 F 3d 1066 (Fed Cir 1994) 7.25

TABLE OF CASES

Golden Pacific Bancorp v Clarke No 85-2384, slip op at 1 (DDC 1986); 837 F 2d 509,
    513 (DC Cir 1988), cert denied, 488 US 890, 109 S Ct 223, 102 L Ed 2d 213 .... 7.25
Goldman Sachs Grp Inc v Ark Teachers Re Sys No 20-222, 594 US (2021) 9.34, 9.36
Gonzales v Oregon 546 US 243 (2006) 3.07, 4.27
Grandon v Merrill Lynch & Co 147 F 3d 184 (2d Cir 1998) 10.33
Great Plains Trust Co v Union Pacific Railroad Co 492 F 3d 986 (8th Cir 2007) 11.60
Greenwich Financial Services Distressed Mortgage Fund 603 F 3d 23 (2d Cir 2010) 11.96
Gregory v FDIC 631 F 2d 896 (DC Cir 1980) 4.65, 4.66
Grey v Federated Group Inc 107 F 3d 730 (9th Cir 1997) 11.60
Griswold v Connecticut, 381 US 479 (1965) 3.12
Guaranty Savings & Loan Association v FHLBB and FSLIC 794 F 2d 1339 (8th Cir 1986) 7.67
Gulf Federal Savings & Loan Association v Federal Home Loan Bank Board 651F2d 259
    (5th Cir 1981) 6.69
Gustafson v Alloyd Co 513 US 561 (1995) 9.41
Gutierrez-Brizuela v Lynch 834 F 3d 1142 (10th Cir 2016) 3.07
Hackettstown National Bank v DG Yuengling Brewing Co 74 (2d Cir 1896) 11.79
Halliburton Co v Erica P John Fund Inc 573 US 258 (2014) 1.14, 9.33, 9.35
Halperin v eBanker USA.com Inc 295 F 3d 352 (2d Cir 2002) 9.27
Handlebar Inc v Utica First Insurance Co 290 A D 2d 633 (3d Dept 2002) 10.111
Hanly v SEC 415 F 2d 589 (2d Cir 1969) 10.32
Heckler v Chaney 470 US 821 (1985) 3.02
Heisley v UIP Engineered Prods Corp (In re UIP Engineered Prods Corp)
    831 F 2d 54 (4th Cir 1987) 11.57
Hempel v Blunt, Ellis & Loewi Inc 123 FRD 313, (ED Wis 1988) 10.34
Herman & MacLean v Huddleston 459 US 375 (1983) 9.23, 9.38–9.40, 9.42, 9.132
Hexion Spec Chemicals v Huntsman Corp 965, A2d 715 (Del Ch 2008) 10.122
Hildene Capital Management v Friedman 11 Civ 5832 (AJN)
    (SDNY 2012) 11.88, 11.96, 11.98, 11.99
Hines v Davidowitz 312 US 52 (1941) 12.04
Hoffman v FDIC [1990] 912 F 2d 1172 (9th Cir) 6.70
Hooper v Mountain States Securities Corp 282 F 2d 195 (1960) 9.18
Horn v Ray E. Friedman Co 776 F 2d 777 (8th Cir 1985) 10.27
Hoxworth v Blinder, Robinson & Co Inc 903 F 2d 186 (3d Cir 1990) 10.34
Humphrey's Executor v United States 295 US 602 (1935) 4.84
Huntington v Attrill 146 US 657 (1892) 6.79
Hutchison v Deutsche Bank Sec Inc 647 F 3d 479 (2d Cir 2010) 9.42
IBP Inc v Tyson Foods Inc [2001] 789 A 2d 14 (Del Ch) 65 .... 10.122, 10.124
ICI v Clarke 789 F 2d 175 (2d Cir 1986) cert denied, 107 US 422 (1986) 6.38
ICI v Clarke 793 F 2d 220 (9th Cir 1986) cert denied 107 US 422 (1986) 6.38
ICI v Conover 790 F 2d 925 (DC Cir 1986) cert denied 107 US 421 (1986) 6.38
ICI v FDIC 815 F2d 1540 (DC Cir 1987) cert denied, 484 US 847 (1987) 6.38
Independent Bankers Association v Heimann [1979] No 78-0811
    (DDC 29 Mar 1979) (mem), rev'd, 627 F 2d 486 (DC Cir 1980) 6.06
Indiana Public Retirement System v SAIC Inc 818 F 3d 85 (2d Cir 2016) 9.28
Ingram Industries Inc. v Nowicki (1981) 527 F Supp 683 .... 9.111
International Multifoods Corp v Commercial Union Insurance Co 309 F 3d 76 (2d Cir 2002) ... 11.107
Investment Company Institute (ICI) v Camp 401 US 617 (1971) 6.23, 6.35–6.37
Irish Bank Resolution Corp, In re, WL 9953792 (Bkr D Del 2014), confirmed on
    appeal in CA No 14-108-LPS (Dist Ct Del) (4 August 2015) 7.93, 7.96, 7.98
Jam v International Finance Corp 139 S Ct 759 (2019) 4.07
Janus Capital Grp Inc v First Derivative Traders 564 US 135, 131 S Ct 2296 (2010) 9.31, 9.129–9.133
Jefferson City School District v Moody's Investors Services Inc 988 F Supp 1341
    (D Colo 1997) 9.96, 9.98
Jefferson County School District No R-1 v Moody's Investor Services Inc
    175 F 3d 848 (10th Cir 1999) 9.98
Jesner v Arab Bank PLC 138 S Ct 1386 (2018) 3.12
JI Case Co v Borak 377 US 426 (1964) 8.18, 9.15–9.17, 9.25, 9.44

Johnson v OTS 81 F 3d 195 (DC Cir 1996) 6.70
Johnson v Robison 415 US 361 (1974) 3.02
Jones v Rath Packing Co 430 US 519 (1977) 3.04
Kardon v National Gypsum Co 69 F Supp 512 (ED Pa 1946) 9.14, 9.20
Kass v E Air Lines Inc Nos 8700, 8701, 8711, 1986 WL 13008 (Del Ch 1986) 11.78
King v Burwell 576 US 473 (2015) 2.41, 3.07, 6.26, 12.51
Kingston Square Associates and Others, In re 214 BR 713 (Bankr SDNY 1997) 11.54, 11.55
Kisor v Wilkie 139 S Ct 2400 (2019) 4.27
Kokesh v SEC 581 US 137, S Ct 1635 (2017) 6.79, 6.80, 6.82
Kowalski v Tesmer 543 US 125 (2004) 4.53
Lacewell v Office of Comptroller of Currency 999 F3d 130 (2021) 4.51, 6.08
LaSalle Bank NA v Nomura Asset Capital Corp 424 F 3d 195 (2d Cir 2005)................ 11.111
LaSalle Bank NA v Paloian 406 BR 299 (ND Ill 2009) 11.15
Lasalle National Bank and Others v Duff & Phelps Rating Co 951 F Supp 1071
    (SDNY 1996)..9.100, 9.102
Lawrence v Texas 539 US 558 (2003) 3.12
LBSF v Bank of America National Association No 17-cv-01224 (SDNY 2018) 553. ......11.42
Lee v FDIC 923 F Supp 451 (SDNY 1996) 4.68
Lehman Bros. Special Fin Inc v Bank of America National Association Ch 11
    Case No 08-13555, Adv No 10-03547, 553 BR 476 (Bankr SDNY 2016)...............11.42
Lehman Brothers Holdings Inc Case No 08-13555 (Bankr SDNY 2009) 10.114
Lehman Brothers Holdings Inc v Ballyrock ABS CDO 2007-1 Ltd, 452 BR 31
    (Bankr SDNY 2011)..11.38
Lehman Brothers Special Financing Inc. v Bank of America National Association
    No 18-1079 (2d Cir 2020) 11.42
Lehman Brothers Special Financing Inc v BNY Corporate Trustee Services Ltd
    No 09-01242 (JMP) US (Bankr Ct SDNY 2010)..11.35
Lehman-Brothers Mortgage-Backed Securities Litigation, In re Nos 10-0712-cv;
    10-0898-cv; and 10-1288-cv (2d Cir 2011) 9.134
Leib v Merrill Lynch, Pierce, Fenner & Smith Inc 461 F Supp 951 (ED Mich 1978)
    aff'd, 647 F 2d 165 (6th Cir 1981) 10.27
Lincoln v Vigil 508 US 182 (1993) 2.41
Litton Industries Inc v Lehman Bros Kuhn Loeb 734 F Supp 1071 (SDNY 1990) 9.51
Litwin v Blackstone Grp LP 634 F 3d 706 (2d Cir 2011) 9.28
Liu v Securities and Exchange Commission 591 US (2020) 6.79, 6.80
Llapa-Singhi v Mukasey 520 F 3d 897 (8th Cir 2008)..6.70
LNC Investments Inc v First Fidelity Bank, National Association 935 F Supp 1333 (1996) 11.95
Lochner v New York 198 US 45 (1905)..3.14
Lorenzo v Securities and Exchange Commission 587 US (2019) 9.130, 9.132
Lowe v SEC 472 US 181, 105 S Ct 2557, 86 L Ed 2d 130 (1985)................................9.98
LTV Securities Litigation, In re (1980) 88 FRD 134 (ND Tex) 9.30
LTV Steel Company Inc, In re 274 BR 278 (Bkrtcy ND Ohio 2002)................... 11.29, 11.31
Lucas v Federal Reserve Bank of Richmond 59 F 2d 617 (4th Cir 1932) 7.26
Lucia v SEC 138 S Ct 2044 (2018) 4.90, 12.09, 13.12
Lujan v Defenders of Wildlife 504 US 555 (1992)...3.10
Lyondell Chem Co, In re 567 BR 55 (Bankr SDNY 2017) aff'd, 585 BR 41 (SDNY 2018) 10.123
MA Schapiro Co v Securities and Exchange Commission 339 F Supp 467 (DDC 1972).........4.65
Mac Donald's Corp v United States [1991] 926 F 2d 1126 (Fed. Cir) 5.09
McCardle, Ex Parte 74 US (7 Wall) 506 (1868) 3.02
McCulloch v Maryland 17 US (4 Wheat) 316 (1819)..3.04
McCullough v FDIC [1980] No 79-1132 (DDC) 4.66
McKinley v FDIC 744 F Supp 2d 128 (DDC 2010)................................... 4.65, 4.66
McLouth Steel Prods Corp v Thomas 838 F 2d 1317 (DC Cir 1988) 4.26
McMahan & Co v Wherehouse Entertainment Inc 859 F Supp 743 (SDNY 1994) 11.60, 11.78
McNary v Haitian Refugee Ctr Inc 498 US 479 (1991).......................................3.02
Major's Furniture Mart Inc v Castle Credit Corporation Inc and Others
    602 F 2d 538 (1979) 11.19

Marblegate Asset Management LLC v Education Management. Corp
   111 F Supp 3d 542 (SDNY 2015); 846 F 3d 1 (2d Cir 2017)................. 11.81, 11.82, 11.96
Marblegate Asset Management v Educ Management Corp 75 F Supp 3d 592
   (SDNY 2014)... 11.80, 11.81, 11.88
Marbury v Madison 5 U.S. 137 (1803) 1.10, 3.02, 3.04
Martin v SEC Doc No 11-2011 (2d Cir 2013) 9.51
Massachusetts v EPA 549 US 497 (2007) 3.10
MCI Telecommunications Corp v AT&T 512 US 218 (1994) 3.07
Meckel v Continental Resources Co [1985] 758 F 2d 811 (2d Cir)................... 11.95, 11.99
MeehanCombs Global Credit Opportunities Funds LP v Caesars Entertainment Corp
   80 F Supp 3d 507 (SDNY 2015)..11.81
Meeker v Lehigh Valley R Co 236 US 412 (1915) 6.79
Melcher, John, Honorable Member, United States Senate, Appellant v Federal Open
   Market Committee and Others 836 F 2d 561 (DC Cir 1987) 4.12, 5.23
Melcher v Federal Open Market Committee 644 F Supp 510 (DDC 1986)............... 4.12, 5.23
Merit Management Group v FTI Consulting 138 S Ct 883 (2018) 11.40, 11.41
Mermelstein v SEC 629 F Supp 672 (DDC 1986) 4.65
Merrill Lynch, Pierce, Fenner & Smith Inc v Cheng 697 F Supp 1224 (DDC 1988).............10.34
Merrill Lynch, Pierce, Fenner & Smith Inc v Dabit 547 US 71 (2006) 9.44
Metlife v FSOC [2016] 1:15-cv-00045-RMC 30, District Court,
   District of Columbia 1.48, 1.50, 1.52, 6.52
Metropolitan Life Ins. Co v RJR Nabisco Inc 716 F Supp 1504 (SDNY 1989)..................11.79
Michigan State Housing Development Authority v Lehman Brothers Derivative
   Products Inc 502 BR 383 (Bankr SDNY 2013) 11.39
Michigan v EPA 135 S Ct 2699 (2015) 1.50, 3.07
Miley v Oppenheimer & Co 637 F 2d 318 (5th Cir 1981) 10.32
Milkovich v Lorain Journal Co 497 US 1, 20, 110 S Ct 2695, 111 L Ed 2d 1 (1990).............9.99
Mills v Electric Auto-Lite Co 396 US 375 (1970) 9.16, 9.17, 9.25, 9.26, 9.44
Mirant Corp, In re WL 2148362 (Bankr ND Tex 2005) 11.57
Momentive Performing Materials (MPM) Silicones LLC, In re Case No 15-1682
   (2d Cir 2017)... 10.113
Morgan Stanley Info Fund Securities Litigation, In re 592 F 3d 347 (2d Cir 2010)..............9.42
Morrison v National Australia Bank 130 S Ct 2869 (2010) 13.53
Morrison v National Australia Bank Ltd 561 US 247 (2010).......................... 8.12–8.14
Motor Vehicle Manufacturers Association v State Farm Auto Mutual Insurance Co
   463 US 29 (1983).. 3.07, 12.51
Mutual Funds Inv Litigation, In re 487 F Supp 2d 618 (D Md 2007) 9.129
Mutual Funds Inv Litigation, In re 566 F 3d 111 (2009)..................................9.129
Natera Securities Litigation, In re No CIV537409 (Cal Super Ct filed 24 March 2016)..........9.49
National Cable & Telecommunications Association v Brand X Internet Services
   545 US 967 (2005) 6.70
National Century Financial Enterprises Inc, In re WL 2849784 (SD Ohio 2006)......... 11.28, 11.96
National Century Financial Enterprises Inc Inv Litigation 580 F Supp 2d 630
   (SD Ohio 2008)...9.100
National Community Reinvestment Coal v National Credit Union Administration
   290 F Supp 2d 124 (DDC 2003) 4.65
National Mining Association v McCarthy 758 F 3d 243 (DC Cir 2014) 4.26
NationsBank v VALIC 513 US 251 (1995)... 6.26, 6.38
NECA-IBEW Health & Welfare Fund v Goldman Sachs & Co 693 F 3d 145 (2d Cir 2012) 9.42
Netshoes Sec Litig, In re NY Slip Op 29219 (Supp Ct, NY County 2019) 9.49
New York Times Co v Sullivan 376 US 254, 84 S Ct 710, 11 L Ed 2d 686 (1964)........... 9.96, 9.97
Newton v Merrill, Lynch, Pierce, Fenner & Smith Inc 135 F 3d 266 (3d Cir 1998).............10.33
NML Capital v Banco Central de la República Argentina 652 F 3d 172 (2d Cir 2011)...........4.06
North American Catholic Educational Programming Foundation Inc v Gheewalla
   [2007] Del LEXIS 227 (Del Supr 2007) 11.57, 12.70
Northern Securities Co v United States 193 US 197 (1904)..................................1.35
Northstar Financial Advisors v Schwab Investments 615 F 3d 1106 (2010) 8.18

Nvidia Corp Sec Litig, In re 768 F 3d 1046 (9th Cir 2014) 9.28
Oakdale Mfg Co Ltd v Garst 18 RI 484, 28 Atl 973 (1894) 8.02
O'Connor & Associates v Dean Witter Reynolds Inc 559 F Supp 800 (SDNY 1983) 9.51
Ohio Bureau of Workers' Compensation v MDL Active Duration Fund 476 F Supp 2d 809 (2007) 10.34
Oil States Energy Services, LLC v. Greene's Energy Group, LLC. Leading Case:
    138 S. Ct. 1365 (2018). 12.09
Olmsted v Pruco Life Insurance Co of New Jersey 283 F 3d 429 (2d Cir 2002). 8.18
Omnicare Inc v Laborers District Council Construction Industry Pension Fund
    575 US 175 (2015) 9.28, 9.42, 9.43, 9.136, 10.30
Oran v Stafford 226 F 3d 275 (3d Cir 2000). 9.28
Owen Equip & Erection Co v Kroger 437 US 365 (1978) 3.02
Owners Corp v Jennifer Realty Co 98 NY 2d 144 (2002). 10.103
Paine Webber, Jackson & Curtis Inc v Adams 718 P2d 508 (Colo 1986) 10.27
Paloian v LaSalle 406 F Supp 2d 299 (ND Ill 2007). 11.26
Paloian v LaSalle Bank NA 619 F 3d 688 (7th Cir 2010) 11.15, 11.27
Pan Am Corp, In re 161 BR 577 (SDNY 1993) 9.98
Pan Am Corp v Delta Air Lines Inc 175 BR 438 (SDNY 1994) 10.123
Paralyzed Veterans of America v DC Arena LP 117 F 3d 579 (DC Cir 1997) 3.07, 4.27
Parkcentral Global Hub Ltd v Porsche Auto Holdings SE 11-397-CV L (2d Cir 2014) 8.15
Parmalat Securities Litigation, In re 376 F Supp 2d 472 (SDNY 2005). 9.120, 9.127, 10.77
Pentagon Fed Credit Union v National Credit Union Admin No 95-1475 (ED Va 1996) 4.65
Perez v Mortgage Bankers Association 135 S Ct 1199 (2015) 4.27
Petron Trading Co v Hydrocarbon Trading & Transport Co 663 F Supp 1153 (ED Pa 1986) 11.20
Philadelphia & Gulf SS Co v Soeffing 59 Pa Super 429 (1915). 8.02
Pierce v SEC [2015] Docket No 14-1079 (DC Cir). 6.100
Pilot Air Freight, LLC v Manna Freight Systems Inc WL 5588671 (Del Ch 2020) 10.103
Pinter v Dahl 486 US 622 (1988). 9.40
Port of Boston Marine Terminal Association v Rederiaktiebolaget Transatlantic
    400 US 62 (1970). 4.38
Press v Chemical Investment Services Corp 166 F 3d 529 (2d Cir 1999). 10.28, 10.30
Prudential Sec Inc Partnerships Litig, In re 930 F Supp 2d 68 (SDNY 1996). 9.27
Pub Employees' Retirement System v Moody's Investor Services Inc
    (2014) 226 Cal App 4th 643, 172 Cal Rptr 3d 238. .... 9.100, 9.102–9.104, 9.112
Public Employees' Retirement System v Moody's Investor Services 226 Cal App.
    4th 643, 172 Cal Rptr 3d 238 (2014). 9.112
Puda Coal Sec Inc Litigation, In re 30 F Supp 3d 230 (SDNY 2014). 9.136
Puda Coal Securities Inc Litigation, In re [2016] No 15-2100 (2d Cir) 9.136
Qimonda AG Bankr, In Re Lit 09-14766-RGM, 09-14766-SSM 433 BR 547;
    462 BRBR 165 Bankr E Dist Vir 7.98
Raichle v Federal Reserve Bank of New York 34 F 2d 910 (2d Cir 1929) 5.08
Ray E Friedman Co v Jenkins 738 F 2d 251 (8th Cir 1984) 10.27
Regents of Univ of Cal v Credit Suisse First Boston (USA) Inc 482 F 3d 372 (CA5 2007) 9.126
Republic of Argentina v NML Capital Ltd [2014] 573 US 134 .... 4.02, 4.03
Republic of Argentina v Weltover Inc 504 US 607 (1992) 4.02
Research Triangle Institute v Board of Governors of the Federal Reserve System
    132 F 3d 985 (4th Cir 1997). 4.12, 5.09
Retail Clerks v Schermerhorn 375 US 96 (1963). 3.04
Revlon Inc v MacAndrews & Forbes Holdings Inc 506 A 2d 173 (Del 1986) 12.70
Rewis v United States 401 US 808 (1971). 2.45
Rhode Island Hospital Trust National Bank v Swartz, Bresenoff, Yavner & Jacobs
    455 F 2d 847 (1972) 9.111
Riegle v FOMC 656 F 2d 873 (DC Cir 1981). 4.12, 5.23
Robertson v Seattle Audubon Society (1992) 4.06
Rodriquez de Quijas v Shearson/American Express 490 US 477 (1989) 10.35
Roe v Wade 410 US 113 (1973). 3.12
Roseton OL LLC v Dynegy Holdings Inc CA No 6689-VCP, 2011 Del Ch LEXIS 113
    (Del Ch 2011) 11.13

Case	Reference
Roth v United States 354 US 476 (1957)	9.97
Ruhrgas AG v Marathon Oil Co [1999] 526 US 574	3.02
Ruiz v Harbor View Community Association 134 Cal App 4th 1456 (2005)	9.104
St Louis County National Bank v Mercantile Trust Co 548 F 2d 716 (8th Cir 1976) cert denied, 433 US 909 (1977)	6.06
Salman v United States 137 S Ct 420 (2016)	9.50
Salzberg v Sciabacucchi (2020) No 346, 2019 (Del)	9.48
San Marino Savings and Loan Association v Federal Home Loan Bank Board 605 F Supp 502 (CD Cal 1984)	7.67
Santa Fe Industries Inc v Green 430 US 462 (1977)	9.21, 9.44, 10.32
Sciabacucchi v Salzberg No 2017-0931-JTL (Del Ch 2018)	9.48
Scott Paper Company Securities Litigation, In re (1992) 145 FRD 366	9.97, 9.98, 9.102
SEC v Capital Gains Research Bureau Inc 375 US 180 (1963)	9.15, 10.26, 10.29
SEC v Clark 915 F 2d 439 (1990) (CA9)	6.79
SEC v First Jersey Secs Inc 101 F 3d 1450 (2d Cir 1996)	9.125
SEC v Fischbach Corp 133 F 3d 170 (1997) (CA2)	6.79
SEC v Luzardo No 01Civ9206 (DC) (SDNY 2004)	9.51
SEC v Texas Gulf Sulphur Co 312 F Supp 77 (SDNY 1970, 1971), aff'd in part and rev'd in part, 446 F 2d 1301 (CA2)	6.79
SEC v Warde 151 F 3d 42 (1998) (CA2)	6.79
SEC v Yun Soo Oh Park 99 F Supp 2d 889 (ND Ill 2000)	10.30
SEC v Zandford 535 US 813 (2002)	9.25
Securities Industry Association (SIA) and Others v FRB 468 US 137 (1984)	6.24, 6.25, 6.37
Securities Industry Association v Board of Governors FRS [1986] 807 F 2d 1052 (DC Cir) cert denied, 483 US 1005 (1987)	6.25, 6.38
Securities Industry v Comptroller of the Currency 577 F Supp 252 (DDC 1983), aff'd, 758 F 2d 739 (DCCir1985) cert denied, 106 S Ct 790 (1986)	6.07
Seidman v OTS 37 F 3d 911 (3d Cir 1994)	6.70
Seila Law LLC v Consumer Financial Protection Bureau 140 S Ct 2183 (2020)	4.50, 4.85–4.87, 4.91, 5.23
Shalala v Guernsey Memorial Hospital 514 US 87 (1995)	4.26
Shapiro v Merrill Lynch, Pierce, Fenner & Smith Inc 495 F 2d 228 (2d Cir 1974)	9.51
Sharon Steel Corp v Chase Manhattan Bank NA 691 F 2d 1039 (2d Cir 1982)	8.29, 10.105, 10.106, 10.112, 10.113, 11.78, 11.82
Shearson/American Express Inc v McMahon 482 US 222 (1987)	10.35
Sheldon v Hill 49 US (8 How) 441 (1850)	3.02
Shell v Hensley 430 F 2d 819 (1970)	9.19
SIA v Board of Governors FRS [1988] 839 F2d 47 (2d Cir) cert denied, 486 US 1059 (1988)	6.25
SIA v Clarke 885 F2d 1034 (2d Cir 1989)	6.25, 6.38
SIA v FHLBB 588 F Supp 749 (DDC 1984)	6.24, 6.37
Siegel v SEC 592 F 3d 147 (DC Cir 2010)	10.32
Sierra Club v Morton 405 US 727 (1992)	3.10
Simpson v AOL Time Warner Inc 452 F 3d 1040 (CA9 2006)	9.126, 9.127
Simpson v OTS 29 F 3d 1413 (9th Cir 1994)	6.70
Skidmore v Swift & Co 323 US 134 (1944)	3.07
Sola Electric Co v Jefferson Electric Co 317 US 173 (1942)	9.16
Southern R. Co v Seaboard Allied Mining Corp 442 US 444 (1979)	3.02
Southern Rock Inc v B&B Auto Supply 711 F 2d 683 (5th Cir 1983)	11.20
Starr International Co v United States 121 Fed Cla 428 (2015)	4.53, 7.25
Starr International Co v United States 856 F 3d 953 (2017)	4.53, 7.25
State ex rel Brown Contracting & Bldg Co v Cook 181 Mo 596, 80 SW 929 (1904)	8.02
State National Bank of Big Spring v Lew, 958 F Supp 2d 127 (DDC 2013)	4.50
State National Bank of Big Spring v Lew 795 F.3d 48 (DC Cir 2015)	4.50
Stoneridge Investment Partners LLC v Scientific-Atlanta Inc 552 US 148 (2008)	9.27, 9.28, 9.31, 9.125, 9.127, 9.130, 9.132
Stratte-McClure v Morgan Stanley 77 F 3d 94 (2d Cir 2015)	9.28

Sunshine State Bank v FDIC [1986] 783 F 2d 1580 (11th Cir). 6.70
Superintendent of Insurance v Bankers Life & Casualty Co 404 US 6 (1971) 9.18, 9.19, 9.25, 9.44
Taberna Preferred Funding IV Ltd, In re 594 BR 576 (Bankr SDNY 2018). 11.67
Talansky v Schulman 2 A D 3d 355, 770 NYS2d 48 (2003) 10.34
Telegraph Savings & Loan Association v Federal Savings & Loan Insurance Corp
    564 F Supp 862 (ND Ill 1981), aff'd 703 F 2d 1019 (7th Cir 1983), cert denied, 464 US 992 . . . . . .7.67
Telegraph Savings & Loan Association v Schilling 703 F 2d 1019 (7th Cir 1983),
    cert denied, 464 US 992, 104 S Ct 484 . . . . .7.67
Tellabs Inc v Makor Issues & Rights Ltd 551 US 308 (2007) 551 US 308 (2007),
    (No 06-484) 437 F 3d 588 (2007) 9.25
Thomas v Comptroller of the Currency 684 F Supp 2d 29 (2010). 4.67
Touche Ross & Co v Redington 442 US 560 (1979) 8.18
Transamerica Mortgage Advisors Inc 444 US 11 (1979) 10.34
Trudeau v Fed. Trade Comm'n 456 F 3d 178 (DC Cir 2006) 3.02
TSC Industries Inc v Northway Inc 426 US 438 (1976) 9.26
Ultramares Corporation v Touche (1932) 174 NE 441. . . . . .9.04, 9.05, 9.109–9.111
Union Pacific R Co v Locomotive Engineers 558 US 67 (2009) 8.12
Union Savings Bank v Augie/Restivo Baking Co Ltd 860 F 2d 515 (2d Cir 1998) 11.24
United Savings Association of Texas v Timbers of Inwood Forest Associates Ltd
    484 US 365 (1988) 11.16
United States v Carolene Products Co 304 US 144 (1938). 3.14
United States v Edmondston 181 US 500 (1901). 7.26
United States v Germaine 99 US 508 (1879) 4.91
United States v Mead Corporation 533 US 218 (2001). 3.07
United States v O'Hagan 521 US 64 (1997) 8.14, 9.50
Universal Camera Corp v NLRB 340 US 474 (1951) 12.51
Unocal Corp v Mesa Petrol Co 493 A 2d 946 (Del 1985). 12.70
US Bank NA v Barclays Bank PLC, No 11 Civ 9199(WHP) 2013 WL 1180414 (SDNY 2013) 10.107
US v O'Hagan 521 US 642 (1997) 9.50
US v Skelly 442 F 3d 94 (2d Cir 2006). 10.27
Utility Air Regulatory Group v Environmental Protection Agency 573 US 302 (2014) 3.07
Valley Forge Christian College v Americans United for Separation of Church and State Inc
    454 US 464 (1982) 3.02
Vander Jagt v O'Neill 226 US App DC 14, 699 F 2d 1166 (1983). 3.10
Vecco Construction Industries Inc, In re 4 BR 407 (Bankr ED Va 1980). 11.24
Veneto Hotel & Casino SA v German American Capital Corp 160 A D 3d 451 (1st Dept 2018). . . . 10.111
Verlinden BV v Central Bank of Nigeria 461 US 480 (1983) 4.02
Vermont Yankee Nuclear Power Corp v Natural Resources Defense Council Inc
    435 US 519 (1978) 4.27
Virginia Pharmacy Bd v Virginia Citizens Consumer Council Inc 425 US 748,
    96 S Ct 1827, 48 L Ed 2d 346 (1976) 9.97
Vullo v Office of Comptroller of Currency, 378 F Supp 3d 271 (SDNY 2019). 4.50, 6.10, 6.08
Vullo v Office of Comptroller of the Currency No 17 Civ 3574, 2017 WL 6512245 (SDNY 2017) 4.51
Waggoner v Barclays PLC 875 F 3d 79 (2d Cir 2017) 9.36
Warth v Seldin 422 US 490, 422 US 498 (1975). 3.02
Washington Federal Savings and Loan Association v Federal Home Loan Bank Board
    526 F Supp 343 (ND Ohio 1981). 7.67
Washington Legal Found v Kessler 880 F Supp 26 (DDC 1995) 4.26
Wells Fargo Bank NA v Wrights Mill Holdings 127 F Supp 3d 156 (SDNY 2015) 11.88
West Virginia v EPA 597 US No 20–1530 (2022) 2.41, 3.07, 4.88, 6.09, 6.26
Whitman v American Trucking Associations 531 US 457 (2001) 2.41
Williams & Connolly LLP v Office of the Comptroller of the Currency
    30 F Supp 3d 82 (DDC 2014) 4.66
Wilmington Savings Fund Society v Cash America International Inc Case
    No 15-CV-5027 (JMF) (SDNY 2016). 10.106, 10.112
Wilson v Comtech Telecomm Corp 648 F 2d 88 (2d Cir 1981). 9.51

Women Office Workers v Bd of Governors of Fed Reserve System 721 F 2d 1 (1st Cir 1983)......4.64
Woods v FHLBB 826 F 2d 1400 (5th Cir 1987)....................................7.67, 7.68
Wright v Ernst & Young 152 F 3d 169 (2d Cir 1998) 9.125
Yates v United States 574 US 528 (2015) 2.43, 2.45
Young, Ex parte 209 US 123 (1908) 3.14
Zais Investment Grade Ltd VII, In re 455 BR 839 (Bkrtcy DNJ 2011) 11.66–11.69
ZZZZ Best Securities Litigation, In re [1994] 864 F Supp 960 (CD Cal) 9.125

Table of Legislation

EUROPEAN UNION

Charter of Fundamental Rights of the
  European Union 3.08, 3.12, 4.07,
    4.09, 4.70, 6.08, 6.54, 7.32, 7.36,
    12.35, 13.56, 13.65, 13.66
  Arts 7–8 . . . . .1.28
  Art 16 . . . . 1.28, 6.54, 7.24
  Art 17 . . . . 4.10, 6.54, 7.24, 7.28, 7.38
  Art 17(2) 7.28
  Arts 20–21 . . . . .1.28
  Art 21(1) 1.28
  Art 23 . . . . .1.28
  Art 27 . . . . .1.28
  Art 41 . . . . 4.93, 6.53, 6.71, 6.85, 6.90,
    7.81, 12.42, 14.14
  Arts 41–42 . . . . .1.28
  Art 42 . . . . 4.82, 13.34
  Art 47 . . . . 1.12, 1.28, 4.78, 4.96, 6.88, 7.24,
    7.38, 7.92, 12.12, 12.42, 13.35, 14.04, 14.14
  Art 48 . . . . .6.88
  Art 51 . . . . .3.13
  Art 51(1) 1.28
  Art 52(1) 6.100
Decision ECB/2015/2464 . . . . .5.15
Decision ECB/2019/21 . . . . .5.15
Directive 82/891, SRB Decision 8/18
  (16 October 2018) 13.28
Directive 93/13 (UCT Directive)
  Art 3 . . . . 10.50
  Art 4(2) 10.50, 12.66
  Art 5 . . . . 10.50
  Ann 10.50
Directive 94/19 on deposit-guarantee
  schemes 4.15, 7.58
  Art 1(3)(i) 4.33
Directive 2001/24 . . . . 7.91, 7.92
  Art 2 . . . . .7.89
  Art 32 . . . . .7.88
Directive 2001/24 (Winding-Up Directive)
  . . . . 7.36, 7.90, 13.28
  Art 1 . . . . .7.89
  Art 2 . . . . .7.89
  Art 9(1) 7.90
  Art 31 . . . . .7.90
  Art 32 . . . . .7.88
Directive 2002/47 on financial collateral
  arrangements 8.05, 11.45
Directive 2002/87 . . . . 4.74, 6.21

Directive 2003/6 (Market Abuse
  Directive) 9.84, 10.22
Directive 2003/71 (Prospectus
  Directive) 9.55, 9.66, 9.72, 9.78, 13.17
  Art 6 . . . . .9.53
Directive 2004/109 (Transparency
  Directive) 9.94
  Art 7 . . . . .9.84
Directive 2004/39
  Art 13(7) and (8) 11.52
  Art 19(9) 10.56
  Art 53 . . . . 13.49
Directive 2006/48 . . . . 13.17
Directive 2006/73 (MIFID Implementing
  Directive), Art 16(2) 11.52
Directive 2007/64, Art 10(4) 6.29
Directive 2008/48 on credit agreements
  for consumers 6.29, 12.64
Directive 2009/110, Art 3(1) 6.29
Directive 2009/138 on the taking-up and
  pursuit of the business of insurance
  and reinsurance (Solvency II), Art 64 . . . . 4.74
Directive 2013/11 on alternative
  dispute resolution 13.44, 13.45,
    13.47, 13.48, 14.21
Directive 2013/36 . . . . .6.56
Directive 2013/36 (Capital Requirements
  Directive) 4.78, 6.19, 6.20, 6.21, 6.28,
    6.29, 6.40, 6.54, 6.55, 6.57, 6.58, 6.95
  Art 3(1)(2) 6.56
  Art 3(1)(7) 6.56
  Art 13, Art 13 . . . . .6.55
  Art 13(1), Art 13(1) 6.55
  Art 29 . . . . .3.11
  Art 53 . . . . 4.74, 4.81
  Art 53(1) 4.74
  Art 65 . . . . .6.86
  Art 67(1)(k) 6.86
  Art 67(2) 6.86
  Art 74 . . . . 6.18, 6.32, 6.59
  Art 74(1) 6.29, 6.31
  Arts 74–95 . . . . .6.32
  Art 88(1) 6.55
  Art 129 . . . . .6.92
Directive 2014/104 . . . . 13.53, 13.54
Directive 2014/17, Art 7(1) 6.29
Directive 2014/49 on deposit
  guarantee schemes 4.15

TABLE OF LEGISLATION

Directive 2014/59 establishing a framework
for the recovery and resolution of
credit institutions and investment
firms (BRRD) 7.03, 7.04, 7.08,
7.16, 7.50, 7.62, 7.90, 9.69
- recital 98.............................4.47
- recital 119 ....7.89
- recital 120 ....9.66
- Art 31.............................7.50
- Art 32(4)(d)..........................4.59
- Art 44...............................7.50
- Art 44(4) 13.28
- Art 44(5) 13.28
- Art 45(4) 13.28
- Art 45ff.............................7.05
- Art 45h............................4.47
- Art 48......................... 13.28
- Art 63ff.............................7.89
- Art 66.............................7.89
- Art 66(3) 7.89
- Art 66(4) 7.89
- Art 102..............................7.14
- Art 103..............................7.14
- Art 104.........................7.14, 7.17
- Art 117..............................7.89
- Arts................................7.14

Directive 2014/65 on markets in financial
instruments (MIFID II)......... 1.06, 4.78,
6.29, 8.18, 13.57
- Art 25(2) 8.18
- Art 76............................4.74
- Art 76(2) 4.74

Directive 2017/1132
- Art 9............................. 10.06

Directive 2017/1132 relating to certain
aspects of company law 8.05

Directive 2019/1023 on discharge of
debt and disqualifications 8.05

ECB Decision 2004/3............... 4.70, 4.73

ECB Decision 2016/810...................5.15

European Stability Mechanism Treaty . 4.09, 4.10

Interinstitutional Agreement between the
European parliament, the Council and
the European Commission on better
Law-Making 1.48

Regulation 2532/98, Art 18(7) 13.08

Regulation 44/2001.....................8.11

Regulation 1049/2001 (Access
Regulation) 4.74, 4.75, 4.73, 4.77,
12.48, 13.31, 13.34, 13.35
- recital 2..............................4.70
- Art 4(1)(a)..........................4.73
- Art 4(3) 4.70, 4.82

Regulation 1/2003, Art 23(5)..............6.81

Regulation 809/2004 ....9.72, 9.140

Regulation 1060/2009 (CRAR)......6.28, 13.58
- recital 35......................... 9.142

- Art 3(2) 6.41, 6.42, 13.21
- Art 5a(1) 9.144
- Art 8(3) 13.22
- Art 16(3) 13.20
- Art 18............................. 13.20
- Art 18(1) 13.20
- Art 35a.........................9.142, 13.57
- Art 35a(4) 9.144
- Art 36e 13.08

Regulation 1093/2010
(EBA Regulation).............. 4.28, 12.10
- Art 1(2) 6.29
- Art 1(3) 6.29
- Art 1(5) 6.29
- Art 8(1)(1bis) and 2 ....6.29
- Art 16..............................6.29
- Art 17(2) 4.20, 4.96
- Art 70(1) and (2)......................4.74

Regulation 1094/2010 (EIOPA
Regulation) 4.28, 4.74, 12.10,
12.40, 13.17, 13.24

Regulation 1095/2010 (ESMA
Regulation) 4.28, 4.74, 6.42, 12.10,
12.40, 13.17, 13.19, 13.21

Regulation 513/2011 ....6.28

Regulation 1257/2012 .... 14.07

Regulation 575/2013 on prudential
requirements for credit institutions and
investment firms (CRR)......6.39, 6.47, 13.22
- Art 7(1) 13.29
- Art 8............................. 13.29
- Art 10.................... 6.19, 6.46, 6.47
- Art 10(1)(a)..........................6.47
- Art 29(2) 6.54
- Art 77..............................6.92
- Art 78..............................6.92
- Art 92..............................6.92
- Art 136(1) and (3)............... 4.43, 13.22
- Art 395..............................6.86
- Art 429(14) 6.63, 6.67
- Art 429(2) 6.63
- Art 429a(1)(j) 6.67

Regulation 1024/2013 conferring specific
tasks on the European Central Bank
concerning policies relating to the
prudential supervision of credit
institutions (SSM Regulation) ... 13.06, 14.17
- recital 30.......................... 14.16
- recital 79.......................... 14.16
- Art 4(3) 12.05, 13.05
- Art 6............................. 13.08
- Art 6(5)(b)..........................4.21
- Art 6(6) 13.05
- Art 14(5) 6.83
- Art 15.............. 4.40, 6.21, 13.06, 13.07
- Art 15(3) 13.07
- Art 15(6) 13.07

Art 18	6.81, 13.08
Art 18(1)	6.91, 13.07
Art 18(5)	13.08
Art 19	14.16
Art 24(11)	13.04
Art 24(7)	4.92
Art 27	4.74
Regulation 241/2014, Art 10	6.54
Regulation 468/2014 (SSM Framework Regulation)	
Art 2(21)(a) and (b)	6.46
Art 2(21)(c)	6.47
Arts 80–84	6.83
Regulation 596/2014 (Market Abuse Regulation)	5.01, 9.84, 13.57
Art 7(1)(a)	9.86
Arts 7–11	5.01
Art 12	9.84
Regulation 806/2014 (SRMR)	4.89, 6.14, 6.81, 7.11, 7.80, 12.59, 14.16
Art 2	13.26
Art 10a	13.29
Art 12(1)	4.47
Art 12(5)	4.47
Art 12h	12.48
Art 12h(1)(8)(c)	13.29
Art 12h(1)(c)	12.49
Art 12i	13.29
Art 15	7.37
Art 18	4.34, 4.44, 4.56
Art 18(1)(c)	4.56
Art 20	7.37, 13.35
Art 20(10)–(11)	13.36
Art 20(11)	7.78, 13.36
Art 20(12)	7.78
Art 20(16)	13.36
Art 20(5)(a)	7.77
Art 34(2)(a)	6.83
Art 65	7.15
Art 85	13.04, 13.29
Regulation 1310/2014	7.15
Regulation 2015/1589	4.59
Art 4(4)	4.60
Regulation 2015/2422	14.02
Regulation 2015/848	8.05
Regulation 2016/1075	4.47
Regulation 2016/1799 laying down implementing technical standards with regard to the mapping of credit assessments of external credit assessment institutions for credit risk	4.43, 13.22
Regulation 2017/1001 (Trademark Regulation)	14.07, 14.20
Regulation 2017/1129 (Prospectus Regulation	9.72
Regulation 2017/1129 (Prospectus Regulation), Art 11	9.53, 9.72
Regulation 2017/2361	13.26, 13.27
Art 2(3)	13.27
Art 5(4)	7.15
Art 8(1)	7.15
Regulation 2017/2394	13.51
Regulation 2019/629	13.14, 14.19
Regulation 2019/980	9.72
Regulation 2019/2175	12.40, 13.19
Regulation 2019/2175 (ESAs Regulations)	4.74, 12.10, 14.16
Art 9(5)	6.26
Art 10	4.28, 4.43
Art 15	4.28, 13.22
Art 16	4.28
Rome Convention	
Art 3(3)	10.18
Rome I Regulation	
Art 3(3)	10.16
Art 9(3)	7.90
Rules of Procedure of the ECB, Art 17	4.28
Statute of the Court of Justice of the European Union	
Art 6	12.14
Protocol No 3	13.14, 14.02
Statute of the European System of Central Banks	
Art 14(4)	5.22
Art 37	4.74
Treaty establishing the ESM	5.04
Treaty on European Union (TEU)	
Art 2	12.12, 12.36
Art 5	1.13, 6.11
Art 5(4)	5.14
Art 7	12.12
Art 13	3.07
Art 19	4.34, 12.12
Art 20	14.07
Protocol 4	
Art 35(1) and (4)	4.13
Art 35(2)	4.13
Treaty on the Functioning of the European Union (TFEU)	14.22
Art 11	12.39
Art 15	4.70, 4.82, 13.34
Arts 63ff	6.54
Art 67	3.05
Art 67(4)	13.66, 14.01, 14.03, 14.04
Art 81	14.05
Art 81(2)	13.66, 14.01, 14.03, 14.04, 14.20
Art 101	13.53
Art 102	13.53
Art 107(2)(b)	4.59
Arts 107ff	4.57
Art 108	4.59
Art 114	4.89, 6.12, 6.26, 6.27, 7.09, 7.11, 14.16
Art 114(1)	7.12

Art 114(2) 7.12
Art 123 .... 4.13, 5.03, 5.07, 5.10, 5.15
Art 123(1) 5.04
Art 125 ....5.04, 5.07
Art 126 ....5.04
Art 127(1) 4.70, 5.03, 5.13, 12.39
Art 127(2) 4.32, 5.22
Art 127(4) 4.10
Art 127(5) 5.03, 5.23
Art 127(6) 4.89, 5.03, 6.12, 6.15
Art 130 .... 4.13, 5.05, 14.16
Art 136 ....5.04
Art 136(3) 5.04
Art 253 .... 12.10
Art 255 .... 12.10
Art 256(3) 14.02
Art 257 .... 12.10, 12.15, 13.66, 14.01,
14.02, 14.15, 14.16, 14.18
Art 261 .... 3.08, 6.91, 12.54, 13.08, 14.19
Art 263 ...... 4.10, 4.30, 4.31, 4.35, 4.36, 4.57,
5.07, 12.46, 13.04, 13.07, 13.22, 14.07
Art 263(1) 3.03
Art 263(4) 3.11, 4.52, 4.56, 13.04
Art 263(5) 12.46
Art 267 ...... 3.11, 4.30, 4.31, 4.35, 4.36, 4.57,
5.10, 6.29, 12.12, 13.24, 13.49, 13.62,
14.02, 14.05, 14.07, 14.19, 14.21
Art 281 .... 14.02, 14.19
Art 281(2) 13.14, 14.02
Art 282(5) 4.10
Art 288(4) 7.58
Art 290 ....3.09
Arts 290–291 ....6.26
Art 291 ....3.09
Art 296 .... 6.76, 12.48, 13.29
Art 340 ....4.10
Art 344 .... 13.62

INTERNATIONAL

Convention on Jurisdictional Immunities
of States and their Property 4.03
Art 21(1)I 4.06
Convention on the recognition and
enforcement of foreign judgments
in civil or commercial matters 13.59
European Convention on Human
Rights (ECHR) 3.13, 6.86, 6.100,
13.62, 13.65, 13.66
Art 6 .... 1.28, 4.54, 6.84, 7.24, 7.74
Art 8 ....1.28
Protocol 1, Art 1 ... 1.28, 4.54, 7.24, 7.28, 7.74
ICSID Convention for investment
arbitration 13.59
New York Convention on the Recognition
and Enforcement of Foreign Arbitral
Awards 13.59

UNIDROIT Convention on
intermediated securities
Art 21 .... 11.48
Art 22 .... 11.48
Art 26(2)(b) 11.48
UPC Agreement 14.06, 14.07

NATIONAL

Argentina

Law 26.961 ....4.06

China

Immunity Act, Order of the President
no 41 [2005] October 28, Art 1 ....4.06

Cuba

Law No 793 (1960), Art 1 ....4.06

Czech Republic

Constitution, Art 10 ....3.05

France

Civil Code
Art 1240 .... 9.06, 9.09
Financial and Monetary Code (FMC) 4.95,
6.19, 6.55, 6.63
Art L. 511–13 .... 6.19, 6.58

Germany

Basic Law 5.10, 6.73
Art 23(1) 14.06
Art 28(2) 10.10
Art 79(2) 14.06
Art 79(3) 3.05
Civil Code 9.02
s 31 ....9.87
s 134 .... 10.13
s 138 .... 10.13, 10.14
s 309 .... 10.90
s 309(12)(1)(b) 10.90
s 309(12)(2) 10.91
s 311 .... 9.114
s 823 .... 9.87, 9.118
s 823(1) 8.19, 9.03
s 823(2) 9.03
s 826 .... 8.19, 9.87, 9.91
Commercial Code
ss 316ff 9.114
s 323 .... 9.114
Investment Products Act 9.59
Securities Prospectus Act 9.59, 9.140
s 23(2)(1) 9.73
s 23(2)(2) 9.73

Securities Trading Act
   ss 97–98 .... 9.87

Italy
Banking Act
   Art 120 .... 12.69
Civil Code 9.06, 10.77
   Art 1411 .... 9.09
   Art 1815 .... 12.69
   Art 2043 .... 9.06, 9.09
Consolidated Financial Act 10.77, 10.91
Law Decree No 394/2000 .... 12.69
Law Decree No 73/2021 .... 12.64
Law No 108/1996 .... 12.69
Legislative Decree No 58/1998 .... 13.49
Legislative Decree No 385/2003 .... 13.49
Legislative Decree No 164/2007 .... 13.49
Legislative Decree No 3/2017 .... 13.56
Penal Code
   Art 644 .... 12.69

Japan
Act on the Civil Jurisdiction of Japan
   with respect to a Foreign State
   Arts 5–6 .... 4.06

Netherlands
Civil Code 10.11
   s 6:194 .... 9.71

Portugal
Civil Code
   Art 437 .... 10.19
   Art 1245 .... 10.19
Decree No 67/2012 of 20 March 2012 .... 13.10
Law no 46/2011 of 21 June 2011 .... 13.10

Spain
Act 1/1999, Additional Provision 3a 11.23
Capital Companies Act 10.06
Civil Code
   Art 1103 .... 9.09
   Art 1257 .... 9.09
   Art 1902 .... 9.06
Constitution
   Art 18 .... 9.96
Organic Law 4/1982 .... 9.96
Royal Decree 1310/2005 .... 9.141
Royal Decree-Law 6/2013 of 23 March ... 12.67

United Kingdom
Bank of England Act
   s 244 .... 4.12
   s 244(3) 4.12

Civil Procedure Rules
   6.20(9) 4.03
Companies Act 2006
   s 750 .... 11.94
   s 994 .... 11.77
Contracts (Rights of Third Parties) Act 1999 .... 9.07
Financial Services and Markets Act
   (FSMA) 2000 .... 8.22, 9.137, 10.67
   s 27 .... 10.88
   s 138D 10.63
   s 150 .... 10.64
Insolvency Act 1986 .... 11.59
   s 6 .... 11.77
   s 123 .... 11.70
   s 123(1) 11.73
   s 123(2) 11.76
Regulated Activities Order (RAO) 2001 ..... 10.67
State Immunity Act 1978
   ss 2–11 .... 4.03
   s 14(4) 4.06
Statute of 13 .... 11.13
Tribunals, Courts and Enforcement
   Act 2007 .... 13.09
Trustee Act 2000
   Sch 1 .... 11.94
Unfair Contract Terms Act 1977
   s 11(1) 10.83

United States
5 USC
   s 552(a)(3) and (b) 4.62
   s 552(a)(4)(B) 4.62
   s 552(b) 4.62
   s 701 .... 3.02, 3.06, 4.18
   s 5491(c)(3) 4.86
11 USC
   s 362(a)(1)(6) 11.16
   s 1112(b) 11.68
   s 1129(b) 11.77
   s 1129(b)(1) 11.77
12 USC
   s 24 .... 5.23, 6.25
   s 36(c)(2) 6.06
   s 241 .... 5.23
   s 263(a) 5.23
   s 302 .... 5.23
   s 304 .... 5.23
   s 343 .... 7.26
   s 1464(d)(6)(A) 7.67
   s 1813(l)(1) 7.51
   s 1819(a) 4.12
   s 3907(a)(2) 6.70
   s 3907(b)(1) 6.70
   s 5229 .... 5.06
   ss 5381 ff 7.03
   s 5491(a) 4.86

TABLE OF LEGISLATION

15 USC
- s 77 . . . . 6.78, 9.42, 9.46, 11.95
- s 77k(e). 9.42
- s 77t(d) 6.78
- s 77z–2 . . . . .9.46
- s 78aa 9.16
- s 78b(2) 8.14
- s 78c(a)(17) 8.14
- ss 78c(f) 6.50
- s 78d–1(a) 4.91
- s 78j(b) 9.12
- s 78n(a) 9.16
- s 78t(e) 9.125
- s 78u-4(2)(A). 13.52
- s 78u-4(3)(A). 13.52
- s 78u-4(b)(2) 9.25
- s 78u-4(b)(4) 9.32
- s 78u-5 . . . . .9.46
- s 78w(a)(2). 6.50
- s 78y(a)(1) 13.12

17 CFR
- s 240.10b-5. . . . . .9.12

18 USC
- Ch 73 . . . . .2.43
- s 1519 . . . . .2.43

22 USC
- s 288(a), (b) 4.07
- s 8772 . . . . .4.06

28 USC
- s 1602 . . . . .4.01
- s 1604 . . . . .4.01
- s 2462 . . . . .6.78

38 USC
- s 211(a). 3.02

Administrative Procedure Act
  (APA) 3.07, 4.12, 4.27, 5.06, 5.09,
    6.50, 7.64, 7.66, 7.67, 7.68, 7.70, 13.12
- s 551(5). 4.26
- s 553(b) and (c) 4.26
- s 702 . . . . 3.02, 4.12
- s 706 . . . . 3.07, 6.49, 12.51
- s 706(2)(a) 2.15

Alien Tort Statute 3.12
Bank Holding Company
  (BHC) Act 6.36, 6.44
- s 4(c)(8) 6.22

Bankruptcy Code
- s 362(b)(17) 10.114
- s 365(e). 11.36
- s 365(e)(1) 11.38
- s 541(c)(1)(B) 11.36, 11.38
- s 546(e). 11.41
- s 548(a)(l)(B). 11.13
- s 560 . . . . 10.114, 11.37

Bankruptcy Reform Act
- s 912 . . . . 11.21

California Code Civ Proc
- s 425.15 . . . . 9.103

Civil Rights Act 8.14
Constitution 2.43, 4.83, 4.87, 4.91, 5.06,
    5.23, 8.03
  Amendment No I 9.96–9.98, 9.103,
    9.104, 9.111, 13.63
  Amendment No V 8.02
  Amendment No XIV
  - s 1 . . . . .8.02
  Art I 12.09, 12.23
  - s 8 . . . . 12.04
  Art II. 13.12
  - s 1 cl 1 . . . . .2.45
  - s 2 cl 2 . . . . .5.23
  - s 2 cl. 2 . . . . .4.91
  Art III. 3.02, 4.02, 12.09
  - s 2 . . . . .3.02
  Art IV, s 1 . . . . .8.02
  Art VI, cl 2 . . . . .3.04

Dodd-Frank Act 4.50, 4.87, 5.21, 6.03,
    6.44, 6.52, 10.25, 13.12
- ss 201-217 . . . . .7.03
- ss 201-217 . . . . .7.03
- s 203(b) 7.03
- s 616(d) 6.44
- s 933 . . . . 9.134
- s 971 . . . . .6.51
- s 1001 . . . . .4.86

Durbin-Delahunt Act. 11.21
Emergency Economic Stabilization Act. 5.06
Employee Abuse Prevention Act. 11.21
Fair Labor Standards Act 3.07
Federal Home Loan Act
- s 5(d). 7.08

Federal Reserve Act .5.05
- s 4 . . . . .5.01
- s 10 . . . . .5.01
- s 13(3). 5.21, 7.26

Federal Tort Claims Act 3.02, 4.12, 7.25
Financial Institutions Reform, Recovery,
    and Enforcement Act 7.69, 7.70
- s 1821(e)(12)(A) 11.32

Foreign Sovereign Immunities
  Act 4.01, 4.02, 4.06, 4.07
Freedom of Information Act 4.62–4.65, 4.69
Glass-Steagall Act 6.03, 6.06, 6.07, 6.22,
    6.23, 6.25, 6.35–6.38
Home Owner Loan Act 7.67
Insider Trading and Securities Fraud
  Enforcement Act. 9.51
Insider Trading Sanctions Act. 9.51
International Organizations Immunities Act 4.07
Investment Advisers Act 1940 . . . . 8.18, 9.15,
    10.24, 10.33
- s 202(a)(11)(A)–(G) 10.25

s 202(a)(11)(C) 10.25	s 10b 1.13, 8.04, 8.13, 8.16, 8.22,
s 203(1) and (2) 10.34	9.11, 9.37, 9.39, 9.54, 9.89, 9.94,
s 206(3) 10.29	9.131, 9.136, 10.34, 10.35, 13.53
s 215 .... 10.34	s 14 .... 9.16, 9.37
McFadden Act 6.06, 6.07, 6.25	s 14(a) 8.18, 9.17
National Bank Act of 1864 (NBA) 6.06, 6.08	s 14a 9.17
Perishable Agricultural Commodities Act (PACA) 11.22	s 15(a) 10.25
	s 15(c) 10.28
Private Securities Litigation Reform Act 1.13, 8.04, 9.24, 9.25, 9.31,	s 20 .... 9.51
9.44, 9.46, 9.47, 9.51, 9.125, 13.52	s 78u-5 .... 9.46
Restatement (Second) on Torts	Securities Litigation Uniform Standards Act 9.44, 9.45
s 552 .... 9.111	s 77p(b) 9.46
Riegle-Neal Interstate Banking and Branching Efficiency Act 6.07	s 77p(c) 9.46
	s 77p(f)(2) 9.46
Sarbanes-Oxley Act	s 77p(f)(3) 9.46
s 806 .... 2.43	Trust Indenture Act 11.65, 11.80–11.83
Securities Act 1933 .... 8.29, 9.37, 9.46, 9.48, 10.35	s 315(a) 11.95
s 11 .... 8.22, 9.38, 9.89, 9.134, 9.136	s 315(d) 11.95
s 12 .... 9.38	s 316(b) 11.60, 11.79, 11.88, 11.111
Securities Enforcement Remedies and Penny Stock Reform Act 6.78	Tucker Act 3.02, 4.12
	Uniform Commercial Code 11.48
Securities Exchange Act of 1934 ..... 1.23, 9.124	Uniform Fraudulent Transfer Act,
s 2(1)(a) 12.04	ss 4(a)(2), 5(a) 11.13
s 3(17) 12.04	Ute Partition Act 9.19

List of Abbreviations

ACER	Agency for the Cooperation of Energy Regulators
ADR	alternative dispute resolution
AIG	American International Group
AML	anti-money laundering
APA	Administrative Procedure Act
ATMs	automatic teller machines
Banxico	Central Bank of Mexico
BHCs	bank holding companies
BoJ	Bank of Japan
BRRD	Bank Recovery and Resolution Directive
CACs	collective action clauses
CBA	cost-benefit analysis
CCPs	central counterparties (
CDOs	collateralized debt obligations
CDSs	credit default swaps
CETA	EU–Canada Comprehensive Economic and Trade Agreement
CFT	countering the financing of terrorism
Charter	EU Charter of Fundamental Rights
CLNs	credit-linked notes, or
CLS	critical legal studies
CMOs	collateralized mortgage obligations
COB	conduct of business
CP	commercial paper
CPC	Community Patents Court
CPVO	Community Plant Variety Office
CRAR	Credit Rating Agencies Regulation
CRR	Capital Requirements Regulation
CST	Civil Service Tribunal
DFS	Directorate of Financial Services
DGS	deposit guarantee scheme
DIS	deposit insurance system
EASA	European Aviation Safety Agency
ECB	European Central Bank
ECHA	European Chemicals Agency
ECHR	European Convention on Human Rights
EDIS	European DIS
EEA	European Economic Area
ELA	emergency liquidity assistance
Eos	executive orders
ESCP	European small claims procedure
ESM	European Stability Mechanism
EUIPO	European Union Office for the Protection of Intellectual Property
FDIC	Federal Deposit Insurance Corporation

FHLBB	Federal Home Loan Bank Board
FinCen	Financial Crimes Enforcement Network
FIRREA	Financial Institutions Reform, Recovery, and Enforcement Act of 1989
FLF	fixed-linked finance
FOLTF	failing-or-likely-to-fail
FOMC	Federal Open Market Committee
FRBNY	Federal Reserve Bank of New York
FSIA	Foreign Sovereign Immunities Act
FSLIC	Federal Savings and Loan Insurance Corporation
FSMA	Financial Services and Markets Act
FSOC	Financial Stability and Oversight Council
FTCA	Federal Tort Claims Act
G-SIFIs	Globally Systemic Financial Institutions
HKMA	Hong Kong Monetary Authority
IFA	independent financial adviser
IRS	interest rate swap
ISDA	International Swaps and Derivatives Association
ITSs	Implementing Technical Standard
LoLR	lender of last resort
MAS	Monetary Authority of Singapore
MBS	mortgage-backed securities
MLCBI	Model Law on Cross-Border Insolvency
MLEGI	Model Law on Enterprise Group Insolvency
MLRIJ	Model Law on Recognition and Enforcement of Insolvency-Related Judgments
MREL	minimum requirements for capital and eligible liabilities
NCAs	national competent authorities
NCWO	no-creditor worse-off
NPLs	non-performing loans
OCC	Office of the Comptroller of the Currency
OLA	Orderly Liquidation Authority
OLAF	European Anti-Fraud Office
OTS	Office of Thrift Supervision
PBoC	People's Bank of China
PONV	point-of-non-viability
PSLRA	Private Securities Litigation Reform Act
RBI	Reserve Bank of India
REIT	real estate investment trust
RFAs	resolution funding arrangement
RTC	Resolution Trust Corporation
RTS	Regulatory Technical Standards
SIV	structured investment vehicle
S&L	savings and loan
SNB	Swiss National Bank
SRB	Single Resolution Board
SRF	Single Resolution Fund
SRM	Single Resolution Mechanism
TARP	Troubled Asset Relief Program
TCEA	Tribunals, Courts and Enforcement Act 2007 (UK)
TLAC	total loss-absorbency capacity
UPC	Unified Patent Court
WTO	World Trade Organization

Authors' Biographies

Marco Lamandini is professor of law at the Alma Mater Studiorum Università degli Studi di Bologna, a vice-chair of the Academic Board of the European Banking Institute (EBI), and a member of the Academic Board of the European Capital Markets Institute (ECMI), a former (the second) President of the Board of Appeal of the European Financial Supervisory Authorities, a member of the Appeal Panel for the Single Resolution Board (SRB), a member of the Italian Arbitro Bancario Finanziario, a member of the Informal Company Law Expert Group (ICLEG) appointed by the European Commission, and an external legal expert to the ECON Committee of the European Parliament on bank resolution matters. He has published extensively, regularly since 2015 with David Ramos Muñoz, on banking and financial law. With OUP he has already published *Capital and Liquidity Requirements for EU Banks*, edited by Bart Joosen, Tobias Tröger, and Marco Lamandini (2022).

David Ramos Muñoz is associate professor of law at Universidad Carlos III de Madrid, and a regular visiting professor at the Alma Mater Studiorum Università degli Studi di Bologna. He is a member of the European Banking Institute (EBI) and European Law Institute (ELI), an alternate member of the Board of Appeal of the European Financial Supervisory Authorities and an alternate member of the Appeal Panel for the Single Resolution Board (SRB), and an external legal expert to the ECON Committee of the European Parliament on bank resolution matters. He has published extensively, regularly since 2015 with Marco Lamandini, on banking and financial law. With OUP he has already published *The Law of Transnational Securitization* (2010).

PART I
THE CONCEPTUAL FRAMEWORK

1
An Introduction to Courts' and Principles-Based Interpretivism

1 Disputes in the law of finance and courts' principles-based interpretivism	1.01	5 Critical views: Rules-based positivism and pragmatism	1.35
2 Principles, financial stability, and interpretation	1.23	6 Principles-based interpretivism versus plausibly similar alternatives in the adjudication of law of finance: the case of cost-benefit analysis and the discourse theory of justice	1.47
3 Principles-based interpretivism, heuristics, and biases	1.29		
4 Principles-based interpretivism and legitimacy	1.31		

1 Disputes in the law of finance and courts' principles-based interpretivism

This book focuses on financial disputes, courts, and the law of finance. In academic and policy-making circles, we speak of 'constitutional law', 'civil law', or 'administrative law', but of 'financial regulation' as if finance's rules and norms were something alien to, or distinct from, 'law'. This emphasizes finance's peculiarities, such as the presence of regulatory norms, the use of soft law, the norm-producing status of administrative authorities, and the relevance of global standard-setting bodies. As a matter of fact, in the law of finance there is, first, a (growing) emphasis on tools that do not fit squarely within traditional conceptions of law: policy statements, press releases, guidelines, memoranda of understanding (MoU), or no-action letters have no obvious legal standing, but to market participants they clearly indicate the official position on legally significant issues. Secondly, in the law of finance there is a prominent role for authorities like central banks or financial supervisors, which seem more norm-producing than norm-accepting, and are sometimes granted so much discretion as to raise the question whether they move within the 'legal' universe, or in a parallel one. Third, the growing importance of global and supranational bodies, which, without any electoral backing, dictate the standards that finance is supposed to abide by. Governmental bodies and agencies are judicially accountable; other, global bodies are not clearly so; and some, like ISDA (the International Swaps and Derivatives Association), are private bodies, which rely on market participants to disseminate their legal standards via private contracting. All these phenomena accelerated after the global financial crisis, raising one pertinent question: are we witnessing law's eclipse in finance? Our answer is a resounding 'no'. Finance presents unique problems for the law, but these need to be answered from inside legal practice.

1.01

1.02 This, in turn, raises several challenges. One, explaining why finance's peculiarities are important for law, and why a legal perspective is important for finance, and finding a conceptual framework that reconciles both sides. Two, to use this conceptual framework to explain how the substantive specialties of finance can be woven together with existing legal practice in concrete practical settings. Three, to explore how this goal could be furthered from a procedural perspective through the use of specialized courts not as a mechanism to replace generalist courts, but to complement them. With all these forces pushing towards specialization, finance's rules may drift away from the logic of law and courts. Is that desirable or inevitable? In our view, neither is inevitable, and, while specialization is desirable, the 'drift' is not. Law and courts provide finance with the certainty it needs to operate, and the elasticity it needs to evolve. This combination of strengths results from law's status as an interpretative construct formed by both rules and principles, which are malleable enough, but can also operate in predictable ways. Yet, these benefits are inextricably linked to the need for consistency across the *whole* legal system. Thus, there will be 'hard cases', where the solution is not preordained by the rules, and where principles collide. This can be a source of drift and instability, but also of evolution and strength. 'Weaving' finance's specificity into the fabric of law's more general questions is essential for both finance and law, and can only be accomplished by courts. We divide the book between Part I, where we explain the theoretical foundations of the role of law and courts; Parts II and III, where we explain how courts have shaped the public law and private law of finance, by combining finance's specific needs with law's broader general principles; and a Part IV, where we make the case for limited specialization of finance justice in the EU. With a note of caution: our scope is functional, and the term 'court' is used throughout this book to encompass also arbitral tribunals and 'quasi-judicial' bodies, to the extent that they render decisions pertaining to the law of finance.

1.03 This book draws comparatively from case law which primarily originates from the European Union (EU), the United Kingdom (UK), and the United States (US), with some references to other jurisdictions, and proposes a taxonomy of cases, both in the public law and in the private law of finance, which highlight finance's specialties. This book also illustrates how the answer to the overwhelming complexity of finance has been a gradual increase in reliance on general principles of law and procedural specialization, and studies its significance.[1]

---

[1] There are excellent books which deal with aspects of regulation and adjudication in the law of finance which are also considered in this book. However, their focus and approach are different from ours and our book is to some extent unique in the existing literature. A recent and excellent book on judicial review in the Banking Union is Chiara Zilioli and Karl-Philipp Wojcik (eds), *Judicial Review in the European Banking Union* (Elgar Financial Law and Practice 2021). Compare also, for a discussion of the case law on the Banking Union, Raffaele D'Ambrosio (ed), *Law and Practice of the Banking Union and of Its Governing Institutions: Cases and Materials* (Quaderni di Ricerca Giuridica della Consulenza Legale No, Bank of Italy, No 88, April 2020); Raffaele D'Ambrosio and others (eds), *Pandectae: Digest of the Case-law on the Banking Union* (Quaderni di Ricerca Giuridica della Consulenza Legale, Bank of Italy, No 92, December 2022). Another excellent book is William Blair, Richard Brent, and Tom Grant, *Banks and Financial Crime: The International Law of Tainted Money* (2nd edn, OUP 2017), which shares with ours the focus on the importance of enforcement through the courts of financial law. Its focus is, however, criminal enforcement. This is also true for Giulia Lasagni, *Banking Supervision and Criminal Investigation, Comparing the EU and US Experiences* (Springer International Publishing 2019); and Silvia Allegrezza (ed), *The Enforcement Dimension of the Single Supervisory Mechanism* (Wolter Kluwer 2020). Thomas Cottier, Rosa M Lastra, and Christian Tietje (eds), *The Rule of Law in Monetary Affairs: World Trade Forum* (CUP 2014) shares with ours a message on the importance of accountability and the rule of law, but it focuses on 'monetary' issues and 'policy' more than on 'disputes' and 'courts'. Christopher Hodges, *Law and Corporate Behaviour: Integrating Theories of Regulation, Enforcement, Compliance and Ethics* (Hart Publishing 2015) also deals, as our book does, with the role of 'law' in constraining financial behaviour, considering, however, corporate law and competition law. Justin O'Brien and George Gilligan, *Integrity, Risk and Accountability in Capital Markets: Regulating Culture* (Hart Publishing 2013) and Gerald Nels Olson, *Money, Morality and Law: A Case for Financial Crisis Accountability* (Kluwer Law International 2019) share with ours a message on the importance of accountability and the rule of law. They do not focus on the fitness of the institutional design for financial disputes adjudication. Joanna

In a field characterized by fluidity and burgeoning activity, both among market practice and **1.04**
regulation, a focus on either gives the impression of a constantly moving target, and yet the
big questions that emerge in financial disputes tend to be surprisingly stable. In the public
law disputes, they concern, for example, the mandates of regulatory and supervisory authorities, their exercise of delegated competences, including enforcement and sanctioning powers and the level of discretion granted to them for assessing facts, or making complex technical assessments or entering the area of policy, which parties have standing to challenge their acts, what acts can be challenged, and how their powers are checked by the fundamental rights of the parties affected by their actions. In private law disputes, they concern an array of different issues concerning, eg, liability for misstatements or misbehaviour, violations of directors' (and other trustees') fiduciary duties, approaches to contract validity and interpretation, and collateral enforcement.

Finance offers important twists when answering all those questions. The exercise of competences is not the same for financial regulators than for other public authorities, and even less so for central banks. In finance, who can challenge a supervisory action becomes a loaded question, for instance when a financial institution's board is replaced with special administrators or trustees appointed by the regulator; at the same time, private law doctrines of tort and contract liability are interspersed with regulatory standards in ways that are often hard to fathom. In turn, fiduciary duties can be decisively shaped by notions of 'financial risk' among others, and collateral enforcement can be extremely challenging when the 'asset' only exists in the imagination or expectations of the parties, and the extremely complex documentation devised by them. This shows that finance's peculiarities are important for law. In turn, however, a legal perspective is important for finance, and both sides need to be reconciled. **1.05**

This requires paying attention to the way financial disputes are handled on their merit in **1.06**
their respective *fora* and see how these decisions, *fora*, and their procedures make use of values, principles, and rules and of their interconnections to respond to the rule of law, and

---

Jemielniak, Laura Nielsen, and Henrik Palmer Olsen, *Establishing Judicial Authority in International Economic Law* (CUP 2018) focuses on the role of 'law' and courts in economic activity, yet it considers WTO disputes, not financial disputes. On the growing number of international courts, a must-read is still Ruth Mackenzie and others (eds), *The Manual on International Courts and Tribunals* (2nd edn, OUP 2010) and, in an historical perspective, Hélène Ruiz Fabri, Michel Erpelding (eds), *The Mixed Arbitral Tribunal 1919-1939, An Experiment in the International Adjudication of Private Rights* (Nomos 2023)Several excellent contributions include Danny Busch, Guido Ferrarini, and Jan Paul Franx (eds), *Prospectus Regulation & Prospectus Liability* (OUP 2020); Danny Busch and Cees van Dam, *A Bank's Duty of Care* (Hart Publishing 2017); Danny Busch, Laura Macgregor, and Peter Watts (eds), *Agency Law in Commercial Practice* (OUP 2016); and more recently Danny Busch, 'The Influence of EU Prospectus Rules on Private Law' (2021) 16 CMLJ 3; 'Self-Placement, Dealing on Own Account and the Provision of Investment Services under MIFID I & II' (2019) 14 CMLJ 4; Danny Busch, 'The Private Law Effect of the EU Market Abuse Regulation' (2019) 14 CMLJ 296; and Danny Busch, 'The Private Law Effect of MIFID: The Genil Case and Beyond' (2017) 13 ERCL 70, as well as the books of Raffaele D'Ambrosio and Stefano Montemaggi (eds), *Private and Public Enforcement of EU Investor Protection Regulation* (Quaderni di Ricerca Giuridica della Consulenza Legale, Bank of Italy, No 90, October 2020), Federico della Negra, *MiFID II and Private Law: Enforcing EU Conduct of Business Rules* (Hart Publishing 2019); Shala F Ali, *Consumer Financial Dispute Resolution in a Comparative Context: Principles, Systems and Practice* (CUP 2013); and Stefan Grundmann and Yeşim M Atamer, *Financial Services, Financial Crisis and General European Contract Law* (Kluwer Law International 2011) analyse systems for financial disputes across the world, but they focus on consumer/investor disputes. Pierre Henry Conac and Martin Gelter (eds), *Global Securities Litigation and Enforcement* (CUP 2019) focuses on 'securities' disputes. On specialized justice, two books stand out in the literature, but with a generalist view see Stephen Legomsky, *Specialized Justice: Courts, Administrative Tribunals, and a Cross-National Theory of Specialization* (Clarendon Press 1990) (although because it was published in 1990, it does not focus on finance in particular, where the argument for specialization is more pressing, and it lacks a practical discussion of cases) and Lawrence Baum, *Specializing the Courts* (University of Chicago Press 2011), which offers a mostly US-based perspective, without a focus on finance.

to help the legal system evolve to adjust to finance's peculiarities. Financial rules' single-mindedness pursuance of one or more overarching values (investor protection, solvency, financial stability) needs to be reconciled with basic legal principles (the rule of law, separation of powers, fundamental rights, property, or contract freedom) and to dispel a wide array of collisions among rules. The symbiosis between law's and financial regulation's principles also applies when the goal at stake is 'stability', and it helps to limit biases and to foster legitimacy. In our view, financial crises provide less an argument for 'suspending' law's role in finance than for strengthening it. In fact, crisis situations are but one example of 'hard cases', ie legal problems that cannot be solved by reference to a single provision and require a deeper reflection over the underpinning legal principles, and the balance between them. For this reason, we claim in this book that courts must rely on principles-based interpretivism to determine the fitness of a certain decision within the law's overall scheme. This requires acknowledging that, in an important number of cases, it does not suffice to discuss the scope of application of a legal rule in isolation, but to understand the considerations of principle supporting that rule, and how they shape its scope and intensity also in relation to other rules and principles. In such exercise, there is a need for greater awareness of the fact that different sets of rules may be inspired by conflicting values and narratives, which need to be considered together, in order to determine whether a specific exercise of authority is legal. A case-by-case analysis can not only result in errors prompted by heuristic biases. It may undermine the integrity of the whole regulatory edifice. This, in turn, requires expert judgment, and thus courts' design has implications for the outcome of the decision-making process.

1.07 Courts are 'curious institutions':[2]

> For some, courts are major decision-makers that function as principals on a par with legislators and executives in developing, monitoring and adapting public policies. Others take quite the opposite view, envisioning courts as more modest institutions whose functions involve arbitrating public and private disputes by doing little more than faithfully interpreting existing law.[3]

For legal realists in the United States, and formalists in civil law jurisdictions[4] courts are a fundamental component of the *trias politica*. For others, however, courts are 'under-funded, under-supported, under-trained and under-protected', and thus 'a neglected branch of government'.[5]

1.08 In this book, we claim that courts are an essential component of the law of finance and, whilst supreme courts at the apex of the judicial systems normally are well-equipped generalist courts which can cope with (mostly episodical, albeit often consequential) case law in financial matters without more,[6] lower courts need to address a wide range of difficult issues of

---

[2] Martin Shapiro, *Courts: A Comparative and Political Analysis* (University of Chicago Press 1981) 1.
[3] Kevin T McGuire, 'The Judicial Process and Public Policy' in RAW Rhodes, Sarah A Binder, and Bert A Rockman (eds), *The Oxford Handbook of Political Institutions* (OUP 2008) 535; Koen Lenaerts, 'The Court's Outer and Inner Selves: Exploring the External and Internal Legitimacy of the European Court of Justice' in Maurice Adams and others (eds), *Judging Europe's Judges* (Hart Publishing 2015) 13; and Joseph HH Weiler, 'Epilogue: Judging the Judges—Apology and Critique' in Maurice Adams and others (eds), *Judging Europe's Judges* (Hart Publishing 2015) 240–41.
[4] Mitchel de S-O-l'E Lasser, *Judicial Deliberations: A Comparative Analysis of Judicial Transparency and Legitimacy* (OUP 2004); Mitchel de S-O-l'E Lasser, 'Transforming Deliberations' in Nick Huls, Maurice Adams, and Jacco Bomhoff (eds), *The Legitimacy of Highest Courts' Rulings* (Asser Press 2009) 33–53.
[5] Hiram E Chodosh, *Global Justice Reform* (New York University Press 2005) 5.
[6] Supreme Courts often count, however, internally, on the specialisation of one or more members in the relevant area of law: compare Chris Hanretty, *A Court of Specialists: Judicial Behavior on the UK Supreme Court* (OUP 2020), in particular 38, 66, 114, 135, 143.

fact and of law and their specialization in the law of finance may hugely help to 'take rights seriously' in finance. We further argue that in Europe courts' specialization may bode well for the new legal order established with the Banking Union,[7] and may decisively contribute to its consistent application, improvement, and expansion under the rule of law.[8] The same is true in the framework of the still developing Capital Markets Union. For this reason, for Europe we advance a proposal for a bespoke mechanism of enhanced judicial cooperation (which may possibly evolve into a dual-court system in the future),[9] which seems to us desirable both from an external and internal perspective[10] and also as a first European response to the ongoing process of 'judicial globalization'.[11]

We argue in this book that in the law of finance courts need to ensure coherence through principled-based interpretivism,[12] one which can occasionally enter the territory of policy.[13] In a sense, we build on an intuition of Katharina Pistor[14] and we consider courts as one of the fundamental 'safety valves of the financial system'. As 'safety valves', courts must then calibrate the interpretation and application of the law of finance 'to adapt it to an inherently unstable financial system' without undermining the credibility of legal certainty and without transforming law in a 'weapon of mass destruction'.[15]

1.09

---

[7] For a discussion whether the European Banking Union is a potential boost to (and blueprint for) integration or a potential blow to democracy see Stefan Grundmann and Hans-W Micklitz (eds), *The European Banking Union and Constitution. Beacon for Advanced Integration or Death-Knell for Democracy?* (Hart Publishing 2019).

[8] Lady Arden of Heswall, 'Foreword' in Chiara Zilioli and Karl-Philipp Wojcik (eds), *Judicial Review in the European Banking Union* (Elgar Edward Publishing 2021) xxvi.

[9] For a seminal proposal dating back to 1990, noting that a new judicial architecture 'should feature as an important item on the agenda' see Jean Paul Jacqué and Joseph HH Weiler, 'On the Road to European Union: A New Judicial Architecture: An Agenda for the Intergovernmental Conference' (1990) 27 CMLR 185.

[10] We use the term 'external' to analyse legal decisions (and their institutional setting) in accordance with criteria external to legal practice, eg whether certain decisions are good for efficiency, expediency, etc. We use the term 'internal' to analyse decisions (and their institutional setting) in accordance with criteria internal to legal practice, eg whether a decision is 'valid' in light of its consistency with precedent and principles. For other authors, an 'internal' view looks not at the outputs of the courts (their decisions), but also at the way courts actually function and their inner working practices and relationships: Jeffrey L Dunoff and Mark A Pollack, 'International Judicial Practices: Opening the 'Black Box' of International Courts' (2018) 40 Michigan J Intl L 40 (comparing the practice of dissent between the ECtHR and the CJEU).

[11] Laurence R Helfer and Anne-Marie Slaughter, 'Towards a Theory of Effective Supranational Adjudication' (1997) 107(2) Yale LJ 273.

[12] Ronald Dworkin, *Taking Rights Seriously* (HUP 1977); compare also Ronald Dworkin, *Justice in Robes* (HUP 2006) 50 (advocating, in praise of theory, a 'theory-embedded approach', whereby 'legal reasoning means bringing to bear on particular discrete legal problems a vast network of principles of legal derivation or of political morality', noting that 'in practice, you cannot think about the correct answer to questions of law unless you have thought through or are ready to think through a vast over-arching theoretical system of complex principles about the nature of tort law, for example'). See also Ronald Dworkin, *A Matter of Principle* (HUP 1995) 119–80.

[13] This is adamant in the policy role of the judiciary in the United States, Arthur R Miller, 'The American Class Action: From Birth to Maturity' (2018) 19 Theoretical Inquiries in Law 1, 9:

> 'No one could be elected President and realistically no political party could secure control of the Congress based on promoting racial equality. That would be politically inexpedient, so it was not surprising that the Supreme Court undertook the task in 1954 in the Brown case. American lawyers understand this and are accustomed to resorting to the courts to press sensitive issues of public policy and to challenge governmental conduct even absent legislative or executive branch guidance. Thus, in many contexts the nation's least democratic branch-in the sense that federal judges are not elected and have lifetime appointments-is asked to formulate policy on various emotional and contentious matters, often because the elected branches are politically paralyzed by a division of viewpoints or political inexpediency ... It is an aspect of American exceptionalism ... [A]nd many judges do not shy away from policy issues.'

[14] Katharina Pistor, 'Towards a Legal Theory of Finance' (2013) ECGI Law Working Paper no 196/2013, 48.

[15] ibid 47.

1.10 We acknowledge that whilst in the US judge-made law has a long tradition in Supreme Court's decisions and this is also true for the Supreme Court in the United Kingdom,[16] in Europe courts, including the Court of Justice of the European Union (CJEU) at the apex of the system, are more prudent in openly asserting their role beyond that of 'saying what the law is':[17]

> If courts go beyond their duty of saying 'what the law is' they lack the legitimacy as they intrude into the political process. By drawing the borderline between law and politics, courts in fact are drawing the contours of their own legitimacy. The imperative need for courts to stand behind that line is by no means a novel question, but it has accompanied them ever since the constitutionalism was born. As Chief Justice Marshall famously articulated more than two hundred years ago, in *Marbury v Madison* [5 U.S. 137 (1803)], whilst '[i]t is emphatically the province and duty of the Judicial Department to say what the law is', acts of a political nature 'can never be examinable by the Courts'.

In this vein, European courts refrain 'from rewriting secondary EU law, even if the latter is outdated or no longer fulfils the objectives it pursues'.[18] Yet, despite this self-perceived modest role, European courts interpret primary EU law 'as a living constitution capable of coping with societal change'[19] and go well beyond 'a formalistic understanding of the rule of law', quietly accepting a 'gap-filling function' meant to 'complete the constitutional lacunae left by the authors of the Treaties' by 'setting the founding principles of the EU legal order by having recourse to the general principles of law'.[20] As Lady Arden recently noted, in the Banking Union 'the case law will connect the dots, and what will appear will be the contours of a developed new legal order, and also opportunities for its application, improvement and expansion'.[21] Thus, courts also exert a maieutic function which helps developing and completing a new legal order in finance.

1.11 In so doing, courts often provide solutions to problems that political institutions could not solve. The establishment of the internal market through the coexistence of positive and negative integration techniques, the former entrusted to the Union political bodies and the latter undertaken by the Court is a landmark example.[22] Thus, as Joseph Weiler noted,[23] 'at a minimum there is a tension' between the statements proclaiming court's self-restraint and its gap-filling function and 'that line between law and politics begs more questions that it resolves'. Indeed:[24]

> [C]ourts can no longer confine themselves to applying the legal rules as established by the legislator. Rather they are increasingly expected to weigh and reconcile the relevant

---

[16] Chris Hanretty, *A Court of Specialists. Judicial Behavior on the UK Supreme Court* (OUP 2020) 17–25. Lord Justice Laws, 'Should Judges Make Law?' in Jeremy Cooper (ed), *Being a Judge in the Modern World* (OUP 2017) 199–212,, 199 (in the 'common law world the interpretation and application of the law are interwoven with its creation, because the judges mediate Parliament's legislation to the people, so that, so far as possible, it conforms to civilized constitutional principles whose guardians are the courts').
[17] Lenaerts (n 3) 13.
[18] ibid 26.
[19] ibid 26.
[20] ibid 15. Reconciliatory interpretation, special attention to the objectives pursued by the legislation and the importance of consistency are described as three interpretative means of paramount importance to this end.
[21] Lady Arden of Heswall, 'Foreword' in Chiara Zilioli and Karl-Philipp Wojcik (eds), *Judicial Review in the European Banking Union* (Edward Elgar Publishing 2021) xxvi.
[22] Lenaerts (n 3) 16.
[23] Weiler (n 3) 238, 241.
[24] Adams and others (n 3) 2.

interests themselves. Also, on ever more frequent occasions, courts must derive appropriate standards from the available rules—i.e. principles of good administration and good governance, demarcations of responsibility, etc.—which may then serve as benchmarks for assessing the extent to which conflicting interests should be protected. For that reason, the process of adjudication will necessarily have to be dynamic—at least, if the law itself is to remain a valued means for channeling social developments.

Courts' fundamental mandate is to ensure the rule of law, so as to preserve the legitimacy of the legal order.[25] The European courts echoed this principle in finance recently in *Banco de Portugal v VR*.[26] The Court was confronted, in the context of the Banco Espirito Santo resolution, with the fact that the appellant had brought an action before the competent national judge in February 2015 against Novo Banco in connection with a liability which was originally transferred to Novo Banco under the original resolution arrangement adopted in Portugal in August 2014 but was subsequently retransferred to Banco Espirito Santo with a retroactive decision of December 2015. The Court held that, although a retransfer of liability from Novo Banco to Banco Espirito Santo was allowed under the original arrangement of 2014, it violated the principle of legal certainty in the first place. Yet, the Court also found that 'the imperative of legal certainty' may have a direct bearing also on the right to effective judicial protection guaranteed by Article 47 of the Charter. The Court concluded, in particular, that the reorganization measures adopted in December 2015 were 'aimed precisely to render inoperative' the judgment delivered in October 2015 by the competent court in the dispute brought by the appellant and that:

1.12

> 63 To accept that reorganisation measure taken by the competent authority of the home Member State subsequent to the bringing of such an action and such a judgment, which have the effect of modifying, with retroactive effect, the legal framework relevant to the resolution of the dispute which gave rise to that action, or even directly to the legal situation which is the subject matter of that dispute, might lead the court seized to reject that action, would constitute a restriction on the right to an effective remedy within the meaning of the first paragraph of Article 47 of the Charter.

Another telling example that legal certainty needs to be ensured in finance no matter the importance of the competing values at stake is offered, in the United Kingdom, by a landmark judgment of the Financial List in *Law Debenture v Ukraine*,[27] where the court concluded that it was compelled to allow for summary judgment in respect of non-payment of Eurobonds issued by the Republic of Ukraine and purchased by Russia, taking account of the tradable nature of such instruments, and irrespective the fact that Ukraine claimed that the non-fulfilment of the payment obligation was caused by Russia's invasion of Crimea, its fuelling and supporting separatist elements and its destabilisation of the political situation in Ukraine, causing huge destruction across eastern Ukraine. Justice Blair, endeavouring to sever the aspects of the human tragedy from those of legal certainty, wrote:

---

[25] One of the 'most underspecified concepts in political theory and social science' according to Weiler (n 3) 235; also compare Adams and others (n 3) 5. For the debate on the legitimacy of strong judicial review in a democracy, when judges can quash primary legislation (as is the case for the CJEU) compare Anthony Arnull, 'Judicial Review in the European Union' in Antony Arnull and Damian Chalmers (eds), *Oxford Handbook of European Union Law* (OUP 2015) 379ff (revisiting the Waldron/Kavanagh debate).
[26] Case C-504/19 *Banco de Portugal, Fundo de Resolucao, Novo Banco v VR* ECLI:EU:C:2021:335, para 51.
[27] Case No FL-2016-00002 *The Law Debenture Trust Corporation PLC v Ukraine* [2017] EWHC 655 reversed on appeal and then referred to the Supreme Court. The Supreme Court delivered its final judgment on 15 March 2023 [2023] UKSC 11 unanimously holding that no summary judgment should be granted.

Ukraine submits that there are compelling reasons to proceed to trial [instead of summary judgment] because the claim is in reality a tool of oppression which includes military occupation, destruction of property, the unlawful expropriation of assets, and terrible human cost. Ukraine submits that these matters should be the subject of the full rigours of a public trial, and that the summary judgment process is not something to which Russia should be entitled to benefit given its egregious conduct. This point was powerfully put by Finance Minister Danyliuk in his evidence, and the court has given it careful consideration. However, ultimately, this is a claim for repayment of debt instruments to which the court has held that there is no justiciable defence. It would not be right to order the case to go forward to a full trial in such circumstances.

1.13 Naturally, courts' role is curtailed by the peculiar process of decision-making in the 'theatre' of justice:

[i]n any given case, two litigants are pitted against one another, each asking for some specific remedy. All else being equal, judges regard it as their responsibility to decide cases as narrowly as possible and develop limited, not expansive rulings'. [Moreover, due to the constraints of this 'theatre'] 'judges who might have particular policy goals must await an appropriate case in which to craft their policy'.[28]

This makes courts' role episodic ('ships passing in the night' in the metaphor of Henry Wodsworth Longfellow[29]), unless 'courts' are apt in constructing a network of supporting precedents. Our finding in this book is that this is what courts do in the law of finance, more than elsewhere. In this sector, caseload is significant and most of the litigants are repeat players who have an abundance of resources, expertise, and access to the best legal representation. This means that, in the law of finance, 'judges are not lacking for legal vehicles in which to develop policy'.[30] Moreover, when courts resort to principles in order to fill in gaps in the legal system or to check administrative discretion, this is an exercise which rarely remains confined to courts' practice and often lends to what has been conceptualized as a 'law-making partnership'. A clear example was the development of the principle of proportionality by the CJEU,[31] which was eventually codified in Article 5 TEU.[32] Another example is offered by US securities fraud litigation.[33] The general antifraud provision of the Securities Exchange Act of 1934, section 10(b), did not expressly provide for any private right of action, nor was this envisaged by Congress. It was the courts which delineated the scope of this judge-made cause of action, and which opened the gates to private securities fraud (class) actions under Rule 10b-5, thereby creating, in the words of the Supreme Court, 'a judicial oak which has grown from little more than a legislative acorn'.[34] Indeed, in its *Basic* judgment[35] the Court created the new 'fraud on the market doctrine' to enable plaintiffs in capital markets transactions to address the 'reliance' requirement in federal securities fraud class actions (reliance can be presumed for securities traded in an efficient market tainted by public misrepresentation), noting that this was necessary to adapt the common law 'reliance'

---

[28] McGuire (n 3) 540.
[29] Sabino Cassese, *A World Government?* (Global Law Press 2018) 252
[30] McGuire (n 3) 543.
[31] Case C-379/87 *Anita Groener v Minister for Education* ECLI:EU:C:1989:599, para 19.
[32] Cassese (n 29) 249.
[33] Jill E Fisch, 'The Development of Securities Litigation as a Law-making Partnership' in Sean Griffith and others (eds), *Research Handbook on Representative Shareholder Litigation* (Edward Elgar Publishing 2018) 12.
[34] *Blue Chip Stamps v Manor Drug Stores* 421 US 723, 737 (1975).
[35] *Basic Inc v Levinson* 485 US 224 (1988).

requirement to the realities of modern securities markets and for 'considerations of fairness, public policy, and probability as well as judicial economy'.[36] However:

> [t]he Court did not act alone in developing the parameters of securities fraud class actions. Congress responded to Basics through explicit statutory provisions that clarified and modified the scope of the class action. In 1995, Congress adopted the PSLRA, which reflected both congressional acceptance of the judicially created private right of action and a reassertion of congressional authority over the scope of that right of action.[37]

These examples also show distinctive features of the 'law-making partnership': **1.14**

> First the original statute must be open-textured so as to contemplate judicial lawmaking through the process of statutory interpretation. Second, Congress and the Court must engage in sequential adjustments, in each case cognizant of, and responding to concerns that are raised in the other forum. Third, Congress and the Court must make these adjustments to further a common objective.[38]

It is a dynamic exercise, and one which is inherently unstable. The Supreme Court was, for instance, presented on several occasions with the question of whether to overrule its prior decision in *Basic*, based upon new evidence on market efficiency, which questioned the assumptions on which *Basic* was grounded.[39] It did not, so far, overrule this doctrine, but it may still do in the future. To some extent, the same occurs in Europe.

Under the rule of law, courts are granted a margin of appreciation to balance conflicting principles, rights, and colliding rules. And, as Katharina Pistor noted:[40] '[l]aw tends to be relatively elastic at the system's apex, but inelastic in its periphery'; therefore, at the apex 'where the very survival of the system is at stake', the 'ultimate backstops abrogate the discretionary power to do what it takes to rescue the system'. Courts may find themselves in the uneasy position to review such decisions as ultimate decision-makers, often to carefully balance values and principles' flexibility with rules' rigidity, preserving the certainty of law. **1.15**

The question then arises on whether, when confronted with hard cases where the survival of the system is at stake, courts are given policy responsibilities of outright political nature and significance.[41] In Europe some have argued that 'the Euro crisis and the legal and institutional responses to it have dramatically increased the powers of the judiciary vis-à-vis the political branches, making economic and monetary affairs in Europe more judicialized than even in a hyper-judicialized system like the US'.[42] Others have argued the opposite, finding that courts are restrained in their ability to adjudicate over 'fiscal rules imposed to constrain policymakers in time of crisis',[43] and that 'have, for the most part, been quite deferential to **1.16**

---

[36] Fisch (n 33) 245.
[37] ibid 15.
[38] ibid 19.
[39] In *Halliburton Co v Erica P John Fund Inc* 134 S Ct 2398, 2408 (2014) the Court reaffirmed *Basic*.
[40] Pistor (n 14) 18.
[41] Sabine Saurugger and Clément Fontan, 'Courts as Political Actors: Resistance to the EU's New Economic Governance Mechanisms at the Domestic Level' (2017) EMU Choices Working Paper Series 5.
[42] Federico Fabbrini, *Economic Governance in Europe: Comparative Paradoxes, Constitutional Challenges* (OUP 2016) 64.
[43] Mitu Gulati and Georg Vanberg, 'Paper Tigers (or How Much Will Courts Protect Rights in a Financial Crisis?)' in Franklin Allen, Elena Carletti, and Mitu Gulati (eds), *Institution and the Crisis* (European University Institute 2018) 113.

the political choices made by their governments and parliaments'.[44] Yet others have contended, in a middle ground, that 'the control exercised by the courts in the post-crisis period has played an important role in reassuring citizens that the fundamental principles stand and must be respected even when decisions need to be taken under pressure; and that the courts, beyond formal barriers, do not hesitate to analyse measures that have an impact on citizens, while exercising judicial restraint and remaining coherent with the fundamental principles of our legal framework and within the constitutional balance of power'.[45]

1.17 The years 2007–2022 have been turbulent ones, and for finance more turbulent than most. The 2007–2009 financial crisis, and its aftermath, with the euro crisis 2010–2013 shaped the economic, political, and legal order like few other events. As if this were not enough, new trends, most notably technological change, and one further accelerated by the pandemic, promise to remake the face of finance yet again. In this fluid environment, legislatures and regulators have seized the opportunity with gusto, passing an overwhelming number of new laws, regulations, rulebooks, or guidelines, to limit future crises, enhance accountability, thoroughly reconsider existing institutions, or simply show that they can keep track with reality. Analyses provide new insights into finance and its legal underpinnings, from perspectives grounded in classical economic or financial theory, behavioural finance, law and economics, institutional economics, political economy, history, as well as the different combinations between them. This has greatly enriched the law of finance as a discipline, and made it more relevant, but it has also made its functioning more complex, in at least two respects. First, the number and complexity of old, new, and proposed rules has made it harder, not easier, to ensure that those rules are consistent. Secondly, the burgeoning supply of theories helps to study finance from more angles than ever before, but there is no instruction manual to use the explanatory theories to draw normative insights, let alone help adjudication to be more robust. This matters because when we add 'law' to a discipline, the stakes are automatically raised, because something 'mistaken' or 'wrong' is not the same as something 'unlawful'. We argue in this book the need of an approach to the law of finance that pays sufficient attention to some intrinsically legal aspects of such law. We synthesize these legal aspects in the role of principles in the interpretation and application of law in the adjudicating financial disputes and in the importance of expert judgment in achieving this result. Some might prefer to call this law's 'open-texture'. However, this would look at law from the 'external' perspective of the economist, sociologist, or member of other disciplines. We think what is needed is an 'internal' perspective, which looks at law's validity, consistency, and integrity, for two reasons. First, because it is only through legal principles that courts, but also agencies and bodies 'make sense' of the law of finance. They may attach some importance to whether their rulings, regulations and decisions are efficient or fair, but they put extra care in ensuring that they are lawful, ie that their sense and meaning is coherent with that of an established set of precedents and principles. Such 'sense' or 'meaning' entails an exercise that is partly linguistic, but also value-laden. Secondly, because legal principles are the gate through which new knowledge and insight from other disciplines, usually in the form of explanatory theories, can acquire normative force and play an effective role in the

---

[44] Bruno de Witte, 'Judicialization of the Euro Crisis? A critical Evaluation' in Franklin Allen, Elena Carletti, and Mitu Gulati (eds), *Institution and the Crisis* (European University Institute 2018) 107.

[45] Chiara Zilioli, 'From Form to Substance: Judicial Control on Crisis Decisions of the EU Institutions (with a Focus on the Court of Justice of the European Union)' in Franklin Allen, Elena Carletti, and Mitu Gulati (eds), *Institution and the Crisis* (European University Institute 2018) 135.

adjudication process, if, and to the extent that, such explanations satisfactorily reflect the balance of criteria for 'good', 'bad', 'right', 'wrong', 'fair', and 'unfair' also present in the law.

In light of this, this book makes a descriptive claim and a normative claim. The descriptive claim is that legal operators, and courts in the first place, use, and need, principles (and the values reflected in such principles) to adopt decisions and ensure their validity, in a way that is often overlooked by rules-based constructs. The normative claim is that such awareness of the role of principles helps to assess the 'rightness' or 'wrongness', the 'fairness' or 'unfairness' of the conduct of private players, of the content of authorities' and courts' decisions, or of new pieces of legislation, by examining whether they are consistent with the fundamental values underpinning our legal system and our society. **1.18**

The above explanation needs to be supplemented by a couple of disclaimers. First, this book does not propose a takeover of the law of finance by moral theory. Whilst we acknowledge the growing narrative emphasis on ethical and moral standards, in the words of a former Governor of the Bank of England, 'to deliver a more trustworthy, inclusive capitalism: one which embeds a sense of the systemic and in which individual virtue and collective prosperity can flourish',[46] we try to keep our analysis as based in norms and practice as possible and exemplify our views with concrete value-considerations. Yet we also think that, in legal terms, it is a mistake to think that the law of finance should be value-neutral (it cannot), that considerations of efficiency are not value-laden (they are), or that they should be the only relevant considerations (they should not and cannot). In our view, the adjudication of financial disputes offers strong evidence of it. Secondly, this book does not make a predictive claim. Being aware of the principles underpinning the rules helps to understand the law of finance better and should help in preventing decisions with a legal content form turning out into 'false positives' or 'false negatives'. That does not mean that courts will always share our views about the relative weight of considerations of principle, or value. But even where they do not, this approach will take them to better engage with fundamental principles and values and to account for them. To do that, this book takes 'hard cases' as the exemplary battlefield. Our view is that hard cases always involve a deep controversy over the principles, policies, and values at stake. We submit that only if this inner controversy is duly acknowledged as part of the legal process and the reasoning of the relevant decision duly substantiates the role that principles play in it, the legal process is made robust enough to effectively serve the public interest. **1.19**

Other authors who depart, like we do, from a criticism of excessive simplification, offer alternative theories, some compatible with ours, because they offer a different viewpoint. Katharina Pistor points out law's 'incomplete' character, and the role that 'culture' or 'enforcement' play for completion purposes.[47] We cannot but agree and this fits within a long tradition that sees 'institutions' as a broader concept, which encompasses all 'humanly devised constraints that structure political, economic and social interaction', constraints that 'consist of both informal constraints (sanctions, taboos, customs, traditions, and codes of conduct), and formal rules (constitutions, laws, property rights)'.[48] Professor Pistor and others **1.20**

---

[46] Mark Carney, 'Inclusive Capitalism: Creating a Sense of the Systemic' (Bank of England, Speech given at the Conference on Inclusive Capitalism, London, 27 May 2014) 10 https://www.bis.org/review/r140528b.htm, cited by W Blair, 'Reconceptualiszing the Role of Standards in Supporting Financial Regulation' in Ross P Buckley, Emilios Avgouleas, and Douglas W Arner (eds), *Reconceptualising Global Finance and its Regulation* (CUP 2016) 443.
[47] Katharina Pistor and Chenggang Xu, 'Incomplete Law' (2003) 35 NYU J Intl L & Policy 931. See also Katharina Pistor, 'The Law and the Non-Law' (2006) 27 Michigan J Intl L 973.
[48] Douglass C North, 'Institutions' (1991) 5 J Econ Perspectives 97.

also focus their criticism on shortcomings of normative institutional analysis that highlight points similar to the ones we make here, such as the lack of discussion of law's indeterminacy of concepts,[49] the connection between legal rules and the system's 'core' features,[50] the role of law as a cognitive institution, and the related 'interdependence' or rules,[51] the 'endogenous' relation between an economic system and its legal system.[52] On this ground, Professor Pistor proposes her compelling *Legal Theory of Finance* (LTF), which emphasizes finance's legal construction, and how this explains its unique characteristics, such as its intrinsic instability, its hierarchy, or the system's varying degrees of 'elasticity' (apex and periphery[53]). This has offered significant progress in the literature's explanatory power. However, by adopting both a viewpoint that is both explanatory, or descriptive,[54] and 'external' to legal practice,[55] the approach runs the risk of offering less insights from a normative and internal perspective. To illustrate this point, if we analyse the role of legal institutions before the 2007–2008 financial crisis, the LTF and approaches based on institutional economics can help us understand better what role in the system was played by legal constructs (eg derivatives regulation, or central banks' policies) or the culture inside central banks and regulators, or why certain (apex) banks were treated differently from (peripheral) banks. However, it cannot help us conclude whether a central bank acted, or not, *lawfully*, whether some banks investors' *rights* were trampled over, or whether bank directors breached their *legal duties*. Institutional economics cannot provide an answer because their goal is to answer pertinent, but different questions. Thus, an 'internal' perspective that considers the arguments from inside legal practice to yield normative conclusions of 'validity' and 'consistency' is still necessary.

1.21 In our view, as we will show throughout this book, this perspective needs to be principles-based in nature. None of the questions above, and similarly difficult ones, can be answered without properly interpreting and weighing the principles underpinning the law of central banks and their operations, supervisory or resolution practice, or investors' role in capital markets regulation, and interpreting what the law is in each case (descriptive claim). A proper interpretation and understanding of these principles, and the way they are interrelated, will establish the framework to assess which conduct is right, fair, and legal (normative claim). This requires, however, expert judgment on facts and complex economic assessments.

1.22 Such principles-based interpretive perspective explains from inside legal practice, what for the external perspective is the 'interdependence' between rules, law's 'incompleteness', or the 'endogeneity' between legal and economic systems, or law's relationship with 'culture'. 'Hard cases' involve questions about what is legally 'right', or 'lawful' which are difficult to answer without appealing to the system's underpinning principles and values. These are inextricably linked to the system's 'cultural' constructs. However, the role and weight of these principles

---

[49] Tamara Lothian and Katharina Pistor, 'Local Institutions, Foreign Investment and Alternative Strategies of Development: Some Views from Practice' (2004) 42 CJTL 101.
[50] Katharina Pistor, 'Rethinking the "Law and Finance" Paradigm' (2009) 6 BYU L Rev 1647.
[51] Katharina Pistor, 'The Standardization of Law and Its Effect on Developing Economies' (2002) 50 AJCL 97.
[52] Pistor (n 50) 1647–70.
[53] Pistor (n 14) 315–30.
[54] ibid 317.
[55] The LTF itself claims to offer an 'explanatory', and not a 'normative' approach. Our classification of it as an 'external' perspective is due to its use by Pistor of concepts outside legal practice (eg 'culture' or 'social norms') or explanations that emphasize the non-legal (eg sociological or economic) logic of legal decisions. See, in particular, Pistor and Xu (n 47). See also Pistor (n 47) 973–83. Saying that culture and social norms influence law is (we believe) true and insightful, but does not help establish the validity of a legal act. Focusing on the legal principles resulting from such culture or norms, however, can do so, and thus offer a normative perspective.

and values in each case will be given by law itself. Thus, its proper recognition needs, in our view, expert judgment. This is not the same as saying that law is 'incomplete', but, rather, a testimony to its 'plasticity', 'flexibility', 'fluidity', or 'adaptability', although it is more accurate to talk about the centrality of principles and law's 'interpretive' nature, which are the source of all these features.

2 Principles, financial stability, and interpretation

Some could argue that 'technical' goals, such as solvency, liquidity, transparency, safety, and soundness, or even financial stability, can be explained by appealing to technical arguments based on the text of the rules and their application, rather than those flaky-ish arguments about 'principles' and 'values'. This would be a mistake. Such rejection of principles would assume a simplified reality that does not exist. Indeed, the general reference to goals such as 'solvency', 'liquidity', 'transparency', 'safety and soundness', or 'stability' obscures the fact that their meaning and inner workings are controversial. The first source of complexity, and controversy, is the 'narrative based' formulation of those goals. That is, any explanation of the pathologies that act as the antonyms for those goals (insolvency, illiquidity, opacity, unsafety and unsoundness or instability etc.) require certain cause-and-effect assumptions about the functioning of markets, which, in turn, illustrate the dynamic sequence of actions and reactions that cause the problems. Every causal connection, thus, needs to be established as a 'story' of sorts, about how different players will behave in the presence of certain constraints and incentives. Solvency rules for banks must assume the existence of some kind of market failure or externality, which explain banks' incentive to accumulate capital cushions that are lower than what is individually or socially optimal;[56] transparency rules for primary and secondary markets must assume that trading platforms and intermediaries, left to their own devices, will produce a less than optimal level of transparency,[57] and so on. These are not 'literary' views of the markets; they are simply a necessity to make sense of facts. When causal explanations about how markets work, and how their forces must be unleashed or constrained, work their way into rules, law lends them its seriousness and validity, but does not regulate controversy away. Such controversy is an intrinsic part of the legal process, as it may affect the 'moral' of the law, ie whether a legal provision is necessary, the 'narrative' of the law, or its justification, and the interplay between the specific rule, and fundamental legal principles. **1.23**

The explanations or 'stories' underpinning the 'moral of the law', or the necessity of the rules, are also the first source of disagreement. In bank regulation, the narrative underpinning the need for intervention is hotly disputed by authors, who posit that transparency levels, or even capital cushions, will be optimal if only market forces are left to work properly,[58] that frictions and inefficiencies introduced by a prior legislative or government intervention, **1.24**

---

[56] See Daniel Tarullo, *Banking on Basel: The Future of International Financial Regulation* (Peterson Institute for International Economics 2008) 16–29 for a discussion of the various arguments.
[57] Joel Seligman, 'The Historical Need for a Mandatory Corporate Disclosure System' (1983) 9 J Corporate Law 1. Contrast with George J Benson, 'Required Disclosure and the Stock Market: An Evaluation of the Securities Exchange Act of 1934' (1973) 63 A Econ Rev 132.
[58] Roberta Romano, 'Empowering Investors: A Market Approach to Securities Regulation' (1998) 107 Yale LJ 2359.

which created the problem in the first place,[59] are removed or that instability cannot be prevented because it is caused by incontrollable market forces, and that restrictive rules will simply hamper the economy's potential level of development.[60] The arguments used in the debate may be 'technical', but their *legal* consequence will be to sow controversy deep down the narrative underpinning the rules, i.e. the 'moral' of the story will, itself, be controversial.

1.25 A second source of complexity is that even if there is agreement about the 'moral' of the story, e.g. about the need for legislative/regulatory intervention, the narratives justifying such intervention may be different and partial, emphasizing different sequences, or the role of different players, ie there may be a disagreement about the decisive, or efficient, cause, and the level of importance that each factor can have in the (construct) of market dynamics. The 2007–2008 financial crisis, and the ensuing 2010–2012 euro zone sovereign debt crisis, have shown an extraordinary literary creativity.[61] Likewise, it is already clear that also the economic disruptions caused by the Covid-19 pandemic, first, and the Russian/Ukrainian war then, will have their toll on the narratives for future reflections of those events into finance.

1.26 Thus, the legal process needs narratives to understand the reality that the law is supposed to regulate and give normative meaning to that law, while it also needs to confront controversy. This is of paramount importance at the stage when courts are called to interpret and apply the law of finance. Indeed, different narratives may inspire a different set of rules, and the *policies* underpinning them.

1.27 Some may argue that the competing narratives or 'themes' are an issue limited to the political process leading to the adoption of the rules, and no further. We believe they are not, for the coexistence between multiple themes can create problems of consistency and interpretation both between each theme and the rules inspired by it, as well as between rules inspired by competing narratives. Part of the problem is in the open-textured nature of the rules, but also in the competing nature of the mandates given to the authorities (eg banks' safety versus investor protection), and the transposition of those mandates into specific rules which in some circumstances may collide. This raises difficult questions about the relative weight and importance of each theme's underpinning principles and values.[62] Problems can be countless, but the general idea is that many cases may require public authorities and the courts that review their acts to make trade-offs between themes and narratives and weigh their importance. The increase of long and detailed rules, rather than mitigating the problem, makes it worse. The sheer numbers of such rules means an increase in the number of interactions between rules, which also increases the probability of inconsistencies and collisions. Also, the need to distribute the entities' legal and compliance departments' attention among a greater

---

[59] Roberta Romano, 'For Diversity in the International Regulation of Financial Institutions: Critiquing and Recalibrating the Basel Architecture' (2014) 31 Yale J on Reg 1.

[60] ibid 52–57.

[61] For one of the best compilations there is about the different narratives see Andrew W Lo, 'Reading about the Financial Crisis: A Twenty Book Review' (2012) 50 J Econ Literature 151.

[62] Only a small portion of the measures originally envisaged by the specific theme may be implemented due to the availability of different options within a single theme, the lack of clarity about the options, the presence of opposing narratives, or sheer political reasons (lobbying, lack of public concern, weakness, or lack of political capital, new 'crises', or problems, etc.) Some authors incorporate an 'interest group' theory to limit the courts' ability to interpret statutes. See eg Frank Easterbrook, 'Statutes' Domains' (1983) 50 U of Chicago L Rev 533. However, using an interest group theory when it comes to statutory interpretation would limit the purpose of having a general law for all, and would be contrary to non-discrimination. Tribe emphasizes the point that even laws contemplating private interests must be susceptible of identifying a broader public interest in protecting the private parties. See Laurence H Tribe, 'Constitutional Calculus: Equal Justice or Economic Efficiency' (1985) 98 Harv LR 614.

number of provisions increases the likelihood of misunderstandings. Finally, the shortening of the rules' shelf life, often as a matter of design,[63] undermines the rules' role as guidance of expected behaviour and hampers the process of settlement that helps gauge the interpretive implications of the new rules.

A final source of controversy arises between the rules and the fundamental rights that protect the individuals and institutions affected by the rules. It is customary to view fundamental rights as hard bulwarks that 'trump' policies in their restricted area,[64] while policy considerations rule in the space left by fundamental rights. This stylized view, however, is simplistic. First, fundamental rights are seldom characterized as 'concrete' rights, but rather behave more like 'abstract' rights, whose content in individual cases needs further specification.[65] The EU fundamental rights texts, such as the EU Charter of Fundamental Rights, talk about rights *and principles*,[66] in order to accommodate legal propositions with varying degrees of generality. Yet even this distinction is not entirely correct, since some of the principles with the greater degree of generality and scope, can also encapsulate some of the hardest rights, such as non-discrimination.[67] Thus, fundamental rights enjoy the double dimension, of both abstract principles and concrete rights. Indeed, some influential views characterize *all* fundamental rights as 'optimization mandates', which are subject to 'balancing' and 'proportionality', when they clash with other rights, policies, or rules, as every open-ended maximization mandate is bound to do.[68] This methodology applies to the fundamental rights normally involved in the law of finance,[69] such as the right to property over tangible and intangible assets (herein included legal titles on shares and creditor status),[70] freedom to conduct a business,[71] privacy rights,[72] procedural rights, during the administrative, and the judicial review procedures,[73] or the right to non-discrimination.[74] Furthermore, in many cases, the rights' protection will be claimed by legal persons, which means that the scope and intensity of the right must be further calibrated.[75] Secondly, not only fundamental rights are

1.28

---

[63] This is the case of the automatic revision clause in many EU rules. These provide that the Commission, on a specified date shall present a report on the implementation of the relevant directive, accompanied, where appropriate, by a proposal for its revision. Very often, the Commission finds that such modification is appropriate.
[64] Ronald Dworkin, 'Rights as Trumps' in J Waldron (ed), *Theories of Rights* (OUP 1984) 153–67.
[65] Ronald Dworkin, 'Hard Cases' (1975) 88(6) Harv LR 1070.
[66] Charter of Fundamental Rights of the European Union [2012] OJ C326, art 51(1) (Charter) provides that the EU institutions, bodies, offices, and agencies, 'shall therefore respect the rights, observe the principles and promote the application thereof in accordance with their respective powers and respecting the limits of the powers of the Union as conferred on it in the Treaties'.
[67] See eg Charter, art 23 (equality between women and men). It is interesting to note that, in Case C-176/12 *Association de Médiation Sociale (AMS) v Union locale des Syndicats* ECLI:EU:C:2014:2 the Court held, with regard to the 'workers' right to information and consultation within the undertaking' that: 'It is therefore clear from the wording of Art 27 of the Charter that, for this article to be fully effective, it must be given more specific expression in European Union or national law,' only immediately to hold that: '[t]he facts of the case may be distinguished from those which gave rise to Kücükdeveci in so far as the principle of non-discrimination on grounds of age at issue in that case, laid down in Article 21(1) of the Charter, is sufficient in itself to confer on individuals an individual right which they may invoke as such'. ibid paras 45–47.
[68] Robert Alexy, *Teoría de los derechos fundamentales* (2nd edn, CEPC 2002).
[69] See generally Marco Lamandini, David Ramos, and Javier Solana, 'The ECB Powers as a Catalyst for Change in EU Law (Part 2): SSM, SRM and Fundamental Rights' (2017) 23(2) Col J Eur L 199.
[70] European Convention on Human Rights (ECHR) art 1 of Protocol 1. See eg *Dennis Grainger and Others v the United Kingdom*, App no 34940/10 (10 July 2012).
[71] Charter, art 16.
[72] See Charter, arts 7–8, or ECHR, art 8.
[73] Charter, arts 41–42, 47, and ECHR, art 6.
[74] Charter, arts 20–21.
[75] Compare judgment of the Italian Constitutional Court No 84/2021 (13 April 2021), implementing CJEU judgment in Case C-481/19 *DB v Consob* ECLI:EU:C:2021:84 on the right (of natural persons) to be silent.

characterisedas principles, or optimization mandates; some of the policies underpinning the law of finance, such as financial stability, tend to be portrayed as 'trumps' themselves. Pitted against such powerful reasons, which can automatically justify a measure's rationale, necessity, appropriateness or proportionality, fundamental rights can be easily trumped over, or, at best, resemble a weak right to make a court 'balance' competing considerations of policy. This may be more difficult to do if the rules applicable operate as an internally coherent whole, where, however, fundamental rights were not, or not sufficiently, taken into consideration, which means that introducing an exception or caveat to a rule via constitutional interpretation creates frictions in the rule's internal structure. Thus, an interpretation needs to be offered, where both the general principles and policy considerations underpinning the rules, and the fundamental rights that operate as their limits, make sense together, and 'fit' within the broader scheme of the legal values that conform the legal system.

3 Principles-based interpretivism, heuristics, and biases

1.29 The third advantage of a principles-based, interpretive perspective to the law of finance has to be formulated cautiously, and with a view deferential to science, but it is important nonetheless. If principles-based interpretivism is necessary, legally, to avoid inconsistent decisions, psychologically it can also help overcome cognitive and decision-making biases, which could deeply affect the adjudicatory process. The literature in the field is vast, but it was pioneered by Kahneman and Tversky, whose experiments alerted about the existence of biases in the way persons process information and make decisions under conditions of uncertainty.[76] These prompt individuals to focus on 'salient' or 'available', if improbable risks,[77] be loss averse,[78] and neglect the role of interventions in an already complex system.[79] Heuristics not only explain probability assessments, but also moral decisions,[80] and can bias them depending on their framing.[81] Given that metaphors and analogical thinking are key in moral, or political decision-making,[82] principles-based interpretation, by forcing courts and agencies to use different frames and openly to address the rules' fundamental questions can help them overcome the bias of a single frame. By superimposing different frames onto a single problem agencies and courts can calibrate the weight of the principles underpinning a specific set of rules, and thus assess their scope and intensity of application. If category-bound thinking is a major source of inconsistency and arbitrariness in judgments,[83] the simultaneous use of different categories can help mitigate those biases. Principles-based

---

[76] Amos Tversky and Daniel Kahneman, 'Judgment under Uncertainty: Heuristics and Biases' (1974) 185 Science 1124.
[77] See Amos Tversky and Daniel Kahneman, 'Judgment under Uncertainty' in Daniel Kahneman, Paul Slovic, and Amos Tversky (eds), *Judgment under Uncertainty: Heuristics and Biases* (CUP 1982) 3.
[78] Daniel Kahneman, Jack Knetsch, and Richard H Thaler, 'Experimental Tests of the Endowment Effect and the Coase Theorem' (1984) 98(6) J Pol Econ 1325; Richard Thaler and others, 'The Effect of Myopia and Loss Aversion on Risk Taking: An Experimental Test' (1997) 112(2) Q J Econ 647.
[79] Richard Dorner, *The Logic of Failure: recognizing and Avoiding Error in Complex Situations* (Metropolitan Books 1996). Most of these were originally identified by Kahneman and Tversky and used by Sunstein as a basis for his criticism. See Cass R Sunstein, *Laws of Fear* (CUP 2005) 34.
[80] Daniel Kahneman and Cass Sunstein, 'Indignation: Psychology, Politics, Law' (2007) U Chicago L School John M Olin Law and Economics Working Paper 346.
[81] Cass Sunstein, 'Moral Heuristics and Moral Framing: Lecture' (2004) 88 Minnesota L Rev 1561.
[82] For a general approach see George Lakoff and M Johnson, *Metaphors We Live By* (University of Chicago Press 1980); George Lakoff, *Moral Politics: How Liberals and Conservatives Think* (University of Chicago Press 2002).
[83] Cass R Sunstein and others, 'Predictably Incoherent Judgments' (2002) 54 Stanford L Rev 1153.

interpretivism is not the antidote to biases, but it is surely a mechanism for limiting some of them.

The above puts forward a *descriptive*, or explanatory claim, and a *normative* argument for principles-based interpretivism in the law of finance. From a descriptive perspective, like Moliere's bourgeois Monsieur Jourdain, who discovered that he had been speaking in prose all his life,[84] principles-based interpretation and application of the law is what courts and other bodies already do or at least try to do (with margins for improvement) and legal theorists have been discussing ever since. We argue, however, that this should be made by courts engaged in financial disputes with more consciousness of the importance of principles-based interpretivism to reconcile law in action with the values inspiring and embedded in the law of finance. From an operational point of view, this should turn into a necessary adjunct to the statement of reasons that shows a straightforward engagement not only with the text of the provisions but also with the general principles inspiring their adoption, their finality and the values embedded in the legislative or regulatory choice. We argue that this also passes through the way the adjudication of financial disputes is organized. 1.30

4 Principles-based interpretivism and legitimacy

Another factor supporting the opportunity of a principles-based interpretivist approach is the need to bridge some logical gaps between issues of validity, and of legitimacy, which are of special importance in the law of finance. By using 'legitimacy' we do not wish to be bogged down in a conceptual quagmire,[85] since we are not trying to explain the concept,[86] but to discuss specific, pressing problems in the law of finance, related to the difficulty to fit the law of finance's decisions, practices, or governance structures within canons of acceptability or justifiability, which is how 'normative legitimacy' is often understood.[87] The problem is one of 'input' legitimacy, which measures the process, as well as of 'output' legitimacy, which measures the success in meeting desired outcomes, i.e. 'delivering the goods'. For institutional purposes, however, 'input/process legitimacy' is more relevant, as it is the parallel concept of 'accountability',[88] understood as a (political) actor's obligation to explain and justify her conduct in a forum, which may be followed by a judgment by the forum, and the ensuing consequences.[89] 1.31

---

[84] Moliére, *Le Bourgeois gentilhomme* (Louandre 1910) scène IV.

[85] In trying to prioritize the concrete legal-political problem over the conceptual problem we share Joseph Weiler's sentiment when he said 'Legitimacy is a notoriously elusive term, over-used and under-specified. So the first thing I will do is to explain the sense in which I plan to use 'Legitimacy' in this essay. Do not, please, argue with me and say: 'That is not legitimacy! It means something else!' See Joseph Weiler, 'In the Face of Crisis: Input Legitimacy, Output Legitimacy and the Political Messianism of European Integration' (2012) 34 Eur Integration 826 and in Joseph Weiler, 'Europe in Crisis: On 'Political Messianism', 'Legitimacy' and the 'Rule of Law' [2012] Singapore J Legal Studies 248, where he makes the exact same remark.

[86] An excellent summary is provided by Fabienne Peter, 'Political Legitimacy' in Edward N Zalta (ed), *The Stanford Encyclopedia of Philosophy* http://plato.stanford.edu/entries/legitimacy/.

[87] Therefore, we would leave aside descriptive accounts of legitimacy, such as Weber's (based on people's actual belief that lends prestige to persons exercising authority). See eg Max Weber, *The Theory of Social and Economic Organization* (Free Press 1964) 382, or accounts that some would classify as 'social', based on empirical assessment of social attitudes of acceptance. See also Weiler, 'In the Face of Crisis' (n 85).

[88] Allen Buchanan, 'Political Legitimacy and Democracy' (2002) 112(4) Ethics 689. See also Giandomenico Majone, 'Transaction-cost Efficiency and the Democratic Deficit' (2010) 17(2) J Eur Pub Pol 150.

[89] Mark Bovens, 'Analysing and Assessing Accountability: A Conceptual Framework' (2007) 13(4) Eur LJ 450. Bovens also offers another distinction of 'accountability' as a 'virtue', which has a normative perspective, and as a

1.32 The reasons why the law of finance poses a particularly acute problem are multiple, but generally stem from finance's complex causal chains, and the fact that, once enacted, the law has to accept such causal chains as a given aspect of its logical structure. This means that, first, when economic effects are far removed from their causes, they may be hard to grasp, and thus unacceptable to citizens, law-makers or judges (inaccessibility); secondly, the 'law of unintended consequences' may be accepted as a valid reason by technocrats or policymakers for not focusing on the more visible aspects of a problem, but it is often less acceptable to citizens, law-makers, or judges as a way to justify a 'wrong' state of affairs only because other options could lead to worse consequences (complexity);[90] thirdly, when adopting new rules legal actors will overlook the tensions between the rationales underpinning these and other rules, and/or inadvertently sacrifice principles or values (dissonance);[91] fourthly, the saliency of a problem may appear to justify granting vast powers to administrative agencies, but the consequences of this may become evident only at a later moment, when the justification that initially seemed obvious is no longer so salient (time-inconsistency); and, fifthly, and as a corollary, the competing forces of the elusive yet ubiquitous 'markets', and the severe and judgmental presence of independent agencies can give the impression that 'people', or 'polities' have their work cut out for them, or, simply, have the decisions made for them (unaccountability). The problem can be particularly acute in the European Union, where a common perception is that the EU itself, and its institutions have a democratic legitimacy problem.[92] Thus, addressing finance's vagaries by transferring more powers to EU institutions can be seen as accumulating one illegitimacy with another, or as a naïve expectation that two illegitimacies, like two negatives, can cancel each other out.

1.33 As a clarification, we are not focusing on 'justice' beyond law, and we limit our concern with legitimacy to the extent that it intersects with legality, because the two are intimately related.[93] If law is an interpretative process, a decision whose process is illegitimate, will tend to be found illegal eventually.[94] Thus, legality (based on principles-based interpretivism) and legitimacy must support each other. Principles-based interpretivism should delineate how to make the decision-making process in the law of finance more legitimate. Consider the role of independent regulatory and supervisory agencies. The legitimacy dimension helps to stress the importance of the *justification* of decisions, or the *reasons* for them, over the *discovery* process, or *motives* leading to that decision.[95] It follows that including justificatory reasons needs to be *institutionalized*, or codified into decision-making, and a lack of such

---

'mechanism', which has a descriptive component. See Mark Bovens, 'Two Concepts of Accountability: Accountability as a Virtue and as a Mechanism' (2010) 33 West Eur Politics 946.

[90] For example, a country's citizens, parliament, or government, may not accept imposing losses on a bank (retail) investors as a means to limit moral hazard or taxpayer losses, or the strict enforcement of defaulted mortgage loans over family homes, as a way to avoid a crisis of non-performing loans (NPLs).
[91] For example, a court enforcing transparency requirements for the marketing of financial instruments among retail investors may not be aware of the effect that his strict interpretation may have on the entities' ability to raise equity capital, and thus their solvency, and the sector's stability and concentration.
[92] Weiler, 'In the Face of Crisis' (n 85); Weiler, 'Europe in Crisis' (n 85) 248.
[93] We agree with Weiler's assertion that 'Legitimacy, normative or social, should not be conflated with legality'. Weiler, 'In the Face of Crisis' (n 85) 827.
[94] Contrast this with a situation where a decision may be found unjust for failing to duly uphold some specific standards of justice, but whose process is legitimate, and will tend to be considered legal. Rawls, for example, argues that, while legitimacy and justice draw on the same political values, legitimacy makes weaker demands for justice, which means that an institution may be unjust, but legitimate. See John Rawls, 'Political Liberalism: Reply to Habermas' (1995) 92(3) J Phil 148.
[95] Giandomenico Majone, *Evidence, Argument and Persuasion in the Policy Process* (YUP 1989) 29.

justification should be a strong prima facie evidence of illegality. Furthermore, not every reason will do. Even if agencies can resort to considerations of policy to make their decisions, considerations of principle, or value, will operate as external limits, and internal, logical constraints, eg requiring any appeal to those principles or values as a justification for agency action to be consistent with the way they are understood by the courts. Secondly, and conversely, the focus on legitimacy should inform a court's use of principles-based legality. On one level it may help courts reflect about their own role in the broader system of checks-and-balances, ie other branches or bodies can obtain a better result in terms of the justification of decisions,[96] courts can consider the availability of such other means, and the multi-faceted nature of 'accountability'[97] (political, administrative, legal) to shape their own standard of review.[98] Both courts, and their standard of review shall remain critical, not because of their intrusiveness, but of their status as the system's keystone, or closing piece and ultimate arbiter. Furthermore, the notion of legitimacy can help the courts to better contextualize the role of fundamental rights in the law of finance, not only as the means to protect the passive victims, but of giving voice to active constituencies who need to be part of the process,[99] a point too often missed when it comes to the law of finance. Thirdly, a principles-based and legitimacy-based view are necessary complements in contexts of polycentric authority, with multiple sources that are not related by hierarchy, or where trying to establish hierarchy may itself be controversial (eg, between the European Union and Member States). In such cases, the pull towards construing a single theory of how different sets of rules, and their unifying principles fit together needs to give way to a construction that acknowledges other systems, and the dialogue between them. Those familiar with EU law will automatically see the connection with 'legal pluralism',[100] grounded on 'discourse theory',[101] and the complex equilibria needed to mitigate the risks of plain 'primacy'.[102]

---

[96] If we put this more formally, it is common to use agency theory, originated in the corporate field, to analyse the action of public agencies. See Giandomenico Majone, 'The Regulatory State and Its Legitimacy Problems' (1999) 22(1) West Eur Politics 1, with reference to Murray Horn, *The Political Economy of Public Administration* (CUP 1995). In its original conception, agency theory can anticipate that under conditions of high monitoring costs, an agent will seek its own interests, rather than the principal's. Michael Jensen and William Meckling, 'Theory of the Firm: Managerial Behavior, Agency Costs and Ownership Structure' (1976) 3 J Fin Econ 305.

[97] Bovens 'Analysing and Assessing Accountability' (n 89) 447–68. See also Deirdre Curtin, *Mind the Gap: The Evolving European Union Executive and the Constitution* (Europa Law Publishing 2004).

[98] Such holistic view of accountability as the reference point to determine the court's standard of review of the legality of a decision, or structure, was at the core of the European Court of Justice's strict review in Case 9/56 *Meroni v High Authority* ECLI:EU:C:1958:7. The specific circumstances, with a semi-private agency, with no clear accountability, and the absence, at that time, of stronger mechanisms of political control did not ensure a robust process of justification, which, in our view, explains the Court's reference to the broader concept of 'institutional balance', as the vantage point to cast judgment.

[99] Some authors have pointed, for example, that the CJEU's case law on the internal market helped to open a direct channel of communication with citizens, by vesting them with individual rights, and thus giving them a stake, and a voice, in the process of European integration. See Miguel Poiares Maduro, *We, the Court: The European Court of Justice and the European Economic Constitution* (Hart Publishing 1998) 27.

[100] See Neil MacCormick, 'Beyond the Sovereign State' (1993) 56 Modern L Rev 1; Miguel Poiares Maduro, 'Interpreting European Law: Judicial Adjudication in a Context of Constitutional Pluralism' (2007) 1(2) Eur J Legal Studies 137. More recently see Klemen Jaklic, *Constitutional Pluralism* (OUP 2014). For some critical views see P Eleftheriadis, 'Pluralism and Integrity' (2010) 23(3) Ratio Juris 365; of Julio Baquero Cruz, 'Another Look at Constitutional Pluralism in the European Union' (2016) 22 Eur LJ 356. For a comprehensive view of the different interactions see Giuseppe Martinico and Oreste Pollicino, *The Interaction between Europe's Legal Systems Judicial Dialogue and the Creation of Supranational Laws* (Edward Elgar Publishing 2014).

[101] Jurgen Habermas, *Between Facts and Norms: Contributions to a Discourse Theory of Law and Democracy* (William Rehg tr, MIT Press 1996).

[102] Bruno de Witte, 'Direct Effect, Primacy, and the Nature of the Legal Order' in Paul Craig and Gráinne de Búrca (eds), *The Evolution of EU Law* (OUP 2011) 323–62.

1.34 The relevance of this approach, however, transcends the European setting, for the law of finance requires increasing coordination on a transnational level, with actions that may result in an intrusion upon principles of the basic legal order. Consider the legal grounds and effects of Memoranda of Understanding (MoU) between authorities, the 'contracts' between central banks, or the use of coordinated supranational structures to decide on joint supervisory or resolution action, which may clash with privacy or property rights, or administrative safeguards. Imagine a resolution action which affects shareholders in third countries. Since different legal orders are mutually aware that each has no absolute power over the other, they are encouraged to engage in a dialogue.[103] Discourse theory provides normative value to what would otherwise be a mere descriptive sociological or political account of how courts interact, but such normative value legitimizes the vessel, and not the content. What renders the acknowledgement of different legal orders 'right', and not merely expedient, is an interpretative approach that can give weight to the principles and values of other legal orders.

5 Critical views: Rules-based positivism and pragmatism

1.35 After having formulated our view of court-based interpretivism, we offer some potential criticisms, and their corresponding replies.

1.36 'Hard cases make bad law' is the catchphrase coined by Oliver Wendell Holmes[104] aimed at cases that enjoy unnecessary public, media, or political attention and stir feelings, in a way that makes the courts go astray from settled law.[105] Formulated this way, this criticism does not concern us, because our 'hard cases' are not hard because they enjoy public attention. They are hard because the problem at stake is a potential inconsistency between the goals and principles inspiring different rules. Some may enjoy public attention, and some not. For those that do, public attention is often a consequence, rather than a cause, of the underpinning clash of goals and principles. Holmes' sentence, however, could be rephrased to make a different argument: hard cases are not a useful example of what 'the law is', because the law has no answer for an entirely new issue, or more mildly put, no clear answer. In our view, this objection would misconstrue the issue, no matter how it is put. In one sense, the objection could be formulated as saying that hard cases solved with an appeal to principles are 'bad law' because they fail the standard of certainty and predictability normally associated with the law. Put in this way, however, the objection barks at the wrong tree, for the 'hardness' of a hard case is not a problem of the method used to find a solution to it, but a problem of the case itself, which cannot be resolved with simpler tools, such as a textual interpretation of specific rules. It is hard because it forces a deeper reflection on the basic criteria lying beneath the rules, criteria that may be controversial, as reflective of competing considerations of principle, or values. Someone following this logic to its last consequences, however, would have to say that the only possible answer in hard cases is 'sorry, but there is no law to solve

---

[103] Maduro (n 99) 31.
[104] The first dated use of the expression was in *Hodgens v Hodgens* [1837] 4 CI Fin 323, quoted by Fred R Shapiro, *The Yale Book of Quotations* (YUP 2006) 614 (Proverbs no 136). The more famous quotation, however, is by Justice OW Holmes' dissenting opinion in *Northern Securities Co v United States* 193 US 197 (1904).
[105] In Justice Holmes' own words: 'Great cases, like hard cases, make bad law. For great cases are called great not by reason of their real importance in shaping the law of the future, but because of some accident of immediate overwhelming interest which appeals to the feelings and distorts the judgment. These immediate interests exercise a kind of hydraulic pressure which makes what previously was clear seem doubtful, and before which even well settled principles of law will bend.'

the problem'. This, however, would be sticking to a reductionist view of the law, which would render it unable to address new, hard cases. There is, however, a third sense of the objection with a deeper meaning. The sentence can also mean that reasonable, knowledgeable jurists can disagree over the *interpretation and application* of the law in concrete, marginal, cases, despite there is agreement as to 'the law' itself. This, in the view of positivists, may be due to discrepancies over the linguistic meaning of terms like 'monetary policy' or 'price stability', 'arbitrary and capricious', 'particular circumstances' and 'financial stability' and 'transparency' just to mention a few examples. Precisely because of this, hard cases are not the best example to illustrate what the 'law' is, something on which most jurists agree most of the time. Formulated in this way, the objection could be an expression of the ideas of Holmes, but also of H.L.A. Hart;[106] in whose view, for the drafter of a specific statute or precedent, it is impossible to anticipate all the *factual* situations that may be encountered in the future, which means that certain provisions need to be open textured,[107] thus leaving room for disagreement and interpretation.

Reframed in this way, however, this view, persuasive as it may appear at first glance, is also unsatisfactory. It would be wrong, and almost disingenuous, to argue that courts spend so much energy in a semantic disagreement over the meaning of 'monetary policy' or 'price stability', or devoting hundreds of pages to ascertain the meaning of 'client money' as a kind of sideshow. They disagreed about what 'the law' for the particular problem was, and what was the right solution, which ensured a construction of the interests at stake that fit within the existing scheme of legal practice, and parties' rights. Thus, hard cases can not only be 'marginal', ie illustrate instances where there is agreement over the *law*, but disagreement over the *application* of that law; they can also be *pivotal* cases, which illustrate deeper disagreements over the law.[108] In this light, the problem is that hard cases are a problem for the neat construction of 'pure' positivists, which is based on a certainty over what is law and what is not.[109] This certainty, in Hart's view, is represented by a 'rule of recognition', which helps to identify what is part of the law, and what is not.[110] The positivist edifice rests upon the *acceptance* of the rule of recognition, which then acts as the source of authoritative criteria for identifying rules of obligation. Disagreements over the law run contrary to the assumption of acceptance of a rule of recognition, which, for some, is a matter of 'convention'. Thus, 'hard cases' are an anomaly, and their role should be marginal. Yet, in our view, any sense of certainty grounded on an idea of 'convention' that overlooks legal principles and controversy is a false sense of certainty. Hart himself revised his position in a postscript, where he acknowledged the importance of principles, and expanded his analysis of the rule of recognition to explain how principles could fit into the overall scheme of the 'law';[111] more modern

1.37

---

[106] HLA Hart, *The Concept of Law* (Clarendon Press 1997) 124.
[107] ibid 128–30.
[108] Ronald Dworkin, *Law's Empire* (Bloomsbury 1998).
[109] In Kelsen's purest positivistic view, this is grounded on a clarity over the body that has promulgated the rules, and the procedure used to promulgate those rules. See Hans Kelsen, *The Pure Theory of Law* (University Presses of California, Columbia and Princeton, 1970).
[110] Hart's 'rule of recognition' is part of the 'secondary rules', which help bring certainty, and move beyond a system based on 'custom' towards a system based on 'law', and also include 'rules of change', and 'rules of adjudication'. See Hart (n 106) 91–100.
[111] In essence, Hart argued, first, that some principles were identified by a convention over the right sources of law, eg the principles that are included in the Constitution, or those that have been repeatedly cited by courts. Second, he also argued that a rule of recognition can be expanded to encompass principles that form part of the legal system not as a matter of their 'pedigree', but as a matter of their content, ie because they belong to a coherent scheme of principles which both fits the institutional history and practices of the system and best justify them, which Hart identifies with a 'soft' positivism. See Hart (n 106) 264–65. In addition to this, Hart also pointed out that Dworkin's discrete, or binary distinction between rules, as legal propositions that apply in an all-or-nothing

positivists follow similar approaches, which try to show that purported disagreements over 'law' are, in reality, disagreements over its 'application'.[112] Indeed, the main disagreements between Dworkinians and positivists are whether the 'law' implies moral judgments, and whether parties disagree over the 'contents' of the law, or over the 'application' of the law. We do not need to answer those questions here to claim a relevant role for principles in the legal system and the adjudication of financial disputes.

1.38 'Hard cases are solved by discretion, not principles'. A second objection postulates that in hard cases, with open textured concepts, where the law provides no clear answer, judges exercise their discretion to solve the problem. In some versions of this idea, like Holmes' legal realism (and rule-scepticism), discretion becomes the norm, and judges weigh considerations of social ends to decide individual cases; the law is not formed by logical deduction from principles or axioms, it is formed by 'predictions' over how the courts will decide on a certain issue.[113] Positivists like Hart argued instead that courts use discretion to decide hard cases;[114] but saw the risk of arbitrariness in this,[115] and also argued that the scope for such arbitrariness is limited by the consensus over the 'core' meaning of certain legal terms, and over the proper role of the courts.[116] This position, however, by relying on the same basic positivist ideas, is vulnerable to the same criticism discussed above: it is difficult to talk about 'convention' or 'consensus' in hard cases, and even more difficult to accept that the controversy is linguistic, rather than 'value based'. The real answer to the objection is that the discretion-based description of how courts solve hard cases is not descriptive at all. Courts do not decide on the basis of discretion, or personal preferences, because doing so would be seen as wrong and capricious. Courts, in hard cases, usually employ long and sophisticated reasoning in an attempt to establish what the law is for the specific problem at hand, a difficult exercise, requiring them to weigh competing objectives, values and propositions of general application, in a construction that makes sense of competing, conflicting, and often seemingly irreconcilable, reasons, a far cry from the massive deployment of discretion proposed by legal realism, or the milder version espoused by some positivists.[117] Furthermore, saying that hard cases are solved by discretion presupposes that discretion is vested in one

---

fashion and principles, which have a dimension of weight and importance, was not of kind, but of degree, since very often rules have also this dimension.

[112] According to Hart, examples of this 'soft' positivism would include EP Soper, 'Legal Theory and the Obligation of a Judge: The Hart/Dworkin Dispute' (1977) 75(3) Michigan L Rev 473; J Coleman, 'Negative and Positive Positivism' (1982) 11(1) J Legal Studies 139; D Lyons, 'Principles, Positivism and Legal Theory' (1977) 87 Yale LJ 415. Professor Coleman re-elaborated his views in J Coleman, *The Practice of Principle: In Defense of a Pragmatist Approach to Legal Theory* (OUP 2001), to argue, in essence, that, in cases where interpreters of the law are called to cast seemingly moral judgments, such as whether a party has acted in 'good faith', or whether a party has behaved 'unreasonably', it is the 'convention' over a rule that includes such terms that makes such judgment 'law'. Dworkin replies that this strategy of 'abstraction' rather than making positivism more robust, signal its demise, and are a trick to recharacterize moral arguments over the content of the law as argument over the application of the law, which also eviscerate the idea of 'convention'. Dworkin, *Justice in Robes* (n 12) 188–94.
[113] OW Holmes, 'The Path of the Law' (1897) 1 The Boston L School Magazine 1. Holmes framed the more famous version of this 'predictive' theory of law, based on the perspective of the 'bad man', who sees no reason for action in moral arguments, but fears punishment.
[114] See Hart (n 106) 141–47.
[115] Hart illustrated this as the 'nightmare' scenario in HLA Hart, 'American Jurisprudence through English Eyes: The Nightmare and the Noble Dream' (1977) 11 Ga L Rev 972.
[116] Hart (n 106) 144–46.
[117] Advocates of the discretion-based view would reply that, in hard cases, courts only 'pretend to be' discussing the law, when they are truly applying their own considerations of justice and morality, in an exercise of discretion, ie having a debate over what the law 'should be'. For a critique see Dworkin (n 108) 37–41, who calls that the 'fingers crossed' defence of positivism.

single body. Yet, in finance there is the discretion of public authorities (central banks, regulators) and the discretion of the courts that review their actions, and then there may be more than one court, eg first instance and appeal, national and supranational etc. Thus, saying that hard cases are solved by discretion begs the question, does not answer it. Consider a case on monetary policy in the EU: the composition of 'discretions' would be impossible. In the EU, the ECB's discretionary monetary policy mandate would be subject to the discretionary interpretation of the CJEU to assess its conformity with EU law, which would, in turn, be subject to the discretionary assessment of national constitutional courts, seeking to establish whether the ECB's, and the CJEU respected the democratic principle of the national constitutions. Thus, the distribution of powers and competences is only admissible if its interpretation is considered a legal exercise, and the decisions where those are allocated are considered 'law', not discretion.[118]

'Principles-based interpretivism is backward looking'. One may claim at this point those philosophical reconstructions of the law are backward-looking and useless; courts should consider the effects of their individual decisions using a forward-looking approach. This objection, based on legal realism,[119] and also in Posner's 'pragmatism',[120] complements the previous criticism, which focused on what courts do, by focusing on what they should do. Admittedly, it is a catchy criticism, prone to sound bites like 'keep it simple', 'focus on the facts', 'decide incrementally and experimentally'. Yet, this provides an attitude, but little guidance. An appeal to deciding cases 'on their own facts', when carefully considered, says nothing about what those facts should say to us. Even if one accepts pragmatism's essentially consequentialist approach, ie the need to focus on the consequences of a legal decision, it is necessary to decide which consequences are 'good' or 'bad', and whether the 'good' consequences outweigh the 'bad' ones, in order to decide whether the decision is 'right'.[121] To do this, one needs to appeal to some kind of theory of value, be it utilitarianism, Rawlsian views, or another moral theory,[122] to rank the different outcomes, which is where the problem is, **1.39**

---

[118] A (cynical) realist could retort that, in such case, the CJEU did not use the law, but only the arguments it found sufficiently persuasive to be accepted by the German BVerfG. But then *why* would their argument (in this case validating the acts of the ECB) be persuasive at all, if not because it would rightly weigh the right principles and values enshrined in the EU Treaties, within the right boundaries of legitimacy conferred by national constitutions?

[119] The consequentialist side of this argument was well-expressed by Holmes when he said that: 'I think that the judges themselves have failed adequately to recognize their duty of weighing considerations of social advantage. The duty is inevitable, and the result of the often proclaimed judicial aversion to deal with such considerations is simply to leave the very ground and foundation of judgments inarticulate and often unconscious, as I have said'. Holmes (n 113) 9. The 'experimental' side of the argument would be synthesized by his '[t]he life of the law has not been logic; it has been experience' in OW Holmes, *The Common Law* (Paulo JS Pereira and Diego M Beltran eds, University of Toronto Law School Typographical Society 2011) 5.

[120] Posner criticized the use of theory as a sound basis for, and deciding cases, because it could be an open door for the judges' imposition of their own personal preferences and proposed a style of 'pragmatic adjudication'. He first did so as an alternative to existing approaches to statutory interpretation. See R Posner, 'Legislation and Its Interpretation: A Primer' (1989) 68 Neb L Rev 431, and then expanded this view as an alternative also to what he saw as an excessively theoretical approach, like Dworkin's. See R Posner, *Overcoming Law* (HUP 1996).

[121] According to Rawls, teleological theories, including utilitarianism, construe the relationship between the 'good', and the 'right', the two main concepts of ethical theories, by arguing that the 'good' can be defined independently from the 'right', eg as 'utility', or 'wealth', and the 'right' can be construed as that which maximizes the 'good'. This, in Rawls' view, has a great intuitive appeal, because it is natural for someone to think that rationality must mean to maximize something. See John Rawls, *A Theory of Justice* (HUP 1971) 21–22.

[122] Dworkin argues that 'pragmatism' at its best simply stood for 'consequentialism' based on utility, wealth maximization, or some other (unspecified) measure of 'good'. This is a theory, not an 'anti-theoretical' view. See Ronald Dworkin, 'In Praise of Theory' (1997) 29 Ariz St LJ 353. Posner objected to this characterization, which led to a thrilling exchange between the two professors. See Richard A Posner, 'Conceptions of Legal Theory: A Response to Ronald Dworkin' (1997) 29 Ariz St LJ 377; Ronald Dworkin, 'In Praise of Theory: Reply' (1997) 29

because this is where the controversy typically lies in the first place, and what makes hard cases hard. Thus, pragmatism so defined, like positivism, would take for granted a non-existent consensus over the hierarchy of values and their relative weight, and attempt to solve the problem by redefining it as a non-problem. This version of pragmatism fails by its own standards. Even if the argument that the positive consequences outweighed the bad ones could be a useful contribution, an engine of the courts' reasoning, this had to be within the path set out by the principles underpinning the relevant set of laws.

1.40 Others claim that 'principles-based interpretivism is too ambitious and impracticable or leads to ossification'. This is another, softer version of pragmatism, espoused by authors like Sunstein and Vermeule, which provides a stronger criticism against a principles-based interpretative approach.[123] Their view is that, first, providing a full fledged theory for every case would be both impractical (since judges do not have the time or ability to do so) and counter-productive, by making consensus more difficult, ie different people may agree on a solution, yet disagree about the theoretical reconstruction that gives rise to it. Secondly, if judges could succeed, nonetheless, it could be even more dangerous, by ossifying existing theories into law, and making evolution more difficult.[124] At its extreme, it may turn legal interpretation into a gnostic exercise, by a court of chosen philosophers. It seems that this is also the core of Posner's objection to what he sees as arrogant theoretical constructs,[125] a concern that is also captured by Isaiah Berlin's qualms about 'hedgehog's views', which try to encompass everything to a single, universal, organizing principle.[126] The truth of these criticisms depends on how far one takes the interpretative exercise.[127]

Ariz St LJ 431; Richard A Posner, 'The Problematics of Moral and Legal Theory' (1998) 111 Harv LR 1637; R Dworkin, 'Darwin's New Bulldog' (1998) 111 Harv LR 1718.

[123] Cass Sunstein and Adrian Vermeule, 'Interpretation and Institutions' (2003) 101 Mich L Rev 885; Cass Sunstein, 'Incompletely Theorized Agreements' (1995) 110 Harv LR 1733.

[124] Sunstein agreed with Dworkin that judges should resolve new cases by relying on parallels from previous cases, and that the way to draw comparisons was by relying on the common principles. He just was more distrustful of the need to derive grand or comprehensive theories to solve every new case, because he considered this well beyond the possibilities of most judges, impracticable given the constraints of time and resources judges normally faced and could also ossify the legal system and render it impervious to change. See Cass R Sunstein, *Legal Reasoning and Political Conflict* (OUP 2000), a point that had been previously stated in Sunstein, 'Incompletely Theorized Agreements' (n 123), and was retaken to formulate a more comprehensive theory of the 'institutional' constraints on interpretation, eg why a generalist court could be compelled to a more formalist interpretation than a specialized agency as a matter of its institutional role. See Sunstein and Vermeule (n 123).

[125] Posner's view can be confusing due to his own personal view of pragmatism. In his view: 'the pragmatist judge regards precedent, statutes, and constitutional text both as sources of potentially valuable information about the likely best result in the present case and as signposts that he must be careful not to obliterate or obscure gratuitously, because people may be relying upon them. But because he sees these "authorities" merely as sources of information and as limited constraints on his freedom of decision, he does not depend on them to supply the rule of decision for the truly novel case. He looks to sources that bear directly on the wisdom of the rule that he is being asked to adopt or modify.' Richard Posner, *The Problematics of Moral and Legal Theory* (HUP 1999) 242. Although his views collide with Dworkin's on a general level, his greater problem seems to be more with some of Dworkin's contributions, such as Ronald Dworkin, *Freedom's Law: A Moral Reading of the American Constitution* (HUP 1997). Posner also criticizes the position of positivism for ossifying the system through its rule of recognition and failing to acknowledge the essence of the common law system of decentralized experimentation.

[126] Isaiah Berlin, *The Hedgehog and the Fox: An Essay on Tolstoy's View of History* (Henry Hardy ed, 2nd edn, Weidenfeld & Nicolson 2014). Not by chance, Dworkin's main contribution to a theory of justice is called Ronald Dworkin, *Justice for Hedgehogs* (HUP 2011). For Dworkin's reply to Berlin's views on moral pluralism see his 'Moral Pluralism' in Dworkin, *Justice in Robes* (n 12) 105.

[127] True, judges or lawyers cannot be expected to have the philosophical training of Dworkin's judge Hercules. Yet, it is equally unrealistic for them to have the insights and experience of Richard Posner or Oliver Wendell Holmes, with the difference that Judge Hercules is an idealization of what 'real' judges do, while Holmes and Posner are real judges themselves.

Of course a new theory is not necessary for every new case, and a principles-based, or **1.41** integrity-based view merely points the direction to follow, not how far to go. Textual interpretation or analogical reasoning will suffice in cases where the similitude between the facts of the case and the hypothesis envisaged in the rule, or decided by precedent, is uncontroversial; in other cases the discussion may focus on whether a different fact calls for the application of a different rule or precedent. As soon as such controversy arises, some criteria will be necessary to accept one analogy or construction and reject another, and these criteria of validity cannot rest on factual similitude alone, but on the correctness of the judgment resulting from such similitude. Legal practice bears this out.

Once we accept the basic idea that, to evaluate conformity with past legal practice, one needs **1.42** to adopt an evaluative perspective that takes into consideration the principles and objectives underpinning applicable precedents or statutes, it is possible to assume that the process of 'justificatory ascent' does not need to exhaust all the legal system every time a problem arises,[128] ie there is no need for a theory, let alone a grand theory for every case. However, there is otherwise no convincing method yet to determine where to stop on an ex ante basis.[129] This largely depends on the specific issue at stake, and the weighing of principles that it required. Indeed, Sunstein subsequently accepted that a principles-based approach does not require grand theories on each case,[130] and that judges who proceed 'one case at a time', are 'highly likely to produce a pattern of outcomes of which they themselves would disapprove'.[131] It seems that, as long as 'theorizing' means imposing different frames to check the solution's consistency with the system's principles and values, it produces more robust outcomes. This also addresses the criticism of ossification of the legal system, which, in any event, is more adequately directed at 'system's theories' that focus on law's self-referenced, or autopoietic, nature.[132] Principles-based interpretative views do not ossify the legal system. First, any new rules adopted by Parliaments or regulatory bodies will form part of the legal system, and thus provide new criteria for interpretation, which can, in turn, change the formulation of higher-level principles. Indeed, a focus on principles, and the need to seek consistency, can help to identify pieces of legislation that should be changed, or reinterpreted, for failing to fit the framework embodied by the new rules. Secondly, in construing certain

---

[128] This could be the so-called 'local priority', by which a court would prioritize the rules or precedents of accepted 'departments' of law, over those from different parts of the legal system. See Dworkin (n 108) 250.

[129] Dworkin's reply to Sunstein and Vermeule clarified that his views did not require a 'grand theory' every time a new case arose, since ordinary lawyers and judges reasoned from the inside-out. See Dworkin, 'In Praise of Theory' (n 122) 370.

[130] See the subsequent exchange in Cass Sunstein, 'From Theory to Practice' (1997) 29 Ariz St LJ 389, 391; Dworkin, 'In Praise of Theory: Reply' (n 129) 445, where Dworkin clarifies that judges reason from the inside-out, and that the reasoning process he very visually defines as 'justificatory ascent', is applied as needed, and that both factors are perfectly compatible with his theory. In fact, Dworkin's own view emphasizes the so-called 'local priority', ie that judges, when looking for a theory that 'fits' a solution within existing legal practice should prioritize the examples of that practice that relate to the legal categories where the new issue belongs, eg 'contract', or 'tort', or, more specifically, 'liability for breach of contract', or 'causation in tort'. Yet he says that such local priority should be abandoned when the distinctions and categories have become mechanical and arbitrary. See Dworkin (n 108) 250 ff.

[131] It is a testimony of Sunstein's elegance, that he is ready to admit, in plain and simple terms, that one of his co-authored studies provides more ammunition for Dworkin than for his own initial approach, ie even if striving for global coherence (which he characterizes as Dworkin's view) may overload the cognitive capacities of judges, 'local coherence' will likely result in inconsistent judgments, which is a reason to promote global coherence as an approach. See Sunstein and others (n 83) 1201. Sunstein has not spared un-nuanced praise for Dworkin's approach, in particular Dworkin's idea of interpretation as a 'chain-novel' exercise, in one of his most recent works, an improbable place to find such reference, since it is an entertainment piece. See Cass Sunstein, *The World According to Star Wars* (Dey Street Books 2016).

[132] Gunther Teubner, *Law as an Autopoietic System* (European University Institute Press Series 1993).

indeterminate concepts the courts (and regulatory bodies) will often have to make considerations of value (dry, technical considerations, such as risk or efficiency would also be included therein), which may be a source of change, if the values underpinning the rules have themselves changed. To sum up, principles-based interpretivism is not an obstacle; it is a major agent of (smooth) change within the area of interaction of predetermined values and the best possible policeman for these values and of their relative consistency at the stage of their implementation by the legal system.

1.43 'The alternative to a system of complex rules is a system of simple decision-making rules'. A seemingly different reaction to current financial regulation, especially after the Great Financial Crisis (GFC) of 2007–2008, cluttered with an excess of legal rules, is to advocate simpler, intuitive, decision-making rules. Although not canonically 'pragmatist', these views embrace part of the pragmatic discourse, since they argue that simple, intuitive rules-of-thumb can best replace complex analysis in the presence of high costs of cognition, excessive complexity, uncertainty, and small samples of data available,[133] while they also posit that complex rules can cause defensive behaviour. Alas, these views also disappoint as soon as one tries to use them as guidance for legal construction. Haldane and Maduros' argument based on the use of 'heuristics',[134] taking the views of Gigerenzer and others, who posit that these are adaptive mechanisms that lead to better decision-making (normative argument) under certain conditions of uncertainty.[135] This goes against the traditional association between 'heuristics' and systematic 'biases' by Tversky and Kahneman,[136] without evidence of why heuristics should work better in this environment.[137]

1.44 Furthermore, it is unclear whether the problem that simple rules try to address is one of models 'overfitting' the data, ie a problem of *prediction*, or one of agencies falling back into 'soft' attitudes as the rules' benefits seem far away on time, while the benefits of ignoring them appear close and certain, a problem of 'time inconsistency' of preferences, or 'self-control', or, in more modern formulations, the 'this time is different' syndrome.[138] This problem can be addressed by strategies of *commitment*,[139] for example, the 2 per cent inflation target of

---

[133] They use the example of a dog catching a Frisbee to illustrate that complex decision-making abilities are not needed to succeed at complex tasks. See Andrew Haldane and Vasileios Maduros, 'The Dog and the Frisbee' (The Changing Policy Landscape: A Symposium Sponsored by the Federal Reserve Bank of Kansas City at Jackson Hole, Wyoming (30 August–12 September 2012) 109–16.
[134] ibid 112.
[135] Gerd Gigerenzer and Henry Brighton, 'Homo Heuristicus: Why Biased Minds Make Better Inferences' (2009) 1 Topics in Cognitive Science 107.
[136] Their seminal article sought to illustrate that 'that people rely on a limited number of heuristic principles which reduce the complex tasks of assessing probabilities and predicting values to simpler judgmental operations. In general, these heuristics are quite useful, but sometimes they lead to severe and systematic errors'. Tversky and Kahneman (n 76) 1124–31. For a more recent criticism of Gigerenzer and Brighton's views see Benjamin E Hilbig and Tobias Richter, 'Homo Heuristicus Outnumbered: Comment on Gigerenzer and Brighton (2009)' (2011) 3 Topics in Cognitive Science 187.
[137] Gigerenzer and others are more nuanced in their conclusions, and do not claim that heuristics work better in all possible environments. See Daniel Goldstein and Gerd Gigerenzer, 'Models of Ecological Rationality: The Recognition Heuristic' (2002) 109 Psych Rev 75.
[138] Carmen M Reinhart and Kenneth S Rogoff, *This Time is Different: Eight Centuries of Financial Folly* (PUP 2009).
[139] Richard Thaler and Hersh Shefrin, 'An Economic Theory of Self-Control' (1981) 89 J Political Econ 392. For a critical survey see also Shane Frederick, George Lowenstein, and Ted O'Donoghue, 'Time Discounting and Time Preference: A Critical Review' (2002) 40 J Econ Literature 351; Robert Henry Strotz, 'Myopia and Inconsistency in Dynamic Utility Maximization' (1956) 23 Rev of Econ Studies 165, for an early example. Thaler exemplifies this taking from Strotz the example of Odysseus in the *Odyssey*, who ordered his men to tie him up to the mast, while they put bee's wax in their ears, so that he could enjoy the sirens' songs without throwing himself overboard. See Richard Thaler, *Misbehaving: The Making of Behavioral Economics* (Norton 2015) 99. Coincidentally, it is exactly

central banks, which helps to overcome time inconsistency.[140] Why does this matter if the answer is still 'simple, clear-cut rules'? It matters because the different nature of the rules requires a different role for discretion. On the one hand, the *predictive* rules are *internal* decision-making rules, ie if we look at the agent from outside, the solution lies in *enhancing* its *discretion*. This seems the type of setting discussed by Haldane and Maduros, who advocate more discretion for public authorities.[141] *Commitment* rules, on the other hand, are generally *external* in nature, because they try to address a problem of self-control and time-inconsistency, and therefore they *curtail* the agent's *discretion*.

When we look at legal rules, it is clear that they resemble more the external kind. However, pre-commitment rules do not fully capture the peculiarities of legal rules, which are not (at least, not just) a way that the agent uses to commit itself to a certain goal or task. They are a standard of *validity* of its actions and carry with them a series of consequences. For example, the fact that a central bank sets a 2 per cent inflation target does not mean that a central bank decision will be rendered invalid, or that it, or its members, will be held liable, or that other consequences will be automatically triggered if the threshold is crossed. Therefore, predictive accuracy is an important part of the decision-making of a public body, such as a central bank, to judge when there is an ongoing inflationary process, an asset bubble, or when an entity is about to become insolvent or illiquid. A pre-commitment to keep inflation low ensures that the body will act upon its predictions. However, when it comes to implementing those decisions by, say, purchasing assets in the market, the problem becomes one of *validity*, which rests on the *legitimacy* of the decision. This will, in turn, heavily rely on the decision's *consistency* with existing rules and past practice, which will be used as ex ante guidance by parties subject to the decisions, and as *ex post* review criteria by courts. **1.45**

Once the distinction is made, the argument in favour of heuristic rules no longer works with legal rules: if the relevant thing is the decision's legitimacy, intuition is not a good justification for the decisions of public authorities or courts. Discretion can be necessary, and thus legally admissible in certain scenarios, but on a wholesale (and unchecked) basis (and oversimplistic rules of thumb only pretend to offer a reasonable check, which in reality they do not) it undermines the decision's legitimacy, and if the problem is one of inaction or defensive behaviour it offers no solution either. That does not mean that complex and lengthy rules are not a problem, especially in hard cases. They truly are. Yet the problem lies in complex rules' susceptibility to increase conflicts and inconsistencies between rules, which means that simple cases may be made hard, and hard cases harder, by piling up the tension between rules *on top of* the tension between principles or policies, typical of hard cases. Yet the superior answer is not to eliminate part of the information or rules for the sake of simplicity, but in seeking the best possible fit within existing rules and practice, and their underpinning policies and values. In this light, a 'simple-rules' approach can be complementary to a principles-based interpretive approach, but not a substitute that can operate on its own. **1.46**

---

the same example used to exemplify the decision-making rules of central banks when they commit themselves to an inflation target.

[140] Finn E Kydland and Edward C Prescott, 'Rules Rather than Discretion: The Inconsistency of Optimal Plans' (1977) 85 J Political Econ 473.
[141] Haldane and Maduros (n 133) 144. They seem to draw an analogy with doctors, who perform better when unencumbered by a complex rulebook.

6 Principles-based interpretivism versus plausibly similar alternatives in the adjudication of law of finance: the case of cost-benefit analysis and the discourse theory of justice

1.47 It is now time to compare our preferred approach to principles with alternatives that are 'plausibly' similar, in the sense that they may 'sound' similar, and/or try to achieve similar goals. We will show where those approaches are compatible with ours, but also that they are not really alternatives to a principles-based interpretation and application of the law of finance by expert courts, but rather complementary to it.

1.48 The clearest example is offered by the use of cost-benefit analysis (CBA), an approach with an important tradition in the United States,[142] which has also been adopted by the European Union as part of its policy-making toolkit.[143] Although CBA was originally related to health and safety or environmental regulation, the debate rapidly moved also to financial regulation, with similarly enthusiastic proponents[144] and critics,[145] engaged in insightful exchange.[146]

1.49 Indeed, the *Metlife v FSOC* case in the United States[147] is a good example where the lack of a CBA was highlighted by the court as an indication that the decision to subject an insurance company to the purview of the Federal Reserve Board was 'arbitrary and capricious', a court decision in the wake of a (controversial) line of case law by D.C. courts that stroke down different SEC regulations for failing to undertake the corresponding CBA.[148] Advocates and critics of CBA have extensively debated the issue, and clarified its advantages, eg clarity

---

[142] Cabinet departments and executive agencies are often required to perform a CBA for major regulations, as a result of executive orders. Of special importance are executive orders (EOs), 12,291 in 1981 by President Ronald Reagan, instructing executive agencies to prepare regulatory impact analyses of their draft proposed and final major rules including a CBA, and to submit them to the Office of Information and Regulatory Affairs (OIRA) within the Office of Management and Budget (OMB); and 12,866 in 1993 by President Clinton, requiring executive agencies to assess costs and benefits of intended regulation. CBA is widely acknowledged as one of the primary tools to anticipate the consequences of rules. See Office of Management and Budget, 'Circular A-4' (17 September 2003) https://www.regulationwriters.com/downloads/Circular-A-4.pdf (accessed 9 September 2022). Although independent agencies have traditionally not been subject to the requirement to undertake a CBA, they were encouraged to do so by a variety of Eos (eg EO No 13,563, 76 Fed Reg 3821 (21 January 2011) (President Obama), and the Administrative Conference of the United States adopted Recommendations suggesting CBA should form part of independent regulatory agencies' policymaking process. See Administrative Conference of the United States (ACUS), 'Benefit-Cost Analysis at Independent Regulatory Agencies' (13 June 2013) https://www.acus.gov/recommendation/benefit-cost-analysis-independent-regulatory-agencies (accessed 9 September 2022).

[143] Interinstitutional Agreement between the European parliament, the Council and the European Commission on better Law-Making [2016] OJ L123/1, recital 5 and point 12; European Commission, 'Better Regulation Guidelines' (7 July 2017) SWD(2017) 350 https://ec.europa.eu/info/sites/default/files/better-regulation-guidelines.pdf (accessed 9 September 2022), Chapter III Guidelines on Impact Assessment, Question 5.

[144] Eric Posner and E Glen Weyl, 'Benefit-Cost Analysis for Financial Regulation' (2013) 103 A Econ Rev 1; Paul Rose and Christopher J Walker, 'The Importance of Cost-Benefit Analysis in Financial Regulation' (2013) Report for US Chamber of Commerce; Committee on Capital Markets Regulation, 'A Balanced Approach to Cost-Benefit Analysis Reform' (October 2013) https://www.capmktsreg.org/2013/10/01/a-balanced-approach-to-cost-benefit-analysis-reform/ (accessed 9 September 2022).

[145] See eg John Coates IV, 'Cost-Benefit Analysis of Financial Regulation: Case Studies and Implications' (2015) 124 Yale LJ 882; Jeffrey N Gordon, 'The Empty Call for Benefit-Cost Analysis in Financial Regulation' (2014) 43 J Legal Studies S351.

[146] The *Yale Law Journal Forum* made it possible for proponents of CBA to reply to John Coates IV article. See Eric Posner and E Glen Weyl, 'Cost-Benefit Analysis of Financial Regulations: A Response to Criticisms' (2015) 124 Yale LJ Rev 246; Cass R Sunstein, 'Financial Regulation and Cost-Benefit Analysis' (2015) 124 Yale LJ Forum 263; Bruce Kraus, 'Economists in the Room at the SEC' (2015) 124 Yale LJ Forum 280. This was followed by the corresponding reply. See Coates IV (n 145) 305–15.

[147] *Metlife v FSOC* [2016] 1:15-cv-00045-RMC 30, District Court, District of Columbia.

[148] *Business Roundtable v SEC* 647 F 3d 1144 (DC Cir 2011); *American Equity Investment Life Insurance Co v SEC* 613 F 3d 166 (DC Cir 2010); *Chamber of Commerce v SEC* 412 F 3d 133 (DC Cir 2005).

about the consequences of rules, and thus wiser, and more rational decision-making,[149] and disadvantages, eg little consideration for values that are hard to quantify, or benefits that are hard to monetize, overestimation of costs, underestimation of future benefits through discount.[150] The debate has moved along similar lines in the field of financial regulation, with critics arguing that CBA is especially implausible due to finance's special features, eg its centrality to the economy, social and political, and non-stationary character, according to Coates;[151] its artificiality and construction by the law, in Gordon's view,[152] while advocates insist that the obstacles are not insurmountable, or that CBA provides alternatives for cases of uncertainty.[153]

There seems to be margin for compromise in practice.[154] While an important part of the debate should focus on whether the conditions to perform CBA are adequate, or on the reforms that would be needed to carry on adequate CBAs.[155] Our point is more basic: regardless of its virtues (or vices) CBA is not an alternative to a principles-based interpretive approach. First, CBA is not a *necessary* part of the law. Recent cases may offer support to the idea that CBA has the status of a transversal principle, such as the US Supreme Court's decision in *Michigan v EPA*,[156] relied upon by *Metlife v FSOC*,[157] where CBA was considered to be an inextricable part of 'rational' analysis, and 'reasonable' interpretation.[158] Yet, such a sweeping statement is misleading, because it was grounded on the purported acceptance by statutory *rules* and agency *practice* of the basic principle. Thus, CBA's scope and intensity must be determined against the backdrop of other legal sources, such as statutory rules or precedents; it is not a meta-principle, let alone *the* meta-principle of legal construction. Indeed, CBA is seen by its advocates as a way to improve the law,[159] not as an inextricable part of what law is, identifiable as such by its mere content.[160] Secondly, CBA is not *sufficient* for purposes of legal construction. Even its advocates accept that CBA works better in some scenarios than

1.50

---

[149] ACUS, 'Recommendation 79-4, Public Disclosure Concerning the Use of Cost-Benefit and Similar Analyses In Regulation' (3 July 1979) 44 Fed Reg 38,826. See also Cass R Sunstein, 'The Office of Information & Regulatory Affairs: Myths and Realities' (2013) 126 Harv LR 1838, 1846.
[150] Frank Ackerman and Lisa Heinzerling, 'Pricing the Priceless: Cost-Benefit Analysis of Environmental Protection' (2001) 150 U Pa L Rev 1557, 1580–81.
[151] Coates IV (n 145) 998–1003.
[152] In Gordon's view, CBA in fields like environmental regulation is possible because it is undertaken over a stable system, which rests on natural constraints, whereas finance is an artificial, legally-constructed field, meaning that non-trivial rule modifications will change the system in ways that are hard to foresee, and thus undercut the value of cost and benefit evidence based on the previous situation. See Gordon (n 145) S351. This explanation could provide an explanation to Coates' claim that finance is non-stationary.
[153] This would be the case of 'breakeven analysis', ie when costs are certain and benefits are not, the analysis needs to determine the minimum benefit that the regulation needs to achieve. See Sunstein (n 146) 263-279; Cass R Sunstein, 'The Limits of Quantification' (2014) 103 Cal L Rev 1369.
[154] Compromise views can focus on CBA's usefulness as a procedural, rather than moral, instrument, which would yield information of moral importance. See eg Donald C Hubin, 'The Moral Justification of Benefit/Cost Analysis' (1994) 10 Econ & Philosophy 169; Coates argues in favour of a 'conceptual CBA' also in procedural terms. See Coates IV (n 145) 1008–1010. CBA's use as a procedural tool would make it possible to accommodate criteria such as deontological rights and other moral values. See Matthew Adler and Eric A Posner, 'Rethinking Cost-Benefit Analysis' (1999) 109 Yale LJ 165.
[155] Richard L Revesz, 'Cost-Benefit Analysis and the Structure of the Administrative State: The Case of Financial Services Regulation' (2017) 34 YJR 545.
[156] *Michigan v EPA* 135 S Ct 2699 (2015).
[157] *Metlife v FSOC* (n 147).
[158] ibid paras 5–7.
[159] See eg Sunstein (n 79).
[160] Strict positivist views failed to capture the fact that certain principles formed part of 'the law' by virtue of their content, something that has led more modern versions of positivism to construe a broader 'rule of recognition' for the elements of the law that does not only appeal to the 'procedure' by which norms were approved, or the 'convention' about their being part of the law, but also to their content.

others, and that it does not exhaust all the possible criteria to construe the law.[161] Focusing solely on CBA would require ignoring harms and benefits that are not quantifiable, eg if they have a moral dimension, despite the fact that they may be embodied in precedents and rules.

1.51 A bank supervisor can use CBA to calibrate capital requirements for each institution, consolidate certain entities within a bank's balance sheet, or subject other entities to prudential rules for banks or funds if and to the extent that the rules, and their underpinning principles, allow so, but cannot ignore those rules and principles, even if it considers that they are not justified by CBA. Indeed, absent such precision, CBA would be *self-defeating*, because, if the conclusion of CBA were that 'an action will be required when justified by CBA, and an action will be invalid when not justified by CBA' this would impose an enormous cost in terms of unpredictability, and the resulting mistrust from the system's lack of legitimacy. This dichotomy is well captured by Rawl's 'two concepts of rules', where he distinguishes between justifying a practice, and justifying a particular action falling under it.[162] Broad theories of justice, such as utilitarianism, or CBA, for that matter, may justify a practice, such as the combination of access to liquidity, deposit guarantee, and bank prudential rules, but a specific supervisory action (or, say, an action to refuse access to liquidity) needs to be justified under the rules themselves.

1.52 This means that, in hard cases, where a question over the applicability of the rules, or the friction between competing sets of rules, also raises questions about the principles and rationale underpinning those rules, any CBA needs to be justified, and circumscribed, by its adoption by applicable rules, and their underpinning principles. It also means that, in cases where the legislature decided to obviate CBA concerns when passing a certain piece of legislation in favour of other considerations, public bodies and courts need to obviate CBA when interpreting and applying the rules, at least in the absence of an overarching mandate to uphold CBA when interpreting the rules, which, right or wrong, was the assumption of the D.C. Court in *Metlife v FSOC*.

1.53 The principles-based interpretative process outlined here could be characterized by some as a theory about the communicative process in law, and more specifically, the law of finance. Our claim could be restated as a claim about what counts as a valid argument, and what does not. In this light, one could see the resemblance with discourse theories of justice, such as Habermas',[163] theories that see argumentation as part of the validation process, such as Rawls' 'reflective equilibrium',[164] or even theories about the policy process that consider argument and persuasion essential in that process.[165] Thus, it is important to identify the parallels, and the differences. In terms of parallels, our argument about the use of principles-based

---

[161] See Sunstein (n 160) 149–74; Andrea Renda and others, 'Assessing the Costs and Benefits of Regulation. A CEPS–Economisti Associati Study for the European Commission' (March 2014) 157 https://ec.europa.eu/smart-regulation/impact/commission_guidelines/docs/131210_cba_study_sg_final.pdf (accessed 9 September 2022).

[162] A 'practice' in Rawls' broader sense, includes any form of activity specified by a system of rules, which define offices, roles, moves, penalties, defences, which give the activity its structure. See John Rawls, 'Two Concepts of Rules' (1955) 64 The Philosophical Rev 3.

[163] Habermas (n 101).

[164] Rawls (n 121). Rawls describes reflective equilibrium as a process of mutual adjustment between considered judgments, which operate as the initial 'fixed points', and the principles that are selected as an explanation of those considered judgments. Sometimes the principles will alter our considered judgments, and other times the principles will be considered as an unsatisfactory explanation of our considered judgments and will have to be adjusted themselves. When the principles match our considered judgments, duly pruned and adjusted, we reach 'reflective equilibrium'. See ibid 18, 42–43.

[165] Giandomenico Majone, *Evidence, Argument and Persuasion in the Policy Process* (YUP 1989).

claims as valid claims can be rephrased as a claim about the validity of arguments, and the enabling procedural mechanisms that facilitate the identification of the relevant principles can be justified by a theory of discourse. Thus, a process that favours the exchange of views, where authorities and courts have to give reasons for their actions, and which is iterative, in the sense that it provides opportunities to review arguments, is better than a process without exchange, reasons, iteration or review. The latter will be illegitimate, which, in our view, provides a strong prima facie claim of illegality.

The differences stem from the scope and reach of each inquiry. Ours is not a theory as ambitious as Rawls', or Habermas'. We do not try to provide a holistic answer to the question of 'justice' in a political society, or for a top-down structuring of communication and discourse. Our goal is to illustrate the controversies that lie at the core of seemingly accepted concepts, and the tensions between vast pieces of financial legislation, and between these and basic fundamental rights, to stress the perils of an overly simplified 'one problem at a time' approach, and to examine the way courts approach the identified tensions and controversies in hard cases, and distil some criteria from that practice, which should be used to discuss problems of legality. Our principles-based interpretive approach fits well with some elements of a discourse theory of law and ethics but does not need to answer their broader questions to be operational. At the same time, all-encompassing theories of justice, or law, like Rawls' or Habermas', due to their level of generality, are inspirational, but not operational, in a field as concrete as the law of finance, at least not without an important process of specification, and are only useful to the extent that the concrete problem can be related back to their basic premises, but not when the problem lies elsewhere. A procedural decision, or rule, that curtails dialogue and exchange, will fall short of a discourse theory's normative standard. Yet if the controversy lies in making sense of a conflict between financial stability, and the avoidance of moral hazard, on one hand, and investor protection and property rights, on the other, all in a context where administrative discretion is in tension with judicial review, authorities and courts will find little comfort in discourse theories, and their indeterminacy. **1.54**

It is time for some stock-taking. In our view the role of principles for courts' interpretation and application of the law of finance is key. First, they are critical to understand both how positive legal 'institutions' are or can be connected with a society's broader 'values', and how these institutions are deployed by courts and public bodies, as well as to understand the potential frictions in both processes. Secondly, in the law of finance's increasingly complex landscape, principles are essential to arbitrate between the competing narratives, and themes, supporting the different sets of rules, as well as to calibrate the scope and intensity of rules, the degree of discretion left to public bodies to exercise their powers, and the role that fundamental rights play as limits to those powers. In this sense we make two claims. The first is that principles-based interpretivism is part of the process by which courts and public bodies apply the law of finance. The second is that this dimension needs to be properly acknowledged to provide better evaluative criteria about whether a decision is right or wrong. **1.55**

Principles-based interpretation is obviously a reality in the practice of courts that adjudicate financial disputes, which need to constantly appeal to the rules' rationale, purpose, objectives, fill in the open-textured concepts left by the legislature, or mediate between potentially inconsistent rules in order to establish the parties' *rights*. This can be seen in all kinds of hard cases, no matter whether present in the field of monetary policy and financial stability, supervision, or insolvency and bank resolution. Yet our claim is not merely descriptive, but normative. Being aware of the importance and role **1.56** of principles-based interpretation provides courts and public bodies with guidance on how to determine what the law *is*. In relation to this, a principles-based, interpretivist approach also helps to understand the proper place of criteria such as the cost-benefit analysis (CBA), whose use, widespread as it is, needs a previous normative habilitation. That is, even if such principles inform the legislative process, and can also be useful interpretative tools, they are not all-encompassing, or self-sufficient, and their use is conditional upon their presence among the values that inform a specific legal practice (rule or precedent) and, as such, compete with other considerations of value. Principles-based interpretivism does not advocate complexity for its own sake, nor does it postulate 'grand theories' as the answer to every problem. It rather helps public bodies and courts to contextualize the problems they examine and use more than one framework to look at them. This does not require those bodies and courts to theorize 'all the way to the top' in each case, but to understand the precedential effect, and implications, that a specific decision could have beyond the immediate field where it applies, and thus understand, to a better extent, the demands of consistency, or integrity, and to see the impact that specific rulings or reasoning can have in the values underpinning the specific institutional framework.

1.57 The above considerations have relevant implications for the role of judicial review, and more specifically for expert adjudication of financial disputes and accountability. The first, and more evident, is that courts have to rely on principles-based interpretivism to determine the fitness of a certain decision within the law's overall scheme. This requires acknowledging that, in an important number of cases, it does not suffice to discuss the scope of application of a legal rule in isolation, but to understand the considerations of principle supporting that rule, and how they shape its scope and intensity. Such exercise needs to be aware that different sets of rules may be inspired by conflicting narratives, which need to be considered together, in order to determine whether a specific exercise of authority is legal. A case-by-case analysis can not only result in errors prompted by heuristic biases. It may undermine the integrity of the whole regulatory edifice. This, in turn, requires expert judgment. Secondly, the law of finance needs to integrate fundamental rights and values properly as part of its overall narrative. Imagine a legislative process where goals are set first, a certain narrative determining a specific cause-and-effect relationship is selected, which inspires a specific set of rules; fundamental rights and values are often examined at the end, as the inconvenient red lines that must not be crossed but are not conceived as principles inspiring the rules. If such shortcomings are present in the legislative process, they cannot be present in the interpretative process. As a matter of hierarchy and interpretative value, they are the more basic sources of legal authority, which means that a greater theoretical effort is needed to blend them within the narratives of monetary and financial stability, or investor protection.

1.58 Thirdly, principles-based interpretivism allows a better understanding of the role of simple rules, as part of a better law-making process, but no substitute for principles-based interpretation (clarity and consensus as to meaning are convenient illusions, but illusions after all). It also helps to understand better the role of transversal interpretative criteria, such as cost-benefit analysis (CBA). A court confronted with a cost-benefit argument needs to consider, first, whether the relevant legal sources are conceived with such criterion in mind, or a different one, and whether other sources that are inspired by different considerations of justice clash with or trump over them. Even if a specific set of prudential rules is inspired by CBA considerations and the supervisory authority is vested with discretionary power to make such CBA, the decision over whether the application of those rules interferes with other rules, say, investor protection rules, or with the fundamental right of privacy, is a legal decision, to be adopted by the court.

Fourthly, among the relevant legal principles, courts need to be more aware of their expert role within the system of governance, where they may be the ultimate arbiters of validity, but they are also accompanied by other parameters that set limits for their role and help put it in context. A court considering whether the act by a supervisory agency is legal or not cannot oscillate between the opposite poles of acknowledging the agency's 'discretion', as a blank check, or ascertaining whether it reached 'the' correct answer. It needs to examine, with expert judgment, first, what was the legal mandate with which it was vested by the relevant rules, and how that mandate has to be examined in light of its finality. Then, it has to examine that mandate in relation with other, potentially competing, mandates by the same agency, or other agencies whose activity may overlap with it. Then, it should analyse what are the legal reasons for vesting the agency with the ability to set goals, and interpret the corresponding provisions, and examine the specific scope of 'discretion' in light of those reasons. Even within the scope of discretion it should examine whether the mechanisms of accountability, consisting in transparency duties, duties to give reasons, or the parties' right to be heard, ensured the robustness of the decision-making process. If the conclusion is compliant, the court should simply declare the decision valid. In case of doubt, it could well ask the agency for more information, or examine the arguments of the parties that may be affected by the decision. Finally, deeper analysis is needed in order to establish the reasons why courts and public bodies in one country should treat soft law of supranational bodies, or legal practice from other countries, as a source of authority for decision-making, other than the fact that 'it works'. **1.59**

'Works for now, until it does not' could be the answer. It is unclear whether the answer may be in states' duty to enhance the legitimacy of their acts, which leads them to incorporate international law as part of the law of the land, in the assumption of an internationally shared notion of human dignity that transcends national borders, at least in what concerns fundamental rights, in broader notions of 'political community', 'shared sovereignty', or 'legal pluralism', which go beyond the nation state and comity, or in a combination of them. Yet we cannot but see that the current system of polycentric exercise of authority in financial matters, by lacking a clear legal, principles-based foundation, is the proverbial giant with clay feet. **1.60**

All this may sound more theoretical than it would be in reality. In the practice of the courts we constantly see interpretative exercises that closely resemble the one that we have just described. Not every hard case requires a full, all-encompassing theory, least of all in a polycentric system. Yet, even if we keep that in mind, the introductory analysis offered here is not trivial, because it stresses the need for greater awareness of the processes going on in courts' interpretation and application of the law of finance and helps to point out that the law's internal consistency, and, beyond that, its coherence with a set of shared values, is its major source of legitimacy. If, in the words of Lord Justice Laws, in the act of construing statutes, judges very often develop, refine, and apply constitutional [and other foundational] principles', interpretation is an autonomous creative process, and one which is 'not just a matter of filling in gaps the legislature would itself have filled, if the legislators had thought about it' but rather a purposively interpretation and application where statutory text is taken **1.61** to mean what it should in light of basic foundational principles.[166] However, to achieve this, as Lord Justice Ryder noted,[167] we need specialist skills and knowledge, because 'judges will have to understand their caseload to a greater extent than in the past; be able to identify the features of cases that are out of the ordinary; and be able to predict, react to and actively direct cases in order to try and achieve the best-quality outcome in each case'.

---

[166] Lord Justice Laws (n 16) 201–203.
[167] Lord Justice Ryder, 'Improving the Delivery of Justice in the Shadow of Magna Carta' in Jeremy Cooper (ed), *Being a Judge in the Modern World* (OUP 2017) 133.

2
Finance, the Rule of Law, and the Courts

1 Legal institutions and financial development	2.01	2.2 Courts, crises, and biases: reframing urgency, seeking consistency, transitioning to 'normalcy'	2.30
2 Law, finance, and crises	2.12	3 Courts and finance beyond crises: hard cases	2.39
2.1 (Rule of) law and (financial) emergencies: expediency, stability, and legitimacy: The role of courts and legal principles	2.13	3.1 Courts beyond financial crises: hard cases, interstitial, and pivotal role	2.40
		3.2 Courts and finance: from back seat to front seat	2.43

1 Legal institutions and financial development

2.01 If we are discussing the role of courts and expert judgment in the field of finance we should start from the basics, for example by asking ourselves whether courts' role in finance is positive, under what circumstances is it positive, and whether it is special and why. There are different arguments that can be explored to address these questions and, in this chapter, we offer an overview of them. First, we begin by analysing the role law and courts can play in financial development. Secondly, we analyse the specific relationship between courts and financial crises, both *at* the time of crisis, when 'expediency' rather than 'coherence' characterizes both market developments and policy reforms, and in *post*-crisis settings, where courts are left with the task of making sense of the whole system of rules. Thirdly, taking a step forward from our introductory remarks in Chapter 1, we discuss the reasons why courts have a special role to play in the law of finance.

2.02 Law is important for financial market development. This statement may seem obvious for a lawyer, but it was overlooked for a long time. When stylized models based on utility maximization carried the day, market players would find an equilibrium if they were left to their own devices, and the law's most important role was to stay out of the way as much as possible. Such theoretical models ignored the richness and complexity of the institutional structures underpinning financial markets,[1] which were also responsible for making them work in the first place. Even in parcels characterized by self-regulation (eg broker–dealer interactions) transactions ran smoothly because market parties could rely on a consensus over basic concepts, such as 'security', 'money', or 'derivative', based on statutory/regulatory definitions, distinctions, such as between 'statement' and 'opinion', or general canons of what was acceptable behavior, and what was not. Financial markets have since their origins been characterized

---

[1] John Stuart Mill, *Utilitarianism* (first published 1863, BLTC 1995); Jeremy Bentham, *An Introduction to the Principles of Morals and Legislation* (first published 1781, BLTC 1995).

by a deep socio-legal embeddedness.[2] Only in this way can market participants concentrate on maximizing a narrower set of variables, because they could take for granted that all the others were not up for discussion, and that all other market participants shared this view.

2.03 Naturally, some academic economists had been stressing the importance of 'institutions' for a long time,[3] but this idea had not become mainstream in economics, and even less so in finance. It jumped to the forefront thanks to ideological, policymaking and academic developments. Ideologically speaking, the 1980s were characterized by the predominance of a decisively pro-market stance in the United States and the United Kingdom (among others), which strongly relied on the ideas of the Austrian school and the Chicago school, some of which (especially in the Austrian school) were vocationally 'institutional' in nature, and understood economic freedoms within a broader context of constitutionally granted freedoms.[4] These views were always hotly contested, but influential.

2.04 In policy-making levels, institutionally based arguments were decisively promoted by multilateral institutions like the International Monetary Fund (IMF) and the World Bank. The two institutions began to concentrate significant energy in promoting what they considered to be the institutional drivers of financial stability and economic development. Critics, however, would counter that their focus on 'property rights' and similar institutions in isolation from other institutions could result in privatizations without sufficient accountability,[5] though this view remains contested, and multilateral institutions use now a complete toolkit that emphasizes the rule of law and accountability checks.

2.05 In academic circles, the connection between institutions and financial development was promoted by several articles by La Porta, López de Silanes, Shleifer, or Vishny,[6] which were followed by others like eg Zingales[7] and Hart.[8] The issue was placed front and center partly because the authors made the provocative claim that common law countries had a superior set of laws, and that this is why they enjoyed greater financial markets development. Given the boldness and broadness of the claim, the evidence put together to support it was shockingly limited (at least for a jurist): in essence, the authors identified a series of corporate law provisions as protective towards investors (one-share-one-vote, pre-emptive rights, anti-director rights, etc.) and then checked whether they were present in corporate statutes around the world. This approach has been extensively criticized for its narrowness, or its

---

[2] Mark Granovetter, 'Economic Action and Social Structure: The Problem of Embeddedness' (1985) 91 AJS 481; Oliver Williamson, 'Markets and Hierarchies: Some Elementary Considerations' (1973) 63 AER 316.
[3] Oliver Williamson, *Markets and Hierarchies, Analysis and Antitrust Implications: A Study in the Economics of Internal Organization* (Free Press 1975); Douglass C North, 'The New Institutional Economics' (1986) 142 JITE/ Zeitschrift Für Die Gesamte Staatswissenschaft 230.
[4] Friedrich A Hayek, *The Constitution of Liberty* (first published 1960, The University of Chicago Press 1978); Ludwig von Mises, *Human Action: A treatise on Economics* (Liberty Funds 2007).
[5] Philip Keefer, 'Governance and economic growth' in Alan Winters and Shahid Yusuf (eds), *Dancing with Giants* (2007) World Bank and the Institute of Policy Studies (Singapore) 211–243; Frank Upham, 'Chinese Property Rights and Property Theory' (2009) 39 HKLJ 611; Frank Upham, 'From Demsetz to Deng: Speculations on The Implications of Chinese Growth for Law and Development Theory' (2009) 41 NYU J of Intl L 551.
[6] Rafael La Porta and Others, 'Legal Determinants of External Finance' (1997) 3 J of Fin II 1131; see Rafael La Porta and others, 'Law and Finance' (1998) 106 JPE 1113.
[7] Alexander Dyck and Luigi Zingales, 'Private Benefits of Control: An International Comparison' (2004) 59(2) The J of Fin 537.
[8] Oliver Hart, 'Incomplete Contracts and the Theory of the Firm' (1988) 4 J of L Econ and Org 11; Oliver Hart and John Moore, 'Foundations of Incomplete Contracts'(1999) 66 The Rev of Econ Studies 115.

inability to get causation right.[9] Yet, no one seems to dispute the claim that law is important for financial market development.

Needless to say, it is not possible to capture all the forces at play during this time, ranging from the 1980s to the late 1990s. The important thing to bear in mind is that the existence of a strong link between financial markets and the law was increasingly stressed by the proponents of the dominant, pro-market ideas, and even as the tide turned on the latter, the former stayed. **2.06**

Yet, even if the importance of legal rights stayed, it did not do so in the narrow form of its early advocates. Institutional economics, for instance, has expanded since those early times. 'Institutions' are now considered by many, if not most, specialists as *the* main driver (or at least one of the main drivers) of economic development.[10] Yet, some of the more well-known proponents of the role of economic institutions in promoting financial development do not highlight such institutions as 'property rights' in the abstract, but emphasize the importance of their connection with political institutions, and the need that political institutions are *inclusive* in order to foster economic institutions that are also inclusive.[11] **2.07**

More to the extreme, authors like Piketty[12] have shifted the debate towards inequality, and the need to dispose of an ideology that entrenches capital, and capital owners, at the expense of workers. Yet, far from undermining the link between law and capital (including finance) if anything they emphasize it even more: if we accepted that ideology drove the legal changes that entrenched the power of capital-holders, changes towards a more egalitarian ideology would need to be accompanied by legal changes (in the laws of property, taxation, etc.) to ensure that balance was effectively restored. **2.08**

More specifically, the 'Law and Finance' approach by La Porta et al. has been contested by other proposals, of which possibly the legal theory of finance (LTF) may be the one with the more defined contours.[13] This view, proposed as already noted in Chapter 1 by Katharina Pistor, postulates that a key driver of finance is its need to deal with uncertainty and liquidity volatility, which are a source of inherent instability, and that finance is 'legally constructed', ie financial assets are a series of promises defined by the law, which means that the law shapes the rights and expectations they confer.[14] 'This legal construction has a paradoxical relationship with finance, since it is a precondition to enjoy legal certainty, but at the same time, at times of uncertainty, if all promises are strictly enforced, it may precipitate the collapse of the system'.[15] The way this problem is resolved is by shaping finance as a hierarchical system with varying flexibility, rigid in the periphery, but elastic at the core, to ensure that the system itself is preserved. Pistor's other contribution tackles another angle of the law-finance relationship, such as the use of the law to 'code' capital, by insulating sources of wealth as 'assets', allocating them to their 'owners', and ensuring their durability.[16] Since this level of skill and **2.09**

---

[9] Katharina Pistor and others, 'Evolution of Corporate Law: A Cross-Country Comparison' (2002) 23 U Pa J Intl L 791.
[10] Dani Rodrik, Arvind Subramanian, and Francesco Trebbi, 'The Primacy of Institutions' (2004) 9 J of Econ Growth 131.
[11] ibid. See also Stephan Haggard and Lydia Tiede, 'The Rule of Law and Economic Growth: Where Are We?' (2011) 39(5) World Development 673.
[12] Thomas Piketty, *Le capital au XXIe siècle* (Sevil 2013).
[13] Katharina Pistor, 'Towards a Legal Theory of Finance' (2013) European Corporate Governance Institute Working Paper 196/2013, 1–51; Katharina Pistor, 'A Legal Theory of Finance' (2013) 41 J of Com Econ 303.
[14] Pistor, 'Towards a Legal Theory of Finance' (n 13) 8–12.
[15] ibid 12–32.
[16] Katharina Pistor, *The Code of Capital: How the Law Creates Wealth and Inequality* (PUP 2020).

ingenuity is only accessible to a select cohort of lawyers, the result of this capital codification process is to entrench inequality.

2.10 Other authors have argued instead that actual capitalism needs to be saved from capitalists, and simply needs to be faithful to its principles.[17] What is noticeable about some of these efforts is that, when compared with their forebears, they show greater awareness of the importance of the legal dimension of financial issues, and thus they emphasize the importance that investors enjoy *actual* freedom of choice, instead of assuming that profit maximization is their ultimate goal (or, at least, the only goal that is realizable[18]), or that contracts (like those subscribed with employees and suppliers) are generally incomplete, and thus it is not obvious that *all* decision-making rights should be allocated to residual claimants, and that businesses can cause externalities.[19] Notably, the scholars who hold these views tend to attach particular importance to law and institutions, and their role in contracts, corporate governance, and financial markets.[20] Courts are one, and not the less important, of those institutions.

2.11 Therefore, economics and finance have gradually evolved to attach increasing importance to the role of law and institutions in making financial markets work. Crucially, this view is shared between authors who may otherwise disagree in professing more 'pro-market' or 'pro-state' views.

2 Law, finance, and crises

2.12 Crises have played a role in strengthening the link between law, courts and finance. In times of economic bonanza, the focus on legal institutions was more circumscribed to relatively narrow views on property rights, market freedom and deregulation. Crises and market failures, on the other hand, have been instrumental to expand the role of the law in finance and of its application by courts. However, this has happened in more obvious and more subtle ways, which is important to differentiate. First, in a more obvious way, market failures have resulted in an increased tolerance for government intervention. There are important arguments justifying the need for greater government intervention, which link to the literature on law and emergencies. However, these views tend to overestimate the virtues of government intervention, and to underestimate their biases. In this sense, crisis measures are framed by urgent issues, which makes it necessary to reframe them in light of the rest of the system, and its fundamental values, a job courts are uniquely well-suited to do.

---

[17] See Raghuram Rajan and Luigi Zingales, *Saving Capitalism from the Capitalists* (PUP 2004); or Luigi Zingales, *A Capitalism for the People: Recapturing the Lost Genius of American Prosperity* (Basic Books 2014).

[18] Oliver Hart and Luigi Zingales, 'Companies Should Maximize Shareholder Welfare Not Market Value' (2017) 2(2) J of L Fin & Accounting 247.

[19] David Frydlinger and Oliver Hart, 'Overcoming Contractual Incompleteness: The Role of Guiding Principles' (2019) NBER Working Paper No 24265 https://scholar.harvard.edu/hart/publications/overcoming-contractual-incompleteness-role-guiding-principals (accessed 12 September 2022). See also Maija Halonen-Akatwijuka and Oliver Hart, 'Continuing Contracts' (2020) 36 JLEO 284.

[20] A more recent collection of essays by prominent academics, policymakers and intellectuals that considered Milton Friedman's 1970 essay 'The Social Responsibility of a Business Is to Increase its Profits' in the *New York Times* 50 years later is noticeably conscious of the importance of laws in shaping ideas like corporate purpose, fiduciary duties, corporate responsibility: Luigi Zingales, Jana Kasperkevic and Asher Schechter, *Milton Friedman 50 Years Later* (Promarket–Stigler Center 2020).

2.1 (Rule of) law and (financial) emergencies: expediency, stability, and legitimacy. The role of courts and legal principles

2.13 Crises are emergencies, and emergencies confront the law with a basic dilemma: should one assume that the situation of emergency is covered by existing law, on the face of evidence suggesting that legislators were far from contemplating and regulating it in legal provisions, or should one accept that it falls outside the law, with the consequence that the actions of the executive will be adopted without judicial review? This question was famously discussed by Carl Schmitt. His thesis was that liberal democracies that adhere to the rule of law have no theory of exceptional states, because they cannot anticipate what will count as an emergency, nor what procedures should be used to allocate powers in such an emergency:[21] emergencies are, by definition, unanticipated, and any plan is bound to be revised. Liberal legalism can only aspire to determine who is the sovereign power that can determine whether there is an exception.

2.14 Schmitt's strongest theses are deeply controversial, and some authors, like Dyzenhaus, argue that they conflate the 'rule by law', which consists in abiding by whatever positive laws there may be, with the 'rule of law', understood as a broader set of principles that a legal system needs to fulfil in order to be called such.[22] These principles, identified by authors such as Lon Fuller, do not ensure that the rule of law fulfils a demanding set of criteria in the sense of a 'morality of aspiration', but the narrower set of criteria normally associated with a 'morality of duty', ie, the basic principles of certainty, publicity, non-retroactivity, etc. that a law needs to be susceptible of imposing duties to the citizenry.[23]

2.15 However, other authors, like Vermeule, propose a milder version of these ideas, at least for administrative law (which would encompass a large part of financial regulation), by making the claim that, at least American administrative law is 'Schmittian' in nature, because it is built around a series of 'black holes' and 'grey holes' that are integral to its structure, and because this cannot be otherwise, for institutional and practical reasons.[24] Vermeule's examples come exclusively from the field of national security, which makes his statements narrow at best. However, the main problem is that, whereas his descriptive statement (ie, American courts are Schmittian, as they leave many black holes and grey holes) is clear enough, his normative statement (ie that such black/grey holes are inevitable) is much less clear. He claims to differentiate between 'holes' (of non-reviewability) and open 'standards', like 'arbitrary and capricious',[25] or 'substantial evidence'[26] (where the intensity of review can be dialled up or down[27]) but provides no clear explanation about why the 'slippery slope' of growing deference to the executive at times of emergency is an inevitability.

2.16 In a different work, Posner and Vermeule suggest a different line of argumentation, more based on the superior ability of the executive to act quickly in emergency situations, a role

---

[21] Carl Schmitt, *Politische Theologie. Vier Kapitel zur Lehre von der Souveränität* (first published 1934 English Edition: CJ Miller (tr)) *Political Theology. Four Chapters on the Concept of Sovereignty* (Antelope Hill Publishing 2020).
[22] David Dyzenhaus, *The Constitution of Law: Legality in a Time of Emergency* (CUP 2006).
[23] Lon Luvois Fuller, *The Morality of Law* (YUP 1969).
[24] Adrian Vermeule, 'Our Schmittian Administrative Law' (2009) 122 Harv LR 1095.
[25] Administrative Procedure Act, s 706(2)(a).
[26] *Citizens to Preserve Overton Park Inc v Volpe* 401 US 402, 416–17 (1971).
[27] Vermeule (n 24) 1106.

for which it needs sweeping powers.[28] However, to imply from this that executive action should go unchallenged, or not subject to court review is a *non sequitur*. Ensuring swift and effective action may be the executive's prerogative and responsibility, but it is not obvious why ensuring lawful action (the judiciary's prerogative) should be any less important. In fact, sometimes fostering trust in the system boils down to a single point in time, where a court is capable of saying and doing the right thing when it is the hard thing to say or do. In reality, when assessing the respective roles of the executive and the judiciary at times of crisis it is important to not conflate two different things. One is the standard of review, ie, whether courts will be deferential with executive action. Another is the timing, or speed of the review, ie, whether court can, or will, review executive acts as fast as the executive can produce them. The second aspect has obvious implications, for reasons that stem from the institutional underpinnings of both mechanisms. The executive has more resources, and is more accountable to the public, which expects it to act quickly. Furthermore, the usefulness of courts is less in their swiftness than in the fairness of their process, and the argumentative nature of their decision-making (things that do not match well with urgency). Yet, whereas it is obvious that court actions will be less swift (and less sweeping) than the executive ones in times of crisis, this does not mean that they have to be more deferential.

2.17 Authors like Zaring point out that courts played a relatively discrete role during the Great Financial Crisis (2007–2008) and its subsequent stages.[29] However, he does not present this as an inevitable, and even less as a desirable, outcome. It was the result of a specific set of circumstances, which included the difficulty of the requirement of 'standing' when the government was the defendant, the unwillingness to proceed with some claims that were hard to prove, when the government acted as plaintiff, and a clear preference for settled outcomes in private disputes. This, however, prevented courts from exercising some important and useful functions.

2.18 Pistor's *Legal Theory of Finance*, although not centred on court deference, can provide a different perspective to understand it, especially in the financial context. In her view, finance is legally constructed, because finance is formed by legally embedded promises; those promises are, implicitly, what the law says they are.[30] Since, as already noted, finance has to confront a structural problem of uncertainty and liquidity[31] (promises are made with the uncertainty of whether there will be enough liquidity to fulfil them all) the law has a paradoxical relationship with finance: on one hand, it is a necessary underpinning (remove the law, and promises will not be enforceable); on the other hand, it is a source of fragility (strictly enforce all promises, and at times of shortage and uncertainty, the system may collapse), and thus the system needs to be rigid in its periphery (when strict enforcement does not endanger the system) and flexible at the apex (when it does). An extension of this would be to hold that courts will be reluctant to strictly enforce private rights when this may endanger the stability of the whole system, and will be deferential towards those better positioned to assess such threats, typically the public authorities.

2.19 The LTF is both provocative and enlightening, but it is a theory for complex environments, and thus should not be boiled down to simple conclusions. First, it cannot be synthesized into

---

[28] Richard Posner and Adrian Vermeule, 'Crisis Governance in the Administrative State: 9/11 and the Financial Meltdown of 2008' (2010) 76 U Chi L Rev 1613.
[29] David Zaring, 'Litigating the Financial Crisis' (2014) 100 Virginia L Rev 1405.
[30] Pistor, 'A Legal Theory of Finance' (n 13) 327.
[31] ibid 317–18.

a 'plain deference' argument: the 'flexibility-for-stability' argument also justifies extending deference to some private arrangements, or not granting it to public authorities. Consider the instances where a specific type of financial instrument takes hold and becomes (or is perceived as) crucial for the functioning of the financial system. Any action that threatens that instrument may trigger market turmoil or precipitate a crisis. Thus, deference may be given in such case to *private* arrangements, even if they may be controversial. This may explain the reluctance to challenge the patrimonial separation between sponsors and Special Purpose Vehicles (SPVs[32]), the bankruptcy privilege of derivatives or repos, or the fact that the determination of 'Events of Default' in derivatives is entrusted to a Determinations Committee with a majority of members representing large dealer banks, and does not withstand scrutiny under principles like independence and impartiality.[33] Indeed, under this premise, the centrality of certain instruments could result in courts reining in public authorities if, eg they may jeopardize the functioning of those instruments, and thus financial markets.

2.20 Secondly, the LTF is a descriptive theory of what the law normally does to confront uncertainty. It is not a predictive theory, which helps us foresee precisely what courts may do in a given case (that would depend on what is perceived as the more immediate danger to stability); nor is it a normative theory, which tells us how courts *should* behave to fulfil their role properly.

2.21 In summary, different perspectives on the issue of 'law and emergencies' hold important truths but have two main limitations. One, they foster a deceptively simple narrative when in fact a large part of the problem in many public and private litigations lies in determining what is the graver threat, and to whom should deference be granted, at the expense of whose deference. Two, they tend to be anchored in considerations of political economy, or institutional economics. This is important to identify the incentives of the parties involved (courts, executive, or private actors) from a perspective *outside* the law itself, ie, the law as described from its observable output. Yet, this does not describe *how law actually works on the inside*, by weighing, choosing, and discarding arguments on the basis of their strength. This also means that, even if judges, seen as individuals with their own utility preferences, wish to be deferential to a specific authority or private arrangement, *the law sets limits on how to do it, and on how far they can go*. These limits are important as well, and, dare we say it, are more important actually to understand the legal process, and the role of courts in the financial system, even at times of crisis, which is less focused on outcomes than on process.

2.22 An important factor that should not be overlooked or even dismissed is the idea of legitimacy, which includes at least 'sociological' legitimacy, which focuses on whether the relevant public regards a decision as justified, appropriate, or deserving of support for reasons beyond fear of sanctions or hope for reward, and 'legal' legitimacy, which normally focuses on whether the decision follows acceptable norms of interpretation.[34] Thus, the sociological legitimacy of a court decision (ie, how it will be perceived, and what consequences it will be on an external sphere) is important, but should not be conflated with legal legitimacy, nor should legal legitimacy be altogether dismissed. Different theories of jurisprudence

---

[32] David Ramos, 'Bankruptcy-remote Transactions and Bankruptcy Law: A Comparative Approach (Part 1): Changing the Focus on Vehicle Shielding' (2015) 10 CMLJ 256.
[33] David Ramos and Javier Solana, 'Bank Resolution and Creditor Distribution: The Tension Shaping Global Banking (Part 1): 'External and Intra-Group Funding' and 'Ex Ante planning v. Ex Post Execution' Dimensions' (2020) 28 U Miami Bus L Rev 1.
[34] Richard H Fallon Jr, 'Legitimacy and the Constitution' (2005) 118 Harv LR 1787. See also Richard H Fallon Jr, *Law and Legitimacy in the Supreme Court* (HUP 2018). We leave aside 'moral' legitimacy.

have dealt with this issue, to explain the rationale of rule-of-law's basic ideas, even at times of crisis. Lon Fuller, in his *Morality of Law* (at the basis of Dyzenhaus' critique of the 'law of emergencies') uses a procedural logic to justify those ideas as enabling legal duties to be communicated effectively. The problem, as a positivist like Hart pointed out, is that some of Fuller's criteria to define 'law' would be 'open-ended', and thus do not help precisely to define what is law, and what it is not.

2.23 Hart's positivism, for its part, tries to define 'law' without the constraints of systems that abide by the rule of law, which explains his emphasis on 'primary' and 'secondary' norms.[35] The problem is that his answer to the cases where rules or precedents do not provide an explicit solution, as would be the case in a (financial) crisis or emergency, is for judges to use 'discretion' to decide. *This does not properly capture the role of courts*. If it did, a court deciding in a situation of crisis would simply state that 'the law has no answer to this, so I prefer outcome A'. Such opinion would be considered illegitimate, legally, for failing to follow accepted interpretative canons, and, quite possibly, sociologically, for being arbitrary, and thus would not bolster, but undermine, the confidence in the system. Furthermore, this view is even less descriptive when there are several layers of decision-making, as there are, for example, in a banking crisis, where there is a bank's board, a supervisory authority (and maybe a bank resolution authority), and the court. In such situations the problem is not to exercise discretion or not, but to allocate discretion between decision-making levels, and to do so based on some acceptable criteria.

2.24 As we noted already in Chapter 1, Dworkin's answer to this problem would lie in his distinction between 'rules', or legal propositions that apply in an 'all-or-nothing' fashion, and 'principles', which have a dimension of weight and importance;[36] *and* his emphasis on 'integrity' as a determinant of the (legal) legitimacy of a decision.[37] In this sense, courts' role in a crisis would be a reconstructive one: they would look at the different sources of law (statutes, regulations, precedents) to see how they relate, taking into account not only the rules, but also the principles underpinning the system, and, in light of this, select the solution that provides a better 'fit' within the system.

2.25 By differentiating between 'policies' (or goals) which are the domain of legislative and executive (and, to the extent that these goals are delegated to agencies, of the agencies themselves) and 'principles', which are the domain of courts, the point is that discretion must be exercised within the confines of the goals specified in the relevant legislation, subject to a review that may focus on the process used to reach the decision, the justification of such decision, and, occasionally, the content of that decision. Even in the private sphere the issue is not that different, since board discretion must be exercised within the confines of the business judgment rule (BJR), or other fiduciary duties, and contract rights must be exercised within the confines of contract provisions, which will often be interpreted under a canon of reasonableness (and, in some jurisdictions, of good faith). Thus, examining the relevant legal principles, determining the scope these principles leave for discretion, weighing available evidence, and determining whether discretion was properly exercised is a much more accurate description

---

[35] HLA Hart, *The Concept of Law* (first published 1961, OUP 2012).
[36] Ronald Dworkin, *Taking Rights Seriously* (first published 1977, Bloomsbury 2019).
[37] See also Ronald Dworkin, *Law's Empire* (HUP 1986). However, a similar conclusion may be reached within Hartian positivism, if one sees courts' decisions not as discretion-based, but as limited by the 'rule of recognition'. See Richard Fallon Jr., 'Constitutional Precedent Viewed through the Lens of Hartian Positivist Jurisprudence' (2008) 86(5) NC Law Rev, 1152.

of how courts would see their own role, and, in our view, a more useful perspective to understand why they are important for financial markets.

There is no reason to change this view for emergencies and crises. Courts will examine the action of public authorities or private agents from the lenses of the law, and not political economy, and the deference, should it be granted, will have to be framed in accordance with available legal tests for 'arbitrary and capricious' action, 'proportionality', or 'good faith' and 'absence of conflict'. The point is that the solution does not come perfectly delineated in rules or precedents, but that does not simply open the door for improvisation and blank deference. Different principles and policies need to be weighed. If the system's stability or integrity is at stake, this can, and will be acknowledged in a legal principle, which means that the courts will not situate themselves outside of the law, or outside their regular role: it will simply be harder and more delicate to find a solution that fits within the system. **2.26**

In fact, reasoning from principles and precedents to facts and evidence will also provide a surer path for courts. Theories that rely on political economy and institutional economics arguments to spawn a theory of 'deference', 'discretion', or 'flexibility' in times of emergency or crisis only offer a false sense of security. Public perceptions of whether a certain judicial outcome may avert a crisis, or trigger it will be on the judge's mind. However, those outside perceptions can easily change, and often do not offer any reliable guidance as to how to proceed. Even a court whose main goal is to avoid trouble, and please the crowd will still seek to fit the decision within existing rules, principles and precedents, if only because it is the safest path, and will balk at making a ruling that can in no way be properly justified in light of pre-existing sources. Even in the extreme case of a judge who writes a 100-page opinion to justify a preordained conclusion that took her five minutes to reach, because the system's stability was at stake, the 100 pages, and the fact that the judge thought that she had to write them *are still relevant* to define the court's role. **2.27**

For the above reasons, our approach to explain the role of courts in the law of finance, consists in taking the point of view of inside legal practice, ie, to look at the content of the opinions themselves, the principles being used, the reasons given, taking the arguments at face value, rather than a point of view from outside legal practice, which tries to explain court decisions on the basis of hidden motives. This has the advantage of being more faithful to the task the way judges themselves would see it, and to rely on observable evidence, rather than speculation. In our view, cases decided in crisis times may be 'hard cases', where deeper reflection may be needed to identify the legal answer. That answer may come sometime after other branches of government have acted. However, that does not make the answer non-legal, nor does it require it to be inevitably deferential. **2.28**

Finally, focusing on courts' role as one of reasoning and argumentation that seeks an outcome coherent with preceding decisions is not only useful to analyse judges' role the way themselves see it from the inside perspective of legal practice. It is also useful to understand their benefits from the outside perspective of society at large. These benefits are related to the courts' ability to help take legal acts adopted at times of crisis where there was a narrow focus on the issues, and adapt them to the situation where those acts sit together with a myriad of other rules. In this sense, in our view, courts' main role is one of recontextualizing rules, and the policies and principles underpinning them, to help see them in light of a broader legal landscape where they have to coexist, and be woven together with other rules, policies and principles, a task that we define as 'reframing', and which can operate in both 'interstitial' and 'pivotal' cases. **2.29**

2.2 Courts, crises, and biases: reframing urgency, seeking consistency, transitioning to 'normalcy'

2.30 The rationale for courts' crucial role, even in crises (and post-crisis) times is related to the way the human mind works, and how different government branches react to the demands and strains that a crisis puts on them. There are good reasons why other branches of government, typically the executive (including agencies) and then the legislative are the 'first responders' in a crisis: they have the resources, as well as the mandate to be proactive, and it is logical for them to be more directly entrusted with the responsibility of putting in place the necessary measures.

2.31 However, members of the executive and the legislative branches are (just) human, and we must assume that they are affected by humans' cognitive biases.[38] Psychology has long studied the effect that some such biases can have in the human mind, especially when making judgments under uncertainty. Since crises are characterized by uncertainty (actual or perceived) one may surmise that the public will be more prone to such biases, and so will be the rules adopted to respond to such uncertainty, if they (and the legislators who make them) participate of the general sentiment. If we follow Kahneman and Tversky, among others,[39] humans are prone to 'attribute substitution', ie people rely on a limited number of heuristic principles which reduce the complex tasks of assessing probabilities and predicting values to simpler judgmental operations.[40] One such heuristics is the so-called 'availability heuristic', where individuals assign a higher or lower probability to an event (including a risk) depending on how easily comes to mind, ie how 'available', familiar, or salient it is. Another is the 'representativeness' heuristic, where the probability that event A originates from process B, that process B will generate event A, is assessed based on the similarity between A and B, in accordance with the subject's stereotyped vision of A.[41] Another is the 'anchoring' effect, where people make estimates by starting from an initial value that is adjusted to yield the final answer. This also means that a choice may vary hugely, depending on how the situation or problem is framed.[42] Furthermore, and crucially for legal problems, the process of attribute substitution works both for technical, probabilistic judgments, but also for moral ones, with studies showing that individuals given the task of determining the severity of a punishment tend to solve this complex problem by consulting the intensity of their outrage.[43]

2.32 If one assumes that these biases affect the executive and legislative, and not just ordinary citizens, new rules and policy actions adopted in the midst of a crisis are expected to

---

[38] See ch 1, paras 1.29 ff.

[39] Also Sunstein's assimilation of their views in the legal domain. Cass R Sunstein, *Laws of Fear* (CUP 2005) 34. It must be also stated that the views expressed by Kahneman and Tversky on heuristics and 'biases' is contested by authors like Gigerenzer, who argue that such heuristics equip us with tools that can yield very good results in daily situations where an accurate calculation would be extremely difficult to conduct. See Gerd Gigerenzer, *Adaptive Thinking: Rationality in the Real World* (OUP 2000). However, we do not need to discuss whether the science of one side is better than the other's, but to simply acknowledge that legislators and regulators, with the skills and resources available to them, are in a position to improve the results achieved by mere heuristic judgments.

[40] Daniel Kahneman and Amos Tversky, 'Prospect Theory: An Analysis of Decisions Under Risk' (1979) 47 Econometrica 263.

[41] Daniel Kahneman and Amos Tversky, 'Judgment under Uncertainty: Heuristics and Biases' (1974) 185 Science 1124.

[42] Amos Tversky and Daniel Kahneman, 'The Framing of Decisions and the Psychology of Choice' (1981) 211 Science 453.

[43] Daniel Kahneman and Shane Frederick, 'Representativeness Revisited: Attribute Substitution in Intuitive Judgment' in Thomas Gilovich, Dale Griffin, and Daniel Kahneman (eds), *Heuristics and Biases: The Psychology of Intuitive Judgment* (CUP 2002).

(i) overrepresent the more 'salient' risks, regardless of the strength of the causal link between them and the crisis, or the probability of their reoccurrence; (ii) focus on market actors or transactions that are seen as sufficiently representative of the phenomenon, rather than on the phenomenon as a whole; and (iii) to exact punishments that are commensurate with the indignation generated by the phenomenon, rather than a balanced assessment of all relevant factors.

Preliminary evidence seems to bear this out. If we focus on the last two financial crises on both sides of the Atlantic, one was a milder crisis, characterized by corporate scandals in 2001–2002; the other, a systemic crisis, with much graver consequences, between 2007 and 2008, accompanied in Europe by an ulterior stage in the form of a sovereign debt crisis. Both gave rise to the flurry of policy activity that one expects when legislatures are being responsive to public sentiment. In both, we see a similar pattern, where legal reforms tried to provide a response to the more salient concerns of the time, rather than a calmer, comprehensive rethinking of the whole system. **2.33**

What is the role of courts with regard to such regulatory responses? The more obvious one, of course, is to apply them. But the view of courts as passive spectators, or mere go-betweens in a process that involves public outrage, leading to statutory law, leading to its application, would be mistaken. Courts have the responsibility to ponder how the new provisions (adopted in the wake of crises and scandals) fit within the broader context of laws, some of them unrelated to the newly adopted ones, some of those with constitutional significance. **2.34**

This role is crucial for another reason. An effect of the attribute substitution, and the availability heuristic or representativeness biases, is the so-called 'system neglect', defined by authors as the tendency to assume that the changes resulting from an intervention (eg a regulatory intervention) will change the part at issue, but not other parts, and that there are no trade-offs between the measures adopted and the risk that they try to prevent, and other risks that may materialize as a result of the new provisions.[44] This problem expands if we take into consideration that humans (and legislators and regulators seem no exception) attach greater value to the things or advantages they already have and may lose, than to the opportunities lost as a result of a certain course of action, the so-called *status quo* bias, or 'loss aversion'.[45] Courts cannot fully correct these biases, but they can try to control their more pernicious effects. In the case of system neglect, they must check for instances where the new provisions treat like situations in an unequal manner, in a way that is unjustifiable, or disproportionate. They may also check that provisions created to protect the *status quo* of one party (say, an investor in a certain kind of instrument) do not impinge on some fundamental aspect of the *status quo* of another party, in a way that does not compensate for the loss. **2.35**

In fact, this role is essential to facilitate a transition from a crisis time to a non-crisis time. Political and administrative authorities, which prioritize responsiveness to the crisis, can function with an on/off switch, meaning that the new measures may acquire a prominence to the detriment of almost everything else, a deep focus that may be followed by an equally swift loss of focus. Courts, on the other hand, do not have an on/off switch: they are expected to consider the broader context and system on a constant basis. This makes them better suited to pilot smoother transitions. **2.36**

---

[44] Cass R Sunstein, 'Beyond the Precautionary Principle' (2003) 151 U of Pen LR 1003, especially at 1010–11.
[45] ibid 1008–10, 1036–55.

2.37 Finally, apart from the substance of the reframing of crisis measures in a way that seeks consistency, ensures respect for fundamental values, and facilitates transition, there is another factor that makes courts particularly useful, and is more related to their *methodology*. As said before, the 'attribute substitution' bias not only affects probabilistic judgments (eg substituting the more salient risk for the more probable one) it also affects moral ones, by substituting the level of moral outrage for the apportionment of blame, or determination of penalties.[46] This does not bode well for legal systems characterized by due process safeguards. Thus, courts' methodology, based on a careful examination of relevant evidence, fair hearing, and impartial adjudication in a publicly available and reasoned ruling is useful to provide 'closure' on matters.[47] Public outrage can feed on disinformation and subjectivity, and lacks nuance. Although courts cannot pick their cases, once the dispute is submitted to them, they are uniquely positioned to assess the conflict in a dispassionate manner, and throw some light on whether moral indignation should be accompanied by legal redress, and by setting responsibility they may help to reassess moral responsibility.

2.38 In summary, whereas the more political branches of government have a more direct responsibility in being responsive to situations of crisis, and addressing the more urgent issues, courts have the responsibility of examining those measures with more distance and broader lenses, to recontextualize the new legal provisions in light of the pre-existing system of rules, precedents, doctrines and principles, to ensure that there is a proper fit. Naturally, courts cannot correct all frictions that they see, since democratically elected bodies are entitled to their own biases.

3 Courts and finance beyond crises: hard cases

2.39 Unlike authors who focus on 'crises', we do not believe that there are two separate roles for courts in crises times and in good times. Their key role remains the same and it consists in addressing 'hard cases' requiring courts to weigh competing principles, interests and considerations within the acceptable canons of judicial interpretation. Crisis times, almost by definition, present plenty of such situations, and thus crisis cases will often be 'hard cases'. Thus, courts' role may easily move from backseat to front seat. This role, however, is by no means solely for crisis times.

3.1 Courts beyond financial crises: hard cases, interstitial, and pivotal role

2.40 The psychological or economic standpoint for the relevance of this role has its own (purely legal) counterpart. In the previous section we discussed the different theories given to the role of courts in cases where the solution is uncertain. Dworkin and his theory of 'hard cases'

---

[46] Kahneman and Frederick (n 43).
[47] This point would be more related to the so-called 'expressive function' of law. See Cass R Sunstein, 'On the Expressive Function of Law' (1996) 144 U of Penn L Rev 2021; Elizabeth S. Anderson and Richard H Pildes,' Expressive Theories of Law: A General Restatement' (2000) 148 U Pa L Rev 1503, 1531. Admittedly, authors often exemplify this by referring more to the moral and social significance or eg condemnation coming from a court. Our view is different, as we consider that the methodical process of examining evidence, weighing principles, and making precise statements also has an expressive role, perhaps the most important of all.

seems to offer a good perspective of the way courts see their role. A crisis situation confronts the court with a 'hard case', which cannot be solved by mere subsumption into a specific rule, and needs looking at the whole picture to find an adequate solution. In fact, a similar reasoning explains the role of reframing and recontextualizing legal provisions adopted during a time of crisis when that crisis has passed: judges will need to appeal to the scope and content of the provision often in light of the finality of that provision, and ask themselves whether it is 'fit' to decide a new issue that is outside what the authorities contemplated at the time when the provision was adopted. Sometimes this will involve a 'borderline' case, where the problem lies in applying an uncontroversial legal test to a limit case, and sometimes a 'pivotal' case where the problem lies in agreeing on the correct test.

At least three aspects of this theory are controversial. First, Dworkin's suggestion that there is 'one right answer' has been hotly contested by some authors,[48] although, as we said earlier, the debate on this issue has little practical relevance for our purposes. Secondly, his suggestion that courts engage in a 'justificatory ascent', where, upon a potential clash of principles, they will move 'upwards' in levels of abstraction to seek a relevant argument that acts as a tie-breaker, and determines that one solution is a better fit than another, is contested by authors like Sunstein and Vermeule, who propose instead a theory of 'incompletely theorized arrangements', where courts will not seek the perfect fit, but only engage in the theorizing that is strictly necessary, using analogy instead.[49] However, in our view, reasoning from principles to facts or reasoning by analogy are just two ways of defining what is at heart the same approach. Thus, in our view these debates on theory are not too relevant to an analysis of the role of courts in practice (in finance or otherwise). Thirdly, Dworkin's distinction between 'borderline' and 'pivotal' cases, is contested as arbitrary.[50] We agree that this distinction is not easy to make, and that sometimes a case that seems 'borderline' when looked at from the level of rules may pose pivotal problems when looked at the level of principles. However, there are reasons why the distinction is useful and should be kept. One is that courts themselves consider this distinction (or variations of it) as legally relevant. The US Supreme Court, for example, when examining whether an issue is subject to an agency's discretionary decision, attaches relevance to whether the issue is 'interstitial', in which case it is ready to presume that it has been left to the discretion of the agency (provided its interpretation is reasonable) or 'fundamental', in which case the presumption is that the law does not intent to leave it to the agency to decide.[51] Thus, in cases where the application of the act is delegated in a two-pronged fashion, including courts and agencies, these have to work out a system to delineate the respective scopes of action, and seem to have chosen the distinction as a relevant element to do so.

2.41

---

[48] For example, Joseph Raz, 'Legal Principles and the Limits of Law' (1972) 81 Yale LJ 823 and more recently Joseph Raz, 'Interpretation Without Retrieval' in A Marmor (ed), *Law and Interpretation* (Clarendon Press 1995); Joseph Raz, 'On the Nature of Law' (1996) 82 Archive fur Rechts und Sozialphilosophie 1; HLA Hart (n 35); Andrei Marmor, *Interpretation in Legal Theory* (Hart Publishing 1990); Jules Coleman, 'Negative and Positive Positivism' (1982) 11 J Legal Studies 139; Jules Coleman, 'The Conventionality Thesis' (2001) 11 Philosophical Issues 354; Jules Coleman, 'Beyond Inclusive Legal Positivism' (2009) 22 Ratio Juris 359; Jules Coleman, 'Tort Law and the Demands of Corrective Justice' (1992) 67 ILJ 349; Richard A Posner, 'Conceptions of Legal Theory: A Response to Ronald Dworkin' (1997) 29 ASLJ 377; Richard A Posner, 'Reply to Critics of the Problematics of Moral and Legal Theory' (1998) 111 Harv LR 1638.

[49] Cass R Sunstein, 'Incompletely Theorized Agreements' (1995) 108 Harv LR 1733; Cass R Sunstein, 'Incompletely Theorized Agreements in Constitutional Law' (2007) University of Chicago Public Law & Legal Theory Working Paper No 147; Adrian Vermeule, 'Many-Minds Arguments in Legal Theory' (2009) 1 JLA 1.

[50] Raz, 'Legal Principles and the Limits of Law' (n 48).

[51] *Lincoln v Vigil* 508 US 182 (1993); *Whitman v American Trucking Associations* 531 US 457, 474–75 (2001). More recently see *King v Burwell* 576 US 473 (2015); or *West Virginia v EPA* 597 US __ (2022).

2.42 Another reason is that this distinction helps to explain how the role of courts in 'reframing' laws and acts adopted in crisis times can work at different levels. Sometimes, the courts' role will consist in determining whether the scope of application of a specific provision adopted in times of crisis must be extended to a case whose facts could fit within the literal language of the provision, but clearly involves a situation that was far from the minds of the legislators when they adopted the provision, and may be better covered by a different provision. Put in this way, such case would be 'borderline', or 'interstitial', since the court's job simply consists in 'making sense' of the scope of a provision in light of a set of circumstances not envisaged by the law-makers, and to 'weave it together' with other legal provisions whose link with the new provisions was not considered by those legislators either. However, in some cases, what appears to be a job of statutory construction at first glance, may, upon closer look, touch upon a fundamental principle that is central for the scheme of the statutory text, or upon a fundamental value of constitutional significance. We will admit that whether and when this occurs cannot be delineated with full precision. Sometimes courts will *choose* to characterize the issue as interstitial in order to avoid the debate over principles and values, and sometimes they will decide that the case must be resolved by going one level up the 'justificatory ascent' ladder. Given that courts have much leeway in the way they decide to *frame* an issue, the distinction between one and another type of case is not set in stone. However, it is important to understand the significance of the difference between 'interstitial' or 'borderline' problems, and 'pivotal' or 'fundamental' ones, and the different methodology applied for their solution, when courts decide to characterize them in one way or another.

3.2 Courts and finance: from back seat to front seat

2.43 A final question is whether the actual court practice bears this out. We believe it does. Consider first how courts dealt with some of the 2000–2001 crisis provisions, something that mostly happened in the United States with some of the Sarbanes Oxley Act (SOX) provisions. In *Free Enterprise Fund v PCAOB*[52] the US Supreme Court held that the appointment and removal mechanism for members of the Accounting Oversight Board (PCAOB) was unconstitutional, as it went against the 'Appointments Clause' in the Constitution, by limiting the powers of appointment and removal of the President of the United States, but rejected the broader constitutionality claim against the whole system of appointment/removal, by considering the unconstitutional clause severable. Then, in *Lawson v FMR LLC*, the Court provided an expansive interpretation of the SOX whistle-blower protection provisions,[53] by considering the plaintiffs, who worked for private companies that provided services for Fidelity mutual funds, ie, they worked for private companies, but served as contractors to the publicly-held mutual funds, which have no employees of their own, as protected by those provisions. Then, in *Yates v United States*,[54] the Court held that a commercial fisherman operating in the Gulf of Mexico who ordered his crew to throw overboard the ship's catch, which, apparently, included undersized red grouper (a kind of fish)

---

[52] *Free Enterprise Fund v Public Company Accounting Oversight Board* 561 US 477 (2010).
[53] SOX 'anti-retaliation' provisions prohibit a public company or an 'officer, employee, contractor, subcontractor, or agent of such company' from 'discharging, demoting, suspending, threatening, harassing, or in any other manner discriminating' against 'an employee,' because that employee blew the whistle on fraudulent activities. See SOX s 806, modifying USC s 1514A.
[54] *Yates v United States* 574 US 528 (2015).

in contravention of the orders of a federal agent conducting an offshore inspection, could not be charged under 18 USC §1519, a provision introduced by SOX, which punishes the falsification, alteration or destruction of records, documents or 'tangible objects' to obstruct a federal investigation,[55] since, the Court considered that the reference to 'tangible object' had to be understood in the context of a provision that referred to record-keeping objects. We should add *Arthur Andersen v United States*,[56] where the Court overturned the lower courts' rulings upholding a jury verdict of guilt towards the auditing firm Arthur Andersen. Although the relevant statute predated SOX,[57] it was interpreted in light of the circumstances of the Enron collapse. In the Court's view, the jury instructions were so vague as to allow a finding of guilt based on much less culpability than the criminal statute actually required.

2.44 At first glance, these cases may seem to have little in common. One concerns appointments, another whistle-blower protections, another the concept of 'knowingly... corruptly', another the concept of 'object'. Yet, all of them illustrate the role that courts play in reframing, and recontextualizing legislation that may have been adopted in a specific moment in time, with its own 'availability', or 'representativeness' biases, and applying it in a broader context, where other interests are also at stake, not the least the need to temper outrage and provide closure. Courts cannot completely de-bias legislation, because some biases, for better or worse, are part of the clear language and legislative intent of the specific statute. However, it is also the duty of courts to ensure that, besides the sentiment of the time when they were adopted, statutes 'make sense' in a broader context, and are not too overbearing. It is also their role to ensure that such crisis statutes are anchored by the more fundamental principles of the legal system. Some cases had to be resolved at the level of constitutional or other foundational principles, and were 'pivotal', in others the issue was more 'interstitial', and some cases could have been resolved at either level, or courts possibly chose the level that they deemed less problematic.

2.45 The important point is that, in each and every case, the Court's explicit role of interpreting the statute was accompanied by a no less important role of framing the problem, to weigh the text and its finality properly, but also broader considerations, including rule-of-law principles. In *Free Enterprise Fund v PCAOB* the concern was not the suitability of the PCAOB adequately to monitor the auditing profession, but the separation of powers that grants the President of the United States the power to 'take care that the laws be faithfully executed'.[58] In *Lawson* the key issue was the proper scope of a provision to be faithful to the Congressional intent to tackle cases of widespread fraud, in a context where contractors' complicity had been key.[59] *Arthur Andersen* was key to weigh the text of the SOX provision in light of established doctrines of mens rea, and provide a careful analysis of the actual involvement of the auditing firm in the cover-up, and temper its implications. In *Yates* the issue was the proper 'framing, and anchoring' of a provision that was decidedly punitive and severe, but

---

[55] 18 USC s 1519.
[56] *Arthur Andersen LLP v United States* 544 US 696 (2005).
[57] Chapter 73 of Title 18 of the USC regulates criminal sanctions for obstruction of justice.
[58] US Constitution, art II, s 1 cl 1.
[59] In the Enron scandal that prompted the SOX Act, contractors and subcontractors, including the accounting firm Arthur Andersen, participated in Enron's fraud and its cover-up. When employees of those contractors attempted to bring misconduct to light, they encountered retaliation by their employers. The SOX Act contains numerous provisions aimed at controlling the conduct of accountants, auditors, and lawyers who work with public companies.

aimed at cases of corporate and financial fraud. Thus, *Free Enterprise Fund* was framed in a pivotal way, while *Lawson* and *Yates* were framed more as interstitial cases, but one could still argue that the proper role of whistle-blowing protections was central to the statutory scheme, while in *Yates* the underpinning issue was whether punitive statutes should have an extended scope, which may undermine the principle of lenity.[60] Thus, we believe that, even if these categories cannot be precisely delineated, they capture a relevant part of the role of courts and this justifies their adoption in this book.

---

[60] Justice Ginsburg's plurality opinion acknowledged this, since, after having reasoned that the definition of 'object' in the act did not include fish, using linguistic and purposive interpretation canons, it held that: 'Finally, if our recourse to traditional tools of statutory construction leaves any doubt about the meaning of "tangible object," as that term is used in § 1519, we would invoke the rule that "ambiguity" concerning the ambit of criminal statutes should be resolved in favor of lenity. *Cleveland v United States*, 531 US 12, 25 (2000) (quoting *Rewis v United States* 401 US 808, 812 (1971)).' *Yates v United States* (n 54).

PART II
PUBLIC LAW DISPUTES IN THE LAW OF FINANCE

3
An Anatomy of Issues in Public Law Disputes

1 Courts, horizontal separation, and vertical allocation of powers	3.02	2 Independent authorities/agencies and discretion	3.06
		3 The individuals within the system: Standing to sue and fundamental rights	3.10

This chapter provides a roadmap to navigate through case law. Hard cases in the public law of finance pivot around three main 'themes': first, separation, or balance of powers, including horizontal separation between courts and the executive, and their vertical allocation in federal (US) or supranational (EU) structures; secondly, the role of independent agencies to accomplish legislative or constitutional purposes; and, thirdly, the role of individuals in the system of judicial review. **3.01**

1 Courts, horizontal separation, and vertical allocation of powers

Both the United States and the European Union rely on executive and regulatory decisions to stabilize, monitor, and manage or prevent crises in the financial system, some adopted at a federal/supranational, some at a state/Member State level. This presents courts with hard questions. Starting with challenges of (horizontal) separation of powers, in the United States constitutional separation of powers and judicial review have a long history. Federal courts are courts of limited jurisdiction, restricted to matters entrusted to them by Congress.[1] In *Marbury v Madison*, the epitome of judicial review, the Supreme Court *rejected* its jurisdiction because the Judiciary Act had expanded it in a manner impermissible by the Constitution, according to Article III section 2.[2] This provision also states that Congress may provide exceptions to court jurisdiction,[3] and although this 'jurisdiction stripping' power is controversial,[4] 'political' matters are excluded from court **3.02**

---

[1] *Bowles v Russell* 551 US 205, 212 (2007); *Owen Equip & Erection Co v Kroger* 437 US 365, 374 (1978).
[2] *Marbury v Madison* [1803] 5 US (1 Cranch) 137, paras 177–78.
[3] Article III s 2 of the US Constitution provides that: '[T]he judicial Power shall extend to all Cases, in Law and Equity, arising under this Constitution, the Laws of the United States, and Treaties' and that, within those cases, the Supreme Court has jurisdiction over some (narrowly defined) categories, and appellate jurisdiction in all the other Cases 'with such Exceptions, and under such Regulations as the Congress shall make'. Thus, Congress may exercise its power to exclude the jurisdiction of federal courts (*Sheldon v Hill* 49 US (8 How) 441, 448–49 (1850)) or the Supreme Court (*Ex Parte McCardle* 74 US (7 Wall) 506, 513–14 (1868)).
[4] It is controversial whether matters can be excluded from *any* kind of judicial review. Lawrence Gene Sager, 'Foreword: Constitutional Limitations on Congress' Authority to Regulate the Jurisdiction of the Federal Courts' (1981) 95 Harv LR 42; Laurence H Tribe, 'Jurisdictional Gerrymandering: Zoning Disfavored Rights Out of the Federal Courts' (1981) 16 H Civil Rights Civil Liberties L Rev 139. Some authors argued that the Constitution prevents Congress from simultaneously curtailing the jurisdiction of *all* federal courts. See eg Akhil Reed Amar, 'A Neo-Federalist View of Article III: Separating the Two Tiers of Federal Jurisdiction' [1985] Bus L Rev 65, or even

jurisdiction.[5] Thus, statutory texts must *expressly* provide for federal courts' subject-matter jurisdiction,[6] or waive sovereign immunity.[7] The Administrative Procedure Act (APA) *presumes* judicial review, but this can be modified by statute.[8] Non-reviewability may result from the express statutory language,[9] or be implied from 'the structure of the statutory scheme, its objectives, its legislative history, and the nature of the administrative action involved'.[10] Judicial review may be excluded if an issue is 'committed to the discretion' of an agency,[11] and/or a statute's terms are so broad that there is 'no law to apply'.[12] Obstacles to judicial review are looked at restrictively, however.[13]

3.03 In the European Union, EU institutions' democratic legitimacy is disputed,[14] and a blanket exclusion of 'political' issues from review would not be acceptable. Thus, the CJEU sees itself as the ultimate guarantor of the system. In *Les Verts* the Court of Justice held that the Union is a 'Union of law', and that there is a direct link between respect for the 'rule of law', and court-reviewability of even legislative acts, by the CJEU.[15] The Court has found that it lacked jurisdiction in *annulment* proceedings only where this did not close the avenues for judicial review.[16] Conversely, the Court has rendered administrative agencies' acts reviewable by initially attributing them to the European Commission,[17] and then, in *Sogelma* by reaffirming its *Les Verts* case law to hold that agency acts must be reviewable,[18] a principle now expressly stated in Article 263(1) TFEU.

the jurisdiction of the Supreme Court. Steven G Calabresi and Gary Lawson, 'The Unitary Executive, Jurisdiction Stripping, and the Hamdan Opinions: A Textualist Response to Justice Scalia' (2007) 107(4) Col L Rev 1002.

[5] Article III of the Constitution confines the federal courts to adjudicating 'cases' and 'controversies'. See *Valley Forge Christian College v Americans United for Separation of Church and State Inc* 454 US 464, 454 US 471–76 (1982). The several (limiting) doctrines are 'founded in concern about the proper and properly limited role of the courts in a democratic society': *Warth v Seldin* 422 US 490, 422 US 498 (1975).
[6] See eg *Ruhrgas AG v Marathon Oil Co* [1999] 526 US 574, 583. 28 USC s 1331 provides for a relatively general clause for subject-matter (original) jurisdiction.
[7] The APA is one of them, after its 1976 amendments (5 USC s 702), the Federal Tort Claims Act (FTCA) is another, for claims for torts committed by employees (28 USC s 2679), and the Tucker Act, for contract and other non-tort claims (28 USC ss 1346, 1491).
[8] *Abbott Labs v Gardner* 387 US 136, 152–53 (1967).
[9] *Johnson v Robison* 415 US 361, 365 (1974), where 38 USC s 211(a) expressly excluded review of the Administrator of the Veterans Administration.
[10] *Block v Community Nutrition Institute* 467 US 340 (1984), with reference to *Southern R. Co v Seaboard Allied Mining Corp* 442 US 444, 442 US 454–63 (1979).
[11] 5 USC s 701.
[12] *Citizens to Preserve Overton Park Inc v Volpe* 401 US 402, 410 (1971). Also if courts lack a legal standard to review the exercise of discretion. *Heckler v Chaney* 470 US 821, 830 (1985).
[13] *McNary v Haitian Refugee Ctr Inc* 498 US 479, 498 (1991); *Johnson v Robison* 415 US 361, 367 (1974) (for preclusion). In *Trudeau v Fed. Trade Comm'n* 456 F 3d 178, 185 (DC Cir 2006) the courts held that 28 USC s 1331 could provide a sufficient basis for subject-matter jurisdiction on non-statutory and constitutional claims.
[14] For some courts democracy lies with Member States. German Federal Constitutional Court (Bundesverfassungsgericht or BVerfG) 2 BvR 2134/92, 2 BvR 2159/92 (12 October 1993) 155 (Maastricht Treaty) https://iow.eui.eu/wp-content/uploads/sites/18/2013/04/06-Von-Bogdandy-German-Federal-Constitutional-Court.pdf (accessed 12 September 2022).
[15] In Case C-294/83 *Les Verts* ECLI:EU:C:1986:166, para 23: '[t]he Treaty established a complete system of legal remedies and procedures designed to permit the Court of Justice to review the legality of measures adopted by the institutions'.
[16] Order in Case T-148/97 *Keeling v OHIM* ECLI:EU:T:1998:114, paras 27–29. See also Case C-160/03 *Spain v Eurojust* ECLI:EU:C:2005:168, paras 41–42. The General Court and the CJEU rejected their jurisdiction under the specific action sought by the applicants but held that other avenues were available.
[17] Case T-123/00 *Thomae v Commission* ECLI:EU:T:2002:307, following the principle enounced in Joined Cases 32/58 and 33/58 *SNUPAT Snupat v High Authority* ECLI:EU:C:1958:16, para 141.
[18] Case T-411/06 *Sogelma* ECLI:EU:T:2008:419. A more recent, and complementary, technique to promote thorough review of agencies' decisions has been to provide Union agencies with internal administrative review bodies (boards of appeal) that have the necessary technical and legal expertise to address appeals concerning technical or scientific decisions. In Case C-46/21 *ACER v Aquind* ECLI:EU:C:2023:182, para 73 the Court has ruled

3.04 A second dimension of the balance of powers is the 'vertical' allocation of powers between federal/supranational and state/Member State level. In the US the supremacy of federal law is grounded on the Constitution[19] and widely accepted, and so is the doctrine of 'pre-emption' of state law by federal law.[20] Conflicts focus more on *whether* a specific federal law pre-empts an issue regulated by state law, in light of the legislative intent,[21] or the compatibility between statutes.[22]

3.05 In the EU the CJEU's case law espouses the doctrine of supremacy (or primacy) of EU law,[23] and holds that EU acts cannot be reviewed in their validity by domestic courts.[24] Member States differ, however. Some rely on the supremacy of *international* obligations[25] (ie not constitutional supremacy) while others hold that EU law prevails over statutory law, but not over national constitutions.[26] This hybrid between 'supremacy' and 'spheres of competence' requires diplomacy and inter-court dialogue, through the preliminary reference procedure, where domestic courts ask the CJEU to rule on questions of EU law.[27] Outcomes vary. Sometimes domestic courts have accommodated the Court of Justice's views,[28] sometimes (much less often) the opposite.[29] In other cases, domestic courts have stressed their supremacy on matters of national constitutional law. Perhaps the most noteworthy example, the German Federal Constitutional Court (FCC) originally declined to review EU acts *if there is an equivalent fundamental rights protection*,[30] *and the EU did not manifestly exceed*

---

that the ACER board of appeal cannot limit its scope of review to merely manifest errors of assessment. For an analogous finding see Case T-125/17 *BASF Grenzach v ECHA* ECLI:EU:T:2019:638, paras 87–89, 124.

[19] US Constitution, art VI cl 2.
[20] *Marbury v Madison* 5 US 137 (1803) (judicial review of legislative acts); *Martin v Hunter's Lessee* 14 US 304 (1816); *Cohens v Virginia* 19 US 264 (1821) (Supreme Court's power to review the decisions of state courts) or *McCulloch v Maryland* 17 US (4 Wheat) 316 (1819) (Supreme Court annulled a Maryland tax on the federally incorporated Bank of the United States).
[21] *Jones v Rath Packing Co* 430 US 519, 525 (1977); *Altria Group v Good* 555 US 70 (2008). Congress' intent is the ultimate touchstone in pre-emption cases. See *Retail Clerks v Schermerhorn* 375 US 96, 103 (1963). However, courts will preferably accept the reading that does not result in pre-emption. See *Bates v Dow Agrosciences LLC* 544 US 431, 449 (2005).
[22] *Edgar v MITE Corp* [1982] 457 US 624 (the Supremacy Clause is activated when compliance with both state and federal law is impossible and/or '[S]tate law stands as an obstacle to the accomplishment and execution of the full purposes and objectives of Congress'.
[23] See eg Case 6/64 *Costa v ENEL* ECLI:EU:C:1964:66.
[24] Case C-314/85 *Foto-Frost v Hauptzollamt Lübeck-Ost* ECLI:EU:C:1987:452.
[25] See eg article 10 of the Czech Constitution. In France, see *Administration des Douanes v Société 'Cafes Jacques Vabre'* Cour de cassation [1975] 73-13556 and *Raoul Georges Nicolo v commissaire du gouvernement*, Conseil d'Etat [1989] no 108243.
[26] In Spain, see eg decision by the Spanish Constitutional Court (SCC) *Sentencia del Tribunal Constitucional* (STC) 64/1991 (22 March 1991), ground no 4 decision by the Polish Constitutional Court, K 18/04 (11 May 2005), or decision by the Lithuanian Constitutional Court in Case no 17/02-24/02-06/03-22/04 (14 March 2006), s 9.4.
[27] TFEU, art 267.
[28] See eg Case C-399/11 *Stefano Melloni v Ministerio Fiscal* ECLI:EU:C:2013:107 (incompatibility of Spanish Constitutional Court doctrine with maximum harmonization measure) followed by decision SCC STC 26/2014 (13 February 2014) (restriction of fundamental rights to accommodate less protective 'maximum harmonization' rules).
[29] Case C-42/17 *MAS and MB* ECLI:EU:C:2017:936 (*Taricco II*), where the Court corrected its previous view of Case C-105/14 C-105/14 *Taricco and Others* ECLI:EU:C:2015:555 (*Taricco I*) due to the consequences this would have from a domestic constitutional perspective.
[30] After *Internationale Handelsgesellschaft v Einfuhr und Vorratsstelle für Getreide und Futtermittel* (29 May 1974) BVerfGE 37, 271 2 BvL 52/71 (*Solange I*), the German Court varied its position in *Wünsche Handelsgesellschaft* (22 October 1986) BVerfGE 73, 339 2 BvR 2, 197/83 (*Solange II*) (German courts need not review the conformity of EU acts with fundamental rights if the protection is equivalent).

2 Independent authorities/agencies and discretion

3.06 Related to separation of powers is the (hard) question of how far financial decisions can be entrusted to independent (and thus undemocratic) agencies/authorities. In the US, there is wider acceptance of limited jurisdiction, and thus of an issue being 'committed to the discretion' of the specific agency,[33] while in the European Union agency acts *must* be reviewable (according to *Sogelma* and *Les Verts*). Nonetheless, in the law of finance, courts normally review the exercise of specific sets of tasks contained within a 'mandate', entrusted to an 'independent' authority, often through 'delegation' of tasks under the logic of 'technical expertise'. These ideas weigh heavily on the courts' review, and the corresponding 'discretion' granted to the authorities.

3.07 In the United States delegated regulation by administrative agencies expanded during the New Deal and after, to shield them from political pressures.[34] The Supreme Court provided a gradually generous interpretation of a 'legitimate delegation' with 'adequate standards' of legislative guidance (*Fahey v Malone*[35]). Eventually, courts granted increasing deference to such agencies, but using different standards of review. The best-known is the *Chevron* standard,[36] for an agency's interpretation of a statute it administers, which considers (step one), whether Congress indicated a clear intent (ie has 'directly spoken to the precise question at issue'); and (step two), if such intent is silent or ambiguous, 'whether the agency's answer is based on a permissible construction of the statute'.[37] This bases deference on a theory of Congress' implicit delegation,[38] which applies most clearly to agency acts 'with the force of law' that follow formal procedures, eg notice-and-comment or adjudication.[39] Courts have found exceptions eg over 'fundamental' issues, because they are less likely to have been delegated.[40] The *Seminole Rock* or *Auer* standard applies to an agency's interpretation of *its own regulations*, which will prevail unless it is 'plainly erroneous or inconsistent with the regulation',[41] and is similar to

---

[31] Maastricht Treaty (n 14); Case 2 BvR 2661/06 (6 July 2010), BVerfGE 126, 286 (*Honeywell* case); Cases 2 BvE 2/08, 2BvE 5/08, BVerfG 2 BvR 1010/08, 2 BvR 1022/08, 2 BvR 1259/08 and 2 BvR 182/09123, 267 (*Treaty of Lisbon case*).

[32] German Basic Law, art 79(3). See eg *Treaty of Lisbon case* (n 31).

[33] 5 USC s 701.

[34] Cass Sunstein, 'Constitutionalism after the New Deal' (1987) 101 Harv LR 439.

[35] *Fahey v Malone* 332 US 245 (1947).

[36] *Chevron USA Inc v NRDC* 467 US 837 (1984).

[37] ibid 843.

[38] *United States v Mead Corporation* 533 US 218, 229 (2001). This angle of *Chevron* was developed in Stephen Breyer, 'Judicial Review of Questions of Law and Policy' (1986) 38 Admin LR 363. See also Cass Sunstein, 'Chevron Step Zero' (2006) 92 Va LR 187.

[39] They 'foster the fairness and deliberation that should underlie a pronouncement of such force'. *United States v Mead Corporation* 533 US 218, 229–30 (2001).

[40] *FDA v Brown & Williamson Tobacco Corp* 529 US 120 (2000); *MCI Telecommunications Corp v AT&T* 512 US 218 (1994).

[41] *Bowles v Seminole Rock & Sand Co* 63. 325 US 410, 414 (1945). In *Auer v Robbins* 519 US 452 (1997) the Supreme Court upheld the Department of Labor's interpretation of a concepts embodied in the Fair Labor Standards Act regulations.

Chevron.⁴² It applies to acts that are not formal rules,⁴³ but not eg to regulations that simply 'parrot or paraphrase' the text of statutory rules.⁴⁴ There is also the APA's 'arbitrary and capricious' standard of review,⁴⁵ developed in *State Farm*, to assess the *rationale* for agency action,⁴⁶ which may sometimes be more demanding than *Chevron*, or used to assess its 'step two', or the less deferential *Skidmore* doctrine,⁴⁷ that *an* agency's interpretation is 'not controlling' upon the court, but depends on the 'thoroughness evident in its consideration, the validity of its reasoning, its consistency with earlier and later pronouncements, and all those factors which give it power to persuade'.⁴⁸ These doctrines contrast with the 'no deference', or '*de novo* review', a full review by the court, where an agency interprets a law that it has *no specific responsibility* to administer, eg APA or Title VII, or the Constitution.⁴⁹ The Supreme Court's view is not static. In *Michigan v EPA* it used the *State Farm* 'arbitrary and capricious' test when the EPA failed to conduct a cost-benefit analysis (CBA).⁵⁰ Then, in *King v Burwell* it refused *Chevron* deference in case of 'major questions',⁵¹ a doctrine given continuity in *Utility Air Regulatory Group v EPA*, where it held that including greenhouse gases within 'air pollutants' definition resulted in 'enormous and transformative expansion in EPA's regulatory authority without clear congressional authorization'.⁵² *West Virginia v EPA* is a recent addition to this line of case law.⁵³ The variety of doctrines, however, does not so often result in a divergence of judicial outcomes in practice.⁵⁴

EU law differentiates between Treaty 'institutions'⁵⁵ and 'agencies and bodies'. Most CJEU's case law on 'discretion' refers to acts by Treaty institutions. The CJEU has used ambiguous terminology, like 'discretion',⁵⁶ 'margin of discretion/appreciation',⁵⁷ 'power/margin of appraisal',⁵⁸ but the standard of review is based on the authority's 'manifest **3.08**

---

⁴² *Capital Network Systems Inc v FCC* 28 F 3d 201, 206 (DC Cir 1994) (even greater deference in case of *Auer*); *Paralyzed Veterans of America v DC Arena LP* 117 F 3d 579, 584 (DC Cir 1997).
⁴³ *Auer v Robbins* 519 US 452, 462 (1997) (statements made during the course of litigation); *Coeur Alaska Inc v Se Alaska Conservation Council* 557 US 261, 277–82 (2009) (internal memorandum).
⁴⁴ *Gonzales v Oregon* 546 US 243, 256–57 (2006).
⁴⁵ 5 USC s 706.
⁴⁶ *Motor Vehicle Manufacturers Association v State Farm Auto Mutual Insurance Co* 463 US 29, 43 (1983) ('if the agency has relied on factors which Congress has not intended it to consider, entirely failed to consider an important aspect of the problem, offered an explanation for its decision that runs counter to the evidence before the agency, or is so implausible that it could not be ascribed to a difference in view or the product of agency expertise').
⁴⁷ *Skidmore v Swift & Co* 323 US 134, 140 (1944). It was considered superseded by *Chevron* until the Court brought it back in *Mead*, for when the agency is not empowered to act 'with the force of law'.
⁴⁸ ibid 140.
⁴⁹ *Crowell v Benson* 285 US 22, 46 (1932).
⁵⁰ *Michigan v EPA* 135 S Ct 2699 (2015).
⁵¹ In *King v Burwell* 135 S Ct 2480 (2015).
⁵² *Utility Air Regulatory Group v Environmental Protection Agency* 573 US 302 (2014). In light of this case law, some have questioned whether *Chevron* is still valid law. Michael Herz, 'Chevron Is Dead; Long Live Chevron' (2015) 115 Col L Rev 1867. Supreme Court Justice Gorsuch suggested overruling *Chevron* in his concurring opinion in *Gutierrez-Brizuela v Lynch* 834 F 3d 1142, 1152 (10th Cir 2016) Catherine M Sharkey, 'Cutting in on the Chevron Two-Step' (2018) 86 Fordham L Rev 2359 argues that the Court's standard seems a hybrid between *Chevron* and *State Farm*.
⁵³ *West Virginia v EPA* 597, US (2022).
⁵⁴ The Supreme Court validated agency action in around a 70–75 per cent of cases where it used a 'canonical' doctrine (in *Auer* it was at 91 per cent) and it showed similar results in cases where it did not expressly refer to any doctrine. See William Eskridge and Lauren E Baer, 'The Continuum of Deference: Supreme Court Treatment of Agency Statutory Interpretations from Chevron to Hamdan' (2018) 96 Georgetown LJ 1083.
⁵⁵ TEU, art 13.
⁵⁶ See eg Case C-441/07 P *Commission v Alrosa* ECLI:EU:C:2010:377.
⁵⁷ See eg Case C-272/09 P *KME Germany AG* ECLI:EU:C:2011:810.
⁵⁸ See eg C-269/90 *Technische Universität München* ECLI:EU:C:1991:438; Case T-22/97 *Kesko v Commission* ECLI:EU:T:1999:327.

error of assessment'. Some scholars have classified case law depending on the source of discretion.[59] Others[60] distinguish between (i) 'discretion proper' or 'power of appraisal', or *delegation*-based discretion, relying on the law's text and context, where more deference is warranted, as in state aid, agricultural policy, decisions not to act etc., and (ii) 'technical discretion' or 'margin of appraisal', *complexity*-based discretion, based on courts' self-restraint, and more dependent on context, and the decision-making process. Yet, the standard in 'complex assessments' is fluid,[61] and EU courts do not resist annulling some decisions where they question the substance, even if they are informed by 'discretion proper'.[62] One difference with the US is that the open-textured nature of a statutory rule does not, by itself, justify delegation-based discretion, which means that, in practice, this will be less common in the EU. Also, criminal penalties are subject to full review[63] and the concept of 'criminal' penalty is also broad[64] and encompasses most sanctioning measures under financial supervision rules.[65]

3.09 The delegation to *agencies* also raises fundamental constitutional issues. In *Meroni*, an early case (of similar significance to the pre-*Fahey v Malone* era in the US), the Court of Justice said that the Treaties' 'balance of powers' acted as a 'guarantee' to the individuals affected by decisions: balance was respected in a delegation to a non-Treaty entity if it encompassed 'clearly defined executive powers', 'subject to strict review'.[66] In the specific case, the delegation entailed 'a wide margin of discretion', and little supervision from the delegating institution,[67] and was thus illegal.[68] In *Romano*, another old case the Court held that an agency 'may not be empowered by the Council to adopt acts having the force of law'.[69] The two were

---

[59] Need for expert knowledge, the need to weigh different interests and policies, to make of complex economic (or social) assessments, or value judgments. Alexander Fritzsche, 'Discretion, Scope of Judicial Review and Institutional Balance in European Law' (2010) 47 CMLR 361.
[60] Miro Prek and Silvère Lefèvre, '"Administrative Discretion", "Power of Appraisal" and "Margin of Appraisal" in Judicial Review Proceedings before the General Court' (2019) 56 CMLR 339.
[61] Compare Joana Mendes, 'Discretion, Care and Public Interests in the EU Administration: Probing the Limits of Law' (2016) 53 CMLR 419; in the Banking Union context, Niamh Moloney, 'Banking Union and the Charter of Fundamental Rights' in Chiara Zilioli and Karl-Philipp Wojcik (eds), *Judicial Review in the European Banking Union* (Elgar Financial Law and Practice 2021) 220; Michael Ioannidis, 'The Judicial Review of Discretion in the Banking Union: From 'Soft' to 'Hard(er)' Look?' in Chiara Zilioli and Karl-Philipp Wojcik (eds), *Judicial Review in the European Banking Union* (Elgar Financial Law and Practice 2021) 130–45.
[62] For example, some bank supervision cases. See Case T-733/16 *Banque Postale v ECB* ECLI:EU:T:2018:477; Case T-745/16 *BPCE v ECB* ECLI:EU:T:2018:476; Case T-757/16 *Société Générale v ECB* ECLI:EU:T:2018: 473; Case T-758/16 *Crédit Agricole v ECB* ECLI:EU:T:2018:472; Case T-751/16 *Confédération national de Crédit mutuel v ECB* ECLI:EU:T:2018:475 (hereafter T-751/16 *Crédit mutuel*) and Case T-768/16 *BNP Paribas v ECB* ECLI:EU:T:2018:471; for an analysis see (n 61) 138–42. Case T-504/19 *Crédit Lyonnais v European Central Bank* ECLI:EU:T:2021:185, by the General Court, was overruled by the Court of Justice in Case C-389/21 P *ECB v Crédit Lyonnais* ECLI:EU:C:2023:368.
[63] In line with TFEU, art 261. See *A and B v Norway*, App nos 24130/11 and 29758/11 (15 November 2016).
[64] Case C-537/16 *Garlsson Real Estate and Others* ECLI:EU:C:2018:193, paras 33–37, and Case C-524/15 *Menci* ECLI:EU:C:2018:197, paras 35–39.
[65] Raffaele D'Ambrosio, 'Due Process and Safeguards of the Persons Subject to SSM Supervisory and Sanctioning Proceedings' in Raffaele D'Ambrosio (ed),. *Law and Practice of the Banking Union and of its governing Institutions (Cases and Materials)* (Quaderni di Ricerca Giuridica della Consulenza Legale, Bank of Italy, No 88, 2020) 74, 48–49. See also Silvia Allegrezza and Olivier Voordeckers, 'Investigative and Sanctioning Powers of the ECB in the Framework of the Single Supervisory Mechanism. Mapping the Complexity of a New Enforcement Model' (2015) 4 Eucrim 151 https://eucrim.eu/articles/investigative-and-sanctioning-powers-ecb-framework-single-supervisory-mechanism/#docx-to-html-fn79 (accessed 12 September 2022); Giulia Lasagni, *Banking Supervision and Criminal Investigation. Comparing the EU and US Experiences* (Springer & Giappichelli Cham 2019).
[66] Case 9/56 *Meroni v High Authority* ECLI:EU:C:1958:7, para 152.
[67] In this case, it was the High Authority, whose functions were later taken over by the European Commission.
[68] *Meroni* (n 66) 153–54.
[69] Case 98/80 *Romano v INAMI* ECLI:EU:C:1981:104, para 20.

peculiar cases: in *Meroni* the power was delegated to a 'private law body', based on the Coal and Steel Community framework, not the comprehensive EC/EU Treaties, and in *Romano* the Court's opinion was too succinct to draw proper inferences.[70] However, both presented major obstacles for modern agencies. Furthermore, Articles 290 and 291 TFEU introduced by the Treaty of Lisbon (2009) contemplate the exercise of 'delegated' and 'implementing' competences *by the Commission* with no reference to the possibility of delegation to other bodies. In its landmark *ESMA short selling* case[71] the Court held that Article 291 TFEU was intended to regulate the exercise of delegated competences by the Commission, but did not exclude delegation to other agencies or bodies. Furthermore, it held that ESMA's ample powers on short-selling were not contrary to *Meroni,* as they were exercised following legally stipulated criteria, and subject to judicial review, even if those criteria were broadly defined and open-textured, nor to *Romano* of which the Court made short shrift. Yet, the Court did not openly overrule *Meroni*, leaving it as a sort of failsafe device, in case (financial) regulators' go too far.

3 The individuals within the system: Standing to sue and fundamental rights

Courts in the US can only decide over 'cases' or 'controversies'. What is a 'case' or 'controversy' is determined by the doctrines of 'ripeness', 'mootness' and the 'political question'.[72] These also give context to the requirement of 'standing'. To show 'standing to sue' a plaintiff must demonstrate that he or she has suffered an 'injury in fact' that is 'fairly traceable' to the acts of the defendant, and which will likely be redressed by a favorable decision.[73] The US action normally comprises a damages claim, which must show an injury 'concrete and particularized', and actual or imminent, and a 'fairly traceable' causal connection.[74] The courts' try to leave out grievances that should best be addressed through political bodies,[75] and do not let plaintiffs assert another person's rights, nor adjudicate generalized grievances, and demand that the plaintiff's complaint fall within the zone of interests protected by the law invoked.[76]

3.10

In the EU the action of *annulment* is available to individuals who show a 'direct and *individual* concern' in the act in question,[77] a concept interpreted restrictively under the

3.11

---

[70] See eg Merijn Chamon, 'EU Agencies: Between Meroni and Romano or the Devil and the Deep Blue Sea' (2011) 48 CMLR 1055; Edoardo Chiti, 'An Important Part of the EU's Institutional Machinery: Features, Problems and Perspectives of European Agencies' (2009) 46 CMLR 1420.
[71] Case C-270/12 *United Kingdom v Parliament and Council* ECLI:EU:C:2014:18.
[72] *Massachusetts v EPA* 549 US 497, 516 (2007). These doctrines are related: '[T]o an idea, which is more than an intuition but less than a rigorous and explicit theory, about the constitutional and prudential limits to the powers of an unelected, unrepresentative judiciary in our kind of government.' *Allen v Wright* 468 US 737, 750 (1984), citing the concurring opinion of Judge Bork in *Vander Jagt v O'Neill* 226 US App DC 14, 26–27, 699 F 2d 1166, 1178–79 (1983).
[73] *Bennet v Spear* 520 US 154, 162 (1997).
[74] *Lujan v Defenders of Wildlife* 504 US 555 (1992); *Sierra Club v Morton* 405 US 727, 735 (1992).
[75] *Allen v Wright* (n 72) 750.
[76] ibid 751. This is completed with the requirement that the plaintiff has a 'cause of action', ie that he 'is a member of the class of litigants that may, as a matter of law, appropriately invoke the power of the court'. *Davis v Passman* 442 US 228, 239 (1979).
[77] TFEU, art 263(4).

Plaumann standard,[78] which the Court has refused to modify.[79] Although the Lisbon Treaty allows 'regulatory acts' to be challenged by showing only a 'direct', but not an 'individual' concern,[80] 'regulatory acts' has been interpreted as acts 'of general application apart from legislative acts'.[81] To be challengeable acts must be directly applicable, without requiring any 'implementing measures'.[82] Alternatively, litigants may challenge (domestic) measures implementing an EU measure, and then request domestic courts to make a preliminary reference to the CJEU, asking about the validity of the EU measure (Article 267 TFEU). Alternatively, plaintiffs may use the liability (damages) action (Article 340 TFEU). Yet, for composite decisions (EU measure implemented by domestic measures) EU courts have insisted that the measure be declared unlawful first, ie individuals must challenge domestic measures, then request the court to make a preliminary reference to the Court of Justice,[83] then request damages.[84] Plaintiffs almost never succeed.

3.12 A second dimension of individuals' role in the process hinges on the relevance of fundamental rights for judicial review of action by public (financial) authorities. In the US the Fourteenth Amendment ensures the equal protection, which, among other things, means that no person can be deprived of life, liberty or property without due process of law. This encompasses the Bill of Rights and rights implicit in the due process clause in state action.[85] Federal authorities would be invariably subject to these clauses. The US Supreme Court was

---

[78] In the famous formulation: '[P]ersons other than those to whom a decision is addressed may only claim to be individually concerned if that decision affects them by reason of certain attributes which are peculiar to them or by reason of circumstances in which they are differentiated from all other persons and by virtue of these factors distinguishes them individually just as in the case of the person addressed.' Case 25/62 *Plaumann & Co v Commission* ECLI:EU:C:1963:17. For a recent application in the banking sector, with regard to the locus standi of shareholders of a bank put into temporary administration in accordance with art 29 CRD and its national implementation see Case T-502/19 *Francesca Corneli v ECB* ECLI:EU:T:2022:627, paras 74–75 (currently on appeal in Joined Cases C-777/22 P and C-789/22 P); for the lack of locus standi of a bank's shareholders against the ECB failing or likely to fail assessment and the SRB decision on the public interest assessment which concluded that resolution was not necessary see Case C-364/20 P *Ernests Bernis v SRB and ECB* ECLI:EU:C:2022:115; for the lack of locus standi against the withdrawal of the bank's licence see Joined Cases C-663/17 P, C-665/17 P and C-669/17 P *BCE v Trasta Komercbanka* ECLI:EU:C:2019:923.

[79] See the attempt of AG Jacobs to persuade the Court in Case C-50/00 *Unión de Pequeños Agricultores v Council* ECLI:EU:C:2002:462, followed in Case T-177/01 *Jégo-Quéré & Cie SA v Commission* ECLI:EU:T:2002:11, para 51. The Court of Justice overturned the General Court's finding in Case C-263/02 *Commission v Jégo-Quéré & Cie SA* ECLI:EU:C:2004:210, paras 29–39.

[80] TFEU, art 263(4).

[81] In Case T-18/10 *Inuit Tapiriit Kanatami & Others v European Parliament & Council* ECLI:EU:T:2011:419, upheld on appeal in Case C-583/11 *Inuit Tapiriit Kanatami v Parliament and Council* ECLI:EU:C:2013:625, paras 38–40 the General Court and the CJEU held that a *regulation* adopted by the Council and the Parliament through the ordinary or special legislative procedure constitute legislative acts, while 'regulatory act' encompasses various categories of legal acts, including, inter alia, delegated acts and implementing acts of general application.

[82] In Case C-274/12 *Telefónica SA v Commission* ECLI:EU:C:2013:852, para 58 a Commission ruling declaring the Spanish aid programme to the telecommunications sector illegal was not challengeable, as it did not entail 'specific consequences' for individual companies.

[83] Case C-217/81 *Compagnie Interagra SA v Commission* ECLI:EU:C:1982:222; Case 12/79 *Hans-Otto Wagner GmbH Agrarhandel KG v Commission of the European Communities* ECLI:EU:C:1979:286.

[84] There is a direct claim if the measure (and the fault) is entirely attributable to the EU (Case T-52/99 *T Port GmbH & Co KG v Commission* ECLI:EU:T:2001:97) or if domestic procedures would not afford the litigant an adequate remedy (Case 281/82 *Unifrex v Council and Commission* ECLI:EU:C:1984:165). Yet, the precise scope of this exception is not fully clear. In some cases the CJEU has heard claims in damages without fully explaining why. See eg Case C-352/98 P *Laboratoires pharmaceutiques Bergaderm SA and Jean-Jacques Goupil v Commission of the European Communities* ECLI:EU:C:2000:361. Furthermore, the damages claim for *legislative/regulatory* acts requires a *flagrant* violation of a *superior* rule of law for the protection of the individual (Case 5/71 *Zuckerfabrik Schoeppenstedt v Council* ECLI:EU:C:1971:116).

[85] Most notable of the non-enumerated rights is the right to privacy. See *Griswold v Connecticut* 381 US 479 (1965); *Roe v Wade* 410 US 113 (1973) (now overturned, however, on 24 June 2022 in *Dobbs v Jackson Woman's Health Organization* 597 US ___ (2022); *Lawrence v Texas* 539 US 558 (2003).

also recently called to consider to what extent banks can be responsible for human rights violations arising out of their activities, and although it concluded in *Jesner v Arab Bank*[86] that a foreign bank could not be sued in the US for alleged complicity in human rights violations under the Alien Tort Statute, it is clear that 'human rights review is becoming integral to the legal and regulatory framework that governs banking sector activity'[87], and beyond.

In the European Union, the EU Charter on Fundamental Rights applies to 'the institutions and bodies of the Union', such as the ECB, SRB, European Commission, or European Supervisory Authorities (and specifically ESMA as regards its mandates of direct supervision), and to Member States when 'implementing Union law',[88] which, it seems, should encompass cases where national authorities operate under largely harmonized law, as in the Single Supervisory Mechanism (SSM) or the Single Resolution Mechanism (SRM).[89] The European Convention on Human Rights (ECHR) is the other relevant text. The European Court of Human Rights (ECtHR), which administers it, however, lacks jurisdiction over any EU institution or body, because the EU is not a party to the ECHR. Yet, the ECtHR would have jurisdiction over decisions by national authorities, if these enjoy some degree of discretion when implementing EU decisions.[90] Absent such discretion, the ECtHR could claim jurisdiction, and declare the EU act contrary to the ECHR, but it has never done so, referring to declare that the EU legal framework provided sufficient safeguards to consider the action ECHR-compliant.[91]

3.13

An important difference between US and European fundamental rights review[92] is the different role of 'proportionality' and 'balancing'.[93] In the EU 'proportionality' has been aptly characterized as a 'matrix principle', which promotes effectiveness and legitimacy,[94] and is key in fundamental rights analysis.[95] 'Balancing' in American law is a 'tool' or 'technique', to weigh rights against policies, and, although used often,[96] it is not as respectable as proportionality is in Europe.[97] This difference may be due to several reasons. For one, the US is an older constitution, focused on narrow, but more categorical 'negative rights',[98] while

3.14

---

[86] *Jesner v Arab Bank PLC* 138 S Ct 1386 (2018).
[87] Moloney (n 61) 210.
[88] EU Charter of Fundamental Rights, art 51 (emphasis added).
[89] Case C-617/10 *Åklagaren v Hans Åkerberg Fransson* ECLI:EU:C:2013:105. In contrast see Case C-206/13 *Siragusa* EU:C:2014:126 (EU environmental protection rules and Italian landscape conservation rules insufficiently connected).
[90] *Matthews v United Kingdom*, App no 24833/94 (29 October 1997). See also *Bosphorus Airways v Ireland*, App no 45036/98 (30 June 2005).
[91] See eg *Bosphorus Airways v Ireland* (n 90). For a more detailed analysis see Marco Lamandini, David Ramos, and Javier Solana, 'The European Central Bank (ECB) as a Catalyst for Change in EU Law (Part 2): SSM, SRM and Fundamental Rights' (2016) 23 Col J of Eur L 199, 207.
[92] Michel Rosenfeld, 'Constitutional Adjudication in Europe and the United States: Paradoxes and Contrasts' (2004) 2 ICON 633; Günter Frankenberg, 'Comparing Constitutions: Ideas, Ideals, and Ideology: Toward a Layered Narrative' (2006) 4 ICON 439.
[93] Jud Mathews and Alec Stone Sweet, 'Proportionality Balancing and Global Constitutionalism' (2009) 47 CJTL 73; Moshe Cohen-Eliya and Iddo Porat, 'American Balancing and German Proportionality: The Historical Origins' (2010) 8 ICON 263.
[94] Koen Lenaerts, 'Proportionality as a Matrix Principle Promoting the Effectiveness of EU Law, and the Legitimacy of EU Action' in 'Continuity and Change: How the Challenges of Today Prepare the Ground for Tomorrow' (ECB Legal Conference 2021) 27.
[95] Robert Alexy, 'Constitutional Rights, Balancing, and Rationality' (2003) 16 Ratio Juris 131; Robert Alexy, *A Theory of Constitutional Rights* (OUP 2010).
[96] T Alexander Aleinikoff, 'Constitutional Law in an Age of Balancing' (1987) 96 Yale LJ 943; Mark S Kende, 'The Unmasking of Balancing and Proportionality Review in U.S. Constitutional Laws' (2017) 25 JICL 417.
[97] Vicki C Jackson, 'Constitutional Law in an Age of Proportionality' (2015) 124 Yale LJ 3094; Moshe Cohen-Eliya and Iddo Porat, 'The Hidden Foreign Law Debate in Heller: The Proportionality Approach in American Constitutional Law' (2009) 46 San Diego L Rev 367; Cohen-Eliya and Porat (n 93) 263–86.
[98] That is, freedom from state interference, and not 'positive obligations'. See *Ex parte Young* 209 US 123 (1908); *Cruz v Beto* 405 US 319, 322 (1972).

European countries are heirs to the post-Second World War expansion in the number and scope of rights. Rights are often depicted as 'optimization mandates',[99] which eventually collide with other rights and policies. The solution is weighing rights against rights, or policies. Moreover, proportionality has a better pedigree in Europe, as it evolved as part of the Prussian Supreme Administrative Court's attempt to rein in the state's police powers,[100] and filled the gap of a very limited parliamentary accountability.[101] Also, it was seen as a formal judicial test, and not as a disguised way for judges to dictate policy,[102] and was a safer option than the more open balancing of interests advocated by von Jhering's,[103] or the *Freirechtschule*. In the United States, 'balancing' was advocated by legal realism, but was never so mainstream[104] to be used as judicial guidance, and never did take root in the United States as proportionality did in Continental Europe. Finally, in countries like Germany society tended to have a benign, even optimist, view, of the courts' role as a means to do law without politics,[105] in contrast with the United States, where distrust of excess does not spare the courts,[106] and the use of 'balancing' of policies and rights has been deemed 'judicial activism' when it has curtailed government action,[107] or enabled it.[108] Thus, in American law court review should be based on more categorical definitions. In practice, this means that economic rights are seen in light of the terms set out in the corresponding regulation, which, in practice, means a greater degree of deference towards the legislature, whereas legislation within specific constitutional prohibitions, such as those of the Bill of Rights, legislation restricting the political process, or discriminating against 'discrete and insular minorities' would be subject to a greater degree of scrutiny.[109] It also means that, in US law, finding that a right has been violated is generally the end of the inquiry, while in Europe this would be the step prior to a proportionality analysis. In practice, elements analysed under the proportionality test in Europe could be used in the United States to delineate the scope of the right, or procedural protections, eg the requiring a justification in terms of costs and benefits.[110]

---

[99] Alexy, *A Theory of Constitutional Rights* (n 95).
[100] Cohen-Eliya and Porat (n 93) 271–72. The initial application of proportionality did not include the three-pronged, or four-pronged version of the test that has later become commonplace.
[101] ibid 272.
[102] ibid.
[103] Rudolph von Jhering, 'In the Heaven of Legal Concepts: A Fantasy' (Charlotte L Levy trs, Foreword by John M Lindsey) (1985) 58 Temp LQ 799.
[104] Legal realism may have been influenced by the German *Freirechtschule*, which was anti-establishment. James E Herget and Stephen Wallace, 'The German Free Law Movement As the Source of American Legal Realism' (1987) 73 Va L Rev 399. Critics of formalism included prominent scholars like Roscoe Pound, 'Mechanical Jurisprudence' (1908) 8 Col L Rev 605; Oliver Wendell Holmes, 'The Path of the Law' (1897) 10 Harv LR 457; or Benjamin Cardozo, *The Nature of the Judicial Process* (YUP 1921). However, they were advanced minds more than mainstream ones. Other, more radical branches, included the critical legal studies (CLS) movement. See Duncan Kennedy and Karl E Klare, 'A Bibliography of Critical Legal Studies' (1984) 94 Yale LJ 461.
[105] Cohen-Eliya and Porat (n 93).
[106] John Hart, Ely *Democracy and Distrust* (HUP 1980). See also Jackson, 'Constitutional Law' (n 97); Cohen-Eliya and Porat, The Hidden Foreign Law Debate (n 97) 396.
[107] *Lochner v New York* 198 US 45 (1905) (property and due process rights).
[108] *Dennis v United States* 341 US 494 (1951) (government restrictions on free speech rights).
[109] *United States v Carolene Products Co* 304 US 144, 152 (1938).
[110] For example, Thoma Cottier and Petros C Mavroidis, *The Role of the Judge in International Trade Regulation. Experience and Lessons for the WTO* (The University of Michigan Press 2003). See also Robert Alexy, 'The Construction of Constitutional Rights' (2010) 4 L & Ethics Hum Rts 26; Alexy, 'Constitutional Rights, Balancing, and Rationality' (n 95) 131–40.

4
A Matter of principles: Justiciability and accountability in the public law of finance

1 Justiciability challenges of monetary and financial stability decisions	4.01	2.3 Soft law acts in financial regulation and supervision: justiciability, legal relevance, and control of shadow legislation	4.25
1.1 Immunity of sovereign debtors, central banks, and international organizations	4.01	2.4 Challengeability of acts in complex proceedings	4.38
1.2 Justiciability of financial stability and crisis management decisions in the EU	4.08	2.5 Standing to challenge decisions	4.49
1.3 Justiciability of central banks' decisions	4.11	3 Accountability beyond justiciability: access to documents, appointments, and quasi-judicial review	4.62
2 Justiciability issues in regulatory, supervisory, and crisis management decisions	4.14	3.1 Transparency and access to documents	4.62
2.1 Exclusions and limitations of liability	4.15	3.2 Independence and appointment of members of financial regulatory bodies	4.83
2.2 Agency discretion, justiciability, and the legitimacy of delegation	4.18	3.3 The relationship between court review and administrative review	4.90

1 Justiciability challenges of monetary and financial stability decisions

1.1 Immunity of sovereign debtors, central banks, and international organizations

Maintaining financial stability requires governments and central banks to operate in the market, eg by issuing debt, purchasing assets, administering funds, etc., which exposes them to lawsuits and raises the question of sovereign immunity. The major issues are (i) courts' self-perceived role in the context of international relations vis-à-vis foreign states (typical in sovereign debt cases), (ii) the treatment of central bank assets as autonomous (or not), (iii) and the treatment of multilateral organizations, like the IMF or the World Bank. **4.01**

The US is a very experienced jurisdiction on claims against foreign sovereigns. From an initial position based on the Act of State doctrine, which reserved foreign policy to the executive branch,[1] there was a gradual openness to exercise jurisdiction,[2] until the matter was regulated by the Foreign Sovereign Immunities Act (FSIA[3]), which grants foreign sovereign governments immunity,[4] subject to exceptions, including for actions based on commercial **4.02**

---

[1] *Banco Nacional de Cuba v Sabbatino* 376 US 398 (1964) (federal courts lack jurisdiction over disputes of a country taking property within its own territory, even if it violates international law).
[2] *First National City Bank v Banco Nacional de Cuba* 406 US 759 (1972) (claim by the Cuban national bank for excess collateral pledged to secure a loan with an American bank, who counterclaimed to offset it against its property expropriated in Cuba expropriated without compensation).
[3] 28 USC s 1602.
[4] ibid s 1604.

activity with a sufficient nexus with the United States.[5] The FSIA and its 'commercial activity' exception allocated immunity decisions to courts, and opened the door to litigation without knowing whether courts would weigh the kind of policy arguments that had been the domain of the executive. Cases like *Verlinden v Central Bank of Nigeria* confirmed that the FSIA's 'restrictive' approach, and the 'commercial activities' exception were not an violation of separation of powers under Article III of the US Constitution,[6] while *Republic of Argentina v Weltover Inc*[7] (a default by Argentina on bonds payable in New York),[8] held that an act would be considered 'commercial' based on its 'nature', not its 'purpose', and that the bond offering was 'commercial' because

> [t]hey are in almost all respects garden-variety debt instruments: They may be held by private parties; they are negotiable and may be traded on the international market (except in Argentina); and they promise a future stream of cash income.[9]

4.03 The subsequent case of *Republic of Argentina v NML Capital*[10] originated in Argentina's swap of more than 90 per cent of its debt for new securities paying twenty-five cents on the dollar. NML Capital, Ltd. ('NML') a hedge fund, purchased some bonds, rejected the exchange, and sued for the full amount before the Southern District of New York, which ruled in favour of NML, which sought discovery of Argentina's global assets. Argentina had waived immunity of jurisdiction in Fiscal Agency Agreement (FAA) in the bonds, but the question was whether US courts could order discovery for Argentina's *global* assets, given that they lacked the authority to execute judgments against the assets held abroad. The US Supreme Court held that any immunity defence 'made by a foreign sovereign in an American court must stand on the Act's text. Or it must fall'. Since the FSIA said nothing of discovery, the Court held that no exception could be inferred, and even global discovery could be ordered. The Opinion held that even the immunity of execution (eg diplomatic or military property) did not result in immunity from discovery, which sought to determine where there may be assets subject to execution.[11] The Argentinian government's argument that the Court's ruling could turn US courts into a 'discovery clearinghouse' for global assets was dispatched by holding that this was a 'riddle' for Congress to solve.[12] NML sought to enforce the New York judgment in other countries, testing their respective frameworks. In the UK's *NML v Argentina*[13] the UK State Immunity Act 1978 (SIA) includes as exceptions to sovereign immunity where a foreign state has submitted to the English courts' jurisdiction and consented to enforcement, while Section 31 of the Civil Jurisdiction and Judgments Act (CJJA) 1982, provided that a judgment by a foreign court against a state could be recognized and enforced if it would be so recognized and enforced had it not been given against a state, and the court would have

---

[5] ibid s 1605(a)(2).
[6] *Verlinden BV v Central Bank of Nigeria* 461 US 480 (1983).
[7] *Republic of Argentina v Weltover Inc* 504 US 607 (1992).
[8] The bonds funded the 'Bonods' transaction, where the Argentine government would sell US dollars to domestic borrowers against Argentine currency. Upon a shortage of US dollar reserves, Argentina sought unilaterally to reschedule its debt. In the Court's view, 'when a foreign government acts, not as regulator of a market, but in the manner of a private player within it, the foreign sovereign's actions are "commercial" within the meaning of the FSIA'. *Argentina v Weltover* (n 7) 615. See also *Alfred Dunhill of London Inc v Republic of Cuba* 425 US 682 (1976).
[9] *Argentina v Weltover* (n 7) 616, 618.
[10] *Republic of Argentina v NML Capital Ltd* [2014] 573 US 134.
[11] ibid para 10: '[T]he reason for these subpoenas is that NML does not yet know what property Argentina has and where it is, let alone whether it is executable under the relevant jurisdiction's law.'
[12] 'Could the 1976 Congress really have meant not to protect foreign states from post-judgment discovery "clearinghouses"? The riddle is not ours to solve (if it can be solved at all) ... [t]he question ... is not what Congress "would have wanted" but what Congress enacted in the FSIA.' *Argentina v NML Capital Ltd* (n 10) 11.
[13] *NML Capital Ltd v Republic of Argentina* [2011] UKSC 31.

had jurisdiction if it had applied the rules in accordance with the SIA.[14] The Court of Appeal held that the SIA and CJJA applied cumulatively, and that the SIA exceptions did not apply, because the enforcement proceedings were not 'relating to a commercial transaction', and the waiver of immunity in the bonds could not be read as a submission by Argentina to the jurisdiction of English courts.[15] The UK Supreme Court overturned this, finding that the CJJA was an *alternative* regime for foreign judgments,[16] but the lords were split on the 'commercial' exception. To some, it sufficed that the New York judgment related to a commercial transaction (the bonds[17]); to others, reading the exception as encompassing 'proceedings relating to a judgment which itself relates to a commercial transaction' 'stretched the language beyond the admissible'.[18] However, they agreed that the waiver of immunity in the bonds conferred jurisdiction on English courts when immunity was the only bar to such jurisdiction.[19] This contrasts with the French rulings *NML v Argentina*,[20] where the Supreme Court (*Cassation*) held that the matter should be decided in accordance with customary international law, relying on the UN Convention (not in force[21]). It then reasoned that the assets (receivables held by private companies) were tax liabilities, and thus linked to the government's execution of its sovereignty, which, in turn, required, under the Convention, a waiver of immunity that was express and univocal, and that the waiver of immunity in the bonds' Fiscal Agency Agreement could not be read as comprising such waiver.[22]

The contrast between the judgments is perplexing. Formally speaking, none of them weighed foreign policy considerations. However, it is hard not to read some (value-laden) irritation with Argentina in the FSIA's formalistic reading by the US Supreme Court, and its nonchalant dismissal of the risk of creating a 'clearinghouse for information' as 'not its problem'. The UK Supreme Court's readiness to read the waiver of immunity in the bonds as a submission to English courts was plausible, but also convenient to execute the judgment of a court from a close ally. The French court's request of an 'express' and 'univocal' waiver to immunity of execution, when such requirement is nowhere to be found in the UN Convention, could be a way to channel concerns about opening the floodgates. This controversy clearly shows the challenges to the rule of law which may originate by the silence or the ambiguity (at best) of applicable rules, by parallel uncertainties in the proper identification of the principles which should govern the matter within the legal framework and by the exposure of courts

4.04

---

[14] '(a) it would be so recognised and enforced if it had not been given against a state; and (b) that court would have had jurisdiction in the matter if it had applied rules corresponding to those applicable to such matters in the United Kingdom in accordance with ss 2-11 of the [SIA].'
[15] *NML Capital Ltd v Republic of Argentina* [2010] EWCA Civ 41.
[16] *NML Capital Ltd v Argentina 2011* (n 13) paras31, 47 (Philips LJ).
[17] ibid paras 31, 38–42 (Philips LJ, joined by Clarke LJ).
[18] ibid paras 31, 86 (Mance LJ, joined by Collins LJ and Walker LJ).
[19] 'If a state waives immunity it does no more than place itself on the same footing as any other person. A waiver of immunity does not confer jurisdiction where, in the case of another defendant, it would not exist. If, however, state immunity is the only bar to jurisdiction, an agreement to waive immunity is tantamount to a submission to the jurisdiction. In this case Argentina agreed that the New York judgment could be enforced by a suit upon the judgment in any court to the jurisdiction of which, absent immunity, Argentina would be subject. It was both an agreement to waive immunity and an express agreement that the New York judgment could be sued on in any country that, state immunity apart, would have jurisdiction. England is such a country, by reason of what, at the material time, was CPR 6.20(9)'. *NML Capital v Argentina 2011* (n 13) 31, 59 (Philips LJ).
[20] *Société NML Capital (Iles Caïmans) v Etat d'Argentine*, Cour de Cassation (1ère Chambre Civile) no 10-25/938, 11-10/450, and 11-13/323 (28 March 2013). The three rulings were issued on the same date.
[21] The UNC Convention on Jurisdictional Immunities of States and their Property, 2004 was also cited as reflective of customary international law in the case *Jurisdictional Immunities of the State (Germany v Italy)* [2012] ICJ Rep 99 (3 February 2012); and the EctHR in Application 34869/05 *Sabeh El Leil v France* ECLI:CE:ECHR:2008:1021DEC003486905.
[22] ibid.

4.05 More recently, the London High Court, Financial List in *The Law Debenture Trust v Ukraine*[23] granted summary judgment (ie judgment without trial, when a party shows that the other has no real prospect of success) to the claimant, a company bringing proceedings under the direction of Russian Ministry of Finance for the non-payment of Eurobonds issued by Ukraine, governed by English law, and held by Russia. Ukraine alleged that Russia applied unlawful economic (trade) and political pressure on Ukraine in 2013 to deter it from signing an Association Agreement with the European Union, and to force it to accept Russian financial support (in the form of the Eurobond transaction) instead; that this pressure amounted to duress under English law, and that this justified non-payment. The High Court held that, while Ukraine had made a strong case of Russian economic pressure, the question whether this pressure could amount to duress in English law was not justiciable. In the High Court view, municipal courts were barred under the foreign act of state doctrine because they: 'cannot have the competence to adjudicate upon or to enforce the rights arising out of transactions entered into by independent sovereign states between themselves on the plane of international law'.

The court also rejected the claim that some treaties/agreements identified by Ukraine, yet not incorporated into English law could prevail over the domestic law rights by the Trustee under the Eurobond transaction. The Court of Appeal upheld the High Court's decision but held that the duress defence was in fact justiciable even against a sovereign state.[24] Instead of using a treaty governed solely by international law, Russia chose the structure of a Eurobond, choosing English law and English courts as the forum. Thus:

> [t]he strong willingness of English courts to apply rule of law standards to do substantive justice between parties to a contract governed by English law is well known (emphasis added). At the point of contracting, Russia chose to submit by any claim by Law Debenture to the jurisdiction of the English court and hence has taken the risk with its eyes open that the court would apply the English law of duress as a substantive matter. This is a materially different context from one in which a third state has its actions called into question in litigation between two different parties.

Further, the court held that the foreign act of state doctrine reflects a principle of respect for comity between states, but 'comity points in both directions' and Russia and Ukraine wished opposite things, and thus 'there is nothing inherently non-justiciable or unmanageable' in applying the duress defence in this context'. Nor there is scope for the constitutional concern that in a matter relating to the conduct of the United Kingdom's foreign affairs 'the courts should be astute not to usurp or cut across the proper role of the executive government, which has the primary responsibility for carrying on those affairs'. The Court of Appeal's test for duress focused on whether the conduct was 'morally or socially unacceptable'. The Supreme Court held that the issue of duress was justiciable, but rejected the Court of Appeal's broad test, holding that instead the courts should focus on the link between duress and equitable doctrines, like unconscionability, ie whether the behaviour in question would 'render the enforcement of a contract unconscionable'.[25] On that basis, whereas Ukraine's

---

[23] *Law Debenture Trust Corporation PLC v Ukraine* [2017] EWHC 655 (Comm) (Justice Blair).
[24] *Ukraine v The Law Debenture Trust Corporation Plc (Rev 1)* [2018] EWCA Civ 2026.
[25] See The Law Debenture Trust Corporation v Ukraine, [2023] UKSC 11.

defence of duress based on threats of physical violence against armed forces and civilians, and of damage against property, could not be determined without a trial, and summary judgment was denied, the economic pressure alleged by Ukraine was not illegitimate under English law, and thus insufficient to establish duress.

4.06 The second issue concerns the treatment of central bank assets.[26] The 'commercial activities' exception can be extremely dangerous, since central banks' activities could, in many ways, be described as 'commercial in nature'. Thus, some laws offer an absolute, or reinforced, immunity for central bank assets.[27] In Germany, the Supreme Court applied a 'finality' test, holding that, when central bank assets serve 'sovereign purposes' they are subject to immunity of execution.[28] In an enforcement action against assets of the central bank of Mongolia held by the Bundesbank, the Court held that whether an asset serves a sovereign purpose depends on whether it is to be used for a sovereign activity (a different approach from US courts[29]). Relying on the UN Convention as customary law the Court held that, even if held under private law arrangements, the currency reserves of a state managed in foreign accounts serve sovereign purposes, and were immune from execution. The US for its part grants immunity to a central bank's assets 'held for its own account', but this raises the question of when central bank assets are not their own. In the US the doctrine of 'instrumentalities' was initially part of the 'act of state' doctrine,[30] but continued to be relevant after the doctrine took second stage. In *First National City Bank v BANCEC*[31] the Cuban revolutionary government established Bancec as '[a]n official autonomous credit institution for foreign trade ... with full juridical capacity ... of its own',[32] but the government owned all of its stock, supplied all its capital, received its profits, and Ernesto 'Che' Guevara served as its president. Following expropriations ordered by Guevara against its local branch, Citibank kept some money owed to Bancec in an account balance as compensation.[33] The Circuit Court upheld Bancec's complaint,[34] but the US Supreme Court overturned,[35] applying its doctrine of 'instrumentalities' as a sort of 'veil piercing', based on equitable principles common to federal common law and international law.[36] It held that the matter could not be decided under Cuban law, because it could be used to circumvent the FSIA's waiver of immunity,[37] and that Bancec was an 'alter ego' of the Cuban government, which exercised extensive control, including over its day-to-day operations, and 'fraud and injustice' would result if the doctrine were not applied (the Cuban government had dissolved Bancec, and appropriated

---

[26] See Ingrid Wuerth, 'Immunity from Execution of Central Bank Assets' in Tom Ruys and Nicolas Angelet (eds), *Cambridge Handbook on Immunities and International Law* (CUP 2018).
[27] UN Convention on Jurisdictional Immunities of States and their Property, art 21(1)I; UK SIA, Section 14(4); Act on the Civil Jurisdiction of Japan with respect to a Foreign State, arts 5–6; China Immunity Act, Order of the President no 41 [2005] October 28, art 1; Argentina Law 26.961. See Wuerth (n 26).
[28] BGH (4 July 2013) VII ZB 63/12.
[29] ibid, citing BGH (1 October 2009) VII ZB 37/08.
[30] *First National City Bank v Banco Nacional de Cuba* (n 2).
[31] *First National City Bank v Banco para el Comercio Exterior de Cuba* 103 S Ct 2591 (1983).
[32] Cuban Law No 793 (1960) art 1.
[33] See Mark Anderson Finklestein, 'First National City Bank v Banco para el Comercio Exterior de Cuba: Act of State and Choice of Law Aspects of Suing Foreign Governmental Corporations' (1983) 9 NC J Intl L & Com Reg 147.
[34] It held that the central bank had not had a 'key role' in the expropriations. See *First National City Bank v Banco para el Comercio Exterior de Cuba* [1981] 658 F.2d 913, 919 (2d Cir.).
[35] *First National City Bank v Banco para el Comercio Exterior de Cuba 1983* (n 31).
[36] The Court referred to the *Case Concerning the Barcelona Traction, Light & Power Co* [1970] ICJ Rep 3 https://www.icj-cij.org/public/files/case-related/50/050-19700205-JUD-01-00-EN.pdf.
[37] On this, the US Supreme Court drew an analogy between Cuban law, used in this case, and the use of Delaware law in *Anderson v Abbott* 321 US 349 (1944).

its assets[38]). The issue arose again in *EM Ltd NML v Banco Central de la República (BCRA*[39]*)*, a part of the *NML v Argentina* saga (see above) where two distressed debt funds sought to enforce judgments[40] against Argentina's central bank assets. Argentina's president had decreed that BCBA's reserves above the amounts needed to support Argentina's monetary base ('unrestricted reserves') be used to pay obligations to the IMF. Plaintiffs unsuccessfully tried to attach BCBA's account with the Federal Reserve Bank of New York (FRBNY), arguing that the decrees had transferred ownership of BCRA's assets to Argentina (property theory),[41] and then tried to argue that Argentina 'controlled BCRA itself' (instrumentality theory).[42] The courts were unconvinced, holding that BCRA's FRBNY account was immune, as it was 'held for its own account'. Thus, plaintiffs argued that, under the *alter ego* theory they could seize BCRA's assets *anywhere in the world* (ie outside the US) and that BCBR's FRBNY account was a 'commercial activity' in the United States.[43] To the Circuit Court the plaintiffs failed to meet either of the two prongs of the *Bancec* test. First, the government's acts to undermine central bank independence were not enough to satisfy the 'extensive control' required for the *alter ego* theory, which requires control of daily operations,[44] Secondly, on the 'fraud and injustice' prong, the Court distinguished cases where states tried to avoid liability (eg in *Bancec* Cuba dissolved Bancec and absorbed its assets), from this case, where Argentina tried to use BCRA's funds to pay the IMF, a 'preferred' creditor, and BCBR was not a 'sham' to hide Argentina's assets. The 'commercial activity' exception was also rejected, since BCRA did not sign the bond instrument, nor adopt the decision to stop paying. BCRA's holding of an account with the FRBNY to purchase dollars was 'entirely incidental' to the merit's claim.[45] Using it to expand sovereign immunity exceptions would also endanger New York's role as a financial centre.[46] The case *Bank Markazi*[47] presented the opposite problem. Parties who had obtained judgments against Iran for its role in state-sponsored terrorism tried to enforce their claims against an Iran's central bank (Bank Markazi) account held with European

---

[38] *First National City Bank v Banco para el Comercio Exterior de Cuba* 1983 (n 31).

[39] *EM Ltd v Republic of Argentina* 473 F 3d 463, 466 n 2 (2d Cir 2007); *NML Capital v Banco Central de la República Argentina* 652 F 3d 172 (2d Cir 2011); *EM Ltd v Banco Central de la República Argentina* 800 F 3d 78 (2015).

[40] Creditors succeeded in enforcing such judgments in some cases. See *NML Capital Ltd v Republic of Argentina* 680 F 3d 254, 260 (2d Cir 2012), or *NML Capital Limited v Republic of Argentina 2010* (n 15) (assets transferred to Argentina, or assets held in trust for Argentina).

[41] '[T]he Decrees did not alter property rights with respect to the FRBNY Funds' because they 'did not create an attachable interest on the part of [Argentina] in the FRBNY Funds'. *BCRA I* (n 39).

[42] The Circuit Court left this door open in *First National City Bank v Banco para el Comercio Exterior de Cuba 1983* (n 31).

[43] They won in the District Court (*EM Ltd v Republic of Argentina* 720 F Supp 2d 273 (SDNY 2010)) but lost in the Circuit (s 1611(b)(1)). See *BCBRA II* (n 39).

[44] For the court, the hiring and firing of board members or officers is an exercise of power incidental to ownership, but this is not synonymous with control over day-to-day operations. Governments exercise some control over instrumentalities, much like parent corporations control certain aspects of otherwise independent subsidiaries. *BCBRA III* (n 39). The court also rejected that such extensive control resulted from the government's use of BCBRA for financing operations, or from the coordination between the two, because these were normal features of the relationship between governments and central banks, and courts should not second-guess matters of policy. *BCBRA III* (n 39).

[45] 'Whatever adverse consequences plaintiffs allegedly suffered from the BRA's loans to Argentina, they would have suffered the same consequences had BCRA used any other bank account in the United States or abroad.' *BCBRA III* (n 39).

[46] Given New York's role as a financial centre, every country and every central bank would be at risk of losing their sovereign immunity on this basis ... weakening the immunity from suit or attachment traditionally enjoyed by the instrumentalities of foreign states could lead foreign central banks, in particular, to 'withdraw their reserves from the United States and place them in other countries. Any significant withdrawal of these reserves could have an immediate and adverse impact on the US economy and the global financial system'.

[47] *Bank Markazi v Peterson* 578 US 212, 136 S Ct 1310 2016).

intermediaries. The central bank alleged several defences, and Congress passed a bill to exclude those defences[48] even identifying the lawsuit by docket number. Bank Markazi alleged that this was an unconstitutional breach of the separation of powers, by dictating the result in a particular case. The Supreme Court, however, held that the statute 'changed the law by establishing new substantive standards' the standard being that, if Iran owned the assets, those assets would be available for execution, citing precedents of *ad hominem* laws that identified cases by docket number.[49] Furthermore, although FSIA transferred the authority over foreign states' sovereign immunity, 'it remains Congress' prerogative to alter a foreign state's immunity'.[50] This bizarre exercise of legislative power was criticized by Chief Justice Roberts' dissent, joined by Justice Sotomayor, as a blow to the separation of powers, and no different from a law that, in a hypothetical (*Smith v Jones*) case said 'Smith wins'.[51]

A third issue is the immunity of international organizations that may play a substantial financial role, like the IMF and the World Bank. In *Jam and Others v International Finance Corporation (IFC)*,[52] the IFC (the financial arm of the World Bank) entered into a loan agreement with Coastal Gujarat Power Limited, a company based in India, to finance the construction of a coal-fired power plant in Gujarat. Petitioners, a community of Indian fisherfolk, represented by an NGO and a legal clinic, sued before US courts, claiming that pollution from the plant harmed the surrounding air, land, and water. The US Supreme Court granted certiorari. At stake was the foundation of the immunity of international organizations. For the International Court of Justice (ICJ) the immunity of states is based on 'sovereign equality',[53] while the immunity of international organizations is based on 'functional necessity', ie to enable international organizations to operate autonomously and effectively, without interference from states.[54] The International Organizations Immunities Act (IOIA) text linked the immunity of international organizations to that of states,[55] because an expansive view of states' immunity was present when the IOIA was drafted, while the more restrictive approach was adopted later. The relevant precedent for the District and Circuit Court was *Atkinson v Inter-American Development Bank*, where courts held that Congress had delegated to the President the responsibility for updating the immunities of international organizations, and not left it to be automatically updated in accordance with developments in the law of the immunity of sovereigns.[56] Under this system the IOIA had not been updated, nor incorporated changes to the law of state immunity (eg the restrictive approach for commercial activities), and kept the preceding, absolute immunity approach.[57] The District and Circuit Courts upheld this absolute immunity.[58] However, the Supreme Court held

4.07

---

[48] It was codified as 22 USC s 8772.
[49] *Bank Markazi v Peterson* (n 47), citing *Robertson v Seattle Audubon Society* (1992).
[50] ibid.
[51] ibid (Roberts dissenting).
[52] *Jam v International Finance Corp* 139 S Ct 759 (2019).
[53] *Jurisdictional Immunities of the State (Germany v Italy)* (n 21) 123, para 57.
[54] Yohei Okada, 'The Immunity of International Organizations Before and after Jam V IFC: Is the Functional Necessity Rationale Still Relevant?' (2020) 72 Q J Intl L 29.
[55] 22 USC s 288(a), (b): 'International organizations, their property and their assets, wherever located, and by whomsoever held, shall enjoy the same immunity from suit and every form of judicial process as is enjoyed by foreign governments, except to the extent that such organizations may expressly waive their immunity for the purpose of any proceedings or by the terms of any contract.'
[56] *Atkinson v Inter-American Development Bank* 156 F 3d 1335 (DC Cir 1998).
[57] 'In light of this text and legislative history, we think that despite the lack of a clear instruction as to whether Congress meant to incorporate in the IOIA subsequent changes to the law of immunity of foreign sovereigns, Congr'ss' intent was to adopt that body of law only as it existed in 1945—when immunity of foreign sovereigns was absolute.' *Atkinson v Inter-American Development Bank* (n 56).
[58] *Jam and Others v International Finance Corporation* 860 F 3d 703 (DC Cir 2017).

that the IOIA intended to link the immunity of international organizations to that of sovereign states, and thus develop them 'in tandem'.[59] Using the 'functional' logic, expanding the waiver of immunity beyond what was needed by the organization's goals could undermine its mission. The IFC's allegations that this ruling could expose it to a flood of litigation were dismissed, holding that the IOIA were mere 'default rules', and that, if the organization's mission were endangered, its charter could be amended to expand its immunity. In fact, the Court compared the statute of the United Nations and the IMF, both of which include quite expansive immunities, with that of the IFC's, which is relatively narrow.[60] Furthermore, acknowledging the IFC's concern in part, it held that it is unclear that the IFC's *lending* activity would necessarily be classified as 'commercial', since it is conducted with governments, and is not commercial in nature.[61] As if to allay the World Bank's concerns, in 2020, on remand from the Supreme Court, the District Court for the District of Columbia (DC) upheld the immunity of the IFC.[62]

1.2 Justiciability of financial stability and crisis management decisions in the EU

4.08 EU law on financial stability and crisis management is not characterized by sovereign immunity, but by other jurisdictional issues such as the justiciability by European courts of non-EU law acts; or of acts with unclear legal status, such as Memoranda of Understanding (MoUs); or problems with the judicial remedy or attribution of the act.

4.09 First, the European Union is a limited Union, based on the principle of conferral. Member States sometimes adopt multilateral treaties which are separate from EU Treaties, but seek to further EU goals, such as financial stability, and employ EU institutions, such as the ECB and the Commission. EU countries, taking inspiration in the IMF framework, adopted the ESM Treaty, and accompanied it by a reform of the EU Treaties, to expressly habilitate Eurozone Member States to conclude specific arrangements for mutual assistance. The *Pringle* case determined that this arrangement was valid, but that acts under the ESM Treaty were not subject to the EU Treaties, including the Charter of Fundamental Rights.[63] In *Ledra Advertising*, under the ESM Treaty, a Memorandum of Understanding (MoU) requiring Cypriot authorities to enforce a write-off and conversion of capital and debt instruments, including non-guaranteed deposits was concluded between, on one side, Cyprus, and on the other side, the

---

[59] ibid 10: 'The IOIA's reference to the immunity enjoyed by foreign governments is a general rather than specific reference. The reference is to an external body of potentially evolving law—the law of foreign sovereign immunity—not to a specific provision of another statute. The IOIA should therefore be understood to link the law of international organization immunity to the law of foreign sovereign immunity, so that the one develops in tandem with the other.'
[60] 'The IFC's concerns are inflated. To begin, the privileges and immunities accorded by the IOIA are only default rules. If the work of a given international organization would be impaired by restrictive immunity, the organization's charter can always specify a different level of immunity ... Notably, the IFC's own charter does not state that the IFC is absolutely immune from suit.' *Jam and Others v IFC* (n 58) 14.
[61] 'Nor is there good reason to think that restrictive immunity would expose international development banks to excessive liability. As an initial matter, it is not clear that the lending activity of all development banks qualifies as commercial activity within the meaning of the FSIA. To be considered "commercial", an activity must be "the type" of activity "by which a private party engages in" trade or commerce ... As the Government suggested at oral argument, the lending activity of at least some development banks, such as those that make conditional loans to governments, may not qualify as "commercial" under the FSIA.' *Jam and Others v IFC* (n 58).
[62] *Jam and Others v International Finance Corporation* [2020] US District Court of the District of Columbia, 1:15-CV-00612-JDB.
[63] Case C-370/12 *Thomas Pringle v Government of Ireland and Others* ECLI:EU:C:2012:756.

ESM, formally, but the Commission (and, to a lesser extent, the ECB) in practice. The plaintiffs sued for breach of the EU Charter, seeking annulment of their acts, and, alternatively, compensation for damages. For the General Court the claims were outside the European courts' jurisdiction.[64] The Court of Justice reversed the General Court.[65] While acknowledging that the actions were adopted formally by the ESM, and thus were not subject to the annulment action, which was inadmissible,[66] the ECB and the Commission did not cease to be Treaty institutions even if they were 'borrowed' by the ESM, and were subject to their Treaty obligations, in particular the Commission, as the guardian of the Treaties,[67] and thus damages claim was considered admissible.

4.10 Secondly, some financial stability measures are formalized in 'soft law' acts,[68] which are hard to classify, and thus it is unclear which act, if any, should be challenged. The presence of non-reviewable acts is not easy to accept for European courts that have emphasized that the EU is a Union of law. Thus, even if some of these acts may not be challengeable under the annulment procedure under Article 263 TFEU, which is conceived for acts intended to produce legal effects vis-à-vis third parties,[69] leaving out opinions and recommendations, it is still possible to use the preliminary reference procedure, where, by answering questions from domestic courts on matters of EU law, the Court of Justice can revise (and annul) any legal acts by EU institutions, agencies and bodies[70] more generally,[71] and the actions in damages, which is also relatively open.[72] The use of MoUs is widespread for reasons of pragmatism, since they can address technical problems without the formalities of Treaties and other instruments,[73] but for this same reason, ie since they are not formal acts, their justiciability is challenging, as it depends on their content: they may simply be declarations of good intentions, but also contemplate serious commitments on relevant matters of policy. EU courts have used a 'substance over form' approach since early cases, considering an 'administrative agreement' between the Commission and the United States, for the application of their respective competition laws as an 'international Treaty' with 'legal effects', and thus null for lack of competence by the Commission,[74] while some 'guidelines' on barriers to trade lacked any legal effect.[75] MoUs are often used to outline the measures that must be adopted by the recipients of financial assistance, and thus can have legal relevance. In *Florescu* the Court of Justice analysed an MoU concluded between the European Union, represented by the Commission, and Romania, to lay down the terms and conditions to grant

---

[64] Case T-289/13 *Ledra Advertising Ltd v European Commission and European Central Bank (ECB)* ECLI:EU:T:2014:981, 45: '[A]lthough the ESM Treaty entrusts the Commission and the ECB with certain tasks relating to the implementation of the objectives of that Treaty, it is apparent from the case-law of the Court of Justice that the duties conferred on the Commission and the ECB within the ESM Treaty do not entail any power to make decisions of their own and, moreover, that the activities pursued by those two institutions within the ESM Treaty solely commit the ESM (Case C-370/12 Pringle [2012] ECR, paragraph 161).'
[65] Joined Cases C-8/15 P to C-10/15 P *Ledra Advertising v Commission and ECB* [2016] ECLI:EU:C:2016:701.
[66] ibid para 53.
[67] ibid paras 57–60.
[68] Compare Niamh Moloney, 'Banking Union and the Charter of Fundamental Rights' in Chiara Zilioli and Karl-Philipp Wojcik (eds), *Judicial Review in the European Banking Union* (Edward Elgar Publishing 2021) 209–20.
[69] Consolidated version of the Treaty on the Functioning of the European Union (TFEU) [2012] OJ C326, art 263.
[70] ibid art 267.
[71] Case C-322/88 *Salvatore Grimaldi v Fonds des maladies professionnelles* [1989] ECLI:EU:C:1989:646, para 8.
[72] TFEU (n 69) art 340.
[73] For a sharp and succinct analysis see Alberto De Gregorio Merino, 'Memoranda of Understanding: A Critical Taxonomy' (ECB Legal Conference 2019) 253.
[74] Case C-327/91 *French Republic v Commission of the European Communities* EU:C:1994:305.
[75] Case C-233/02 *France v Commission of the European Communities* EU:C:2004:173.

financial assistance to a non-Euro country facing difficulties with its balance of payments.[76] It held that:

> [T]he Memorandum of Understanding gives concrete form to an agreement between the EU and a Member State on an economic programme, negotiated by those parties, whereby that Member State undertakes to comply with predefined economic objectives in order to be able, subject to fulfilling that agreement, to benefit from financial assistance from the EU', and was thus 'an act by an EU institution'.[77]

The MoU was, thus, justiciable. In *Ledra* the MoU between the ESM and Cyprus was subject to the ESM Treaty (a non-EU treaty) and not reviewable by the Court of Justice,[78] but when *consenting* to the MoU on behalf of the ESM the Commission was subject to the Treaties, and could not sign if the MoU was contrary to them.[79] Nonetheless, the Court held that an act by the Commission as part of the ESM was formally an ESM act, and not attributable to the Commission for purposes of an annulment action,[80] and the Court did not clarify the scope and limits of this non-attributability,[81] and any action against a MoU affecting the rights of individuals (eg investors) would still need to clear the *Plaumann* test on standing. If a MoU leaves a state discretion as to how to implement the measures, individual plaintiffs will lack a 'direct and individual concern' in the measures.[82] This problem also arises outside MoUs. In *Steinhoff*[83] the General Court considered the restructuring of the Greek public debt, including a 'haircut' (ie reduction in nominal value of the credit) in accordance with the applicable collective action clause (CAC) on all bondholders including the non-consenting minority. The ECB had provided an Opinion under Article 127(4) and Article 282(5) TFEU to Greece, supportive of such restructuring. Minority bondholders sued the ECB for failing to alert Greece that the restructuring would breach their fundamental right to property (Article 17 of the Charter), and the General Court dismissed the action finding the restructuring necessary of securing the stability of the Euro Area banking system, and not disproportionate. The subsequent appeal was dismissed by the CJEU as being, in part, manifestly inadmissible and in part manifestly unfounded.[84]

---

[76] Case C-258/14 *Florescu and Others* ECLI:EU:C:2017:448, 33.
[77] ibid 34–35: 'The Memorandum of Understanding gives concrete form to an agreement between the EU and a Member State on an economic programme, negotiated by those parties, whereby that Member State undertakes to comply with predefined economic objectives in order to be able, subject to fulfilling that agreement, to benefit from financial assistance from the EU … As an act whose legal basis lies in the provisions of EU law mentioned in paragraphs 31 to 33 of the present judgment and concluded, in particular, by the European Union, represented by the Commission, the Memorandum of Understanding constitutes an act of an EU institution.'
[78] *Ledra 2016* (n 65) 50.
[79] ibid para 53.
[80] ibid para 55: '[T]he duties conferred on the Commission and ECB within the ESM Treaty, important as they are, do not entail any power to make decisions of their own. Further, the activities pursued by those two institutions within the ESM Treaty solely commit the ESM.' See *Pringle* (n 63) 161.
[81] Dariusz Adamski, 'Judicial Review of Economic and Financial Governance MoUs: Between Legal Impeccability and Economic Flaws' (ECB Legal Conference, Building Bridges: Central Banking Law in an Interconnected World 2019) 267 https://www.ecb.europa.eu/pub/pdf/other/ecb.ecblegalconferenceproceedings201912~9325c45957.en.pdf (accessed 21 September 2022).
[82] ibid 269.
[83] Case T-107/17 *Steinhoff and Others v ECB* ECLI:EU:T:2019:353.
[84] Case C-571/19 *EMB Consulting and Others v ECB* ECLI:EU:C:2020:208.

1.3 Justiciability of central banks' decisions

Liability of central banks is often presented, from a financial stability perspective, as a threat to independence and the proper performance of central bank functions.[85] Yet, how realistic is this prospect, if it fails to acknowledge that there may be important nuances? In general, courts are deferential towards central banks' monetary policy decisions. Excluding liability of individual members for monetary policy decisions, and promoting self-restraint in general, may be desirable. Conversely, a blanket exemption from justiciability may undermine central banks' legitimacy if judicial review is an important part of accountability.

4.11

Studies suggest that a large number of central bank laws exclude or limit central bank liability,[86] although they are less detailed as to what kind of liability (criminal, civil, administrative).[87] Immunity often encompasses the 'central bank' itself, and more often the 'members' of decision-making bodies, or 'staff'.[88] Yet, details matter to understand how exemptions are construed. The Bank of England (BoE) Act treats the BoE (including directors, officers, employees, or agents) as having immunity in its monetary and financial stability functions,[89] but not for acts in bad faith, or in contravention of human rights.[90] In the United States, the federal government has sovereign immunity and cannot be sued unless it has waived its immunity and consented to be sued. General statutes like the Federal Tort Claims Act (tort lawsuits), or the Tucker Act (contract lawsuits) are partial, not blanket waivers. Many statutes also waive immunity with 'sue or be sued' clauses,[91] and the Administrative Procedure Act provides a general waiver for agency acts.[92] Contract lawsuits have been rejected on the basis of (non-waived) immunity, against Federal Reserve Banks,[93] which are not considered 'agencies' (and thus not covered by the APA's waiver). Federal courts tend to consider lawsuits against the Federal Open Market Committee (FOMC) as non-justiciable, for lack of standing or other doctrines. In *Bryan v FOMC*, the plaintiff challenged the FOMC as an unwarranted delegation of powers by Congress; the court held that the plaintiff had not shown an injury different from that of any other citizen.[94] In *Riegle* the court could not deny standing to the plaintiff, a senator, but threw the complaint out using the doctrine of equitable discretion,[95] because he could still sue as a private plaintiff. Yet, in *Committee for Monetary Reform*, the courts applied a new, more restrictive tests for standing to sue and denied standing to a private plaintiff.[96] Then, in *Melcher v FOMC*, the D.C. District Court reconciled both rulings, thus denying standing to the plaintiff as a private citizen, but granting it to him as a legislator disapplying the doctrine of equitable discretion.[97] However, on appeal

4.12

---

[85] BIS, 'Issues in the Governance of Central Banks: A Report from the Central Bank Governance Group' (2009) 138; Asraf Khan, 'Legal Protection: Liability and Immunity Arrangements of Central Banks and Financial Supervisors' (IMF WP/18/176).
[86] ibid 17–18.
[87] ibid para 21.
[88] ibid para 22.
[89] BoE Act, s 244.
[90] ibid s 244(3).
[91] See eg 12 USC s 1819(a) (FDIC may 'sue and be sued ... in any court of law or equity').
[92] APA, s 702.
[93] *Research Triangle Institute v Board of Governors of the Federal Reserve System* 132 F 3d 985, 988 ff (4th Cir 1997).
[94] *Bryan v Federal Open Market Committee* 235 F Supp 877, 882 (D Mont 1964).
[95] *Riegle v FOMC* 656 F 2d 873 (DC Cir 1981).
[96] *Committee for Monetary Reform v Board of Governors* No 83-1730 (DDC 26 October 1983) aff'd, 766 F 2d 538 (DC Cir 1985).
[97] *Melcher v Federal Open Market Committee* 644 F Supp 510 (DDC 1986).

the Circuit Court applied equitable discretion, and considered the case non-justiciable.[98] In the Circuit Court's view, considerations of principle on the separation of powers, and courts' limited jurisdiction, at the core of equitable discretion, were unaffected by justiciability concerns.

4.13 A third example is the ECB, created as a supranational institution, but not referred to as an 'EU institution' in the Treaties, which together with other features (eg financial independence) questioned whether it could be a body outside EU Traties. In the *OLAF* case the issue was whether the ECB could be subject to the European Anti-Fraud Office (OLAF) dependent of the European Commission.[99] The Court held that it was subject to it, as it 'falls squarely within the Community framework'.[100] While the ECB's 'privileges and immunities' were those necessary for the performance of its tasks, its independence did not mean 'separation',[101] and its accountability should not affect its ability to perform its functions independently.[102] The ESCB Protocol subjects the ECB (i) to judicial review by the CJEU, and to damages claims like other institutions,[103] (ii) to national courts in its dealings with debtors and creditors;[104] and (iii) to the CJEU the disputes over the fulfilment of their duties by national central banks. The ECB is subject to the Privileges and Immunities of the EU and, like other EU institutions, its acts cannot be reviewed by national courts (but it is treated like any other institution). A recent discussion of the liability regime of national central banks in light of the principle of ECB independence and of the prohibition of monetary financing was centre stage in *Banka slovenije*,[105] where the Grand Chamber of the CJEU concluded that a liability regime under which a national central bank is required to pay compensation for losses arising as a result of the exercise of (non-monetary policy) statutory powers (in the Slovenian case: banks' crisis management) is not in itself incompatible with the principle of independence pursuant to Article 130 TFEU, unless such a liability regime ultimately affects the central bank's ability to perform its ESCB tasks effectively, by potentially depriving the central bank of a substantive part of its resources or profits. The Court also held that a central bank's liability regime which may be triggered even if the central bank had fully complied with the rules, and thus without the need to prove a serious breach of the duty of case violates the prohibition of monetary financing under Article 123 TFEU. Finally, although plaintiffs are subject to the strict test of standing if they bring an annulment claim, the same does not happen if they bring proceedings before national courts, and then raise a question over the validity of ECB acts, which gives rise to a preliminary reference before the Court of Justice. This has resulted in extremely important cases (which will be considered in next sections).

---

[98] *John Melcher, Honorable Member, United States Senate, Appellant v Federal Open Market Committee, and Others* 836 F 2d 561 (DC Cir 1987).
[99] Case C-11/00 *Commission of the European Communities v European Central Bank* ECLI:EU:C:2003:395.
[100] ibid para 92.
[101] ibid 144: 'recognition that the ECB has such independence does not have the consequence of separating it entirely from the European Community and exempting it from every rule of Community law'. ibid 135.
[102] ibid paras 137–39, 181. The Court also held that an ECB decision on fraud prevention, where it arrogated to itself the sole power to pursue such matters (internally) was unlawful, as it 'established a separate system peculiar to the ECB'.
[103] Article 35.1 and 35.3 Protocol 4.
[104] Article 35.2 Protocol 4.
[105] Case C-45/21 *Banka Slovenije and Republic Slovenije* ECLI:EU:C:2022:670.

2 Justiciability issues in regulatory, supervisory, and crisis management decisions

Regulatory, supervisory, and crisis management acts are a more conventional exercise of public authorities' powers than financial stability or monetary measures, but they raise their own challenges. These result from (i) the exclusions and limitations of liability, (ii) the exercise of agency discretion, (iii) the legal nature of soft law acts and (iv) the difficulty of meeting the test of standing to sue. **4.14**

2.1 Exclusions and limitations of liability

EU case law has focused on when national limitations of the liability of public (financial) authorities can go against EU law general principles, and undermine the effectiveness of EU legal provisions.[106] The cases *Paul and Others*,[107] and especially *Kantarev v Balgarska Narodna Banka*,[108] and *BT v Balgarska Narodna Banka*,[109] all involved liability for the defective transposition of the EU framework of Deposit Guarantee Schemes (DGS).[110] The specific substantive issues will be dealt with in a subsequent chapter, but one specific challenge was the constraints posed by German law (*Paul and Others*) and Bulgarian law (*Kantarev* and *BT*) for bringing liability claims against national authorities. In *Paul and Others* the client of a bank that did not adhered to any DGS sued national authorities, and, after a brief (perhaps too brief) analysis, the Court held that the DGS Directive did not impose obligations of result, but of means, and did not oppose national norms limiting the liability of *supervisory* authorities which should have made sure that the bank adhered to a DGS.[111] In *Kantarev* the Court distinguished the facts from those of *Paul and Others*, because here the bank (KTB) did form part of a DGS, and the EU law provision stated that depositors could make their claim when deposits became 'unavailable' (not when the bank's licence was withdrawn, as alleged by national authorities). The Court explained that individuals would have a right to reparation if three conditions were met: (i) the rule of EU law infringed must be intended to confer rights on them; (ii) the breach of that rule must be sufficiently serious; and **4.15**

---

[106] Compare for the Banking Union Martina Almhofer, 'The Liability of Authorities in Supervisory and Resolution Activities' in Chiara Zilioli and Karl-Philipp Wojcik (eds), *Judicial Review in the European Banking Union* (Elgar Financial Law and Practice 2021) 221–35; Martina Almhofer, *Die Haftung der EZB für rechtswidrige Bankenaufsicht* (Mohr Siebeck 2018); Phoebus Athanassiou, 'Non-Contractual Liability under the Single Supervisory Mechanism: Key Features and Grey Areas' (2015) 7 JIBLR 391; Raffaele D'Ambrosio, 'The Liability Regimes within the SSM and SRM' in Raffaele D'Ambrosio (ed), *Law and Practice of the Banking Union and of its governing Institutions (Cases and Materials)* (Quaderni di Ricerca Giuridica della Consulenza Legale, Bank of Italy, No 88, 2020) 527.

[107] Case C-222/02 *Paul and Others* ECLI:EU:C:2004:606.

[108] Case C-571/16 *Kantarev v Balgarska Narodna Banka* ECLI:EU:C:2018:807.

[109] Case C-501/18 *BT v Balgarska Narodna Banka* ECLI:EU:C:2021:249.

[110] Directive 94/19/EC of the European Parliament and of the Council of 30 May 1994 of the European Parliament and of the Council on deposit-guarantee schemes [30 May 1994] OJ L135 (applicable Case C-222/02 *Peter Paul, Cornelia Sonnen-Lütte and Christel Mörkens v Bundesrepublik Deutschland* ECLI:EU:C:2004:606 and *Kantarev* (n 108)) later repealed by Directive 2014/49/EU of the European Parliament and of the Council on deposit guarantee schemes [2014] OJ L173 (applicable in *BT v Balgarska Narodna Banka* (n 109)).

[111] Some authors note that the principle held in *Paul and Others* was dependent on the limited harmonization of deposit protection at the time and doubt that the same principle would still hold today Almhofer (n 106) 227; Danny Busch and Stef Keunen, 'Is the Statutory Limitation of Liability of the AFM and DNB Contrary to European Union Law' (4 March 2019) https://ssrn.com/abstract=3346240 or http://dx.doi.org/10.2139/ssrn.3346240 (accessed 21 September 2022).

(iii) there must be a direct causal link between that breach and the loss or damage sustained by the individuals'.[112] National courts had to apply those criteria, following the guidelines from the Court of Justice.[113] The Court also held that (i) the EU law provisions were unconditional and sufficiently precise, and thus had direct effect,[114] *and* that they conferred rights on individuals, as they were intended for the protection of depositors, and the determination of the unavailability of deposits 'triggers the deposit-guarantee mechanism and, accordingly, the reimbursement of depositors'.[115] (ii) The seriousness of the breach had to be assessed pursuant to a standard of a 'manifest and grave disregard by the Member State for the limits set on its discretion'. This depended on several factors: 'the clarity and precision of the rule breached, the measure of discretion left by that rule to the national authorities, whether any error of law was excusable or inexcusable, whether the infringement and the damage caused was intentional or involuntary', or the fact that the position taken by an EU institution may have contributed' to the national measures.[116] In the case at hand, the Court held that the discretion left by the DGS rules was quite circumscribed: the unavailability of deposits had to be expressly declared within five days,[117] and the actions of the central bank (Balgarska Narodna Banka, or BNB) suggested that it had doubts on the bank's ability to repay the deposits.[118] Despite this, neither the BNB nor other authorities had made a declaration of unavailability. After rejecting some allegedly attenuating circumstances raised by the national court,[119] the Court concluded that prima facie there appeared to be a sufficiently serious breach of EU law,[120] then leaving for the national court to assess the causal link between breach and harm.[121]

4.16 In *BT v Balgarska Norodna Banka* the problem were national (Bulgarian) legislation provisions, which subjected individuals' right to obtain compensation for damage caused by national authorities (a) first, to the prior annulment of the act or omission causing the damage, (b) secondly, to the intentional nature of the damage and, (c) thirdly, to the obligation for the individual to prove the existence of real and certain material damage at the time of bringing the action for compensation'.[122] The Court used *Kantarev's* test as a basis, namely (i) right-conferring provisions, (ii) sufficiently serious breach, and (iii) causal link, and held that national law could impose less onerous conditions, but not additional constraints.[123] As held in *Kantarev*, the DGS Directive provisions conferred individual rights, and there seemed to be a sufficiently serious breach.[124] Under the principle of procedural autonomy it is for national courts to determine the procedures to make good on the claim, *subject to* the principles of equivalence and effectiveness.[125] The principle of effectiveness examines 'whether a national

---

[112] *Kantarev* (n 108) 94.
[113] ibid para 95.
[114] ibid para 100.
[115] ibid para 103.
[116] ibid para 105.
[117] ibid paras 106–108.
[118] ibid para 109.
[119] *Kantarev* (n 108) paras 111–14. For the Court of Justice, to establish liability for breach of EU Law it was irrelevant (i) whether the DGS-Fund had sufficient resources to pay back all depositors, (ii) whether the deposits had been repaid after the restructuring measures, and (iii) whether the deposits had been repaid with interest accrued during the period when payment was suspended (June 2014–November 2014) (this was relevant for the actual harm, but not to establish the breach of EU Law).
[120] *Kantarev* (n 108) para 115.
[121] ibid para 116.
[122] *BT v Balgarska Narodna Banka* (n 109) para 112.
[123] ibid paras 113–14.
[124] ibid para 115.
[125] ibid para 116.

procedural provision makes it impossible or excessively difficult to exercise the rights conferred on individuals by the legal order of the Union.[126] Since the plaintiff could not fulfil first national law requirement, ie the annulment of the act giving rise to liability, because the individual lacked standing to challenge general acts, this was unreasonable, and contrary to the principle of effectiveness.[127] So was the second national law requirement, ie an intentional act, since EU law precludes national legislation requiring intentional harm in addition to a sufficiently serious breach of Union law[128] The third requirement, ie the 'reality and certainty of the harm' was admissible, but that it was apparent that the applicant had 'clearly quantified the damage which it allege[d] to have suffered', which was the interest on deposits from the suspension of payments and the amounts above the guaranteed amount.[129] For the Court, the loss above guaranteed amounts were not hypothetical because bankruptcy proceedings had not yet finished, as this affected the quantity of losses, not their reality for purposes of making the claim admissible.[130] Damages claims could encompass 'imminent damage foreseeable with sufficient certainty, even if the damage cannot yet be precisely assessed'.[131]

4.17 What do these cases have in common? First, DGS provisions are peculiar, because a faulty application can be linked to depositors' loss quite clearly. Secondly, the contrast between the Court's view in *Paul and Others* and in *Kantarev* and *BT* shows the growing assertiveness of the Court, as the DGS framework became more harmonized. Also, the last two cases show the Court's reckoning that respecting Member States' procedural autonomy can sometimes endanger EU law's effectiveness, a finding that is becoming increasingly recurring in the most recent case law of the European courts in the law of finance (and will be further discussed in next chapters of this book). Damages claims are detail-intensive, and sometimes finding that an EU provision grants 'rights to individuals' is not enough. Leaving the interpretation of open-textured concepts like 'serious breach' to national courts may leave the rules toothless. Here the Court all but plainly stated that Bulgarian authorities were liable, and that national limitations could not be used to effect a de facto exclusion of liability. This growing assertiveness on remedies to ensure harmonization of rights can be observed in other fields, such as the law of liability arising from false statements.[132]

2.2 Agency discretion, justiciability, and the legitimacy of delegation

4.18 Agency discretion can potentially affect the *justiciability* of regulatory and supervisory acts, or the standard of review applicable to them (as discussed in Chapter 3). In the US's experience, agency discretion cannot be so easily dissociated from the idea of 'limited jurisdiction', which may happen when an act is 'committed to discretion' of an agency,[133] and it is widely admitted that agencies can exercise *regulatory* discretion and many landmark cases involve the exercise of regulatory competences.

---

[126] ibid para 117.
[127] ibid paras 118–19.
[128] ibid para 121.
[129] ibid paras 122–23.
[130] ibid paras 124–25.
[131] ibid para 126.
[132] Compare Marco Lamandini and David Ramos Muñoz, 'Bankia: Can You Have a Capital Markets Union without Harmonised Remedies for Securities Litigation?' *EULawLive* (19 June 2021) 16–24.
[133] 5 USC s 701.

4.19 The position of European courts is different. First, there are considerations of principle. In the EU an act's 'regulatory' or 'supervisory' nature affects its justiciability through the doctrine of standing. Beyond that, in the *ESMA Short selling* the Court of Justice revised its doctrine of agency discretion, making it more flexible, and holding that agencies can be delegated powers (even regulatory powers) that entail the application of relatively open-textured provisions.[134] Yet, such delegation cannot entail 'broad discretion'. The element of distinction is the presence of legal constraints to agency action that make the decision amenable to judicial review.[135]

4.20 Yet, these considerations do not fully capture EU courts' approach to the justiciability of discretionary acts. In *SV Capital v EBA*, for example, the EBA adopted a decision *not to* investigate the Finnish and Estonian banking authorities. The Board of Appeal (BoA)[136] held that the EBA's broad discretion under the relevant provisions meant that the appeal was unfounded, but that it was, nonetheless, admissible.[137] Yet, the General Court held that the appeal was inadmissible, and that the BoA had acted beyond its competence when it found the action admissible.[138] The Court applied by analogy the case law in actions for annulment of Commission decisions refusing to initiate infringement proceedings, holding that, if the EBA is not bound to initiate proceedings, but had discretion to do so, the persons who lodge a complaint cannot challenge the decision not to investigate, unless those persons have special procedural rights.[139] Thus, in this context, the presence of discretion was used as a basis for the non-justiciability of the act, and for the annulment of the Board of Appeal's act stating otherwise. After the reform of the provisions in the EBA Regulation,[140] the BoA expressed some doubts about the impact of the new language on the admissibility of appeals against decisions not to investigate,[141] but the General Court in a later case preferred not to address those doubts and firmly maintained that such actions are inadmissible,[142] and the BoA subsequently followed this view.[143]

4.21 As another variation, one should look at the *Satabank* and *Pilatus Bank* cases. In *Satabank* the direct supervision of a 'less-significant' bank corresponded to national (Maltese) authorities, which had appointed a 'competent person' to oversee the business of said bank, but the appellant requested the ECB to exercise direct supervision over the bank, and to give instructions to such 'competent person'.[144] The ECB can use its initiative to take over direct supervision of smaller banks from national authorities to ensure 'consistent application of

---

[134] Case C-270/12 *United Kingdom v Parliament and Council* ECLI:EU:C:2014:18.
[135] ibid.
[136] *SV Capital v EBA*, BoA 2013-008; Ref EBA C 2013 002 (24 June 2013).
[137] Article 17(2) of the EBA Regulation stated that: 'Upon a request from one or more competent authorities, the European Parliament, the Council, the Commission or the Banking Stakeholder Group, or on its own initiative, and after having informed the competent authority concerned, *the Authority may investigate* the alleged breach or non-application of Union law.'
[138] Case T-660/14 *SV Capital v European Banking Authority* EU:T:2015:608, 46–50 (inadmissibility), 66–72 (BoA's lack of competence).
[139] *SV Capital* (n 138) 47–48, and authorities cited.
[140] The new text of art 17(2) of the EBA Regulation states that: 'Upon request from one or more competent authorities, the European Parliament, the Council, the Commission, the Banking Stakeholder Group, or *on its own initiative*, including *when this is based on well-substantiated information from natural or legal persons*, and after having informed the competent authority concerned, *the Authority shall outline how it intends to proceed with the case and, where appropriate, investigate* the alleged breach or non-application of Union law.'
[141] *Decision of A v ESMA*, D 2021 02 (12 March 2021).
[142] Order of the General Court of 10 August 2021 in Case T-760/20 *Jakeliūnas v ESMA*, EU:T:2021:512, 26–40.
[143] *Decision of C v EBA*, BoA-D-2022-01 (7 July 2022).
[144] Order of the General Court in Case T-494/20 *Satabank v ECB* ECLI:EU:T:2021:797.

high supervisory standards',[145] and it enjoys broad discretion, and here the appellant's ultimate goal was to make the ECB give instructions to the competent person *in order to* allow the bank shareholders' lawyer to have access to its premises and resources to perform representation duties, ie it bore no relationship with the need to 'ensure high supervisory standards'.[146] Yet, the Court examined the substance of the pleas without ruling first on admissibility for lack of ECB's competence to give instructions to the competent person given the link between admissibility and merits, and the action's manifest lack of foundation in law. In *Pilatus* the General Court dismissed the appellant's allegation that the ECB should have exercised direct supervision over a Maltese bank, because failing to do so meant that the licence withdrawal had not truly been an ECB decision, but a fait accompli of Maltese authorities;[147] the Court held that the ECB's competence to exercise direct supervision was an option, not an obligation, to be exercised to ensure the consistency of 'high supervisory standards', and the appellants had not substantiated why not acting had resulted in a breach of those standards.[148]

4.22 The reverse example is *Landeskreditbank* where direct supervision corresponded to the ECB because the bank was a 'significant institution', but the bank nonetheless alleged that the ECB should have exercised its discretion to leave supervision to national authorities due to its 'special circumstances'.[149] EU Courts, instead of finding the decision non-reviewable, manifestly inadmissible, or exercising a cursory review, took the opportunity to develop some basic principles of the multi-level exercise of competences in the Banking Union.

4.23 Finally, at the other extreme, in the *Banque Postale* cases, where the ECB had discretion to exclude certain exposures from the denominator of the leverage ratio, the General Court used a finalistic interpretation of the specific provisions to effectively 'flip' them, by forcing the ECB to justify its refusal to exclude the exposures, with a relatively demanding evidentiary burden to do so (notably, however, the General Court took this approach one step further in *Crédit Lyonnais I*, but this was appealed, and annulled by the Court of Justice in *Crédit Lyonnais II*, which means that the tip of the scale is not fully clear).[150] This sits in contrast with a more pro-agency approach followed in the *ABLV v SRB*[151] case, where the General Court first recalled its standard of review of complex economic assessments, then qualified it by noting that the fact that 'the SRB does have a margin of discretion [in taking its final determination on the failing or likely to fail of a credit institution] does not mean that the EU courts must refrain from reviewing the SRB's interpretation of the economic data on which the decision is based', and the courts must establish 'not only whether the evidence relied on was factually accurate, reliable and consistent, but also whether the evidence contained all the relevant information which must be taken into account in order to assess a complex

---

[145] SSM Regulation, art 6(5)(b).
[146] *Satabank* (n 144) paras 32–35.
[147] Case T-27/19 *Pilatus Bank v ECB* EU:T:2022:46; at the time of writing the appeal is pending in Joined Cases C-750/21 P and C-256/22 P, *Pilatus Bank plc v ECB* but Advocate General Kokott, adopting an (overly, in our view) wide notion of preparatory acts (including prior national decisions to suspend voting rights, to impose a moratorium on the authorisations of bank transactions and to appoint a competent person) in composite proceedings concerning the withdrawal of the bank's license in her Opinion delivered on 25 May 2023 ECLI:EU:C:2023:431 (paras 95 and 103), proposed that the Court should set aside the judgment of the General Court..
[148] ibid 49–54.
[149] Case T-122/15 *Lendeskreditbank Baden-Württemberg v ECB* EU:T:2017:337; Case C-450/17 P *Lendeskreditbank Baden-Württemberg v ECB* EU:C:2019:372.
[150] Case T-733/16 *Banque Postale v ECB* ECLI:EU:T:2018:477. See also Case T-504/19 *Crédit Lyonnais v ECB* ECLI:EU:T:2021:185 and Case C-389/21 P *ECB v Crédit Lyonnais* ECLI:EU:C:2023:368.
[151] Case T-280/18 *ABLV Bank AS v SRB* ECLI:EU:T:2022:429, paras 91–94.

situation and whether it was capable of substantiating the conclusion drawn from it', but then concluded that in order to establish a manifest error of assessment such as to justify the annulment of the contested decision, 'the evidence adduced by the applicant must be sufficient to make the factual assessments used in the decision in question implausible'.

4.24 In summary, European courts' position on the justiciability of discretionary acts is more pragmatic than doctrinal. The intricacies of each case weigh more heavily than any theory of delegation and separation of powers. As a matter of principle, delegating to agencies is lawful, as long as the applicable provisions are precise enough to allow for court review (*ESMA Short selling*). However, an agency's decision *not to* exercise initiative to investigate may be non-reviewable, unless the complaint is filed by some privileged plaintiffs (*SV Capital*). Yet, for the ECB's decision *not to* exercise its power of initiative to 'flip' the default distribution of supervisory powers, the Courts may opt to declare a complaint 'manifestly unfounded', or even to use the case to lay out considerations of principle and finality (*Landeskreditbank*). Such finalistic approach may be even used to curtail discretion in practice (*Banque Postale*), despite a well-established approach to respect in the review the outcome of such discretion in the assessment of complex economic situations, unless such assessments prove implausible (*ABLV v SRB*). All this despite the ESAs and the SRB are 'agencies' and the ECB is a Treaty 'institution'. Since EU law of finance is a work-in-progress, and US numerous doctrines of discretion have not led to greater clarity or predictability, this may not be a bad approach.

2.3 Soft law acts in financial regulation and supervision: justiciability, legal relevance, and control of shadow legislation

4.25 Soft law acts present a pervasive problem in financial regulation and supervision. Typically, acts formally recognized as directly binding must undergo long procedures. Thus, public authorities will resort to guidelines, memoranda, notes, letters, and a plethora of other tools where the authority or its staff declare how they interpret the law, and intend to apply it. The two main problems are (i) whether these acts are challengeable, (ii) what are their legal effects, and (iii) whether courts can consider them as a circumvention of the more onerous procedural requirements for other acts.

4.26 In the United States, courts have dealt with the problem of reviewability using the 'ripeness' requirement and similar tests. Generally, 'legislative rules' have the 'force and effect of law',[152] are adopted pursuant to the procedure envisaged in the specific statute, or the Administrative Procedure Act (APA), typically following notice-and-comment, and can be reviewed.[153] 'Interpretive rules,' by contrast, are issued 'to advise the public of the agency's construction of the statutes and rules which it administers',[154] do not require notice-and comment rulemaking, and 'do not have the force and effect of law'. Agencies have often successfully argued that soft law acts, such as 'interpretative rules', 'letters', etc. are not challengeable

---

[152] *Chrysler Corp v Brown* 441 US 281 S Ct (1979).
[153] The Administrative Procedure Act (APA) defines a 'rule' as 'an agency statement of general or particular applicability and future effect designed to implement, interpret, or prescribe law or policy' and regulates the procedure for 'rule making' 5 USC s 551(5). The APA distinguishes between two types of rules: So-called 'legislative rules' are issued through notice-and-comment rulemaking, see sections 553(b), (c), and have the 'force and effect of law'.
[154] *Shalala v Guernsey Memorial Hospital* 514 US 87, 99 (1995).

because they are not 'final',[155] and 'binding'.[156] What is 'final' and 'binding', however, is not easy to determine for soft law instruments. Sometimes guidance documents have been considered not 'final' or 'binding',[157] while in other cases, courts have weighed carefully the acts' practical effect,[158] holding that, whereby if the agency treats the rule as a legislative rule, ie as controlling in the field, as a basis for enforcement action, this can be also challengeable.[159]

On the second problem (circumvention), acts that are not formal rules, eg interpretative rules, statements made in the course of a litigation, etc.[160] are granted '*Auer* deference', similar or even greater than the '*Chevron* deference',[161] granted to legislative rules. Since agencies can use interpretations to circumvent the notice-and-comment procedure needed for legislative rules,[162] the D.C. Circuit, in *Paralyzed Veterans of America*[163] began to ask agencies to go through notice-and-comment when they changed their interpretations. However, this doctrine was overturned in *Perez, Secretary of Labor and Others v Mortgage Bankers Association*.[164] In a unanimous opinion, the Supreme Court used a textualist analysis to indicate that the APA's text excluded interpretative rules from 'notice-and-comment' procedures;[165] such exclusion also applied to the procedure to amend those rules, and the Circuit Court could not introduce new requirements in light of a reconstruction of the concept of 'rule'.[166] To the Supreme Court, the APA imposes *minimum* procedural requirements on agency acts, and the agencies themselves can impose further (or *maximum*) procedural requirements that courts can control.[167] This, however, left an even more important question, ie the revision of the *Auer* doctrine, which grants much leeway to agencies to change its own interpretations of its rules. Justice Sotomayor's Opinion held that courts had means to control the exercise of such interpretive powers,[168] but other justices, although concurring

4.27

---

[155] *Dietary Supplemental Coalition Inc v Kessler* 978 F 2d 560, 563 (9th Cir 1992); *Washington Legal Found v Kessler* 880 F Supp 26, 28 (DDC 1995). See Lars Noah, 'Administrative Arm-Twisting in the Shadow of Congressional Delegations of Authority' 5 Wis L Rev 983, 987 (1997).
[156] *Dalton v Specter* 511 US 462, 469–70 (1994); *Franklin v Massachusetts* 505 US 788, 798 (1992). Recommendations did not bind the President.
[157] *National Mining Association v McCarthy* 758 F 3d 243, 247 (DC Cir 2014).
[158] *McLouth Steel Prods Corp v Thomas* 838 F 2d 1317, 1321 (DC Cir 1988).
[159] *Appalachian Power Co v EPA* 208 F 3d 1015, 1022–23 (DC Cir 2000)
[160] *Auer v Robbins* [1997] 519 US 452, 462 (statements made during the course of litigation); *Coeur Alaska Inc v Southeast Alaska Conservation Council* 557 US 261, 277–82 (2009) (internal memorandum). Not granted eg to regulations that simply 'parrot or paraphrase' the text of statutory rules (*Gonzales v Oregon* 546 US 243, 256–57 (2006)).
[161] *Capital Network Systems Inc v FCC* 28 F 3d 201, 206 (DC Cir 1994) (*Auer* warrants even greater deference).
[162] Compare 5 USC s 553 (2012) and s 553(b)(3)(A).
[163] *Paralyzed Veterans of America v DC Arena LP* 117 F 3d 579, 584 (DC Cir 1997).
[164] *Perez v Mortgage Bankers Association* 135 S Ct 1199 (2015).
[165] ibid: 'The text of the APA answers the question presented ... states that unless "notice or hearing is required by statute", the Act's notice-and-comment requirement "does not apply ... to interpretative rules".' § 553(b)(A). This exemption of interpretive rules from the notice-andcomment process is categorical, and it is fatal to the rule announced in *Paralyzed Veterans of America v DC Arena LP* (n 163).
[166] *Perez v Mortgage Bankers Association* (n 164), citing *FCC v Fox Television Stations Inc* 556 US 502, 515 (2009). To the Circuit Court's focus on § 1 of the Act, which defines 'rule making' to include not only the initial issuance of new rules, but also 'repeal[s]' or 'amend[ments]' of existing rules', the Supreme Court held that the Circuit reading 'conflates the differing purposes of §§ 1 and 4 of the Act. Section 1 defines what a rule-making is. It does not, however, say what procedures an agency must use when it engages in rulemaking. That is the purpose of § 4. And § 4 specifically exempts interpretive rules from the notice-and-comment requirements that apply to legislative rules'.
[167] *Perez v Mortgage Bankers Association* (n 164), citing *Vermont Yankee Nuclear Power Corp v Natural Resources Defense Council Inc* 435 US 519, 524 (1978).
[168] *Perez v Mortgage Bankers Association* (n 164) (Sotomayor J): 'Even in cases where an agency's interpretation receives Auer deference, however, it is the court that ultimately decides whether a given regulation means what the agency says. Moreover, Auer deference is not an inexorable command in all cases' since courts can correct it when it is plainly erroneous, there are reasons to suspect that it does not reflect the agency's considered judgment, or conflicts with a previous interpretation.'

in the final ruling, were less sanguine, finding that the APA text, as interpreted in *Perez* plus *Auer*, gave agencies' control of the scope of the notice-and-comment requirement.[169] The Supreme Court's new justices have expressed their desire to limit deference, and curtail, if not eliminate, *Auer* deference.[170]

4.28 The US experience is enlightening, since the EU is now dealing with its own soft law challenges, including European Commission Communications or Guidelines, European Supervisory Authorities (ESAs) Regulatory Technical Standards (RTS)[171] and Implementing Technical Standards (ITS)[172] Guidelines and Recommendations,[173] or the Guidelines of the ECB[174] or SRB,[175] in supervision and resolution. The CJEU does not have an established 'doctrine', like *Chevron* or *Auer*, and views are more case-to-case, but agencies' interpretations are not binding on the courts, and agency 'discretion' is more constrained than '*Chevron* deference' or '*Auer* deference'.

4.29 In *Kotnik*[176] the Court of Justice adjudicated on the European Commission 'Banking Communication', which stated that the Commission would make the legality of Member State's use of public resources in financial assistance mechanisms for troubled financial institutions, under the EU State aid regime, conditional on the existence of burden-sharing by shareholders and creditors. The Court evaluated the legality of the Communication in a preliminary reference procedure, ie domestic courts asked a question to the Court of Justice. With regard to the deference granted, the Court held that:

> [t]he Commission enjoys wide discretion, the exercise of which involves complex economic and social assessments' and 'may adopt guidelines in order to establish the criteria on the basis of which it proposes to assess the compatibility, with the internal market, of aid measures envisaged by the Member States.[177]

Thus, the guidelines' effect was the Commission's self-limitation, since:

> In adopting such guidelines and announcing by publishing them that they will apply to the cases to which they relate, the Commission imposes a limit on the exercise of that discretion and cannot, as a general rule, depart from those guidelines, at the risk of being found to be in breach of general principles of law, such as equal treatment or the protection of legitimate expectations.

---

[169] *Perez v Mortgage Bankers Association* (n 164) (Scalia J). To him, as long as: 'the agency does not stray beyond the ambiguity in the text being interpreted, deference compels the reviewing court to 'decide' that the text means what the agency says'. To Justice Sotomayor's statement that 'deference is not an inexorable command in all cases', Scalia quipped that: 'Of course, an interpretive rule must meet certain conditions before it gets deference—the interpretation must, for instance, be reasonable—but once it does so it is every bit as binding as a substantive rule.'
[170] *Kisor v Wilkie* 139 S Ct 2400, 2425 (2019). *Auer* deference was 'saved' by the votes of the then four more liberal justices, and Chief Justice Roberts (5:4 majority).
[171] See art 10 of the Regulation 2019/2175: Amendment of Regulation (EU) No 1093/2010 establishing a European Supervisory Authority (European Banking Authority), Regulation (EU) No 1094/2010 establishing a European Supervisory Authority (European Insurance and Occupational Pensions Authority), Regulation (EU) No 1095/2010 establishing a European Supervisory Authority (European Securities and Markets Authority) (hereafter ESAs Regulations).
[172] ESAs Regulations (n 171) art 15.
[173] ibid art 16.
[174] Rules of Procedure of the ECB, art 17 https://eur-lex.europa.eu/legal-content/EN/TXT/?uri=legissum%3A01020302_1 (accessed 21 September 2022).
[175] SRB, 'About', https://www.srb.europa.eu/en/about (accessed 21 September 2022).
[176] Case C-526/14 *Kotnik and Others* ECLI:EU:C:2016:767.
[177] ibid para 80.

Conversely, Member States could rely on exceptional circumstances *other than* those contemplated in the guidelines, and the Commission had a duty to examine the circumstances case by case.[178] Thus, the guidelines were binding on the Commission, but could not impose 'independent obligations' on Member States.[179] In spite of this clever framing, in practice the Commission guidelines imposed additional criteria to comply with the State aid regime.

In *Kotnik* the Commission's guidelines were 'justiciable' via the preliminary reference procedure of dialogue between courts, under Article 267 TFEU. There the Court applies the more flexible *Grimaldi* test, under which the Court considers that Article 267 TFEU confers on the Court jurisdiction to decide on the *validity* and *interpretation* of *all* acts of EU institutions and bodies 'without exception', including non-binding acts.[180] Conversely, if the guidelines had been directly challenged by, eg banks, or investors, under an *annulment* action under Article 263 TFEU, which leaves out 'opinions and recommendations,'[181] their justiciability would have been subject to the more demanding '*ERTA* test' for acts 'intended' to have legal effects,[182] which the Court has applied to guidelines,[183] codes of conduct,[184] communications,[185] or letters.[186] In *Belgium v Commission*, despite pressure to revise its position, the Court maintained that: **4.30**

> [A]ny provisions ... whatever their form, which are intended to have binding legal effects are regarded as 'challengeable acts' ...' and, in order to determine this, 'it is necessary to examine the substance of that act and to assess those effects on the basis of objective criteria, such as the content of that act, taking into account, as appropriate, the context in which it was adopted and the powers of the institution which adopted the act.[187]

The Court disregarded the AG Opinion, which advised to the Court to consider factors that, resulted in the act's 'having legal effects', even if it was not binding.[188]

Thus, to the Court (i) the justiciability of a soft law act is bifurcated, with two separate tests for the preliminary reference, and the annulment procedure; and (ii) soft law acts are not binding, for the Court, or Member States' authorities. Yet, the weaknesses of this framework are evident. First, the bifurcation of admissibility tests clashes with the Court's own *TWD* doctrine, whereby if a person who *'undoubtedly'* has standing under the annulment procedure (Article 263 TFEU) does not make use of that procedure, it cannot later make use of the preliminary reference procedure (Article 267 TFEU) for the same purpose,[189] ie treating **4.31**

---

[178] ibid para 41: 'The adoption of a communication such as the Banking Communication does not therefore relieve the Commission of its obligation to examine the specific exceptional circumstances relied on by a Member State, in a particular case.'
[179] ibid paras 43–44.
[180] *Grimaldi* (n 71) para 8. See also *Florescu* (n 76) para 1.
[181] TFEU (n 69) art 263 states that: '[T]he Court of Justice of the European Union shall review the legality of legislative acts, of acts of the Council, of the Commission and of the European Central Bank, *other than recommendations and opinions*.'
[182] Case C-22/70 *Commission v Council* ECLI:EU:C:1971:32.
[183] Case C-366/88 *France v Commission* ECLI:EU:C:1990:348 and C-443/97 *Spain v Commission* ECLI:EU:C:2000:190.
[184] Case C-303/90 *France v Commission* ECLI:EU:C:1991:424.
[185] Case C-325/91 *France v Commission* ECLI:EU:C:1993:245 and C-57/95 *France v Commission* ECLI:EU:C:1997:164.
[186] Case C-308/95 *Netherlands v Commission* ECLI:EU:C:1999:477.
[187] Case C-16/16 P *Belgium v Commission* ECLI:EU:C:2018:79, 31–32.
[188] See ibid Opinion of AG Bobek ECLI:EU:C:2017:959.
[189] Case C-188/92 *TWD Textilwerke Deggendorf* EU:C:1994:90. See more recently Case C-135/16 P *Georgsmarienhütte and Others v Bundesrepublik Deutschland* ECLI:EU:C:2018:582.

both proceedings as part of a *unified* system of remedies. Secondly, if soft law measures are perceived as binding, and applied as such, they can be used to circumvent formal procedures, or the absence of regulatory competence altogether. Case law shows that European courts have been pragmatic, and grant legal relevance to soft law measures when it was expedient, but without a clear wish to address the shortcomings of their framework.

4.32 In *United Kingdom v European Central Bank*[190] the Court annulled the Eurosystem Oversight Policy Framework published by the ECB in July 2011, which imposed a 'location requirement' on central counterparties (CCPs), ie CCPs settling euro-denominated transactions should be incorporated in the euro area and have full managerial control and responsibility over core functions exercised from within that area. The Court held that, to determine whether an act is capable of having legal effects, and thus can be challenged under an annulment action, it is necessary to examine its wording and context, its substance, and the intention in a way in which the parties concerned could reasonably have perceived that act to be assessed. The policy framework used mandatory wording and was specific enough to be directly applicable, and since its addressees, ie Eurozone Member States' regulatory authorities could conclude that they were required to enforce compliance with the location requirement, a CCP not meeting the location criteria could be denied access to other operators in the processing chain for securities transactions, the Framework should be considered as having legal effects. Furthermore, the formulation of a location requirement for CCPs was 'equivalent to the addition of a new rule in the legal order', which was not in any pre-existing legal provision. The Court held that the 'location requirement' went beyond mere oversight and was tantamount to regulation, and the ECB competence over 'payment systems' under Article 127(2) TFEU did not extend to securities clearing and settlement systems. Thus, when the use of soft law was seen as a clear way to circumvent mandates and procedures.

4.33 In *BT v Balgarska Narodna Banka*,[191] a preliminary reference procedure, the Court found that the Bulgarian measures on deposit guarantees were incompatible with EU rules on Deposit Guarantee Schemes (DGS), and could give rise to state liability against plaintiffs who lost their right to immediate refund of their bank deposits, following its previous *Kantarev* case law.[192] However, given the non-compliance by Bulgarian law and authorities with EU deposit guarantees rules, the EBA had intervened, issuing a recommendation on measures to comply with EU rules on DGS.[193] The Court considered that the recommendation was an act that *had to be taken into consideration* by national authorities, and could be relied upon by the plaintiff, even if it was not directed to it,[194] and also a justiciable act under the preliminary reference procedure.[195] However, the recommendation stated, possibly to enhance expediency that, whereas the 'unavailability of deposits' required an express act, it could also be *implied* in other acts, such as the intervention of the institution.[196] This was said before *Kantarev*, where the Court had held that deposit 'unavailability' required *a formal act* and an express declaration. Thus, the Court held that the EBA's view was contrary to the Court's

---

[190] Case T-496/11 *United Kingdom v European Central Bank* ECLI:EU:2015:133.
[191] *BT v Balgarska Narodna Banka* (n 109).
[192] The Court also found that limitations imposed by Bulgarian law on state liability were also illegal.
[193] EBA, *Recommendation to the Bulgarian National Bank and Bulgarian Deposit Insurance Fund on action necessary to comply with Directive 94/19/EC* (EBA/REC/2014/02, 17 October 2014).
[194] *BT v Balgarska Narodna Banka* (n 109) paras 78–82.
[195] ibid paras 82–83.
[196] ibid: '[I]n the absence of an explicit act establishing the unavailability of KTB's deposits within the meaning of Article 1(3)(i) of Directive 94/19, the decision taken by the BNB to place KTB under special supervision and to suspend KTB's obligations was tantamount to such a finding.'

finding in *Kantarev*,[197] and thus invalid to that effect, and the national court could not rely on that premiss to assess compliance with EU law.[198]

In *Crédit Mutuel*[199] the ECB exercised consolidated supervision over a financial group of co- **4.34** operative entities with a central body that was not a credit institution, and one of the group entities challenged the decision before the Administrative Board of Review (ABoR) and the General Court. The ABoR largely relied on the guidelines issued by the European Committee of Banking Supervisors (ECBS) the predecessor of the European Banking Authority (EBA) in its (key) finding that the status of the central body as a credit institution was not a requirement to exercise consolidated supervision. The Court considered that such guidelines could be relevant to establish the interpretative 'context' of the relevant legislative provision.[200] However, it also clarified that:

> The interpretation of the relevant legislation by an administrative authority cannot bind the EU Courts which have exclusive jurisdiction to interpret EU law, under Article 19 TEU',[201] and thus, that 'although the ECBS guidelines are an aspect which might be taken into account by the EU Courts, they cannot be accorded any particular weight.[202]

Likewise, in *ABLV v SRB* the General Court examined the issue whether the failing or likely to fail assessment performed by the ECB and the SRB under Article 18 of the SRM Regulation was compliant with the EBA Guidelines promoting convergence of supervision and resolution practices regarding the interpretation of the different circumstances when an institution shall be considered failing or likely to fail, and concluded that, although such Guidelines list several factors that in most cases need to be taken into consideration, it is not incompatible with the guidelines that 'there might be situations where meeting just one condition, depending on its severity and prudential impact, would be sufficient to trigger resolution'.[203] In turn in the *Tercas* case[204] the fact that the Commission had adopted a state aids decision in compliance with a provision of its Banking communication on state aids in the banking sector which made also relevant as state aids, under certain conditions, the interventions of DGS did not preclude the European courts from annulling the state aids decision.

The more frontal challenge to the Courts' approach to soft law came in *Fédération Bancaire* **4.35** *Française (FBF) v Autorité de contrôle prudentiel et de résolution (ACPR)*,[205] where the French Banking Federation (FBF) sought the annulment before the Conseil d'État (Council of State) of a notice by the French Authority for Prudential Supervision and Resolution (ACPR) stating that it would comply with the European Banking Authority (EBA) Guidelines on

---

[197] ibid paras 96–99.
[198] ibid paras 100–101.
[199] Case C-152/18 P *Crédit Mutuel Arkéa v ECB* ECLI:EU:C:2019:810. Compare Francesco Martucci, 'The Crédit Mutuel Arkéa Case: Central Bodies and the SSM, and the Interpretation of National Law by the ECJ' in Chiara Zilioli and Karl-Philipp Wojcik (eds), *Judicial Review in the European Banking Union* (Edward Elgar Publishing 2021) 504–509.
[200] *Crédit Mutuel* (n 199) 74.
[201] ibid para 75.
[202] ibid para 78.
[203] *ABLV Bank AS v SRB* (n 151) para 113.
[204] Joined Cases T-98/16, T-196/16 and T-198/16 *Italy v Commission* ECLI:EU:2019:T:2019:167 and Case C-425/19 *Commission v Italy, Fondo Interbancario di tutela dei depositi, Banca d'Italia and Banca Popolare di Bari* ECLI:EU:C:2021:154.
[205] Case C-911/19 *Fédération bancaire française (FBF) v Autorité de contrôle prudentiel et de résolution (ACPR)* ECLI:EU:C:2021:599.

product oversight and governance arrangements for retail banking products.[206] The FBF alleged that the EBA's guidelines were invalid because the EBA lacked competence to issue them, and the French court made a preliminary reference to the Court of Justice, asking whether a challenge against the guidelines was admissible and whether the guidelines were invalid. In his Opinion, AG Bobek advised the Court to consider the Guidelines as 'challengeable acts', under a broader interpretation of Article 263 TFEU,[207] by considering acts that, taking into account the broader context, produced legal effects (in this case on the individual banks). This In the AG's view, would help to mitigate the effects of the *TWD* doctrine, and address other frictions arising from the duality of actions (annulment under Article 263 TFEU, and preliminary reference under Article 267 TFEU).[208] The AG was also very clear that he was concerned that allowing the Union agencies and bodies to issue non-binding measures with little judicial control would only 'encourage a further spread of 'crypto-legislation' in the form of soft law in the Union', raising problems of legitimacy, and overlapping quasi-regulation.[209]

4.36 The Court did not heed the AG's advice. It used its traditional approach to establish what measures create binding legal effects. By analysing the measures' language, and the fact that national authorities could refuse to abide by them, if they provided a justification, it concluded that these were neither binding measures for national authorities;[210] nor for financial institutions, since these only had to explain their reasons for non-compliance with the guidelines.[211] Thus, they could not be subject to an annulment procedure under Article 263 TFEU.[212] The Court also found that the Guidelines were valid, as their 'product governance' focus was sufficiently related to the 'corporate governance' provisions they allegedly used as a basis, which showed the Court's readiness to trust the EBA. The Court trusted all control over soft law acts to the fact that under the preliminary reference procedure ex Article 267 TFEU, they could be reviewed even though they lacked binding effect,[213] and the plaintiff needed not be 'directly and individually concerned' by the act,[214] as under the annulment procedure.

4.37 By way of summary, soft law acts are slippery, and a matter of concern on both sides of the Atlantic. Regulatory authorities succeed most of the time in rendering them non-justiciable, save for limited cases. However, whereas in the US, a long period where doctrines of deference have proliferated has given way to a reconsideration of the need for courts to rein in administrative discretion, in the EU the Courts are walking in the opposite direction, with limited justiciability coupled with a readiness to trust the agencies' judgment, although they have yet to meet in the middle (US Courts still grant greater deference to agencies). The majority in both the US Supreme Court and the Court of Justice still sufficiently trusts each

---

[206] Another French Banking Federation's challenge to EBA's guidelines, and notably EBA's loan origination guidelines (EBA/GL/2020/06), their interplay with the Mortgage Credit Directive 2014/71/EU as well as the French Prudential Supervision and Resolution Authority (ACPR) compliance with them, was subsequently dismissed by the Council of State, with decision on 22 July 2022, without the need for a further referral to the CJEU: compare *EU Law Live* (4 August 2022).
[207] Case C-911/19, *FBF v ACPR*, Opinion of AG Bobeck ECLI:EU:C:2021:294.
[208] ibid paras 112–19, 134.
[209] ibid paras 85–88.
[210] *FBF v ACPR* (n 205) paras 39–45.
[211] ibid para 46.
[212] This made it unnecessary to consider the issue of standing: the acts would not be subject to annulment action, and thus no question arose of the preliminary reference procedure being precluded.
[213] *FBF v ACPR* (n 205) paras 52–57.
[214] ibid paras 58–65.

court's ability to exercise proper review, and thus curtail abuses, but in both cases the court's position is not uncontested.

2.4 Challengeability of acts in complex proceedings

4.38 The problem of a formal lack of 'binding nature' spans beyond soft law, and is more pervasive in the presence of complex procedures, involving multiple steps. In the United States, to be binding, and thus reviewable, an act must mark the 'consummation' of the agency's decision-making process,[215] it must not be of a merely tentative or interlocutory nature,[216] and the action must be one by which 'rights or obligations have been determined,' or from which 'legal consequences will flow'.[217]

4.39 The approach is very similar in the EU, where 'only measures the legal effects of which are binding on, and capable of affecting the interests of, the applicant by bringing about a distinct change in his legal position are acts or decisions which may be the subject of an action for annulment'.[218] In this vein, 'intermediate measures' whose aim is to prepare the final decision are not, in principle, subject to an action for annulment, because, if EU courts adjudicate on a 'provisional opinion' they would decide on matters where the administrative authority has not yet had 'an opportunity to state its position and would as a result anticipate the arguments on the substance', confusing procedural stages both administrative and judicial, in a way contrary to the division of powers.[219] Furthermore, EU courts also consider 'confirmatory' or 'implementing' acts as not subject to challenge, ie those that contain 'no new factor' as compared with a previous measure.[220] This raises several issues, depending on whether the procedure involves (i) national and EU authorities (vertical procedures); (ii) several EU authorities (horizontal procedures); or (iii) a combination of both.

4.40 In vertical procedures the leading case is *Berlusconi Fininvest* case (*Berlusconi I*).[221] Mr Berlusconi, through Fininvest, held a qualifying holding in Mediolanum SpA, a financial holding company that controlled Banca Mediolanum. At the time of the original acquisition Mediolanum was not a bank, and no authorisation was required for qualifying holdings, but as this was extended also financial holding companies (in 2014), Fininvest and Mr Berlusconi applied, and were rejected by Italian authorities on grounds of suitability (ie 'fit-and-proper') requirements due to Mr Berlusconi's tax fraud convictions in 2013, but the decision was annulled by the Consiglio di Stato, who rejected the retroactive application of fit-and-proper requirements to holding companies, a decision that became *res judicata*. Later, however, a

---

[215] *Chicago & Southern Air Lines Inc v Waterman SS Corp* 333 US 103, 113 (1948).
[216] *Bennett v Spear* 520 US 154 (1997).
[217] *Port of Boston Marine Terminal Association v Rederiaktiebolaget Transatlantic* 400 US 62, 71 (1970).
[218] Case C-131/03 P *Reynolds Tobacco v Commission* ECLI:EU:C:2006:541, para 55; Case 60/81 *IBM v Commission* ECLI:EU:C:1981:264, para 9; Case C-123/03 P *Commission v Greencore* ECLI:EU:C:2004:783, para 44.
[219] Joined Cases C-463/10 P and C-475/10 P *Deutsche Post AG v Commission* [2011], ECLI:EU:C:2011:656, paras 50–51. See also case C-415/15 P *Stichting Woonpunt and Others v Commission* ECLI:EU:C:2017:216, and case law cited therein.
[220] Case C-334/17 P *Estonia v Commission* EU:C:2018:914,para 46; Case C-224/12 P *Commission v Netherlands and ING Groep* ECLI:EU:C:2014:213, para 69.
[221] Case C-219/17 *Silvio Berlusconi and Finanziaria d'investimento Fininvest SpA (Fininvest) v Banca d'Italia and Istituto per la Vigilanza Sulle Assicurazioni (IVASS)* ECLI:EU:C:2018:102. See the commentary by Filipe Brito Bastos, 'Judicial Review of Composite Administrative Procedures in the Single Supervisory Mechanism: Berlusconi' (2019) 56 CMLR 1355.

reverse merger between Mediolanum and Banca Mediolanum allowed a second assessment under the Single Supervisory Mechanism (SSM) rules[222] which involved a proposal by Bank of Italy, which proposed to reject the application for a qualifying holding, and a decision by the ECB, which followed the proposal (albeit not bound by it). Mr Berlusconi challenged the ECB act before the General Court, Bank of Italy's preparatory act before Italian courts, and also filed an 'azione di ottemperanza' also before the Italian Consiglio di Stato, to force compliance with the previous ruling. The Consiglio di Stato made a preliminary reference, which resulted in the ruling. The Court of Justice explained that there were two possible approaches in composite procedures: if EU authorities were not bound by the national authorities' decision, EU courts would control the legality of the final act (*Sweden v Commission*[223]), and if the EU authority was bound by the national decision, national courts would control the legality of the national act (*Borelli*[224]). The Court applied the *Sweden v Commission* test, and held that, in controlling the legality of the final act, the Court would also examine any irregularities in the preparatory act which may potentially render unlawful the final decision, because, where EU law does not divide between national and EU powers, but allocated 'exclusive decision-making power' to the latter, EU Courts have exclusive jurisdiction, which also means examining 'any defects vitiating the preparatory acts or the proposals of the national authorities that would be such as to affect the validity of that final decision',[225] ie EU courts are *exclusively competent to decide on the national leg of the procedure*.[226] The decision by the general Court (*Berlusconi II*) is examined in a subsequent section.[227] However, it is worth noting here that the General Court dismissed all appellant's pleas alleging about the illegality of the preparatory act, under the national leg of the procedure, because those pleas had been submitted before the European court only after *Berlusconi I* was decided, and thus after the application for annulment in *Berlusconi II* was lodged, and this could not be considered a new element of law, as it only confirmed a legal situation of which the appellant was aware at the time when he brought his appeal.

4.41 The CJEU has later confirmed these views. In *Iccrea Banca*[228] several decisions by Bank of Italy concerning the bank's contributions to the Single Resolution Fund (SRF) were challenged before Italian administrative courts, which considered themselves competent, because, in their view, Italian authorities played 'an active and decisive role' first during the determination and then during the raising of such contributions.[229] However, in the ruling following a preliminary reference by those courts, the CJEU reiterated its previous doctrine: the Single Resolution Board (SRB), the EU resolution agency, had exclusive competence to determine the contributions, and thus EU courts have exclusive jurisdiction to review the SRB acts.[230] Then, in *Portigon* the General Court came across a somewhat reverse

---

[222] SSM Regulation, art 15.
[223] Case C-64/05 P *Sweden v Commission* ECLI:EU:C:2007:802.
[224] Case C-97/91 *Oleificio Borelli v Commission* ECLI:EU:C:1992:491.
[225] *Berlusconi* (n 221) para 44.
[226] In this case, the final ruling of the Consiglio di Stato no 2890/2019 (3 May 2019) declared the action inadmissible.
[227] One of the authors was the external lawyer retained by the European Central Bank in this case (our comments on the judgment are therefore limited to a minimum). Compare also Giorgio Buono, 'Banking Authorisations and the Acquisition of Qualifying Holdings as Unitary and Composite Procedures and Their Judicial Review' in Chiara Zilioli and Karl-Philipp Wojcik (eds), *Judicial Review in the European Banking Union* (Elgar Financial Law and Practice 2021) 251–284.
[228] Case C-414/18 *Iccrea Banca v Banca d'Italia* ECLI:EU:C:2019:1036.
[229] ibid para 24.
[230] ibid paras 37–42.

problem, because the determination of the SRF's *ex ante* contributions by the SRB, as an act, was not directed to the bank, but to the National Resolution Authorities (NRAs) which had to issue their own acts to render it effective.[231] Nonetheless, the General Court found that the determination was a final, not a preparatory act, and thus the applicant bank had standing to sue, because, even if it was not 'directly' concerned (as the act was not directed to it) it was 'individually' concerned.[232]

4.42 Horizontal procedures, where different EU authorities are entrusted with different steps of the procedure also present their own issues. The easiest case concerns procedural, or interlocutory measures. In *Pilatus Bank v ECB*[233] the General Court considered that a challenge against *an ECB's email* requesting the applicant to direct its communications via a specifically appointed 'competent person'[234] was inadmissible, because the email did not produce legal effects distinct from the licence withdrawal decision, only limited effects typical of an intermediate procedural measure, without substantive effects.[235]

4.43 Other acts are more challenging. Despite the *ESMA Short selling* case arguably expanded the *Meroni* doctrine (as we already discussed in a Chapter 3), EU legislators are wary of delegating discretionary and/or regulatory competences to EU agencies. Thus European Supervisory Authorities (ESAs) only elaborate draft Regulatory Technical Standards (RTSs) or Implementing Technical Standards (ITSs) which, after endorsement by the Commission, become delegated regulations[236] or implementing regulations.[237] Intermediate measures with 'independent legal effects' can be challenged in an action for annulment only if the illegality cannot be remedied in an action brought against the final decision.[238] Otherwise, EU Courts can control both the legality of the agency's assessment *and* the Commission's discretion in reviewing the final act (*Artegodan*).[239] Although the CJEU has not decided on the justiciability of RTS or ITS, the Board of Appeal of the ESAs did in *Creditreform Rating AG v EBA*,[240] where it considered inadmissible the challenge by a rating agency of a draft ITS on the mapping of credit assessments by credit rating agencies,[241] as a preparatory act, based on the General Court's case law. Although not independently challengeable, the legality of the ITS could be reviewed with the final act since it had a 'decisive importance' for the Commission's decision.[242]

---

[231] Case T-365/16 *Portigon v SRB* ECLI:EU:T:2019:824.
[232] ibid paras 75–81.
[233] Case T-687/18 *Pilatus Bank v ECB* ECLI:EU:T:2019:542.
[234] ibid para 22.
[235] ibid paras 23–25.
[236] ESAs regulations (n 171), art 10.
[237] ibid art 15.
[238] Case C-650/18 *Hungary v Parliament* ECLI:EU:C:2021:426, 46, with references to Cases C-312/90 *Spain v Commission* EU:C:1992:282, 21 and 22; C-47/91, *Italy v Commission* EU:C:1992:284, 27 and 28; and C-463/10 P and C-475/10 P *Deutsche Post and Germany v Commission* EU:C:2011:656, paras 53, 54, 60.
[239] Case T-40/00, *Artedogan and Others v Commission* ECLI:EU:T:2002:283, 197–99.
[240] *Creditreform Rating AG v EBA*, BoA-D-2019-05 https://www.eba.europa.eu/about-us/organisation/joint-board-of-appeal/decisions.
[241] Draft implementing technical standards amending Implementing Commission Implementing Regulation (EU) 2016/1799 laying down implementing technical standards with regard to the mapping of credit assessments of external credit assessment institutions for credit risk in accordance with Articles 136(1) and 136(3) of Regulation (EU) No 575/2013 of the European Parliament and of the Council (Text with EEA relevance) (7 October 2016) on the mapping of ECAIs' credit assessments under Article 136(1) and (3) of Regulation (EU) No 575/2013.
[242] *Creditreform Rating AG v EBA* (n 240) 64. The BoA relied on *Artegodan* (n 239), as well as on Case T-725/15, *Arysta LifeScience Netherlands v European Food Safety Authority* ECLI:EU:T:2018:977 and Case T-311/06 *FMC Chemical SPRL v EFSA* ECLI:EU:T:2007:67.

4.44 Another scenario where horizontal procedures can reach extraordinary complexity is the implementation of a bank resolution scheme, where (i) the supervisory authority (eg the ECB) declares the bank as 'failing-or-likely to fail' (FOLTF), (ii) the resolution authority (eg the SRB) adopts a resolution scheme *or* may also decide that resolution is *not* in the public interest, *and* in the Single Resolution Mechanism (SRM) (iii) the Commission *endorses* the SRB decision, to make it binding, yet another residue of *Meroni*-related concerns about delegating discretionary competences, and (iv) the resolution scheme is addressed to the NRAS.[243] Thus, the question is which of these steps are challengeable.

4.45 In *ABLV Bank v ECB*, the ECB found the bank FOLTF, but resolution was *not* required by the public interest, and the bank was subject to liquidation under national insolvency law. The General Court held that the separate challenge of the FOLTF assessment by the ECB was inadmissible,[244] and the Court of Justice confirmed its decision.[245] The FOLTF assessment was a preparatory, or 'intermediate measure',[246] which lacked direct legal effects,[247] as it was only one of the elements pertaining to the adoption of the resolution scheme, not binding on the resolution authority.[248] The SRB could disagree with the ECB, or find an irregularity, and although this was unlikely, it was important to differentiate between the ECB's *auctoritas*, and the SRB's *potestas*.[249] Also, the FOLTF assessment was not analogous to the withdrawal of the banking licence by the bank supervisor.[250] The issue was taken a step forward in *ABLV v SRB*, where the General Court was asked to clarify whether the SRB, when finally adopting its decision whether or not to apply resolution following the ECB's FOLTF, was entitled to solely rely on the ECB's FOLTF assessment, without carrying out its own examination. The Court, somewhat formalistically (in our view), concluded that the SRB could indeed rely on such assessment without more, 'having regard to the broad discretion enjoyed by the SRB in accordance with case law … since the ECB was the institution best placed to carry out the FOLTF assessment'.[251] At the same time, the *ABLV* cases identified a red-line in composite proceedings which are both horizontal and vertical, clarifying eg that the proceeding leading to the determination whether or not resolution is in the public interest starts with the ECB FOLTF and ends with the SRB determination, which, even if it is a decision *not to* place the bank in resolution, is justiciable, but if the SRB decides that resolution is not in the public interest, the subsequent liquidation of a bank for which resolution is considered not in the public interest 'sits outside of any resolution scheme' and does not arise from the SRB decision on the non-application of the resolution.[252]

---

[243] Article 18 of Regulation 306/2014 (SRM Regulation) provides for the ECB's FOLTF assessment (no (1) paras 2–4), the SRB's adoption of a resolution scheme), and the Commission's endorsement and the communication to the NRAs.

[244] Case T-281/18 *ABLV Bank v ECB* EU:T:2019:296 and Case T-283/18 *Bernis and Others v ECB* ECLI:EU:T:2019:295; on appeal, Joined Cases C-551/19 P and C-552/19 P *ABLV and Others v ECB* ECLI:EU:C:2021:369. Compare Anna Gardella, 'Judicial Control of the Interface between the ECB and the SRB in the SRM' in Chiara Zilioli and Karl-Philipp Wojcik (eds), *Judicial Review in the European Banking Union* (Edward Elgar Publishing 2021) 461–72.

[245] *ABLV v ECB* (n 244). The judgment followed the Opinion of AG Campos Sanchez-Bordona (Joined Cases C-551/19 P and C-552/19 P *ABLV v ECB* [2021] Opinion of AG Sánchez-Bordona ECLI:EU:C:2021:16).

[246] *ABLV v ECB* (n 244) para 39.

[247] ibid paras 45–48.

[248] ibid paras 60–69.

[249] ibid paras 68–71.

[250] ibid paras 74–75.

[251] *ABLV Bank AS v SRB* (n 151) para 108.

[252] ibid para 51; *ABLV v ECB* (n 244) para 49; Case T-282/18, *Bernis and Others v SRB* ECLI:EU:T:2020:209, paras 39–45.

4.46 Then, in *Fundación Tatiana Pérez de Guzmán*,[253] part of the *Banco Popular* saga, the General Court held that the SRB's decision to adopt a resolution scheme of Banco Popular was independently reviewable, despite the resolution scheme needs to be endorsed by the Commission to be enforceable. In the Court's view, the Commission's endorsement could not deprive the resolution scheme of its autonomous legal effects,[254] and the fact that it could endorse it or object to it present objections to its discretionary elements did not mean that it could claim for itself the SRB's competences, nor modify the resolution scheme, or its legal effects.[255] Furthermore, in light of the SRM framework, the objective of the adoption of the resolution scheme was not to prepare the Commission's decision.[256]

4.47 One of the most complicated examples arose in the decision on admissibility in Case 1/2022 by the SRB Appeal Panel.[257] The act challenged was an SRB decision on Minimum Requirements on Capital and Eligible Liabilities (MREL), the cushion of equity and debt to facilitate resolution strategies such as bail-in. The MREL decision was adopted through a resolution college formed by the resolution authorities of the banking group. Resolution colleges lack independent decision-making powers,[258] so the MREL decision, where the parent company of the group is under the supervision of SRB, is adopted by the group resolution authority (the SRB), and signed in agreement by all other resolution authorities sitting in the college,[259] in this case the SRB, on behalf of Member States participating in the SRM, *and* authorities of the non-participating Member States.[260] Subsequently, the SRB issued *its own* separate MREL decision replicating the contents of the previous decision adopted in the college, and adding the instructions to the relevant national resolution authorities of the Banking Union (NRAs).[261] The Appeal Panel held that the joint decision of the college adopted by the group resolution authority and signed by all the authorities was a bundle of individual decisions with the same content, and thus binding and challengeable, because it was a final decision, and could not be considered a preparatory act for the subsequent SRB decision,[262] which was, instead, confirmatory, except in what concerned the instructions to the NRAs.

4.48 By way of summary, the test underpinning the review of acts in complex proceedings is similar in the US and the EU, but the EU presents unique challenges due to the high level

---

[253] Case T-481/17 Fundación *Tatiana Pérez de Guzmán el Bueno v SRB* ECLI:EU:T:2022:311. Compare also Case T-510/17 *Del Valle Ruiz and Others v Commission and SRB* ECLI:EU:T:2022:312; Case T-523/17, *Eleveté Invest Group and Others v Commission and SRB* ECLI:EU:T:2022:313; Case T-570/17 *Algebris (UK) and Anchorage Capital Group v Commission* ECLI:EU:T:2022:314 and Case T-628/17, *Aeris Invest v Commission and SRB* ECLI:EU:T:2022:315.
[254] *Tatiana Pérez* (n 253) paras 127–30.
[255] ibid 132.
[256] ibid 137.
[257] Appeal Panel Decision on Admissibility, case 1/22, June 2022. Both authors acted as Co-Rapporteurs in this decision (our comments to the decision therefore limited to a minimum).
[258] Recital (98) of Directive 2014/59/EU establishing a framework for the recovery and resolution of credit institutions and investment firms [2014] OJ L173.
[259] Case 1/22, Appeal Panel Decision on Admissibility (June 2022) para. 69.
[260] Commission Delegated Regulation (EU) 2016/1075 supplementing Directive 2014/59/EU of the European Parliament and of the Council with regard to regulatory technical standards specifying the content of recovery plans, resolution plans and group resolution plans, the minimum criteria that the competent authority is to assess as regards recovery plans and group recovery plans, the conditions for group financial support, the requirements for independent valuers, the contractual recognition of write-down and conversion powers, the procedures and contents of notification requirements and of notice of suspension and the operational functioning of the resolution colleges [2016] OJ L184 (hereafter Commission Delegated Regulation 2016/1075).
[261] SRM Regulation (n 243) art 12(1), (5).
[262] Case 1/22, Appeal Panel Decision (n 259) 66–76. See also BRRD (n 258) art 45h and Commission Delegated Regulation 2016/1075 (n 260) arts 86–93.

of complexity resulting from (i) multi-level system of governance, with the involvement of national and EU authorities; and (ii) the division between 'technical' aspects, assessed by agencies, and 'policy' or 'discretionary' assessed by Treaty institutions. The challenge ability of these acts is still a complex matter, but it is essential for the rule of law.

2.5 Standing to challenge decisions

4.49 The doctrine of 'standing' takes into consideration mostly the plaintiffs' relative position with regard to the challenged act. This presents problems in lawsuits against regulatory measures, and lawsuits against supervisory or crisis management measures by the bank's shareholders.

4.50 Starting with regulatory decisions, in the US, 'standing' comprises requirements such as the existence of an 'injury in fact', or the 'ripeness' of the claim. In *State National Bank of Big Spring v Lew* private plaintiffs and states challenged the Dodd-Frank Act's provisions. The District Court granted the government's motion to dismiss, considering the complaints 'premature', which required to guess how the authorities would exercise their powers.[263] In a unanimous Opinion by Judge Kavanaugh, the Circuit affirmed in part and reversed in part. The plaintiffs' challenge against the provisions on the Consumer Financial Protection Bureau (CFPB), which provided for the appointment of a single director (instead of a board), as contrary to the Appointments Clause of the Constitution satisfied the requirements of standing and ripeness[264] because the plaintiff was a regulated entity (standing), and because it challenged the lawfulness of the entity itself, and not its acts, and asking the plaintiff to wait for an unlawful act would be tantamount to 'require plaintiffs to bet the farm'.[265] Conversely, the claim against the Financial Stability and Oversight Council (FSOC) power to designate an entity as systemically important (SIFI), for violating principles of nondelegation and separation of powers was dismissed for lack of standing, since the plaintiff was not a SIFI, and its allegations that the designation as a SIFI was more beneficial were 'simply too attenuated and speculative'.[266] The court also dismissed the claim that the Orderly Liquidation Authority (OLA), which permits regulators, led by the Federal Deposit Insurance Corporation (FDIC) to put a firm in receivership and wind it down, as contrary to the Constitution's Bankruptcy Clause and due process clause because it was too premature to consider 'the legality of how the Government might wield the orderly liquidation authority in a potential future.[267] The CFPB issue was picked up later in *Seila Law*.[268]

4.51 US courts were confronted again with a similar issue in *Vullo v OCC*[269] and *Conference of State Bank Supervisors (CSBS) v OCC*, where state regulators, led by New York's Directorate of Financial Services (DFS), challenged the decision by the Office of the Comptroller of the Currency (OCC) to grant special purpose national bank ('SPNB') charters (non-depository charters) to FinTech companies ('FinTech charter'). The complaints were dismissed for lack of standing and ripeness when the OCC had not begun accepting charters,[270] they were filed

---

[263] *State National Bank of Big Spring v Lew* 958 F Supp 2d 127, 166 (DDC 2013).
[264] *State National Bank of Big Spring v Lew* 795 F.3d 48 (DC Cir 2015).
[265] ibid, citing *Free Enterprise Fund v Public Co Accounting and Oversight Board* 130 S Ct 3138, 3151 (2010).
[266] *State National Bank of Big Spring v Lew* 2015 (n 264) 55.
[267] ibid.
[268] *Seila Law LLC v Consumer Financial Protection Bureau* 140 S Ct 2183 (2020).
[269] *Vullo v Office of Comptroller of Currency* 378 F Supp 3d 271, 279 (SDNY 2019).
[270] *Vullo v Office of Comptroller of the Currency* No 17 Civ 3574, 2017 WL 6512245 (SDNY 2017); *CSBS v Office of the Comptroller of the Currency* 313 F Supp 3d 285, 299 (DDC 2018).

again once the OCC announced that it would accept applications for SPNB charters, and were dismissed again because of lack of standing and ripeness as the DFS concerns (federal pre-emption, undermining of New York laws, to the loss of revenue) were considered too speculative and thus 'failed to allege that the OCC's decision caused it to suffer an actual or imminent injury in fact'.[271]

In the EU, to have 'standing' an act must be of 'direct and individual concern' to the applicant, ie it must affect it for its special characteristics,[272] and the Court has refused to expand the test, to encompass instances of 'substantial adverse effect' test.[273] For regulatory acts, the act need only be of 'direct concern' to the applicant, but in *Inuit* the Court clarified that 'regulatory acts' do not comprise legislative acts,[274] which, considering that EU financial authorities' have very limited regulatory powers, is very restrictive. **4.52**

In supervisory or crisis management decisions, a major issue is the standing to sue of a financial institution's shareholders who challenge supervisory or crisis measures against the institution. In the US, in *Starr v United States* the Federal Reserve Bank of New York (FRBNY) decision to lend American International Group (AIG) US$85 billion to save the insurance giant from insolvency, in exchange for a 79.9 per cent equity stake in the company was challenged by one of AIG's major shareholders. The Court of Federal Claims considered the transaction an illegal exaction,[275] but the Court of Appeals for the Federal Circuit dismissed the complaint for lack of standing.[276] Even assuming that the plaintiff fulfilled the general conditions of 'actual or imminent injury-in-fact', 'concrete and particularized', a 'causal connection between injury and conduct' and 'likely redressability by a favorable decision', the plaintiff could not satisfy the requirement that it was not raising a third-party's legal right,[277] and thus the Court held that it was not a 'direct', but a 'derivative' claim.[278] Bailouts using public funds, like the 2009 Troubled Asset Relief Program (TARP) had similar luck. In *Re Chrysler* shareholders sued against the bail-out of the car manufacturer, unsatisfied by the (allegedly low) price paid its assets, arguing that TARP funds were unlawfully used because manufacturers, such as Chrysler, were not 'financial institutions' (which seems to be a strong argument) but the case was dismissed for lack of standing.[279] **4.53**

In Europe the issue was analysed by the European Court of Human Rights (ECtHR). In *Credit and Industrial Bank v Czech Republic*[280] the combined effect of replacing the board with an administrator appointed by the authorities, depriving bank representatives of powers of representation, the adoption of the decision without the presence of the bank, and the fact that it **4.54**

---

[271] *Lacewell v Office of Comptroller of Currency* Docket [2021] No 19-4271 (Maria Vullo had been replaced by Linda Lacewell as Superintendent of the DFS).
[272] TFEU (n 69) art 263(4), as understood in Case 25/62 *Plaumann v Commission* ECLI:EU:C:1963:17.
[273] Case C-50/00 P *Union de Pequeños Agricultores (UPA)* ECLI:EU:C:2002:462. More recently, it dismissed for lack of standing in a 'climate responsibility' case. Case C-565/19 P *Armando Carvalho and Others v European Parliament and Council* ECLI:EU:C:2021:252.
[274] Case C-583/11 P *Inuit Tapiriit Kanatami and Others v European Parliament and Council of the European Union* ECLI:EU:C:2013:625.
[275] *Starr International Co v United States* 121 Fed Cla 428 (2015).
[276] *Starr International Co v United States* 856 F 3d 953 (2017).
[277] ibid, citing *Kowalski v Tesmer* 543 US 125, 128–29 (2004).
[278] ibid. The court discussed precedents in federal law and Delaware law (where the entity was domiciled) on the distinction between 'direct' and 'derivative' claims, which focused on who suffered the harm, and who would receive the benefit of recovery.
[279] In *Re Chrysler Inc* 405 BR 79, 83 (Bankr SDNY 2009).
[280] *Credit and Industrial Bank v the Czech Republic*, App no 29010/95 (21 October 2003).

was not subject to appeal was a breach of due process rights.[281] In *Capital Bank v Bulgaria*[282] the bank was declared insolvent, and deprived of its licence, and wound up, and the decision was unchallengeable before the Courts, and this too was a breach of due process rights.[283] Yet, the test in *Agrotexim v Greece*[284] is that only a person whose rights have been directly affected can sue as a 'victim', and shareholders cannot be identified with their company, and are not victims unless the interference *directly* violates their rights.[285] This happened when the shares themselves were cancelled,[286] or the state took over a bank.[287] In *Albert and Others v Hungary*[288] the mandatory integration of some well-functioning banks into a scheme controlled by the state, subjecting some strategic and day-to-day decisions to state-controlled bodies. The banks' shareholders appealed, arguing that some decisions affected them directly (eg restrictions on dividends), but the measures were found lawful by the Hungarian Constitutional Court. The ECtHR, in a Chamber judgment, dismissed the case for lack of standing,[289] and a Grand Chamber Panel accepted the case into the Grand Chamber, only to confirm the dismissal or lack of standing. The measures could interfere with the rights of the banks, but not directly with the rights of shareholders,[290] these could not be identified with the banks, since they did not hold 100 per cent of the shares[291] (although they held 98.28 per cent of one and 87.65 per cent of another), and there were no exceptional circumstances justifying veil piercing. Finally, shareholders failed to show that their shares had lost value as a result of the integration scheme, and that they were *individually* affected as such shareholders. The Court acknowledged that in *Credit and Industrial Bank v Czech Republic* and *Capital Bank v Bulgaria* there were 'exceptional circumstances' eg a bank could not bring a complaint on its own.[292] More recently, in *Korporativna Targovska Banca AD v Bulgaria*[293] the Court held that Bulgaria violated the bank's shareholders' and executive rights to a fair trial under Article 6 of the Convention and the protection of property under Article 1 of Protocol no 1, because its Supreme Administrative Court refused to examine the claims raised by shareholders and executives of a bank after the withdrawal of its licence, holding that only the bank itself could challenge the decision to withdraw its licence.

4.55 The Court of Justice also decided on this issue in *Trasta Komercbanka*,[294] where Trasta's licence (a Latvian bank), was withdrawn by the ECB at a proposal of the Latvian bank

---

[281] ibid paras 69–72. According to the ECtHR's findings, in the process of review envisaged in the procedural laws, the courts could not examine the substantive reasons for the imposition and extension of compulsory administration, the procedure was exclusively written, with no hearing, and no possibility of opposition by the bank's management.
[282] *Capital Bank AD v Bulgaria*, App no 49429/99 24 (24 November 2005).
[283] *Credit v Czech Republic* (n 280) para 69; *Capital Bank AD v Bulgaria* (n 282) paras 27–33.
[284] *Agrotexim v Greece*, App no 14807/89 (7 July 2002).
[285] See Dolores Utrilla, 'Banking Restructuring and Shareholders' Property Rights: On Standing and Substance' *EU Law Live* (7 July 2020).
[286] *Olczak v Poland*, App no 30417/96 (7 July 2002).
[287] *Süzer and Eksen v Turkey*, App no 6334/05 (23 October 2012).
[288] *Albert and Others v Hungary*, App no 5294/14 (7 July 2020). Compare Utrilla (n 285).
[289] *Albert and Others v Hungary* (n 288).
[290] ibid paras 127–34.
[291] ibid paras 135–37.
[292] ibid para 144.
[293] Applications nos 46564/15 and 68140/16 (30 August 2022).
[294] Order of the General Court in Case T-247/16 *Trasta Komercbanka AS* ECLI:EU:T:2017:623, and appeal in Joined Cases C-663/17 P, C-665/17 P and C-669/17 P *ECB v Trasta Komercbanka and Others* ECLI:EU:C:2019:923. See the summaries by René Smits of the Advocate General's Opinion https://ebi-europa.eu/wp-content/uploads/2019/05/Challenging-a-banks-license-withdrawal-by-the-ECB-can-the-bank-act-or-can-its-shareholders_280419_def_.pdf (accessed 24 September 2022). See also Giorgia Marafioti, 'The Trasta Komercbanka Cases: Withdrawals of Banking Licences and Locus Standi' in Chiara Zilioli and Karl-Philipp Wojcik (eds), *Judicial Review in the European Banking Union* (Edward Elgar Publishing 2021) 521–29.

supervisor, and the liquidator, appointed at the request of that authority revoked all powers of attorney issued by the bank's board, which was confirmed in a Latvian court decision against which no appeal was possible. A corrected decision was issued after the Administrative Board of Review (ABoR) issued an opinion. Both decisions were challenged. The General Court dismissed the first as inadmissible but considered the shareholders' claim as admissible,[295] and the court's order was appealed by the ECB, the European Commission and Trasta and its shareholders. The Court of Justice held that the bank had standing to sue, and the shareholders had not.[296] The Court emphasized the 'Union of law', and the principle of judicial protection,[297] which was ensured by the right of the person affected by the withdrawal decision to challenge the decision.[298] To do so, it is 'necessary to show that the person concerned has indeed made the decision to bring the action and that the lawyers who claim to represent that person have in fact been authorised to do so'. National law determines who can act on behalf of the bank, subject to institution, subject to their obligation to ensure the right to an effective remedy[299] which would be infringed if:

> [a] liquidator empowered to take such decisions were to be appointed on the basis of a proposal from a national authority which took part in the adoption of the act adversely affecting the legal person concerned and which resulted in its going into liquidation. Having regard to the relationship of trust between that authority and the appointed liquidator which is involved in such an appointment procedure and to the fact that a liquidator's task is to carry out the final liquidation of the legal person which has gone into liquidation, there is a risk that that liquidator may avoid challenging, in court proceedings, an act which that authority has itself adopted or which has been adopted with its assistance and which has led to the legal person concerned going into liquidation.[300]

Given the liquidator's potential conflict of interest, he could not be granted the responsibility for the revocation of the power of attorney granted to the bank's lawyer.[301] Conversely, shareholders lacked standing to contest the withdrawal of a bank's licence, for lack of 'direct concern'. The contested measure did not 'directly affect'[302] the shareholders because the licence withdrawal 'had been issued to Trasta Komercbanka itself and not to its shareholders ad personam'.[303] The Court of Justice rejected the General Court's insistence on the 'intensity' of the effects' ie that shareholders' right to dividend became 'illusory'[304] for focusing on economic effects, not whether there were direct *legal* effects.[305] Shareholders' legal rights had not been affected.[306] Furthermore, the withdrawal of the licence did not 'directly affect shareholders' right to participate in the company's management of that company', because

---

[295] *Trasta Komercbanka* (n 294).
[296] ibid.
[297] ibid paras 54–55.
[298] ibid para 56.
[299] ibid paras 57–59.
[300] ibid para 60.
[301] ibid para 75.
[302] ibid para 103.
[303] ibid para 104.
[304] ibid para 106.
[305] ibid paras 108–109.
[306] ibid para 111: '[t]he negative effect of that withdrawal is economic in nature; the right of shareholders to receive dividends, just like their right to participate in the management of that company, if necessary by changing its object, has in no way been affected by the decision at issue'. For a different factual finding, compare however, more recently, Case T-502/19 *Francesca Corneli v ECB* ECLI:EU:T:2022:627, paras 38–54, 78–82 (on appeal also on this point of law in Joined Cases C-777/22 P and C-789/22 P).

the liquidation following the licence withdrawal was a matter of Latvian law.[307] Although the Court's reasoning on the standing of the bank, and its bodies is sound, the arguments on the standing of shareholders seem a bit formalistic. Maybe the Court had in mind a scenario where *only one* party should challenge, and the bank was the better choice. However, it is unclear why this is preferable to grant *both* the bank *and* the shareholders legal rights. For the moment, however, the matter has been clarified.

4.56 This restrictive position has been maintained in the context bank resolution cases. In *Liaño Reig v SRB*[308] the Court of Justice considered inadmissible an action for annulment of the decision to adopt a resolution scheme for Banco Popular. In *Algebris v SRB*,[309] where a shareholder of Banco Popular Español challenged only the part of the resolution scheme concerning the conversion of Tier 2 instruments (BPEF bonds) into newly issued shares (arguing that this was the one that affected it directly) the Court held that it could not partially annul a resolution decision, because the challenged part could not be separated from the other elements of the resolution scheme without altering the substance of that resolution decision, and dismissed the case. As to measures different from the resolution scheme itself, shareholders challenged the Single Resolution Board (SRB) decision *not to* conduct an ex post valuation. EU bank resolution rules require a provisional valuation as a pre-requisite for resolution tools (Valuation 1), a second *ex post* valuation (Valuation 2) and a valuation to determine whether creditors were treated worse than under regular insolvency/liquidation rules (Valuation 3), and the SRB decided not to conduct Valuation 2 because the resolution instrument (the sale-of-business) yielded a market price, thus making a second valuation redundant. The General Court declared the action inadmissible for lack of standing, as shareholders lacked a 'direct concern'.[310] Valuation 2 seeks to (i) ensure that any asset losses 2 are fully recognised in the books of accounts of the entity, all the Banco Popular shares were transferred to Banco Santander, and it was for Banco Santander 'to ensure that any losses incurred were reflected in its consolidated accounts, and (ii) to inform the decision to write back creditors' claims or to increase the value of the consideration paid in case Valuation 2 yielded a *higher* value than Valuation 1, but only under the bail-in tool, the bridge bank tool,[311] or the asset separation tool,[312] not the sale of the business tool.[313] Thus, the applicants lacked a direct concern to them, since they could not obtain any compensation',[314] as they ceased to be Banco Popular shareholders when their shares were transferred to Banco Santander. This view is a bit formalistic, since, after all, shareholders were affected by a write-down of their shares, only it was executed immediately before applying the sale-of-business tool.[315] More reasonably, there is a specific valuation (Valuation 3) directed at determining any unfair treatment, and the resulting compensation, and thus there was no need to use

---

[307] *Trasta Komercbanka* (n 294) paras 113–14. Thus, the second requirement for direct effect, ie that implementation is purely automatic and resulting from EU rules alone without the application of other intermediate rules' did not apply either.
[308] Case T-557/17 *Carmen Liaño Reig v SRB*, ECLI:EU:T:2019:771; on appeal, Case C-947/19, *Carmen Liaño Reig v SRB* ECLI:EU:C:2021:172.
[309] Order in Case T-2/19 *Algebris v SRB* ECLI:EU:T:2019:741. Parallel proceedings were Case T-599/18 *Aeris Invest v SRB* ECLI:EU:T:2019:740 and Case T-512/19 *Del Valle Ruiz and Others v SRB* ECLI:EU:T:2022:331.
[310] *Algebris* (n 309) 39.
[311] ibid para 46.
[312] ibid para 47.
[313] ibid paras 48–50.
[314] ibid para 55.
[315] Decision SRB/EES/2017/08 (7 June 2017) art 5, no 5.2 concerning the adoption of a resolution scheme for Banco Popular.

Valuation 2 for that purpose. In the *ABLV Bank* cases, following the ECB failing or likely to fail (FOLTF) assessment of ABLV Latvia and ABLV Luxembourg, the SRB adopted decisions not to take resolution actions with regard to these two entities, holding that resolution was not necessary in the public interest pursuant to Article 18(1)(c) of the SRM Regulation. These SRB decisions were challenged both by ABLV Bank[316] and by its shareholders.[317] In *ABLV v SRB* the General Court held that the SRB's decision whether or not to adopt a resolution scheme in respect to a credit institution is an act that is open to challenge, because that decision 'definitely establishes the position of the SRB at the end of the complex administrative procedure provided for in Article 18 SRM Regulation' and has implications on the tools available to resolve the crisis of the credit institution (some of which, if adopted, may enable the bank to continue part of its activity), producing therefore 'binding legal effects such as to affect the interest of the bank'.[318] In contrast, the General Court considered that the parent company ABLV Bank AS to had no standing to challenge the parallel decision adopted by the SRB in respect to its subsidiary ABLV Luxembourg. In *Ernests Bernis v SRB*[319] the European courts dismissed the case as inadmissible finding that the 'no resolution' decision adopted with respect to ABLV Latvia and Luxembourg does not directly concern their shareholders in the sense required by Article 263(4) TFEU.

4.57 Finally, the issue of a plaintiff's standing to challenge an EU decision has also arisen in state aid proceedings. The Commission's requirement of 'burden sharing' by shareholders and debtholders as a precondition to declare state aid lawful under Articles 107 ff TFEU expressed in its Commission Banking Communication[320] (before there was any EU framework on bank resolution) resulted in challenges against the Banking Communication itself, which raised problems typical of soft law (eg *Kotnik*) as well as against individual Commission decisions approving measures of financial assistance subject to burden sharing, or declaring others as illegal state aid. Unlike *Kotnik*, which was a preliminary reference under Article 267 TFEU challenges against individual decisions were *annulment* actions, under Article 263 TFEU, which had to satisfy a more demanding standard of standing. In *BPC Lux 2 Sàrl v Commission*,[321] the plaintiffs were holders of Tier 2 subordinated bank bonds issued by Banco Espirito Santo (BES) which was subject to the most important resolution procedure in Portugal, involving a bridge bank, and the approval of aid worth of EUR 4,899 million for its initial capital. As a condition to approve it, the Commission required that 'no claim of shareholders and holders of subordinated debt or any hybrid instruments could be transferred to the Bridge Bank', and that BES would be liquidated shortly. The General Court found that the plaintiffs 'did not have an interest in bringing proceedings for annulment of the contested decision'.[322]

4.58 On appeal, the Court of Justice set aside the order of the General Court, holding that, for the complaint to be admissible, the plaintiffs should have an 'interest' in the contested measure, ie 'the annulment of that measure must be capable, in itself, of having legal consequences and that the action, if successful, may procure an advantage for the party which has brought

---

[316] *ABLV Bank AS v SRB* (n 151).
[317] *Bernis* (n 252); on appeal Case C-364/20 P *Bernis and Others v SRB* ECLI:EU:C:2022:115. Edoardo Muratori, 'Ernests Bernis (appeal) and Judicial Review by the CJEU of Non-Resolution Decision in the EU Banking Union: No Standing for the Shareholders of the Relevant Entity' (2022) 7 European Papers 327.
[318] *ABLV Bank AS v SRB* (n 151) para 34.
[319] *Bernis* (n 317) and *Bernis 2022* (n 317).
[320] *BT v Balgarska Narodna Banka* (n 109).
[321] Case C-544/17 P *BPC Lux 2 Sàrl v European Commission* ECLI:EU:C:2018:880.
[322] Order of the General Court in T-812/14 *BPC Lux 2 and Others v Commission* EU:T:2017:560 (not published).

that action'.[323] Even if the national proceedings and the EU proceedings had, formally, a 'different subject matter' (as held by the General Court) the national proceedings had to decide whether, in transferring BES's operational segments to the bridge bank, the investors 'left behind' in BES, a bank without licence, ready for liquidation, received a treatment worse than under Portuguese insolvency law. A win in the domestic action would reverse the resolution decision, and the bonds' loss of value. Since resolution and state aid decision were 'inextricably linked', if the Commission's decision were ruled illegal, this would 'significantly increase the likelihood of success of the judicial review proceedings' before the Portuguese courts against the resolution decision'.[324] Thus, EU Courts must not evaluate whether the domestic action was well founded, but whether the action for annulment could benefit the plaintiff.[325]

4.59 In *Anthony Braesch v Commission*.[326] the applicant represented the holders of subordinated bonds ('FRESH bonds'[327]) in Monte dei Paschi Siena (MPS), the Italian bank, which, after several attempts to raise private capital with different restructuring plans, it was subject to public financial support (guarantee of senior liabilities) and precautionary recapitalization. The latter is an exception to avoid a FOLTF assessment, which, unlike resolution tools, can be used to inject funds in a solvent entity[328] to avoid resolution.[329] The Commission considered the measures compliant with the state aid and bank resolution frameworks,[330] given that they included sufficient burden-sharing measures. This included the cancellation of the FRESH bond contracts. Holders of bonds challenged the contract cancellation before Luxembourg courts, and the state aid decision before EU Courts. The General Court stayed the proceedings until *BPC Lux* was decided. Then, it relied on the broad definition of 'interested party' in the rules of procedure for approval of state aid measures,[331] holding that, as 'interested parties' in the state aid proceedings the bondholders would also have an 'interest' in bringing the annulment action, because it would force the Commission to re-open the procedures, and give the investors the opportunity to submit their comments.[332] Furthermore, in line with *BPC*, a finding of (i)legality in the state aid procedure by EU Courts could influence the national procedure,[333] and EU Courts' job was not to decide whether such procedure was

---

[323] *BPC Lux* (n 322) para 28, citing Judgment of 4 June 2015 in Case C-682/13 P *Andechser Molkerei Scheitz v Commission*, not published, EU:C:2015:356 and case law cited there.

[324] ibid para 35. The plaintiffs had sufficiently proven the link between both outcomes. See *BPC Lux* (n 322) 36. '[T]he annulment of the contested decision by the General Court would, first, support the arguments which they had already put forward in the national proceedings, according to which the resolution of BES was disproportionate in Portuguese law, and, second, make it possible to put forward, again in the context of those proceedings, the argument that, in the absence of the State aid at issue, the resolution of BES could not have achieved the objective of preventing its insolvency.'

[325] ibid para 56, citing Judgment of 17 September 2015, Case C-33/14 P *Mory and Others v Commission* EU:C:2015:609, para 76.

[326] Case T-161/18, *Anthony Braesch and Others v European Commission* ECLI:EU:T:2021:102. See Kathrin Blanck, 'State Aid and Bank Resolution Law before the European Court of Justice' in Chiara Zilioli and Karl-Philipp Wojcik (eds), *Judicial Review in the European Banking Union* (Edward Elgar Publishing 2021) 473–93.

[327] The financial structure of the transaction was complex, and one of the authors was involved as counsel in some of the pending cases concerning the transaction. Thus, we skip most details. Holders of FRESH bonds were made subject to burden-sharing measures.

[328] This was confirmed by an ECB letter sent to the Commission. See *Anthony Braesch* (n 326) 9.

[329] BRRD (n 258) art 32(4)(d).

[330] TFEU (n 69) art 107(2)(b).

[331] Council Regulation 2015/1589 laying down detailed rules for the application of Article 108 of the Treaty on the Functioning of the European Union [2015] OJ L248, art 1(h) ('any Member State and any person, undertaking or association of undertakings whose interests might be affected by the granting of aid, in particular the beneficiary of the aid, competing undertakings and trade associations').

[332] *Anthony Braesch* (n 326) para 51.

[333] ibid para 52: '[T]he Court requested the parties to state whether the cancellation of the FRESH contracts arose from BMPS's restructuring plan. In its response, the Commission submitted that the cancellation of those contracts arose from the restructuring plan in conjunction with Decree-Law 237/2016 and that the Italian

well-founded. could not substitute their criterion for that of national courts on whether such actions were well-founded.[334]

Thus, the plaintiffs not only had an 'interest' in bringing proceedings, but also 'standing'. **4.60** The Commission had decided not to raise objections, but, if there were doubts about the aid package, the Commission had to open a formal investigation procedure, where all 'interested parties' could participate. This rendered such interested parties 'directly and individually concerned', giving them standing.[335] It is interesting to note, first, that the opening of a formal investigation by the Commission is prompted by 'doubts as to the compatibility with the internal market' of a state measure,[336] but this should happen if the measure introduces unnecessary distortions because it is too generous, which should be mitigated by *more* burden sharing measures. Here the bondholders suggested that the outcome should be less burden-sharing, which seems unlikely. Secondly, the General Court followed the Court of Justice in *BPC Lux*, and read 'direct and individual concern' broadly in cases of state aid. The paradoxical result is that a bank's shareholders and bondholders can challenge the assessment of the compatibility with state aid rules of burden sharing measures in a bank's restructuring plan, but not the restructuring plan itself. Although this anomaly can be explained by the greater openness of state aid procedures, it is important to monitor the situation, to see if the Court of Justice corrects the General Court, to align the standing test in state aid along the stricter lines.

In conclusion, in principle EU Courts' test of 'standing' under the 'direct and individual' **4.61** concern seems stricter than US Courts' test. However, in practice US courts have restricted the actions by bank shareholders under the more specific doctrine of 'third-party actions' (ie excluding complaints where a party in reality represents the interests of a different party) in line with EU Courts' view or even stricter. This, together with the more flexible view of EU Courts on the idea of 'standing' in state aid procedures *and* the use of the preliminary reference procedure to palliate the strictures of the annulment procedure[337] have resulted in a rebalancing of the situation overall.

3 Accountability beyond justiciability: access to documents, appointments, and quasi-judicial review

3.1 Transparency and access to documents

3.1.1 The experience in the United States
In the United States, lawsuits seeking the disclosure of relevant information and documents **4.62** are a well-established practice, with a firm statutory basis: the Freedom of Information Act (FOIA) provides that administrative agencies must make reasonable efforts to search for the

---

authorities and BMPS worked closely together when drafting that plan, which formed part of the commitments offered by the Italian authorities during the examination of the aid measures by the Commission. By contrast, in their response to that question, the applicants stated that that restructuring plan assumed expressly that the FRESH contracts were ineffective and unenforceable.'

[334] ibid para 53.
[335] ibid para 59.
[336] Regulation 2015/1589 (n 331), art 4(4).
[337] *Anthony Braesch* (n 326) paras 59–60.

requested information *unless* one of nine exceptions apply.[338] These comprise (1) matters of national security, (2) internal personnel rules and practices, (3) information prohibited/exempted from disclosure by another act, (4) trade secrets and commercial or financial information obtained from a person and privileged or confidential; (5) inter-agency or intra-agency memorandums or letters that would not be available by law to a party other than an agency in litigation with the agency, (not applicable after twenty-five years), (6) personnel and medical files and similar files, (7) records or information compiled for law enforcement purposes, with some limitations, (8) contained in or related to examination, operating, or condition reports prepared by, on behalf of, or for the use of an agency responsible for the regulation or supervision of financial institutions, and (9) geological and geophysical information and data, including maps, concerning wells.[339] A 'separation criterion' applies, ie if an exception applies, the agency will disclose a separable part of the document.[340] More important, the agency bears the burden of proving that one of the exceptions applies,[341] and the courts have the power to review the matter *de novo*, ie strict standard of review, and to examine the information *in camera*.[342] When it comes to evaluating public authorities' reasons for non-disclosure, it suffices that their assertions are 'logical' or 'plausible', but parties requesting disclosure can bring contrary evidence.[343]

4.63 The FOIA has been used as a basis to request information from the Federal Reserve,[344] and financial supervisors. In *Federal Open Market Committee v Merrill Lynch* the Supreme Court considered the FOMC as an 'agency' for FOIA purposes, and construed narrowly the exemptions under the Act (especially Exemption 5 of inter-agency and intra-agency documents), with much attention to detail. The Court admitted that a limited withholding of information is acceptable during periods of time when the information is critical to ongoing negotiations or government functions.[345] However, it rejected the FOMC's contention that:

> Exemption 5 confers general authority upon an agency to delay disclosure of intra-agency memoranda that would undermine the effectiveness of the agency's policy if released immediately', because 'Such an interpretation of Exemption 5 would appear to allow an agency to withhold any memoranda, even those that contain final opinions and statements of policy, whenever the agency concluded that disclosure would not promote the 'efficiency' of its operations or otherwise would not be in the 'public interest'. This would leave little, if anything, to FOIA's requirement of prompt disclosure, and would run counter to Congress' repeated rejection of any interpretation of the FOIA which would allow an agency to withhold information on the basis of some vague 'public interest' standard.[346]

---

[338] 5 USC s 552(a)(3) and (b).
[339] 5 USC s 552(b).
[340] 5 USC s 552(b) 2nd para.
[341] *Ball v Board of Governors of Federal Reserve System* 87 F Supp 3d 33 (DDC 2015).
[342] ibid: 'On complaint, the district court of the United States in the district in which the complainant resides, or has his principal place of business, or in which the agency records are situated, or in the District of Columbia, has jurisdiction to enjoin the agency from withholding agency records and to order the production of any agency records improperly withheld from the complainant. In such a case the court shall determine the matter *de novo*, and may examine the contents of such agency records in camera to determine whether such records or any part thereof shall be withheld under any of the exemptions set out in subsection (b) of this section, and the burden is on the agency to sustain its action.'
5 USC s 552(a)(4)(B).
[343] *Ball v Board of Governors* (n 341).
[344] See eg Kara Karlson, 'Checks and Balances: Using the Freedom of Information Act to Evaluate the Federal Reserve Banks' (2010) 60 AUL Rev 213.
[345] *Federal Open Market Committee (FOMC) v Merrill* [1979] 443 US 340 (1979).
[346] ibid para 355.

More recently, in the midst of the 2007–2008 financial crisis, several news organizations from **4.64** the Board of Governors of the Federal Reserve and the FOMC information about bail-outs (eg details about loans, borrower banks, and collateral). The Board of Governors refused, alleging that the information was exempted under Exemptions 4 and 5. It also alleged that it lacked information about the loans' collateral, which was held by the Federal Reserve Bank that made each loan, and their records were separate from the Board's records, and thus no search for documents was conducted. The requesting parties appealed. In *Fox News v Board of Governors* the district court ruled in favour of the Board, holding that the Board's records were fell under FOIA Exemption 4 (not discussing Exemption 5) and the case was appealed.[347] In *Bloomberg v Board of Governors* the District Court rejected the Board's objections,[348] and both the Board and the Clearinghouse Association, a group of banks that asked to intervene as defendant, appealed, abandoning the argument of Exemption 4. The Circuit Court ruled on the two appeals on the same date (19 March 2010). In *Bloomberg* held that the information requested did not fall under Exemption 4,[349] because the information on loans, borrowers, collateral, etc. was not 'obtained from' other banks, and thus it was not necessary to determine whether that information was 'privileged and confidential'. Contrary to what the Board stated, Reserve Banks did not simply receive information from borrowers and granted the loans, but they evaluated the loans and collateral, and decided on granting or not. The Court also dismissed the Board's attempt to extend the 'program effectiveness' exception, ie that disclosure would hinder the program 's effectiveness, as it would 'impair its mission to furnish critical infusions to distressed banks on a confidential basis' and thereby prevent loss of confidence and bank runs,[350] as equivalent to the 'public interest' test, rejected in *Merrill*. As the Court eloquently put it 'The arguments are plausible, and forcefully made. But a test that permits an agency to deny disclosure because the agency thinks it best to do so (or convinces a court to think so, by logic or deference) would undermine 'the basic policy that disclosure, not secrecy, is the dominant objective of [FOIA]'.[351] Building on *Bloomberg*, the Circuit Court in *Fox News* held that, although Federal Reserve Banks did not act 'by delegation of' the Board of Governors,[352] the Board's records also included the records maintained for in official files 'in any division or office of the Board or any Federal Reserve Bank in connection with the transaction of any official business'.[353] Thus, it was ordered that the records be searched and disclosed.

Supervision of financial institutions is a different matter, as it has its own Exemption 8. During **4.65** the FOIA's first years the main case was *M.A. Schapiro v SEC*,[354] where courts construed the reference to 'financial institutions' narrowly, not encompassing broker–dealers. Later, courts have changed this, extending the exemption to information on stock exchanges,[355]

---

[347] *Fox News Network LLC v Board of Governors of the Fed Reserve System* 639 F Supp 2d 384 (SDNY 2009).
[348] *Bloomberg LP v Bd. of Governors of the Fed. Reserve System* 649 F Supp 2d 262 (SDNY 2009).
[349] *Bloomberg LP v Board of Governors of the Fed. Reserve System* F 3d, No 09-4083-cv (2d Cir 2010).
[350] This test, adopted by the First and District of Columbia Circuits, 'allows agencies to withhold6information as confidential under Exemption 4 if they believe that withholding it 'serves a valuable purpose and8is useful for the effective execution of its statutory responsibilities'. *Bloomberg LP v Board* (n 349), citing *Women Office Workers vBd of Governors of Fed Reserve System* 721 F 2d 1, 11 (1st Cir 1983).
[351] *Bloomberg LP v Board* (n 350).
[352] *Fox News Network LLC v Board of Governors* (n 347).
[353] ibid, citing 12 CFR § 261.2(i)(1)(ii).
[354] *MA Schapiro Co v Securities and Exchange Commission* 339 F Supp 467, 470 (DDC 1972).
[355] *Mermelstein v SEC* 629 F Supp 672, 673–75 (DDC 1986). Mermelstein corrected the previous interpretation in Shapiro, and was relied on by *Feshbach* and *Berliner* (see next footnotes).

broker–dealers, and self-regulatory organizations (eg the NASD)[356] or financial advisers.[357] Courts have considered that the exemption serves two purposes: first, and primarily, to 'ensure the security of financial institutions', which could be endangered by runs on banks caused by the disclosure of 'candid evaluations';[358] secondly (and secondarily), to protect the relationship between banks and agencies, to foster cooperation,[359] which could be jeopardized if eg information were made available to competitors.[360] Therefore, courts have construed the exception broadly.[361]

4.66 In *Consumers Union of United States Inc v Office of the Comptroller of the Currency* (OCC) the Circuit Court for the District of Columbia held that Exemption 8 excluded 'documents relating to the extent of compliance by certain national banks with the Consumer Credit Protection Act', because 'if Congress has intentionally and unambiguously crafted a particularly broad, all-inclusive definition, it is not our function ... to subvert that effort'.[362] Courts have applied the Exemption to cases where the institution had been defunct for several years,[363] to bank examination reports, including reports assessing compliance with consumer rules,[364] or records of examinations conducted by Federal Reserve Banks for the Board of Governors of Federal Reserve System.[365] Courts have also accepted the non-disclosure of 'related documents',[366] including 'real time information' received by agencies.[367] In *Abrams v OCC* the OCC investigated a Surety Bank (a Texas bank) for not charging Abrams, the bank's CEO, the normal transaction fee in wire transfers. The OCC prepared an examination report ('the Report'), notified Abrams that it was conducting a formal investigation of him, and issued an Order of Investigation, which was considered confidential. Abrams sought disclosure of the Order. The court, after an *in camera* review of the Order, concluded that it was 'related to' the examination report, and within Exemption 8. The OCC had not waived protection under Exemption 8 by disclosing the Order of Investigation when serving subpoenas.[368]

4.67 Some cases comprised questions disguised as requests for documents. In *Thomas v Comptroller of the Currency* the plaintiff submitted a FOIA request to the Comptroller of the

---

[356] '[T]he term "financial institutions" encompasses brokers and dealers of securities or commodities as well as self-regulatory organizations, such as the [National Association of Securities Dealers].' *Feshbach v SEC* 5 F Supp 2d 774, 781 (ND Cal 1997).

[357] '[I]nvestment advisors, as a matter of common practice, are fiduciaries of their clients who direct, and in reality make, important investment decisions.' *Berliner, Zisser, Walter & Gallegos v SEC* 962 F Supp 1348, 1351 n 5 (D Colo 1997).

[358] *Gregory v FDIC* 631 F 2d 896, 898 (DC Cir 1980); *National Community Reinvestment Coal v National Credit Union Administration* 290 F Supp 2d 124, 135–36 (DDC 2003).

[359] See also *Fagot v FDIC* [1984] 584 F Supp 1168, 1173 (DPR); *McKinley v FDIC* 744 F Supp 2d 128, 144 (DDC 2010).

[360] *Consumers Union of the US Inc v Heimann* 589 F Supp 531, 533 (DC Cir 1978).

[361] See eg *Pentagon Fed Credit Union v National Credit Union Admin* No 95-1475 (ED Va 1996).

[362] *Consumers Union v Heimann* (n 360).

[363] *Gregory v FDIC* 631 F 2d 896, 898 (DC Cir 1980); *Berliner, Zisser, Walter & Gallegos v SEC* (n 357).

[364] Even if the contents originate with consumers, and not financial institutions or regulations. *Consumers Union v Office of the Comptroller of Currency* No 86-1841, slip op at 2–3 (DDC 1988).

[365] *Clarkson v Greenspan* No 97-2035, slip op at 14–15 (DDC 1998).

[366] *McCullough v FDIC* [1980] No 79-1132 (DDC). In *Williams & Connolly LLP v Office of the Comptroller of the Currency* 30 F Supp 3d 82, 90 (DDC 2014) the court held that communications between the agency's attorneys and supervisory employees and the Banks, their proposed independent consultants, and proposed independent counsel as well as internal agency and inter-agency discussion of the vetting of independent consultants and independent counsel were 'related to' a bank examination and were protected.

[367] *McKinley v FDIC* (n 359).

[368] *Abrams v OCC* [2006] No 3:05-CV-2433-N ECF, affirmed in *Abrams v Dep't of Treasury*, 243 F App'x 4, 6 (5th Cir 2007).

Currency seeking 'various bonding information' relating to himself (a convict in prison). The Court found that:

> It is clear that the information he requested is not the type of information the OCC maintains. Moreover, because the OCC's files are arranged by the name of the supervised national bank, federal branch or agency, defendant could not reasonably be expected to conduct a search of its records without the name of such an entity.[369]

4.68 Some doubtful cases concern the disclosure of 'purely factual materials'. Some courts have held that, absent any controlling case law supporting a 'distinction between factual versus analytical or deliberative material' withholding both factual and other material better safeguards the 'public appearance' of financial institutions and encourages cooperation between financial institutions and agencies.[370] Other courts have refused to extend the protection to purely factual material.[371]

4.69 The only explicit statutory exception to Exemption 8 is in the Federal Deposit Insurance Corporation Act of 1991, which requires all federal banking agency inspector generals to conduct a review and to make a written report when a deposit insurance fund incurs a material loss with respect to an insured depository institution,[372] and save for the information that would reveal the identity of any customer of the institution, the federal banking agency 'shall disclose any report on losses required under this subsection, upon request' under the FOIA, and cannot exclude any information about the insured depository institution' under Exemption 8.[373]

3.1.2 The EU legal framework ... or patchwork on access to documents

4.70 The EU lacks a single framework for transparency and disclosure of documents held by public authorities, and offers something closer to a patchwork quilt of rules. The general provisions are Article 15 TFEU, and access to documents is subject to Regulation 1049/2001 (Access Regulation),[374] which applies to agencies like the ESAs or the Single Resolution Board (SRB). The ECB[375] as a Treaty institution, has its own Decision ECB/2004/3 to regulate access to documents,[376] approved when the ECB was solely a monetary institution (in fact, its 'constitutional' (or Treaty) status is primarily based on its monetary mandate under Article 127(1) TFEU), and, although recital (59) of the Single Supervisory Mechanism (SSM) Regulation states that the Access Regulation should *also* apply ECB supervisory to documents, the ECB, contrary to this, insists in regulating *all access to documents requests* under its Decision. Legally dubious, this is extremely convenient for the ECB, because the ECB Decision, although inspired by the Access Regulation, presents clear differences,[377] as the following table shows.

---

[369] Also that: '[A]gencies are not required to maintain their records or perform searches which are not compatible with their own document retrieval systems'. *Thomas v Comptroller of the Currency* 684 F Supp 2d 29 (2010), citing *Assassination Archives Research Ctr Inc v Cent Intelligence Agency* 720 F Supp 217, 219 (DDC 1989).
[370] *Bloomberg v SEC* 357 F Supp 2d 156, 170 (DDC 2004).
[371] *Lee v FDIC* 923 F Supp 451, 459 (SDNY 1996).
[372] USC s 1831o(k) (1).
[373] USC s 1831o(k) (4).
[374] Regulation (EC) No 1049/2001 of the European Parliament and of the Council regarding public access to European Parliament, Council and Commission documents [2001] OJ L145.
[375] Compare Daniel Sarmiento, 'Confidentiality and Access to Documents in the Banking Union' in Chiara Zilioli and Karl-Philipp Wojcik (eds), *Judicial Review in the European Banking Union* (Edward Elgar Publishing 2021) 165–93.
[376] European Central Bank Decision ECB/2004/3 (4 March 2004) on public access to European Central Bank documents as modified by ECB Decisions ECB/2011/6 and ECB/2015/1.
[377] For a general (critical) approach towards the ECB/2004/3 see eg Päivi Leino-Sandberg, 'Public Access to ECB Documents: Are Accountability, Independence and Effectiveness an Impossible Trinity?' (ECB Legal Conference Proceedings 2019) 195.

Table 4.1: Comparison between Access Regulation and ECB Access Decision

Item	Access Regulation	Decision ECB/2004/3
General provision	Article 1 Regulation's goal to define *principles, conditions and limits* of access to information, and has the goal of establishing rules ensuring the *easiest possible exercise* of this right, and to promote good administrative practice on access to documents.	Article 1 Decision's goal to define *conditions and limits* for access to documents and to promote good administrative practice on public access to such documents.
Absolute exceptions	Article 4.1 Short list of 'public interest' exceptions No reference to 'confidential information'.	Article 4.1 Long list of 'public interest' exceptions 'Confidential information' expressly protected
Relative exceptions	Analogous treatment in ECB/2004/3 Decision	Articles 4.2 Access Regulation and 4.2
Internal documents and deliberations	Article 4.3 Conditional exception	Article 4.3 Unconditional exception for documents part of internal deliberations

4.71 There are three main differences. First, the Access Regulation is framed as a norm on the 'principles of access', as well as the 'conditions and limits', whereas the ECB Decision is framed as a norm of 'conditions and limits'. Thus, the general rule is 'access' in one case, and 'restriction' in the other. This is reinforced by the Access Regulation's express reference to the Charter of Fundamental Rights,[378] in contrast with the ECB Decision's reference the ECB protocol and statute.[379] Thus, 'access to documents' seems an individual right in one case, and a matter of good administrative practice in the other. Secondly, in both texts access to documents is subject to 'relative exceptions' in case of commercial interests, court proceedings and inspections, investigations and audits, which apply 'unless there is an overriding interest in disclosure'. However, on the absolute exceptions, where institutions 'shall refuse' access, with no exceptions, the two texts differ widely. The Access Regulation has limited exceptions, including public security, defence and military matters, international relations, and the financial, monetary or economic policy of the Community or a Member State. The ECB Decision has a much longer list, which also includes protecting the integrity of euro banknotes, public security, international financial, monetary or economic relations, the stability of the financial system in the Union or in a Member State, the Union's or a Member State's policy relating to the prudential supervision of credit institutions and other financial institutions, the purpose of supervisory inspections, the soundness and security of financial market infrastructures, payment schemes or payment service providers, as well as the

---

[378] Access Regulation (n 374) recital 2.
[379] ECB/2004/3 Decision (n 376) recital 3.

confidentiality of information protected as such under EU law.[380] This longer list, together with the open textured nature of some of its items (eg 'stability', 'prudential supervision policy' etc.) transforms the ECB rules into a framework of 'confidentiality', not 'access'.

Thirdly, on internal documents, under the Access Regulation disclosure can be refused only **4.72** if this would seriously undermine the institution's decision-making process,[381] while the ECB Decision excepts internal documents without requiring that this may also undermine the institution's decision-making. This requirement is added only for documents reflecting exchanges of views between the ECB and other authorities (then, access can only be refused if disclosure seriously undermines the ECB's effectiveness in performing its tasks[382]).

It is interesting to note that, in contrast with the US, monetary policy and financial stability **4.73** are considered 'absolute exceptions',[383] whereas financial supervision of credit institutions is considered as a relative exception in the Access Regulation,[384] and only as an absolute exception in the ECB Decision.

Crucially, to complete the picture one must consider that, in addition to the 'access texts' (the **4.74** Access Regulation and ECB Decision), different EU laws define what information is 'confidential' or subject to professional secrecy, for banks (CRD IV),[385] investment firms (MiFID II),[386] insurance undertakings (Solvency II),[387] European Supervisory Authorities (ESAs[388]), or the ECB itself.[389] As pointed out by Smits and Badenkoop,[390] the basic principle is the same in CRD IV, Solvency II and MiFID II, but details differ, for example in the exceptions to non-disclosure (with some important differences between MiFID II, on one side, and CRD IV and Solvency II on the other[391]). Then, the ESAs Regulations do not include some exceptions to non-disclosure present in other rules,[392] while the ECB rules provide for a general standard of secrecy without much specification or exceptions. More importantly, unlike the

---

[380] ECB/2004/3 Decision (n 376) art 4.2.
[381] Access Regulation (n 374) art 4.3.
[382] ECB/2004/3 Decision (n 376) art 4.3.
[383] Access Regulation (n 374) art 4(1)(a); ECB Decision, art 4(1)(a) 2nd and 7th exceptions.
[384] The 'purpose of inspections, investigations and audits' is considered a relative exception in both art 4(2) of the 3rd Access Regulation (n 374) and art 4(2) 3rd of the ECB/2004/3 Decision (n 376), but after a 2015 amendment the ECB decision also added among its absolute exceptions ' the Union's or a Member State's policy relating to the prudential supervision of credit institutions and other financial institutions,' and '— the purpose of supervisory inspections,' which de facto make devoid of purpose the relative exception.
[385] Article 53 of Directive 2013/36/EU of the European Parliament and of the Council on access to the activity of credit institutions and the prudential supervision of credit institutions and investment firms, amending Directive 2002/87/EC and repealing Directives 2006/48/EC and 2006/49/EC [2013] OJ L176CRD IV.
[386] Directive 2014/65 of the European Parliament and of the Council of 15 May 2014 on markets in financial instruments and amending Directive 2002/92/EC and Directive 2011/61/EU (recast) [2014] OJ L173 (MiFID II) art 76.
[387] Directive 2009/138/EC of the European Parliament and of the Council of 25 November 2009 on the taking-up and pursuit of the business of Insurance and Reinsurance [2009] OJ L335 (Solvency II Directive) art 64.
[388] See art 70(1) and (2) of Regulations 1093/2010 (EBA Regulation), 1094/2010 (EIOPA Regulation), and 1095/2010 (ESMA Regulation).
[389] Statute on the European System of Central Banks (ESCB) art 37; SSM Regulation, art 27.
[390] René Smits and Nikolai Badenhoop, 'Towards a Single Standard of Professional Secrecy for Supervisory Authorities: A Reform Proposal' (2019) 3 Eur LJ 295.
[391] For example, CRD IV (n 385) art 53(1), MiFID II (n 386) art 76(2) and Solvency II (n 387) art 64(1) contemplate the possibility of disclosing information in summary or aggregate form, but this disclosure should be made in a way that does not permit to identify 'individual credit institutions' (CRD IV), 'individual insurance or reinsurance undertakings' (Solvency II) or 'individual investment firms, market operators, regulated markets *or any other person*' (MiFID II). Conversely, all of them contemplate an exception for the disclosure of information in the context of 'criminal proceedings', but MiFID II also includes 'tax proceedings'.
[392] For example, they make no mention to the possibility of disclosing information in bankruptcy and winding-up proceedings. See Smits and Badenkoop (n 390).

Access Regulation, here the basic interpretative principle is 'confidentiality', which makes interpretation difficult. This is even more so for national competent authorities (NCAs), that may be subject to national constitutions that require more transparency than the EU framework (which is not difficult) or the ECB framework (which is very easy).[393]

4.75 The first key for evolution, in our view, is 'convergence' first between the ECB framework, and its insistence on secrecy, with the general principle of transparency in the Access Regulation, which would not affect the ECB's independence, and then between different standards of confidentiality. The second is 'consistency' between the principle of 'access' and that of 'confidentiality' since the approach should be the same no matter the side from which one approaches the issue. Courts' role is crucial in this endeavor.

3.1.3 The case law on access to documents in the SSM and SRM

4.76 The CJEU has examined questions of access to documents of banking supervision in *Espirito Santo I*,[394] *Baumeister*,[395] *UBS Europe*,[396] *Buccioni*,[397] *Espirito Santo II*,[398] and *Di Masi and Varoufakis v ECB*.[399] These cases have gone some way to reconcile the different regimes on 'access' to documents, and 'confidentiality'.[400] Fortunately, the CJEU has not followed the compartmentalized approach of EU rules, although we cannot have full consistency without statutory changes. In *Banco Espirito Santo* the General Court, deciding in the context of the ECB Access Decision, considered the petition to access the Governing Council decision to suspend access by Banco Espirito Santo to credit instruments, and to set the ceiling for the provision of emergency liquidity that could be provided by Banco de Portugal to *Banco Espirito Santo*. The Court rejected the ECB's contention that this would undermine the confidentiality of the Governing Council proceedings.[401] However, the Court accepted its argument that such disclosure could undermine financial or monetary policy.[402]

4.77 In *Baumeister* the Court of Justice considered the meaning of MiFID confidentiality provisions in light of the Access Regulation. The facts of the case concerned a firm, Phoenix, which basically ran a scheme to defraud investors. The plaintiff spent years before German courts, which gave him conflicting answers, and sued the government, going all the way up to the Federal Supreme Court, which made a preliminary reference to the Court of Justice, asking whether all information communicated to the supervisory authority fell within the scope of 'confidential information', without any further qualification.[403] The Court (not following the expansive definition of 'confidential information' proposed by the Advocate General) held that the exchange of information between supervisory authorities is necessary for the effective supervision, and that this requires confidentiality, but that this cannot operate as a general presumption that all information relating to a supervised entity be deemed to be confidential.[404]

---

[393] This can give rise to conflicts between the duties of national officials under their domestic laws, and under EU law. See Leino-Sandberg (n 377) 210.
[394] Case T-251/15 *Espirito Santo Financial v European Central Bank* EU:T:2018:234.
[395] Case C-15/16 *BaFin v Ewald Baumeister* ECLI:EU:C:2018:464.
[396] Case C-358/16 *UBS Europe and Alain Hondequin and Others v DV and Others* ECLI:EU:C:2018:715.
[397] Case C-594/16 *Enzo Buccioni* ECLI:EU:C:2018:717.
[398] Case T-730/16 *Espirito Santo Financial Group v European Central Bank* ECLI:EU:T:2019:161.
[399] Case T-798/17 *Fabio De Masi and Yanis Varoufakis v ECB* ECLI:EU:T:2019:154.
[400] See Smits and Badenhoop (n 396). Compare Sarmiento (n 375) 165–93.
[401] *Banco Espirito Santo* (n 394) paras 77–83.
[402] ibid paras 88–108.
[403] Smits and Badenhoop (n 396).
[404] *Baumeister* (n 395) paras 33–35.

In *Buccioni* the Court of Justice had to assess the meaning of confidentiality provisions. **4.78**
It is important to note that, although the problem was based on CRD IV provisions, the
Court used a general approach, which interpreted the provisions of CRD IV and MiFID
on confidentiality together, and referred to *Baumeister* (based on MiFID) as a precedent
that could be applied by analogy. This is so despite the fact that the MiFID II provisions
show relevant differences (especially with regard to the exceptions to non-disclosure) with
CRD IV. Nevertheless, despite the fact that it framed the problem in the context of the right
to an effective remedy/judicial protection (Article 47 of the Charter) the Court was relatively cautious, and allowed supervisory authorities and national courts much leeway to balance an applicant's right to access and the public interests involved in the confidentiality of
information.[405]

In *UBS Europe*, the Court held that two persons who had been deemed no longer 'fit and **4.79**
proper' to perform functions in the financial market could not have copies of the correspondence from the national supervisory authority, because this was, according to the Court,
not a case 'covered by criminal law'[406] (which provides an exception to the non-disclosure of
documents). The Court read the provisions in the context of the right to judicial protection
(like it previously did in *Buccioni*), which includes the right of access to the file, but held that
this right was not unfettered, and has to be balanced by other interests, and that national
courts are the ones that can do such balancing.[407]

In *Di Masi and Varoufakis* the General Court considered the ECB's refusal to grant access **4.80**
to the documents of the legal advice for its decision of the supply of emergency liquidity by
the Greek central bank to Greek banks, within the framework of the ECB Access Decision,
accepting the ECB's characterization that these were documents 'for internal use', and thus
confidential,[408] which the ECB had duly motivated in its decision,[409] and rejecting the petitioners' arguments about the existence of an overriding public interest.[410]

In *Malacalza Investimenti v ECB*[411] the applicant, the main shareholder of Banca Carige, **4.81**
requested access to the ECB decision to place the said entity in temporary administration
under resolution rules, its annexes, and other decisions on Banca Carige. The ECB rejected
the request in its entirety under Article 4(1)(c) of its Access Decision, on 'the confidentiality
of information that is protected as such under Union law'. In its view, this 'contained a general presumption of confidentiality covering all cases coming within the scope of the prudential supervision task entrusted to it' (referring to Article 27 SSM Regulation and Article
53 CRD IV) ie a general rule in itself, rather than an exception.[412] Yet, since the ECB lodged
its defence seven days late the Court entered judgment by default, as the action was 'neither
manifestly inadmissible nor manifestly lacking any foundation in law'.[413] The Court stated
expressly that 'the applicant rightly submits that the existence of such a general presumption of confidentiality, derived from Article 4(1)(c) of Decision 2004/258, has not hitherto

---

[405] *Buccioni* (n 397) paras 27–33.
[406] *UBS Europe* (n 396) paras 46–48.
[407] ibid paras 68–70.
[408] *De Masi and Varoufakis* (n 399) paras 45–52.
[409] ibid paras 53–58.
[410] ibid paras 67–72.
[411] Case T-552/19 *Malacalza Investimenti v ECB* ECLI:EU:T:2020:294.
[412] ibid paras 18–21.
[413] ibid para 58.

been recognized or established by the case law'.[414] This principle was then reiterated and such presumption of confidentiality excluded in *Aeris Invest v ECB*[415] where the Court annulled the ECB decision rejecting access to ECB documents pertaining to the resolution of Banco Popular Español and in *Corneli v ECB*[416] where again the Court annulled the ECB decision rejecting access to its decision to place Banca Carige under special administration.

4.82 For the SRM, the Appeal Panel has decided numerous cases on access to documents,[417] mostly as a result of the Banco Popular resolution, yet more recently also in respect to Sberbank resolution and ABLV liquidation. The question was whether, in light of the right that 'any citizen' has under the Public Access Regulation to access documents, the SRB had granted adequate access to Banco Popular's shareholders and subordinated bondholders to the documents supporting the SRB's resolution decision. The Appeal Panel's answer was 'not nearly enough', since the SRB had refused disclosure of key documents, such as the resolution decision, the valuation report and the resolution plan in their entirety. Key to the Appeal Panel decisions were the arguments that: (i) the conferral of powers to Union agencies is conditional upon respecting fundamental rights and judicial review; and (ii) administrative safeguards, including access to documents are instrumental to both. Thus, the Appeal Panel held that the SRB erred in law when refusing to access the valuation report in its entirety. The report was a critical part of the resolution decision, and thus had to be at least partially disclosed. The SRB was only partly entitled to refuse access to other documents: the resolution decision, some parts of the resolution plan and other relevant documents could be disclosed in a redacted, non-confidential form, without endangering financial stability, since months had passed since the resolution decision.[418] In successive rounds of appeals the Appeal Panel could provide more nuanced answers and develop a stable framework of analysis to balance the competing interests based on the following principles: (a) The right of access is a transparency tool of democratic control available to all Union citizens irrespective of their interests in subsequent legal actions;[419] (b) The principle is that all documents of the institutions should be accessible to the public, since the Public Access Regulation implements Article 15 of the TFEU, and a fundamental right under Article 42 of the Charter of Fundamental Rights of the European Union, although certain public and private interests are also protected by way of exceptions and the agencies must be able to protect internal deliberations to safeguard their ability to carry out their tasks; (c) Exceptions to public access to documents must be applied and interpreted narrowly;[420] (d) For certain categories of documents the Union institutions, bodies and agencies can rely on a general presumption that their disclosure would undermine one of the interests protected by the Public Access

---

[414] ibid para 51.
[415] Case T-827/17 *Aeris Invest v ECB* ECLI:EU:T:2021:660 (on appeal in Case C-782/21 P pending).
[416] Case T-501/19 *Corneli v ECB* ECLI:EU:T:2022:402.
[417] For a similar finding and a wider discussion, see Aeris (n 415) (currently on appeal in Case C-728/21 P). It is also disputed in pending cases before the General Court, still awaiting decision (eg Cases T-62/18 *Aeris Invest v SRB*; T-496/18, *OCU v SRB* OJ C 352; and T-514/18 *Del Valle Ruiz* OJ C427 challenging Appeal Panel decisions in Case T-16/19 *Activos y Inversiones Monterroso*, challenging the SRB's revised confirmatory decision). Case T-480/18 *Ontier España* ECLI:EU:T:2018:871 has already been dismissed on purely procedural grounds.
[418] The Appeal Panel agreed with the SRB that documents exchanged with the ECB or the European Commission were protected as part of the deliberation process, under art 4(3) of the Access Regulation (n 374).
[419] Case C-60/15 *Saint-Gobain Glass Deutschland* ECLI:EU:C:2017:540, 60–61 and Case T-376/13 *Versorgungswerk der Zahnärztekammer Schleswig-Holstein v European Central Bank* ECLI:EU:T:2015:361, para 20.
[420] Case C-280/11 *Council v Access Info Europe* ECLI:EU:C:2013:671, para 30.

Regulation.[421] The vast majority of these Appeal Panel's decisions have been accepted by the parties and have become final; a few have been challenged before the General Court and are awaiting judgment.[422]

3.2 Independence and appointment of members of financial regulatory bodies

Although our primary focus is on the role of courts, and thus on legal (or judicial) accountability, courts also act as enforcers when the accountability is exercised by other actors, including political bodies. One particular line of case law of the US Supreme Court, on the Appointments Clause of the US Constitution, has special significance for financial regulatory bodies, as it has enhanced accountability and democratic legitimacy at the expense of independence.

The first case was *Free Enterprise Fund v PCAOB*,[423] where the members of the newly established Public Company Accounting Oversight Board (PCAOB) enjoyed a double protection to enhance their independence, since they could only be removed 'for good cause shown' by the officers of the Securities and Exchange Commission (SEC), who, in turn, could only be removed for 'inefficiency, neglect of duty, or malfeasance in office'. The Supreme Court held that 'the Constitution has been understood to empower the President to keep executive officers accountable—by removing them from office, if necessary'. Although the Supreme Court had accepted the constitutionality of the removal 'for cause' to protect independence,[424] in all those cases 'only one level of protected tenure separated the President from an officer exercising executive power. The President—or a subordinate he could remove at will—decided whether the officer's conduct merited removal under the good-cause standard'.[425] Therefore:

> Without the ability to oversee the Board, or to attribute the Board's failings to those whom he can oversee, the President is no longer the judge of the Board's conduct … If Congress can shelter the bureaucracy behind two layers of good-cause tenure, why not a third? … The diffusion of power carries with it a diffusion of accountability. The people do not vote for the 'Officers of the United States' … They instead look to the President to guide the 'assistants or deputies … subject to his superintendence' … Without a clear and effective chain of command, the public cannot 'determine on whom the blame or the punishment of a pernicious measure, or series of pernicious measures ought really to fall.[426]

The Court also downplayed the argument of technical competence and expertise that justifies independent agencies, in quite vehement, political terms, holding that:

> [w]here, in all this, is the role for oversight by an elected President? The Constitution requires that a President chosen by the entire Nation oversee the execution of the laws. And the 'fact that a given law or procedure is efficient, convenient, and useful … will not save

---

[421] Case C-404/10 *Commission v Edition Odile Jacob* ECLI:EU:C:2012:393; C-514/07 P *Sweden and Others v API and Commission* ECLI:EU:C:2010:541; C-365/12 P *Commission v EnBW* EU:C:2014:112; C-514/11 P and C-605/11 P *LPN and Finland v Commission* EU:C:2013:738; C-562/14 P *Sweden v Commission* EU:C:2017:356.
[422] Compare Case T-514/18, *Del Valle Ruiz and Others v SRB*; Case T-62/18 *Aeris Invest v SRB*; Case T-62/18 *Aeris Invest v SRB* (n 417); more recently Case T-290/23 *Sberbank v SRB* (action brought on 24 May 2023).
[423] *Free Enterprise Fund v Public Company Accounting Oversight Board* 561 US 477 (2010).
[424] *Humphrey's Executor v United States* 295 US 602 (1935).
[425] *Free Enterprise Fund* (n 423).
[426] ibid.

it if it is contrary to the Constitution', for '[c]onvenience and efficiency are not the primary objectives—or the hallmarks—of democratic government' … The growth of the Executive Branch, which now wields vast power and touches almost every aspect of daily life, heightens the concern that it may slip from the Executive's control, and thus from that of the people. This concern is largely absent from the dissent's paean to the administrative state.[427]

4.86 Several years later in *Seila Law LLC v CFPB*,[428] the US Supreme Court assessed the lawfulness of the appointment and removal system for the director of the Consumer Financial Protection Bureau (CFPB) a federal consumer protection and product regulation agency,[429] headed not by a board, like other agencies, but by a director, appointed by the President, with the advice and consent of the Senate, and removable only 'for cause'.[430] The Supreme Court held that the structure of one director, removable only for cause, was a historical anomaly and, unlike the (debatable) historical examples of other bodies, this one enjoyed vast powers.[431] In the Court's view, the US constitutional system concentrated power in no single body except for the President, which, in turn, was the most democratically accountable. Thus, all agencies had to be accountable to the President, who, in turn, was accountable to the people, and

> [T]he CFPB's single-Director structure contravenes this carefully calibrated system by vesting significant governmental power in the hands of a single individual accountable to no one. The Director is neither elected by the people nor meaningfully controlled (through the threat of removal) by someone who is.[432]

4.87 Next, in *Collins v Yellen*[433] the Supreme Court considered unconstitutional the removal clauses of the Federal Housing Finance Agency (FHFA), which oversees the US mortgage giants (or Government-Sponsored Enterprises—GSEs), Fannie Mae and Freddie Mac. The FHFA's Acting Director in 2008 put the GSEs into conservatorship, and negotiated with Treasury a capital injection by Treasury, in exchange for the subscription of senior preferred shares.[434] The conservatorship powers was considered lawful but the removal protections were considered unconstitutional, since the Supreme Court had already stated in *Seila Law* that the FHFA was another historical anomaly,[435] prompted by the Dodd-Frank Act, like the CFPB. Thus, the interest was on the Court's treatment of the *amicus brief* arguments, which tried to distinguish the FHFA from the CFPB. First, it held that, the FHFA's more limited powers did not call for a different result (although in *Seila Law* one of the problems was that the CFPB's powers were vast) because the President's control fulfilled an important role, regardless of the agency's function, and the Court was not in a good position to

---

[427] ibid.
[428] *Seila Law* (n 268).
[429] USC 12 USC s 5491 (a) introduced by Section 1001 of the Dodd-Frank Act.
[430] USC 12 USC s 5491(c)(3) stated that: 'The President may remove the Director for inefficiency, neglect of duty, or malfeasance in office.'
[431] *Seila Law* (n 268) 21, n 8: 'the CFPB … acts as a mini legislature, prosecutor, and court, responsible for creating substantive rules for a wide swath of industries, prosecuting violations, and levying knee-buckling penalties against private citizens'.
[432] *Seila Law* (n 268) 23.
[433] *Collins v Yellen* 141 S Ct 1761 (2021).
[434] ibid para 2.
[435] *Seila Law* (n 268) para 20.

weigh the differences in powers[436] (although in *Seila* it had declared that the vastness of the CFPB had been a major part of the problem). Secondly, it rejected that the FHFA's position as a 'receiver' turned it into a private agent, which justified removal protections, because the FHFA's powers stemmed from a specific statute, which granted powers greater than those of a regular conservator, and allowed it to subordinate private interests to public interest.[437] Thirdly, even if the GSEs were not purely private entities, the President's removal powers still had an important role to play, and GSEs could have an impact in the lives of millions of Americans.[438] Finally, on the objection that the removal 'for cause' was a 'modest' restriction (unlike the CFPB's), the Court held that:

> [T]he Constitution prohibits even 'modest restrictions' on the President's power to remove the head of an agency with a single top officer' because The President must be able to remove not just officers who disobey his commands but also those he finds 'negligent and inefficient'… those who exercise their discretion in a way that is not 'intelligen[t] or wis[e]'… those who have 'different views of policy'… those who come 'from a competing political party who is dead set against [the President's] agenda'… and those in whom he has simply lost confidence.[439]

The removal clauses were severable from the rest of the law, but the case cemented the Court's new doctrine: the sprawling administrative state can prevent accountability; technical expertise and independence are matters of convenience; agency heads are 'subordinates' of the President, who should be able to remove them without cause. This adds to the gradual tendency to erode doctrines of administrative discretion in cases where the issue involves a 'major question' or 'political significance'.[440] US agencies seem to be heading towards an era of greater judicial, and even more political, control. **4.88**

This case law provides a counterpoint to the EU, which is still undergoing its own process of agencification, and has buttressed the independence of agencies from the European Commission, which itself lacks direct democratic legitimacy. Such shortcomings are often remedied by making the agencies directly accountable to the European Parliament. Yet, this has already raised conflicts with national constitutional courts. The German Federal Constitutional Court (FCC) ruled in 2019 on the constitutionality of the Banking Union's Single Supervisory Mechanism (SSM), Single Resolution Mechanism (SRM) and Single Resolution Fund (SRF). The FCC held that the 'constitutional' basis of the SSM (Article 127(6) TFEU), and SRM (Article 114 TFEU) rendered them constitutional *provided that they were interpreted restrictively*.[441] More importantly, the FCC held that the independence of the ECB and the Single Resolution Board (SRB) undermined democratic legitimacy,[442] a **4.89**

---

[436] *Collins v Yellen* (n 433) para 29.
[437] ibid paras 29–30.
[438] ibid paras 30–31: 'This argument fails because the President's removal power serves important purposes regardless of whether the agency in question affects ordinary Americans by directly regulating them or by taking actions that have a profound but indirect effect on their lives. And there can be no question that the FHFA's control over Fannie Mae and Freddie Mac can deeply impact the lives of millions of Americans by affecting their ability to buy and keep their homes.'
[439] *Collins v Yellen* (n 433) paras 31–32.
[440] *West Virginia v EPA* 597 US No 20–1530 (2022).
[441] 30 July 2019, 2 BvR 1685/14, 2 BvR 2631/14, paras 167–69, 233, 242, 245–46, 258, 265.
[442] ibid para 210 ('the ECB's independence is in clear conflict with the principle of the sovereignty of the people') and at 279 ('While domestic law initially provided for comprehensive democratic legitimation and oversight of measures relating to bank resolution (see (a) below), the SRM Regulation results in a diminished level of democratic legitimation').

problem that needed to be balanced by more accountability of the ECB and SRB, including administrative review by the ECB's Administrative Board of Review (ABoR), and the SRB's Appeal Panel, judicial review by EU Courts, or political accountability by the European Parliament and Council, and national parliaments, and the accountability of NCAs and NRAs, before national parliaments and courts.[443] In the FCC view, the federal government could also influence EU bodies 'indirectly' through its presence in the Council, and the national parliament could participate in this process if it was duly informed.[444] Although the FCC's position could seem strict to critics, it still showed some appreciation for the role of independence and technical expertise, and sought to justify the SSM/SRM without delving much deeper on the extent to which national governments and parliaments were involved in the process, and/or how agency heads could be appointed or removed. Thus, when gauging the optimal level of accountability of EU agencies, EU Courts and political bodies need to be conscious of the competition presented by Member States.

3.3 The relationship between court review and administrative review

4.90 Administrative review bodies are conceived to enhance agency accountability beyond judicial review, but they, in turn, add complexity, as courts need to manage the relationship between administrative and judicial review.

4.91 In the US, the case *Lucia v SEC*[445] discussed the status of administrative law judges (ALJs). The SEC instituted administrative proceeding against Raymond Lucia and his investment company for allegedly misleading investors. To enforce securities laws the SEC can preside over administrative proceedings,[446] or (typically) delegate the task to an ALJ, using a special appointment procedure.[447] In *Lucia* the ALJ Cameron Elliot found a violation of the Act in one of the claims, and imposed sanctions; the SEC remanded the case for factfinding on the other three claims,[448] and the ALJ issued a revised decision, with the same sanctions. Lucia alleged that judge Elliot's appointment (by SEC staffers) violated the Appointments Clause of the Constitution, where only the President, 'Courts of Law,' or 'Heads of Departments' can appoint 'Officers'.[449] To the SEC and the D.C. Circuit Court ALJs were 'employees', not 'officers', but the Supreme Court disagreed. Following its recent, but now consolidated doctrine on the Appointments Clause,[450] and *Freytag v Commissioner*, where the Court declared that the Special Trial Judges' (STJs) of the United States Tax Court held 'significant authority',[451] in light of their ongoing, not episodical, role, and the 'significant discretion' they exercised.[452]

---

[443] SSM/SRM (n 441) paras 213, 214, 216–17, 224, 229 (SSM), 275, 276, 281–83, 288–89 (SRM).
[444] ibid 272–73 (SRM).
[445] *Lucia v SEC* 138 S Ct 2044; 201 L Ed 2d 464 (2018).
[446] 17 CFR s 201.110 (2017).
[447] ibid. 15 USC s 78d–1(a). The SEC had five ALJs. Other staff members, rather than the Commission proper, selected them all.
[448] In the SEC's view, an ALJ's 'personal experience with the witnesses' places him 'in the best position to make findings of fact' and 'resolve any conflicts in the evidence.'
[449] US Constitution, art II, s 2 cl. 2.
[450] *Free Enterprise Fund* (n 423); *Seila Law* (n 268); *Collins v Yellen* (n 433).
[451] *Freytag v Commissioner* 501 US 868 (1991). See also *United States v Germaine* 99 US 508, 510 (1879).
[452] *Freytag v Commissioner* (n 451).

The ALJs were 'carbon copies' of the STJs, who held a permanent position, and exercised the same 'significant discretion' when carrying out 'important functions', with authority similar to those of judges (hold hearings, take testimony, examine evidence, and issue decisions with factual findings, legal conclusions, and remedies). The differences between STJs and ALJs (more limited powers to enforce discovery, and the possibility of the SEC to decide against court review of ALJs decisions) were considered minor, and thus ALJs were 'officers', whose appointment had to conform to the Appointments Clause of the Constitution.

4.92 European courts have mostly focused on the characterization of administrative review bodies, and the deference granted to their decisions. There is variation between these bodies: the Single Supervisory Mechanism (SSM) Administrative Board of Review (ABoR) issues 'opinions', which are not binding for the ECB,[453] but the Appeal Panel for the Single Resolution Board (SRB), or the Board of Appeal (BoA) for the European Supervisory Authorities (ESAs) issue 'decisions' that are binding on the authorities, and are closer to quasi-courts.

4.93 EU courts have placed ABoR Opinions not as issued by a separate body, but within the ECB's 'internal' structure, thus attributing ABoR Opinions to the ECB, eg if the ECB did not sufficiently justified a supervisory decision, but the ABoR did, the decision complied with the duty to state reasons.[454] In *Landeskreditbank*, the ECB exercised its supervisory competence over the applicant bank as a 'significant' institution;[455] the bank challenged the decision before the ABoR, and then before the General Court, which held that in so far as the decision followed the ABoR's Opinion:

> The Administrative Board of Review's Opinion is part of the context of which the contested decision forms a part and may, therefore, be taken into account for the purpose of determining whether that decision contained a sufficient statement of reasons.[456]

4.94 In the *Crédit Mutuel Arkea* case,[457] which decided whether the ECB could exercise consolidated supervision over a group whose central body was not a credit institution, the General Court held that:

> [A]lthough the reasons for the ECB's decision to organise the consolidated prudential supervision of the Crédit Mutuel group through the CNCM do not expressly appear in the contested decision, the Board of Review provided a statement of reasons in that respect ... In so far as the ECB ruled in the contested decision in conformity with the Board of Review's opinion, which forms part of the context of that decision, it must be considered

---

[453] SSM Regulation, art 24(7). See also Marco Lamandini and David Ramos Muñoz, 'Administrative Pre-Litigation Review Mechanism in the SRM: the SRM Appeal Panel' in Chiara Zilioli and Karl-Philipp Wojcik (eds), *Judicial Review in the European Banking Union* (Edward Elgar Publishing 2021) 44–58.
[454] EU Charter of Fundamental Rights, art 41 (rights of good administration).
[455] Case T-122/15 *Landeskreditbank v ECB* ECLI:EU:T:2017:337.
[456] ibid para 125.
[457] Case T-751/16 *Confédération nationale du Crédit mutuel v ECB* ECLI:EU:T:2018:475. The case was appealed, and the Court of Justice in *Crédit Mutuel* (n 199), largely confirmed the General Court decision. The same circumstances were examined in another case, Case T-52/16, which resulted in a quasi-identical ruling. See the summary by René Smits (who also acted as a voting member of the ABoR) https://ebi-europa.eu/wp-content/uploads/2019/01/Note-on-the-Arke%CC%81a-judgments-for-publication-final.pdf (accessed 24 September 2022).

that the ECB endorsed the reasons set out in the opinion and that the merits of the contested decision may be examined in the light of those reasons.[458]

4.95 In *Caisse regionale du Crédit Agricole* the General Court cited with approval the ABoR Opinion, which found lawful the ECB decision to approve four candidates as chairmen of the boards of four regional banks, but rejected their appointments as 'effective director', as against the 'four eyes' principle, which requires the separation between management and supervision of decisions.[459]

4.96 The interplay between administrative and judicial review is not always so smooth. In *SV Capital v EBA* SV Capital appealed a decision by the EBA *not to* investigate the Finnish and Estonian banking authorities,[460] and the Board held the appeal unfounded after declaring it admissible.[461] In annulment proceedings, the General Court (GC) held the action against the EBA inadmissible as time-barred,[462] but held the action against the Board admissible. The GC raised the issue of admissibility, finding that the Board had acted ultra vires by finding the appeal admissible. Since the EBA's refusal to undertake an investigation did not fall strictly within the list of 'decisions' subject to appeal, the Board had exceeded its competences.[463]

---

[458] Case T-751/16 *Crédit mutuel* (n 457) para 51.

[459] Joined Cases T-133/16–T-136/16 *Caisse régionale de crédit agricole mutuel Alpes Provence and Others v ECB* ECLI:EU:T:2018:219. The ABoR interpreted the relevant provisions of the French Financial and Monetary Code as meaning that an 'effective director' has an executive mandate, the chairperson is non-executive, and executive mandate and supervision must be separate.

[460] The authorities had refused to investigate a breach of suitability requirements by two persons from the Estonian branch of a Finnish bank.

[461] *SV Capital* (n 138).

[462] The two months since the EBA decision was notified had passed. In the Court's view, the applicant should not have waited until after the decision of the Board of Appeal, but brought the action before the GC as a precautionary measure. See *SV Capital* (n 138) para 44.

[463] ibid paras 67–69. The GC also held that the applicant was not one of the entities specifically listed in EBA Regulation, art 17(2). In so finding, the Court paid no heed to the arguments regarding fair trial rights under art 47 of the Charter that the plaintiff raised.

5
Courts' review of monetary and financial stability decisions

1 Introduction: monetary and financial stability and their legal challenges	5.01	3 Monetary policy decisions		5.08
2 Financial stability and fiscal backstops	5.06	4 Open issues: lender of last resort (LoLR) and appointment of central bank members		5.21

1 Introduction: monetary and financial stability and their legal challenges

5.01 Courts will review decisions concerning monetary or financial stability decisions only if they find that there has been a clear disregard by monetary and financial stability authorities of the legal framework that regulates their mandate and operations. The core institutions of stability are central banks, which evolved from private or semi-private entities,[1] or private sector solutions,[2] into policy-making institutions[3] in the twentieth century, with a 'core' mandate of price stability or exchange stability and other additional objectives (secondary or not[4]).

5.02 Price stability, or stability, is a 'core' objective of monetary policy,[5] which is normally executed by setting interest, and by conducting operations like asset purchases or repos in financial markets, with counterparties like dealer banks.[6] Many central banks in emerging economies focus on foreign exchange rates instead,[7] and execute purchases or sales or foreign currency

---

[1] Rosa Lastra, *International Financial and Monetary Law* (OUP 2015) ch 2; Charles Goodhart, *The Evolution of Central Banks* (MIT Press 1985).

[2] Gary Gorton, 'Clearinghouses and the Origin of Central Banking' (1985) 45 J Econ Hist 277.

[3] Tomaso Padoa Schioppa, 'Central Banks and Financial Stability: Exploring the Land in Between' in Vítor Gaspar, Philip Hartmann, and Olaf Sleijpen (eds), *The Transformation of the European Financial System* (European Central Bank 2002) https://www.ecb.europa.eu/pub/pdf/other/transformationeuropeanfinancialsystemen.pdf (accessed 24 September 2022), 269. Federal Reserve Act, ss 4, 10.

[4] See eg Diego Valiante and Others (including the two authors of this book), , *Study on exemptions for third-country central banks and other entities under the Market Abuse Regulation and the Markets in Financial Instruments Regulation MARKT/2014/069/G3/ST/OP* (2015) https://www.ceps.eu/wp-content/uploads/2017/10/Study%20on%20exemptions%20for%20third-country%20central%20banks%20and%20other%20entities%20under%20MAR%20and%20MiFIR.pdf (accessed 24 September 2022). This is more marked in the case of the Hong Kong Monetary Authority (HKMA), the Monetary Authority of Singapore (MAS), or the Central Bank of Mexico (Banxico), but it also presents in the People's Bank of China (PBoC), the Bank of Japan (BoJ), the Reserve Bank of India (RBI), the Banco Central do Brasil, or the Swiss National Bank (SNB).

[5] Bank of International Settlements Markets Committee, 'Monetary Policy Frameworks and Central Bank Market Operations' (2019) https://www.bis.org/publ/mc_compendium.htm (accessed 24 September 2022).

[6] Frederick Mishkin, 'The Transmission Mechanism and the Role of Assets in Monetary Policy' (2001) NBER Working Paper Series Working Paper 8617; Valiante (n 4) nos 2.1.2–2.1.4, 2.3.

[7] Not all countries, in effect, distinguish between price stability and currency stability. See Valiante (n 4) no 1.1.2.

in foreign exchange (FX) markets, or invest in foreign (normally fixed-income) assets[8] (in the US or the EU central banks manage foreign reserves, but do not normally intervene in the FX market[9]). The years following the 2007–2008 financial crisis saw the emergence of 'unconventional' policies of asset purchases and expansion of central banks' balance sheets and of eligible collateral,[10] and also the establishment of bilateral currency swap agreements to supply the necessary liquidity in foreign currency.[11] The result is that central banks' mandates allows them to act both as policy-makers (setting policy rates) and private institutions (transacting in the market) and also to manipulate the market, things that present challenges to courts for deciding what is justiciable, and what is appropriate, in light of the fact that, for central banks, the means (instruments, operations) are secondary to the ultimate goal: price or exchange stability.

5.03 The crisis also resulted in a stronger focus on financial stability, to ensure that there is no sharp deviation between asset prices and fundamentals, nor credit distortions.[12] Failing to treat financial stability as part of their mandate[13] was later criticized as too narrow an approach in the wake of the 2007–2008 financial crisis.[14] Thus, central banks expanded their toolkit to support financial markets through emergency liquidity lines, and restructuring private entities (both as authorities and as creditors),[15] and some added competences in financial supervision. The ECB's role in both supporting the markets and assuming supervisory competences was controversial in the European Union, since the ECB's mandate is defined in relatively narrow terms, ie price stability,[16] accompanied by a prohibition of financial assistance to Member States,[17] and the references to both financial stability and prudential supervision, albeit present in the TFEU, are more limited.[18]

5.04 Apart from central banks, fiscal capacity is needed to buttress stability, which may have judicial implications depending on the institutional setting. The United States relies on the dollar as the ultimate reserve currency, and a centralized Treasury. Thus, during the 2007–2008 crisis there were numerous programmes and initiatives coordinated between the Federal

---

[8] Madhusudan Mohanty, 'The Transmission of Unconventional Monetary Policy to the Emerging Markets' (2014) BIS Papers 78.
[9] Valiante (n 4) no 1.1.2.
[10] Leonardo Gambacorta, 'The Effectiveness of Unconventional Monetary Policy at the Zero Lower Bound: A Cross-Country Analysis' (2014) 46 J of Money, Credit and Banking 615; Brett Fawley and Christopher Neely, 'Four Stories of Quantitative Easing' (2013) 95 Federal Reserve Bank of St Louis Review 51.
[11] B di Mauro, B Weder, and Jeromin Zettelmeyer, 'The New Global Financial Safety Net: Struggling for Coherent Governance in a Multipolar System' (2017) CIGI Essays in International Finance 4; Daniel Gros and Angela Capolongo, *Global Currencies During a Crisis: Swap Line Use Reveals the Crucial Ones* (ECON Committee In-depth study PE 648.809, 2020).
[12] Roger Ferguson, *Should Financial Stability Be An Explicit Central Bank Objective?* (Challenges to Central Banking from Globalized Financial Systems Conference at the IMF in Washington DC 2020) https://www.imf.org/external/pubs/ft/seminar/2002/gfs/eng/ferguson.pdf (accessed 24 September 2022).
[13] The so-called 'Greenspan doctrine' that central banks should not try to spot asset bubbles but simply provide monetary stimulus once they burst was very influential. Alan Greenspan 'Opening Remarks' (2002) Federal Reserve Bank of Kansas City Economic Symposium Rethinking Stabilization Policy,1-. Compare with Claudio Borio and Philip Lowe, 'Asset Prices, Financial and Monetary Stability: Exploring the Nexus' (2002) BIS Working Paper 114.
[14] Frederic S Mishkin, 'Monetary Policy Strategy: Lessons after the Crisis' (2011) NBER Working Paper 16755.
[15] See Valiante (n 4) 2.3.
[16] Consolidated version of the Treaty on the Functioning of the European Union OJ C326 (TFEU) art 127(1).
[17] ibid art 123.
[18] ibid art 127(5) (The ESCB 'shall contribute to the smooth conduct of policies pursued by the competent authorities relating to … the stability of the financial system') and (6) (The Council may confer 'specific tasks upon the ECB concerning policies relating to the prudential supervision of credit institutions and other financial institutions with the exception of insurance undertakings').

Reserve System and the Treasury through the Troubled Asset Relief Program (TARP).[19] The EU has a Monetary Union, but no fiscal union, and there are limits to financial assistance (i) between Member States;[20] (ii) and from the ECB to Member States or the European Union;[21] and (iii) rules to ensure fiscal discipline[22] and limit excessive deficits.[23] Thus, the financial crisis of 2007–2008 led to a sovereign debt crisis, and financial assistance facilities, leading to the European Stability Mechanism (ESM) through a Treaty outside EU Treaties,[24] and an amendment of the TFEU.[25] Covid-19 crisis responses were less 'financial', and more focused on the real economy, small businesses or municipal governments,[26] and also involving fiscal capacity in the EU, something unprecedented at this size, including grants to Member States, through the Next Generation EU Fund (Next Gen EU) and the Recovery and Resilience Facility, with a goal of stabilization and transformation (digitalization and sustainability[27]). Yet, the more limited institutional framework for financial assistance in the EU means that political objections can easily turn into legal challenges.

By way of introduction, central banking and monetary and financial stability have not traditionally been particularly litigious due to three main factors: first, the asymmetry of expertise between central banks and courts, which makes the latter reluctant to challenge the former openly; secondly, the emphasis on independence in central banks' basic legal,[28] or even constitutional[29] texts, which makes courts wary of being seen as interfering with it; and, thirdly, the definition of central banks' mandate through open-ended goals like price stability, full employment and economic development, currency or financial stability,[30] and the lack of a single way in which central bank *instruments* can be used to achieve them. Thus, central bank decisions may be controversial, but seldom 'unlawful', 'grossly negligent' or 'unjustifiable'. The case is similar for financial stability measures. As long as procedures have been correctly followed, the challenges to the substance of the measures will be left to the political branches of government. Yet, the degree of court scrutiny may still differ between each side of the Atlantic.[31] EU Courts are deferential, but analyse the matter, while US courts tend to often find that it is 'not their place' to adjudicate over certain decisions.

5.05

---

[19] For a comprehensive analysis see Xiaoxi Liu, 'The Costs of Bailouts in the 2007-08 Financial Crisis' (2017) 22 Fordham J of Cor & Fin L 417.

[20] TFEU (n 16) art 125.

[21] ibid art 123(1).

[22] ibid art 126.

[23] ibid art 136(3).

[24] Treaty establishing the ESM (signed on 2 February 2012) https://www.esm.europa.eu/legal-documents/esm-treaty (accessed 24 September 2022).

[25] TFEU (n 16) art 136 was amended to add a new section (3), which now reads: '[T]he Member States whose currency is the euro may establish a stability mechanism to be activated if indispensable to safeguard the stability of the euro area as a whole. The granting of any required financial assistance under the mechanism will be made subject to strict conditionality.'

[26] See a summary in the IMF, 'Policy Responses to COVID-19 Policy Tracker' https://www.imf.org/en/Topics/imf-and-covid19/Policy-Responses-to-COVID-19#U (accessed 24 September 2022).

[27] European Commission, 'Negotiation process of the 2021-2027 long-term EU budget & NextGenerationEU' https://ec.europa.eu/info/strategy/eu-budget/long-term-eu-budget/2021-2027/negotiations_en#commission-proposal-may-2020 (accessed 24 September 2022); European Commission, 'Recovery and Resilience Facility' https://ec.europa.eu/info/business-economy-euro/recovery-coronavirus/recovery-and-resilience-facility_en (accessed 24 September 2022).

[28] Federal Reserve Act 1913.

[29] TFEU (n 16) Art 130.

[30] Valiante and Others (n 4) nos 1.1.1–1.1.3; BIS, 'Monetary Policy Frameworks and Communication (2019–2022)' (2019) https://www.bis.org/am_office/rsn/mpfac.htm (accessed 24 September 2022).

[31] See Stefanie Egidy, 'Judicial Review of Central Bank Actions: Can Europe Learn from the United States?' (ECB Legal Conference 2019 'Building Bridges: Central Banking Law in an Interconnected World') 56–57.

2 Financial stability and fiscal backstops

5.06 Public interventions to protect financial stability were common, and massive, during the Great Financial Crisis (2007–2009) and the subsequent sovereign debt crisis in Europe (2010–2012) and after. In the United States the most important initiative was the TARP. The Emergency Economic Stabilization Act (EEEA) expressly provided for the possibility of judicial review, and only excluded injunctive 'or other form of equitable relief' against the Treasury Secretary, thus leaving the possibility of 'arbitrary and capricious' review under the Administrative Procedure Act (APA).[32] Yet, legal challenges to TARP or other bail-out measures were extremely rare,[33] and the only case, *Chrysler*, where the car manufacturer alleged that the TARP had been unlawfully used since the entity was not a 'financial institution' was dismissed for lack of standing. Most other complaints alleged a violation of the Takings Clause or Due Process Clause of the US Constitution, and will thus be analysed in that context.[34] Yet, the general view is that bail-outs to preserve financial stability attract little judicial scrutiny.

5.07 The situation is different in the European Union. First, although individual plaintiffs may lack standing for an action of annulment,[35] 'privileged' plaintiffs like Member States have it, and individual plaintiffs may sue before national courts, and then ask those courts to make a preliminary reference to the Court of Justice, which will adjudicate on the legality of the measures. This happened in *Pringle*,[36] where the Court examined the legality of the European Stability Mechanism (ESM). The Court ruled (correctly, in our opinion) that the ESM did not increase the Union competences in the Treaties,[37] did not encroach on the Union's exclusive competence on monetary policy,[38] nor breached the limits of the 'no bail-out clause' for states.[39] Yet, the Court concluded that the ESM did not encroach on the Union's monetary policy competence *because* this competence was linked to the European System of Central Banks' (ESCB) narrow objective of price stability, and thus monetary policy could be distinguished from economic policy.[40] Then, to justify that the ESM did not breach the constraints on mutual financial assistance between Member States the Court compared these *constraints* (less strict) with the *prohibition* of financial assistance for the ECB or National Central Banks (NCBs).[41] Both findings would be later used by the German Federal Constitutional Court

---

[32] 12 US Code, s 5229 (2012). Emergency Economic Stabilization Act of 2008, Public Law No 110-343, s 119 of the EESA stated that '[A]ctions by the Secretary pursuant to the authority of this Act … shall be held unlawful and set aside if found to be arbitrary, capricious, an abuse of discretion, or not in accordance with law'. Then, the act excluded injunctive or other forms of equitable relief, but although arbitrary and capricious can be considered 'equitable relief', it made no sense for the Act to provide for review, and then exclude it. Thus, the reference was interpreted narrowly as encompassing only interim injunctive relief. See eg Steven Davidoff and David Zaring, 'Regulation by Deal: The Government's Response to the Financial Crisis' (2009) 61 Admin L Rev 463, 520.

[33] The very comprehensive review in David Zaring, 'Litigating the Financial Crisis' (2014) 100 Va L Rev 1421, only found in the case *In re Chrysler Inc* 405 BR 79, 83 (Bankr SDNY 2009).

[34] Zaring (n 33).

[35] TFEU (n 16) art 263.

[36] Case C-370/12 *Thomas Pringle v Government of Ireland* ECLI:EU:C:2012:756.

[37] *Pringle* (n 36) paras 46 ff.

[38] ibid paras 92 ff.

[39] ibid paras 129 ff.

[40] ibid para 96.

[41] ibid para 132: 'Article 123 TFEU, which prohibits the ECB and the central banks of the Member States from granting "overdraft facilities or any other type of credit facility", employs wording which is stricter than that used in the "no bail-out clause" in Article 125 TFEU. The difference in the wording used in the latter article supports the view that the prohibition stated there is not intended to prohibit any financial assistance whatever to a Member State.'

(FCC) to challenge the legality of the ECB's 'unconventional' monetary policies. *Pringle*, however, only shows some of the strains in a system of financial stability that has been built in instalments, and has not yet overcome all of its contradictions.[42]

3 Monetary policy decisions

5.08 US courts grant an extraordinary level of deference to monetary authorities. *Raichle v Federal Reserve Bank of New York*,[43] a Great Depression case, is still an authoritative precedent, where a plaintiff's claim that the Fed's monetary policy caused him losses in his property (stocks and bonds) without due process, by 'spreading propaganda' about a shortage of money, was dismissed out of hand by a Court of Appeals that considered that it was not its place to adjudicate on monetary policy:

> [I]t would be an unthinkable burden upon any banking system if its open market sales and discount rates were to be subject to judicial review. Indeed, the correction of discount rates by judicial decree seems almost grotesque, when we remember that conditions in the money market often change from hour to hour, and the disease would ordinarily be over long before a judicial diagnosis could be made ... We can see no basis for the contention that it is a tort for a Federal Reserve Bank to sell its securities in the open market, to fix discount rates which are unreasonably high, or to refuse to discount eligible paper, even though its policy may be mistaken and its judgment bad. The remedy sought would make the courts, rather than the Federal Reserve Board, the supervisors of the Federal Reserve System, and would involve a cure worse than the malady.[44]

5.09 So far, no court has disagreed with this rationale.[45] Rather than mere deference, monetary policy decisions do not seem 'fit' for judicial review, and some suggest that they fall outside the scope of the APA.[46] Courts have rejected claims of unconstitutionality for lack of standing,[47] or used the doctrine of 'sovereign immunity' to dismiss claims against the Fed's regulation of the monetary system.[48] The only dormant threat in *Raichle* is the reference by the court to the hypothetical adoption of monetary policy made 'in bad faith'. This old proviso could be dusted off in case of a rapid deterioration of public trust, or a court willing to ingratiate itself with the public. As things stand today, the threat still looks remote.

5.10 The contrast between the US and the EU is stark. In the US, a blanket reference to central bank discretion by the courts is relatively uncontroversial. In the EU, *Gauweiler* and *Weiss*, both cases of judicial review of monetary policy decisions, stand out as some of the most important precedents in the law of finance. Why? The difference is due to the presence of

---

[42] Marco Lamandini, David Ramos Muñoz, and Violeta Ruiz Almendral, 'The EMU and Its Multi-Level Constitutional Structure' (2020) 47 Legal Issues of Economic Integration 295.
[43] *Raichle v Federal Reserve Bank of New York* 34 F 2d 910, 912 (2d Cir 1929).
[44] ibid.
[45] David Zaring, 'Law and Custom on the Federal Open Market Committee' (2015) 78 L & Contemp Probs 157.
[46] ibid.
[47] *Bryan v Federal Open Market Committee* 235 F Supp 877 (D Mont 1964).
[48] In *Research Triangle Institute v Board of Governors of the Federal Reserve System* 132 F 3d 985 (4th Cir 1997), the court rejected the plaintiff's attempt to extend the waiver of sovereign immunity of Federal Reserve *banks* to the Federal Reserve *Board*, and the parallel attempted by the plaintiff with *Mac Donald's Corp v United States* [1991] 926 F 2d 1126 (Fed. Cir), where the court extended the waiver of sovereign immunity from Navy's exchanges to the Navy Resale and Services Support Office (NAVRESSO), for its close association with the exchanges.

'vertical' tensions between constitutional texts: the EU Treaties, on one side, and national constitutions (the German *Grundgesetz* or Basic Law in both cases) on the other. *Gauweiler* was decided after the 2012 sovereign debt crisis,[49] where speculation about public finances led to rate increases in government bonds in several EU countries, putting the very existence of the euro at risk. Mario Draghi, the ECB President pledged to do 'whatever it takes to save the euro' and announced the Outright Monetary Transactions (OMT) programme, to buy an open-ended quantity of bonds from troubled euro countries in secondary markets. A group of German citizens challenged this policy before the German Federal Constitutional Court (FCC) arguing that OMT (i) was an ultra vires act outside the ECB-ESCB mandate; (ii) violated the prohibition of monetary financing under Article 123 TFEU; and (iii) undermined the principle of democratic legitimacy in the German Basic Law, and German constitutional identity.[50] The FCC made a preliminary reference procedure to ask the Court of Justice[51] about (i) and (ii) before deciding on (iii).

5.11   On a superficial level, the complaint looks similar to that under *Raichle*, but its circumstances were very different. There was no 'policy' to speak of, only the announcement of one (the plaintiffs had challenged a press release); the policy was 'unconventional'. Also, the ECB is part of the European *System* of Central Banks (ESCB, or Eurosystem), a two-level structure where National Central Banks (NCBs) are still present, and implement the decisions by the ECB's Governing Council, and the ESCB has a narrower mandate (price stability only) than the Federal Reserve. Thus, the German plaintiffs were appealing not solely to EU law, but to national law, and national sensitivities. Consequently, the FCC's first-ever preliminary reference was also very 'unconventional'. Rather than asking a question to the Court of Justice, it stated that, in its view, the ECB acts were unlawful, and asked the Court of Justice to confirm this, and hinted that it might only follow the ruling in such case.

5.12   The seriousness of the case cautioned against dismissing the preliminary reference as hypothetical (or, in US terms, 'unripe') despite the fact that the policy had not been adopted.[52] On substance, the Court of Justice used *Pringle* as its interpretative framework. There the Court had concluded that the ESM did not encroach on the Union's monetary mandate because that mandate was defined in the strict terms of price stability, and did not encompass economic policy. In *Pringle* the Court had also said that the ESM did not violate the Treaties' constraints to financial assistance between Member States *because* these were just that, constraints, and not prohibitions, like the one imposed on the ECB. The FCC used this to argue that, in light of this, OMT was 'economic policy', and thus unlawful, and to argue that it breached the absolute prohibition of monetary financing. Why such a confined reading? Because, in the FCC's view, the ECB's independence could otherwise encroach upon democratic legitimacy.

---

[49] For a more detailed analysis see Marco Lamandini, David Ramos, and Javier Solana, 'The ECB as a Catalyst for Change in EU Law (Part 1): The ECB Mandate' (2016) 23 Col J of Eur L 2.

[50] See Case C-62/14 *Gauweiler and Others* ECLI:EU:C:2015:400, para 6. On these grounds, the applicants alleged that the German Federal Government and the German Bundestag had not complied with their duty to work towards the repeal of the OMT decision or, at least, to prevent its implementation. See Bundesverfassungsgericht [BVerfG, Federal Constitutional Court], Case No 2 BvR 2728/13 (14 January 2014), para 5. An English translation of the decision is available at http://www.bundesverfassungsgericht.de/en/index.html (accessed 24 September 2022).

[51] The preliminary reference procedure is based on article 267 TFEU (n 16), and it epitomizes the 'dialogue between courts'. Based on its own established case law, the FCC considered itself competent to examine whether European institutions and agencies had trespassed their powers and violated the principle of conferral, or impinged on the constitutional identity of the German Basic Law. See *OMT* (n 50) paras 22–31. This was the first time the FCC made a reference to the CJEU. See Udo Di Fabio, 'Karlsruhe Makes a Referral' (2014) 15 German LJ 107.

[52] See *Gauweiler* (n 50) paras 19–30 for the arguments of several Member States against admissibility.

The German FCC's long-established doctrine warned that the basic democratic principle lied with nation states, and that it formed part of Germany's basic democratic identity, which could not be altered by integration in the EU. This, in its view, justified a restrictive reading of the ECB's mandate. Thus, the framing of the problem could be 'interstitial' for EU law, but was 'pivotal' for the FCC, and this changed the approach and raised the stakes.

5.13 The Court of Justice's ruling combined diplomacy and ingenuity. OMT was 'monetary' and not 'economic policy', because 'monetary policy' includes actions to restore the 'monetary policy transmission mechanism', and ensure the 'singleness of monetary policy'.[53] If certain impediments undermined the effectiveness of monetary policy, the ESCB should be able to adopt the actions necessary to remove those impediments. On financial assistance prohibitions, the Court said that the Treaties prohibited 'direct' financial assistance, eg bond purchases in primary markets, and measures with equivalent effect.[54] The finality of the provision was to ensure Member States' sound budgetary policy, and the OMT programme would purchase bonds from States undergoing structural adjustment programmes, ie not to undermine a sound budgetary policy.[55]

5.14 The thornier issue was the standard of review, because the Court of Justice could not use the (German) principle of democratic legitimacy, but could not simply fail to scrutinize the ECB's actions either. Borrowing from the Advocate General (AG) Opinion the Court used the principle of proportionality,[56] which helped to reconcile the ECB's 'broad discretion', with judicial review.[57] Proportionality was also a reliable term for a German (or continental European) tradition, to assess whether a measure is appropriate to achieve the stated goal, and whether it goes beyond what was necessary[58] in a flexible way. Notably, the Court of Justice did not use the proportionality test of its case law on fundamental rights, or EU Treaty freedoms (hard proportionality), but that of Article 5(4) TEU, which refers to Union action, and is relatively deferential[59] (soft proportionality) more based on the duty of the institution to give reasons for its actions.[60] This helped the Court to stay within EU law principles, while facilitating some common ground for the national court. The FCC's final decision in *Gauweiler* took on board the Court of Justice's decision,[61] but objected to what it saw as a lax approach on the assessment of the facts, the distinction between 'monetary' and 'economic'

---

[53] 'The ability of the ESCB to influence price developments by means of its monetary policy decisions in fact depends, to a great extent, on the transmission of the 'impulses' which the ESCB sends out across the money market to the various sectors of the economy. Consequently, if the monetary policy transmission mechanism is disrupted, that is likely to render the ESCB's decisions ineffective in a part of the euro area and, accordingly, to undermine the singleness of monetary policy. Moreover, since disruption of the transmission mechanism undermines the effectiveness of the measures adopted by the ESCB, that necessarily affects the ESCB's ability to guarantee price stability. Accordingly, measures that are intended to preserve that transmission mechanism may be regarded as pertaining to the primary objective laid down in Art 127(1) TFEU.'

[54] *Gauweiler* (n 50) para 102.

[55] ibid paras 112–18.

[56] ibid paras 66 ff.

[57] ibid para 69: '[W]here an EU institution enjoys broad discretion, a review of compliance with certain procedural guarantees is of fundamental importance. Those guarantees include the obligation for the ESCB to examine carefully and impartially all the relevant elements of the situation in question and to give an adequate statement of the reasons for its decisions.'

[58] ibid para 67.

[59] Ibid para 67 'the principle of proportionality requires that acts of the EU institution be appropriate for attaining the legitimate objectives pursued by the legislation at issue and do not go beyond what is necessary to achieve those objectives' The institutions of the Union shall apply the principle of proportionality as laid down in the Protocol on the application of the principles of subsidiarity and proportionality.

[60] *Gauweiler* (n 50) paras 69–71.

[61] Judgment of 21 June 2016, 2 BvR 2728/13, 2 BvE 13/13, 2 BvR 2731/13, 2 BvR 2730/13, 2 BvR 2729/13 (*Gauweiler II*).

policy, and the prohibition of monetary financing.[62] Nonetheless, the FCC concluded that the ECB had not 'manifestly' exceeded its competences[63] as the FCC's ultra vires test requires, and found some solace in the fact that the Court of Justice, by using a proportionality analysis and the duty to state reasons, had provided a modicum of judicial review.[64]

5.15 The underlying problem did not go away, however, and as the sovereign debt crisis morphed into an economic crisis with deflationary pressures, the ECB's Governing Council adopted a series of 'unconventional' monetary policy programs,[65] including, from January 2015, its Public Sector Purchase Program (PSPP) for the purchase of government bonds from *all* Member States[66] (not just specific countries, as in OMT) by National Central Banks (NCB). In its preliminary reference the German FCC again express its dissatisfaction with what it perceived to be a potentially illegal act. In *Weiss* the FCC used *Gauweiler* to argue that: (i) PSPP's had 'direct economic effects' on banks' balance sheets or sovereign states, which put it outside 'monetary' policy; (ii) there was no adequate statement of reasons to justify PSPP, nor a proportionality assessment by the ECB about potential side effects; and (iii) the PSPP's violated the prohibition of monetary financing under Article 123 of the TFEU.[67] The Court of Justice upheld the PSPP.[68] PSPP consisted in bond purchases, and these are considered ECB 'instruments'; the fact of having an impact in banks' balance sheets or sovereign finances could not immediately place them outside 'monetary policy'.[69] Furthermore, the measure was not vitiated by a manifest error of assessment, the existence of deflationary pressures was well-established, and PSPP sought to counter it,[70] and the measure did not go beyond what was necessary, since it was not obvious that a different measure could have achieved a similar outcome,[71] the measure was temporary,[72] and there were criteria to limit the eligible securities and amounts purchased.[73] Also, there was evidence that the ECB had weighed potentially negative side effects, and that it had adopted measures to limit potential losses.[74] Finally, the Court of Justice also held that the PSPP did not breach the prohibition of monetary financing, since it did not consist in purchases in the primary market,[75] and the 'blackout' waiting period it imposed before purchasing bonds, and other design conditions ensured that Member States could not rely on PSPP when making their offerings, nor banks when making their purchases.[76] The temporary and quantitative limits of the policy were

---

[62] ibid paras 181–89.
[63] ibid para 190.
[64] ibid paras 193–94.
[65] These included the Asset-backed Securities Purchase Programme (ABSPP), the third Covered Bond Purchase Programme (CBPP3), and the fourth Corporate Sector Purchase Programme (CSPP), as well as a new Targeted Long Term Refinancing Operation /TLTRO). This was further extended by Decision 2016/810 (ECB/2016/10) (OMRLT-II) and, with respect to seven targeted refinancing operations, by Decision 2019/1311 (ECB/2019/21) (OMRLT-III). See Marco Lamandini and David Ramos Muñoz, 'Monetary policy judicial review by 'hysteron proteron'? In praise of a judicial methodology grounded on facts and on a sober and neutral appraisal of (ex ante) macro-economic assessments' *EU Law Live* (20 May 2020).
[66] The PSPP was implemented initially to run until September 2016 for a monthly amount of €60 billion euros, and then expanded until the end of 2017 (ECB/2015/2464) and further increased to a maximum amount of €80 billion until March 2017 (ECB/2016/702 and ECB/2017/100).
[67] Case C-493/17 *Weiss and Others* ECLI:EU:C:2018:1000.
[68] ibid.
[69] ibid paras 53–70.
[70] ibid paras 75–78.
[71] ibid paras 80–83.
[72] ibid paras 84–87.
[73] ibid paras 87–90.
[74] ibid paras 94–99.
[75] ibid paras 101–108.
[76] ibid paras 109–28.

also considered sufficient to conclude that the policy would not deter Member States from pursuing a sound budgetary policy.[77]

5.16 The FCC's subsequent decision (*Weiss II*)[78] following the Court of Justice's was harsh, holding that both the ECB *and* the Court of Justice had acted ultra vires, because the Court's proportionality analysis failed to set any meaningful limit on the ECB's actions,[79] and the ECB had not offered any evidence to justify the *necessity* of the measure, or its side effects. The FCC judged the Court of Justice's proportionality analysis 'incomprehensible'.[80] In our view, the FCC was wrong. One can very well disagree with the rationale for the ECB measures, and yet admit that a court should not adjudicate economics.[81] However, the main problem with the FCC decision is that it did not challenge the rationale so much as say that 'there was no evidence' that the ECB had considered its alternatives (necessity) and side effects (proportionality).[82] This was untrue, as there was overwhelming evidence that the ECB had considered the PSPP's necessity, side effects and alternatives.[83] Fortunately, the FCC left the door open to be offered more evidence that justified that a proportionality exercise had been conducted, which was done through the presentation of documents by the Bundesbank and through parliamentary questions.[84]

5.17 The second problem in the FCC's decision is its grasp of monetary policy. To the FCC, both the Court of Justice and the ECB disregarded 'economic policy effects' such as those on 'public debt, personal savings, pension and retirement schemes, real estate prices and the keeping afloat of economically unviable companies'.[85] To build its theory, the FCC focused on the difference in the Treaty between monetary policy (conferred to the ESCB) and economic policy (to Member States). Yet, to infer a stark distinction between 'monetary policy objectives' and 'economic policy effects'[86] is a *non sequitur*.[87] At the risk of stating the obvious: monetary policy means that certain instruments (eg interest rates, bond purchases)

---

[77] ibid paras 129–43. The Court dismissed as too hypothetical the question of whether it would be contrary to the financial assistance prohibitions to give rise to a situation where the losses in government bonds forced the recapitalization of a national central bank, and other central banks shared the losses. ibid paras 159–66.

[78] BVerfG 2 BvR 859/15, 2 BvR 1651/15, 2 BvR 2006/15 and 2 BvR 980/16 (5 May 2020) (*Weiss II*); see Filippo Annunziata, Marco Lamandini, and David Ramos Muñoz, 'Weiss and EU Union Banking Law: A Test for the Fundamental Principles of the Treaty' (2020) EBI Working Paper Series 67 for a more detailed analysis.

[79] *Weiss II* (n 78) paras 127, 136, 140–44, 146.

[80] ibid para 116.

[81] In fact, the Court of Justice acknowledged that the economic arguments could be disputed, but that this did not suffice to establish a 'manifest error of assessment'. ibid para 91.

[82] ibid paras 137–49.

[83] For a synthesis of these see eg Lamandini and Ramos Muñoz (n 65); Annunziata, Lamandini, and Ramos Muñoz (n 78) 46–52. Maybe the FCC considered that the ECB should have stated those reasons in the text of the decisions themselves adopting the PSPP (Decisions 2015/2464 and 2017/100). Paragraphs 132–36 of *Weiss II* suggest that the German court's primary source was the text of the decisions themselves. However, in paras 137–49 the Court suggested also that there was no evidence beyond the decisions. Nor did the FCC challenge the Court of Justice premise (at 33) that compliance with the duty to state reasons must 'be assessed by reference not only to the wording of the measure but also to its context and to the whole body of legal rules governing the matter in question' nor contested the Court of Justice's careful analysis of text and context in paras 34–41 (with numerous examples of the ECB's balancing exercise). Since some ECB sources were referred to in the Court of Justice's decision, the FCC statement looks even more bizarre.

[84] European Parliament, 'Parliamentary Questions on the Judgment of the German Constitutional Court on the PSPP' (13 May 2020) https://www.europarl.europa.eu/doceo/document/E-9-2020-002957_EN.html (accessed 24 September 2022).

[85] *Weiss II* (n 78) 139.

[86] ibid 159.

[87] In *Gauweiler* the Court of Justice seemed to accept the FCC's distinction as a premise, something that we criticized. See Lamandini, Ramos Muñoz, and Solana (n 49) 17–18. Fortunately, in *Weiss* (n 67) the Court of Justice pointed to the futility of attempting to differentiate between monetary goals and economic effects.

are used to *cause economic effects* (in asset prices, wages, imports/exports, etc.) that ultimately lead to the monetary policy objective (price stability).[88] These economic effects are foreseeable, well-known, and sought by the policy. If this, in the FCC's view, renders the policy illegal, then *every* monetary policy action would be illegal;[89] even a by-the-book intervention that raises interest rates to fight inflation and causes a recession, or at the other extreme of the spectrum a by-the-book intervention that keeps interest rates low and causes bubbles and inflation would be unlawful and/or disproportionate.

5.18 Finally, the argument pervading the FCC judgment and approach is that democratic legitimacy was at stake. This is one of the principles of Germany's 'eternity clause of the Constitution', which in some aspects cannot be altered, and puts a limit to integration, and highlights the principle of conferral to control EU integration.[90] Since the ECB is an independent institution lacking democratic legitimacy, it must be subject to a stricter scrutiny.[91] Yet, this is based on an unfortunate and disputable, in our view theory that the ultimate *demos*, or depositary of democratic legitimacy is only the nation state.[92] This demands a stricter scrutiny from the Court of Justice, and, at the same time, makes the Court 'unworthy' to discuss arguments of democratic legitimacy, since only the national highest courts could speak of them with authority.

5.19 Despite the FCC's judgment many flaws, at least two elements invite reflection. First, if an issue is characterized as 'pivotal' or 'fundamental', it will be hard for courts to dodge the technicalities of the case. In this context courts risk criticism for endangering separation of powers, and for taking over a task they are unsuitable to do.[93] Yet, if the alternative is a constitutional crisis, courts must be prepared to weigh narratives and expected effects more assertively. The Court of Justice did this convincingly in these cases, but in future cases it may need to be willing to challenge the narratives of public authorities, and possibly require expert evidence when needed. A second lesson is that, in these cases, the discussion about 'monetary versus economic', 'statement of reasons', or 'proportionality' was a surrogate for the real argument, which was about democratic legitimacy and accountability. And this may be the point where the Court of Justice's reasoning in *Gauweiler* and *Weiss* could have been better fine-tuned.[94] Even if the ECB's actions were justified, the fact is that a central bank is credible because it has at its disposal an unlimited ability to create money and purchase assets, and thus saying that the programmes were proportionate because they were limited, like the ECB and the Court of Justice did, is not fully convincing. The exercise of such power presents a risk for central bank independence, in the form of greater political pressure,[95] once the central bank's balance sheet is loaded with government bonds.

---

[88] *Weiss* (n 67) paras 64–66.
[89] ibid para 67: '[I]f the ESCB were precluded altogether from adopting such measures when their effects are foreseeable and knowingly accepted, that would, in practice, prevent it from using the means made available to it by the Treaties for the purpose of achieving monetary policy objectives.'
[90] See eg *Weiss II* (n 78) paras 100–103, 106, 113, 142–43.
[91] ibid paras 157–59.
[92] This view comes from the FCC's cases BVerfGE 89, 155 (12 October 1993); and Cases 2 BvR 2134/92, 2 BvR 2159/92 (12 October 1993) (Maastricht) and BVerfG, 2 BvE 2/08 (30 June 2009) (Treaty of Lisbon).
[93] See eg Matthias Lehmann, 'Varying standards of judicial scrutiny over central bank actions' (ECB Legal Conference 2017) 112, 126 ff; and also Matthias Lehmann, 'The End of 'Whatever it takes'? – The German Constitutional Court's Ruling on the ECB Sovereign Bond Programme' Oxford Business Law Blog (7 May 2020) https://www.law.ox.ac.uk/business-law-blog/blog/2020/05/end-whatever-it-takes-german-constitutional-courts-ruling-ecb (accessed 24 September 2022).
[94] Lamandini, Ramos, and Solana (n 49) 16–17.
[95] *Weiss II* (n 78) para 161.

5.20 The *answer*, however, is not to declare the measure illegal, but to acknowledge the risk, and the need for greater democratic accountability, not to undermine, but to protect independence. In this sense, *Gauweiler* and *Weiss* must be read not only in light of *Pringle*, but also of the *SSM/SRM* ruling[96] on bank supervision. There the General Court and the Court of Justice adopted a relatively centralizing approach, and side-stepped issues of accountability, thus leaving the FCC dissatisfied, and also as the sole standard bearer of democracy. Instead of this, the Court of Justice could have offered an alternative (and compelling) narrative, where democratic legitimacy is vested both in national parliaments and the European Parliament, and accompanied by accountability tools. The ECB routinely gives explanations before the European Parliament for its monetary and its supervisory tasks, and even if this form of accountability can be improved,[97] the European Parliament typically does a better job than national parliaments, which tend to show no interest on these matters. Finally, matters susceptible of constitutional collision could be resolved with a more imaginative use of inter-court dialogue.[98]

4 Open issues: lender of last resort (LoLR) and appointment of central bank members

5.21 Having seen the matters that have been tested before the courts, it remains to see what matters are still untested. These include central banks' lender of last resort (LoLR) functions, and the appointment of central bank members. LoLR has not been challenged in the US or the EU (where, however, access to the unredacted content of LoLR decisions has been a litigated issue in the wake of banks' failures and the adoption of crisis management measures).[99] In the US, one likely setting could be the Federal Reserve's emergency lending authority under Section 13(3). Its initially broad language said that the Board of Governors 'in unusual and exigent circumstances' could lend money to individuals or corporations if it is a last resort, and the loan is 'secured to the satisfaction of the Federal Reserve Bank',[100] a proviso used to (controversially) refuse a loan to Lehman Brothers.[101] The provision was restricted by the Dodd-Frank Act in 2010.[102] Section 13(3) now requires that the borrower is a 'participant in any programme or facility with broad-based eligibility', and that assistance was required 'for

---

[96] BVerfG 2 BvR 1685/14, 2 BvR 2631/14 (30 July 2019). Compare Raffaele D'Ambrosio and Donato Messineo (eds), *The German Federal Constitutional Court and the Banking Union* (Quaderni di Ricerca Giuridica della Consulenza Legale Bank of Italy, No 91, 2021) 7–117 (and an English translation of relevant excerpts of the judgment at 255).

[97] Marco Lamandini and David Ramos Muñoz, 'Banking Union's accountability system in practice: A health check-up to Europe's financial heart' (2022) Eur Law J volume 28, issue 4-6, 187-217–; Marco Lamandini and David Ramos Muñoz, 'SSM and SRB Accountability at European level: What Room For Improvements?' Study requested by the ECON Committee of the European Parliament, PE 645.711 (April 2020).

[98] See Lamandini, Ramos Muñoz, and Ruiz Almendral (n 42).

[99] Compare e.g. Case T-251/15 *Espirito Santo Financial (Portugal) v ECB* ECLI:EU:T:2018:234 and on appeal Case C-442/18 *ECB v Espirito Santo Financial (Portugal)* ECLI:EU:C:2019:1117.

[100] Federal Reserve Act, s 13(3) (before 2010); more recently Case T-827/17 *Aeris Invest v ECB* ECLI:EU:T:2021:660.

[101] The Board argued that it *could not* lend. Authors have debated this. Some argue that the Board could lend because it had enough powers, but could also refuse. Peter Conti-Brown, *The Power and Independence of the Federal Reserve* (PUP 2016); Laurence M Ball, 'The Fed and Lehman Brothers' NBER Monetary Economics Program (14 July 2016) 218. Others defend the Board's position. Philip Wallach, *To the Edge. Legality, Legitimacy, and the Responses to the 2008 Financial Crisis* (Brookings Institution Press 2015).

[102] See Marc Labonte, 'Federal Reserve: Emergency Lending Congressional Research Service' (2020) R44185 https://crsreports.congress.gov (accessed 24 September 2022).

the purpose of providing liquidity to the financial system, and not to aid a failing financial company'[103] (ie system-wide, and not individual ad hoc liquidity assistance), and precludes lending to an insolvent firm, or lending 'to remove assets from the balance sheet of a single and specific company', and requires the loans to be secured 'sufficient[ly] to protect taxpayers from losses', and any programme 'to be terminated in a timely and orderly fashion'. It is unclear, however, who is the ultimate authority to interpret these concepts, ie the courts or the Federal Reserve.

5.22 In the European Union, the ECB has declared that it lacks the legal basis for LoLR (or Emergency Liquidity Assistance—ELA), which, under the decentralized ESCB system, belongs to national central banks (NCBs),[104] although it has a veto power over the exercise of ELA functions by National Central Banks.[105] This position is debatable,[106] and presents a similar problem to the Fed's refusal to lend to Lehman Brothers: a legal provision used to justify a policy decision that is controversial. In the recent case of *Del Valle Ruiz v Spain*, an international investment arbitration tribunal ruled that the Bank of Spain did not exceed its discretion in not granting ELA to Banco Popular, a failed bank, but the decision also showed that the ELA process involves close coordination between the ECB and NCBs, while ultimately it is the NCB alone that faces scrutiny.[107] This also involves risks, as a national court or international investment tribunal may hinder the effectiveness and coherence of what should function as an EU-based scheme. In our view,[108] the ECB could exercise ELA/LoLR functions if they can be related to its 'price stability' mandate (including financial stability), its role 'to promote the smooth operation of payment systems', or to contribute to the smooth conduct of prudential supervision and financial stability policies by competent authorities.[109]

5.23 The second open issue is the appointment and removal of central bank members. In the Federal Reserve System, the latent threat lies in the constitutionality of the appointment of Presidents and Vice-Presidents of Reserve Banks. The seven members of the Board of Governors, its most important governing body, are appointed by the President, and

---

[103] Federal Reserve Act (current), s 13(3).
[104] ECB, ELA Procedures (the procedures underlying the Governing Council's role pursuant to Article 14.4 of the Statute of the European System of Central Banks and of the European Central Bank with regard to the provision of ELA to individual credit institutions) https://www.ecb.europa.eu/pub/pdf/other/201402_elaprocedures.en.pdf (accessed 24 September 2022).
[105] 'Article 14.4 of the Statute of the European System of Central Banks and of the European Central Bank (Statute of the ESCB) assigns the Governing Council of the ECB responsibility for restricting ELA operations if it considers that these operations interfere with the objectives and tasks of the Eurosystem'. ECB ELA Procedures (n 104).
[106] Compare eg in the same volume of ECB Legal Conference 2015: From Monetary Union to Banking Union, on the Way to Capital Markets Union https://www.ecb.europa.eu/pub/pdf/other/frommonetaryuniontobankingunion201512.en.pdf. (accessed 24 September 2022) the contributions by Chiara Zilioli, 'Introduction' 49; Christos V Gortsos, 'Last Resort Lending to Solvent Credit Institutions in the Euro Area before and after the Establishment of the Single Supervisory Mechanism (SSM)' 53; and R Lastra, 'Reflections on Banking Union, Lender of Last Resort and Supervisory Discretion' 154.
[107] *Del Valle Ruiz and Others v The Kingdom of Spain* (2023) Case No 2019-17, Final Award, https://www.italaw.com/cases/6822 (accessed 12 August 2023), paras. 604-659.
[108] Lamandini, Ramos, and Solana (n 49) 21–22.
[109] TFEU (n 16) Art 127(2) (payment systems) and 127(5) (contribution to smooth conduct of prudential supervision and financial stability policies). If payments systems like Target2 are used. See Francesco Purificato and Caterina Astarita, 'TARGET2 Imbalances and the ECB as Lender of Last Resort' (2015) 3 Int J Fin Stud 482; Ulrich Bindseil and Philipp Johann König, 'The Economics of Target 2 Balances' (2011) Discussion Paper 2011-035, SFB 649. If the ECB could contribute to prudential supervision and/or financial stability policies when competent authorities were in Member States, it should be able now that the ECB itself is the main competent prudential authority in the Banking Union.

confirmed by the Senate,[110] but the regional Federal Reserve Banks were traditionally private entities, with directors appointed by the owning banks, directors which, in turn, appointed the Presidents and Vice-presidents in each Federal Reserve Bank.[111] The Federal Open Market Committee (FOMC), the fed's most important policy-making body, is formed by *both* the seven members of the Board of Governors *and* the five members chosen from the Presidents and Vice-Presidents of the regional banks. Thus, some argue that this could be contrary to the Appointments Clause of the US Constitution,[112] especially since, in cases of vacancies, the banking industry could have control over the FOMC.[113] In *Riegle v FOMC* senator Riegle challenged the constitutionality of the appointment mechanism, but the court excluded the lawsuit on grounds of equitable discretion, and courts have tended to deny standing to all plaintiffs, and render these issues de facto non-justiciable.[114] In *Melcher* the district court considered that this was illogical, as 'the result is that section 263(a) is immune from constitutional attack',[115] but concluded that the 'balance of public and private elements' meant that FOMC members were not 'officers' of the United States, and thus did not need to be appointed subject to the Appointments Clause.[116] On appeal, however, the Circuit Court maintained that the equitable discretion doctrine in *Riegle* applied, even if this ruled out the possibility of judicial challenges.[117] Although this seems to close access to judicial review, a recent line of case law by the US Supreme Court has put increasing pressure on the need that the appointments of agencies (especially independent agencies) complies with the Appointments Clause.[118] This increases the chance that courts may revise past precedents (the Supreme Court denied certiorari in *Melcher*, for example).

In the EU, the challenges for the appointment of central bank members arose in *Rimšēvičs v Latvia and ECB v Latvia*,[119] where the governor of a Latvian bank was 'relieved from office' for alleged corruption, which also meant Latvia's removal as an ECB member. Even if the ECB had only requested the Court to find that Latvia had infringed Article 14(2) of the Statute of the ESCB, the Court of Justice went further and held that it was competent to review a national legal act affecting the ECB's independence, and to annul such measure, because that article derogated from the general distribution of powers between the Court and national courts, and the ESCB, by combining NCBs with the ECB resulted in 'a less marked distinction between the EU legal order and national legal orders.[120] **5.24**

---

[110] 12 US Code s 241.

[111] 12 US Code ss 263(a), 302, 304.

[112] US Constitution, art II, s 2 cl 2, states that '[the President] shall nominate, and by and with the Advice and Consent of the Senate, shall appoint ... all other Officers of the United States'.

[113] Conti-Brown (n 101) See also Peter Conti-Brown, 'The Institutions of Federal Reserve Independence' (2015) 32 YJR 257.

[114] In *Riegle* the court used equitable discretion to dismiss an appeal by a senator, assuming that private plaintiffs could sue, but in *Committee for Monetary Reform v Board of Governors* 766 F 2d 538 (DC Cir 1985) private plaintiffs were denied standing.

[115] *Melcher v Federal Open Market Committee* 644 F Supp 510, 516–17 (DDC 1986).

[116] ibid 523–24.

[117] *John Melcher, Honorable Member, United States Senate, Appellant v Federal Open Market Committee and Others* 836 F 2d 561 (DC Cir 1987).

[118] *Free Enterprise Fund v Public Company Accounting Oversight Board* 561 US 477 (2010); *Seila Law LLC v Consumer Financial Protection Bureau* 140 S Ct 2183 (2020); *Collins v Yellen* 141 S Ct 1761 (2021).

[119] Cases C-202/18 *Ilmārs Rimšēvičs v Republic of Latvia* ECLI:EU:C:2019:139 and C-238/18 *European Central Bank v Republic of Latvia*, Opinion of AG Kokott ECLI:EU:C:2018:1030; Joined Cases C-202/18 and C-238/18 *Rimšēvičs v Latvia and European Central Bank v Republic of Latvia* EU:C:2019:139.

[120] René Smits, 'ECJ Annuls a National Measure against an Independent Central Banker' (*European Law Blog*, 26 February 2019) https://europeanlawblog.eu/2019/03/05/ecj-annuls-a-national-measure-against-an-independent-central-banker/ (accessed 24 September 2022).

6
Courts' Review of Regulatory and Supervisory Decisions

1 Introduction: regulatory and supervisory frameworks and their legal challenges	6.01	4.2 Financial groups	6.42
2 Vertical allocation of powers and judicial review in regulatory and supervisory decisions	6.06	5 A comparative assessment of courts' standard of review	6.47
2.1 The experience in the US: branching restrictions, FinTech, and administrative discretion	6.06	5.1 US courts' 'arbitrary and capricious' standard: the 'demanding' version, and its challenge to the substantive application of the law	6.48
2.2 EU law: constitutional frictions, composite procedures, and EU authorities' application of national laws	6.10	5.2 EU Courts' substantive-leaning and finalistic review: Their role as ultimate authorities in defining key concepts of the law of finance	6.52
3 Horizontal separation of powers and judicial review in regulatory and supervisory decisions	6.22	5.3 US courts' 'arbitrary and capricious' standard and procedural safeguards	6.66
4 Courts and the regulatory perimeter: shadow banking, parallel unregulated activities, and banking groups	6.33	5.4 EU Courts' process-based review and procedural safeguards	6.69
4.1 Shadow banking and parallel activities	6.34	6 Enforcement measures, sanctions, and penalties: safeguards and standard of review	6.75

1 Introduction: regulatory and supervisory frameworks and their legal challenges

Unlike the authorities entrusted with monetary policy and financial stability, regulatory and supervisory authorities are supposed to exercise more strictly rule-bound competences, which courts must review. In practice, this depends on the text, context, logic, and finality of the legal frameworks devising those competences, the presence of open-textured provisions, and the discretion granted to the agencies. Thus, 'vertical' tensions, between federal/supranational and state/national levels, and 'horizontal' tensions, mostly between executive agencies and judiciary, will be the background of many disputes. **6.01**

In addition, the first set of 'design' considerations to bear in mind is linked to the regulatory model, and its relevance for the perimeter of regulated institutions, and the allocation of competences between regulators/supervisors. The models are the 'sectoral' (banking, securities, insurance), 'single regulator', or 'twin peaks' (prudential and market conduct).[1] This **6.02**

---

[1] Michael W Taylor, 'Twin Peaks: A Regulatory Structure for the New Century' (1995) Centre for the Study of Financial Innovation, Paper No 20; J Kremers, D Schoenmaker, and P Wierts, 'Cross–Sector Supervision: Which Model?' in R Herrings and R Litan (eds), *Brookings Wharton Papers on Financial Services* (Brookings Institution Press 2003).

is important to define the 'regulatory perimeter', ie the definition of 'regulated entities', and the power to bring unregulated (or lightly regulated) entities within the purview of competent authorities. The most recent example was 'shadow banking', where non-bank financial institutions engaged in 'maturity transformation',[2] giving rise to the works of the Financial Stability Board (FSB) to define shadow banking 'functions', and identify its risks.[3] Courts will bear in mind the logic of the rules when determining whether public authorities can bring entities inside, or leave them outside, the regulatory perimeter.

6.03 A second, related consideration concerns financial groups. Sometimes the parent company of the group may not be a licensed institution (despite a more recent regulatory trend to license as financial or mixed financial holding companies also the parent company of a financial group), but regulatory authorities may consider that it poses a risk to the group. Courts will have to decide whether the rules allow the authorities to bring such parent companies within their purview. In other cases, there may be 'structural' measures in place, which may limit the exposure of certain regulated entities (eg banks) to other entities (risky activities, from 'investment', under the Glass-Steagall Act, to certain hedge funds or proprietary trading, under the Volcker Rule in the Dodd-Frank Act). Courts will have to decide whether authorities enforce these restrictions properly.

6.04 A third 'design' consideration concerns the exercise of regulatory or supervisory powers for macroprudential reasons, which means addressing a system-wide problem by means of measures that affect individual institutions. This makes economic sense,[4] but courts need to be extra cautious that the usual tests of 'arbitrary and capriciousness', 'giving reasons' or proportionality.

6.05 Prudential considerations are also relevant, as they impose restrictions on financial institutions to ensure their solvency and liquidity,[5] which financial institutions have an incentive to evade, by trying to rely on their own assessment of risks. This 'cat and mouse' game has resulted in the Basel Framework going from the originally scant thirty pages to the unreasonably (if 'better regulation' has to be taken seriously) more than 700, with the logical increase in complexity. This poses challenges on the treatment of certain 'capital' instruments, the risk weights of certain exposures, or financial firms' need for robust governance systems, and/or remunerations systems that do not incentivize risk.

2 Vertical allocation of powers and judicial review in regulatory and supervisory decisions

2.1 The experience in the US: branching restrictions, FinTech, and administrative discretion

6.06 In the US, there is ample experience with 'vertical' tensions between federal and state levels due to the 'dual banking system' with federal and state charters. At some point,

---

[2] Paul McCulley, 'Teton Reflections' (2007) PIMCO Global Central Bank Focus.
[3] FSB, *The Financial Crisis and Information Gaps. Second Phase of the G-20 Data Gaps Initiative (DGI-2)* (2017) https://www.imf.org/external/np/g20/pdf/2017/092117.pdf.
[4] Markus Brunnermeier and Others, 'The Fundamental Principles of Financial Regulation' (2009) 11 Geneva Reports on the World Economy xv.
[5] Daniel K Tarullo, *Banking on Basel: The Future of International Financial Regulation* (Peterson Institute for International Economics 2008) 33–34.

state-chartered banks could open branches in some states, depending on applicable state laws, while federally chartered banks were forbidden to do so by federal statute.[6] This placed federally chartered banks at a competitive disadvantage, and federal authorities tried to stretch federal acts to their limit, and were challenged before the Supreme Court.[7] In *First National Bank of St. Louis v Missouri ex rel Barret* the Supreme Court annulled the Attorney General's interpretation that national banks' 'incidental powers' allowed them to open 'teller windows'.[8] Congress' reacted by passing the McFadden Act,[9] later amended by the Glass-Steagall Act,[10] to allow federally-chartered banks to open branches on the same conditions as state-chartered banks.[11] This created a problem when federal authorities tried to be more flexible than state laws. In *Walker* the Supreme Court held that the OCC had to comply with a Utah statute that only allowed branching through the acquisition of existing banks,[12] and in *Dickinson* the Court invalidated OCC rulings authorizing national banks to operate 'mobile messenger services' and off-premises 'deposit machines' as part of their 'incidental powers', holding that 'branch' was a term of federal law (and could not be determined by state law) *but* these activities were against the branching prohibition.[13] Crucially, the Court reached that conclusion in light of the Act's goal of competitive equality, which prohibited advantaging some banks over others.[14] The district courts used this approach to provide an expansive interpretation of the term 'branch', which included drive-in facilities,[15] offices for trust services,[16] loan production offices,[17] or even automatic teller machines (ATMs),[18] in a way that constrained the attempts by federal authorities to ease branching restrictions. The approach changed in the 1980s, where the courts adopted a more deferential approach towards administrative agencies.

The important thing is that, although the issue of branch restrictions presented sociological or political economy implications,[19] and the debates of the McFadden and Glass-Steagall

6.07

---

[6] The National Bank Act of 3 June 1864, ch 106, 13 Stat 101 (in different sections of 12 US Code) did not mention the opening of 'branches' among the incidental powers of nationally chartered banks.

[7] See Michelle L Odorizzi, 'Customer-Bank Communication Terminals and the McFadden Act Definition of a 'Branch Bank' (1975) 42 The U of Chicago L Rev 362.

[8] *First National Bank v Missouri* 263 US 640, 659 (1924).

[9] House of Representatives 2, 69th Cong, 1st Sess (18 June 1926).

[10] Banking Act of 1933, ch 89, 48 Stat 162 (Glass-Steagall Act).

[11] National and state banks could open branches in the state to the extent that this was 'authorized to State banks by the statute law of the State in question by language specifically granting such authority affirmatively, and not merely by implication or recognition'. See ss 23(c)(2) 12 US Code s 36(c)(2) (1970).

[12] *First National Bank of Logan v Walker Bank & Trust Co* 385 US 252 (1966). It dismissed the OCC interpretation that held that, once a state permitted branching in some way, branching conditions had to be those under federal law.

[13] The Court made short shrift of the OCC argument that, under the banks' contracts, the monies would not be deemed 'deposited' until brought to the teller at the main bank. *First National Bank in Plant City v Dickinson* 396 US 122, 137 (1969).

[14] See *First National Bank of Logan* (n 12) 262, and *Dickinson* (n 13) 137–38, where the Court held that: 'Unquestionably, a competitive advantage accrues to a bank that provides the service of receiving money for deposit at a place away from its main office; the convenience to the customer is unrelated to whether the relationship of debtor and creditor is established at the moment of receipt or somewhat later.'

[15] *Dakota National Bank v First National Bank & Trust Co* 414 F Supp 1161 (DND 1976), rev'd, 554 F 2d 345 (8th Cir 1977) cert denied, 434 US 877 (1977). North Dakota's law, which governed the bank expansion, could be read as allowing one drive-in facility as an 'extension', but more than one would violate McFadden restrictions.

[16] *St Louis County National Bank v Mercantile Trust Co* 548 F 2d 716 (8th Cir 1976) cert denied, 433 US 909 (1977).

[17] *Independent Bankers Association v Heimann* [1979] No 78-0811, slip op at 1 n 1 (DDC 29 Mar 1979) (mem), rev'd, 627 F 2d 486 (DC Cir 1980) (hereafter *Independent Bankers Association v Heimann*). The Circuit Court reversed, but only because it considered the claim barred under the doctrine of *laches*.

[18] *Independent Bankers Association v Heimann* (n 17).

[19] See eg Raghuram G Rajan and Rodney Ramcharan, 'Land and Credit: A Study of the Political Economy of Banking in the United States in the Early 20th Century' (2011) 66 The J of Fin 1895.

Acts were rich on economic arguments about competition or stability,[20] the courts' focus was very different. First, the courts appealed to Act's *finality* of competitive equality. In a second stage, courts deferred to agencies to determine how the Act should be interpreted. In *SIA v OCC*, for example, the district and circuit courts held that an OCC authorization to two national banks to establish brokerage subsidiaries violated the McFadden Act,[21] but the Supreme Court reversed, holding that the Act's restrictions applicable to 'the general business of banking' could *plausibly* be read (like the OCC did) to cover only core banking functions.[22] Thus, the courts made a first pivot from a 'vertical' conflict between state and federal levels to a conflict of interpretation, where they claimed the ultimate power to determine the statute's meaning and goals. Subsequently, by re-framing the problem as one of deference to an agency's 'plausible' interpretation on the face of ambiguous statutory language,[23] they made a second pivot, ceding this interpretative power to the agencies. Thus, although the issue of branching restrictions faded away,[24] the underpinning legal arguments remained.

6.08 These arguments were subsequently picked up in the 'FinTech charter' cases. Under the National Bank Act (NBA) of 1864 the Office of the Comptroller of the Currency (OCC) regulates federally chartered national banks in their *'business of banking'*, and, once such banks receive a federal charter, they can 'exercise ... all such incidental powers as shall be necessary to carry on the business of banking; by discounting and negotiating promissory notes, drafts, bills of exchange, and other evidences of debt; by receiving deposits; by buying and selling exchange, coin, and bullion; by loaning money on personal security; and by obtaining, issuing, and circulating notes'. In 2003, the OCC amended federal regulations to issue Special Purpose National Bank (SPNB) charters, for national banks engaging in a limited list of banking activities, eg lending, but not deposit-taking.[25] Then, Comptroller Thomas Curry announced in late 2016 that the OCC would consider issuing SPNB charters for FinTech firms.[26] This was opposed by some states, especially New York, which argued that this was a form of pre-empting state law, and lowering consumer protection standards on, eg usury, payday loans or, predatory lending, and also that they would lose revenue as firms migrated from state to federal chartering. In 2018,[27] the OCC announced that it would

---

[20] See *First National Bank of Logan* (n 12) 259–61 for a description of the arguments of Senators McFadden and Glass, among others.

[21] *Securities Industry v Comptroller of the Currency* 577 F Supp 252 (DDC 1983), aff'd, 758 F 2d 739 (DCCir1985) cert denied, 106 S Ct 790 (1986).

[22] The Supreme Court denied certiorari on the issue of the application of the Glass Steagall separation of commercial and investment banking but it decided the issue of the McFadden Act under the case named *Clarke v SIA* 479 US 388, 404 (1987).

[23] ibid para 404.

[24] They were eliminated under the Riegle-Neal Interstate Banking and Branching Efficiency Act of 1994 HR 3841, 103rd Congress (1993–1994).

[25] The OCC-chartered firm could 'be a special purpose bank that limits its activities to fiduciary activities or to any other activities within the business of banking'. 12 CFR s 5.20(e)(1)(i), adding that 'special purpose bank that conducts activities other than fiduciary activities must conduct at least one of the following core banking functions: Receiving deposits, paying checks, *or* lending money' (emphasis added).

[26] The OCC published a white paper, entitled 'Supporting Responsible Innovation in the Federal Banking System: An OCC Perspective' (2016), later followed by a Proposed Rule-making, Receiverships for Uninsured National Banks, 81 Fed Reg 62,835, 62,837 (13 September 2016), and later (December 2016) by another white paper 'Exploring Special Purpose National Bank Charters for Fintech Companies' (2016), concluding that it could be 'in the public interest' for the OCC to grant FinTech charters.

[27] Two initial lawsuits, by the New York Director of Financial Services (DFS) and the Conference of State Bank Supervisors (CSBS) were dismissed for lack of 'ripeness' (there was no actual harm, since no SPNB charter had been issued). *Vullo v Office of Comptroller of Currency* 378 F Supp 3d 277 (2017); *CSBS v Office of the Comptroller of the Currency* 313 F Supp 3d 285, 299 (2018).

accept SPNB applications,[28] and the New York DFS brought a new lawsuit, arguing that the OCC had exceeded its authority by granting charters to non-deposit-taking institutions. The District Court in *Vullo v OCC* set aside the OCC decision,[29] concluding that the meaning of the 'business of banking' in the statutory text was 'unambiguous', pursuant to dictionaries, modern and old, and thus left no room for discretion.[30] The court also reasoned that the result would be a federal pre-emption of fintech entities, a 'dramatic disruption of federal-state relationships in the banking industry', a 'fundamental revision' of the NBA, a question of 'deep economic and political significance', 'central to the statutory scheme', which was unlikely to have been left to agency discretion.[31] However, the Second Circuit set aside the District Court decision for lack of standing/ripeness, as the DFS failed to allege an 'actual or imminent injury', and its concerns were 'too speculative', since they would arise only after the OCC actually received SPNB charter applications.[32]

6.09 It is debatable whether the court's conclusion that the complaint came 'too early' condemned any subsequent judicial remedy to arrive 'too late', but in the end it seems that New York and other states were trying to create a deterrence effect. The OCC announced later a revision of its policies,[33] and the regulatory and legal uncertainty made it less likely that many FinTechs would apply for the new federal charter. Yet, the main point is that in the US the tension between federal and state rights has, for the moment, taken second place, to the issue of administrative discretion. The question is whether the current Supreme Court, which is less deferential to administrative agencies, and more conscious of state rights,[34] will extend this logic to financial regulation, to find that a decision that upsets a regulatory scheme's balance between state and federal powers is a 'major question', not to be left to an administrative agency.

2.2 EU law: constitutional frictions, composite procedures, and EU authorities' application of national laws

6.10 In the EU, vertical tensions are more important, since the doctrine of supremacy of EU law is not uniformly accepted by national supreme (or constitutional) courts, some of which, like the German Federal Constitutional Court (FCC), have collided with the Court of Justice on

---

[28] OCC, 'Policy Statement on Financial Technology Companies' Eligibility to Apply for National Bank Charters', and the 'Comptroller's Licensing Manual Supplement: Considering Charter Applications from Financial Technology Companies' both of 31 July 2018.

[29] *Vullo v Office of Comptroller of Currency* 378 F Supp 3d 271 (SDNY 2019).

[30] Also, the evolution of the Act, with two amendments, in 1978 and 1982 to allow the chartering of 'trust banks' and 'bankers' banks', suggested, *a contrario*, that the OCC could not charter a non-depository institution absent a statutory amendment. *Vullo v Office of Comptroller of Currency 2019* (n 29) 294–95.

[31] *Vullo v Office of Comptroller of Currency 2019* (n 29), 297, citing the Supreme Court case law about agency discretion on the face of 'significant questions'.

[32] At this time, no non-depository fintech has applied for—let alone been granted—an SPNB charter, and, as DFS concedes, no state law or regulation has been preempted as a result of the Fintech Charter Decision. Thus, there is currently no non-depository fintech that can claim federal preemption engaging in any practice that may give rise to the regulatory harms that DFS alleges, such as charging interest rates that exceed New York's statutory cap. Moreover, the Fintech Charter Decision merely indicates that the OCC intends to begin accepting SPNB charter applications from non-depository fintechs; it is not a guarantee that those applications will be granted ... Moreover, even if the OCC grants an SPNB charter to some non-depository fintech, it is not entirely clear that the regulatory disruption that DFS fears will actually occur'. *Lacewell v Office of Comptroller of Currency* 999 F3d 130 (2021).

[33] ibid.

[34] Most recently see *West Virginia v EPA* 597 US No 20–1530 (2022).

monetary policy cases like *Gauweiler* in 2015, and *Weiss*, in 2020, where the FCC went (in our opinion) one step too far in its ruling, its tone, and its assessment of the facts (Ch 5 s 3). A key point often overlooked is that, although *Gauweiler* and *Weiss*' are very closely linked in substance and arguments, in the interlude between them were the parallel decisions of *Landeskreditbank*, by the General Court and the Court of Justice,[35] and the *SSM/SRM* decision, by the German Constitutional Court.[36] These two are the missing piece that shows how the German Constitutional Court had begun its frictions with the Court of Justice before *Weiss*.

6.11 The *Landeskreditbank* case was a superficially simple case, and a 'hard case' deep down. The ECB had classified *Landeskreditbank* as a 'significant' credit institution, based on its assets (larger than €30 billion). The appellant alleged that the provision of the SSMR and the Framework Regulation excluded ECB supervision in case of 'particular circumstances'. In the appellant's view, this required interpreting the concept of 'significant' institution in light of the principles of proportionality and subsidiarity.[37] This meant that supervision by the ECB was not 'necessary' or 'appropriate', since due to the bank's low-risk model supervision by the national authority (Bundesbank) was sufficient. The General Court accepted that the relevant provision had to be interpreted in light of its text, but also 'its context and of the objectives pursued by the set of rules of which it forms a part',[38] and upheld the ECB position. The 'specific factual circumstances' could exclude ECB supervision of a 'significant' institution only if direct supervision by German authorities 'would be better able to ensure the attainment of the objectives' of the SSM framework,[39] but it was the appellant's burden to prove that, something it had failed to do. Yet, the Court went one step further, holding in an *obiter* fashion, that SSM did not distribute supervisory powers between national authorities and the ECB, but created a single mechanism, which exclusively vested *all* competences on the ECB, while NCAs exercised them by re-delegation from the ECB,[40] or 'assisted' the ECB in performing its tasks.[41] The Court of Justice confirmed both the final conclusion (that it was the bank's burden to prove the 'special circumstances', which it had failed to do), and also the General Court's doctrine of 'exclusive power, decentralized (and subordinate) implementation' (instead of 'shared competences').[42]

---

[35] Case T-122/15 *Landeskreditbank Baden Württemberg v ECB* ECLI:EU:T:2017:337; on appeal Case C-450/17 P *Landeskreditbank Baden Württemberg v ECB* ECLI:EU:C:2019:372. See Raffaele D'Ambrosio and Marco Lamandini, 'La "prima volta" del Tribunale dell'Unione Europea in materia di Meccanismo Unico di Vigilanza' (2017) Giur Comm II 577; Raffaele D'Ambrosio and Marco Lamandini, 'La sentenza del 30 luglio 2019 del BverfG sull'Unione bancaria e il difficile dialogo tra Karlsruhe e Lussemburgo' (2020) Giur Comm II 962.

[36] 30 July 2019, 2 BvR 1685/14, 2 BvR 2631/14 (*SSM/SRM*). Compare Raffaele D'Ambrosio and Donato Messineo (eds), *The German Federal Constitutional Court and the Banking Union* (Quaderni di Ricerca Giuridica della Consulenza Legale, Bank of Italy No 91 2021) 7–117 (and an English translation of relevant excerpts of the judgment at 255).

[37] Treaty of the European Union (TEU), art 5. We note that this was the primary basis for the proportionality analysis by the Court of Justice in *Gauweiler* and *Weiss*.

[38] Case C-450/17 P *Landeskreditbank* (n 35) paras 40–41.

[39] Case T-122/15 *Landeskreditbank* (n 35) para 81.

[40] ibid para 54: '[i]t is apparent ... that the logic ... consists in allowing the exclusive competences delegated to the ECB to be implemented within a decentralised framework, rather than having a distribution of competences between the ECB and the national authorities in the performance of the tasks referred to in Article 4(1) of that regulation.' See also at para 59 (subordinated).

[41] Case C-450/17 P *Landeskreditbank* (n 35) paras 38, 41: '[t]he ECB is exclusively competent to carry out the tasks stated in that provision in relation to all those institutions ... The national competent authorities thus assist the ECB in carrying out the tasks conferred on it by Regulation No 1024/2013, by a decentralised implementation of some of those tasks in relation to less significant credit institutions'.

[42] Case C-450/17 P *Landeskreditbank* (n 35).

In the parallel case the plaintiffs alleged before the FCC that the Banking Union's main components ie the SSM, and the ECB's powers; the Single Resolution Mechanism (SRM), and the Single Resolution Board (SRB) powers; and the Single Resolution Fund (SRF) were ultra vires and unconstitutional. The FCC dismissed the complaint, but the key were the arguments used. The FCC concluded that in light of their 'constitutional' basis, both the SSM (Article 127 (6) TFEU), and SRM (Article 114 TFEU) were constitutional *provided* that they were interpreted restrictively.[43] Furthermore, to the FCC both mechanisms established a division of competences where only some tasks were attributed to the ECB, and to the SRB,[44] while substantial tasks were left to NCAs, and NRAs.[45] For the SSM in particular, NCAs tasks were exercised under national law, and not through re-delegation from the EU authorities.[46] The FCC expressly denied any contradiction between this view, and the CJEU's view in *Landeskreditbank*, despite the blatant inconsistencies between them.

6.12

And yet, despite this case opened a potential constitutional conflict, like *Gauweiler* and *Weiss* did in monetary policy, there are notable differences. Where *Weiss* was extreme, *SSM/SRM* was restrained, where *Weiss* (in our view) misinterpreted basic principles of EU law, *SSM/SRM* was deeply attached to the text of the Treaty, and where *Weiss* was confrontational, *SSM/SRM* tiptoed around the contradiction. Rather than a 'good' or 'bad', this would be a 'mixed' example of EU inter-court dialogue.[47]

6.13

Another key aspect of the FCC ruling was its finding that the independence of the ECB's Supervisory Board and the SRB diminished 'democratic legitimacy'.[48] and was a cause for concern,[49] to be mitigated by accountability mechanisms,[50] including the ECB's administrative review by the Administrative Board of Review (ABoR), and the SRB's quasi-judicial review by the Appeal Panel (AP),[51] the judicial review of both ECB and SRB by the General Court and the Court of Justice,[52] or the political accountability before the European Parliament and Council,[53] and national parliaments, to which reporting obligations are also due.[54] Furthermore, national parliaments and courts review the actions of NCAs and NRAs,[55] and in the FCC view the federal government could also influence EU bodies 'indirectly' through its presence in the Council, and the national parliament could participate in this process if it was duly informed.[56]

6.14

---

[43] *SSM/SRM* (n 36) 167–69, 233, 242, 245–46, 258, 265.
[44] ibid paras 173–76 (SSM), 254–56 (SRM).
[45] ibid paras 177–84 (SSM), 261 (SRM).
[46] ibid para 185 (for the SSM).
[47] Marco Lamandini, David Ramos Muñoz, and Violeta Ruiz Almendral, 'The EMU and Its Multi-Level Constitutional Structure' (2020) 47 Legal Issues of Economic Integration 295.
[48] *SSM/SRM* (n 36) 203–30, 267–92.
[49] ibid paras 209–10. In para 210, the BVerfG held that: '[t]he ECB's independence is in clear conflict with the principle of the sovereignty of the people (Art. 20(2) first sentence GG) given that an essential policy area is beyond the reach of the directly and democratically legitimated representatives of the people ... This cannot be justified by the [monetary policy independence] given that ... this provision requires a restrictive interpretation of the ECB's monetary policy mandate and may not simply be applied to other areas'. With regard to the SRM, the BVerfG held, in para 279 that: 'While domestic law initially provided for comprehensive democratic legitimation and oversight of measures relating to bank resolution (see (a) below), the SRM Regulation results in a diminished level of democratic legitimation'.
[50] *SSM/SRM* (n 36) 209, 212, 216, 217, 291, 292.
[51] ibid paras 213 (SSM) and 275 (SRM).
[52] *SSM/SRM* (n 36) 214 (SSM) and 276 (SRM). In addition, national courts have a role in controlling ECB actions such as on-site inspections and entries on business premises. See ibid 215 (SSM).
[53] ibid paras 216–17 (SSM).
[54] ibid paras 218 (SSM), 288 (SRM).
[55] ibid paras 224, 229 (SSM) and 281–83, 289 (SRM).
[56] ibid paras 272–73 (SRM).

6.15 The CJEU's idea of 'exclusive power with decentralised implementation' has been reiterated and used as a basis for other findings. In *Berlusconi II*[57] (see below in this section) the Court held that vesting the ECB with the exclusive competence to evaluate the acquisition of a qualifying holding in a significant credit institution was not contrary to the 'exception of insurance undertakings', excluded from ECB supervision under Article 127(6) TFEU, because the objectives of the provisions on the acquisition of qualifying holdings could not be satisfied if the mere fact that a credit institution also carried out insurance activities had the effect of removing it from ECB control.[58] In *Ukrselhosprom*[59] the General Court used the *Landeskreditbank* doctrine as background to delineate the relationship between competences by national supervisory and resolution authorities and the ECB (see below).

6.16 A second source of vertical tensions due to the complexity of the SSM framework arises from the interaction of EU and domestic procedures, most obvious in 'composite or compound proceedings', with a 'domestic leg' and a 'European leg'. *Berlusconi & Fininvest (Berlusconi I)* is the leading case, and was the prelude to *Berlusconi II*, referred to above.[60] *Berlusconi I* was analysed in chapter 4 s 2.4, for its implications on the justiciability of financial decisions. The Court of Justice held that, in the procedure for the acquisition of a significant holding, where there is a proposal by the national authority (Bank of Italy) and a final decision by the ECB, since the 'national leg' of a proceeding does not determine the conclusion of the European leg, EU courts are exclusively competent to adjudicate on the final decision by EU authorities, including on any illegality present in the national leg, and national courts cannot rule on the preparatory decision by national authorities. Yet, in *Berlusconi II* the General Court considered the appellant's plea about the illegality of the Italian leg of the procedure inadmissible because it was filed after *Berlusconi I* was decided, and thus after the appeal in *Berlusconi II* was lodged. To the General Court, Court of Justice's findings in *Berlusconi I* were not a new element of law that arose during the proceedings, something that would have justified admitting the new plea, but a confirmation of a situation of which the appellant was aware when it filed the appeal, and the ruling's effects were *ex tunc*, ie they dated back to the date of entry into force of the provisions interpreted by the court.[61] The Court also made short shrift of the allegation in *Berlusconi II* that the 'system' of SSM rules may not leave any room for the control of *constitutionality* of national preparatory acts by national courts (for which EU Courts are not competent). Whilst the timing of the decisions was a procedural peculiarity, which only affected this specific appellant, the preclusion of control of constitutionality of national preparatory acts is a latent structural problem, which is bound to resurface.

6.17 However, difficulties can also arise when national and EU levels are only partially interdependent. In *Ukrselhosprom* the General Court affirmed the ECB's exclusive competence to withdraw a bank's authorization.[62] National (Estonian) resolution authorities had declared a bank failing-or-likely-to-fail (FOLTF) *but* considered that resolution was not in the public interest, while, in parallel, the entity was considered not to fulfil the requirements for authorization, due to money laundering violations by both Estonian *supervisory* authorities (which

---

[57] Case T-913/16 *Finanziaria d'investimento Fininvest SpA (Fininvest)/Silvio Berlusconi v ECB* [2022] ECLI:EU:T:2022:279 (on appeal in Joined Cases C-512/22 P and C-513/22 P pending).
[58] ibid para 66.
[59] Joined Cases T-351/18 and T-584/18 *Ukrselhosprom v ECB* EU:T:2021:669.
[60] See also the commentary by Filipe Brito Bastos, 'Judicial Review of Composite Administrative Procedures in the Single Supervisory Mechanism: Berlusconi' (2019) 56 CMLR 1355.
[61] *Berlusconi II* (n 57) paras 250–55.
[62] *Ukrselhosprom* (n 59).

made a proposal to withdraw) and the ECB (which withdrew the authorization). The Court confirmed that, under the resolution framework, resolution authorities are the ones competent to decide on resolution measures, and the FOLTF finding by supervisors is merely preparatory and not binding on them; but that this does not subordinate the ECB's power to withdraw the authorization to the decision of resolution authorities. The vertical and horizontal interplays can be even wider, as shown by the *PNB Banka* saga, where the ECB first took over the supervision of PNB Banka at the request of the Latvian supervisory authority by classifying the same as a significant entity subject to its direct supervision, then concluded an on-site inspection which found substantial provisioning shortfalls and a balance-sheet insolvency, followed by, first, an ECB determination of FOLTF, subsequently by an insolvency declaration from the national competent bankruptcy court, and finally by the ECB decision to withdraw the bank licence, again upon proposal of the national supervisor. All those ECB's decisions were challenged before the General Court, which dismissed the four separate, yet linked, appeals on 7 December 2022.[63]

6.18 Then, there may be EU and national decisions adopted independently, with an interaction not envisaged in the law. In *Anglo Austrian AAB Bank (AAB)* a finding by national authorities that a bank had committed anti-money laundering violations was followed by an ECB decision to withdraw its licence for repeated and serious breaches of the duty to have 'robust governance arrangements' (Article 74 CRD, as transposed by national legislation).[64] The General Court dismissed the bank's allegations that the money laundering violations 'dated back in time, prescribed or were not serious or had been corrected'.[65] The objections about the money laundering findings did not affect the assessment under the provisions on the withdrawal of authorizations,[66] ie the Court did neither revise the findings of national courts (it could not), nor let the nuances of national proceedings predetermine how it would adjudicate on the matter.

6.19 A third source of vertical tension is the application by EU institutions of national law, an institutional novelty of the Banking Union analysed by courts in decisions like *Caisse regionale de crédit agricole v ECB*,[67] and *Crédit Mutuel Arkea*.[68] In *Caisse regionale de crédit agricole*

---

[63] Case T-275/19 *PNB Banka v ECB* (ECB decision of 14 February 2019) ECLI:EU:T:2022:781; Case T-230/20 *PNB Banka v ECB* (ECB decision of 17 February 2020) ECLI:EU:T:2022:782; Case T-301/19, *PNB Banka v ECB* (ECB decision of 1 March 2019) ECLI:EU:T:2022:774; and Case T-330/19 *PNB Banka v ECB* (ECB decision of 21 March 2019) ECLI:EU:T:2022:775.
[64] Case T-797/19 *Anglo Austrian AAB v ECB* ECLI:EU:T:2022:389.
[65] ibid para 27.
[66] ibid paras 58–62, 66, 67–72, 73–91, 124–31, 134–36, 138–47.
[67] Joined Cases T-133/16 to T-136/16 *Caisse régionale de crédit agricole mutuel Alpes Provence and Others v ECB* ECLI:EU:T:2018:219. See the Summary by René Smits (*EBI* 2019) https://ebi-europa.eu/wp-content/uploads/2019/01/Cre%CC%81dit-Agricole-Cases-Summary.pdf; Christos Gortsos, 'The Crédit Agricole cases: banking corporate governance and application of national law by the ECB' in Chiara Zilioli and Karl-Philipp Wojcik (eds), *Judicial Review in the European Banking Union* (Edward Elgar Publishing 2021) 510–20.
[68] Case T-712/15 *Crédit Mutuel Arkea v ECB* ECLI:EU:T:2017:900; on appeal Joined Cases C-152/18 and C-153/18 *Crédit Mutuel Arkea v ECB* ECLI:EU:C:2019:810. See the commentary by Daniel Sarmiento, 'National Law as a Point of Law in Appeals at the Court of Justice. The case of Crédit Mutuel Arkéa/ECB' *EU Law Live* (2019); Francesco Martucci, 'The Crédit Mutuel Arkéa Case: Central Bodies and the SSM, and the interpretation of National Law by the ECJ' in Chiara Zilioli and Karl-Philipp Wojcik (eds), *Judicial Review in the European Banking Union* (Elgar Financial Law and Practice 2021) 504–509. More recently the General Court held that the ECB had mistakenly applied national law in a decision to adopt the early intervention measure of special administration in Case T-502/19 *Francesca Corneli v ECB* ECLI:EU:T:2022:627, para 100; on appeal, in Joined Cases C-777/22 P and C-789/22 P pending, the Court is asked, inter alia, to clarify whether an alleged misinterpretation of national law by the General Court is a question of law or a question of distortion of facts, the scope of the interpretation in conformity of national law and to what extent Article 4(3) SSMR authorises the direct application of the CRD by the ECB, if national law incorrectly implemented CRD.

the problem was the interpretation of the 'four eyes' principle, which requires that the bank is 'effectively directed' by at least two persons. The ECB interpreted the reference to 'effective direction' as comprising executive directors, ie those who combine their directorship with a senior management role, and also read the provision in light of other bank rules, which prohibit the accumulation of the roles of chairperson and chief executive, thus refusing to authorize as 'effective directors' four CEOs who were *also* chairpersons. The relevant EU provision had been transposed by Article L. 511-13 of the French Financial and Monetary Code, which, in turn, had been interpretated by the French *Autorité du Control Prudentielle et resolution* (ACPR) *and* after the complaint had been filed, by a Council of State decision. The General Court combined an analysis of the relevant EU provisions and an analysis of the national provisions and opinions, where it showed deference to national law and authorities. It stated that the ACPR had had an opportunity to clarify that its position was the same as that of the ECB,[69] and with regard to the posterior ruling by the Council of State, it held that:

> [T]he fact that the judgment of the Conseil d'État (Council of State) of 30 June 2016 postdates the contested decisions does not preclude it being taken into account for the purpose of interpreting Article L. 511-13 of the CMF, since the applicants have had the opportunity to present their observations before the General Court.[70]

The Court conferred much importance to the interpretation rendered by the Council of State, which it quoted verbatim in some parts,[71] to confirm that the ECB's interpretation was correct.

In *Crédit Mutuel Arkea*,[72] the issue was the existence of a 'group', for purposes of consolidated supervision in the case of a decentralized number of cooperative entities affiliated to a central body that was not, itself, a credit institution. The ECB concluded that there was, indeed such a group, in light of Article L-511.30 of the French Financial and Monetary Code. The General Court affirmed the ECB's decision, but it held that the national provision was too ambiguous, and it did not seem to impose a degree of commitment by group entities equivalent to the one required by the European provision that it transposed (Article 10 CRR). Shortly after the General Court's decision, a judgment by the French Council of State interpreted the national provision in a sense that clarified that the degree of commitment would be equivalent, and the requirement under the EU provision would be met. Thus, upon appeal before the Court of Justice, the Commission proposed a substitution of grounds, where the Court could validate the ECB act, but this time using the authoritative interpretation of the Council of State. The Court of Justice agreed, and gave the parties an opportunity to amend their positions in light of the new judgment, and then considered its implications. The Court of Justice concluded that the opinion of the Council of State had to be taken into account, and considered it in much detail for its own opinion.[73] Unlike other 'tensioned' cases, this is a positive example of how a constructive engagement between courts can lead to a result that fully acknowledges the importance of both national and EU law. This was helped by the friendly attitude of both the Council of State (which issued an opinion precisely on the issue

---

[69] The judgment was given following an action for misuse of powers in respect of Position 2014-P-07 of the ACPR, in which the ACPR clarified that its interpretation of the concept of 'effective director' was the same as that advocated by the ECB, which referred to Position 2014-P-07 of the ACPR in the contested decisions. *Caisse régionale de crédit agricole* (n 67) 86.
[70] *Caisse régionale de crédit agricole* (n 67) 87.
[71] ibid para 88.
[72] *Crédit Mutuel* (n 68).
[73] ibid paras 103–106.

at hand) and the Court of Justice (which dedicated extensive space to analyse the findings of that opinion). It remains to be seen what the results are when courts are more reluctant to engage and cooperate.

Finally, case law also shows that there are limits to the relevance of national law in EU authorities' decisions. In *AAB*, referred to above, the alleged flaws of the findings of money laundering violations by national authorities, based on national law, did not result in a serious challenge to the ECB's own findings of violations of governance provisions, ie the assessment was based on both the provisions of the CRD and the national legislation transposing it, but did not 'drag along' the bank's allegations based on the national money laundering proceedings. On the specific allegation that the violations 'had not been ascertained in decisions having res judicata authority', as allegedly required under national law, the General Court based its decision not on any requirement under national law, but on EU case law requiring that the decision establishing the guilty violation must be 'final', even if it is an administrative decision,[74] and the Court's assessment of the 'seriousness' of the breach was made on the basis of EU law only. Yet, the Court made a detailed assessment of national legislation (in particular the connection between CRD 'governance' provisions and money laundering prevention) to hold that the ECB did not act beyond its competence when it took money laundering into consideration in finding a breach of governance rules.[75] Nonetheless, it also held that, even if the ECB had chosen the wrong legal basis under national law, this could not result in annulment, as the outcome would not have changed, since there were other provisions to choose from.[76]

6.20

In the origins of the case of *Fininvest & Berlusconi v ECB* (*Berlusconi II*)[77] Fininvest (and Mr Berlusconi) holding in the holding company (Mediolanum) of a significant bank (Banca Mediolanum), albeit acquired many years before, became relevant for regulatory purposes in 2014 once national law started to require the authorization of qualifying holding also for mixed financial holding companies; such acquisition was not authorized by Bank of Italy, out of concern for a prison sentence against Mr Berlusconi for tax fraud, but this decision to reject was annulled by Italian courts due to a transitory provision in the applicable national 'fit and proper' requirements which the Italian Consiglio di Stato interpreted as preventing to give effect to a prison sentence which predated the 2014 inclusion in the regulatory framework of mixed financial holding companies. Subsequently (with the SSM and the CRD in force), a reverse merger between Banca Mediolanum and Mediolanum), by which Fininvest's indirect holding became a direct holding was treated by the ECB as an 'acquisition of a significant holding', to be authorized by the ECB, after a proposal was made by Bank of Italy. In *Berlusconi I* the Court of Justice found that EU courts were exclusively competent to decide because the national 'leg' of the procedure (by Bank of Italy) did not determine the outcome of the 'European leg', by the ECB. Then, the General Court had to decide on the legality of the ECB decision, but the ECB had to apply Italian law. Nonetheless, the General Court held that 'acquisition of a qualified holding' is concept that requires an 'autonomous and uniform' interpretation,[78] because the corresponding provisions in the SSM Regulation and the CRD did not make an express reference to national law to determine the meaning and scope of the

6.21

---

[74] *AAB* (n 64) paras 45–46. For a comment see Enrico Gagliardi and Laura Wissink, 'So Far So Good: The Review of National Law in EU Judicial Proceedings' *EULawLive* (8 July 2022).
[75] ibid paras 105–109 (duty to state reasons) and paras 124–30 (breach of legality).
[76] ibid para 110.
[77] *Berlusconi II* (n 57).
[78] ibid para 44.

reference to the 'acquisition of a qualifying holding',[79] and because making the application depend on the interpretation of the concept under national law could threaten its mandatory (and uniform) application across the Union.[80] The Court also dismissed the fact that, at the time of the contested decision, the CRD provisions (Articles 22–23) had not been fully transposed into Italian law, because the legislative provisions that transposed it had been enacted; only the decrees that were supposed to elaborate the criteria for 'integrity' and 'competence' were not in place,[81] and a transitional provision stated that, while these decrees were not enacted, the norms previously in place, continued to apply.

3 Horizontal separation of powers and judicial review in regulatory and supervisory decisions

6.22 In the United States, the exploration by the courts of the issue of delegation and deference is inextricably linked to the erosion of the Glass-Steagall Act (GSA), and the rise of shadow banking. It is instructive to see how judicial attitudes switched with perceptions about the relative roles of courts and agencies, but also how a case's details could influence the final outcome. In a first stage, courts claimed for themselves the responsibility to determine the meaning and finality of an Act. In *ICI v Camp*[82] the Supreme Court invalidated an OCC Regulation authorizing banks to operate collective investment funds because, although 'courts should give great weight to any reasonable construction of a regulatory statute adopted by the agency charged with the enforcement of that statute', here (i) the OCC had no 'official' position on the Regulation's Glass-Steagall implications, and its counsel's post-hoc rationalizations during the court proceedings were not entitled to the same deference,[83] and the Court held that the Glass-Steagall's finality was to promote a drastic separation, to prevent the 'subtle hazards' of banks' involvement with securities', ie courts were the ultimate guardians of congressional intent.[84] Nonetheless, in *Federal Reserve Board (FRB) v ICI (ICI II)* the Supreme Court held that the Federal Reserve's amended Regulation Y, which expanded the activities 'closely related to banking'[85] and allowed bank holding companies (BHCs) and their nonbanking subsidiaries to act as investment advisers to closed-end investment companies,[86] was valid, because (i) this interpretation was supported by banking practice and a 'normal' reading of the statutory text, (ii) the FRB's determination of banking's 'closely related' activities was entitled to the greatest deference, and that (iii) even if the activity were not permissible to a bank it should be permissible for a BHC's subsidiary.[87]

---

[79] ibid para 45. The provisions were Article 15 of the Council Regulation (EU) No 1024/2013 conferring specific tasks on the European Central Bank concerning policies relating to the prudential supervision of credit institutions [2013] OJ L287 (SSM Regulation) and Directive 2013/36/EU of the European Parliament and of the Council on access to the activity of credit institutions and the prudential supervision of credit institutions and investment firms, amending Directive 2002/87/EC and repealing Directives 2006/48/EC and 2006/49/EC [2013] OJ L176 (Directive 2013/36 or CRD).
[80] *Berlusconi II* (n 57) para 48.
[81] ibid paras 118–22.
[82] *Investment Company Institute (ICI) v Camp* 401 US 617 (1971).
[83] ibid paras 629–30.
[84] See *ICI v Camp* (n 82) 629–34.
[85] Bank Holding Company Act, s 4(c)(8).
[86] *Board of Governors, FRS v Investment Co Inst* 450 US 46 (1981).
[87] ibid 5 paras 7–65.

The second stage took place in 1984, where in *Securities Industry Association (SIA) et al v* **6.23**
FRB (Bankers' Trust I) the Supreme Court annulled the FRB's authorization of banks' commercial paper distribution and other activities, as against the GSA prohibition of 'securities' activities,[88] because (i) its official position was established by its counsel during the proceedings, and was not entitled to 'substantial deference',[89] and commercial paper fell within the 'plain meaning' of 'security'; and the FRB's approach overlooked Glass-Steagall's aim to prevent the 'subtle hazards' of bank's *involvement* with securities.[90] Yet, on the very same date in *SIA v FRB (Schwab)* the Court confirmed the FRB's power to authorize a BHC to acquire a non-banking affiliate principally engaged in retail securities brokerage.[91] These parallel decisions bifurcated the deference granted to regulators: a 'substantial deference' standard for restrictions to BHCs and subsidiaries, and a less deferential (and more controversial) one on restrictions directly applicable to banks, (due to the Court's finalistic interpretation of Glass Steagall section 16).[92]

The third stage completed the crystallization of deference. In *Bankers Trust II*, the Circuit **6.24**
Court for the District of Columbia side-stepped Supreme Court's *Bankers Trust I*, holding that the FRB could authorize banks' private placement of commercial paper, as it was not the 'securities underwriting'.[93] In *SIA v FRB (Citicorp.)* the Second Circuit upheld the FRB's view that BHCs would not be 'engaged principally' in securities underwriting through subsidiaries, if revenues from this did not exceed 10 per cent of gross revenues.[94] In *SIA v Clarke* the Second Circuit upheld the OCC's decision to apply to mortgage-backed securities (MBS) the treatment of mortgage loans, which banks were authorized to originate and sell[95] (instead of treating them as securities).

The Supreme Court certified this shift by denying certiorari in the above cases. Furthermore, **6.25**
in *NationsBank v VALIC* it deferred to an OCC interpretation that annuities were not 'insurance', despite they were typically marketed by insurance companies, and often regulated as insurance products under state law.[96] The Court held that the OCC had discretion to interpret the meaning of 'the business of banking' when issuing authorizations.[97] Annuities were sufficiently similar to bank instruments to treat them within the 'business of banking',[98] and

---

[88] *Securities Industry Association (SIA) and Others v FRB* 468 US 137 (1984) *(Bankers Trust I)*.
[89] At the administrative level, the FRB considered that CP was not a 'security', and thus did not address the potential dangers to the GSA. Only during court proceedings did the FRB try to address them through its counsel. A reviewing court 'must reject administrative constructions of a statute, whether reached by adjudication or by rulemaking, that are inconsistent with the statutory mandate or that frustrate the policy that Congress sought to implement'.
[90] ibid.
[91] *Securities Industry Association (SIA) and Others v FRS*, 468 US, 207 (1984) *(Schwab)*. On that year, the District Court for the District of Columbia held valid the authorization by the Federal Home Loan Bank Board (FHLBB) of an application by three savings and loan (S&L) associations to use a subsidiary to engage in brokerage and investment advisory services. See *SIA v FHLBB* 588 F Supp 749 (DDC 1984).
[92] *Bankers Trust I* had a dissent, which advocated more deference, citing *Camp* (n 82), *Chevron*, *ICI* and the *Schwab* ruling from that same day, and stressed that there was no 'plain meaning' in either section 16 or section 21 that forecloses the Board's interpretation'. See *Bankers Trust I* (n 88) 166–72.
[93] *Securities Industry Association v Board of Governors FRS* [1986] 807 F 2d 1052 (DC Cir) cert denied, 483 US 1005 (1987). The Court held that, unlike in *Bankers Trust I*, the Board had properly justified the absence of the 'subtle hazards' of banks' involvement with securities.
[94] *SIA v Board of Governors FRS* [1988] 839 F2d 47 (2d Cir) cert denied, 486 US 1059 (1988).
[95] *SIA v Clarke* 885 F2d 1034 (2d Cir 1989).
[96] *NationsBank v VALIC* 513 US 251 (1995).
[97] The OCC administered the National Banking Act, 12 US Code s 24, 7th, which stated that 'national banks had the 'To exercise ... all such incidental powers as shall be necessary to carry on *the business of banking*'.
[98] 'By providing customers with the opportunity to invest in one or more annuity options, banks are essentially offering financial investment instruments of the kind congressional authorization permits them to broker'. *NationsBank v VALIC* (n 96) 260.

Congress had not ruled out the OCC's 'functional' interpretation.[99] The power to interpret the GSA and the McFadden Act was handed over to agencies. The Supreme Court, in its current composition, is less deferential to agencies, and has been ready to use the presence of 'major questions' as an increasingly broader exception (among others) to *Chevron* deference.[100] Like *VALIC* assimilated *Chevron* into financial regulation, future decisions may assimilate these new trends.

6.26 In the EU the law of finance has been the testbed to a major revision of the doctrine on the legitimacy of agency discretion. For a long time, *Meroni* seemed to prohibit delegation of discretionary powers to independent agencies,[101] and *Romano*[102] seemed to rule out agencies' power to adopt quasi-legislative acts. In the *ESMA short selling* decision,[103] the United Kingdom challenged the regulation on short selling. The regulation which, combined with Article 9(5) of ESMA founding regulation conferred on ESMA the power to temporarily prohibit or restrict short selling activities,[104] which, the UK alleged, was an exercise of *discretionary* powers, contrary to *Meroni*, an exercise of *regulatory* powers, contrary to *Romano*, an impermissible exercise of delegation beyond post-Lisbon Treaty Articles 290–291 TFEU, which only contemplated delegation to the European Commission, and a misuse of Article 114 TFEU, which authorizes rules for the 'establishment and functioning of the internal market', not the regulation or restriction of it.

6.27 The Court of Justice rejected all the challenges. First, it held that[105] there is a difference between delegating 'discretionary power implying a wide margin of discretion' (an unlawful 'actual transfer of responsibility') and delegating 'clearly defined executive powers', subject to strict review based on objective criteria determined by the delegating authority (lawful). While *Meroni* involved giving 'a degree of latitude which implied a wide margin of discretion', to a private law body, ESMA short selling involved a public agency's exercise of actions constrained by law, as (i) ESMA could only act if there was a threat to financial stability or the orderly functioning/integrity of markets, (ii) it had to consider the measure's side-effects, and (iii) could only adopt specific acts, such as requests of information, or prohibitions. These constraints also made the decision amenable to judicial review, and ruled out a 'very large measure of discretion', in compliance with *Meroni*.[106] The Court treated the *Romano*-based objection against agencies' quasi-legislative acts of general application as another version of the *Meroni* test and dismissed it too.[107] On delegation, the Court held that other Treaty provisions presumed (but not regulated) delegation to agencies Articles 290–291 did

---

[99] *NationsBank v VALIC* (n 96) 262. The Court dismissed VALIC's reliance on state laws that characterized annuities as products sold by insurance companies.
[100] *King v Burwell* 576 US 473 (2015); *West Virginia v EPA* (n 34).
[101] Joined Cases C-9/56 and 10/56 *Meroni & Co Industrie Metallurgiche v High Authority of the European Coal and Steel Community* ECLI:EU:C:1958:7.
[102] Case C-98/80 *Giuseppe Romano v Institut national d'assurance maladie-invalidité*ECLI:EU:C:1981:104.
[103] Case C-270/12 *United Kingdom of Great Britain and Northern Ireland v European Parliament and Council of the European Union* ECLI:EU:C:2014:18. See C Di Noia and M Gargantini, 'Unleashing the ESMA: Governance and Accountability. After the CJEU Decision on the Short Selling Regulation' (2014) 15 Eur Org L Rev 24; R Filler, 'Ask the Professors: Did the ECJ properly Rule by Dismissing the UK's Attempt to Annul ESMA's Regulation Banning Short Selling' (2014) 34 Futures and Derivatives L Report 3.
[104] Article 28(1) of Regulation (EU) No 236/2012 of the European Parliament and of the Council on short selling and certain aspects of credit default swaps of 14 March 2012, and art 9(5) of each of the ESAs Regulations(regs 1093/2010, 1094/2010, 1095/2010).
[105] *ESMA short selling* (n 103) paras 41–54.
[106] ibid.
[107] ibid paras 65–67.

not exhaust all delegation options.[108] Finally, the Court, departing from Advocate General Jääskinen's Opinion,[109] held that the internal market competence under Article 114 TFEU conferred discretion on the EU legislature to choose the appropriate method of harmonization, which included establishing agencies, especially if highly technical and specialized analyses were needed,[110] and regulatory measures addressed to Member States or to individuals,[111] *especially* in exceptional circumstances, such as serious disturbances in financial markets.[112]

ESMA short selling reset the foundations of delegation and agency discretion, but some key statutory rules still reflect a major change. Some, like the ESAs (ESMA, EBA, EIOPA) founding regulations, were enacted before the case was decided; others, like the Banking Union texts, were enacted on the same year, when the case's implications were not clear. Arguably, the ruling itself did not help. It was short in details, conclusory in style, and although it overcame some of *Meroni*'s constraints, it did not make a formal overruling. Its legacy is the following: **6.28**

(i) Delegation to agencies is legitimate *as long as* delegated acts are amenable to judicial review (no delegation without justiciability). Currently EU financial agencies enjoy regulatory and supervisory powers.[113]

(ii) Competences beyond a technical assessment, and eg involving a discretionary weighing of policy, or political, considerations should not be delegated.[114] This explains how, for example in bank resolution the Single Resolution Board (an agency) adopts a resolution scheme, but the European Commission (a Treaty institution) must endorse it to be fully binding.[115] The meaning of 'discretion' and 'policy choices' is unclear.[116]

(iii) When legislating, there is still strict division between agencies' (ESMA, EBA, EIOPA) adoption of the draft, preparatory act (Regulatory Technical Standard—RTS, Implementing Technical Standards—ITS) and the Commission's adoption of the final act through the endorsement of the agencies' acts (delegated regulations for RTS, implementing regulations for ITS). *ESMA short selling* did not clarify how agencies can exercise autonomous regulatory competences, which means that they often do so via soft law acts, which, in turn, raise other justiciability problems.

After *ESMA Short selling*, another big test was *Fédération Bancaire Française (FBF) v Autorité de contrôle prudentiel et de résolution (ACPR)*.[117] The plaintiff, the French Banking federation **6.29**

---

[108] ibid paras 78–86. Also, in this case the whole framework allocated different competences to ESMA and national authorities.
[109] Case C-270/12 *United Kingdom of Great Britain and Northern Ireland v European Parliament and Council of the European Union*, Opinion of Advocate General Jääskinen ECLI:EU:C:2013:562.
[110] *ESMA short selling* (n 103) paras 102–103, citing Case C-217/04 *United Kingdom v Parliament and Council* ECLI:EU:C:2006:279, para 44.
[111] *ESMA short selling* (n 103) paras 106–107, citing Case C-359/92 *Germany v Council* ECLI:EU:C:1994:306, para 37.
[112] *ESMA short selling* (n 103) paras 108–14:
[113] For example, ESMA has direct oversight on credit rating agencies and trade repositories. See Regulation (EU) No 513/2011 of the European Parliament and of the Council amending Regulation (EC) No 1060/2009 on credit rating agencies [2011] OJ L145.
[114] Compare also Case C-507/13 *United Kingdom of Great Britain and Northern Ireland v European Parliament and Council*, Opinion of AG N Jääskinen ECLI:EU:C:2014:2394, para 62 (banks' managers remuneration under Directive 2013/36/EU).
[115] Raising the problem of determining, which act is reviewable.
[116] This affects the standard of review by the Court of Justice.
[117] Case C-911/19 *Fédération bancaire française (FBF) v Autorité de contrôle prudentiel et de résolution (ACPR)* ECLI:EU:C:2021:599.

(FBF) argued before French courts that the European Banking Authority (EBA) Guidelines on product oversight and governance arrangements for retail banking products were invalid, and the French court made a preliminary reference to the Court of Justice under Article 267 TFEU. The Guidelines presented a justiciability challenge, because they were a soft law instrument, as analysed in chapter 4 s 2.3, but the case also raised a key problem on the exercise of powers by agencies. In fact, the European Commission unusually agreed with the plaintiff that the EBA was acting beyond its mandate.[118] By way of background, EBA can issue guidelines and recommendations to harmonize supervisory practices when (i) they fit within the EBA's founding legislation's goals, which include consumer, depositors and investor protection, mitigating financial intermediaries' risk-taking, or promoting consistent, efficient and effective supervisory practices (first step),[119] and (ii) there is a legal basis in the specific legislation (step two).[120] In *FBF v ACPR* the problem was step two. The EBA referenced its Guidelines to various provisions in the Capital Requirements Directive (CRD), the Payment Services Directive (PSD), the e-money Directive, or the Consumer Credit Directive.[121] However, as suggested by the Advocate General Opinion, these norms regulated the *corporate* governance of banks, payment services and e-money firms, etc. and not *product* governance, like the Guidelines did.[122] The difference, in the AG's view, is that one (corporate governance) focuses on transparent organizational structure, allocation of responsibilities, etc. and the other (product governance) on ensuring that products fit the target market, are properly marketed, etc.[123] Product governance is regulated in MiFID,[124] from where, the AG suggested, the EBA may have taken inspiration for the Guidelines,[125] but since MiFID applies to *investment* service providers, the EBA could not formally use it, and thus the EBA chose other legislative acts, which did *not* regulate *product* governance.[126] In the AG's view, being permissive on soft law would be an invitation for a 'crypto-legislation' bypassing the legislative process, raising problems of legitimacy and institutional balance.[127]

---

[118] Case C-911/19 *Fédération bancaire française (FBF) v Autorité de contrôle prudentiel et de résolution (ACPR)*, AG Bobek Opinion ECLI:EU:C:2021:294, para 57.

[119] Article 1(5) and 16 of Regulation 1093/2010 of the European Parliament and of the Council establishing a European Supervisory Authority (European Banking Authority), amending Decision No 716/2009/EC and repealing Commission Decision 2009/78/EC [2010] OJ L331.

[120] Articles 1(2) and (3), 8(1)(1bis) and (2) and 16 of EBA Regulation (n 119).

[121] Article 74(1) of CRD (n 79), Article 10(4) of Directive 2007/64/EC of the European Parliament and of the Council Directive 2007/64/EC of the European Parliament and of the Council on payment services in the internal market amending Directives 97/7/EC, 2002/65/EC, 2005/60/EC and 2006/48/EC and repealing Directive 97/5/EC [2007] OJ L319 (PSD), Article 3(1) of Directive 2009/110/EC of the European Parliament and of the Council of 16 September 2009 on the taking up, pursuit and prudential supervision of the business of electronic money institutions amending Directives 2005/60/EC and 2006/48/EC and repealing Directive 2000/46/EC [2009] OJ L267 and Article 7(1) of Directive 2014/17/EU Directive 2014/17/EU of the European Parliament and of the Council of 4 February 2014 on credit agreements for consumers relating to residential immovable property and amending Directives 2008/48/EC and 2013/36/EU and Regulation (EU) No 1093/2010 [2010] OJ L60 (Consumer Credit Directive).

[122] *FBF v ACPR*, AG Bobek Opinion (n 118) 67. Conceptually speaking, there is a difference between *corporate* governance rules, *conduct* rules, which provide fiduciary-like duties in client-intermediary interactions, and product governance, which try to ensure that such duties are fulfilled by matching them with structural, organizational (and intrusive) rules. Marco Lamandini and David Ramos Muñoz, *EU Financial Law. An Introduction* (Wolters Kluwer 2016) 659, 733.

[123] *FBF v ACPR*, AG Bobek Opinion (n 118) 68.

[124] Directive 2014/65/EU of the European Parliament and of the Council on markets in financial instruments (MiFID II).

[125] *FBF v ACPR*, AG Bobek Opinion (n 118) para 56.

[126] ibid para 69. The Commission said that EBA had exceeded its mandate with regards to CRD (n 79), e-money providers and PSD, but not to the Consumer Credit Directive. To the AG, the Consumer Credit Directive still lacked the detailed structural and procedural provisions typical in a product governance regime. *FBF v ACPR*, AG Bobek Opinion (n 118).

[127] *FBF v ACPR*, AG Bobek Opinion (n 118) para 85–86.

6.30 The Court of Justice, however, used the same two-step test, but reached the opposite conclusion. Both the AG and the Court read the same legal provision, Article 74 (1) CRD, which states that:

> Institutions shall have robust governance arrangements which include a clear organisational structure with well-defined, transparent and consistent lines of responsibility, effective processes to identify, manage, monitor and report the risks they are or might be exposed to, adequate internal control mechanisms, including sound administration and accounting procedures, and remuneration policies and practices that are consistent with and promote sound and effective risk management.

6.31 The AG Opinion focused on the initial reference to 'governance arrangements', as meaning *corporate* governance, and read the rest of the provision in this light. In contrast, the Court began by the subsequent reference to 'effective processes to identify, manage, monitor and report risks'. As long as the Guidelines referred to 'internal processes and structures' (and not to, eg product suitability or intermediaries' duties), they would fall within Article 74 CRD,[128] even if the Guidelines' ultimate goal, ie to ensure client-product 'fit' was not mentioned in the CRD provisions allegedly used as a legal basis.[129] The reasoning used to fit the Guidelines within CRD provisions was applied by analogy to also fit them within the PSD and the e-money Directive.[130] Having surmounted the obstacle of 'step two', it was then easy to conclude that, by promoting consumer protection, they also fit within the EBA's broader mandate[131] (step one). The Court side-stepped the bigger issue raised by the AG's Opinion, ie the threat of bypassing the legislative process.

6.32 The position of US and EU courts vis-à-vis administrative discretion has varied with the concrete moment in history, and also with the circumstances of each case. However, two major differences stand out. First, whereas the delegation of discretionary and/or policy-making powers to agencies is considered perfectly legitimate in the US, it is not in the EU, and even the *ESMA short selling* did not go as far as stating that. Secondly, whereas in the US the 'authority' to interpret a statute may fall on an agency, in the EU such authority and responsibility must necessarily befall on courts. In fact, European courts prefer to support an agency's controversial interpretation of a statute, like the Court of Justice did in *FBF v ACPR*, than to simply say that the agency had acted within its discretion to interpret and apply the statute in one of its possible ways.

4 Courts and the regulatory perimeter: shadow banking, parallel unregulated activities, and banking groups

6.33 'Perimeter patrol', ie determining which entities fall inside and outside the perimeter of regulated institutions is one of the most sensitive tasks for authorities, and courts. It is the quintessential exercise of discretion and, as such, is bound to be controversial. First, we analyse

---

[128] *FBF v ACPR* (n 117) paras 104–10.
[129] ibid paras 111–12. CRD (n 79) arts 74–95.
[130] ibid paras 114–17, 118–21. The fit within the Consumer Credit Directive was justified by the conduct rules in the directive, which require credit providers to behave in an equitable, honest, and transparent manner, which must be based on adequate information on the characteristics of consumers, and the Guidelines ensured that this information was duly taken into account.
[131] ibid paras 125–27.

case law (i) on 'shadow banking' and similar 'parallel' activities, and then (ii) on the treatment of financial groups.

4.1 Shadow banking and parallel activities

6.34 In the US in the years prior to the Great Financial Crisis (GFC) of 2007–2008, three issues were inextricably linked: shadow banking, the erosion of the Glass-Steagall Act (GSA), and judicial doctrines on administrative discretion. 'Shadow banking' is 'credit intermediation involving entities and activities outside the regular banking system'.[132] It was one of the GFC's main causes,[133] linked to regulators' gradually lenient view on the GSA.[134] Yet, courts' role is often overlooked, although in these years the Supreme Court shaped its doctrines on agency discretion. The interplay between industry, regulators and courts shaped the face of shadow banking before the GFC. The GSA forbade banks from undertaking eg 'investment' in 'securities' activities. These loose concepts led to competitive pressures that rendered GSA's wall more porous: when Regulation Q capped bank deposits' interest rates securities firms began offering money-market funds (MMFs[135]), and thrifts, not subject to GSA,[136] began offering 'negotiable order of withdrawal (NOW) accounts.[137] Banks, in turn, began distributing securities-like 'commercial paper', issuing mortgage-backed debt, and setting up Bank Holding Companies (BHC) that acquired non-bank financial firms.[138] Bank regulators, like the Office of the Comptroller of the Currency (OCC) and the Board of Governors of the Federal Reserve (Federal Reserve Board or FRB) gradually showed a more permissive attitude towards banks, while industry bodies representing the interest of the investment community took the issue to courts.

6.35 In the first round, *ICI v Camp*[139] annulled an OCC Regulation authorizing banks to operate collective investment funds, because investment funds were a 'security', if one took into account the 'subtle hazards' of banks' involvement with securities that the GSA tried to prevent,[140] ie courts were open to finalistic interpretation to preserve congressional intent. Yet,

---

[132] FSB, 'Shadow Banking: Strengthening Oversight and Regulation. Recommendations of the Financial Stability Board' (27 October 2011) https://www.fsb.org/wp-content/uploads/r_111027a.pdf (accessed 23 September 2022).
[133] G-20, 'Statement: Seoul Summit Meeting Document' (November 2010) 41; The Financial Crisis Inquiry Commission, *Final Report of the National Commission on the Causes of the Financial and Economic Crisis in the United States* (Pursuant to Public Law 111–21, 2011); Leszek Balcerowicz and Others, *The High-Level Group on Financial Supervision in the EU Report* (2009) 15; FSA, *The Turner Review. A Regulatory Response to the Global Financial Crisis* (2009) 21.
[134] US Senate Financial Crisis Inquiry Report (n 133) 32, 35.
[135] ibid para 32.
[136] Savings banks were excluded from the scope of application of Glass-Steagall and Regulation Q because the long-term nature of their assets and the limitations placed on deposit withdrawals put them among investment banks. See Jan Kregel, 'Can a Return to Glass-Steagall Provide Financial Stability in the US Financial System?' (2010) 63 PSL Q Rev 60.
[137] Alan J Kapan, 'The Negotiable Order of Withdrawal (NOW) Account: "Checking Accounts" for Savings Banks?' (1973) 14 Boston College Industrial and Com L Rev 471.
[138] US Senate Financial Crisis Inquiry Report (n 133) 29–33.
[139] *ICI v Camp* (n 82).
[140] Such hazards included the 'obvious' one that a bank could invest in 'imprudent' investments, and the less obvious risk that the promotional and other pressures by its investment affiliate would compromise the bank's 'fiduciary' position, by making it shore up its securities affiliates, extend credit facilities more easily to firms where its affiliate has invested, push certain securities onto its customers, grant them loans to purchase those securities, or compromise its disinterested financial advice, or suffer reputational contagion if investors lost money through its investment affiliate. See *ICI v Camp* (n 82) 629–34.

later in *FRB v ICI (ICI II)* the Supreme Court allowed the Federal Reserve to expand the activities 'closely related to banking'[141] to allow BHCs and their non-banking subsidiaries to act as investment advisers to closed-end investment companies.[142] Thus, there was a difference between banks and BHCs.

Later, in 1984, in two simultaneous cases the Supreme Court annulled the FRB's authorization of banks' distribution of commercial paper, for being 'securities' (*Bankers' Trust I*)[143] sticking to *Camp*'s finalistic interpretation,[144] but also allowed the FRB to authorize a BHC to acquire a retail securities brokerage as an affiliate (*Schwab*).[145] On the surface, this confirmed the difference between banks and BHCs. In reality, this entrenched the permissive view on BHCs (*Schwab* was a unanimous decision) while the (stricter) finalistic approach was contested and waning (Bankers Trust I had three judges dissenting).[146] Then, in 1986 the Court ruled against the FRB's attempt to bring 'non-bank banks', or entities that acted as functional equivalent of banks,[147] notably industrial banks, and thrifts offering NOW accounts within its purview (*FRB v Dimension Financial*). In spite of the deference granted to the FRB the amended Regulation Y went against the plain text of BHC Act section § 2(c), which applied to entities (i) where the 'depositor has a legal right' to withdraw on demand, which could not apply to NOW accounts, where clients could withdraw 'as a matter of practice' but had no 'legal right'; and to entities (ii) which 'engage in the business of making commercial loans', not 'commercial loan substitutes'.[148] In summary, courts enabled the expansion of non-bank activities through BHCs, (still) limited the expansion of non-bank activities by banks themselves, but curtailed bank regulators' attempt to police functional equivalents of banking activities (ie shadow banks). This drew a roadmap for the rise of competing types of financial conglomerates, resulting from the expansion of commercial banks, or investment banks.

6.36

In the last stage, Circuit Courts de facto overruled *ICI v Camp*, by allowing banks to distribute funds,[149] de facto overruled *Bankers' Trust I*, by allowing banks to do private placement of commercial paper, as something different from the 'underwriting' of securities *I*,[150] while allowing BHCs to engage in securities underwriting through

6.37

---

[141] Bank Holding Company Act of 1956, s 4(c)(8).
[142] *Board of Governors, FRS v Investment Co Inst* 450 US 46 (1981).
[143] *Bankers Trust I* (n 88).
[144] The FRB based its position on its view that CP were not 'securities', and said nothing about the risks that GSA sought to prevent. In the Court's view, CP fell under the 'plain meaning of "security"', but, more important, the "subtle hazards" of mixing banking and investment were very present'.
[145] *Schwab* (n 91) 468 US 207. On that same year, the District Court for the District of Columbia held valid the authorization by the Federal Home Loan Bank Board (FHLBB) of an application by three savings and loan (S&L) associations to have a brokerage and investment advisory subsidiary. See *SIA v FHLBB* (n 91) because GSA prohibitions did not apply equally to BHCs.
[146] *Bankers Trust I* (n 88), O'Connor dissent at para 162.
[147] *Board of Governors of FRS v Dimension Financial* 474 US 361 (1986), fn 3.
[148] ibid paras 366, 368–69.
[149] *ICI v Clarke* 789 F 2d 175 (2d Cir 1986) cert denied, 107 US 422 (1986); *ICI v Conover* 790 F 2d 925 (DC Cir 1986) cert denied 107 US 421 (1986); *ICI v Clarke* 793 F 2d 220 (9th Cir 1986) cert denied 107 US 422 (1986) (OCC decision to authorize the establishment and marketing of 'trusts' or 'funds' pooling assets from Individual Retirement Accounts (IRAs), which, according to ICI, were functionally equivalent to a 'mutual fund', and against GSA). See also *ICI v FDIC* 815 F2d 1540 (DC Cir 1987) cert denied, 484 US 847 (1987) (FDIC authorization of non-member banks to engage in securities underwriting and other activities not permitted to banks).
[150] *Securities Industry Association v Board of Governors FRS* 807 F2d 1052 (DC Cir 1986) cert denied, 483 US 1005 (1987) (*Bankers' Trust II*). The Court held that, unlike in *Bankers Trust I* the Board had properly justified the absence of the 'subtle hazards' resulting from banks' involvement with securities, considered relevant by Congress, by limiting placements to a limited number of (large) institutions. *Bankers' Trust II*, para 1069. However, the Court did not address the Supreme Court's *actual* concerns in *Bankers' Trust I* (n 88) ie the conflict of interest in a bank's involvement in the securities market, or the dilution of the GSA's 'broad prohibition' into an 'administrative regulation'. See *Bankers Trust I* (n 88) at 147, 153–56.

subsidiaries,[151] and banks to issue pass-through mortgage-backed securities (MBS), as equivalent to mortgages, rather than to securities.[152] The Supreme Court also abandoned its role as the ultimate enforcer of the spirit of banking laws, by denying *certiorari* in all these cases. It certified this transition by affirming in *NationsBank v VALIC* that bank regulators were entitled to great deference, even to treat as 'banking' products (annuities) that had traditionally been treated as insurance.[153]

6.38 While the US Supreme Court case law did not cause shadow banking, it enabled it, and, together with regulators, helped to shape its face, in the form of sprawling BHCs in the first place, and then through the growth of bank substitutes, and MBS and commercial paper activities by both investment banks and commercial banks. Shadow banking filled the cracks left by GSA concepts and the doctrines of agency discretion.

6.39 US experience provides a cautionary tale to European courts' still limited experience with 'shadow', or parallel, activities. In *Romanelli*[154] the Romanelli brothers were prosecuted for selling financial instruments representing an amount receivable and immediate repurchased at a price which incorporated the agreed interest, and warrants representing an option to acquire debentures issued by Romanelli Finanzaria SpA. This, authorities alleged, was the regulated activity of credit institutions, and the brothers lacked a banking licence.[155] The Romanelli brothers alleged that the funds raised from the public were not 'intrinsically repayable'; repayment resulted from a separate 'restitution agreement'. The key was how to interpret 'repayable funds' under the Directive.[156] The Court of Justice used a broad interpretation of 'credit institution' and 'repayable funds', since a narrower interpretation 'would undermine the objective of protecting consumers against the harm which they could suffer through financial transactions',[157] given that the banking sector is particularly sensitive 'from the point of view of consumer protection' and consumers must be protected against transactions by 'institutions disregarding the requirements relating to their solvency or whose managers do not have the necessary professional qualifications or integrity'.[158] The case's broader point was strikingly similar to that under the case *FRB v Dimension Finance*, and the NOW accounts, discussed above. It was the details, eg the makeshift (and dubious) arrangement of the Romanellis, as opposed to a whole industry-wide trend in NOW accounts; or the more open-textured definitions in the Directive, as opposed to the stricter language of the American statute, that led the Court of Justice to reach an opposite conclusion, and enable the authorities' efforts to deter parties from undertaking shadow banking activities. Thus, *Romanelli* is still relevant today. However, some elements have changed, and would add further complications. First, some powers have been centralized at an EU level, and thus a case today could involve national authorities, EU authorities, or both. Secondly, the Court's emphasis on 'consumer protection' would have to be tempered now that the EU laws that

---

[151] *Securities Industry Association v. Board of Governors FRS (Citicorp)* 839 F.2d 47 (2d Cir. 1988).
[152] *SIA v Clarke* 885 F 2d 1034 (2d Cir 1989).
[153] *NationsBank v VALIC* (n 96).
[154] Case C-366/97 *Criminal proceedings against Massimo Romanelli and Paolo Romanelli* ECLI:EU:C:1999:71. David Ramos, 'Shadow Banking: the Blind Spot in Banking and Capital Markets Reform' (2016) 13 Eur Company & Fin Law Rev 157.
[155] *Romanelli* (n 154) para 5.
[156] ibid para 7.
[157] ibid para 16, citing the Opinion of AG Fennelly, Case C-366/97 *Romanelli*, Opinion of AG Fennelly ECLI:EU:C:1998:523.
[158] *Romanelli* (n 154) para 11, with reference to Case C-222/95 *Parodi v Banque H Albert de Bary* ECLI:EU:C:1997:345.

regulate banks (the Capital Requirements Directive—CRD and Regulation—CRR) also emphasize prudential goals. Would the Court be equally supportive of, say, efforts by the ECB to treat, eg some kind of credit market hedge funds as 'credit institutions', and subject them to bank capital requirements? We will have to wait for an answer.

6.40 A different perimeter issue was decided by the Joint Board of Appeal in four parallel cases brought against ESMA by *Svenska Handelsbanken AB, Skandinaviska Enskilda Banken AB, Swedbank AB*, and *Nordea Bank Abp* (the 'shadow rating' cases).[159] The case's focal point in law was the concept of a 'rating', as opposed to investment 'research' and 'recommendations'. ESMA's Board of Supervisors found that the four banks' inclusion of 'shadow ratings' in their credit research reports was a negligent infringement of Credit Rating Agency Regulation No 1060/2009 (CRAR), and imposed fines on all four banks, who appealed the decision. Article 3(2) of CRAR is somewhat ambiguous in excluding recommendations and 'investment research' from the definition of 'credit ratings'. In the four cases, 'shadow ratings' included in the banks' investment research and recommendations, were creditworthiness assessments composed by the banks' credit analysts, based in whole or in part on the methodology of the 'official' rating agencies, and using an *alphanumerical rating*. This, to ESMA, put them outside the investment research exemption under CRAR, and within the definition of 'rating', even if the overall reports themselves could be characterized as MiFID investment research. The BoA found no evidence of unlawfulness in the decisions under the principles of legal certainty and due process and upheld ESMA's assessment that the activities of the appellants fell within CRAR provisions. Thus, the banks had to be CRAR-registered to undertake the activity, and absent such registration they had infringed the provisions. In reaching its conclusion, the BoA realized that a literal interpretation was not enough, and the legislative history of the relevant provisions was not very enlightening, but if one considered the purpose of the provisions, the BoA held (§ 262) that upholding the banks' interpretation would allow market participants to circumvent CRAR restrictions

> [s]imply by including credit ratings in documents containing recommendations or investment research or even 'opinions about the value of a financial instrument'. In other words, subject to the market abuse framework, anyone could at least in theory issue credit ratings so long as the ratings were included in a document that fell within the Article 3(2) definitions ... These ratings could not have the regulatory use set out in Article 4 ... but would nonetheless be (and present themselves as) credit ratings.

6.41 However, a second focal point was that the practice was not undertaken by a single institution, but was common across the whole Nordic debt market. Thus, the BoA concluded that, due to the ambiguous wording of Article 3(2) CRAR, and the unusual circumstances in which the banks' practice had been carried out in the Nordic debt markets for many years, without any perception of CRAR impropriety, the infringements were not negligent. Thus, ESMA's Board of Supervisors could not impose fines, and the cases were remitted for the adoption of amended measures, under Article 60(5) of the ESMA Regulation.

---

[159] BoA D 2019 02, BoA D 2019 03, BoA D 2019 04, *Svenska Handelsbanken*, BoA D 2019 01, *Skandinaviska Enskilda Banken v ESMA*, BoA D 2019 05; *Swedbank v ESMA*, BoA D 2019 06, *Nordea Bank v ESMA*, BoA D 2019 07 www.esma.europa.eu/it/page/board-appeal (accessed 23 September 2022). The four cases were conducted in parallel, with a single hearing and four simultaneous decisions drafted in a single document. In *Scandinaviska Enskilda Banken AB v ESMA*, the board had decided first to dismiss a request for suspension of the application of the contested decision with a decision of 30 November 2018.

4.2 Financial groups

6.42 Although corporate and insolvency laws and a large part of financial regulation are entity-centric, financial institutions tend to be inserted in group structures, which present many challenges, namely: (i) how to reconcile the entities' formal independence with the actual interdependence within the group; (ii) how to monitor group entities that, like parent, or central entities, may not be licensed as financial institutions; and (iii) whether to focus on positive features (intragroup support) or negative ones (opacity and contagion).

6.43 In the US, the Board of Governors of the Federal Reserve (Federal Reserve Board—FRB) as the consolidated supervisor under the Bank Holding Company (BHC) Act, interpreted its powers to ensure the 'safety and soundness' of banking groups to refuse approval of merger transaction unless the parent company was a 'source-of-strength' to its subsidiaries including in times of liquidity scarcity.[160] This interpretation was challenged in *First Lincolnwood*, and the US Supreme Court accepted that the Board had the power to impose upon the acquirer of a bank the need to be a source of strength for its subsidiary as a condition for acquisition.[161] Yet, the Fed later used the doctrine to *impose* upon a troubled BHC a duty to recapitalize its bank subsidiaries (using the money from the sale of non-bank subsidiaries). The decision was successfully challenged before the Fifth Circuit in *McCorp*,[162] but the Supreme Court remanded the case, holding that the Circuit Court lacked jurisdiction based on procedural grounds,[163] leaving open the issue about the scope of the Fed's mandate.

6.44 The doctrine was codified by the Dodd-Frank Act.[164] This settled the question of whether bank regulators have authority to require the parent to be a source-of-strength. However, it does not answer the question of how much discretion does this entail, if, eg authorities try to micro-manage intra-group funding structures, or impose on the parent company a duty to financially assist its subsidiaries, even if this compromises the parent's viability, or runs against the views of the parent's board. As we discuss below in s 5.3., in light of the court's 'proceduralised' standard of review, the answer to this would depend on whether the authorities have acted in an 'arbitrary and capricious' manner.

6.45 In the EU, the disputes have centred over the exercise of *consolidated* supervision, when some group entities are not credit institutions. In *Crédit Mutuel Arkea*.[165] Crédit Mutuel was

---

[160] Leonard Bierman and Donald Fraser, 'The Source-of-Strength' Doctrine: Formulating the Future of America's Financial Markets' (1993) 12 Ann Rev Banking L 269. For comparison of former and current approaches see Paul L Lee, 'The Source-of-Strength Doctrine: Revered and revisited: Part I' (2012) 129(9) The Banking LJ 771; and Paul L Lee, 'The Source-of-Strength Doctrine: Revered and Revisited: Part II' (2012) 129(10) The Banking LJ 867.

[161] *Board of Governors of Fed Reserve System v First Lincolnwood Corp* 439 US 234, 238 (1978).

[162] *Board of Governors of the Federal Reserve System v MCorp Financial, Inc.* aff'd in part and rev'd in part 112 S Ct 459 (1991).

[163] According to the Supreme Court, the court could only review the Federal Reserve Board decision when it was a final decision, which the one concerned in the *McCorp* case was not. See *Board of Governors of the Federal Reserve System v MCorp* (n 162).

[164] Section 616(d) of the Dodd-Frank Act adds a new section 38A to the Federal Deposit Insurance Act. Subsection (a) of the new section 38A states that: 'The appropriate Federal banking agency for a bank holding company or savings and loan holding company shall require the bank holding company or savings and loan holding company to serve as a source-of-financial strength for any subsidiary of the bank holding company or savings and loan holding company that is a depository institution.'

[165] Case T-712/15 *Crédit Mutuel* (n 68). The case was appealed, and the Court of Justice in *Crédit Mutuel* (n 68), largely confirmed the General Court decision. The same circumstances were examined in another case, Case T-52/16, which resulted in a quasi identical ruling. See the summary by René Smits (n 67) (who also acted as a voting member of the ABoR) https://ebi-europa.eu/wp-content/uploads/2019/01/Note-on-the-Arke%CC%81a-judgments-for-publication-final.pdf (accessed 23 September 2022).

a non-centralized French banking group, formed by a network of local credit unions, of the cooperative corporate form. Each local mutual credit union was affiliated with a regional federation, and each federation with the Confédération nationale du Crédit Mutuel (CNCM), the network's central body. The group also encompasses Caisse centrale du Crédit Mutuel (CCCM), a public limited cooperative finance company with variable share capital, authorized as a credit institution, owned by the members of the network. The ECB issued a decision where it exercised its powers of consolidated supervision over CNCM and of direct supervision over a number the entities listed in that decision, including the applicant, Crédit Mutuel Arkéa, a public limited cooperative finance company with variable share capital, authorized as a credit institution (the decision set out the prudential requirements for the Crédit Mutuel group). The applicant alleged that the ECB lacked competence for consolidated supervision because the CNMC was not a credit institution. The Single Supervisory Mechanism (SSM) rules on consolidated supervision referred to 'vertical' groups with a parent company that is a credit institution, or a 'mixed financial holding company',[166] but they also contemplated the case of groups formed by entities affiliated to 'a central body which supervises them', provided certain conditions (under Article 10 of the Capital Requirements Regulation—CRR) were met.[167]

6.46 The case exemplifies EU courts' tendency to appeal to the *finality* of legal provisions. To the General Court, consolidated prudential supervision had two aims. First, 'to enable the ECB to identify the risks likely to affect a credit institution which derive not from the institution itself, but from the group of which it forms part'; secondly, 'to avoid the prudential supervision of the entities making up those groups being fragmented between different supervisory authorities'.[168] On this basis, the ECB could treat Crédit Mutuel group's bespoke structure as apt for consolidated supervision, and could only 'waive' it under the conditions of Article 10 CRR, but this was a discretionary decision, and the ECB decided against it.[169] Furthermore, pursuant to those objectives, the proximity between the institutions affiliated to the central body was enough to justify the existence of a group, because, 'if a credit institution were to fail, have the effect of putting the other entities affiliated to the same central body at risk'.[170] Thus, the fact that the central body was not a credit institution was not an obstacle for consolidated supervision. The Court acknowledged that this prevented the ECB from exercising any sanctioning powers, since those are reserved for 'credit institutions, financial holding companies and mixed financial holding companies', but could use other tools, and this was acceptable because consolidated supervision is 'in addition to, not a replacement for, prudential supervision on an individual basis of the credit institutions'.[171] The Court of Justice confirmed the General Court's ruling,[172] taking note of a decision by the French Council of State issued after the General Court ruling (as discussed in s 2.2 the case's other salient feature was the application of national law by EU authorities). The Council of State held that the CNCM held greater responsibilities over the functioning of the group, its cohesive

---

[166] Article 2(21)(a) and (b) Regulation (EU) No 468/2014 of the European Central Bank establishing the framework for cooperation within the Single Supervisory Mechanism between the European Central Bank and national competent authorities and with national designated authorities (SSM Framework Regulation) (ECB/2014/17) [2014] OJ L141.
[167] SSM Framework Regulation (n 166) art 2(21)(c).
[168] Case T-712/15 *Crédit Mutuel* (n 68) 58, 61.
[169] ibid paras 65–70.
[170] ibid para 88.
[171] ibid paras 91–92.
[172] *Crédit Mutuel* (n 68).

operation, technical and financial scrutiny, including the decision to merge branches, and was statutorily responsible for implementing banking system regulations on behalf of the whole group and must, as a 'parent undertaking in the Union', have a recovery plan for that group'.[173] Thus, CNCM was also responsible for issuing binding instructions to branches to ensure that they comply with the provisions applicable to them and to impose the appropriate penalties on them should they fail to comply with those provisions, or to introduce 'binding joint and several liability mechanisms' between network members.[174] All this implied obligations with a 'much more onerous financial impact on that member than the imposition of a mere obligation to transfer capital and liquid assets',[175] and thus, *implied* the existence of an obligation to transfer capital and liquid assets within the group to meet obligations towards creditors, 'with the result that the ECB was justified in taking the view that the condition laid down in Article 10(1)(a) of Regulation No 575/2013 was fulfilled'.[176]

5 A comparative assessment of courts' standard of review

6.47 Courts' standard of review when financial authorities apply the law of finance partly reflects their views about delegation and separation of powers, and about the finality of concrete legal provisions. US courts offer a relatively proceduralized review, under the 'arbitrary and capricious' standard. However, under the cost-benefit analysis (CBA) this can sometimes result in a challenge to agencies' understanding of a provision's substance and finality. In contrast, EU courts openly focus their review on the substance and finality of legislative provisions, which reflects their perception of themselves as the ultimate guarantors of the system's legitimacy (5.2.). Furthermore, courts may also focus on procedural safeguards, also under 'arbitrary and capricious' in the US (5.3.) or under a panoply of specific protections and general principles in the EU (5.4.).

5.1 US courts' 'arbitrary and capricious' standard: the 'demanding' version, and its challenge to the substantive application of the law

6.48 US courts' standard of review of agency decisions is shaped by ideas of delegation and administrative discretion. As discussed earlier in ss 2.1., 3 and 4.1. in some early cases courts appealed to the finality of statutes to interpret concepts such as the 'business of banking', but this approach ceded ground to ideas of deference and discretion. Indeed, theories of process-based review emphasize that courts should not second second-guess other bodies substantive choices, but focus on the decision-making process.[177] Regardless of their shortcomings and criticisms,[178] in a financial setting, court review has gravitated towards the 'arbitrary and capricious' standard (section 706, Administrative Procedure Act (APA)). Although a primarily process-based standard, it is not entirely so. Depending on the substantive regulatory provisions with which it interacts, the more 'demanding' version of the standard, by

---

[173] ibid para 103.
[174] ibid para 104.
[175] ibid para 106.
[176] ibid para 107.
[177] John H Ely, *Democracy and Distrust: A Theory of Judicial Review* (HUP 1980).
[178] See eg Lawrence H Tribe, 'The Puzzling Persistence of Process-Based Constitutional Theories' (1980) 89 Yale LJ 1063.

increasing the agencies' burden of justifying their actions in requiring a cost-benefit analysis (CBA), may, in practice, verge on a challenge to the agency's *substantive* application of the rules. In contrast, as seen later in s 5.3., the same standard can turn into a relatively deferential focus on procedural safeguards.

The requirement of CBA as part of the 'arbitrary and capricious' review has been distinctively used by the D.C. Circuit. In cases against the Securities and Exchange Commission (SEC), the requirement of a CBA resulted from combining 'arbitrary and capricious' with the requirement that the SEC considers the effects of its rules on 'efficiency, competition, and capital formation'.[179] In 2005, in *Chamber of Commerce v SEC* the SEC required mutual funds to have a board with 75 per cent independent directors to benefit from certain exemptions, when 50 per cent was the previous requirement.[180] The SEC was trying to correct abuses in the industry, and based the reform on its experience and comment letters, but not on an empirical study, since available data was conflicting. The Court held that the SEC had violated the APA by failing to take the costs of the decision into account.[181] The decision accepted that an agency did not always have to provide empirical analysis;[182] but it also held that the SEC had to provide cost figures; and rejected the SEC's argument that costs were hard to estimate, due to the different ways in which a fund could satisfy its conditions, holding that it was the SEC's duty to apprise itself, and also Congress and the public, of the regulation's economic consequences.[183] Then, in *American Equity Investment Life Insurance Co. v SEC*,[184] the D.C. Circuit decided on a rule subjecting Fixed Index Annuities (FIA) to disclosure requirements and other investor protections, because, in the SEC's view, FIAs were risky (due to the underlying investments in securities) and lacked adequate protections. Although for the SEC the rule's benefits outweighed its costs (typically, registration and disclosure costs), and it conducted a CBA, the court held that the SEC's analysis was incomplete because it did not measure the rule's effect on efficiency, competition, and capital formation *against the baseline* of those factors under applicable state insurance laws.[185] **6.49**

On *Business Roundtable v SEC*,[186] the D.C. Circuit reviewed the 'proxy access' rule, which addressed the concern of prohibitive costs of distributing proxy materials preventing shareholders from submitting director nominations.[187] The SEC used a Dodd-Frank Act which habilitated it to propose a controversial rule[188] (it passed by a 3:2 vote)[189] to make companies **6.50**

---

[179] 15 US Code ss 78c(f), 78w(a)(2), 80a-2(c). The provision was introduced in 1996.
[180] *Chamber of Commerce v SEC* (2005] 412 F3d 133 (DC Cir).
[181] ibid para 136.
[182] ibid para 142, holding that: '[W]e are acutely aware that an agency need not—indeed cannot—base its every action upon empirical da-ta; depending upon the nature of the problem, an agency may be 'entitled to conduct ... a general analysis based on informed conjecture.'
[183] *Chamber of Commerce v SEC* (n 180) 144.
[184] *American Equity Investment Life Insurance Co v SEC* (2010) 613 F 3d 166 (DC Cir).
[185] '[T]he SEC's analysis is incomplete because it fails to determine whether, under the existing regime, sufficient protections existed to enable investors to make informed investment decisions and sellers to make suitable recommendations to investors. The SEC's failure to analyze the efficiency of the existing state law regime renders arbitrary and capricious the SEC's judgment that applying federal securities law would increase efficiency.' *American Equity Investment Life Insurance Co v SEC* (n 184) 178–79.
[186] *Business Roundtable v SEC* 647 F 3d 1144 (DC Cir 2011). See comment 'Business Roundtable v. SEC. D.C. Circuit Finds SEC Proxy Access Rule Arbitrary and Capricious for Inadequate Economic Analysis' (2012) 125 HLR 1088.
[187] Rachel Benedict, 'Note Judicial Review of SEC Rules: Managing the Costs of Cost-Benefit Analysis' (2012) 97 Minnesota L Rev 286.
[188] Section 971 of the Dodd-Frank Wall Street Reform and Consumer Protection Act, Pub L No 111-203, 124 Stat 1376 (2010) stated that: '[t]he Commission may issue rules [expanding proxy access], under such terms and conditions as the Commission determines are in the interests of shareholders and for the protection of investors'.
[189] Exchange Act Rule 14a-11 (rule 14a-11).

include qualifying shareholder (3 per cent) nominees on proxy ballots. The SEC's economic CBA was substantial and took numerous staff hours. The D.C. Circuit, however, found the SEC's efforts insufficient, and using very harsh language,[190] stroke down the rule based on three premises. First, the SEC underestimated the expenses that directors would incur campaigning against proxies. To the Court, the SEC's view that the rule would improve board performance had 'no basis beyond mere speculation', by relying on 'two relatively unpersuasive studies' instead of 'the numerous studies submitted by commenters that reached the opposite result', and by stating that existing state (corporate) law rights not the SEC rules designed to enforce them, were to blame for potential costs, calling this reasoning 'illogical and, in an economic analysis, unacceptable'.[191] Secondly, although the SEC had only considered, but not 'adequately addressed' the risk that institutional investors like unions and pension funds could manipulate the rule.[192] Thirdly, the court considered the SEC's projections of the frequency of election contest 'internally inconsistent and therefore arbitrary'.[193] Business Roundtable is an outlier, where the court imposed a very high evidentiary bar on the agency as a way to express its disagreement on the underlying substantive and political controversy of proxy fights.

6.51 The case gave the D.C. District Court momentum to adopt a less deferential attitude in a case applying post financial crisis Dodd-Frank Act mandates. In *Metlife v FSOC* the District Court for the District of Columbia reviewed the Financial Stability and Oversight Council (FSOC) decision to subject Metlife, an insurance company, to Federal Reserve Board supervision, after considering its financial distress as 'posing a threat to financial stability'.[194] The court held that the 'arbitrary and capricious' standard (used by the Dodd-Frank Act, which established the FSOC) required taking into account an agency's prior policy if this had 'engendered serious reliance interest' on the supervised entities, which required a special justification by the agency about why the decision was 'necessary' and 'appropriate'. By failing to conduct a CBA, the FSOC had not provided such justification, and had failed to consider 'all the relevant circumstances', and the decision was arbitrary and capricious.[195] The decision remains controversial. Congress' intent was for the FSOC to identify systemic risks, and this required some degree of discretion, and it is not obvious that a CBA is the only way to justify a decision under the 'arbitrary and capricious' standard. Yet, none of these arguments were explored, since the administration decided not to pursue the appeal, and the issue remains open.

5.2 EU Courts' substantive-leaning and finalistic review: Their role as ultimate authorities in defining key concepts of the law of finance

6.52 EU Courts' review shows important differences with US courts' approach. EU courts attach much importance to process-based review, and in some decisions courts do not evaluate

---

[190] *Business Roundtable v SEC* (n 186) 1148–49: '[I]nconsistently and opportunistically framed the costs and benefits of the rule; failed adequately to quantify the certain costs or to explain why those costs could not be quantified; neglected to support its predictive judgments; contradicted itself; and failed to respond to substantial problems raised by commenters.'
[191] *Business Roundtable v SEC* (n 186) 1149–51.
[192] ibid para 1152.
[193] *Business Roundtable v SEC* (n 186) 1153.
[194] *Metlife v FSOC* 1:15-cv-00045-RMC 30 (2016) District Court, District of Columbia.
[195] ibid.

the choices made by EU legislators or Member States, but focus on the factors considered in the decision and its justification.[196] Some provisions, such as Article 41 of the EU Charter of Fundamental Rights provide for the 'duty to give reasons' as a source of scrutiny,[197] and procedural safeguards (referred to in subsequent sections) are very relevant. Also, EU courts acknowledge the importance of 'discretion', and are deferential to administrative authorities. Yet, EU courts do not accept ideas such as that agencies may not be bound by a court's interpretation of a legal term, or that an issue may be 'committed to agency discretion'. EU courts have the ultimate responsibility to interpret EU law, and, in the presence of open-textured concepts and provisions they will discuss whether an agency's interpretation is 'the' reasonable interpretation, rather than 'a reasonable enough' interpretation. In doing so, Courts provide an authoritative interpretation of key concepts of financial law, and incidentally bolster the legitimacy of supranational authorities which could otherwise be contested at a national level.

In *OC and Others v Banca d'Italia*[198] the Court reviewed the concept of 'capital'. Under the Basel-inspired requirements in the Capital Requirements Directive and Regulation (CRD and CRR) and EBA interpretations common shares could be deemed ineligible as 'capital', for purposes of the Core Equity Tier 1 (CET1) or Additional Tier 1 (AT1) ratios,[199] if national company law permitted shares' redemption for non-distribution of dividends,[200] or contemplated a shareholders' right of redemption, unless the redemption/repurchase was made subject to prior supervisory approval.[201] This was problematic for cooperative banks. Article 29(2) CRR acknowledged the principles of variable capital and 'open door' as co-essential to the cooperative form under company law, *but* also provided that the institution should be able to refuse redemption or, where this was prohibited under national (company) law, to limit their redemption.[202] Italian rules[203] provided that, above a certain threshold, (EUR 8 billion) a bank had to convert into a joint-stock company (limited by shares) and to defer/limit share redemption indefinitely. The banks alleged that this interfered with the right to property and freedom to conduct a business under Articles 16 and 17 of the Charter of Fundamental Rights (EU Charter), and with free movement of capital (under Articles 63 ff TFEU). The Italian Constitutional Court dismissed these arguments[204] but,

6.53

---

[196] Koen Lenaerts, 'The European Court of Justice and Process-Based Review' (2012) 31(1) Ybk of Eur L 3.

[197] For example, in decisions subject to a large degree of discretion, such as monetary policy decisions, the Court of Justice has put great emphasis on the European Central Bank's duty to give reasons, and even assessed the 'proportionality' of the measure based on the ECB's reasons. See ch 5.

[198] Case C-686/18 *OC and Others v Banca d'Italia* ECLI:EU:C:2020:567.

[199] Marco Lamandini and David Ramos Muñoz, 'The Definition of Common Equity Tier 1 Capital and of Contingent Capital and the Diversity of Capital Instruments issued by European Credit Institutions' in Bart Joosen, Marco Lamandini, and Tobias Tröger (eds), *Capital and Liquidity for European Banks* (OUP 2022).

[200] EBA, *Report on the monitoring of CET1 instruments issued by EU institutions, Second Update* 21, s 84 https://www.eba.europa.eu/sites/default/documents/files/documents/10180/2551996/51a39b9d-a68d-476a-b2c6-e2c21527a05f/EBA%20Report%20on%20the%20monitoring%20of%20CET1%20instruments%20issued%20by%20EU%20Institutions.pdf?retry=1 (accessed 23 September 2022).

[201] ibid 21, s 83.

[202] The European Commission implemented this principle in art 10 of Commission Delegated Regulation (EU) No 241/2014 supplementing Regulation (EU) No 575/2013 of the European Parliament and of the Council with regard to regulatory technical standards for Own Funds requirements for institutions [2014] OJ L74 (CRR), which specified that the limit to redemption may consist either in the deferral of the redemption or in the limitation of its amount for an unlimited period of time depending on the prudential situation of the institution.

[203] Italian Law-Decree No 3 (24 January 2015), converted into Law 24 March 2015, no 33 (*banche popolari* with assets exceeding 8 Billion Euro had to convert in 18 months into joint stock companies) and regulatory rule by Bank of Italy of 9 June 2017.

[204] The new law was challenged twice: in both cases the Italian Constitutional Court dismissed the challenge (judgments No 287 of 2016, and No 99 of 2018), following a line of interpretation proposed in Marco Lamandini, 'La riforma delle banche popolari al vaglio della Corte Costituzionale' (2017) Le Società 140.

since Italian rules transposed EU rules, the Italian Council of State made a preliminary reference to the Court of Justice. The Court held that the question on the compatibility of the threshold for conversion with property rights was inadmissible, because EU rules did not require Italian law to impose a threshold of conversion; it was a choice by Italy, and thus not a measure 'implementing EU law', nor subject to the EU Charter.[205] The Court then held that the decision on the compatibility of *restrictions over redeemability* with property rights corresponded to national courts, but subject to quite deterministic principles outlined by the Court. Under these principles, the redemption restrictions were not a property deprivation, nor interfered with the essence of freedom to conduct a business; were justified by the goals like ensuring good governance, sector stability, the prudent exercise of banking activities, and preventing systemic risk.[206] For the Court, 'there is a clear public interest in ensuring that core equity investment in a bank is not unexpectedly withdrawn',[207] but it left the proportionality analysis (ie whether the measures constrained the right to property beyond what was necessary) to the referring court.[208] The compatibility of the *threshold measures* with free movement of capital was admissible (because this principle applied also to measures that did not 'implement EU law'), and the Court acknowledged that the measures were 'restrictions', and could dissuade investors from other Member States.[209] However, they were based on a clear public interest, and the analysis of 'necessity' was left for national courts. Interestingly, the Court did not delve deeper on whether property and free movement of capital warranted a similarly demanding (or deferential) review, and also limited itself to arguments of policy (ie the rationale of the interfering measures) not arguments of principle (eg why plaintiffs might consider share redemption co-essential to property rights over *people's* banks' shares) beyond a cursory remark stating that 'cooperative societies conform to particular operating principles'.[210]

6.54 *Caisse regionale de crédit Agricole v ECB*[211] analysed banks' *governance* rules. The ECB, as the group-level competent supervisory authority, approved four candidates for board chairmen of four regional banks of the 'non-centralised' (ie, cooperative) Crédit Agricole group in France, but rejected their appointment as 'effective directors' (*dirigeants effectifs*) as incompatible. The ECB had to approve the appointment pursuant to the Capital Requirements Directive (CRD IV) provisions on 'effective direction' (Article 13 CRD).[212] However, the

---

[205] Case C-686/18 *OC and Others v Banca d'Italia and Others* (n 198), paras 52–53.
[206] ibid paras 90–92. According to the referring court, that legislation is thus intended to make the legal form of people's banks more in line with the specific dynamics of the reference market, to guarantee greater competitiveness for those banks and to promote greater transparency in their organization, operation, and functions. Such objectives, which are capable of ensuring good governance in the cooperative banking sector, the stability of that sector and prudent exercise of banking activities, help to prevent the default of the institutions concerned, or even a systemic risk, and, as a result, help to guarantee the stability of the banking and financial system.
These were clearly objectives of public interest.
[207] *OC and Others* (n 198) para 94: 'there is a clear public interest in ensuring that core equity investment in a bank is not unexpectedly withdrawn, and in thus preventing that bank and the whole of the banking sector from being exposed to instability, from a prudential perspective'.
[208] ibid para 97.
[209] ibid paras 103–104.
[210] ibid para 89.
[211] *Caisse régionale de crédit Agricole* (n 67). See the Summary by René Smits (n 67) https://ebi-europa.eu/publications/eu-cases-or-jurisprudence> (accessed 23 September 2022) and the comment of Christos Gortsos, 'The Crédit Agricole Cases: Banking Corporate Governance and Application of National Law by the ECB' in Chiara Zilioli and Karl-Philipp Wojcik (eds), *Judicial Review in the European Banking Union* (Edward Elgar Publishing 2021) 510–20.
[212] CRD (n 79) art 13(1) states that: '[T]he competent authorities shall grant authorisation to commence the activity of a credit institution only where at least two persons effectively direct the business of the applicant credit institution.'

ECB reasoned that, to be approved, the person also had to comply with the provisions on 'governance arrangements' which prohibit the accumulation of the position of chairperson and CEO (Article 88 CRD) CRD).[213] A further complication was that these provisions had been transposed in the French Financial and Monetary Code (FMC), *and* interpreted by the French Prudential Control and Resolution Authority. The case was heard first by the Administrative Board of Review (ABoR), which confirmed the ECB's interpretation, and then by the General Court.

To the General Court there was no definition of 'persons who effectively direct the business **6.55** of the institution', but a textual analysis showed that '[I]it consists of three elements: first, a reference to the concept of direction, 'at least two persons ... direct', then an adverb qualifying that direction, 'effectively', and, lastly, a reference to the subject of that direction, 'the business of ... the institution'.[214] Although the reference to 'direction' could refer to any member of the management body (board, or management board[215]), the adverb 'effectively', plus the reference to the 'business of the institution' narrowed the definition to executive directors.[216] To supplement this construction the Court used the so-called 'four eyes' principle (under which there must be two sets of eyes to manage and control management in a bank[217]). To the Court, the principle had changed from the first banking directives, where the requirement applied to 'all members' of the board/management body (including non-executives) to subsequent texts, like the CRD, which narrowed it down to executive directors.[218] Finally, under a contextual and finalistic interpretation, although the Court did not find evidence of the 'four eyes' principle's objectives in the CRD recitals, it found it in the corporate governance provisions. In the Court's view:

> [I]n the general scheme of Directive 2013/36, the objective relating to good governance of credit institutions ... requires effective oversight of the senior management by the non-executive members of the management body, which necessitates checks and balances within the management body. It is clear that the effectiveness of such oversight may be jeopardised if the chairman of the management body in its supervisory function, while not formally acting as chief executive officer, is also responsible for the effective direction of the business of the credit institution.[219]

Therefore, although under the initial directives the 'four eyes' principle could be read *inde-* **6.56** *pendently* of good governance provisions (which authorized joint appointments as chairman and CEO), the CRD IV had integrated the 'four eyes' principle as part of good governance, precluding the chairman of the management body in its supervisory function from being also responsible for the effective direction of the business of the credit institution.[220]

---

[213] CRD (n 79) art 88(1) states that: '[T]he chairman of the management body in its supervisory function of an institution must not exercise simultaneously the functions of a chief executive officer within the same institution, unless justified by the institution and authorised by competent authorities.'
[214] *Caisse régionale de crédit Agrícole* (n 67) 56.
[215] ibid para 57. This could be inferred from the reference to CRD (n 79) art 3(1)(7).
[216] It thus rejected the bank's argument that it could also comprise non-executive directors involved in the day-to-day business of the institution, but more focused on the 'oversee[ing] and monitor[ing] [of] management decision-making', which art 3(1)(8) of the directive entrusts to the management body in its supervisory function'. *Caisse régionale de crédit Agricole* (n 67) 59–61.
[217] Summary of the judgment by René Smits (n 67).
[218] *Caisse régionale de crédit Agricole* (n 67) paras 66–67.
[219] ibid para 79.
[220] ibid para 80.

6.57 This conclusion did not depend on type of board (eg single board versus dual-board) because it 'relates only to the organisation of powers within the management body'.[221] The final part of the ruling gave detailed attention to the transposition of CRD IV by French law, and the views of the ACPR and the French Council of State. In particular, the Court quoted the Council of State opinion verbatim, which held that the chairperson of the bank may not be regarded as 'effectively directing' the institution. Thus, neither the French ACPR (as held by the Council of State) nor the ECB (as held by the General Court) had misconstrued the relevant provisions.[222] Under that assumption:

> [o]nly in the event that the chairman of the board of directors of a credit institution had been expressly authorised to have responsibility for its general management that that individual could be appointed 'effective director' of that institution, within the meaning of the second paragraph of Article L. 511-13 of the CMF'.[223]

6.58 Good governance provisions tend to 'sprawl' into other fields. In *AAB*, the General Court upheld the ECB decision to withdraw a bank's licence for breaching the duty to have 'robust governance arrangements' (Article 74 CRD, as transposed by national legislation) after national authorities found violations of anti-money laundering provisions.[224] The Court rejected the appellant's argument that legally required 'governance arrangements' should be restricted to 'financial risks', not money laundering, since the ECB had correctly referred to the governance requirements, and the national provisions on governance made a reference to the need for measures against the risk of money laundering.[225]

6.59 *Berlusconi II*[226] considered the rules on 'fit-and-proper', in the context of the acquisition of qualifying holdings. As already noted in s 2.2., Italian courts had validated Fininvest's (and, indirectly, Mr Berlusconi's) acquisition of shares in the holding company (Mediolanum) of a bank (Banca Mediolanum). Later, the ECB treated the reverse merger between the bank and its holding company, by which Fininvest's (and, indirectly, Mr Berlusconi's) indirect holding became a direct holding in the bank as an 'acquisition', and denied authorisation on grounds that Mr Berlusconi did not fulfil 'fit-and-proper' requirements. The General Court interpreted the concept of 'acquisition of a significant holding' autonomously and independently of national law, and broadly, pursuant to its objective to ensure the *suitability* of the proposed acquirer,[227] because, under a restrictive interpretation, limited to eg 'purchases of shares in the market' the rules could be circumvented.[228] Under this broad, finalistic interpretation a restructuring of an indirect into a direct holding was an 'acquisition', even if the degree of influence by the acquirers has not changed,[229] and allowed the ECB to evaluate Mr Berlusconi also after the transaction had occurred[230]. By treating the reverse merger as a 'new' acquisition,[231] the ECB decision did not entail a retroactive application of the law; nor was it contrary to legal certainty and *res judicata*, because it was not an overruling of the

---

[221] ibid para 82.
[222] ibid para 88.
[223] *Caisse régionale de crédit Agricole* (n 67) para 89 (emphasis added).
[224] *AAB* (n 64).
[225] ibid paras 127–28.
[226] *Berlusconi II* (n 57).
[227] ibid paras 52, 54.
[228] ibid paras 51–55.
[229] ibid paras 57, 59–60.
[230] ibid paras 81–85.
[231] ibid paras 97–98.

original decision by national courts, which, in turn, could not affect the exercise of an exclusive competence by EU authorities.[232]

In *Pilatus Bank* the General Court considered the harsh implications of the 'fit-and-proper' requirement of 'good repute'.[233] A director and shareholder in a Maltese bank was indicted in the United States, on charges of funnelling money to the bank. This led to a massive deposit withdrawal, followed by Maltese authorities' decision to revoke the individual's directorship and suspend his voting rights as a shareholder, followed by the ECB's decision to withdraw the bank's licence, following a proposal from Maltese authorities. The appellants alleged that the ECB had failed to examine the facts, and relied on US authorities' press releases, while the indictment was based on activities that were only 'criminal' in the US (due to the sanctions against the Islamic Republic of Iran) but not in the EU. To the Court, the provisions on withdrawal of authorisation and acquisition of qualifying holdings were connected, and the authorities could withdraw the licence of a bank whose shareholders were considered unsuitable.[234] Then, the Court interpreted the concept of 'good repute' in light of the finality of the provisions, which was prudential and risk oriented, also drawing on EBA documents, concluding that it encompassed a person's conduct, but also the perception of others, and the public's confidence in the financial institution.[235] The indictment and media attention were enough to cast serious doubts about the integrity of the shareholder, and consider him unsuitable, and, since he held 100 per cent of the bank, this led to a massive withdrawal of deposits, an increase of the risk ratio, and a request to terminate its loan by the bank's main borrower, which represented 90 per cent of the bank's loan book and its main source of income (the remaining 10 per cent were either non-performing loans, or had also requested early termination).[236] Thus, regardless of the truth about the allegations, the ECB made an adequate cause-and-effect assessment, and drew the correct prudential implications. Yet, although the Court openly accepted external perceptions as a major source of 'suitability', one should also consider the case's peculiarities: a wholly owned small bank, whose deposit base and loan book heavily depended on its owner.

6.60

A somehow similar line of reasoning was followed by the General Court in *ABLV v SRB*[237] where the US Department of Treasury through the Financial Crimes Enforcement Network (FinCen) announced a draft measure to designate ABLV Bank as an institution of primary money laundering concern pursuant to section 311 of the USA PATRIOT Act. After such announcement the bank was no longer able to make payments in the US dollars and this triggered a liquidity crisis which led the ECB to communicate to the bank that, in order to avoid default, if had to have 1 billion Euro in cash by a set deadline in its account with the Latvian Central Bank. The alleged unlawfulness of the FinCen announcement and thus of the reaction to it by the ECB and SRB and the ECB determination of such amount were challenged by the bank as disproportionate in the context of the application for annulment of the SRB decision based upon the FOLTF assessment made by the ECB, but the claim was rejected by the Court noting that also a liquidity constraint could trigger the failing or likely

---

[232] ibid para 104.
[233] Case T-27/19 *Pilatus Bank plc and Pilatus Holding Ltd v ECB* ECLI:EU:T:2022:46 (currently on appeal in Cases C-750/21 P and C-256/22 P, where AG Kokott delivered her Opinion on 25 May 2023 ECLI:EU:C:2023:431 proposing to the Court to set aside the judgment of the General Court)
[234] ibid paras 63–71.
[235] ibid paras 73–80.
[236] ibid 83–95.
[237] Case T-280/22 *ABLV Bank v SRB* ECLI:EU:T:2022:429.

to fail of a bank and that the appellant had not given evidence of the implausibility of the ECB conclusions.[238]

6.61 The previous cases show how the General Court claims the ultimate authority to determine *the* correct meaning of open-textured provisions according to their finality while maintaining a deferential approach to administrative authorities. Is this merely a sideshow to lend legitimacy to any decision by those authorities? The answer is a clear 'no', as in other cases the Court has disagreed with those authorities, sometimes controversially. In the *Banque Postale—Crédit Agricole* cases (or the 'Livret' cases),[239] and the subsequent *Crédit Lyonnais* case[240] the General Court decided over the ECB's refusal to exclude from the calculation of the leverage ratio the exposures resulting from different types of accounts (Livret A, LEP, LDD).[241] These were special tax-exempt savings accounts regulated by the French Financial and Monetary Code, where a part of the funds received by the banks was held centrally by the Caisse des dépôts et consignations (CDC), a French public financial institution. The leverage ratio is an institution's capital measure divided by *total* liabilities[242] (ie not risk-weighted liabilities, as in the capital ratio). However, there is the possibility of a discretionary exclusion by the ECB from the ratio's denominator of exposures arising from deposits that the bank must transfer to a public sector entity to fund general interest investments.[243] Several French banks sought ECB authorization to exclude the balance of these accounts from the denominator of the leverage ratio, and this was rejected by the ECB. The banks argued that the ECB exceeded its competence or, alternatively, committed an error of law, manifest error of assessment, and violated EU principles. The General Court accepted that, in trying to reconcile the logic of the leverage ratio, which considers a bank's total exposure, and the Commission's objective to exclude certain low-risk exposures that did not reflect an investment choice by the bank, the law granted the ECB ample discretion.[244] Nonetheless, the Court held that the ECB had committed an error in law, because it had exercised its discretion in a way that would deprive the legal provision of any practical effect.[245] The ECB's argument to exclude the exposures was that they were state-guaranteed assets, and thus carried the risk of default by the French State'.[246] Yet, since the provision permitted the exclusion of

> [o]nly exposures to public service entities having a State guarantee, a refusal given on the theoretical ground that a State may be in a payment default situation, without consideration of the likelihood of such a possibility in the case of the State concerned, would

---

[238] ibid paras 94, 116–24.
[239] Case T-745/16 *BPCE v ECB* [2018] ECLI:EU:T:2018:476. Six practically identical cases were decided, and the rulings had a practically identical content, involving the largest French banking groups. These included: *Caisse régionale de crédit agricole* (n 67); Case T-757/16 113 *Société Générale and Crédit agricole Corporate and Investment Bank v European Commission* ECLI:EU:T:2018:73; Case T-751/16 *Crédit mutuel* (n 168); *BPCE v ECB* (ibid); and Case T-733/16 *Banque Postale v ECB* ECLI:EU:T:2018:477. See the summary by René Smits (n 67) https://ebi-europa.eu/wp-content/uploads/2019/01/Summaries-RS.pdf (accessed 23 September 2022). Compare Michael Ioannidis, 'The Judicial Review of Discretion in the Banking Union: From 'Soft' to Hard(er)' Look' in Chiara Zilioli and Karl-Philipp Wojcik (eds), *Judicial Review in the European Banking Union* (Edward Elgar Publishing 2021) 138–42.
[240] Case T-504/19 *Crédit Lyonnais v ECB* ECLI:EU:T:2021:185.
[241] These included the *Livret A* (Savings passbook A), the Livret d'épargne populaire (Popular Savings Passbook) (LEP), and the *Livret de Développement Durable et solidaire* (LDD) accounts.
[242] Article 429(2) of CRR (n 202).
[243] Article 429(14) of CRR (n 202).
[244] *Banque Postale* (n 239) paras 54–55.
[245] ibid paras 74–76.
[246] ibid para 72.

amount to rendering the possibility envisaged by [the relevant provision] virtually inapplicable in practice.[247]

6.62 Furthermore, in the Court's view, the risk of excessive leverage stemmed from the eventual need for a bank to take measures like the distressed selling of assets, which could result in losses and valuation corrections in scenarios of insufficient liquidity.[248] Such fire sales could occur during the time lag (the 'adjustment period') between the bank's position and the CDC position, and, since the ECB had admitted that the adjustment period did not give rise to a liquidity risk, it could not exceed the 'gravely stressed conditions' envisaged by the liquidity ratio.[249] Thus, the ECB could not choose to reject without a thorough examination of the characteristics of the instrument involved.[250] Also, the large volume (or concentration) of the exposures was not enough to exclude them, because this might be relevant only if the bank could not obtain payment, and would have to have recourse to forced sales of assets.[251]

6.63 In the subsequent *Crédit Lyonnais I* case the bank alleged that the ECB had failed to properly implement the Court's previous decisions because it allowed all *Crédit Agricole* group entities to exclude all CDC exposures, except *Crédit Lyonnais*, which the ECB allowed to exclude only a 66 per cent of said exposures.[252] The ECB had offered a methodology for its exclusion, and the Court accepted that it had 'analysed the [French state's] likelihood of default', based on credit ratings (not top ratings) and credit default swaps (with a non-negligible probability of default).[253] The Court also accepted that the ECB had justified the scenarios of 'gravely distressed conditions', with past examples of sudden, massive withdrawals, that, with a non-negligible risk of default, the exposures' size, or concentration could be relevant, and that the ECB's methodology was within its supervisory mandate, and did not result in the exercise of regulatory powers.[254] Yet, the General Court still rejected the ECB's assessment of the risk of withdrawals, followed by distressed sales, as failing to account for some of the accounts' key features, namely: (i) as 'safe investments' they would tend to increase, not decline in a crisis; (ii) unlike regular deposits, which may be invested in any way, the funds under the 'Livréts' were transferred to the CDC, and could not be invested in high-risk or illiquid assets; (iii) rather than deposit insurance, they benefited from a dual guarantee from the French state, which made the analogy with past examples of withdrawals from 'regular' sight deposit accounts unfit,[255] and, in the absence of an assessment based on similar products, the remaining elements, ie the risk of default of the French state, the volume and concentration of exposures, were insufficient to substantiate the ECB's decision,[256] and thus the General Court decided that all the CDC exposures should be excluded from the leverage ratio.[257]

6.64 The case was appealed before the Court of Justice, and in *Crédit Lyonnais II* both the AG Emiliou and the Court found that the General Court had gone one step too far, and

---

[247] ibid para 86. See also para 88.
[248] ibid para 93; *Caisse régionale de crédit agricole* (n 67), paras 70–72.
[249] *Banque Postale* (n 239) 96–98, 106; *Caisse régionale de crédit agricole* (n 67) paras 73–78.
[250] *Caisse régionale de crédit agricole* (n 67) para 81.
[251] *Banque Postale* (n 239) paras 73, 92.
[252] The appellant referred in particular to the case *Caisse régionale de crédit agricole* (n 67).
[253] *Crédit Lyonnais I* (n 240) para 44.
[254] ibid paras 67–68 (past experience of massive withdrawals), para 82 (relevance of size and concentration once there is a non-negligible risk of default), and paras 94–95 (methodology within its supervisory mandate).
[255] ibid paras 107–14.
[256] ibid paras 118–22.
[257] ibid paras 125–26.

substituted its assessment for that of the ECB.[258] EU Courts must assess 'whether the evidence relied on is factually accurate, reliable and consistent but also whether that evidence contains all the relevant information which must be taken into account in order to assess a complex situation and whether it is capable of substantiating the conclusions drawn from it', and apply procedural guarantees, 'including the obligation for that institution to examine carefully and impartially all the relevant aspects of the situation in question'.[259] By that yardstick, the Court of Justice found, the General Court had not questioned the ECB's assessment of the non-negligible risk of massive withdrawals (and thus fire sales) or of the highly liquid nature of the CDCs, which it used as a basis, ie the Court had not questioned the 'material accuracy, reliability and consistency' of the assessment, nor established that the factors considered did not constitute all relevant information.[260] Thus, the General Court did not review the ECB's findings under a 'manifest error' standard, but rather (incorrectly) used the same facts as a basis to reach a different conclusion as to the risk of fire sales, in a context where the ECB had broad discretion, and without establishing how considerations such as that regulated savings deposits could not be invested in risky or illiquid assets, or the dual guarantee mechanism rendered the ECB's assessment manifestly incorrect.[261] The Court of Justice reviewed (and upheld) the ECB's assessment under a 'manifest implausibility' standard: the bank's evidence that these 'safe investments' could accrete in a crisis did not render the ECB's reliance by analogy on past examples of massive withdrawals manifestly implausible; nor did the bank's argument that the transaction was 'structurally balanced' (ie the liability side of funds was matched by the safe investment in the asset side) exclude that the 'deferred adjustment period' between the withdrawal of funds, and the repayment by the CDC could present a risk of distressed sales, not entirely addressed by the liquidity ratio.[262] The *Crédit Lyonnais* action was thus dismissed.

6.65 The saga of *Banque Postale* and *Crédit Lyonnais I* and *II* are a good example of EU Courts' gradual adjustment of their role in the European law of finance, and the difficulty of balancing public authorities' discretion, with an adequate level of scrutiny. Supervisory authorities must have the last say on the *assessment* of facts, eg the risk involved in a certain situation, but Courts can challenge the facts as stated, or the exclusion of certain facts from the assessment. These are matters that can be found in courts in other jurisdictions, eg the US. Crucially, however, EU Courts insist on claiming the ultimate authority to state the finality of a legal provision, and to base their rulings largely on a finalistic, or teleological interpretation of the law, a less common feature. However, *Crédit Lyonnais* is a cautionary tale that this scrutiny can be taken one step too far, and that the boundaries between legal (finalistic) interpretation and risk assessment are not that clear-cut. The leverage ratio is a simpler, non-risk-weighted ratio, which computes *total* exposures in the denominator, something that paints an unflattering picture of banks with large, but low-risk balance sheets. Whether an exposure is risk-free should thus be irrelevant. *Only* where banks acted as a mere go-between for public investments by individual savers, the supervisor *could* (may) exclude exposures arising 'from deposits that the institution is legally obliged to transfer to the public

---

[258] See Case C-389/21 P *ECB v Crédit Lyonnais* ECLI:EU:C:2022:844 (AG Emiliou Opinion of 27 October 2022), and ECLI:EU:C:2023:368 (Court of Justice decision of 4 May 2023).
[259] ibid paras 56–57.
[260] ibid paras 67–70.
[261] ibid paras 71–73.
[262] ibid paras 91–97 (absence of 'manifest implausibility' in the ECB's assessment of risk of massive withdrawals) and 98–107 (arguments on 'structurally balanced' nature of CDC, 'deferred adjustment period' and distressed sales beyond the time horizon of the liquidity ratio).

sector entity ... for the purpose of funding general interest investments'. This was probably perceived by some banks or Member States as a concession to national idiosyncrasies. Yet, the provision did not grandfather national provisions, but granted discretion to the ECB, which rejected the exclusion because it perceived that French banks faced some intermediation risk and that excluding CDCs would not paint an accurate picture. By asking the supervisor to justify why it had not excluded the exposures, the General Court arguably 'flipped' the burden of proof. Furthermore, it focused on the exposures' risk, which, it seems, fits more the logic of the capital ratio than the leverage ratio, and challenged the ECB's extrapolation from past crises as too pessimistic, which not only substitutes the Court's judgment for the supervisor's, but also overlooks the fact that a forward-looking perspective normally requires thinking about risks that have not materialized, and are not reflected in historical data.[263] The provision was amended to make the exclusion of such exposures more automatic, not discretion-based,[264] but the ECB appealed the decision as a matter of principle, to delineate the respective roles of courts and supervisors. The Court of Justice partially corrected what was, perhaps, a decision based on the peculiar features of an individual case, and reiterated a more balanced approach to court review.

5.3 US courts' 'arbitrary and capricious' standard and procedural safeguards

Although US courts occasionally use the 'arbitrary and capricious' standard to impose a demanding requirement of cost-benefit analysis (CBA) on agencies, more frequently the standard is used in a procedural, and deferential way, exemplified in the review of supervisory decisions to ensure financial institutions' 'safety and soundness'. **6.66**

At an early stage, US courts had a more demanding approach. In *Gulf Federal*, the Fifth Circuit reviewed a decision where the FHLBB (the savings bank regulator) found that a federal savings association miscalculation of loans' interest due to the detriment of its borrowers was an 'unsafe and unsound' practice, and issued a cease-and-desist order to recalculate the interest and reimburse borrowers. The Fifth Circuit held that the FHLBB lacked cease-and-desist authority, and that 'unsafe or unsound practice' was a term used only for practices 'contrary to generally accepted standards of prudent operation' which 'created an abnormal risk' and 'threaten the financial integrity of the association'.[265] Later, in *First Bank of Bellaire v OCC*[266] the Fifth Circuit applied the *Gulf Federal* test to a decision by the OCC (the banks' regulator) of a breach of 'law, rule, or regulation' finding that the OCC's evidence was insufficient to sustain its capital order.[267] **6.67**

---

[263] Furthermore, the General Court relied on some reasoning that was not always clear. For example, it stated that 'unlike deposits ... which may be invested in any way ... including in high-risk or illiquid assets, capable of contributing to the creation of excessive leverage ... the present case concerns funds that the applicant is required to transfer to the CDC and which therefore cannot be invested in high-risk or illiquid assets' (*Crédit Lyonnais I* (n 240) para 113). Yet, a bank does not 'invest' existing deposits of money; it *creates* a money deposit when it identifies an investment opportunity (see Michael McLeay, Amar Radia, and Ryland Thomas, 'Money Creation in the Modern Economy' (2014) Q1 Bank of England Quarterly Bulletin 14). Also, risky or illiquid assets do not 'contribute to the creation of excessive leverage'; they are assets, not liabilities.

[264] The provision was formerly Article 429(14) of the CRR (n 202), now Article 429a(1)(j).
[265] *Gulf Federal Savings & Loan Association v Federal Home Loan Bank Board* 651F2d 259 (5th Cir 1981).
[266] *First National Bank of Bellaire v Comptroller of the Currency* 697 F2d 674, 685–87 (5th Cir 1983).
[267] ibid.

6.68 In parallel, however, the Supreme Court in the *De la Cuesta* case,[268] rejected that the FHLBB lacked authority to supervise thrifts' relationships with their borrowers, a key reason for the *Gulf Federal* decision to reject the breach of standards vis-à-vis borrowers as 'unsafe or unsound practice', and Congress passed the International Lending Supervision Act of 1983 (ILSA), which provisions restricted judicial review of capital orders, enhanced bank agencies' discretion, and authorized them to adopt binding capital minimums through notice-and-comment rulemaking.[269] Thus, subsequent cases, like *Sunshine Bank* relied on Congress' intent to defer to bank regulators' opinions within a 'zone of reasonableness'.[270] In *Bank of Coushatta*, the court held that Congress intended to insulate the "independent discretion" of bank regulators from judicial review:[271] there was neither a convincing statutory authorization for judicial review of the capital directives, nor a meaningful review standard.[272] Some cases, like *Hoffman*,[273] *Simpson*,[274] *Seidman*,[275] *Johnson*,[276] or *Llapa-Singhi*[277] formally adhered to *Gulf Federal* restrictive definition of 'unsafe and unsound' as having a 'reasonably direct effect on an association's financial soundness', but the general tendency was to defer to the agency's interpretation. In fact, *In the Matter of Patrick Adams*, the OCC concluded that, unless a judicial construction is based on the plain meaning of a statute, an ambiguous statutory term in a statute an agency is responsible for administering does not preclude the agency from reaching a contrary decision, ie the agency is not bound by a court,[278] a position that would be hard to conceive in the EU. In *Frontier State Bank of Oklahoma*[279] the Court told the long history of the 'safe and sound' standard, and how the reforms had committed it to agency's discretion.[280] The Court's review was limited to the 'arbitrary and capricious' review of the agency's justification of its decision (in the case, a cease-and-desist order that limited the bank's leverage strategy). After the FDIC's repeated interactions with the bank, a six-day hearing before an administrative law judge (ALJ), and the justifications offered by the FDIC, the court dismissed all the objections by the defendant bank.

---

[268] *Fidelity Federal Sav & L Association v De la Cuesta* [1982] 458 US 141.
[269] Each appropriate Federal banking agency shall have the authority to establish such minimum level of capital for a banking institution as the appropriate Federal banking agency, in its discretion, deems to be necessary or appropriate in light of the particular circumstances of the banking institution. 12 US Code s 3907(a)(2). Also, '[f]ailure of a banking institution to maintain capital … as established pursuant to subsection (a) of this section may be deemed by the appropriate Federal banking agency, in its discretion, to constitute an unsafe and unsound practice within the meaning of section 1818 of this title'. 12 US Code s 3907(b)(1).
[270] *Sunshine State Bank v FDIC* [1986] 783 F 2d 1580, 1583–84 (11th Cir).
[271] *FDIC v Bank of Coushatta* 930 F 2d 1122, 1126 (5th Cir 1991), citing the Report from the Senate Committee on Banking, Housing and Urban Affairs, S Rep No 98-122, 98th Cong, 1st Sess 16.
[272] *FDIC v Bank of Coushatta* (n 928) 1128–29.
[273] *Hoffman v FDIC* [1990] 912 F 2d 1172 (9th Cir).
[274] *Simpson v OTS* 29 F 3d 1418, 1425 (9th Cir 1994).
[275] *Seidman v OTS* 37 F 3d 911, 928 (3d Cir 1994).
[276] *Johnson v OTS* 81 F 3d 195 (DC Cir 1996).
[277] *Llapa-Singhi v Mukasey* 520 F 3d 897 (8th Cir 2008).
[278] '[T]he Supreme Court has recognized that a judicial construction of an ambiguous statutory term in a statute that an agency is responsible for administering does not preclude the agency from reaching a contrary statutory interpretation otherwise entitled to deference under the Chevron doctrine so long as the judicial ruling is not based on the plain meaning of the statute. Because "unsafe or unsound practice" has never been determined to have a plain meaning, the Comptroller is not bound by contrary caselaw.' *In The Matter of Patrick Adams*, OCC AA-EC-11-50, #2014-126 Terminates#N11-004 and #N12-001, citing *National Cable & Telecommunications Association v Brand X Internet Services* 545 US 967 (2005).
[279] *Frontier State Bank Oklahoma v FDIC* 702 F 3d 588 (10th Cir 2012).
[280] ibid: 'Each appropriate Federal banking agency shall have the authority to establish such minimum level of capital for a banking institution as the appropriate Federal banking agency, in its discretion, deems to be necessary or appropriate in light of the particular circumstances of the banking institution.'

5.4 EU Courts' process-based review and procedural safeguards

In addition to their distinctive 'substantive' (and finalistic) review, EU courts are also the ultimate guarantors of procedural safeguards. These encompass principles of good administration, such as rights of defence, or the duty to state reasons, examined in this section, as well as general principles like legal certainty or proportionality, examined in the next section, due to their closer connection with enforcement actions. **6.69**

Article 41 of the EU Charter enshrines principles of good administration, including the right to have the affairs handled fairly and impartially, and, more specifically, the rights to be heard, to access the file, or the administration's duty to give reasons. **6.70**

An habitual (if unsuccessful) cause of complaint are the narrow time windows to access the file, and file observations. Although the basic laws of addition and subtraction are universal, appellants and authorities clash about what are the relevant dates, especially in 'composite' proceedings with a 'national leg' and a 'European leg', as EU authorities tend to grant access upon the closing of the national leg, and often refuse access to the draft decision by national authorities. In *Berlusconi II* the appellant alleged that Bank of Italy had granted it access to the file on the expiry date for the filing of evidence, ie 14 September, but in reality the ECB notified its draft decision on October 6, and the appellant could submit its observations by 11 October, ie the appellant had three weeks to look at the evidence, and three days to file observations, and was unable to justify why earlier access was warranted.[281] In *AAB* the Court also focused on the possibility to be heard between the draft and definitive decisions *by the ECB*, and not national authorities.[282] Courts also tend to be deferential to authorities on the right to be heard. In *Berlusconi II*[283] and *AAB*[284] the General Court held that this does not entail the right to a hearing. **6.71**

Another cause for contention is the right of access to the file in cases of confidential information. As in the case of the right 'external' access to documents courts tend to be relatively deferential to authorities' classification of documents as 'confidential', and focus on whether the rights of defence have been impaired. In *Berlusconi II* the General Court concluded that, in light of the clear and exhaustive statement of pleas by the ECB, the rights of defence had not been impaired, and access to internal communications between the ECB and Bank of Italy was not warranted.[285] The same happened in *AAB*, where internal communications between ECB and Austrian authorities did not prevent the appellant from defending itself, also because it had been the addressee of numerous decisions by Austrian authorities and courts on the money laundering charges that were used as a basis to withdraw its licence.[286] **6.72**

Occasionally, appellants may allege other principles, such as 'lack of an independent/impartial assessment by EU authorities, when these rely on findings by national authorities. In *AAB* the General Court dismissed these allegations, merely pointing to the overabundance of evidence of breaches relied upon, and the thoroughness of the ECB's decision.[287] In *Ukrselhosprom* the General Court dismissed out of hand the appellant's allegation that **6.73**

---

[281] *Berlusconi II* (n 57) paras 185–88.
[282] *AAB* (n 64) paras 229–43.
[283] *Berlusconi II* (n 57) 208–209.
[284] *AAB* (n 64) paras 274–79.
[285] *Berlusconi II* (n 57) paras 194–202.
[286] *AAB* (n 64) paras 244–48.
[287] ibid paras 251–73.

the ECB had been led by 'misleading' information by the national authority as a 'bald assertion'.[288] It also dismissed its more specific objection that the ECB had failed to consider the appellant's change in management, because it had done so, and found it insufficient, in light of the shareholders' seemingly enduring influence.[289]

6.74 An important safeguard is the duty to state reasons, ie to motivate the decision, based on Article 296 TFEU. It is a key principle,[290] which, thanks to its flexibility allows courts to undertake a formal review on the surface, but to delve into the arguments used by the authority into certain detail.[291] Its key elements are: (i) it must be appropriate to the measure; (ii) must disclose the reasoning in a 'clear and unequivocal' fashion *in order to enable* (iii) the persons concerned with enough information to know if the decision is vitiated by error, and challenge it; and (iv) the competent courts to review.[292] However, it is distinct from the question of whether the reasons given are correct, ie the substantive legality of the measure.[293] Also, it largely depends on the circumstances of the case, the content of the measure, the nature of the reasons, the interest of the measure's addressees in obtaining explanations, and its context, more than its wording, ie it is not necessary to specify all relevant matters of fact and law.[294] Since context matters, so does courts' treatment. Some decisions show a cursory verification that all the relevant elements were there, like *AAB*,[295] or *Ukrselhosprom*.[296] In *Landeskreditbank* the statement by the ECB itself was limited, but the General Court used the ABoR decision as the ECB's statement of reasons.[297] Another relevant precedent is the *Crédit Agricole* case,[298] but since it was a case of sanctions it will be dealt with in s 6, which will also cover principles like legal certainty and proportionality.

6 Enforcement measures, sanctions, and penalties: safeguards and standard of review

6.75 Enforcement actions present special challenges. Their harshness requires special safeguards. Although enforcement in the law of finance could give rise to a separate treatise,[299] we will briefly concentrate on the more salient issues, which concern: (1) the classification of measures as 'criminal' or 'punitive'; (2) procedural criminal safeguards such as the privilege

---

[288] *Ukrselhosprom* (n 59) paras 214–24.
[289] ibid paras 228–36.
[290] Case T-122/15 *Landeskreditbank* (n 35) para 121.
[291] This is not only a feature of cases on regulation and supervision. It was an important factor in *Gauweiler* and *Weiss* in monetary policy. See ch 5, s 2.
[292] Case T-122/15 *Landeskreditbank* (n 35) para 123.
[293] ibid para 122.
[294] ibid para 124.
[295] *AAB* (n 64) para 110.
[296] *Ukrselhosprom* (n 59) para 384.
[297] Case T-122/15 *Landeskreditbank* (n 35) paras 123–30.
[298] Case T-576/18 *Crédit Agricole v ECB* EU:T:2020:304.
[299] Compare, for the Banking Union, Giulia Lasagni, *Banking Supervision and Criminal Investigation. Comparing the EU and US Experiences* (Springer and Giappichelli 2021); Raffaele D'Ambrosio, 'The Legal Review of the SSM Administrative Sanctions' in Chiara Zilioli and Karl-Philipp Wojcik (eds), *Judicial Review in the European Banking Union* (Edward Elgar Publishing 2021) 316–32; Leo Flynn, 'The Judicial Review of Fines and Penalty Payments Set by the SRB' and Jeanne Poscia, 'The VTB Case: Administrative Penalties and Administrative Measures' both in Chiara Zilioli and Karl-Philipp Wojcik (eds), *Judicial Review in the European Banking Union* (Edward Elgar Publishing 2021) 429–443, 571–78. See also Silvia Alegrezza (ed), *The Enforcement Dimension of the of the Single Supervisory Mechanism (SSM): The Interplay Between Administrative and Criminal Law* (Wolter Kluwer Cedam 2020) 1–665.

against self-incrimination; (3) the review of enforcement and penalties under principles such as legality, 'seriousness'; or (4) proportionality (analysed separately); and (5) specific criminal safeguards, such the presumption of innocence and the *ne bis in idem* principle.[300]

6.76 Punitive, or enforcement measures require special powers and are subject to special safeguards. Thus, classifying them is important. In the US, this issue has been analysed in cases brought by the Securities and Exchange Commission (SEC) for violations of federal securities laws before federal district courts. Initially, the SEC could only seek injunctions barring future violations. Later, Congress authorized the SEC to seek monetary penalties,[301] with a specific five-year limitation for actions 'for the enforcement of any civil fine, penalty, or forfeiture'.[302] In *Gabelli* the US Supreme Court held the provision applicable to monetary penalties.[303]

6.77 Yet, in addition to monetary penalties, in the 1970s the SEC began seeking disgorgement of gains eg in insider trading cases,[304] and continued after the SEC enforcement remedies were expanded. In *Kokesh* the Supreme Court considered whether the five-year limitation was applicable to disgorgement.[305] In the Court's view, the key elements were: (1) 'whether the wrong sought to be redressed is a wrong to the public, or a wrong to the individual' (penal laws apply to offences against the state) and (2) whether they are sought 'for the purpose of punishment, and to deter others from offending in like manner' as opposed to compensation to a victim.[306] The Court found that disgorgement was a 'penalty' subject to the five-year period because it was 'imposed by the courts as a consequence for violating 'public laws', ie wrongs against the United States,[307] *and* 'for punitive purposes', ie deterrence was key, not incidental,[308] and often there was no compensation.[309] The Court also rejected that disgorgement was 'restorative', since it had often exceeded the wrongdoer's profits, comprising third parties' profits (eg tippees in insider trading[310]). The Court left open whether the SEC could seek disgorgement *at all*.

---

[300] For a detailed analysis of the background on these issues see Marco Lamandini, David Ramos, and Javier Solana, 'The European Central Bank (ECB) as a Catalyst for Change in EU Law. Part 2: SSM, SRM and Fundamental Rights' (2016) 23(2) Columbia Journal of Eur L 199.

[301] This was adopted in 1990, as part of the Securities Enforcement Remedies and Penny Stock Reform Act, 104 Stat 932, codified at 15 USC s 77t-(d).

[302] 28 USC s 2462.

[303] *Gabelli v SEC* 568 US 442, 454 (2013). The Court also held that the five-year period began when the fraud occurred, not when it was discovered, rejecting the Circuit Court interpretation (which, in turn, had accepted the SEC's view).

[304] *SEC v Texas Gulf Sulphur Co* 312 F Supp 77, 91 (SDNY 1970, 1971), aff'd in part and rev'd in part, 446 F 2d 1301 (CA2).

[305] A jury found that Kokesh's actions violated several federal statutes. To understand why the SEC sought disgorgement, the court ordered Kokesh to pay a civil penalty of US$2,354,593, while the request for disgorgement was for US$34.9 million, US$29.9 million of which resulted from violations outside the limitations period'. See *Kokesh v SEC* 581 US 137, S Ct 1635 (2017).

[306] ibid, citing *Huntington v Attrill* 146 US 657, 667 (1892); and *Meeker v Lehigh Valley R Co* 236 US 412, 421–22 (1915).

[307] *Kokesh* (n 305): '[w]hen the SEC seeks disgorgement, it acts in the public interest, to remedy harm to the public at large, rather than standing in the shoes of particular injured parties'.

[308] In *Texas Gulf* (n 304) 92, the Court emphasized the need 'to deprive the defendants of their profits in order to ... protect the investing public by providing an effective deterrent to future violations', and later '[t]he primary purpose of disgorgement orders is to deter violations of the securities laws by depriving violators of their ill-gotten gains'. *Kokesh* (n 305), citing *SEC v Fischbach Corp* 133 F 3d 170, 175 (1997) (CA2).

[309] *Kokesh* (n 305), citing *SEC v Fischbach Corp* (n 308): 'As courts and the Government have employed the remedy, disgorged profits are paid to the district court, and it is "within the court's discretion to determine how and to whom the money will be distributed."

[310] *Kokesh* (n 305), citing *SEC v Warde* 151 F 3d 42, 49 (1998) (CA2) ('A tippee's gains are attributable to the tipper, regardless whether benefit accrues to the tipper'); *SEC v Clark* 915 F 2d 439, 454 (1990) (CA9).

6.78 Then, *Liu v SEC*[311] revised the legality of the power to seek disgorgement. The two defendants, Liu and Wang, falsely led investors to believe that their investments qualified for a US programme offering permanent residence status to immigrants who substantially invested in a US enterprise. Courts found them guilty of fraud and in breach of several federal securities provisions, and ordered disgorgement. Liu and Wang argued before the Supreme Court that, in accordance with *Kokesh*, disgorgement was an unlawful 'penalty'. The Court in *Liu* upheld disgorgement as an 'equitable remedy', but subject to restrictions, based on two principles: first, 'equity' practice authorized courts to strip wrongdoers of their ill-gotten gains (the remedy's labels varied, but its substance was the same); secondly, to be an equitable remedy, and not a punitive sanction, the SEC should seek disgorgement not 'in excess of a defendant's net profits' from wrongdoing, and 'for the benefit of investors', ie it could not deposit the funds with Treasury.[312] The Court rejected the SEC's view that the remedy's primary purpose was to deprive the wrongdoers of gains,[313] and left for courts on remand to examine whether it was possible to give effect to the distribution due to eg practical unfeasibility. Finally, the Court declared unlawful the SEC's practice of seeking to impose disgorgement on a wrongdoer 'for benefits that accrue to his affiliates, sometimes through joint-and-several liability' as contrary to the common-law rule of individual liability for wrongful profits'.[314]

6.79 In the EU, classifying a measure as 'criminal' triggers certain safeguards eg the right to silence, or *ne bis in idem*, and enhances others, eg proportionality. Both the ECtHR and the CJEU interpret the term 'criminal' autonomously under the *Engel* test, which takes into account (i) the legal classification of the offence under national law, (ii) the nature of the offence, and (iii) the degree of severity of the penalty.[315] The 'characterization' of the penalty has gradually lost relevance, and both the ECtHR[316] and the CJEU[317] have considered administrative fines as 'criminal' despite statutory language to the contrary.[318] Therefore, the similar language in the SSM and SRM rules[319] is no obstacle to apply criminal safeguards.

6.80 In practice, courts analyse the nature of the offence carefully and use the penalty's severity as a tie-breaker. In *Grande Stevens*, a market abuse case, the ECtHR paid particular attention to (i) the fact that the interests protected were all general interests of society, usually protected by criminal law; (ii) the fact that the penalties were intended to punish and deter, not to compensate (two aspects common with *Kokesh* or *Liu*); and (iii) the severity of the penalties that

---

[311] *Liu v Securities and Exchange Commission* 591 US ___ (2020).
[312] ibid. The equitable nature of the profits remedy generally requires the SEC to return a defendant's gains to wronged investors for their benefit.
[313] In *Liu v SEC* (n 311) the phrase 'appropriate or necessary for the benefit of investors' must mean something more than depriving a wrongdoer of his net profits alone, else the Court would violate the 'cardinal principle of interpretation that courts must give effect, if possible, to every clause and word of a statute'.
[314] *Liu v SEC* (n 313).
[315] *Engel & Others v Netherlands*, App no 5100/71 (8 June 1976) 82; Case C-617/10 *Åklagaren v Hans Åkerberg* EU:C:2013:105, para 35; Case C-489/10 *Łukasz Marcin Bonda v Commission* EU:C:2012:319, para 37.
[316] *Didier v France*, App no 58188/00 (27 August 2002) (financial markets); *Dubus SA v France*, App no 5242/04 (11 June 2009) (banking rules); *Lilly France SA v France*, App no 53892/00 (3 December 2002) (competition rules).
[317] Joined Cases C-204/00 P *Aalborg Portland A/S*; C-205/00 P *Irish Cement Ltd*; Case C-17/10 *Toshiba & Others v Commission* EU:C:2012:72.
[318] Article 23(5) of the Council Regulation 1/2003/EC on the implementation of the Rules on Competition laid down in Articles 81 and 82 of the Treaty [2003] OJ L1.
[319] SSM Regulation (n 79) art 18; art 110 of the Regulation (EU) No 806/2014 of the European Parliament and of the Council establishing uniform rules and a uniform procedure for the resolution of credit institutions and certain investment firms in the framework of a Single Resolution Mechanism and a Single Resolution Fund and amending Regulation (EU) No 1093/2010 [2014] OJ L225 (SRM Regulation) (referring to 'administrative' penalties).

could be imposed, not those actually imposed.³²⁰ Thus, procedures with a punitive dimension, such as market abuse, are clearly 'criminal'. A similar finding is present in cases by the Court of Justice, such as *Spector Photo Group*,³²¹ or *DB v CONSOB*, where the Court held that 'some of the administrative sanctions imposed by Consob appear to pursue a punitive purpose and to present a high degree of severity such that they are liable to be regarded as being criminal in nature'.³²²

6.81 There are more doubts about *banking supervision* measures. The above rationale could classify as 'criminal' all administrative penalties, since they protect general interests and must be 'dissuasive',³²³ but also measures that are not even 'penalties', eg withdrawing a bank's licence, or rejecting the suitability of a director or shareholder.³²⁴

6.82 Courts do not necessarily classify such measures as 'criminal'. In *Capital Bank v Bulgaria*,³²⁵ an ECtHR case, the withdrawal of a bank's licence was examined under the 'civil' procedural safeguards. Yet, since public authorities treated it as an 'administrative' measure, not subject to court review, the ECtHR did not need to challenge this classification to find that there had been a breach of Article 6 ECHR. In some cases, however, the distinction was relevant. In *Pilatus Bank* the General Court held that the decision to withdraw a bank's licence as a result of a criminal indictment of its shareholder in the US, was not 'criminal' in nature, and could not benefit of the presumption of innocence, because the withdrawal decision was taken once the indictment had led to a massive withdrawal of deposits, and the request of early termination of the practical totality of the bank's loans.³²⁶

6.83 Furthermore, in other cases the appellants did not even seek to classify the measures as 'penalties', and this did not prevent them from relying on safeguards common to 'criminal' and non-criminal cases. In *Berlusconi II*, where the ECB refused to authorize the acquisition of a qualified holding in a significant bank, due to the appellant's previous criminal conviction, the appellant alleged principles like non-retroactivity, legal certainty, proportionality and rights of defence, based on CRD and SSM provisions, and Article 41 (good administration) of the EU Charter.³²⁷ In *Anglo Austrian AAB* or *Ukrselhosprom* the appellant banks challenged the withdrawal of their banking licences, alleging breaches of legal certainty, proportionality, effective judicial protection and good administration.³²⁸

6.84 Finally, there may be other relevant distinctions beyond 'criminal-non-criminal'. In *VTB*³²⁹ the Austrian VTB Bank challenged the annulment of a supervisory decision to levy 'absorption' interests for exceeding the large exposure limit (Article 395 CRR) before national courts, which made a preliminary reference to the Court of Justice to ask about the compatibility with EU law of the automatic application of such measure under national law. The Court concluded, contrary to the national supervisor, that such measure was not a

---

[320] *Grande Stevens v Italy*, App no 18640/10, 18647/10, 18663/10, 18668/10 and 18698/10 (4 March 2014) 96–98.
[321] Case C-45/08 *Spector Photo Group* ECLI:EU:C:2009:806.
[322] Case C-481/19 *DB v CONSOB* ECLI:EU:C:2021:84.
[323] Lamandini, Ramos, and Solana (n 300).
[324] SSM Regulation (n 319) art 14(5); SSM Framework Regulation (n 166) arts 80–84; SRM Regulation (n 319) art 34(2)(a). In *Grande Stevens* (n 320), one of the penalties considered 'criminal' was the withdrawal of licenses. However, the Court assessed the severity by considering all the consequences *as a whole* including monetary fines.
[325] *Capital Bank AD v Bulgaria*, App no 49429/99 (24 November 2005) 105.
[326] *Pilatus* (n 233).
[327] *Berlusconi II* (n 57).
[328] *AAB* (n 64).
[329] Case C-52/17 *VTB Bank (Austria) v Finanzmarktaufsichtsbehörde* ECLI:EU:C:2018:648.

non-punitive 'economic control' measure to recover the advantage obtained by breaching the limit of Article 395 CRR, but an *administrative* measure within the meaning of Article 65 CRD IV. Thus, it had to comply with the requirements of Article 67(1)(k) and Article 67(2) CRD IV. These provided conditions for exposures exceeding such limits, which the Court considered incompatible with an automatic application of 'absorption interests'. The case showed that there are legal challenges beyond a classification between 'criminal' and not, for example, between administrative penalties, other administrative measures, and national powers independent from the banking supervision framework, which are useful to draw a line with the sanctions 'à coloration penale' under the ECHR case law.

6.85 Among properly 'criminal' procedural safeguards the 'right to silence', or privilege against self-incrimination (here referred indistinctly as a 'right' or 'privilege') is conceptually the more cumbersome.[330] The Court of Justice was initially very restrictive, not acknowledging its status as a fundamental right (more a safeguard of good administration) in cases that normally involved businesses[331] and the ECtHR recognized it as part of fair trial rights, with some equivocation[332] but *not for legal persons*.[333] The Court of Justice later maintained its restrictive construction,[334] raising doubts about its scope and intensity.

6.86 In *DB v CONSOB*, the Court of Justice clarified that the privilege applied in market abuse cases,[335] *and* is a fundamental right. The Italian Securities Commission (CONSOB) fined DB for insider dealing and for *failure to cooperate* due to his refusal to answer questions during a hearing. DB appealed, reaching the Supreme Court (Cassazione), which referred a question about the constitutionality of the Italian law to the Italian Constitutional Court, which made a preliminary reference to the Court of Justice, on the compatibility of Italian law (based on Directive No. 2003/6 (later and Regulation No. 596/2014)) criminal sanctions for refusing to answer potentially self-incriminating questions during investigations, and the status of the 'right to silence' as a fundamental right under Articles 47 and 48 of the Charter (fair trial rights). Drawing on its case law and on that of the ECtHR, the Court held (i) that the right to silence is not confined to statements of admission of wrongdoing or directly incriminating remarks, but also 'covers information on questions of fact which may subsequently be used in support of the prosecution' and may have a bearing 'on the conviction or the penalty'; but (ii) it cannot justify every failure to cooperate, such as a refusal to appear at a hearing or delaying tactics to postpone it;[336] and (iii) market abuse proceedings prima facie fit the description of 'criminal' proceedings where the right applies, but that it may even apply in investigation proceedings if, pursuant to national law, the evidence obtained in those proceedings may be

---

[330] Lamandini, Ramos, and Solana (n 300).

[331] See Case C-374/87 *Orkem v Commission* EU:C:1989:387.

[332] In *Saunders v United Kingdom*, App no 19187/91 (17 December 1996) the ECtHR held that the right sought to ensure that the prosecution obtained their evidence without coercion, but did not extend to, for example, the obtention through compulsory powers of documents with existence independent of the suspect's will. *Saunders* (n 332) paras 68–69. Yet, it is accepted that the privilege can invalidate documents obtained through compulsion. See eg *Funke*; *JB v Switzerland*, App no 31827/96 (3 May 2001).

[333] This raises complex issues about the privilege's *nature*. See Ronald J Allen and M Kristin Mace, 'The Self-Incrimination Clause Explained and Its Future Predicted' (2004) 94(2) J Crim L & Criminology 243; Ronald J Allen, 'Theorizing about Self-Incrimination' (2008) 30 Cardozo L Rev 247.

[334] See Joined Cases C-293/13 P and C-294/13 P *Fresh del Monte Produce Inc v Commission* EU:C:2015:416; Joined Cases C-125/07 P, C-133/07 P & C-137/07 P *Erste Group Bank & Others v Commission* EU:C:2009:576; Case C-407/04 *Dalmine SpA v Commission* EU:C:2007:53.

[335] Case C-481/19 *DB v CONSOB* (n 322).

[336] ibid paras 40–41.

used in criminal proceedings against that person in order to establish that a criminal offence was committed'.[337]

In light of this, even though a business (undertaking) has a duty to cooperate in investigations: 'that undertaking cannot be compelled to provide answers which might involve an admission on its part of the existence of such an infringement'.[338] Yet, case law based on businesses 'cannot apply by analogy when determining the scope of the right to silence of natural persons' (like DB).[339]

6.87

Therefore, while businesses benefit from what seems a procedural safeguard, arising from principles of good administration,[340] comprising the possibility of 'not providing answers which might involve an admission' of the infringement, natural persons benefit from the right to silence, or privilege against self-incrimination, as a full-blown fundamental right. The Italian Constitutional Court adhered to this *dictum*[341] and declared the national law unconstitutional vis-à-vis the right to silence of natural persons.

6.88

A third, key aspect concerns the courts' standard of review of penalties or enforcement measures. The issue of the standard of review ('legality review' versus 'full review') is relevant in cases where the ECtHR examines the compliance of states with Convention rights.[342] In *Grande Stevens* the Court held that the review by the Turin Court of Appeal of insider dealing penalties imposed by the Italian Securities Commission 'CONSOB' fell short of standards:[343] the court was impartial, independent, and had full jurisdiction, it reviewed the reasons for the decision and reduced some penalties for being disproportionate, but it was unclear whether the hearings were 'public', or whether there was an effective equality of arms between the parties, and the public hearings before the Supreme Court could not make up for this, as it was not a court with 'full jurisdiction'.[344] In the Banking Union the discussion about standard of review of penalties in the early stages of the Banking Union[345] due to Article 261 TFEU's implication that courts had full review, but so far, this relevance has been echoed by case law. Courts tend to do a legality review with varying degrees of intensity, focusing more on the legal principles of such review. In 'penalty' cases EU Courts may have 'full review' powers, in accordance with Article 261 TFEU, but in *VQ v ECB* the General Court held that, even if this were so, that would be strictly limited to the amount of the penalty,[346] and the Court otherwise made a legality review. Furthermore, as discussed above, even though 'penalties' have their own specific provision in the SSM (Article 18(1) SSM Regulation) separate from other measures (eg withdrawal of licence, 'fit-and-proper'), in practice the parties have relied on similar principles, such as legality or proportionality.

6.89

Principles such as *legality* or *legal certainty* have been used by appellants to allege that supervisory or enforcement measures were not based on the breach of applicable legal provisions,

6.90

---

[337] ibid para 44.
[338] ibid para 47, citing *Orkem* (n 331).
[339] *DB v CONSOB* (n 322), para 48.
[340] EU Charter of Fundamental Rights, art 41.
[341] Italian Constitutional Court, Judgment No 84/21 (30 April 2021) (Professor Viganò being the rapporteur).
[342] *Menarini Diagnostics v Italy*, App no 43509/08 (27 September 2011) 63–67. The ECtHR emphasized that *Consiglio* had gone beyond an 'external' review of the consistency of the decision on penalties, and examined the elements resulting in the final determination.
[343] *Grande Stevens* (n 320).
[344] ibid paras 153–55. Public hearings before the *Corte di Cassazione* were not enough, as the court did not have full jurisdiction.
[345] Lamandini, Ramos, and Solana (n 300).
[346] *VQ v ECB* ECLI:EU:T:2020:313, para 94.

or that those criteria were too convoluted. EU Courts tend to sternly dismiss allegations by supposedly sophisticated financial institutions about their inability to comply with legal requirements, as complex as these may be. In *Urkselhosprom* the General Court made short shrift of the bank's allegations that it was given insufficient instructions on what changes to make to comply with governance provisions after several money laundering violations were noticed.[347] In *VQ v ECB*[348] the bank challenged an ECB penalty for repurchasing its own shares without prior ECB authorisation. It alleged that that, although the required prior approval under Article 77 CRR was in force as of 1 January 2014 and directly applicable, Article 78 CRR, which developed the 'supervisory permission', required, as one of the conditions, the authority's satisfaction with the capital requirements (Article 92 CRR), and with the capital conservation buffer (Article 129 of CRD IV), and this one was not in force yet. Yet, the General Court held that the language of Article 77 was clear and unequivocal, and Article 92 requirements were already in force.[349] In *Crédit Agricole*[350] the bank was imposed a penalty for a continued breach of the provisions on classification of capital instruments. The Court rejected the appellant's allegation that it had relied on the EBA classification of the instrument, holding that, under the CRD system the credit institution must obtain an *ex ante* authorization from the supervisor before treating an instrument as Core Equity Tier 1 (CET 1), rather than waiting for the authority to do an ex post check.[351] In *Berlusconi II*, although Italy had not fully transposed the CRD's provisions on 'fit-and-proper' on which the ECB relied upon, and the appellant disputed the application of some guidelines issued by Bank of Italy, in the Court's view the transitional provisions made reference to other domestic legislation that provided a sufficient basis for the assessment that a past conviction for tax fraud was sufficient to establish a lack of 'good repute'.[352]

6.91 Occasionally, the parties have attempted to argue that the rules were too complex, and/or the bank's interpretation was acceptable through the argument of 'negligence'. In *Crédit Agricole* the Court also dismissed the bank's allegation that it was not 'negligent', because it followed the EBA's listing of certain instruments as 'capital'. The Court held that a financial institution could deduce the scope of its obligations from an attentive reading of the provisions, also because one thing were the rules establishing the eligibility of a financial instrument as 'capital', and another the 'verification' rules,[353] and that the inclusion of the instruments among the EBA list was not definitive (nor binding on the ECB). However, in some cases the argument may succeed. In the *Nordic Banks* 'shadow ratings' case the Board of Appeal of the ESAs considered that the activity of several banks fit within the regulated activity, and not as 'investment advice', but held, in light of the fact that such an activity was the market practice long before the EU rating agency rules were adopted, that the breach of the rules was not negligent.[354]

6.92 A related argument, straddling between legality and proportionality, in proceedings with a national and a European 'leg', or where EU authorities apply national law, is to argue that the

---

[347] *Ukrselhosprom* (n 59) paras 273–87.
[348] *VQ* (n 346). See also Case T-203/18 *VQ v ECB* ECLI:EU:T:2018:261. Compare Laura Wissink, 'The VQ Case T-203/18: Administrative penalties by the ECB under judicial scrutiny' in Chiara Zilioli and Karl-Philipp Wojcik (eds), *Judicial Review in the European Banking Union* (Edward Elgar Publishing 2021) 542–50.
[349] *VQ* (n 346) paras 46–54.
[350] See *Crédit Agricole* (n 298).
[351] ibid paras 53–63.
[352] *Berlusconi II* (n 57) paras 118–26.
[353] *Crédit Agricole* (n 298) paras 80–84.
[354] *Svenska Handelsbanken AB and Others v ESMA* BoA D 2019 01-04 (27 February 2019).

breach of national provisions was neither 'serious' enough, nor established with enough certainty, to justify the enforcement measures. In *Anglo Austrian* the appellant (unsuccessfully) alleged that, under Austrian law, sanctions for serious violations of money laundering rules could be only imposed under administrative criminal or criminal law by judicial proceedings with the force of res judicata, not administrative sanctions. To the General Court, states transposing EU rules had to provide appropriate *administrative* sanctions. Thus, although states were free to also introduce criminal sanctions, the nature of the sanction (criminal-administrative) could not be decisive to qualify the violation as 'serious'.[355] Furthermore, what mattered for EU law was not whether there was a judicial decision with *res judicata* effects, but whether the decision establishing the violation was 'final', which happened to a decision by an administrative authority not challenged by the applicant.[356]

6.93 Perhaps the most common allegation is about *proportionality*, including supervisory measures, enforcement measures and penalties. In *Berlusconi II* the General Court dismissed the appellant's allegation that the ECB's refusal of the acquisition of a significant holding due to concerns about the acquiror's 'good repute was disproportionate, because it imposed a forced sale, holding that (i) the ECB decision contained no *order* to dispose of the shares (CRD provided for the suspension of voting rights); and that (ii) the ECB had no margin of discretion, because the applicant's past tax fraud convictions automatically meant that he could not fulfil the 'good repute' requirement.[357] In *AAB*, the General Court held that the withdrawal of the licence pursued objectives of general interest and was suitable to end violations. It also rejected the appellant's argument about the *necessity* of the measure, holding that the fact that the ECB adopted the decision seven months after the proposal by the national authority was justified in light of the documentation (the decision and the bank's letters contesting it) and that lesser measures (injunctions and fines) had been used, without corrective measures being adopted.[358] Alternative measures, such as AAB's self-liquidation, or the temporary cessation of its banking activities, were insufficient to remedy the breaches,[359] and if side-effects towards depositors or investors were to result in a measure's disproportionality, it would be impossible to withdraw the licence.[360] In *Ukrselhosprom* the General Court highlighted the structured and comprehensive proportionality analysis, where the ECB considered (and rejected) other alternatives, and held that, specifically in relation with one of the appellants, contrary to its allegations, the ECB had not based its decision on a mere breach of passporting rules (whereby the appellant set up a branch in Latvia without notification) but on other, and repeated breaches, notably related to anti-money laundering.[361]

6.94 Proportionality analysis is not too different in pure 'penalty' cases, despite the fact that courts may arguably have a 'full review'. In *VQ v ECB* General Court dismissed the applicant's allegation that the penalty was disproportionate: the legal provisions were clear and unequivocal, and the applicant continued with its behaviour in breach of the rules after being warned by the Joint Supervisory Team (JST).[362] Supervisory measures were not an alternative, since the

---

[355] *AAB* (n 64) paras 39–42.
[356] ibid paras 43–48.
[357] *Berlusconi II* (n 57) 171–79. These arguments also meant that there was no violation of the rights to property and freedom to conduct a business.
[358] *AAB* (n 64) paras 172–78, 184–89.
[359] ibid paras 189–92.
[360] ibid paras 194–97.
[361] *Ukrselhosprom* (n 59) paras 311, 314–18.
[362] *VQ* (n 346) paras 63–65. The Court also rejected the appellant's allegation that alternative supervisory measures could have been imposed, holding that the purpose of those measures was to ensure compliance with prudential requirements, not to punish the infractors. ibid 66.

purpose of those powers was to ensure compliance with prudential requirements, and not to punish.[363] The Court also dismissed the applicant's interim request to suspend the publication of the decision, or, alternatively, to anonymize it, since the Court held that the standard of a 'serious and irreparable harm',[364] because pecuniary damage was not irreparable save in exceptional circumstances, if, eg it imperilled the bank's viability.[365] It also rejected that the publication had caused 'disproportionate damage' to the bank: a literal, contextual and finalistic interpretation of the rules showed that publication was the norm, and anonymisation should apply in exceptional circumstances in light only of the harm caused by the publication, and not of other factors, such as the (lesser) gravity of the offence,[366] and any harm would not be 'irreversible', since the annulment decision could equally be published.

6.95 Indeed, even though the *theoretical* possibility of full review of penalties by courts may be key to ensure proper safeguards, courts may be wary to exercise it *in practice*. A clear example is the *Crédit Agricole* case. There the Court rejected the bank's allegations that the penalty lacked a legal basis, or that the breach had not been 'negligent' (the content of the provisions should have been clear enough) but it annulled in part the administrative penalty. Yet, instead of holding that the penalty was 'disproportionate', which could have been criticized for substituting its views for those of the ECB, it emphasized that the ECB had a 'wide discretion' to determine the amount of the penalty, and thus, in view of the wide discretion, and the substantial amount of the penalty, *the duty to state reasons was particularly important*.[367] In the case, the decision was not adopted following an opinion of ABoR, there was no prior practice with regard to imposition of penalties, and the ECB had not published its methodology to determine the amount of penalties.[368] Furthermore, the statement of reasons listed the different relevant considerations, but did neither allow the bank to understand the methodology, nor the Court to review it,[369] and, finally, although the penalty was imposed on a bank, the ECB referred to the size of the group as a factor.[370]

6.96 Finally, there is also a role for specific 'criminal' safeguards. The presumption of innocence was considered in the *Spector Photo Group* case, where the Court of Justice held that the presumption of the 'mental element' by insider dealing rules, which permitted to assume the intention of the breaching party was not contrary to the principle of the presumption of innocence, as long as it stayed within reasonable boundaries, ie 'that presumption is open to rebuttal and the rights of the defence are guaranteed'.[371] In *Pilatus Bank* the General Court rejected the existence of a breach of the right to the presumption of innocence in a case where the ECB withdrew a bank's licence partly as a consequence of the criminal indictment of one of its shareholders in the United States, and the resulting loss of confidence by depositors and investors: the Court held that the measure (withdrawal of licence) was not criminal in nature, and the ECB had based its assessment of the shareholder's 'good repute' on 'allegations', without accepting them as true, and thus the fact that it failed to examine the allegations was not a breach of the safeguards.[372] In *VQ v ECB* the General Court held, with regard

---

[363] *VQ* (n 346) para 66.
[364] *VQ v ECB Order* (n 348) paras 13–14.
[365] ibid paras 15–16.
[366] *VQ* (n 346) paras 79–91.
[367] *Crédit Agricole* (n 298) paras 133–34.
[368] ibid para 139.
[369] ibid 144–47.
[370] ibid 151–55.
[371] *Spector* (n 321) para 44. See also paras 39–42.
[372] *Pilatus* (n 233).

to the publication of penalties, that the text of the regulation was very clear in that penalties must be published as a general rule, and the interpretation of legal provisions in light of fundamental principles cannot result in an interpretation *contra legem*.[373]

6.97 An equally important criminal safeguard is the *ne bis in idem* principle.[374] EU courts have sometimes been flexible in competition cases[375] and required (i) identity of facts, (ii) unity of the offender, and (iii) unity of the legal interests protected, thus allowing the existence of parallel competition proceedings and sanctions at EU and national levels.[376] The General Court has merely held that the latter penalty must take the former into account as a matter of 'natural justice'.[377] On the other hand, the ECtHR has adopted a more protective approach and prohibited not only the trial of the 'same offences', but of different offences with the same material facts.[378]

6.98 Market abuse cases like *Menci*,[379] *Di Puma*,[380] and *Zecca*, as well as *Garlsson*[381] considered the compatibility of duplicate proceedings and penalties with the *ne bis in idem* principle. The Court of Justice found that there could be a duplication of criminal and administrative proceedings against the same person with respect to the same acts, although such limitation of the *ne bis in idem* was to be evaluated as a limitation of fundamental rights, subject to Article 52(1) of the Charter, and thus national legislation had to (i) pursue an objective of general interest; (ii) establish clear and precise rules identifying the circumstances subject to duplication; (iii) ensure that the proceedings are coordinated to limit disadvantages, and (iv) ensure that the severity of all of the penalties imposed is limited to what is strictly necessary vis-à-vis the seriousness of the offence, factors to be verified by national courts, which should also ensure that the provisions also comply with the ECHR. In *Garlsson* the Court held that the objective of guaranteeing the integrity of the financial markets of the EU and public confidence in financial instruments could justify a duplication of proceedings,[382] and there was coordination of proceedings, but the duplication seemed to go beyond what was strictly necessary (ie lack of proportionality[383]).

6.99 In joined cases *Di Puma* and *Zecca*, the Court found no infringement of EU law, in light of the *res judicata* principle, holding that, in presence of a (final) decision of acquittal, a subsequent proceeding for administrative fines of a criminal nature would be contrary to the *ne bis in idem* principle, and, although a duplication of proceedings might be possible in theory to protect the integrity of the financial markets of the EU and public confidence in financial instruments, but should strictly comply with proportionality, and, given the facts, would clearly exceed what was necessary for such purpose. Thus, in several of these judgments the principle of proportionality, in conjunction with considerations of a public interest nature,

---

[373] VQ (n 346) paras 88–90.
[374] Lamandini, Ramos, and Solana (n 300).
[375] When a first decision was annulled for procedural reasons, the courts have permitted the resumption of enforcement proceedings. See Case T-24/07 *ThyssenKrupp Stainless AG v Commission* EU:T:2009:236.
[376] The controversial argument is that the two types of proceedings view restrictions from different angles. See *Toshiba & Others* (n 317).
[377] See Case T-322/01 *Roquette Frères v Commission* EU:T:2006:267.
[378] See Case C-17/10 *Toshiba & Others v Commission*, Opinion of Advocate General Kokott ECLI:EU:C:2011:552, paras 121–23.
[379] Case C-524/15 *Luca Menci v Procura della Repubblica* ECLI:EU:C:2018:197.
[380] Joined Cases C-596/16 and C-597/16 *Enzo di Puma v Consob* ECLI:EU:C:2018:192.
[381] Case C-537/16 *Garlsson Real Estate v Consob* ECLI:EU:C:2018:193).
[382] ibid paras 44–47.
[383] ibid paras 53–59.

provided again the check against which deviations from the *ne bis in idem* principle could be justified.

6.100 In *Pierce v SEC*, US courts examined similar issues under other doctrines.[384] Pierce sold shares of stock in a corporation (Lexington, Inc.) through offshore bank accounts located in Liechtenstein, failing to comply with SEC registration requirements. He transferred the stock through a personal account, and two corporate accounts of entities where he was the beneficial owner, and lied during the SEC's investigation about his interest in the corporate accounts and the transactions through them. The SEC initiated a (first) enforcement action seeking disgorgement of unlawful profits only from the personal account, and tried to expand the action after receiving documents from Liechtenstein evidencing transactions through the corporate accounts, but the administrative law judge (ALJ) declined, and a second action was initiated. Pierce did not object to the facts, but alleged res judicata, judicial estoppel, equitable estoppel, and waiver. The DC District Court held that the second enforcement action could proceed:[385] Pierce lied during the first proceeding, which made specious his assertions that the charges arising from the sales out of the corporate accounts had been 'actually asserted' in the first action. The SEC was under no obligation to amend its initial action, or seek review of the ALJ's finding on the inadmissibility of further evidence.[386] The Court rejected Pierce's other arguments (estoppel, judicial estoppel, or waiver) on similar grounds.

---

[384] *Pierce v SEC* [2015] Docket No 14-1079 (DC Cir).

[385] It is not entirely clear that the Commission's disposition rests on principles of res judicata that are 'entirely consistent with the application of res judicata in the federal courts,' but this is a matter of no consequence in this case. It is well understood in administrative law that a reviewing court will uphold an agency action resting on several independent grounds if any of those grounds validly supports the result. '[I]n other words, the point is that if the result in a case is obvious, based on the record before the court and the rationale offered by the agency, 'the best course is for the reviewing court to simply apply the obvious result.' We do not quibble with an agency because we do not agree with every ground upon which it has justified its decision. *Pierce v SEC* (n 384) para 12.

[386] *Pierce v SEC* (n 384) para 15. In sum, Pierce's assertion that the charges arising from the unlawful sales of Lexington stock out of the corporate accounts were 'actually asserted' in the first proceeding is specious. The division did not obtain the pertinent information regarding Pierce's unlawful trading through the corporate accounts until after the record had been closed in the first enforcement action. The fact that reference was made to the corporate accounts proves nothing because it was too late for the division to include the charges in the OIP. Thus, there is no merit to Pierce's argument that the Commission could not rely on the fraudulent concealment exception to foreclose the application of res judicata in the second enforcement action.

7

Courts' Review of Crisis Management Decisions

1	Introduction: crisis management frameworks and the courts	7.01	3.5 Substantive review beyond 'property' (III): EU state aid cases' implications for shareholders and creditors	7.59
2	The legitimacy of crisis management frameworks	7.07	4 Procedural safeguards: 'Arbitrary and capricious', 'good administration' and judicial protection	7.63
	2.1 Delegation and accountability of enforcement powers and funding schemes	7.08	4.1 US safeguards under the 'arbitrary and capricious' standard	7.64
	2.2 Crisis management funding: deposit guarantees and resolution funds	7.14	4.2 EU process review and procedural safeguards	7.73
3	Substantive review: 'property' and other rights	7.23	4.3 A brief mention to investment treaties arbitration	7.83
	3.1 Substantive safeguards in bank crises	7.24	5 Cross-border recognition and cooperation	7.87
	3.2 Substantive safeguards in sovereign crises	7.39	5.1 The regional (EU) context	7.88
	3.3 Substantive review beyond 'property': conditions for intervention	7.44	5.2 The international context	7.93
	3.4 Substantive review beyond 'property' (II): cases involving depositors	7.50		

1 Introduction: crisis management frameworks and the courts

Crisis management often involves actions by monetary or fiscal authorities (examined under 'financial stability) and actions by authorities such as the US Federal Deposit Insurance Corporation (FDIC) or the European Single Resolution Board (SRB) or national resolution authorities as well as of the supervisory authorities, consisting in taking control of financial institutions, allocating losses among their creditors, and withdrawing their licence. **7.01**

A swift takeover of the troubled institution, and allocation of losses among creditors is an efficient way to avoid contagion and minimize taxpayer support,[1] but raises major issues of fairness and equity towards shareholders and, even more importantly, creditors, which have a public policy, and even constitutional significance, and jurisdictions differ as to the scope and extent of powers by specialist administrative authorities, and the interference with creditors' rights.[2] Standards for creditor treatment[3] are inspired by different considerations from resolution frameworks for systemically important banks, which does not render them inconsistent, but introduces a source of tension.[4] **7.02**

---

[1] FSB, 'Key Attributes of Effective Resolution Regimes' (October 2011) 1 https://www.fsb.org/wp-content/uploads/r_111104cc.pdf (accessed 21 September 2022).
[2] David Ramos and Javier Solana, 'Bank Resolution and Creditor Distribution: The Tension Shaping Global Banking (Part I): 'Individual Bank v GROUP' and "ex ante v ex post" Dimensions' (2020) 28 Miami J Bus L 1.
[3] Insolvency and Creditor Rights Standard (ICR) formed by the Bank's Principles and the UNCITRAL Guide http://siteresources.worldbank.org/INTGILD/Resources/ICRStandard_Jan2011_withC1617.pdf (accessed 21 September 2022).
[4] Ramos and Solana (n 2).

7.03 Such tension arises in relation with the tools to deal with bank failure. The US ample experience is based on the powers and practice of the FDIC,[5] which were topped-up by the Dodd-Frank Act's introduction of the Orderly Liquidation Authority (OLA)[6] to deal with companies whose failure could cause financial instability.[7] The EU made a massive overhaul of the system in 2014, with the Bank Recovery and Resolution Directive (BRRD)[8] and the Single Resolution Mechanism (SRM),[9] which provides for centralized decision-making on resolution schemes over significant institutions. This raises general problems related to the constitutional legitimacy of authorities that have such ample powers and tools, and also specific problems related to the specific deployment of those tools. Inspired by a logic of avoiding contagion and systemic risk, resolution authorities can take control of financial institutions *before* they are fully insolvent (ie when a bank is 'failing or likely to fail (FOLTF)'), and impose a write-down or conversion of capital and debt instruments (bail-in), while leaving out claims that would rank *pari passu* with ordinary claims, because this is important to preserve the bank's critical functions and/or keep the bank operational.[10] This raises legal challenges associated to the 'triggers', eg whether a bank was actually FOLTF, and with the treatment parallel to, and different from what creditors and shareholders would receive in insolvency or liquidation proceedings, which raises the problem of discrimination.[11]

7.04 A second pillar in crisis management is funding and liquidity, by means of deposit insurance systems (DIS), or deposit guarantee schemes (DGSs). In the EU, in addition to the DGS, there is 'resolution funding', with the resolution funding arrangement (RFAs) regulated in the BRRD and the Single Resolution Fund (SRF) as part of the Banking Union, which has special importance in the absence of a European DIS (EDIS). Leaving aside matters of design,[12] the key challenges are to determine coverage (ie what entities and/or deposits are covered) and contributions (ie how the contributions to the DIS or the SRF are determined, whether the system is clear and transparent, whether there is any discrimination, etc.).

7.05 A third factor is resolution planning, which seeks to avoid a potentially messy crisis by making, or asking banks to make 'living wills' that ensure their orderly resolution without any public financial assistance. At least for the largest globally systemic financial institutions (G-SIFIs) the tendency is to plan for a resolution strategy involving the bail-in of capital and debt, which requires them to issue easily bail-inable instruments, the so-called total loss-absorbency capacity (TLAC)[13] or minimum requirements for capital and eligible liabilities

---

[5] FDIC, *The First Fifty Years: A History of the FDIC* 1933-1983 (Federal Deposit Insurance Corporation 1984) 84 ff https://www.fdic.gov/resources/publications/first-fifty-years/index.html (accessed 15 August 2023).
[6] Dodd-Frank Act, Title II, ss 201–217, 12 USC ss 5381 ff.
[7] Dodd-Frank Act, s 203(b), 12 USC ss 5383(b).
[8] Directive 2014/59/EU, establishing a framework for the recovery and resolution of credit institutions and investment firms [2014] OJ L173.
[9] Regulation (EU) No 806/2014 establishing uniform rules and a uniform procedure for the resolution of credit institutions and certain investment firms in the framework of a Single Resolution Mechanism and a Single Resolution Fund [2014] OJ L225. See also European Commission, 'Banking Union' http://ec.europa.eu/finance/general-policy/banking-union/single-resolution-mechanism/index_en.htm (accessed 21 September 2022).
[10] Deposits, clients' assets, and short-term liabilities and others that ensure continuity of critical functions. See eg FSB (n 1) 3 (Preamble), nos 2.3, 3.2–3.4. (deposits and critical functions), and 4.1 and Appendix II, Annex 3 (clients assets).
[11] Ramos and Solana (n 2).
[12] For a further discussion see Marco Lamandini and David Ramos Muñoz, *EU Financial Law: An Introduction* (Wolters Kluwer 2016) 835.
[13] See eg FSB, 'Total Loss-Absorbency Capacity Standard' (6 November 2014) https://www.fsb.org/2015/11/total-loss-absorbing-capacity-tlac-principles-and-term-sheet/ (accessed 21 September 2022). On the relationship between TLAC standard and MREL add-on calibrations for EU G-SIIs, compare the Appeal Panel decision in Case 1/22, *A v SRB* (14 April 2023).

(MREL) in the EU.[14] Determining the level of instruments to be issued promises to be controversial, as the determination of capital requirements.

A fourth factor in crisis management is its cross-border dimension.[15] Cross-border cooperation, information exchange, and recognition of actions adopted by other authorities is critical for the smooth execution of crisis management in large, and less large financial institutions and groups. Yet, there is no single blueprint for that. The UNCITRAL framework opts for a rules-based model of unified universalism and mutual recognition, suitable for court-based systems,[16] while the FSB Key Attributes focus more on a series of good practices and cooperation, and the 'giving effect' to cross-border action,[17] adequate for systems based on administrative authorities. The legal challenges are quite abundant, and include the application of the rules to determine jurisdiction and applicable law (eg if more than one jurisdiction may declare itself competent) the application of rules on recognition and cooperation, and the 'fair' treatment of creditors and shareholders, especially if the ranking and hierarchy rules differ between jurisdictions.

2 The legitimacy of crisis management frameworks

Is it legitimate to habilitate an administrative authority with far-reaching powers to take over a not-fully-insolvent institution and impose losses upon its shareholders and creditors? Is it legitimate to fund such crisis management systems by levying a mandatory contribution on financial institutions? These questions are less easy than they may appear at first glance, and courts have had to deal with them before discussing more concrete issues.

2.1 Delegation and accountability of enforcement powers and funding schemes

In the US, the legitimacy of its federal bank crisis management system was tested a few years after it was established. In *Fahey v Malone*[18] the Federal Home Loan Bank Board (FHLBB) appointed a conservator for a savings and loan (S&L) association, for 'conducting its affairs in an unlawful, unauthorized, and unsafe manner' and having an 'unfit and unsafe' management'. The plaintiffs alleged an unconstitutional seizure of property without due process of law, in malice and ill-will. A specially formed three-judge district court declared the relevant section of the Act unconstitutional, removed the conservator, restored the institution to its former management, and enjoined the authorities 'from ever asserting any claims, right, title

---

[14] BRRD (n 8) art 45 ff (MREL).
[15] David Ramos and Javier Solana, 'Bank Resolution and Creditor Distribution: The Tension Shaping Global Banking (Part II): The Cross-border Dimension' (2020) 28 Miami J Bus L 245 ff; Rosa M Lastra (ed), *Cross-Border Bank Insolvency* (OUP 2011) 166; Jonathan M Edwards, 'A Model Law Framework for The Resolution of G-SIFIs' (2012) 7 CMLJ 131; Matthias Haentjens, 'Private Law in Banking Union Litigation' and Jens-Hinrich Binder, 'Resolving a Bank: Judicial Review with Regard to the Exercise of Resolution Powers' both in Chiara Zilioli and Karl-Philipp Wojcik (eds), *Judicial Review in the European Banking Union* (Edward Elgar Publishing 2021) 59–76, 367–94.
[16] UNCITRAL Model Law on Cross-Border Insolvency (MLCBI); Model Law on Recognition and Enforcement of Insolvency-Related Judgments (MLRIJ); and Model Law on Enterprise Group Insolvency (MLEGI), as well as the Legislative Guide on Insolvency. See https://uncitral.un.org/en/texts/insolvency.
[17] FSB (n 1).
[18] *Fahey v Malone* 332 US 245 (1947).

or interest' in or to the Association's property'.[19] On appeal, the Supreme Court examined whether this was an 'unconstitutional delegation of legislative powers' without adequate standards of action or guides to policy.[20] Unlike the district court's precedents, which referred to delegations of powers to turn certain acts into federal crimes, without previous state practice, this case involved regulatory, not 'penal provisions', dealt with S&L associations 'created, insured, and aided by the federal government', and their problems of 'insecurity and mismanagement which are as old as banking enterprise', and included remedies which were not 'unknown to existing law to be invented by the Board in exercise of a lawless range of power'.[21] The FHLBB's appointment of conservator was based on rules which were 'sufficiently explicit, against the background of custom, to be adequate for proper administration and for judicial review if there should be a proper occasion for it'.[22] The S&L's organizational charter expressly indicated its subjection to the relevant statute:[23] if shareholders benefited from a statute including certain limitations for public protection, they were estopped from alleging the unconstitutionality of those limitations.[24] Thus, after an initial hesitance, the courts' view softened, allowing the rise of the administrative state.

7.09 In the EU, the bank resolution framework (BRRD plus SRM) dates from 2014, so early challenges are recent. One was the case decided by the German Federal Constitutional Court (FCC) in 2019 on the constitutionality of *both* the SSM *and* the SRM framework (*SSM/SRM*).[25] The plaintiffs alleged that the SRM was ultra vires and contrary to the EU Treaties' principle of conferral of powers, and undermined democratic legitimacy. The FCC expressed concern about the use of the competence for the approximation of laws on the internal market (the internal market competence) to create agencies, also in light of the Court of Justice's recent openness to delegate powers to them.[26] This, it held, did not find clear support in the text of the Treaty (Article 114 TFEU), a systematic analysis (based on conferral and a multi-level system of administrative cooperation[27]), or a teleological analysis, which called (in its view) for a strict interpretation of enforcement powers.[28]

7.10 However, the FCC accepted the SRM and the agency (Single Resolution Board—SRB), *within narrow limits*.[29] In the FCC's view, the SRB satisfied this test, provided the transferred tasks and powers were interpreted strictly.[30] It harmonized bank crisis management, centralized

---

[19] ibid 248.
[20] Section 5(d) of the Federal Home Loan Act gave the Board 'full power to provide in the rules and regulations herein authorized for the reorganization, consolidation, merger, or liquidation of such associations, including the power to appoint a conservator or a receiver to take charge of the affairs of any such association, and to require an equitable readjustment of the capital structure of the same, and to release any such association from such control and permit its further operation'.
[21] *Fahey v Malone* (n 18) 250.
[22] ibid 254.
[23] ibid 255.
[24] 'It is an elementary rule of constitutional law that one may not 'retain the benefits of the Act while attacking the constitutionality of one of its important conditions.' *Fahey v Malone* (n 18).
[25] 2 BvR 1685/14, 2 BvR 2631/14 (30 July 2019) (*SSM/SRM*). Compare Raffaele D'Ambrosio and Donato Messineo (eds), *The German Federal Constitutional Court and the Banking Union*, Quaderni di Ricerca Giuridica della Consulenza Legale, Bank of Italy No 91 (March 2021) 7–117 (and an English translation of relevant excerpts of the judgment at 255).
[26] *SSM/SRM* (n 25) 236–39.
[27] ibid 242–45.
[28] ibid 245.
[29] ibid 246. The transfer of powers that are not clearly defined or cannot be sufficiently reviewed, of essential decisions on the strategic direction of a policy area and of other fundamental decisions as well as the delegation of legislative powers is ruled out.
[30] *SSM/SRM* (n 25) 247.

decision-making, linked with the SSM, and improved the internal market, by limiting spillovers into non-participating states.[31] SRB powers and tasks were sufficiently defined and accompanied by adequate safeguards,[32] and the SRB lacked exclusive decision-making competence (eg the Commission also intervened) and it had power only over significant institutions.[33] To the FCC this is acceptable if the SRB tasks and powers 'are not extended through interpretation'.[34]

Furthermore, to the FCC the independence of both the SRB and national resolution authorities (NRAs) results in a diminished level of democratic legitimacy.[35] However, this was balanced by political accountability mechanisms, including vis-à-vis national parliaments, which, in the FCC's (arguably mistaken) view meant that German political bodies could 'at least indirectly influence' the SRB's actions,[36] and sufficed to avoid an encroachment on the principles of democratic legitimacy and popular sovereignty.[37] Also important is the system of administrative review, by the Appeal Panel, and especially judicial review, by the CJEU.[38] Finally, the 'bank levy' (contributions to the Single Resolution Fund—SRF) was not ultra vires either, because, although to the FCC Article 114 does not authorize the EU to impose taxes or levies,[39]

7.11

> [t]he bank levy ... imposition is not based on the SRM Regulation, but on domestic law ... Likewise, it is not the SRM Regulation, but the relevant Intergovernmental Agreement that provides for the transfer of the revenue generated by the bank levy.[40]

This finding rests on flawed premises:[41] SRF contributions are grounded on EU law, not national law, and the assessment of what is lawful or not should not be based on a national (ie German) conception of 'tax or contribution'. Yet, it raises valid points. From an EU law perspective, the Treaties' 'internal market competence', which follows the ordinary legislative procedure, with qualified majority is apt for 'regulatory' schemes, while tax harmonization measures require 'special procedure', with unanimity.[42] Yet, creating contributions to fund European agencies under the internal market competence is lawful *if* the levying of compulsory contributions is treated as consideration for a service, and forms part of the logic and functioning of the specific harmonized (resolution) regime, *or if* the 'special procedure' provisions requiring unanimity do not apply if there is a regulatory scheme for the approximation of laws in the internal market, which includes an agency, *and* the levy is key for the scheme, eg because it bolsters the agency's independence.[43] From a national law perspective,

7.12

---

[31] ibid 249–51.
[32] ibid 253–58.
[33] ibid 259–61.
[34] ibid 265.
[35] ibid 279, 282, 283.
[36] ibid 272–73.
[37] ibid 285–92.
[38] ibid 275–76.
[39] ibid 300.
[40] ibid 303, 306.
[41] For a more detailed analysis see Marco Lamandini, David Ramos Muñoz, and Violeta Ruiz Almendral, 'The BVerfG's Assessment on the Contributions to the Single Resolution Fund and Article 114 TFEU' in Raffaele D'Ambrosio and Donato Messineo (eds), *BVerfG's Ruling on the Banking Union* (Quaderni di Ricerca Giuridica della Consulenza Legale della Banca d'Italia 2021) 103; Marco Lamandini, David Ramos Muñoz, and Violeta Ruiz Almendral, 'The BVerfG's Assessment on the Contributions to the Single Resolution Fund' (2021) 21 Quaderni di Ricerca Giuridica della Consulenza Legale 1.
[42] TFEU, art 114, paras (1) and (2).
[43] Lamandini, Ramos Muñoz, and Ruiz Almendral, 'The BVerfG's Assessment on the Contributions to the Single Resolution Fund' (n 41).

an EU-level independent agency with control over its funding entails a loss of democratic legitimacy, which needs to be balanced by enhanced accountability, and the rise of independent authorities is only permissible if there is a sufficient combination of political, administrative, and *legal* checks on their action.[44]

7.13 The legitimacy of the SRM was challenged again before the General Courts in a flood of cases following the resolution of Banco Popular, of which the General Court chose five pilot cases (the 'pilot cases') *Tatiana Pérez*,[45] *Del Valle*,[46] *Eleveté*,[47] *Algebris*,[48] and *Aeris*[49] to deal with the majority of legal issues. Apart from the substantive and procedural challenges, examined in subsequent sections, the appellants challenged the SRB role as an unlawful delegation of powers. Based on the *Meroni* doctrine, reinterpreted by the *ESMA Short Selling* case, the Court distinguished between the (unlawful) delegation of a discretionary power, and the (lawful) delegation of a clearly defined executive power, amenable to judicial review.[50] In the Court's view, the SRM scheme fell under the second category: the initial proposal (of direct exercise of SRB powers) was modified out of concerns by the Council to introduce an endorsement (and thus control) by the Commission of whether the resolution was 'required by the public interest' (the more 'discretionary' element of the resolution scheme), and this made the delegation lawful.[51] As per the use of specific resolution tools, such as the sale of business and write-off and conversion of capital instruments, the Court held that the Commission's assessment also encompassed the choice of resolution tools, and whether they are adequate to resolution objectives,[52] to the point of even stating that the resolution tools did not entail a delegation of autonomous competences[53] (which is debatable). The short time for the Commission to endorse or not (24 hours) was not seen as an impediment by the Court, since, in its view, the Commission is duly informed of any actions in preparation for resolution.[54]

2.2 Crisis management funding: deposit guarantees and resolution funds

7.14 In the EU resolution funding financing arrangements are set out in Articles 99–107 of the BRRD, which contemplate a target level of 1 per cent of covered bank deposits,[55] to be met through ex ante contributions by financial institutions to the resolution funds[56] (extraordinary ex post contributions may be raised if funds are insufficient).[57] Banks must also contribute to the SRB's administrative expenses. Both have been contentious and highly litigated.

---

[44] For a more extensive treatment see Marco Lamandini and David Ramos, 'Banking Union's Accountability System in Practice. A Health Check-Up to Europe's Financial Heart' (2022) Eur LJ volume 28, issue 4-6, 187-217.
[45] Case T-481/17 *Tatiana Pérez de Guzmán v SRB* ECLI:EU:T:2022:311.
[46] Case T-510/17 *Del Valle Ruiz v Commission & SRB* ECLI:EU:T:2022:312.
[47] Case T-523/17 *Eleveté v Commission & SRB* ECLI:EU:T:2022:313.
[48] Case T-570/17 *Algebris v Commission & SRB* ECLI:EU:T:2022:314.
[49] Case T-628/17 *Aeris Invest Sàrl v Commission & SRB* EU:T:2022:315.
[50] ibid paras 123–27; *Del Valle* (n 46) paras 209–11.
[51] *Aeris* (n 49) paras 128–34. *Del Valle* (n 46) paras 212–19.
[52] *Aeris* (n 49) paras 136–42, 143–45.
[53] ibid paras 146–48.
[54] *Del Valle* (n 46) paras 230–31.
[55] BRRD (n 8) art 102.
[56] ibid art 103.
[57] ibid art 104.

In administrative litigation before the Appeal Panel for the SRB[58] most conflicts involved a **7.15**
tension between 'certainty' and 'proportionality' in cases of 'change of status', ie entities alleged that they no longer qualified for contribution. In some decisions, after being subject to resolution measures, the entity had ceased to be 'banks', and were not included in the list compiled by the ECB.[59] The Appeal Panel had doubts about the validity of some rules,[60] but could not declare them invalid, as it is an administrative appeal body, and not an EU Court,[61] and thus read them in light of their finality to avoid validity challenges. In other cases, it found that entities subject to liquidation procedures under national law, which ceased to be subject to the SRM and no longer required the SRB's 'services', were still subject to the contributions in the particular year because at the moment of the calculation the entity was still a credit institution;[62] that a group's parent company still qualified as the 'contribution debtor' despite after a restructuring it had ceased to be the parent company;[63] and that an entity was still a licensed credit institution at the time of the calculation despite it had undergone a comprehensive restructuring and claimed that 2020 was the planned time for closure of its voluntary winding up process.[64]

Such 'change of status' problems were also present in the court case *State Street Bank*,[65] where **7.16**
an Italian bank had been merged with its parent company in Germany at a time where Italy had not fully transposed the BRRD. The Court held, first, that that the relevant provisions on 'change of status' had to be interpreted as including a transaction:

> [B]y which an institution ceases, in the course of a year, to be under the supervision of the national resolution authority following a cross-border merger through acquisition by its parent company, and as a result that transaction has no impact on the institution's obligation to pay in full the ordinary contributions due for the contribution year in question.

Then, the relevant provisions had to be considered applicable to a situation like the one **7.17**
at hand, where the merger and dissolution took place in 2015, despite Italy having not yet

---

[58] See Marco Lamandini and David Ramos Muñoz, 'Law and Practice of Financial Appeal Bodies (ESAs' Board of Appeal, SRB Appeal Panel): A View from the Inside' (2020) 57 CMLR 119.

[59] The SRB sent a letter in March 2015 requesting payment to all the banks included in a list of significant credit institutions under ECB direct supervision under Regulation 1024/2013, published by the ECB itself on its website on 4 September 2014. One addressee contested this, as it had ceased to be a bank (in Germany) in July 2015.

[60] A literal reading made Commission Delegated Regulation (EU) No 1310/2014 on the provisional system of instalments on contributions to cover the administrative expenditures of the Single Resolution Board during the provisional period [2014] OJ L354 potentially incompatible with the SRMR (n 9).

[61] A regulation is presumed to be lawful and only the CJEU has the power to declare it invalid. Case C-362/14 *Maximillian Schrems v Data Protection Commissioner* ECLI:EU:C:2015:650, para 61; Case C-188/10 *Aziz Melki (C-188/10) and Sélim Abdeli (C-189/10)* ECLI:EU:C:2010:2016, para 54; C-101/78 *Granaria* (1979) ECLI:EU:C:1979:38, paras 4 and 5; Case C-63/87; C-533/10, *CIVAD* EU:C:2012:347, para 43; Case F-128/12 *CR v Parliament* ECLI:EU:F:2014:38, paras 35, 36, 40; Case T-218/06 *Neurim Pharmaceuticals v OHIM* ECLI:EU:T:2008:379, para 52; Case T-120/99, *Kik v OHIM* (2001) ECLI:EU:T:2001:189, para 55.

[62] Appeal Panel decision in Case 4/2018 *A v SRB* (13 August 2018).

[63] In Appeal Panel decision in case 5/2018 *A v SRB* (20 July 2018) the appellant alleged that taking data on 31 December 2016 instead of September 2017 was 'disproportionate and not appropriate', but the Appeal Panel held that the SRB must raise contributions from the 'contribution debtor' under arts 8(1) and 5(4) of Commission Delegated Regulation 2361/2017, which, in groups, it is the same as the 'fee debtor' of SSM supervisory fees, which the entity was.

[64] In Appeal Panel decision in case 6/2018 the appellant said that, since it had received money from the Deposit Guarantee Scheme, by failing to take the alleged specific circumstances into account the SRB was indirectly imposing a burden on the other German banks members of the DGS, which also contributed to the SRB administrative expenses pursuant to SRMR, art 65.

[65] Case C-255/18 *State Street Bank International GmbH v Banca d'Italia* ECLI:EU:C:2019:967. More recently, a change of status to the effect of a reimbursement request following the withdrawal of licence was centre stage in Case C-202/21 P *ABLV Bank v SRB* ECLI:EU:C:2022:734.

formally established either the national resolution authority or the national fund and the contributions having not yet been calculated. Nonetheless, the entity was not obliged to pay the extraordinary contributions (under Article 104 BRRD) because it merged with its parent company on a date prior to the establishment of an extraordinary contribution by Italy's national resolution authority.

7.18 Courts have also analysed the calculation of ex ante contributions by financial institutions beyond such transitional situations.[66] In a first batch of cases (*Portigon, Banco Cooperativo Español*), the General Court dismissed some appeals as manifestly inadmissible,[67] but it also annulled the contributions by several banks,[68] a finding that continued in a second batch of rulings (*Landesbank Baden-Württemberg v SRB, Vorarlberger Landes- und Hypothekenbank v SRB, Portigon v SRB*[69]). Some grounds were formal and ad hoc, eg holding that SRB decisions were not properly authenticated. Yet, more importantly, the General Court also held that the SRB did not comply with the duty to state reasons. The decisions contained the list of factors used in the calculation, but no information that permitted to verify the calculations, since the 'risk-adjusted' factors were based on aggregate data from individual institutions, which were not disclosed.[70] This rendered the method 'inherently opaque' and adversely affected the individual bank's ability effectively to challenge the calculation.[71] In fact, the Court held that not only the SRB calculation, but also the method of calculation of the contributions envisaged in the Commission Delegated Regulation was opaque, and declared it illegal,[72] and susceptible of undermining judicial protection.[73]

7.19 The decision was appealed and the Court of Justice fully *rejected* the General Court's reading.[74] On the issue of authentication of the decision, the General Court had raised the point of its own motion, without giving the SRB the opportunity to respond properly, thus violating the right to be heard (*audi alteram partem*[75]).

7.20 More important, the duty to state reasons had to be appraised in light of the legal nature of each act, and of the interest of each person in obtaining an explanation, to enable him to understand the scope of the act concerning him.[76] Unlike 'tax-like' contributions, where the Court had required that they 'comprise an exact and detailed statement of account of the elements of the claim' as a precondition for judicial review,[77] ex ante contributions had

---

[66] Compare Concetta Brescia Morra and Federico Della Negra, 'Overview on the Litigation on the 'ex ante Contributions to the SRF: The Strict Standard of Review Adopted by the Court to Ensure Effective Legal Protection' in Chiara Zilioli and Karl-Philipp Wojcik (eds), *Judicial Review in the European Banking Union* (Edward Elgar Publishing 2021) 551–63. There are about 80 cases pending regarding ex-ante contributions to the SRF based upon decisions adopted after 2018.

[67] Orders in Case T-661/16 *Credito Fondiario v SRB* ECLI:EU:T:2018:806, confirmed by Court of Justice judgment of 5 March 2020; Case C-69/19 P *Credito Fondiario v SRB* ECLI:EU:C:2020:178; Case T-14/17, *Landesbank Baden Württemberg v SRB* ECLI:EU:T:2018:812; Case T-42/17 *VR-Bank Rhein-Sieg v SRB* ECLI:EU:T:2018:813.

[68] Case T-365/16 *Portigon v SRB* ECLI:EU:T:2019:824; Case T-323/16 *Banco Cooperativo Español v SRB* ECLI:EU:C:2013:856.

[69] Judgments of 23 September 2020, Case T-411/17 *Landesbank Baden-Württemberg v SRB* ECLI:EU:T:2020:435; Case T-414/17 *Vorarlberger Landes- und Hypothekenbank v SRB*, ECLI:EU:T:2020:437; and Case T-420/17 *Portigon v SRB* ECLI:EU:T:2020:438.

[70] Case T-411/17 *Landesbank Baden-Württemberg* (n 69) 97–98.
[71] ibid paras 100–102.
[72] ibid paras 129–40.
[73] ibid paras 127–43.
[74] Joined Cases C-584/20 P and C-621/20 P *Landesbank Baden-Württemberg* ECLI:EU:C:2021:601.
[75] ibid paras 56–78.
[76] ibid paras 104.
[77] ibid paras 106.

an 'insurance-based' logic, and the SRB calculation had to use data provided by the banks which were 'business secrets'.[78] The Court rejected the argument that the SRB could have used other calculation methods not involving business secrets, since the legislature enjoys broad discretion to design the calculation methods,[79] and drew an analogy with the calculation of contributions to DGS, which are lawful.[80] Thus:

> [T]he obligation to state reasons must be regarded as fulfilled where the persons concerned by a decision fixing ex ante contributions to the SRF, while not being sent data which are business secrets, have the method of calculation used by the SRB and sufficient information to understand, in essence, how their individual situation was taken into account, for the purposes of calculating their ex ante contribution to the SRF, relative to the situation of all the other financial institutions concerned.[81]

7.21 With regard to the finding of illegality of the applicable (Commission) rules, the Court of Justice held that most factors (eg the bank's assets) were not problematic. The problem was the risk adjustment factor, which sought to make a *comparative* risk assessment of the institution vis-à-vis other institutions. This was done by allocating each institution to a 'bin', or discrete category of similar institutions, assigning a common value for a rescaled indicator, consolidating all indicators into a composite indicator (weighing different risk pillars) and then calculating the risk adjusting multiplier according to a rescaling of the composite indicator.[82] Thus, the institution could not be given 'data enabling it to verify fully the accuracy of the value of the risk adjusting multiplier attributed to it' as it would require disclosing business secrets, but it could have access to data '[i]n summary or collective form such that entities concerned cannot be identified', such as 'the limit values of each 'bin' so that the entity could be satisfied that its category matched its economic situation, or that the discrete category was consistent with the methodology in the delegated regulation.[83] Such 'statement of reasons' does not enable to 'systematically' detect any error' but is sufficient to satisfy the entity that the information it provided was included in the calculation, and/or to identify any use of manifestly incorrect information.[84] Thus, the Commission Delegated Regulation was considered lawful and, since the General Court's finding of a breach of judicial protection was based on a mistaken reading of the duty to state reasons, the SRB actions were also lawful.[85]

7.22 Also part of this litigation are the 'irrevocable payment commitments' (IPCs) cases. IPCs are part of the mechanism for banks to comply with their obligation to contribute to deposit guarantee schemes and resolution funds. Some of the largest French banks, including *Société Générale, BNP Paribas, Crédit Agricole,* or *Crédit mutuel*,[86] following a concerted

---

[78] ibid paras 113–14.
[79] ibid paras 117–18.
[80] ibid para 119.
[81] ibid para 122.
[82] ibid paras 132–34.
[83] ibid paras 136–37. Furthermore, 'the other stages of the methodology for calculating *ex ante* contributions to the SRF are based, as the Advocate General stated in point 149 of his Opinion, on aggregate data from the institutions concerned, which may be disclosed in collective form without infringing the SRB's obligation to respect business secrets'. ibid para 138.
[84] *Landesbank Baden-Württemberg* (n 74) para 140.
[85] ibid paras 143–49.
[86] Case T-143/18 *Société Générale v ECB* ECLI:EU:T:2020:389. The Court decided several cases with quasi-identical pleas. These included Cases T-144/18 *Crédit Agricole and Others v ECB* ECLI:EU:T:2020:390 ; Case T-145/18 *Confédération nationale du Crédit mutuel and Others v ECB* ECLI:EU:T:2020:391; Case T-146/18 *BPCE and Others v ECB* ECLI:EU:T:2020:392; Case T-149/18 *Arkéa Direct Bank and Others v ECB* ECLI:EU:T:2020:393; and Joined Cases T-150/18 and T-345/18 *BNP Paribas/BCE* ECLI:EU:T:2020:394.

pattern appealed an ECB decision, which had required all IPCs to be deducted from the figure of Core Equity Tier 1 (CET1) capital. The applicants argued that the ECB had promulgated a new prudential rule (ie a sort of amendment to 'Pillar 1' Basel Framework capital requirements) and thus acted beyond its mandate (limited to Pillar 2, Supervisory Review and Evaluation Process—SREP measures), that it had erred in law, rendering the legal provisions on IPCs ineffective, and committed a manifest error, by failing to appraise the IPCs *individually* for each institution. The General Court upheld the ECB's competence to require specific provisioning or prudential policies to institutions,[87] and to exercise supervisory powers with regard to off-balance sheet items.[88] Yet, it sided with the appellants in finding that the deduction of IPCs from CET1 capital was a *general* position, whilst the SREP must involve the supervisory cycle for individual institutions, and thus the ECB failed to consider each institution individually, and annulled the corresponding part of the ECB decisions.[89]

3 Substantive review: 'property' and other rights

7.23 Crisis management measures normally entail a serious interference with property, when authorities wrest control over the entity's operations, transfer its assets and/or liabilities to an acquiror, a 'bridge bank', or a 'bad bank', or write-down or convert its equity or debt. In all these cases a pertinent question is whether any of these measures amounts to an 'expropriation' or an unlawful interference with property. Such complaints can also arise in sovereign crises where haircuts are applied to sovereign bonds. Then, we focus on courts' review beyond the protection of property rights, including cases that examine the 'triggers' for action, and cases determining other substantive protections for depositors and holders of shares and subordinated debt.

3.1 Substantive safeguards in bank crises

7.24 US cases have dealt with these questions under the Fifth Amendment (the 'Takings Clause'), reserved for cases of expropriation.[90] The key question is whether crisis measures have gone 'too far', become an expropriation (if not, *procedural* safeguards, to be examined in s 4, apply). In Europe, under the European Convention on Human Rights (ECHR), and the EU Charter of Fundamental Rights (Charter), substantive protections encompass both 'expropriation' as well as of 'interference with' property,[91] besides the more procedural protections.[92] As we are about to see, however, the availability of standards does not translate into a strong practical challenge to the action of public authorities, and courts do not seem too comfortable addressing substantive protections, either in the US or in Europe.

7.25 In the US, in the *Fahey v Malone* case[93] discussed in a previous section, the parties raised the 'Takings' clause of the Constitution, but the courts focused on the legitimacy of the

---

[87] *Société Générale v ECB* (n 86) paras 46–50.
[88] ibid paras 51–61.
[89] ibid paras 64–74.
[90] The Fifth Amendment states that 'private property [shall not] be taken for public use without just compensation'.
[91] ECHR, art 1 Protocol 1; Charter, arts 16, 17.
[92] ECHR, art 6; Charter, art 47 (judicial protection) and art 41 (good administration).
[93] *Fahey v Malone* (n 18).

regulatory scheme and the appointment of a conservator. 'Takings' claims were discussed in *American Continental Corp*.[94] the Saratoga case (*California Housing*),[95] or *Golden Pacific Bancorp*.[96] The line of reasoning, set in *American Continental Corp* was that a compensable regulatory taking did not exist when public authorities' actions promoted the public interest in a sound banking system, and did not interfere with the investment-backed expectations of the bank.[97] In the *Saratoga* case the court examined carefully the whole regulatory architecture, and concluded that, as a result of operating voluntarily in such a regulated environment, the S&L 'held less that the full bundle of property rights'.[98] In *Golden Pacific*, where an investigation by the Office of the Comptroller of the Currency (OCC) unveiled that an instrument ('yellow certificates of deposit') treated as 'non-book' investments made on its clients' behalf was, in reality, deposits, without assets to match, leading to the FDCIC's appointment as receiver. The courts dismissed the complaints under the 'arbitrary and capricious' standard and the Federal Tort Claims Act (FTCA),[99] and the 'Takings' complaint. A 'Takings' could arise in two ways: first, as a result of a regulatory scheme, a property owner may suffer a physical invasion or permanent occupation of his or her property; secondly, a regulatory scheme may also result in a compensable taking without a physical invasion or occupation of property when regulations go 'too far' and impinge on private freedom. Yet, on the physical occupation basis, the court reaffirmed the Saratoga case's holding that, in a highly regulated industry Golden Pacific lacked the full bundle of property rights, especially the right to exclude others from its property. The second basis, ie whether the scheme went 'too far' required an ad hoc assessment, but courts normally considered 'the character of the governmental action, its economic impact, and its interference with *reasonable investment-backed expectations*'.[100] On the basis of this third element the court held that, given 'the highly regulated nature of the banking industry ... Golden Pacific could not have had a historically rooted expectation of compensation' because it 'could not have reasonably expected that the government 'would fail to enforce the applicable statutes and regulations',[101] nor could the OCC's previous inaction be construed as a 'commitment' to accept the yellow certificates of deposit in the future.[102]

In *Starr v United States*, the Court of Federal Claims[103] addressed an alleged 'takings' claim committed not in regulatory, but in 'transactional' form. Starr was a shareholder of American International Group (AIG), a large insurer, which played a major role in the credit default swaps (CDSs) market, by protecting against the risk of default of securitized assets. The securitisation market collapse created a liquidity problem for the group, and the Federal Reserve Bank of New York (FRBNY) relied on Section 13 (3) of the Federal Reserve Act[104] to

7.26

---

[94] *American Continental Corp* 22 Cl Ct (1991).
[95] *California Housing Securities* 959 F 2d 955 (Fed Cir 1992).
[96] *Golden Pacific Bancorp and Miles P Jennings, Jr v United States* 15 F 3d 1066 (Fed Cir 1994).
[97] *American Continental Corp* (n 94).
[98] *California Housing* (n 95) 955–56.
[99] *Golden Pacific Bancorp v Clarke* No 85-2384, slip op at 1 (DDC 1986); 837 F 2d 509, 513 (DC Cir 1988), cert denied, 488 US 890, 109 S Ct 223, 102 L Ed 2d 213.
[100] *Golden Pacific v US* (n 96).
[101] 'Indeed, Golden Pacific's expectations could only have been that the FDIC would exert control over the Bank's assets if the Comptroller became satisfied that the Bank was insolvent and chose to place it in receivership.' *Golden Pacific v US* (n 96).
[102] *Golden Pacific v US* (n 96).
[103] *Starr International Co v United States* 121 Fed Cl 428 (2015) (*Starr International 2015*); *Starr International Co v United States* Docket No 1:11-cv-00779-TCW (DC Cir 2017) (*Starr International 2017*).
[104] Section 13(3) of the Federal Reserve Act, 12 USC s 343. That statutory provision allowed the Federal Reserve Board, '(I)n unusual and exigent circumstances', to authorize a Federal Reserve Bank to provide an interest bearing

grant AIG a large loan to AIG in exchange for 79.9 per cent of its equity (later converted into AIG common stock), and the replacement of the CEO.[105] AIG's Board accepted the loan's terms as a better alternative than bankruptcy, but Starr alleged that the transaction was (1) an illegal exaction, because the FRBNY lacked the authority to acquire AIG's equity (due process claim), and (2) an illegal taking (a Takings claim). The Court of Federal Claims agreed with the plaintiff on the illegal exaction claim,[106] holding that, since the government had no obligation to confer a benefit, if it decided in its discretion to confer it, it could not demand the surrender of rights it lacked the authority to demand.[107] The court rejected the objection that the Act authorized the FRBNY to grant the loan 'subject to such limitations, restrictions, and regulations as the Board of Governors of the Federal Reserve System may prescribe', holding that the express language of the Act did not contemplate the possibility of demanding consideration beyond an interest rate, and the FRBNY's 'incidental powers cannot be greater than the powers otherwise delegated to it by Congress'.[108] Also, the favourable vote of AIG's Board was irrelevant to the court, as voluntary acceptance is not a defence in the case of an illegal exaction.[109] Nonetheless, despite upholding the 'illegal exaction' claim, the court awarded zero damages, because AIG's choice was ultimately between the loan and bankruptcy, and rejected the Takings claim, because this required 'authorized government action', and an illegal exaction was *unauthorized* government action.[110]

7.27 However, the case was appealed, and the Circuit Court dismissed the complaint for lack of standing, since the complaint was brought by the shareholders, who were raising third party (ie the corporation's) rights.[111] This precluded a definitive finding on the substance of the claims. Yet, the Circuit Court made some interesting pronouncements of substance. It eg distinguished 'between a new issuance of equity and a transfer of existing stock from one party to another', since a new issuance diluted all shares, and did not operate over the shareholders' shares, and rejected that the FRBNY was the 'controlling party', because its strong bargaining position was not tantamount to the position of a majority shareholder who owes fiduciary duties.[112]

---

loan to a qualifying entity, 'subject to such limitations, restrictions, and regulations as the (Federal Reserve Board) may prescribe'. See *Starr International 2017* (n 103).

[105] 'The $85 billion loan was, and remains, the largest s 13(3) loan ever granted. It is also the only instance in which the Government obtained equity as part of a s 13(3) loan.' *Starr International 2017* (n 103).
[106] *Starr International 2015* (n 103).
[107] ibid.
[108] ibid. This, in the court's view, was supported by different Acts of Congress, which limited the government's ability to take over the control of corporations, and turn them into government agencies without congressional authorization, while the precedents cited by the government (*Lucas v Federal Reserve Bank of Richmond* 59 F 2d 617 (4th Cir 1932)) referred to instances where the federal reserve banks had asked for collateral as part of the conditions of the loans.
[109] *Starr International 2015* (n 103), citing *American Airlines Inc v United States* 551 F 3d 1294, 1302 (Fed Cir 2008) or *Finn v United States* (1970) 192 Ct Cl 814, 820, 428 F 2d 828, 831, among other numerous authorities. *United States v Edmondston* 181 US 500 (1901) held that 'voluntariness' was only a defence when there had been a mutual mistake of law.
[110] *Starr International 2015* (n 103) citing *Alves v United States* 133 F 3d 1454, 1456–58 (Fed Cir 1998); *Figueroa v United States* 57 Fed Cl 488, 496 (2003).
[111] *Starr International 2017* (n 103). See also ch 4 s 2.5.
[112] ibid: 'Outside third parties with leverage over a transaction, even in a take-it-or-leave-it scenario, do not necessarily have a responsibility to protect the interests of a counterparty, less so the interests of a counterparty's constituents. Starr has not shown that the Government, through its alleged leverage, owed any fiduciary duties to Starr at the time of the equity acquisition.'

7.28 In Europe, property protection is three-pronged: one general principle, a requirement of expropriation with compensation, and a prohibition of disproportionate interference.[113] Courts have an expansive view of 'property rights', which include absolute *and* relative rights over immovable and intellectual property,[114] financial instruments,[115] businesses,[116] pensions, or entitlements.[117] The courts' vision of the protection against interferences with property over financial instruments is clear in form, but less so in substance.

7.29 In *Grainger* the ECtHR[118] decided over the crisis management of Northern Rock. The bank was nationalized, making it necessary to calculate shareholders' compensation. The independent valuer was expressly instructed to assume that *no financial assistance would be granted* to the bank, and thus concluded that compensation should be zero. The shareholders (a hedge fund) sued before English courts, which dismissed all the claims, and before the ECtHR, which also dismissed the complaint: the government had a wide margin of appreciation in this field, zero compensation resulted from the bank's losses, not from government intervention, public authorities were not obliged to cover the debts of a private institution, and the government's decision, was justified by the need to avoid moral hazard, and was thus far from being 'manifestly without reasonable foundation'. The Court tiptoed around the claim that Northern Rock had been treated a differently from other, systemically important banks, like RBS and HBOS, which were bailed-out. The argument would have complicated things, since the Court should have openly accepted that discretion permits discrimination without justification, or that one valid justification can be systemic importance (which would mean admitting that the system tolerates, if not promotes, moral hazard).

7.30 In *Kotnik*[119] and *Dowling*[120] the Court of Justice analysed the Commission's Banking Communication, which, in case of government assistance to banks required burden-sharing (ie absorption of losses by shareholders and creditors) as a matter of *policy* to consider the assistance not contrary to state aid, a position that, sometimes, went against years or practice by public authorities, which favoured bail-outs over bail-ins. Yet, the Court of Justice rejected that this could be the basis of any 'legitimate expectation' by shareholders or debtholders, because this:

> [P]resupposes that precise, unconditional and consistent assurances, originating from authorised, reliable sources, have been given to the person concerned by the competent authorities of the European Union. That right applies to any individual in a situation in which an institution, body or agency of the European Union, by giving that person precise assurances, has led him to entertain well-founded expectations.[121]

---

[113] ECHR, art 1, Protocol 1, Charter, art 17 of the. See *Sporrong and Lönroth v Sweden*, App no 7151/75, 7152/75 (23 September 1982).
[114] Charter, art 17(2); *Anheuser-Busch Inc v Portugal*, App no 73049/01 (11 January 2007).
[115] *Bramelid and Malmström v Sweden*, App nos 8588/79 and 8589/79 (12 December 1983).
[116] *Traktörer Aktiebolag v Sweden*, App no 10873/84 (7 July 1989).
[117] *Kjartan Ásmundsson v Iceland*, App no 60669/00 (12 October 2004).
[118] *Dennis Grainger and Others v United Kingdom*, App no 34940/10 (10 July 2012). More recently, in *Freire Lopes v Portugal*, App no 58598/21 (23 February 2023), the ECtHR addressed the question of the alleged violation of art 1 of Protocol 1 (protection of property) of the resolution of Banco Espirito Santo in August 2014, finding the application inadmissible, finding that Banco de Portugal had a degree of discretion in determining what measures to take in relation to Banco Espirito Santo failure.
[119] Case C-526/14 *Tadej Kotnik and Others v Drzavni zbor Republike Slovenije* ECLI:EU:C:2016:570. See also Ch 4 s 2.3.
[120] Case C-41/15 *Gerard Dowling and Others v Minister for Finance* ECLI:EU:C:2016:836.
[121] '[E]conomic operators are not justified in having a legitimate expectation that an existing situation which is capable of being altered by the EU institutions in the exercise of their discretion will be maintained.' *Kotnik* (n 119) para 62 and case law cited.

7.31 Since investors had not been given any 'precise, unconditional and consistent assurance', they had no legitimate expectation, and thus there was no need for a transitional period to adjust to the new framework.[122] Furthermore, burden-sharing was not an illegal interference with property rights, because shareholders' losses came from the bank, and not an authorities' distributional decision, and the no-creditor worse-off (NCWO) principle ensured that creditors would be no worse-off than under regular insolvency/liquidation. Although investors in bank shares and bonds cannot expect the government to bail out the bank, the sweeping rationale used by the Court would mean that *any* intervention would be legitimate unless there were a series of 'precise, unconditional and consistent assurances, originating from authorised, reliable sources'. Thus, the Court would not analyse the regulatory scheme and context to see if it could give rise to such expectations.

7.32 In *Mallis*[123] and *Ledra*[124] the Court of Justice examined the impact of measures adopted by Cyprus and previously agreed with the European Stability Mechanism (ESM) within an aid package, where the Commission and the ECB were the main players inside the ESM. In *Mallis* the Court dismissed the annulment action because the conduct could not be attributed to EU authorities, but to the ESM; but in *Ledra* the Court considered the *damages* complaint against the Commission and ECB justiciable, as, even when 'borrowed' by the ESM, they continued to be Treaty institutions, subject to the Charter. Yet, given this landmark ruling on justiciability, the case's substance was a bit underwhelming. On the measures, consisting in a write-down and conversion of debt instruments, including the conversion of a 37.5 per cent of Cyprus Popular Bank's uninsured deposits into shares, with the promise of a buy-back of shares if the bank went overcapitalized, the Court held that:

> In view of the objective of ensuring the stability of the banking system in the euro area, and having regard to the imminent risk of financial losses to which depositors with the two banks concerned would have been exposed if the latter had failed, such measures do not constitute a disproportionate and intolerable interference impairing the very substance of the appellants' right to property.[125]

7.33 The problem is not that the measures were unreasonable, but the difficulty to understand *why* they were reasonable since there was no clear rationale or justification (perhaps the complaint was not very elaborate on these grounds). Burden-sharing is not ruled out by property rights, and insolvency is a good benchmark to measure investors' acceptable losses (no-creditor worse off principle). Beyond that, however, it is hard to draw further guidance.

7.34 These points are not academic. Differences in treatment between creditors led the Austrian Constitutional Court[126] to annul the Austrian Federal Act on Restructuring Measures for Hypo-Alpe-Adria-Bank International AG (HaaSanG), which provided that supplementary capital and subordinate debt instruments held by third parties would expire *provided* they matured before June 30, 2019, together with all their guarantees (by the State of Carinthia). The Court held that the authorities were entitled to discretion (as in *Grainger*), that the

---

[122] ibid 68. Even if there had been such an expectation, the objectives financial stability, avoiding excessive public spending and minimizing distortions of competition would qualify as 'overriding policy interests' justifying the absence of transitional period.
[123] Case C-105/15 *Mallis* ECLI:EU:C:2016:702.
[124] Joined Cases C-8/15 and C-10/15 *Ledra Advertising and Others v Commission* ECLI:EU:C:2016:701. See also ch 4 s 1.2.
[125] ibid para 74.
[126] Austrian Constitutional Court, G-239/14, AUT-2015-1-002 (3 July 2015).

measures (eg the alteration of maturities) were not per se an expropriation (as in *Ledra*), and it used insolvency as the benchmark to establish the value of claims (as in *Kotnik*), but found the distinction between claims untenable.

A subsequent case decided by the General Court, *Pavvlika/Chrysostomides*, was a follow-up to *Ledra*, in that it analysed Cyprus' crisis-management measures.[127] The complaint was more comprehensive, as it also reviewed a sale of Greek bank branches, and probably more thorough, which rendered the General Court's reasoning equally so. The Court explained that the measures were proportionate because the bail-in was based on a clear and accessible legal framework with creditor safeguards,[128] suitable to the end sought,[129] and proportionate,[130] like the sale of branches.[131] Official communications could not generate legitimate expectations for a 'prudent and circumspect' reader,[132] and there was no discrimination.[133] The Court explained common sense market facts in plain terms, holding that bank deposits are not risk-free, that investors' harm must be assessed based not on securities' nominal value, but their 'true' market value, and against the alternative of a liquidation process.[134] It also held that the ECB enjoys broad discretion in emergency liquidity assistance (ELA) operations, and the absence of constrains meant that there could not be any 'legitimate expectations'.[135] **7.35**

In *BT v Balgarska Narodna Banka*[136] the Court of Justice answered a preliminary reference from Bulgarian courts on the compatibility of Bulgarian law with the Deposit Guarantee Schemes (DGS) Directive. The directive required (i) a finding that deposits had become 'unavailable' within a short timeframe through an express declaration by the authorities; (ii) a determination of which deposits were due and payable; and (iii) the DGS' repayment of deposits. Bulgaria made repayment contingent on the bank's 'insolvency' or the withdrawal of its licence, which meant a much longer time, and included other constraints on reimbursement, which prompted depositors' liability claim, one of whose grounds was the violation of property rights. The Court held that Bulgarian authorities were subject to the Charter because the Directive on the Winding Up of Credit Institutions applied.[137] It was for the national court to determine whether the measures constituted 'a disproportionate and intolerable interference with the very substance of the applicant's right to property', but the Court **7.36**

---

[127] Case T-786/14 *Bourdouvali and Others v Council and Others* ECLI:EU:T:2018:487. The Court decided on the same date Case T-680/13 *Chrysostomides K & Co and Others v Council and Others* ECLI:EU:T:2018:486. Since its text is a verbatim copy of *Bourdouvali and Others*, references will be made to the former.

[128] *Bourdouvali and Others* (n 127) paras 268–84. Creditors could not be put in a worse position than if the entity had been liquidated, while the urgency of the situation (and the fact that the measures were not 'penalties') justified the lack of opportunity to object.

[129] ibid paras 285–98. There was no manifest error of assessment in the diagnosis of Cyprus' economic situation, or the opinion that converting deposits into equity to achieve a 9 per cent core capital ratio, and separating a 'bad' bank could stabilize (and trim) the system.

[130] ibid paras 299–324, 329. The parliament in Cyprus had rejected less intrusive measures, a full state bail-out would have made public debt unsustainable, bank recapitalization by the ESM was not an option, and the applicants could not prove that other alternatives could have been less harmful, equally effective, or more swiftly executed.

[131] ibid paras 331–60. The measures reduced contagion risk, not doing so would have increased financial assistance beyond the committed amounts, and the sale was open and transparent.

[132] ibid paras 403–38.

[133] In relation to other creditors, depositors of Greek branches, deposits below €100,000, or other countries' creditors, or against members of cooperative banks. *Bourdouvali and Others* (n 127) paras 439–508.

[134] ibid paras 313, 317, 320.

[135] ibid paras 361–402.

[136] Case C-501/18 *BT v Balgarska Narodna Banka* ECLI:EU:C:2021:249.

[137] Winding-Up Directive. The directive applied even in a situation that was purely internal to a Member State. See *BT v Balgarska Nadorna Banka* (n 136) para 104.

aided in such determination, by providing grounds on which to justify the interference. The domestic court should consider:

> [i]f, in view of the imminent risk of financial loss to which the depositors with KTB would have been exposed in the event of KTB's bankruptcy, other less restrictive measures, such as a partial suspension of payments or a partial limitation of KTB's activities, would have achieved the same results. It is apparent from the request for a preliminary ruling that the supervisory measures at issue in the main proceedings were limited in time and that, during that period, in accordance with national law, contractual interest accrued on the suspended pecuniary commitments. Moreover, in addition to the fact that the guaranteed amount of the deposits with KTB was repaid to the applicant in the main proceedings through the FGVB, the amount of its deposits exceeding the guaranteed amount remains recoverable in the context of the bankruptcy proceedings instituted in respect of that bank.[138]

7.37 The above principles were confirmed in the Banco Popular cases, decided over the largest bank crisis administered by EU authorities, where one of the claims repeated by the appellants was that the resolution scheme over Banco Popular constituted an intolerable interference with their property. The General Court relied on *Kotnik*, *Ledra*, or *Chrysostomides* to emphasize that property is 'not an absolute right', and can be subject to restrictions, which must be: (a) provided for in legal provisions (legality); (b) necessary to pursue EU objectives of general interest (necessity) and; (c) proportionate to those objectives (proportionality), that bank crisis management measures typically fulfil those requirements, and it is widely admitted that shareholders bear first losses, and their investment carries risks.[139] In the specific context, the measures were (a) provided for in the SRMR,[140] (b) necessary to ensure financial stability and prevent contagion,[141] and (c) proportionate to the ends sought, because the SRB justified why it used the sale of business and discarded other alternatives,[142] there was no discrimination, because shareholders are not comparable to depositors,[143] and the NCWO principle prevented a worse treatment than under liquidation.[144] Claims of a 'lack of compensation' were misdirected against resolution measures, as they would result from the official valuation specifically oriented at establishing any compensation right,[145] or unjustified, because property rights do not guarantee immediate payment, or payment if there is no harm.[146] Furthermore, any compensation should take as counterfactual the shares' value in a *liquidation*, calculated pursuant to a specific valuation procedure for such purpose, ie not their market value at the moment of intervention,[147] nor their value in case of a hypothetical

---

[138] *BT v Balgarska Narodna Banka* (n 136) paras 109–10.
[139] *Tatiana Pérez* (n 45) paras 482–99 ; *Del Valle* (n 46) paras 488–99 ; *Algebris* (n 48) paras 391–402; *Eleveté* (n 47) paras 159–74.
[140] The fact that a definitive valuation (Valuation 2) was finally not undertaken was no breach of legality. *Del Valle* (n 46) paras 504–506. Nor was there any breach of legality in the Commission's endorsement of the decision. *Algebris* (n 48) paras 406–408.
[141] The Court rejected the appellants' claim that, unlike *Kotnik* (n 119), *Ledra* (n 124) etc., this was not a 'systemic' crisis, but one circumscribed to a specific entity, because, the Court held, distress can easily propagate from one bank to another. *Tatiana Pérez* (n 45) para 501.
[142] *Tatiana Pérez* (n 45) paras 502–505; *Del Valle* (n 46) para 501; *Eleveté* (n 47) paras 182–89.
[143] *Eleveté* (n 47) paras 194–95.
[144] *Tatiana Pérez* (n 45) paras 502–505; *Del Valle* (n 46) para 511; *Algebris* (n 48) paras 413–17; *Eleveté* (n 47) paras 199–208.
[145] *Tatiana Pérez* (n 45) paras 512–21; *Algebris* (n 48) para 417. The NCWO and the valuation are regulated, respectively, in SRMR, arts 15, 20.
[146] See eg *Algebris* (n 48) paras 416–21.
[147] *Tatiana Pérez* (n 45) paras 522–25; *Algebris* (n 48) paras 423–27.

private solution,[148] nor their value under a hypothetical 'definitive valuation'[149] which has a different purpose, and was (lawfully) not carried out in this case. Finally, property rights do not grant their holders a right to be heard beyond what was granted by procedural safeguards,[150] and, in any event, its restriction was proportionate in light of the objectives sought (financial stability and preventing contagion) which required adopting the decision in an extremely short time period.[151]

Case law shows, in our view, the 'evanescence' of property rights over banks' financial instruments (shares or bonds) in crisis contexts. This is intransigent also in the most recent findings of the Court of Justice in *Banco Santander v JAC and MCPR*, where Banco Popular shareholders claimed that they were mis-sold the bank's shares by way of a false prospectus[152] and the bank had hidden the real financial situation of the bank in a public offer consummated only one year before the resolution of the bank; to safeguard the proper functioning of resolution, the Court of Justice concluded nonetheless that, where there is a potential clash, the public interest in resolution had to prevail over investor protection and that therefore shareholders whose shares were cancelled in resolution could not claim damages for the previous mis-selling of such shares nor the retroactive annulment of their original investment decision and the restitution of their moneys. The Court noted that the right of property under Article 17 of the Charter, as well as the right to an effective judicial protection under Article 47 of the Charter, are not absolute rights.[153] However, the Court also conceded that these litigious claims based on securities law should be considered in the evaluation of the compensation, if any, due to shareholders and creditors in resolution, by adding their value in the comparison of the shareholders' treatment in resolution with the one they would have received in liquidation[154] (something that has, in our view, important practical implications on the way such evaluation needs to be done). By way of conclusion, since banks and their owners operate in a highly regulated sector, courts conclude that they accept from the outset the eventuality of intervention. This makes it difficult to provide a 'baseline' of what property rights would be like absent regulatory intervention, which is a source of interference, but also of stability. Furthermore, courts seem uncomfortable with a broad-based 'balancing' of rights against public interests, and prefer to focus on the details of the regulatory scheme. This means that a precise claim of the breach of a concrete provision has more prospects than a broader claim of breach of property rights. Finally, when assessing the necessity and proportionality of the interference, courts tend to focus on the process by which the decision was adopted, and its justification, ie the focus is on procedural safeguards. If we take out the *legality* protection based on concrete provisions, and the *procedural* safeguards, it is hard to identify any added protection dispensed by property rights, which may be why applicants use property rights as an ancillary plea, not their 'core' claim.

7.38

---

[148] *Algebris* (n 48) para 422.
[149] *Del Valle* (n 46) paras 511–26.
[150] *Tatiana Pérez* (n 45) 527–30; *Del Valle* (n 46) 533.
[151] *Del Valle* (n 46).
[152] Case C-410/20 *Banco Santander SA v JAC and MPCR* ECLI:EU:C:2022:351.
[153] ibid para 47.
[154] ibid paras 48–50.

3.2 Substantive safeguards in sovereign crises

7.39 Financial stability involves a strong link between banks' and sovereign finances. Unsurprisingly, crisis management measures often affect not only banks' instruments, but also sovereign instruments, eg through cuts in 'entitlement' expenditures, or bond haircuts. Although not the core of our analysis, it is useful to observe the parallels. In *Florescu* the Court of Justice examined the proportionality of cuts to pensions and other entitlements. The Court of Justice held that a proprietary interest over a social benefit could exist 'where legislation provides for the automatic payment' of that benefit,[155] but that cuts would be proportionate because they furthered general interest goals (rationalize public spending), were exceptional and temporary, states have broad economic discretion, and the burden was reasonable (the beneficiary could choose between a pension and a public salary[156]). *Florescu* referred to the ECtHR's more abundant case law[157] on property rights over pensions and entitlements. Why is this relevant? Because we can again observe the courts' hesitance to provide a 'baseline' for rights that, in essence, have their origin in regulation, and cannot exist without it.[158] And it is not by coincidence that in deciding *Banco Santander* the Court made express reference to *Florescu*.[159]

7.40 Cases on sovereign debt present similar difficulties, as shown by the Greek debt restructuring cases. On the face of the unsustainability of Greek sovereign debt the ECB temporarily suspended the application of its collateral framework to avoid excluding Greek debt as eligible collateral, which would have sent it spiralling down. Yet, to complete this temporary fix a restructuring of Greek debt was needed, which was achieved using collective action clauses (CACs), only after the ECB had swapped its debt for new and be spared the haircut. These transactions were challenged in *Accorinti v ECB*,[160] where the plea was one of non-contractual liability. The General Court, however, dismissed the claim, holding that:

> [T]the fact remains that, where a prudent and circumspect economic operator is able to foresee the adoption of an EU measure likely to affect his interests, he cannot rely on that principle if the measure is adopted. Nor can economic operators have a legitimate expectation that an existing situation which is capable of being altered by the EU institutions in the exercise of their discretion will be maintained, especially in an area such as monetary policy, the subject-matter of which is constantly being adjusted according to variations in the economic situation.[161]

7.41 In the Court's view, the statements by ECB officials opposing such restructuring could not be read as creating a legitimate expectation, because they were too general, in spite of them

---

[155] Including the 'rights resulting from the payment of contributions to a social security scheme' but does not entitle 'a person to a pension of a particular amount'. Case C-258/14 *Eugenia Florescu and Others v Casa Judeţeană de Pensii Sibiu and Others* ECLI:EU:C:2017:448, para 50.

[156] Ie the measures cut pension rights for beneficiaries who did paid work for public entities.

[157] In *Florescu* (n 155) the CJEU cited *Kjartan Ásmundsson v Iceland* (n 117) 39. See also *Gaygusuz v Austria*, App no 39/1995/545/631 (23 May 1996) 1142, paras 39–41, or *Bellet, Huertas and Vialatte v France*, App nos 40832/98, 40833/98, and 40906/98 (27 April 1999), or *Skórkiewicz v Poland*, App no 39860/98 (1 June 1999).

[158] The ECtHR has said in some cases that the interference must be assessed by reference to the income before the intervention (*Kjartan Ásmundsson* (n 117) 45; *Apostolakis v Greece*, App no 39574/07 (22 October 2009)) or pursuant to the situation in which the recipient is left (*Koufaki v Greece*, App nos 57665/12 and 57657/12 (7 May 2013)).

[159] *Banco Santander* (n 152) para 47.

[160] Case T-79/13 *Accorinti v ECB* ECLI:EU:T:2015:756.

[161] ibid para 76.

restructuring remained a possibility, and the ECB lacked the power to impose a restructuring of Greek sovereign debt.[162] Perhaps the most interesting aspect of the case was the application of the standard of a 'prudent and circumspect operator', who assumes that every investment carries a risk.[163]

This view had continuity in the ECtHR case *Mamatas v Greece*,[164] where the restructuring itself was challenged. The Court held that the involuntary haircut was *not* a *deprivation* of, but an *interference* with, property, accomplished through a lawful measure, which pursued the general interest, and was proportionate to the ends sought.[165] More important, the Court engaged with well-known substantive arguments, eg that every investment, including sovereign bonds, entails a risk,[166] a bond's nominal value does not represent its market value. Finally, the Court held that collective action clauses (CACs) used to bind the non-participating (and unwilling) investors are habitual market practice to avoid the 'holdout problem', and thus were the lesser evil from a transactional (ie not just public interest) perspective.[167] **7.42**

'Sovereign' cases confirm that, regardless of the context, courts are deferential to authorities, and uncomfortable balancing private rights and public interests in cases where the object of property is created by law, and thus necessarily with strings attached. **7.43**

3.3 Substantive review beyond 'property': conditions for intervention

Since courts are relatively permissive of interferences with property provided the conditions for intervention are fulfilled, the existence of such conditions is a key, and contested matter. In the *Banco Popular* cases, the General Court had to examine the application of a resolution scheme to said bank. The ECB found that Banco Popular was failing-or-likely-to-fail (FOLTF) due to a serious liquidity crisis, resulting from excessive deposit outflows, the speed of such outflows, and the bank's inability to generate further liquidity, but nonetheless that it could not be clearly established whether it was also FOLTF based on its capital position, ie its solvency, and the SRB followed the ECB conclusions, declaring the bank FOLTF and applying a resolution scheme. **7.44**

The Court refused to depart from its typical standard of review, based on the ideas of (i) limited review and broad discretion in cases of complex economic assessments; and (ii) manifest error of assessment, although completed with a process-based review,[168] with an emphasis on the factual elements relied upon by the SRB.[169] Yet, beyond that, in practice the Court also made a substantive review, appraising the SRB's interpretation of the relevant provisions, especially those establishing the conditions for resolution. **7.45**

---

[162] ibid para 78.
[163] *Accorinti* (n 160) para 82.
[164] *Mamatas and Others v Greece*, App nos 63066/14, 64297/14, and 66106/14 (21 July 2016).
[165] ibid 91–94, 96–100, 101–105, 106 ff.
[166] This demanded a standard of 'prudent and circumspect' investors (*Mamatas* (n 164) 117–18) also a central point in *Accorinti* (n 160) 82, 121, which scrutinized the ECB's being spared from the haircut.
[167] *Mamatas* (n 164) 109–16.
[168] Koen Lenaerts, 'The European Court of Justice and Process-Based Review' (2012) 31 Ybk Eur L 3.
[169] *Tatiana Pérez* (n 45) paras 167–71; *Del Valle* (n 46) paras 107–10; *Eleveté* (n 47) paras 111–15; *Algebris* (n 48) paras 105–109; *Aeris* (n 49) paras 115–19.

7.46 The General Court upheld the SRB's interpretation. It held that a FOLTF finding over a solvent, yet illiquid institution was permitted by (i) the text of the relevant law, which allowed a FOLTF declaration over an entity with the inability or potential inability in the near future to pay debts as they fall due, while 'balance sheet insolvency' was a separate, and independent cause for making such FOLTF declaration; (ii) the context, including the recitals, which supported this interpretation; (iii) the EBA's Guidelines, which referred to a breach of liquidity requirements as a cause for a FOLTF finding, and listed adverse liquidity developments among the relevant factors.[170]

7.47 In light of this framework, the SRB decision properly weighed the relevant factors. First, Banco Popular had breached liquidity requirements, and was unable to restore compliance at the date when the resolution scheme was implemented, ie its liquidity problems were not temporary.[171] Secondly, the SRB correctly concluded that there were no alternatives, such as supervisory or private sector measures. The appellants could not clearly indicate which alternatives were available other than emergency liquidity assistance (ELA), but granting ELA was not within the SRB's power and, although the ECB approved it, it was deemed insufficient to meet the liquidity shortfall and was eventually withdrawn by the Bank of Spain.[172] Early intervention measures were not the competence of the SRB.[173]

7.48 Likewise, the bank's liquidity position had not left enough time for a private transaction. Even the entity's board acknowledged that the bank was failing, and was unable to mobilize enough resources through contingency measures to avoid failure.[174] A capital increase was considered initially, but this was before the liquidity position worsened, and there was no clear evidence that a sale of assets was considered, or could have been effective; there was no time for a merger or acquisition, given the dire situation, and a private sale process had not resulted in any solution.[175] Finally, the Court found no error of assessment in the existence of a public interest in resolution: an ordinary insolvency proceeding would have resulted in greater losses for creditors, and the losses sustained by shareholders and subordinated creditors were outweighed by the preservation of critical functions, and financial stability.[176]

7.49 Likewise, in *ABLV v SRB*[177] the US Department of Treasury through the Financial Crimes Enforcement Network (FinCen) announced a draft measure to designate ABLV Bank as an institution of primary money-laundering concern pursuant to section 311 of the US Patriot Act. After such announcement, the bank was no longer able to make payments in US dollars and this triggered a liquidity crisis which led the ECB to communicate to the bank that, in order to avoid default, it had to have €1 billion in cash by a set deadline in its account with the Latvian Central Bank. The ECB determination of such amount, and the subsequent finding that the bank was failing or likely to fail (FOLTF) for failing to deposit the cash was challenged by the bank as disproportionate. The claim was rejected by the Court, which concluded (i) that the SRB, although not bound by the ECB's assessment, could rely on such assessment; (ii) that a situation of illiquidity could trigger the failing or likely to fail (FOLTF) of

---

[170] See eg *Tatiana Pérez* (n 45) paras 373–75, 384–88; *Del Valle* (n 46) paras 332–34, 341–45; *Eleveté* (n 47) paras 129–31, 141–45.
[171] *Tatiana Pérez* (n 45) paras 379–83; *Del Valle* (n 46) paras 337–40; *Eleveté* (n 47) paras 148–58.
[172] See eg *Tatiana Pérez* (n 45) paras 394–407; *Del Valle* (n 46) paras 368–77; *Eleveté* (n 47) paras 154–58.
[173] *Tatiana Pérez* (n 45) paras 453–54.
[174] ibid paras 367–68; *Del Valle* (n 46) paras 328–29, 362.
[175] *Tatiana Pérez* (n 45) paras 408–19; *Del Valle* (n 46) paras 363–66, 381–401; *Eleveté* (n 47) paras 193–231.
[176] *Tatiana Pérez* (n 45) paras 434–40; *Eleveté* (n 47) paras 239–55.
[177] Case T-280/22 *ABLV Bank v SRB* ECLI:EU:T:2022:429.

a bank (regardless of whether other conditions for a FOLTF assessment, eg insolvency were present); (iii) that the ECB assessment of the short-term liquidity needs of the bank could not be reversed by the court because the FOLTF finding should not be constrained by the regulatory definition of 'liquidity' but by the overall assessment that the entity would, in the near future, be unable to pay its debts or liabilities as they fell due; (iv) that this assessment of facts disregarded whether the reasons giving rise to the illiquidity situation (ie whether the US indictments were legitimate or not); and (v) that in this regard, the appellant had not given evidence of the implausibility of the ECB conclusions.[178]

3.4 Substantive review beyond 'property' (II): cases involving depositors

Given property's evanescence as a substantive right, creditors may prefer more specific substantive protections, especially if they are depositors, who in many jurisdictions are granted preferential rights[179] and are protected as a matter of public policy.[180] A 'deposit' and its 'payability' are legal concepts, which means that courts' role is key to ensure the system's soundness. **7.50**

US cases have considered the scope of protected deposits. In *FDIC v Philadelphia Gear Co* the US Supreme Court had the opportunity to analyse whether a standby letter of credit was an 'insured deposit'.[181] The FDIC's long-standing interpretation had been that a contingent promissory note was not an insured 'deposit' because it represented no hard assets, and thus was not 'money or its equivalent' under federal law, but the Act was not entirely clear, and the creditor was successful before the district and circuit courts.[182] The Supreme Court analysed the Act in light of its historical context and finality: it was adopted 'in the throes of an extraordinary financial crisis', and tried 'to safeguard the hard earnings of individuals against the possibility that bank failures would deprive them of their savings'.[183] Successive amendments had not changed the finality, and the purpose of 'safeguarding assets and 'hard earnings'' was not furthered by treating transactions not involving 'no such surrender of assets or hard earnings to the custody of the bank' as 'money or its equivalent' and extending deposit insurance to them.[184] Nor had Congress overruled the FDIC's long-standing interpretation excluding **7.51**

---

[178] ibid paras 94–95, 101, 104, 108, and 116–24.
[179] See eg art 108 (preferential treatment in insolvency) and BRRD (n 8) art 44 (exclusion from bail-in).
[180] BRRD (n 8) arts 31 and 34.
[181] *FDIC v Philadelphia Gear Corp* 476 US 426 (1986). The standby was opened, the bank was declared insolvent, and FDIC (receiver) rejected payment of the standby. The respondent sued the FDIC, alleging that the standby letter of credit was an insured 'deposit'.
[182] Title 12 USC s 1813(l)(1) provides: 'The term "deposit" means—(1) the unpaid balance of money or its equivalent received or held by a bank in the usual course of business and for which it has given or is obligated to give credit, either conditionally or unconditionally, to a commercial . . . account, or which is evidenced by . . . a letter of credit or a traveler's check on which the bank is primarily liable . . . Philadelphia Gear Corp successfully argued before the lower courts that the standby was a "deposit" because the bank was primarily liable, and the promissory note evidenced the receipt by the bank of "money or its equivalent". *FDIC v Philadelphia Gear* (n 181).
[183] *FDIC v Philadelphia Gear* (n 181).
[184] Philadelphia Gear, which now seeks to collect deposit insurance, surrendered absolutely nothing to the bank. The letter of credit is for Philadelphia Gear's benefit, but the bank relied upon Orion to meet the obligations of the letter of credit, and made no demands upon Philadelphia Gear. Nor, more importantly, did Orion surrender any assets unconditionally to the bank.

standbys,[185] which despite not being contained in a regulation, deserved 'a great deal of deference'.[186]

7.52 In the EU, where there is still no single European Deposit Insurance Scheme (EDIS) consistency of concepts is key to grant a uniform protection. In *Peter Paul* the Court of Justice of the EU considered the potential liability of the German government for its alleged failure promptly to implement the Deposit Guarantee Directive (94/19, later reformed in 2014), which, the plaintiffs argued, led to German supervisory authorities' inadequate supervision of the bank (which was not subject to any DIS system). The Court held that deposit insurance systems did not grant depositors a *specific* right to have their governments adopt supervisory measures,[187] and EU DGS rules did not impose an obligation to supervise (indemnification, if any, was through the deposit insurance system[188]). EU rules did not oppose German law's position that supervisory measures were exercised in the *general* interest, not in depositors' *particular* interest, and thus imposed obligations of means, not results.[189]

7.53 Subsequently, in the *Icesave* case, the EFTA Court[190] decided over extraordinary measures adopted by Iceland during the 2007–2009 crisis, which left accounts opened by the Dutch and British branches of the Icelandic bank Landsbanski without coverage.[191] The EFTA Court held that, in contrast with the amended directive (in 2009) which established an obligation of *ends*,[192] the (applicable) 1994 Directive provided an obligation of *means* and of supervision.[193] More surprising was the finding that foreign depositors were not discriminated, despite *only domestic* deposits were transferred to the 'good bank' (New Landsbanski). For the Court, non-discrimination was restricted to the absence of a difference in treatment of depositors 'by the guarantee itself and the way it uses its funds', and 'the transfer of domestic deposits—whether it leads in general to unequal treatment or not—does not fall within the scope of the nondiscrimination principle as set out in the Directive'.[194] Thus, by considering recovery and compensation measures as being 'outside deposit insurance' a government could, in practice, discriminate between depositors. In the *Aresbank* case, also decided by the EFTA court,[195] a Spanish bank's loan to Landsbanski was not treated by the latter as a deposit (not entered as such in the books, nor were special documents issued, nor were premiums paid to the DGS[196]) and would have been an interbank deposit ineligible for repayment. And yet, when the Icelandic financial supervisory authority (FME) set up a bridge bank to take over 'of the branches of Landsbanki in Iceland due to deposits from financial undertakings' etc., the EFTA Court held that it should be transferred to the bridge bank.

---

[185] *FDIC v Philadelphia Gear* (n 181): Committee Reports on the 1960 amendments likewise give no indication that the amendments' phrasing was meant to effect any fundamental changes in the definition of deposit; those Reports state only that the changes are intended to bring into harmony the definitions of 'deposit' used for purposes of deposit insurance with those used in reports of condition, and that the FDIC's rules and regulations are to be incorporated into the new definition.

[186] *FDIC v Philadelphia Gear* (n 181) citing *Chevron v Natural Resources Defense Council Inc* 467 US 837 (1984).

[187] Case C-222/02 *Peter Paul and Others v Germany* ECLI:EU:C:2004:606.

[188] ibid paras 30–31.

[189] ibid paras 40–47.

[190] Case E-16/11 *EFTA Surveillance Authority v Iceland* (28 January 2013).

[191] ibid paras 27–29. Since they were opened through bank branches, they were subject to the Icelandic deposit guarantee scheme.

[192] *EFTA Surveillance Authority v Iceland* (n 190) paras 138–40.

[193] EEA states had to introduce a DGS and fulfil certain supervisory tasks, but not to ensure the payment of aggregate deposits in all circumstances. See *EFTA Surveillance Authority v Iceland* (n 190) para 135. A state guarantee would be contrary to state aid rules and would promote moral hazard. ibid paras 165, 167.

[194] *EFTA Surveillance Authority v Iceland* (n 190) paras 209, 216.

[195] Case E-17/11 *Aresbank SA and Landsbankinn hf, Fjármálaeftirlitið (the Financial Supervisory Authority) and Iceland* (22 November 2012).

[196] ibid paras 47.

In *Kantarev v Balgarska Narodna Banka* and *BT v Balgarska Narodna Banka*, the Court of **7.54** Justice, in preliminary references made by Bulgarian courts, as a result of the crisis of KTB Bank analysed the concept of 'unavailable deposit', which triggers the obligation of repayment, and the constraints imposed by Bulgarian authorities.[197] In *Kantarev* Bulgarian law subjected the 'unavailability' of deposits, and their reimbursement to the bank's insolvency and/or the withdrawal of its licence, which considerably delayed the repayment, and, in the appellant's view, was contrary to the DGS Directive, and gave rise to the state's liability. According to the Court of Justice:

> [T]he necessary and sufficient condition for determining whether a deposit that is due and payable has become unavailable is that, in the view of the relevant competent authority, a credit institution appears to be unable for the time being, for reasons which are directly related to its financial circumstances, to repay the deposit and to have no current prospect of being able to do so. In addition ...... determination must be made, by that relevant competent authority, 'as soon as possible' and 'no later than five working days after first becoming satisfied [that the credit institution in question] has failed to repay deposits which are due and payable'.[198]

Therefore, 'the determination that deposits of a credit institution have become unavailable **7.55** cannot depend on the insolvency of the credit institution in question or on the withdrawal of its banking licence'.[199] This was contrary to the provision's text and purpose, which was 'both to protect depositors and to ensure the stability of the banking system, by preventing massive withdrawal of deposits not only from a credit institution in difficulties but also from healthy institutions following a loss of public confidence in the soundness of the banking system'.[200] Thus, it was imperative that the DGS intervened within a 'very short period' as soon as a credit institution's deposits became unavailable.[201] Furthermore, the 'unavailability of deposits' must be determined by the authorities' express act, because it is expressly stated by the norm, as such unavailability starts the clock for reimbursement,[202] and because clarity of information is essential in the interest of deposit(or) protection and financial stability.[203] Such 'unavailability' could not be deduced from other acts (eg placing a bank under administration) which do not entail the kind of assessment about the unavailability of deposits. Nor could it be subjected to conditions such as the account holder's making an unsuccessful request.[204]

On the issue of state liability, the Court tempered its doctrine in *Paul and Others*, holding **7.56** that the lack of an obligation of results did not preclude the possibility of a state liability for incorrect transposition or implementation of a directive.[205] Although it was for the national court to assess the state's liability, the Court of Justice provided the main elements for such assessment. First, the DGS Directive had direct effect, since:

---

[197] Case C-571/16 *Nikolay Kantarev v Balgarska Narodna BankaKantarev* ECLI:EU:C:2018:807; *BT v Balgarska Narodna Banka* (n 136).
[198] *Kantarev* (n 197) paras 49–50.
[199] ibid para 51.
[200] ibid para 56.
[201] ibid para 57.
[202] ibid para 72.
[203] ibid paras 74–75.
[204] ibid paras 79–87.
[205] ibid para 89.

[B]y stating that the relevant authority must determine whether deposits are unavailable as soon as possible and in any event no later than five working days after first becoming satisfied that a credit institution has failed to repay deposits which are due and payable, that provision lays down an unconditional and sufficiently precise obligation with which it is for the BNB, the authority designated for determining whether deposits are unavailable, to ensure compliance within the course of its responsibilities,[206]

7.57 Also, it conferred *individual rights*.[207] Secondly, to assess the existence of a 'sufficiently serious breach' of EU law, the national court could decide, but with limited latitude,[208] and suggested that the circumstances seemed to indicate the existence of a breach.[209]

7.58 *BT v Balgarska Narodna Banka* was also a case of state liability, involving similar facts. The Court clarified that, despite ruling in *Kantarev* that an incorrect transposition of the DGS Directive could give rise to state liability, the directive did not cover non-deposit liabilities, ie damages for the late payment or incorrect supervision were not covered by the DGS.[210] Yet, the text and intent of the directive precluded national legislation *or* contract clauses (eg the conditions of participation in the DGS) that subjected deposit repayment to the withdrawal of the bank's licence, and/or the depositor's request of repayment. Reiterating *Kantarev*, repayment was triggered when deposits became 'unavailable', and this affected *all* the deposits at the specific institution.[211] In the meantime the EBA, after an investigation procedure of the specific case adopted some recommendations,[212] which concluded that the national authorities had not complied with the directive, by failing to make a declaration of unavailability within five days, *but also concluded* (possibly to avoid a legal limbo) that, absent such declaration, the decision to place the bank under special supervision and suspend payment obligations *amounted to* such declaration. The Court considered that, although the EBA's recommendations were not a 'binding' act,[213] national courts had to 'take them into consideration with a view to resolving the disputes submitted to them',[214] and thus the Court could evaluate their validity. On the substantive issue, the problems, very well summarized by AG Campos Sánchez-Bordona, were that *Kantarev* had clarified that the process of claiming DGS compensation is quite mechanistic: first, there is an express declaration by state authorities; second, the national authority must decide which deposits are to be repaid, a decision that affects *all* the deposits of the credit institution; third, the repayment takes place.[215] Thus, one could not *assimilate* another act, eg declaration of insolvency, withdrawal of licence, or

---

[206] ibid para 100.
[207] ibid paras 101–103.
[208] ibid para 106.
[209] ibid para 109: the supervisory measures taken by the BNB show that it harboured doubts, in the light of the financial situation of KTB Bank, concerning the ability of KTB Bank to repay the deposits quickly. In addition, the measures taken by the BNB for the suspension of KTB Bank's payments and transactions prevented KTB Bank from repaying the deposits.
[210] *BT v Balgarska Narodna Banka* (n 136) paras 49–60.
[211] ibid paras 61–75.
[212] EBA, 'Recommendation to the Bulgarian National Bank and Bulgarian Deposit Insurance Fund on action necessary to comply with Directive 94/19/EC EBA/REC/2014/02' (17 October 2014) https://www.eba.europa.eu/sites/default/files/documents/10180/856039/40ad5eae-beef-4f55-a7d0-272b9cf38586/EBA%20REC%202014%2002%20%28Recommendation%20to%20the%20BNB%20and%20BDIF%29.pdf?retry=1 (accessed 21 September 2022).
[213] *BT v Balgarska Narodna Banka* (n 210) para 79, referring to TFEU, art 288(4) and Regulation No 1093/2010, art 17(3), as well as to its previous case law, Case C-16/16 P *Belgium v Commission* ECLI:EU:C:2018:79, para 26.
[214] *BT v Balgarska Narodna Banka* (n 213) para 80.
[215] Case C-501/18, *BT v Balgarska Narodna Banka*, Opinion of AG Campos Sánchez-Bordona ECLI:EU:C:2020:729, 39–63 (*BT v Balgarska Narodna Banka*, AG Opinion).

suspension of payments to the declaration of unavailability.[216] The Court agreed, declaring that part of EBA recommendation invalid.[217]

3.5 Substantive review beyond 'property' (III): EU state aid cases' implications for shareholders and creditors

If depositors are type of creditors who enjoy special protection, shareholders and ordinary creditors are the ones who are subjected to burden-sharing. They are thus essential, if not willing, actors in making the system work. This is tricky. Ordinary creditors, absent a depositor privilege, may rank *pari passu* with depositors, and subordinated creditors or shareholders also benefit from safeguards. In the EU, before resolution frameworks were adopted, this balance between burden-sharing and safeguards was stricken in the EU Commission Banking Communication 2013, which applied the framework on EU state aid. Apart from issues of justiciability and substantive protection under 'property rights' they raise other relevant issues, as seen below. **7.59**

An example is the Grand Chamber judgment in *Commission v Italy*, also known as the *Banca Tercas* case,[218] where the issue was the imputability to the Italian state of acts undertaken by the Fondo Interbancario di Tutela dei Depositi (FITD) a private law-based consortium of banks established in 1987 to guarantee their members' bank deposits. Participation to the fund is mandatory under national law. Due to Banca Tercas' financial difficulties, a decision was made by the FITD, and authorized by Bank of Italy, to intervene Banca Tercas with an injection of funds to cover certain exposures, followed by a write-down of 'old', and issuance of 'new' capital.[219] The Commission, however, declared the intervention a case of illegal state aid, which was contested by the Italian government, aided by Bank of Italy. **7.60**

The General Court held that the measures were not an illegal state aid, because the FITD intervention was not attributable to the Italian state.[220] When the measure is adopted by a private entity the Commission is subject to a stricter standard to demonstrate that it was adopted under the actual influence or control of public authorities than in case of measures by a public undertaking,[221] and the Commission did not satisfy that standard.[222] and also failed to demonstrate that the intervention concerned resources 'controlled' by the Italian state, and therefore at its disposal.[223] On appeal the Court of Justice confirmed the General Court's ruling. It held that, even in case of aid by public entities, the Commission must establish that there was actual involvement of public authorities in the decision to grant aid.[224] In contrast, in cases of aid by a private undertaking, the state lacks the more obvious way (ownership) to exercise control. The authorization by Bank of Italy was insufficient to establish **7.61**

---

[216] ibid paras 118–19.
[217] *BT v Balgarska Narodna Banka* (n 214) paras 99–101.
[218] Joined Cases T-98/16, T-196/16 and T-198/16, *Italy, Banca Popolare di Bari SpA (formerly Banca Tercas), Fondo intercbancario di tutela die depositi v Commission* ECLI:EU:T:2019:167; Case C-425/19 P *Commission v Italy, Banca Popolare di Bari SpA (formerly Banca Tercas), Fondo intercbancario di tutela die depositi* ECLI:EU:C:2021:154.
[219] Case T-198/16 *Banca Tercas* (n 218) paras 19–20.
[220] ibid.
[221] ibid paras 68–69, 89–91.
[222] ibid paras 114–31.
[223] ibid paras 139–60.
[224] C-425/19 P *Banca Tercas* (n 218) 62.

influence, because, conversely, there was no legal mechanisms to *force* the FITD to extend aid, and its indications to reach a 'balanced agreement' could not be read as an instruction.[225] The Court dismissed the Commission's argument that such a strict standard of attribution facilitated the circumvention of the bank resolution framework, by making it impossible to consider a DGS intervention as state aid. This was a case-by-case exercise.[226] The Court also upheld the General Court's rejection of the Commission's argument that the FITD used 'state resources': FITD funds were private, the intervention was voluntary, and Bank of Italy reviewed the measure's compliance with the law, not its appropriateness or opportunity.[227]

7.62 In the *Banca delle Marche* case[228] the General Court dismissed the complaint against the Commission by shareholders and subordinated creditors of Banca delle Marche, an Italian bank that was placed under extraordinary administration on account due to 'serious ... deficiencies and irregularities' and then resolved under national resolution rules implementing the BRRD in November 2015 through a bridge bank tool. The Commission initiated of its own motion a preliminary examination of the support measures by FITD in favour of Banca Tercas and Banca delle Marche itself. Later, the Commission drew attention to the possible existence of state aid in the case of Banca delle Marche, and requested Italian authorities to provide it with updated information and to refrain from implementing any FITD measures receiving a decision from the Commission. After a second attempt to give support to the bank by the FITD, the Commission stressed to Italian authorities that using the DGS to recapitalize a bank was subject to the state aid rules, and thus Bank of Italy had no other choice than initiate a resolution procedure, notifying its draft decision to the Commission, noting that the FITD had been unable to recapitalize the bank without a 'prior positive assessment by the Commission' with regard to state aid rules. Shareholders alleged that, by means of unlawful instructions sent to Italian authorities, the Commission had prevented the Banca delle Marche's rescue/recapitalisation and sought non-contractual liability. The Court dismissed the applicants' action on the ground that they have not established a causal link between the Commission's allegedly unlawful conduct and the alleged damage, with the result that the conditions for the European Union to incur non-contractual liability are not fulfilled.

4 Procedural safeguards: 'Arbitrary and capricious', 'good administration' and judicial protection

7.63 Given the limited practical effect of substantive safeguards, shareholders and creditors have often relied on procedural safeguards, which present specific challenges for banks. These have crystallized under the 'arbitrary and capricious' standard in the US (4.1) while they are still evolving in the EU (4.2) and have been subject to limited case law in international investment arbitration (4.3).

---

[225] Case T-198/16 *Banca Tercas* (n 218) paras 114, 115–19, 127; Case C-425/19 P *Banca Tercas* (n 218) paras 74–76. The Court rejected the application of doctrines such as the 'emanation of the state', in case law on state liability, to the context of state aid. Case C-425/19 P *Banca Tercas* (n 218) para 77.
[226] Case C-425/19 P *Banca Tercas* (n 218) para 78.
[227] ibid para 98; Case T-198/16 *Banca Tercas* (n 218) 133–61.
[228] Case T-635/19 *Fondazione Cassa di Risparmio di Pesaro and Others v Commission* ECLI:EU:T:2021:394.

4.1 US safeguards under the 'arbitrary and capricious' standard

In the US the judicial review of bank crisis management actions is based on the 'due process' clause of the Constitution, and, more specifically (and based on recent case law) on the Administrative Procedure Act (APA). In *Fahey v Malone* the Supreme Court dealt with the due process allegation that the conservator was appointed without an ex ante hearing. The Court held that:

7.64

> This is a drastic procedure. But the delicate nature of the institution and the impossibility of preserving credit during an investigation has made it an almost invariable custom to apply supervisory authority in this summary manner. It is a heavy responsibility, to be exercised with disinterestedness and restraint, but, in the light of the history and customs of banking, we cannot say it is unconstitutional.[229]

In the specific case, the hearing was prevented by the plaintiffs' injunction, and the solution could not consist in letting the entity (S&L) continue its activity 'undisciplined and unchecked';[230] nor could it be presumed that an administrative (ie, not judicial) hearing would not be fair and impartial, or that the administrative hearing would foreclose all form of judicial review.[231]

7.65

Later case law refined the analysis, based on subsequent Supreme Court caselaw on the standard of review for non-regulatory, ie supervisory or crisis management actions, such as *Citizens to Preserve Overton Park*[232] and similar cases,[233] as well as the APA 'arbitrary and capricious' standard. This is generally a limited review but may be a *de novo* review 'when the action is adjudicatory in nature and the agency factfinding procedures are inadequate' and 'when issues that were not before the agency are raised in a proceeding to enforce non adjudicatory agency action'.[234]

7.66

The matter was raised during the 1980s' savings and loan (S&L) crisis, and the interventions by the Federal Home Loan Bank Board (FHLBB), the Office of Thrift Supervision (OTS), which succeeded it, and the Federal Savings and Loan Insurance Corporation (FSLIC, equivalent to the FDIC for S&L) typically, appointed as receiver. Some district courts saw the need for *de novo* review, to give plaintiffs the opportunity to present evidence outside the administrative record,[235] but the Circuits clarified that 'classic' standards would be applicable. In *Guaranty Savings & Loan Association v FHLBB*[236] the plaintiff, an S&L which engaged in an expansionist strategy with brokered deposits, and risky loans for real estate acquisitions was required by the FHLBB to establish adequate reserves for these loans. This resulted in negative equity, but the FHLBB appointment of the FSLIC as receiver was challenged by the S&L. The Circuit Court referred to the APA's 'arbitrary and capricious' and to *Overton Park*

7.67

---

[229] *Fahey v Malone* (n 18) 254.
[230] ibid para 255.
[231] ibid para 257.
[232] *Citizens to Preserve Overton Park v Volpe* (1971) 401 US 402.
[233] See eg *Camp v Pitts* 411 US 138 (1973).
[234] *Overton v Volpe* (n 232) with reference to 5 USC s 706(2)(F).
[235] *Fidelity Savings & Loan Association v Federal Home Loan Bank Bd* 540 F Supp 1374, 1377–78 (ND Cal 1982), rev'd on other grounds, 689 F 2d 803 (9th Cir) cert denied 461 US 914 (1983), 103 S Ct 1893, 77 L Ed 2d 283; *Telegraph Savings & Loan Association v Federal Savings & Loan Insurance Corp* 564 F Supp 862, 868–70 (ND Ill 1981), aff'd sub nom *Telegraph Savings & Loan Association v Schilling* 703 F 2d 1019 (7th Cir 1983), cert denied, 464 US 992, 104 S Ct 484, 78 L Ed 2d 681.
[236] *Guaranty Savings & Loan Association v FHLBB and FSLIC* 794 F 2d 1339 (8th Cir 1986).

as the standard of review,[237] and rejected that a provision in the Home Owner's Loan Act, indicating that courts would review the decision to appoint a receiver 'upon the merits',[238] should defined the scope of review. Then, absent a definition of the *scope* of review, the court should limit review to *the administrative record*, without any *de novo* proceeding.[239] The 'arbitrary and capricious' *standard* required considering the relevant factors and whether there had been a 'clear error of judgment', and that despite the fact inquiry must be careful, the review should be 'narrow'; and, on this basis, the Court held that the decision to appoint a receiver was not arbitrary or capricious.[240]

7.68 A similar approach can be found in *Woods v FHLBB* decided the year after.[241] Again a S&L's expansion through brokered deposits and real estate investments was followed by supervisory intervention (an 'adverse rating report', followed by a special examination, followed by a 'cease and desist' order for 'unsafe and unsound' practices) and the appointment of the FSLIC as receiver,[242] which was challenged. The Circuit Court on appeal relied on *Guaranty*, and the Supreme Court precedents used there, to hold that, absent an explicit indication, the scope of review should be limited to the administrative record, and not comprise a *de novo* review, and the standard of review should be the (limited) 'arbitrary and capricious' standard under the APA. The Court added that this conclusion, drawn in *Guaranty*, was supported by the 'strong congressional intent for swift, effective regulatory action'[243] which favoured limited review. The Court put this in the context of the *superiority* of the public over private interest, and the nature of shareholders' rights as 'limited':

> Woods' and Western's private interests are obviously subordinate to those of the government. When Woods acquired Western, he was aware of the extensive regulatory system and the possibility of continuous, in-depth supervision by Bank Board examiners.[244]

7.69 In *Franklin Savings Association v OTS*[245] the plaintiff, a S&L association, expanded its liabilities side, through brokered deposits, and its asset side, through investments in mortgage-backed securities (MBS), collateralized mortgage obligations (CMOs) and other complex and speculative assets,[246] off-balance sheet transactions (with eerie resemblance to the practices that later led to the Great Financial Crisis). The OTS repeatedly expressed its concerns, and then made specific findings of Franklin's 'unsafe and unsound condition', and appointed the Resolution Trust Corporation (RTC) as receiver. Franklin challenged the decision, and the district court allowed the entity to submit evidence outside the administrative record, and develop facts about the statutory grounds for the appointment of the receiver, characterized

---

[237] *Guaranty Savings & Loan Association* (n 236) with reference to *San Marino Savings and Loan Association v Federal Home Loan Bank Board* 605 F Supp 502, 508 (CD Cal 1984) and *Washington Federal Savings and Loan Association v Federal Home Loan Bank Board* 526 F Supp 343, 350 (ND Ohio 1981).

[238] 12 USC s 1464(d)(6)(A) provided that, in the event of the appointment of a receiver the S&L could bring an action 'and the court shall *upon the merits* dismiss such action or direct the Board to remove such (...) receiver' (emphasis added).

[239] *Guaranty Savings & Loan Association* (n 236).

[240] ibid.

[241] *Woods v FHLBB* 826 F 2d 1400 (5th Cir 1987). The legislative intent was that mandated by 12 USC s 1464(d)(6)(A) (again, the Home Owner Loan Act 1933).

[242] *Woods v FHLBB* (n 241).

[243] ibid, also citing its previous opinion in *Alliance Federal Savings and Loan Association v Federal Home Loan Bank Board (FHLBB)* 782 F 2d 490, 493, modified on other grounds, 790 F 2d 34 (5th Cir 1986).

[244] *Woods v FHLBB* (n 241).

[245] *Franklin Savings Association v OTS* 934 F 2d 1127 (8th Cir 1991).

[246] These included deeply discounted securities, reverse repurchase agreements, long call and put options and strips (both interest only and principal only), derivative securities (entitle the holder to receive only part of the mortgage payments), and junk bonds.

the case as 'a dispute over accounting practices', and held that the director lacked a factual basis for its decision, and ordered the removal of the receiver.[247] The Circuit Court provided one of the most clear and detailed analyses of both the *scope* of review, ie the evidence that the court examines, and the *standard* of review, ie, how it examines the evidence.

On the *scope* of review, the relevant Act (Financial Institutions Reform, Recovery, and Enforcement Act of 1989 (FIRREA)) included no explicit mention of the scope of review, but the court relied on *Overton Park* and other cases to hold that *ex novo* review was pertinent only if one of the exceptions in those cases applied, eg where the administrative record fails to disclose the factors considered by the agency,[248] where it is necessary for background information or for determining whether the agency considered all relevant factors including contrary evidence,[249] or to explain technical terms or complex subject matter.[250] Unlike *Overton*, where review was based on limited evidence,[251] in this case the record was detailed and voluminous. FIRREA indicated that the receiver's appointment would be based on the OTS director's 'opinion', which meant that the director should 'review only such information as he deems necessary or desirable to enable him to arrive at an informed and fair opinion'; otherwise the Act's purpose of 'prompt' action would be defeated. The record should permit the court to determine whether the director had a 'rational basis' to appoint the receiver,[252] and if there were elements missing, which were considered by the director, they should be included, but no extended review should result. The Court concluded that the evidence was sufficient to form an informed opinion. **7.70**

On the *standard* of review, the Court relied on *Guaranty* and *Woods*, and the APA's 'arbitrary and capricious'. Overturning the district court's finding, the Circuit held that, on the assets' side, the district court had failed to understand the director's concern with Franklin's lack of diversification, which was not remedied by more risk monitoring or limited divestment; and, on the liabilities side, that the district court, by focusing on the (low) cost of funding for the entity, failed to understand the director's actual concern about liquidity risk.[253] Thus, given that the concept of 'unsafe and unsound' practices is relatively open, and subject to evolution, the authorities' judgment, especially those of 'predictive' nature, about the institution's risk of failure should be granted deference. On the ground of 'capital depletion', the Circuit court held that there was ample evidence that Franklin had continued distributing dividends and paying bonuses despite orders to stop growing, and that it had dismissed OTS warnings. Thus, the district court had erred in law by relying on Franklin's accounting methods, instead of the OTS's: its role was to check whether the decision, within the agency's area of expertise, was supported by evidence, and fell within the bounds of reason.[254] The same happened with **7.71**

---

[247] *Franklin Sav Association v Director of Office of Thrift Supervision* 742 F Supp 1089 (D Kan 1990), citing *Collie v FHLBB* 642 F Supp 1147 (ND Ill 1986). This was called a 'hybrid standard of review' by the Circuit court.
[248] *Franklin Savings v OTS* (n 245) citing *Overton v Volpe* (n 232) 825.
[249] *Franklin Savings v OTS* (n 245), citing *Thompson v United States Dept of Labor* (1989) 885 F 2d 551, 555 (9th Cir).
[250] *Franklin Savings v OTS* (n 245), citing *Animal Defense Council v Hodel* 867 F 2d 1244, 1244 (9th Cir 1989) and *Animal Defense Council v Hodel* 840 F 2d 1432, 1436 (9th Cir 1988).
[251] *Franklin Savings v OTS* (n 245). Overton revolved around a statutory prohibition against building highways through a public park where a feasible and prudent alternate route exists. The Secretary authorized the construction of a six-lane highway through a public park. The Secretary failed to make any factual findings as to why he believed there was no feasible and prudent alternate route. The Supreme Court held formal findings were not required (...) We believe Overton is thus distinguishable and does not dictate an expanded scope of review.
[252] *Franklin Savings v OTS* (n 245) 1127. To require the director to have reviewed and relied on all working papers, synopses of all conversations, and other minutiae, would defeat FIRREA's objective requirement of prompt supervisory action.
[253] *Franklin Savings v OTS* (n 245).
[254] ibid.

other grounds. Thus, by dismissing OTS' accounting practices as 'too conservative' and accepting Franklin's, the district had failed to understand the basic idea of review:

> The proper inquiry under the arbitrary and capricious standard is not which expert is more impressive, or even if the reviewing court agrees with a particular view over another. Rather, the appropriate inquiry of the reviewing court is whether a reasonable person considering the matters on the agency's table could find a rational basis to arrive at the same judgment as made by the director.[255]

7.72 The Circuit thus concluded, in strong terms, that there was clear evidence of a mismanaged entity, identified by the OTS, which was the entity supposed to exercise expertise, while courts had to show deference, in accordance with congressional intent,[256] and that the district court had failed to understand this in exercising full, or *de novo* review.

4.2 EU process review and procedural safeguards

7.73 Compared with the US the 'procedural' standard of review of crisis management measures in EU law is still at a very early stage, but nonetheless presents many similarities. We must differentiate between the situation before the *Banco Popular* cases, and after.

7.74 Before *Banco Popular* some ECtHR cases,[257] such as *Credit and Industrial Bank v Czech Republic*[258] and *Capital Bank v Bulgaria*,[259] focused on *procedural* safeguards. Facing a financial crisis, Czech and Bulgarian authorities adopted extraordinary intervention measures over individual banks, (Credit and Industrial Bank and Capital Bank) to mitigate insolvency's spill-over effects. Capital Bank was declared insolvent, deprived of its licence, and wound up, and applicable rules rendered the intervention unchallengeable before the Courts.[260] Credit and Industrial Bank's board was replaced with an insolvency administrator appointed by administrative authorities, which meant that the former directors/representatives lacked standing to lodge an appeal on behalf of the bank.[261] In both cases, the ECtHR focused on procedural rights[262] and concluded that there had been a breach. In *Credit and Industrial Bank*, the deprivation of representative powers had rendered review practically impossible, as the decision was adopted without the presence of the bank, and was not subject to appeal.[263] In *Capital Bank*, the decision had been notified after its adoption, but Courts

---

[255] ibid.
[256] ibid. 'The ultimate question underlying this dispute is: Who is vested with the responsibility for determining the quality of assets, the proper levels and types of assets and liabilities, appropriate accounting standards, and the numerous other questions relating to the safe and sound condition of a financial institution? Congress has answered this question by enacting FIRREA, which clearly vests this responsibility in the director.'
[257] See eg Marco Lamandini, David Ramos, and Javier Solana, 'The European Central Bank (ECB) Powers as a Catalyst for Change in EU Law (Part 2): SSM, SRM and Fundamental Rights' (2016) 23 Col J of Eur L 199.
[258] *CME Czech Republic BV v The Czech Republic* (2003) Award by Wolfgang Kühn, Stephen Schwebel, and Ian Brownlie under UNCITRAL Rules.
[259] *Capital Bank AD v Bulgaria*, App no 49429/99 (24 November 2005).
[260] *Credit v Czech Republic* (n 258) 69; *Capital Ban AD v Bulgaria* (n 259) 27–33.
[261] *Credit v Czech Republic* (n 258) 58.
[262] The applicants challenged the measures on grounds of a breach of ECHR, art 6 (access to court) and art 1 of Protocol 1 (right to property), but in *Credit v Czech Republic* (n 258) the arguments were the same, and the ECtHR declined to examine the 'property' claim after finding a breach of art 6. In *Capital Bank v Bulgaria* (n 259) the ECtHR used a procedural approach for both art 6, art 1 of Protocol 1.
[263] *Credit v Czech Republic* (n 258) 69–72. According to the ECtHR's findings, in the process of review envisaged in the procedural laws, the courts could not examine the substantive reasons for the imposition and extension of compulsory administration. The procedure was exclusively written, with no hearing, and no possibility of opposition by the bank's management.

had not acted as 'courts with full jurisdiction'.[264] Moreover, the hearing before the Central Bank, an administrative body, could not replace the lack of judicial review.[265] Interestingly, in *Capital Bank*, the ECtHR found the measures disproportionate in spite of the peculiarities of the 'banking business' and the public interest in financial stability: the need for urgency could justify stricter time limits, not absence of review, and the need to avoid panic did not justify the absence of a hearing on the withdrawal of the licence, which was adopted months after the bank was intervened.[266]

In the Banco Popular cases the General Court had to deal with practically all kinds of procedural claims, which will shape EU procedural safeguards in bank crisis management for years to come. **7.75**

When discussing its standard of review the Court refused to depart from its case law on 'complex assessments', which focuses on the existence of a 'manifest error' or misuse of powers,[267] but added that this standard required the court also to examine the accuracy, reliability, and consistency of the SRB's evidence, ie a 'process-based review', although leaving the appellant the burden to produce evidence that made the SRB's factual assessment appear *implausible*.[268] **7.76**

An important part of the decision to put the entity in resolution was the valuation process. This was composed of a valuation prepared by the SRB on 5 June 2017 under Article 20(5)(a) SRMR, to determine whether the conditions for resolution were met (valuation 1), and another valuation prepared by an appointed independent expert on 6 June 2017 (Valuation 2). The General Court rejected the appellants' argument that Valuation 1 was not carried out by an independent person as required by the SRMR as a general rule, holding that the urgency of the situation enabled the SRB to carry the valuation itself, and that such valuation was rendered obsolete (and could thus be 'trumped') by the ECB's FOLTF assessment on 6 June 2017, which relied on more updated information on deposit withdrawals.[269] The Court also dismissed all the allegations,[270] including about the expert's alleged lack of independence,[271] the methodology used, which, the Court confirmed, was based on a correct methodology,[272] conducted under important uncertainty and time constraints,[273] and yet compliant with applicable technical criteria (which the Court discussed in extensive detail[274]). The Court also found that it was 'reasonable, prudent and realistic' despite the divergence between scenarios, which was not that large (7 per cent of BPE's balance sheet; also, the divergence between scenarios resulted from a category-by-category approach for each class of assets/liabilities), or with Valuation 1, which purpose was different, ie to determine the conditions of resolution.[275] In any event, the valuation is supposed to provide technical information to the authority, not to dictate the action that it should follow. **7.77**

---

[264] *Capital Bank v Bulgaria* (n 259) 109, 135.
[265] ibid 105–109, 134–35.
[266] ibid 113, 137.
[267] *Tatiana Pérez* (n 45) 167–69; *Del Valle* (n 46) 107–108; *Eleveté* (n 47) 111–12; *Algebris* (n 48) 105–106; *Aeris* (n 169) 115–16.
[268] *Tatiana Pérez* (n 45) 170–71; *Del Valle* (n 46) 109–10; *Eleveté* (n 47) 114–15; *Algebris* (n 48) 108–109; *Aeris* (n 49) 118–19. For a similar conclusion compare also *ABLV v SRB* (n 184) paras 94 and 116–24.
[269] *Tatiana Pérez* (n 45) 562–73; *Del Valle* (n 46) 263–67; *Eleveté* (n 47) 293–303.
[270] See eg *Tatiana Pérez* (n 45) 576–620; *Aeris* (n 49) 602–68.
[271] *Eleveté* (n 47) 305–27.
[272] ibid 331–45.
[273] ibid 348–53.
[274] ibid 354–93.
[275] ibid 394–411.

7.78 The appellants' argument that the SRB had not conducted an ex post definitive valuation, as required by Article 20(11) SRMR had already been rejected in the *Aeris* and *Algebris* cases by the General Court and the Court of Justice, which accepted the SRB's opinion that the valuation would have served no practical purpose, and that it was not required by the SRMR, since Article 20(12) mentions the valuation if bail-in, bridge bank, or asset separation tools are used, but does not mention the 'sale of business' tool; the logic being that, in case that tool is used, the right valuation is the one resulting from the market price, in a lawful tender procedure.[276] The General Court also rejected the appellants' objections to the tender process (Banco Popular was sold to Santander for €1), holding that the process was transparent, the SRB addressed the five entities that had shown an interest in the sale.[277] The process sought to strike a balance between the sale procedural requirements and resolution objectives. Any deviations from the procedure (eg admitting Santander's offer even after the deadline set) were justified by resolution objectives (the urgency of the situation, and the need to avoid an uncontrolled insolvency, and the danger to financial stability), resulting in an adjudication to Banco Santander for €1, as it was the only entity who made an offer.[278]

7.79 The Court also rejected the allegations concerning the duty to state reasons. The SRB was not obliged to give reasons on the sale process, since this was conducted by the Spanish FROB, nor on the price, which resulted from a competitive process.[279] The SRB justified thoroughly the conditions of resolution and the choice of tool,[280] and provided a copy of the resolution scheme, which was redacted in the confidential parts.[281] Since the SRB justified the alternative chosen, it was not obliged to consider any hypothetical alternative, eg a segregation accompanied by liquidity provision, as suggested by one appellant, which did not substantiate why such solution would have been viable, or how it reconciled the minimal destruction of value (which was its aim) with fulfilling resolution objectives, such as the continuity of critical functions (something that the sale of business did[282]). The Court also dismissed the allegations that the Commission simply endorsed the SRB's decision, without giving its own reasons: the law only requires the Commission either to endorse the SRB decision or to object to its discretionary aspects and, in any event, the duty to give reasons must be appraised in light of the circumstances of the case, which include the urgency of the situation.[283]

7.80 The General Court also considered (and rejected) the allegations concerning the breach of procedural safeguards. The appellants alleged that they were deprived of their right to be heard by both the SRMR provisions, and the SRB. On the SRMR provisions on resolution tools, the Court held that the measures adopted under these are *addressed* to the bank, although shareholders may be negatively affected (eg by a write-down of instruments[284]). Then, their right of audience is not absolute, but may be limited if justified by objectives of general interest, such as those protected by resolution.[285] In particular, resolution requires

---

[276] Cases C-874/19 P *Aeris* EU:C:2021:1040; and C-934/19 P *Algebris* EU:C:2021:1042. Yet, even the invalidity of the ex post valuation could not affect the validity of the resolution decision, since it was an act posterior to it.
[277] See eg *Tatiana Pérez* (n 45) 630–53.
[278] ibid 654–700.
[279] *Eleveté* (n 47) 538–40.
[280] ibid 541–58.
[281] ibid 560–69.
[282] *Aeris* (n 48) 669–97.
[283] *Del Valle* (n 46) 550–62; *Algebris* (n 48) 149–55.
[284] *Tatiana Pérez* (n 45) 201–203.
[285] *Tatiana Pérez* (n 45) 209–21; *Del Valle* (n 46) 136–50; *Eleveté* (n 47) 446–66; *Algebris* (n 48) 341–58; *Aeris* (n 49) 231–50.

the adoption of urgent measures, whose effectiveness may need a certain 'surprise effect', which would be hindered (and the objectives thwarted) if a right of audience were granted to shareholders.[286]

7.81 The principle of effective judicial protection was also respected from the moment that shareholders could file an annulment action (among others), since this principle does not grant a right to challenge measures *before* they are adopted, nor requires the possibility for the court to undo the act.[287] Finally, the Court rejected the appellants' allegations concerning their lack of access to the documents used by the SRB for its decision. The right of access to the file (Article 41 of the Charter) is exercised during the administrative proceedings, and is restricted to the entity subject to resolution, ie the bank, and not its shareholders.[288] Furthermore, it cannot comprise confidential information, eg facilitated by third parties (who must be able to trust that the information will remain confidential[289]), and, in any event, the appellants were facilitated non-confidential versions of several of the relevant acts.[290] The Court reached analogous conclusion when the access was claimed as part of the appellants' right of judicial protection.[291]

7.82 Finally, the Court rejected the appellants' allegations about a breach of confidentiality, based on the SRB Chair's interview with Bloomberg, followed by an Article by Reuters, which cited an anonymous source at the Commission or SRB. Their combined effect, according to the appellants, was to cause the liquidity crisis, and precipitate the resolution. Yet, in the Court's view, in her interview the SRB Chair made relatively general remarks, and did not disclose any confidential information, while the appellants were unable to substantiate that the cited 'official' was, in fact, someone at the Commission or SRB (and the information about the troubles of Banco Popular was already public). Even if there had been a breach of confidentiality, this could not have led to the annulment of the resolution decision because the absence of a leak would not have changed the decision, which was based on the fulfilment of the conditions for resolution, and because the decision was not in any event caused by the leak, but by a combination of multiple events, related to Banco Popular's financial situation.[292]

4.3 A brief mention to investment treaties arbitration

7.83 Protection under investment treaties[293] originated in cases of blatant expropriation and abuse, but has significantly evolved under standards like 'most favoured nation' (MFN), 'Fair and Equitable Treatment', or 'Full Protection and Security',[294] to be assimilable to (or stronger than) constitutional or administrative protections.[295]

---

[286] *Tatiana Pérez* (n 45) 222–42; *Del Valle* (n 46) 151–85; *Eleveté* (n 47) 467–93; *Algebris* (n 48) 359–87; *Aeris* (n 49) 251–72.
[287] *Del Valle* (n 46) 187–99.
[288] *Tatiana Pérez* (n 45) 321–31; *Del Valle* (n 46) 456–64; *Eleveté* (n 47) 495–504.
[289] *Tatiana Pérez* (n 45) 332–37; *Del Valle* (n 46) 466–80; *Eleveté* (n 47) 505–23.
[290] *Del Valle* (n 46) 481–83; *Eleveté* (n 47) 524–26.
[291] *Del Valle* (n 46) 441–55.
[292] *Eleveté* (n 47) 603–27; *Algebris* (n 48) 156–213; *Aeris* (n 49) 431–49.
[293] See Lamandini, Ramos, and Solana (n 257).
[294] For criticism of the unpredictability that this causes see Susan D Franck, 'The Legitimacy Crisis in Investment Treaty Arbitration: Privatizing Public International Law Through Inconsistent Decisions' (2005) 73 Fordham L Rev 1521, 1558.
[295] See Thomas Eilmansberger, 'Bilateral investment treaties and EU Law' (2009) 46 CMLR 383.

7.84 For our purposes the more relevant standards are: (a) the doctrine of *indirect expropriation* and (b) the 'fair and equitable treatment' standard. The former distinguishes between regulatory intervention, which the investor has to endure, and expropriation, which carries compensation corresponding to the severity or economic impact of the measure.[296] The 'Fair and Equitable Treatment' (FET) standard protects the investor's 'legitimate expectations'[297] about the legal environment when the investment was made, or the procedural 'fairness' with which the investor is treated, including administrative due process and similar safeguards.[298] This standard does not prevent states from passing new rules, but it recognizes the right of investors to compensation in the face of certain changes in regulation or licensing, even 'crisis' measures.

7.85 Two cases illustrate these points further. In *Saluka Investments v Czech Republic*[299] the arbitral tribunal held the respondent to be in breach of the FET standard because, in the midst of a systemic debt problem, the state provided financial assistance *only* to three of the four biggest banks and left out the entity in which the plaintiffs had invested. The tribunal considered that the problem was generalized and therefore concluded that the reasons alleged by the state did not justify denying assistance to one entity while providing it to others.[300] In *Del Valle Ruiz v Spain*[301] the claimants alleged that Spain had breached its investment treaty obligations, especially the FET standard, during the crisis of Banco Popular, a large Spanish bank. The case presented a major jurisdictional problem because the Mexico-Spain investment treaty did not cover acts by EU authorities, and the decision that the bank was failing or likely to fail (FOLTF) was adopted by the ECB, the bank's resolution scheme with the sale to Banco Santander was adopted by the SRB (EU resolution authority), and only executed by the Spanish resolution authority (FROB) (the challenges of these measures before European courts are analysed at 7.13, 7.37 or 7.73), and the decision not to grant Emergency Liquidity Assistance (ELA) was adopted by the Bank of Spain in coordination with the ECB. For the rest, Spain, in the claimants' view, had not so much 'acted' to harm the bank, as failed to act to correct the acts of other parties in order to arrest the bank's fall. The tribunal adopted a compromise solution. It declared itself competent to decide on Spain's actions, but took into account all the above elements as a factual context. Thus, the tribunal held that Spain was not under a duty to end deposit withdrawals, or correct public officials' statements, or enact a

---

[296] See eg *Metalclad Corp v United Mexican States* (2000) ICSID Case No ARB(AF)/97/1; *Metalclad Corporation v The United Mexican States* (2002) 5 ICSID Rep 209, 225; *CME v Czech Republic* (2001) Partial Award http://www.italaw.com/sites/default/files/case-documents/ita0178.pdf (accessed 21 September 2022). This can include the appointment of a manager if that manager interferes with the property involved. See *Tippets, Abbett, McCarthy, Stratton v TAMS-AFFA Consulting Engineers of Iran* (1984) 6 Iran-US Cl Trib Rep 219. The test also includes the existence of a purpose or intention to expropriate, but this is not essential, and it is not necessary to prove it. *Metalclad Corp*, 5 ICSID Rep 225, para 101.

[297] See eg *Metalclad* (n 296) 225.

[298] If the investor relied on such legal environment when the investment was made, it may give rise to a legitimate expectation that needs to be protected. *BG Group plc v Republic of Argentina* (2007) Final Award http://www.italaw.com/sites/default/files/case-documents/ita0081.pdf (accessed 21 September 2022). See also *Waste Management Inc v The United Mexican States* (2004) ICSID Case No ARB(AF)/00/3, 6 ICSID Rep 538 (procedural fairness); *International Thunderbird Gaming Corporation v United Mexican States* (2006) Arbitral Award, 200 http://www.italaw.com/sites/default/files/case-documents/ita0431.pdf (accessed 21 September 2022) (procedural safeguards).

[299] *Saluka Investments BV v Czech Republic* (2006) Case No 2001-04, Partial Award, PCA Case Repository (Perm Ct Arb) https://pcacases.com/web/sendAttach/880 (accessed 21 September 2022).

[300] ibid paras 327–47. The conduct was only aggravated by regulatory changes, which modified the rules for provisioning of loan losses. The tribunal held this was a consequence of a lack of adequate protection of creditors in the enforcement of security interests, which was the responsibility of the state.

[301] *Del Valle Ruiz and Others v The Kingdom of Spain* (2023) Case No 2019-17, Final Award, https://www.italaw.com/cases/6822 (accessed 12 August 2023).

short-sales ban (and the decision not to do so was neither arbitrary nor discriminatory); that in the ELA process the Bank of Spain did not exceed its discretion in assessing the adequacy of collateral or applying haircuts, and the ultimate decision not to grant ELA was precipitated by the bank's board's assessment that the bank was FOLTF; and that the FROB neither 'push' the SRB to use the sale of business tool, nor organised a flawed auction process.[302] In conclusion, the tribunal held that Spain did not breach the FET standard, nor the standards of national treatment or expropriation, and categorically dismissed all the claimants' allegations, to the point of making an award of costs to the respondent, unusual in investment arbitration.

7.86 The elements of *Saluka* suggest that there was clear discrimination between the domestic-held and foreign-held entities, and those of *Del Valle* that investment arbitration tribunals can also be deferential in cases where the assessments were technical and justified. However, what matters most is that an international arbitration tribunal engaged with the actual facts. In this regard, the *Banco Popular* decisions by the General Court are as detailed as the *Del Valle* award. Other court decisions are less so. It is likely that actions like those adopted in *Golden Pacific Bancorp* or *Woods* in the US, or *Grainger*, *Kotnik*, or *Ledra* in the EU[303] would be found valid under the FET or expropriation standards. The point is that the arbitral tribunal did not simply condone the government actions in the name of financial stability but evaluated the measures in light of the objectives pursued, in terms of substance and procedure. In this sense, the best guarantee that investment treaties will not raise any surprises is to ensure that substantive and procedural safeguards remain adequate.

5 Cross-border recognition and cooperation

7.87 Sometimes crisis measures require the recognition or cooperation of foreign authorities and courts, which presents special challenges.[304] We differentiate between the regional (EU) context and the international context.

5.1 The regional (EU) context

7.88 In the regional (EU) context, mutual recognition of insolvency action must be 'automatic' and without objections under the Winding Up of Credit Institutions Directive. As an early example, in Case C-85/12 *LBI*, two attachment orders against an Icelandic bank succeeded despite the measures being based on legislative provisions rather than acts of administrative or judicial authorities.[305] The EFTA Court for the European Economic Area (EEA) also

---

[302] Ibid paras. 528-539 (deposit withdrawals), 546-570 (public statements), 576-591 (short-sales ban), 604-659 (ELA), 670-709 (sale to Santander).
[303] See section 2.2.2.
[304] See eg Ramos and Solana (n 15).
[305] Case C-85/12 *LBI hf v Kepler Capital Markets SA and Frédéric Giraux* ECLI:EU:C:2013:697. The measures adopted in Iceland (a moratorium of enforcement) through legislation were conditional upon judicial or administrative action, and were subject to automatic recognition in France, because there had been such judicial measures. The attachment orders were considered 'enforcement actions' and thus subject to the home Member State jurisdiction rather than 'lawsuits pending' subject to the law of the state where the lawsuit is pending. ibid 51–58, with reference to art 32 of Directive 2001/24/EC on the reorganisation and winding up of credit institutions (2001) OJ L125.

upheld the principle of automatic recognition in E-28/13 *LBI hf v Merrill Lynch International Ltd*[306] relying on *LBI* to hold that all states must recognize that the home state and its law determine the validity or voidability of detrimental acts, and that this must be subject to narrowly construed exceptions, which did not apply in a case where Icelandic law determined the avoidance of bond payments despite the agency agreement, the bonds and their payment coupons being subject to English law.[307]

7.89 BRRD rules superimpose themselves to the Winding Up Directive's scheme, which subjects resolution measures to its mutual recognition,[308] thus reinforcing the mutual recognition principle.[309] Yet, recognizing measures that may be controversial is difficult,[310] and the BRRD limits the recourse of shareholders and creditors to mechanism of challenge and redress.[311] In *Goldman Sachs v Novo Banco*[312] Banco de Portugal (BdP), the resolution authority for Banco Espirito Santo (BES), a major Portuguese bank, made a series of decisions to transfer *some* of BES' assets and liabilities to a bridge bank, Novo Banco (NB), and *not transfer* others. In a first decision (August decision), BdP indicated the types of liabilities that would be transferred. Later, in a December decision it clarified that a loan facility subscribed by BES with Oak Finance Luxembourg (Oak) would not be transferred to the bridge bank. The loan facility was expressly subject to English law and to the jurisdiction of English courts. Goldman Sachs, as assignee of Oak's claim under the loan facility, sought repayment of the loan from NB arguing that English courts had jurisdiction to determine whether NB was a party to the loan facility entered into by BES as its predecessor, despite NB was not a signatory. Goldman also argued that that the December decision was equivocal because, while it purported to 'transfer', it merely declared a 'no transfer', which, Goldman Sachs argued, was not within the express powers granted to BdP under the BRRD. The commercial court found for Goldman Sachs, holding that the BES' liability under the loan facility had been transferred to NB and that the latter was therefore bound by the English jurisdiction clause. The judge based its decision on the Brussels I Regulation on civil disputes, holding that the case was a contractual matter, and only then did it turn to the BRRD. The court adopted a narrow formal interpretation of the term 'transfer' under Article 66 BRRD and found that the December decision fell outside its scope.[313] This narrow interpretation was overturned by the Court of Appeal, which held that the December decision was a 'reorganisation measure' in the sense of the Bank Winding-Up Directive and thus fell within the scope of mutual recognition.[314] Thus, the December decision had to be given effect by the

---

[306] E-28/13 *LBI hf v Merrill Lynch International Ltd* (17 October 2014).
[307] ibid 73. The contention was over art 30(1) of the Winding Up Directive (n 305), which refers to the validity and voidability of acts detrimental to creditors. The defendant would have needed to prove the non-voidability of the acts pursuant to the English laws that would be applicable in the case (including insolvency law, contract law, statutes of limitation, etc).
[308] See new no (4) of art 1, and art 2 of the Winding-Up Directive (n 307), introduced by art 117 of BRRD (n 8). See also BRRD (n 8) recital 119.
[309] BRRD (n 8) arts 63 ff directly regulate the powers of resolution authorities and the applicable safeguards instead of relying on national law. BRRD, art 66, which regulates the power to enforce crisis management measures or crisis prevention measures by other Member States, provides a broad principle of effectiveness and recognition.
[310] BRRD (n 8) art 66(4) provides for the recognition of bail-in measures.
[311] BRRD (n 8) art 66(3), (5), and (6) subject the safeguards applicable to transfers or bail-in measures, and the rights of shareholders, creditors, or third parties to challenge them, to the laws of the resolution authority's state and excludes any right to challenge under the laws of their own jurisdictions.
[312] *Goldman Sachs v Novo Banco* [2015] EWHC 2371 (Comm).
[313] ibid 94.
[314] See Case No A3/2015/3007 & A3/2015/3008, *Guardians of New Zealand Superannuation Fund and Others v Novo Banco* [2016] EWCA Civ 1092, paras 24–34. The UK Court of Appeals relied on the broader interpretation of 'reorganisation measures' under art 2 of Directive 2001/24 laid out in the decision of the Court of Justice of the European Union of *Kotnik* (n 119).

English courts and NB was 'not a party' to the loan facility extended to BES at the time of the August decision.[315] This decision was recently upheld by the UK Supreme Court in even more rotund terms.[316]

Another European precedent concerned the resolution of Heta, a specific entity created in 2014 **7.90** by an ad hoc act to manage the crisis of the Hypo Alpe Adria group.[317] The ad hoc act provided for the annulment of certain financial obligations. Once the BRRD was transposed into Austrian law, the Austrian legislature passed another act to resolve Heta despite it was not a credit institution, also cancelling or introducing a fifteen-month moratorium to some debt instruments issued by Hypo Alpe and Heta as a precondition for the valuation of the entity and the application of resolution tools. Bayern LB, a holder of such instruments, challenged the Austrian decision before the Münich court, which refused to grant cross-border recognition[318] because, first, these were not 'reorganisation' or 'recapitalisation' measures but 'liquidation' measures, and they did not concern a bank but another institution;[319] and, secondly, because the administrative act adopting the measures merely transposed a *legislative* act, which was not among the acts subject to recognition. Having rejected the application of BRRD or the Winding Up Directive, the court also refused to grant the measure the status of a public policy measure under Article 9(3) of the Rome I Regulation since its purpose was not to protect financial stability, but, rather, Austrian public finances, to the detriment of German creditors.[320] These are puzzling arguments. The view that a court can subject recognition to a sort of 'pedigree' test, where it examines the purposes for which the measures are used, seems at odds with the automatic recognition system at the core of the BRRD and the Bank Winding Up Directive.[321] The objection based on the legislative nature of the act had been explicitly rejected by the CJEU in *LBI*.[322] Protecting public funds is a public policy goal of the BRRD.[323] Unfortunately, since the specific act was annulled by the Austrian Constitutional Court on grounds that it unfairly discriminated between creditors,[324] there was no appeal and the German decision became final.

The Court of Justice had the opportunity to rule on these matters in *Banco de Portugal and* **7.91** *Novo Banco Spain v VR*,[325] which, again, concerned the resolution of BES, and the transfer of obligations to the bridge bank Novo Banco. VR had a contract with BES Spain (the BES branch in that country) for the purchase of preferred shares in the Icelandic bank Kaupthing Bank. Novo Banco had maintained the relationship with VR as a client.[326] Then, VR sued

---

[315] See *Guardians and Others v Novo Banco 2015* (n 314) 36–39.
[316] See *Goldman Sachs v Novo Banco* [2018] UKSC 34, 27, 28.
[317] Heta's purpose was to wind down Hypo Alpe's assets. See Matthias Lehmann, 'Bail-In and Private International Law: How to Make Bank Resolution Measures Effective across Borders' (2017) 66 Intl & Com LQ 1, 133.
[318] Regional Court, Munich I, *BayernLB v Hypo Alpe Adria* [2015] BeckRS 2015, para 15096 http://www.gesetze-bayern.de/(X(1)S(fngr2brnlkwonln4pai0cuz3))/Content/Document/Y-300-Z-BECKRS-B-2015-N-15096?hl=true&AspxAutoDetectCookieSupport=1 (*HETA* case).
[319] ibid.
[320] *HETA* case (n 318).
[321] Aside from covering 'winding up' proceedings, pursuant to art 9(1) of the Directive these encompass 'winding up proceedings *concerning a credit institution*', which could cover Heta proceedings, because they concerned Hypo Alpe, ie a bank.
[322] *LBI hf v Kepler and Others* (n 305).
[323] Article 31 includes among 'resolution objectives' the need '(b) to avoid a significant adverse effect on the financial system, in particular by preventing contagion, including to market infrastructures, and by maintaining market discipline'; and (c) to protect public funds by minimising reliance on extraordinary public financial support'.
[324] See Lehmann, 'Bail-In and Private International Law' (n 317) 133.
[325] Case C-504/19 *Banco de Portugal and Novo Banco Spain v VR* ECLI:EU:C:2021:335.
[326] ibid 10.

Novo Banco, arguing that the contract for the purchase of shares was null and void. To that complaint, Novo Banco opposed that it lacked the capacity to be sued, since the liabilities under the contract were not among the ones listed in the Annexes, which indicated the liabilities transferred to it. Furthermore, and in any event, the liabilities would have been retransferred retroactively from Novo banco to BES, following a subsequent decision by the competent Portuguese authorities, which indicated that liability arising from the performance of investment advisory services.[327] The Spanish courts made a preliminary reference, asking whether principles of judicial protection and legal certainty applied in this context.[328] The Court of Justice considered the BES/Novo Banco resolution measures as reorganization measures under the Directive 2001/24, and analysed the case in light of one of the exceptions to the general rule of the applicability of the *lex concursus*, such as that of 'pending proceedings', where the substantive and procedural effects are determined by the law of the state where those proceedings are pending,[329] Spanish law would be the one applicable to the effects of the lawsuit by the plaintiff.

7.92 Furthermore, and what is more remarkable, the Court held that 'such interpretation is also required in the light of the general principle of legal certainty and the right to effective judicial protection guaranteed by the first paragraph of Article 47 of the Charter'.[330] In particular, with regard to legal certainty the Court held that, even though VR may have had the relevant information to decide whether to bring the lawsuit, she was not in a position to anticipate, once the action was brought, the impact of the re-transfer decision, and its retroactive effect, and thus subjecting the effects of the lawsuit to the *lex concursus* was contrary to legal certainty.[331] Crucially, the Court held that this result was required by the principle of effective judicial protection. Since VR had obtained a judgment, she had a right to have recognition for that judgment, and the retroactive application of the resolution measures simply negated this possibility. Even though the Court acknowledged the possibility of adopting crisis management measures with retroactive effect,[332] in this case, the reorganization measures sought to deprive of effects a decision by a judicial body from another country,[333] and thus, in the Court's view:

> To accept that reorganisation measures taken by the competent authority of the home Member State subsequent to the bringing of such an action and such a judgment, which have the effect of modifying, with retroactive effect, the legal framework relevant to the resolution of the dispute which gave rise to that action, or even directly to the legal situation which is the subject matter of that dispute, might lead the court seised to reject that action, would constitute a restriction on the right to an effective remedy within the meaning of

---

[327] ibid 19.
[328] ibid 24.
[329] ibid 36–49, with reference to art 32 of the Winding Up Directive (n 305).
[330] *Banco de Portugal and Novo Banco Spain v VR* (n 325) 50.
[331] ibid 53–54: VR was not in a position, once her action had been brought but before a final decision had been adopted, to anticipate the implementation of the latter option and to make arrangements accordingly. Thus, the recognition, in the main proceedings, of the effects of the decisions of 29 December 2015 in so far as it is capable of calling into question the judicial decisions already taken in favour of VR, which are still the subject of a pending lawsuit, and which has the result, with retroactive effect, that the defendant can no longer be sued for the purposes of the action brought by the applicant, is incompatible with the principle of legal certainty.
[332] *Banco de Portugal and Novo Banco Spain v VR* (n 325) 61.
[333] ibid 62: '[t]hose decisions aim precisely to render inoperative the judgment of [Spanish court], by calling into question the interpretation that that court had made of the decision of August 2014. As is clear [... [they refer expressly to the action brought by VR in order to establish, counter to that judgment, that the liability that might arise from that action had not been transferred from BES to Novo Banco.'

the first paragraph of Article 47 of the Charter, even if such measures are not in themselves contrary to Directive 2001/24 ...[334]

5.2 The international context

The framework of international coordination, recognition and enforcement of bank crisis management raises the dilemma of whether it is better to adhere to principles that work in cross-border insolvency, eg the UNCITRAL Model Law on Cross-Border Insolvency (Model Law) at the price of losing precision for banks, or to use a more precise framework, like bank resolution, and lose the support of well-established principles for mutual recognition (typically for court-based models). Managing this tension often requires considerable diplomacy. **7.93**

In *re Irish Bank Resolution Corporation Ltd*[335] Irish Bank Resolution Corporation (IBRC) was a bridge bank that succeeded two Irish private banks (Anglo Irish Bank Corporation and Irish Nationwide Building Society) after they suffered severe liquidity crises and were nationalized by the state. The winding up of IBRC was ordered in the IBRC Act 2013, which also changed an important part of Ireland's corporate liquidation rules. The foreign representatives who sought recognition were special liquidators appointed under public authority and were supervised by the Irish Finance Minister and the High Court of Ireland. US courts recognized the Irish proceedings as 'main proceedings' under the framework, based on the Model Law. They dismissed the argument about the non-applicability of Chapter 15 to 'banks' tiptoeing over whether IBRC was a bank and focusing instead on the fact that it had closed its branches in the US before the request of recognition.[336] Thus, banks' specialties are not insurmountable. Recognition may be more problematic if bank crisis management seek to protect specific interests. **7.94**

In *Stanford International Bank*, UK courts refused to recognize proceedings ordered by a Texas court, which appointed the SEC as receiver. Courts in Antigua and Barbuda, the place of the bank's registered office, had applied and been granted such recognition first. Thus, the English court considered that (i) the US receiver had to prove and did not try to prove that the entity's COMI was in the US; and, more crucially, (ii) the proceedings were not 'pursuant to a law relating to insolvency' because they were not collective proceedings seeking to protect all creditors but were rather instituted to prevent fraud and detriment to *US* investors.[337] One could draw a parallel with bank resolution, which seeks to avoid systemic risk and contagion, protect taxpayers and mitigate moral hazard, or preserve critical functions, and conclude that some of its key differences with insolvency, may justify non-recognition rules. **7.95**

Conversely, proceedings where the finality is not skewed towards (or against) certain classes of creditors need not present that problem. The courts of *re Irish Bank Resolution Corporation Lt* (cited above) rejected the objection that the proceedings were directed by the Irish Finance Ministry, holding that the proceeding was 'administrative or judicial in nature', **7.96**

---

[334] *Banco de Portugal and Novo Banco Spain v VR* (n 325) 63.
[335] *In re Irish Bank Resolution Corp*, WL 9953792 (Bkr D Del 2014), confirmed on appeal in CA No 14-108-LPS (Dist Ct Del) (4 August 2015).
[336] ibid 7.
[337] *Re Stanford International Bank Ltd* [2010] EWCA Civ 137.

as required by the Model Law, that provisions on corporate liquidation applied, and that any creditor could seek a court ruling on issues arising during the proceeding.[338] Despite the Finance Minister could in theory give priority to any assets to the Irish State, this did not mean that the Proceedings were not collective in nature. In fact, the IBRC Act 2013 adopted the priority and distribution scheme set out in the Companies Act and creditors of the same rank distributed proceeds *pari pasu*.[339]

7.97 One field for potential conflict are the provisions on creditor ranking and priorities, which touch on core policies.[340] There are not two ranking and priority systems exactly alike,[341] and these differences can be a source of friction that hinders cross-border cooperation.[342] Model law provisions on foreign creditors treatment are particularly nuanced to balance the demands of non-discrimination with the need to respect the domestic system of priorities.[343]

7.98 Some cases exemplify the potential for cooperation. In *HIH Casualty and General Insurance*[344] an insurer declared insolvent in Australia had substantial assets in the UK (reinsurance claims corresponding to reinsurance policies taken out in the London market). English courts, including the House of Lords, ordered the transfer of those assets to satisfy insolvency priorities under Australian law, which, unlike UK law, accorded preferential treatment to insurance creditors.[345] Yet, aside from Lord Hoffmann's universalist proclamation, there were other factors at play that made it convenient for UK courts to do without assets located in their territory.[346] In normal circumstances, local authorities would apply their local priority system and lack tools to grant foreign creditors preferential status, other

---

[338] *In re Irish Bank Resolution Corp* (n 335).

[339] ibid 14.

[340] José María Garrido, 'The Distributional Question in Insolvency: Comparative Aspects' (1995) 4 Intl Insolvency Rev 25.

[341] Jose María Garrido, 'No Two Snowflakes the Same: The Distributional Question in International Bankruptcies' (2011) 46 Texas Intl LJ 459.

[342] This situation is well summarized by Westbrook. From a broad policy perspective, the differences are not crucial, yet each one represents a contentious result in a particular case because one party or another will be advantaged or disadvantaged. Meaningful cooperation among courts will often require that one or the other priority system prevails. The question is whether a court will feel so bound by the local system so as to prevent cooperation with a foreign court. See Jay Lawrence Westbrook, 'Priority Conflicts as a Barrier to Cooperation in Multinational Insolvencies' (2009) 27 Penn State Intl L Rev 869.

[343] Article 13 of the UNCITRAL Model Law on Cross-Border Insolvency provides that (i) foreign creditors should not be treated worse than local creditors; (ii) this non-discrimination should not affect the local system of priorities; and (iii) this notwithstanding, the application of such system should not lead to foreign creditors ranking lower than ordinary local creditors. Lest the non-discrimination principle should be emptied of its meaning by provisions giving the lowest ranking to foreign claims, paragraph 2 establishes the minimum ranking for claims of foreign creditors: the rank of general unsecured claims.' Guide to Enactment and Interpretation of the UNCITRAL Model Law on Cross-Border Insolvency, para 119.

[344] *HIH Casualty and General Insurance Ltd* [2008] UKHL 21.

[345] ibid (1), (35). The differences that resulted from the application of either the UK system of priorities or the Australian one were listed in a table in (53).

[346] Namely, (i) Australia was one of the jurisdictions included by the Secretary of State among those qualified to receive special assistance; (ii) due to the implementation of EU insurance rules, Britain was about to enact an insurance creditors' priority similar to the Australian, which made the divergence temporary, and thus, arguably, not a matter of policy; (iii) protection of foreign creditors enhanced London's pre-eminence as an insurance centre; and (iv) the conflict in the case was between foreign priorities and the local *pari passu* principle (protective of unsecured creditors), which, in a taxonomy of priority conflicts, would be of a less intense kind than that between foreign and local priorities. See Garrido (n 341) 463–65.

than local law categories. Nevertheless, courts in one country would be ready to grant recognition to resolution action if creditors were treated fairly. As the court in *re Irish bank* made clear, the key is whether creditors are subject to the foreign country's system of ranking and priorities and whether creditor treatment is roughly similar to the local system.[347] A public policy exception is reserved for serious deviations that leave key interests unprotected.[348]

---

[347] 'Appellants suggest (largely through a series of questions see DI 34 at 1 18) that the Irish Proceeding discriminates against US creditors and deprives them of due process and other unspecified constitutional rights, in favor of the Irish government. As Appellees persuasively respond, the provisions objected to by Appellants parallel provisions in laws adopted by the United States in response to the global financial crisis.' *In re Irish Bank Resolution Corp* (n 335).

[348] *In Re Qimonda AG Bankr* Lit 09-14766-RGM, 09-14766-SSM 433 BR 547; 462 BRBR 165 Bankr E Dist Vir. US courts considered that the German procedure insufficiently protected the rights of the licensee under an IP licensing contract (US provisions would grant the licensee a choice, whilst the foreign representative indicated its intention not to perform the contracts).

PART III
PRIVATE LAW DISPUTES IN THE LAW OF FINANCE

8
An Anatomy of Issues in Private Law Disputes

1 Private disputes and vertical allocation of powers	8.01	3 Vertical, horizontal tensions, and private plaintiffs: regulatory provisions and private law doctrines	8.16
2 Beyond verticality: private law disputes, jurisdiction, and applicable law	8.08	4 Access to justice and collective redress	8.23
		5 Contract interpretation: party autonomy, boilerplate, or hard cases?	8.25

1 Private disputes and vertical allocation of powers

Underpinning private disputes between individuals or corporations are often questions about which territorial unit can provide the rules for such disputes, especially in the case of federal states (like the US) or supranational unions (like the EU). The interplay between levels is normally shaped by two ideas: first, 'primacy' or 'supremacy', discussed in Chapter 3. We will see it present in securities law liability (based on federal provisions) in the US, or prospectus liability in the EU. A second idea is that of 'free movement' and 'competition', where the process of harmonization is not top-down, but 'bottom-up'. This, however, requires companies and services to move freely across the area, without constraints, and such constraints may sometimes reflect public policy principles. Such tension is present in both the US and the EU. **8.01**

US financial law enjoys a clearer division between federal securities and bankruptcy law, and state corporate and contract law, which enabled it to reap the benefits of large, deep, liquid securities markets with some harmonized rules, and some competition. There is no unanimity as to whether this competitive process is beneficial or harmful;[1] it has been defining for the US current status quo, where the big winners have been Delaware for corporate laws and New York for contract law (at least for financial contracts). Conversely, however, state securities laws have been an important feature of the potential overlaps and divergences have been limited by the 'commerce clause'.[2] This empowers Congress to legislate, and puts limits on state legislation that hinders interstate commerce ('negative' or 'dormant' commerce clause), **8.02**

---

[1] See eg US Supreme Court, 'Records and Briefs of the United States Supreme Court' (1942) 10, 22; Paul G Mahoney, 'Securities Regulation by Enforcement: An International Perspective Manning' (1990) 7 YJR 305; G Warren, 'Reflections on Dual Regulation of Securities: A Case Against Preemption' (1984) 3 Boston College L Rev 1 Jonathan R Macey, 'Corporate Law and Corporate Governance. A Contractual Perspective' (1993) 18 J Corp L 185;Roger J Dennis and Patrick J Ryan, 'State Corporate and Federal Securities Law: Dual Regulation in a Federal System' (1992) 22 Publius 21; SEC, 'The Advantages of a Dual System: Parallel Streams of Civil and Criminal Enforcement of the U.S. Securities Laws' (September 1998) https://www.sec.gov/news/speech/speecharchive/1998/spch222.htm (accessed 29 September 2022).

[2] David Ramos Muñoz, *The Law of Transnational Securitization* (OUP 2010) 9.05–9.07; Elvin R Latty, 'Pseudo-Foreign Corporations' (1955) 65 Yale LJ 137, 145.

an effect reinforced by the equal treatment clause, the due process clause or the 'full faith and credit' clause.³ Courts have held that there is no mandatory principle against 'pseudo-foreign' corporations,⁴ and have accepted that entities incorporated in and with the centre of interest in one state can operate in other states,⁵ even in breach of 'host' corporate laws,⁶ and even when they were incorporated in one state to avoid the laws of another state.⁷

8.03 In *Edgar v MITE* the US Supreme Court struck down an Illinois statute that subjected the tender offer in a takeover to the approval of the Secretary of State,⁸ because this could prevent the efficient allocation of resources through the market for corporate control, restrict interstate commerce, and upset the neutrality of the US Constitution between shareholders, managers, and offerors.⁹ The restriction was not justified by investor protection or, in any event, was outweighed by the harm caused.¹⁰ Further generations of anti-takeover statutes approached the issue from the perspective of investor protection (as blue-sky statutes) by increasing disclosure requirements or imposing formalities on the offeror (after gaining control), and stripping him of voting rights if non-compliant.¹¹ In *CTS Corp v Dynamic Corp of America*,¹² the Supreme Court examined a vote-stripping provision for non-compliance with shareholder approval requirements, which had been declared unconstitutional by the Seventh Circuit's Judge Posner, who held that the market for corporate control protected shareholders' interests, and any restriction of it would be an intolerable interference with interstate commerce. The Supreme Court reversed, holding that the statute did not 'discriminate against' interstate commerce,¹³ nor did it unduly restrict it by, for example, creating 'an impermissible risk of inconsistent regulation by different States'¹⁴ and, in any event, Indiana had a legitimate interest in promoting stable relations between corporate constituencies and shareholder voice,¹⁵ which could balance interstate commerce.¹⁶ The approach resembled the proportionality analysis of EU courts (in the US, 'balancing' is less frequent, or less openly carried out, as discussed in Chapter 3).

8.04 Beyond these cases where the 'dormant' commerce clause was in play, as we discuss in Chapter 9, tensions between federal and state levels were present where federal courts initially 'created' a damages claim out of a federal regulatory statute (section 10b of the Securities and Exchange Act, and SEC rule 10b-5) which were not intended for such purpose, and this claim asserted itself against the more 'natural' alternatives of actions for breach of corporate fiduciary duties (among other examples). Once the federal claim was well-established, the Supreme Court worked on some constraints, and Congress passed the Private Securities

---

³ US Constitution, Constitutional Amendment No XIV, s 1, Amendment V, or art IV, s 1.
⁴ *Demarest v Flack* 128 NY 205, 28 NE 645, 649 (1891).
⁵ *Oakdale Mfg Co Ltd v Garst* 18 RI 484, 28 Atl 973 (1894) (enforce contract); *Philadelphia & Gulf SS Co v Soeffing* 59 Pa Super 429 (1915) (enforce stock subscription).
⁶ *Commonwealth Acceptance Corp v Jordan* 198 Cal 618, 246 Pac 96 (1926) (non-compliance with equal voting laws).
⁷ *State ex rel Brown Contracting & Bldg Co v Cook* 181 Mo 596, 80 SW 929 (1904). See Latty (n 2) 145.
⁸ *Edgar v MITE Corp* 457 US 624 (1982).
⁹ ibid.
¹⁰ ibid.
¹¹ Arthur R Pinto, 'Takeover Statutes: The Dormant Commerce Clause and State Corporate Law' (1987) 41 Miami L Rev 474.
¹² *CTS Corp v Dynamics Corp of America* (1987) 481 US 69.
¹³ ibid paras 87–88.
¹⁴ ibid paras 88–89.
¹⁵ ibid paras 89–93.
¹⁶ ibid paras 93–94.

Litigation Reform Act (PSLRA[17]) with this aim. Eventually, plaintiffs would begin taking the opposite path, ie choosing state venues to claim breaches of federal statutes, which led to further multi-level dynamics. In any event, these tensions have not hindered markets because the core unstated assumption has always been that rules should be interoperable, and allow cross-border corporate and securities activities, leading to impressive market development. Thus, courts could limit themselves to take a step back, and apply the law without having to further the efforts towards market construction. Once the default attitude was positive, and not reluctant towards firms operating across borders, the market could take care of itself, without much help from the Constitution.

This contrasts with the EU, where the state of civil justice is far from perfect.[18] Contract and property law are Member States' competence. Securities laws, although also state-level, have been largely harmonized, and so is a large part of company law,[19] as well as many (financial) contract and property provisions,[20] and some corporate insolvency provisions,[21] which are also subject to automatic cross-border recognition.[22] **8.05**

Furthermore, in company law the Court of Justice has been more active than the US Supreme Court in setting limits to Member States' regulatory powers. Despite initially stating that corporations were creatures of Member States, which could constrain their 'exit' (*Daily Mail*[23]) the Court then adopted a more assertive tone, accepting that corporations could incorporate outside their 'real seat', and prohibiting 'host' authorities in their 'real seat' from refusing to register a secondary establishment (*Centros*[24]), denying them capacity to act in legal proceedings (*Überseering*[25]), or making it unjustifiably difficult to merge (*SEVIC*[26]). 'Exit' restrictions continued to be acceptable (*Cartesio*[27]) but the Court has also found that this, too, has limits (*Polbud*[28]). **8.06**

And yet, when it comes to applying common, harmonized EU financial laws in private-to-private relationships, courts in each Member State often reason from their (un-unharmonized) domestic law doctrines 'upward', rather than from the common EU rules 'downward', and without assuming that rules have to be interoperable and restrictions limited. The result is that private application of financial laws is probably the single greatest obstacle standing in the way of EU-wide financial markets. Private enforcement **8.07**

---

[17] John W Avery, 'Securities Litigation Reform: The Long and Winding Road to the Private Securities Litigation Reform Act of 1995' (1996) 51 Business Lawyer 335, 335–36, 348, 357–58.
[18] For an insightful description see Burkhard Hess, 'The State of the Civil Justice Union' in Burkhard Hess, Maria Bergström, and Eva Storskrubb (eds), *EU Civil Justice: Current Issues and Future Outlook* (Hart Publishing 2016) 1–19.
[19] Directive (EU) 2017/1132 of the European Parliament and of the Council relating to certain aspects of company law [2017] OJ L169.
[20] See eg Directive 2002/47/EC on financial collateral arrangements [2002] OJ L168.
[21] Directive (EU) 2019/1023 of the European Parliament and of the Council on preventive restructuring frameworks, on discharge of debt and disqualifications, and on measures to increase the efficiency of procedures concerning restructuring, insolvency and discharge of debt, and amending Directive (EU) 2017/1132 (2019) OJ L172 (hereafter Directive on restructuring and insolvency).
[22] Regulation (EU) 2015/848 of the European Parliament and of the Council on insolvency proceedings [2015] OJ L141.
[23] Case C-81/87 *The Queen v Treasury and Commissioners of Inland Revenue, ex parte Daily Mail* and *General Trust plc* ECLI:EU:C:1988:456.
[24] Case C-212/97 *Centros* ECLI:EU:C:1999:126.
[25] Case C-208/00 *Überseering* ECLI:EU:C:2002:632.
[26] Case C-411/03 *SEVIC* ECLI:EU:C:2005:762.
[27] Case C-210/06 *Cartesio* ECLI:EU:C:2008:723.
[28] Case C-106/16 *Polbud* ECLI:EU:C:2017:804.

mechanisms 'have not traditionally formed part of EU securities and markets regulation' and thus 'Member States differ considerably with respect to the design of causes of action and the extent to which private enforcement is engaged'.[29] In our view, the problem is less one of *predictable divergence* than one of *unpredictable levels of similitude*.

2 Beyond verticality: private law disputes, jurisdiction, and applicable law

8.08 Sometimes the tension is not between federal/supranational and state levels, but between a determination of the applicable law and jurisdiction that is 'unilateral' (or asymmetric), typical in public law, where courts are part of the state's powers, and the 'bilateral' (or symmetric) determination, more typical in private law, where courts (should) apply conflict of law rules which (should) work similarly regardless of which is the court that applies them.

8.09 Symmetry is harder where disputes involve regulatory rules, with strong considerations of public policy. Such disputes, however, are more frequent in some contexts than others. Contract disputes allow a more symmetrical assessment, and also for the parties' choice of law and jurisdiction. Disputes over *property* have a clear connecting factor, the location of the assets, which is also a proxy of the state's enforcement power. The problem is that financial assets (i) are normally 'claims', which (ii) must be satisfied by a debtor, are (iii) often based on a contract, and (iv) often 'securitized' to facilitate their circulation, and (v) often represented by book entries in the accounts or registry of a financial intermediary, which may, in turn, be linked to the book entries of another intermediary or central registry. Thus, the issue depends on the characterization of the issue as a 'contract', 'debt', 'proprietary', or 'custody' or 'deposit' problem as each may point to a different connection. This may be further complicated if the conflict is enmeshed in insolvency disputes, where the neutral rule gets entangled with the public policy goal of treating creditors fairly. Cross-border insolvency rules have improved their certainty by emphasizing connecting factors like the 'centre of main interest' (COMI) and exceptions (eg rights *in rem*), but public policy and the temptation of unilateralism continue to be strong.

8.10 Finally, tort-like disputes, eg for breach of securities laws, may have rules that can apply 'symmetrically', such as the place of the harmful conduct or the occurrence of the harm, but these can yield to 'unilateralist' approaches, as soon as a court weighs heavily aspects such as, eg investors' residence. This can lead to overlaps, inconsistencies, and questions about the limits of unilateralism. The risk of overlaps and inconsistencies is illustrated by the *Kolassa* case,[30] where an investor domiciled in Austria claimed damages from a bank domiciled in the UK for contractual, pre-contractual, and tortious liability of the bank as a result of loss in value of a financial instrument issued by the bank but acquired on the secondary market by the investor from a third party. The Court held that the jurisdictional provisions for consumer contracts (consumer's domicile) or for contracts in general (place of performance), could not be relied upon to claim a breach of the bond conditions and the prospectus if the bond was acquired from a third party (jurisdiction on contract issues[31]). On tort matters, the

---

[29] Niamh Moloney, *EU Securities and Financial Markets Regulation* (OUP, Second Edition, 2014) 968 (the quotation is not present, as such, in the Third Edition 2023, but for a similar finding see 28–30).
[30] Case C-375/13 *Harald Kolassa v Barclays Bank plc* ECLI:EU:C:2015:37.
[31] ibid paras 20–35 (jurisdiction on consumer contracts) and 36–41 (jurisdiction on contracts).

mere fact that the applicant has suffered financial loss does not suffice for the attribution of jurisdiction to the courts of the investor's domicile if both the event causing the loss and the loss occur in another Member State.[32]

8.11 Since determining where 'the events giving rise to the loss took place' or 'the loss occurred' can be difficult, the Court based its decision on the allegation that the harm was sustained as a result of the 'management of the funds in which the money from the issue of those certificates had been invested', and 'the actions or omissions alleged against Barclays Bank with respect to its legal information obligations'. Thus, since no evidence suggested that the loss events had taken place in a state other than the state where the issuer had its seat,[33] this should dictate the criterion of the court. As for the 'the place where the loss occurred', the Court attached weight to the location of the applicant's bank account.[34] This, in the Court's view, 'strengthened legal protection' by letting the applicant identify *easily*, and the defendant *reasonably* to foresee the competent court.[35] The Court was not asked in that case to look at the potential complications that could occur: the securities account could well have been located in a third country, or be an *omnibus* account with multiple securities from multiple parties. The statements could have been made by the issuer, and/or distributed by other parties involved in the transaction, etc. We will have to wait to see how such complications play out in practice.

8.12 The limits to unilateralism and extraterritorial application of laws are exemplified by *Morrison v National Australia Bank Ltd*, decided by the US Supreme Court.[36] The National Australia Bank, whose 'ordinary shares' were not traded on any US exchange, purchased HomeSide Lending, a mortgage servicing company headquartered in Florida in 1998, and later had to write down the value of its assets, causing the National Australia Bank's share price to fall. Australian investors sued the National Australia Bank, HomeSide, and their officers in the US for violating federal securities laws (on securities fraud). The respondents moved to dismiss for lack of subject-matter jurisdiction, which was granted by the district and Second Circuit. The case was brought to the Supreme Court, which held that the Circuit Court erred when it considered the extraterritorial reach of section 10(b) as an issue of subject-matter jurisdiction,[37] holding that the District Court had subject-matter jurisdiction. However, the Supreme Court considered it unnecessary to remand the case because the rules on territorial jurisdiction[38] justified dismissal.

8.13 The Court relied on the *Aramco* case to hold that it is a 'longstanding' principle of American law that 'legislation of Congress, unless a contrary intent appears, is meant to apply only

---

[32] ibid paras 42–49.
[33] ibid paras 51–53.
[34] 'The courts where the applicant is domiciled have jurisdiction, on the basis of the place where the loss occurred, to hear and determine such an action, in particular when that loss occurred itself directly in the applicant's bank account held with a bank established within the area of jurisdiction of those courts.' See *Kolassa* (n 30) para 55.
[35] *Kolassa* (n 30) para 56: 'The place where the loss occurred thus identified meets, in circumstances such as those referred to in paragraph 51 of this judgment, the objective of Regulation No 44/2001 of strengthening the legal protection of persons established in the European Union, by enabling the applicant to identify easily the court in which he may sue and the defendant reasonably to foresee in which court he may be sued ... given that the issuer of a certificate who does not comply with his legal obligations in respect of the prospectus must, when he decides to notify the prospectus relating to that certificate in other Member States, anticipate that inadequately informed operators, domiciled in those Member States, might invest in that certificate and suffer loss.'
[36] *Morrison v National Australia Bank Ltd* 561 US 247 (2010).
[37] Subject to r 12(b)(1), which refers to 'a tribunal's power to hear a case'. See *Union Pacific R Co v Locomotive Engineers* 558 US 67, 81 (2009).
[38] See r 12(b)(6).

within the territorial jurisdiction of the United States'.[39] This reversed decades of precedent in Circuit Courts, which, like the Second Circuit here, took the Exchange Act's silence about section 10(b)'s extraterritorial application as a mandate on the courts to 'discern' whether Congress would have wanted the statute to apply. In the Court's view, courts must begin with a presumption *against* extraterritoriality, and then reason that, when a statute gives no clear indication of an extraterritorial application, it has none. To the Court, the lower courts' disregard of the presumption had created 'a collection of tests for divining what Congress would have wanted, complex in formulation and unpredictable in application',[40] which 'demonstrate the wisdom of the presumption against extraterritoriality'.[41] Such presumption permits a clear application in all cases as a background, against which Congress can legislate with predictable effects.[42] Thus, section 10(b) does not provide a cause of action to foreign plaintiffs suing foreign and American defendants for securities traded on foreign exchanges.

8.14 Then, since SEC rule 10b–5 was promulgated under section 10(b), it did 'not extend beyond conduct encompassed by section 10(b)'s prohibition',[43] and thus, if one was not extraterritorial, neither was the other. The Court also held that the general reference to 'foreign' commerce in the definition of 'interstate commerce'[44] could not defeat the presumption against extraterritoriality,[45] and the fact that the Exchange Act's reference among its purposes to 'prices established and offered in such transactions are generally disseminated and quoted throughout the United States and foreign countries',[46] did not suggest an extraterritorial purpose.[47] Thus, although some HomeSide executives carried out some of their activities in Florida, and some misleading statements were made there, the case lacked all contact with United States territory,[48] if one prioritized the connection of US securities exchanges.[49] If Congress intended a foreign application 'it would have addressed the subject of conflicts with foreign laws and procedures'.

8.15 Lower courts applied this new approach in cases like *Absolute Activist Value Master Fund* to consider a transaction of securities not listed in US exchanges 'domestic' if 'irrevocable liability is incurred or title passes within the United States'.[50] In *Parkcentral Global Hub* the same circuit held that 'while a domestic transaction or listing is necessary to state a claim under § 10(b), it may not be sufficient'. Thus, a claim against foreign defendants based on 'largely foreign conduct, for losses incurred by the plaintiffs' based on 'price movements of foreign securities' constitutes an impermissible extraterritorial application of the statute.[51]

---

[39] *Morrison v National Australia Bank Ltd* (n 36), citing *EEOC v Arabian American Oil Co*, 499 US 244, 248 (1991) (*Aramco*).
[40] *Aramco* (n 39) para 256.
[41] ibid para 261.
[42] ibid.
[43] *Aramco* (n 39) para 262, citing *United States v O'Hagan* 521 US 642, 651 (1997).
[44] 15 USC § 78c(a)(17).
[45] Citing *Aramco* (n 39) 251
[46] 15 USC § 78b(2); *Morrison v National Australia Bank Ltd* (n 36).
[47] *Morrison v National Australia Bank Ltd* (n 36). Nothing suggests that this national public interest pertains to transactions conducted upon foreign exchanges and markets. The fleeting reference to the dissemination and quotation abroad of the prices of securities traded in domestic exchanges and markets cannot overcome the presumption against extraterritoriality.
[48] Comparing this case with *Aramco* (n 39), in this second case the plaintiff had been hired in Houston and was an American citizen, and the Court concluded that the 'focus' of congressional concern in Title VII of the Civil Rights Act of 1964 was neither that territorial event nor that relationship, but *domestic* employment. See *Morrison v National Australia Bank Ltd* (n 36).
[49] The Act's prologue, and the fact that the Act's registration requirements apply only to securities listed on national securities exchanges, as well as by s 30(a) and (b).
[50] *Absolute Activist Value Master Fund Ltd v Ficeto* 677 F 3d 60, 67 (2d Cir 2012).
[51] *Parkcentral Global Hub Ltd v Porsche Auto Holdings SE* 11-397-CV L (2d Cir 2014).

3 Vertical, horizontal tensions, and private plaintiffs: regulatory provisions and private law doctrines

The rule declaring that it shall be *unlawful* to 'use or employ, in connection with the purchase **8.16** or sale of any security' a 'manipulative or deceptive device or contrivance in contravention of such rules and regulations as the [SEC] may prescribe',[52] or the rule stating that:

> When providing investment advice or portfolio management the investment firm shall obtain the necessary information ... so as to enable the investment firm to recommend to the client or potential client the investment services and financial instruments that are suitable for him and, in particular, are in accordance with his risk tolerance and ability to bear losses"[53]

look straightforward enough, until one asks 'what happens if someone breaches them?' This is a loaded question, which encapsulates three different, but interrelated ones. First, is the breach determined by federal/supranational or state authorities? Secondly, is the breach determined by regulatory agencies, who penalize the wrongdoer, or by courts? Thirdly, should aggrieved parties have a direct right to enforce the breach, ie does the regulatory provision confer rights on private parties?

The three questions will be linked by the logic and purpose of the concrete regulatory provisions, which courts must apply. Yet, courts may sometimes go beyond the original purpose and create a private right of action, or use the rule to shape already existing private law doctrines, as seen in Chapter 9. The court's choice will not only affect private-to-private relationships, but also the vertical balance between territorial units and the horizontal balance between agencies and courts. **8.17**

In the US, courts' views have changed, including the US Supreme Court. From an initial **8.18** approach where the courts' role was to 'provide such remedies as are necessary to make effective the congressional purpose',[54] the Court adopted a more restrictive stance, requiring the presence of clear legislative intent to favour a class of citizens and to create a private right of action.[55] The initial idea of strengthening the relevance of federal law and courts for securities disputes was subsequently balanced by the need to acknowledge states' competences in corporate or contract law (first question). In the UK, a very different setting, courts try to identify the legislative intent to protect *a limited class of citizens* as the basis for a private right of action[56] and, if a statute provides other means of enforcement, this is taken as evidence

---

[52] Securities and Exchange Act 1934, s 10b.
[53] See art 25(2) of Directive 2014/65/EU on markets in financial instruments and amending Directive 2002/92/EC and Directive 2011/61/EU Text with EEA relevance [2014] OJ L173 (MiFID II).
[54] See *JI Case Co v Borak* 377 US 426, 433 (1964), where the Court held that there was a private right of action implied under § 14(a) of the Securities and Exchange Act 1934 (false or misleading proxy statements) in view of the congressional purpose of the Act.
[55] In *Cort v Ash* 422 US 66, 78 (1975); *Touche Ross & Co v Redington* 442 US 560, 576 (1979) (the question was not whether the Court thought that it could improve upon the statutory scheme, but to determine legislative intent); *Alexander v Sandoval* 532 US 275 (2001). This led to the dismissal of private rights of action in lawsuits for breach of duties under the Investment Advisers Act 1940. See eg *Olmsted v Pruco Life Insurance Co of New Jersey* 283 F 3d 429, 433 (2d Cir 2002); *Northstar Financial Advisors v Schwab Investments* 615 F 3d 1106 (2010) (where the District Court's finding of a private right of action was subsequently overruled by the Ninth Circuit).
[56] *Roe v Sheffield City Council (No 1)* [2004] QB 653 Court of Appeal (Civil Division), citing *X (Minors) v Bedfordshire County Council* [1995] 2 AC 633, 731.

contrary to such right.⁵⁷ No private right arises from statutes creating a regulatory system for the benefit of the public at large.⁵⁸

8.19 The German system of torts presents similarities through a different path: non-contractual liability arises from 'unlawful' damage, which may result from the violation of a right enjoying absolute protection (life, integrity, property),⁵⁹ the intentional infliction of damage *contra bonos mores*,⁶⁰ or the violation of a statutory rule.⁶¹ Economic loss does not per se give rise to liability, and law-makers wanted to avoid its entry by the back door of statutory breach. Thus, statutory breaches *only* give rise to damages when the statute is *intended to protect another person*.⁶² Thus, statutes that protect general interests cannot be the basis for a tort action,⁶³ and a person cannot claim damages for breach of statute if she does not belong to the group of people protected by the rule's scope.⁶⁴

8.20 The issue is different in countries with a 'general clause' tort (Spain, France, Italy, Belgium). In France or Belgium, the breach of a statutory standard can give rise to 'fault' (*faute*) if committed freely and consciously (*librement et consciemment*),⁶⁵ and the law does not require, in principle, that the stated aim of the statute is to protect the specific plaintiff since French law rejects the 'relativity' of duties (*relativité aquilienne*) and emphasizes the absolute character of statutory duties.⁶⁶ In Spain, however, scholars and case law have construed the 'general clause' in the sense that the breach of a specific statutory standard of care only gives rise to liability when the *purpose of the rules* was to *avoid the harmful result*, or the avoidance of the harmful result was within the 'protective scope' of the norm.⁶⁷ In Italy, the law requires 'unlawful' damage (*danno ingiusto*), which is reminiscent of the German system, but this 'unlawfulness' is often linked to 'negligence' or, more frequently, with 'causation'.

8.21 In the EU, such approaches must be complemented by the Court of Justice case law on non-contractual liability of Member States for breach of rules that *confer rights on individuals* (as opposed to 'avoiding the harmful result').⁶⁸ Rules that seek to find common ground, such as the European Draft Common Framework of Reference define 'negligence' as either the breach of a 'general' standard of care or a 'particular' standard of care provided by a statutory provision 'whose purpose is the protection of the person suffering the damage from that damage'.⁶⁹ Yet, the Court of Justice has abstained from imposing its own doctrine of damages liability on Member States, preferring to interpret EU provisions, while deferring to Member States on private law doctrines. The Court, however, reserves the power to control the outcome to ensure that the protection is not 'less favourable than those concerning

---

[57] *Cutler v Wandsworth Stadium Ltd* [1949] AC 398; *Lonrho Ltd v Shell Petroleum Co Ltd (No 2)* [1982] AC 173.
[58] *Groves v Wimborne* [1898] 2 QB 402 (Lord Browne-Wilkinson).
[59] German Civil Code, s 823 I.
[60] ibid s 826.
[61] ibid s 823 II.
[62] ibid.
[63] Cees van Dam, *European Tort Law* (2nd edn, OUP 2013) 244.
[64] ibid.
[65] Christian von Bar, *Non-Contractual Liability Arising out of Damage Caused to Another* (Otto Schmidt/De Gruyter European Law Publishers 2009) 596; Van Dam (n 63) 245.
[66] ibid.
[67] Luis Díez Picazo, *Derecho de daños* (Civitas 1999) 360; STS (27 April 1992) no appeal 560/1990, RJ 1992/3414.
[68] See ch 4, para 4.33. See also Van Dam (n 63) 247–48, as well as Joined Cases C-6 and 9/90 *Francovich and Bonifaci v Republic of Italy* ECLI:EU:C:1991:428; Joined Cases C-46/93 and C-48/93 *Brasserie du Pêcheur, Factortame III* ECLI:EU:C:1996:79; Joined Cases C-178, 179, 188, 189 and 190/94 *Dillenkofer and Others v Federal Republic of Germany* ECLI:EU:C:1996:375.
[69] See Draft Common Frame of Reference (DCFR) art 3:102 (*Negligence*) (a).

similar claims based on provisions of national law' (equivalence) nor 'arranged to make the exercise of rights conferred by the EU legal order practically impossible' (effectiveness). It also insists on giving concepts in EU law an autonomous and uniform interpretation, taking into account the context and purpose of the provision.[70]

8.22 Determining 'legislative intent' and whether it 'intends' to confer private rights is a highly case-specific task, although courts seem to follow three approaches. The first approach is the *determinative* approach, where *regulatory* provisions *directly* support *private* claims, shaped through a self-referenced interpretation of the regulatory provisions themselves. This is the approach of US federal courts on securities fraud claims under section 10b of the Exchange Act 1934, or prospectus liability under section 11 of the Securities Act 1933. The second approach is the 'compartmentalized' approach, where financial regulatory provisions and actions under private law walk parallel but separate paths, and even if the breach of regulatory rules can result in liability claims, those claims are independent from general claims under contract or tort. This appears to be the case of UK courts, where damages claims under the Financial Services and Markets Act (FSMA) are kept separate from actions under the tort of negligence or 'misrepresentation'. The third approach is the *symbiotic* approach, where regulatory provisions are used by courts to reshape private law concepts such as 'negligence' or 'good faith' duties, and/or their *finality* is used to interpret the defendants' defences under private law. This is the case of courts in some EU jurisdictions on prospectus liability or the duties of financial intermediaries, as seen in Chapters 9 and 10.

4 Access to justice and collective redress

8.23 Collective redress mechanisms are discussed elsewhere, eg Chapters 9 and 13, but we can outline some general ideas here. First, collective redress is key to bridge the gap between regulatory goals and private remedies. While individual actions hinge on the peculiarities of the particular case, class actions emphasize common patterns, which help to detect widespread pathologies, give weight to the purposive interpretation of regulatory provisions, and ensure that the court ruling has a market-wide impact.

8.24 Secondly, for this reason, to shape collective redress apart from providing the procedural mechanisms for the formation of a 'class', substantive rules must allow the presentation of a complaint that emphasizes the commonalities. For example, a strict focus on the requirement that plaintiffs establish *individual reliance* on a statement would defeat this (Chapter 9). Likewise, *clauses in contract documentation* may exclude reliance by the investor. If they must be examined as individual occurrences, even when they are boilerplate, and their text is the same, this may defeat the idea of collective or class (Chapter 13).

---

[70] Case C-343/13 *Modelo Continente Hipermercados* ECLI:EU:C:2015:146; compare also Case C-279/12 *Fish Legal and Shirley* ECLI:EU:C:2013:853, para 42.

5 Contract interpretation: party autonomy, boilerplate, or hard cases?

8.25 Parties use financial contracts which include complex clauses as an instrument of precision to achieve a transaction's goals.[71] To achieve them, however, parties need courts to uphold their intent without appealing to a 'policy' that may be alien to the parties' intent. Sometimes such policy may operate as a matter of mandatory law. However, more often the problem will be one of determining what 'the parties' intent' really means and/or what the 'default' rule is.

8.26 Simply put, the very idea of 'enforcing the parties' will' takes for granted that *all* the parties share the *same* understanding of *all* transaction terms and *all* their implications in *all* scenarios. The reality is that parties do not envisage every scenario, let alone a solution for each of them. The literature in law-and-economics and the economics of contracts has examined the problem of contractual 'gaps' and 'background/default rules',[72] accepting the idea of 'incomplete contract' as the working hypothesis,[73] and proposing as potential solutions: (a) a 'majoritarian' rule, ie a gap should be filled by the term that most parties would choose;[74] (b) the 'individually efficient' rule, ie a gap should be filled by the term that is efficient in the particular case[75] (eg 'reasonableness' standard[76]); (c) the 'plain meaning' rule, ie in case of a gap, courts should enforce the contract terms according to their ordinary or 'plain meaning', without trying to ascertain the individual parties' intentions or 'special meaning';[77] and (d) the 'penalty' rule, ie a gap will be filled by a rule that the majority of the parties would not choose, incentivizing the parties to contract around this gap in the future, which provides valuable guidance.[78]

8.27 Yet, these views do not fully capture the courts' dilemma, which (i) is often to determine whether there is a gap in the first place, and (ii) is less related to 'deliberate gaps', ie solutions left open by the parties because the cost is high, and more to 'unintended gaps' and inconsistencies between complex contract clauses, which are not a 'known unknown', where a market standard can be extrapolated, but an 'unknown unknown'.[79] Some scholars

---

[71] For a broader approach see David Ramos Muñoz, 'Can Complex Contracts Replace Bankruptcy Principles? Why Interpretation Matters' (2018) 92 Am Bankruptcy LJ 4.
[72] See eg Ian Ayres and Robert Gertner, 'Filling Gaps in Incomplete Contracts: An Economic Theory of Default Rules' (1989) 99 Yale LJ 87; Ian Ayres and Robert Gertner, 'Strategic Contract Inefficiency and the Optimal Choice of Default Rules' (1992) 101 Yale LJ 729.
[73] For legal scholars, including law-and-economics scholars, a contract is incomplete if the obligations arising out of it are not specified for all situations or, as some put it, for all 'states of the world'. For economists, a contract is incomplete if it fails to provide for the efficient set of obligations in each state of the world. See Robert Scott and George Triantis, 'Incomplete Contracts and a Theory of Contract Design' (2006) 56 Case W Res L Rev 187, 190–91. We are here primarily concerned with the law-and-economics inquiry, ie the optimal default rules in the case of a gap in contract provisions.
[74] See Charles Goetz and Robert E Scott, 'The Limits of Expanded Choice: An Analysis of the Interactions Between Express and Implied Contract Terms' (1985) 73 Cal L Rev 261.
[75] Eric E Posner, 'Economic Analysis of Contract Law after Three Decades: Success or Failure?' (2003) 112 Yale LJ 829, 840; Ian Ayres, 'Preliminary Thoughts on Optimal Tailoring of Contractual Rules' (1993) 3 S Cal Interdisc LJ 1.
[76] For example, the solution may be specific for the parties, but the principle that permits it needs to be more general. See L Kaplow, 'Rules versus Standards: An Economic Analysis' (1992) 42 Duke LJ 557.
[77] See Alan Schwartz and Robert Scott, 'Contract Theory and the Limits of Contract Law' (2004) 113 Yale LJ 541, 594–609.
[78] Ayres and Gertner, 'Strategic Contract Inefficiency' (n 73) and Ayres and Gertner, 'Filling Gaps' (n 73).
[79] Ramos Muñoz (n 71). For examples of unintended gaps and inconsistencies, see Claire Hill, 'Why Contracts Are Written in "Legalese"' (2001) 77 Chicago-Kent L Rev 59. See also Claire Hill, 'Bargaining in the Shadow of the Lawsuit: A Social Norms Theory of Incomplete Contracts' (2009) 34 Del J Corp L 191.

suggest that courts should rely on a self-referenced interpretation of the contract, and assume an intent to derogate from default rules.[80] Yet, if the contract content is convoluted or leads to absurd results this may be harder to justify as 'reasonable' than a well-known rule, which explains the phenomenon of 'sticky' default rules.[81] Even leaving this phenomenon aside, scholars tend to underestimate the difficulty of an integrative, self-referenced interpretation of a contract. In complex transactions, the parties' intent may be elusive, or a post-hoc construct.

Given that contract interpretation, when the meaning of terms is disputed, requires courts to look at the parties' goal, and the transaction's function and finality, it is not that different from statutory and legal interpretation in 'hard cases'. This should not be surprising. A rule is no less 'legal' because it is agreed between few (eg two) parties, and, when its 'true' meaning is elusive, there are limited options: one can use its 'regular', 'contextual', or 'finalistic' meaning. As in the case of statutory or precedent-based interpretation, there may be cases where the parties disagree about whether a specific provision applies to the facts (borderline problem) or more deeply about the sense that such provision has (pivotal problem). In 'pivotal' problems, determining what the contract language means cannot be made without determining what the clause does in the broader context of the ensemble of clauses where it is inserted, which requires a deeper understanding of the contract's finality and 'principles'. Such functional or finalistic interpretation may occasionally draw analogies with legal provisions solving similar problems, eg courts interpreting a term that may allocate decision-making rights to a majority of creditors (in creditor coordination cases) may check whether the solution is 'oppressive' in light of corporate or insolvency law. **8.28**

The tendency towards a functional interpretation is stronger in case of boilerplate contract provisions, which repeat themselves across the market, and thus a court decision will have an impact far beyond the individual case, as happens with the International Swaps and Derivatives Association (ISDA) documentation for derivatives. In *Sharon Steel Corp v Chase Manhattan Bank NA*[82] New York courts held that the interpretation of boilerplate language is a matter of law, not of fact, and must thus be uniform to ensure predictability and to foster efficient capital markets (a public policy interest).[83] The Delaware courts adopted this same view in *Bank of New York Mellon v Liberty Media Corp*.[84] Some scholars argue that there should be consistency beyond the specific transaction.[85] Others draw from the experience of sovereign debt markets, suggesting that some boilerplate clauses are so widely used that they **8.29**

---

[80] Put differently, courts should make default rules of interpretation easy to circumvent, unless the difficulty in doing so serves some socially desirable purpose, such as giving guidance to facilitate posterior decision-making by parties or courts, protecting the uninformed, or facilitating different negotiated solutions for different parties. See Ayres and Gertner, 'Filling Gaps' (n 73) 123–25; Lon Fuller, 'Consideration and Form' (1941) 41 Col L Rev 799, 800–801.

[81] Ayres and Gertner, 'Filling Gaps' (n 73) 120–23; Goetz and Scott (n 74). Schwartz and Scott also make a similar point. See Schwartz and Scott (n 77) 564.

[82] *Sharon Steel Corp v Chase Manhattan Bank NA* 691 F 2d 1039 (2d Cir 1982).

[83] ibid 1051.

[84] *The Bank of NY Mellon Trust Co v Liberty Media Corp* 29 A 3d 225 (Del 2011).

[85] David V Snyder, 'Language and Formalities in Commercial Contracts: A Defense of Custom and Conduct' (2001) 54 SMU L Rev 617.

constitute a sort of market norm, akin to statutory interpretation, and interpreters should rely on the original drafter's intent.[86] Yet, such an approach raises important issues, from the risk of oversimplifying the partis' intent[87] to the difficulty of tracing back every clause to its original drafter. In any event, the intuition behind such proposals remains valid: when interpreting contracts, context and finality matter, sometimes beyond the particular parties' relationship.

---

[86] The original intention of the parties who first used the clause would be, in a way, the genuine 'meeting of the minds'. See Stephen J Choi and Mitu Gulati, 'Contract as Statute' (2006) 104 Mich L Rev 1130. The authors have also done extraordinary work in tracking the evolution of specific boilerplate clauses in sovereign debt contracts. See Stephen Choi, Mitu Gulati, and Eric A Posner, 'The Dynamics of Contract Evolution' (2013) 88 NYU L Rev 1; Mitu Gulati and Robert Scott, *The Three and a Half Minute Transaction: Boilerplate and the Limits of Contract Design* (University of Chicago Press 2013).

[87] Ramos Muñoz (n 71). It is one thing to liken contract interpretation to statutory interpretation, as Choi and Gulati suggest, and another to consider that statutory interpretation consists in ascertaining the original intention of the drafters of the statute. 'Originalism' is a respected but by no means majoritarian approach to statutory interpretation. For one of the most popular and bright originalists see Antonin Scalia, *A Matter of Interpretation: Federal Courts and the Law* (PUP 1998). For an overview of the different approaches to interpretation in constitutional law see Jack M Balkin, 'Framework Originalism and the Living Constitution' (2009) 103 Nw L Rev 549.

9
Courts and the Law of Liability for Misstatements in Securities Offerings

1 Introduction: liability for misstatements and pure economic loss in private law 9.01
2 The development of a statute-based liability system: the US Exchange Act and Securities Act 9.11
  2.1 Implying a private right of action, and federalizing securities litigation 9.12
  2.2 Determining what investors deserve protection: materiality, reliance, and class actions. 9.26
  2.3 Section 10b and rule 10b-5 and defendants (renvoi) 9.37
  2.4 Registration statement and prospectus liability under the Securities Act 1933 9.38
  2.5 Section 10b, rule 10b-5, and vertical balance: Summary and latest developments 9.44
  2.6 Insider trading: a major source of criminal liability, a relatively secondary source of private law liability 9.50
3 The creeping codification of securities liability for misstatements in the EU 9.52
  3.1 Prospectus liability: an EU provision with doctrinal traction 9.53
  3.2 Courts' steps towards harmonizing prospectus remedies: scope, damages, and invalidity. 9.58
  3.3 The dawn of a doctrine of 'reliance' and 'fraud-on-the-market' in domestic and EU courts? 9.70
  3.4 Liability beyond prospectus: other disclosures and failures to disclose (market abuse) 9.84
4 Specialties of 'secondary actor' and gatekeeper liability 9.95
  4.1 Constitutional dimension: statements versus opinions and free speech in US law 9.96
  4.2 Private law considerations 9.106
  4.3 Regulatory dimension (I): secondary actors as 'makers' of statements? 9.122
  4.4 Regulatory considerations (II): Liability under securities laws and gatekeeper regulation in EU countries 9.137

1 Introduction: Liability for misstatements and pure economic loss in private law

A keystone in the private law of finance is the liability for economic loss caused by false information disseminated in the market. The inquiry to determine whether a party has made a 'statement' or 'opinion', 'omitted', or 'concealed' relevant information it was supposed to disclose, and whether the plaintiff is entitled to rely on the information intersperses issues of 'pure' private law of contract and tort, and regulatory issues (and, occasionally, constitutional protections). **9.01**

The starting point for private law is that a person A cannot be liable to just *any* person B for *any* damage resulting from *any* statement, but different legal systems use different ideas to 'enclose' the circle of plaintiffs and defendants. **9.02**

9.03 The German Civil Code (BGB) states that compensable damages result from an injury to 'the life, body, health, freedom, property or another right',[1] ie they rely on a 'list' of protected interests, based (1) on the Roman *LexAquilia*, which did not draw a sharp distinction between civil and delictual responsibility and ignored 'wealth' as an interest worthy of protection, hence the exclusion of 'pure economic loss' from compensable damages; and (2) on the 'jurisprudence of concepts' (*Begriffsjurisprudenz*).[2] Yet, the codification helped to systematize the law of torts, and the *nature* of the damage itself ceded ground to the *unlawfulness* of the damage.[3] Thus, damage is compensable if 'unlawful', because it injures one of the interests in the 'list', breaches a statutory rule,[4] or intentionally inflicts damage on another person in a manner contrary to 'common decency', or public policy.[5]

9.04 Traditional English law relied on a number of 'torts', and UK (and US) courts were reluctant to compensate for pure economic loss,[6] which may obey different rationales.[7] Some argue that limiting damages for 'pure economic loss' would miss the point that old English precedents excluded it as a way to limit the number of plaintiffs, not to exclude 'economic' losses per se.[8]

9.05 Yet, the 'torts' system was upended by the introduction of the tort of 'negligence', which allowed the compensation of damages resulting from the breach of a duty of care,[9] and now constitutes the basis of a majority of tort cases in the UK. In cases of misstatements, the 'unlawfulness' now depended on a 'duty of care' which is relative, ie depends on an assumption of responsibility by the person making the statements, which renders the situation 'akin to contract',[10] and/or the parties' 'proximity' or special relationship,[11] and a 'policy' analysis, which determines whether imposing such duty of care can be oppressive for the defendant.[12] Throughout this change, courts acknowledged that it was not sensible to restrict damages for 'economic loss' to cases of physical harm,[13] but others limited such economic loss to misrepresentation cases.[14]

---

[1] Section 823(1) of the German Civil Code provides that: 'A person who, intentionally or negligently, unlawfully injures the life, body, health, freedom, property or another right of another person is liable to make compensation to the other party for the damage arising from this.'

[2] James Gordley, 'The rule against recovery in negligence for pure economic loss: an historical accident?' in Mauro Bussani and Vernon Valentine Palmer (eds), *Pure Economic Loss in Europe* (CUP 2003) 36–46.

[3] Gordley (n 2) 39ff; Basil Markesinis, *The German Law of Torts* (Hart Publishing 1994) 68.

[4] German Civil Code, s 823 (2).

[5] ibid s 826.

[6] See eg *Ultramares Corporation v Touche* (1932) 174 NE 441 and *Caparo Industries PLC v Dickman* [1990] UKHL 2.

[7] One argument is rooted in Weir's distinction between policy aims: tort law is protective, and makes a person liable for making things worse, while contract law is productive, acts in furtherance of a person's interests; and, as such, makes a person liable for failing to make things better. Thus, economic losses belong in contract law. Yet, distinguishing between 'making things worse' and 'making things better' is not easy. See eg *Junior Books v Veitchi* [1983] 1 AC 520. See Basil S Markesinis and Simon Deakin, *Tort Law* (4th edn, Clarendon Press 1999) 9–12. Furthermore, this creates a difference between interests protected by tort and unprotected, or between property and wealth or the expectation of profit, which are hard to justify. See *Canadian National Railway v Norsk Pacific Steamship Co* 91 DLR (4th) 289, 383 (1992) (Stevenson J).

[8] Bernstein says that, while some cases categorically excluded 'economic' loss from the loss of third-party property, others acknowledged that the rationale for this was pragmatic, ie to avoid that claims may be indefinitely multiplied. See Robby Bernstein, *Economic Loss: General Principles* (2nd edn, Sweet & Maxwell 1998) 11–12 and case law cited. See also Gordley (n 2) 46–52.

[9] *Donoghue v Stevenson* [1932] All ER Rep 1, [1932] AC 562.

[10] *Hedley Byrne & Co Ltd v Heller & Partners Ltd* [1964] AC 465.

[11] *Caparo Industries PLC v Dickman* (n 6).

[12] ibid. See also *Ultramares Corporation v Touche* 174 NE 441 (1932).

[13] There was 'neither logic nor common sense' in granting recovery only when a financial loss was caused by physical injury. See *Hedley Byrne* (n 10) (Lord Devlin).

[14] *SCM (United Kingdom) Ltd v WJ Whittall & Son Ltd* [1971] 1 QB 337; *Spartan Steel & Alloys Ltd v Martin & Co (Contractors) Ltd* [1973] 1 QB 27 (Lord Denning).

In contrast with the German and common law systems, (1) tort laws in France, Spain, or Italy **9.06**
do not limit the type of damages that may be compensated (there is a general reference to
'damages'[15]); and (2) tort liability is based on a 'general clause'; where there is compensation
for damages *caused* wilfully or with 'fault' (*faute*, *culpa*, or *colpa*[16]). France and Spain do not
explicitly require 'unlawfulness',[17] while Italy has a mixed system,[18] requiring 'unjust damage'
(*danno ingiusto*)[19] (some scholars argue that Spanish law also requires 'unlawfulness').[20]

A second element of comparison is the division between contract and tort. In common law **9.07**
systems, for example, contract law is shaped by the idea of *consideration*: if a party gave no
consideration (ie did not suffer a detriment nor conferred a benefit on the promisor) she
cannot enforce the promise, nor claim liability from the promisor.[21] This rigidity led to an
'escape into' tort law for matters that could have been regulated by contract principles,[22] including liability for misstatements.[23]

Conversely, German law restricted the damages redressable by tort liability, which, in turn, **9.08**
led to the expansion of contract liability to (1) cases of *culpa in contrahendo* in the pre-
contractual phase of negotiations;[24] and (2) cases where a party should be within the protective sphere of the contract;[25] and (3) in cases of negligent misstatements.[26]

Civil law systems in France, Spain, or Italy contemplate both a flexible notion of contract (in- **9.09**
cluding third-party beneficiaries[27]) *and* a general clause of fault-based tort liability,[28] which
makes it harder to classify liability for misstatements as 'tort' or 'contract'.[29] Yet, even if included under 'contract', the duty of the person giving information is one of means, and a
breach revolves around the subjective element of 'fault'.[30]

These relatively basic principles must provide the basis for the very complex environment **9.10**
of liability for misstatements by parties who issue or offer financial instruments, and secondary actors who participate in that offer. Different jurisdictions have coped with this
phenomenon using different approaches, and this chapter analyses their 'hits and misses'.
First, we analyse the challenges of *creating* a wholly new liability system, based on regulatory

---

[15] French Civil Code, art 1240, Spanish Civil Code, art 1902, Italian Civil Code, art 1223.
[16] ibid. See also Italian Civil Code, art 2043.
[17] See art 1240 of the French Civil Code, and art 1902 of the Spanish Civil Code.
[18] Mauro Bussani and Vernon Valentine Palmer, 'The Liability Regimes of Europe: Their Façades and Interiors' in Mauro Bussani and Vernon Valentine Palmer (eds), *Pure Economic Loss in Europe* (CUP 2003) 133–35.
[19] Italian Civil Code, art 2043.
[20] José Manuel Busto Lago, *La antijuridicidad del daño resarcible en la responsabilidad civil extracontractual* (Tecnos 1998) 17 ff. Yet, since an 'unlawful' damage depends on the breach of a conduct rule, and the conduct rule is general (ie 'harm no one') the unlawfulness would be hard to differentiate from the assessment of 'fault', except if a valid defence excludes liability (eg legitimate exercise of rights, consent of the aggrieved person, legitimate defence or state of necessity). ibid 246.
[21] Sir Guenter Treitel, *The Law of Contract* (11th edn, Sweet & Maxwell 2003) 67. This even annulled contract provisions for the benefit of third parties, requiring the Contracts (Rights of Third Parties) Act 1999.
[22] See *Ross v Caunters* (1980) Ch 297; *Junior Books Ltd v Veitchi Co Ltd* [1983] 1 AC 520.
[23] *Hedley Byrne* (n 10).
[24] Reichsgericht (Sixth Civil division) RGZ 78, 239, JW 1912, 191 (7 December 1911).
[25] See Bundesgerichtshof, BGHZ 66, 51, NJW 1976, 712 (28 January 1976).
[26] BGH 1979, 548, NJW 1979, 1595 (12 February 1979).
[27] Spanish Civil Code, art 1257, Italian Civil Code, art 1411. See B Nicholas, *The French Law of Contract* (OUP 1992) 181 ff.
[28] French Civil Code, art 1240, Spanish Civil Code, art 1103, Italian Civil Code, art 2043.
[29] See eg Frances Donato Busnelli, 'Itinerari europei nella 'terra di nessuno tra contratto e fatto illecito': la responsabilità da informazioni inesatte' in F Busnelli and S Patti, *Danno e responsabilità civile* (Giappichelli 1997) 222.
[30] ibid.

provisions using the US as an example. Secondly, we analyse the challenges in the EU countries, which have tried to adjust tort doctrines under private law to the purpose and finality of regulatory provisions, ie seeking convergence of outcomes, while preserving autonomy of means or procedure. Finally, we separately analyse the role of liability of 'secondary actors', including 'gatekeepers', where private law principles are combined with constitutional considerations and regulatory goals.

2 The development of a statute-based liability system: the US Exchange Act and Securities Act

9.11 US law by far has the most developed law of securities law liability. First, we will see how section 10b of the Securities and Exchange Act (hereafter: Exchange Act), and its accompanying rule 10b-5, developed by the Securities and Exchange Commission (SEC) which regulate statements made in secondary markets spearheaded the creation of the current 'system' largely through path-dependent choices that helped establish a private *federal* right of action (section 2.1) then limit the instances where this would be available (section 2.2) and the circle of defendants (section 2.3) Then, we will complete the picture by analysing the role of sections 11 and 12 of the Securities Act, which regulate liability for the registration statement (section 2.4) the subsequent role of state law (section 2.5) and the limited role of insider trading provisions (section 2.6).

2.1 Implying a private right of action, and federalizing securities litigation

9.12 Section 10(b) makes it unlawful to 'use or employ, in connection with the purchase or sale of any security' a 'manipulative or deceptive device or contrivance in contravention of such rules and regulations as the [SEC] may prescribe'.[31] The SEC's implementing regulation, rule 10b-5, further elaborates this statutory language, rendering 'unlawful', 'in connection with the purchase or sale of any security' to: [e]mploy any device, scheme, or artifice to defraud; make any untrue statement of a material fact or to omit to state a material fact necessary in order to make the statements made not misleading; or engage in any act, practice, or course of business which operates or would operate as a fraud or deceit upon any person'.[32] Both rules are a 'legislative acorn' from where a proverbial oak tree grew,[33] since case law applying both provisions is far more abundant than case law applying all other securities law provisions combined.

9.13 Yet, an obvious observation is that neither provision talks about private plaintiffs' rights of action. Legislators drafted section 10b as a broad provision enabling the SEC to regulate securities markets, but has been circumscribed to 'disclosure' cases,[34] and section 10b-5,

---

[31] 15 USC s 78j(b).
[32] 17 CFR s 240.10b-5.
[33] See Chief Justice Rehnquist in *Blue Chip Stamps v. Manor Drug Stores*, 421 U.S. 723, 737 (1975). The English proverb reads 'great oaks from little acorns grow'.
[34] Steve Thel, 'The Original Conception of Section 10(b) of the Securities Exchange Act' (1990) 42 Stanford L Rev 385.

drafted somewhat hastily,[35] did not have in mind the subsequent flood of *private* litigation.[36] Thus, in a way both provisions are narrower than originally intended,[37] but in another way, their impact in private securities law has been impressive, thanks largely to the role of courts.

Key to this has been the combination between (i) the 'horizontal' issue of the respective roles of agencies (part of the executive) and courts; (ii) the 'vertical' issue of the respective roles of state corporate law (as well as contract law or fiduciary principles); and (iii) the respective roles of government (again, through its agencies) and individuals in spearheading the legal debate by acting as the relevant plaintiffs. In securities lawsuits under section 10b and rule 10b-5 the issues have been inextricably intertwined.

9.14

Although lower courts had implied a private right of action relatively early,[38] the US Supreme Court tackled securities laws' private right of action relatively late, and its first decisions did not refer to section 10b. In *SEC v Capital Gains Research Bureau*[39] the Supreme Court held that under the *Investment Advisers Act* the SEC could obtain an injunction compelling a registered investment adviser to disclose to his clients his practice of purchasing shares of a security for his own account *shortly before recommending* that security for long-term investment only to sell it immediately after at a profit, as 'a fraud or deceit upon any client'. To the Court the Act had to be construed flexibly, to protect its remedial purpose,[40] its goal of full and frank disclosure,[41] intended to 'substitute a philosophy of disclosure for the philosophy of *caveat emptor*'.[42]

9.15

Next year, the Court decided *JI Case Co. v Borak* (*Borak*).[43] Overturning the finding of lower courts, the Supreme Court held that, in a case of breach of state fiduciary laws, the plaintiff could also allege a breach of federal securities laws[44] on proxy solicitation statements, under section 14 of the Exchange Act, and federal courts could award not only declaratory relief, but also equitable relief, as the provision permitted a private cause of action, and federal courts could provide remedies.[45] Although the provision did not refer expressly to private actions, this could be considered implicit in its finality of 'investor protection' and 'broad remedial purpose', including both direct and derivative actions.[46] Thus: 'When a federal statute condemns an act as unlawful, the extent and nature of the legal consequences of the condemnation, although left by the statute to judicial determination, are nevertheless federal questions, the answers to which are to be derived from the statute and the federal *policy* which it has adopted.'[47]

9.16

---

[35] ibid 462, citing Conference on Codification of the Federal Securities Laws, 22 Bus Law 793, 921–23 (1967) (recollections of Milton Friedman).
[36] See eg American Bar Association (ABA) 'Rule 10b-5' https://www.americanbar.org/groups/business_law/publications/the_business_lawyer/find_by_subject/buslaw_tbl_mci_rule10b5/ (accessed 30 September 2022).
[37] Thel (n 34) 463 and fns 3–12 and accompanying text.
[38] See eg *Kardon v National Gypsum Co* 69 F Supp 512 (ED Pa 1946).
[39] *SEC v Capital Gains Research Bureau Inc* 375 US 180 (1963).
[40] ibid.
[41] ibid.
[42] ibid.
[43] ibid.
[44] The complaint sought rescission or damages to a corporate stockholder with respect to a consummated merger where he was deprived of pre-emption rights, and which was authorized pursuant to the use of a proxy statement alleged to contain false and misleading statements.
[45] Section 14, 15 USC s 78n(a), and s 27, 15 USC s 78aa.
[46] *JI Case Co v Borak* 377 US 426, 433 (1964).
[47] ibid, citing *Sola Electric Co v Jefferson Electric Co* 317 US 173, 317 US 176 (1942).

9.17 In *Mills v Electric Auto-Lite Co* (*Mills*)[48] lower courts had dismissed a complaint by minority shareholders under corporate law to set aside a merger, because, they held, the terms were 'fair', and the shareholders had to rebut the presumption of fairness. Yet, the plaintiffs alleged, the merger had been prompted by a false or misleading proxy statement, which failed to disclose that some corporate directors of one of the merging corporations were nominees of, and controlled by, the other corporation.[49] The Supreme Court reversed, holding that dismissing the complaint would contravene the purpose of proxy solicitation rules by bypassing shareholders,[50] and leaving shareholders the burden of rebutting the presumption of fairness would discourage them from privately enforcing proxy rules that 'provides a necessary supplement to Commission action'.[51] Thus, instead of letting the federal issue of transparency be absorbed within the 'fairness' of the merger under state corporate laws, the Court affirmed federal securities law's independence, and the need for a separate cause of action. These early cases show that securities fraud case law was enabled by precedents on different provisions (on proxy statements) which helped build causes of action independent of state *corporate* and/or *fiduciary* standards.

9.18 Only in the early 1970s did the Supreme Court address private causes of action under section 10b. In *Superintendent of Insurance v Bankers Life & Casualty Co.* (*Bankers Life*)[52] the plaintiffs alleged that a corporation's sole stockholder had misappropriated sale proceeds.[53] Lower courts had dismissed, holding that no investor was harmed, and that the securities transactions themselves were unobjectionable.[54] The Supreme Court disagreed. Even if the transactions arguably did not undermine securities markets, there was an 'act' or 'practice' under rule 10b-5, and section 10b,[55] because the reference to 'in connection with' a sale of securities had to be construed broadly, and:

> [t]he fact that the transaction is not conducted through a securities exchange or an organized over-the-counter market is irrelevant to the coverage of § 10(b) ... Likewise irrelevant is the fact that the proceeds of the sale that were due the seller were misappropriated.[56]

9.19 Most relevant, the Court confirmed lower courts' view that rule 10b-5 implied a private cause of action.[57] This was reaffirmed next year in *Affiliated Ute Citizens v United States* on the sale of shares in a corporation that managed tribal assets and

---

[48] *Mills v Electric Auto-Lite Co* 396 US 375 (1970).
[49] The petitioners, minority shareholders of respondent Electric Auto-Lite Co, brought this action derivatively and on behalf of minority shareholders as a class to set aside a merger of Auto-Lite and the Mergenthaler Linotype Co (which, before the merger, owned over half of Auto-Lite's stock). The petitioners charged that the proxy solicitation for the merger by Auto-Lite's management was materially misleading, and violated s 14(a) of the Securities Exchange Act of 1934 and rule 14a-9 thereunder, in that the merger was recommended to Auto-Lite's shareholders by that company's directors without their disclosing that they were all nominees of and controlled by Mergenthaler. *Mills v Electric Auto-Lite Co* (n 48).
[50] Securities Exchange Act of 1934, s 14(a) and r 14a-9.
[51] *Mills v Electric Auto-Lite Co* (n 48), citing *JI Case Co v Borak* (n 46) 432.
[52] *Superintendent of Insurance v Bankers Life & Casualty Co* 404 US 6 (1971).
[53] The petitioner (liquidator of Manhattan Casualty Co) alleged that the company's sole owner sold to a person who conspired with others to use Manhattan's own Treasury bonds to pay for the shares; the bonds were sold and the proceeds used in the purchase of the stock, thus depleting Manhattan's assets. This was concealed by a purported transfer (in exchange for the bond sale proceeds) of a certificate of deposit which, in fact, had been assigned by Manhattan's new president, a co-conspirator, to another corporation, and by it used as collateral for a loan.
[54] '[N]o investor [was] injured' and that the 'purity of the security transaction and the purity of the trading process were unsullied'. *Pehowic v Erie Lackawanna Railroad Company* 430 F 2d 361 (1970).
[55] *Superintendent of Insurance v Bankers Life & Casualty Co* (n 52).
[56] ibid 11, citing *Hooper v Mountain States Securities Corp* 282 F 2d 195, 201 (1960).
[57] *Superintendent of Insurance v Bankers Life & Casualty Co* (n 52) 14, citing *Shell v Hensley* 430 F 2d 819, 827 (1970).

rights,[58] which also discussed the issue of investor *reliance* (see s 2.2), and reaffirmed again in *Blue Chip Stamps v Manor Drugs*,[59] where the Court also confirmed lower courts' longstanding *Birnbaum* doctrine[60] that only purchasers of securities could file a claim under rule 10b-5.

Thus, in *Ernst & Ernst v Hochfelder*[61] the Supreme Court relied on the weight of precedent, and openly acknowledged that: **9.20**

> Although § 10(b) does not, by its terms, create an express civil remedy for its violation, and there is no indication that Congress, or the Commission when adopting Rule 10b-5, contemplated such a remedy, the existence of a private cause of action for violations of the statute and the Rule is now well established ... During the 30-year period since a private cause of action was first implied under § 10(b) and Rule 10b-5, a substantial body of case law and commentary has developed as to its elements.[62]

Courts' social norm about the respective roles of federal and state laws had changed enough to openly acknowledge that this was not Congress' plan after all. The Court could then concentrate on polishing the details of the nascent securities fraud doctrine, as it did in the next cases. **9.21**

In *Santa Fe Industries*[63] minority shareholders who opposed a short-form merger, instead of seeking compensation of their fair value through a second appraisal (corporate law remedy) alleged that their stock had been fraudulently appraised, under section 10b and rule 10b-5. The Court held that federal provisions were only actionable for 'manipulation or deception', which was not present (shareholders were given the necessary information[64]), the transaction's 'fairness' was not important for the Act, which focused on disclosure,[65] and, crucially: **9.22**

> A second factor in determining whether Congress intended to create a federal cause of action in these circumstances is 'whether *the cause of action [is] one traditionally relegated to state law*' ... The result would be to bring within the Rule a wide variety of corporate conduct traditionally left to state regulation. In addition to posing a 'danger of vexatious litigation ... this extension of the federal securities laws would overlap and quite possibly interfere with state corporate law.

---

[58] *Affiliated Ute Citizens of Utah v United States* 406 US 128 (1972). The Ute Partition Act enabled the partition and distribution of the tribe's assets between mixed-blood and full-blood members, and the joint management of assets not practicably distributable. Ute Distribution Corp (UDC) was created to jointly manage oil, gas, and mineral rights, it issued 10 shares and made First Security Bank of Utah (the bank) UDC's stock transfer agent. There were several federal court cases, and in one (*Reyos*) some mixed-bloods sued the bank, alleging breaches of Rule 10b_5.
[59] *Blue Chip Stamps* (n 33).
[60] *Birnbaum v Newport Steel Corp* 193 F 2d 461 (1952).
[61] *Ernst & Ernst v Hochfelder* 425 US 185 (1976). An accounting firm was retained to audit a brokerage firm's books and records, whose customers invested in a fraudulent scheme by the firm's president and principal stockholder. Customers sued the accounting firm under section 10(b) as having 'aided and abetted' the fraud by failing to uncover it (the brokerage firm was bankrupt, its president committed suicide).
[62] *Ernst & Ernst v Hochfelder* (n 61) 197, citing *Blue Chip Stamps* (n 33), *Affiliated Ute Citizens of Utah* and lower courts' *Kardon v National Gypsum Co* 69 F Supp 512 (ED Pa 1946).
[63] *Santa Fe Industries Inc v Green* 430 US 462 (1977).
[64] *Castaneda v Partida* 430 US 473–77 (1977).
[65] the Court repeatedly has described the 'fundamental purpose' of the Act as implementing a 'philosophy of full disclosure'; once full and fair disclosure has occurred, the fairness of the terms of the transaction is, at most, a tangential concern of the statute. *Castaneda v Partida* (n 64) 478.

9.23 In *Aaron v SEC*,[66] the Court reaffirmed the requirement of 'scienter' in lawsuits seeking injunctive relief. Yet, in *Herman & MacLean v Huddleston*[67] it held that section 10b's fraud action was compatible with the more specific action for misstatements in the *registration statement*,[68] and that plaintiffs had to satisfy the 'preponderance of evidence' standard, and not the more exacting 'clear and convincing evidence' standard of civil fraud under state laws, because federal securities statutes sought to remedy common law remedies' deficiencies in securities markets, not reproduce them.[69]

9.24 Thus, from a habilitation for the SEC to regulate securities markets section 10b was transformed into a habilitation for court-enforced civil remedies. This also allowed courts to model the provision and adjust the process.

9.25 Yet, Congress was not fully comfortable with this, and passed the Private Securities Litigation Reform Act (PSLRA) to enact a heightened pleading standard: securities fraud claims would need to *specify* each misleading statement, its maker, time, and place, the elements of the false representation *and* what its maker obtained, and explain why the statement was misleading. On scienter, plaintiffs must 'state with particularity facts giving rise to a strong inference that the defendant acted with the required state of mind'.[70] The PSLRA thus opened a new chapter of Congress-Court interaction. Thus, in *SEC v Zandford*[71] the Court held that a stockbroker's sale of his customer's securities and use of proceeds for his own benefit was a fraud 'in connection with the purchase or sale of any security',[72] giving continuity to earlier precedents like *Borak*, *Mills*, or *Bankers Life*, holding that, although not every fraud involving securities falls under section 10(b), a 'scheme in which the securities transactions and breaches of fiduciary duty coincide' may give rise to liability under the statute.[73] Yet, in *Tellabs, Inc. v Makor*,[74] the Court openly acknowledged that the PSLRA's demanding pleading requirements were 'among the control measures Congress included in the PSLRA', to curb 'abusive litigation by private parties', and interpreted the reference to strong inference[75] as meaning 'more than merely plausible or reasonable'.[76] Since the PSLRA finality was to increase the plaintiffs' pleading burden, a 'complaint would survive ... only if a reasonable person would deem the inference of scienter cogent and at least as compelling as any opposing inference one could draw from the facts alleged'.

2.2 Determining what investors deserve protection: materiality, reliance, and class actions

9.26 After sculpting a private claim from the breach of regulatory provisions, US courts also shaped the process in a second way. Once a court determines that the Act seeks to protect investors, and this justifies a private right of action, the immediate next step is to determine

---

[66] *Aaron v SEC* 446 US 680 (1980).
[67] *Herman & MacLean v Huddleston* 459 US 375 (1983).
[68] See sections 2.3 and 2.4.
[69] *Herman & MacLean v Huddleston* (n 67) 387–91.
[70] 15 USC s 78u-4(b)(2).
[71] *SEC v Zandford* 535 US 813 (2002).
[72] ibid 815, 818.
[73] ibid 820, 825.
[74] *Tellabs Inc v Makor Issues & Rights Ltd* 551 US 308 (2007).
[75] Which created a split among Circuits. *Bowles v Russell* 551 US 314 (2007).
[76] *Tellabs Inc v Makor Issues & Rights Ltd* (No 06-484) 437 F 3d 588 (2007).

what kind of investor deserves protection. This means establishing what kind of facts, if false, can result in a cause of action (*materiality* of *omissions* and *opinions*), and what behaviour is expected from investors (*reliance*). The issue arose in *Mills*[77] where the Court held that the Circuit should not have required shareholders to prove that the allegedly false proxy statement 'had a decisive effect' on the vote, holding that it sufficed that it 'might have been' considered important by a 'reasonable person'.[78] Yet, the point was not central for the decision, because courts had considered the requirement to be met. Thus, in *TSC Industries, Inc. v Northway, Inc.*[79] a minority shareholder alleged that the proxy statement where shareholders were recommended to vote in favour of a merger with liquidation was false and materially misleading,[80] the Supreme Court rejected the '*might* consider important' standard, holding that an omitted fact would be 'material' when there is a 'substantial likelihood that a reasonable investor would consider it important', because it would see it as affecting the 'total mix of information made available'.[81]

9.27 The standard was imported into securities fraud cases in *Basic Inc. v Levinson*,[82] a landmark case on the treatment of 'omissions' and investors' 'reliance'. On omissions the Court held that 'silence, absent a duty to disclose, is not misleading under rule 10b-5'.[83] Lower courts used this holding to dismiss 'vague and non-specific' statements as mere 'puffery', and thus non-actionable,[84] even to hold that a statement or omission is not 'material' if the market already possesses said information,[85] or to consider immaterial representations made in the presence of 'cautionary language' in the same offering ('bespeaks caution' doctrine)[86] except if the defendant fails to disclose that the risk has transpired.[87]

9.28 On the other hand, in *Stoneridge Investment Partners*[88] the Supreme Court followed *Basic* and *Affiliated Ute Citizens*,[89] to conclude that, in a securities fraud claim where there are 'material' omissions, there is a presumption of reliance.[90] Thus, lower courts had to deal with the question of when there is a duty to disclose, which is of special relevance in the disclosure of 'known trends and uncertainties' under Item 303 of Regulation S-K. Courts in the Third,

---

[77] *Mills v Electric Auto-Lite Co* (n 48).
[78] *Mills v Electric Auto-Lite Co* (n 48) 385–86: 'Where the misstatement ... has been shown to be 'material', as it was found to be here, that determination itself indubitably embodies a conclusion that the defect was of such a character that it might have been considered important by a reasonable shareholder ... There is no need to supplement this requirement, as did the Court of Appeals, with a requirement of proof of whether the defect actually had a decisive effect on the voting.'
[79] *TSC Industries Inc v Northway Inc* 426 US 438 (1976).
[80] Among other factors, National Industries (National) acquired 34 per cent of TSC, and replaced its board with National nominees, including its president and vice-president, and proposed a merger with liquidation of TSC, without disclosing who were National's nominees in the proxy statement. *TSC Industries Inc v Northway Inc* (n 79).
[81] ibid 450: This standard is fully consistent with *Mills*' general description of materiality as a requirement that 'the defect have a significant *propensity* to affect the voting process'. It does not require proof of a substantial likelihood that disclosure of the omitted fact would have caused the reasonable investor to change his vote.
[82] *Basic Inc v Levinson* (1988) 485 US 224.
[83] ibid n 17: 'To be actionable, of course, a statement must also be misleading. Silence, absent a duty to disclose, is not misleading under Rule 10b-5. "No comment" statements are generally the functional equivalent of silence.'
[84] Recently see eg *Geffner v Coca-Cola Co* 928 F 3d 198, 200 (2d Cir 2019).
[85] *In re Convergent Techs Sec Litig* 948 F 2d 507 (9th Cir 1991).
[86] *Halperin v eBanker USA.com Inc* 295 F 3d 352, 357 (2d Cir 2002); *Rombach v Chang* 355 F 3d 164, 174 (2d Cir 2004).
[87] *Halperin* (n 86) para 173, ie there is 'no protection to someone who warns his hiking companion to walk slowly because there might be a ditch ahead when he knows with near certainty that the Grand Canyon lies one foot away'. In re *Prudential Sec Inc Partnerships Litig* 930 F Supp 2d 68, 72 (SDNY 1996).
[88] *Stoneridge Investment Partners LLC v Scientific-Atlanta Inc* 552 US 148 (2008).
[89] *Affiliated Ute Citizens of Utah v United States* 406 US 128, 154 (1972).
[90] *Stoneridge Investment Partners LLC v Scientific-Atlanta* (n 88) 159.

Ninth, and Eleventh Circuit seemed to find that non-compliance with Item 303 cannot be the basis for securities fraud claims, because 'materiality' under Item 303 is based on the standard that the disclosures are 'reasonably likely' to have an impact on sales, revenue etc., while section 10b is based on a 'substantial likelihood' standard.[91] Conversely, some Second Circuit cases suggested that, in line with *Stoneridge*, non-compliance with Item 303 could be a basis for a claim[92] *if* a trend or uncertainty is presently known to management, reasonably likely to have material effects on the registrant's financial conditions, and there is 'a substantial likelihood that the disclosure of the omitted fact would have been viewed by the reasonable investor as having significantly altered the total mix of information made available' considering quantitative and qualitative factors.[93] Although in *Leidos*, a case where the Supreme Court could have clarified this, the parties settled (*Leidos, Inc. v Ind. Pub. Ret. Sys.*, No. 16-581); the Supreme Court may settle the issue in *Macquarie Infrastructure Corp. v Moab Partners* (No. 22-1165).

9.29 Courts have also dealt with the question of *'opinions'*, the authority being *Omnicare*,[94] not a section 10b case, but a section 11 (registration statement) case, where the Supreme Court held that a pharmaceutical company's registration statement, including declarations 'believed' to be in compliance with the law, could not give rise to a claim, and that the (reversed) Circuit decision had conflated 'statements' and 'opinions'. Nor did the registration statement contain omissions that could render the opinions untrue, because this would only happen if (i) material facts were omitted, which (ii) would conflict with what a reasonable investor would take from the statement itself,[95] which has become a standard for subsequent decisions by lower courts.[96]

9.30 The 'reliance' requirement was explored in *Basic Inc. v Levinson* with an interesting plot twist. The case concerned a merger, the companies' representatives publicly denied the ongoing merger talks, and Basic's shareholders who sold their shares between the 'denial' and the suspension of trading filed a class action lawsuit. Class certification requires that *common* questions of fact or law *predominate* over individual plaintiffs' particular questions,[97] and the defendants alleged that securities fraud requires investor 'reliance' to establish the causal connection between misrepresentation and injury',[98] and the need to establish *individual reliance* defeated class certification. Yet, the Supreme Court held that, important as it was, reliance was not the only way to show causal connection: against the causation in 'face-to-face' transactions of early precedents, investors currently transacted by going to the market, which priced the securities.[99] Thus, since presumptions were useful devices to allocate the burden of proof, *and* Congress 'relied on the premise that securities markets are affected by information' one could use a 'fraud-on-the-market' theory, to *presume* reliance. The

---

[91] *Oran v Stafford* 226 F 3d 275, 287 (3d Cir 2000); *In re Nvidia Corp Sec Litig* 768 F 3d 1046 (9th Cir 2014); *Carvelli v Ocwen Fin Corp* 934 F 3d 1307, 1331 (11th Cir 2019).
[92] *Indiana Public Retirement System v SAIC Inc* 818 F 3d 85 (2d Cir 2016); *Stratte-McClure v Morgan Stanley* 77 F 3d 94 (2d Cir 2015).
[93] See *Litwin v Blackstone Grp LP* 634 F 3d 706, 716–17 (2d Cir 2011); *Ganino* 228 F 3d 154 (2d Cir 2000).
[94] *Omnicare Inc v Laborers District Council Construction Industry Pension Fund* 575 US 175 (2015).
[95] ibid 12.
[96] *Abramson v Newlink Genetics Corp* 965 F 3d 165, 175 (2d Cir 2020); *Fogel v Vega* 759 F App 18, 24 (2d Cir 2018); *City of Dearborn Heights Act 345 Police & Fire Ret Sys v Align Tech Inc* 856 F 3d 605, 610 (9th Cir 2017).
[97] Fed Rule Civ Proc, s 23(b)(3).
[98] *Basic v Levinson* (n 82).
[99] Between seller and buyer the market transmits information in the form of a market price, performing a substantial part of the valuation process as the investor's 'unpaid agent'. *Basic v Levinson* (n 82) citing *In re LTV Securities Litigation* (1980) 88 FRD 134, 143 (ND Tex).

presumption could be rebutted by showing that the misleading information did not lead to price distortions, or that an individual plaintiff would have traded even knowing the falsity, eg market-makers privy to the information, or if the information had somehow reached the markets, and was reflected in the price, or if investors would have divested for other reasons.

Fraud-on-the-market led to class-actions and litigation in great numbers, and then to subsequent attempts to limit it. Some scholars objected that the surge of class actions in the 90s and 2000s failed to fulfil the two main *Basic* objectives: to compensate investors, since many investors' diversification strategies accounted for the risk already, and class actions resulted in redistribution among investors, and to deter from fraud.[100] The PSLRA increased the burden of pleading requirements, and, in its initial drafting, would have excluded the *Basic* presumption altogether, but this was ultimately kept.[101]

9.31

The debate moved then to the courts[102] in *Dura Pharmaceuticals*,[103] where investors alleged that the company's managers' and directors' statements about future Food and Drug Administration approval of a new asthmatic spray device fraudulently led investors to purchase Dura securities at an artificially inflated price,[104] the Supreme Court held that 'an inflated purchase price' will not by itself constitute or proximately cause the relevant economic loss needed to allege and prove 'loss causation'. The Court drew a parallel between section 10b and common law torts of deceit and misrepresentation, to conclude that 'economic loss' and 'loss causation' were requirements of both, and the Ninth Circuit's 'inflated price' theory was mistaken. First, at the moment of purchase 'there has been no loss ... yet, and the link with subsequent loss is not invariably strong', since it will depend, eg on the price of sale.[105] Given 'the tangle of factors affecting price', misrepresentation may sometimes 'touch upon', but does not necessarily 'cause' a loss.[106] Secondly, the 'inflated price' theory overlooked that securities statutes sought to 'maintain public confidence in the marketplace ... by deterring fraud', 'not to provide investors with broad insurance against market losses, but to protect them against those economic losses that misrepresentations actually cause'.[107]

9.32

The cumulative discontent with the surge of class actions probably emboldened Supreme Court plaintiffs' (typically defendants in lower courts) ultimately unsuccessful attempt to persuade the Supreme Court to overrule *Basic* in the *Halliburton* cases. These cases concerned the merger of Halliburton and its competitor Dresser industries, promoted as a win–win by Halliburton's CEO (and former US Vice-President) Dick Cheney, without disclosing Dresser's massive asbestos liabilities. Halliburton's price dropped 72 per cent

9.33

---

[100] Paul G Mahoney, 'Precaution Costs and the Law of Fraud in Impersonal Markets' (1992) 78 Va L Rev 623, 650–51; John C Coffee Jr, 'Reforming the Securities Class Action: An Essay on Deterrence and Its Implementation' (2006) 106 Colum L Rev 1534, 1556–61; Amanda M Rose, 'The Multienforcer Approach to Securities Fraud Deterrence: A Critical Analysis' (2010) 158 UPA L Rev 2173, 2179–80.
[101] John W Avery, 'Securities Litigation Reform: The Long and Winding Road to the Private Securities Litigation Reform Act of 1995' (1996) 51 The Business Lawyer 335, 335–78.
[102] Some cases tried to restrict the number of defendants, as we will see below. *Central Bank Of Denver NA v First Interstate Bank Of Denver NA and Jack K Naber* 511 US 164 (1994) no 92-854; *Stoneridge Investment Partners LLC v Scientific-Atlanta* (n 88); *Janus Capital Grp Inc v First Derivative Traders* 564 US 135, 131 S Ct 2296 (2010).
[103] *Dura Pharmaceuticals Inc v Broudo* 544 US 336 (2005).
[104] 15 USC s 78u–4(b)(4). The District Court dismissed, for lack of pleading 'loss causation'; the Circuit reversed, based on 'fraud-on-the-market'.
[105] *Dura Pharmaceuticals v Broudo* (n 103): 'Shares are normally purchased with an eye toward a later sale. But if, say, the purchaser sells the shares quickly before the relevant truth begins to leak out, the misrepresentation will not have led to any loss. If the purchaser sells later after the truth makes its way into the market place, an initially inflated purchase price *might* mean a later loss. But that is far from inevitably so.'
[106] *Dura Pharmaceuticals v Broudo* (n 103).
[107] ibid.

post-disclosure, leading investors to sue, although the district and circuit dismissed, holding that causation had not been proven.[108] The Supreme Court held that 'fraud-on-the-market' applied to 'common reliance', and thus investors did not need to prove loss causation for class certification purposes.[109] Upon remand, the district and circuit certified the class ('causation/reliance' arguments belonged in the trial stage[110]), leading to another petition to the Supreme Court. In the meantime, in *Amgen*[111] the Court dismissed a different line of attack on *Basic*. The Court rejected the petitioners' view that the 'predominance of common questions' requirement required plaintiffs to prove 'materiality' (only material misrepresentations should affect prices in an efficient market) holding that the assessment of 'materiality' belonged in the trial stage, not upon class certification.[112] Eventually, in *Halliburton II* the Court reaffirmed *Basic*,[113] admitting that 'fraud-on-the-market' was a judicial creation, but rejecting the petitioners' reasons to overrule it. The Court dismissed the plaintiffs' behavioural economics and empirical evidence contradicting the 'efficient capital markets hypothesis', holding that *Basic* was not based on a 'robust view' of market efficiency, but on the more modest premise that 'market professionals generally consider most publicly announced material statements about companies, thereby affecting stock market prices'.[114] The Court also rejected the plaintiffs' criticism of *Basic*'s assumption that most investors rely on prices because they cannot outperform the market (with the counterexample of 'value investors'[115]) holding that 'value investors' are not indifferent to prices either. The Court also rejected petitioners' broader point that the logic of recent cases, which sought to narrow down securities fraud actions *not intended by Congress* by reducing the circle of defendants led to overruling *Basic*, holding that the need to constrain the circle of defendants would have meant to eviscerate the requirement of proving plaintiffs' reliance, while *Basic* 'provides an alternative means of satisfying it'.[116] Ultimately, the Court held, the risk and cost of excessive litigation were matters best left for Congress.

9.34 After *Halliburton* rejected a plain overruling, the plaintiffs concentrated on nibbling at the edges of *Basic*, as in *Goldman Sachs v Arkansas Teachers*,[117] where Goldman's shareholders brought securities fraud action against the bank and its executives, alleging that in the period 2006–2010 Goldman misrepresented its conflicts-of-interest procedures, and the integrity and honesty of its practices (Goldman had conflicts in the structuring and marketing of Collateralized Debt Obligations) making the stock price 'to remain inflated by preventing pre-existing inflation from dissipating from the stock price' ('inflation maintenance theory'),[118] until a SEC enforcement action corrected it. The district court and Circuit

---

[108] *Archdiocese of Milwaukee Supporting Fund Inc v Halliburton Co* 597 F 3d 330 (5th Cir 2010).
[109] *Erica P John Fund Inc v Halliburton Co* 563 US 180 (2010) (*Halliburton I*).
[110] ibid.
[111] *Amgen Inc v CT Ret Plans & Trust Funds* 568 US 455 (2013).
[112] In the Court's view: '[F]ailure to present sufficient evidence of materiality to defeat a summary-judgment motion or to prevail at trial would not cause individual reliance questions to overwhelm the questions common to the class. Instead, the failure of proof on the element of materiality would end the case for one and for all; no claim would remain in which individual reliance issues could potentially predominate. However, in the class certification stage, plaintiffs need not, at that threshold, prove that the predominating question will be answered in their favor.' *Amgen* (n 111).
[113] *Halliburton Co v Erica P John Fund Inc* 573 US 258 (2014) (*Halliburton II*).
[114] *Halliburton II* (n 113), citing *Basic v Levinson* (n 82) para 247.
[115] ibid, citing *Amgen* (n 111).
[116] ibid.
[117] *Goldman Sachs Grp Inc v Ark Teachers Re Sys* No 20-222, 594 US (2021).
[118] ibid, citing *FindWhat Investor Group v FindWhat.com* 658 F 3d 1282, 1315 (CA11 2011).

certified,[119] and rejected Goldman's assertion that the misstatements were 'too general' to maintain price inflation,[120] as a way of 'smuggling materiality into Rule 23' (a view rejected in *Amgen*, cited above). The Supreme Court held that, by then, the plaintiffs accepted that 'a more-general statement will affect a security's price less than a more-specific statement on the same question'. The Court agreed, holding that courts 'should be open to all probative evidence', 'regardless whether the evidence is also relevant to a merits question like materiality'.[121] Price impact, under the 'inflation-maintenance' theory would be the amount that the stock's price would have fallen 'without the false statement'.[122] This could be indirectly inferred by observing how ulterior disclosures made the price drop, and assuming that it previous misstatement maintained the price high. And yet:

> [T]hat final inference—that the back-end price drop equals front-end inflation—starts to break down when there is a mismatch between the contents of the misrepresentation and the corrective disclosure. That may occur when the earlier misrepresentation is generic (eg, 'we have faith in our business model') and the later corrective disclosure is specific (eg, 'our fourth quarter earnings did not meet expectations'). Under those circumstances, it is less likely that the specific disclosure actually corrected the generic misrepresentation, which means that there is less reason to infer front-end price inflation—that is, price impact—from the back-end price drop.[123]

Thus, the Court remanded the case for 'all record evidence relevant to price impact' to be considered, 'regardless whether that evidence overlaps with materiality or any other merits issues'. Secondly, Goldman also alleged that, since *Basic*'s presumption switched the burden of proof, should Goldman produce evidence of lack of price impact the burden should switch back. The Court rejected this as contrary to *Basic* and *Halliburton II*, holding that defendants may rebut the presumption only by making any 'showing that severs the link between the alleged misrepresentation and ... the price received (or paid) by the plaintiff'.[124] Yet, the Court held that this would not be of much consequence, because if, according to the first issue, the district court must simply 'assess all the evidence of price impact', then the defendant's 'burden of persuasion will have bite only when the court finds the evidence in equipoise—a situation that should rarely arise'. 9.35

In *Goldman* the Supreme Court framed the issue as 'interstitial', ie the Court said that *Amgen* and *Halliburton* did not prohibit district courts from 'examining all the evidence', including, eg a statement's generic nature at class certification. Yet, it could have 'pivotal' consequences, as circuits decide what 'examine all the evidence' means. In fact, by holding that the *Basic* presumption 'will have bite only when the court finds the evidence in equipoise' the Court suggested that it perceived the district courts' task as a thorough one, which may undermine *Amgen*'s finding that 'materiality' should not be assessed upon class certification. Thus, the 9.36

---

[119] The district court initially certified the class, but the Second Circuit vacated the order, holding that the district had failed to apply the 'preponderance of the evidence' test to determine whether Goldman had rebutted the presumption in *Basic*, and had not considered some evidence on the absence of price impact. On remand, the district weighed both parties' evidence, concluding that Goldman had failed to rebut the presumption. A divided Second Circuit affirmed.
[120] These included relatively generic statements in the SEC filings and annual reports, such as: 'We have extensive procedures and controls that are designed to identify and address conflicts of interest, "Our clients" interests always come first' or 'Integrity and honesty are at the heart of our business.'
[121] *Goldman Sachs v Arkansas Teachers* (n 117).
[122] Citing *Glickenhaus & Co v Household International Inc* 787 F 3d 408, 415 (2020) (CA7).
[123] *Goldman Sachs v Arkansas Teachers* (n 117).
[124] ibid.

Court signalled its openness to hear new arguments on an evolving issue of principle *as long as* it is made through claims of detail, which enable the Court to 'control the discourse'. This nuanced view was visible not only on the Court's final ruling, but also in the contrast between the Supreme Court indication that the validity of the 'inflation maintenance' theory was not in dispute then, and the Court would not decide on the issue, and the decision by the Second Circuit to decertify the class, when it applied the Supreme Court ruling, concluding that the defendants had rebutted the presumption of reliance by showing the 'mismatch' between the generic statements used as a basis for the action, and the company's highly specific disclosure, which was enough t 'sever the link' between statements and stock price drop[125]. This suggests that the Court could further look into these issues in the future. Considering the relevance of inflation-maintenance theory,[126] this is no small thing.

2.3 Section 10b and rule 10b-5 and defendants (renvoi)

9.37 The third issue in the evolution of securities fraud is who can be a defendant, but since this issue was shaped by theories on 'secondary actor liability', and their impact on gatekeepers and third parties, the issue will be discussed below (see section 4).

2.4 Registration statement and prospectus liability under the Securities Act 1933

9.38 US securities law liability has been shaped by section 10b of the Exchange Act, and rule 10b-5, but not only. Provisions on proxy statements (section 14 of the Act) were crucial in early case law. The other main provisions are sections 11 and 12 of the Securities Act 1933, which cover liability for misstatements in the securities' registration statement and prospectus, and inspired European 'prospectus liability' rules. Unlike section 10b, section 11's liability is more specific about the documents, and persons, that are relevant, but conversely it does not require 'scienter'.

9.39 In *Herman & MacLean v Huddleston*[127] investors brought a federal securities fraud class action against participants in a securities offering, including the accounting firm which issued an opinion on the financial statements and a *pro forma* balance sheet contained in the registration statement and prospectus. The Supreme Court held that the more specific remedy under section 11 of the 1933 Act did not preclude actions under section 10(b) of Exchange Act,[128] because both acts 'constitute interrelated components of the federal regulatory scheme governing transactions in securities',[129] and the two provisions create distinct

---

[125] On the issue of principle of the inflation-maintenance theory, the Court held that 'Although some Courts of Appeals have approved the inflation-maintenance theory, this Court has expressed no view on its validity or its contours. We need not and do not do so in this case.' *Goldman Sachs v Arkansas Teachers* (n 117) n 1. For the findings of detail of the rebuttal of the presumption, see *Arkansas Teachers Retirement System v. Goldman Sachs Group* No. 22-484 (2d Cir. Aug. 10, 2023).
[126] Some suggest that inflation-maintenance was relied upon in a 71 per cent of class actions, and plaintiffs succeeded at meeting the *Basic* presumption most of the time. Note, Congress, the Supreme Court, and the Rise of Securities-Fraud Class Actions, 132 Harv L Rev 1067, 1077 (2019). See also *Waggoner v Barclays PLC* 875 F 3d 79, 104 (2d Cir 2017); *Glickenhous & Co v Household International Inc* 787 F 3d 408, 419 (7th Cir 2015); *FindWhat Investor Grp v FindWhat.com* (n 118).
[127] *Herman & MacLean v Huddleston* (n 67).
[128] ibid paras 380–87.
[129] ibid para 381, citing *Ernst & Ernst v Hochfelder* 425 US 185, 425 US 206 (1976).

causes of action, intended to address different types of wrongdoing: section 11, more limited in scope (purchasers of securities against specific parties for misstatements in specific documents), but placing a minimal burden on the plaintiff; section 10(b) a 'catch all' provision (*any* purchaser of *any* security against *any* person using *any* manipulative device) carrying a heavier burden (eg to prove scienter),[130] a logic was reinforced by a finalistic interpretation, since in the Court's view:

> Exempting such conduct from liability under § 10(b) would conflict with the basic purpose of the 1933 Act: to provide greater protection to purchasers of registered securities. It would be anomalous indeed if the special protection afforded to purchasers in a registered offering by the 1933 Act were deemed to deprive such purchasers of the protections against manipulation and deception that § 10(b) makes available to all persons who deal in securities.[131]

The Court relied on *Ernst & Ernst v Hochfelder*, and its 'scienter' requirement.[132] Otherwise, should negligence-based claims be admissible under section 10b, this general provision would side-step specific provisions, like section 11. Yet, this also meant that both actions should not be mutually exclusive,[133] a finding confirmed by the fact that securities laws' reforms had left this aspect untouched.[134] Sections 11 and 12 thus had a more limited scope and circle of defendants, aspects revisited in subsequent cases. **9.40**

In *Pinter v Dahl*[135] the Court assessed who could be a defendant under section 12(a)(1), which refers to anyone who offers or sells a security in violation of registration requirements. The Court held that this includes the 'owner who passes title' and anyone who successfully solicits a purchase 'motivated at least in part by a desire to serve his own financial interests or those of the securities owner',[136] which extends to underwriters, broker-dealers, etc. participating in the securities offering, even if they never had title to the security. In *Gustafson v Alloyd Co.*,[137] the Court determined that the scope of section 12(a)(2), referred to the 'prospectus', which 'is a term of art referring to a document that describes a public offering of securities by an issuer or controlling shareholder' and does not include 'private contracts of sale' not held out to the public.[138] **9.41**

Lower courts have characterized sections 11(a) and 12(a)(2) as 'Securities Act siblings with roughly parallel elements', where section 11 imposes "virtually absolute' liability" on *issuers*, while other defendants under ss 11 and 12(a)(2) 'may be held liable for mere negligence'.[139] Using the assertion in *Herman & Maclean* that a need not prove that the issuer acted with any intent to deceive or defraud[140] as a basis, they have elaborated on the standard required under these sections. Thus, '[A] plaintiff relying on section 11 must establish one of the following bases of liability: (1) a material misrepresentation; (2) a material omission in contravention of an affirmative legal disclosure obligation; or (3) a material omission **9.42**

---

[130] *Herman & MacLean v Huddleston* (n 67) paras 383–84.
[131] ibid para 384.
[132] See section 2.2.1.
[133] *Herman & MacLean v Huddleston* (n 67) para 385.
[134] ibid para 385.
[135] *Pinter v Dahl* 486 US 622 (1988).
[136] ibid para 647.
[137] *Gustafson v Alloyd Co* 513 US 561 (1995).
[138] ibid para 584.
[139] *In re Morgan Stanley Info Fund Securities Litigation* 592 F 3d 347, 359 (2d Cir 2010).
[140] *Herman & MacLean v Huddleston* (n 67) 381–82.

of information that is necessary to prevent existing disclosures from being misleading'.[141] 'Section 12(a)(2) provides similar redress where the securities at issue were sold using prospectuses or oral communications that contain material misstatements or omissions.'[142] They have also held that section 11 "imposes strict liability on issuers and signatories, and negligence liability on underwriters", for material misstatements or omissions in a registration statement'.[143] Thus, unlike section 10b actions, a plaintiff need not establish 'scienter, reliance, or loss causation'.[144] However, a defendant may avoid liability by proving 'negative loss causation', ie that the alleged misstatement or omission did not lead to a decline in the company's stock price.[145] To succeed in this, a defendant must prove that 'the risk that caused the losses was not within the zone of risk concealed by the misrepresentations and omissions', or that 'the subject of the misstatements and omissions was not the cause of the actual loss suffered'.[146]

9.43 In *Omnicare*[147] the Supreme discussed liability for relevant omissions in statements formally presented as 'opinions'. Omnicare's registration statement contained the company's opinion that it was in compliance with federal and state laws, but it was later sued by the federal government for alleged kickbacks from pharmaceutical manufacturers. Investors (pension funds) sued under section 11, the district dismissed, the circuit reversed, and the Supreme Court overturned it, holding that an opinion is not an 'untrue statement of fact' because it proves wrong. Yet, the Court also said that a statement of opinion could be false if the person knew facts that would render a reasonable person incapable of believing that opinion, or if the opinion contained supporting statements of fact that proved false.[148] None of these was possible in the case, which involved 'pure' statements of opinion.[149] Furthermore, the Court held that certain omissions can render a statement of opinion false, if the opinion conveys facts about how the opinion was formed, ie its basis, but the real facts are otherwise, and not disclosed, eg an investor expects a statement about a firm's compliance with the law to be based on some meaningful legal inquiry, 'rather than, say, mere intuition, however sincere',[150] bearing in mind, however, the perspective of a 'reasonable investor'.[151] Finally,

---

[141] *Hutchison v Deutsche Bank Sec Inc* 647 F 3d 479, 484 (2d Cir 2010).
[142] *Morgan Stanley Info Fund Securities Litigation* (n 139).
[143] *Federal Housing Finance Agency for Federal National Mortgage Association v Nomura Holding Am Inc* 873 F 3d 85, 99 (2d Cir 2017), quoting *NECA-IBEW Health & Welfare Fund v Goldman Sachs & Co* 693 F 3d 145, 156 (2d Cir 2012).
[144] *Morgan Stanley Info Fund Securities Litigation* (n 139).
[145] '[T]he defendant proves that any portion or all of such damages represents other than the depreciation in value of such security resulting from [the alleged misstatement or omission], such portion of or all such damages shall not be recoverable.' 15 USC s 77k(e).
[146] *Federal Housing Finance v Nomura* (n 143) 154.
[147] *Omnicare v Laborers District Council* (n 94).
[148] In the Court's example: 'Suppose the CEO in our running hypothetical said: "I believe our TVs have the highest resolution available because we use a patented technology to which our competitors do not have access." That statement may be read to affirm not only the speaker's state of mind, as described above, but also an underlying fact: that the company uses a patented technology.' *Omnicare v Laborers District Council* (n 94) 9.
[149] 'To simplify their content only a bit, Omnicare said in each that "we believe we are obeying the law." And the Funds do not contest that Omnicare's opinion was honestly held.' *Omnicare v Laborers District Council* (n 94) 9.
[150] *Omnicare v Laborers District Council* (n 94) 11–12.
[151] ibid 13: 'An opinion statement, however, is not necessarily misleading when an issuer knows, but fails to disclose, some fact cutting the other way. Reasonable investors understand that opinions sometimes rest on a weighing of competing facts; indeed, the presence of such facts is one reason why an issuer may frame a statement as an opinion, thus conveying uncertainty ... A reasonable investor does not expect that every fact known to an issuer supports its opinion statement.'

excluding 'opinions' would be contrary to the finality of the Act, which was to make issuers tell 'the whole truth' to investors.[152]

2.5 Section 10b, rule 10b-5 and vertical balance: Summary and latest developments

In early US cases the substantive issue of liability could not be dissociated from the issue of the 'vertical' balance between federal and state levels, as the Supreme Court tried to carve out a role for federal securities law among dominant state corporate, contract and fiduciary laws.[153] Subsequently, as securities fraud was more established, the Supreme Court began to seek some limits, not through a 'theory' of what falls within state 'corporate' law, and federal 'securities' law (as there was room for overlap), but pragmatically, as a matter of restraint.[154] And then, as securities fraud was further restricted by the PSLRA[155] and the Court itself, through its case law on secondary actor liability,[156] state courts began to look more promising as enforcers of *securities* laws. To minimize the risk of inconsistencies and 'drift', Congress passed the Securities Litigation Uniform Standards Act (SLUSA), to preclude certain state law class actions involving 'a misrepresentation or omission of a material fact in connection with the purchase or sale of a covered security'. SLUSA defined 'covered security' to include only securities traded on a national exchange or issued by investment companies, but did not answer the question whether *federal* laws could be enforced at a state level.

9.44

In *Merrill Lynch*,[157] the Supreme Court held that SLUSA precludes covered state law claims where the alleged fraud dissuades a potential buyer from purchasing a security or prevents an investor from selling. The Court reasoned that the 'requisite showing ... is deception in connection with the purchase or sale of any security, not deception of an identifiable purchaser or seller', based on a broad reading of SLUSA, noting that a narrow reading would be contrary to its purpose, ie to prevent the restrictions on federal securities class actions from being thwarted by using state securities class actions.[158] Class actions brought by holders (as opposed to purchasers or sellers) 'pose a special risk of vexatious litigation', and it would be 'odd' if SLUSA did not pre-empt 'that particularly troublesome subset of class actions'.[159] However, in *Chadbourne & Parke*[160] the Court held that SLUSA did not preclude state law class actions not involving 'covered securities', such as, as it happened in the case, certificates of deposit not traded on any national exchange (which, in the case, were falsely represented as being backed by covered securities)'.[161] SLUSA did not apply, since the plaintiffs did not

9.45

---

[152] *Omnicare v Laborers District Council* (n 94) 17: Congress adopted § 11 to ensure that issuers 'tell the whole truth'... literal accuracy is not enough: An issuer must as well desist from misleading investors by saying one thing and holding back another. Omnicare would nullify that statutory requirement for all sentences starting with the phrases 'we believe' or 'we think'. But those magic words can preface nearly any conclusion.
[153] *Superintendent of Insurance v Bankers Life & Casualty Co* (n 52); *JI Case Co v Borak* (n 46); *Mills v Electric Auto-Lite Co* (n 48).
[154] *Santa Fe Industries* (n 63).
[155] See sections 2.1 and 2.2.
[156] See sections 2.2 and 2.3.
[157] *Merrill Lynch, Pierce, Fenner & Smith Inc v Dabit* 547 US 71 (2006).
[158] ibid para 85.
[159] ibid para 86.
[160] *Chadbourne & Parke LLP v Troice* 571 US 377 (2014).
[161] ibid para 387.

'allege that the defendants' misrepresentations led anyone to buy or to sell (or to maintain positions in) covered securities'.[162]

9.46 Yet, in *Cyan Inc.*[163] the Court held that SLUSA does not pre-empt actions before state courts based on the Securities Act, nor does it empower defendants to remove such actions from state to federal court. Investors in an IPO brought a class action against Cyan, alleging 1933 Act violations before the California Superior Court. The Court held that the Act created private rights of action, granting *both* federal and state courts jurisdiction, unlike the Exchange Act, which conferred exclusive jurisdiction to federal courts. The subsequent PSLRA *substantive* reforms applied in all courts,[164] but its *procedural* reforms only applied in federal courts. Since plaintiffs sought to side-step these constraints by using state courts SLUSA pre-empted some types of class actions through the 'state-law class action bar', which excluded 'covered class actions' over 'covered securities' under state law,[165] and defined 'covered securities' and 'covered class actions' to disallow sizable class actions founded on state law respecting a nationally traded security's purchase or sale.[166] SLUSA also[167] provided for the removal of certain class actions to federal court, and their dismissal. This left the 'jurisdictional provision', which had two exemptions (or 'conforming amendments'). The more relevant provided that state and federal courts shall have [concurrent] jurisdiction over 1933 Act cases, 'except as provided in section 77p … with respect to covered class actions' (the 'except clause'). Cyan alleged that the 'except clause' stripped state courts of power to adjudicate 1933 Act claims in 'covered class actions'. The Court disagreed. In its view, the statute 'does not say what it does not say', ie it did not deprive state courts of jurisdiction over 1933 Act claims.[168] It was still not clear whether the combined reading of the 'except clause' and the 'state law bar' also barred actions before state courts based on the Securities Act. In the Court's view:

> The critical question for this case is therefore whether §77p limits state-court jurisdiction over class actions brought under the 1933 Act. It does not. As earlier described, §77p bars certain securities class actions based on *state* law … as a corollary of that prohibition, it authorizes removal of those suits so that a federal court can dismiss them. See §77p(c); *supra,* at 4–5. But the section says nothing, and so does nothing, to deprive state courts of jurisdiction over class actions based on *federal* law. That means the background rule of §77v(a)—under which a state court may hear the Investors' 1933 Act suit—continues to govern.[169]

9.47 The Court rejected Cyan's reading of the reference to § 77p in the 'except clause' as referring *only* to the definition of 'covered class actions' in that provision (§ 77p(f)(2)), which

---

[162] ibid para 381.
[163] *Cyan Inc v Beaver County Employees Retirement Fund* 583 US ___ (2018).
[164] For instance, the statute created a 'safe harbour' from federal liability for certain 'forward-looking statements' made by company officials. 15 USC s 77z–2 (Securities Act of 1933); s 78u–5 (Securities Exchange Act 1934).
[165] Section 77p(b) stated that: 'No covered class action based upon the statutory or common law of any State … may be maintained in any State or Federal court by any private party alleging—(1) an untrue statement or omission of a material fact in connection with the purchase or sale of a covered security; or (2) that the defendant used or employed any manipulative or deceptive device or contrivance in connection with the purchase or sale of a covered security.'
[166] 'According to SLUSA's definitions, the term 'covered class action' means a class action in which 'damages are sought on behalf of more than 50 persons'. § 77p(f)(2). And the term 'covered security' refers to a security listed on a national stock exchange. § 77p(f)(3) (cross-referencing § 77r(b))'.
[167] ibid s 77p(c).
[168] *Cyan v Beaver County Employees Retirement Fund* (n 163).
[169] ibid.

comprised all actions seeking damages on behalf of more than 50 persons (both under state and federal law). Cyan could not simply 'cherry pick' one part of § 77p. Doing so would deprive state courts of jurisdiction over actions with no national interest.[170] This result was not contrary to congressional intent, which was primarily to prevent lawsuits before state courts from becoming the way to circumvent the substantive restrictions introduced by the PSLRA.

Thus, some companies adopted strategies to restrict the jurisdiction of state courts, for example by amending their charters to include provisions removing cases to federal courts. In *Salzberg v Sciabaccuchi*[171] the Delaware Chancery Court considered the provision invalid, holding that one such provision 'cannot bind a plaintiff to a particular forum when the claim does not involve rights or relationships that were established by or under Delaware's corporate law',[172] but the Delaware Supreme Court upheld the formal validity of the clause, holding that Federal Forum Provisions (FFP) involve securities claims, and, since registration statements is 'an important aspect of a corporation's management of its business affairs and of its relationship with its stockholders', the FFP involves 'intra-corporate' litigation, the 'management of the business' and the 'conduct of the affairs of the corporation', and is thus, facially 'valid under Section 102(b)(1)'; a doctrinal trend followed by the California Court of Appeals in *Wong* and *Simonton* which found that the forum selection clause was neither contrary to the Securities Act nor an 'uncnscionable' clause imposed by a party with superior bargaining power.[173] Courts in other states could follow different criteria, and lower courts could still find such a clause invalid in specific circumstances.

9.48

Plaintiffs' incentives to 'forum shop' will depend on the consistency between federal law and state courts. So far, state courts seem to be following federal doctrine. In *Netshoes*,[174] investors in an IPO brought claims against a Brazilian sports and lifestyle online retailer under ss 11, 12(a)(2), and 15 of the 1933 Act. The Opinion relied on federal criteria, such as the in-actionability of 'opinions', the 'bespeaks caution' doctrine, or the non-liability for forward-looking statements as insufficiently material. Other rulings, like *Natera* (California) emphasized the need for consistency between federal and state courts after *Cyan*.[175]

9.49

2.6 Insider trading: a major source of criminal liability, a relatively secondary source of private law liability

Insider trading cases are a major exponent of US criminal liability, and courts' role in criminal securities law, with landmark cases like *Chiarella v United States*,[176] where the Supreme Court laid out insider trading's 'traditional' or 'classical' theory, where section 10(b) and rule 10b-5 are violated '[W]hen a corporate insider trades in the securities of his corporation

9.50

---

[170] *Cyan v Beaver County Employees Retirement Fund* (n 163).
[171] *Salzberg v Sciabacucchi* (2020) No 346, 2019 (Del). The provision read: 'Unless the Company consents in writing to the selection of an alternative forum, the federal district courts of the United States of America shall be the exclusive forum for the resolution of any complaint asserting a cause of action arising under the Securities Act of 1933. Any person or entity purchasing or otherwise acquiring any interest in any security of [the Company] shall be deemed to have notice of and consented to [this provision].'
[172] *Sciabacucchi v Salzberg* No 2017-0931-JTL (Del Ch 2018).
[173] *Salzberg v Sciabacucchi* 2020 (n 171); *Wong v Restoration Robotics, Inc.*, 78 Cal. App. 5th 48 (Cal. Ct. App. 2022); *Simonton v Dropbox, Inc.* No. A161603 (Cal. Ct. App. May 13, 2022).
[174] *In re Netshoes Sec Litig* NY Slip Op 29219 (Supp Ct, NY County 2019).
[175] *In re Natera Securities Litigation* No CIV537409 (Cal Super Ct filed 24 March 2016).
[176] *Chiarella v United States* 445 US 222 (1980).

on the basis of material, non-public information',[177] and that trading 'on such information qualifies as a 'deceptive device' under § 10(b) because 'a relationship of trust and confidence [exists] between corporate shareholders and the insiders who obtained confidential information by reason of their position.[178] In *Dirks v SEC*[179] the Court held that the 'tippee' (who receives information tips) had a 'fiduciary duty' towards shareholders not to trade on information to his personal gain when the insider had breached its own duty by disclosing it, and the tippee knew the breach,[180] in *United States v O'Hagan*,[181] it accepted that fraud could result from a person's misappropriating confidential information ('misappropriation theory'),[182] and in *Salman v United States*[183] it extended the idea of 'personal' gain' to cases where the tipper makes a 'gift' to a trading relative or friend.

9.51 Yet insider trading cases have not been a major source of civil liability. Such liability was admitted relatively early in *Shapiro v Merrill Lynch*[184] but it is not that prominent. Possibly, the active role played by the SEC and public prosecutors leaves private plaintiffs putative actions *after* public prosecution has finished. Furthermore, some acts in the 1980s (the ITSA and ITSFEA) expanded the scope for civil remedies, but with less incentive for private plaintiffs.[185] The PSLRA prevented the recovery of attorneys' fees in certain cases and heightened pleading requirements,[186] while the ITSFEA codified the *Shapiro* requirement that the aggrieved party trades 'contemporaneously' with the insider,[187] and limited damages to a single disgorgement of profits made or loss avoided. Finally, the Fair Fund provision of the Sarbanes-Oxley Act of 2002 provided for the distribution of amounts disgorged by defendants to the SEC, which limits recovery to investors who either traded on the same day as the insider or were on the opposite side of the trade from the insider.[188] Furthermore, the total amount of damages imposed against any person under insider trading must be 'diminished by the amounts, if any, that such person may be required to disgorge, pursuant to a court order obtained at the instance of the Commission'.[189] Thus, once ill-gotten gains are disgorged, there can be no double recovery, and once the SEC has obtained disgorgement, this could eliminate the recovery by private plaintiffs (including punitive damages[190]) and may even deprive them of standing.[191]

---

[177] ibid.
[178] ibid.
[179] *Dirks v SEC* 463 US 646 (1983).
[180] ibid.
[181] *US v O'Hagan* 521 US 642 (1997).
[182] ibid.
[183] *Salman v United States* 137 S Ct 420 (2016).
[184] *Shapiro v Merrill Lynch, Pierce, Fenner & Smith Inc* 495 F 2d 228 (2d Cir 1974).
[185] The Insider Trading Sanctions Act of 1984 (ITSA) and the Insider Trading and Securities Fraud Enforcement Act of 1988 (ITSFEA) were enacted after mounting public concern over insider trading increased criminal and civil penalties for insider trading violations. ITSA authorizes the SEC to seek hefty monetary damages but moneys would be payable into the US Treasury. ITSFEA enhanced civil sanctions for the SEC, although it added an express private right of action for contemporaneous trading.
[186] The PSLRA amended s 20 of the Securities Exchange Act 1934 to bar the payment of attorneys' fees or expenses incurred by private parties out of disgorgement funds created by an SEC action, and heightened pleading requirements for private actions and instituted an automatic stay of discovery pending determination of a motion to dismiss.
[187] This led to litigation on the concept of 'contemporaneously'. Plaintiffs trading three to four days after the trade can have standing (*Shapiro*, 495 F 2d 241) but those trading one month later not (*Wilson v Comtech Telecomm Corp* 648 F 2d 88, 94–95 (2d Cir 1981)). See also *O'Connor & Associates v Dean Witter Reynolds Inc* 559 F Supp 800, 803–804 (SDNY 1983) (plaintiffs who had allegedly traded less than a week after the defendant traded were 'sufficiently contemporaneous').
[188] *SEC v Luzardo* No 01Civ9206 (DC) (SDNY 2004).
[189] Pub L No 100-704, 102 Stat 4677 (1988).
[190] *Litton Industries Inc v Lehman Bros Kuhn Loeb Inc* 734 F Supp 1071, 1076 (SDNY 1990).
[191] *Martin v SEC* Doc No 11-2011 (2d Cir 2013).

3 The creeping codification of securities liability for misstatements in the EU

9.52 In light of US experience, some limitations in a nascent European law of securities liability are evident: national courts are the ones directly determining issues of liability, while the Court of Justice can only decide when it is asked a question, via preliminary reference procedure. However, some progress is undeniable. The prospectus liability provision has 'doctrinal traction', and there has been significant development through the case law in some jurisdictions and by the Court of Justice itself on the elements of a liability action (section 3.2) *and*, crucially, the contours of a doctrine of *reliance* (section 3.3).

3.1 Prospectus liability: an EU provision with doctrinal traction

9.53 If one had to surmise what provision of EU law presents the kind of potential to become the starting point for an EU doctrine of securities law liability, it would be Article 11 of the Prospectus Regulation,[192] which, in terms similar to its predecessor (Article 6 of the Prospectus Directive[193]) states that:

> Member States shall ensure that responsibility for the information given in a prospectus, and any supplement thereto, attaches to at least the issuer or its administrative, management or supervisory bodies, the offeror, the person asking for the admission to trading on a regulated market or the guarantor, as the case may be. The persons responsible for the prospectus, and any supplement thereto, shall be clearly identified in the prospectus by their names and functions or, in the case of legal persons, their names and registered offices, as well as declarations by them that, to the best of their knowledge, the information contained in the prospectus is in accordance with the facts and that the prospectus makes no omission likely to affect its import.

9.54 To manage expectations, one must acknowledge that Article 11 differs from US provisions in that it can neither be directly enforced by EU authorities, nor before EU Courts, it leaves Member States options to delineate the circle of defendants, and the objective and subjective basis for a complaint, and it is about *prospectus* liability, which is narrower than the liability for misstatements under section 10b of the Exchange Act.[194] Yet, the US experience shows that section 10b was not even intended as a liability provision, but the basis for regulatory schemes by the SEC; courts made it what it is today. Thus, judicial interpretation can be a major transformative force.

---

[192] Regulation (EU) 2017/1129 of the European Parliament and of the Council on the prospectus to be published when securities are offered to the public or admitted to trading on a regulated market, and repealing Directive 2003/71/EC(Text with EEA relevance) [2017] OJ L168.

[193] Directive 2003/71/EC of the European Parliament and of the Council on the prospectus to be published when securities are offered to the public or admitted to trading and amending Directive 2001/34/EC [2003] OJ L345.

[194] See section 2.1.

9.55 The provision on prospectus liability has several things going for it. First, it expressly refers to *civil* liability, ie it does not give the option to omit civil liability altogether to the benefit of public enforcement. Secondly, it provides a basis for court-construed doctrines on several fronts,[195] including:

- Defendants: Liability must attach to 'at least the issuer or its administrative, management or supervisory bodies, the offeror, the person asking for the admission to trading on a regulated market or the guarantor'. Thus, Member States cannot exempt all of these parties from liability, but can choose to include other parties within the circle of defendants.
- Scope: Parties may be liable for the *prospectus*, not its summary (with exceptions).
- Objective/subjective standards,[196] where the provision can influence:
    - 'Materiality': the rules habilitate a mechanism by which the competent authorities authorize certain omissions[197])
    - Imputability, or attributability: the *persons responsible* shall include in the prospectus a declaration 'that, to the best of their knowledge, the information contained in the prospectus is in accordance with the facts and that the prospectus makes no omission likely to affect its import', which makes it difficult to exclude liability for facts a party is required, or expected to know (it also frames the issue in terms similar to the 'due diligence defence' of US law[198]).
    - Relativity/proximity: Member States could not exclude liability of a party listed as defendants for lacking 'proximity' with the plaintiff (investor) as this would go against the text of the Regulation.[199]

9.56 Member States have transposed the norm in different ways.[200] The majority enacted a specific prospectus liability regime; others left the matter to the courts and their civil law doctrines.[201] There are some identifiable trends. Most states include a list of specific persons responsible for the information in the prospectus, and provide for joint and several liability,[202] and most require 'negligence', and limit the list of plaintiffs to 'investors'.[203] However, some countries provide for joint *or* several liability,[204] or differentiate between negligent and intentional liability,[205] or provide for strict liability,[206] or limit plaintiffs to original purchasers of securities.[207] Crucially, presumptions of 'fault' or 'causal link' may also vary. Therefore, prospectus

---

[195] Member States have transposed the provision differently, while maintaining some minimum harmonization, which can give rise to common principles. For an excellent and comprehensive study on the issue see Danny Busch, Guido Ferrarini, and Jan Paul Franx (eds), *Prospectus Regulation and Prospectus Liability* (OUP 2020).
[196] Danny Busch, 'The Influence of the EU Prospectus Rules on Private Law' (2021) 16 CMLJ 3.
[197] Thus, a party responsible for prospectus information who omits it could be forced to explain why it did not seek authorization for such an omission. See Busch (n 196) 13–14.
[198] ibid 15. Such due diligence defence is available under eg Dutch law or Spanish law.
[199] Busch (n 196) 24.
[200] ESMA, *ESMA Report. Comparison of liability regimes in Member States in relation to the Prospectus Directive* (30 May 2013) ESMA/2013/619 (ESMA Report).
[201] ibid 12, para 26.
[202] ibid 12, paras 28–30.
[203] ibid 13, paras 35, 39.
[204] Belgium provides for joint liability; Luxemburg for several liability. ESMA Report (n 200) 12, paras 32–33.
[205] Cases of France, or the United Kingdom. See ESMA Report (n 200) 13, paras 36–37.
[206] ESMA Report (n 200) 13, para 37.
[207] Case of eg Belgium, Hungary, or Slovenia (in Belgium financial intermediaries may also sue). ESMA Report (n 200) 13, para 40.

liability will 'have bite', if courts develop common interpretations *at the level of principle*, ie beyond the mere text of the rules, adapting private law doctrines when needed, to align them with the provision.

This must be made under the so-called principles of 'equivalence and effectiveness', framed by precedents in consumer law,[208] or investment firms' conduct duties[209] as meaning that 'they must not be less favourable than those concerning similar claims based on provisions of national law or arranged in such a way as to make the exercise of rights conferred by the EU legal order practically impossible'.[210] These broad principles can be an insipid formulism that presides over large national divergences, or become a driving force of doctrinal harmonization through dialogue between national courts and the Court of Justice. EU courts can leverage, if they wish, on their settled case law to hold that a uniform application of EU law under 'equality' or 'effectiveness' requires giving EU law provisions an 'autonomous' meaning, which must take into account the provision's context and purpose.[211] Pressure will mount for a more substantive, hands-on approach to national laws. **9.57**

3.2 Courts' steps towards harmonizing prospectus remedies: scope, damages, and invalidity

Court experience suggests that prospectus liability is still in a relatively early stage, and courts are trying to fit securities regulation goals within private law principles. In Italy, the Supreme Court (*Corte di Cassazione*) in 2010[212] held that the law requires that the market interaction of supply and demand be driven by truthful information released by the securities' issuer or offeror, and if such information is not truthful, supply and demand interact at a different price level, which causes damage recoverable in *tort*. By the same token, a false statement or omission is 'material' if it is susceptible of causing such price alteration. **9.58**

In Germany,[213] there are two kinds of prospectus liability: the specific, or statutory prospectus liability (*spezialgesetzliche Prospekthaftung*) pursuant to the Securities Prospectus Act (*Wertpapierprospektgesetz* WpPG) or the Investment Products Act (*Vermögensanlagengesetz* 'VermAnlG')), and the prospectus liability according to civil law (*zivilrechtliche Prospekthaftung*), which often applies to investments not covered by statutory prospectus liability. This led German courts to create a prospectus liability based on the concept of *culpa in contrahendo*.[214] Then, courts distinguish between prospectus liability in a narrower sense (*Prospekthaftung im engeren Sinne*), for initiators, founders, management and persons with **9.59**

---

[208] See eg European Commission, An evaluation study of national procedural laws and practices in terms of their impact on the free circulation of judgments and on the equivalence and effectiveness of the procedural protection of consumers under EU consumer law https://op.europa.eu/en/publication-detail/-/publication/531ef49a-9768-11e7-b92d-01aa75ed71a1/language-en (accessed 30 September 2022).

[209] Case C-604/11, *Genil 48 SL and Others v Bankinter SA and Others* ECLI:EU:C:2013:344.

[210] ibid.

[211] Case C-343/13 *Modelo Continente Hipermercados SA v Autoridade para as Condições de Trabalho—Centro Local do Lis (ACT)* ECLI:EU:C:2015:146; compare also Case C-279/12 *Fish Legal and Shirley* EU:C:2013:853, para 42, and Case C-201/13 *Deckmyn and Vrijheidsfonds* EU:C:2014:2132, para 14.

[212] Decision by Cassation Court No 14056 (11 June 2010). See the discussion in Paolo Giudici, 'Italy' in Danny Busch, Guido Ferrarini, and Jan Paul Franx (eds), *Prospectus Regulation and Prospectus Liability* (OUP 2020) 505.

[213] Sebastian Mock, 'Germany' in Danny Busch, Guido Ferrarini, and Jan Paul Franx (eds), *Prospectus Regulation and Prospectus Liability* (OUP 2020).

[214] See eg Federal Supreme Court (BGH) decision of 24 May 1982, Ref: II ZR 124/81, where the Court considered the liability of the trust limited partner in a public limited partnership towards the capital investors recruited by issuing prospectuses due to negligence in contract negotiations.

particular influence on the issuing company, and participating in the prospectus in externally recognizable ways; and general prospectus liability (*Prospekthaftung im weiteren Sinne*) for persons not connected to the issuing company, but personally involved in providing the prospectus, eg who adopt the prospect as their own. Courts have considered the existence of prospectus liability in the broader sense, for example, in the case of marketing and distribution of funds,[215] applying more general principles of civil law, with less influence of regulatory provisions.[216] Nonetheless, courts have also interpreted the 'narrower sense' liability relatively broadly to encompass persons with specific economic interest and a major influence on the prospectus such as a controlling shareholder ordering a subsidiary's offering, or and a major shareholder issuing his or her shares,[217] although this case law involved securities not admitted to trading.[218] In the famous *Rupert-Scholz* decision the Federal Supreme Court extended the prospectus liability under civil law even to public statements of a former minister of the federal government, since he advertised (as a member of the supervisory board) as a sound investment the securities of a firm that later failed.[219] In the Court's view, 'narrower' prospectus liability also applies to those who, from a position of professional and/or economic prominence or professional expertise, assume a 'guarantor' position, and, through their involvement in the offering prospectus, create a special, additional condition of trust and submit declarations.[220] Likewise, courts have tended to use a relatively broad definition of the 'statements' included within prospectus liability, which comprise market-related written statements containing relevant information for the evaluation of the investment. The broad approach is a consequence of the principle of effectiveness, under EU law.

9.60 Another important aspect are the *remedial* consequences of a breach of prospectus rules, and the 'fit' between EU securities rules' goals, and domestic private law principles. The 'neater' way to do this is through a damages claim. However, some jurisdictions consider that false information can induce an 'error' or 'mistake', and the remedy is the annulment of the contract. This is a 'messier' solution. It is unclear whether this would result in the nullity of the contract for *subscription* or for the *purchase* of the instrument. If the *subscription* contract, would this void the contract with all the subscribers? Would a 'cure' be possible? If the *purchase* contract eg for an investor who acquired the shares in the secondary market, from a financial intermediary like a bank, the investor would be suing a party who did not cause the mistake. If the instruments are shares, there would still be the *company* contract, ie the contract in the articles of incorporation/bylaws, although the nullity would be limited to the newly subscribed shares. In both the subscription contract and the company contract the consequence of the annulment, ie the reimbursement of funds, would contravene of EU company law rules on 'capital', which prohibit, or severely limit, restitution to shareholders.[221]

---

[215] See eg BGH, judgment II ZR30/10M (23 April 2012); BGH, judgment II ZR 30/10 (23 April 2012); BGH, judgment II ZR82/11 (23 October 2012); BGH, judgment II ZR 82/11 (23 October 2012); BGH judgment II ZR 252/11 (5 March 2013).
[216] See eg BGH, judgment II ZR211/09 (23 April 2012), where the Court held that founding shareholders are liable to the investor joining through a trustee for damages from prospectus liability in the broader sense if the trustor is to be treated as a directly joining partner according to the articles of association.
[217] BGH, XI ZR 344/11 (18 September 2012).
[218] Mock (n 213).
[219] BGH- III ZR103/10 (17 November 2011).
[220] ibid.
[221] Miguel Iribarren Blanco, *Responsabilidad Civil por la Información Divulgada por las Sociedades Cotizadas: su aplicación en los mercados secundarios de valores* (2008) 2 Revista del Mercado de Valores 61 ff.

Courts in countries like Austria and Spain,[222] as well as the Court of Justice, have tried to **9.61** cope as best as possible, with limited success. The Austrian Supreme Court held that prospectus liability rules would take precedence over capital maintenance rules, as *lex posterior* because payments under prospectus liability are made to investors not in their capacity as shareholders (*causa societatis*), but in the same way as those made to any other creditor with a claim against the corporation.[223] This position of Austrian courts prompted *Hirmann v Immofinanz*,[224] where Mr Alfred Hirmann purchased shares of Immofinanz AG ('Immofinanz'), a public company ('Aktiengesellschaft') through a broker on the secondary market (there was no new issuance) Aviso Zeta AG ('Aviso Zeta'), which deposited the shares in a custody account held by Aviso Zeta in Mr Hirmann's name. Mr. Hirmann sued Immofinanz alleging that the prospectus was misleading, because it did not state that the proceeds from an equity issue were used to buy shares in Immofinanz to manipulate and speculate with the price of the stock, resulting in a risk greater than that indicated in the prospectus (this among other allegations of fraud and embezzlement). This resulted in a 'mistake', which should lead to the annulment of the contract. Immofinanz disputed this, but also claimed that the remedy (annulment) sought was incompatible with company law principles, such as capital maintenance, or the non-refundability of capital contributions, which have also been harmonized by EU company law directives. The Court distinguished between the scope of company law and securities law provisions, holding for the former that: 'their purpose is to regulate only the legal relationships established between the company and its shareholders which derive exclusively from the memorandum and articles of association and that they are directed solely to internal relations within the company concerned'.[225] Thus, provisions on securities liability were not contrary to company law principles, because:

> [T]he liability of the company concerned to investors, who are also its shareholders, by reason of irregular conduct on the part of that company prior to or at the time of the purchase of its shares, does not derive from the memorandum and articles of association and is not directed solely at the internal relations of that company. The source of the liability at issue in such a case is the share purchase contract.[226]

Furthermore, those provisions were not contrary to the principle of equal treatment of **9.62** shareholders,[227] nor was the company's duty to reimburse the price subject (or contrary) to the provisions on treasury shares (a company's acquisition of its own shares[228]), or on company nullity and liquidation.[229] Capital markets provisions sought to determine liability for breach of capital markets rules, not to regulate corporate relations. Thus, the compensation paid to an investor need not be limited to the securities' purchase price.[230]

In light of this, national provisions determining 'liability' (damages, restitution) imple- **9.63** mented the EU Prospectus, Transparency and Market Abuse norms' provisions on 'penalties'. Each Member State shall set the criteria for determining 'penalties' subject to the principles of equivalence and effectiveness,[231] which require measures to be 'effective, proportionate

---

[222] For a comparative analysis see Iribarren Blanco (n 221).
[223] OGH judgment 7 Ob 77/10i (30 March 2011) and 6 Ob 28/12d (15 March 2012).
[224] Case C-174/12 *Alfred Hirmann v Immofinanz AG* ECLI:EU:C:2013:856.
[225] ibid para 27.
[226] ibid para 29.
[227] ibid paras 30–32.
[228] ibid paras 34–35.
[229] ibid paras 52–54 and also paras 65–67.
[230] ibid para 66.
[231] ibid para 40.

and dissuasive',[232] but otherwise leave wide discretion to Member States.[233] The concrete measures constituted 'an appropriate remedy for the harm suffered by the investor and for the failure of the issuing company to comply with the information requirements', and were capable of deterring issuers from misleading investors.[234] The Court's conclusions were sound, as are *some* of their premises. Provisions on securities liability (prospectus, insider trading, etc.) are not contrary to company law, and protect different interests; prospectus liability combines compensation to investors and deterrence, and these goals should, in principle, not be roadblocked by technicalities of domestic company law; company law directives should be interpreted to be compatible with EU securities law, and, in case of doubt, the latter may prevail as *lex specialis*. This prevalence of 'ends' (ie ensuring payment, compensation and deterrence) should still allow company and contract law work out the 'means' to accommodate it. However, the Court went further than that, sometimes unnecessarily. To distinguish between capital markets rules and company law 'capital maintenance' rules it seemed to suggest that rules restricting a company's acquisition of its own shares seek primarily to prevent artificial increases in the share price,[235] when one of the main goals (if not the main) of the rules (which, in fact, apply to both listed and non-listed companies) is to give creditors security. Then, to differentiate between the scope of company law and capital markets law, the Court distinguishes between a company's 'internal' relations, deriving from the 'memorandum and articles of association' (company law)[236] and rules concerning 'not internal' relations, and derived from the 'purchase contract' (capital markets).[237] Many would object that company law regulates elements beyond 'internal' relations, eg creditor protection, or that it goes beyond a contract between shareholders, or would argue that capital markets provisions cover not only 'the purchase contract', eg if an investor subscribes for the shares, and does not purchase them in the secondary market. Should investor protection be subordinated to company law capital maintenance rules in that case? Most likely it should not. Maybe the Court was not very comfortable with matters of private or company law, but the distinction should not be used in future cases.

9.64 The Court's approach led to further conflicts, like the first *Bankia* rulings by the Spanish Supreme Court in February 2016 (the contents of the two rulings were very similar, and will be collectively referred to as *Bankia I*[238]) on investors' purchase of shares of Bankia, one of the largest Spanish IPOs, involving one of the country's largest banking groups, which resulted from the merger of several savings banks, in an attempt to spawn a more solvent group, which ultimately failed: the extra provisioning required by regulators fatally undermined the group's capital position. The plaintiffs were retail investors, who purchased shares from their banks, and claimed (among other things) that they were misled in subscribing the shares. The case was peculiar. Instead of claiming mis-selling from the bank, resulting

---

[232] ibid para 39.
[233] ibid para 41.
[234] ibid para 43.
[235] ibid para 24: In turn, the fourth recital in the preamble to the Second Directive indicates that the aim of that directive is to maintain the capital, which constitutes the creditors' security, in particular by prohibiting any reduction by distribution to shareholders where the latter are not entitled to it and by imposing limits on a company's right to acquire its own shares. The latter constraint is due, in particular, to the need to ensure the protection of shareholders and creditors against market behaviour which might reduce a company's capital and cause the prices of its shares artificially to rise. The issue may be in the drafting, but it seems to suggest that preventing artificial increases is the way to protect shareholders and creditors interests.
[236] *Hirmann* (n 224) para 27.
[237] ibid.
[238] Supreme Court decisions nos 23/2016, and 24/2016 (3 February 2016).

in damages (as provided by Spanish rules on prospectus liability), investors requested the nullity of the contract for the subscription of the shares.[239] Furthermore, since the falsities in Bankia's prospectus were also analysed in a criminal procedure, Bankia staked a large part of its procedural defence on the 'preference' of these, when the evidentiary standard is different in criminal and civil law, and the cases could proceed in parallel. Thus, criminal courts found no crime in the misstatements,[240] while the Supreme Court held that there was a 'mistake', which resulted in the annulment of the contract.[241] Leaving aside matters the Court's assessment of the 'falsities',[242] on the doctrinal issue of 'error/mistake' the Court dismissed the opinions of courts and scholars who considered the annulment of the subscription incompatible with the rules on company nullity, and relied on *Immofinanz* to hold that securities provisions take precedence over company law provisions, and investors, even if they are shareholders, must be treated like a third party, as their claim does not have *causa societatis*, and creditors are not protected by capital maintenance rules if these may thwart investor compensation. Thus, even when prospectus rules provide that damages are the consequence of a breach of prospectus rules, it is also possible to request the annulment in cases where, *as in the case of retail investors*, such mistake is substantial and excusable, and determined their consent;[243] because, although it is not a compensatory action, it has equivalent effect.[244] The problems begin once one asks *how* should the issuer execute the ruling: is the capital increase and share issuance considered null without any further action? Should the company adopt a new shareholders resolution to undo the capital increase with regard to *all* shareholders? Or to the affected shareholders only? Once restitution operates, how should the entity treat the shares it received, as treasury shares or otherwise? One could go on and on. Damages claims allow compensation to investors, and present no such disadvantages. The Court of Justice could have suggested as much, in the name of equivalence and effectiveness. Fortunately, a subsequent decision by the Spanish Supreme Court in 2021 focused on a claim for damages.

The Court of Justice discussed prospectus liability again in *Banco Santander*.[245] Investors subscribed for shares in a public offering by Banco Popular. Some months later, the bank was subjected to resolution measures, consisting in the write-off of the shares, then sold to Banco Santander for €1. Investors sued Banco Popular, and sought (and obtained in the first instance) the invalidity of the contract as a result of misinformation in the prospectus; Banco Santander appealed, and the Spanish court of appeal made a preliminary reference.

9.65

The Court of Justice concluded that the EU provisions on the Bank Recovery and Resolution Directive (BRRD Directive 2014/59/EU) excluded the possibility of an action for breach of prospectus rules, reasoning as follows: BRRD recitals indicate that its rules constitute precise

9.66

---

[239] The doctrine of mistake was greatly expanded by Spanish courts in recent years. Lower courts in this case had rejected that there was a relationship of 'advice', and upheld the plea of contract invalidity for 'mistake'. The plaintiffs may thus have decided to drop the alternative claim.

[240] See *Sentencia de la Audiencia Nacional (SAN)* 2347/2020 of 29 September 2020, ECLI:ES:AN:2020:2347.

[241] STS nos 23/2016 and 24/2016 (n 238).

[242] The Supreme Court referred to the restating of the financial statements of 2011, while the financial statements used in the IPO were those of the first quarter of 2011, they leave aside the fact that the revision of the financial statements of Bankia's *parent* company resulted in part of the placement of the shares in Bankia's IPO at a significantly lower price than that expected, they do not weigh the fact that Spain had a W-shaped crisis, and 2012 represented the second 'V', something that could not be easily anticipated; nor could one anticipate the royal decrees in 2012 that increased capital needs. For a careful analysis of these arguments, see Manuel Conthe, 'Las sentencias del Supremo sobre Bankia' (2016) 21 El Notario del Siglo 66. The decision by the *Audiencia Nacional* confirmed this reading of the facts.

[243] STS nos 23/2016, Ground of Decision Third and 24/2016, Ninth Ground of decision (n 238).

[244] Supreme Court decision no 24/2016, Ninth Ground of decision (3 February 2016).

[245] Case C-410/20 *Banco Santander v JAC and Others* ECLI:EU:2022:351.

exceptions to EU company law rules for the protection of shareholders and creditors; the Prospectus Directive is 'materially' comprised within said company law directives, ergo BRRD constitutes an exception to it.[246] Furthermore, a claim of prospectus liability constitutes one of the claims subject to write-off and conversion, and the same happens to the claim of invalidity, since both seek compensation from the entity subject to resolution.[247]

9.67 One can sympathise with the Court's concern, ie granting 'finality' and 'closure' to bank crisis management measures. However, the Court's conclusion is questionable, and the arguments used dubious. Prospectus liability rules cannot 'materially' be squeezed within 'Union company law directives', the concept used by recital 120 of the BRRD. Nor does fit within the logic of said recital, which says that '[i]n a situation where resolution authorities need to act rapidly, those rules may hinder effective action'. This may be the case of, for example, rules requiring approval by company bodies (which operate ex ante) but not of liability rules, which operate ex post, and thus do not hinder the expediency of crisis management measures. Indeed, the logic of prospectus liability is not to protect shareholders per se, but to protect them against falsities in the prospectus. In this light, the 'exception' logic used by the Court clearly does not fit: one can suspend shareholder protection by replacing it with crisis management rules, which include some safeguards (eg the no creditor worse off (NCWO) principle acknowledged by the Court), but one cannot suspend the truth (or falsity) of statements in a prospectus, their materiality, etc.

9.68 The Court's last argument, ie that the claim for invalidity is a claim seeking compensation, and thus one subject to write-off and conversion is no less puzzling. Under private law, claims of contract invalidity seek restitution, not compensation. Even if we leave this point aside (and it is not a minor one), taking the Court's view to its last consequences, should we conclude that a prospectus liability claim ranks *pari passu* with a shareholder claim? What if the plaintiff is a senior bondholder? Should we say instead that the claim has the same ranking of the instruments issued? If so, should *prospectus liability* vary with the instrument? This does not seem to square out with prospectus rules or private law rules, where a liability claim is (or should be) a damages claim, normally ranking *pari passu* with ordinary claims. This has moreover quite intractable implications for the resolution process itself, because it implies that such damages need to be taken into consideration in the valuation which is performed to determine what compensation need to be granted to affected shareholders and creditors under the NCWO principle.

9.69 The Court of Justice's case law has treated prospectus liability in concentric circles: company law rules outside, then prospectus liability rules, then BRRD, all without touching domestic remedies. This approach looks increasingly untenable, and results in bad inter-court dialogue. Spanish courts should have asked whether a remedy like invalidity is compatible with the logic of the write-off and conversion (it does not seem to be), or whether BRRD rules were relevant to assess elements like 'falsity', 'materiality' or 'reliance'. Yet, the Court of Justice could have invited further questions, or raised these issues of its own motion. Instead, it gave the impression that, rather than deferential, it is still uncomfortable with private remedies. The solution is greater engagement, to foster convergence of the law. The next point shows examples of how this can be achieved.

---

[246] ibid paras 39–40, with reference to recital 120 of Directive 2014/59/EU BRRD.
[247] *Santander* (n 245) paras 41–43.

3.3 The dawn of a doctrine of 'reliance' and 'fraud-on-the-market' in domestic and EU courts?

Once a cause of action is established, a key aspect to harmonize the substance of securities liability is the 'causal' link, including the element of 'reliance', and the distribution of the evidentiary burden through presumptions, as seen in the 'fraud-on-the-market' theory. As we will see, this is also key in the EU. **9.70**

An important national example is the *World Online* case, decided by the Dutch Supreme Court (Hogue Raad).[248] Investors sued the internet company World Online for losses allegedly suffered as a consequence of the prospectus released in the IPO, since the company's top person (Nina Brink) had sold her shares through a controlled legal entity weeks before the IPO for a price much lower than that of the offering, and no express statement was made on this. The Supreme Court held that, by not disclosing the information on the price of the sale in the prospectus, the company and the investment banks in the offering acted wrongfully towards subscribers of shares in the IPO, and subsequent subscribers. The Supreme Court assessed concepts such as 'misleading', and 'wrongful' within section 6:194 of the Dutch Civil Code, using as a reference point the expectation of an averagely informed, cautious and observant ordinary 'reference investor', who is prepared to go deeply into the information, but lacks specialist knowledge and experience (except if the information is specifically targeted to that audience[249]). Thus, if the statement, in its context, would reasonably be of the essence for the 'reference investor', ie, its inaccuracy or incompleteness could reasonably affect his economic behaviour, the statement will be misleading and wrongful, regardless of whether the investor actually read the prospectus.[250] **9.71**

Even if the information is misleading, the company may not have to compensate damages absent a *causal link* between the information and the actual investment decision, which can take into account the investor's circumstances. The causal link test is the so-called *conditio sine qua non* test, which does not require absolute certainty, but the judges' conviction of a high probability of the link. Since an investor may be guided by a multitude of factors, it would be impossible to prove that he was actually influenced by the misleading statement under normal evidentiary rules. Such influence could be experienced indirectly, through the state of opinion created by the statement.[251] However, in the Court's view, the requirement of causation had to be interpreted *in light of* the Prospectus Directive (the predecessor of the Prospectus Regulation) goal to provide 'effective legal protection', which meant a presumption that the *conditio sine qua non* link was present.[252] This was a rebuttable presumption, like the one in *Basic*,[253] which may be countered by proving that the decision to purchase was not influenced by the misleading statements (if, eg took place before these were made); or if the investor was a professional investor with knowledge and experience, it may be justified to exclude the presumption and apply ordinary rules, and require the investor to prove the causal link (also if the ordinary investor was assisted by a professional investor). Yet, the Court's distinction between retail and wholesale investors could create friction with EU prospectus **9.72**

---

[248] Hoge Raad, Dutch Supreme Court HR, nr 07/11104 (27 November 2009) ECLI:NL:HR:2009:BH2162 (*World Online*).
[249] ibid para 4.10.3.
[250] ibid para 4.10.4.
[251] ibid para 4.11.1.
[252] ibid para 4.11.2.
[253] See section 2.2.2.

rules,[254] which differentiate between retail and sophisticated investors in some cases, such as offers of non-equity securities,[255] not in others. Should courts reject liability, eg if securities are offered only or primarily to sophisticated investors, this could send the message that such information is 'mandatory but not quite'. If securities are distributed to both sophisticated and retail investors with no distinction in the rules (eg an IPO of equity securities) excluding liability could fail to provide an 'effective, proportionate and dissuasive' remedy. However, the Dutch Supreme Court did not rule out a further balancing of factors, nor suggested that investors' sophistication would automatically lead to a different treatment. The matter needs further development in the courts.

9.73 In Germany, the courts have created a doctrine similar to the US 'fraud-on-the-market' doctrine (the so-called *Anlagestimmung*[256]), by which, if the prospectus created a positive environment, or 'investment atmosphere', for the reception of the securities, investor reliance, and the causal link, is presumed; a presumption that can be rebutted if it is proven that the plaintiff purchased the securities without knowing the incorrect or incomplete information,[257] or that the facts, once disclosed, did not contribute to a reduction in the securities price.[258] Such presumption is based on the standard of the 'average investor',[259] who lacks specialized knowledge, but may understand financial statements,[260] although the Federal Supreme Court held in another decision (of securities distributed to inexperienced investors) that such average investor lacks the ability to understand financial statements.[261]

9.74 In Italy, the courts have made a relatively brief analysis of causation and reliance, often using an assessment of materiality to presume investor reliance (reminding of US courts), and with some possible influence from German doctrine of 'investment atmosphere',[262] but without conceptualizing the point too much. In its leading prospectus case, the Supreme Court's excluded a requirement of proof of reliance, noting that the prospectus has an essential role in informing investors, and thus an untrue prospectus creates an alteration of investors' decision-making.[263] Unless the false facts or omissions are immaterial, reliance is presumed, a holding maintained by the lower courts.[264]

9.75 In Spain, courts have gone in the same direction, although with frictions resulting from their recourse to both 'mistake' and 'damages'. In the *Bankia I* cases,[265] although not involving a claim of damages, but of contract annulment, the defendant bank's main objection was that the courts of appeal (*Audiencia Provincial*) had not established the causal link between the prospectus' false statements and the contract. In one case, it was even established that the plaintiffs (retail investors) had not read the prospectus.[266] The Supreme Court rejected this

---

[254] Busch (n 196) 25.
[255] See eg Commission Delegated Regulation (EU) 2019/980 supplementing Regulation (EU) 2017/1129 of the European Parliament and of the Council as regards the format, content, scrutiny, and approval of the prospectus to be published when securities are offered to the public or admitted to trading on a regulated market, and repealing Commission Regulation (EC) No 809/2004 [2019] OJ L166.
[256] Mock (n 213) 20.48, 485, and case law cited therein.
[257] Securities Prospectus Act, s 23(2)(1).
[258] ibid s 23(2)(2).
[259] Mock (n 213) 20.34, 479.
[260] Federal Court of Justice II ZR 172/81, NJW 1982, 2827 (12 July 1982).
[261] Federal Court of Justice XI ZR 344/11, BGHZ 195, 1, n. 25 = NJW 2013, 539 (18 September 2012). See, however, the summary of the criticism in Mock (n 213) 20.34–20.36, 479–80.
[262] Giudici (n 212) 22.27.
[263] Italy Cassation Court No 14056 (11 June 2010).
[264] Milan Court of Appeal, 15 January 2014 and Milan Tribunal (17 January 2014) Le Società (2015) 849.
[265] STS 23/2016 and 24/2016 (n 241). See section 3.2.
[266] Supreme Court decision no 24/2016 (3 February 2016).

reasoning, highlighting several ideas. The first was that the assessment of investors' 'mistake' in the IPO was based on the Court's doctrine of mistake in mis-selling cases.[267] The second was that the causal link held even if the investors did not actually read the prospectus, because its information was 'disseminated', creating the 'disposition' to invest,[268] and/or 'creating an opinion' on the entity's economic prospects.[269] The third idea was the fact that the cases involved retail investors was key for the causal link, because they lacked alternative sources to balance the pro-investment disposition or state of opinion; *especially* because the bank was not only the issuer, but also the intermediary that sold the shares (or belonged to the same group).[270] This also helped to conclude that the mistake was 'excusable'. Fourth, such interpretation was compatible with company law principles in light of the *Hirmann v Immofinanz*.[271]

9.76 Thus, the doctrine of Spanish courts, of *World Online*, or the German *Anlagestimmung*, or Italian courts' approach include a presumption of reliance and thus of causal link. This could be the basis of a common principle, which could be the substantive basis of an EU-wide securities class action, as long as procedural rules accompany it.

9.77 However, it is also important to acknowledge the main obstacles. First, all courts emphasize the retail-non-retail distinction, which may require non-retail investors to prove reliance. Secondly, some countries (Spain, Austria, and Germany) contemplate both damages *and* annulment, whereas, to be feasible, EU-wide (class) actions should be based on the same remedies.

9.78 The *Bankia* saga has been key to begin confronting these obstacles, through a subsequent Spanish Supreme Court rulings (*Bankia II*[272] and *Bankia IV*)[273] on *damages*, and two days after *Bankia II*, a decision by the Court of Justice (*Bankia III*[274]). The plaintiffs' damages claim was decided with a reasoning analogous to the *Bankia I* claims on 'mistake', but there were key differences. The plaintiff was a retail investor who subscribed shares in the IPO, *and* later purchased shares on the days before the revision of financial statements. Bankia did not contest the primary market subscription; only the secondary market purchases, and unlike the *Bankia I* cases, (i) the appellate court dismissed the complaint for lack of causation; (ii) the court deciding the parallel criminal case against Bankia and its directors (*Audiencia Nacional*), sternly rejected all the public prosecution's claims.[275] The Supreme

---

[267] In its decision 23/2016 it explained its doctrine of mistake, recently restated as a result of the flood of misselling cases (see section 3.1), which included a causal link between the mistake and the finality intended when concluding the contract. In its decision 24/2016 the Supreme Court made a shorter summary of its recent doctrine of mistake, and emphasized that its criterion was aligned with the Principles of European Contract Law (PECL).

[268] Supreme Court decision no 23/2016 (3 February 2016) Third ground of decision, no 2.

[269] Supreme Court decision no 24/2016 (3 February 2016) Ninth ground of decision.

[270] The two decisions differed on some aspects, due to lower courts' different assessment of the causal link. Decision 23/2016 highlighted that Bankia was previously unlisted, and lacked a history of trading and listing price, and the prospectus was an essential (mandatory) requirement. Thus, the prospectus information was the *decisive element* for 'small' (retail) investor, especially since they were advised by the very employees of the issuing entity, under a relationship of personal and commercial trust. See Supreme Court decision of 3 February 2016, no 23/2016, Third ground of decision, no 2. In decision 24/2016, the Court held that the court of appeals had sufficiently established causation by relying on decisions of other courts in analogous cases (the Bankia IPO was very litigious) and by showing investors' mistaken representation. The fact that plaintiffs were small (retail) investors made the mistake excusable, since they lack other means to obtain the economic information of the company. See Supreme Court decision of 3 February 2016, no 24/2016, Ninth ground of decision.

[271] See section 2.3.2.

[272] Spanish Supreme Court judgment no 380/2021 (1 June 2021) ECLI:ES:TS:2021:2251 (*Bankia II*).

[273] STS 2150/2022 ECLI:ES:TS:2022:2150 (2 June 2022).

[274] Case C-910/19, *Bankia v Union Mutua Asistencial de Seguros (UMAS)* ECLI:EU:C:2021:433 (*Bankia III*).

[275] *Audiencia Nacional* Judgment no 13/2020 (29 September 2020).

Court's construction was structured and precise. It downplayed the criminal case's relevance, which had a different evidentiary standard, and decided different issues.[276] Then, it offered a finalistic interpretation of prospectus rules, based on the goal of 'full disclosure',[277] as a basis to establish the plaintiff's standing and decide on causation, because, although it is not a matter regulated in the EU rules, and left to Member States, it is subject to the principles of equivalence and effectiveness.[278] On this basis, the Court reiterated that the causal link resulted from the dissemination of information, and the creation of opinion and investment trends among the public. Thus, there was not even a need to read the prospectus. This element fulfilled the *factual*, or 'phenomenological' element of causation, but also the *legal* element of 'objective imputation', ie Bankia, by distributing the misleading prospectus, *created the risk* that, upon materializing, fell within the protective scope of the norm (the Prospectus Directive[279]). The fact that, before the purchase, some new facts were known that affected the share price did not affect the conclusion. In case of good faith purchases (as the case seemed to be) the new events did not sever the causal link, but merely affected the figure of damages (the differential between purchase price and post-revision price was lower than with the subscription price).[280]

9.79 The *Bankia III* case, decided by the Court of Justice, involved Bankia and a mutual insurance company. Bankia's offering had included a (prospectus-based) tranche for retail investors, employees and directors, and a book building-based 'institutional tranche' for qualified investors (without prospectus).[281] Both tranches were offered after the registration of the prospectus on 29 June 2011, but after the revision of financial statements, the shares lost almost all their value, and were suspended from trading. The institutional investor sought the annulment of the share purchase order, alleging 'mistake/error', and, alternatively, damages liability for issuing a misleading prospectus. The appeal court (Audiencia Provincial) dismissed the annulment claim, but upheld the damages claim, and Bankia appealed to the Spanish Supreme Court which made a preliminary reference to the Court of Justice, which addressed key issues on qualified investors protection and reliance.

9.80 First, the Court of Justice noted that prospectus rules do not exclude qualified investors from filing a liability claim:[282] a prospectus-based civil liability claim may be brought by any investor, whatever its condition.[283] This followed Advocate General De la Tour's Opinion,[284] which clarified the extent to which an investor can successfully claim to have 'relied' on the prospectus to bring a damages claim. This solves a latent contradiction between the stated aim of the norm, which justifies the mandatory production of information on the need to protect retail investors, while omitting a reference to qualified investors, and the reality of the market, where retail investors seldom care about the prospectus information, while qualified

---

[276] See *Bankia II* (n 272) Fifth Ground of Decision. Although the Court relied on its previous ruling no 24/2016 to discard the relevance of the criminal procedure for the civil complaints, this one had special relevance, given that the decision had already been rendered.
[277] *Bankia II* (n 272) Sixth Ground of Decision nos 1–8.
[278] ibid Sixth Ground of Decision no 21.
[279] ibid Sixth Ground of Decision nos 22–25.
[280] ibid Sixth Ground of Decision nos 26–28.
[281] For further reference see Marco Lamandini and David Ramos Muñoz, 'Bankia: Can You Have a Capital Markets Union without Harmonised Remedies for Securities Litigation?' *EU Law Live* (19 June 2021).
[282] *Bankia III* (n 274) paras 27–33.
[283] ibid 34–38.
[284] Case C-910/19 *Bankia v UMAS*, Opinion of AG Richard de la Tour ECLI:EU:C:2021:119, paras 38–41.

investors care (or at least pretend to care) for it. Truth in securities can be told to people who can understand it, something that can normally be presumed of professional investors.

The second (and harder) issue was whether in deciding on liability courts should assess to **9.81** what extent qualified investors were aware of the issuer's economic situation beyond what was stated in the prospectus, based on their legal and commercial relations, eg being shareholders or members of the issuer's management bodies, etc. The Court held that prospectus rules grant Member States broad discretion to determine the elements of a damages claim, *subject to* the principles of equivalence and effectiveness.[285] Thus, national laws may ask a court to consider an investor's awareness (or its duty to be aware) of the issuer's economic situation, but that those national rules cannot be less favourable than other national rules governing similar actions (equivalence), and cannot in practice have the effect of making it impossible or excessively difficult to bring that action, which the referring court must determine on a case-by-case basis.[286]

This is in line with *Hirmann* and other cases, but in sticking to this position the Court of **9.82** Justice increasingly seems to walk a tightrope between past and future. In our opinion, harmonized primary rights in the law of finance is of limited consequence without a harmonization of secondary rights, or remedies, and a Capital Markets Union that seeks to guarantee investors uniform protection is not possible without more harmonized civil remedies. EU institutions' attempts to nudge Member States towards more convergence have been timid,[287] and unsuccessful. Greater harmonization is desirable, and, we believe, inevitable.[288] One can only surmise whether this process will be prompted by the Court of Justice's negative harmonization, eg declaring certain national remedies incompatible with EU law, by positive harmonization from the co-legislators, or both. The US experience offers useful lessons about the role of courts in filling open-textured provisions with meaning, while EU cases show the Court of Justice ill-at-ease having to deal with concepts of tort law or corporate law to determine their 'equivalence' and 'effectiveness'. Yet, some future case will present a decision where domestic courts' conclusion is impeccably consistent with their private law doctrines, yet grants investors a protection that is sub-standard, inaccessible, or both, ie there comes a point where Member States' procedural autonomy impairs EU law equivalence and effectiveness, and something has got to give. The Court of Justice will have to decide whether to limit itself to dictating a different outcome, leaving domestic courts full freedom to find the best interpretation to get there from within their laws, or to acknowledge that sometimes EU law goals and domestic law too deeply interwoven to compartmentalize interpretation, as the Spanish Supreme Court did with the 'causation/reliance' element. Legislative solutions

---

[285] *Bankia III* (n 274) paras 42, 45.
[286] ibid paras 46–48.
[287] There is, so far, one EU remedy in case of credit rating agencies (*Infra* paras 4.113 ff) and a Recommendation inviting Member States to establish collective redress mechanisms Commission Recommendation of 11 June 2013 on common principles for injunctive and compensatory collective redress mechanisms in the Member States concerning violations of rights granted under Union Law.
[288] As noted by Professor Merritt B Fox, 'Initial Public Offerings in the CMU: A US Perspective' in Danny Busch, Emilios Avgouleas, and Guido Ferrarini (eds), *Capital Markets Union in Europe* (OUP 2018) 296: 'no Member State's law has as strict a regime as that under US s 11. Moreover, Member States' liability rules vary as to the extent that they fall short of this standard and which country's regime applies with respect to an action by any particular investor against any particular issuer depends on the choice of law rules of the various countries involved. The resulting crazy quilt of potential liability for issuer misstatements and omissions is thus a suboptimal deterrent ... This suggests that an EU-wide civil liability regime resembling that section 11 should ultimately be a component of the CMU.' Compare also Paul Davies, 'Damages Actions by Investors on the Back of Market Disclosure Requirements' in Danny Busch, Emilios Avgouleas, and Guido Ferrarini (eds), *Capital Markets Union in Europe* (OUP 2018) 326.

would provide a more certain roadmap, but EU co-legislators may prefer to let the Court force the decision upon them, and thus lend them extra legitimacy. Following the preliminary ruling, in *Bankia IV* the Supreme Court decided on damages. The plaintiff was a retail investor who acquired the securities on the secondary market. The Court declared the termination of the purchase contract with restitution effects. In contrast to *Bankia II*, here the Court examined the alleged misrepresentation in the prospectus as a breach of contract. The main differences between *Bankia IV* and *Bankia II* were, on the one hand, that the restitution effects in *Bankia IV* resulted from a breach of an essential contractual obligation and therefore they had effects only between the parties in the dispute. On the other hand, the Court placed value on the lack of compliance of the promise by the issuer rather than on the validity of the consent given by the investor. The Court first stated that the prospectus regime protects not only the investors who subscribe to a public offering for subscription or sale of securities (primary market), but also those who acquire marketable instruments on the secondary market, as the prospectus is intended to preserve 'the legal certainty necessary to guarantee the confidence of investors and operators in the financial markets'.[289] Secondly, the Court held that, in the business reality of public offerings of sale or subscription of negotiable securities, the information contained in the prospectus is a substantial element of the subscription or purchase contract. In other words, the Court affirmed that such information is integrated into the contract itself as an essential part of it.[290] Therefore, a damages action does not derive strictly speaking from a breach of the pre-contractual information obligation imposed by the securities regulations, but from a breach by Bankia of its contractual obligation to deliver what it promised under the purchase or subscription agreement.[291] As, in accordance with the Court, providing misleading information in the prospectus constituted a breach of the 'essential obligation' of the issuer and frustrates the investors' expectations,[292] the ruling declared the termination of the contract with restitution effects. In doing so, the Court applied the principle of 'full reparation'[293] in order to reestablish the patrimonial situation prior to the causation of the damage, and ensure that the creditor does not suffer any loss, but neither any enrichment, as a consequence of the compensation.

9.83 Indeed, as seen above, Member States' courts seem to be converging on the basic contours of a theory of liability, namely: (i) if a prospectus contains 'material' false statements and omissions, there is a presumption that the information will be disseminated in the market, and create a 'state of opinion' or 'investing climate'; (ii) this provides the basis for a presumption of reliance by retail investors; (iii) such presumption is nonetheless subject to c'ontrary evidence, and this depends on the circumstances of the case (although, generally speaking, reversing the presumption will be difficult in the case of retail investors); (iv) sophisticated investors can bring a claim for false information in the prospectus, but they cannot expect the same treatment, and the assessment of reliance depends more on the factual circumstances; sometimes this will suffice to turn the presumption on its head, sometimes it will be

---

[289] STS 2150/2022 ECLI:ES:TS:2022:2150 (2 of June 2022) Fifteenth Ground of Decision 8–9 (STS 2150/2022).
[290] ibid.
[291] ibid Fourteenth Ground of Decision, 8. In accordance with art 1461 of the Civil Code, shares of a company that is not a party to the contract. 1461 CC): shares of a company with the solvency and profitability ratios derived from the accounting, financial and equity information reflected in the prospectus, first included in the contractual offer and then in the contract itself.
[292] ibid Fifteenth Ground of Decision, 3.
[293] ibid Fourteenth Ground of Decision, 12. The court held that the compensation for damages (deriving from both contractual and non-contractual negligence) entails the economic compensation of the damage caused to the injured party.

an added element to be weighed by courts. There is less clarity or consensus about the doctrinal importance of qualified investors, but this is something the Court of Justice can help with. Otherwise, by acknowledging the parallel developments of Member States' courts, and their alignment with EU rules' interpretation, the Court of Justice can take a step similar to decisions like *Bankers' Life* or *Basic*.[294]

3.4 Liability beyond prospectus: other disclosures and failures to disclose (market abuse)

Beyond prospectus rules, the EU provisions that can be a clearer basis for liability[295] are the Transparency Directive provisions[296] providing for the responsibility of information periodically and specifically by listed companies,[297] and the provisions of the Market Abuse Regulation (MAR),[298] and Directive (MAD),[299] which do not refer to civil liability, but partially harmonize criminal procedures and sanctions,[300] and prescribe extensive duties of disclosure to 'insiders',[301] as well as restrictive rules on market manipulation.[302] 9.84

Court of Justice case law has been based on market abuse norms[303] in cases of criminal liability and safeguards, which were analysed in earlier chapters. Yet, the Court has also interpreted the concepts that give rise to liability. In *IMC Securities* it held that market abuse rules did not require, in order for the price of one or more financial instruments to be considered to have been fixed at an abnormal or artificial level, that that price must maintain an abnormal or artificial level for more than a certain duration.[304] 9.85

In *Geltl*,[305] the Court held that the concept of 'inside information', which must be of a 'precise nature'[306] encompasses, in the case of a 'protracted process' intended to bring about a particular result not only the information about that result (once it happens), but also the intermediate steps of that process which are connected with bringing about that future 9.86

---

[294] *Bankers Life & Casualty Co v Crenshaw* 486 US 71 (1988); *Basic v Levinson* (n 82).
[295] Except for the case of rating agencies, considered separately. See section 4.
[296] Directive 2004/109/EC of the European Parliament and of the Council on the harmonisation of transparency requirements in relation to information about issuers whose securities are admitted to trading on a regulated market and amending Directive 2001/34/EC [2004] OJ L390 (Transparency Directive).
[297] Article 7 of the Transparency Directive (n 296) states that: 'Member States shall ensure that responsibility for the information to be drawn up and made public in accordance with Articles 4, 5, 6 and 16 lies at least with the issuer or its administrative, management or supervisory bodies and shall ensure that their laws, regulations and administrative provisions on liability apply to the issuers, the bodies referred to in this Article or the persons responsible within the issuers.'
[298] Regulation (EU) No 596/2014 of the European Parliament and of the Council on market abuse (market abuse regulation) and repealing Directive 2003/6/EC of the European Parliament and of the Council and Commission Directives 2003/124/EC, 2003/125/EC and 2004/72/EC [2014] OJ L173 (Market Abuse Regulation or MAR).
[299] Directive 2014/57/EU of the European Parliament and of the Council on criminal sanctions for market abuse [2014] OJ L173 (Market Abuse Directive (MAD)).
[300] ibid.
[301] See eg MAR (n 298) arts 7–11.
[302] See eg ibid art 12.
[303] There have been no cases on the Transparency Directive, save for the *Hirmann* case (n 224), where the questions on liability formulated by the Austrian court, although more centred on the existence of a prospectus, also encompassed liability for breach of the Transparency Directive and the market abuse norms.
[304] Case C-445/09 *IMC Securities* ECLI:EU:C:2011:459.
[305] Case C-19/11 *Markus Geltl v Daimler AG* ECLI:EU:C:2012:397.
[306] See eg MAR (n 298) art 7(1)(a).

circumstance or event.[307] The finding was incorporated in a subsequent amendment of market abuse rules,[308] and while the case involved the resignation of a board member, the finding could also apply to other processes, such as merger talks. In the controversial *Lafonta* case,[309] the Court of Justice held that in order for information to be regarded as being of a 'precise nature' for purposes of insider dealing, it need not require the person receiving the information to understand the particular direction in which the market price might be affected, ie up or down in the understanding that it would be possible to speculate with the variability of prices itself, eg through derivatives.

9.87 Domestic case law has also developed these provisions. Germany is one of the more active enforcers in cases of false or misleading information or non-publication of inside information,[310] *and* offers some relevant examples of civil liability.[311] Initially, liability under general tort law (section 823 of the German Civil Code) was excluded, with the exception (rarely successful) of wilful acts against *bonos mores* (section § 826 German Civil Code).[312] Yet, in the 2004 leading case of *Infomatec*, the Federal Supreme Court held that the *wilful* dissemination of false information was immoral, and thus contrary to *bonos mores*, and granted damages under section 826 BGB against the managers of Infomatec,[313] and later, in 2005, in *EMTV*, it held that a company is responsible for the *wilful* actions of its managers under section 31 of BGB.[314] Nonetheless, in *Comroad* the Court held the need to establish a causal link between the misstatement (or incorrect notification) and the purchase decision.[315]

9.88 Further litigation was facilitated by the provisions in the Securities Trading Act (WpHG, sections 97–98),[316] which explicitly regulate civil liability for inside information-related wrongful conduct, including non-publication or publication of false information. The standard of proof is generally reversed, and issuers need to prove that the non-disclosure, or the unawareness were not deliberate or resulted from gross negligence.[317] Yet, if the plaintiff exercises a restitution-based remedy (reimbursement of the price) she needs to prove that she would not have purchased the shares if the information duties had not been breached.[318]

---

[307] See *Geltl* (n 305). The Court also held that: '[T]he notion of a set of circumstances which exists or may reasonably be expected to come into existence or an event which has occurred or may reasonably be expected to do so' refers to future circumstances or events from which it appears, on the basis of an overall assessment of the factors existing at the relevant time, that there is a realistic prospect that they will come into existence or occur. However, that notion should not be interpreted as meaning that the magnitude of the effect of that set of circumstances or that event on the prices of the financial instruments concerned must be taken into consideration.

[308] See the drafting of MAR (n 298) art 7(2).

[309] Case C-628/13 *Jean-Bernard Lafonta v Autorité des marchés financiers* ECLI:EU:C:2015:162.

[310] See eg Marco Ventoruzzo, 'Comparing Insider Trading in the United States and in the European Union: History and Recent Developments' (European Corporate Governance Institute (ECGI) Law Working Paper No 257/2014, 2014).

[311] See Lars Röh and Tobias de Raet, 'The Securities Litigation Review: Germany' (7 June 2021) https://thelawreviews.co.uk/title/the-securities-litigation-review/germany#footnote-105-backlink (accessed 30 September 2022).

[312] Carsten Gerner-Beuerle, 'Underwriters, Auditors, and Other Usual Suspects: Elements of Third Party Enforcement in US and European Securities Law' (2009) 6 Eur Co and Fin L Rev 503. See also Philip Koch, 'Section 19. Disclosure of Inside Information' in Rüdiger Veil (ed), *European Capital Markets Law* (Rebecca Schweiger tr, Hart Publishing 2017).

[313] BGH Case No II ZR 218/03, BGHZ 160 (19 July 2004).

[314] BGH, Case No II ZR 187/02, NZG 2005 (9 May 2005).

[315] BGH, Case No II ZR 80/04, NZG 2007 (guidance order of 28 November 2005).

[316] Section 97 Liability for damages due to failure to publish inside information without undue delay; s 98 Liability for damages due to publication of untrue inside information.

[317] Section 97(2) states that 'Issuers who can prove that the failure to publish was not deliberate or an act of gross negligence are not liable for damages', and s 98(2) states that: 'Issuers who can prove that they were not aware of the inaccuracy of the inside information and that the lack of awareness does not constitute an act of gross negligence are not liable for damages'.

[318] BGH, NJW 2012 (13 December 2011).

The landmark case *Hypo Real Estate* (HRE) dealt with the veracity of quarterly results and projections, as well as press releases, and alleged non-disclosures (or late disclosures) by a large German property lender, about the valuation and risks of its pool of collateralized debt obligations (CDOs) based on US real estate loans, which were subject to major revisions.[319] The Munich Higher Regional Court made a sample decision, holding that there were breaches of the duty to inform in connection with the press releases, and the effects of the US crisis, but limiting the *dies a quo* from where the duty to inform began to apply.[320]

On appeal, the Federal Supreme Court[321] upheld the Higher Regional Court's finding that there was no breach of duty to provide information before August, and that the earnings forecast based on previous quarterly results was not legally objectionable, providing an extensive discussion of the standard applicable to *forecasts*, reminiscent of US courts' case law on 'material omissions' in the disclosure of 'trends and uncertainties'.[322] The German Court was ready to find liability for a failure to disclose, and was demanding with the accuracy of the factual background concerning forecasts.[323] It also upheld the lower court finding that the August press release contained untrue and incomplete information. However, the Supreme Court overturned the Higher Regional Court's finding that HRE was obliged to correct the statements in the press release by means of an ad hoc announcement. In the Court's view, the duty to make ad *hoc* disclosures arises not merely because it renders the earlier information inaccurate, but because it leads to inside information subject to disclosure, and the lower court had not clarified *which* specific facts were supposed to have been concealed by the press release, and thus it was not clear that there should have been a corrective ad hoc disclosure about the composition of the US CDO portfolio.[324] The Federal Supreme Court also upheld the determination that the ad hoc announcement of 15 January 2008 was not 'published immediately', and thus breached the duty to release inside information because a duty to disclose already existed on 8 January 2008 (when the information became known) and HRE was not exempt from the obligation to publish.

9.89

Subsequently, the *Volkswagen* cases involve the auto manufacturer's use of a 'defeat device' in diesel cars, which helped reduced emissions of nitrogen oxide during the cars' testing. Product liability lawsuits were filed in parallel with securities lawsuits for false information and non-disclosure (under section 97 WpHG). The latter are conducted by the Higher Regional Court of Brunswick, although some cases against Porsche, Volkswagen's largest

9.90

---

[319] The CDO portfolio's cumulative nominal value was around €1.5 billion. Standard & Poor's and Moody's announced on 10 July 2007 that certain CDOs would be subject to closer examination. Then, HRE announced in July quarterly earnings of €183 million and increased its 2007 Management Board's earnings forecast from €680 to €710 million. IKB Deutsche Industriebank AG bail-out was known on 30 July . HRE confirmed its forecast on 3 August 2007 (press release) and disclosed the size of her US CDO portfolio. On 7 November HRE released its quarterly financial statements, and a press release announced its CEO's assessment that the HRE Group had emerged stronger from the market crisis. A downgrade of CDO by Fitch Ratings Inc on 12 November also affected securities held by the HRE Group, and they revised their model for CDO ratings. On 15 January 2008, HRE announced that a revaluation of the US CDO portfolio led to large expenses and income adjustments (€290 million) leading to a drop in stock price from €33.10 to €21.64 by the close of the day.

[320] The Munich Court held that there were breaches of the duty to inform in the press releases of 3 August 2007 and 7 November 2007, the effects of the US real estate crisis from 15 November 2007 and the ad Hoc notification dated 15 January 2008. It did not determine any breaches of the duty to inform before August 3, 2007. OLG Munich decision KAP 3/10 (15 December 2014).

[321] BGH judgment II ZB 31/14 (17 December 2020) ECLI: DE: BGH: 2020: 171220BIIZB31.14.0 (*BGH Hypo*).

[322] See sections 2.2 and 2.4, and the Circuit split on whether omissions from Item 303 of S-K can give rise to liability under ss 10b (Securities Exchange Act 1934) and 11 (Securities Act 1933).

[323] *BGH Hypo* (n 321) 6.

[324] ibid para 130.

shareholder, were decided by the Higher Regional Court of Stuttgart, which held that the parent holding company could be obliged to make an *ad hoc* announcement, especially if the operating subsidiary has not done so, but that knowledge of inside information concerning the subsidiary could not without more be attributed to the parent, even if some Volkswagen board members were also Porsche board members, since (Volkswagen) board members were subject to confidentiality duties, and these were not waived by Volkswagen's board.[325] On product liability cases, the Federal Supreme Court found in favour of the plaintiffs in a 2020 case,[326] with no final word on the securities lawsuits.

9.91 In contrast, the Supreme Court curtailed plaintiffs' options on claims of *market manipulation* with a holding that these provisions were intended to safeguard the market at a 'macro' level, and not individual investors, and thus tort liability would fall for the absence of a specific (relative) duty from defendants to plaintiffs,[327] leaving only public enforcement, and actions under section 826 of the Civil Code. This was confirmed by cases on the Volkswagen/Porsche takeover, where Porsche announced its intent to acquire 50 per cent of Volkswagen's shares, and to not acquire a 75 per cent. This announcement was followed by short sales, but Porsche continued its stakebuilding in Volkswagen up to a 74.1 per cent, and announced that it would reach 75 per cent, leading to a sharp price increase, and to losses by short-sellers', who sued Volkswagen and Porsche for market manipulation. Courts showed little sympathy for short-sellers, and held that provisions on market manipulation could not be a basis to compensate investors, and that Porsche's incorrect press releases could not qualify as wilful causation of damage under sections 826 and 31 of the Civil Code.[328]

9.92 In the United Kingdom, most efforts seem to have focused on the administrative and criminal side of insider dealing, with *R v McQuoid* an important precedent on sentencing criteria.[329] On market manipulation, however, the courts had the opportunity to adjudicate on the private law consequences of the LIBOR scandal.[330] So far, private plaintiffs have focused on complaints for misrepresentation or fraud, and the results are (doctrinally speaking) unremarkable. In the *Boyse v Natwest* case[331] the court dismissed a complaint for fraudulent misrepresentation as time-barred under the statute of limitations. The High Court was satisfied that a reasonably diligent person in the claimants' position would have been aware of LIBOR's developments. The Financial Service Authority's (FSA) Final Notice on LIBOR manipulation in 2013 should have offered the claimant a sufficiently clear picture to plead for fraudulent misrepresentation. Thus, its complaint, more than six years later, was time-barred.

9.93 The most important case has been *Property Alliance Group (PAG) v Royal Bank of Scotland (RBS)*,[332] but it involved mostly *contract* claims, for four LIBOR-referenced swaps between

---

[325] The Higher Regional Court of Stuttgart held that the claims against Porsche were identical to those against Volkswagen (resolution of 27 March 2019 (Case No 20 Kap 2 – 4/17)) but was overruled by the Federal Supreme Court, which declared the claims admissible. See BGH Case No II ZB 10/19 (16 June 2020). The Higher Regional Court of Stuttgart decided the claims in its decision of 23 March, 2023 Case No 20 Kap 2/17. The case is pending before the Federal Supreme Court, in case BGH II ZB 9/23.
[326] BGH judgment Case No VI ZR 252/19 (25 May 2020).
[327] BGH Case No XI ZR 51/10) NJW 2012 (13 December 2011).
[328] OLG Stuttgart Case No 2 U 102/14 (26 March 2015) BeckRS 2015, 05690; upheld by the Supreme Court BGH, Case No KZR 73/15 (15 November 2016) BeckRS 2016, 21465.
[329] *R v McQuoid* [2009] EWCA Crim 1301; *R v McQuoid* [2009] 4 All ER 388.
[330] See eg David Hou and David Skeie, 'LIBOR: Origins, Economics, Crisis, Scandal, and Reform' (Federal Reserve Bank of New York Staff Report No 667 (March 2014)).
[331] *Boyse (International) Ltd v NatWest Markets plc and Another* [2021] EWHC 1387 (Ch).
[332] *Property Alliance Group Limited v The Royal Bank of Scotland PLC* [2018] EWCA Civ 355.

PAG and RBS and as such are considered I a subsequent chapter.[333] Yet, one of PAG's contract claims concerned the LIBOR manipulation. The Court acknowledged that the LIBOR manipulation was well known, and accepted that, when it sold LIBOR-linked products, RBS was impliedly representing that LIBOR was an honest, and not a dishonest or manipulated, rate. However, the Court dismissed the complaint because, while RBS had accepted that it had manipulated both Swiss franc and Japanese Yen LIBOR, it had not admitted manipulating sterling LIBOR, and the High Court had found no evidence of it. Therefore, it upheld the High Court's dismissal. On the particular issue of the High Court's failure to consider the correctness of the FSA's findings, the Court of Appeal held that this was, perhaps, unfortunate, but did not invalidate the conclusion, because the correctness of the FSA's findings did not affect the conclusion that the implied representation (that RBS was not manipulating sterling LIBOR) was not a false representation, because findings about the manipulation of one currency could not be used to infer manipulation of a different currency.[334] The Court of Appeal allowed the appeal as a test case to set the tone for subsequent litigation, ie a public and well-documented scandal was insufficient to substantiate any claim, which needed to be precisely referred to the specific product.

9.94 By way of summary, in Europe civil liability doctrine is more developed on prospectus liability than in other securities provisions. Domestic case law standards may evolve and converge in the future, perhaps aided by the Court of Justice, but are not there yet. So far, the Court of Justice has clarified some insider trading concepts, but in 'criminal' cases, which far exceed civil cases. Meanwhile, the Transparency Directive still lacks a clear presence, which presents a large contrast with, eg US section 10b of the Exchange Act. Yet, some key doctrinal developments are taking place in countries like Germany, where courts have jointly insider trading provisions to give 'teeth' to disclosure obligations, finding that a case of material omissions may be reinforced if 'inside' information was not disclosed.

4 Specialties of 'secondary actor' and gatekeeper liability

9.95 The previous sections analysed cases where it was not in doubt that the defendant 'made' a statement and/or she *had to* make a truthful statement. In this section we examine cases where one or both these premises are disputed. There are 'secondary actors' involved in the drafting, making and dissemination of documents and statements that aid in the distribution of financial instruments, such as accountants, analysts, technical experts (eg engineers) broker-dealers or financial intermediaries etc. Some safeguard market integrity (gatekeepers). Yet, they would claim that they issue mere 'opinions' that are protected by free speech, or not actionable if false, or that they are mere secondary players, and other parties 'make' or 'own' the statements. This presents a *constitutional* dimension, based on the protection of 'opinions' as speech (section 4.1), a *private law* dimension, based on the application of tort or contract doctrines to opinions or statements (section 4.2), and a *regulatory* dimension, based on whether secondary actors can attract primary liability of securities laws as 'makers' of statements (section 4.3), or secondary liability, as a result of the specific rules applicable to them (section 4.4).

---

[333] See sections 3.1 and 3.2.2.
[334] *PAG v RBS* (n 332) 150.

4.1 Constitutional dimension: statements versus opinions and free speech in US law

9.96 Free speech protects gatekeepers like rating agencies who, through their ratings cause harm to issuers, who sue for defamation, libel, slander, etc.[335] or torts against honour/image in some civil law countries.[336] Rating agencies in the US have cited the First Amendment, which protects free speech. The basis is *Gertz*,[337] where, in a libel lawsuit against a publisher involving matters of public concern, the Supreme Court held that the First Amendment prohibited awards of presumed and punitive damages for false and defamatory statements.[338]

9.97 The question, then, was what were 'matters of public concern'. In *Dun & Bradstreet v Greenmoss Builders*[339] (*Dun*) the agency Dun & Bradstreet sent a confidential report to five subscribers indicating that the respondent, a construction contractor, had filed for bankruptcy. The report turned out to be false, and grossly misrepresented the respondent's assets and liabilities, but it reached the company when it discussed financing options with its bank, and asked for a correction and the names of the recipients of the false report. The agency issued a corrective notice to the five addressees of the report, but refused to provide their names, and the company sued the agency. The US Supreme Court held that (a) constitutional protection of free speech was not absolute, but required a balancing with the states' interest in protecting a person's reputation,[340] which, in case of a private person,[341] was more important, ie it was a 'strong and legitimate' interest. This could still not outweigh the constitutional interest in free speech on matters of public concern, but (b) 'not all speech is of equal First Amendment importance'.[342] Public speech linked to 'interchange of ideas for the bringing about of political and social changes desired by the people',[343] is 'the essence of self-government'.[344] Other types of speech do not trigger such overwhelming protection, including 'commercial speech'[345] and 'matters of private concern',[346] where the state's interest was 'substantial' while the incidental effect of remedies on speech have significantly less constitutional interest.[347] Whether a speech involves matters of public concern

---

[335] See eg *Dun & Bradstreet Inc v Greenmoss Builders Inc* 472 US 749, 105 S Ct 2939 (1985); *Jefferson City School District v Moody's Investors Services Inc* 988 F Supp 1341 (D Colo 1997).

[336] See eg art 18 of the Spanish Constitution, or Organic Law 4/1982, which regulates in Spain the civil actions for acts that violate the right to one's honour, privacy, or self-image.

[337] *Gertz v Robert Welch Inc* 418 US 323, 94 S Ct 2997, 41 L Ed 2d 789 (1974). The First Amendment was considered as a limit to the state defamation laws in *New York Times Co v Sullivan* 376 US 254, 84 S Ct 710, 11 L Ed 2d 686 (1964) for 'major public issues'.

[338] The exception is when the plaintiff proves 'actual malice', ie knowledge of falsity or reckless disregard for the truth'. See *Gertz v Robert Welch Inc* (1974) 418 US 323, 94 S Ct 2997, 41 L Ed 2d 789. The test also originated in *New York Times v Sullivan* (n 337).

[339] *Dun v Greenmoss Builders* (n 335).

[340] See *Dun v Greenmoss Builders* (n 335) 2944–45, citing *Gertz* (n 338) 3008: 'These protections, we found, were not "justified solely by reference to the interest of the press and broadcast media in immunity from liability". Rather, they represented "an accommodation between [First Amendment] concern[s] and the limited state interest present in the context of libel actions brought by public persons"'.

[341] *Dun v Greenmoss Builders* (n 335) 2945, citing *Gertz* (n 338) 3009.

[342] ibid 2945.

[343] *Roth v United States* 354 US 476, 484 (1957); *New York Times v Sullivan* (n 337).

[344] *Garrison v Louisiana* 379 US 64, 74–75, 85 S Ct 209, 215–16, 13 L Ed 2d 125 (1964).

[345] *Dun v Greenmoss Builders* (n 335) 2946 (citations omitted): the most prominent example of reduced protection for certain kinds of speech concerns commercial speech. Such speech, we have noted, occupies a 'subordinate position in the scale of First Amendment values' … It also is more easily verifiable and less likely to be deterred by proper regulation … Accordingly, it may be regulated in ways that might be impermissible in the realm of non-commercial expression.

[346] ibid paras 2946–47.

[347] ibid para 2947.

'must be determined by [the expression's] content, form, and context ... as revealed by the whole record'.³⁴⁸ Thus, the rating agency's speech was solely in the individual interest of the speaker and its specific business audience,³⁴⁹ and lacked special protection if it was false and damaging to the victim's reputation. Moreover, the report was only distributed to five subscriptors, who, under the agreement, could not disseminate it further.³⁵⁰ Finally, the profit motive made it harder to claim constitutional protections, and ensured a control by the market (ie an inaccurate rating was of little use for investors or creditors) thereby decreasing the risk of 'any incremental 'chilling' effect of libel suits'.³⁵¹

Lower courts in *Re Scott Paper Company*³⁵² granted a rating agency journalist (qualified) privilege in a motion to compel discovery made by investors (plaintiffs) suing a rated issuer for securities fraud, emphasizing that rating agency publications were directed to the general public. The court saw no reason why disseminators of corporate financial information should not have as strong a claim to First Amendment protection as do disseminators of other kinds of information;³⁵³ and referred to an unrelated case (*Lowe v SEC*³⁵⁴), but not to *Dun*. In *Re Pan Am Corp*, the court granted journalist privilege to S&P because it rated virtually all public debt financing and preferred stock issues.³⁵⁵ **9.98**

*Jefferson City School District v Moody's*³⁵⁶ was more similar to *Dun & Bradstreet*. The plaintiff had refinanced part of its debt issuing refunding bonds, and chose Fitch and Standard & Poor's to rate it, not Moody's; nor did it provide Moody's with information about its financial condition. Moody's issued a so-called 'unsolicited opinion' raising concerns over the plaintiff's ability to meet its commitments, with a significantly negative effect. The plaintiff claimed interference with contractual relations and injurious falsehood. The court did not mention *Dun*, but focused on the 'statements-opinions' distinction,³⁵⁷ concluding that the report was a constitutionally protected 'opinion'. **9.99**

Subsequent cases such as *Enron*,³⁵⁸ or *Compuware Corp. v Moody's*³⁵⁹ used the First Amendment to automatically shield rating agencies from suits by *purchasers of securities*, because (they held) ratings were made public, or distributed 'to the world'.³⁶⁰ An exception applies when ratings are distributed 'privately' to a 'limited' and/or 'select' group of 'qualified' investors, as in *Lasalle National Bank*,³⁶¹ National Century **9.100**

---

³⁴⁸ ibid para 2947, citing *Connick v Myers* 461 US 147–48, 103 S Ct 1690 (1981).
³⁴⁹ *Dun v Greenmoss Builders* (n 335) 2948.
³⁵⁰ As such, it cannot be said that the report involves any 'strong interest in the free flow of commercial information'. *Dun v Greenmoss Builders* (n 335) 2948, citing *Virginia Pharmacy Bd v Virginia Citizens Consumer Council Inc* 425 US 748, 764, 96 S Ct 1827, 48 L Ed 2d 346 (1976).
³⁵¹ *Dun v Greenmoss Builders* (n 335) 2948.
³⁵² *In re Scott Paper Company Securities Litigation* (1992) 145 FRD 366.
³⁵³ ibid para 370.
³⁵⁴ In *Lowe v SEC* 472 US 181, 105 S Ct 2557, 86 L Ed 2d 130 (1985) the US Supreme Court declined to determine whether investment newsletters had First Amendment protection as 'press', but the lower court 'believed' that 'the Supreme Court would be likely to hold ... that the investment newsletters involved there would also be protected'. *Scott Paper Company Securities Litigation* (n 352) 371.
³⁵⁵ *In re Pan Am Corp* 161 BR 577, 580–82 (SDNY 1993).
³⁵⁶ *Jefferson City School District v Moody's Investors Services Inc* (1997) 988 F Supp 1341 (D Colo); *Jefferson County School District No R-1 v Moody's Investor Services Inc* 175 F 3d 848, 856 (10th Cir 1999).
³⁵⁷ The 'statement-opinion' distinction was based on the test in *Milkovich v Lorain Journal Co* 497 US 1, 20, 110 S Ct 2695, 2706, 111 L Ed 2d 1 (1990).
³⁵⁸ *In re Enron Corp Securities, Derivative & 'ERISA' Litig* 511 F Supp 2d 742, 820 (SD Tex 2005).
³⁵⁹ *Compuware Corp v Moody's Investor Services Inc* 499 F 3d 520, 529 (6th Cir 2007).
³⁶⁰ *Enron* (n 358).
³⁶¹ *Lasalle National Bank and Others v Duff & Phelps Rating Co* 951 F Supp 1071 (SDNY 1996).

Financial,³⁶² *Abu Dhabi Commercial Bank*,³⁶³ *Anschutz v Merrill Lynch*,³⁶⁴ or *Calpers v Moody's*.³⁶⁵

9.101 Thus, lower courts expanded the protection from defamation suits brought by issuers to securities lawsuits brought by investors, despite the fact that both have different rationales and, for example, punitive damages are common in the former but not in the latter. They also side-stepped the US Supreme Court's balanced approach in *Dun & Bradstreet*. The Court's emphasis on 'self-government', or the 'interchange of ideas for the bringing about of political and social changes' as the justification of the protection is absent. Instead *Dun's* argument about the restricted distribution of the statement (to few subscribers) has become the rule of thumb to differentiate 'public' and 'commercial' speech. Yet, the five-subscribers argument in *Dun* was introduced by a 'moreover', ie it was a side argument, because, to the Supreme Court, whether a speech was of 'public concern' must be determined by the 'content, form, and context . . . as revealed by the whole record', and not by the number of addressees. Indeed, in *Dun & Bradstreet* the Court concluded that the rating agency's statement was solely in the individual interest of the speaker and its specific business audience.³⁶⁶ In fact, it is unclear why a widely disseminated rating should cease to have a commercial purpose.

9.102 Thus, it would be more consistent with *Dun* to distinguish between statements that only have business relevance to investors, and those relevant to a wider audience. In *Lasalle National Bank*³⁶⁷ or *Re Fitch*³⁶⁸ the rating agencies (Duff & Phelps and Fitch) were denied journalist privilege for the purposes of discovery of evidence³⁶⁹ with the argument that, unlike actual journalists, who cover 'newsworthy' (ie 'public interest') issues, rating agencies rated issuances based on the client's request, ie client's interest.³⁷⁰ This distinction could still have dangerous side-effects,³⁷¹ but it correctly emphasizes the predominantly private nature of the interest guiding the ratings.

9.103 Another authority is *CalPERS v Moody's*,³⁷² where the state court of San Francisco denied First Amendment protection because ratings had the limited purpose of making money,³⁷³ and because ratings directed to a restricted number of investors (citing *Abu Dhabi* as precedent). On appeal, the Court of Appeals analysed Moody's special motion, based on an

---

³⁶² *National Century Financial Enterprises Inc Inv Litigation* 580 F Supp 2d 630 (SD Ohio 2008).
³⁶³ *Abu Dhabi Commercial Bank and Others v Morgan Stanley & Co Incorporated and Others* 651 F Supp 2d 155 (SDNY 2009).
³⁶⁴ *Anschutz Corp v Merrill Lynch & Co* WL 1134321 (ND Cal 2010) 23–24.
³⁶⁵ *Pub Employees' Retirement System v Moody's Investor Services Inc* (2014) 226 Cal App 4th 643, 172 Cal Rptr 3d 238 (*Calpers v Moody's*).
³⁶⁶ *Dun v Greenmoss Builders* (n 335) 2948.
³⁶⁷ *Lasalle National Bank and Others v Duff* (n 361).
³⁶⁸ *In re Fitch* 330 F 3d 104 (2nd Cir 2003).
³⁶⁹ In this sense, compare with *Scott Paper Company Securities Litigation* (n 352).
³⁷⁰ See eg *Fitch* (n 368) 110.
³⁷¹ First, it protects the biggest rating agencies, since they are the only ones that, in the words of the court in *re Fitch* (n 368) (referring to S &P) rate 'virtually all public debt financing and preferred stock issues whether they were done by . . . clients or not'. See *In re Fitch* 330 F 3d 104 (2nd Cir 2003) 109. As such, it creates very important entry costs, with the consequent anti-competitive effect. Secondly, it creates an incentive for rating agencies to issue unsolicited rating opinions only to claim journalist privilege, regardless of whether or not the agency has at its disposal the necessary information and expertise to rate the securities.
³⁷² *California Public Employees' Retirement System (Calpers) v Moody's Corp* CGC-09-490241 (Super Ct Cal, SF County 2010).
³⁷³ *CalPERS v Moody's* (n 365) 8: 'The right to free speech allows us to give our opinions on things of public concern. The issuance of these SIV ratings is not, however, an issue of public concern. Rather, it is an economic activity designed for a limited target for the purpose of making money. That is not something that should be afforded First Amendment protection and the Defendants are not akin to members of the financial press.'

anti-SLAPP statute, conceived to strike meritless lawsuits intended to curtail free speech.[374] The motion based on the anti-SLAPP statute required the defendant to show that its acts were performed 'in furtherance of its constitutional right' to free speech, in which case the burden shifted to the plaintiff to establish a probability of prevailing on the merits.[375]

Relying on Fourth Circuit precedent, the court downplayed the fact that the statements were directed to a limited class of investors,[376] holding that, in spite of this: **9.104**

> [T]he ratings themselves concerned an ongoing discussion regarding the financial well-being of a significant investment opportunity that was of interest to a definable portion of the public—to wit, the large group of QIBs/QPs eligible to invest millions of dollars or more on behalf of an even greater number of individual pensioners or investors.[377]

Since the defendant showed a prima facie case of First Amendment speech, the burden shifted to the plaintiffs, who had to show a probability of prevailing on the merits, which it did, to the court's satisfaction, based on private law considerations, as we will see in the next section. **9.105**

4.2 Private law considerations

The liability of 'secondary actors' and gatekeepers under private law can be described as liability for false statements, or for 'pure economic loss', with different legal basis depending on the jurisdiction.[378] The UK presents a 'dual track', with the tort of 'deceit', applicable to fraudulent misrepresentations in prospectuses and securities documents,[379] and the tort of negligence,[380] applicable to negligent misstatements,[381] which requires a duty of care, owed *only* when there is an 'assumption of responsibility' 'akin to contract'[382] (which also means that the party concerned can also disclaim the liability). Neither option typically applies to 'gatekeepers' like auditors (or rating agencies). Courts have sternly rejected a duty of care from auditors towards investors.[383] The law was summarized in *Customs and Excise Commissioners v Barclays Bank*,[384] where Lord Bingham stated that there were three tests developed by courts: **9.106**

> The first is whether the defendant assumed responsibility for what he said and did vis-à-vis the claimant, or is to be treated by the law as having done so. The second is commonly known as the threefold test [in Caparo]: whether loss to the claimant was a reasonably foreseeable consequence of what the defendant did or failed to do; whether the relationship between the parties was one of sufficient proximity; and whether in all the circumstances it is fair, just and reasonable to impose a duty of care on the defendant towards the claimant (… 'policy'). Third is the incremental test, based on the observation … that: 'It is preferable,

---

[374] California Code Civ Proc, s 425.16 (anti-SLAPP section).
[375] *Calpers v Moody's* (n 365).
[376] ibid, citing *Ruiz v Harbor View Community Association* 134 Cal App 4th 1456, 1468 (2005).
[377] *Calpers v Moody's* (n 365).
[378] See section 1.
[379] *Derry v Peek* [1889] UKHL 1.
[380] *Donoghue v Stevenson* (n 9).
[381] *Hedley Byrne* (n 10).
[382] ibid.
[383] *Caparo Industries PLC v Dickman* (n 6).
[384] *Customs and Excise Commissioners v Barclays Bank plc* [2006] UKHL 28, [2007] 1 AC 181.

in my view, that the law should develop novel categories of negligence incrementally and by analogy with established categories, rather than by a massive extension of a prima facie duty of care restrained only by indefinable 'considerations which ought to negative, or to reduce or limit the scope of the duty or the class of person to whom it is owed'.[385]

9.107 Also relevant is *SAAMCO*,[386] a lawsuit against a negligent property valuer after the crash of the early 1990s left owners with too high valuations with negative equity as prices tumbled, where Lord Hoffmann set the parameters for the *scope* of liability for professional opinions: for breach of statutory duty, 'the question is answered by deducing the purpose of the duty from the language and context of the statute'; for tort, 'it will similarly depend upon the purpose of the rule imposing the duty' (exemplified with *Caparo* for auditors); and, for implied contract duty, 'the nature and extent of the liability is defined by the term which the law implies', which means construing 'the agreement as a whole in its commercial setting'.[387] In general, '[r]ules which make the wrongdoer liable for all the consequences of his wrongful conduct are exceptional and need to be justified by some special policy',[388] an idea that he illustrated with his famous 'mountaineer example':

> A mountaineer about to undertake a difficult climb is concerned about the fitness of his knee. He goes to a doctor who negligently makes a superficial examination and pronounces the knee fit. The climber goes on the expedition, which he would not have undertaken if the doctor had told him the true state of his knee. He suffers an injury which is an entirely foreseeable consequence of mountaineering but has nothing to do with his knee.[389]

9.108 Thus, the Court of Appeal's decision was against common sense, because it made the defendant liable for consequences which, although foreseeable, did not have 'a sufficient causal connection with the subject matter of the duty'.[390] A person providing information should be responsible only for the consequences of the information being wrong.[391] *SAAMCO* is less valid for determining *when* a party has assumed responsibility for a statement, than for determining the scope of responsibility once it has been assumed.[392]

9.109 US courts, for their part, have perhaps the earliest example of gatekeeper (non) liability for negligent misstatements in *Ultramares v Touche*,[393] where Cardozo's well-known opinion held that the evidence suggested that the accountants' statements could very well involve negligence, but there was no duty of care: accountants had a duty to do their work without fraud, but not without negligence, because to do so would 'expose accountants to a liability in an indeterminate amount for an indeterminate time to an indeterminate class'.[394] The

---

[385] ibid para 4. Bingham also acknowledged that the three tests overlapped, and were not fully reconcilable, so he considered all three. See ibid para 8.
[386] *South Australia Asset Management Corporation v York Montague Ltd (SAAMCO)* [1996] 3 WLR 87 (*SAAMCO*) and *Banque Bruxelles Lambert SA v Eagle Star Insurance Co Ltd* [1996] UKHL 10.
[387] *SAAMCO* (n 386) para 15.
[388] ibid para 18.
[389] ibid para 19.
[390] ibid para 22.
[391] ibid para 23:[A] person under a duty to take reasonable care to provide information on which someone else will decide upon a course of action is, if negligent, not generally regarded as responsible for all the consequences of that course of action. He is responsible only for the consequences of the information being wrong.
[392] *SAAMCO*'s authority was reaffirmed in *BPE Solicitors v Hughes-Holland* [2017] UKSC 21.
[393] *Ultramares Corporation v Touche* 174 NE 441 (1932).
[394] ibid: 'If liability for negligence exists, a thoughtless slip or blunder, the failure to detect a theft or forgery beneath the cover of deceptive entries, may expose accountants to a liability in an indeterminate amount for an indeterminate time to an indeterminate class. The hazards of a business conducted on these terms are so extreme as to enkindle doubt whether a flaw may not exist in the implication of a duty that exposes to these consequences.'

plaintiffs could bring an action for fraud or deceit, but lacked 'privity' of contract to make a claim of negligence.[395]

9.110 Not all decisions in common law countries flatly reject gatekeeper liability, however. In *Bathurst*,[396] by the Federal Court of Australia, local councils sued ABN Amro, which created a structured credit product (constant proportion debt obligations or CPDOs), Standard & Poor's (S&P) which rated it AAA and Local Government Financial Services (LGFS) which aided ABN Amro in creating Australian CPDOs, known as Rembrandt Notes, which fell in value after the financial crisis. The first instance court found for the plaintiffs.[397] S&P acknowledged the rating's flaws, but argued on appeal that it owed no duty of care, relying on *Hedley*, *Caparo*, or *Ultramares*. The Federal Court dismissed all the grounds of appeal. On S&P's argument that this would impose 'indeterminate liability' the Court held that liability for the Rembrandt Notes was not indeterminate because S&P may not have known the precise identity of investors, but it knew that they were members of a class (ie, investors who purchased Rembrandt Notes) which was narrow, in light of the size of the issue and the minimum level of subscription (around eighty) and that liability would also be limited in time, ie as long as the rating was retained or the notes' maturity (these were ten-year notes).[398] On the argument that sophisticated investors needed no protection by a duty of care, the Court held that an investor's 'reasonable reliance' on the statement determined the vulnerability of that investor, not the opposite (ie first, the investor's vulnerability, then reliance), and neither LGFS nor the councils could 'second-guess' S&P's rating, and thus they had to rely on it.[399] S&P's disclaimers did not exclude liability.[400] The Court also rejected the argument that there were no direct dealings between S&P and LGFS: requiring direct or contractual dealings was inconsistent with the principle of 'determinacy that a duty can be owed to a class' used by the court as a principle, and the fact that the authorities supported the finding that a duty could exist even where there has been no direct relationship between the person who owed the duty and the person to whom the duty was owed.[401]

9.111 In the US, *Ultramares* is still good law in New York,[402] but courts in other states have been less demanding on liability for negligence. Courts in Rhode Island have held that liability can arise for careless misstatements relied upon by the plaintiffs.[403] The Supreme Court of California in *Bily v Arthur Young & Co*.[404] examined different precedents in detail, and decided to follow *Ultramares* in its decision to not impose a general duty of care on accountants as to the conduct of audits that extended to parties other than the accountants' client. However, the Court also accepted that an accountant can be held liable to third parties under a negligent misrepresentation theory.[405] Thus, an investor who assumed the company's

---

[395] *Ultramares v Touche* (n 393): Something more must then appear than an intention that the promise shall redound to the benefit of the public or to that of a class of indefinite extension. The promise must be such as to 'bespeak the assumption of a duty to make reparation directly to the individual members of the public if the benefit is lost'.

[396] *ABN AMRO Bank NV v Bathurst Regional Council* [2014] FCAFC 65.

[397] *Bathurst Regional Council v Local Government Financial Services Pty Ltd (No 5)* [2012] FCA 1200. Possibly knowing how controversial it would be, the judge issued an opinion of more than 1,400 pages.

[398] ibid paras 591–95.

[399] ibid paras 599–601.

[400] ibid paras 602–13.

[401] ibid para 613.

[402] *Credit Alliance Corporation v Arthur Andersen & Co* (1985) 483 NE 2d 110.

[403] *Rhode Island Hospital Trust National Bank v Swartz, Bresenoff, Yavner & Jacobs* 455 F 2d 847, 851 (1972).

[404] *Bily v Arthur Young & Co* 3 Cal 4th 370, 834 P.2d 745, 11 Cal Rptr 2d 51 (1992).

[405] This was under s 552 of the Restatement (Second) on Torts. In *Ingram Industries Inc. v Nowicki* (1981) 527 F Supp 683 a federal court used this as a basis for the liability standard.

solvency could not sue the accountants, but an investor who requested, read, and relied upon the accountants' audit report could.

9.112 On rating agency liability, apart from First Amendment cases,[406] a notable case is *CalPERS v Moody's*,[407] the defendant rating agency alleged an anti-SLAPP statute (which seeks to strike meritless lawsuits against free speech) and succeeded in showing a prima facie defence of free speech which required the plaintiff to show a probability that it would prevail on the claim. The plaintiff did, in the court's view. Relying on *Bily* (above), the court held that, although statements regarding future events are deemed 'opinions', expressions of professional opinion may be treated as representations of fact, when a party possesses or holds itself out as possessing superior knowledge, and bases its assertions also on past and present events. Furthermore, the Court accepted that the plaintiffs had offered sufficient evidence to prove a prima facie case that the rating agencies lacked a reasonable basis to believe the accuracy or truthfulness of their ratings.[408] On the duty of care the Court used the *Bily*'s standard 'that looks to the specific circumstances to ascertain whether a supplier of information has undertaken to inform and guide a third party with respect to an identified transaction or type of transaction',[409] finding that it was satisfied because:

> Quite simply, this is not a case where it is alleged the defendant 'merely knew' of the possibility its professional opinions were being shared with third parties. This is a case where CalPERS alleges the Rating Agencies, first, helped create the underlying products and, second, assigned and published ratings on those products that were then prominently featured in marketing materials given to investors interested in purchasing them.[410]

9.113 The plaintiff had also provided sufficient evidence that it had actually 'relied' on the ratings. As to whether this was 'reasonable' (or, in this case, 'justifiable') reliance, the court held that: 'CalPERS' sophistication, on our record, does not preclude a finding of justifiable reliance. CalPERS has presented evidence that the SIV market existed in a 'shroud of secrecy' and very few persons, even within the Agencies themselves, were privy to the SIVs' composition.'[411] The Court also rejected that the claim under state common law was pre-empted by the Credit Rating Agency Reform Act 2006, since there was a presumption against pre-emption for actions in negligence and deceit (traditionally the domain of states) and the Act's content did nothing to contradict such presumption.

9.114 In Germany, there are several legal bases on which to base liability of secondary actors and gatekeepers, all of them difficult.[412] First, plaintiffs may establish a contract between investors and gatekeepers, which is difficult given the misalignment of interests between the issuer and the investor (it is hard to justify a contract-based claim in favour of both) or the investor's specific vulnerability.[413] Another possibility could be to rely on section 311

---

[406] See section 4.1.
[407] *Public Employees' Retirement System v Moody's Investor Services Inc* 226 Cal App. 4th 643, 172 Cal Rptr 3d 238 (2014).
[408] Expert testimony and the transaction's financial incentives supported that 'the Agencies were only paid if the SIV deal closed, which would only happen if a top rating was assigned to the deal'.
[409] *Calpers v Moody's* (n 365), citing *Glenn K Jackson Inc v Roe* 273 F 3d 1192, 1200, fn 3 (9th Cir 2001), quoting *Bily*, Cal 4th, 410.
[410] *Calpers v Moody's* (n 365).
[411] ibid.
[412] See eg Brigitte Haar, 'Civil Liability of Credit Rating Agencies: Regulatory All or-Nothing Approaches between Immunity and Overdeterrence' (2013) SAFE White Paper No 1; Matthias Lehmann, 'Civil Liability of Rating Agencies: An Insipid Sprout from Brussels' (LSE Law, Society and Economy Working Papers 15/2014, 2014).
[413] Haar (n 412) 4.

no. 3.2 of the German Civil Code, which makes a person liable for inspiring *confidence*, thus influencing contract negotiations or conclusion. Yet, this may require some direct contact between the parties. Also, some precedents contemplate auditors' liability if plaintiffs were included within the *protective scope* of the audit contract. In 1998 the Federal Supreme Court decided[414] a case where the bankruptcy administrator of a company that had acquired the shares of another company from its sole shareholder sued the auditors commissioned by the sole shareholder to carry out a compulsory (statutory) audit,[415] which (wrongly) validated a surplus higher than under earlier financial statements, in light of accounting irregularities emerged later (in reality there was an important deficit). The Supreme Court accepted the principle that an auditor's duty of care is owed to the company that hires the auditor,[416] and there is normally no duty towards third parties, but this should not be read as a full exclusion of liability vis-à-vis third parties. This may arise, for example, if a contract displays protective effects towards third parties, which may happen if a client commissions a report or expert opinion from a person with specialist knowledge recognised by the state (eg publicly appointed expert, auditor, tax adviser) to use it vis-à-vis a third party. There the report's purpose is to induce trust, and to have evidentiary value for the third party, and a conflict of interest between client and third party is not an obstacle to incorporate the latter into the protective scope.[417] Nor is there an obstacle to apply these principles to a *statutory* audit, *provided that* it is sufficiently clear to the auditor that a particular work product is wanted from the auditor, to be used with a third party who trusts in his expert knowledge.

9.115 Thus, the Court distinguished the general principle (to limit liability towards an unknown number of parties), and the 'trustee' or 'expert' liability, where the auditor is made aware that the audit would be used for the specific purpose[418] of generating trust in a third party, to be the basis of an economic decision, and these aspects (identifiable third parties, and the kind of decision to be made) are recognizable by the expert.[419] This 'direct contact' touches on ideas similar to the 'proximity' required by *Caparo* or US case law, and seeks to ensure that the gatekeeper can calculate its risk when concluding the contract (and, if necessary, insure it). Conversely, the expert should not be liable towards third parties if, in light of the contract's purpose, he cannot be expected to accept the risk of extended liability without additional remuneration.[420] This turns on the interpretation of the contract and its surrounding circumstances.

9.116 Subsequent case law has included, for example, the shareholder and managing director of a GmbH (limited liability company) within the protective scope of a contract between the GmbH and a tax adviser, which seeks to assess the GmbH's risk of bankruptcy,[421] or determined the scope of protection of contracts for legal advice,[422] but the approach is generally

---

[414] BGH III ZR 245/96 (2 April 1998).
[415] In accordance with HGB, ss 316ff.
[416] Pursuant to HGB, s 323 (especially para 1, sentence 3).
[417] BGH III ZR 245/96 (n 414).
[418] In the case at hand, the lower court deduced the existence of such awareness, and thus the protective scope, from a letter of 9 October 1992 from the attention of the accountant that was consulted by the company that was later subject to administration by the plaintiff, stating that the now current annual accounts would not be changed by them and could be confirmed by them.
[419] BGH, judgments X ZR 250/02 (20 April 2004); III ZR 256/04 (6 April 2006); III ZR 277/08 (7 May 2009) (BGH, III ZR 277/08).
[420] BGH, III ZR 277/08 (n 413).
[421] BGH, IX ZR 145/11 (14 June 2012) or BGH, judgment III ZR 156/13 (24 April 2014).
[422] BGH, IX ZR 252/15 (21 July 2016). If the subject of a legal advice contract concluded is advice on decisions for the client, the lawyer contract generally has no protective effects in favour of the (legal) representative of the client.

restrictive. The Supreme Court has also framed the issue using regulatory provisions on securities prospectuses,[423] or its doctrine on prospectus liability 'in a broader sense', for securities not traded on an organized market,[424] holding that accountants, lawyers, and other experts mentioned in a (voluntary) prospectus can be held liable, because they contribute to the creation of trust for investors.[425] However, the Court has also held that auditors can only be held liable if they do not merely act as (mandatory) auditors but if they explicitly guarantee the correctness of the prospectus' (financial) information.[426]

9.117 Case law on rating agencies is still developing. In some 2020 decisions the Berlin Regional Court (LG)[427] used principles like the doctrine of 'expert' or 'trustee' liability, and of contracts with protective effects towards third parties, as well as the requirements of 'proximity' to assess liability.[428] The court highlighted that the *registered* rating agency qualified as an 'expert',[429] that it did not rate an 'issuer' (which could expose it to incalculable liability) but an 'issue', ie specific bond issuance, thus satisfying the requirement of proximity or direct contact,[430] and that the rating agency knew the amount of the bond (thus making the harm calculable) and the fact that its rating would be used to facilitate the distribution of the bond. It is still early to conclude whether this assessment will hold.

9.118 Absent contract and quasi-contract claims, the general provision on tort liability excludes pure economic loss-based harm.[431] This leaves the provision on claims for acts contrary to public policy,[432] which requires a violation of public policy, scienter, and reliance. This has been used to claim liability against third parties such as lawyers, but requires a high burden of proof, which succeeds only in case of clear mistakes, where the defendant does not verify information despite clear concerns.[433] These requirements have been applied even when the liability of the third party (eg auditor) was sought in the context of a securities offering, where regulatory provisions are applicable.[434]

9.119 In countries like France, Spain, or Italy, tort liability is based on a general, non-restrictive clause. The Spanish Supreme Court has issued several judgments on auditors' *contract* liability.[435] In contrast with US, UK, or German decisions, they have not cautioned against liability, but simply assessed the breach of a general duty of care (based on the *lex artis*) as the initial requirement. To limit liability, the Court has used a two-step *causation* test, including 'factual' causation, under a *conditio sine qua non* test, and 'legal' causation, under an 'objective imputation' test, which seek to identify the normative criteria determining that a negligent act 'caused' a harmful result.[436] In a 2008 decision, the Court held that there was

---

[423] BGH, IX ZR 245/12 (6 February 2014).
[424] See sections 2.3.1 and 2.3.2.
[425] Mock (n 213) and authorities cited.
[426] BGH VII ZR 232/17 (21 November 2018); Mock (n 213).
[427] LG Berlin judgment 11 O 5/19 (5 May 2020).
[428] ibid, with references to BGH, judgments of 20 April 2004, X ZR 250/02; 6 April 2006, III ZR 256/04; 7 May 2009, III ZR 277/08.
[429] It distinguished this from the case where a non-registered entity could not be presumed to have the requisite expertise (OLG Dresden of 6 March 2019, 5 U 1146/18).
[430] The court distinguished this from the OLG Düsseldorf from 02/08/2018, 6 U 50/17.
[431] German Civil Code, s 823 only contemplates harm to life, physical integrity, or property.
[432] ibid s 826.
[433] Haar (n 412) 5–6, and authorities cited.
[434] See eg BGH judgment VII ZR 236/19 (12 March 2020).
[435] See eg Spanish Supreme Court decision no 338/2012 (7 June 2012) or no 520/2018 (21 September 2018).
[436] Spanish Supreme Court decisions no 869/2008 (14 October 2008) (RJ 2008/6913); Spanish Supreme Court Roj. 5445/2008 (9 October 2008) no 115/2009 (5 March 2009) or no 355/2009 (27 May 2009).

no causal link between the audit report and investors' losses, because they admitted that they did not read the audit report, and did not base their investment decision on it, and rejected the plaintiffs' argument that, had the auditors properly performed their duties, the losses would have been detected, and the actions causing the harm (an intervention by the securities commission) avoided.[437] In a 2016 decision, the Court found, first, that there had been breaches of the *lex artis*, and thus *fault* in the auditors' accounting of inventories, but the Court distinguished between the harm consisting in the disappearance of (stolen) inventoried goods from the port, where there was no causal link (the harm was caused by the party who stole the goods) and the resulting (wrongful) recording of profits, and the incorrect calculation of tax liabilities. This approach shows some similarities with the 'protective scope' of a legal norm, or contract, under German law, and is reminiscent of the 'policy' element of US or UK law, but unlike them it has no sharp exclusionary effect, and is administered more flexibly. Since no precedent has involved a listed company, the potential number of plaintiffs has always been limited. So far, this 'liberal' approach has not led to a flood of cases.

Italy offered some early cases on rating agency liabiilty by the courts in Rome (*Lehman Brothers*[438]) and Milano (*Parmalat*).[439] The Rome court rejected the argument that ratings could be considered mere 'opinions', protected by free speech, and accepted that they were meant to instil trust among investors.[440] Any harm was caused to the plaintiffs' freedom of contract, by influencing their decision to invest, and thus belonged to the field of tort liability.[441] The decision also considered aspects like the causal link, or investors' reliance, and the distinction between professional and retail investor, but the key aspect was the breach of the duty of care, which should be assessed in light of the standard of professional care applicable to the rating agencies.[442] It was on this point that the complaint failed to satisfy the court that, in light of the information in possession of the rating agency, it should have reached a different conclusion about the solvency of the instruments.[443] In contrast, the decision by the Milano Court focused on the rating agency's *contractual* liability vis-à-vis the issuer, where the issue was the duty of care, since in this case there were no issues with regard to proximity or causality towards third parties.[444] An opinion by higher courts may help consolidate the elements of liability.

9.120

The previous analysis presents similarities and differences. Although all jurisdictions accept liability for 'fraud', wilful conduct is extremely difficult to prove, and thus the majority of claims are negligence-based. Then, plaintiffs need to prove the causal link, and some form of 'reliance' on the statements. The greatest contrast is in negligence claims, where some jurisdictions rely on 'policy-like' arguments to exclude liability (US), others on quasi-contract constructions based on 'assumption of responsibility', proximity, etc. (UK) or on a broad understanding of contract liability, including trust-inducing and protective effects towards third parties (Germany), while others do not limit liability ex ante but use the elements of contract or tort liability to make case-by-case assessments (Spain, Italy) without apparently opening the 'floodgates' of liability.

9.121

---

[437] Spanish Supreme Court decision Roj 5445/2008 (9 October 2008).
[438] Tribunale di Roma, n 6827 (27 March 2015).
[439] Tribunale Milano, sezione VI n 8790 (1 July 2011).
[440] Tribunale di Roma *n 6827* (27 March 2015).
[441] ibid.
[442] ibid.
[443] ibid.
[444] Tribunale Milano *n 8790* (n 434). Chiara Picciau *Diffusione di giudizi inesatti nel mercato finanziario e responsabilita' delle agenzie di rating* (Egea 2018).

4.3 Regulatory dimension (I): secondary actors as 'makers' of statements?

9.122 The question whether gatekeepers and third parties can be sued by investors has been shaped by decisions on who can be a defendant under section 10b and rule 10b-5, where the Supreme Court showed its reluctance to expand civil liability in a succession of cases from the 90s onwards. First, in *Central Bank of Denver*[445] the petitioner (Central Bank of Denver) was the indenture trustee in a bond issuance by a public building authority to finance public improvements in a development, secured by landowner assessment liens. Bond covenants required land subject to the liens to be worth at least 160 per cent of the bonds' outstanding principal and interest, and required the developer (Am West Development) to report annually to Central Bank on the compliance with the 160 per cent test. Bond purchasers sued the authority, the bonds' underwriters, and land developer for violating section 10b, and Central Bank, for 'aiding and abetting' a section 10b fraud. The Supreme Court granted *certiorari*, because some circuits held that civil liability could also be imposed for 'aiding and abetting'.

9.123 The Supreme Court overruled them, and differentiated two issues:[446] first, the scope of prohibited conduct; secondly, the elements of private liability, including, eg reliance. The Court suggested that, since courts had created the private rights of action under section 10b and rule 10b-5, the correct approach was to at least not expand liability beyond the text of the provisions. The statutory text made no reference to 'aiding or abetting', and this could not be implied. Nor could one rely, as suggested by the SEC, on the reference under 10b to those who 'directly or indirectly' engage in the proscribed conduct to encompass those who 'aid or abet'. In the Court's view:

> The problem, of course, is that aiding and abetting liability extends beyond persons who engage, even indirectly, in a proscribed activity; aiding and abetting liability reaches persons who do not engage in the proscribed activities at all, but who give a degree of aid to those who do. A further problem with respondents' interpretation of the 'directly or indirectly' language is posed by the numerous provisions of the 1934 Act that use the term in a way that does not impose aiding and abetting liability.[447]

9.124 The Court used by analogy the cases where it had used the statutory references to 'manipulation and deception' to limit liability to cases of fraud, to refuse to extend the scope of the statute to 'acts that are not themselves manipulative or deceptive within the meaning of the statute'.[448] The Court reinforced this conclusion using as context the whole text of the Act, which did not use 'aiding and abetting' language, thus suggesting that there could be no liability for aiding and abetting in breach of *any* of those provisions.

9.125 *Central Bank* led to calls for amending the Exchange Act to include a cause of action for 'aiding and abetting', but instead Congress, in the PSLRA,[449] directed prosecution of aiders and abettors by the SEC.[450] Lower courts interpreted the Supreme Court ruling with variations: some used a bright-line test, which requires the party to be 'credited with making the

---

[445] *Central Bank of Denver* (n 102).
[446] ibid paras 174–76.
[447] *Central Bank of Denver* (n 102).
[448] ibid paras 177–78.
[449] Section 104, 109 Stat 757.
[450] 15 USC s 78t(e).

statement';[451] others a 'substantial participation test', ie a *significant* or *substantial* role in the statement;[452] and others a 'creator test', where the person simply needs to *create* the misrepresentation by writing misstatements that will be incorporated in a document, given to investors.[453] Financial intermediaries could be held liable if they 'controlled' the statement, but 'control person liability' is used more for cases of a parent company, or inside directors.[454] Some of these theories were disallowed by subsequently Supreme Court case law, as we are about to see.

More than ten years after *Central Bank* came *Stoneridge Investment Partners*,[455] where a cable operator (Charter) engaged in fraudulent practices so meet Wall Street expectations for cable subscriber growth and operating cash flow in quarterly statements, apparently aided by the suppliers of the digital cable converter (set top) boxes, Scientific-Atlanta and Motorola (respondents): Charter would overpay for the boxes, and the respondents would purchase advertising from Charter, which would record advertising revenues, and capitalize expenses in set top boxes, thus fooling the auditor (Arthur Andersen). The respondents appeared to connive,[456] but had no role in preparing or disseminating Charter's financial statements, and their own financial statements booked the transactions as a wash, under generally accepted accounting principles. Investors sued the respondents, alleging that they knew Charter's scheme and investors' reliance, or acted with reckless disregard. The District Court granted the respondents' motion to dismiss for failure to state a claim, and the Circuit affirmed.[457]

9.126

The Supreme Court affirmed, concluding that investors could not sue the respondents because they had not relied upon their statements or representations. As stated in *Central Bank*, the Act did not contemplate liability for 'aiding and abetting' and thus a 'secondary actor' must satisfy each of the elements for liability'.[458] Yet, the Court also overruled the Circuit's view that 'only misstatements, omissions by one who has a duty to disclose ... are deceptive within the meaning of the rule', holding that 'it would be erroneous' to find that 'there must be a specific oral or written statement' for liability to follow. Under causation and reliance, whether respondents had made a 'statement' was less relevant than whether they had caused the harm. Here the key was that the plaintiffs could neither prove that they had relied on the respondents' statement/conduct, nor any circumstances to presume reliance, eg material omissions by a party obliged to disclose, or a disclosure of information to the public ('fraud-on-the-market' theory[459]). The Court also rejected 'scheme liability' and

9.127

---

[451] *Anixter v Home-Stake Prod Co* 77 F 3d 1215, 1225 (10th Cir 1998); *Wright v Ernst & Young* 152 F 3d 169 (2d Cir 1998).
[452] *In re ZZZZ Best Securities Litigation* [1994] 864 F Supp 960, 967 (CD Cal).
[453] This was proposed by the SEC in the amicus brief presented to the *Enron* case, and eventually adopted by the *Enron* court. See *Enron* (n 358).
[454] See eg *SEC v First Jersey Secs Inc* 101 F 3d 1450, 1472 (2d Cir 1996).
[455] *Stoneridge Investment Partners LLC v Scientific-Atlanta* (n 88).
[456] At Charter's request, Scientific-Atlanta sent documents to Charter stating—falsely—that it had increased production costs, raising the price for set top boxes. Charter also agreed to purchase from Motorola a specific number of set top boxes and pay liquidated damages for each unit not taken (and would pay said damages). Scientific-Atlanta and Motorola also signed contracts with Charter to purchase advertising time for a price higher than fair value, and the new set top box agreements were backdated to make it appear that they were negotiated a month before the advertising agreements.
[457] *In re Charter Communications Inc Securities Litigation* 443 F 3d 987 (2006). Circuit decisions conflicted as to whether an investor could sue under § 10(b) a party that made no public misstatement but had participated in a scheme to violate § 10(b). *Simpson v AOL Time Warner Inc* 452 F 3d 1040 (CA9 2006) with *Regents of Univ of Cal v Credit Suisse First Boston (USA) Inc* 482 F 3d 372 (CA5 2007).
[458] *Stoneridge Investment Partners LLC v Scientific-Atlanta* (n 88).
[459] See section 2.2.

similarly broad theories espoused by some courts,[460] which would hold defendants liable for engaging in conduct with the purpose of creating a false appearance of material fact to further a scheme to misrepresent a company's revenue.[461] In the Court's view, such device could not obviate that 'reliance is tied to causation, leading to the inquiry whether respondents' acts were immediate or remote to the injury'. Respondents' acts were not disclosed to the investing public, and too remote to satisfy the requirement of reliance. Charter, not respondents, misled its auditor and filed fraudulent financial statements; nothing respondents did made it necessary or inevitable for Charter to record the transactions as it did.[462] Furthermore, the Court advised against using broad theories to federalize well-functioning fields like sate contract law,[463] or incorporate common law fraud under section 10b,[464] in contravention of Congress' intent to limit causes of action for 'aiding and abetting' to lawsuits brought by the SEC.[465]

9.128 *Stoneridge* went beyond *Central Bank*'s textualism, and anchored the exclusion of secondary actor civil liability in the Court's precedents. The exclusion of liability did not result from the Court's timidity to expand liability beyond express statutory language, but from its own very theories of causation and reliance that engendered class actions in the first place. Thus, relatively expansive views of reliance under 'material omissions', 'fraud-on-the-market', etc. also excluded liability in the absence of reliance on statements or conduct. The Court also considered the need for restraint 'vertically' (to limit federalization of state-law issues), and 'horizontally' (to respect Congressional intent).

9.129 With civil liability out for 'secondary actors' as such the next battle was to determine who is a 'maker' of a fraudulent a statement, in *Janus Capital Group*.[466] Janus Capital Group, Inc. (JCG), was a publicly traded company that created the Janus family of mutual funds, organized in a Massachusetts business trust, the Janus Investment Fund (the Fund), which retained JCG's subsidiary, Janus Capital Management (JCM) as investment adviser and administrator. The Fund was a separate legal entity owned by mutual fund investors, but JCM provided 'the management and administrative services necessary for the operation', and all the Fund's officers were also JCM officers, but only one of the Fund's board of trustees' members was associated with JCM. A complaint by the New York Attorney General against JCG and JCM alleging 'market timing' in several funds run by JCM, led to investors' withdrawals, thus reducing JCM's management fees and JCG's income and value. Owners of JCG stock sued JCG and JCM under section 10b and rule 10b–5, alleging that JCG and JCM 'caused mutual fund prospectuses to be issued for Janus mutual funds and made them available to the investing public, which created the misleading impression' that JCG and JCM would implement measures to curb market timing in the funds. The District Court dismissed the

---

[460] *Enron* (n 358) ('scheme liability'); *In re Parmalat Securities Litigation* 376 F Supp 2d 472, 509 (SDNY 2005); *Simpson v AOL Time Warner Inc* 452 F 3d 1040 (CA9 2006).
[461] *Stoneridge Investment Partners LLC v Scientific-Atlanta* (n 88) 552.
[462] ibid para 552.
[463] *Stoneridge Investment Partners v Scientific-Atlanta* (n 88): 'Were the implied cause of action to be extended to the practices described here, however, there would be a risk that the federal power would be used to invite litigation beyond the immediate sphere of securities litigation and in areas already governed by functioning and effective state-law guarantees. Our precedents counsel against this extension.'
[464] Just as s 10(b) 'is surely badly strained when construed to provide a cause of action ... to the world at large'... it should not be interpreted to provide a private cause of action against the entire marketplace in which the issuing company operates'. *Stoneridge Investment Partners v Scientific-Atlanta* (n 88).
[465] *Stoneridge Investment Partners v Scientific-Atlanta* (n 88).
[466] *Janus Capital Group Inc v First Derivative Traders* 564 US 135 (2010).

claim,⁴⁶⁷ but the Fourth Circuit reversed, holding that the plaintiffs had sufficiently alleged that JCG and JCM 'made' the misleading statements.⁴⁶⁸ The Supreme Court reversed. The opinion, by Clarence Thomas, stated that section 10b and rule 10b-5 did not intend to create a cause of action, and thus the Court should give 'narrow dimensions' to a right of action Congress did not authorize when it first enacted the statute and did not expand when it revisited the law'.⁴⁶⁹ In Thomas' characteristic textualism, one 'makes' a statement by stating it. When 'make' is paired with a noun expressing the action of a verb, the resulting phrase is 'approximately equivalent in sense' to that verb'.⁴⁷⁰ Thus:

> [T]he maker of a statement is the person or entity with ultimate authority over the statement, including its content and whether and how to communicate it. Without control, a person or entity can merely suggest what to say, not 'make' a statement in its own right. One who prepares or publishes a statement on behalf of another is not its maker ... This rule might best be exemplified by the relationship between a speechwriter and a speaker. Even when a speechwriter drafts a speech, the content is entirely within the control of the person who delivers it. And it is the speaker who takes credit—or blame—for what is ultimately said.⁴⁷¹

9.130 The Court drew from *Central Bank* that parties who 'contribute 'substantial assistance' do not actually 'make' the statement,⁴⁷² and from *Stoneridge* that, ultimately, 'nothing [the defendants] did made it necessary or inevitable for [the company] to record the transactions as it did'.⁴⁷³ Hence *Janus*' emphasis on the 'authority over the content of the statement and whether and how to communicate it' and its refusal to treat the 'creator' of a statement as its 'maker' as linguistically unsound, and inconsistent with *Stoneridge*. The Court also dismissed the 'well-recognized and uniquely close relationship between a mutual fund and its investment adviser': the fund had a board of directors, and formalities were respected. Attributing responsibility to advisers was Congress' decision, not the courts'. Finally, the plaintiffs' theory would broaden the 'control person liability' doctrine under section § 20 (a) of the Act.⁴⁷⁴ It is unclear whether the Court meant this brief remark as an invitation to delve deeper in a relatively obscure provision, which has not been too popular among securities plaintiffs.

9.131 Then, in *Lorenzo v SEC*,⁴⁷⁵ the Supreme Court handed a rare victory to the SEC (and to securities plaintiffs). Lorenzo was the director of investment banking at a registered broker-dealer (Charles Vista LLC, or Vista) with a single investment banking client, Waste2Energy Holdings, Inc., a company developing technology to convert 'solid waste' into 'clean renewable energy'. Waste2Energy stated in a public filing a figure of total assets, including intangible (IP) assets that made Lorenzo sceptical, because, in his view, they were a 'dead asset'

---

⁴⁶⁷ *In re Mutual Funds Inv Litigation* 487 F Supp 2d 618, 620 (D Md 2007).
⁴⁶⁸ *In re Mutual Funds Inv Litigation* 566 F 3d 111, 121 (2009).
⁴⁶⁹ *Janus Capital Group* (n 466).
⁴⁷⁰ ibid.
⁴⁷¹ ibid.
⁴⁷² *Janus Capital Group* (n 466) n 6 and text.
⁴⁷³ ibid n 7 and text.
⁴⁷⁴ *Janus Capital Group* (n 466): Congress also has established liability in §20(a) for '[e]very person who, directly or indirectly, controls any person liable' for violations of the securities laws. 15 USCA § 78t(a). First Derivative's theory of liability based on a relationship of influence resembles the liability imposed by Congress for control. To adopt First Derivative's theory would read into Rule 10b–5 a theory of liability similar to—but broader in application than, see *post*, at 9—what Congress has already created expressly elsewhere.
⁴⁷⁵ *Lorenzo v Securities and Exchange Commission* 587 US (2019).

because the technology 'didn't really work'. Waste2Energy hired Vista to sell debentures to investors, and later Waste2Energy publicly disclosed, and told Lorenzo that the IP was worthless. Yet, shortly thereafter Lorenzo sent two e-mails to prospective investors referring to the firm's 'confirmed assets', without discussing Waste2Energy's public statements, at the direction of his boss, who supplied the content and 'approved' the messages, but signing his own name, as 'Vice President—Investment Banking', and inviting the recipients to 'call with any questions'. The SEC instituted proceedings against Lorenzo, under rule 10b-5, section 10(b) of the Exchange Act, and section 17(a)(1) of the Securities Act, by sending false and misleading statements to investors with intent to defraud. Lorenzo appealed, arguing an absence of scienter, rejected by the Circuit, and not discussed further, and an absence of liability under rule 10b-5(b), under *Janus*. The Circuit upheld this,[476] but held that Lorenzo could still be liable under rule 10b-5(a) and (c), and sections 10b and 17(a)(1). The question was whether someone who was not the 'maker' of a statement could nonetheless be held liable under other provisions of the Act, when the only conduct consisted in making a statement.

9.132 The Supreme Court agreed with the SEC, holding that dissemination of false or misleading statements with intent to defraud can fall within rules 10b–5(a) and (c), and other statutory provisions, even if the disseminator fell outside rule 10b–5(b) because he did not 'make' the statements. The Opinion by Breyer (the dissenter in *Janus Capital*, while Thomas dissented in *Lorenzo*) held that rule 10b-5's language was broad enough to encompass a 'statement' within the definition of other types of fraudulent conduct,[477] a conclusion reinforced by the dictionary. There could be doubts in 'borderline cases' with people only incidentally involved in the communications, but there was 'nothing borderline about this case', where the petitioner 'sent false statements directly to investors, invited them to follow up with questions, and did so in his capacity as vice president of an investment banking company'.[478] The Court also rejected Lorenzo's (and the dissent's) view that the Act's 'liability for statements' and 'scheme liability' were mutually exclusive, holding that Court precedents supported that different provisions could overlap, and refer to the same conduct.[479] Thus, '[e]ach succeeding prohibition' was 'meant to cover additional kinds of illegalities—not to narrow the reach of the prior sections'.[480] To hold otherwise would exempt conduct like the dissemination of false statements to promote the purchase of securities, which epitomizes the idea of 'fraud', and which Congress showed no intent to exclude. The Opinion held that this would not render *Janus* 'dead letter', because *Janus* referred to the 'making' of statements, while *Lorenzo* referred to the 'dissemination' of statements. The Court saw no problem in holding the maker of a single statement subject to primary liability under letters (a) and (c) of the rule *and* to secondary liability under letter (b) (if the SEC, not precluded by the exclusion of

---

[476] ibid.
[477] *Lorenzo v SEC* (n 475) 5–6: 'It would seem obvious that the words in these provisions are, as ordinarily used, sufficiently broad to include within their scope the dissemination of false or misleading information with the intent to defraud. By sending emails he understood to contain material untruths, Lorenzo "employ[ed]" a "device", " scheme ", and "artifice to defraud" within the meaning of subsection (a) of the Rule, §10(b) and §17(a)(1). By the same conduct, he " engage[d] in a[n] act, practice, or course of business" that " operate[d] ... as a fraud or deceit" under subsection (c) of the Rule.'
[478] ibid p 6.
[479] 'The premise of this argument is that each of these provisions should be read as governing different, mutually exclusive, spheres of conduct. But this Court and the Commission have long recognized considerable overlap among the subsections of the Rule and related provisions of the securities laws.' *Lorenzo v SEC* (n 475) 7, citing *Herman & MacLean* (n 140) para 383 to be discussed below, in the context of prospectus liability.
[480] *Lorenzo v SEC* (n 475) 9, citing *United States v Naftalin* 441 US 768, 774 (1979).

'aiding and abetting' liability, like private plaintiffs, brought the complaint under (b)). This was not contrary to *Central Bank's* aim to draw a 'clean line' between rule 10b-5's primary and secondary violations, nor to *Stoneridge's* focus on *undisclosed* deceptions.

9.133 Despite these arguments, *Lorenzo* was a victory for plaintiffs, who, if failing to show that a secondary actor 'made' a statement, could still argue that he employed a 'device, scheme, or artifice' to defraud, or engaged in an 'act, practice, or course of business' to commit fraud or deceit, rather than arguing 'control person liability', as suggested in *Janus*. A field that seemed barren suddenly looked alive again.

9.134 Beyond actions under general securities fraud provisions, the perception that rating agencies needed to be more accountable (after the 2007-2009 Great Financial crisis) led to an amendment by the Dodd-Frank Act to facilitate rating agencies' liability for false information in the prospectuses.[481] However, the result was that rating agencies refused to have their ratings included in prospectuses and offering documents for asset-backed securities. Since US rules *required* the inclusion of such ratings, this led to the paralysis of the market until the SEC issued a no-action letter, indicating its intention not to pursue enforcement actions.[482] Courts, in turn, maintained a reluctant approach. In *re Lehman Brothers*,[483] investors in SEC-registered mortgage pass-through certificates sued the rating agencies. They alleged that the agencies had an active role in the structuring and securitization process, since investment banks designed the composition of loan pools, certificate structures and credit enhancements to achieve desirable credit ratings, in direct communication with the agencies, and this made the latter strictly liable under sections 11 and 15 of the Securities Act.

9.135 The Second Circuit made a textual analysis of both sections, holding that, to qualify as an 'underwriter' under section 11, a party must 'participate in the underwriting, offering, sale or purchase of securities', and it is not enough to 'facilitate' the offering of securities to the public,[484] although it kept an open mind with respect to their potential liability as 'experts' after the Dodd-Frank reforms. Then, the Court rejected that rating agencies could qualify for 'control person liability' under section 15, because control means 'the power to direct or cause the direction of the management and policies of [the primary violators], whether through the ownership of voting securities, by contract or otherwise', and the agencies, at the most, they had an advisory role. Since section 15 requirements were not met, the Court did not analyse 'control person liability' under section 20 (fraud cases), which also requires a 'culpable participation' in the fraud by the controlled person.

9.136 A final consideration is whether gatekeepers' liability for their statements of 'opinion' may also be excluded under the *Omnicare* standard.[485] In *Puda Coal*[486] the plaintiffs were investors in Puda Coal, and alleged that the firm's auditors, Moore Stephens Hong Kong, failed to discover a fraudulent scheme orchestrated by the company insiders to transfer the company's assets to themselves.[487] The district court considered the audit a 'statement of

---

[481] Section 933 of Dodd-Frank Act repealed rule 436(g) of the Securities Act 1933, and subjected rating agencies to 'expert liability' for misleading statements in registration statements under s 11 of the Securities Act 1933.
[482] Haar (n 412) 9.
[483] *In re Lehman-Brothers Mortgage-Backed Securities Litigation* Nos 10-0712-cv; 10-0898-cv; and 10-1288-cv (2d Cir 2011).
[484] ibid.
[485] *Omnicare v Laborers District Council* (n 94).
[486] *In re Puda Coal Securities Inc Litigation* [2016] No 15-2100 (2d Cir).
[487] Puda Coal Inc was a coal company based in China and publicly traded in the United States. The company conducted its operations through Shanxi Puda Coal Group Co, indirectly owned by Puda. In 2009, Puda's chairman Ming Zhao, and his brother Yao Zhao, orchestrated the fraudulent transfer of Puda's entire interest in

opinion', finding no evidence that Moore Stephens disbelieved its own opinions.[488] This was confirmed by the Second Circuit on appeal.[489]

4.4 Regulatory considerations (II): Liability under securities laws and gatekeeper regulation in EU countries

9.137 In the EU gatekeepers' liability can result from extending liability under securities provisions, eg on liability for the prospectus, or periodic disclosures or specific statements, or from specific regulatory provisions, eg on rating agency liability.

9.138 In the UK, the Financial Services and Markets Act (FSMA) 2000 and implementing regulations make liable the parties who 'accept responsibility' for the prospectus,[490] 'authorize' its contents,[491] or 'offer' the securities.[492] Generally, only the issuer and its directors customarily take responsibility for the prospectus, and it is generally understood that mere participation as the underwriter does not qualify an entity to 'authorize the contents' of the prospectus, but the status of the lead underwriter is problematic.[493] Then, it is difficult to conclude whether underwriters can be 'offerors', and still they could benefit from the exemption for when the prospectus was 'primarily' drafted by the issuer.[494]

9.139 German law, for its part, attaches liability 'in a specific/narrow' sense to certain parties, including those who *assumed responsibility* for the prospectus, and who *initiated* the issue of the prospectus. Although these concepts may give rise to expansive and restrictive views,[495] it is normally understood that auditors or rating agencies do not fall within this definition, because they 'lack an economic interest'.

9.140 Yet, this does not fully exclude their potential liability. In a 2004 decision, the Federal Supreme Court held that an auditor can be subject to prospectus liability towards capital investors as a so-called guarantor *and* also be liable under a contract with protective effect towards third parties.[496] In a subsequent 2014 decision,[497] the Court held that an auditor which approved a profit forecast then included in a prospectus subject to EU rules[498] could be liable towards

---

Shanxi to Ming Zhao, and 49 per cent of Shanxi to a state-owned private equity fund, making Puda's financial statements false. Moore Stephens Hong Kong did not discover the scheme until a research report in 2011 exposed it, and investors filed a class action under s 11 Securities Act 1933 and s 10b Exchange Act.

[488] *In re Puda Coal Sec Inc Litigation* 30 F Supp 3d 230, 259 (SDNY 2014).
[489] *In re Puda Coal Securities Inc Litigation* (n 486).
[490] FSA Prospectus Rule, s 5.5.3(2)(c).
[491] ibid s 5.5.3(2)(f).
[492] ibid s 5.5.3(2)(d)(i).
[493] Gerner-Beuerle (n 312) 494. Olga Skripova, *Civil Liability as an Enforcement Tool of Securities Underwriter Gatekeeping Duty* (Erasmus Unniversiteit 2012).
[494] Gerner-Beuerle (n 312) 494–95. For the exemption see rule 5.5.7.
[495] See section 2.1. The reference to the parties that 'initiate the issue', which is considered to be directed to the parties that control the prospectus' content and publication, is interpreted by some as encompassing the underwriters, while others consider that the legislative intent was to exclude them (or most of them) as not fulfilling one of two conditions: a central role and a direct financial interest. Gerner-Beuerle (n 312) 501–502.
[496] BGH, judgment X ZR 283/02 (8 June 2004). The latter claim expires in accordance with the rules applicable to the auditor's contractual liability.
[497] BGH, judgment III ZR156/13 (24 April 2014).
[498] art 3 and Annex I No 13.2 of Regulation (EC) No 809/2004 implementing Directive 2003/71/EC of the European Parliament and of the Council as regards information contained in prospectuses as well as the format, incorporation by reference and publication of such prospectuses and dissemination of advertisements [2004] OJ L149.

investors. Interestingly, although based on regulatory provisions under German and EU law, the Court's reasoning was based on private law doctrines, such as that of contracts with protective effects towards third parties, and required that the 'expert' opinion or appraisal must be intended to foster a third party's trust, as a basis for an economic decision, and be recognizable as such by the expert.[499] Yet, a 2018 decision was more restrictive, holding that auditors can only be held liable if they explicitly guarantee the correctness of the prospectus' financial information.[500] Courts have also held that prospectus liability can extend to those who, due to their special professional and economic position or specialist knowledge (eg banks), assume a guarantor's position, because they are involved in the prospectus' design or in the distribution, and/or create conditions of trust and make declarations. However, using a bank's 'good name' in the prospectus does not justify trust-based liability if there are no further circumstances that place it in a guarantor position.[501]

9.141 Other countries, like Spain, regulate separately the responsibility for the issuer and the offeror, the guarantor and the 'directing entity' (typically, the lead underwriter), and specify the items for which each responds.[502] This restricts the possibility of finding an underwriter liable as 'offeror'. Yet, the 'general' clause of tort liability for *fault* in countries like Spain, France, or Italy (see section 4.2 above) permits a more open approach, especially if plaintiffs allege the breach of statutory provisions, and are within their protective scope. In this context, specific provisions may have the effect of *limiting* liability for secondary actors and gatekeepers.

9.142 In light of potential divergences, and the (seen as unacceptable) liability exclusion in some jurisdictions, EU rules have partly harmonized rating agency liability under the amended Article 35a of CRAR. The initial CRAR hoped that its clarity would facilitate civil actions, which could rely on Member States' domestic laws.[503] However, in practice domestic laws prevented investors from suing, or widely diverged between themselves. Thus, after a high-debate, high-pressure process, and a watering-down of the initial proposal, the provision was amended in 2013 and now states that: 'Where a credit rating agency has committed, intentionally or with gross negligence, any of the infringements listed in Annex III having an impact on a credit rating, an investor or issuer may claim damages from that credit rating agency for damage caused to it due to that infringement.' The basic elements are: (i) a breach of rules; (ii) intention or commit gross negligence; and (iii) the breach's 'impact' on the credit rating.

9.143 The requirement of wilful conduct or 'gross' negligence is more restrictive than some national laws, but (iv) the rule does not require any contract between plaintiff and rating agency, and provide that liability 'shall only be limited in advance where that limitation is: (a) reasonable and proportionate; and (b) allowed by the applicable national law' (Article 35a(3)). This seems to exclude *Caparo*-like, or German law contract-based liability, requirements. Yet, (v) the rule maintains *causation/reliance* and supplements it with different requirements,

---

[499] See section 4.2.
[500] BGH VII ZR 232/17 (21 November 2018); Mock (n 213).
[501] BGH Order II ZB 18/17 (22 January 2019).
[502] The provisions are included in Royal Decree 1310/2005 of 4 November on Admission to Listing and Prospectus (RD Listing and Prospectus). Article 33 regulates the liability for the issuer and offeror, without introducing restrictions, art 34 regulates the liability of the guarantor, which is responsible only for the information it elaborates and art 35 the liability of the directing entity, which is responsible for performing diligently the checks on the truthfulness and accuracy of the information that are customary in market practice.
[503] Regulation No 1060/2009 on credit rating agencies (CRAR) [2009] OJ L302, recital 35.

depending on the plaintiff. Thus, while an investor may claim damages if 'it establishes that it has reasonably relied, in accordance with Article 5a(1) or otherwise with due care, on a credit rating for a decision to invest into, hold onto or divest from a financial instrument covered by that credit rating', an issuer may claim damages 'where it establishes that it or its financial instruments are covered by that credit rating and the infringement was not caused by misleading and inaccurate information provided by the issuer to the credit rating agency, directly or through information publicly available'.

9.144 This helps harmonize causation/reliance, and replaces an ex ante liability exclusion with an ex post calibration of liability, and is complemented by provisions seeking to *reduce* reliance on ratings, especially by financial intermediaries (Article 5a(1) CRAR). Finally, the provision respects national traditions: terms such as 'damage', 'intention', 'gross negligence', 'reasonably relied', 'due care', 'impact', 'reasonable', and 'proportionate' shall be interpreted in accordance with national law, as will matters not covered by the regulation, eg jurisdiction[504] and the provision does not exclude further civil liability claims under national law.[505] Some suggest that the provision's level of harmonization is insufficient, given national courts' leeway to interpret open-textured concepts in light of their own national traditions, and that there should be more guidance about those concepts.[506] Even then, as long as courts anchored in different liability doctrines have the last word about the meaning of the provision, such provision will not be uniform. In fact, Article 35a CRAR's criteria were already present in many Member States. Having the same word is not the same as having the same language, however, which needs a more active role by courts or quasi-courts, or a more intense dialogue between national courts and the Court of Justice. This could help use the principle of equality and effectiveness require terms not expressly referring to the law of the Member States for their meaning and scope must normally be given an *autonomous and uniform* interpretation across the EU, based on the provision's context and purpose.[507]

---

[504] C Desogus, 'La responsabilità extracontrattuale da rating errato: la Cassazione si esprime sulla competenza giurisdizionale' (2013) Giurisprudenza Commerciale 1009.
[505] CRAR (n 503) art 35a(4).
[506] DJ Verheij, *Credit Rating Agency Liability in Europe: Rating the Combination of EU and National Law in Rights of Redress* (Eleven International Publishing 2020).
[507] Case C-343/13 *Modelo Continente Hipermercados SA v Autoridade para as Condições de Trabalho—Centro Local do Lis (ACT)* ECLI:EU:C:2015:146; compare also Case C-279/12 *Fish Legal and Shirley* EU:C:2013:853, para 42; and Case C-201/13 *Deckmyn and Vrijheidsfonds* EU:C:2014:2132, para 14.

10
Courts and Financial Contract Disputes

1 Introduction	10.01	3.3 Regulatory requirements and private law duties in the EU (I): Fashioning private remedies for breach of regulatory duties	10.49
2 Validity disputes: the (un)enforceability of complex/speculative financial transactions in light of corporate 'capacity' and public policy	10.06	3.4 Regulatory requirements and private law duties in the EU (II): causal link, reliance, and basis clauses.	10.82
3 Disputes about intermediaries' duties and representations	10.24	4 Financial contracts' interpretation: express versus implied duties, specificity versus coherence	10.93
3.1 Duties of advisers and broker–dealers in the US, and their significance in private actions	10.25	4.1 Contract interpretation: reasonableness, express, and implied terms	10.94
3.2 Banks' marketing duties under private law, absent advisory relationships	10.37	4.2 Contract interpretation: general considerations, events of default and valuation	10.105
		4.3 Materially adverse events	10.122

1 Introduction

Parties to financial contracts collide on a myriad of issues. However, in terms of legal doctrine, their disputes largely fit within three large groups: there are disputes about the *validity* of the agreement, there are disputes about representations and duties, and there are disputes about the interpretation and enforcement of the contract. **10.01**

In the first kind of dispute, it is typical for the 'financial party', a bank or financial intermediary, to rely on the agreement's express terms, and for the non-financial party, typically a client, to rely on some objection to such enforceability. They may ground this objection on the allegation that the contract exceeded the 'capacity' of the non-financial party, an issue that arises in case of legal persons, or on the allegation that the contract, by its substance and nature, was contrary to a public policy, an issue that arises in case of 'speculative' contracts. We cover this in section (2). **10.02**

In the second type of dispute, clients (or debtors) allege that the bank, or financial intermediary, was either obliged by some kind of duty to inform or give advice, and/or gave certain representations about the financial contract, product, or instrument, which were then ignored. We cover these disputes in section (3). **10.03**

The third type of dispute is the more 'purely contractual' in nature, as it concerns the construction, application, and enforcement of contract terms. However, given the nature of industry-wide 'standard terms' of many financial agreements (eg derivatives subject to the **10.04**

ISDA documentation) court decisions have an impact far beyond the specific case. We cover these disputes in section (4).

10.05 Although the three types of disputes are different, some common themes emerge. One is the role of banks and financial intermediaries in the system. In the extreme, they may be subject to absolute public policy principles, which may affect contract validity, but more often they will be subject to duties toward their client or counterparty, resulting from general private law principles or regulatory rules. A second theme is the balance between 'precision' and 'reasonableness'. Contracts are carefully drafted documents, and their precise language matters. Yet, contracts are inevitably, or at least typically incomplete, and language does not exist in a vacuum, and often the courts will need to understand the logic of the transaction to choose one meaning or another. This need will be greater when the documentation is 'boilerplate' and its use widespread across the market and/or the transaction follows a certain structure that is replicated in multiple other transactions.

2 Validity disputes: the (un)enforceability of complex/speculative financial transactions in light of corporate 'capacity' and public policy

10.06 Can a legal person conclude contracts that exceed its own 'capacity'? Harmonized provisions of EU company law provide an expansive view of corporate 'capacity': a company cannot rely on limitations to the powers of its representatives vis-à-vis third parties, but states can limit the validity of acts beyond the company's object.[1] In the UK, for example, the contractual capacity of a company was limited by a statutorily mandated 'objects clause' in the company's memorandum of association, which had to state the objects for which the company was incorporated, thus rendering any acts exceeding those objects ultra vires, and void *ab initio*.[2] Reforms in 2004 changed this default rule, and attributed full capacity to a company to undertake any business activity or conclude any transaction, but left companies the option of including an 'objects clause'. In some civil law countries, eg Spain, Italy or Germany, corporate entities are considered to have full general capacity, but their acts had to be concluded by organs such as directors, whose power of representation extends to all the acts within the corporate object. Should they exceed them, they would be null, *except* if the third parties relying on the acts acted in good faith.[3] Courts tend to interpret the reference to acts 'within the object' broadly, comprising those acts that are incidental or ancillary (eg English courts[4]) and 'auxiliary' or 'neutral' (eg Spanish courts[5]).

---

[1] Article 9 of Directive 2017/1132 relating to certain aspects of company law [2017] OJ L 69, provides that: '1. Acts done by the organs of the company shall be binding upon it even if those acts are not within the objects of the company, unless such acts exceed the powers that the law confers or allows to be conferred on those organs. However, Member States may provide that the company shall not be bound where such acts are outside the objects of the company, if it proves that the third party knew that the act was outside those objects or could not in view of the circumstances have been unaware of it. Disclosure of the statutes shall not of itself be sufficient proof thereof. 2. The limits on the powers of the organs of the company, arising under the statutes or from a decision of the competent organs, may not be relied on as against third parties, even if they have been disclosed.'
[2] *Ashbury Railway v Riche* (1875) LR 7 HL 653, 671.
[3] The current formulation is included in arts 233–34 of the Spanish Capital Companies Act.
[4] *Rolled Steel Products (Holdings) Ltd v British Steel Corp* [1982] Ch 478.
[5] Spanish Supreme Court decision RJ 2009/4449 (19 June 2009).

However, there are more doubts in the case of entities other than for-profit corporations. **10.07**
Local governments are considered 'corporations' in some countries. In the 1990s English
local governments concluded interest-rate swaps with banks, where they lost a lot of money.
District auditors questioned whether they had the capacity to conclude such transactions,
and the House of Lords held they did not in *Hazell v Hammersmith*.[6]

More recently, in *Haugesund Kommune and Another v Depfa ACS Bank*[7] UK courts de- **10.08**
cided over the validity of swap contracts concluded by *Norwegian* municipal governments
(*Kommunes*) with an Irish bank, which was a subsidiary of a German bank, in contravention of Norwegian laws on local authorities (the swap was a convoluted way of extending
financing to the Kommunes). The contracts were governed by English law, but local authorities were 'corporations' under Norwegian law, and the English court held that the issue of
the corporations' capacity to conclude legal acts was subject to Norwegian law, which rendered them invalid.[8] On appeal, one question was what fell within the concept of 'capacity',
because, the bank alleged, the High Court had conflated 'corporate capacity', 'substantive
power' to conclude a contract and the transactions 'unlawfulness'.[9] To the bank, even if
Norwegian law might limit 'power', or make the transactions unlawful, the *Kommunes* had
capacity because they were analogous to English corporations created by Royal Charter, like
Oxford and Cambridge.

However, to the Court of Appeal the concept of 'capacity' had to be given a 'broad, inter- **10.09**
nationalist interpretation': there is a difference between the Anglo-American tradition,
where 'capacity' is conceived with a purpose in mind, and the continental tradition, where
the legal entity's 'power of law' is universal, and thus constraints do not result from a doctrine of ultra vires, but from other limits (eg the impact on third parties, and the extent to
which those parties can rely on it).[10] Thus, matters that in other laws fell under 'power' were
matters of 'capacity' under English law. Likewise, the Court interpreted broadly the concept of a corporation's 'constitution', as encompassing all relevant sources of its powers, including constitutional documents *and* relevant laws.[11] In light of this, under the relevant
laws, *Kommunes* lacked 'capacity' (power) to conclude loan contracts, a concept broad
enough to include the swaps, which were considered void. The outcome was not positive for
the Kommunes, though, since the consequence of voidness was the restitution of the sums
paid by the bank.

The 'capacity' and validity of swaps concluded by municipalities was also analysed by **10.10**
German courts. The Federal Supreme Court has held that legal persons under *public law*
cannot effectively act legally outside the area of responsibility and activity assigned to them
by law or the statutes, and the legal acts carried out by them outside this area are null and
void.[12] In a 2015 case, the Court applied this doctrine to a derivative concluded by the municipality of *North-Rhine Westphalia*.[13] The Court held that there was no need to resort to the
doctrine of acts beyond the legal capacity, since the swap concluded was well within the local

---

[6] *Hazell v Hammersmith and Fulham London Borough Council* [1992] 2 AC 1
[7] *Haugesund Kommune v Depfa ACS Bank* [2010] EWCA Civ 579.
[8] ibid.
[9] ibid paras 30–35.
[10] ibid paras 38–47.
[11] ibid paras 48–49.
[12] BGH, judgment I ZR84/54 (28 February 1956) BGHZ 20, 119, 122 ff; decision NotZ 3/69, BGHZ 52, 283, 286 (15 July 1969).
[13] BGH, judgment XI ZR 378/13 (28 April 2015).

governments' sphere of activity.[14] In the Court's view, Article 28(2) of the German basic law guarantees municipalities a comprehensive power of self-administration, including financial autonomy for the conclusion of financial futures transactions.[15] Whether the plaintiff's swap contracts were concluded for hedging or speculative purposes was irrelevant, and even if the municipality had breached budgetary law principles and acted unlawfully, this would still not be 'ultra vires'.[16]

10.11 Then, in *Credit Suisse International v Stichting Vestia Groep*,[17] UK courts analysed the capacity of a Dutch Social Housing Association (SHA), a kind of foundations (ie no shareholders, only a board) subject to the Dutch Civil Code, which own a large part of the real estate portfolio of the Dutch residential rental market. Their activities are restricted to social housing, and subject to important constraints: under their Financial Regulations they could enter derivatives to manage borrowing costs, ie hedging, but not for speculation. The Court concluded that the articles of association and Civil Code provisions, where SHAs had the core object 'to operate exclusively in the field of social housing', restricted Vestia's capacity to conclude the swaps.[18] Outside their object, a SHA could still conclude 'secondary acts', which served the interest of the corporate entity, ie not those of a different party. Such interest was understood in an objective sense, ie in light not of the act's ultimate finality, but its substance, and not their formal label.[19] The Court held that a SHA was a non-profit entity, operating in a highly regulated field,[20] and thus that Vestia had the capacity to enter into some swap contracts, but not others, called the *ultra vires* transactions.[21] However, the court found that Vestia was estopped from alleging its lack of capacity, because, apart from the derivative, it had also concluded an ISDA Master agreement with a 'warranty of capacity'. Yet another example where English courts mitigated the harmful impact for the bank.

10.12 In *Santander Totta v Companhia de Carris de Ferro de Lisboa* (which, in turn, relied on the previous case, *Standard Chartered v Ceylon Petroleum*[22]) the debtors, Portuguese public transport companies which run the metro, bus and tram services of Lisbon and Porto, concluded 'exotic' swaps, different from 'plain vanilla' swaps.[23] The corporations' argument was that they had the capacity to conclude swaps for hedging, but not speculative purposes. The English court (Blair J) considered Portuguese law implications, with competing expert testimonies. The court rejected the debtor companies' argument that the corporations' capacity depended on whether the transaction *helped* the company fulfil the ends of 'contributing to the economic and financial balance of the public sector as a whole and in achieving adequate levels of satisfaction in meeting the community's needs', or, alternatively, that the capacity depended on the 'object' clause of the articles of association, and that the validity of

---

[14] ibid para 63.
[15] ibid paras 65–68.
[16] ibid paras 68–69.
[17] *Credit Suisse v Vestia* [2014] EWHC 3103 (Comm).
[18] ibid paras 188–90.
[19] ibid paras 196–203, also 206.
[20] ibid paras 208–209.
[21] ibid paras 228–53.
[22] *Santander Totta v Companhia de Carris de Ferro de Lisboa* [2016] EWHC 465 (Comm), and [2016] EWCA Civ 1267; *Standard Chartered v Ceylon Petroleum Corporation (CPC)* [2011] EWHC 1785 (Comm), [2012] EWCA Civ 1049.
[23] *Santander Totta* (Comm) (n 22) 6: 'What makes the swaps unusual was the incorporation of a "memory" feature. Speaking generally, once the reference interest rates (EURIBOR and sometimes LIBOR) moved outside upper or lower "barriers", the fixed rate payable by the Transport Companies had a "spread" added to it. The spread was cumulative at each payment date, and was subject to leverage (in all but one swap), hence the swaps being described as "snowball" swaps.'

secondary or ancillary activities beyond the clause depended on whether the transaction was 'appropriate' ie 'necessary' or 'convenient' for its power to borrow, in pursuit of its objective of running a collective transportation system' . In the judge's reasoned view, this was not a workable test in practice for a third party, and at best would introduce unbearable uncertainty on the corporations' capacity, and the transactions' validity, and was thus rejected as a correct expression of Portuguese law, because, in the Court's view, the clauses about 'objectives' were not 'capacity' or 'objects', but 'good management' principles which bound internally, but not externally.[24] However, the situation became even more complicated with swap cases concerning Italian local authorities after the Italian Supreme Court decided in *BNL v Cattolica* that, although swaps (and derivatives) are presumed valid as they are not 'futile bets', but 'rational bets', this presumption held only if the client (local authority) understood the swap's mark-to-market value and probabilistic scenarios, and also held that local administration laws prevented Italian local authorities from concluding swaps contracts for 'speculative purposes' (and were otherwise void); the *Cattolica* judgment led to cases where English courts tried to determine whether *Cattolica* was expressive of Italian 'validity provisions', which could not affect swaps subject to English law (*deutsche Bank v Busto Arsizio*) or Italian law on 'capacity', in which case even a swap subject to English law could be invalidated (*Intesa v Commune di Venezia*).[25]

10.13 Debtors have raised other defences. In Germany or Portugal, they have alleged the contracts' unlawfulness for being contrary to statutory prohibitions,[26] 'immoral', eg contrary to the prohibition of usury (Germany), or void for lack of *causa* (Portugal).[27] In the *North-Rhine Westphalia* case (cited above), the Court held that whether the swap violated a prohibition was a matter for the municipal law of North-Rhine Westphalia, but this did not include the circulars of the regional Ministry of the Interior; only ordinances, statutes, and common law, which did not include any prohibition against speculation,[28] and that the 'profitability principle' bound municipalities internally, but could not bind third parties.[29]

10.14 As for 'immorality', in Germany a legal transaction is immoral and void within section 138 of the German Civil Code (BGB) if its overall character, inferred from the summary of content, motivation and purpose, is not compatible with basic legal/moral principles, while in Portugal one (isolated) Supreme Court case deemed several swaps void for lack of *causa*, because there was no underlying risk to cover.[30] For the doctrine of 'usury', German courts hold that a 'noticeable disproportion' exists if the effective contractual rate exceeds the effective customary market rate customary by around 100 per cent or 12 percentage points, but other

---

[24] *Santander Totta* (Comm) (n 22) paras 312–14, 328. Furthermore, the companies were not able to furnish a clear test for when a company could be considered a 'public company' since this depended on the degree of state ownership, which would introduce further uncertainty.
[25] Decision by the Italian Supreme Court, cass civ (12 May 2020) n 8770; *Banca Intesa Sanpaolo SPA & Anor v Comune Di Venezia* [2022] EWHC 2586 (Comm); *Deutsche Bank AG London v Commune di Busto Arsizio* [2021] EWHC 2706 (Comm) (Cockerill J).
[26] German Civil Code, s 134.
[27] ibid s 138 (Germany). In Portugal, Supremo Tribunal de Justiça SSTJ, Procedure no. 531/11.7TVLSB.L1.S1, 29 January 2015.
[28] BGH, judgment XI ZR 378/13 (28 April 2015) 72–75.
[29] ibid 76.
[30] In Germany, BGH, judgments V ZR 437/99 (19 January 2001) BGHZ 146, 298 (19 January 2001) 301 and from XI ZR 378/13, BGHZ205, 117 Rn. 69 (28 April 2015). In Portugal, see SSTJ Procedure no. 531/11.7TVLSB. L1.S1 (n 27). Compare with SSTJ, Procedure no. 876/12.9TVLSB.L1, 26 January 2016, which held the swaps valid, and is a clearer expression of the Court's

circumstances may be considered in differences between 90 per cent and 100 per cent,[31] and the loan's special features must also be considered.[32] However, on derivatives contracts, the BGH in the *North-Rhine Westphalia* case held that in contracts with an element of 'chance', 'betting', or speculation, deviations from market values does not per se result in immorality, especially after the reforms of the securities acts[33] excluded financial futures from the prohibition of 'gambling' contracts.[34]

10.15 Conversely, the BGH case law holds that a swap transaction is immoral only if it is *designed* to put the bank's counterparty without a chance from the outset.[35] In a 2017 case, the Court held that, despite there was a speculative element, ie the rate was linked to the evolution of exchange rate against the Swiss franc, at the moment of conclusion, the contractual interest was below the market rate, and although due to market developments the payable interest ended being several times the market rate, this was not foreseeable to either party, and thus not 'usurious'. The 'speculative' or even 'gaming' character did not per se result in the contract's immorality, and the structured loan did not put the plaintiff 'without a chance'.[36]

10.16 In the UK courts have analysed these matters in cross-border cases, subject to English law pursuant to a choice-of-law clause, but where clients' alleged that the contract was subject to their country's mandatory laws under Article 3(3) of the Rome Regulation I, which states that:

> Where all other elements relevant to the situation at the time of the choice are located in a country other than the country whose law has been chosen, the choice of the parties shall not prejudice the application of provisions of the law of that other country which cannot be derogated from by agreement.

10.17 In *Dexia Crediop SpA v Comune di Prato*[37] the court applied Article 3(3) to interest rate swaps under an ISDA Master Agreement with an English law choice of law clause. The contract parties were both incorporated in Italy, the swaps were entered into in Italy, and performed in Italy. The bank contended that there were two 'elements relevant to the situation' not connected with Italy. First, the ISDA standard form was drafted by international working groups and used in international derivative transactions to promote certainty. Secondly, for each swap, the bank entered into a back-to-back hedging swap with a bank outside Italy in the international market using the same standard documentation.[38] However, the court was unimpressed, and held that using an international agreement was not an 'element of the situation' connected with a country outside Italy, and the back-to-back transaction, even if relevant to the bank, was not so to the client, although subsequently the Court of Appeal reversed, following instead the approach of Blair J in *Santander* (see next paragraph), thus leaving the High Court's view as an example of a defunct doctrinal approach.[39]

---

[31] BGH judgments III ZR217/85 (15 January 1987) XI ZR 252/89 (13 March 1990) or XI ZR 220/10 (29 November 2011).
[32] BGH, decision III ZR 201/88 (13 July 1989).
[33] In particular, § 37e Sentence 1 WpHG.
[34] BGH Judgment XI ZR 378/13 (n 28) para 81.
[35] BGH judgments XI ZR 93/09 (9 March 2010) or XI ZR 28/09 (13 July 2010).
[36] BGH judgment Ref. no XI ZR 152/17 (19 December 2017) paras 29–30.
[37] *Dexia Crediop SpA v Comune di Prato* [2015] EWHC 1746 (Comm).
[38] ibid para 209.
[39] ibid para 211: '[E]ven if the standard form itself were shown to have a connection with another country, that would not in the present case be an 'element relevant to the situation' as it existed at material times. Throughout the relevant period everything relevant to the use of the form happened in Italy. As to Dexia's decision in each

10.18 The currently dominant approach in English courts was shaped by *Santander Totta v Companhia de Carris de Ferro*, mentioned above, where the High Court and subsequently the Court of Appeal reached the opposite conclusion to the High Court in *Prato*. Article 3(3) was characterized as an anti-avoidance provision, but one that did not require 'intent' to avoid, or bad faith, simply that *all* relevant aspects were connected to a country.[40] Bank clients relied on *Dexia*, pointing out that 'Portugal was where both parties were incorporated, where the parties communicated with each other, where the swaps were entered into, and where the obligations under the swaps had to be performed'. However, the court held that Article 3(3) had to be interpreted restrictively in commercial transactions,[41] and distinguished between cases where the court has to look for the connecting factors to establish the applicable law, and cases where there is already a choice of law, which must be overcome. Thus, it sufficed that *some* relevant elements pointed to a different jurisdiction, which happened if one looked beyond the contract, and to 'the situation' more broadly.[42] Thus:

> [B]ecause of the right to assign to a bank outside Portugal, the use of standard international documentation, the practical necessity for the relationship with a bank outside Portugal, the international nature of the swaps market in which the contracts were concluded, and the fact that back-to back contracts were concluded with a bank outside Portugal in circumstances in which such hedging arrangements are routine, the court's conclusion is that Article 3(3) of the Rome Convention is not engaged because all the elements relevant to the situation at the time of the choice were not connected with Portugal only. In short, these were not purely domestic contracts. Any other conclusion, the court believes, would undermine legal certainty.[43]

10.19 The court also held that the contracts would have been valid even if it had applied Portuguese law prohibition of 'games of chance', or the 'change of circumstances' doctrine. The court held that, since the provisions transposing the Investment Services Directive had recognized 'derivatives' as a valid financial instrument, and swaps as a form of derivatives, the Civil Code Article 1245 prohibition of 'games of chance' should be construed as leaving out said derivatives, also in of Supreme Court of Justice and lower courts case law.[44] However, the court accepted the bank clients' expert testimony on the mandatory nature of Article 437 of the Portuguese Civil Code, on the 'change of circumstances' doctrine, and accepted that, under Portuguese law, the parties cannot fully derogate the principle on an ex ante basis.[45]

10.20 The position of Italian courts contrasts with these views. In a decision of 12 May 2020,[46] relying on principles already set out in a decision by the Court of Appeal of Milan,[47] the Italian Supreme Court (*Cassazione*) set out the conditions for the validity of the interest rate

case to choose a non-Italian counterparty for its back to back hedging swap ... Whether or not Dexia entered into a hedging swap is a matter for Dexia alone: to Prato it is immaterial.' The Court of Appeal reversed. See *Dexia Crediop SpA v Comune di Prato* [2017] EWCA Civ 428.

[40] *Santander Totta* (Comm) (n 22) 373.
[41] ibid para 374.
[42] *Santander Totta* (Comm) (n 22) 395.
[43] ibid para 411.
[44] The court made reference to Decisions of the Supreme Court of Justice 531/11.7TVLSB.L1.S1 (n 27) (which annulled the swaps) and 309/11.8TVLSB.L1.S1 (11 February 2015) (which considered the swap as lawful) and concluded that the Court's favorable view towards the swaps validity was established in the SSTJ in procedure 876/12.9TVLSB.L1 (n 30).
[45] *Santander Totta* (Comm) (n 22) paras 503–23.
[46] Italian Supreme Court Decision Cass civ n 8770 (n 25).
[47] Decision by the Court of Appeal of Milan n 3459 (18 September 2013).

swap (IRS) contract subscribed to by Italian municipalities. According to the Court, IRSs are a kind of 'differentiated bet', which may have a hedging *or* a speculative function. Being a sort of 'rational' bet, they are prima facie valid, unlike pure or futile bets, which would be invalid but only if the contract's risk is 'reasonable'. A risk is 'reasonable' if the investor (in this case, the municipalities) is able to understand the mechanics of the contract, and the economic advantage or disadvantage arising from the transaction, as well as the degree of risk taken.

10.21 In many civil law jurisdictions, consent, *object*, and *causa* are a validity requirement. In the Court's view, only a reasonable risk can be part of the contract's causa, and the risk information is necessary to determine the contract's object. Absent these, the contact will be invalid. To ensure its validity the bank must inform the client of the mark-to-market value of the contact, and the 'probabilistic scenarios', ie the likely return of the interest rates flowing from bank to client and back, in light of the forecast curves and future perspectives of interest rate trends. In the absence of these, the contracts would be declared null and void, and the banks ordered to return the moneys received during the contract duration. One must note that the line of reasoning is not very different from that of the Italian Constitutional Court in *BNL v Cattolica* (above), which makes it difficult to determine whether it pertains the concept of *causa*, of 'object', of 'capacity' in the case of public entities, or simply some form of public policy consideration. Some lower courts subsequently expressed views contradictory with the Supreme Court's,[48] declaring that the IRS contracts could not be declared invalid for lack of causa because they included an adequate causal characterization of the risk hedging; nor can they be declared invalid for having an indetermined object, because the 'object' is not the mark-to-market, but the exchange of differentials (the mark-to-market represents the replacement value). Thus, it was not mandatory to disclose it, especially since the contract contained the elements to calculate the mark-to-market value, such as duration, payment dates, notional, fixed rate, etc., nor the probabilistic scenarios, since the courts found that these were based in publicly available data. One factor in the lower courts' ruling could be that the swaps in those cases were relatively simple, but in the meantime the official position of the highest court is relatively tipped against financial institutions.

10.22 A final consideration of the private remedies resulting from a breach of public policy rules is illustrated by the *Quinn v Irish Bank Resolution Corp.*, decided by Irish courts.[49] Some loans guaranteed by Quinn family members for Sean Quinn's payment obligations for his contracts for difference and the purchase of shares in Anglo Irish Bank to unwind his position in the bank were allegedly in contravention of the market abuse rules transposing the then Market Abuse Directive 2003/6/EC. None of the regulations stipulated any private remedies for breach of said provisions. The court, siding with Anglo, held that the breach of such provisions would not render the contracts invalid, because a court must consider 'whether the requirements of public policy and the legislation concerned' require the additional sanction of voidness or unenforceability. In such assessment, the court should consider factors such as whether: (i) the contract carries out the act that the legislation seeks to prevent, (ii) the statute's wording implies that it suffices with the consequences stipulated therein, (iii) the policy is designed to apply equally to both contracting parties, or only one, (iv) voidness or unenforceability may be counterproductive to the statutory aim itself, (v) in light of the

---

[48] See eg the decision by the Court of Appeal of Milan n 2003 (28 July 2020) or Tribunal of Milan n 6224 (14 October 2020).
[49] *Quinn v Irish Bank Resolution Corp* [2015] IESC 29. See the excellent analysis by Blanaid Clarke, 'Ireland' in Danny Busch and Cees Van Dam (eds), *A Banker's Duty of Care* (Hart Publishing 2019) 315.

statutory purpose, if the range of express adverse consequences may be considered sufficient, (vi) the imposition of voidness or unenforceability may be disproportionate to the seriousness of the conduct.

This is a model approach to assess the effects of public policy provisions. Instead of focusing only on the 'relevance' of the provisions, it seeks to find the meaning and finality of those provisions, and to assess the coherence of the private remedy with that finality. This kind of seamless integration between public regulatory law and private remedies is needed, but often missed in the approach of courts. **10.23**

3 Disputes about intermediaries' duties and representations

The clients of banks and other financial intermediaries often claim that these have breached some kind of duty to 'disclose' or 'give advice', which raise the issue of the interplay between regulatory standards and private law, echoing the cases on the liability of issuers/offerors of securities against investors discussed in Chapter 9. First, we consider the case of US broker–dealers and advisers as an example (section 3.1) and then we analyse the duties of financial intermediaries in selected EU jurisdictions under private law doctrines (section 3.2) and the impact of regulatory rules on consumer protection and intermediaries' duties (section 3.3) and the intermediaries' defences, such as 'causation' and 'reliance' (section 3.4). **10.24**

3.1 Duties of advisers and broker–dealers in the US, and their significance in private actions

US investment advisers are subject to the 1940 Investment Advisers Act, which contemplates a relatively broad definition of 'adviser'.[50] It omits certain brokers, dealers, and banks and bank holding companies,[51] including any broker or dealer: (i) whose performance of its investment advisory services is 'solely incidental' to the conduct of its business as a broker or dealer; and (ii) who receives no 'special compensation' for its advisory services.[52] A separate, special compensation, for the advisory service means that a broker–dealer must be also considered an investment adviser. Broker–dealers must register with the SEC under the Exchange Act,[53] and become members of a self-regulatory organization (SRO), like FINRA, and of the Securities Investor Protection Corporation (SIPC). **10.25**

---

[50] An adviser is 'any person who, for compensation, engages in the business of advising others, either directly or through publications or writings, as to the value of securities or as to the advisability of investing in, purchasing, or selling securities, or who, for compensation and as part of a regular business, issues or promulgates analyses or reports concerning securities'. Section 202(a)(11).

[51] Advisers Act, s 202(a)(11)(A)--(G).

[52] ibid s 202(a)(11)(C). See also SEC Advisers Act Rule 202(a)(11)-1. However, the DC Circuit in *Financial Planning Association v SEC* 482 F 3d 481 (DC Cir 2007) vacated the original Advisers Act Rule 202(a)(11)-1, holding that the SEC did not have the authority to exclude broker-dealers that offered fee-based brokerage accounts from the 'investment adviser' definition.

[53] Section 15(a) provided that they effect securities transactions or induce or attempt to induce purchase/sale of such securities transactions

10.26 Courts[54] have held that Investment Advisers Act rules establish a federal fiduciary standard for advisers, which governs their conduct.[55] This is less clear for broker–dealers. The rules do not characterize the relationship as 'fiduciary', nor impose a fiduciary duties, but courts may find the existence of fiduciary duties in certain circumstances.[56] Fiduciary duties may arise under state (common) law in circumstances involving the exercise of discretion over clients' assets, or a relationship of trust and confidence.

10.27 In *Davis v Merrill Lynch*[57] the Circuit did not reverse the trial court instruction that the jury should find a breach of fiduciary duty by the investment bank: the applicable state law (South Dakota) lacked precedents on the existence of fiduciary duties by broker–dealers, but this was still a matter for state law, and the Circuit refused to follow precedents that directly rejected the existence of a fiduciary duty in non-discretionary accounts (as was the case[58]). Typically, courts found fiduciary duties when a broker had discretionary authority over a customer's account.[59] They focused on the circumstances, eg whether there was de facto authority (even in a non-discretionary account) and whether the customer was sophisticated,[60] to establish the degree of trust and confidence in the broker.[61] Yet, in general, in non-discretionary accounts, a broker–dealer, absent special circumstances, has no duty to give ongoing *advice*.[62] It may still be subject to fiduciary duties, but restricted to the specific matters entrusted to them.[63]

10.28 Broker–dealers are subject to the 'duty of fair dealing', because, by hanging out its sign, or 'shingle', a broker–dealer is deemed to be making the implied representation that it will deal fairly with its customers ('shingle theory'). This results in certain duties and limits, and the disclosure of 'unfair' actions.[64] Finally, section 15(c) of the Exchange Act prohibits misstatements and omissions and manipulative acts. Thus, one needs to look at the differences in each specific context.

10.29 One of the adviser's key duties applies in case of conflicts of interest. An investment adviser must *fully* disclose to its clients all *material* information intended to 'eliminate, or at least expose, all conflicts of interest which might incline an investment adviser—consciously or unconsciously—to render advice which was not disinterested', and the non-disclosure

---

[54] See the excellent SEC Study SEC, 'Study on Investment Advisers and Broker-Dealers as Required by Section 913 of the Dodd-Frank Wall Street Reform and Consumer Protection Act' (January 2011) https://www.sec.gov/news/studies/2011/913studyfinal.pdf (accessed 5 October 2022).

[55] See eg *SEC v Capital Gains Research Bureau* 375 US 180, 84 S Ct 275 (1963) with regard to the Act's s 206(1) and (2).

[56] SEC, 'Inspection Report on the Soft Dollar Practices of Broker-Dealers, Investment Advisers and Mutual Funds (22 September 1998) (SEC Report).

[57] *Davis v Merrill Lynch, Pierce, Fenner & Smith Inc* 906 F 2d 1206 (8th Cir 1990).

[58] *Davis v Merrill Lynch*, citing *Horn v Ray E. Friedman Co* 776 F 2d 777, 779 (8th Cir 1985) (Horn) (applying Arkansas law); *Ray E Friedman Co v Jenkins* 738 F 2d 251, 254 (8th Cir 1984).

[59] *US v Skelly* 442 F 3d 94, 98 (2d Cir 2006). Not when it lacked such discretion because the customer had the final say. See *Associated Randall Bank v Griffin, Kubik, Stephens & Thompson Inc* 3 F 3d 208, 212 (7th Cir 1993).

[60] *Leib v Merrill Lynch, Pierce, Fenner & Smith Inc* 461 F Supp 951, 953-954 (ED Mich 1978) aff'd, 647 F 2d 165 (6th Cir 1981).

[61] *Paine Webber, Jackson & Curtis Inc v Adams* 718 P2d 508 (Colo 1986) (practical control of an account indicative of trust and confidence placed in the broker).

[62] 'A nondiscretionary customer by definition keeps control over the account and has full responsibility for trading decisions.' *De Kwiatkowski v Bear, Stearns & Co Inc* 306 F 3d 1293 (2d Cir 2002).

[63] *Press v Chemical Investment Services Corp* 166 F 3d 529 (2d Cir 1999) (under New York law).

[64] *Charles Hughes & Co v SEC* 139 F 2d 434 (2d Cir 1943).

of which may result in the commission of a *fraud* by the adviser.[65] Advisers' duty is broad, and not mechanical.[66] The Investment Advisers Act also restricts an adviser from acting as principal in a transaction with a client without previously disclosing this to the client, and obtaining her consent.[67] The approach is less strict if the adviser is matching a client's order with another client's order (ie no need to disclose each transaction).[68]

A broker's duty is more fact-specific, and depends on the relationship and situation. **10.30** Disclosure duties are limited, and refer just to the execution of the transaction when the broker is not recommending securities, which means that it may keep its self-interest in the transaction to itself.[69] However, if a broker recommends a security everything changes, and the information must be 'honest and complete'.[70] This includes 'material adverse facts', eg acting as a market maker for the security,[71] or being paid to promote a fund to its customers.[72] The balance between the right not to speak, and the duty to be honest when one chooses to speak echoes the *Omnicare* discussion on omissions.[73] In extreme cases, the conflict of interest may result in fraud, as in 'scalping', ie, where a broker recommends a security to a client, and immediately sells it at a profit 'riding the wave' of the rise in price.[74]

Another key issue is suitability. Advisers must make a reasonable determination that invest- **10.31** ment advice is suitable based on the client's financial situation and objectives, and to make a reasonable investigation that it is not basing recommendations on materially inaccurate information.[75]

Broker–dealers' 'suitability' duty is part of their duty of fair dealing (above), ie they must **10.32** make recommendations in the client's interest, and to 'reasonably believe' that they are suitable. Sometimes, 'suitability' was assessed under anti-fraud provisions,[76] but these require 'scienter',[77] and thus a breach of fiduciary duty eg an unsuitable recommendation is not a 'fraud'.[78] Broker–dealers may commit fraud without making statements through practices like 'churning', ie buying and selling securities for a customer solely for generating commissions.[79] Otherwise, 'suitability' is subject to FINRA rules and disciplinary actions.[80] To find the existence of a 'recommendation', courts have assessed whether the statements made constituted a 'call to action', which could 'influence' the client.[81] The more individualized the statement, the likelier it will be seen as a 'recommendation'.[82] Finally, a breach of FINRA

---

[65] *SEC v Capital Gains Research Bureau* (n 55).
[66] SEC Report (n 56). It must include, for example, the 'soft dollar' benefits received by the adviser.
[67] Investment Advisers Act, s 206(3).
[68] ibid rule 206(3).
[69] *Press v Chemical* (n 63); *Carras v Burns* 516 F 2d 251, 257 (4th Cir 1975).
[70] *De Kwiatkowski v Bear, Stearns & Co Inc* 306 F 3d 1293 (2d Cir 2002).
[71] *Chasins v Smith, Barney & Co* 438 F 2d 1167 (2d Cir 1970).
[72] *In re AIG Advisor Group* 390 Fed Appx 495 (2d Cir 2009).
[73] See ch 9, sections 2.1–2.2.
[74] *SEC v Yun Soo Oh Park* 99 F Supp 2d 889 (ND Ill 2000) (if a relationship of trust and confidence between broker and client).
[75] SEC Report (n 56).
[76] *Hanly v SEC* 415 F 2d 589 (2d Cir 1969).
[77] See section 2.
[78] Thus, there is a tension between *federal* securities fraud, and *state* fiduciary law. See *Santa Fe Indus Inc v Green* 430 US 462 (1977).
[79] *Miley v Oppenheimer & Co* 637 F 2d 318, 324 (5th Cir 1981).
[80] *Siegel v SEC* 592 F 3d 147, 150, 158 (DC Cir 2010).
[81] *Siegel v SEC* (n 80): 'Siegel's communication "reasonably could have been viewed as a call to action" and reasonably would influence an investor to trade a particular security or group of securities.'
[82] As we will see, very similar to the test of 'financial advice' framed by courts in EU jurisdictions, following EU regulatory rules. See sections 3.1.4 and 3.1.5.

suitability duties does not require 'scienter', and a broker is not relieved of its duty to make suitable recommendations if it obtains the client's consent, but this breach is typically enforced through arbitration.[83]

10.33 Other duties include best execution, or custody. For advisers, best execution means selecting a broker–dealer for their customers' account, such that the total costs are the most favourable. This may include the possibility of aggregating orders *if* this contributes to best execution by, eg reducing execution costs. Custody requires having controls to protect clients' assets from loss, misuse, misappropriation, etc.[84] Broker–dealers are also bound by 'best execution',[85] and must *execute* trades in the more favourable terms for their customers, taking into account the terms reasonably available.[86] When they deal with customers on a principal basis, a broker–dealer may violate Exchange Act rule 10b-5 if it knowingly sells a security to a customer at a price not reasonably related to the prevailing market price.[87] Apart from 'best execution', brokers are required to charge 'fair' or reasonable fees and prices, ie reasonably related to market prices.[88]

10.34 Although the duties applicable to advisers and broker–dealers are very important, remedies are less impressive. For investment advisers, there is first a limited right to void the adviser's contract, and obtain restitution of fees,[89] but no private right to damages or monetary relief.[90] Sections 206(1) and (2) of the Advisers Act provide a fraud-based action enforceable by the SEC. Secondly, a client can bring a claim under section 10b of the Exchange Act and rule 10b-5[91] but cannot simply allege the breach of the adviser's duties, and has to fulfil those provisions' onerous requirements, which works only in egregious cases (eg 'scalping' cases above). Thirdly, the client may rely on state law remedies for breach of fiduciary duties,[92] negligence,[93] or common law fraud.[94] Broker–dealers, for their part, are subject to more limited federal law duties. Clients have framed their breaches of duties as securities fraud actions, under sections 10b and rule 10b-5, 15(c), or 17(a),[95] while breaches of FINRA rules are normally enforced via FINRA disciplinary procedures. It is unclear whether a breach of FINRA rules gives rise to a private law cause of action.[96] Some courts were in favour, if the rule was meant for the direct protection of investors and the conduct was tantamount to fraud,[97] while others dismissed the claims.[98] However, the court may take into account a breach of these duties as evidence of fraud, negligence, or breach of fiduciary duty.[99]

---

[83] SEC Report (n 56) 63.
[84] Investment Advisers Act, r 206(4)-2.
[85] *Newton v Merrill, Lynch, Pierce, Fenner & Smith Inc* 135 F 3d 266 (3d Cir 1998).
[86] SEC Report (n 56) 69:The Commission has stated that broker-dealers should also consider at least six additional factors: (1) the size of the order; (2) the speed of execution available on competing markets; (3) the trading characteristics of the security; (4) the availability of accurate information comparing markets and the technology to process the data; (5) the availability of access to competing markets; and (6) the cost of such access.
[87] *Grandon v Merrill Lynch & Co* 147 F 3d 184, 189–90 (2d Cir 1998). See SEC Report (n 56) 69.
[88] SEC Report (n 56) 66.
[89] Investment Advisers Act, s 215.
[90] *Transamerica Mortgage Advisors Inc* 444 US 11, 17 (1979).
[91] Securities Exchange Act of 1933, s 10b and r 10b-5.
[92] *Carl v Galuska* 785 F Supp 1283 (ND Ill 1992).
[93] *Talansky v Schulman* 2 A D 3d 355, 770 NYS2d 48 (2003).
[94] *Ohio Bureau of Workers' Compensation v MDL Active Duration Fund* 476 F Supp 2d 809 (2007).
[95] See *Aaron v SEC* 446 US 680 (1980) for the discussion on the requirement of scienter in some actions.
[96] SEC Report (n 56) 83.
[97] *Hempel v Blunt, Ellis & Loewi Inc* 123 FRD 313, (ED Wis 1988).
[98] *Gilman v Shearson/American Express Inc* 577 F Supp 492 (DNH 1983).
[99] *Hoxworth v Blinder, Robinson & Co Inc* 903 F 2d 186, 200 (3d Cir 1990) (fraud); *Merrill Lynch, Pierce, Fenner & Smith Inc v Cheng* 697 F Supp 1224, 1227 (DDC 1988) (negligence).

10.35 Nonetheless, claims against broker–dealers are typically subject to arbitration, even Exchange Act (including section 10b) claims. Such arbitration clauses were considered valid by the US Supreme Court in *Shearson v McMahon*[100] for claims under section 10b of the Exchange Act, and in *Rodriquez de Quijas v Shearson/American Express*[101] for claims under the Securities Act 1933, *and* under state law in *Dean Witter v Byrd*.[102] Although enforcement is healthy and robust, this parcel of securities law is less shaped by court precedents.

10.36 In summary, US law shows the difficulty of striking the right balance between private law doctrines and regulatory provisions contained in mandatory rules or self-regulatory norms. Courts' habitual solution is to assert the independence of private law rights of action or doctrines, ie 'legal autonomy', while at the same time letting industry-specific standards operate as a relevant basis of fact with legal significance, but not outcome-determinative strength.

3.2 Banks' marketing duties under private law, absent advisory relationships

10.37 The existence, and content, of banks' duties towards their clients absent an advisory relationship or regulatory duties, has been explored extensively in the UK, where courts have insisted on looking at the issue in a 'purely contractual' light. As a general rule, a bank owes a duty of care to not make negligent misstatements to its client *only if* it has made an 'assumption of responsibility'.[103] Bank clients often allege that they were 'induced' to contract by the bank's misrepresentations, but the contracts' sweeping disclaimers normally exclude this. Thus, clients try to persuade the courts that the bank was under a duty 'not to' misstate, or to 'explain', or that there were 'additional' representations beyond the written document. One of the scant authorities favourable to the client is *Cornish v Midland Bank*,[104] where a bank manager described to a wife a second mortgage in favour of her husband as 'just like a building society mortgage', omitting that the mortgage would secure any future borrowing by the bank to the husband. The manager could have (a) advised the customer to seek independent advice, or (b) explained the matter fully. This developed into the idea that there is a sort of an 'advisory spectrum of duties' that a bank might owe to its customer, which could include a 'mezzanine' or 'intermediate' duty, less onerous than a 'duty to advise' but more demanding than the 'duty not to misstate'.

10.38 Another is *Bankers Trust International Plc v Dharmala*,[105] where the court held that, in principle, a bank owes 'no duty to explain'. However, 'if the bank does give an explanation' or advice then it owes a duty to give it accurately and properly, and in the case the bank volunteered an explanation, but failed to explain its clients fully the effects ad risks of the swaps. In more recent cases plaintiffs made 'mis-selling' claims, sometimes under the Misrepresentation Act, without success. In *Peekay*[106] a customer asserted that it had not understood the investment it was acquiring because it had been described incorrectly to him by the defendant bank in a

---

[100] *Shearson/American Express Inc v McMahon* 482 US 222 (1987).
[101] *Rodriquez de Quijas v Shearson/American Express* 490 US 477 (1989).
[102] *Dean Witter Reynolds Inc v Byrd* 470 US 213 (1985).
[103] *Hedley Byrne & Co Ltd v Heller & Partners Ltd* [1964] AC 465. See ch 9, s 4.
[104] *Cornish v Midland Bank* [1985] 3 All ER 513.
[105] *Bankers Trust International v PT Dharmala Sakti Sejahter* [1996] CLC 518.
[106] *Peekay Intermark v Australia and New Zealand Banking Group* [2006] EWCA Civ 386.

conversation before he contracted to purchase the investment. The customer's agent signed a risk disclosure statement which indicated that the customer understood the transaction, and the bank assumed the client's awareness of the risks, practices, and transaction suitability. Thus, the Court of Appeal held that the client was estopped from asserting different facts.[107]

10.39 *Peekay* set the tone for other mis-selling cases on banks' (non)duties in cases of complex products, including *IFE Fund*,[108] *Springwell*,[109] *Titan Steel*,[110] *Raiffeisen (RZB)*,[111] *Cassa di Risparmio*,[112] *Bank Leumi*,[113] or *MTR*.[114] The courts rejected the existence of a duty to inform, and/or the existence of the alleged representations by the bank,[115] and the clients' reliance on such representations to conclude their contracts.[116] They also held that the boilerplate clauses in the contract[117] were binding and determined the *basis* for contracting (so-called 'basis' clauses) instead of excluding liability (exclusion clauses[118]), since treating the clauses as liability exclusions would have subjected them to a test of 'unfairness', which could render them void. There was no appreciable difference between the cases where the client was a financial institution, eg *Peekay*, *IFE*, *RZB*, or *Cassa di Risparmio* and those where it was not, eg *Springwell* or *MTR Bailey v Barclays*, or between cases where the bank acted as a lender, promoting a syndicated loan, eg *RZB v RBS*, or *MTR Bailey*, or where it sold, or executed an investment, eg *Peekay*, *IFE v Goldman Sachs*, *Springwell*, and *Cassa di Risparmio*.

10.40 Of these, *Raiffeisen* involved a special purpose entity set up by Royal Bank of Scotland (RBSFT) to purchase shares in an Enron subsidiary. Enron Corp, which was engaging in accounting malpractice, gave oral assurances to RBS that it would ensure that RBS would receive its equity back, plus an attractive return,[119] but RBS marketed the loan using an information memorandum (IM) that made no reference to the oral assurances. RZB alleged that it had entered the transaction believing RBS representation that it had invested 'unsupported equity' in it, as a way to 'monetise' Enron's investment, and that it was led to believe that the transaction complied with accounting principles. The Court rejected that these

---

[107] *Peekay* (n 106) para 57: 'It is common to include in certain kinds of contracts an express acknowledgement by each of the parties that they have not been induced to enter the contract by any representations other than those contained in the contract itself. The effectiveness of a clause of that kind may be challenged on the grounds that the contract as a whole, including the clause in question, can be avoided if in fact one or other party was induced to enter into it by misrepresentation. However, I can see no reason in principle why it should not be possible for parties to an agreement to give up any right to assert that they were induced to enter into it by misrepresentation, provided that they make their intention clear, or why a clause of that kind, if properly drafted, should not give rise to a contractual estoppel.'
[108] *IFE Fund SA v Goldman Sachs International* [2006] EWHC 2887 (Comm).
[109] *Springwell Navigation Corp v JP Morgan Bank* [2008] EWHC 1186 (Comm) and also [2008] EWHC 1793 (Comm). Some points were appealed in *Springwell Navigation Corp v JP Morgan Bank* [2010] EWCA Civ 1221.
[110] *Titan Steel Wheels Limited v Royal Bank of Scotland Plc* [2010] EWHC 211 (Comm).
[111] *Raiffeisen Zentralbank Osterreich AG v The Royal Bank of Scotland Plc* [2010] EWHC 1392 (Comm).
[112] *Cassa Di Risparmio Della Repubblica Di San Marino Spa v Barclays Bank Ltd* [2011] EWHC 484 (Comm).
[113] *Bank Leumi (UK) Plc v Wachner* [2011] EWHC 656 (Comm).
[114] *MTR Bailey Ltd v Barclays Bank plc* [2014] EWHC 2882 QB.
[115] *IFE v Goldman Sachs* (n 109) paras 67–71; *MTR Bailey Ltd v Barclays Bank* (n 115) paras 82–90 (fiduciary duty).
[116] The test for 'inducement' was formulated in *Dadourian v Simms and Others* [2009] EWCA Civ 169 (paras 99, 101).
[117] See eg *Cassa Di Risparmio Della Repubblica Di San Marino* (n 113) paras 512–16, 527–32. In *Titan Steel Wheels v RBS* (n 111) para 82, David Steel J applied estoppel to an agreement about the future, where Titan were to seek independent advice if required. In *Bank Leumi (UK) Plc v Wachner* (n 114) paras 183–84 Flaux J applied the doctrine to a term, 'You agree that you will rely on your own judgment for all trading decisions'.
[118] See the long analysis in *RZB v RBS* [2010] EWHC 1392 (Comm) paras 250–314.
[119] Enron's accounting malpractice with Special Purpose Entities (SPEs) were exposed in the Report by the Special Investigative Committee of the Board of Directors of Enron Corp by William C Powers Jr (2002) (Powers Report). In this case, RBSFT allowed Enron to record a profit selling shares, without recording any liability to RBSFT under the total return swap, which was permitted under US GAAP, if at least 3 per cent of the substantive equity in RBSFT was 'at risk'. If Enron made the representations in writing, there was no 'at risk', because RBS was covered, and this (apparently) did not happen with oral representations.

representations constituted the 'real and substantial' cause of RZB entering the contract.[120] Furthermore, the alleged representations were not in the IM or related documents.[121]

In *Springwell*[122] the plaintiff brought claims against JP Morgan for misrepresentation and breach of contractual, tortious, and fiduciary duties in advising Springwell for heavy losses on derivative products exposed to Russian sovereign debt.[123] The court dismissed the misrepresentation claims. The statement that the investments were 'conservative' and 'liquid' were not false in the context of a sophisticated investor who understood the market's risks. Furthermore, any misrepresentations would not have been actionable, since Chase's employee was merely giving his 'opinions' as a salesman to a sophisticated investor, not stating any facts. Even under a 'low level' duty of care not to make negligent misstatements and to use reasonable care not to recommend a risky investment without pointing out such riskiness,[124] the investors' knowledge, and the absence of a duty to advise, ruled out the existence of actionable misstatements, let alone negligent ones.[125] Although in *Springwell* the specific context was key, some of the Court's views, eg that there was no financial advice if there was no payment for it, or that a 'salesman' cannot provide advice, or be subject to a duty to inform, have precedential value.

10.41

In *Crestsign*[126] the court rejected that there was any advisory duty, and that common law duties should be influenced by regulatory standards, but found that there could be a 'mezzanine' duty' or context-specific duty to explain.[127] However, this was not a duty to explain all available products, nor a 'duty to educate' or to ensure that the information was properly understood. It was enough to give summary information of the products' basic attributes, or state that the break-up costs would be 'substantial' for the client. The judge held that, if there had been a duty to advise, it would have been breached, but that the 'mezzanine duty' was not (just). Yet, even this mild attempt at an intermediate range of duties was rejected in *Thornbridge v Barclays*,[128] where the judge held that, in non-advised sales, there was not even a duty to explain.

10.42

Recently, in *PAG v RBS*,[129] PAG entered into four LIBOR-referenced swaps with RBS, incurred substantial break costs and brought many claims. The High Court dismissed all the claims, and the Court of Appeal largely confirmed the findings. On the specific issue of a 'duty to inform', PAG relied on *Bankers Trust* to argue that, in non-advice claims, a duty not

10.43

---

[120] *RZB v RBS* (n 119) para 215.
[121] ibid 132. In particular, one could not conclude that RBS's equity investment was 'entirely unsupported', and any statement about the 'monetization' of Enron's investment did not assure the transaction's lawfulness, or compliance with accounting principles: 'monetization' is not a technical *accounting* term, and the statement was not made by accountants or lawyers.
[122] *Springwell* (n 109). Some points were appealed in *Springwell 2010* (n 109).
[123] Springwell was the investment vehicle for a group of shipping companies owned and controlled by a Greek shipping family (Adamandios Polemis (AP) and his family) with a long-standing relationship with JP Morgan Chase. Springwell invested heavily in Russian debt, especially derivative instruments called GKO-linked notes (the GKO LNs) brought down by the Russian financial crisis in 1998.
[124] *Springwell* (n 109) paras 78, 123.
[125] ibid para 124.
[126] *Crestsign Ltd v National Westminster Bank Plc & Anor* [2014] EWHC 3043 (Ch). The case also referred to later to illustrate different court attitudes towards the relationship between regulatory provisions and private law doctrines. See sections 3.1.4 and 3.1.5.
[127] *Crestsign* (n 126) paras 36, 42.
[128] *Thornbridge v Barclays* [2015] EWHC 3430 (QB).
[129] *PAG v RBS* [2018] EWCA Civ 355.

to misstate under *Hedley Byrne* applies. The Court of Appeal held that *Bankers Trust* was best seen as an application of *Hedley Byrne* in specific circumstances, rather than a new standard, because in *Bankers Trust* the bank had put forward an explanation that entering into the proposed substitute swap would improve the risk exposure of the customer.[130] Furthermore, the expression 'mezzanine' duty or intermediate (in *Crestsign*) should be best avoided, and parties should concentrate instead on the assumption of responsibility in the case.[131] Only '[i]n some exceptional cases, a defendant may assume a responsibility to speak',[132] exemplified by *Cornish v Midland Bank*.[133]

10.44 Thus, the bank did not make a negligent misstatement by failing to present the full picture. It was enough to say that early termination would carry adverse consequences, and that their calculation would depend on the difference between the floating rate payable by RBS, and the fixed interest rate payable by PAG. The bank's calculation of break-up costs under its internal models was the bank's subjective opinion, and PAG never asked to see the internal models, nor did this factor 'induce' it to conclude the contracts.[134] PAG's fraudulent representation claim also failed. Barclays' staff characterized the transaction as a 'hedge', despite the fact that it protected against rate increases, but not against all interest movements.[135] However, PAG was aware of the terms of the transaction,[136] and nothing suggested that RBS staff used the term 'hedge' without believing that it was such hedge.[137] Finally, the Court rejected that RBS was obliged to exercise its contractual right to request a valuation of PAG's portfolio in a 'reasonable' manner.[138]

10.45 The exception to this pattern are cases of fraud, such as *Parabola Investments*,[139] where the court was fully convinced that the bank's agent's fraudulently represented that, despite some losses, his client's overall position was profitable, and this this led to a series of disastrous investments by the plaintiff (Mr Gill), which satisfied the test of 'inducement'.[140]

10.46 For German courts in principle a lender does not owe a duty of care to its client (typically, a borrower) to ensure the viability of the loan, or to explore the borrower financial capacity.[141] However, there are relevant scenarios where the existence of such a duty can be inferred from the circumstances, notably if the lender has a significantly superior knowledge of the loan-funded investment's risks, the bank is in a situation of conflict of interest, or the bank went beyond the typical role of lender, and promoted the investment.[142] The first scenario is relatively extreme, and the bank needs to have a clear knowledge with regard to the risks,

---

[130] ibid para 66.
[131] *PAG v RBS* (n 129) 67. The expression 'mezzanine' duty or intermediate duty, first coined in *Crestsign* (n 126), is best avoided. It appears to reflect the notion that there is a continuous spectrum of duty, stretching from not misleading, at one end, to full advice, at the other end. Rather, concentration should be on the responsibility assumed in the particular factual context as regards the particular transaction or relationship in issue.
[132] *PAG v RBS* (n 129) para 65.
[133] *Cornish v Midland Bank* (n 104).
[134] *PAG v RBS* (n 129) paras 80–85.
[135] ibid paras 89–92.
[136] ibid paras 93–96.
[137] ibid paras 99–111.
[138] See section 3.2.1.
[139] *Parabola Investments Ltd & Another v Browallia CAL Ltd & Others* [2009] EWHC 901 (Comm).
[140] *Parabola Investments* (n 139) para 102: 'It is perfectly obvious that Mr Gill is not some manic or compulsive trader who would have driven himself, lemming like, over the cliff if he had known the true position. I accept that he is rational and sensible and that he is particularly sensitive to making losses. If during the Man period he was less rational and sensible than at other times, that demonstrates how effectively he was being deceived by the fraud.'
[141] BGH judgments II ZR 393/02 (14 June 2004); XI ZR 255/03 (26 October 2004).
[142] See the excellent summary in Jens-Heinrich Binder, 'Chapter 3: Germany' in Danny Busch and Cees van Dam (eds), *A Bank's Duty of Care* (Hart Publishing 2019) 65.

or at least behave in a grossly negligent way, which may arise in case of a long-term relationship.[143] The second scenario arises in cases where the bank, by granting the loan, may be trying to protect its previous involvement in the investment, and fails to disclose that circumstance to the borrower.[144] The third scenario arises in cases where the bank acts as a sort of co-sponsor.[145]

10.47 In Italy, the validity of derivatives contracts for breach of mandatory provisions has been discussed in a multitude of cases and recently also in a 2020 case, already considered in section 2, decided by the Italian Supreme Court (*Corte di Cassazione*[146]) concerning interest rate swaps (IRSs) entered into by local public authorities and financial institutions. Since the reasoning is focused on the *validity* of the contract the case is discussed in the next point. Nonetheless, the reasoning of the Court implies the existence of a duty by the bank to disclose the mark-to-market and probabilistic scenarios, and, if it fails to do so, the contract lacks *causa* and lacks a determined *object*, and is thus invalid.

10.48 In other jurisdictions the courts' standards have been shaped by the use of regulatory provisions as a reference point, as seen in the next sections.

3.3 Regulatory requirements and private law duties in the EU (I). Fashioning private remedies for breach of regulatory duties

10.49 Chapter 9 sections 3.2 and 3.3 showed that the Court of Justice has been shy in using regulatory provisions to fashion private law remedies in the liability for misstatements in the prospectus and elsewhere. Yet, this contrasts with the Court's case law on unfair contract terms in *consumer* loans.

10.50 On unfair contract terms, the UCT Directive (93/13/EC) provided the following: (i) a substantive control of 'unfair' clauses (Article 3 and Annex); (ii) the exclusion of substantive control over clauses that define the contract's main object, or establish the balance between price and the goods or services (Article 4 (2)); and (iii) the requirement that clauses must be drafted in a 'plain, intelligible' language (Article 5). On 'remedies' unfair clauses were considered non-binding, but Member States were granted some flexibility on how to implement this, and nothing was expressly said about the consequences of the control over the object and price.

10.51 The 'dialogue' between domestic courts and the Court of Justice shifted this substantive and procedural balance in a decidedly pro-consumer way. In *Caja Madrid v Ausbanc*, a case decided over variable interest loans' clauses that 'rounded up' to the next quarter of a percentage point, the Court of Justice held that the directive did not preclude national legislation (in Spain) that did not transpose Article 4(2), and thus allowed the judicial review of the clauses related to the main object or the price, even if these were plain and intelligible.[147] In its subsequent *Banesto* decision the Court further insisted in a finalistic interpretation of the directive to foster consumer protection, and in the importance of nullity as a remedy, as opposed to the reinterpretation of unfair clauses, due to its 'dissuasive effect'.[148]

---

[143] BGH judgment XI ZR 204/04 (19 September 2006).
[144] BGH judgment XI ZR 414/04 (20 March 2007).
[145] BGH judgment XI ZR 322/03 (6 November 2007).
[146] Italian Supreme Court judgment n 8770 (n 25).
[147] Case C-484/08 *Cajamadrid v Ausbanc* ECLI:EU:C:2010:309.
[148] Case C-618/10 *Banesto* ECLI:EU:C:2012:349, para 69.

10.52 Subsequently, the Spanish Supreme Court chose not to heed the *Caja Madrid* advice, concluding that courts should not revise the 'price clause'.[149] Yet, it also subjected a 'floor clause', ie of minimum interest rate, included in a mortgage loan (ie a 'price' clause) to the 'plain, intelligible' test, and held that such test encompassed the 'formal transparency', of how the clause was incorporated into the contract, but also the 'material transparency' of the clause, using a doctrine also present in Germany. The consequence of the clause not meeting such material transparency was its 'unfairness', and invalidity. Yet, the Court limited the invalidity's remedial effects to make it non-retroactive, possibly conscious of the effects it could have in banks' already delicate financial position (the case was decided after the Great Financial Crisis, and Europe's sovereign debt crisis).

10.53 Then, the Court of Justice, in several decisions such as *Kásler*[150] and *Matei*,[151] adopted the 'material transparency' test, a twist that enabled a de facto substantive control over clauses that regulated the contract's main object and price. Furthermore, the Court also expanded this 'transparency' test to encompass the precontractual stage, transforming it into a requirement to provide the consumer with sufficient information in *RWE*, *Kásler* or *Matei*.[152] Morphing the separate checks of 'substantive control + unfairness' and 'transparency control + *contra proferentem*' into a check of 'material transparency + invalidity' helped the Court to assert a finalistic interpretation whereby the consumer is in a weaker position, and consumer law helps replace the contract's formal balance with an effective balance, as stated in *Gutiérrez Naranjo*.[153] In *BNP Paribas* the Court reiterated the transformation of the 'plain and intelligible' test into a requirement to provide 'sufficient and accurate information to enable the average consumer, who is reasonably well informed and reasonably observant and circumspect, to understand the specific functioning of the financial mechanism in question and thus to evaluate the risk of potentially significant adverse economic consequences of such terms on his or her financial obligations throughout the term of the agreement'.[154]

10.54 In parallel to its expansion of the 'substantive' protections under the Directive, the Court also asserted itself in the field of *remedies*. In *Mostaza Claro*,[155] *Pannon*,[156] *Asturcom*,[157] *Aziz*,[158] or *Adikko Bank*[159] the Court held that due to the public policy nature of consumer protection rules domestic courts had to assess, of their own motion, the clauses' 'unfairness' (typically in loan contracts), even if consumers did not allege it, and even if the procedure was not a 'declaratory procedure', where substantive issues were discussed, but a procedure for the execution of an arbitral award (*Mostaza*, *Asturcom*) or an enforcement procedure, typical in some jurisdictions for mortgage loans (*Aziz*, *Adikko*), ie not suspending the procedure to examine the validity of clauses was contrary to EU law. Subsequently, in *Gutiérrez Naranjo* the Court rejected the Spanish Supreme Court's limitation of invalidity effects, making it retroactive, and confirmed that, although the Directive does not expressly provide for any separate remedy for breach of the 'plain and intelligible' requirement, other than the interpretation

---

[149] Spanish Supreme Court decisión 241/2013 ECLI:ES:TS:2013:1916 (9 May 2013).
[150] Case C-26/13 *Kásler* ECLI:EU:C:2014:282.
[151] Case C-143/13 *Matei* ECLI:EU:C:2015:127.
[152] Case C-92/11 *RWE* ECLI:EU:C:2013:180, 44, *Kásler* (n 150) paras 69–70; Case C-143/13 *Matei* (n 151) paras 73–75.
[153] Case C-154/15 *Gutiérrez Naranjo* ECLI:EU:C:2016:980.
[154] Joined Cases C-776/19 to C-782/19 *BNP Paribas Personal Finance* ECLI:EU:C:2021:470.
[155] Case C-168/05 *Mostaza Claro* ECLI:EU:C:2006:675, para 38.
[156] Case C-243/08 *Pannon* ECLI:EU:C:2009:350, para 32.
[157] Case C-40/08 *Asturcom* ECLI:EU:C:2009:615, para 53.
[158] Case C-415/11 *Aziz* ECLI:EU:C:2013:164, para 64.
[159] Case C-407/18 *Adikko Bank* EU:C:2019:537, para 50.

contra proferentem (see Article 6), the Court applies by analogy the remedy of the 'unfair terms', ie invalidity. Thus, the idea of 'material transparency' conjoined the 'transparency' and 'substantive' tests into one. Furthermore, in *BNP Paribas* the Court rejected domestic law time limits for the national court to assess the clauses' invalidity. Lately, in *Unicaja*, *Ibercaja Banco Desio*, and *Impuls Leasing* the Court held that not even national procedural principles, like *res judicata*, can limit national courts' duty to assess the validity of potentially unfair contract terms.

The state of play described above for consumer law contrasts with the case law on the duties of financial intermediaries under MiFID. Leaving aside 'near misses' like *Khorassani*, *Länsförsäkringar* or *Banif Genil* was the case[160] where the Court of Justice analysed the application of MiFID to a financial contract, specifically a swap contract that protected the bank's client against rises in variable interest rates (Euribor) but made it pay when rates did not rise. The bank allegedly did not assess the 'suitability' and 'appropriateness' of the products for its client, which sought to have the contacts declared void *ab initio*. The Spanish court asked the Court of Justice (i) whether there was a relationship of 'advice' requiring a 'suitability' assessment, (ii) whether a swap contract was a 'complex' product, requiring an 'appropriateness' assessment, and (iii) whether failing to perform either test resulted in the contract's voidness. **10.55**

The Court held that the assessment of 'suitability', in case of investment 'advice', and 'appropriateness', for other cases, are excluded for 'not complex' products. However, a swap was a complex product, and the assessment could not be excluded.[161] The assessment can also be excluded if 'an investment service is offered as part of a financial product',[162] and the swaps were related to loan contracts with the same bank. The Court of Justice analysed the different language versions of MiFID, concluding that 'an investment service is offered as part of a financial product within the meaning of Article 19(9) of Directive 2004/39 only if it forms an integral part of that financial product at the time it is offered to the client'.[163] This was a matter of fact for the domestic court, but the Court of Justice indicated that: **10.56**

> [T]he fact that the duration of the financial instrument to which that service relates is greater than that of the product, that a single financial instrument applies to different financial products offered to the same client or that the instrument and the product are offered in different contracts are indicia that that service does not form an integral part of the financial product in question.[164]

Furthermore, although the standards applicable to the swap and the underlying product (loan) need not be equivalent, given the objective of investor protection, to exclude MiFID **10.57**

---

[160] Case C-604/11 *Genil 48 SL v Bankinter* ECLI:EU:C:2013:344. Case C-678/15 *Khorassani* ECLI:EU:C:2017:451 (MiFID not applicable to activity of brokering with a view to concluding a contract covering portfolio management services, as this was not 'reception and transmission of orders' in relation to 'one or more financial instruments'); Case C-542/16 *Länsförsäkringar Sak Försäkringsaktiebolag* ECLI:EU:C:2018:369 (financial advice relating to capital placement in context of insurance mediation and capital life assurance not subject to MiFID, but to insurance mediation directive); Case C-312/14 *Banif Plus Bank Zrt* ECLI:EU:C:2015:794 (MiFID not applicable to foreign exchange transactions under foreign currency denominated loan).
[161] *Genil* (n 160) paras 34–35.
[162] ibid para 37.
[163] ibid para 42.
[164] ibid para 44. Furthermore, in order to determine whether the assessments under MiFID would be excluded, the domestic court also asked whether it should take into consideration whether the provisions or standards the domestic court asked relating to assessment or information, referred to in art 19(9) of Directive 2004/39, to which the financial product concerned is already subject must be similar to the obligations provided in art 19(4) and (5), it is clear that art 19(9) does not state that such a similarity is a requirement.

standards the standards applicable to the underlying product 'must enable there to be a risk assessment of clients and/or include information requirements, which also encompass the investment service which forms an integral part of the financial product in question'.[165]

10.58 On the existence of 'advice', the Court relied on statutory definitions, which referred to the existence of a 'personal recommendation', made 'to a person in his capacity as an investor or potential investor and if it is presented as suitable for that person or based on a consideration of the circumstances of that person', without including recommendations disseminated solely through distribution channels or intended for the public, and thus the characterization of the relationship did not depend on the financial instrument, but on the way it is marketed.[166]

10.59 Finally, on the key issue of the private law consequences of the breach of MiFID rules on suitability (if there was advice) or appropriateness (if there was not) the Court offered some guidance, but was perhaps too cautious, noting that MiFID provided for the imposition of administrative penalties, but not for the contractual consequences of non-compliance. Thus, it held that 'it is for the internal legal order of each Member State to determine the contractual consequences of non-compliance with those obligations, subject to observance of the principles of equivalence and effectiveness'.[167] This very brief conceptual roadmap for domestic courts[168] includes several ideas: one, Member States' laws must determine '*the* contractual consequences', two, there must be *some* consequences, three, the principles of 'equivalence' and 'effectiveness' will be the yardstick to determine compliance. Yet, this still led to different perceptions in Member States, with .

10.60 The UK exemplifies an approach where private law is 'detached' from MiFID rules, and based on doctrines of misrepresentation and liability for misstatements.[169] Yet, courts have held that financial 'advice' creates 'special' duties for intermediaries, since the Financial Services Act of 1986. In *Martin v Britannia Life Ltd*[170] an agent for an insurance group suggested to the claimants to re-mortgage of their home, surrender a number of life policies as collateral, and to take out of a new endowment policy and pension policy, and the charging of the endowment policy as security for the re-mortgage. Contrary to the defendant's allegation, the court held that, although the suggestion to remortgage was 'investment business', 'investment advice' comprehended all financial advice given to a prospective client, not only in relation to an 'investment', but also as to any ancillary or associated transaction, even if outside the Act's definition of 'investment business'.[171]

10.61 This view was followed in *Walker v Inter-Alliance Group*,[172] where the client attended meetings with an independent financial adviser (IFA) some accompanied by a Mr Boakes, and transferred his former company's pension scheme into a self-administered personal pension scheme, which he left very dissatisfied, and sued for damages for wrongful advice. The High Court relied on the FSA 1986, and the rules by the Securities Investments Board (SIB) and self-regulatory organizations (SROs), holding that 'any element of comparison or evaluation

---

[165] *Genil* (n 160) para 47.
[166] ibid 52–53.
[167] ibid para 57.
[168] This was echoed in later decisions, such as Case C-174/12 *Hirmann* ECLI:EU:C:2013:856.
[169] See section 2.
[170] *Irvani v Irvani* [2000] Lloyd's Rep 412.
[171] *Martin v Britannia Life Ltd* [2000] Lloyds Rep 412, para 5.4.5.
[172] *Walker v Inter-Alliance Group plc* [2007] EWHC 1858 (Ch).

or persuasion is likely to cross the dividing line' from information to advice', and concluded (the italics are ours) that:

> Mr Boakes' repeated statements of *what he would do if he were in Mr Walker's position constituted the giving of investment advice.* The same is true, in my opinion, of *his statements comparing and evaluating the benefits available* to Mr Walker under [the different schemes], and of *his promotion of* the concept of drawdown as embodied in Scottish Equitable's Retirement Control product which I am satisfied *went far beyond the mere provision of factual information in a neutral way.*[173]

10.62 In short, Mr Boakes breached the principle of polarization, and Scottish Equitable's own compliance manuals, by giving investment advice when he should not have done, and that this was not 'vague' or 'ambiguous'.[174]

10.63 As MiFID-based rules entered into force, breaches of conduct of business (COB) rules became actionable, but this did not apply to business clients.[175] Thus, courts' case law on bank–client relationships not covered by the new MiFID rules proceeded without taking notice of them. Cases referred to in the previous section, like *Peekay, Springwell, Raiffeisen*, etc.[176] are based on private law principles. The new COB rules are seen as confined to their scope of application, with no broader relevance in terms of principle.

10.64 This contrasts with cases where COB rules were applicable. In *Rubenstein v HSBC*[177] a retail client (Rubenstein) sold his home and was looking for a safe investment while searching for a new property. An HSBC financial adviser gave him details of a fund in an insurance-based product with AIG Life, reassuring him that the fund's risk was *the same* as cash in a deposit account and the only risk was AIG Life's risk of default. Rubenstein invested but failed to find a property, and on the weekend before Lehman Brothers collapsed, and AIG Life's parent (AIG) wobbled, he withdrew his money, receiving less than he had invested, suing the bank for wrongful advice, negligence, breach of contract, and breach of (regulatory) statutory duties.[178] The High Court found that the bank had given negligent advice, which the investor Rubenstein had relied on, but that the loss was caused by unprecedented and unforeseeable market turmoil, and was too remote to be compensated. The appeal[179] will be discussed in the next section.[180]

---

[173] ibid para 96.
[174] ibid para 97: '[t]he concept of investment advice is broad enough to include any communication with the client which, in the particular context in which it is given, goes beyond the mere provision of information and is objectively likely to influence the client's decision whether or not to undertake the transaction in question ... Mr Boakes' statements to Mr Walker constituted investment advice, even if the precise words that he used cannot now be reconstructed'.
[175] FSA Act 2000, s 138D.
[176] *Peekay* (n 106); *Springwell* (n 109); *Raiffeisen* (n 111).
[177] *Rubenstein v HSBC Bank plc* [2011] EWHC 2304 (QB), [2012] EWCA Civ 1184.
[178] In particular for breach of the FSA's applicable COB rules pursuant to s 150 of the Financial Services and Markets Act 2000.
[179] *Rubenstein v HSBC* [2012] EWCA Civ 1184.
[180] See section 3.4.

10.65 It is noticeable how UK courts are cautious with the idea of expanding the scope of regulatory rules, or mixing them with private law. In *Forsta v Bank of New York Mellon*,[181] the court held a custodian responsible towards its *institutional* clients for failing properly to disclose the riskiness of certain investments, comparing the treatment of these investors and the better treatment given to other clients,[182] but the decision focused on the fact and common law precedents, making only a cursory reference to COB rules. In *Green and Rowley*[183] the judge expressed a clear distinction between the common duty of negligence and the regulatory COB rules' duties.[184] Yet, in *Crestsign*[185] the judge considered that the bank provided no 'advice' because there was a clause clearly excluding such advice,[186] and that COB rules did not apply because the client was a limited company carrying on a business. Yet, the court rejected the bank's argument that the client was trying to 'thinly disguise' a claim of breach of COB rules as a breach of a common law duty, holding that:

> I agree with the banks that the two sets of duties are not to be treated as co-terminous and that breach of a COBS duty is not necessarily common law negligence; on the other hand, it does not follow that breaches of COBS duties ... cannot also be negligent at common law. Nor is the content of the COBS duties wholly irrelevant in a common law claim brought by a person unable by statute to sue for breach of a COBS duty. The COBS duties are likely to be relevant to determining the standard of care required of a reasonably careful and skilled adviser, since a reasonably skilled and careful adviser would not fall short of the standard required to meet relevant regulatory requirements.[187]

10.66 In *Ramesh Parmar v Barclays*,[188] a bank's long-standing clients sued for breach of COBS rules on advised sales (rule 10) or, alternatively, for non-advised sales (rule 9). The court dismissed marketing materials about 'Barclays Capital's unrivalled depth of expertise', 'corporate risk advisory', 'bespoke', 'our more popular solutions', and 'tailoring the protection' as evidence of advice, finding that the sale was non-advised. The bank had breached the rules for non-advised sales because some words on the calculation of cancellation costs were misleading, but there was no liability because the clients were not misled.[189]

10.67 *Adams v Options* examined the provision of 'advice' without a licence.[190] Mr Adams contracted with an unregulated intermediary, CLP Brokers Sociedad Limitada (CLP), which persuaded him to cash out his pension fund and invest in a self-invested personal pension (SIPP), a regulated instrument ('relevant investment'), operated by Carey (later, Options) a regulated intermediary, which invested in 'storepods', unregulated investments that included (risky) leases of units in a storage facility in Blackburn. After the investments went badly,

---

[181] *Forsta AP-Fonden v Bank of New York Mellon* [2013] EWHC 3127 (Comm). Although the case was decided in the context of a custodian's relationship, the damages were granted for failure to disclose investment in risky instruments.

[182] For example, it applied the standard of *The Achilleas* [2008] UKHL 48, [2009] 1 AC of whether the damage was within the reasonable contemplation of the parties, but without limitations pursuant to theories of 'assumption of responsibility', as in *Haugesund Kommune v Depfa* [2011] EWCA Civ 33.

[183] *Green and Rowley v Royal Bank of Scotland plc* [2012] EWHC 3661 (QB).

[184] ibid para 82: 'The duty to take care not to mis-state is much narrower than the advisory duty ... The Hedley Byrne duty does not include any duty to give information unless without the statement is misleading. Equally the duty under Rule 5.4.3 [of COB] to take reasonable steps to ensure that the counterparty to a transaction understands the nature of its risks is well outside any notion of a duty not to misstate.'

[185] *Crestsign* (n 126).

[186] ibid.

[187] ibid.

[188] *Ramesh Parmar & Another v Barclays Bank plc* [2018] EWHC 1027 (Ch).

[189] See section 3.4 on banks' defences.

[190] *Russell David Edward Adams v Options UK Personal Pensions LLP* [2021] EWCA Civ 474.

Mr Adams sued under the FSMA, alleging that the defendant had engaged in a 'regulated activity' under the Regulated Activities Order (RAO) 2001, without an authorization, and that it had breached COB rules, by failing to 'act honestly, fairly and professionally in accordance with the best interests of its client' (a MiFID-based provision[191]). Since the claim itself was based on a breach of regulatory provisions the courts made extensive reference to those, as well as other sources, such as the FCA Perimeter Guidance (PERG) Manual. The High Court dismissed all the claims,[192] holding that the storepods were not regulated investments, and that the SIPP was, but Options had given advice on the storepods, but not on any SIPP. Thus, Options had acted as a 'bare introducer', but not given 'advice'. The Court of Appeal overturned,[193] and relying on *Walker v Inter-Alliance Group*[194] or *Rubenstein v HSBC*[195] on 'advice' held that:

> [T]he simple giving of information without any comment will not normally amount to 'advice'. On the other hand ... the provision of information which 'is itself the product of a process of selection involving a value judgment so that the information will tend to influence the decision of the recipient' is capable of constituting 'advice' ... 'any element of comparison or evaluation or persuasion is likely to cross the dividing line' ... A communication to the effect that the recipient ought, say, to buy a specific investment can amount to 'advice on the merits' without elaboration on the features or advantages of the investment.[196]

10.68 The Court relied on the FCA's Guidance Manual to conclude that the advice related to a 'particular investment' because the advice 'can relate to a number of 'particular investments'.[197] Thus, CLP's encouragement to invest in storepods, combined with the introduction to Carey, was precise enough. Even if investing in a SIPP (regulated) was just the means to invest in storepods (unregulated) there had been a breach of regulatory rules. The Court also found CLP liable of engaging in the regulated activity of 'making arrangements' in investments, because CLP's actions had the 'causal potency' to lead to a deal (this is discussed in the next point).[198]

10.69 In summary, UK case law offers varying examples of the incidence of regulatory rules in private law ranging from the null or negligible (*Peekay, IFE, Springwell*, etc.) to *Ramesh* or *Adams* where the claim was based on a breach of regulatory provisions. 'Mixed' cases either refer to regulatory provisions to affirm private law independence from them, like *Thornbridge* or *Crestsign*, or to seek a sensible integration, like *Walker* or *Rubenstein*. The limited presence of *Rubenstein*-like cases suggests a still-compartmentalized view.

10.70 Civil law countries also offer a variety of approaches on the relationship between private law doctrines and regulatory provisions. These include cases of 'independent' approaches, but also 'symbiotic' approaches, where regulatory provisions have been instrumental for major changes in private law doctrines.

10.71 Courts in Germany have followed 'independent' approaches. In Germany it is long established that a bank advising a customer about a financial product enters a separate legal

---

[191] Based on MiFID, art 19(1).
[192] *Adams v Options Sipp UK LLP and Financial Conduct Authority* [2020] EWHC 1229 (Ch).
[193] *Adams v Options* (n 190).
[194] *Walker v Inter-Alliance Group* (n 172).
[195] *Rubenstein v HSBC* (n 180).
[196] *Adams v Options* (n 190) para 75.
[197] ibid paras 76–78.
[198] See section 3.4.

relationship, subject to enhanced good faith duties, where it must advise the client in in a way commensurate with the financial product, and the client's qualifications and readiness to take risks (*Bond* judgment).[199] The German Federal Supreme Court (BGH) has applied this approach in many cases. In 2011, the Court analysed the scope of an advisory bank's duty to inform about the Issuer's insolvency risk (Lehman Brothers) for 'basket certificates' or 'index certificates',[200] holding that, if the bank had already indicated that, in case of issuer or guarantor insolvency, the investor would lose all capital (general issuer risk), the bank was not bound to provide additional information about the failure of de-posit guarantee systems to intervene.[201]

10.72 In another 2011 case the Court held that, in marketing a 'spread ladder swap' to a producer of hygiene products the bank breached these duties and had to pay damages, since it failed to disclose that, at the time of contracting, the swap had a negative value (ie the expectation was that future payments would favour the bank).[202] In the Court's view, a bank must inquire about the investor's willingness to take risks before making a recommendation, unless it is already familiar with this aspect as a result of a long-term business relationship or the investor's previous investment decisions. In the case of a highly complex product, such as the swap, the information must ensure that the investor has essentially the same level of knowledge with regard to the risk of the transaction as the bank advising him, because only then it is possible to identify an independent decision. The bank does not need to explain that it is making profits with the products (as this is obvious), and there is generally no duty to disclose. However, the swap's negative market value created a serious conflict of interest, and the risk that the advice would not be made in the client's interest, and thus had to be disclosed. The Supreme Court has clarified, however, that the disclosure obligation of the negative market value does not arise when the advisory bank is not a party to the speculative swap transaction.[203]

10.73 Subsequent cases have also dealt with the duty to disclose specific circumstances that put the parties in an 'adversarial' position, or otherwise give rise to a conflict of interest. For example, in a case where index certificates were sold in a proprietary trading transaction (section 2(3) sentence 2 WpHG), the advising bank did not have to disclose its profit margin,[204] nor inform the customer that the certificate is acquired as part of the bank's proprietary trading.[205] However, there is an obligation of the advising bank to inform about payments received when selling media funds,[206] or about the receipt of hidden fees, regardless of their amount.[207]

10.74 German courts have also dealt with the issue of when the parties conduct their actions on the basis of a relationship of advice (*Anlageberatungsvertrag*), and when the intermediary will be acting as a securities broker (*Anlagevermittlungsvertrag*). They have treated this as a matter

---

[199] BGH, judgment Ref No XI ZR 12/93 (6 July 1993).
[200] BGH, judgments no XI ZR178/10 and no XI ZR182/10 (27 September 2011).
[201] BGH judgment no XI ZR182/10 (27 September 2011).
[202] BGH judgment no XI ZR 33/10 (22 March 2011).
[203] BGH, judgment XI ZR316/13 (20 January 2015) with reference to BGH judgment no XI ZR 33/10 (22 March 2011).
[204] BGH judgment no XI ZR182/10 (27 September 2011). This is not contradicted by the German Federal Supreme Court case law on the disclosure of hidden internal fees or on the need to clarify the existence of reimbursements contradicts this. See BGH judgment XI ZR 191/10, WM2011, 925 Rn 20 ff (9 March 2011).
[205] BGH judgment no XI ZR182/10 (27 September 2011).
[206] BGH, decision XI ZR510/07 (20 January 2009).
[207] BGH, judgment XI ZR147/12 (3 June 2014).

of contract interpretation,[208] but with a different approach from that of English courts. They have treated the advisory relationship as a 'contract of advice' independent from the contract for the specific product or service and, most important, they have relied on the existence of a request of information by the client and the bank's awareness that the client would place special trust in that information to find the existence of 'advice', and treated other factors, eg whether it was the customer's initiative or the bank's, whether a fee was agreed, etc. as secondary.[209]

Nonetheless, a brokerage relationship can also result in liability. The Supreme Court has held that an investment broker owes the investor a correct and complete information about the factual circumstances that were of particular importance for the investment decision of the interested party,[210] and must also check the investment concept about which he is providing information, including the *plausibility* of the statements made, in particular about economic viability.[211] In the contract initiation meeting, the broker may give the client a prospectus, instead of a verbal explanation of the investment, if this is suitable in form and content, and the information is truthful and conveyed in an understandable way *before* the conclusion of the contract.[212] Then, the broker must assess the prospectus' plausibility, to ensure that it gives a coherent overall picture of the investment, and objectively complete and correct information; and, if no plausibility check has been carried out, the broker must also point this out to the client.[213] Thus, courts have required brokers to perform plausibility checks to a prospectus for an investment in wind turbines,[214] or to the models to calculate a real estate fund's profitability facilitated by the fund initiator to the broker, which he facilitated to the client.[215] Investment brokers may also have to disclose the internal fees paid for sales that was not listed in the prospectus.[216]

10.75

Although courts acknowledge the importance of regulatory provisions like MiFID in framing and modulating private law duties, because their finality is investor protection, they have also insisted in the independence of private law duties,[217] and the fact that regulatory provisions do not create *independent duties* under private law.[218] They have applied this general principle in rejecting, for example, that regulatory restrictions on the acceptance of inducements from third parties in relation to the provision of investment services may be binding in private, contract-based, relationships of advice.[219] This may raise difficulties[220] if the Court of Justice takes *Genil's*[221] broad statement further, to mean that Member States have discretion to determine 'what', but not 'whether' private law consequences result from a breach of regulatory rules.

10.76

---

[208] Binder, 'Chapter 3: Germany' (n 142) para 68.
[209] ibid para 69 and authorities cited.
[210] BGH judgment III ZR 145/06- NJW-RR 2007 (12 July 2007).
[211] BGH judgments III ZR 413/04 (12 May 2005) III ZR 62/99 (13 January 2000).
[212] BGH judgments from III ZR 145/06 NJW-RR 2007 (12 July 2007); and III ZR 218/06 NJW-RR 2007 (22 March 2007).
[213] ibid.
[214] BGH judgment no III ZR 17/08 (5 March 2009).
[215] BGH, judgment III ZR144/10 (17 February 2011).
[216] BGH, judgment III ZR218/06 (22 March 2007) Real estate fund.
[217] Binder, 'Chapter 3: Germany' (n 142) 73.
[218] BGH judgment XI ZR 56/05 (19 December 2006).
[219] Bundesgerichtshof, XI ZR 332/12 (19 December 2013).
[220] Binder, 'Chapter 3: Germany' (n 142) 73.
[221] *Genil* (n 160).

10.77 Other civil law countries exemplify 'symbiotic' approaches, since their courts have used regulatory provisions to reformulate private law duties and doctrines. Italy was a relatively early adopter of regulatory provisions as guidance for private law duties.[222] In a first wave of litigation over bonds issued by sovereigns (Argentina) and corporates (Cirio and Parmalat), the courts helped to accommodate the new standards in traditional private law doctrines, including precontractual liability, contractual liability, avoidance based on 'mistake/error' (relative nullity), and avoidance for breach of mandatory rules (absolute nullity).[223] In a 2008 decision, the Supreme Court held that the duties imposed by the Consolidated Financial Act provided for more intense duties than the Civil Code, which should be construed according to their finality (investor protection).[224] It was followed by other decisions, where courts enabled the transition by declaring that regulatory duties were an expression of the principle of good faith.[225] These comprise a duty properly to inform the client, a duty to draft clauses in a relatively simple language,[226] or the duties to assess the 'suitability' and 'appropriateness', a common source of complaints.[227]

10.78 Nonetheless, in 2007 the Supreme Court also limited this expansion, holding that COB rules are not 'mandatory rules', which give rise to annulment actions, but admitting that their breach could give rise to precontractual liability, and to damages for breach of contract.[228] This contrasts with the approach consisting in rendering the contract void, like that of courts in Spain, or Italian case law on swaps concluded by municipalities.[229]

10.79 In Spain, case law on 'mis-selling' of financial products was relatively scant before MiFID, and courts tended to see the issue in purely contact terms, to the benefit of banks and investment firms. In late 2012, a case decided by the Spanish Supreme Court considered the swap valid and binding under a traditional application of the doctrine of 'mistake',[230] because, although the swap was not a hedge, but speculative, 'the client was aware of such speculative nature'. There was no 'mistake' because there was no 'malicious concealment' of information, and because the client understood the *nature* of the transaction (the *alea*, or risk).

10.80 Then, it all changed. In January 2014, in another swap case, the Supreme Court accepted a doctrine developed by the lower courts, which, in essence, posited that the breach of mandatory provisions on the classification of clients (suitability and appropriateness) constituted prima facie evidence of 'mistake', which resulted in the contract's annulment.[231] Although by itself, the failure to comply with information duties did not necessarily entail an 'error', the regulatory provisions, based on the bank-client informational asymmetry, could influence the assessment of a 'mistake'. Furthermore, the doctrinal requirement that the 'mistake' must fall over the *object* of the contract should be interpreted as comprising the mistake over the 'specific risks' of the swap. Thus, given the mandatory requirement to provide information,

---

[222] Federico della Negra, 'The Private Enforcement of the MiFID Conduct of Business Rules: An Overview of the Italian and Spanish Experiences' (2014) 10 ERCL 571. See also Filippo Rossi and Marco Garavelli, 'Chapter 6: Italy' in Danny Busch and Cees van Dam (eds), *A Bank's Duty of Care* (Hart Publishing 2019) 139.
[223] See della Negra (n 222).
[224] Italian Supreme Court decision, Cass Civ n 17340 (25 June 2008).
[225] Court of Appeal of Milan Decision n 1094 (15 April 2009). See Rossi and Garavelli (n 222) 1406.
[226] Italian Supreme Court judgment 5 April 2004, n 7776. See Rossi and Garavelli (n 222) 146.
[227] See Rossi and Garavelli (n 222) 147.
[228] Italian Supreme Court Plenary judgments n 26724 and 26725 (19 December 2007). See della Negra (n 222) 582.
[229] See section 2.
[230] Spanish Supreme Court decision no 683/2012, RoJ 7843/2012 ECLI:ES:TS:2012:7843 (21 November 2012).
[231] Spanish Supreme Court decision no 840/2013 ECLI:ES:TS:2014:354, (20 January 2014).

one could assume that such information, including the 'guidance and warnings about the risks associated with such instruments', are essential for the retail customer to give a valid consent, and that ignoring such specific risks was prima facie evidence that consent was based on a wrong mental representation or 'error'; 'essential' because it affected the main cause of the contracting. To the Court, the duties to assess the suitability and/or appropriateness of the product for the client were also relevant to assess the 'mistake'. The Court concluded that there was a relationship of financial advice, and the lower court was correct in annulling the swap contract, and it expanded the doctrine of 'mistake', to encompass not only the general idea of risk, but also the specific product's risks. There and in subsequent rulings[232] the Spanish Supreme Court relied in *Genil*[233] to limit the scope of 'execution only' relations, making it extremely difficult, if not impossible, for a bank to rely on this regime when selling a complex product, like a swap, especially to retail clients.

10.81 In conclusion, mandatory provisions can influence the substance and remedies of domestic private law very much, or very little. In the EU the Court of Justice acts as an arbiter, using the principle of effectiveness to foster convergence when needed. Yet, it is hard to believe that a single principle can give rise to such seemingly different approaches. The Court has used the principle boldly in the field of consumer protection, creating a 'material transparency' test, expanding it into a bank's duty to provide precontractual information that makes the consequences understandable for the consumer, and attaching to the breach of this duty the same remedy as to the unfairness of the clause itself, ie the invalidity of the clause itself. None of these steps was preordained; they have been doctrinal choices by the Court, which has not hesitated to push back on domestic law when it threatened these choices. The Court has not done anything comparable in the field of capital markets law. In the field of prospectus liability the Court has taken some tentative steps despite national courts seem to be converging in some respects (see Chapter 9, section 3.2). In the field of financial intermediaries' duties under MiFID, the Court has been even more prudent still, at least for the moment. Part of the reason for this contrast may be that the Unfair Contracts Directive makes express to 'invalidity', which has given the Court of Justice a remedial entry point. Be it as it may, there is currently an asymmetry between transparency duties under consumer law, where right and remedy are relatively comprehensive and harmonized, and under financial law, where lack of harmonization of remedies hinders the protection of rights. This is ironic, considering that MiFID regulates intermediaries' duties more extensively than consumer rules do.

3.4 Regulatory requirements and private law duties in the EU (II): causal link, reliance, and basis clauses

10.82 In fashioning a private right of action for breach of regulatory provisions, 'creating' the plaintiff's right is as important as delineating the defendant's defences (see eg Chapter 9, section 3.2). In particular, the causal link, the investor reliance, and the courts' *presumptions* and allocation of the burden of proof, are essential, and a major point of contention in some cases. Defendants tend to argue that investors did not rely on the information given, or that

---

[232] Spanish Supreme Court decisions n 384/2014 ES:TS:2014:2659 (7 July 2014); n 385/2014 ES:TS:2014:2660 (8 July 2014); n 387/2014 ES:TS:2014:2666 (8 July 2014).
[233] *Genil* (n 160).

they signed clauses stating that the investor 'is aware' of, or 'understands' the risks ('basis' clauses). Regulatory provisions can shape these defences, and vice-versa the defences can bolster regulatory rules, or deprive them of effectiveness. This, in turn, is a task for the courts.

10.83 Courts in the UK have extensive experience enforcing 'basis clauses' or 'non-reliance clauses'.[234] *Peekay*,[235] *Springwell*,[236] or *Raiffeisen*[237] are a benchmark of comparison, as they involved sophisticated investors, and no regulatory provisions. In such case, if parties agree on a particular state of affairs as the basis of their transactions, they are estopped from asserting different facts (*Peekay*); or relying on certain views as 'representations' (in *Springwell* they were characterized as 'opinions', but a 'non reliance' clause estopped the client from relying on them).[238] In *Raiffeisen* Clarke J reasoned that whether a non-reliance clause could be deemed a clause excluding or restricting liability, potentially invalid under section 11(1) of the Unfair Contract Terms Act 1977, depended on 'whether the clause attempts to rewrite history or parts company with reality'. In his view, in the case of sophisticated commercial parties, the clause was an agreement on the information used by the partis as a basis for contracting, and not an exclusion of liability. In *Crestsign*[239] the bank recommended specific swap structures, and its employee was referred to as an 'expert', to explain them to the client; the judge found that the banks owed a duty to use reasonable skill,[240] acknowledged 'the disparity in knowledge and expertise', which made it 'reasonable to rely' on the bankers' skill and judgment, and referred to the possibility of a 'mezzanine' duty to inform (beyond basic duties, but not reaching 'advisory duties'). He also held that the bank would have been negligent *had there been advice*. And yet, the contract clauses disclaiming the existence of advice, [241]led the court to rely on *Henderson v Merrett Syndicates*[242] to hold that 'an assumption of responsibility may be negatived by an appropriate disclaimer', and on *Raiffeisen* to consider that the clauses were not liability exclusion clauses, but 'basis' clauses, because 'they defined the relationship as one in which advice was not being given', which, in itself, erased the basis for liability. In *obiter* fashion, the court mentioned that, had the clauses been liability exclusions, they would have been null, for being 'unreasonable' under section 2 of the Unfair Contract Terms Act 1977 (UCTA).

10.84 In *Rubenstein v HSBC*[243] the outcome was different. The High Court rejected the bank's allegation that the client had contracted on an 'execution only' basis, because the protocols for 'execution only' services' were not followed, and the exchange between bank employee and client suggested a relationship of advice.[244] Then, on the customer's 'reliance', the court held

---

[234] See section 3.3.
[235] *Peekay* (n 106).
[236] Springwell (n 109) and also [2008] EWHC 1793 (Comm). Some points were appealed in *Springwell 2010* (n 109).
[237] *Raiffeisen* (n 111).
[238] *Springwell* (n 109) paras 171, 186. Also, the clients were not passive investors, and the investment decisions reflected their preferences.
[239] *Crestsign* (n 126).
[240] Citing *Hedley Byrne* (n 103).
[241] The terms of business for retail clients included, in bold the clause: 'We will not ... provide you with advice on the merits of a particular transaction or the composition of any *account ... in relation to any transaction or account*.' The clause was brought to Mr Parker's attention in a cover letter to the terms of business for retail clients and standalone derivate terms documents sent to Crestsign two days before the transaction completed, and they were also repeated in other transaction documents.
[242] *Henderson v Merrett Syndicates Ltd* [1995] 2 AC 145.
[243] See section 2.4 for a discussion of the facts.
[244] *Rubenstein v HSBC* (n 177) para 73. The instruction form for the non-advised sales process was not used and no-one ticked the non-advice box for Mr Rubenstein. The absence of a know-your-customer (KYC) form was not enough evidence to contradict this finding. ibid 75–76.

that, unlike *Peekay* or *Springwell* there had been no non-reliance form or clause, and that the important thing was whether the advice had been negligently provided (it was) and whether the client understood the risks (he did not).[245] Yet, despite concluding that there was advice, negligently provided and relied upon, the judge held that the damage was not 'caused' by the advice on a product, but by the exceptional market turmoil following the collapse of Lehman Brothers (a large investment bank), and the 'unthinkable' run on AIG (an insurer), and, relying on *SAAMCO*, that the timescale of the investment (one year) meant that the bank's scope of liability did not extend to facts happening long after the advice was given;[246] the damage was too remote.[247]

10.85 The Court of Appeal disagreed, because the bank had advised to invest in the specific product.[248] Crucially, the correct approach was not to separate between liability in negligence and contract, on one side, and regulatory provisions on the other side: under *SAAMCO*, the *scope* of the duty in tort depended on the purpose of the rule, in contract on the nature and extent of liability under the implied term, and in case of statutory duty on the statute itself, and thus 'the position in negligence and contract will fall in behind the statutorily discerned purpose'.[249] The Court held that FSMA COB rules sought to strengthen consumer protection, thus 'what connected the erroneous advice and the loss was the combination of putting Mr Rubenstein into a fund which was subject to market losses while at the same time misleading him by telling him that his investment was the same as a cash deposit, when it was not'.[250] The investment's timescale was not determinative of the scope of liability, because in practice the investment was made while Mr Rubenstein found a new home (and thus depended on how quickly he found it[251]), and the difference between one and three years was not too great for a cash deposit-equivalent, which is what the bank had advised.[252]

10.86 In *Ramesh Parmar v Barclays*,[253] the High Court rejected the existence of advice, and the breach of regulatory rules, but, in a moral victory for the plaintiff, it held that the bank could not rely on its 'basis clause'. The regulatory rules (COBS 2.1.2) prevented firms from 'seeking to (1) exclude or restrict; or (2) rely on any exclusion or restriction of; any duty or liability it may have to a client under the regulatory system'. The court rejected the bank's argument that this provision was equivalent to s3 of UCTA, holding that COBS 2.1.2 went further than section 3 UCTA, because it prevents 'a party creating an artificial basis for the relationship, if the reality is different'. Thus, had the bank been giving advice, it could not have relied on the basis clause.

---

[245] *Rubenstein v HSBC* (n 177) para 99: 'The adviser's skill lies in matching the product to the client's needs and circumstances. If the wrong product is recommended, and loss is suffered because the client chooses to invest in it, it does not follow that the recommendation did not cause the loss simply because the client said that he understood its key features ... Mr Rubenstein's understanding of the key features of the EVRF is not what matters. What matters is whether he properly understood the risk. It was Mr Marsden's obligation to make sure that he did.'
[246] The judge relied on *SAAMCO*, and Lord Hoffmann's 'mountaineer example'. See ch 9, s 4.1.
[247] *Rubenstein v HSBC* (n 177) paras 108–16.
[248] On the use of *SAAMCO*'s 'mountaineer example', the Court of Appeal in *Rubenstein v HSBC Bank Plc* [2012] EWCA Civ 1184 held, at 103: 'The doctor did not advise, let alone recommend, his patient to go mountaineering: he merely told him that his knee was in good shape. Mr Marsden, however, not only advised Mr Rubenstein on the investment of his capital, but also recommended a particular investment.'
[249] ibid para 114.
[250] ibid para 118.
[251] ibid para 95.
[252] ibid paras 121–22.
[253] *Ramesh Parmar & Another v Barclays Bank plc* [2018] EWHC 1027 (Ch).

10.87 Then, in *Adams v Options*,[254] the Court of Appeal found the existence of 'advice' in the case of an unregulated entity (CLP), who advised on unregulated products (storepods) *through* an investment in regulated instruments (SIPP) in a regulated financial intermediary (Carey) and thus found a breach of the 'general prohibition' to undertake regulated activities (financial advice) without a licence.[255] The court also found that CLP had also engaged in the regulated activity of 'arranging deals' in investments. The relevant statutory text excluded from the definition of the regulated activity the 'arrangements which do not or would not bring about the transaction to which the arrangements relate'. Using precedents and the FCA's Guidance Manual, the court held that there had to be a 'causal connection' between the acts and the investment, but that a *conditio sine qua non*, or 'but for' test, could include too much, ie cases where the investment resulted from different interventions, all necessary, and too little, ie cases where arrangements 'do not necessarily result in anything further happening', but could potentially bring about a transaction.[256] Thus, the idea to 'bring about' required a 'causal potency' test.[257] The defendant met this test, because it had procured letters of authority, partially completed the application forms, instructed the company to identify pods to be sold, etc.,[258] and thus had breached the prohibition.

10.88 However, the way the arrangement was conducted, CLP (unlicensed party) brought the investors to Carey (licensed party) which would sign them up for the (unregulated) investments under an 'execution only' agreement, which excluded 'advice'. Even if a firm had breached the prohibition to undertake regulated activities without a licence, the FSMA allowed the court to respect the agreement '[i]f the court is satisfied that it is just and equitable in the circumstances of the case', and, for this purpose, regard should be had to 'whether the provider knew that the third party was (in carrying on the regulated activity) contravening the general prohibition'. To the Court, the reference to 'knew' meant *actual* knowledge, and Carey did not have actual knowledge of CLP's breaches.[259] And yet, although the provider's *knowledge* is a relevant factor, it 'by no means dictates the conclusion that … discretion must be exercised in its favour'.[260] Thus, the Court held that, in light of all circumstances, discretion should not be exercised in the intermediary's favour, because this created moral hazard.[261] The concurring opinion by Lady J Andrews put it eloquently:

> As the unhappy history of the transfers of small personal pensions into SIPPs holding high risk investments related in that judgment illustrates, the liberalisation of the pension regime in 2006 brought with it fresh opportunities for unscrupulous entities to target the gullible, the greedy or the desperate. There is nothing to prevent a regulated SIPP provider such as Carey from accepting instructions from clients recommended to it by an unregulated person, and from doing so on an 'execution only' basis. But the basis on which they

---

[254] *Adams v Options* (n 190).
[255] See sections 3.1.1, 3.1.3, 3 1.4.
[256] *Adams v Options* (n 190) para 95.
[257] ibid para 97.
[258] ibid paras 98–100, with reference to para 48, describing the steps.
[259] ibid paras 108–10.
[260] ibid para 111. It may still be appropriate to deny relief if there are other factors present, such as whether 'the provider should reasonably have known that the general prohibition was being contravened'.
[261] There were many reasons supporting the Court's conclusion, among them: (i) a key aim of the FSMA was consumer protection (which ran contrary to the intermediary's assertion that the plaintiff caused his own losses); (ii) s 27 FSMA placed the risk of accepting introductions from unregulated sources on the regulated providers (a sort of anti-moral hazard provision); and (iii) in a six-month period, 580 of Carey's clients invested in storepods, despite their being high risk and non-standard investments, most of them via CLP, and there were hints that many clients were neither rich nor sophisticated (due to the relatively low amounts); (iv) Carey learned that CLP was receiving high fees from the storepods providers. See *Adams v Options* (n 190) para 115.

contract with their clients will only go so far to protect them from liability. If they accept business from the likes of CLP, they run the risk of being exposed to liability under section 27 of the FSMA.[262]

By way of summary, although they eloquently empathise with investors' plight, when it comes to ruling UK courts generally rely on contract clauses, even boilerplate ones, to establish the basis on which the parties agree. Thus, in practice bank clients face important obstacles when trying to allege misselling, and may only be protected in cases where the conduct falls squarely within concrete regulatory provisions. **10.89**

German courts have a different approach. The existence of 'advice' depends not only on the written contract, but also on the parties' communications. Furthermore, and on the issue of causation, reliance, and other defences, courts have often reversed the burden of proof, requiring the financial institution who breached disclosure duties to prove that the damage would have occurred anyway, ie that the client would have ignored the advice.[263] The trial court must still question the plaintiff if the defendant alleges that the product would have been acquired anyway, and look at all the facts to make such determination.[264] Yet, courts have rejected some banks' strategies to establish non-reliance, break the causal link, or balance their alleged breach of duties, such as allegations about the professional qualification of an investor's employee as a graduate economist,[265] or about the fact that the investor did not read the subscription slip which was briefly given to him for signature *after* the advice was given (thus, not detecting the contradiction between the advice and the investment description was not grossly negligent[266]). Also, a financial intermediary should not have automatically concluded from the fact that an investor refused to accept an issue prospectus as 'too thick and heavy' and just 'paperwork' that he was not interested in any other risk information, nor did this restrict advisory duties, eg risk and other sensitive information.[267] Boilerplate 'basis' clauses stating that the investor took note of risk information have been considered ineffective.[268] Indeed, acknowledgement of receipt of such provisions must be signed separately from the rest of the contract, and not include other declarations.[269] **10.90**

In Italy, the courts' assimilation of regulatory standards into private law doctrines was accompanied by an adaptation of the rules on the distribution of burden of proof, and thus on causation and reliance. The leading cases decided by the Supreme Court in 2007 discussed in the previous point,[270] relied on the text of the Consolidated Financial Act, which went beyond MiFID provisions, by stipulating a reversal of the burden of proof, which also meant **10.91**

---

[262] ibid para 131 (Andrews LJ).
[263] BGH judgment XI ZR 214/92 (16 November 1993) BGHZ 124, 151, 159 ff. This does not depend on whether or not an investor would have faced a decision-making conflict if properly advised. Focusing on the potential decision-making conflict is not compatible with the protective purpose of reversing the burden of proof. BGH, judgment XI ZR 262/10 (8 May 2012). See also BGH judgment III ZR 176/18 (16 May 2019).
[264] BGH, judgment XI ZR 262/10 (8 May 2012).
[265] BGH, judgment XI ZR33/10 (22 March 2011). The fact that one of the investor's employees was a graduate economist cannot establish a presumption that he understood the specific risks of a complex product like a CMS spread ladder swap.
[266] BGH, judgment III ZR93/16 (23 March 2017). The fact that the investor has failed to read through the issue prospectus presented to him does not entail gross negligence. BGH, judgment III ZR249/09 (8 July 2010).
[267] BGH judgment III ZR 498/16 (7 February 2019).
[268] Under s 309 No 12 Clause 1 Letter b of the German Civil Code (BGB). See BGH judgment of III ZR 109/17 (10 January 2019).
[269] Furthermore, the question of whether the investor has had enough time to take note of a prospectus made available to him for information about the risks of the investment, among other things, depends on the specific circumstances of the individual case. There is no standard deadline. BGH judgment of 10 January 2019 III ZR 109/17.
[270] See s 309 No 12 Clause 2 BGB.

that, in case of breach of MiFID provisions, it was for the financial intermediary to prove the lack of causal link and/or the client's non-reliance.

10.92 The Spanish Supreme Court after its change of doctrine,[271] clarified that what vitiates the consent by 'error/mistake' is not the failure to inform, or assess the suitability or appropriateness, but the lack of knowledge of the contracted product and its specific risks, ie the wrong mental representation about the contract's object. Thus, there could be a breach of regulatory duties and still no 'mistake', if, for example, the client already knew the information. Yet, a failure to inform leads to presume the existence of mistake, and also the 'excusability' of the error (another private law requirement), because if the retail customer needed this information and the financial institution was obliged to provide it, not knowing the product's risks is excusable to the client.

4 Financial contracts' interpretation: express versus implied duties, specificity versus coherence

10.93 'Pure' contract disputes require courts to 'enforce the terms of the contract'. This is harder than it looks. In practice, as they seek to ascertain the contract's meaning, courts have to balance at least two types of tensions. First, in many disputes that are not allegedly about the 'marketing' process (as analysed in previous sections), parties (clients, typically) allege that the contract rested on some shared understanding that went beyond its letter, which introduces a tension between express terms and implied terms and/or reasonableness, or good faith (section 3.1). Secondly, courts' interpretation has to balance the need to ascertain the meaning of the concrete contract terms (specificity) with the need to ensure coherence in the solution to conflicts that are functionally similar, typically about whether a 'default' has occurred and its consequences (section 3.2) and the enforcement, including material adverse events (section 3.3).

4.1 Contract interpretation: reasonableness, express, and implied terms

10.94 As we move past cases where regulatory duties are involved, banks', and financial intermediaries' clients claims about the breach of 'standards' do not subside. They just mutate. Instead of claiming a breach of mandatory provisions, clients allege breaches of implied terms, or a conduct considered 'unreasonable', or in breach of 'good faith'. This means that standards of contract interpretation must be analysed together with implied duties.

10.95 In the UK there is no implied duty of good faith,[272] which means that claims focus on the existence of implied duties of reasonableness and common sense, or contract interpretation. In *Investors Compensation Scheme (ICS) Ltd*[273] investors were persuaded to mortgage their property and buy equity-linked bonds with the cash, lost money, and were compensated by the ICS, to which they assigned their claims, but with a section 3(b) excluding 'Any claim

---

[271] Spanish Supreme Court decision no 840/2013 (n 231).
[272] *Walford v Miles* [1992] 2 AC 128. However, see *Yam Seng Pte v International Trade Corp* [2013] EWHC 111 (QB).
[273] *Investors Compensation Scheme Ltd v West Bromwich Building Society* [1997] UKHL 28.

(whether sounding in rescission for undue influence or otherwise) that you have or may have against the West Bromwich Building Society'. ICS sued, and West Bromwich alleged that the 'or otherwise' excluded damages, and not only rescission claims, while ICS argued that 'or otherwise' comprised rescission-based, but not damages claims. The House of Lords concluded that the damages claim had been assigned (unlike the rescission claims), but more importantly, Lord Hoffman set an influential standard,[274] which held that contract interpretation (1) is the ascertainment of the meaning which the document would convey to a reasonable person having all the background knowledge reasonably available to the parties in the situation in which they were at the time of the contract; (2) that background comprises the so-called 'matrix of fact', which includes anything affecting how the language of the document would have been understood by a reasonable man; but (3) excludes the previous negotiations of the parties and their declarations of subjective intent (admissible only in an action for rectification) for reasons of practical policy (to limit litigation); then, according to the *meaning* of the document to a reasonable person, (4) this is not the same thing as the meaning of its words; the latter is a matter of dictionaries and grammars; the meaning of the document is what the parties using those words against the relevant background would reasonably have been understood to mean;[275] and (5) the 'rule' that words should be given their 'natural and ordinary meaning' reflects the common sense proposition that we do not easily accept that people have made linguistic mistakes, particularly in formal documents.[276]

Contracting parties may differ about what is 'reasonable', and in the financial context, sophisticated parties tend to insist on the contract's literal language. Whether and how far was discussed by the Supreme Court in *Rainy Sky SA and Others v Kookmin Bank*,[277] an acquisition by a ship owner (Rainy Sky) of vessels from a South Korean shipbuilder (Jinse) under a performance bond subscribed with Kookmin Bank to guarantee the repayment of the buyer's money. Rainy Sky made two payments, Jinse entered insolvency, and Rainy Sky sought payment of the bond. Kookmin Bank objected, since the bond clause stated, that: 'Pursuant to the terms of the Contract, you [Rainy Sky] are entitled, upon your rejection of the Vessel in accordance with the terms of the Contract, your termination, cancellation or rescission of the Contract or upon a Total Loss of the Vessel, to repayment of the pre-delivery instalments.' However, in paragraph [3] it stated that 'we hereby ... undertake to pay to you ... all such sums due to you under the Contract'. Thus, the bank argued that the bond only covered 'rejection of the vessel' and 'termination, cancellation or rescission of the contract', not Jinse's insolvency. **10.96**

The High Court found in Rainy Sky's favour, focusing on the reference in paragraph [3] to 'all such sums', but the Court of Appeal, relying on *ICS*'s 'matrix of facts' supported Kookmin's interpretation,[278] holding that 'all *such* sums' (emphasis added) referred to the sums under paragraph [2], since the alternative 'robs paragraph 2 of any purpose or effect'.[279] This was 'commercially reasonable' for the Court because[280] the interpretation, although unfavourable to **10.97**

---

[274] ibid.
[275] ibid, citing *Mannai Investments Co Ltd v Eagle Star Life Assurance Co Ltd* [1997] 2 WLR 945 ('background may not merely enable the reasonable man to choose between the possible meanings of words which are ambiguous but even ... to conclude that the parties must ... have used the wrong words or syntax').
[276] *ICS v West* (n 273).
[277] *Rainy Sky SA and Others v Kookmin Bank* [2011] UKSC 50, 1 All ER (Comm) 1.
[278] *Kookmin Bank v Rainy Sky SA and Others* [2010] 1 CLC 829, [2010] EWCA Civ 582, [2011] 1 All ER (Comm) 18, 130 Con LR 19.
[279] ibid para 49.
[280] ibid paras 39–41, citing *Wickman Machine Tools Sales Ltd v Schuler AG* [1974] AC 235; *Antaios Compania Naviera SA v Salen Rederierna AB* [1985] AC 191; and *Chartbrook Ltd v Persimmon Homes Ltd* [2009] 1 AC 1101.

Rainy Sky, was not 'absurd or irrational' or 'so extreme as to suggest that it was unintended'.[281] The Supreme Court, however,[282] held that if the parties have not used unambiguous language,[283] it was necessary 'to strive to attribute to it a meaning which accords with business common sense'.[284] In case of a poorly drafted contract:

> [T]he poorer the quality of the drafting, the less willing the court should be to be driven by semantic niceties to attribute to the parties an improbable and unbusinesslike intention, if the language used, whatever it may lack in precision, is reasonably capable of an interpretation which attributes to the parties an intention to make provision for contingencies inherent in the work contracted for on a sensible and businesslike basis.[285]

10.98 In other words, even when poorly drafted, a contract's language must be enforced, but courts will not go to decipher an obscure clause by attributing to it an 'unbusinesslike commercial result'.[286] Thus, although acknowledging that construing clause [A] in the way suggested by Rainy Sky made clause [B] a bit pointless, the Court held that excluding the payment of the bond would lead to 'the surprising and uncommercial result' that the Buyers would not be able to call on the Bonds on the Builder's insolvency, which would be most likely to require the first class security'.[287]

10.99 Since contract language comes first, and common sense is secondary, clients often argue that contract included *implied* terms, which are needed to make sense of the contract language, or result from representations by the other party, or default rules applicable to the contract, or from the existence of *discretion*. In *Paragon Finance*,[288] the Court of Appeal found that a mortgagee with the power to set interest rates under a variable rate mortgage (and who refused to lower it, in line with other market rates), was subject to an implied term not to impose unreasonable or extortionate rates, nor to act with an 'unreasonable, improper, dishonest or capricious purpose', but held that such duty had not been breached, since the rates were not 'extortionate' in light of the time when the bargain was made, and were justified by commercial considerations, nor were they 'unreasonable', in the sense of a conduct or decision that no reasonable person would subscribe.

10.100 In *Socimer v Standard Bank*,[289] Socimer had purchased from Standard a portfolio of emerging market debt, whose value, after Socimer went into liquidation, was to be determined by Standard Bank, which was hard, given that some securities were particularly illiquid. Socimer argued that there was an implied term to engage in an 'honest attempt at

---

[281] ibid para 51.
[282] *Rainy Sky SA and Others v Kookmin Bank* (n 277).
[283] ibid para 23, in which case the court must apply if, even if unreasonable.
[284] ibid para 24, citing *International Fina Services AG v Katrina Shipping Ltd (The Fina Samco)* [1995] 2 Lloyd's Rep 344.
[285] *Rainy Sky SA and Others v Kookmin Bank* (n 277) 26, the quote was from *Gan Insurance Co Ltd v Tai Ping Insurance Co Ltd* [2001] CLC 1103, 1118–19; [2011] EWCA Civ 1047; [2001] 2 All ER (Comm) 299, which, in turn, was citing *Sinochem International Oil (London) Ltd v Mobil Sales and Supply Corp* [2000] CLC 878 at p 885, which was citing *Mitsui Construction Co Ltd v A-G of Hong Kong* [1986] 33 BLR 14.
[286] For such 'reasonableness-based' or 'commonsensical' approach the Court referred to *Barclays Bank plc and Others v HHY Luxembourg SARL and Another* [2010] EWCA Civ 1248; *In the Matter of Golden Key Ltd (In Receivership)* [2009] EWCA Civ 636; *In Re Sigma Finance Corporation (in administrative receivership)* [2009] UKSC 2; [2010] 1 All ER 571,.
[287] *Rainy Sky SA and Others v Kookmin Bank* (n 277) para 41.
[288] *Paragon Finance plc v Nash and Others* [2001] EWCA Civ 1466, [2002] 1 WLR 685.
[289] *Socimer International Bank Ltd v Standard Bank London Ltd* [2008] Bus LR 1304, [2008] 1 Lloyd's Rep 558, [2008] EWCA Civ 116.

a valuation which most fairly and reasonably reflects the value of the Designated Asset in question at the termination date',[290] but the opinion by Rix distinguished between 'a duty to act reasonably', eg a duty to arrive at a reasonable price, which 'is intended to be entirely mutual and thus guided by objective criteria', and in case of dispute, 'the decision-maker becomes the court itself';[291] and 'a duty to not act unreasonably',[292] applicable here, following *Paragon*,[293] which is subject to concepts of 'honesty, good faith and genuineness', and the 'absence of arbitrariness, capriciousness, perversity and irrationality',[294] which allows a party to look after its interest.

The *Socimer* standard was followed in many cases.[295] In *Torre v The Royal Bank of Scotland*[296] Sales J held that the discretion of an agent bank with the duties owed to the mezzanine lenders in a structured loan facility,[297] only to find that, although an event of default had not been notified, there was no breach of the duty because no one in the RBS team believed that such default had existed, and the bank was not 'aware of any default'. Sales J also rejected that there could be an implied duty to communicate relevant information as arising from the law of agency, since the duties were defined by the documents.[298] Nor was such duty implied in such documents. First, it was not *necessary* to imply it. Secondly, the contract clause provided that, absent instructions from lenders, the agent 'may act (or refrain from taking action) as it considers to be in the best interest of the Lenders', which, under the *Socimer* standard, would conflict with the implied duty suggested by the plaintiffs. Finally, the occurrence of an event of default 'may involve difficult evaluative judgments', and the contract indicated that the agent would not be responsible for such judgments'.

10.101

In the US, courts consider that debt contracts (including indentures) are subject to the general rules of contract interpretation. In *Chesapeake Energy Corp. v Bank of New York*[299] the court held that, when interpreting an indenture's terms one should assume that 'the intent of the parties must be found within the four corners of the contract'. Only if a reasonably intelligent person looking at the contract objectively could interpret the language in more than one way, the court could deem the text ambiguous and consider extrinsic evidence. However, what is 'ambiguous' can be, itself, ambiguous, and in *Chesapeake* the lower court found that the language of the indenture 'unambiguously' authorized Chesapeake (the issuer) to redeem the notes at the special price by giving notice of redemption during the special early redemption period,[300] and the appellate court found that the terms of the indenture unambiguously terminated Chesapeake's right to redeem the notes at the special price (thus finding in favour of the noteholder plaintiffs).[301]

10.102

---

[290] ibid para 45.
[291] ibid para 66.
[292] ibid paras 64, 66, 73, with references to *Associated Provincial Picture Houses Ltd v Wednesbury Corporation* [1948] 1 KB 223.
[293] ibid para 64.
[294] ibid paras 66, 73.
[295] These range from High Court cases (eg *Lehman Brothers International (Europe) v JFB Firth Rixson* [2010] EWHC 3372, or *LBI EHF v Raiffeisen Zentral Bank Osterreich* [2017] EWHC 522) to Supreme Court cases (eg *Braganza v BP Shipping* [2015] UKSC 17).
[296] *Torre v The Royal Bank of Scotland* [2013] EWHC 2670 (Ch) [2013] WLR(D) 343, 35.
[297] ibid para 37.
[298] ibid para 142.
[299] *Chesapeake Energy Corporation v Bank of New York Mellon Trust Company NA* [2013] 57 F Supp 2d 316 (SDNY).
[300] ibid.
[301] *Chesapeake Energy Corp v Bank of New York Mellon Trust Co NA* No 13-1893 (2d Cir 2014).

10.103 Contract law in some US states may differ from English law on implied duties. New York's law, the most popular for financial contracts, acknowledges that 'all contracts imply a covenant of good faith and fair dealing in the course of performance',[302] with similar views in the law of California,[303] although in Delaware courts seem to require the existence of a 'gap' in the contract to apply the duty,[304] which bears some resemblance with English courts' emphasis on 'commercial reasonableness' and 'business common sense' when there is lack of clarity. The duty of good faith, however, is not a duty to act in 'subjective good faith', and does not prevent opportunistic breach,[305] nor does it create new contract rights, or defeat express contract provisions.[306] In *Fesseha* the court rejected the plaintiffs' claim that the defendant violated the covenant of good faith and fair dealing in liquidating his securities without notice and opportunity to cure, holding that:

> While the covenant of good faith and fair dealing is implicit in every contract, it cannot be construed so broadly as effectively to nullify other express terms of a contract, or to create independent contractual rights … Here, the Customer Agreement expressly granted TD Waterhouse the right to liquidate plaintiff's positions 'when it deem[ed] it necessary for its protection' and nothing in the Truth in Lending Disclosure Statement limited that right.[307]

10.104 In civil law countries, the duty of good faith binds the parties *in addition to* express contract duties, and is reminiscent of 'implied terms' doctrines. In some European countries the duty of good faith in financial contracts and transactions has been shaped bearing in mind the scope of regulatory provisions applicable to the bank-client relationships, which may affect relationships of advice, but not only them,[308] while in others the doctrine of good faith (especially, although not only in pre-contractual situations) has developed independently from the regulatory provisions, although taking them into consideration.[309] Thus, in those jurisdictions the focus is often the configuration of express, and especially implied, obligations, in light of the representations made during the process of formation of the contract, which in turn depend on the duties applicable to the financial intermediary.

4.2 Contract interpretation: general considerations, events of default and valuation

10.105 The 'theme' underpinning the cases in this and the next point is the difficulty to reconcile 'contract precision' with 'market-wide consistency'. Financial transactions are risk-sensitive, and parties want to be certain when they can pull out of a transaction, and/or enforce its terms. Yet, this is trickier than it seems. On one hand, parties legitimately want courts to focus on the specific language of contract documents drafted for the specific transaction. On the other hand, a court determination that a 'default' has occurred will have an impact in transactions using similar contract terms, or terms having the same function, an effect that must

---

[302] *Owners Corp v Jennifer Realty Co* 98 NY 2d 144, 153 (2002).
[303] *ADE Systems Inc v Energy Labs Inc* 183 A D 3d 791 (2d Dept 2020).
[304] *Pilot Air Freight, LLC v Manna Freight Systems Inc* WL 5588671, paras 18–19 (Del Ch 2020).
[305] Adrienne B Koch, 'A Narrow Lane: Navigating Claims for Breach of the Duty of Good Faith and Fair Dealing' [2020] NYLJ 16 November 2020 https://katskykorins.com/a-narrow-lane-navigating-claims-for-breach-of-the-duty-of-good-faith-and-fair-dealing/ (accessed 5 October 2022).
[306] *Fesseha v TD Waterhouse Investment Services* 305 A D 2d 268 (1st Dept 2003).
[307] ibid.
[308] See section 3.2 for the references to Italian law or Spanish law.
[309] See sections 3.2, 3.3., and 3.4. for the references to German law.

also be weighted by the court. This effect is exacerbated when contract documents are based on 'boilerplate' terms, or contract documentation that is standardized across the market. In *Sharon Steel*,[310] although admitting that debt contracts should be construed under general principles of contract interpretation, the court also held that the interpretation of boilerplate language is a matter of law, not of fact, and courts need to pursue a uniform interpretation to ensure predictability and to foster efficient capital markets (a 'policy-driven' argument).

This balance between precision and consistency is present in cases about 'events of default'. In the US, despite *Sharon Steel* openly acknowledged that there were market-wide considerations at stake, courts are not always willing to go beyond the contract's express language. In *Eternity v Morgan*[311] the court did, finding that a 'voluntary exchange' of debt offered by the Argentinian government was, in reality, a 'mandatory transfer', which amounted to a 'restructuring', and thus a credit event.[312] Yet, in *Aon Financial Products v Société Générale*, the court found that there was an event of default in a credit default swap (CDS) between BSIL and Aon, hedging against a default by the Philippines Government Service Insurance System (GSIS), but not in another CDS between Aon and Société Génerale against a default by the 'Government of the Philippines'. Despite both contracts seemed to be concluded back-to-back, the court refused to overlook the formal language, under which a default by GSIS was not a default of the 'Government of the Philippines', and thus did not treat both contracts as a seamless transaction.[313] In *Wilmington Savings Fund Society v Cash America International Inc.*[314] the indenture provided that an 'event of default' would include 'prohibited transactions', whereby 'the aggregate book value of the properties' would exceed ten percent of the company's 'Consolidated Total Assets'.[315] Cash America spun off a subsidiary, Enova, and the court found an event of default, by making the assessment over total assets, leaving outside liabilities.

10.106

In other cases, courts went on to analyse the transaction's structure and objectives, and the clauses' function. In the CDO in *Deutsche Bank v Elliot International*, enforcement events triggered an extra-judicial administration and liquidation of the securitized asset pool. Yet, the trustee had filed an interpleader action (where a trustee who holds property on behalf of someone else seeks to establish to whom it should be transferred) the trustee 'short-circuited the Indenture's remedial procedures'. Thus, the court looked at what the parties intended, and concluded that an enforcement event had occurred.[316] In *U.S. Bank National Association v Barclays* the court stressed that it should construe the contract 'so as to give full meaning and effect to all of its provisions', and held that there was no event of default because the principal amounts that the trustee had failed to pay to Barclays had not yet become due and payable,[317] as part of its broader judgment on the trustee's diligence.

10.107

---

[310] *Sharon Steel Corp v Chase Manhattan Bank NA* 691 F 2d 1039 (2d Cir 1982).
[311] *Eternity Global Master Fund Ltd v Morgan Guar Trust Co of NY* 375 F 3d 168 (2d Cir 2004).
[312] ibid. The district court held that the term 'mandatory transfer' was 'ambiguous' and susceptible to more than one interpretation, and did not grant summary judgment. In further hearings, the court held that a 'mandatory transfer' could encompass debt exchanges offered in a way involving economic coercion.
[313] Although extrinsic evidence suggested that the protection buyer was trying to cover itself against the risk of the first contract, the court stuck to the express language of the agreements, which referred to different debtors and instruments. See *Aon Financial Products v Société Générale* 476 F 3d 90 (2d Cir 2007).
[314] Case No 15-CV-5027 (JMF) (SDNY 2016).
[315] ibid.
[316] The portfolio manager's acquisition of assets that did not meet the stated maturity requirements was a breach of R&W, and resulted in a notice of default by the 'Controlling Class' of Noteholders (Class A). *Deutsche Bank Trust Co Americas v Elliot International LP*, No 09 Civ 5242(WHP) 2011 WL 2421297 (SDNY 2011) on reconsideration in part, 2011 WL 10901798 (SDNY 2011).
[317] *US Bank NA v Barclays Bank PLC*, No 11 Civ 9199(WHP) 2013 WL 1180414 (SDNY 2013).

10.108 Courts in the UK show a similar balance between form and function. In *Grupo Hotelero Urvasco SA (GHU) v Carey*[318] GHU had two banking facilities, with Banco Bilbao Vizcaya Argentaria (BBVA), the group's main lender, and with Carey, a new lender once GHU began having difficulties with its bank finance. GHU sued Carey for failing to advance funding for the development of a hotel and apartments,[319] at a time of tight credit. Blair J, however, found for the bank.[320] The agreement sought to balance the interests of the creditor to protect itself in case of insolvency, and of the borrower in not imposing upon itself impractical restrictions. In light of this, it held that customary dealings over GHU's indebtedness would not, by itself, amount to a 'rescheduling' event of default, because they did not entail a 'formal deferment'.[321] However, since the lending agreement with Carey considered 'default' a default under the BBVA agreement, and this one provided that 'an event of default occurs if the company *begins* negotiations with *any* creditor for the rescheduling of any of its indebtedness', 'by reason of actual or anticipated financial difficulties' (this was the transaction's 'factual matrix'),[322] Blair concluded that there were several defaults. Growing financial difficulties forced the borrower to negotiate with its creditors beyond rescheduling in an ordinary course of business, or beyond the liquidity issues Carey was already aware of. Thus Carey was not estopped from relying on such facts.[323] Then, although BBVA waived other defaults in its loan (to persuade Carey to join the funding)[324] GHU's late payment to contractors met the loan clauses' 'materiality threshold', as it affected the borrower's ability to achieve Practical Completion by the Long Stop Date. Then, the state of the project's certification had been *forzado* (which could mean 'forced' or 'twisted') to show progress but in reality did not meet the requirements,[325] and also there had been a failure to advance the money to the project company.[326]

10.109 In *Torre Asset Funding*[327] junior mezzanine lenders sued the agent bank, Royal Bank of Scotland (RBS), which was also a senior lender in a structured financing deal to a property company (Dunedin), which became insolvent, leaving several funding tiers unpaid, the plaintiffs included. RBS Property Ventures (PV) Team acted both as Agent for B1 lenders and for RBS as lender at the junior subordinated mezzanine (or B2) level *and* as equity participants holding loan notes at the bottom of the finance structure. Dunedin's discussion with the PV team of a rolling up of interest for B2 lenders were considered an event of default, because 'by reason of actual or anticipated financial difficulties' Dunedin had commenced negotiations with one of its creditors (RBS was also a lender). Sales J relied on *Grupo Hotelero Urvasco*, since the event of default provisions were similarly worded, and its 'matrix of facts' to assess the seriousness of the dealings. In a highly leveraged transaction with tight financial covenants, Dunedin's inability to pay the interest in full for B2 and

---

[318] *Grupo Hotelero Urvasco SA v Carey Value Added SL* [2013] EWHC 1039.
[319] The development should take place on a prime site on the corner of Aldwych and the Strand in central London (the site of the old Marconi Building) bought in 2004 by Urvasco Ltd, an English subsidiary of GHU set up as the vehicle for the development. Various agreements were entered into on 21 December 2007, including a loan agreement. Had the agreements run their course, at completion, Carey would have acquired the property under a share purchase agreement, subject to a leaseback to GHU, which would have had an option to repurchase after seven years.
[320] The existence of a material adverse effect is analysed in section 3.3.
[321] *Grupo Hotelero Urvasco SA v Carey Value Added* (n 318) paras 573–74.
[322] ibid para 575.
[323] ibid paras 595–98.
[324] ibid paras 599–612.
[325] ibid paras 730–34. Nonetheless, Blair J rejected as a separate ground the inability to reach completion by the long stop date, since practical completion *could* have been achieved.
[326] *Grupo Hotelero Urvasco SA v Carey Value Added* (n 318) paras 822–24.
[327] *Torre v RBS* (n 296).

M1 mezzanine, all things being equal, unless there was a roll-up of the B2 interest equivalent to 7–8 per cent of the overall amount of interest to be serviced (considered substantial), the roll-up proposal was considered an event of default.[328] However, the court rejected that RBS (or PV) had a duty to communicate these developments to the junior mezzanine lenders.[329]

10.110 The events of default related to 'insolvency' are discussed in chapter 11 on insolvency, property, and creditor coordination cases.[330]

10.111 Once the 'event' itself has materialized, its consequences also matter, including the potential checks on the non-defaulting party's power to behave opportunistically. In *lending* agreements banks normally insist on having ample powers to act post-default. One example are the so-called 'notwithstanding' clauses, ie 'notwithstanding' is normally considered a trumping word that 'controls over any contrary language',[331] in case of conflict between clauses.[332] In *Veneto Hotel v German American Corp.*[333] a loan and security agreement was subscribed between Veneto Hotel & Casino, S.A. ('Veneto'), a Panamanian corporation owning a hotel in Panama City (the Hotel), and German American Capital Corp. (GACC). GACC loaned money to Veneto in 2007, under a loan that was subsequently amended. The hotel revenues were deposited in a 'holding account' by the account trustee, HSBC Bank, to be distributed to other accounts, such as those funding operating expenses, including (after section 3.1.7(a)(v) was amended) once an event of default happened. Yet, section 3.1.11(a), upon an event of default, allowed GACC to instruct the trustee not to fund those accounts. In January 2015, GACC sent Veneto a default notice, and the whole loan became due and payable, followed by an instruction to the trustee to stop funding Veneto. Veneto sued, arguing that the fund's freeze prevented it from paying operating expenses like wages and taxes, leading to the suspension of its gambling licence, and claiming a breach of contract, and breach of covenant of good faith, since section 3.1.7(a)(v) required the funding of operating expenses even post-default. Yet, the court held that section 3.1.11(a) was a 'notwithstanding' clause, a 'trump card', and an implied duty of good faith could not prevail over it.

10.112 In *indenture* provisions,[334] some cases have discussed the conflict between clauses (i) allowing the issuer to redeem the notes 'prior to the maturity date' in exchange for a 'make whole' redemption price (principal + accrued interest + redemption premium) and clauses that, in case of default, allow acceleration as a non-exclusive remedy.[335] It was often assumed that, upon a default, noteholders would accelerate and claim the principal plus accrued interest, but not the premium. However, even in the 1980s, in *Sharon Steel* (referred to above), the court held that:

---

[328] *Torre v RBS* (n 296) para 136: 'The interests of lenders were sufficiently detrimentally affected by this level of slippage from the original business plan as to make it reasonable to infer that the parties intended that such a situation should be covered by the phrase "financial difficulties" in clause 23.5(a) and so capable of triggering the acceleration and enforcement mechanisms set out in the various facility agreements (with the practical effect that lenders would then be drawn into a negotiation to see if the financial difficulty could be resolved without the need to bring those mechanisms into operation).'
[329] See ch 11, s 6.
[330] See ch 11, s 5.
[331] *Handlebar Inc v Utica First Insurance Co* 290 A D 2d 633, 635 (3d Dept 2002).
[332] *Cisneros v Alpine Ridge Group* 508 US 10, 18 (1993).
[333] *Veneto Hotel & Casino SA v German American Capital Corp* 160 A D 3d 451, 452 (1st Dept 2018).
[334] Adrian JS Deitz and others, 'Indented: Recent Court Decisions on New York Law-Governed Indentures and Their Impact' (2019) Butterworths J Intl Banking and Fin L 245.
[335] *Sharon Steel Corp v Chase Manhattan Bank* NA, 691 F 2d 1039 (2d Cir 1982).

where 'acceleration provisions of the indentures are explicitly permissive and not exclusive of other remedies' and the debtor does not 'find … itself unable to make required payments', there is 'no bar … to [the lender] seeking specific performance of the redemption provisions' … In such circumstances, 'the redemption premium' must be paid.[336]

10.113 In *Wilmington Savings Fund Society v Cash America International Inc*.[337] the spin-off of a subsidiary amounted to an event of default, and the court relied on *Sharon Steel* and differentiated between cases where acceleration resulted from involuntary actions, like bankruptcy, and cases where it resulted from the issuer's voluntary actions, as in the case, where noteholders could seek *specific performance* of the optional redemption provisions since, to execute the spin-off the issuer should have first redeemed the notes paying the premium. In *Re Energy Future Holdings*,[338] the issuer filed for bankruptcy and sought to repay some notes at principal plus interest and to refinance a part of the notes; but the indenture trustees sued, seeking a declaration that the refinancing of the notes triggered the obligation to pay the amount with premium. The Delaware District Court rejected the noteholders' claim, but the Circuit Court reversed, holding that the attempt to refinance triggered acceleration, making the notes immediately payable, but this did not exclude the premium; in fact, the subsequent refinancing constituted a redemption, thus triggering the requirement to pay with premium. The Court surprisingly dismissed the issuer's distinction between 'acceleration' and 'redemption' because: 'Rather than "different pathways", together they form the map to guide the parties through a post-acceleration redemption.'[339] However, in *Re Momentive Performing Materials (MPM) Silicones LLC*[340] the debtors' reorganization plan gave the two classes of noteholders the choice between accepting the reorganization plan and receiving cash for the outstanding principal and interest (and no premium) or reject the plan and receive replacement notes, with a principal equal to the 'make-whole' amount, to the extent determined by the court. The noteholders rejected the plan; the bankruptcy court confirmed it, but the Circuit Court held that the issuance of replacement notes *after* the automatic acceleration (after the bankruptcy filing) was not a 'redemption', which was reserved for pre-maturity repayments, since upon acceleration the maturity moves to the acceleration date, and replacement notes were not issued at the issuer's 'option'.[341]

10.114 Post-default tensions also arise in derivatives contracts. Since a large part of derivatives contracts are based on the standard ISDA documentation, court rulings can have a market-wide impact, which raises the stakes. A series of past cases had to decide what happens where there is an event of default and the non-defaulting party (NDP) is 'out-of-the-money', ie it owes money to the defaulting party (DP) 'in-the-money', and decides not to terminate, or tries to minimize the bill. ISDA's 'flawed asset provision' (Master Agreement section 2(a)(iii)) subjects a party's payment and delivery obligations to a series of conditions precedent,

---

[336] ibid 1047–53.
[337] Case No 15-CV-5027 (JMF) (SDNY 2016).
[338] *In re Energy Future Holdings Corp* 842 F 3d 247 (3d Cir 2016).
[339] ibid.
[340] *In re Momentive Performing Materials (MPM) Silicones LLC* Case No 15-1682 (2d Cir 2017).
[341] *In re Momentive Performing Materials (MPM) Silicones LLC* (n 340): '[A]cceleration brought about by a bankruptcy filing changes the date of maturity of the accelerated notes to the date of the petition … Therefore, any payment on the accelerated notes following a bankruptcy filing would be a post-maturity payment … the 'plain meaning of the term "redeem" is to "repay … a debt security … at or before maturity" … Here, Debtors' payment was post-maturity, not 'at or before' maturity … even assuming MPM's issuance of the replacement notes was a "redemption", it would not have been "at [MPM's] option" … Rather, the obligation to issue the replacement notes came about automatically by … the automatic acceleration clauses. A payment made mandatory by operation of an automatic acceleration clause is not one made at MPM's option.'

including the absence of an 'event of default'. Thus, if a party defaults, the condition precedent is not fulfilled, and the obligation is suspended, but the contract does not provide whether this situation can be prolonged indefinitely, or whether there is an implied term requiring it to end. Courts have generally answered that it can go on indefinitely, and there are no implied limits. In *Enron Australia*[342] Enron tried to force TXU to call an early termination date, but the Supreme Court of New South Wales upheld TXU's right simply to suspend payment as long as default continued.[343] However, in *Metavante* the New York Bankruptcy Court decided that Metavante, the non-defaulting party, had to either continue to make payments under an interest rate swap or terminate the transaction and pay amounts due to the defaulting party, and could not rely on section 2(a)(iii) simply to sit and wait. Yet, this finding was based on bankruptcy rules, which mandate a stay of enforcement of contractual rights, and prohibit *ipso facto* clauses, which vary the debtor's rights upon its bankruptcy. The rules include a safe harbour for swaps, repos, and master netting agreements, but this encompasses only *termination,* ie not suspension or variation, and the legislative intent was merely to permit a *prompt* termination (*Metavante* had waited for one year).[344] Thus, finalistic interpretation prevailed because it concerned statutory rules, not contract clauses.[345]

10.115 English courts, however, less constrained by bankruptcy rules[346] have relied primarily in the text of the ISDA master agreement, but this still required several High Court and Court of Appeal decisions to clarify the matter. In *Marine Trade SA v Pioneer*[347] the High Court (Flaux J) suggested obiter that section 2(a)(iii) was a 'one time' provision for calculating whether an amount is payable; thus, if no payment obligation existed on the settlement date, the payment obligation would be extinguished, and would not revive. Yet, this was not followed by other cases. The 'extinction' of the payment obligation was questioned in *Lomas and Others v JFB Firth Rixson*,[348] and *Lehman Brothers Special Financing (LBSF) v Carlton Communications*,[349] where Lehman Brothers' bankruptcy was an event of default, but the counterparties did not terminate and opted to withhold payments under section 2(a)(iii). Briggs J held that section 2(a)(iii) suspended (not extinguished) payments, but this lasted only until the transaction terminated or expired at its maturity date, whereupon the payment obligation was extinguished and the non-defaulting party was permanently released. There was no implied term that the suspension could only last for a 'reasonable time' or that the non-defaulting party had to designate an 'early termination date'. The two decisions were appealed, together with other two decisions, *Pioneer Freight v Cosco*[350] and *Britannia Bulk,*[351] on a different issue (see next paragraphs). The Court of Appeal in *Lomas v JFB Rixon* upheld *Lomas* and *LBSF*[352] on the 'suspension' and the absence of an implied term of 'reasonableness', or the duty to designate an early termination date. However, it held that payment

---

[342] *Enron Australia Finance Pty Ltd (in liq) v TXU Electric Ltd* (2003) 48 ACSR 266 (NSW). See S Farrell, 'Court Upholds ISDA's Flawed Asset Provision' (2004) 23 Intl Fin L Rev 33.
[343] ibid.
[344] *In re Lehman Brothers Holdings Inc* Case No 08-13555 (Bankr SDNY 2009). See s 362(a) (prohibition) and ss 362(b)(17) and 560 (exception) of the US Bankruptcy Code.
[345] See section 4.1.5 for an analysis of the case law on the prohibition of *ipso facto* clauses and the bankruptcy safe harbour.
[346] See also section 4.1.5.
[347] *Marine Trade SA v Pioneer Freight Futures Co Ltd BVI and Another* [2009] EWHC 2656 (Comm).
[348] *Lomas and Others v JFB Firth Rixson Inc and Others* [2010] EWHC 3372 (Ch).
[349] *Lehman Brothers Special Financing Inc v Carlton Communications Ltd* [2011] EWHC 718 (Ch).
[350] *Pioneer Freight Futures Company Ltd v Cosco Bulk Carrier Company Ltd* [2011] EWHC 1692 (Comm).
[351] *Britannia Bulk plc v Pioneer Navigation Ltd and Others* [2011] EWHC 692 (Comm).
[352] *Lomas v JFB Rixson* [2012] EWCA 419.

obligations continued suspended while the condition precedent remained unfulfilled, and were not extinguished at the transaction's maturity date, and the amounts continued to accrue (and could even be netted) a situation that could be prolonged indefinitely, and these obligations will revive if the default is cured, or if the NDP terminates the transaction.[353]

10.116 Apart from the 'suspension versus extinction', another major post-default issue was the method for calculating termination payments. Under the 1992 ISDA, parties could choose between the 'market quotation' method, based on reference market-makers' quotations, ie the amount these would pay (if negative) or ask (if positive) to enter a 'replacement transaction', while the 'loss' method considered the termination currency equivalent of the amount that the party determines as its total associated loss (or gain; 'loss' can be negative). These two mechanisms were combined with the first method (which limited payments to the defaulting party, in a way reminiscent of damages for breach of contract) or the second method (with no such limitation).

10.117 Yet, the 'market quotation' method gave rise to major disparities in illiquid markets. In *Peregrine Fixed Income v Robinson Department Store*[354] Robinson (the non-defaulting party) survey of market-makers resulted in an amount considerably lower than Peregrine's loss,[355] because market-makers considered that Robinson was in a restructuring process, and the court accepted the right to challenge the market quotation if it was 'commercially unreasonable'.[356] In *Enron Australia* the court criticized the three experts' approach as 'commercially unreasonable',[357] showing preference for a valuation mechanism that had not been contemplated by any of the parties.

10.118 *Pioneer Freight v TMT (TMT)*[358] and *Britannia Bulk*[359] analysed whether an out-of-the-money non-defaulting party would owe money to a defaulting party and whether the 'loss' methodology would limit that, while in *Anthracite Investments*[360] Briggs J summarized the 1992 ISDA approach.[361] The cases were appealed, and the issue was relevant enough for the Court of Appeal to concentrate all the appeals in a 'doctrinal' decision, *Lomas v JFB Rixson*,[362] where it confirmed the findings in *Britannia Bulk*, and cited favourably the decision in *Anthracite*. In summary: 'market quotation' and 'loss' sought to achieve roughly the same outcome, but, importantly, the loss and second method provisions were a deliberate departure from common law principles on damages for breach of contract.[363] Thus, parties

---

[353] ibid para 25 (accrual of debts, not of payment obligation), para 62 (possibility to prolong the situation indefinitely), and para 38 (no implied term requiring termination within reasonable time).
[354] *Peregrine Fixed Income v Robinson Department Store* [2000] EWHC 99 (Comm).
[355] Market-makers' quotations were US$750,000, US$9.5 million, and US$25.5 million. In case of disparities the middle quotation (US$9.5 million) had to be selected, but this compared poorly with the payments that Peregrine should have received from Robinson as a result of its losses (around US$87.3 million).
[356] *Peregrine Fixed Income v Robinson Department Store* (n 354).
[357] The market was so illiquid that the parties replaced the 'reference market-makers' language with 'experts', but did not replace the method (i.e. still based on a replacement transaction). The quotations relied on bid and offer prices but did not discount the effect of a highly illiquid market (thus the price spread was very wide) and relied on averages (although the non-defaulting party would always choose the highest bid price and lowest offer price). *Enron Australia Finance Pty Limited (in liquidation) v Integral Energy Australia* [2002] NSWC 753.
[358] *Pioneer Freight v Cosco Bulk Carrier Company* (n 350).
[359] *Britannia Bulk plc v Pioneer Navigation Limited and Others* [2011] EWHC 692 (Comm).
[360] *Anthracite Rated Investments (Jersey) Ltd v Lehman Brothers Finance SA* [2011] EWHC 1822 (Ch).
[361] ibid para 116.
[362] *Lomas v JFB Rixson* [2012] EWCA 419.
[363] These two ideas were already present in *Anthracite*, where Briggs J had also held that the 'loss of bargain' by the non-defaulting party requires assuming that the transaction will proceed until its conclusion, and all conditions will be fulfilled, no matter how improbable this may be (the 'clean value' as opposed to 'dirty valuation' approach).

willing their approach to be close to common law principles could choose the first method, to ensure one-way payments from the out-of-the-money *defaulting* party to the non-defaulting party, but not the opposite. However, in light of the controversy ISDA changed the approach in its 2002 Agreement, to bind the parties to *a single* (although more *flexible*) method based on 'replacement cost', which mixes market quotation and loss approaches.[364]

10.119 *Lomas v JFB Rixon* (appeal) decided another issue, raised in *TMT*,[365] *Pioneer Freight v Cosco*[366] (*Cosco*) and *Britannia Bulk*.[367] In those cases the non-defaulting party was out-of-the-money, but unlike *Lomas* or *LBSF*, the transaction was terminated, and not just suspended, because the parties had incorporated the Automatic early termination provisions, there was no issue about 'suspension'; the transactions were terminated.[368] Thus, the issue was whether the calculation of the settlement amount should include the payments scheduled *after* the event of default, ie payments that would have become due absent section 2(a)(iii). NDPs argued that section 2(a)(iii) had a 'one-off effect', and thus excluded any payments scheduled to be paid to the defaulting party between the event of default and the early termination ('retrospective nil loss' argument[369]) and after the early termination ('prospective nil loss'). The High Court in *TMT*, breaking with *Marine Trade* (above) held that[370] the ISDA 'system' was pro-netting, both during the life of the agreement and after termination, and the 'payable' amounts to be included should not be restricted to amounts satisfying the conditions precedent, ie absent default; insisting on the payment of 'gross' rather than 'net' amounts would have no 'commercial justification', and would be 'wholly contrary to the ethos' of ISDA.[371] However, in *Cosco* the High Court held, in line with *Marine Trade* (above), that payments scheduled between the event of default and the automatic early termination would be *excluded* from net payments calculations, because 'suspended' payment obligations did not survive the transaction's natural expiry date, ie they were not transactions 'outstanding' or 'in effect'. In *Britannia Bulk* the High Court held that the ISDA model sought a 'clean' calculation 'assuming satisfaction of each condition precedent', and thus not factoring in the event of default.[372]

10.120 *Lomas v JFB Rixson*[373] solved the split confirming the criterion in *Britannia Bulk*, rejecting *Cosco*'s, and citing *TMT* with favour. In the Court's view, the ISDA model seeks settlement during the life of the agreement, and upon termination. If the NDP wishes to enforce the defaulting party's payment obligations, it must give credit for *all* the sums due on its part, *including* those with suspended payments, ie a transaction's maturity date does not extinguish payment obligations, which continue to be in existence. However, this would only apply to

---

[364] They also clarify some issues that arose in the cases examined, such as the need to bear in mind, in calculating the replacement cost, the party's current creditworthiness (*Peregrine*) market liquidity (*Enron*) cost of funding (rejected as a criterion in *Peregrine*).

[365] *Pioneer Freight Futures Company Limited v TMT Asia Limited* [2011] EWHC 778 (Comm).

[366] *Pioneer Freight v Cosco Bulk Carrier Company* (n 350).

[367] *Britannia Bulk plc v Pioneer Navigation Limited and Others* [2011] EWHC 692 (Comm).

[368] The contracts were freight forward agreements (FFAs) derivatives where one party pays the other the difference between a fixed price and the actual freight price published by the Baltic Exchange. Yet, the FFAs were governed by the FFABA terms, which incorporated by reference the 1992 ISDA Master Agreement, the automatic early termination, and the loss method.

[369] The label was used in *Pioneer v TMT (No 2)* [2011] EWHC 1888 (Comm).

[370] See Stephen H Moller, Anthony RG Nolan, and Howard M Goldwasser, 'Section 2(a)(iii) of the ISDA Master Agreement and Emerging Swaps Jurisprudence in the Shadow of Lehman Brothers' (2011) 7 JIBLR 313.

[371] ISDA, 'International Swaps and Derivatives Association Inc 2002 Master Agreement' https://www.sec.gov/Archives/edgar/data/1355515/000127727706000388/exh43to8kpsa_lb20063.pdf (accessed 5 October 2022).

[372] *Britannia Bulk v Pioneer* [2011] EWHC 692 (Comm).

[373] *Lomas v JFB Rixson* [2012] EWCA 419.

amounts payable on the same date in respect of the same transactions, ie the defaulting party could not set off sums it owed in one month against sums owed in another month.[374]

10.121 It is remarkable that an issue as basic as whether termination is up to the NDP or happens anyway, the calculation of the settlement and the amounts to be included needed a detail analysis by experienced judges. In general, though, the 'narrow' and 'literal' approaches (eg the focus on 'payable' in *Cosco*) were less robust than those that sought a more comprehensive grasp of the transaction's 'commercial rationale', the 'financial structure of the relationship', or even the 'ethos' of the transaction.[375] Thus, contract interpretation and statutory interpretation are different because the interests at stake are different, not because methodologically speaking the exercise is different. Despite the fixation of some market participants on the 'literal meaning', words do not exist in a vacuum, and, if considered so, solutions can easily turn absurd and harmful to the market. If operators are frustrated with some judicial misunderstandings of the sense of some clauses, as opposed to the insider's view, they have only themselves to blame for the complexity of the text, whose clarity should be commensurate to its relevance.

4.3 Materially adverse events

10.122 Material adverse events (MAE) clauses (also known as MACs) are customarily included in acquisition (M&A) and financial agreements. In the seminal case, *IBP v Tyson Foods*,[376] concerning a transaction between beef and pork distributors, whose economic prospects suffered as a result of a harsh winter, Tyson tried to walk away from the agreement, arguing that IBP had suffered a 'materially adverse' effect, due to its poor results in two quarters. However, the court held that:

> [A] buyer ought to have to make a strong showing to invoke a Material Adverse Effect exception to its obligation to close. Merger contracts are heavily negotiated and cover a large number of specific risks explicitly. As a result, even where a Material Adverse Effect condition is as broadly written as the one in the Merger Agreement, that provision is best read as a backstop protecting the acquiror from the occurrence of unknown events that substantially threaten the overall earnings potential of the target in a durationally-significant manner. A short-term hiccup in earnings should not suffice; rather the Material Adverse Effect should be material when viewed from the longer-term perspective of a reasonable acquiror. In this regard, it is worth noting that IBP never provided Tyson with quarterly projections.[377]

10.123 *Hexion Specialty Chemicals v Huntsman Corp*.[378] confirmed the view based on the 'knowledge' (by the party alleging the MAE), 'magnitude', and 'duration' of the event, which has prevailed among American courts, also in lending agreements. In *Pan Am Corp v Delta*, for example, the courts considered valid a lender's termination of a loan based on a MAE clause,[379] despite the relatively short period (ie three months) due to the 'rapid deterioration' of the

---

[374] The court also decided some insolvency issues. See ch 11.
[375] *Pioneer Freight v TMT* (n 365) para 44.
[376] *IBP Inc v Tyson Foods Inc* [2001] 789 A 2d 14 (Del Ch) 65.
[377] ibid.
[378] *Hexion Spec Chemicals v Huntsman Corp* 965, A2d 715 (Del Ch 2008).
[379] *Pan Am Corp v Delta Air Lines Inc* 175 BR 438 (SDNY 1994).

borrower's revenue. Likewise, in *Re Lyondell Chem*[380] the borrower claimed breach of contract for its lender's refusal to fund under a revolving line of credit. Yet, the lender alleged that the borrower's situation due to a major recession, extreme weather events (hurricanes), and an accident at one of its facilities, plus its conversations with lenders for a bankruptcy filing and its hiring of restructuring advisers, amounted to a MAE. In line with *Tyson Foods*, the court held that MAC clauses must be read 'in the context of the entire agreement and in conjunction with other evidence of the parties' intent' to determine whether the MAC 'was within the contemplation of the parties at the time of the agreement', within their control, as well as its magnitude. Applying New York law, the court held that the lender had breached the contract:[381] there was no precedent to support that insolvency constitutes a MAC, and the representation of solvency was required by the bank when the loan was made, but not for subsequent draw repayments.

English courts dealt with MAE clauses in *Grupo Hotelero Urvasco SA (GHU) v Carey*.[382] The **10.124** clause was a representation that: 'There has been no material adverse change in its financial condition (consolidated if applicable) since the date of this Loan Agreement.' The loan agreement cross-referenced a BBVA credit agreement providing that an event of default in this constituted a default under the loan agreement, and included a similar MAC provision relating to the guarantor.[383] Carey argued that the words 'financial condition' of the borrowers had to be interpreted broadly, including its economic prospects. However, Blair J held that the assessment should begin with the position shown in the financial statements, and not include the prospects of the company, or external economic or market changes. He compared the MAC's reference to 'financial condition', with the reference in the 'event of default' clause of the BBVA credit agreement to the borrower's 'business'. Yet, the inquiry need not be limited to financial statements, and the borrowers' ceasing to pay bank debts, anticipating a rescheduling, was relevant. On 'materiality', the Court, again, agreed with the borrower's standard, which focused on whether changes in the balance sheet position were relevant to a borrower's ability to meet its payment obligations. The key was the 'significance' of the change; otherwise a lender could easily call a default or suspend lending, precipitating insolvency. Finally, on the relevance of pre-existing conditions, ie whether the borrower's financial difficulties could constitute a MAE if they predated the loan, Blair J cited *IBP v Tyson Foods* with approval on the 'knowledge' element, holding that circumstances known at the moment of drafting the contract cannot constitute a MAE.[384] Yet, although rejecting the existence of a MAE, the court found an event of default.

---

[380] *In re Lyondell Chem Co* 567 BR 55 (Bankr SDNY 2017) aff'd, 585 BR 41 (SDNY 2018).
[381] ibid para 123.
[382] *Grupo Hotelero Urvasco SA v Carey Value Added* (n 318) para 4.452 for its discussion of the existence of a 'default' by the borrower.
[383] A misrepresentation about the financial condition would have been a default under the BBVA credit agreement if made at a relevant point in time.
[384] 'General and/or sectoral economic decline that was known to, or should have been foreseen by, the party relying on the clause when he entered into the contract is unlikely to be held to constitute a material adverse change unless the wording of the clause is particularly clear on the point.' *Grupo Hotelero Urvasco SA v Carey Value Added* (n 318) para 361, citing Richard Hooley, *Material Adverse Change Clauses After 9/11*, ch 11 of Sarah Worthington (ed), *Commercial Law & Commercial Practice* (Hart Publishing 2003) and '[t]he lender cannot trigger the clause on the basis of circumstances of which it was aware at the date of the contract since it will be assumed that the parties intended to enter into the agreement in spite of those conditions, although it will be possible to invoke the clause where conditions worsen in a way that makes them materially different in nature'. *Grupo Hotelero Urvasco SA v Carey Value Added* (n 318) para 362, citing Philip Rawlings, 'Avoiding the Obligation to Lend' [2012] JBL 89.

11
Courts in insolvency, collateral, and creditor coordination disputes

1 Introduction	11.01	5.2 Limiting bankruptcy filing by creditors: non-petition and non-recourse clauses, and other mechanisms	11.59
2 Special purpose vehicles (SPVs) insolvency and claw-back risk	11.11		
2.1 Structured transactions risks in theory: avoidance, recharacterization, and substantive consolidation	11.12	6 Inter-creditor coordination disputes in collective enforcement, liquidation, and restructuring	11.71
2.2 Structured credit and claw-back risks in practice: interim asset control in insolvency, and the treatment of bespoke transactions	11.29	6.1 Collectively enforcing claims: 'insolvency events' clauses and their hybrid (contract-statutory) construction by courts	11.72
3 Derivatives disputes in insolvency	11.37	6.2 Restructuring claims and inter-creditor conflict: disenfranchisement and oppression	11.77
4 Disputes over financial collateral: characterization, custody, and segregation	11.43	7 Inter-creditor coordination disputes and the role of agents and trustees	11.89
4.1 Classifying complex collateral arrangements as a recognizable security	11.44	7.1 The role of agent banks	11.90
4.2 Custody, intermediation, and segregation risk	11.48	7.2 Creditor coordination and the role of trustees (I): Duties and responsibilities	11.93
5 Inter-creditor disputes ensure bankruptcy remoteness (shielding the assets from formal bankruptcy proceedings)	11.53	7.3 Creditor coordination and the role of trustees (II): Discretion and discretion-constraining clauses	11.101
5.1 Limiting bankruptcy filing by SPV directors, and fiduciary duties	11.54	8 Inter-creditor disputes over the distribution of proceeds	11.106

1 Introduction

11.01 Chapter 11 analyses courts' role in inter-creditor conflicts. This differs from the subject matter in Chapter 10, where 'contract' disputes typically involved bank-client or creditor–debtor relationships. In those disputes the dominant questions were, first, whether contractual rights and obligations are, or should be determined by the letter of the contract, or by considerations of 'fairness', or 'asymmetry' between the parties, which could enter the relationship via 'public policy' doctrines, and 'voidness' claims, in extreme cases, or through 'implied' duties of disclosure, care, or loyalty, or of 'misrepresentations', in the majority of cases; and, secondly, whether courts adhere to the 'plain meaning' of contract terms, even if this leads to odd results, or are/should be open to considerations of 'good faith' or 'reasonableness', which seek to achieve an outcome that respects the letter, but also the 'logic' and 'finality' of the contract.

11.02 Disputes in this Chapter 11 revisit these issues, but with clear differences. Disputes between creditors, especially 'financial' creditors like banks and other intermediaries involve sophisticated parties who can adequately assess and negotiate their contract terms. Thus, 'interference' with these terms in the name of 'fairness' or 'asymmetry' is harder to justify. Yet, 'public policy' considerations are present in bankruptcy cases, where the question is not whether the 'adjusting' creditors, who negotiated their position, may be negatively affected by the contract terms, but whether the enforcement of such terms whisks the collateral assets away from other creditors.

11.03 Section 2 shows that such policy considerations may justify the transaction avoidance, recharacterization (eg of a 'transfer' into a 'secured' transaction), or even in the 'substantive consolidation' of the vehicle where the assets were placed. There we analyse how courts' prudent use of their powers does not prevent them from achieving pragmatic results behind the cloak of the 'specific' facts of the case, or the 'bespoke' nature of the transaction. Section 3 covers the related issues of financial derivatives. While in Chapter 10 we saw how 'pure contract' disputes over derivatives are largely influenced by standard (ie ISDA) documentation, ISDA has also succeeded in convincing legislators that derivatives enforcement (through close-out netting) should be protected from bankruptcy through an exception, or 'safe harbour' from bankruptcy principles, which promote *pari passu* distribution, and prohibit so-called *ipso facto* clauses (which modify contract rights upon a party's insolvency) or creditor 'deprivation'. Yet, while legislators may have weighed the policy reasons before adopting such exceptions, courts have been left the task of navigating the disputes where the question is whether the court should apply the exception, or general bankruptcy rules, and to 'fit' policy arguments with the intricacies of each transaction.

11.04 Section 4 closes the 'pack' of insolvency issues with disputes over 'collateral', custody, and segregation. Simplifying much: the internal 'plumbing' of financial institutions and groups is complex, and 'collateral', including money and securities, are essential to ensure liquidity. Financial groups seek to mobilize assets inside the group, or to even use their clients' assets, using specific arrangements that serve their needs. Yet, such arrangements need to fit within recognizable categories of 'property' or 'security' arrangements, and/or respect conditions for the 'segregation' of, and/or 'control' over the assets. Courts confronted with bespoke arrangements must 'characterize' the transaction in a way that fits the facts, and balances principles of creditor 'fairness' *and* the protection of secured creditors' (or investors') expectations.

11.05 Section 5 analyses conflicts that straddle 'insolvency' and 'contract' disputes. In these cases creditors seek not only to insulate a pool of collateral assets from the insolvency of the debtor who originated them (as seen in section 1) but also to shield them from being subject to enforcement actions by individual creditors, or from entering insolvency proceedings altogether by, for example, placing the collateral in a special purpose vehicle –(SPV) and constraining both the power of directors to file for bankruptcy, and individual creditors' rights of action through no-action clauses. Creditors trust more their contractually agreed mechanisms for liquidation and distribution, but individual creditors may challenge such arrangements, arguing that stopping 'voluntary' bankruptcy filings is contrary to directors' duties, or bankruptcy principles, or that no-action clauses cannot (or should not) fully constrain creditors from filing certain claims.

11.06 Sections 6–8 analyse 'purer' contract disputes, where courts had to interpret and enforce creditors' arrangements for restructuring debt, seizing, administering, and liquidating assets, and distributing the proceeds from liquidation. In principle, there cannot be a context more 'sterilized' from considerations of policy and principle. And yet, if we look at the full picture, courts, even the most deferential, cannot rule out such considerations altogether, because contracts are seldom 'complete'; they leave matters for interpretation, and courts need to fill such 'gaps'.

Section 6 analyses inter-creditor conflicts. Some conflicts are about the existence of a 'credit event' that activates the collective seizure and liquidation of assets. If this is an 'insolvency event', considerations of insolvency policy will be imported into contract interpretation. That section also analyses conflicts between creditors' 'majority' and 'minority', where the latter alleges 'oppression' or 'unfairness', raising questions about the scope of good faith duties, or even about the possibility of applying 'fairness' principles of corporate and insolvency law by analogy. **11.07**

Section 7 analyses disputes where creditors use third parties, such as agent banks or trustees, to coordinate their rights. Very often, contract documents leave a large gap between the (substantial) role that the third party is *supposed* to play, eg in monitoring, seizing, administering, liquidating, etc. if the transaction is to function well, and the (minimum) duties formally stipulated in the contract. Courts must balance a strict contract interpretation with more 'functional' approaches, where the 'implied' duties of the third party are based on the role it plays in the transaction. **11.08**

Finally, section 8 analyses the cases where trustees, following court instructions, must distribute proceeds among different creditor classes. Even here, courts may interpret complex contract clauses negotiated and signed by sophisticated parties, but it is surprising how often courts will be faced with gaps and conflicts, which force courts to find the 'purpose' and 'rationale' of the contract-based distribution system to find a 'reasonable' solution. Such a solution is, very often, analogous to the one that would result from applying insolvency principles like *pari passu*; and, when it is not, it tends to be because not only is the contract language explicit but the rationale and purpose of the contract structure is also clear. **11.09**

None of these considerations is surprising if we view of courts' role as shaped by 'principles-based interpretation'. This does not mean that courts can substitute their view for that of the parties in private law any more than they could substitute their view for that of public authorities in private disputes. Yet, courts are required by law to ensure that their decisions are coherent with precedent, statute ... and contract. This normally goes beyond a pure linguistic exercise, and comprises a fuller understanding of the contract 'meaning', 'rights' and 'obligations, and the 'logic' or 'finality' underpinning them. No matter which logic the court seeks to ascertain, whether that of the parties or the legislator, the task of interpretation is about 'meaning', a task where principles are instrumental. **11.10**

2 Special purpose vehicles (SPVs) insolvency and clawback risk

Structured transactions like securitization require the transfer of assets into a SPV) or a special purpose entity (SPE), which then issues notes backed by those assets. This requires protecting the separate pool in the SPV. The risk in theory are that the assets will be clawed-back **11.11** or consolidated into the estate of the originator/transferor (section 2.1) Yet, as we will see, while these risks are relatively negligible, the risks in practice are different (section 2.2).

2.1 Structured transactions risks in theory: avoidance, recharacterization and substantive consolidation

11.12 It is customary to consider the risk of avoidance of the transfer of assets to the SPV, its recharacterization as a secured transaction, or the SPV's consolidation with the originator under doctrines of substantive consolidation or veil piercing. Reality shows, however, that courts are extremely cautious on this front.[1]

11.13 On 'avoidance' risk, in the US a transaction can be unwound if the debtor has not received 'fair value' in the exchange[2] ('constructive fraud' doctrine[3]). Yet, its relevance is low in securitization, where consideration for the assets transferred is typically a 'fair value'.[4] Some scholars have argued that the doctrine should apply in its broader version (so-called 'non-hindrance' policy variant)[5] and threaten securitization, because no transaction should be shielded from bankruptcy, no matter its importance for the market. Yet, the cases relied upon for the theory were quite unique, and there is no clear common rationale,[6] and the idea that fraudulent transfer law allows insolvency courts to use a 'policy analysis' does find clear support in case law, and could give rise to unbound discretion in securitization, factoring, secured loans, asset sales or corporate spin-offs. Thus, courts have abstained from policy analysis, and focused on traditional circumstances, such as the 'fairness' of the transaction terms.

11.14 In *Roseton OL LLC v Dynegy Holdings*[7] the Delaware Court of Chancery dismissed the plaintiffs' motion to restrain the transfer by the defendant (DHI) of its coal- and gas-fired power plants from existing subsidiaries to new insolvency remote subsidiaries controlled by DHIs' wholly owned subsidiary (the entities would then receive a new credit facility). The court held that the reorganization would not transfer any value from its corporate structure, would improve DHI's liquidity (with the new credit facility), and DHI was not insolvent. Thus, the request could not succeed in the absence of evidence that DHI had an actual intent to prevent the plaintiffs from collecting payment if the subsidiary-lessees defaulted.[8]

11.15 In the *Doctors Hospital* saga the bankruptcy court and district court rejected a fraudulent transfer to an insolvency-remote special purpose vehicle,[9] but the Seventh Circuit vacated,

---

[1] See David Ramos Muñoz, 'Bankruptcy-remote Transactions and Bankruptcy Law: A Comparative Approach (Part 1): Changing the Focus on Vehicle Shielding' (2015) 10 CMLJ 239.
[2] Bankruptcy Code, s 548(a)(l)(B); Uniform Fraudulent Transfer Act, ss 4(a)(2), 5(a).
[3] The origins are in the Statute of 13 in Elizabethan England. See Kenneth Kettering, 'Securitization and Its Discontents: The Dynamics of Financial Product Development' (2008) 29 Cardozo L Rev 1585.
[4] Steven L Schwarcz, *Structured Finance: A Guide to Asset Securitization* (Practising Law Institute 2002) s 4.7; Jason Kravitt (ed), *Securitization of Financial Assets* (Aspen Publishers 1995) 5.05[H].
[5] Kettering (n 3). See the criticism in Thomas Planck, 'Sense and Sensibility in Securitization: a Prudent Legal Structure and a Fanciful Critique' (2009) 30 Cardozo LL Rev 617 and the reply in Kenneth Kettering, 'Pride and Prejudice in Securitization: a Reply to Professor Planck' (2009) 30 Cardozo L Rev 1977.
[6] See the discussion in Ramos Muñoz (n).
[7] *Roseton OL LLC v Dynegy Holdings Inc* CA No 6689-VCP, 2011 Del Ch LEXIS 113 (Del Ch 2011).
[8] ibid. In this case, the assets would not leave DHI's control. The court considered the insolvency-remote nature of the entities as an important factor in assessing the existence of a fraudulent transfer.
[9] *Doctors Hospital of Hyde Park Inc v Desnick and Others* 360 BR 787, 811–12 (Bankr ND Ill 2007); *LaSalle Bank NA v Paloian* 406 BR 299, 366 (ND Ill 2009).

asking the lower courts whether the vehicle had separate existence.[10] The court held that there was no fraudulent transfer, even though the SPV was fully owned by the hospital and the hospital's owner (Desnick), because the hospital received consideration for the receivables (in the form of a cancelation of debts) and the court accepted that the companies were separately represented as evidence of arm's length execution,[11] holding that directors were able to 'change hats' to represent two corporations.[12] The implications for 'substantive consolidation' are discussed below.

11.16 The risk of 'recharacterization' of a transfer into a secured loan tends to be referred to as a clearer danger to structured transactions,[13] because enforcement could be subject to a stay[14] or even invalidated if the security is subject to registration. Yet, cases show that here, too, the risk is quite low.

11.17 In the UK, the elements to distinguish a sale from a secured transaction in *Re George Inglefield Ltd*[15] were: (i) the assignor's *equity of redemption*, ie the right to recover the collateral, absent in a sale; (ii) the assignor's right to the surplus in the sale of collateral to third parties; and (iii) the assignee's right to claim against the assignor the difference if the collateral value is insufficient, all absent in a sale (recourse).[16] This approach was refined in *Orion Finance Ltd*,[17] where the court held that (i) one, to ascertain the parties' intention the court would first consider the existence of a 'sham'; and only after discarding this it would analyse whether the 'label' corresponded to the parties' real intent (ie the bar to discard a sham is relatively low); (ii) two, to ascertain that intent requires a seeing if the language of contract provisions is consistent with their legal effect.[18] What is 'inconsistent', depends on multiple factors, ie courts must interpret the agreement as a whole, and even assess the whole contractual 'architecture'. In *Orion* the assignment was done as part of a security package to finance the acquisition of computer equipment,[19] a conclusion reinforced by the use of language suggesting a security right,[20] and was thus recharacterized. Yet, *Orion* remains an isolated example, and its elements are not normally present in structured transactions.

---

[10] *Paloian v LaSalle Bank NA* 619 F 3d 688, 695, 696 (7th Cir 2010).
[11] *In re Doctors Hospital of Hyde Park Inc* WL 5524696 (Bankr ND Ill 2013).
[12] ibid para 216, and authorities cited.
[13] See Thomas E Plank, 'The True Sale of Loans and the Role of Recourse' (1991) 14 Geo Mas U L Rev 287; Thomas E Plank, 'The Security of Securitization and the Future of Security' (2004) 25 Cardozo L Rev 1655; Robert D Aicher and William J Fellerhoff, 'Characterization of a Transfer of Receivables as a Sale or a Secured Loan upon Bankruptcy of the Transferor' (1992) 65 Am Bankr LJ 186– ff; Lois R Lupica, 'Asset Securitization: The Unsecured Creditor's Perspective' (1998) 76 Tex L Rev 595; Stephen J Lubben, 'Beyond True Sales: Securitization and Chapter 11' (2005) 1 NYU J L & Bus 94; Vijay Selvam, 'Recharacterisation in 'True Sale' Securitizations: The 'Substance over Form' Delusion' [2006] J Bus L 637; Alan Berg, 'Recharacterisation after Enron' [2003] J Bus L 216.
[14] 11 USC s 362(a)(1)(6) (2006) (automatic stay); *United Savings Association of Texas v Timbers of Inwood Forest Associates Ltd* 484 US 365, 382 (1988).
[15] *In Re George Inglefield Ltd* [1933] Ch 1.
[16] ibid.
[17] *Orion Finance Ltd v Crown Financial Management Ltd* [1996] BCC 621.
[18] Millett LJ in *Orion Finance Ltd v Crown Financial Management Ltd* [1996] BCC 621, 627: 'The substance of the parties' agreement must be found in the language they have used; but the categorization of a document is determined by the legal effect which it is intended to have, and if when properly construed the effect of the document as a whole is inconsistent with the terminology which the parties have used then their ill-chosen language must yield to the substance.'
[19] Orion leased computer equipment to Atlantic, who leased it to its customers, and Atlantic assigned to Orion all the receivables from its clients' future payments, as part of Atlantic's security package.
[20] The assignment clause read: 'The hirer (Atlantic) as security for its obligations hereunder, shall assign to the owner (Orion)...all moneys...payable...to the intent that they be charged with the payment of all moneys...except that such a security and assignment will not encumber.'

11.18 Other common law courts, such as Canada's, apply a similar approach. In *Metropolitan Widows*[21] the court laid down a number of relevant factors (the parties' intent, the transfer of ownership risk and level of recourse; the ability to identify the assets sold or to calculate the purchase price; the right to retain surplus collections or to repurchase the assets; the responsibility for collection of the accounts receivable; or the originator's ability to extinguish the purchaser's rights from sources other than the collection of the receivables), but also stressed that these were not a mechanical checklist, and that the most important was the parties' intention.[22] On this basis, it held that the transfer to an SPV in a securitization was a 'sale'. The Hong Kong court in *Incorporated v Yun Choy Ltd and the Standard Chartered Bank (Hong Kong) Ltd* were more formalistic, and assimilated the parties' intent with the contract's formal language, and despite the numerous elements that kept the assets' risk in the transferor's hands,[23] found that the transfer was a 'sale'.

11.19 Courts in the US are more open to follow a 'substance over form' approach and to look at the economics of the transaction directly. In *Major's Furniture*[24] a furniture company (assignor) sold the receivables to a financing company (assignee) under terms that left all the risk of default to the furniture company. The furniture company claimed from the assignee the surplus, arguing that it was a 'security' assignment.[25] The court, under UCC Article 9, held that 'the question for this court then is whether the nature of the recourse, and the true nature of the transaction are such that the legal rights and economic consequences of the agreement bear a greater similarity to a financing transaction or to a sale'.[26] The existence of recourse, in itself, was not enough to classify the transaction as security, but enough was the fact that the assignor had retained all the receivables' conceivable risk, and the assignee had unilaterally modified the financing conditions (ie as in a secured credit line).[27] Such economic analysis was also present in *Endico Potatoes*,[28] where the court held that, regardless of the 'label attached to the transaction', 'the root of all of these factors is the transfer of risk'.[29] The court relied on the contract language, where the fund provider stated being 'pleased to confirm the terms and conditions under which we shall make loans and advances to you upon the security of your accounts receivable'.[30]

11.20 Another relevant factor was the continuous involvement of the assignor in the servicing of the receivables, although recharacterization normally happened in the presence of other elements, such as the non-notification of rights to the account debtor and the retention of rights to ask the account debtor for price adjustments, the commingling of funds, or the existence

---

[21] *Metropolitan Toronto Police Widows and Orphans Fund v Telus Communications Inc* (2005)75 OR (3d) 784 (CA).
[22] Yet the ultimate goal was to 'give legal effect to the intention of the parties as expressed in the language of the agreement'. *Metropolitan Toronto Police Widows v Telus Communications* (n 21) 796.
[23] *Incorporated v Yun Choy Limited and the Standard Chartered Bank (Hong Kong) Limited* [2012] 1 HKLRD 396. The company retained the risk of non-repayment of debt by its customers, it had a right to the surplus of the receivables and, if the amount received from the receivables fell short, the bank could recover the balance from the company.
[24] *Major's Furniture Mart Inc v Castle Credit Corporation Inc and Others* 602 F 2d 538 (1979).
[25] The UCC gave the surplus to the assignee in a 'sale' of receivables, and to the assignor, in a sale for the purposes of security. See *Major's Furniture* (n 24) 543–44.
[26] *Major's Furniture Mart* (n 24) para 545.
[27] ibid paras 543–44. The court was also careful to distinguish between warranties of quality or validity (which could coexist with a true sale treatment) and warranties of collectability, which transferred the receivables' intrinsic risk.
[28] *Endico Potatoes Inc v CIT Group/Factoring Inc* 67 F 3d 1063, 1066–67 (2d Cir 1995).
[29] ibid.
[30] ibid.

of recourse,[31] and other courts have rejected that an assignment can be recharacterized as a secured transaction for including a separate collection fee.[32]

In *Doctors Hospital*, the bankruptcy court classified a transfer of receivables from a hospital to an SPV as a 'sale', despite the assignor receiving the vehicle's equity, not a cash price, because the transaction gave the vehicle no recourse for the unpaid receivables, nor did it 'permit or require the hospital to repurchase or substitute other receivables or property if the obligors did not pay'.[33] **11.21**

Despite this reduced risk reforms to protect securitization were proposed at a federal level[34] and adopted at a state level.[35] Yet, the *Endico* court above resolved the case using the reference to 'sale' in the federal Perishable Agricultural Commodities Act (PACA), despite the fact that Texas had an anti-recharacterization provision.[36] Courts tend to respect the transfer, and are reluctant to recharacterize, but they focus on the transaction's details, and statutes that determine the outcome based on other (policy) considerations disturb this interpretative exercise. **11.22**

In civil law countries, Spanish courts[37] hold that the recourse against the transferor is not enough to recharacterize the transfer,[38] but is a relevant element in the few cases that applied a 'substance-over-form' test to find a security assignment.[39] In those few cases, the courts' approach did not focus primarily on the economic effects, but on the contract language.[40] A statutory reform was passed in 1999 to provide insolvency protection to certain financial assignments (typically factoring).[41] Such sectoral rules have not changed the general principles applicable beyond the scope of the Act,[42] but they provide a safe harbour to assignments complying with the statute. The new provisions, thus, created a duality of approaches: one, generally applicable, where courts focus mostly on form (though they could **11.23**

---

[31] *Petron Trading Co v Hydrocarbon Trading & Transport Co* 663 F Supp 1153, 1159 (ED Pa 1986) (in addition to servicing payments, the assignor prepared the invoices for contract payments, did not notify the account debtor, and reserved itself the right to ask the debtor for price adjustments); *Southern Rock Inc v B&B Auto Supply* 711 F 2d 683, 685 (5th Cir 1983) (servicing and commingling of funds); *Ables v Major Funding Corp* 82 BR 443, 448 (Bankr ,SD Tex 1987) (servicing, commingling, and recourse).

[32] *Bear v Coben (In re Golden Plan of Calif. Inc)* 829 F 2d 705, 709 (9th Cir 1986).

[33] *Doctors Hospital of Hyde Park* (n 11).

[34] Successive attempts were made to modify bankruptcy law, first to protect securitizations as 'true sales', with s 912 US Bankruptcy Reform Act; 107th Congress s 912 (2001); House of Representatives 333, and afterwards (with Enron's demise, and the bad press for SPVs) to recharacterize them, with the Employee Abuse Prevention Act 2002, or Durbin-Delahunt Act.

[35] Reforms precluding recharacterization were adopted in Texas, Louisiana, Delaware, Nevada, and Alabama. See Kenneth Kettering, 'True Sale of Receivables: A Purposive Analysis' (2008) 16 ABI L Rev 511, 519 ff.

[36] It is unclear whether such state statutes would apply in the presence of federal bankruptcy law. Federal bankruptcy law must respect state law property rights (*Butner v United States* 440 US 48 (1979)) unless 'a federal interest requires a different result'. See Kettering (n 35) 557–58.

[37] For further detail see David Ramos Muñoz, *Transacciones Trascendentes. Operaciones fuera de balance, disociación de la propiedad y problemas regulatorios, patrimoniales y de gobierno* (2012) 125 RDBB 201, 201 ff.

[38] Spanish Supreme Court Decision of 11 February 2003 (RJ 2003/938) (the transferor's assumption of insolvency risk does not affect the legal nature of the transaction, unless the assignment is done for the mere purposes of servicing). See also Decision 2 February 2001 (RJ 2001/1685). Nevertheless, the Decision of 4 December 2007 (RJ 2007/8897) associated disparate factors, such as the recourse, servicing, and *pro solvendo* assignment with the absence of a transfer of property.

[39] Decisions of 2 February 2001 (RJ 2001/1685) and 4 December 2007 (RJ 2007/8897).

[40] References to language such as 'we have transferred' were taken to justify sale effects (Supreme Court Decision of 11 February 2003 (RJ 2003/938); and of assignment *salvo buen fin*, to justify the absence of a true sale (Supreme Court Decision of 27 June 2003 (RJ 2003/4313).

[41] Additional Provision 3a of the Act 1/1999 (5 January 1999) about venture capital entities.

[42] The 1999 reform was a reaction to the harsh insolvency regime of 'retroaction'. The regime was eliminated in 2003 but the privilege was kept. See José Ramón García Vicente, *La Prenda de Créditos* (Civitas 2006) 181.

potentially focus on substance, if it is very obvious);[43] another, specifically applicable to financial transactions, which primarily focuses on whether the assignee is a registered/regulated entity.[44]

11.24 'Substantive consolidation' of the vehicle is the other risk analysed in structured transactions, but is the concern justified? The answer seems to be 'no'. 'Substantive consolidation', as a doctrine, is only known in the US,[45] where it evolved as an outgrowth of the bankruptcy court's broad equity powers in cases where insolvent debtors transferred assets to subsidiaries to keep them insolvency-proof.[46] In *Re Vecco* the court tried to systematize its elements: (1) difficulty in segregating individual assets and liability; (2) presence of consolidated financial statements; (3) profitability of consolidation at a single physical location; (4) commingling of assets and business functions; (5) unity of interests and ownership between various corporate entities; (6) existence of parent and intercorporate guarantees on loans; (7) transfer of assets without formal observance of corporate formalities.[47] This is similar to piercing the corporate veil, but requires an 'equitable' weighing of pros and cons. In any event, it is an exceptional remedy for cases of commingled estates or creditors dealing with the entities as a single economic unit.[48]

11.25 Structured transactions like securitization are unlikely to give rise to these elements. SPVs are often not subsidiaries of the sponsor and typically comply with so-called 'separateness covenants', which require them to respect formalities, conduct business in their own name, pay debts out of their own funds, keeping separate books, etc.[49] Furthermore, the marketing of securitized products emphasizes that the investor will be exposed to risks other than the originator's/sponsor's. Evidence in the US suggests that courts respect such separateness. In *Re CEIDCO* debtors filed for bankruptcy and requested substantive consolidation to strengthen their bargaining position against the secured creditor (Lehman Brothers) but the court refused absent creditors' approval,[50] relying on the entities' separateness.[51]

11.26 In *Doctors Hospital*, the central issue was whether the securitization vehicle (MMA Funding LLC (MMA)) had separate 'real existence'. The transaction was quite complex.[52] The same man, Desnick, owned the originator of the receivables, a hospital, the company owning the hospital's land (HPCH), and controlled the vehicle, MMA. The hospital would transfer the

---

[43] Supreme Court Decision RJ 2004/1811 (5 March 2004) (the Court examined the substance of the agreement to decide who had ownership over the receivables and the right to surplus).
[44] Supreme Court Decisions RJ 2004/3553 (28 May 2004) and 2004/5986 (6 October 2004); and RJ 2003/938 (11 February 2003).
[45] Peter J Lahny IV, 'Asset Securitization: A Discussion of the Traditional Bankruptcy Attacks and an Analysis of the Next Potential Attack, Substantive Consolidation' (2001) 9 Am Bankr Inst L Rev 815; Michael J Cohn, 'Asset Securitization: How Remote Is Bankruptcy Remote?' (1998) 26 Hofstra L Rev 929; Maria Elizabeth Kors, 'Altered Egos: Deciphering Substantive Consolidation' (1998) 59 U Pitt L Rev 381.
[46] See Kors (n 45).
[47] See *In re Vecco Construction Industries Inc* 4 BR 407, 410 (Bankr ED Va 1980) See also the thorough study of other checklists in Kors (n 45) 400–402.
[48] *Alexander v Compton (In re Bonham)* 229 F 3d 750 (9th Cir 2000); *Union Savings Bank v Augie/Restivo Baking Co Ltd* 860 F 2d 515, 518 (2d Cir 1998). See also David Ramos Muñoz, *The Law of Transnational Securitization* (OUP 2010) 89.
[49] Standard & Poor's, 'Structured Finance: Auto Loan Criteria' 47–48 https://www.spglobal.com/ratings/en/sector/structured-finance/structured-finance-sector (accessed 14 October 2022).
[50] In this regard the court relied on *Bruce Energy Centre Ltd v Orfa Corp of America (In re Orfa Corp of Philadelphia)* 129 BR 404 (Bankr ED Pa 1991), which represents a restrictive approach to substantive consolidation, by requiring the affirmative vote of each class of creditors.
[51] *In Re Central European Industrial Development Company (CEIDCO) LLC d/b/a Ceidco* 288 BR 572 (Bankr ND Cal 2003) 576.
[52] See Ramos Muñoz (n 1); Ramos Muñoz (n 48) 192–93.

receivables in exchange for equity in MMA, and MMA would transfer them to Daiwa (bank) which would transfer loan advances to MMA. A posterior loan from Nomura to HPCH complicated the deal even more, requiring an intercreditor agreement, and a cash collateral agreement between creditors to ensure that the Nomura loan would be paid out with the funds from the Daiwa loan, and that Desnick (through Doctors' Hospital) controlled MMA. Doctors' Hospital went bankrupt, and the trustee alleged that the transfer of receivables to Daiwa was fraudulent because MMA had no separate legal existence, and the receivables had always been the property of Doctors' Hospital. The bankruptcy court and the district court dismissed the claim,[53] but the Circuit remanded the case for a determination whether MMA had 'valid existence' as a 'legitimate bankruptcy remote vehicle', because:

> MMA Funding lacked the usual attributes of a bankruptcy-remote vehicle. It was not independent of Desnick or the Hospital; ... and MMA Funding operated as if it were a department of the Hospital. It did not have an office, a phone number, a checking account, or stationery; all of its letters were written on the Hospital's stationery. It did not prepare financial statements or file tax returns. It did not purchase the receivables for any price (at least, if it did, the record does not show what that price was). Instead of buying the receivables at the outset, MMA Funding took a small cut of the proceeds every month to cover its (tiny) costs of operation.... The Hospital continued to carry the accounts receivable on its own books, as a corporate asset ...There is scarcely any evidence in this record that MMA Funding even existed, except as a name that Daiwa's and Desnick's lawyers put in some documents.[54]

11.27 Thus, the problem was not the use of a bankruptcy-remote securitization vehicle, but the *deviations* from market practice. Even so, the bankruptcy court held that MMA complied with the Court of Appeals' more demanding requirement that the vehicle 'buy assets' and 'manage assets', 'in its own interest rather than the debtor's',[55] because the lack of an address or stationary were less important than the segregated accounts, paying for the receivables in subordinated notes or equity was 'normal', and the vehicle respected corporate formalities, kept separate records, and had separate operations.[56] The court also held that it was difficult to apply a 'substance-over-form' test, because bankruptcy-remote vehicles have 'no purpose and no substantial effect' beyond excluding bankruptcy law, and 'it can hardly be argued that all secured loans are subject to attack for that reason'.[57] Furthermore, the bank relied on MMA's status as a bankruptcy-remote entity when making the loan because 'There is good reason to avoid judicial disruption of commercial transactions based on a balancing of factors susceptible to subjective interpretation'.[58]

11.28 Outside the US the probability of consolidation is slimmer still, since 'substantive consolidation' does not exist, only 'reverse' veil piercing, and is seldom used.[59] Veil piercing is exceptional for cases normally involving creditor fraud[60] or confusion.[61] In securitization,

---

[53] *Doctors Hospital of Hyde Park* (n 11); *Paloian v LaSalle* 406 F Supp 2d 299 (ND Ill 2007).
[54] *Paloian v LaSalle* 619 F 3d 688, 696 (2010).
[55] *Doctors Hospital of Hyde Park* (n 11).
[56] ibid paras 220–25.
[57] ibid para 202.
[58] ibid para 232.
[59] Karen Vandeckerckhove, *Piercing the Corporate Veil* (Kluwer Law International 2007) 405, 452, 474, 498 concludes that substantive consolidation is even more exceptional than veil piercing.
[60] See eg the Spanish Supreme Court decision RJ 2013\1628 (3 January 2013), where the Supreme Court consolidated the patrimonies of several subsidiaries with that of the parent company.
[61] Vandeckerckhove (n 59) 380–527.

unless the sponsor/originator siphons out resources from the vehicle,[62] there is no ground for intervention. In *Re Polly Peck*[63] investors in the securities issued by the vehicle sued the parent company (in substantive consolidation creditors of the parent would seek to consolidate the subsidiary), but court flatly rejected the claims under all veil piercing theories (agency, cipher, façade, or alter ego) holding that the existence of a single economic unit could not result in veil piercing, since 'substance means legal substance, not economic substance (if different)', and, that 'the separate legal existence of group companies is particularly important when creditors become involved'.[64]

2.2 Structured credit and claw-back risks in practice: interim asset control in insolvency, and the treatment of bespoke transactions

11.29 Although courts seldom have the appetite to engage with 'grand' theories like fraudulent transfers or substantive consolidation, in the US they have been more interested in threatening bankruptcy-remoteness in practice by granting *temporary possession/control* rights.[65] In *Re LTV Steel*,[66] LTV had set up two subsidiaries to securitize its rights over accounts receivable and inventory. However, when it filed for bankruptcy, it received permission by an interim order to use the proceeds from those receivables to continue its activity. One of the subsidiaries' creditors' (Abbey) motion to modify the interim order was overruled. The court held that it should not decide on whether the receivables were part of the debtor's estate in the interim order, as this required an evidentiary hearing, but it added that (1) the debtor had an *equitable* interest in the property, which provided a sufficient basis for the interim order, because:

> [t]o suggest that Debtor lacks some ownership interest in products that it creates with its own labor, as well as the proceeds to be derived from that labor, is difficult to accept'; and that (2) 'granting Abbey National relief from the interim cash collateral order would be highly inequitable', considering the consequences for employees and retirees.[67]

Thus, the court was ready to balance arguments of equity, as long as this was an interim decision without precedential value.

11.30 A similar pattern can be seen in so-called 'indirect' or de facto consolidation cases, where insolvency-remote SPVs and their sponsors enter insolvency simultaneously; and, while formally keeping separate estates, the sponsor is authorized to use the entities' assets.[68] In *Re General Growth Properties*[69] the court dismissed the motion to dismiss the bankruptcy filing of several SPVs by several secured creditors, who alleged that the filing was to the detriment of secured debtors, and to the benefit of the sponsor and parent, which benefitted from the automatic stay, by using the cash that would have gone to pay the SPVs' loans to

---

[62] . See *In re National Century Financial Enterprises Inc* WL 2849784 (SD Ohio 2006).
[63] *Re Polly Peck International plc (In Administration) (No 4)* [1996] 2 All ER 433, [1996] BCC 486.
[64] ibid 498.
[65] See Ramos Muñoz (n 1) 239–74.
[66] *In re LTV Steel Company Inc* 274 BR 278 (Bkrtcy ND Ohio 2002).
[67] ibid 286.
[68] Forrest Pearce, 'Bankruptcy-Remote Special Purpose Entities and a Business's Right to Waive Its Ability to File for Bankruptcy' (2012) 28 Emory Bankr Devs J 507, 514; Jason Lynch, 'Reevaluating Bankruptcy Remoteness: Transfers of Risk, Implications of the GGP Reorganization' (2010) 29 Am Bankr Inst J 58.
[69] *In re General Growth Properties* 409 BR 43 (Bankr SDNY 2009).

pay for its reorganization. The court held that since each SPV's bankruptcy would be kept separate, with no risk of substantive consolidation, and that, despite the 'inconvenience' to secured creditors, directors *should* take into consideration the *interest of the group* in deciding whether to file for bankruptcy.[70]

11.31 Thus, broader policy debates (eg on consolidation) can miss important details: under US law the control, or possession, over the assets, can trump ownership in the short-term, and transform a property right in a guarantee of 'adequate protection', which relies on the court's conclusion about the revenue-generating capacity of the use of the assets of the bankrupt firm.[71] In many cases what matters is whether a certain measure implies de facto consolidation in the short term. In *re Pacific Lumber*[72] the issue was the procedural (not substantive) consolidation and joint administration of the bankruptcy of six affiliated entities, including Palco, the operating company and Scopac, a Delaware SPV, wholly-owned by Palco, which issued notes secured by timberland transferred by Palco (both worked as an integrated company.[73] Two competing reorganization plans were presented to the court: one, by Bank of New York, as Indenture Trustee (rejected), one, by a creditor (Marathon) and a competitor (MRC) (accepted) to dissolve all six entities, cancel intercompany debts, and create two new entities, Townco and Newco. Almost all of Palco's assets would be transferred to Townco, while Timberlands and sawmill assets of the sawmill would be placed in Newco,[74] with a contribution by MRC and Marathon to pay claims against Scopac (SPV). The trustee appealed the plan as a de facto substantive consolidation. The court considered substantive consolidation an 'extreme and unusual remedy',[75] and the dangers of its use for 'securitized lending through a bankruptcy-remote special purpose entity like Scopac',[76] but dismissed the complaint.[77] Thus, absolute separation is harder to maintain when the SPV depends on the sponsor for servicing and collection of debt, and the sponsor depends on the SPV for collateral.

11.32 In *Bank of New York v FDIC*[78] (*NextBank I*) NextBank NA securitized its receivables through an SPV/SPE, with several interrelated transaction documents: a Trust Agreement, an Administration Agreement, a Transfer and Servicing Agreement, and a master indenture. When NextBank entered receivership, the Federal Deposit Insurance Corporation (FDIC) was appointed receiver, which should have activated an acceleration clause in the master indenture,[79] but the FDIC refused to activate it, and kept the transaction going, using noteholders' capital to purchase new credit card receivables, and paying interest pursuant to

---

[70] ibid 70.
[71] In *LTV Steel Company* (n 66) 286–87 the court held that: 'It is true that the pre-petition receivables are being used by Debtor to purchase and manufacture more steel. However, Debtor's use of the pre-petition receivables will inevitably lead to an increase in the value of post-petition receivables and inventory, in which Abbey National has a security interest.'
[72] *Bank of New York Trust Co v Official Unsecured Creditors' Committee* 584 F 3d 229 (2009).
[73] 'One of Scopac's three directors sat on Palco's board, and the companies had the same CEO, CFO, and General Counsel for substantially all of the relevant period. Palco had the sole right to harvest Scopac's timber, which Palco then processed and sold. Scopac was to repay the noteholders with proceeds from its sales to Palco'. See *Bank of NY Trust Co v Official Unsecured Creditors* (n 72) 238.
[74] ibid.
[75] ibid 250. In so doing it referred to *In re Gandy* 299 F 3d 489, 499 (5th Cir 2002).
[76] *Bank of NY Trust Co v Official Unsecured Creditors* (n 72) 251.
[77] 'Its only other evidence of substantive consolidation is based on the erroneous contention that the plan commingled inter-company administrative claims.' *Bank of NY Trust Co v Official Unsecured Creditors* (n 72) 250–51.
[78] *Bank of New York v FDIC* 453 F Supp 2d 82 (DDC 2006) aff'd 508 F 3d 1 (DC Cir 2007) (hereafter *Bank of New York v FDIC* or *NextBank* I).
[79] Master Indenture, art V, § 5.01. *Bank of New York v FDIC* (n 78) 87.

the non-accelerated schedule. BNY, as trustee sued the FDIC. The lawfulness of the FDIC's action depended on whether NextBank had 'entered into' the master indenture agreement, pursuant to section 1821(e)(12)(A) of the Financial Institutions Reform Recovery and Enforcement Act (FIRREA).[80] The parties wielded their dictionaries before the district and circuit courts, to determine what 'enter into' means.[81] Leaving this aside, District Judge Huvelle concluded that NextBank was a party to the master indenture (despite the fact that it had not signed under the heading 'parties' in that document, as it did in the other three, but under the heading 'acknowledged and accepted') because, it held, the four separate documents could be construed as a single, joint agreement.[82] Two noticeable aspects are that (i) even if legal personalities are separate, separation can be blurred through contract and statutory interpretation, and (ii) instead of repudiating or avoiding transactions, the FDIC used its powers to 'enforce transactions', and keep them going, despite the acceleration clause. This placed the trustee in the uncomfortable position of making a policy-based argument in favour of extending the application of the rules in order to preserve securitization, a policy argument that was rejected by the court.[83] The saga did not end here, and investors eventually took control over the assets,[84] but this case is yet another example of details trumping doctrine. When the SPV/SPE, in substance, depends for servicing cash management on its sponsor, if this sponsor becomes insolvent it will have little incentive to work for the interest of the insolvency-remote creditors, rather than its own creditors'.[85]

11.33 The existence of practical risks to the vehicle's separateness increases in bespoke, and thus untested, transaction structures. In the *Perpetual Trustee* saga, the transaction was a synthetic securitization:[86] unlike 'cash' securitizations, instead of transferring the property over the receivables a derivative contract, typically a credit default swap (CDS) is subscribed between the swap counterparty (which occupies the 'originator-like' role), who acts as the 'protection buyer' (here, Lehman Brothers Special Financing, or LBSF), and the SPV, which acts as the 'protection seller', over securitized assets (reference obligations, held, in the case, by a Lehman Brothers' entity).[87] The vehicle raises the funds by issuing credit-linked notes

---

[80] Under s 1821(e)(12)(A): '[T]he FDIC as receiver [has] the authority to enforce contracts entered into by [a] depository institution in receivership notwithstanding any contract clause providing for termination, acceleration or default solely by reason of insolvency or the appointment of the receiver.' *Bank of New York v FDIC* (n 78) 90.

[81] *Bank of New York v FDIC* (n 78) 93, and, on appeal, 508 F 3d 1 (DC Cir 2007) 4–5.

[82] The court held that 'enter into' was an autonomous concept in a federal statute, and need not, as suggested by BNY, be interpreted under state contract law.

[83] BNY argued, first, that the regulatory limitation, restricted to the FDIC's use of its power to repudiate transactions, should be interpreted broadly, as 'a statement that the agency would not interfere with any of the [investor] risk-reduction elements of a securitization'. The court dismissed the argument that FDIC powers because the limitation of the FIDC's powers was narrow and restricted. See *Bank of New York v FDIC* (n 78) 98, and, on appeal, 508 F 3d 1 (DC Cir 2007) 5–6. Then, the court dismissed BNY's argument that the FDIC's move threatened the assets' 'legal isolation' needed for their treatment as a 'transfer', because such treatment should be granted as long as the FDIC could not 'recover or reclaim' the transferred assets. See ibid at 97–98.

[84] After NextBank I, BNY argued in *FDIC v Bank of New York* 479 F Supp 2d 1 (DDC 2007) (*NextBank II*) that the *ipso facto* clause was still enforceable against the trustee, and this had to be resolved through an interpleader action in New York (possibly a more accommodating venue for noteholders' interest). Judge Huvelle held that the *ipso facto* clause was unenforceable, as contrary to FIRREA. The Circuit confirmed NextBank I and II in *Bank of New York v FDIC* [2007] 508 F 3d 1 (DC Cir) but it also held that matters concerning the maturity of the notes had not been decided; noteholders instructed BNY as trustee, to seize the collateral assets, and BNY, arguing that it faced conflicting claims (and probably coordinated with the noteholders) sought an interpleader dispute before New York courts, where noteholders' finally prevailed in the instance and on appeal. See *Bank of New York v First Millennium* 607 F 3d 905 (2010).

[85] Ramos Muñoz (n 48) 77–85.

[86] ibid.

[87] See *Perpetual Trustee Co Ltd v BNY Corporate Trustee Services Ltd* [2009] EWCA Civ 1160, [2010] Bus LR 632, [2010] BCC 59, [2010] BPIR 174 for more details.

(CLNs) and investing the proceeds in safe assets. In *Perpetual*, Lehman would pay the sums owed to noteholders (the excess between the collateral assets and Reference Obligations was a risk or insurance 'premium'). If there was a default in the reference obligations, the protection buyer could seize the collateral assets. However, the priority would 'flip' over to the noteholders[88] in case of bankruptcy of LBSF or its parent, Lehman Brothers Holdings Inc (LBHI). Both LBHI and LBSF entered bankruptcy and the validity of the 'flip' was discussed both before UK and US courts.

Courts in the UK decided the case on the basis of the general 'anti-deprivation' doctrine, which states that there cannot be a valid contract that a man's property shall remain his until bankruptcy, and on the happening of that event go over to someone else, and be taken from his creditors.[89] The Court of Appeal held that the priority-flip was valid pursuant to the anti-deprivation principle because: (1) collateral assets had been acquired with the noteholders' money; (2) the 'effect of the 'flip' provisions was thus not to divest LBSF of monies, property, or debts; but, rather, merely to change the order of priorities in which the rights were to be exercised in relation to the proceeds of sale of the collateral in the event of a default';[90] (3) as the security right granted to LBSF included, from its inception, the 'priority flip' right had always been a contingent one; (4) the priority flip clause was activated not by the insolvency of LBSF (the entity that would have been 'deprived') but the insolvency of its parent, LBHI; which occurred before LBSF filed for insolvency.

11.34

Not all arguments are equally solid. The first one does not seem relevant or supported by precedent;[91] the second interprets the concept of 'divestment of property' in a formalistic way which could render the doctrine ineffective.[92] The third is more subtle, but some scholars argue that parties could not create a contingent right, because this is possible only in case of proprietary interests, which can *only* and *necessarily* be defined in a time limited way (subject to the parties' design), such as leases, and *all other* interests, including charges, as in the case,[93] where a time limit does not shape the right, but effects a deprivation.[94] In civil law, the *numerus clausus* doctrine restricts the creation of rights *in rem* beyond those contemplated by the law,[95] and the alteration of their basic characteristics.[96] In any event, the fourth argument, ie that the clause was activated *before* the debtor's bankruptcy precluded the application of the British anti-deprivation doctrine.[97]

11.35

In the US, the court[98] decided the case under the specific statutory prohibitions of *ipso facto* clauses, i.e. clauses that seek to 'terminate or modify' the contract, or 'any right or obligation'

11.36

---

[88] Sarah Worthington, 'Insolvency Deprivation, Public Policy and Priority Flip Clauses' (2010) 7 Intl Corp Rescue 28.
[89] *In re Harrison* [1880] 14 Ch D 19, 26 (Cotton LJ). See also *Money Markets International Stockbrokers Ltd v London Stock Exchange Ltd* [2002] 1 WLR 1150, 87.
[90] *Perpetual Trustee* (n 87) 62.
[91] See Worthington (n 88) 31, and authorities cited. It would draw an artificial distinction between funded and unfunded synthetic securitizations.
[92] Not very consistent with the anti-deprivation nature of back-up doctrine.
[93] See Worthington (n 88) 37, with reference to *Money Markets International Stockbrokers Ltd v London Stock Exchange Ltd* [2002] 1 WLR 1150, 37, 118; *Ex parte Jay, re Harrison* [1879] 14 Ch D 19, 26, and the authorities cited in *Perpetual Trustee* (n 87).
[94] Worthington (n 88) 37–38.
[95] Luis Díez-Picazo, *Fundamentos del Derecho Civil Patrimonial: III Las relaciones jurídico-reales: El Registro de la Propiedad. La posesión* (Civitas 2008) 131 ff.
[96] ibid 132–33.
[97] Worthington (n 88) 38.
[98] *Lehman Brothers Special Financing Inc v BNY Corporate Trustee Services Ltd* No 09-01242 (JMP) US (Bankr Ct SDNY 2010) (Peck J).

under the contract as a result of the beginning of 'a case', ie bankruptcy.[99] Judge Peck held (unlike his British counterparts) that the clause was invalid because, pursuant to the transaction documents, it was LBSF's insolvency, not LBHI's (its parent's) that triggered the clause.[100] However, he also held that the result would have been the same if the clause had been triggered by LBHI's insolvency, because the reference to '*a* case', rather than '*the* case' meant that the statute invalidated clauses that were activated with the bankruptcy of related parties.[101] The functioning of the Lehman entities as an 'integrated enterprise' meant that 'the financial condition of one affiliate affects the others' thus treating their bankruptcy filings as a 'singular event for purposes of interpreting this *ipso facto* language', and 'the first filing at the holding company level' as a valid application of the reference to 'a' case. Judge Peck carefully stressed that nothing in the decision should affect 'issues of substantive consolidation, the importance of each of the separate petition dates for purposes of allowing claims against each of the debtors or any other legal determination', so as not to open a 'can of worms'. The parties subsequently settled the issue,[102] preventing clarification, although subsequent case law has shown that this reading is no longer good law (see section 3).

3 Derivatives disputes in insolvency

11.37 The diverging treatment by the courts in the *Perpetual Trustee* cases analyzed above in section 2.2 partly resulted from the judge's perception that the contract sought a bespoke solution contrary to bankruptcy mandatory rules. Other cases have interpreted the prohibition of *ipso facto* clauses showing much more deference to standard market documentation, like the ISDA Model Agreement, including cases on the so-called 'bankruptcy safe harbour', in section 560 of the US Bankruptcy Code.

11.38 Judge Peck, who decided the *Perpetual* case in the US ruled again on the validity of 'flip' clauses in synthetic securitizations in *Ballyrock*,[103] in a credit derivative between Lehman Brothers Special Financing (LBSF) as protection buyer, and Ballyrock (the vehicle) as protection seller, over collateralized debt obligations (CDOs) and mortgage-backed securities (the reference obligations). The contract was covered by an ISDA master agreement, and included a guarantee from LBHI (Lehman's parent holding) and a credit support annex designating LBHI as a 'credit support provider' to LBSF. Wells Fargo Bank NA was trustee in the indenture agreement. Ballyrock issued several classes of notes to investors, which would receive money based on a payments waterfall arrangement, based on insolvency ranking. Termination payments for the party 'in the money' ranked high, *except* if the payments were owed by the defaulting party.[104] Therefore, termination payments owed to LBSF could rank

---

[99] Bankruptcy Code, ss 365(e) and 541(c)(1)(B). The wide scope of the provision, which refers to 'modification', left no room to discuss the 'divestment of property' concept, as under English law.

[100] *In re Lehman Brothers Holdings Inc* (n 98) 16–17.

[101] Earlier versions of ss 365(e)(1) and 541(c)(1)(B) referred, respectively, to 'the commencement of a case under this Act *by or against the debtor*', and 'the commencement of a case under this title *concerning the debtor*', references suppressed in favour of a more generic reference to 'a case'.

[102] Joseph Checkler, 'Lehman Ends Suit with BNY Mellon, Perpetual Trustee' (*The Wall Street Journal* (15 December 2010) http://online.wsj.com/article/SB10001424052748704098304576021560555088914.html (accessed 14 October 2022).

[103] *Lehman Brothers Holdings Inc v Ballyrock* ABS CDO 2007-1 Ltd, 452 BR 31 (Bankr SDNY 2011).

[104] Unpaid termination payments were granted high priority within the waterfall arrangement, before senior noteholders. However, the documents indicated that, in case of a default by LBSF or LBHI, the termination

as third-priority position or 'drop to precipitously in rank to nineteenth place in the waterfall if LBSF is the defaulting party'.[105] Following LBHI's bankruptcy, Ballyrock notified an early termination, liquidated its assets, and planned to distribute to the senior noteholders, according to the documentation. LBSF sought a declaration that the priority shift violated New York law and bankruptcy law. Bankruptcy Code provisions invalidate *ipso facto* clauses, which terminate or modify an agreement as a result of the commencement of bankruptcy.[106] The court held that the ruling in *Perpetual Trustee* would render ineffective the changes in the waterfall arrangement resulting from activation of the termination payment clause, and that the clause did not benefit from the safe harbour protections for non-defaulting swap counterparties' rights to liquidate, terminate, or accelerate one or more swap agreements. The judge said that it would be incorrect to expand the section beyond the plain meaning of 'liquidation, termination, or acceleration', and thus the clause 'deprived' LBSF of valuable property rights upon designation by the non-debtor counterparty of an early termination date. The defaulted synthetic termination payment provision substantially lowered the priority of payment within the waterfall arrangement, effectively nullifying LBSF's entitlement to termination payments.[107]

11.39 However, Judge Peck later decided *Michigan State Housing v Lehman Brothers Derivative Products (LBDP)*,[108] concerning an ISDA master agreement between LBDP and the Michigan State Housing Development Authority, as an umbrella for twenty interest rate swaps. After Lehman's parent's bankruptcy, the contracts were assigned to Lehman Brothers Special Financing (LBSF) and amended to include the market quotation method for settlement if LBSF filed for bankruptcy, and the mid-market quotation method otherwise.[109] LBSF filed for bankruptcy,[110] and Michigan Housing determined that LBSF owed more than US$36 million under market quotation; LBSF alleged that the amendment was an illegal *ipso facto* clause (under the mid-market method Michigan Housing would owe more than US$59 million). The Court held that the contractual method of liquidation was 'safe harboured' under section 560. The Court used a dictionary to ascertain the meaning of 'liquidation' under section 560, concluding that the right to cause liquidation must include the right to determine the exact amount due and payable as a result of that liquidation, ie both were 'inextricably linked'. The Court rejected LBSF's narrower construction, which would only protect the right to cause liquidation, but not the methodology, holding that:

> The phrase 'the exercise of any contractual right,' when combined with 'to cause the liquidation, termination, or acceleration' indicates that the liquidation, termination, or acceleration must be performed in accordance with a contractual provision of the swap agreement. The contractual provision determines the method, and without that method, the right to liquidate has no practical meaning.[111]

---

payment would be designated as a 'defaulted synthetic termination payment', and subordinated to the senior noteholders, and capped in the amount of US$30,000. *Lehman Brothers v Ballyrock* (n 103) 35–36.

[105] ibid 37.
[106] Bankruptcy Code, ss 365(e)(1), 541(c)(1)(B).
[107] *Lehman Brothers v Ballyrock* (n 103).
[108] *Michigan State Housing Development Authority v Lehman Brothers Derivative Products* Inc 502 BR 383 (Bankr SDNY 2013).
[109] ibid. See Chapter 10 section 4.2 for cases analyzing 'market quotation' and valuation methods.
[110] This was a default under s 5(a)(vii) of the ISDA master.
[111] *Michigan State Housing Development Authority v Lehman Brothers* (n 108).

11.40 The Court distinguished this case from *Perpetual Trustee* and *Ballyrock* because the *ipso facto* clauses there were not included in the swap agreement, but in related indentures, and did not fall within section 560, as they did not directly deal with liquidation, acceleration, or termination.

11.41 The, the Supreme Court ruled on the safe harbour protection in *Merit Management Group v FTI Consulting*,[112] a case where the owner of a racetrack (Valley View) sought to buy a competing racetrack (Bedford), and made payments to that effect, including to Bedford's shareholder (Merit). Valley View entered bankruptcy, and FTI, the trustee, sought to avoid the transfer by Valley View to Merit, but the transaction had been executed through their agent banks, using derivatives, and Merit argued that it benefitted from the safe harbour, for transactions 'made by or to' financial institutions,[113] and there was a Circuit split on whether the safe harbour applied to cases where such financial institutions were mere 'conduits'. The unanimous opinion by Justice Sotomayor held that the safe harbour did not exclude the rules on fraudulent transfers in cases where the financial institution was not the beneficiary. Since section 546(e) (safe harbour) read 'Notwithstanding' the sections that contemplated the trustee's avoidance powers, the safe harbour was an exception to the trustee's power, and thus the 'relevant transfer' to assess the safe harbour was the transaction the trustee sought to avoid, ie once the trustee has properly identified the transfer, the court has no reason to examine the relevance of component parts to limit the avoiding power.[114] In the Court's view, this solution had the benefit of being straightforward: FTI sought to avoid the Valley-to-Merit transfer, and the Court had to look at this transfer, which did not meet the safe harbour criteria because it did not happen between financial institutions.[115] Thus, by anchoring the safe harbour in the 'avoidance' provisions, the Court let bankruptcy trustees some leeway to strategically define the transaction subject to avoidance to not fall within the safe harbour.

11.42 The background of *Michigan* and *Merit* helped to overrule *Perpetual* and *Ballyrock*, in *Lehman Brothers Special Financing (LBSF) v Bank of America,* which analysed a 'flip' clause similar to that of *Ballyrock*. LBSF sought to recover from noteholders, issuers, and trustees under forty-four synthetic CDOs the moneys distributed as 'termination payments' after LBSF and LBHI went bankrupt. The trust indenture's priority clauses gave LBSF priority *except* if Lehman's default triggered termination, in which case the priority 'flipped' to noteholders. LBSF alleged that these were unenforceable *ipso facto* clauses. However, Judge Peck, the author of the *Perpetual* and *Ballyrock* opinions had retired, and Judge Chapman[116] dismissed LBSF's claim, holding that (i) the priority provisions did not modify any existing LBSF upon bankruptcy; (ii) that any modification would have occurred *before* LBSF's bankruptcy,[117] and, most consequentially, that (iii) even if the clauses were *ipso facto* clauses, they would be protected by section 560's safe harbour, which, given the 'unambiguously sweeping text of section 560' required a 'broad and literal' interpretation.[118] The district court confirmed, relying on the literal meaning of section 560 and several dictionaries to hold that

---

[112] *Merit Management Group v FTI Consulting* 138 S Ct 883 (2018).
[113] Bankruptcy Code, s 546(e).
[114] *Merit Management Group v FTI Consulting* (n 112) 13–14.
[115] *Merit Management Group v FTI Consulting* (n 112) 18–19.
[116] *Lehman Bros. Special Fin Inc v Bank of America National Association* Ch 11 Case No 08-13555, Adv No 10-03547, 553 BR 476 (Bankr SDNY 2016).
[117] Judge Chapman declined to follow *Perpetual*, where Judge Peck relied on the broad language of *ipso facto* prohibitions, which referred to 'a case' of bankruptcy (not, eg 'the' case) to render unlawful a 'flip' activated with the bankruptcy of an entity in the same group as the contract signatory.
[118] *LBSF v Bank of America National Association* No 17-cv-01224 (SDNY 2018) 553.

'liquidate' meant 'bring[ing] the swap agreement to an end by distributing the [c]ollateral pursuant to the priority provisions'.[119] The fact that the trustee, and not investors themselves, exercised the (flip) right was no problem, because the safe harbour 'requires only the exercise "of" a swap participant's contractual right, but that right need not be exercised "by"' the swap participant'.[120] *Perpetual* and *Ballyrock* were not controlling authorities and, anyway, in those cases the 'flip' was not part of the swap agreement.[121] The Circuit affirmed.[122] It relied on (i) a broad interpretation of 'swap', which encompassed all the terms incorporated in it, such as the priority provision, and (ii) a broad interpretation of 'liquidation', which 'must include the disbursement of proceeds from the liquidated collateral', a view that openly overruled *Perpetual* and *Ballyrock*, and (iii) confirmed the district's view that what was needed was the enforcement 'of', and not 'by' a swap participant.[123] Market practice had found its way into bankruptcy policy.

4 Disputes over financial collateral: characterization, custody, and segregation

11.43 Financial institutions need collateral assets to ensure liquidity, and often use bespoke arrangements to make it possible for such collateral to be used, and circulate quickly; which sometimes includes using their clients' assets. This, however, faces courts with the problem of classifying said bespoke arrangement within existing categories of 'property' and 'security' (section 4.1) and, in cases where clients' assets are used without proper segregation, striking a balance between protecting clients and protecting general creditors (section 4.2).

4.1 Classifying complex collateral arrangements as a recognizable security

11.44 Complex collateral arrangements can create tensions with insolvency principles, because, being exceptions to *pari passu*, courts need to classify them as a recognizable form of property or security arrangement in order to enforce them. This present the parties the dilemma of choosing a bespoke arrangement tailored to their specific needs with the risk that it may be misinterpreted, or even disregarded by the courts.[124]

11.45 This tension was clear in the '*Extended Liens*' case, also part of the Lehman Brothers saga.[125] Here there was a group-level arrangement for the centralized management of cash and instruments. Under this arrangement the group parent in Europe, Lehman Brothers International Europe (LBIE) would act as custodian, and hold property on trust for other group entities. Yet, another group entity, Lehman Brothers Finance SA (LBF) would also have a 'general lien' over assets, in respect of monies owed *by* LBF *to* LBIE, *and to* any other Lehman group

---

[119] ibid. LBSF more restrictive view of 'liquidate' as 'calculating' the amounts due would ignore the provision's context, and render it a nullity.
[120] ibid 7–8.
[121] *LBSF v Bank of America* (n 118) 7.
[122] *Lehman Brothers Special Financing Inc. v Bank of America National Association* No 18-1079 (2d Cir 2020).
[123] ibid 23, 25.
[124] See Marco Lamandini and David Ramos Muñoz, *EU Financial Law* (CEDAM/Kluwer 2016).
[125] *In Lehman Brothers International (Europe) (in administration)* [2012] EWHC 2997 (Ch)).

affiliate, hence the 'extended liens' name.[126] This made it possible that the parent would act as custodian, but that one of the subsidiaries could freely operate over the collateral, and perform some group treasury functions. However, when the different group entities entered insolvency proceedings, the question was whether there was some form of security enforceable in insolvency. The court recharacterized the purported 'lien', which is a security interest only applicable to goods susceptible of physical possession, as a 'floating charge'.[127] This made the arrangement unenforceable, since charges (including floating charges) require registration to be valid. There was an exception to the registration requirement under the statutory rules transposing the Financial Collateral Directive,[128] which admitted the possibility of a valid and enforceable security over collateral that is 'substituted' by the provider. However, this required that such collateral remained under the 'possession' or 'control' of the collateral taker.[129] Briggs J used the legislative history to conclude that the provision had to be interpreted restrictively, to exclude floating charges where the collateral provider can substitute the collateral on a regular basis until the charge 'crystallizes'.[130]

11.46 This opened the question of the enforceability of forms of 'floating' or 'rotating' security in other jurisdictions, eg in Italy the *pegno rotativo* was accepted because it was argued that the English floating charge (which inspired the *pegno rotativo*) was admitted under the Financial Collateral Directive,[131] a conclusion discredited by the *Extended Liens* case.

11.47 In another Lehman case, *Lomas v RAB Market Cycles*,[132] the question was whether the prime broker agreement (charge version) (the PB Agreement) concluded by LBIE, the group's European parent entity, was a 'trust' that would make LBIE a trustee and thus give its clients proprietary protection in the event of LBIE's insolvency. Unsecured creditors objected on grounds that, although the PB Agreement described LBIE as trustee of the assets for the benefit of its clients, it gave LBIE rights to substitute and use its clients' assets. This, unsecured creditors alleged, was incompatible with a trust and should have deprived clients of any proprietary rights in the assets in insolvency.[133] Despite recognizing certain anomalies,[134] the court concluded that, taken as a whole, the PB Agreement did disclose a sufficient intention to make LBIE the trustee over the client's assets or their substitute.[135]

---

[126] The clause read: 'The Client [LBF] agrees that the Custodian [LIBE] shall have a general lien on all ... Property held by it under this Agreement until the satisfaction of all liabilities and obligations of the Client (whether actual or contingent) owed to the Custodian or any Lehman Brothers entity under any other arrangement entered into with any Person in the Lehman Brothers organisation. In the event of failure by the Client to discharge any of such liabilities and obligations when due ... the Custodian shall be entitled to sell ... or otherwise realize any such Property ... and to apply the proceeds of such sale or realisation in the satisfaction of such liabilities and obligations.'
[127] *In Lehman Brothers International (Europe) 2012* (n 125).
[128] Directive 2002/47/EC of the European Parliament and of the Council of 6 June 2002 on financial collateral arrangements [2002] OJ L168.
[129] ibid arts 2(2), 8(3)(b) and recitals 9, 10.
[130] Briggs J was also persuaded by the exclusion from the English statutory rules that transposed the Directive of arrangements granting collateral-providers control rights over the collateral beyond the right to substitute collateral or to withdraw excess collateral. See *In re Lehman Brothers International (Europe) 2012* (n 125). This holding was in line with the previous decision of *Re F2G Realisations Ltd: Gray v GTP Group Limited* [2011] 1 BCLC 313, but was much more detailed about its reasons, which gives it greater precedential value.
[131] E Gabrielli, *Il pegno* (UTET 2005) 261, and E Gabrielli, 'Contratti di garanzia finanziaria, stabilità del mercato e procedure concorsuali' (2005) Riv dir priv 517.
[132] *Lomas v RAB Market Cycles (Master Fund) Limited* [2009] EWHC 2545 (Ch).
[133] ibid 20.
[134] ibid 49–52.
[135] ibid 53–63. The court found the existence of a trust 'notwithstanding the conferral of rights on LBIE in relation to it which would have made a 19th century trust lawyer turn in his grave'. See Mr Justice Briggs, 'Has English Law Coped with the Lehman Collapse?' [2013] Butterworths J Intl Banking and Fin L 132.

4.2 Custody, intermediation, and segregation risk

11.48 Financial transactions also present 'custody risk', ie the risk of the intermediary not properly acting as a go-between between investors and issuers ('disconnecting'), or of not properly segregating securities or money from the intermediary's own assets.[136] The UNIDROIT Convention on intermediated securities seeks to solve these issues, by combining the 'no upper-tier attachment' rule, ie no right against intermediaries up the custody chain,[137] with a specific priority right over the securities held by the intermediary;[138] and, in case of a shortfall, a pro-rata share in the intermediary's accounts of each type of security.[139] Absent this complete framework, courts in different jurisdictions have had to deal with these risks in their own way.

11.49 The risk of 'disconnecting' arose in *Eckerle v Wickeder Westfalenstahl GmbH*,[140] where a company incorporated in England, which operated from Germany and was listed there (DNick Holding plc), adopted a shareholders' meeting resolution to discontinue listing and become a private company, which was opposed by three minority shareholders, who sought annulment or an appraisal (ie paid 'exit') right. Yet the names of those shareholders were not in the shareholder register, which mentioned the Bank of New York Depository (Nominees) Ltd which held the shares on trust for Clearstream AG, which kept accounts for its accounts holders, which were banks and other financial institutions, which, in turn held the accounts for the investors (or for other institutions which held the accounts for the investors). The company's articles of incorporation tried to address the problem of registered shareholders being different from the ultimate beneficial owners. However, they merely indicated that 'Clearstream holders' could direct the registered holder of shares how to exercise the vote. These 'holders' were financial entities. The ultimate investors, who were still at least one or several layers away, could not exercise their rights, as they were not considered 'shareholders'.

11.50 The risk of segregation arose in the *Lehman Brothers Clients Assets Sourcebook* cases.[141] UK rules, a transposition of MiFID safekeeping rules, required money to be deposited in clients' segregated accounts, but instead of segregating upon receipt, LBIE used the 'alternative approach', permitted by the rules, whereby money was paid into LBIE accounts and then segregated into client accounts after a (daily) 'reconciliation process'. The last reconciliation took place days before the bankruptcy, leaving a shortfall, and some funds were not segregated at all, leaving a total shortfall of US$1 billion, a failure to comply with segregation duties 'on a truly spectacular scale'.[142]

11.51 Courts had to answer three issues: (i) whether clients' statutory trust over account 'moneys' was established when the money was received, or only when it was segregated in separate accounts; (ii) whether the specific recovery procedure envisaged in regulatory rules, involving

---

[136] See Lamandini and Ramos Muñoz (n 124); David Ramos and Javier Solana, 'Bank Resolution and Creditor Distribution: The Tension Shaping Global Banking (Part I): "External and Intra-Group Funding" and "ex ante Planning v. ex post Execution" Dimensions' (2020) 28 Miami J Bus L 1.
[137] UNIDROIT Convention, art 22; Uniform Commercial Code, art 8 s 8-503.
[138] UNIDROIT Convention, art 21; Uniform Commercial Code, art 8 s 8-503(a).
[139] UNIDROIT Convention, art 26(2)(b); Uniform Commercial Code, s 8-503(b).
[140] *Eckerle and Others v Wickeder Westfalenstahl GmbH & Another* [2013] EWHC 68 (Ch).
[141] *In re Lehman Brothers International (Europe)* [2009] EWHC 3228 (Ch); *In re Lehman Brothers International (Europe)* [2010] EWCA Civ 917; *In re Lehman Brothers International (Europe) 2012* (n 125). Lehman Brothers International Europe (LBIE) was the principal trading subsidiary in Europe of a US bankrupt bank, which held large amounts of money on behalf of their customers.
[142] *Lehman Brothers International (Europe) 2009* (n 141).

a primary pooling event, or PPE, of client moneys, as a previous step to effect a quick transfer, would include the moneys actually segregated or also the moneys that should have been segregated; (iii) whether clients would participate in the pool if they had claims to client money or only if they had contributed to the pool.

11.52   In first instance Briggs J found that clients could benefit from a trust, which arose upon receipt of moneys. However, he found that the specific recovery procedure with the PPE only included the moneys actually segregated, and clients whose moneys had actually been contributed. This left the sole remedy of 'tracing' under trust law, ie clients would be entitled to a proprietary claim, but only if they could trace the assets, something that, in case of money, was quite an ineffective solution. The Court of Appeal and the Supreme Court upheld the finding on the 'trust', but reversed the conclusion on the applicability of PPE rules. The Court of Appeal relied on a finalistic interpretation of Article 16(2) MiFID Implementation Directive,[143] and its aim to provide a 'high level of protection to all clients' to hold that clients shared in the pool if their money ought to have been segregated, regardless of whether it was actually segregated. The Supreme Court confirmed this in a 3:2 decision (Lords Walker and Hope dissented).[144] The problem is that this (i) could suggest that the existence of property rights largely depends on the belief, or expectation, by clients, of such existence; (ii) allocates property rights based on a finalistic interpretation of a rule that focuses on safekeeping duties; and (iii) by trying to grant equal protection to all clients the courts granted an equal delay in the recovery of funds.

5 Inter-creditor disputes ensure bankruptcy remoteness (shielding the assets from formal bankruptcy proceedings)

11.53   Sophisticated creditors often seek to control collateral assets.[145] To do this, creditors not only protect collateral assets from the insolvency of their originator (section 5.2) but try to ensure that such collateral assets are not subject to individual enforcement actions by any individual creditor, nor subject to formal bankruptcy proceedings, as we see here.[146] To this aim, creditors place the assets in a SPV, and constrain the power of directors voluntarily to file for bankruptcy, as well as creditors' rights to file individual claims against the SPV. Courts, however, must analyse whether such arrangements are consistent with directors' duties (section

---

[143] Article 16(2) of MiFID Implementing Directive (Commission Directive 2006/73/EC implementing Directive 2004/39/EC of the European Parliament and of the Council as regards organisational requirements and operating conditions for investment firms and defined terms for the purposes of that Directive [2006] OJ L241) states that: 'If, for reasons of the applicable law, including in particular the law relating to property or insolvency, the arrangements made by investment firms in compliance with paragraph 1 to safeguard clients' rights are not sufficient to satisfy the requirements of Article 13(7) and (8) of Directive 2004/39/EC on markets in financial instruments amending Council Directives 85/611/EEC and 93/6/EEC and Directive 2000/12/EC of the European Parliament and of the Council and repealing Council Directive 93/22/EEC [2004] OJ L145, Member States shall prescribe the measures that investment firms must take in order to comply with those obligations.'

[144] Thus, what mattered was whether the clients had a 'money claim'. Since the rules provided that distribution would be made to those who had a 'client money entitlement', the problem was surmounted by holding that this concept referred to a 'contractual entitlement'. *Lehman Brothers International (Europe) 2010* (n 141); *Lehman Brothers International (Europe) 2012* (n 125).

[145] See Ramos Muñoz, 'Can Complex Contracts Replace Bankruptcy Principles?' (2018) 92 American Bankruptcy LJ 417. See Ramos Muñoz, 'Insolvency-remote Transactions in a Comparative Perspective (Part 2)' (2015) 10 Capital Markets LJ 362

[146] See Ramos Muñoz (n 1); and Ramos Muñoz 'Part 2' (n 145).

5.1) and whether there are limits to the enforcement of no-action, non-petition, and non-recourse clauses (section 5.2).

5.1 Limiting bankruptcy filing by SPV directors, and fiduciary duties

The more obvious way the assets of a project may enter bankruptcy is if the SPV that holds **11.54** them files for bankruptcy. Thus, parties may arrange the transaction, for example, to require a unanimous vote for voluntary filing and/or instilling on directors the importance of not filing. The question is whether such constraints may go against directors' fiduciary duties.

The issue arose in two US cases, *Re Kingston Square*[147] and *Re General Growth Properties*.[148] **11.55** *Re Kingston Square* involved real estate financing: each SPE controlled one piece of property and was controlled by the same three directors: A, a sort of 'sponsor', his own straw man (B), and an independent director (C). The properties were refinanced by a loan from Chase Manhattan Bank and by REFG, a securitization SPV owned by the DLJ Group. After a default, Chase and REFG, as secured creditors, began foreclosure proceedings. A convinced unsecured creditors with claims arising from ancillary services to file for bankruptcy,[149] but the bankruptcy petitions were not ratified by directors. Transaction documents required unanimous directors' consent to file for bankruptcy; the independent director, C, abstained. The court held that C had not fulfilled his fiduciary duties towards unsecured creditors; which, in the court's view, put into question his independence.[150] Unfortunately, the court did not explain why such fiduciary duties were owed *precisely* to unsecured creditors, and not to other constituencies, thus leaving the bigger issues unanswered.

General Growth Properties (GGP) concerned a real estate investment trust (reit) presiding **11.56** over an extremely complex corporate structure. When GGP could not roll-over its debt, it filed for bankruptcy, and its entities 'were in varying degrees of financial distress'.[151] A team of advisers was hired to do an analysis of the entire group and each separate entity to classify them from A to G, according to the convenience of bankruptcy. Bankruptcy filing required the unanimous vote in each board, including independent directors, who, in exercising their fiduciary duties, were supposed to consider the company's interest including its respective creditors.[152] Two independent directors were supplied by Corporation Service Company (CSC) and served in the board of more than 150 project-specific entities, before being replaced 'without any prior indication' by two other independent directors, who voted affirmatively to the bankruptcy filing, including for entities not in default. Secured creditors filed

---

[147] *In re Kingston Square Associates and Others* 214 BR 713 (Bankr SDNY 1997).
[148] *In re General Growth Properties* 409 BR 43 (Bankr SDNY 2009).
[149] *In re Kingston Square Associates and Others* (n 147).
[150] ibid.
[151] ibid 58.
[152] Some clauses stated that: '[I]n the case ... the Independent Managers shall consider only the interests of the Company, including its respective creditors, in acting or otherwise voting on the matters referred to in Article XIII (p).' Article XIII (p) required the 'unanimous written consent of the Managers of the Company, including both of the Independent Managers' in order for the SPE to file for bankruptcy. The Operating Agreements indicated that: '[I]n exercising their rights and performing their duties under this Agreement, any Independent Manager shall have a fiduciary duty of loyalty and care similar to that of a director of a business corporation organized under the General Corporation Law of the State of Delaware.' See *In re General Growth Properties* 409 BR 43, (Bankr SDNY 2009) 64.

a motion to dismiss, arguing that bankruptcy petitions had been filed in bad faith, but the court dismissed their allegations.

11.57 The court held, first, that the entities were part of a group (and, for example, depended on the parent for a bail-out), and since the group's financial structure was seriously imperilled,[153] this could be a decisive factor.[154] Secondly, it held that directors' fiduciary duties in corporate law required them to take creditors' interests into consideration after the company became insolvent; before that they had to consider only shareholders' interests;[155] ie the parent company's, and sternly rejected the idea that directors should serve creditors' interest:

> As the Delaware cases stress, directors and managers owe their duties to the corporation and, ordinarily, to the shareholders. Seen from the perspective of the group, the filings were unquestionably not premature.[156]

11.58 The logic and functioning of an SPV are very different from those of an operational company. An SPV is supposed to execute the transaction in a mechanical way, and, if there is a default, to follow the steps envisaged in the transaction documents. Still, these cases show that this may be difficult when the steps are not clearly preordained, and directors are subject to fiduciary duties.

5.2 Limiting bankruptcy filing by creditors: non-petition and non-recourse clauses, and other mechanisms

11.59 'No-action', or 'non-petition' clauses[157] may be included to ensure that none of the secured parties is to institute any form of bankruptcy or insolvency proceedings against the company,[158] normally by vesting a trustee with the sole power to file claims. If an SPV has been set up, this will include most, or even *all* creditors, which will ensure a vehicle's 'bankruptcy remoteness'.[159] An alternative way to block individual enforcement actions is by means of 'limited recourse' provisions, which, instead of excluding *procedural* rights to sue, limit

---

[153] The court held that: 'There is no question that the SPE structure was intended to insulate the financial position of each of the Subject Debtors from the problems of its affiliates, and to make the prospect of a default less likely. There is also no question that this structure was designed to make each Subject Debtor "bankruptcy remote." Nevertheless, the record also establishes that the Movants each extended a loan to the respective subject debtor with a balloon payment that would require refinancing in a period of years and that would default if financing could not be obtained by the SPE or by the SPE's parent coming to its rescue. Movants do not contend that they were unaware that they were extending credit to a company that was part of a much larger group, and that there were benefits as well as possible detriments from this structure. If the ability of the Group to obtain refinancing became impaired, the financial situation of the subsidiary would inevitably be impaired.'

[154] The court drew heavily on *Heisley v UIP Engineered Prods Corp (In re UIP Engineered Prods Corp)* 831 F 2d 54 (4th Cir 1987); and *In re Mirant Corp* WL 2148362 (Bankr ND Tex 2005).

[155] In holding so the court referred to *North American Catholic Educational Programming Foundation Inc v Gheewalla* [2007] Del LEXIS 227 (Del Supr 2007); and to *Credit Lyonnais Bank Netherland NV v Pathé Communications Co* [1991] Del Ch (Dec).

[156] *In re General Growth Properties* 409 BR 43 (Bankr SDNY 2009) paras 65–66.

[157] See Ramos Muñoz (n 48) 98–100.

[158] *In the Matter of Golden Key Ltd (In Receivership) v In the Matter of the Insolvency Act 1986* [2009] EWHC 148 (Ch).

[159] One of the SIV receivers in *Golden Key* described it as follows: It is an essential feature of the SIV structure that it is 'insolvency remote' in the sense that the Company's creditors have agreed, by way of various different contractual mechanisms, only to look to the assets secured …, and then only in accordance with the terms of the Limited Recourse provisions set out in the documentation governing the Company's operations. See *In the Matter of Golden Key Ltd* (n 158).

creditors' *substantive* rights to a specific asset pool, excluding further claims against the debtor. This may be useful to achieve 'bankruptcy remoteness' in an SPV.

Are these clauses enforceable in all circumstances, including to prevent bankruptcy filing? In the United States the enforceability of no-action clauses is admitted.[160] However, in the case of debenture offerings, section 316(b) of the Trust Indenture Act (TIA) 1939 provides that a holder of indenture securities has an individual right to sue for payment of principal and interest on the (or after) due dates set out in the note.[161] This mandatory provision[162] implies that a bondholder's debt cannot be reduced, or its term extended, without that debtholder's consent,[163] which shows a concern against retail bondholders being forced to relinquish part of their rights in out-of-court debt restructurings.[164] The individual petition right, which cannot be excluded, can be a money-collection claim, or, according to some courts, a bankruptcy petition.[165]

11.60

Also, the case *Audax Credit Opportunities v TMK*[166] (the TriMark litigation) showed that contractual ingenuity to limit individual enforcement has its limits. TriMark, a restaurant company heavily hit by the pandemic and in need of refinancing issued new senior debt to the defendants, securing it with the same collateral that secured TriMark's existing first-lien debt. Yet, TriMark and the new creditors agreed on a plan to put the defendants' interest before that of pre-existing creditors, where the defendants (having more than 50 per cent of first-lien debt) allegedly voted to change the terms of that debt, stripping it of some of its protections, and subsequently TriMark exchanged the new lenders' first lien debt for a new class of super-senior debt, with a higher priority order, thus effectively pushing plaintiffs' (non-participating lenders) debt from first lien to third lien. Such exchange was made on a dollar-for-dollar, despite the first lien debt traded at 78 cents on the dollar (thus, there was a net transfer of value). The amendments in the debt covenants that predated the exchange stripped non-participating lenders of information rights, and expanded the no-action clause in the original agreement to preclude lenders from 'tak[ing] or institute[ing] any actions or proceedings, judicial or otherwise, for any ... right or remedy or assert[ing] any other cause of action,' against TriMark, *or* against the lender defendants.[167] The non-participating lenders brought a claim for voidness of the amendments, breach of (the original) contract, and breaches of the implied covenant of good faith and fair dealing. The defendants alleged that under the no-action clause the plaintiffs lacked standing, because the clause required them to request the administrative agent to initiate litigation. The Court rejected the defendants' arguments, reasoning that no-action clauses are generally enforceable 'because they reflect an *ex ante* agreement to sacrifice certain individual rights for the "salutary purpose" ' of 'benefiting the venture as a whole'. However, taking the plaintiffs' allegation as true, there

11.61

---

[160] *Akanthos Capital Management LLC v Compucredit Holdings Corp* F 3d, 2012 WL 1414247, 1 (11th Cir 2012); *In re Enron Corporation Securities and ERISA Litigation* (Not Reported in F Supp 2d) WL 744823, 70 Fed R Serv 3d 113 (SD Tex 2008); *McMahan & Co v Wherehouse Entertainment Inc* 859 F Supp 743, 749 (SDNY 1994); *Feldbaum v McCrory Corp* WL 119095 (Del Ch 1992). This Includes claims for fraudulent conveyance.
[161] See s 316 (b) TIA 1939. See George W Shuster Jr, 'The Trust Indenture Act and International Debt Restructurings' (2006) 14 Am Bankr Inst L Rev 432.
[162] *Enron and ERISA* (n 160); *Great Plains Trust Co v Union Pacific Railroad Co* 492 F 3d 986, 991 (8th Cir 2007); *Cruden v Bank of NY* 957 F 2d 961, 968 (2d Cir 1992).
[163] Shuster (n 161) 442.
[164] ibid 439.
[165] *Envirodyne Indus Inc v Conn Mut Life Co (In re Envirodyne Indus Inc*, 174 BR 986, 996 (Bankr ND Ill 1994); *Grey v Federated Group Inc*, 107 F 3d 730, 733 (9th Cir 1997). See Shuster (n 161) n 14 and accompanying text.
[166] *Audax Credit Opportunities Offshore Ltd v TMK Hawk Parent Corp* No 2021-50794 (NY Sup Ct 2021).
[167] ibid.

was 'no ex ante agreement to the no-action provisions *or* salutary benefit' (emphasis in the original).[168]

11.62 Courts in the UK also generally enforce no-action clauses.[169] In *Elektrim SA v Vivendi Holdings 1*, the case turned on an interpretation of the scope of the clause,[170] not its validity. The High Court interpreted the clause broadly, holding that the claimed loss assumed Elektrim's bankruptcy, and that proving in bankruptcy was one of the species of proceedings under the exclusive control of the trustee. This was confirmed on appeal.[171]

11.63 In *Elliott International et al v Law Debenture Trustee* the Court allowed individual debtors to appear before a French court in the context of insolvency (*sauvegarde*) proceedings.[172] This in itself should raise no problem for the enforceability of no action clauses under English law because the issue concerned the interpretation of the clause, the trustee agreed with bondholders' appearance, whose purpose was to opposed the French proceedings, and to seek a declaration by the French court that it was not competent. Yet the court also concluded that:

> Even if the opposition proceedings are to be regarded as part and parcel of the safeguard proceedings (much as an application within a company insolvency in this court could properly be viewed as part of the same proceedings), the safeguard proceedings themselves are not proceedings to enforce the terms of the bonds; rather they are proceedings the purpose of which is to achieve or assist in achieving a restructuring of the Issuer's debt[173].

11.64 The court's distinction between 'enforcement' and 'restructuring' is debatable. If used as precedent, it could lead to the conclusion that a no-action clause only bars individual enforcement proceedings, but not a filing for bankruptcy/insolvency. It also shows the uncertainty of a case-by-case approach towards interpreting clauses that may enjoy widespread use in the market.

11.65 The implied assumption of some courts seems to be that individual enforcement and/or filing are replaced with collective (court-based) enforcement proceedings, where the trustee acts on behalf of all bondholders.[174] Yet, in bankruptcy-remote transactions claims by

---

[168] *Audax v TMK* (n 166): 'Here, taking Plaintiffs' allegations as true, there was no ex ante agreement to the no-action provisions or salutary benefit. Plaintiffs signed on to the substantially narrower no-action provisions in the Original Agreement and did not consent to the amendment. Moreover, the amended provisions lack any semblance of arm's-length agreement because the Lender Defendants allegedly crafted them with a view to immediately exiting the contract, thus gaining the protective benefit of the no-action provisions' amended terms without ever having to abide by them as parties to the contract. Even assuming the Original Agreement permitted (or at least did not expressly prohibit) "Required Lenders" to amend the no-action provision in some respects, it cannot reasonably be construed to give Defendants carte blanche to make it exorbitantly expensive, if not impossible, for Plaintiffs to enforce their un-amendable consent rights under Section 9.02 [b] of the Original Agreement.'

[169] *In the Matter of Golden Key Ltd* (n 158) 47; *Elektrim SA v Vivendi Holdings 1 Corp Law Debenture Trust Corp plc v Vivendi Holdings 1 Corp* [2008] EWCA Civ 1178, 92–94, and 100; *Highberry Ltd v Colt Telecom Group Plc (No 1)* [2002] EWHC 2503 (Ch).

[170] The case was part of the legal battle between Deutsche Telekom and Vivendi for the control of a Polish telecommunications company (PTC). Elektrim was going to transfer its holding in PTC to Vivendi, but eventually transferred it to DT. DT paid the price to Elektrim, which agreed to transfer the money to the bondholders' trustee. Vivendi acquired the bonds from a bondholder and sued before the Florida courts to undo the money transfer. The trust deed and the debt document were subject to English law and courts, and they ruled against Vivendi, based on the no-action clause.

[171] *Elektrim SA v Vivendi Holdings 1* (n 169).

[172] *Elliott International LP and Others v Law Debenture Trustees Limited* [2006] EWHC 3063 (Ch) para 47.

[173] ibid para 47.

[174] In *Elektrim SA v Vivendi Holdings 1* (n 169) for example, the acted in the Polish proceedings until they requested the hearings to be adjourned as a result of DT's payment to Elektrim, and Elektrim's composition proposal, and subsequent payment to the trustee, on behalf of bondholders.

individual bondholders may be precluded, but the alternative may consist in the seizure and liquidation of the assets by the trustee, and a subsequent distribution of proceeds, with little court supervision, in the form of directions voluntarily sought by the trustee.[175] In *Golden Key* the English court tiptoed around this issue.[176]

In the US, offerings subject to the Trust Indenture Act (TIA) protect individual bondholders' **11.66** right to not suffer the modification of basic indenture terms without their consent. Thus, no-action clauses are admissible. Yet, the courts have shown that bankruptcy-remoteness need not mean bankruptcy-proof in all cases.

In *re Zais Investment Grade Limited VII* senior creditors filed a bankruptcy petition for a se- **11.67** curitization SPV used for a CDO squared[177] because they could not achieve the two-thirds majority vote the indenture required to approve any debt restructuring plan. Their plan was to liquidate the assets and give the cash to senior creditors (the amount of assets left barely covered their claims). The debtor SPV did not contest the bankruptcy filing. Junior creditors opposed (in bankruptcy they lost the advantage of the requisite majorities under the indenture), and asked the court to abstain itself and dismiss the case, because Zais was incorporated in the Cayman Islands, and because section 305(a)(1) of the Bankruptcy Code permits dismissal of a bankruptcy petition when 'the interests of creditors and the debtor would be better served by such dismissal'. The court rejected these. The entity had no actual presence in the Cayman Islands, and could be a debtor in the US.[178] Then, there were no other proceedings pending; the out-of-court settlement had been brought to a stalemate; and the option letting the assets run off was rejected too, because a plan had been suggested: if the plan was inequitable, as suggested by junior creditors, that should be decided in the confirmation stage, but not by prematurely dismissing the bankruptcy filing.[179] In the *First Millennium* case, although not involving a bankruptcy petition, the Second Circuit rejected the FDIC arguments that the notes were 'limited by recourse only to the collateral' (and, since there were no collateral assets left, the FDIC could take over the amounts identified as 'transferor interest') and gave noteholders full recourse to 'transferor interest', ie funds held by the trustee for the benefit of the originator, because the 'limited recourse' clause was inconsistent with other clauses, which provided an 'absolute and unconditional' right by noteholders, under a 'Notwithstanding' clause.[180]

---

[175] Ramos Muñoz (n 48) 100. See *BNY Ltd v Eurosail plc* [2011] EWCA Civ 227 (CA). See *In the Matter of Golden Key Ltd* (n 158); *In re Cheyne Finance plc (In Receivership)* [2007] EWHC 2402 (Ch), [2008] Bus LR 1562, [2008] 2 All ER 987, [2008] BCC 182, [2008] 1 BCLC 741; *The Bank of New York v Montana Board of Investments, Party A, Party B*, [2008] EWHC 1594 (Ch); *Re Whistlejacket* [2008] EWHC 463 (Ch); *In Re Sigma Sigma Fin Corp (in administration) Re* [2008] EWHC 2997.

[176] *In the Matter of Golden Key Ltd* (n 158):the usual rights of an unsatisfied creditor to initiate insolvency proceedings are ousted in favour of the rights, whether sounding in contract or trust, provided by the documentation. No party has submitted that there is any objection, from a public policy point of view, in investors agreeing to make their investment upon such a basis.

[177] Zais was incorporated in the Cayman Islands. It issued secured notes in the Irish Stock Exchange and used the money to acquire securities, which were pledged for its obligations against noteholders, with Bank of New York Mellon being appointed as trustee. The vehicle also issued junior 'income' notes, which were unsecured, and treated as 'equity' in the indenture. *In re Zais Investment Grade Ltd VII* 455 BR 839 (Bkrtcy DNJ 2011).

[178] For this point the court relied on *re Bear Stearns High-Grade Structured Credit Strategies Master Fund Ltd* 374 BR 122 (Bankr SDNY 2007) aff'd 389 BR 325 (SDNY 2008).

[179] *In re Zais Investment Grade Ltd VII* 455 BR 839 (Bkrtcy DNJ 2011) 847.

[180] 'Notwithstanding any other provision in this Indenture, each Holder of a Note shall have the right which is absolute and unconditional to receive payment of the principal and interest'. See *Bank of New York v First Millennium* (n 84) For a further reference of 'Notwithstanding' clauses, and how they may 'trump' other clauses see ch 10, s 4.2.

11.68 In contrast, in *re Taberna Preferred Funding*[181] (*Taberna*) three holders of senior notes issued by an SPV (CDO) filed a bankruptcy petition, which was opposed by the SPV debtor (Taberna), its collateral manager, and five junior creditors. The court held that the senior creditors were ineligible, ie they failed to make a prima facie case that they 'held claims' against the debtor, because their notes were non-recourse. Even if they had been eligible, the court would have dismissed anyway, because it was 'in the best interest of creditors and the estate'.[182] The court found that it would be unjust to find that the petitioners, sophisticated creditors, would be prejudiced by the transaction's liquidation terms that they analysed and bargained for. Furthermore, the filing served no bankruptcy purpose (neither an 'equitable distribution', nor a debtor's rehabilitation). The CDO was a non-operating company, there was no risk of dissipation of assets, senior creditors' rights were protected, and they only sought to liquidate the collateral for their benefit. In *Zais* the debtor did not oppose the petition, which, the court found, was filed in good faith, to realize the maximum value without negatively impacting junior creditors (which, in *Taberna*, would be 'out-of-the-money' in a bankruptcy liquidation, but not necessarily so outside bankruptcy).

11.69 By comparing *Taberna* with *Zais* and *GGP* one can see courts' difficult task. This means acknowledging eg that 'bankruptcy is historically a creditors' remedy allowing for the orderly liquidation of assets for the collective benefit of all creditors',[183] but may also require a careful balancing of equity principles and the enforcement of contract terms as in *Taberna*.

11.70 A slight variation of non-recourse were the 'post enforcement call option' (PECO) agreements,[184] where, in case of enforcement over collateral assets and these were insufficient, a company associated with the issuer would have a call option over all the notes at a nominal price; the note purchaser would not enforce them, and an issuer who owes nothing cannot be insolvent. A PECO clause was examined in the UK in *Eurosail*.[185] The High Court and the Court of Appeal differentiated between the debtor vehicle's 'statutory' insolvency, and the (contractual) insolvency 'event of default' in the document which they had to examine,[186] finding that the entity was not 'unable to pay its debts', and thus not insolvent.[187] Yet, in *obiter* the Court of Appeal distinguished between 'insolvency remoteness', and 'bankruptcy remoteness',[188] holding that the PECO clause could prevent the entity from entering bankruptcy proceedings, but not from being insolvent.[189] Noteholders' rights were full recourse until the security was enforced and the collateral was found insufficient, which activated the PECO clause. It was at that point where the insolvency 'event of default' was assessed to serve enforcement notice.[190] Otherwise, the courts seemed to have no prima facie objection to a PECO clause depriving the parties of access to insolvency proceedings.

---

[181] *In re Taberna Preferred Funding IV Ltd* 594 BR 576 (Bankr SDNY 2018).
[182] 11 USC § 1112(b).
[183] *In re Zais* (n 179) 847.
[184] The rationale was tax-based. Limited recourse implied the levy of stamp duty on the issue, and compromised the deductibility of interest paid on the securities. This was modified with the Taxation of Securitisation Companies Regulations 2006.
[185] *BNY Corporate Trustee Services Ltd v Eurosail-UK 2007-3BL plc and Others* [2010] EWHC 2005 (Ch) (Morritt J); *BNY Corporate Trustee Services Ltd v Eurosail-UK 2007-3BL plc and Others* (*BNY Ltd v Eurosail plc* (CA)) [2011] EWCA Civ 227.
[186] *BNY Corporate Trustee Services Ltd 2010* (n 185) para 41.
[187] Pursuant to Insolvency Act 1986, s 123.
[188] *BNY Corporate Trustee Services Ltd* 2011 (n 185) para 28.
[189] ibid paras 28 and 90.
[190] Otherwise, the whole insolvency test, and the event of default provision, would not have made much sense. *BNY Corporate Trustee Services Ltd* 2011 (n 185) para 100 (Neuberger LJ).

6 Inter-creditor coordination disputes in collective enforcement, liquidation, and restructuring

Even if creditors manage to steer clear of formal bankruptcy proceedings this does not end their disputes. The alternative to formal bankruptcy is contract-based liquidation (or, occasionally, restructuring). However, as in bankruptcy, creditors will have different preferences as to when to activate the mechanism through an 'insolvency event' (6.1.) and when and how to restructure, including conflicts between majority and minority creditors where the latter allege 'oppression' (section 6.2). **11.71**

6.1 Collectively enforcing claims: 'insolvency events' clauses and their hybrid (contract-statutory) construction by courts

Contract triggers based on the 'insolvency' of a debtor vehicle present special challenges.[191] First, can a bankruptcy-remote vehicle be insolvent when there are clauses designed to prevent insolvency? Can courts use the interpretation of statutory insolvency provisions as background rules or principles to fill the gaps in contract-insolvency clauses? **11.72**

In *Cheyne*, a structured investment vehicle (SIV) suffered a 'major capital loss and an enforcement event', and the Bank of New York, as security trustee, appointed receivers. In a first decision (*Cheyne I*),[192] the court interpreted the insolvency event clause, which applied a 'cash flow test', ie the vehicle would not be insolvent unless it was unable to pay its debts as they became due.[193] The court construed this provision, together with its reference to section 123(1) of the English Insolvency Act 1986, as excluding the 'balance-sheet test' under section 123(2),[194] and adopted the receivers' view that Cheyne was not insolvent.[195] **11.73**

Subsequently, in *Cheyne II*, the court had to decide again whether the vehicle was insolvent.[196] This time Cheyne would not be able to pay its senior debts in full by letting the investments run to maturity: it would have to sell its assets before maturity in an uncertain market with discounts between 0 per cent to 7 per cent, or otherwise default on its payments earlier. To the receivers, a sale of the whole portfolio would improve the prospect of paying all senior debts in full, but not in time. The question was whether Cheyne was unable to 'pay its debts as they fell due', as stated in the documents. This mirrored the statutory 'cash flow' **11.74**

---

[191] See Ramos Muñoz, 'Part 2' (n 145), citing Paris Commercial Court (3 November 2008) RG no 2008077996, Dame Luxembourg and RG no 2008077997, SAS Coeur de La Defense; Paris Court of Appeal 25 February 2010, RG no 09/22756, Coeur de La Défense (HOLD); French Supreme Court (Cour de cassation) – Commercial financial and economic chamber (Chambre commercial, financière et économique) decision no 240 of 8 March 2011 (10-13.988/10-13.989/10-13.990)).

[192] *In re Cheyne Fin Plc* [2008] 1 BCLC 732.

[193] The clause in the transaction documents read: 'Insolvency Event means a determination by the Manager or any Receiver that the Issuer is, or is about to become, unable to pay its debts as they fall due to Senior Creditors and any other persons whose claims against the Issuer are required to be paid in priority thereto, as contemplated by Section 123(1) of the United Kingdom Insolvency Act 1986 (such subsection being applied for this purpose only as if the Issuer's only liabilities were those to Senior Creditors and any other persons whose claims against the Issuer are required under the Security Trust Deed to be paid in priority thereto).' ibid. On the cash-flow test see Roy Goode and Kristin van Zwieten, *Principles of Corporate Insolvency Law* (5th edn, Sweet & Maxwell 2018); Vanessa Finch, *Corporate Insolvency Law: Perspectives and Principles* (2d edn, CUP 2009) 146–47.

[194] *In re Cheyne II* (n 192) 7.

[195] The controversy was more about the distribution of monies. See section 7.

[196] *In re Cheyne* (n 175).

test, but did not expressly refer to future debts. Yet, the court interpreted the contract clause in light of the statutory provisions on insolvency and their history, which used an 'overall approach,' until 1985, when the 'cash flow' and 'balance sheet' tests were separated, and relied on case law and academic commentary[197] on section 123 to hold that the 'cash flow test' permitted 'an element of futurity'. Finding that Cheyne was insolvent, Briggs J held:

> [c]ash-flow or commercial insolvency is not to be ascertained by a slavish focus only on debts due as at the relevant date. Such a blinkered review will, in some cases, fail to see that a momentary inability to pay is only the result of a temporary lack of liquidity soon to be remedied, and in other cases fail to see that due to an endemic shortage of working capital a company is on any commercial view insolvent, even though it may continue to pay its debts for the next few days, weeks or even months before an inevitable failure.[198]

11.75 The case shows, yet again, the difficulty of interpreting a contract clause according to its 'plain meaning', especially if it uses language that has a background and context.

11.76 The issue arose again in *Eurosail*,[199] an SPV used to issue notes by Lehman Brothers, the subsequently bankrupt bank. Pre-enforcement rules used a 'pay-as-you-go' approach (favourable to short-term creditors) until (1) the trustee's enforcement notice; or (2) an event of default, which included both the 'cash flow' insolvency, and 'balance sheet 'insolvency under section 123(2) of the Insolvency Act 1986. The vehicle hedged its interest rate and currency risk through Lehman entities, which no longer could perform their part, thus raising the question about the vehicle's (contract) insolvency.[200] Both the Chancery Court (Morritt C), and the Court of Appeal (Neuberger J) held that a contract provision incorporating a statutory concept should be interpreted in light of its statutory meaning.[201] As to section 123(2), both courts held that, when assessing a company's ability to pay its debts, one needs to take into account its current assets, not prospective or contingent assets, while the duty to consider contingent liabilities did not imply the need to aggregate them at face value with current liabilities, including a conversion at the applicable spot exchange rate.[202] The courts held that harmful effects would follow if section 123(2) allowed a winding-up of a company every time that liabilities exceeded assets.[203] The balance-sheet test should prevent current and short-term creditors from being paid at the expense of creditors who gave credit after the point of no return.[204] The Court of Appeal sought to reconcile this with *Cheyne*'s view that cash-flow insolvency should not 'slavishly focus' on debts due, holding that both tests are distinct, and one focuses more on the future than the other. Section 123(2) does not impose a wholly new, relatively mechanical 'assets-based' test. The Court of Appeal also held

---

[197] See eg *Jacobs J and Taylor Australia and New Zealand Banking Group Ltd* [1988] 6 ACLC 808, 811; or Goode and van Zwieten (n 193); Ian Fletcher, *The Law of Insolvency* (3d edn, Sweet & Maxwell 2002) and other authorities cited.
[198] *In re Cheyne* (n 175) 39. The view was enhanced by reference to posterior statutory reforms that supplemented the reference 'as they become due' with the addition of 'and payable'. See *Cuthbertson & Richards Sawmills Pty Ltd v Thomas* (1998) 28 ACSR 310, 319 (Einfeld J); *Southern Cross Interiors Pty Ltd v Deputy Commissioner of Taxation* (2001) 39 ACSR 305 (Palmer J); or *Lewis v Doran* (2005) 219 ALR 555.
[199] *BNY Corporate Trustee Services Ltd 2011* (n 185).
[200] Most assets were sterling-denominated mortgages; most liabilities were dollar or euro-denominated notes. See *BNY Corporate Trustee Services Ltd 2011* (n 185) 19.
[201] The Court of Appeal referred to *Enviroco Ltd v Farstad Supply A/S* [2010] Bus LR 1008, paras 53–54, as authority. See *BNY Corporate Trustee Services Ltd 2011* (n 185) para 34.
[202] For an analysis of the respective assets and liabilities see Ramos Muñoz, 'Part 2' (n 145). See also *BNY Corporate Trustee Services Ltd 2011* (n 185) 76–80.
[203] *BNY Corporate Trustee Services Ltd 2011* (n 185) para 46.
[204] ibid para 48.

that insolvency law should not prevent a 'reasonable business person' from trying to trade through a difficult period.[205] This ignored the fact that, in structured finance, an SPV is not a 'reasonable businessperson', and the 'debtor' has no interest worthy of protection. The only question should have been whether favouring the interest of short-term creditors with a pay-as-you-go system was justified.[206] The case shows that, even if using statutory concepts to interpret contract clauses is a good starting point, sometimes the interests protected by the statute are not present in the contract documentation, and courts may need to do the adjustment.

6.2 Restructuring claims and inter-creditor conflict: disenfranchisement and oppression

Inter-creditor conflicts in bankruptcy law are solved through provisions that facilitate majority decisions and mitigate the holdout problem.[207] The same happens in corporate law. The idea is to allow majority decision-making, while ensuring that minorities are not treated unfairly,[208] which is often achieved through the use of open-textured principles, such as 'fairly', or 'equitably' in bankruptcy law, or the prohibition of 'oppression' in corporate law.[209]

11.77

Outside these, it depends on contract provisions, and their enforceability. Collective action clauses (CACs) have been discussed in connection with sovereign bonds issued by Latin American countries under English or New York law[210] or EU countries affected by the sovereign debt crisis.[211] CACs are also a regular feature in corporate debt offerings, although they have received less attention in relation to insolvency-remote structures.[212] Such clauses are included routinely in trust indentures to avoid collective action problems.[213] The clauses do not pose validity issues in the laws of the UK,[214] the US,[215] or Canada.[216] German law was reformed in 2009 (the New Bondholder Act), to allow the exercise of collective rights (matters that could be decided by the representative, matters that could be decided by a majority

11.78

---

[205] ibid paras 57–58.
[206] The issue is discussed again in relation to the distribution of proceeds. See section 7.
[207] In the US, see eg 11 USC s 1129(b) (the provision on 'cramdowns'). See Jennifer Payne, 'Debt Restructuring in English Law: Lessons from the U.S. and the Need for Reform' (2013) Oxford Legal Research Paper Series No 89.
[208] See eg 11 USC s 1129(b)(1) for the requirements to override a dissenting class.
[209] 11 USC s 1129(b)(1) and (2) (requirement of treating nonconsenting, impaired classes 'fairly and equitably.') In corporate law, see eg John Coffee Jr, 'The Mandatory/Enabling Balance in Corporate Law: An Essay on the Judicial Role' (1989) 89 Col L Rev 1688. In the UK, s 6 of the Insolvency Act 1986 allows a challenge of a CVA if it 'unfairly prejudices' a creditor. See also *Re Charnley Davies Ltd (No 2)* [1990] BCLC 760, and s 994 Companies Act 2006 enshrines the 'unfair prejudice' remedy.
[210] Joy Dey, 'Collective Action Clauses: Sovereign Bondholders Cornered?' (2009) 15 L & Bus Rev of the Americas 485; Sergio J Galvis and Angel L Saad, 'Collective Action Clauses: Recent Progress and Challenges Ahead' (2004) 35 Geo J Intl L 713; Elmar B Koch, 'Collective Action Clauses: the Way Forward' (2004) 35 Geo J Intl L 665; Elmar B Koch, 'Collective Action Clauses: Theory and Practice' (2004) 35 Geo J Intl L 693 Elmar B Koch, 'The Use of Collective Action Clauses in New York Law Bonds of Sovereign Borrowers' (2004) 35 Geo J Intl L 815.
[211] Jason B Gott, 'Addressing the Debt Crisis in the European Union: The Validity of Mandatory Collective Action Clauses and Extended Maturities' (2012) 12 U Chi J Intl L 201.
[212] See, however, Nancy P Jacklin, 'Addressing Collective-Action Problems in Securitized Credit' (2010) 73 L & Contemp Prob 175.
[213] See eg *Elektrim SA v Vivendi Holdings 1* (n 169) 2–3.
[214] *Acevedo v Imcopa Importacao* [2012] EWHC 1849 (Comm); *Elektrim SA v Vivendi Holdings 1* (n 169); *Elliott International LP and Others v Law Debenture Trustees Limited* (n 172); *Highberry Ltd v Colt Telecom Group Plc (No 1)* (n 169).
[215] *Akanthos Capital Management LLC v Compucredit* (n 160); *McMahan & Co v Wherehouse Entertainment Inc* 859 F Supp 743, 749 (SDNY1994); *Feldbaum v McCrory Corp* (n 160).
[216] *Casurina Ltd Partnership v Rio Algom Ltd* [2004] 40 BLR (3d) 112.

of bondholders, and matters requiring a super-majority),[217] while in Japan a mandatory regime in the Commercial code applies for bonds subject to Japanese law.[218] Even if majority decision-making is allowed, the question is whether open-textured principles are applicable. The problem arises when the contract may not successfully address all possible contingencies. Delaware and New York courts have explored these issues in corporate debt offerings.[219] In Delaware courts the standard was set in *Katz v Oak Industries*,[220] a junk-bond era case. An investor agreed to buy Oak's stock, upon condition that its debt be reduced, but this was prohibited by the bond covenants. Bondholders agreed to vote to remove the covenants and then exchange their bonds for 'payment certificates' that promised less than the bonds' face value, but more than their market value. Losing bondholders sued to enjoin the exchange, arguing that it was 'coercive'. The court held that the issuer-bondholders relationship is contractual, not fiduciary in nature, and that an offer had to be 'wrongfully' coercive, to be invalidated, which requires a breach of a contract term, or bad faith, which did not happen if the parties would have approved of the behaviour if it had been presented to them when they agreed to the bond terms.[221]

11.79 New York courts followed a similar approach in practice in *Sharon Steel*,[222] although there they held that the interpretation of boilerplate language was a matter of law, not fact, and courts should seek to ensure certainty and predictability for the good functioning of markets.[223] On this basis, in *Metropolitan Life v Nabisco* in an acquisition leveraged with junk bonds where the acquiror planned to push down the debt on the target, to the detriment of the target's original bondholders, the courts refused to recognize the existence of implied duties by the debtor/issuer towards bondholders that could prevent it from accepting the offer.[224] There are, however, some older precedents holding that the majority bondholders owe a duty of good faith to minority bondholders,[225] but the meaning of this duty remains unclear.

11.80 Other courts have discussed similar issues under the Trust Indenture Act (TIA). Section 316(b) of the TIA states that the modification of 'core' terms, eg the right to payment, is subject to unanimity, while other terms are not. Thus, it has been habitual to threaten a modification of protective covenants eg subordination of debt, waiver of a parent guarantee, etc. to obtain the consent of all bondholders.

11.81 In *Marblegate Asset Management*[226] the court dismissed the request for a temporary injunction against a restructuring plan for failure to establish irreparable harm, but held that the

---

[217] Jason Grant Allen, 'More Than a Matter of Trust: The German Debt Securities Act 2009 in International Perspective' (2011) 7 Cap Mkts LJ 55 ff.
[218] IMF, *Design and Effectiveness of Collective Action Clauses* (6 June 2002) 8 https://www.imf.org/external/np/psi/2002/eng/060602.htm (accessed 14 October 2022).
[219] See Keegan S Drake, 'The Fall and Rise of the Exit Consent' (2014) 63 Duke LJ 1602.
[220] *Katz v Oak Industries Inc* 508 A2d 873, 878 (Del Ch 1986).
[221] ibid 880. This test was also applied in *Kass v E Air Lines Inc* Nos 8700, 8701, 8711, 1986 WL 13008 (Del Ch 1986).
[222] As held in *Sharon Steel Corp v Chase Manhattan Bank NA* 691 F 2d 1039 (2d Cir 1982).
[223] See ch 10, s 3.2.
[224] See *Metropolitan Life Ins. Co v RJR Nabisco Inc* 716 F Supp 1504 (SDNY 1989).
[225] See *Hackettstown National Bank v DG Yuengling Brewing Co* 74 . 110, 110 (2d Cir 1896). The conclusion in *Hackettstown* was partly due to the peculiar circumstances of the case, ie the bondholder who voted to delay payments was also a shareholder, which means by voting on the delay its position would be strengthened, a blatant conflict of interest. Thus, it is unclear how egregious the conduct would need to be to be considered in breach of the implied duty of good faith.
[226] *Marblegate Asset Management v Educ Management Corp* 75 F Supp 3d 592, 595 (SDNY 2014).

minority bondholders had shown a likelihood of success on the merits because the Trust Indenture Act afforded broad protection against *non-consensual* debt reorganizations. Following *Mechala*,[227] the court analysed the text, history, and context of section 316(b), concluding that the requirement of unanimous consent not only protects the formal right to payment, but also the practical ability to receive payment. Thus, the unanimity requirement should apply to amendments that impair such practical ability, eg protective covenants,[228] modifications that effectively 'disinherit the dissenting minority', including subordination, waiver of parent guarantees, etc.[229] This *dictum* was reiterated in *Marblegate II*[230] and followed by other courts in *Meehancombs Global Credit Opportunities Funds*[231] and *Caesars Entertainment*.[232]

11.82 Some market players reacted with concern,[233] some commentators questioned *Marblegate's* historical analysis.[234] On appeal, a split Second Circuit reversed.[235] It concluded that the legislative history and context of section 316(b) supported the protection against modifications to the formal right to receive payment. It would be difficult to distinguish which transactions constitute an out-of-court debt restructuring designed to eliminate a non-consenting holder's ability to receive payment, since this would require looking at subjective intent, which would be contrary to the uniform interpretation of boilerplate provisions since *Sharon Steel*.[236]

11.83 In corporate debt (as opposed to securitized and structured debt, analysed below) the question of 'sacred rights' that require individual consent also arises in cases outside the TIA, such as loan-based financings. This was the case of the TriMark litigation, considered above, where the debtor and the defendant lenders agreed on the provision of new funding by the latter, in the form of first-lien debt, and, through a series of seemingly orchestrated steps, the new lenders (defendants) voted to change the terms of the original credit agreement, weakening some of its covenants, and subsequently transferred their first lien debt to the debtor, swapping it for newly issued, and more senior debt.[237] The changes were denounced as 'cannibalistic assault', 'lender-on-lender violence', and outright 'theft', by the plaintiffs, who were the non-participating lenders (ie those affected by the amendments, and not benefitting from the debt swap). The court held that the contract language provided that holders of more

---

[227] *Federated Strategic Income Fund v Mechala Group Jamaica Ltd* No 99 CIV 10517 HB, 1999 WL 993648 (SDNY 1999).

[228] According to Judge Fallia, the legislative intent of the Trust Indenture Act 1939 was bondholder protection. Restructurings should go into bankruptcy when unanimity could not be achieved, and 'evasion of judicial scrutiny of the fairness of debt-readjustment plans' should be avoided. *Marblegate* (n 226) 613.

[229] ibid 615.

[230] *Marblegate Asset Management LLC v Education Management. Corp* 111 F Supp 3d 542 (SDNY 2015),, overruled by *Marblegate Asset Management LLC v Educ Management Corp* 846 F 3d 1 (2d Cir 2017).

[231] *MeehanCombs Global Credit Opportunities Funds LP v Caesars Entertainment Corp* 80 F Supp 3d 507, 510 n 31 (SDNY 2015).

[232] *BOKF NA v Caesars Entertainment Corp* 144 F Supp 3d 459 (SDNY 2015), invalidated by *Marblegate 2017* (n 230).

[233] Including major law firms. See Baker Botts LLP and Others, 'Opinion White Paper' (25 April 2016) https://www.friedfrank.com/files/PressHighlights/TIA%20316_b_%20Opinion%20White%20Paper%20-%20Execution%20Copy_7524787_27_NY_.pdf (accessed 14 October 2022); US Chamber of Commerce's and Loan Syndications and Trading Association's *amicus brief* urging the Court of Appeals for the Second Circuit to reverse. See US Chamber Litigation Center, *Marblegate Asset Management LLC v Education Management Finance Corp* (September 2015) http://www.chamberlitigation.com/cases/marblegate-asset-management-llc-v-education-management-finance-corp (accessed 14 October 2022).

[234] Harald Halbhuber, 'Debt Restructurings and the Trust Indenture Act' (2017) 25 Am Bankr Inst L Rev 1.

[235] *Marblegate 2017* (n 230) 1.

[236] ibid.

[237] *Audax v TMK* (n 166). See section 5.2.

than 50.0 per cent of the loans could amend the terms of the agreement, and the fact that the defendants subsequently transferred their rights to the debtor in exchange for new, super-senior debt was not relevant. However, the court acknowledged that the contract identified certain 'sacred rights', which could only be modified with 'the written consent of each Lender directly and adversely affected', and that plaintiffs had stated a viable claim that defendants could not place a tranche of debt above the plaintiffs' place in the waterfall, even if the order of distribution remained facially unaffected (the court did not conclude that this was *the* more reasonable interpretation, but 'viable' enough to survive the motion to dismiss). As a consequence the claims of breach of contract also survived the motion to dismiss. The court, however, dismissed the claims for breach of good faith, because good faith could not go against the contract's terms, nor impose obligations beyond those express terms. Thus, the court preferred to rely on an interpretation of the meaning of the priority provisions in the lending agreement than to expressly open the door to considerations of good faith.

11.84 In the UK, a majority of bondholders may alter *any* of the debenture terms, including the right to payment. Some early cases held that majority bondholders could not oppress the minority and had to exercise their rights in good faith,[238] but in other cases the standard was relatively low.[239] More recently, in *Azevedo v Imcopa Importaçao*,[240] the issuer offered consent payments to bondholders who would agree to postponed interest payments. The court held that consent was valid, and these payments were not a bribe, because they were made openly and did not prevent the exercise of voting rights; nor were contrary to the *pari passu* principle, because this principle applied in full in the context of insolvency, and outside insolvency it applied only to the amounts passing through the hands of the trustee, which was not the case with the exit consent payments.[241]

11.85 In *Assénagon Asset Management SA*[242] the court invalidated the consent. Some aspects of the *Assénagon* terms were more coercive: *Azevedo* proposed postponing interest payments; *Assénagon* substituting new notes for the old ones; *Azevedo* offered payment to those voting in favour, *Assénagon* threatened that those voting against would receive nominal consideration, ie lose everything; *Azevedo*'s offer was made by the issuer made; *Assénagon*'s by the majority of noteholders; *Azevedo*'s offer could be beneficial to all noteholders, as it facilitated the reconstitution of the issuer; *Assénagon*'s wiped-out the note value; *Azevedo*'s plaintiff only alleged 'bribery'. *Assénagon*'s alleged 'oppression' (yet, the offer was available to all bondholders, and its terms were transparent, as in *Azevedo*[243]). Beyond factual aspects, the court's approach was different. The court accepted that, even if very little value had been offered for the exchange, this was admissible, as permitted by contract provisions, as long as

---

[238] In *Mercantile Inv & General Trust Co v International Co of Mexico* [1893] 1 Ch 484 the court held that majority bondholders had their power 'on trust' and were subject to a fiduciary duty to exercise that power for the benefit of the bondholder class as a whole. See Stephen Moverly Smith and Heather Murphy, 'Challenges to Collective Action Clauses: Can Any Parallel Be Drawn with Unfair Prejudice Petitions and Oppression of the Minority?' (2012) 27(8) Butterworths J Intl Banking & Fin L 479.

[239] *Redwood Master Fund Ltd v TD Bank Europe Ltd* [2002] All ER (D) 141. The majority lenders did not negotiate in bad faith because their motivation was not to improve their position at the expense of the other bondholders, nor was it vindictive or malicious towards them. Good faith sought to evaluate whether a reasonable person could see the restructuring as being in the interest of all the lenders as a group, but did not mean that any change prejudicial to one class of lenders could not be in the interest of all lenders.

[240] *Azevedo v Imcopa Importaçao* [2012] EWHC 1849 (Comm); [affd] [2013] EWCA Civ 364.

[241] [2012] EWHC 1849 (Comm). This begs the question of what would have happened if the payments had passed through the hands of the trustee.

[242] *Assénagon Asset Management SA v Irish Bank Corp Ltd* [2012] EWHC 2090 (Ch).

[243] ibid para 83.

procedural safeguards (eg enhanced quorum) were respected.²⁴⁴ Then, the court combined a literal reading of the contract with a functional interpretation.²⁴⁵ The court considered a 'disenfranchisement' clause which stated that '[n]either the Issuer nor any Subsidiary shall be entitled to vote at any meeting in respect of Notes beneficially held by it or for its account', which tried to address the risk of conflict of interest if the debtor became its own creditor, and interpreted it very broadly, forbidding the issuer from voting those notes *even after* they were surrendered by noteholders who had expressly consented to vote for the restructuring. Then, the court considered the allegation that the majority noteholders owed a duty of good faith to the minority holders in light of the contract itself, but also of the principles that govern majority-minority disputes in cases of partners, shareholders, and bondholders, distilling a general principle that majority power must be directed in good faith for the benefit of all the company's interest holders.²⁴⁶ In light of this, the court concluded that the consent was invalid.

11.86 Majority-minority creditor conflicts present additional complexities if the debtor is a bankruptcy-remote SPV. Unlike operating companies, SPVs hold assets, and there is less a risk of destructing value in case of liquidation, and there is no 'debtor interest', only creditors' interests at stake. Furthermore, the offeror of the amendment may vary: it may be the originator of the assets, the arranger of the transaction, the servicer, a seller of the notes, or even a swap counterparty (in synthetic transactions). Furthermore, notes are 'tranched' in different seniority levels, which exacerbates the conflicts between creditor groups, but creditors are normally sophisticated parties.

11.87 In *Citicorp Trustee Co. v Barclays*²⁴⁷ the circumstances were complex, and not fully clarified in the ruling: Barclays held securitized notes (Barclays notes),²⁴⁸ and, using different arrangements, was entitled to direct the vote of notes held by Rabobank (Rabobank notes), but since Barclays had subscribed a credit derivative with a Swap Counterparty, Ambac, to hedge its exposure on the notes, Ambac was entitled to direct Barclays and Rabobank notes' vote.²⁴⁹ The issue was whether Barclays, Rabobank, or both were disenfranchised from voting. The court relied on *Assénagon* and held that neither was disenfranchised.²⁵⁰ On the Barclays notes, Barclays and other arrangers were precluded from voting by the contract's disenfranchisement provision *only* when they acted as sellers of the notes (this sought to prevent the conflict of interest). When they held notes acquired in a different capacity, such as a purchaser of them on the open market, then they were entitled to vote.²⁵¹ On the Rabobank notes, Barclays' power to direct Rabobank's vote, and Ambac's power to direct Barclays' vote, did not turn either of them into beneficial owners.²⁵² The court was stymied from adopting

---

²⁴⁴ ibid paras 52, 54–55.
²⁴⁵ ibid paras 39–49. The court also introduced an interesting reasoning, whereby the *debt* contract not only creates duties between lender and borrower, but also between lenders themselves.
²⁴⁶ *Assénagon* (n 242) paras 72–73.
²⁴⁷ *Citicorp Trustee Co Ltd v Barclays Bank Plc* [2013] EWHC 2608 (Ch).
²⁴⁸ ibid para 32. Apparently, the notes were held for investors who preferred to remain anonymous, but were deposited at Clearstream, which established Barclays' property rights over the notes. Thus, '[t]he entries on the screen' are 'conclusive and binding'.
²⁴⁹ *Citicorp Trustee* (n 247) paras 43–44.
²⁵⁰ The relevant provision read: 'Those Notes (if any) which are for the time being held *by or on behalf of or for the benefit for the Issuer or each of the Sellers*, any holding company of any of them or any other Subsidiary of any such holding company, in each case as beneficial owner, shall (unless and until ceasing to be so held) be deemed not to remain outstanding.' *Citicorp Trustee* (n 247) 49 (the italics are ours).
²⁵¹ *Citicorp Trustee* (n 247) paras 69–95.
²⁵² ibid paras 96–114.

a more functional approach by the overly complex nature of the transaction[253] and the inability of the parties to explain the *purpose* of the contract provisions,[254] and was also frustrated by Barclay's change in position, first arguing that its notes were not disenfranchised, and then shortly thereafter arguing that they were disenfranchised.[255] Again, it was hard to rule on disputes solely on the basis of contract language, without understanding its logic.

11.88 In the US majority-minority issues in bankruptcy-remote transactions have arisen sporadically.[256] In *Wrights Mill Holdings* the documents allowed a majority of junior investors ('Preferred Shareholders') to direct the Trustee to effect a sale of collateral at the best price, provided there were at least two offers.[257] Preferred Shareholders had little chance of recovery because the underlying assets 'catastrophically, failed to perform', and, when they received two offers, accompanied by a 'consent payment' to the Preferred Shareholders, the majority holder of the junior notes directed the trustee to accept one of those offers.[258] There may have been collusion between offerors and noteholders,[259] but the court did not expressly rely on this ground to hold that the offer was not an 'offer' according to the contract, because the consent payment rendered it illegal, and thus 'incapable of being accepted'. In the court's view: (i) parties exercising discretion, like the preferred shareholders, were subject to the duty of good faith; (ii) the purpose of the transaction was to benefit senior noteholders, not to enrich junior ones at their expense; and (iii) the fact that junior investors had no 'skin in the game' made them conflicted. This reasoning is at odds with that of *Marblegate Asset Management*, but the court's reasoning, which seemed to rely on open-textured duties, was couched in the language of contract provisions.

7 Inter-creditor coordination disputes and the role of agents and trustees

11.89 Creditors may adopt some crucial decisions by majority, but in most cases they rely for the management of collateral assets on third parties, raising questions about the status of those parties and their duties. Some cases have analysed the role of agent banks (7.1.) others the role of trustees, both in general (section 7.2) and in the context of clauses that restrict their discretion and liability (section 7.3).

---

[253] ibid para 30 ('The set up and structure of the various transactions seems to a simple-minded property lawyer to be Byzantine in the extreme').
[254] *Citicorp Trustee* (n 247) paras 52–54: 'Consequently, if they are disenfranchised the junior Note holders' powers are promoted. Why should this happen? The most startling fact in this case is that nobody was able to give me any clear basis for the *purpose* of the provision. Further if either Barclays or Rabobank's Disputed Notes are disenfranchised that will have a significant impact on Ambac which could find the debts being rescheduled to its detriment but be powerless to control how they should be voting because the Notes are disenfranchised. The junior Noteholders of course want them to be disenfranchised as it promotes their position.'
[255] Ironically referred to as 'Barclay's Sommersault'. See *Citicorp Trustee* (n 247) 69. Barclays' exposure was hedged by Ambac. Thus, any negative effect of disenfranchisement would be suffered by Ambac. This justified granting Ambac the power to direct Barclays' vote in the first place.
[256] *Bank of New York v First Millennium* (n 84) the court concluded that cl 5.08 of the indenture, modelled after s 508 of the Model Trust Indenture, modelled after s 316(b) TIA, sought to protect bondholders' core rights to payment from amendment by the majority, but the case hinged on the relationship between the clauses on 'limited recourse' and 'unconditional' right to payment. Supra section 5.2.
[257] *Wells Fargo Bank NA v Wrights Mill Holdings* 127 F Supp 3d 156 (SDNY 2015).
[258] The case relied on the account of facts in the related case of *Hildene Capital Management v Friedman* 11 Civ 5832 (AJN) (SDNY 2012). See section 7.2.
[259] *Wells Fargo Bank* (n 257) paras 162–63.

7.1 The role of agent banks

11.90 Agent banks occupy a key role in syndicated financing,[260] raising questions about the scope of their duties towards other syndicate banks. US courts case law was shaped by cases of loan participations. In *Banco Español de Crédito*, or *First Citizens* courts held that: '[I]n the case of arm's length transactions between large financial institutions, no fiduciary duty exists unless one was created in the agreement.'[261] This was confirmed in the *Banque Arabe* cases.[262] However, in the famous case *Chemical Bank v Security Pacific*,[263] the Ninth Circuit reversed the district court decision, finding that Security Pacific had disclaimed liability *except* for gross negligence and wilful misconduct, which had not happened, but the court also held that the agent bank owed fiduciary duties to other syndicate members, because, in the court's view, the 'very meaning of being an agent is assuming fiduciary duties to one's principal'.[264] Thus, the court accepted liability disclaimers and interpreted them broadly, but in its view, fiduciary duties were linked to the bank's role, and not to the parties' obligations in the contract documentation.

11.91 In the UK, the case *Torre Asset Funding Ltd*,[265] the transaction was a structured financing to a property company, Dunedin, which became insolvent, leaving several tiers of debt unpaid, including the junior mezzanine (B1) lenders. These sued Royal Bank of Scotland (RBS), which was agent bank for the B1 lenders *and* lender in other tiers of the transaction. The transaction included loan facility agreements for each tier, similar in drafting and an inter-creditor deed (the ICD). The junior mezzanine facility agreement (JMFA) was based on standard documentation of the Loan Market Association (LMA), including the clause for the agent bank's duties. RBS' property venture (PV) team engaged with the junior mezzanine noteholders and with the borrower, which sought to renegotiate its financial commitments by, for example, rolling up interest payments due to 'financial difficulties'. This was an 'event of default',[266] which the plaintiffs claimed that RBS was aware of, or should have been aware of, and did not communicate to the other banks. They also claimed that it failed to provide copies of the business plan and cash flow spreadsheets facilitated by the borrower, and that, when it sought the plaintiffs' consent to roll up interest payments, it misstated the reasons for doing so; had it been forthcoming, the lenders would have sold their positions, or agreed to a restructuring. One contract provision described the agent bank's duties as 'solely mechanical

---

[260] Agasha Mugasha, *The Law of Multi-Bank Financing: Syndicated Loans and the Secondary Loan Market* (OUP 2008).
[261] *Banco Espanol de Credito v Security Pacific National Bank* 763 F Supp 36, 45 (SDNY 1991), aff'd 973 F 2d 51 (2d Cir1992); *First Citizens Federal Savings and Loan Association v Worthen Bank and Trust Co* 919 F 2d 510, 513–14 (9th Cir 1990).
[262] *Banque Arabe et Intern d'inv v Maryland National Bank* [1993] 819 F Supp 1282 (SDNY 1993); *Banque Arabe et Internationale v Maryland National Bank* 57 F 3d 146 (2d Cir 1995).
[263] *Chemical Bank; National Westminster Bank, USA v Security Pacific National Bank* [1994] 20 F 3d 375 (9th Cir 1994). Security Pacific granted a US$15 million loan to a borrower, and later agreed with the two plaintiffs to grant a syndicated loan, and filed a financing statement to perfect a security interest for the first loan, but not for the second loan. The borrower filed for bankruptcy, and the syndicated banks were unsecured creditors, while Security Pacific was a secured creditor for its first loan, where the statement was filed. The documents included a condition precedent that the agent bank and its counsel should receive executed UCC financing statements of the borrower's inventory and accounts receivable, and broad disclaimer clauses, excluding Security Pacific's liability 'except for gross negligence or wilful misconduct', including for 'the effectiveness, enforceability, validity or due execution' of contract documentation. See Agasha Mugasha, 'The Agent Bank's Possible Fiduciary Liability to Syndicate Banks' (1996) 27 Can Bus LJ 403.
[264] *Chemical Bank* (n 263).
[265] *Torre Asset Funding v RBS* [2013] EWHC 2670. See also chapter 10 sections 4.1. and 4.2.
[266] ibid.

and administrative in nature', but the judge held that this should be read in light of the more specific provisions, which imposed duties to, or conferred discretion on the agent. This is relevant in light of the *Socimer* standard, which, when an agent has discretion, requires acting with 'reasonableness', which implies honesty, good faith, and genuineness, and must not be 'arbitrary, capricious, perverse or irrational'.[267]

11.92 Yet, this duty was limited. Sales J rejected that a duty to notify resulted from the law of agency, since any duties under the law of agency would be those defined in the financing agreements. Nor could a term be implied, because the parties could not reasonably understand that the agreement contained such a term.[268] The term under which RBS, when acting without instructions from the lenders, 'may act (or refrain from taking action) as it considers to be in the best interest of the Lenders', although subject to *Socimer*, could not conflict with the express terms of the agreement. Under the contract's express terms, and precedents on contract interpretation and 'commercial reasonableness' and 'business common sense'.[269] RBS was not subject to a duty to evaluate the situation, to see whether there was, or not, an event of default.[270] Finally, a duty to inform could not be implied in the Intercreditor Deed, since it would conflict with other contract provisions, which only expected the Agent to act when something amounting to an event of default was brought home to him.[271] Thus, Sales J concluded that the PV team was not 'aware of any default', since 'they were very far from believing that any event of default... had occurred; and they had good grounds for believing that the matter would be resolved without difficulty'.[272] Thus, the court emphasized certainty over 'fairness' towards creditors.

7.2 Creditor coordination and the role of trustees (I): Duties and responsibilities

11.93 In case of multiple parties and a debt offering, a trustee is appointed to look after debenture holders' interests, including to enforce their claims.[273] In bankruptcy-remote transactions, an Enforcement Event may result in the trustee taking over the assets to administer and liquidate them and distribute the proceeds.[274]

---

[267] *Torre v RBS* (n 265) para 162 '[A]n Agent may be assigned duties which require it to act in a reasonable manner, and the fact that the model for clause 26 includes exemption clauses contemplates that an Agent may have wider duties imposed on it than simply to act as a postal service, in respect of which such exemption from liability may be required.' *Torre v RBS* (n 265) 30.
[268] *Torre v RBS* (n 265) paras 152–56, citing *AG of Belize v Belize Telecom Ltd* [2009] UKPC 10.
[269] Including *In Re Sigma* (n 175); *Rainy Sky and Others v Kookmin Bank* [2011] UKSC 50.
[270] *Torre v RBS* (n 265) para 163: 'Apart from receipt of such a notice, by virtue of clause 26.6(b)(i) the Agent is entitled to make the assumption that no Default has occurred, unless again it has actual knowledge of a special class of case of Default which is obvious and calls for no major evaluative judgment to be made (there may be a need to make some minor evaluative judgment, since there is a very limited exception) namely failure to pay a sum due under any facility agreement (the limited exception is if the failure to pay 'is caused by administrative or technical error' and payment is made within three business days of the due date).'
[271] *Torre v RBS* (n 265) para 163.
[272] ibid para 201.
[273] See David Ramos Muñoz, 'In Praise of Small Things: Securitization and Governance Structure' (2010) 5 CMLJ 388.
[274] Normally a series of notices from the servicer to the trustee, and from the trustee to the SPV formalize the change of control. See *Re Whistlejacket Cap Ltd* (n 175). The trustee may have a veto right over certain transactions, or directly manage the assets.

Trustees' duties are contract-based in the UK, where contract clauses can also exclude liability except in cases of fraud (*Armitage v Nurse*[275]). The Trustee Act 2000 imposes a duty of care, which, in debenture offerings, applies to the appointment of agents, and can be shaped by contract.[276] The Companies Act 2006 limits the possibility of liability exemptions, but still indicates that the trustee's duties, whose breach give rise to liability, are shaped by 'the provisions of the trust deed conferring on him any powers, authorities or discretions'.[277]

US courts focus on the contract (or trust deed), but in construing the contract they also take into consideration statutory rules, such as the Trust Indenture Act (TIA[278]), and common law (courts have often treated the TIA as a crystallization of common law duties[279]). On this basis, they tend to distinguish between trustees' pre-default duties (totally shaped by contract) and post-default ones, where the trust document is still the primary, but not the only source.[280] There are, however, differences. In corporate debt transactions some courts are more inclined to rely on contract terms,[281] while others refused to confine the trustee's duties to those strictly delineated under the indenture, despite the existence of disclaimer clauses.[282]

In securitization and structured finance courts have resisted imposing implied duties on the trustee and majority bondholders,[283] but they have otherwise assimilated the trustee's position and duties to those in corporate debt offerings.[284] In *Ellington Credit Fund*, the trustee was accused of breaching the pre-default duty to monitor the underlying assets and funds to avoid their depletion, a duty similar to the corporate indenture trustee's duty to monitor the issuer. The court held that pre-default duties are shaped by the indenture and that no breach of fiduciary duty existed.[285] Although the trustee held a position of trust and confidence, where it enjoyed some control and responsibility over the asset pool, this was insufficient to override the principle that those duties are ministerial and determined by the contract.[286]

Despite this formulaic approach, much still depends on the specific role of the trustee. In *Galena Street Fund v Wells Fargo*[287] the trustee had to take over servicing duties from the servicer. The plaintiffs alleged that it breached the servicing agreement by failing to stop

11.94

11.95

11.96

11.97

---

[275] [1998] Ch 241.
[276] Trustee Act 2000, Sch 1.
[277] Companies Act 2006, s 750.
[278] 15 USC s 77.
[279] *Re EF Hutton Southwest Properties II Ltd v Union Planters National Bank* 953 F 2d 963 (5th Cir 1992); *Meckel v Continental Resources Co* [1985] 758 F 2d 811 (2d Cir).
[280] *Hutton* (n 279). The strict contract approach in *Meckel* (n 279) and *Elliot Association v J Henry Schroder Bank & Trust Co* 838 F 2d 66 (2d Cir 1988) can be explained because both involved alleged breaches of duty committed in the pre-default stage. *LNC Investments Inc v First Fidelity Bank, National Association* 935 F Supp 1333, 1347 (1996). Even in a pre-default stage, the trustee must (1) avoid conflicts of interest and (2) perform all basic, non-discretionary, ministerial tasks with due care. These are not fiduciary duties, but obligations, whose breach may give rise to tort liability. Statutory rules (TIA) limit contract clauses, which cannot exempt the trustee from liability for 'willful misconduct, negligent action, or negligent failure to act'. Trust Indenture Act 1939, s 315(a). Section 315(d) insulates the trustee for errors of judgment in good faith, in line with case law. See *Hutton* (n 279) 963.
[281] See *AG Capital Funding Partners LP v State Street Bank & Trust Co* 896 N E 2d 61 (NY 2008).
[282] See eg *Becker v Bank of New York Mellon Trust Co* NA, 172 F Supp 3d 777 (ED Pa 2016).
[283] See *Marblegate 2017* (n 230).
[284] *Greenwich Financial Services Distressed Mortgage Fund* 603 F 3d 23, 29 (2d Cir 2010); see *Ellington Credit Fund v Selected Portfolio Serv* 837 F Supp 2d 162, 192 (SDNY 2011); *Hildene Capital Management v Friedman* (n 258).
[285] *Ellington Credit Fund* (n 284) 193.
[286] ibid 194 and authorities cited. See also *In re National Century Financial Enterprises* WL 2849784 (SD Ohio 2006) and *Ellington Credit Fund* (n 284) para 162.
[287] *Galena Street Fund v Wells Fargo* [2013] No 12-cv-006870-BNB-KMT, 2013 WL 2114372 (D Colo).

reimbursements and by continuing to pass on the losses to the trusts. The judge did not dismiss the claim because, despite the existence of a limitation clause, he could not find categorically that the trustee had not assumed any obligations prior to the transfer of the servicing obligations.[288] The court restated the *Ellington* view that trustees in securitizations are comparable to (corporate) indenture trustees, and that the only 'implied duties in a pre-default setting were a general duty of care and a duty to avoid conflicts of interest.[289] Yet the court held that the plaintiffs had sufficiently stated a claim for a conflict of interest, because the trustee was also acting as a servicer, and was thus monitoring itself.[290] This illustrates the difficulty of reconciling the trustee's formal contract duties with its 'function' in the transaction.

11.98 Avoiding conflicts of interest is even more difficult in 'creditor-creditor' conflicts. In theory, trustees are subject to an undivided duty of loyalty, especially present post-default.[291] However, the scope of this duty may be less clear in cases of conflict between classes of creditors.

11.99 In *Hildene Capital Management v Friedman*,[292] senior investors sued the trustee and junior investors (preferred shareholders) for an alleged breach of fiduciary duty in connection with a CDO offering, because the trustee presented junior investors with an offer that included an 'inducement', or side payment, and there were allegations (although no definitive evidence) of collusion. The plaintiffs (senior investors) claimed that the trustee had breached its duties by forwarding an offer 'not authorized' by the contract.[293] The breach of contract claim survived a motion to dismiss because the clause was ambiguous,[294] and rejected the claims for (pre-default) breach of (strictly defined) fiduciary duties,[295] *but* did not dismiss the claim for conflict of interest.[296] Unlike past situations of conflicting claims over collateral assets in the same transaction, this time the trustee had not filed an interpleader action to seek court clarification. Thus, even when the parties' try to limit court intervention this may be impossible if there is a conflict between classes of creditors, and seeking directions from the court is seen as an implied duty, or often a necessity by the trustee itself, which seeks to be protected from liability.

---

[288] ibid para 10. The court also held that the no-action clause requiring notification to the trustee as a prerequisite for judicial action was inapplicable in this context, for it would have required the trustee to sue itself. ibid 11–12.
[289] *Galena Street Fund v Wells Fargo* (n 293) paras 13–14.
[290] ibid 14.
[291] See *BNP Paribas Mortgage Corp v Bank of America NA* 778 F Supp 2d 375 (SDNY 2011): 'After an event of default, the indenture trustee's fiduciary duties expand by operation of New York common law, [such that] fidelity to the terms of an indenture does not immunize an indenture trustee against claims that the trustee has acted in a manner inconsistent with his or her fiduciary duty of undivided loyalty to trust beneficiaries') (internal citations omitted).
[292] *Hildene Capital Management v Friedman* (n 258).
[293] See section 6.2 above for the treatment of 'inducement' payments and similar mechanisms in majority–minority conflicts.
[294] ibid 1. Clause 10(3)(d) read: 'The Trustee [Wells Fargo] on behalf of the Issuer shall notify the Holders of the Preferred Shares of any Portfolio Collateral that is subject to an Offer. If no Event of Default has occurred and is continuing, and subject to the provisions of Article XII hereof, the Holders representing at least 66–2/3% of the Preferred Shares may direct the Trustee to release from the lien of this Indenture such Portfolio Collateral in accordance with the terms of the Offer in each case against receipt of payment therefor.' The trustee argued that this clause authorized a sale if instructed by the necessary majority of junior investors, while the plaintiffs argued that the clause gave a veto to junior creditors, and that contract provisions sought to prohibit any disposition. The language ('release collateral from the lien') was unclear.
[295] The court referred to *Elliot* (n 280) and *Meckel* (n 279).
[296] *Hildene Capital Management v Friedman* (n 258) 13–14.

U.S. courts impose more exacting post-default duties on trustees. In *BNP Paribas Mortgage* **11.100**
Corp v Bank of America[297] Bank of America had to act as trustee, custodian, and depositary, and had a duty to notify events of default and potential events of default. The documents limited the trustee's liability unless and until it received notification of an event of default from the issuer (SPV), and the trustee alleged that any breaches were caused by the issuer. Yet, the court held that the trustee's role was to monitor, screening, and approving the actions of the issuer,[298] holding that it was under a duty to notify interested parties and to shut down the transaction when it had actual knowledge of an event of default.[299] On the claims for breach of fiduciary duty, which referred to post-default conduct the court held that fiduciary duties 'expand by operation of New York common law' in a post-default context.[300] Thus, the court denied defendant's motion to dismiss.[301] This is another example of how a court used a functional interpretation of contract provisions to determine the parties' rights and duties. It focused on how a trustee's function and duties expand in a post-default context, despite the restrictive language of the contract's clauses.

7.3 Creditor coordination and the role of trustees (II): Discretion and discretion-constraining clauses

Difficulties also arise in determining the extent of implied open-textured duties, such as the **11.101**
duty to exercise discretion, good faith, and fairness towards beneficiaries, despite contractual provisions that attempt to limit those duties. In *Citibank v MBIA*[302] a Dutch-incorporated vehicle (fixed-linked finance (FLF)) had acquired some junior (Tier 3) tranches of the Channel Tunnel debt and issued securities. QVT, a hedge fund, acquired some of the bottom tranches. MBIA Assurance SA provided direct credit enhancement for senior tranches. Citibank was the trustee. After several Eurotunnel companies went into French insolvency (*sauvegarde*) proceedings the trustee sought court guidance on a proposal for debt restructuring (replacing Tier 3 notes with hybrid notes). The trustee could instruct FLF and determine the result for all noteholders,[303] but under the trust deed it was bound to follow MBIA's instructions, as 'Note Controlling Party', MBIA had instructed Citibank to vote in favour of the plan. QVT alleged that Citibank actually had to consent to the plan, which meant using its own judgment and discretion.[304] The court relied entirely on the contract documentation,[305] holding that the broad language employed to define the trustee's powers allowed it to

---

[297] *BNP Paribas Mortgage Corp* (n 291).
[298] ibid.
[299] ibid. Some of the breaches of covenants by the issuer were not events of default but potential events of default, and thus were not covered by the clause that limited the trustee's liability to cases where it had received written notice. Furthermore, according to the clause, the trustee had to notify when it had 'actual knowledge' of the event, which could happen not only when the trustee received notice. Finally, the court relied on cl 9.1's language that '[n]otwithstanding anything in this Base Indenture to the contrary, in the event that an Indenture Event of Default [occurs]', the trustee had a duty to shut down the facility. The Court asked, rhetorically, that '[i]f an indenture trustee is under no enforceable obligation to act prudently to preserve and manage the trust assets in the event of default, and so to provide some reasonable assurance that the bondholders eventually receive their due, it may be asked whether the indenture does in fact secure the payment of anything'. ibid 400. On the relevance of 'notwithstanding anything' clauses see section 3.4.1.
[300] *BNP Paribas Mortgage Corp* (n 291) para 401.
[301] ibid 402–408.
[302] *Citibank NA v MBIA* (CA) [2007] All ER (D) 141.
[303] ibid para 21.
[304] ibid. QVT alleged that, if Citibank used its discretion, it would reject the plan, which would impair value.
[305] *Citibank NA v MBIA* (n 302) para 34: 'In truth this is not a case turning on authorities. It turns on the effect of particular provisions of particular documents, and authority is of little assistance.'

instruct FLF to accept the restructuring. Such powers were not limited by the trustee's role as a mortgagee,[306] and the trustee's exercise of the issuer's rights was not affected by MBIA's note-controlling party status. Even if the trustee were acting for the exclusive benefit of the note controlling party and to the detriment of investors as a whole, the trustee's acts would nevertheless be valid in light of the language of the trust deed. The court also relied on a trust deed clause, which provided that, when acting in accordance with the note controlling party's instructions, the trustee need not act in the interest of noteholders as a whole.[307] In the court's view, this provision did not affect the trustee's 'irreducible core' of duties, despite surrendering all its discretion to MBIA.[308]

11.102 The court followed the language of the clauses, rather than looking at the function of the trustee or the default rules that apply under trust law. This decision is consistent with the general holding of *Armitage v Nurse*,[309] which also granted a great deal of leeway to the contracting parties. Yet, the court noted that the enterprise was clearly insolvent, some form of restructuring was necessary, and QVT was obviously holding out to extract a more advantageous proposal. Had the facts been different, the existence of a procedure biased by design might have warranted a different result.

11.103 Another question is whether creditors who have signed no-action clauses can be considered as adequately represented by the trustee. Some court decisions show deference to the contract. In *NextBank II*[310] the court acknowledged that '[b]ondholders are not necessary parties to litigation wherein an indenture trustee under a bond issue is a party and exercises in good faith and without neglect his contractual authority to represent and assert the lien securing the issue'.[311] Only under limited circumstances will the interests of absent beneficiaries be considered not properly represented by a trustee. Yet these include cases 'when a single trustee represents beneficiaries with conflicting interests', or if there is evidence that the trustee has assumed an 'antagonistic' attitude toward certain beneficiaries and their legal position.[312] In *Nextbank*, it was clear that there were 'no division[s], no differences, no disagreements, no quarrels' among the noteholders, and, therefore, BNY's fiduciary obligations were clear.[313] Yet, the case might have been decided differently if the interests of the noteholders had diverged, eg if the 'note controlling party' had been aligned with, for example, the interests of some creditor class.

---

[306] According to counsel for QVT, the mortgagee can only preserve the mortgaged property while the mortgagor is performing its obligations. According to the court, however, what a mortgagee can or cannot do depends on the terms of the mortgage. *Citibank NA v MBIA* (n 302) 43. The court also rejected the argument that consent to the restructuring would destroy the commercial nature of the bond, transforming it from a securitization investment into a cash investment.

[307] *Citibank NA v MBIA* (n 302) para 7. See cl 10.4 of the trust deed: 'When acting in accordance with the instructions of MBIA while it is the Note Controlling Party pursuant to these presents and the other Transaction Documents, the Trustee shall not (subject to Clause 14.1.7) be required to have regard to the interests of the Noteholders and the other Issuer Secured Creditors ... When giving any instructions, consents or waivers under the Transaction Documents, MBIA (if MBIA is the Note Controlling Party) need have no regard to the interests of the Noteholders.'

[308] *Citibank NA v MBIA* (n 302) para 34. In the words of the Court, '[t]he position would look less unusual if the directions were to come from the G Noteholders (who are likely to have similar interests to MBIA) but would still be in substance the same.' The court held that the trustee's functions would be increased if MBIA decided not to give any directions.

[309] *Armitage v Nurse* [1998] Ch 241.

[310] *FDIC v Bank of New York* 479 F Supp 2d 1, 10 (DDC 2007). For more on the *NextBank I* and *II* (n 84) litigation see section 3.2.2.

[311] ibid.

[312] ibid paras 10–11.

[313] ibid para 11.

As an example of a more functional approach of trustees' duties by UK courts on the face **11.104**
of conflict between creditor classes is *Bank of New York v Montana Board of Investment*.[314]
The case involved Orion, a Cayman-incorporated SIV, which had issued senior notes, senior subordinated notes, and capital subordinated notes. The security agreement, under New York law, appointed Bank of New York as security trustee. In 2007, the SIV experienced downgraded ratings that triggered an Automatic Enforcement Event.[315] Thus, the notes became due and payable and the assets were under the full control of the trustee.[316] Creditors' interests diverged and restructuring proposals were rejected. Senior noteholders directed the trustee to sell the collateral, while subordinated noteholders asked the trustee to refrain from liquidating any collateral until market values recovered. The court applied general principles of New York law on contract interpretation as directed by the contract,[317] and also relied on legal principles on secured transactions and trust law. It first referred to New York's UCC, which provides that the secured creditor has a duty to dispose of collateral in a commercially reasonable manner,[318] which includes waiting to dispose of the assets when prices are low as a result of a market collapse.[319] It also held that, unlike the ministerial pre-default duties, a trustee's post-default duties require prudent judgment in dealing with trust assets to preserve and not waste them.

The court distinguished the trustee's obligation to enforce the security interest for the benefit **11.105**
of senior creditors from the execution of that obligation, where senior noteholders had no right to direct the trustee as to the time, place, or manner of sale.[320] The court held that the trustee's 'exclusive control' of the collateral and 'exclusive right' to exercise rights over it were incompatible with a power by senior creditors to dictate the manner of sale.[321] If the trustee's duty was to conduct a sale in a commercially reasonable manner, it had to exercise its own discretion and judgment as to the best means to accomplish this. It could not simply rely on the dictates of the senior creditors. 'It cannot surrender [its] discretion or any part of it to any individual class of creditor.'[322] Thus, in *Bank of New York v Montana Board of Investment*, even if the contract clause gave priority to the interests of senior noteholders, the court relied on a functional interpretation of the trustee's role and sought to adjust the clause's language to the logic of that function. The court reached a conclusion that was similar to what would have resulted from bankruptcy or corporate principles. Perhaps the court's functional

---

[314] *Bank of NY v Montana Board Investments* [2008] EWHC 1594 (UK).
[315] Security Agreement, cl 5.1.1(b).
[316] The trustee sent an enforcement notice and an 'exclusive control notice' to the custodian, and could dispose of the assets.
[317] Those principles were summarized by the English court as follows: (i) the interpretation must give effect to the parties' intention as expressed in the words of the written agreement; (ii) the court cannot add or excise terms, or distort their meaning to make a new contract for the parties; (iii) the court must decide whether the agreement is clear or ambiguous; (iv) if clear and complete, the court must enforce it as written according to its plain meaning, but if ambiguous, the court can resort to extrinsic evidence; (v) the security agreement had to be interpreted in an objective and uniform manner, as securities were widely held by investors and the agreement did not result from a specific lender-borrower relationship or a particularized intention of the parties. *Bank of NY v Montana Board Investments* (n 314) para 32.
[318] New York UCC, art 9-610 provides that: '(b) Commercially reasonable disposition. Every aspect of a disposition of collateral, including the method, manner, time, place and other terms, must be commercially reasonable.'
[319] The court referred to the committee notes of the UCC drafters, which stated: '[T]his Article [ie 9-610] does not specify a period within which a secured party must dispose of collateral ... It may, for example, be prudent not to dispose of goods when the market has collapsed.' *Bank of NY v Montana Board Investments* (n 314) para 36.
[320] ibid para 42.
[321] ibid para 56.
[322] ibid paras 56–58. The language used was suggestive, because it stated that the trustee *cannot* surrender its discretion (as if this were a defining feature of its position) and also made a reference to the 'benefit of all creditors', a view parting from that of the court in *Citibank NA v MBIA* (n 302).

approach was explained by its application of New York law, rather than by a variation from UK relatively formal approach. In any event, this decision shows to balance creditors' rights as a matter of *substance* and the need to preserve *procedural* fairness. Even if the contract gives one class 'controlling' status, if there is scope for the exercise of trustee discretion courts will seek to enforce it, and this can greatly impact the solution given.

8 Inter-creditor disputes over the distribution of proceeds

11.106 The distribution of proceeds from liquidation can create conflict where the sequence of acts (when to liquidate, when to distribute and how) is disputed. There are (1) cases of strict enforcement of the contract language; (2) cases where courts appeal to 'commercial reasonableness', 'business common sense', reaching solutions similar to those under insolvency law; and (3) cases where courts apply the *logic* of contract provisions, which is sufficiently clear, and different from the logic of insolvency rules. We consider them in sequence.

11.107 There are numerous cases where courts have enforced the specific order of priority stipulated in contract clauses. In *LaSalle Bank v BNP Paribas* and in *Bank of America v AIG Financial Products*[323] different contract clauses offered led to diverging results on the priority of different classes of creditors, but one of the clauses read '[a]nything in this indenture to the contrary notwithstanding'.[324] This same clause was also consistent with the transaction's logic, which sorted out the notes into classes A-1, A-2, B, C, or D.[325] This was consistent with the clause regulating the failure of a coverage test. To the judge's view, 'failure of a coverage test, like an event of default, signals that trouble lies ahead and that the trustee may not be able to make payments to all of the noteholders' and thus 'the most reasonable interpretation of the indenture' was 'to require sequential distribution in the event that a coverage test is not satisfied'.[326] In *Bank of New York v First Millennium*[327] the court relied on a similar clause stating '[n]otwithstanding any other provision in this Indenture'[328] to hold that held that noteholders' rights were unconditional and with unlimited recourse, and prevailed over the 'limited recourse' clause, and thus noteholders could claim the moneys held by the trustee for the Transferor Interest, which would have otherwise been appropriated by the FDIC as receiver. The 'notwithstanding' clause was also contained in the note instrument, while the limited recourse was included in the indenture and incorporated into the notes.[329] Thus, apart from the strict language, the court relied on the logic of the contract documentation.

11.108 If contract language is unclear courts tend to rely on 'commercial reasonableness', 'business common sense' and similar formulae,[330] which often leads to principles of 'fairness' towards creditors, such as *pari passu*. In *Re Whistlejacket*, a case involving a Jersey-incorporated

---

[323] 08-Civ-6134-LAP (SDNY 2010); *Bank of America v AIG Fin Prod Corp* WL 5065477 (SDNY 2013) aff'd in part, 509 F App'x 24 (2d Cir 2013) as amended.
[324] See also ch 10, s 4.2.
[325] *Bank of America*, 2010 WL 5065477, 4 (*Bank of America*, 2010 WL 5065477). The clause also included a clause subordinating other classes to class A-1 notes.
[326] ibid para 3.
[327] *Bank of New York v First Millennium Bank* (n 84).
[328] ibid para 916. The court relied on *International Multifoods Corp v Commercial Union Insurance Co* 309 F 3d 76 (2d Cir 2002) as authority to hold that the 'notwithstanding' clauses trump conflicting provisions.
[329] The Court of Appeals held that '[w]here there is a conflict between the terms of the note and ancillary documents, the terms of the note control'. ibid para 919.
[330] See sections 3.2.1 and 4.2.2.

SIV[331] the questions were whether an insolvency acceleration event had accelerated the payment date for notes and postponed the payment of notes matured before that date, and whether the security trust deed (STD) created a de facto order of priority between senior creditors with debts 'due and payable' and those whose debts were not yet 'due and payable'. The lower court found that there was such an order of priority, and the receivers should distribute proceeds to senior creditors with matured debts,[332] but the Court of Appeal reversed, holding that the STD did not contemplate any order of priority between senior creditors.[333] Transaction documents made no express distinction between senior creditors, nor mentioned the timely payment nor of the trustee's duty to secure it.[334] Any construction leading to a priority within the senior creditors class was untenable because, 'the effect is likely to be haphazard, arbitrary and unpredictable'.[335] Thus, the court construed the clause as providing for two 'states' for the vehicle: (1) prior to insolvency, the assets could be presumed to be enough to meet liabilities and sums were to be paid as they became due; and (2) after insolvency, receivers had some discretion to refuse payment to a creditor whose debt had not yet become due, but they were subject to the obligation 'to pay each class of creditors pro rata and *pari passu*, including for any debts due but not yet payable'. In that second state, holding the receivers liable to pay sums as they became due would give rise to 'anomalous and problematical consequences'.[336] Thus, the court examined the clauses' function, the outcomes resulting from each interpretation, and what it perceived as the more reasonable outcome, ie *pari passu* was seen as a yardstick of normalcy and predictability.

A similar approach was followed in *Sigma Finance Corp.*, which involved another SIV issuing medium term notes (MTNs) to fund the purchase of asset-backed securities. It was badly hit by the 2008 financial crisis, the trustee took control and appointed receivers.[337] The rival interpretations of the Security Trust Deed were that: (1) moneys should be distributed on a 'pay-as-you-go' basis; (2) debts due and payable in (or prior to) the realization period should be part of a single pool, within which Sigma's remaining assets were to be distributed (the 'mixed' approach); or (3) Sigma's assets should be allocated equitably between short and long-term liabilities, on a *pari passu* basis.[338] Clause 7.6 of the STD provided that: 'During the realisation period, the trustee shall so far as possible discharge on the due dates, therefore any short term liabilities falling due for payment during such period, using cash or other realisable or maturing Assets of the Issuer.' Both the Companies Court and the Court of Appeal found in favour of the pay-as-you-go approach,[339] holding that the clause had to be interpreted according to its natural and ordinary meaning, which provided that the Security Trustee had to continue paying maturing notes in full during the realization period, until there were no more assets, because an event of default did not trigger *pari passu*

11.109

---

[331] *Re Whistlejacket* (n 175). The SIV had issued US medium term notes (USMTNs) under an indenture governed by New York law but the security trust deed (STD) was governed by English law. An enforcement event transferred control to the trustee (who appointed receivers) and was soon followed by an insolvency acceleration event.
[332] *Re Whistlejacket* (n 175).
[333] ibid.
[334] ibid para 48.
[335] ibid para 58 (adding that such holding would accept that an action on the side of the company as debtor could, by choosing to shorten or extend the period before notifying the events leading to 'insolvency' influence the respective priorities within the class of senior creditors).
[336] *Re Whistlejacket* (n 175) para 59.
[337] *In Re Sigma* (n 175).
[338] ibid.
[339] *In Re Sigma* (n 175) 1303; *In Re Sigma Sigma Corp* [2009] BCC 393.

distribution.[340] This solution could strike someone as 'unfair', but the courts' role was to ascertain what the parties' bargain was.[341]

11.110 On appeal, the UK Supreme Court[342] did not limit its interpretation to the clause's 'so far as possible' language, but warned against excessively focusing on a specific sentence and emphasized the relevance of the document as a whole to search for consistency and to interpret each clause in light of its relative importance in the overall framework[343] (ie a systematic, rather than literal, interpretation). Thus, the court focused on the *system* of distribution envisaged in the trust deed, which asked the trustee to group assets into long- and short-term pools and match them with liabilities to calculate the pro-rata distribution, giving the trustee great discretion in doing so[344] (ie a 'functional' interpretation). The court concluded that the pay-as-you-go approach followed by lower courts put too much weight on an ancillary provision on the discharge of debts, which was inconsistent with the overall scheme of the document.[345] If the goal was to create several pools to discharge debts according to their maturity, the 'pay-as-you-go' system, by depleting the asset pool that should otherwise be used to pay the other classes would, in practice, prevent the mechanism from operating, or upset the balance between short- and long-term pools of liabilities.[346] This would give creditors with 'due and payable' debts preferential treatment over long- and short-term classes. Thus, the court held that the 'so far as possible' language applied only to the scenario when the vehicle was solvent.[347] Thus, the assumption that same-class creditors are treated equally absent evidence to the contrary 'trumped' the clause's express language. *Pari passu* was not applied by, for example, extending the logic of bankruptcy law, but by holding that this was the understanding of a 'reasonable person',[348] which prevented arbitrary solutions.[349] This is an example of how the logic underpinning certain bankruptcy principles is pervasive and

---

[340] ibid. The words 'so far as possible' were construed as referring to the practicality of paying on the due dates in light of the assets available. 'So far as possible' was, in the court's opinion, not a way of subordinating the 'pay as you go' to the general principle of *pari passu* distribution. *Sigma Sigma Fin Corp 2009* (n 339). The Court of Appeal added that the ambiguity of 'so far as possible' could mean that short term liabilities had to be satisfied on their due date, but that the trustee could not be made responsible if they were paid a day or more late.

[341] *Sigma Sigma Fin Corp* (n 339). The court's holding was: 'I think it likely that many lawyers may be instinctively surprised at such a conclusion, since the culture with which they will be familiar is one ordinarily providing for a pari passu sharing in an insolvency. The notion of first come first served, or pay as you go, is alien to that culture and so cannot be right. I too had an instinctive initial sympathy with the case advanced by [senior creditors whose debts were not due and payable], since when the available pot is too small to pay everyone in full, a pari passu distribution has an obvious appeal. But we are not here concerned to apply any conventional insolvency regime. The STD [Security Trust Deed] reflects a commercial bargain made between, or on behalf of, the interested parties and our task is to interpret what that bargain was.' See *Sigma Sigma Fin Corp* (n 339) 92. The court also relied on *Cheyne II* (n 192).

[342] ibid.

[343] See eg references to *Investors Compensation Scheme Ltd v West Bromwich Building Society* [1998] 1 WLR 896. See section 3.2.1 (contract interpretation); *Miramar Maritime Corp v Holborn Oil Trading Ltd* [1984] 1 AC 676; *Charter Reinsurance Co Ltd* [1997] AC 313.

[344] *In re Sigma Fin Corp 2009* (n 339).

[345] ibid para 12.

[346] ibid paras 17–19. Distinguishing between realization period debts and other short-term liabilities was artificial because, if paid earlier, they would enjoy preference, and, if not, they would just swell the general body of short term liabilities, without special priority (arbitrary) would send the trustee conflicting messages (to meet realisation period debts, and to ensure balanced and equitable pools for all creditors).

[347] *In re Sigma Fin Corp 2009* (n 339) paras 23–24.

[348] Compare paras 29 and 32 in *Sigma Sigma Fin Corp 2009* (n 339).

[349] ibid para 21. Lord Mance stated: '[I]t remains in my view improbable that commercial parties would contemplate that, after so important an occurrence as an Enforcement Event, priority would be conferred even to a modest extent and in the short-term on a particular group of creditors on the basis of the chance of their indebtedness falling due, or being capable of being made to fall due, during the Realisation Period.'

how courts tend to lean back on it as a yardstick of the normalcy or soundness of a contract solution.

Courts do not always fall back on principles like *pari passu* as soon as terms are ambiguous. **11.111** In other cases, courts sought the logic of the parties' agreement and enforced it, even if contrary to *pari passu*. *Bank of New York v First Millennium*[350] (US) was an interpleader action for the distribution of assets in a credit card receivables securitization. The case was referred to among those where contract clauses provided a 'clear' solution, because the court relied on the 'notwithstanding' clause. Yet, the court also appealed to the logic of the transaction to decide between the FDIC and the noteholders competing theories about the allocation of proceeds. The FDIC argued that the transaction envisaged a complex system of allocation of funds once a part of unpaid receivables were classified as 'unreimbursed investment charge-offs'.[351] This was allocated to each series of notes, reducing distributions and principal. To the FDIC, the remaining funds should be allocated to the 'transferor interest', and thus paid to the FDIC as receiver. The court sided with the noteholders, who argued that all the funds resulting from receivables collection should be available to them, since the note's unpaid principal, called the note principal balance, became due and payable,[352] and also held that noteholders' rights were not limited to the collateral because the clause included the 'notwithstanding' reference, and defined noteholders' rights as 'unconditional rights', but also because the court should seek to apply 'all' contract clauses.[353] The Noteholders argued that the 'unconditional rights' clause still permitted nonrecourse notes if the noteholders consented to it,[354] and thus, the 'limited recourse' clause was not deprived of meaning.

In *Cheyne I*, a UK case, receivers applied for directions as to how they should apply moneys **11.112** during the period between the Enforcement Event and the Insolvency Event.[355] There were two rival interpretations of the clause on distribution of proceeds, a 'pay as you go' and a 'pari passu' approach. In finding in favour of the 'pay as you go' interpretation, the court interpreted the distribution clause in light of another clause that, between the Enforcement Event and the Insolvency Event, required receivers 'to manage the Company's assets with the express objective of achieving the timely payment in full of debts to Senior Creditors as and when they fall due for payment.'[356] The 'pay as you go' approach was consistent with this, and the pari passu approach at odds with it.[357]

The most interesting case of this group may be *Golden Key*,[358] due to its partial contradiction **11.113** with *Sigma Finance*. Like *Sigma*, it involved another SIV. In *Golden Key*, the notes became

---

[350] *Bank of New York v First Millennium* (n 84).
[351] ibid para 552.
[352] *Bank of New York v First Millennium* (n 84) paras 557–58. Thus, unreimbursed charge-offs affected the periodic distributions, but did not result in permanent principal write-offs affecting the final maturity.
[353] ibid para 556 (citing *LaSalle Bank NA v Nomura Asset Capital Corp* 424 F 3d 195, 206 (2d Cir 2005) and *Galli v Metz* 973 F 2d 145, 149 (2d Cir 1992).
[354] Such consent was present in the case of class D noteholders. *Bank of NY*, 598 F. Supp. 2d 550 (SDNY 2009) at 561–64. Conversely, the FDIC's argument that the 'unconditional rights' clause was restricted to preserving noteholders' rights from majority amendment, according to section 316(b) of the Trust Indenture Act, ran against the categorical language of the clause, which was not limited to the scenario envisaged in section 316(b).
[355] *In re Cheyne Finance Plc* [2007] Ch D 17 (*Cheyne I*).
[356] *Cheyne II* (n 192) cl 10.2.
[357] Furthermore, the full provision for senior obligations was not a condition precedent for the payment of obligations as they fell due. The conflict between senior creditors did not end here and was revisited in *Cheyne II* (n 192). In *Cheyne II*, by finding that the vehicle was 'insolvent', the court triggered a procedure contemplating *pari passu* distribution.
[358] *In re Golden Key Ltd (in receivership)* [2009] EWHC 148 (Ch) 95.

automatically due and payable when they reached maturity date and had to be paid if there were funds available, but all notes would become due and payable if a mandatory acceleration event occurred.[359] In the court's view, this created a vested right of noteholders whose notes had already become due and payable, which had to be redeemed on a 'pay as you go' basis, while the acceleration provision could not be construed backwards to delay the due date of the notes already due.[360] In reaching this conclusion, the court relied on the 'carefully delineated system of operating states' contained in the collateral trust and security agreement (CTSA), which distinguished between pre-wind down and post-wind down states, where maturing notes would be paid on a pay-as-you-go basis, as opposed to the post-acceleration-redemption date, where payment would be made on a pro-rata and *pari passu* basis.[361] The court rejected the *Re Whistlejacket* court's approach, holding that the structure there was simpler, 'with a single unified priority regime which, importantly, did not provide explicitly for payment of maturing notes on a pay as you go basis'.[362]

11.114 More importantly, the court differentiated between the logic of the transaction and the logic of bankruptcy principles: here the system relied not on the financial status of the vehicle, but on formal acts, such as notices of Wind-Down, Acceleration, or Insolvency, which enhanced certainty, regardless of its inherent fairness.[363] The court considered the alleged 'unfairness' towards creditors of the same class, acknowledging that one might expect *pari passu* distribution in case of imminent insolvency. Yet, since the parties had devised a 'bankruptcy-remote' structure, drawing analogies from insolvency law was not appropriate,[364] and recourse to the contract's express language should be the preferred option.[365] The Court of Appeal affirmed on other grounds.[366] It relied on 'commercial reasonableness' as the primary criteria for contract construction,[367] but it did not go as far as to say what logic supported the distinction between creditors with debts 'due and payable'.[368] The court framed the issue as a matter of 'postponement' and found that, absent explicit language, it was unreasonable for the notes that had become due and payable by reaching maturity to be postponed and to rank *pari passu* with the notes that had become due and payable only as a result of their acceleration.[369]

---

[359] ibid paras 91–93.
[360] ibid paras 93–94.
[361] ibid para 97.
[362] ibid para 101.
[363] In re Golden Key Ltd (n 358) para 98: 'I accept the submission of counsel for the Shorts that the structure established by the CTSA is one that depends on written notification of defined and (for the most part) clearly ascertainable events in order to bring about a change of operating state. A structure of that sort has the merits of being clear, certain and relatively simple to operate, all of which are in themselves desirable commercial objectives.'
[364] Since the parties had sought to exclude insolvency proceedings via no-action clauses 'the degree of assistance which can be obtained, in construing the documentation, from analogies with the general law of insolvency is limited'. In re Golden Key Ltd (n 358) para 48.
[365] In re Golden Key Ltd (n 358) 98. The machinery of *pari passu* distribution had less force in this case, 'because the parties have all agreed to sign up to an investment structure which is "insolvency remote"'.
[366] ibid 1–69. See also the concurring opinion by Lloyd J, at 70–148 (who had also delivered the opinion in Re Whistlejacket (n 175)).
[367] In re Golden Key Ltd (n 358) paras 27–29.
[368] The court stated that: '[I]t has not been suggested that this is a case where the parties have contributed to some collective investment, and thus suffered some common misfortune which would be a factor favouring a pari passu distribution.' In re Golden Key Ltd (n 358) para 63. However, one wonders why the making of a 'collective investment' should be the only, or preferred, argument in favour of *pari passu* distribution.
[369] The Court held that the language of the contract was not sufficiently explicit to justify the postponement. In the Matter of In re Golden Key Ltd (n 368) paras 34–62. The problem with this literal or plain meaning interpretation, unlike the self-referenced one of the high court, is that it would suffice if the issue had been framed as one of priority, as it was in Sigma Finance.

The Chancery Court pointed that there were differences between *Golden Key* and *Re* **11.115**
Whistlejacket, but relied heavily on the Court of Appeal's analysis in *Sigma Finance*,[370] which
was later overturned by the Supreme Court. Had the Court of Appeal in *Golden Key* also
relied on *Sigma Finance*, the Supreme Court's holding would have rendered *Golden Key* an
invalid precedent. Instead, the Court of Appeal in *Golden Key* focused on the documentation
and dismissed the usefulness of *Sigma*'s interpretation as pertaining to a 'very different' question.[371] This renders compatible two seemingly contrasting (some would say inconsistent)
approaches to very similar contract documentation.

---

[370] *In re Golden Key Ltd* (n 358) para 103.
[371] ibid para 67.

PART IV
TOWARDS BETTER JUSTICE IN FINANCE: THE CASE FOR SPECIALIZED COURTS IN EUROPE

12
Dispute Resolution in Finance and Its Shortcomings: Europe as a Test Case

1 Courts' fragmentation in the law of finance	12.01	5 Courts and inter-institutional 'dialogue' (I): the exercise of discretion and the standards of review	12.44
2 Courts' independence and impartiality	12.08		
3 Courts' expertise and specialization	12.16	6 Courts and inter-institutional 'dialogue' (II): inter-court coordination (or lack thereof) and its systemic effects	12.55
3.1 An 'external' perspective	12.17		
3.2 An 'internal' perspective	12.30		
4 Courts' organization and procedure	12.41	6.1 The 'threshold' issue	12.56
		6.2 The 'linearity' issue	12.62

1 Courts' fragmentation in the law of finance

The previous chapters show (i) that courts have to rely on principles-based interpretivism to fit a new decision within law's overall scheme, (ii) that this requires expert judgment, and (iii) that courts' design has implications for decision-making. In light of this, the goal of a 'complete system of effective judicial protection' in the law of finance has substantive, but also procedural implications. These help us identify some shortcomings in the European system, which we analyse as a test case in this chapter, to base our claim that slightly revisiting the court system for the law of finance would be a desirable complement to the Banking Union and Capital Markets Union.[1]

Europe is an interesting test case, because it arguably offers a '*complete judicial system*': the different *fora* are rather random components of a loose and informal network, where fragmentation reigns among disparate judicial, quasi-judicial, arbitral, and conciliatory venues. These venues compete, *yet their cooperation and convergence is insufficient*, despite the efforts of the CJEU at the apex of the system to ensure the primacy of EU law. The lack of an orderly design, specialization, and coordination causes many, if not all, nodes to show vulnerabilities.[2] In public law, quasi-courts have been created to cope with finance's need for expediency, yet their design is far from perfect; regulators' expertise and coordination is not matched by a court review that is coordinated and/or specialized. In private law, specialization and delocalization of disputes are taking court justice into uncharted waters, whilst

---

[1] As early as in 1990. See Jean Paul Jacqué and Joseph HH Weiler, 'On the Road to European Union: A New Judicial Architecture: An Agenda for the Intergovernmental Conference' (1990) 27 CMLR185 argued that a new judicial architecture 'should feature as an important item on the agenda'.

[2] Properly designed accountability networks are in principle better suited to ensure effective accountability in any system of multilevel governance: Carol Harlow and Richard Rawlings, 'Promoting Accountability in Multilevel Governance: A Network Approach' (2007) 13 ELJ 542.

mass, small-ticket litigation engages quasi-courts as an effective alternative dispute resolution tool; yet responses are still fragmented and uncoordinated.

12.03 A complete picture needs also to take account of arbitration, both for private-commercial and public-investment disputes, which shows vulnerabilities of its own. An approach based solely on the identification of the competent *fora* and applicable laws can facilitate the emergence of one or more preferred venues, but not a harmonized and convergent interpretation and application of the law of finance across Europe, a problem that becomes structural if arbitration is the preferred mechanism, and awards are not public. This fosters a 'silos' outcome, where each of the prevailing adjudicatory venues develops and settles its own case law, with very little horizontal dialogue with competing venues. There is also a limited vertical dialogue with the Court of Justice via preliminary rulings, because in arbitration such dialogue is delayed to the stage of enforcement of the award before the competent national court, and is highly episodical. For London courts, which have acted as the preferred forum for a long time up to Brexit, dialogue has now become unviable. All this is depriving Europe of one of the fundamental means and methods of legal unification: courts.

12.04 In the US federalism, the 'harmony without unity'[3] of the laws of the country is reflective of its dual court system, a feature deeply embedded in the nation's political roots. Although also in the United States uniformity of law is only relative, due to the concurrence of federal and state powers and difficulties of coordination,[4] Article VI, section 2 of the Constitution provides that federal law is supreme ('Supremacy Clause') and the Supreme Court has used this provision to clarify that federal law can pre-empt state law any time 'it stands as an obstacle to accomplishment and execution of the full purposes and objectives of the Congress'.[5] This happens in case of open conflict, but also if federal law supersedes state legislation, including cases where federal regulation is so dominant that state laws on the same subject should not operate.[6] In addition, the Commerce Clause[7] enables federal regulation not only on commercial deals but any time there is a material effect on interstate commerce or an instrumentality of interstate commerce, including the mails.[8] This has turned federal courts, and the Supreme Court, at the apex of the federal system, into a powerful instrument of legal unification also in the law of finance. The Supreme Court 'renders opinions in only about 80 cases a year',[9] but this increases state courts' need for dialogue with federal law, in order to avoid collisions that may reach the Supreme Court. This is achieved through federal appellate courts. Even though their opinions are only binding on other federal courts (which may decide in first instance) and in state matters only the state supreme courts have the last word, the presence of informal means for coordinating state courts and the presence of appellate courts help to enhance the consistency of the system.[10]

---

[3] James R Maxeiner, 'United States Federalism: Harmony Without Unity' in Daniel Halberstam and Mathias Reimann (eds), *Federalism and Legal Unification: A Comparative Empirical Investigation of Twenty Systems* (Springer 2014) 491.
[4] ibid 500. For fact-finding compare Jason A Cantone, *Report on Federal-State Court Cooperation: A Survey of Federal Chief District Judges* (Federal Judicial Center 2016).
[5] *Hines v Davidowitz* 312 US 52, 67 (1941).
[6] *English v General Electric Company* 496 US 72, 79 (1990).
[7] Congress has the power to legislate 'to regulate commerce with foreign nations, and among the several states and the Indian tribes': art I, s 8 of the US Constitution.
[8] See eg Securities and Exchange Act 1934, ss 2(1)(a), 3(17).
[9] Maxeiner (n 3) 502.
[10] ibid.

12.05 There are other interesting differences. First, whilst the CJEU is called to interpret national law as part of the Banking Union rule book (pursuant to Article 4(3) of the SSM Regulation), the US Supreme Court is not authorized to interpret state law and 'only exceptionally—and then against substantial criticism—does it do so'.[11] Secondly, the concern that state courts would not properly enforce federal law led to a dual court system in the United States, where 'there are parallel state and federal courts in both first and appellate instances', something not required by the Constitution.[12] It would be unfair to suggest that Member States' courts show now reluctance to enforce European law under the control of the CJEU. Yet, the American experience still holds a valuable lesson: as interconnectedness grows, there is a need for more 'bridges', or open channels of communication, beyond the existing channels of the requests for preliminary ruling. In the US, for instance, most states permit federal courts and the highest courts of sister states to 'certify' to their state's highest courts questions of state law that may determine a cause and for which there is no controlling state law precedent'.[13] This enables a horizontal channel for an open dialogue on the interpretation and application of national law. This open dialogue would prove extremely useful at the European level to ensure effective convergence in the interpretation and application of state law implementing directives in the law of finance. This, however, is still missing.[14]

12.06 As we discussed in Part II, in the context of public law disputes divergent interpretations of European principles and rules can easily scale up into blunt challenges to the system's legitimacy. This can occur if eg the ECB is called to interpret and apply different national laws implementing EU directives,[15] which may lead to diverse outcomes ('fit and proper' requirements have been an example).[16] This also occurs where the European courts are called to interpret such national laws (and their implementing administrative regulations of general application[17]). Such interpretations are not binding beyond the single case, and yet their authority would be undeniable. When the interpretation of national law cannot rely on a settled case law of national supreme courts, the exercise of interpretation made by European courts may enter into 'unchartered waters' and may even require, in pivotal cases,

---

[11] See *Bush v Gore* 531 US 98 (2000).
[12] Maxeiner (n 3) 516.
[13] ibid.
[14] In a different context (horizontal coordination of courts at the international level) see Mads Andenas and Johann Ruben Leiss, 'The Systemic Relevance of Judicial Decisions in Article 38 of the ICJ Statute' (2017) 77 ZaörV 907, noting that, partly due to a lack of political action to resolve contradictions and fragmentation, courts have been left with a central role, and have to work out ways to acknowledge each other's opinions and address conflicts, thus contributing to a 'custom-based', instead of 'hierarchy-based' system.
[15] Compare Florin Coman-Kund and Fabian Amtenbrink, 'On the Scope and Limits of the Application of National Law by the European Central Bank within the Single Supervisory Mechanism' (2018) 33 Banking & Fin L Rev 133; Andreas Witte, 'The Application of National Banking Supervision Law by the ECB: Three Parallel Modes of Executing EU Law?' (2014) 21 MJ 89; Andrea Magliari, 'Il Single Supervisory Mechanism e l'applicazione dei diritti nazionali da parte della Banca Centrale Europea' [2015] Riv It Dir Pubbl Comun 1348; Alexander Kornezov, 'The Application of National Law by the ECB: A Maze of (Un)Answered Questions' ECB Legal Conference 2019, *Building Bridges: Central Banking Law in an International World* (ECB 2019) 136–51; for an application compare Joined Cases C-152/18 and C-153/18 *Crédit mutuel Arkéa v ECB* ECLI:EU:C:2019:810; Joined Cases T-133/16 to T-136/16, *Caisse Régionale Crédit agricole mutuel Alpes Provence v ECB* ECLI:EU:T:2018:219; Case T-913/16 *Fininvest and Silvio Berlusconi v ECB* ECLI:EU:T:2022:279; Case T-797/19 *Anglo Austrian AAB v ECB* ECLI:EU:T:2022:389.
[16] See eg ECB, 'Guide to Fit and Proper Assessments. Updated in May 2018 in line with the joint ESMA and EBA Guidelines on suitability' (May 2018) 7 https://www.bankingsupervision.europa.eu/ecb/pub/pdf/ssm.fap_guide_201705_rev_201805.en.pdf (accessed 24 September 2022).
[17] Compare Miro Prek and Silvère Lefèvre, 'The EU Courts as "National" Courts: National Law in the EU Judicial Process' (2017) 54 CMLR 369; Vittorio Di Bucci, 'Quelques questions concernant le controle jurisdictionnel sur le mécanisme de surveillance unique' in Roberto Adam, Vincenzo Cannizzaro, and Massimo Condinanzi (eds), *Liber Amicorum Antonio Tizzano* (Giappichelli 2018) 316–31.

the European court preliminarily to refer a constitutionality question[18] to the competent national Constitutional Court (if the state adopts a concentrated constitutionality review)[19] or otherwise to engage directly in a constitutionality review of the applicable national law. Thus, the potential and, dare we say it, the necessity for coordination in the law of finance between the European and national levels are no longer unidirectional but have become (at least) bi-directional. Further, fragmentation can also occur in relation to interpretations of national law by national courts, and by European courts, if the General Court, or the Court of Justice, as part of the reasoning to reach a conclusion on matters of EU law, has to reach a conclusion as to the meaning and content of national law.

12.07 Another example materializes, for example, when national courts are competent to review sanctions and other administrative measures based on national law, but subject to a degree of harmonization. There is no formal judicial coordination among Member States and each national court acts on a self-referenced law, save for the rare preliminary references to the Court of Justice. Finally, fragmentation occurs horizontally in the coordination between European courts and quasi-courts, since the latter cannot make preliminary references to the Court of Justice, including if there are doubts about the legality of European law which are central for their decision.[20] The same is true for small-ticket, mass litigation alternative dispute resolution (ADR) mechanisms, although the vast majority of their rulings in the law of finance are, if not legally, factually final.

2 Courts' independence and impartiality

12.08 A consequence of the fragmentation of dispute resolution *fora* is that there is no single 'identity' for a court for the law of finance, which results in different appointing systems, and their implications for independence, impartiality, and expertise. This is not specific for Europe, nor new. One other example is the World Trade Court, ie the WTO Appellate Body, a permanent, independent, international tribunal that can uphold, modify or reverse the legal findings and conclusions of WTO panels' reports.[21] The Appellate Body is formed of seven judges appointed by the Dispute Settlement Body composed of all WTO members

---

[18] Di Bucci (n 17) 330; Mario Martini and Quirin Weinzierl, 'Der Vollzug nationalen Rechts durch di EZB und seine ungelösten Folgeprobleme' (2017) NVwZ 177; Christoph Grabenwarter and others, 'The Role of Constitutional Courts in the European Judicial Network' (2021) 27 European Public L 43 in particular at 59. The issue was raised as a (new) ground of appeal during the proceedings of *Berlusconi/Fininvest v ECB* (n 15) but was considered inadmissible for procedural reasons (the case is currently on appeal: *Crédit mutuel* (n 15)).

[19] The growing dialogue between CJEU and national Constitutional Courts is one of the defining factors of current enforcement of EU law, also beyond the law of finance: compare Juan A Mayoral and Marlene Wind, 'Introduction. National Courts vis-à-vis EU law: New Issues, Theories and Methods' in Bruno de Witte and others (eds), *National Courts and EU Law: New Issues, Theories and Methods* (Edward Elgar Publishing 2016) 3, n 11; Darinka Piqani, 'The Simmenthal Revolution Revisited: What Role for Constitutional Courts?' in Bruno de Witte and others (eds) *National Courts and EU Law: New Issues, Theories and Methods* (Edward Elgar Publishing 2016) 26–48. For a positive example, compare recently Italian Constitutional Court, judgment no 84/2021 of 13 April 2021 implementing the preliminary ruling of the CJEU in Case C-481/19 *DB v Consob* ECLI:EU:C:2021:84 on the right to be silent; the dialogue may also take place out of the formal channels of the preliminary ruling: for an application see Italian Constitutional Court no 267 of 17 December 2017.

[20] Case C-31/85 *Foto Frost (Firma) v Hauptzollamt Lübeck-Ost* EU:C:1987:452.

[21] Peter Van den Bossche, 'The Appellate Body of the World Trade Organization' in Geert De Baere and Jan Wouters (eds), *The Contribution of International and Supranational Courts to the Rule of Law* (Edward Elgar Publishing 2015) 189. The Appellate Body is often referred to as the 'World Trade Court': compare Claus-Dieter Ehlermann, 'Six Years on the Bench of the 'World Trade Court': Some Personal Experiences as Member of the Appellate Body of the WTO' (2002) 36 J of World Trade 605.

for a four-year term (renewable once) among 'persons of recognized authority, with demonstrated expertise in law, international trade and the subject matter of the covered agreements'. Members must be also broadly representative of membership in the WTO, but must be unaffiliated with any government and be independent and impartial.[22] However, currently the Appellate Body is unable to review appeals given its ongoing vacancies, after the expiry of the last sitting members on 30 November 2020 and the inability of WTO members to agree on the new appointments due to the United States refusal, based on claims of 'judicial overreach'. Thus, once a well-functioning, impartial and rules-based binding dispute settlement system ceases to operate, and appeals fall 'into the void', it becomes extremely difficult for WTO members to enforce WTO obligations and trade conflicts become intractable political quagmires. It also shows the costs of courts' independence when governments subject to their jurisdiction shy away from their duties and obligations under the rule of law. A second example is the International Court of Justice (ICJ), possibly the most important international court. The ICJ consists of fifteen judges of different nationalities which, under Article 9 of its Statute, must 'represent the main forms of civilization and of the principal legal systems of the world', and are elected through the participation of the United Nations' General Assembly and the Security Council.[23] It is notable that, although all state parties have the right to propose candidates, those proposals are not made by the governments but by the members of the Permanent Court of Arbitration, and thus by the four jurists who are designated as such by each state in the context of the Permanent Court of Arbitration. Thus, in the context of state-to-states dispute, international arbitration and international courts compete no less than cooperate and there are even interlinkages on court appointment and independence.

12.09 Moving to the national level, in the United States the identity of a 'court' is slippery, most notably due to the shifting lines between different types of federal 'courts'. Article III of the Constitution protects the judicial power of the United States from political influence through appropriate incentives (such as lifetime salaries and tenure), but 'does not specify what adjudications may be heard only in Article III courts'.[24] Therefore, in principle, it is the Congress that decides what settlement of disputes is 'styled as judicial'[25] and how.[26] Yet, this also finds its way in the case law of the Supreme Court, which distinguished (as we do in this book) between 'public' and 'private' rights and:

> [b]lessed non-Article III resolution of public rights, which historically arose between the government and persons subject to its authority, while insisting on varying levels of Article III involvement for private questions involving the liability of one individual to one another under the law.[27]

This is a point more recently reiterated by the Supreme Court in *Oil States Energy Services, LLC v Greene's Energy Group, LLC*.[28] There the Court held that the administrative patent

---

[22] Van den Bossche (n 21) 192.
[23] Philippe Couvreur, 'The International Court of Justice' in Geert De Baere and Jan Wouters (eds), *The Contribution of International and Supranational Courts to the Rule of Law* (Edward Elgar Publishing 2015) 93.
[24] 'Oil States Energy Services, LLC v. Greene's Energy Group, LLC. Leading Case: 138 S. Ct. 1365 (2018)' (2018) 132 HLR 307 https://harvardlawreview.org/2018/11/oil-states-energy-services-llc-v-greenes-energy-group-llc/ (accessed 24 September 2022).
[25] ibid.
[26] For a critique (also based on legislative history) see F Andrew Hessick, 'Consenting to Adjudication Outside the Article III Courts' (2018) 71 Va L Rev 715.
[27] HLR (n 24) quoting *Cromwell v Benson* 285 US 22, 51 (1932).
[28] HLR (n 24).

judges sitting on the Patent Trail and Appeal Board of the United States Patent and Trademark Office are 'squarely within the public-rights doctrine' when they are given the right to adjudicate disputes between patent holders and private challengers to the effect of cancelling previously issued patents, because the franchise granted by the patent is public, and patents are 'creatures of statute law'. However also Article I administrative law judges (ALJs) are 'officers of the United States subject to the Appointments Clause', as clarified in *Lucia v SEC*,[29] following *Freytag v Commissioner*[30] (US Tax Court special trial judges are 'officers with significant authority') and must be appointed by qualified appointing authorities, including the Administration (in response to *Lucia* the Trump administration issued an executive order exempting all ALJs from competitive civil servants hiring requirements and the department head retroactively appointed the five SEC ALJs).[31]

12.10 In Europe courts' appointment is inspired by a variety of different modes, sometimes controversial.[32] The appointment of EU courts and quasi courts is grounded on selection procedures where professional skills and reputation are first checked for compliance with high standards,[33] but then the appointing authority is left the final say and quite some leeway in the ultimate selection of the candidates. The appointing authorities are also different: (i) national governments, through a common accord after a hearing and a suitability opinion of an independent advisory panel for the appointment of CJEU judges, according to Article 255 TFEU; (ii) the Council, though a decision under Article 257 TFEU for judges sitting in a specialized court attached to the GCEU; (iii) the European Commission and/or the European agencies for the appointment of the members of the boards of appeal. At national level, independence ought to be in line with the 2010 Council of Europe Recommendation on judges (paras 46–47), which suggests that 'the authority taking decisions on the selection and career of judges should be independent of the executive and legislative powers' and 'at least half of its members should be judges chosen by their peers'.

12.11 In *Guðmundur Andri Ástráðsson v Iceland*[34] the Grand Chamber of the ECtHR rendered a landmark judgment on the interplay between judicial independence, appointment modes, and rule of law. The Court recalled, first, that several international sources set out the

---

[29] ibid.
[30] *Freytag v Commissioner* 501 US 868 (1991).
[31] HLR (n 24) 287 and 291.
[32] Compare Joseph HH Weiler, 'Epilogue: Judging the Judges—Apology and Critique' in Maurice Adams and others (eds), *Judging Europe's Judges* (Hart Publishing 2015) 251, noting that: '[T]he possibility of reappointing judge and advocate general at the end of their term of office is an ongoing scandal unknown in all respectable jurisdictions. It compromises the appearance of independence of judges (since their reappointment would depend on their own government).'
[33] 'Qualifications required for appointment to the highest judicial office in their respective countries or who are jurisconsults of recognised competence' for the judges of the CJEU under art 253 TFEU; 'persons whose independence is beyond doubt and who possess the ability required for appointment to judicial office' for specialized judges under art 257 TFEU; 'individuals of a high repute with a proven record of relevant knowledge and professional experience, including supervisory experience, to a sufficiently high level in the fields' concerned (banking, securities, insurance, and pensions) by the specific regulations for members of the Boards of Appeal of the ESAs under art 58 of the Regulations 1093/2010 Regulation (EU) of the European Parliament and of the Council establishing a European Supervisory Authority (European Banking Authority), amending Decision No 716/2009/EC and repealing Commission Decision 2009/78/EC [2010] (EBA Regulation) 1094/2010 of the European Parliament and of the Council establishing a European Supervisory Authority (European Insurance and Occupational Pensions Authority) amending Decision No 716/2009/EC and repealing Commission Decision 2009/79/EC [2010] (EIOPA Regulation) and 1095/2010 of the European Parliament and of the Council establishing a European Supervisory Authority (European Securities and Markets Authority) amending Decision No 716/2009/EC and repealing Commission Decision 2009/77/EC [2010] COM/2018/646 final (hereafter ESMA Regulation) (together, ESAs Regulations).
[34] *Andri Ástráðsson v Iceland*, App no 26374/18 (1 December 2020).

principle of independence of judges as an essential component of the right to a fair trial, including the United Nations (UN) Basic Principles on the Independence of the Judiciary. The Court also noted that the 2007 Report on Judicial Appointments adopted by the European Commission for Democracy Through Law (Venice Commission) acknowledged that 'no single non-political 'model' of appointment system exists, which can fully secure independence of the judiciary. The court then recalled landmark cases of the Grand Chamber of the Court of Justice in *Simpson and HG*,[35] *A.K. and Others (Independence of the Disciplinary Chamber of the Supreme Court of Poland*,[36] and *Commission v Poland*,[37] as well as precedents of the EFTA Court[38] and of the Inter-American Court of Human Rights. The ECtHR considered thus, in the first place, that any judicial body needs 'to satisfy the requirements of independence—in particular from the executive—and of impartiality', because lacking such a prerequisite it may not even be characterized as a 'tribunal' for the purposes of Article 6 § 1 of the Convention. Secondly, it underlined 'the paramount importance of a rigorous process for the appointment of ordinary judges to ensure that the most qualified candidates—both in terms of technical competence and moral integrity—are appointed to judicial posts' (and 'the higher a tribunal is placed in the judicial hierarchy, the more demanding the applicable selection criteria should be'). The ECtHR further found that non-professional judges could be subject to different selection criteria, particularly when it comes to the requisite technical competence. Yet, in the Court's view, a "merit-based selection not only ensures the technical capacity of a judicial body to deliver justice as a 'tribunal', but it is also crucial in terms of ensuring public confidence in the judiciary and serves as a supplementary guarantee of the personal independence of judges". The ECtHR could then conclude that:

> 230 ... the Court is well aware that there are varying judicial appointment systems across Europe, and the mere fact that the executive, in particular, has decisive influence on appointments—as is the case in many States Parties, where the restraints on executive powers by legal culture and other accountability mechanisms, coupled with a long-standing practice of selecting highly qualified candidates with an independent state of mind, serve to preserve the independence and legitimacy of the judiciary—may not as such be considered to detract from the characterisation of a court or tribunal as one established by 'law'. The concern here relates solely to ensuring that the relevant domestic law on judicial appointments is couched in unequivocal terms, to the extent possible, so as not to allow arbitrary interferences in the appointment process, including by the executive.

and could later find, in another landmark case (*Xero Flor w Polsce sp. Zoo v Poland*[39]) concerning the alleged unlawful appointment of a constitutional judge, that the participation of unlawfully appointed judges in rulings would amount to a violation of Article 6(1) of the Convention. The case law of the ECtHR under Article 6(1) of the Convention is telling also

---

[35] Joined Cases C-542/18 RX-II and C-543/18 RX-II *Réexamen Simpson v Council* ECLI:EU:C:2020:232.
[36] Joined Cases C-585/18, C-624/18 and C- 625/18 *A.K. and Others (Independence of the Disciplinary Chamber of the Supreme Court)* ECLI:EU:C:2019:982.
[37] Case C-619/18 *Commission v Poland (Independence of the Supreme Court)* ECLI:EU:C:2019:615.
[38] Case E-21/16 *Pascal Nobile v DAS Rechtsschutz-Versicherungs AG* [2017] EFTA ct. Rep. 554 and also accessible at www.eftacourt.int
[39] *Xero Flor w Polsce sp Zoo v PolandApplication*, App no 4907/18 (7 May 2021); compare Jacub Jaraczewski, 'From Boars to Courts: The Landmark ECtHR Case *Xero Flor v Poland*' *EU Law Live* (11 May 2021). More recently, the Court of Appeal of Krakow lodged a request for preliminary ruling to the CJEU asking whether judgments issued by a non-independent and non-impartial court of final instance are binding on ordinary courts or whether they can be set aside by these (Case C-225/22, pending).

on other aspects of detail.[40] In *Campbell and Fell v United Kingdom*[41] the Court held that appointment procedure and duration of term for judges are a key factor to assess their independence and impartiality from the executive power. In *Henrik Urban and Ryszard Urban v Poland*[42] the ECtHR—in parallel with the Polish Constitutional Court[43]—found that a temporary judge (an assessor) appointed in a Polish court did not meet the standards of fair trial because it could be removed from office by the Ministry of Justice and there were no sufficient guarantees against a possible arbitrary exercise of such power by the ministry.[44] In contrast, in *Ringeisen v Austria*[45] the Court held that the appointment of a member of a court presided by a professional judge by an industry association would not run counter the independence of the court, because there was evidence that the appointee was free from industry's influence or pressure when carrying out the function.[46] The same was held for members of administrative courts.[47] Courts need not only to be independent, but also impartial. According to the ECtHR, impartiality refers to the subjective position of the court and its members in respect to the parties.[48] Appearance of impartiality is also essential[49] and can be jeopardized for instance where persons external to the sitting court could take part to the deliberations (also without any active role in it).[50] Independence and impartiality are requirements 'closely linked'.[51]

12.12 European courts have followed a similar path. In its Opinion 1/17 of 30 April 2019[52] the CJEU held that independence entails two aspects: (i) an external aspect, which presupposes that the body functions wholly autonomously, without hierarchical constraints, subordinations, or taking orders (ie protected against external pressures), which requires certain guarantees, eg against removal, and commensurate level of remuneration; and (ii) an internal aspect, linked to impartiality, and seeking to ensure that an equal distance is maintained from the parties and their interests, which requires objectivity and the absence of any interest in the outcome of the proceedings. Independence and impartiality require rules on the body's composition, appointment, length of service, grounds for abstention, rejection, dismissal, to dispel 'any reasonable doubt in the minds of individuals as to the imperviousness of that body to external factors and its neutrality with respect to the interests before it'. These requirements—first elaborated in *Graham J. Wilson v Ordre des avocats du barreau de Luxembourg*[53] and further specified in *Associacao Sindical dos Juizes Portugueses v Tribunal de Contas*[54]—are now at the heart of a long string of cases concerning (mostly) Poland,

---

[40] Gabriele Steinfatt, *Die Unparteilichkeit des Richters in Europa im Lichte der Rechtsprechung des Europäischen Gerichtshofs für Menschen* (Nomos 2012) 25 ff.
[41] *Fell v United Kingdom*, App nos 7819/77 and 7878/77 (19 March 1981).
[42] *Henryk Urban and Ryszard Urban v Poland*, App no 23614/08 (30 November 2010).
[43] Case SK 7/06 (24 October 2007) https://trybunal.gov.pl/fileadmin/content/omowienia/SK_7_06_GB.pdf (accessed 24 September 2022).
[44] Karol Pachnik and Jakub Krajewski, 'The European Concept of a Fair Trial and the Legal Admissibility of Assessors in the Polish Judicial System' in Elzbieta Kuzelewska and others (eds), *European Judicial Systems as a Challenge for Democracy* (Intersentia 2015) 233 ff.
[45] *Ringeisen v Austria*, App no 2614/65 (16 July 1971).
[46] *Flux (No 2) v Moldova*, App no 31001/03 (3 October 2007); *Affaire Zolotas v Grece*, App no 38240/02 (2 June 2005).
[47] See *Majorana v Italy*, App no 75117/01 (26 May 2005).
[48] Steinfatt (n 40) 39–55.
[49] *Langborger v Sweden*, App no 11179/84 (22 June 1989). Compare Steinfatt (n 40) 55 ff.
[50] *Lormines v France*, App no 65411/01 (9 November 2006); *Tedesco v France*, App no 11950/02 (10 May 2007).
[51] *Siglfirdingur Ehf v Island*, App no 34142/96 (7 September 1999).
[52] Opinion 1/17 *Accord ECG UE-Canada* ECLI:EU:C:2019:341.
[53] Case C-506/04 *Graham J Wilson v Ordre des avocats du barreau du Luxembourg* ECLI:EU:C:2006:587. Compare also Case C-199/11 *Europese Gemeenshap v Otis* ECLI:EU:C:2012:684, para 64.
[54] Case C-64/16 *Associação Sindical dos Juízes Portugueses* ECLI:EU:C:2018:117.

including *A.K. and Others (Independence of the Disciplinary Chamber of the Supreme Court of Poland* and in *Commission v Poland*.[55] The court considers judicial independence a fundamental component of the rule of law one of the fundamental values protected by Article 2 TEU[56] and a prerequisite for effective judicial protection referred to in Article 19 TEU and for the right to an effective remedy before a tribunal enshrined in the Charter of Fundamental Rights of the EU (Article 47). This means that a court must always 'act as a third party' in relation to the dispute[57] and all EU institutions are committed to ensure courts' independence.[58] Also in the EU context, independence and impartiality are a characterizing factor for a 'court'. Notably, the (perhaps) most important of the several *Vaassen*[59] criteria which must be fulfilled by any dispute resolution body to qualify as 'court or tribunal of a Member State' for making a reference for preliminary ruling under Article 267 TFEU is that it must be permanent and independent.[60]

12.13 There are, however, margins of flexibility left by European courts to the design of courts, which may prove particularly helpful for discussing expert courts in the law of finance. An interesting precedent is once again the CJEU Opinion 1/17 on CETA courts where the court offered precious guidance on several aspects of detail concerning the design of a specialized court such as duration of appointment (full-time or part-time), expertise, remuneration (fixed, retainer fee; hourly fees):

> 223   As regards the external aspect of the requirement of independence, ... the Members of the CETA Tribunal *will be appointed for a fixed term and will have to possess specific expertise (emphasis added)* [and] [t]he CETA ensures ... that the Members will receive a level of remuneration commensurate with the importance of their duties. The CETA guarantees, last, the protection against removal of those Members ... For the same reason, it must be held that it was open to the Parties, without adversely affecting the requirement of independence, to stipulate, in Article 8.27.12 of the CETA, that the amount of the monthly retainer fee to ensure the availability of the Members of those Tribunals will be determined by the CETA Joint Committee and, in Article 8.27.15, *that that body may decide to transform that retainer fee and fees and expenses into a regular salary, and decide applicable modalities. (emphasis added)*. As the Advocate General stated in points 260 and 261 of his Opinion, the fact that those provisions concerning the remuneration of Members of the CETA Tribunal and Appellate Tribunal are intended to evolve cannot be perceived as constituting a threat to the independence of those Tribunals, *but conversely permits the gradual establishment of a court composed of Members who will be employed full-time* (emphasis added).

---

[55] Joined Cases C-585/18, C-624/18 and C-625/18 *AK and Others (Independence of the Disciplinary Chamber of the Supreme Court)* (n 36) and Case C-192/18 *Commission v Poland (Independence of ordinary courts)* ECLI:EU:C:2019:924. For an overview of recent judgments on judicial independence see Rafal Manko, *European Court of Justice Case Law on Judicial Independence*, (Briefing from the EPRS: European Parliamentary Research Service July 2021, PE696.173).

[56] Such values are, in turn, protected through the sanctions listed in Art 7 TEU: for a discussion of the applicability of art 7 in the context of the PiS Party's reform bills in Poland threatening judicial independence, compare eg Michael Hoffmann, '[PiS]sing off the Courts: The PiS Party's Effect on Judicial Independence in Poland' (2018) 51 Va J of Trans L 1153.

[57] Koen Lenaerts, Ignace Maselis, and Kathleen Gutman, *EU Procedural Law* (Janek T Nowak ed, OUP 2015) 54, n 36; Case C-516/99 *Schmid* ECLI:EU:C:2002:313, paras 34–44.

[58] Communication from the Commission, 'EU Law: Better Results through Better Application' (2017/C 18/2) [2017] OJ C18.

[59] Case C-61/65 *Vaassen (neé Göbbels)* ECLI:EU:C:1966:39.

[60] Case C-54/96 *Dorsch Consult* EU:C:1997:413, para 23; Case C-517/09 *RTL Belgium* ECLI:EU:C:2010:82.

The Opinion also leaves that some degree of flexibility in the rules on courts' appointment is acceptable, yet it finds its limit in the fundamental respect of independence and impartiality, which, no matter how different the appointing methods are,[61] needs to be ensured under all appointing systems as a prerequisite of the rule of law and the legitimacy of the court.

12.14 Yet this is more easily said than done. Which institutional incentives may foster judicial independence is a quagmire in the academic debate. Professor Richard Posner[62] identified a paradox:

> [A]t the heart of economic analysis of law is a mystery that is also an embarrassment: how to explain judicial behavior in economic terms, when almost the whole thrust of the rules governing compensation and other terms and conditions of judicial employment is to divorce judicial action from incentives, to take away the carrots and stick, the different benefits and costs associated with different behaviors, that determine human action in an economic model.[63]

Public choice[64] acknowledges that judicial independence may depend on how court members are selected, for how long they are given their tenure, how they got paid and on their accountability and thus on matters of institutional design. In other terms, 'under the right conditions judicial independence can be part of an incentive-compatible system',[65] one which formally recognizes an independent status, provides fixed and commensurate remuneration, and a reasonably long tenure, and contemplates the possibility for sitting judges of being dismissed during their term of office only for serious ground and by unanimous decisions of their peers.[66] Collective and secret decision-making procedures,[67] high reputation and professional requirements as a precondition to appointment are additional devices which can be conducive to the desired outcome.[68] Yet public policy also cares to admit that such formal institutions cannot be 'the whole answer'. 'Substantive independence' depends also on the willingness of political actors to respect courts' role in the first place, and on the incentives for judges and political actors to pursue, on an ongoing basis, such independence. Fleck and Hanssen note that:

> [J]udges are not—and cannot conceivably be—entirely independent of the world around them. The formal institutions that govern procedures for retention, promotion, compensation, discipline and so forth provide means by which other actors can attempt to influence judicial behavior. At the extreme formal rules can be altered (or ignored) in order to undo judicial decision. That said, judicial institutions are usually designed with the specific goal of insulating judges from this kind of influences.[69]

---

[61] For a US perspective on the 'conventions of judicial independence' (and a cautionary tale about the fragility of judicial independence, particularly at a time when government officials seem willing to depart from other long-standing norms) see Tara Leigh Grove, 'The Origins (and Fragility) of Judicial Independence, (2018) 71 Va L Rev 465.

[62] William M Landes and Richard A Posner, 'The Independent Judiciary in an Interest Group Perspective' (1975) 18 J L & Econ 877.

[63] Richard A Posner, 'What Do Judges and Justices Maximize? (The Same Thing Everybody Else Does)' (1993) 3 Supreme Court Econ Rev 1, 3.

[64] Robert K Fleck and F Andrew Hanssen, 'Judges: Why Do They Matter?' in Michael Reksulak and others (eds), *The Elgar Companion to Public Choice* (2nd edn, Edward Elgar Publishing 2013) 233, in particular 237.

[65] ibid 246.

[66] Compare to this effect art 6 of the Statute of the CJEU.

[67] Robert Schütze, *European Union Law* (CUP 2015) 200, n 94.

[68] For an empirical work identifying measures meant to bring about, de iure or de facto, judicial independence, compare Lars P Feld and Stefan Voigt, 'Economic Growth and Judicial Independence: Cross-country Evidence Using a New Set of Indicators' (2003) 19 Eur J Political Econ 497.

[69] ibid 242.

The thrust of the problem is that independence and impartiality are, at the very end, states of mind. Thus, there is no simple normative solution. A problem further exacerbated by the fact that there is no simple consensus on what independent and 'optimal' court decisions are either.

12.15 Our focus, however, are courts that settle financial disputes, and whether they meet these standards. We believe there is margin for improvement, as we use quasi-courts as an example. As we will discuss more extensively in a next section, their appointment is delegated to the authority whose decisions they must review, the renewal of their five-years term depends *again* on the authority's governing body. This may flip the court's incentives to challenge the authority's decisions, or contradict the appearance of independence. Remuneration is based on hourly fees and becomes therefore episodical if workload is not continuous, with a risk of transforming the membership in an honorary one. These are faulty lines in the design of internal boards of review which at the end may jeopardize their role as courts and they emerge as distinct, organizational weaknesses as such even more so if only one compares them with the appointment and status requirements for specialized courts under Article 257 TFEU.

3 Courts' expertise and specialization

12.16 A different, but related, set of considerations concerns professional skills. This raises a question: to what extent element of courts' specialization are necessary in the law of finance? Should a court settling financial disputes be composed not only of generalist judges but also experts in the law of finance, and/or in finance, in economics and in prudential matters? This requires a short digression on pros and cons of judicial specialization in both 'interstitial' and 'pivotal' cases. We start to address this question by considering pros and cons of courts' specialization in general terms. Then we move on to consider existing shortcomings in Europe.

3.1 An 'external' perspective

12.17 A World Bank study portrayed a few years ago[70] court specialization as a growing trend worldwide (including the United States and Europe). In the study, the most distinctive elements of courts specialization are found, first, in that 'certain types of cases are handled by the judiciary somewhat differently, possibly even separately from the rest' and, second, that this responds to 'the increasing specialization of the law and the growing complexity of the topics'.[71]

12.18 Court specialization is not new.[72] Illustrative examples are, eg in the United States, the Delaware Chancery Court, which dates back to 1792, and in Europe the English courts

---

[70] Heike Gramckow and Barry Walsh, 'Developing Specialized Court Services: International Experiences and Lessons Learned' (2013) Justice and Development Working Paper Series no 24/2013.
[71] Working Party of the Consultative Council of European Judges (CCEJ) *Report of the 22nd Meeting, Strasbourg,* (CCJE, 22–28 March 2012).
[72] Specialization was rooted in medieval particularism. Compare for example Alain Wijffels and CH Van Rhee (eds), *European Supreme Courts: A Portrait Through History* (Third Millenium Publishing 2013); however, as noted in CCEJ (n 71) 32 in the *ancien régime* particularism was reflected in the special systems of particular courts (based either on the local outreach of the jurisdiction, or on the legal status of a particular transaction, or of one's personal status), whereas in modern judicial systems courts are homogenous in that they are part of the same national legal and judicial system. See also Willem Theus, ' There and Back Again From Consular Courts through Mixed Arbitral

specialized in maritime law, which date back to the fourteenth century. In continental Europe, specialized merchant courts in Italian medieval times served as a blueprint for the '*jurisdiction consulaire*' of the Paris Merchant Courts under Carl IX, which then turned into the specialized '*Tribuneaux de commerce*' established under Article 631 of the Commercial Code of 1807, still a remarkable example of courts composed by experts whose collective expertise is far beyond the law. Yet 'the more complex and specific the legal framework becomes and the more sophisticated the economic environment, the greater the calls for specialization'.[73] Specialized courts have also become a defining feature of modern dispute resolution, including financial disputes.

12.19 The World Bank offers a matrix for an 'external view' of court specialization, that helps to assess its advantages and disadvantages:[74] greater efficiency, higher quality decisions especially in complex areas, and greater uniformity are some of specialization's strengths. Yet, these must be weighed against risks of capture, threats to the unity of the judiciary, inequality in access to justice at the geographical periphery (specialized courts operate only in main centres), or compartmentalization of knowledge which could hinder quality and flexibility.[75] Thus, specialized courts can be deemed superior only if (i) their area of expertise (and subject-matter jurisdiction) can be clearly defined and separated from all other disputes, (ii) there is a sufficiently high volume of cases, (iii) there is a preponderance of technical issues that require expert judgment, (iv) uniformity in the adjudication of any particular matter may be actually expected, (v) the need for specialization is not contingent or temporary and (vi) there are pilot tests showing the case for specialization in any relevant field.[76] To sum up, the World Bank's study spells out four prerequisites for judiciary specialization: (i) complex legal requirements calling for specialist knowledge, (ii) need for additional services and/or separate processes, (iii) case type volume and (iv) external demand (ie complaints/concerns about process inefficiencies or quality issues in the subject matter or an assessment of the importance for societal good that specialization is ensured). All of these prerequisites seem to be in place with public and private disputes in the law of finance.

12.20 The World Bank's study offers in turn a taxonomy of different models of specialization, including separate courts at one end, and generalist courts with one specialist member at the other end. A middle ground is a specialist division or bench within a generalist court. The World Bank further notes that specialized procedures, including supporting services, are a necessary component of any specialized court system.

12.21 These findings are largely in line with academic literature and practice. In the US dual-court system, specialized court are common, yet not for the law of finance.[77] Salient examples are

---

Tribunal to International Commercial Courts' in Hélène Ruiz Fabri, Michel Erpelding (eds.), *The Mixed Arbitral Tribunals, 1919-1939* (Nomos, 2023), 29-64.

[73] Gramckow and Walsh (n 70) 4.
[74] In principle, 'the burden of proof that the benefits of specialization outweigh the costs [stays] on those promoting specialization': David Rottman, 'Does Effective Therapeutic Jurisprudence Require Specialized Courts (and Do Specialized Courts Imply Specialized Judges)?' (2000) 37 Court Review 25; Holger Fleischer, Sebastian Bong, and Sofie Cools, 'Spezialisierte Spruchkörper im Gesellschaftrecht' (2017) 81 RabelsZ 610.
[75] The matrix is further developed including practical aspects highlighted by the US Congress as early as the 90s. See Federal Reports Study Committee, 'Report of the Federal Courts Study Committee' (1990) 22 Connecticut L Rev 4; Edward Cazalet, *Specialized Courts: Are they a Quick Fix or a Long-Term Improvement in the Quality of Justice* (World Bank 2001).
[76] Gramckow and Walsh (n 70) 15.
[77] Markus B Zimmer, 'Overview of Specialized Courts' (2009) 2 Intl J Court Administration 46.

the US Tax Court, the Bankruptcy Courts, the US Court of Appeals for the Federal Circuit, the US Court of International Trade at the federal level; and commercial courts, administrative courts, and small claims courts at state level. A balance of their experience is positive and shows, to our purposes, that specialized courts reduce 'conflicts in the interpretation and application of the law in their field(s) of jurisdiction', and 'limit the forum shopping'.[78] Moreover, 'independent specialized review tribunals with judges who understand and are familiar with the intricacies of the law and regulations that govern administrative agency activity and services are much better positioned to adjudicate appeals of agency decisions than are general-jurisdiction judges'.[79]

A comprehensive book published by Lawrence Baum[80] in 2011 addressed judicial specialization in the United States, building on Martin Shapiro's insights on patent policy and law[81] and on courts[82] of the late 1960s and early 1980s, and on Stephen Legomsky's wider analysis.[83] Professor Baum notes the tension between an embedded tradition 'of a generalist judiciary' and the 'belief in the specialization which permeates society as a whole'.[84] He identifies what he calls 'neutral virtues' of specialization such as quality of decisions, efficiency and uniformity in the law, and notes that 'it is reasonable to posit that judicial specialization enhances these virtues, but the empirical evidence of this enhancement is remarkably slim'.[85] He concedes, however, that:

12.22

> [G]ains in efficiency could be countered by the need to litigate jurisdictional boundaries between generalist and specialized courts and the inconvenience to litigants of bringing cases to a geographically centralized court. Concentration of judges could reduce efficiency if it means that some judges are assigned exclusively to a category of cases does not fully occupy their time in certain periods ... The uniformity gained from concentrating cases in a single court could have a corresponding cost, the absence of diverse decisions on an issue that ultimately produce better policy.[86]

In turn, he identifies 'non-neutral effects' on the substance of judicial policy, and notes that specialization of courts may also change 'the ideological content of their polices or their support for competing interests in a field'.[87] Finally, in a cross-country comparison, Professor Baum notes that many civil law countries in Europe feature greater court specialization than common law countries, and most notably Germany, because:

> Germany stands out for its level of specialization: subject-matter specialization is the foundation of the judicial structure. Alongside the ordinary courts in Germany are separate hierarchies of courts, spanning the state and federal systems, for labor, public and administrative law, taxes and social insurance. Within the ordinary courts there is additional subject-matter specialization at the trial and appellate level.[88]

---

[78] ibid 47.
[79] ibid 48.
[80] Lawrence Baum, *Specializing the Court* (University of Chicago Press 2011).
[81] Martin Shapiro, *The Supreme Court and Administrative Agencies* (New York Free Press 1968). Consider that the first work of Lawrence Baum: Lawrence Baum, 'Judicial Specialization, Litigant Influence and Substantive Policy: The Court of Customs and Patent Appeals' (1977) 11 L & Society Rev 823.
[82] Martin Shapiro, *Courts: A Comparative and Political Analysis* (University of Chicago Press 1981).
[83] Stephen Legomsky, *Specialized Justice: Courts, Administrative Tribunals, and a Cross-National Theory of Specialization* (OUP 1990).
[84] Baum (n 80) 2.
[85] ibid 4.
[86] ibid 33–34.
[87] ibid (for examples in the tax domain see 147–54; in the corporate practice of the Delaware courts, 186–91).
[88] ibid 23.

12.23 Exemplary of the tensions between specialized and generalist courts are the US history and practice of the Tax Court.[89] The first federal tax court was established in 1924 as Board of Tax Appeals, an independent agency; it adopted the 'court' title in 1942, but remained an executive-branch agency, and finally gained the status of an Article I court in 1969. The Tax Court is just *an alternative forum* for income tax disputes: the government, and taxpayers can file, at their choice, a lawsuit also in a district court or the Court of the Federal Claims (where however they must first pay the disputed amount and then bring the action; which may explain why most cases are filed with the Tax Court).[90] In this context, thus, 'a highly specialized court, a moderately specialized court, and a set of generalist courts hear cases in the same field'.[91]

12.24 Three historic features of the tax courts offer interesting lessons. First, the tax court was originally established as an administrative board within the executive-branch and not as a court because 'uncertainty whether the new body would function well militated in favour of an administrative board that could be abolished with relative ease'. Only after the board gained a foothold[92] was it converted into a specialized court. Secondly, although the Tax Court is based in Washington D.C., tax judges travel nationwide to conduct trials in various designated cities, ie it is not appreciably less convenient than a district court. The Tax Court also developed a small tax case procedure for cases involving claims of US$50,000 and less.[93] This exemplifies the kind of flexible arrangements which may be necessary to accommodate a centralized specialized court to the convenience of its users. Thirdly, although the Tax Court is composed of nineteen presidentially appointed members, trial sessions are conducted also by senior judges serving on call and by special trial judges, all with special expertise in tax law and a past career in the tax government or in private practice. This also poses the question if past careers in the government translate into courts' inclinations in favour of the government itself.[94] Some studies find that 'taxpayers have substantially higher winning percentages in the district courts' than in the Tax Court, but this is not conclusive evidence that these judges are pro government.[95]

12.25 The European academic debate is in line with these conclusions. A 2017 special issue of RabelZ[96] which comprehensively considered different patterns of judicial specialization focusing on special chambers of the judiciary adjudicating on specific subject matters concluded that specialized courts respond to actual needs, yet with nuances and not without resistance in certain contexts, the most notable being the US Courts of Appeals, which still proudly characterize themselves as courts of generalist judges.

---

[89] ibid 148.
[90] ibid 148.
[91] ibid 150.
[92] ibid 149.
[93] ibid 148.
[94] Compare, however, Mark P Altieri and others, 'Political Affiliation of Appointing President and the Outcome of Tax Court Cases' (2001) 84 Judicature 310.
[95] Baum (n 80) 152–54.
[96] Holger Fleischer, 'Spezialisierte Gerichte: Eine Einführung' (2017) 81 RabelsZ 497 ff (where additional references to previous literature). Compare also Holger Fleischer, 'Gerichtspezialisierung im Gesellschaftsrecht: Die Erfolgsgeschichte des Delaware Court of Chancery' in Helmut Siekmann (ed), *Festschrift für Baums* (Mohr Siebeck 2017) 416–431; Holger Fleischer and Nadja Danninger, 'Die Kammer für Handelssachen: Entwicklungslinien und Zukunftperspeckiven' (2017) ZIP 205; Holger Fleischer and Nadja Danninger, 'Comparing Commercial Courts in France and Germany: Tribunaux de commerce and Kammern für Handelssachen' (2017) 3 Rev Trim Dr Fin 48 (also in German in (2017) *RIW* 549).

An 'external' perspective on specialized courts thus offers mixed results, yet with benefits **12.26** that often outweigh the costs. This is also confirmed by the 'economics of judicial behavior', a strand of literature developed within the so-called 'positive political theory'.

Starting from Adam Smith's say, that 'commerce and manufacturers can seldom flourish **12.27** long in any state which does not enjoy a regular administration of justice',[97] positive political theory has analysed 'judicial games' in light of 'hard institutional rules' such as procedure and game sequencing, and of 'softer micro-analytic aspects of judicial decision-making, such as legal doctrines'.[98] This strand of literature acknowledges, first, that courts, through legal doctrine and precedent, are a fundamental part of the legal order, because law is '[w]hat emerges within the political-institutional competition between courts, agencies and legislatures'[99] and courts mostly develop the legal order through the margin of judicial appreciation granted to them in the interpretation and application of standards or general principles. Secondly, courts compete in different 'theaters of justice', such as (a) the horizontal theatre, where judges interact with other institutions, in principle on an equal standing, in a policy struggle where no one institution has complete control over the others (consider eg the 'dialogues' between supreme courts and legislatures), (b) the vertical theatre, best represented by the judicial hierarchy between higher and lower courts and (c) the internal theatre (judges sitting together on a judicial panel).[100] Competition can often take place in more than one theatre at a time.

A first claim of positive political theory, from an 'external' standpoint, is that, *if* courts matter **12.28** for economics, commerce, and, critically, finance, *if* courts' role is shaped not only by hard institutional rules, but also by soft ones, such as legal doctrines, and *if* these are shaped by the patterns that determine the horizontal, vertical, and internal organization of courts, the only conclusion is that judicial organization has a key role to play in the development of the law.

Quantitative studies confirm the preference for *commercial* specialization. Case studies published by Doing Business in 2012 and 2019 find for instance that specialized commercial courts, or specialized commercial sections within generalist courts—'tend to improve efficiency' and result 'in faster and less costly contract enforcement'.[101] Similar findings are reached by OECD cross-country stock-taking exercises,[102] considering factors like trial length, appeal rates, budget allocated to the court, case-flow management, using metrics in line with those developed by the International Consortium for Court Excellence, a quality

---

[97] Adam Smith, *An Enquiry into the Nature and Causes of the Wealth of Nations* (first published 1776, Edwin Cannan ed, Methuen & Co Ltd 1904) 752.
[98] Emerson H Tiller, 'The Law and Economics of Judicial Decision-making' in Francesco Parisi (ed), *The Oxford Handbook of Law and Economics*, vol I, *Methodology and Concepts* (OUP 2017) 223.
[99] ibid.
[100] ibid 225.
[101] World Bank, *Enforcing contracts* (Doing Business 2012) 5 https://www.doingbusiness.org/content/dam/doingBusiness/media/Annual-Reports/English/DB12-Chapters/Enforcing-Contracts.pdf (accessed 24 September 2022). World Bank, 'Enforcing Contracts and Resolving Insolvency. Training and Efficiency of the Judicial System (Doing Business 2019)' 54 https://elibrary.worldbank.org/doi/10.1596/978-1-4648-1326-9_Case4 (accessed 24 September 2022).
[102] Giuliana Palumbo and others, 'Judicial Performance and Its Determinants: A Cross-country Perspective' (2013) OECD Economic Policy Papers no 5, in particular, 26; Giuliana Palumbo and Others, 'The Economics of Civil Justice: New Cross-Country Data and Empirics' (2013) OECD Economics Department Working Papers no 1060.

management system for courts.[103] No specific indications on the efficiency of specialized courts are offered, on the contrary, by the EU Justice Scoreboard.[104]

3.2 An 'internal' perspective

12.30 An 'external' perspective normally focuses on court specialization's impact on efficiency. Yet, one should connect efficiency considerations with arguments of validity and consistency, ie an 'internal' perspective, which looks at the law of finance from inside legal practice. Thus, once we have reflected on the (social, economic, or political) benefits and risks from outside legal practice, an 'internal' perspective must look at 'law' as an interpretative body of rules and principles, the relevance of 'hard cases' for its development, and the impact of courts' specialization in that process. Our claim is that some elements of courts' specialization may also play an important role in the law of finance's 'internal' perspective, and more specifically, for the proper implementation and development of the Banking Union and of the Capital Markets Union.

12.31 As we noted in previous chapters, 'hard' cases involve 'pivotal' problems, where the controversy about the adequate solution masks a deeper disagreement over the criteria to be employed to reach such solution, ie a disagreement over the law itself.[105] Such cases often imply collisions of rules and principles and are difficult to square within a formally positivistic framework, which assumes the existence of a 'rule of recognition' that determines which is the law applicable to the case.[106] In 'hard' or 'pivotal' cases, the semantic problem of determining what a legal concept means is inextricably linked with the resolution of the problem at hand. The relevance of the distinction between 'pivotal' and 'interstitial' cases constitutes a first argument in favour of some elements of judicial specialization. In areas characterized by a complex subject matter, a convoluted set of facts and norms, and seemingly arcane legal issues, expertise is critical not just to understand the problem, but to differentiate marginal, or borderline and pivotal cases. The final decision (eg on appeal) over pivotal questions corresponds to the highest courts, typically generalist courts, but unless a specialist court has helped absent a process of analysis that helps 'depurate' the matters of detail, and dig up the deeper issue, the case's focal point may often be missed.

12.32 Secondly, hard cases are resolved by using arguments of policy and arguments of principle, but arguments of policy belong primarily in the realm of legislative, executive, and administrative bodies, because they operate under the prerogative of discretion, while arguments of principle belong primarily in the realm of judicial bodies, because the claims presented before them are claims of 'right'. Even when courts use arguments of policy, eg the legislative intent of a certain provision (budget discipline, consumer protection, etc.), or weigh the consequences of a certain decision on a collective goal, their ultimate aim is to determine the scope of a certain right (or power or responsibility). Even if judges internally weigh other

---

[103] Compare Liz Richardson, Pauline Spencer, and David Wexler, 'The International Framework for Court Excellence and Therapeutic Jurisprudence: Creating Excellent Courts and Enhancing Wellbeing' (2016) 25 J Judicial Administration 148.
[104] Compare for 2018, Communication from the Commission to the European Parliament, the Council, the European Central Bank, the European Economic and Social Committee and the Committee of the Regions the 2018 EU Justice Scoreboard (28 May 2018) COM(2018) 364 final.
[105] Ronald Dworkin, *Law's Empire* (HUP 1986) 42.
[106] HLA Hart, *The Concept of Law* (first published 1961, OUP 2012) 91–100.

considerations, the acceptable justification for their decisions must be based on arguments of principle and right. Thus, principles-based interpretivism in the law of finance needs to be 'operationalized' and translated into a necessary adjunct to the motivation supporting any relevant decision in the application of the rules and standards, showing a straightforward engagement of the decision-maker not only with the literary text of the relevant provisions but, more importantly, with their finality, and the principles and values inspiring their adoption.

This gives us a second argument to support specialization. The premise is that courts are circumscribed by the kind of arguments that they can use, which is what differentiates their role from that of political or administrative bodies. Courts may not uphold a solution simply because it is more efficient, or equitable, or accords more with a collectively desirable goal. They must fit, or 'weave' the new decisions into the fabric of existing statute and precedent, to ensure consistency, and the integrity of the legal system, ie that like cases are treated alike. In the law of finance integrity-consistency and equal treatment become the most important objective at times where the normative framework has acquired such depth and complexity. Thus, specialized courts can not only separate 'marginal' from 'pivotal' cases. They can also better identify the features of a case that make it similar to (or different from) another case. **12.33**

To this one may object that judges cannot, and should not, formulate a full-blown, comprehensive, theory every time a new case arises: they should limit themselves to 'incompletely theorized arrangements'.[107] Yet, how can a court determine the level of theorization ex ante? The answer is 'it cannot'. A court first needs to see the specific facts and classify the legal problem, and then determine the 'optimal level of theorization'. This exercise is similar to the 'principles-based interpretivism' that, in our view, is the defining feature of the role of courts. Using 'analogy' is just a way of using 'principles-based interpretivism' when the parallel is clear. If one disputes the analogy, or offers an alternative, reasoning by exact analogy may not suffice, but principles-based interpretivism does. It is what defines the exercise as 'legal'. This also shows the advantages of specialized courts, which range from sieving through the case details to help draw the proper analogy, to testing the broader reasons that prevent analogy in truly pivotal cases and pave the way for a final decision. **12.34**

The third step in our reasoning begins by pointing out a feature overlooked by legal philosophers, but is critical in the law of finance, such as the relationship between courts and agencies in interpreting law, and implementing policy. Sometimes, defenders of principles-based interpretivism, like Dworkin, suggest that there is 'one right answer';[108] ie a party either has or has not a right. Yet, in the law of finance considerations of 'right' are also mixed with considerations of policy, as well as with considerations of 'power' and 'responsibility', or 'mandates' of monetary, supervisory, or resolution authorities.[109] Such brand of hard cases need special attention (and expert judgment) because they entail two types of difficulties. One is that the court needs to understand the policies, or goals, pursued by the statute, to understand the scope and limits of the agency's mandate, to differentiate between reviewing (the court's role) and substituting (not the court's role). Another is that, in such exercise, courts need a special self-awareness, because even when they are expected to determine what the law is impartially, courts are also a party in the 'institutional balance' of powers. This requires **12.35**

---

[107] See Cass Sunstein and Adrian Vermeule, 'Interpretation and Institutions' (2003) 101 Michigan L Rev 885; Cass Sunstein, 'Incompletely Theorized Arrangements' (1995) 108 Harv LR 1733.
[108] Ronald Dworkin, *Taking Rights Seriously* (first published 1977, Bloomsbury 2019) 24.
[109] Wesley Newcomb Hohfeld, 'Some Fundamental Legal Conceptions as Applied in Judicial Reasoning' (1913) 23 Yale LJ 1, 30.

a reflexive self-restraint coded into their institutional DNA.[110] This is a task that specialized courts are uniquely placed to undertake, and a task that is particularly needed in the current context of the EU law of finance. If one considers the examples of courts lenient towards administrative authorities, as courts tend to be in the US, they often rest on a tacit assumption that the authority's decision-making process is legitimate, partly because it is based on well-settled, predictable practice. Contrast this with the current European law of finance, which is new, and has operated a drastic re-distribution of competences in favour of newly established supervisory and resolution authorities with extensive, open-textured, goal-oriented mandates. Not only anchoring the legitimacy of these authorities inside national laws and EU law is a key priority. Doing it wrong poses an existential threat to the whole system. Thus, courts cannot limit themselves to an attributive role. They need to top it up with a discursive one: aside from delineating the respective roles of the authorities and themselves, courts also need to engage in a constructive dialogue with the authorities, where eg the different elements of the proportionality test (especially the 'necessity' and 'appropriateness') are used to understand the difference between an exercise of powers that is proper, from one that is excessive. EU Courts seem to be partly aware of this, and rather than granting deference, they engage in purposive interpretation, most of the time to legitimize the authorities' views.

12.36 As a fourth, and final, step in our reasoning, while courts enforce 'laws', and do not enact them, in 'hard cases' courts will often find themselves delving into the 'values' that pervade the social order underpinning the legal order.[111] The relevance of such value-based dimension is often overlooked, as it is the broader question of how to shape justice in the European Union,[112] a concept surprisingly neglected in the Treaties (where there is no express reference to it as a foundational value in Article 2 TEU).[113] More specifically, in our view case law confirms the finding of Floris de Witte that 'European Union law generates ... 'conflicts of justice' on a continuous basis throughout its territory' and this is so because there are differences 'between how Member States and the EU understand justice, in both institutional and normative terms'.[114] In turn, 'these 'conflicts of justice' can be overcome by articulating' forms of transnational solidarity that reflect the connections between citizens in the EU across borders'. As de Witte has argued:

> [T]he EU's tiered institutional settlement offers a novel and fascinating way of extending the values of social justice beyond the nation state. It does so by standing on the shoulders of the national welfare state construction and adding a transnational dimension to its values. Such a tiered understanding of the idea of justice in Europe, however, raises three issues: (1) it challenges us to think beyond the contractarian reflex that equates justice with

---

[110] Chiara Zilioli, 'From Form to Substance: Judicial Control on Crisis Decisions of the EU Institutions' in Franklin Allen, Elena Carletti, and Mitu Gulati (eds), *Institutions and the Crisis* (EUI 2018) 146 (also noting at 142 the distinction between principles and rights to the effect of the applicability of the Charter in the law of finance, also in light of judgment in Case C-414/16 *Egenberger* EU:C:2018:257). For a different view see Mitu Gulati and Georg Vanberg, 'Paper Tigers (Or How Much Will Court Protect Rights in a Financial Crisis?)' in Franklin Allen, Elena Carletti, and Mitu Gulati (eds), *Institutions and the Crisis* (EUI 2018) 111.

[111] Giulio Itzcovich, 'On the Legal Enforcement of Values: The Importance of the Institutional Context' in Andras Jakab and Dimitry Kochenov (eds), *The Enforcement of EU Law and Values* (OUP 2017) 32, 36–39, comparing how the 'noble dreams' and the 'nightmares' of both neo-constitutionalism and legal positivism, enforcement of values and strict constructionism, *Wertjurisprudenz*, and *Gesetzpositivismus* interact with the idea of the judicial role.

[112] Our reference is to Floris De Witte, *Justice in the EU: The Emergence of Transnational Solidarity* (OUP 2015).

[113] However, the Amsterdam Treaty made justice an objective in its own right in the area of justice, freedom and security and made judicial cooperation a political target.

[114] De Witte (n 112) 1.

political self-determination of a demos; (2) it demands that we create a tiered institutional and normative model, involving both the nation state and the EU, that can make sense of the new ties between individual citizens that the process of European integration, and in particular its norms of free movement, continue to generate; and (3) it requires that we construct novel concept of transnational solidarity that help us understand what those new ties—which may come in economic, social or political forms—tell us about our transnational obligations of justice.[115]

12.37 In this book we build on this intuition and develop these concepts further. The goal is also to show how properly framing the institutional architecture of justice in the law of finance would be a major contribution, on several fronts. First, in the handling of both national and cross-border cases, to improve courts' effectiveness and more uniform and consistent responsiveness in adjudicating complex disputes with significant impact in a highly harmonized context. Secondly, specifically for Europe, in cases with a pan-European or cross-border dimension, to further 'disentangle the pursuit of justice from the structures of the nation state'.[116] This can favour a more cooperative and consistent interpretation and application of European law and an administration of justice that is responsive to the values common to the European project.

12.38 In conclusion, we believe that some elements of courts' specialization are the most suited to address the overwhelming complexities of the Banking Union and the Capital Markets Union. First, the law of finance is formed by an assemblage of disparate rules and chunks of legislation that follow different logics and goals, but no unifying plan, which makes the effort of ex post reconciliation through interpretation extraordinarily important. Secondly, those goals or 'policies' have to be reconciled, in turn, with other propositions with a dimension of weight and importance, such as the more concrete 'principles', which may formulate rights and duties, or the more abstract 'values', which are supposed to cut across the legal order and inform all policy-making. Thirdly, the application of rules and policies is not only entrusted to courts, but also to administrative authorities, which means that, on top of making sense of the whole ensemble, courts have to leave room for spaces of discretionary decision-making. Fourth, those same courts have to also respect the vertical division of competences between national and supranational levels. Thus, a look from the inside of legal practice shows that the challenges of the EU law of finance are especially daunting, in a way that is hardly matched in any other discipline. An applicative dimension is insufficient without an interpretative one, which is crucial to draw the pivotal cases from the simply factually complex. In addition, an iterative dimension, where certain problems are revisited on a regular basis is also crucial to delineate the contours of rights (eg consumer and investors' rights), but also mandates and

---

[115] ibid 4. In a similar line of thinking, which acknowledges the centrality for democratic legitimacy of transnational solidarity within the Banking Union, Pedro Gustavo Teixeira, 'The Future of the European Banking Union: Risk-Sharing and Democratic Legitimacy' in Mario Pilade Chiti and Vittorio Santoro (eds), *The Palgrave Handbook of European Banking Union Law* (Palgrave Macmillan 2019) 135–52, arguing that the exercise of banking supervision and resolution competences have also distributive consequences within the Union and the perceived legitimacy of such distributive effects is key to prevent the risk of disintegration and ensure future sustainability of the Banking Union. An interesting test case for such value-based dimension of the role of courts may prove in due course the 'greening' of the Euro monetary policy (as announced in the press release of the Governing Council of the ECB of 4 July 2022), its reliance on art 11 TFEU in coordination with art 127(1) TFEU: an anticipation could be seen in the case, lodged in April 2021 and withdrawn in November 2022, *ClientEarth v Belgian National Bank* before Belgian courts (first instance and appeal) and in the German Constitutional Court Order of 24 March 2021 on the *Bundes-Klimaschutzgesetz* (1BvR 2656/18, 1 BvR 288/20, 1 BvR 96/20, 1BvR 78/20) (see Press Release no 31/2021 of 29 April 2021 www.bundesverfassungsgericht.de).
[116] De Witte (n 112) 207.

powers bit by bit, like a sculptor's chisel. A look from the outside shows that the financial sector needs certainty and predictability, but also that the new financial architecture, and the institutions that conform it, need legitimacy and accountability, and courts have a major role to play in it. Their expert judgment is therefore key.

12.39 That the resolution of disputes in the law of finance may require a court which is composed by experts in the law of finance, in finance, in economics and in prudential matters is an underpinning of the regulations establishing the joint Board of Appeal of the European Financial Supervisory Authorities and the SRB Appeal Panel.[117] Specialization is also present in some courts for private law disputes, like the expert judges of hybrid commercial courts or non-legal experts as member of the panel of the court in the Paris Commercial Tribunal and in PRIME arbitration courts in the Hague. This is not new. An interesting parallel can be drawn with tax courts in Victorian England, as well as with the Special Commissioners and the members of the Board of Internal Revenue which had often no legal training and this was regarded by some commentators of the time as 'illogical' and 'anomalous' because none of the stringent requirements for the appointment of a county court judge applied to them despite their 'unlimited jurisdiction' on the tax matters attributed to their adjudication.[118] Nonetheless, their role was long preserved, because tax laws could only be administered by specialists:[119]

> [T]ax law was acknowledged as being particularly complex and technical. Illogical arrangements, ambiguous language, poor drafting, innumerable amendments, the practice of reading a number of sections in different Acts as one and the invariable tradition of incorporating earlier Acts into a new taxing Act merely by reference, meant that tax Acts were notoriously long, obscure and complex. Furthermore, there existed a large body of material incorporating the interpretation of tax legislation by the central boards, instructions to tax officials as to how they were to deal with certain cases or groups of taxpayers, regulations issued by the boards and countless circulars and orders embodying the daily implementation of tax law. This practice of the revenue departments was central to the implementation of the tax law, and was utterly inaccessible to anyone outside the closed circles of the central revenue boards.

Yet, aside from the parallels, one should be conscious of the differences as well. In Victorian England the specialist tax expertise was needed to ensure 'a more precise knowledge' of the cases, but 'tax was not perceived as law in the generally accepted sense of the term' and 'administrative bodies with merely incidental judicial powers [were deemed] not exercising the power of the state, so they were not courts and could not be constituents of the judicial system. Context was everything'.[120] In the current context of the law of finance, the subject matter is equally complex, but the expertise is needed not to create a 'law within the law', but fully to appreciate the nature of the issue, and its exact legal implications, to separate

---

[117] Article 58 of the ESAs' regulations sets out, for instance, that the Board of Appeal is composed of six members and six alternates '[w]ho shall be individuals of high repute with a proven record of relevant knowledge and professional experience, including supervisory, experience to a sufficiently high level in the fields of banking, insurance, occupational pensions, securities markets or other financial services, excluding current staff of the competent authorities or other national or Union institutions involved in the activities of the Authority.'

[118] Chantal Stebbings, 'Bureaucratic adjudications: The internal appeals of the Inland Revenue' in Paul Brand and Joshua Getzler (eds), *Judges and Judging in the History of the Common Law and Civil Law. From Antiquity to Modern Times* (CUP 2015) 159.

[119] ibid 166.

[120] ibid 167, 172.

marginal, borderline cases based on minute details from truly pivotal ones, which test the system's internal consistency and to ensure coherence also in 'interstitial' cases with a principles-based interpretation and application of the law of finance. This is why, as much as we advocate a court system characterized by some elements of specialization, we do so with the caveat that such a system must be closely connected with generalist courts (and with the CJEU at the apex of the system), to ensure that there is no 'drift effect'.

12.40 This raises three issues. First, it makes it necessary to consider whether the fact that the law of finance is 'law', there should be a requirement that all court's members have a legal background. To some extent, this is suggested by the recent 2019 ESAs reform by Regulation (EU) 2019/2175, which introduced a new requirement for all members of the Board of Appeal to have a proven record of 'relevant knowledge of Union law'.[121] Yet, we believe that a limitation only to lawyers by education of the eligibility criteria to sit as member of a financial court would be a mistake, as it would be disproportionate and would deprive the court of the interdisciplinary expertise necessary to have 'more precise knowledge' internal to the court of the cases, something that an expert witness can only provide to some extent and from outside the court, and proved so far of limited help in the CJEU practice. This raises a second, and more practical, issue: how members of a financial court with no legal background can properly deliver on their duties if they lack the ability to draft decisions using legal terminology. While acknowledging that this could pose an intractable issue with monocratic courts, with a single-member, or composed by members all with the same background, we consider that collegial work and appropriate secretarial support should in principle be enough to handle the matter.[122] What really matters to identify a case's knot is the acumen and full understanding of the substance of the matter, rather than the mastery in the arcane art of legal writing. Thirdly, from what constituency should members of the courts in the law of finance best be recruited? The experience, so far, of the Board of Appeal of the ESAs, the Administrative Board of Review of the ECB, and the Appeal Panel of the SRB offers preliminary indications as to the importance of a mixed background and on how members who are academics or were former central bankers and/or high officials in supervisory authorities or financial institutions could contribute well to the work of their boards.

4 Courts' organization and procedure

12.41 Courts do not, and cannot, work, internally, in a vacuum. They need organizational support, including research assistance, and their performance reflects to some extent also the effectiveness of such support. Yet, there is no single model of secretarial support to a court.

---

[121] Regulation (EU) 2019/2175 of the European Parliament and of the Council amending Regulation (EU) No 1093/2010 establishing a European Supervisory Authority (European Banking Authority) Regulation (EU) No 1094/2010 establishing a European Supervisory Authority (European Insurance and Occupational Pensions Authority) Regulation (EU) No 1095/2010 establishing a European Supervisory Authority (European Securities and Markets Authority) Regulation (EU) No 600/2014 on markets in financial instruments, Regulation (EU) 2016/1011 on indices used as benchmarks in financial instruments and financial contracts or to measure the performance of investment funds, and Regulation (EU) 2015/847 on information accompanying transfers of funds [2019] OJ L334/I. It is unclear, however, if this will preclude the appointment of experts in the fields of banking, insurance, occupational pensions, securities markets or other financial services who are not lawyers by education; we consider that it probably will not, if they could show the requested 'relevant knowledge of Union law'.

[122] Although tax was not considered a part of the law in full, tax adjudicators of Victorian England—to continue with our historical parallel—'had free and constant recourse to their own legal department'. Stebbings (n 118) 68.

The Appellate Body of the WTO is eg assisted by a Secretariat, which is separate by the WTO Secretariat and comprises more than a dozen of lawyers.[123] The International Court of Justice has a staff of more than twenty lawyers, several of them being seconded to the judges. The Board of Appeal of the ESAs, the Administrative Board of Review of the ECB and the Appeal Panel of the SRB have a Secretariat which is functionally independent from other functions of the agency, but with no budgetary autonomy. This may be a consequence of the relative youth of these agencies, but it is unfortunate. Although it is fair to acknowledge that, for example, the Appeal Panel Secretariat has been progressively strengthened in resources, the difference is still striking if one compares with the resources and the judicial clerks traditionally assigned eg to federal judges in the United States, to the UK Supreme Court, to the German Federal Constitutional Court and the German federal courts, to the Supreme Court of the Netherlands, or to the members of the CJEU and their key role in practice in promoting good quality of the judgments.

12.42 Another important set of considerations concerns the *procedural* angle. Due process and the right to be heard are the golden rule across the board, but in different ways. The most visible difference is between courts and quasi-courts in the EU. Indeed, only formal courts are subject to the more exacting requirements of fair trial under Article 47 of the Charter, while internal review bodies, being of an administrative nature, are only bound by the principle of good administration under Article 41 of the Charter.[124] This translates into different procedural rules, time limits, rules on the taking of evidence and oral hearings, but also on case management. However, the relevance of fundamental rights of procedural nature in all adjudicatory proceedings in the law of finance cannot be understated. Case law clearly shows that whenever individual substantive fundamental rights are weighed against the public interest and have to yield to such public interest (as occurs, for instance, where financial supervisors take intrusive administrative measures affecting property rights), courts are very careful in ensuring that at least all procedural rights have been properly respected. This is a point famously emphasized by the Court of Justice in *Gauweiler*. Even in the context of monetary policy, which is the perfect example of an issue where courts fear to tread, the Court held that both the principle of conferral by which an authority exercises its mandate and the legality of its discretionary exercise are conditional upon the existence of judicial review,[125] and precisely when the authority is granted broad discretion 'a review of compliance with certain procedural guarantees is of fundamental importance'.[126]

12.43 Another aspect of procedure which is highly EU-specific is the language of the proceedings. Under Regulation No. 1 1958 European citizens are in principle entitled to use their language in their relationship with European institutions.[127] The CJEU has accepted deviations from this general principle only in exceptional circumstances and if duly motivated. As AG Maduro noted in *Spain v Eurojust*:[128]

---

[123] Van den Bossche (n 21) 192.
[124] Case C-119/15 *Biuro Podrozy Partner v Prezes Urzedu Ochrony Konkurencji I Konsumentow* ECLI:EU:C:2016:987; Fabrizio Cafaggi, 'Towards Collaborative Governance of European Remedial and Procedural Law' (2018) 19 Theoretical Inquiries in L 252.
[125] Case C-62/15 *Peter Gauweiler v Deutsche Bundestag* ECLI:EU:C:2015:400, paras 41, 68.
[126] ibid para 69.
[127] For a comprehensive discussion of the multi-linguist approach in the EU and its implications, Friederike Zedler, *Mehrsprachigkeit und Methode* (Nomos 2014) in particular as to the procedural languages, 93–103.
[128] Case C-160/03 *Kingdom of Spain v Eurojust*, Opinion of Advocate General (AG) Poiares Maduro ECLI:EU:C:2004:817, paras 37–38.

As is clear from the judgment in *Kik v OHIM*, the references to the use of languages in the European Union contained in the Treaty 'cannot be regarded as evidencing a general principle of Community law that confers a right on every citizen to have a version of anything that might affect his interests drawn up in his language *in all circumstances*'. There are circumstances in which that right cannot be applied. But those circumstances can but be limited and they must be justified on every occasion. In any event, the Union institutions and bodies have a duty to respect the principle of linguistic diversity.

This has practical implications mostly for quasi-courts, which must in principle operate under the same multi-linguistic arrangement of the CJEU, but without having the same resources for translation. This can result in delays and difficulties in the delivery of judgments in the language of the procedure and in the management of hearings in languages other than English.

5 Courts and inter-institutional 'dialogue' (I): the exercise of discretion and the standards of review

12.44 Courts sit atop the justice system, but they are not the only institutions entrusted with the application of the law of finance. Monetary, supervisory and resolution authorities also have important rules-based mandates to fulfil, and the need that such mandates are executed under conditions of independence and technical expertise requires that they be granted a margin of appreciation, and in some cases broad discretion in the assessment of complex economic issues. European courts have used in the law of finance a formula previously used in cases where EU authorities, typically the Commission, make 'complex economic assessments', whereby they should be granted relatively broad discretion.[129] The fact that the Court decides to 'anchor' that discretion in the existence of complex technical assessments is justified by the assumption that the Commission has a superior level of technical (economic) competence to the Court, and that interfering with its technical decisions could do more harm than good. This takes us back to some of our core arguments, because the moment this assumption does not fully work, the argument for discretion is severely weakened.

12.45 To clarify our position fully, the presence of elements of specialization in the court system does not mean that the presence of complex technical assessments no longer justifies giving leeway to the institution or agency. Yet, it means that the argument on 'discretion' is no longer 'black and white'. An agency may still have the ability to make factual inferences that are technically complex (eg whether a specific factor may have an impact on financial stability), and as long as it is properly justified a court (including a specialized court) should not substitute its judgment for that of the agency making a 'de novo assessment'. However,

---

[129] See eg Case C-56/64 *Consten and Grundig v Commission* ECLI:EU:C:1966:41, para 347; Case C-42/84 *Remia BV and Others v Commission of the European Communities* ECLI:EU:C:1985:327, para 34. More recently see Case C-386/10 P *Chalkor AE Epexergasias Metallon v European Commission* ECLI:EU:C:2011:815, para 54. Compare Alexander Fritzsche, 'Discretion, Scope of Judicial Review and Institutional Balance in the European Law' (2010) 47 CMLR 361; Andriani Kalintiri, 'What's in a Name? The Marginal Standard of Review of Complex Economic Assessments in EU Competition Enforcement' (2016) 53 CMLR 1282–1316; Joana Mendes, 'Discretion, care and public interests in the EU Administration: Probing the limits of law' (2016) 53 CMLR 419; in the EU law of finance, Matthias Lehmann, 'Varying Standards of Judicial Scrutiny over Central Bank Actions' (ECB Legal Conference 2017 –Shaping a new legal order for Europe: a tale of crises and opportunities, 4–5 September 2017) https://www.ecb.europa.eu/pub/pdf/other/ecblegalconferenceproceedings201712.en.pdf (accessed 24 September 2022).

a specialized court can determine more accurately when the reasoning is flawed, or the justification insufficient, in light of the applicable legal framework that is supposed to limit agencies' decision-making in a way that makes their margin of appreciation acceptable. In simpler terms: the actual deployment of technical expertise is a very fact-specific task, as is its justification. Specialized courts are better placed to examine those specific decisions because they may better understand the meaning and implications of both factual, technical circumstances and of the legal provisions that limit the agency's ability to make inferences from them. Scrutiny may be more granular, and thus 'discretion', or 'technical leeway' more credible and acceptable. This is not because specialized courts are infallible, or cannot get it wrong, far from it; but because, having been selected on the basis of their expertise, they can be presumed to understand the technical issues, and the way they interact with the relevant regulatory framework, so they can legitimately engage with both in more detail. Thus, a decision stating that an agency measure was disproportionate or insufficiently justified, regardless of its technical accuracy, is legally more robust, because it is more legitimate for such a court to dig deeper into the agency's decision.

12.46 This takes us to the opposite of discretion, which is judicial review,[130] a field that reinforces the opinion in favour of some elements of specialization in the court system, and completes the arguments made so far. The standard of review of regulatory/supervisory action which must be applied by the courts and quasi-courts at work in the law of finance is seemingly uncertain. This relates, in the first place, to appeals against supervisory decisions.[131] It is unclear, for instance, whether the proceedings before the CJEU have the same scope of the appeals before the ESAs' Board of Appeal or the SRB Appeal Panel. In one decision[132] the Board of Appeal—quite incidentally—seemed to acknowledge that an appeal could allow, at least in some circumstances, a somewhat wider consideration on the merit, beyond the legality review applied by the CJEU. In the literature[133] some have gone much farther and have argued that the board is vested with unlimited, full review jurisdiction that could take the board to reconsider all aspects of the merit of the decision. Others argue that, since the board of Appeal noted that an appeal is a very different procedure to a court review under Article 263 TFEU, 'the impact of this is that market participants will have greater opportunity to challenge ESMA for a failure to act than is possible for other forms of EU (in)action'.[134] Another author[135] suggests, however, that (i) since appeals are grounded on the legal basis of Article 263(5) TFEU, (ii) the 2019 reform of the CJEU Statute which acknowledges the role of some Boards of Appeal is premised on the assumption that the administrative review of those Boards of Appeal already offers a first instance legality review, and (iii) the appealable decisions are bound in their content by the rule of law, the standard of review should be the same as the one of the CJEU under Article 263 TFEU. Yet another interpretative proposal regarding the SRB Appeal Panel puts forward that, although the Panel's administrative review

---

[130] For a comparative view see Tim Koopmans, *Courts and Political Institutions. A Comparative View* (CUP 2003) 108, 129–62; Shapiro (n 82) 111–25, 153–54.
[131] Andreas Witte, 'Standing and Judicial Review in the New EU Financial Markets Architecture' (2015) 2 OJFR 1.
[132] BoA 2014 05 *Investor Protection Europe v ESMA* (10 November 2014).
[133] Matteo Gargantini, 'La registrazione delle agenzie di rating e il ruolo della Commissione di ricorso delle Autorità europee di vigilanza finanziaria (nota a Commissione di ricorso delle Autorità europee di vigilanza finanziaria, 10 gennaio 2014)' (2014) Rivista di Diritto Societario 416.
[134] Ryan Murphy, 'The effective enforcement of economic governance in the European Union: brave new world or a false dawn?' in Sara Drake and Melanie Smith (eds), *New Directions in the Effective Enforcement of EU Law and Policy* (Edward Elgar Publishing 2016) 316 citing BoA decision *Investor Protection Europe v ESMA* (n 132).
[135] Ginevra Greco, *Le Commissioni di ricorso nel sistema di giustizia dell'Unione Europea* (Giuffré 2020) 170.

must remain a legality review, and the Appeal Panel 'may not be at liberty merely to substitute its own appraisal to that of the SRB', 'the applicable standard of review at the level of the Appeal Panel is that of the 'error of assessment', meaning that 'the error need not be manifest in the same manner as it does before the CJEU; because of its mixed composition the Appeal Panel can be expected to investigate more thoroughly whether the economic assessment made by the SRB was not erroneous'.[136]

Opinions are still not settled on this. European courts, relying precisely on the legal and scientific competences of the members of the Boards of Appeal, have showed, more recently, a preference for a scope and intensity of the review extended to 'error' of assessment (and thus beyond the idea of 'manifest error'), at least for Boards of Appeal established within European agencies outside the law of finance.[137] Those findings have also been supported by the Court of Justice, holding that otherwise the appellant could not appeal the agency decision before the EU judicature, while General Court would be carrying out a limited review of a decision which is itself the result of a limited review, against the principle of effective judicial protection.[138] The Court's findings concerned the Boards of Appeal of ECHA and ACER, whose defining feature is to be in functional continuity with the authority itself, in the sense that those two Boards of Appeal expressly enjoy the same powers as those available to the body of the agency that adopted the appealed decision. It is hard to fathom whether the Court will apply the same reasoning by analogy to the ESAs Board of Appeal and the SRB Appeal Panel, which are not in a similar functional continuity and do not expressly enjoy the same power of the governing bodies of the relevant agencies. Unlike other boards of appeal which can exercise on appeal any power which lies within the competence of the agency or remit the case, they can only confirm or remit the appealed decision. Such difference cautions against any automatic inference by analogy. Also, the argument that the administrative appeal bars the appellant from challenging the decision of the agency before the EU judicature and that, therefore, there should not be a 'limited review of a 'limited review', in violation of the principle of effective judicial protection is not entirely convincing. The example of composite proceedings is useful, since there the pleas for annulment may also concern preparatory acts which are part of the proceedings leading to the adoption of the final decision.[139] Likewise, to the extent that errors of the agency's decision may have determined the manifest illegality of the Board of Appeal decision, the application for annulment of a Board of Appeal decision may also concern such errors of the agency's decision. If this is so, then the General Court would be able to subject to its limited review also the agency decision, and the risk 'of a limited review of a limited review' as described by the court would dissolve. In practical terms, it does not appear that European courts confine themselves to such a narrow understanding of their role.

12.47

---

[136] Yves Herinckx, 'Judicial Protection in the Single Resolution Mechanism' in Robby Houben and Werner Vandenbruwaene (eds), *The Single Resolution Mechanism*, vol 2 (Intersentia 2017) para 26.

[137] Case T-125/17, *BASF v ECHA* ECLI:EU:T:2019:638, paras 60, 65, 87–89; the appeal in Case C-565/17 *BASF v ECHA* ECLI:EU:C:2018:340 was dismissed with order of the Vice-President of the Court of 28 May 2018; Case T-735/18 *Aquind v ACER* ECLI:EU:T:2020:542, paras 50–70; on appeal, C-46/21 P *ACER v Aquind* ECLI:EU:C:2023:182.

[138] Case C-46/21 P *ACER v Aquind*, ECLI:EU:C:2023:182, paras 58-73, especially para 67 (see also the Opinion of 15 September 2022 in Case C-46/21 P *ACER v Aquind* ECLI:EU:C.2022:695, and Case T-125/17, *BASF v ECHA* ECLI:EU:T:2019:638, para 58).

[139] Filipe Brito Bastos, 'Derivative Illegality in European Composite Administrative Procedures' (2018) 55 CMLR 101.

12.48 So far, the ESAs Board of Appeal and the SRB Appeal Panel have considered that their review cannot lead to a *de novo* evaluation and needs to respect the margin of appreciation which the applicable rules confer upon the agency and its governing bodies. In *Scope Rating v ESMA*[140] the Board of Appeal clarified that it is not 'in functional continuity with the ESMA's Board of Supervisors', noting that '(unlike other boards of appeal of European agencies, eg EUIPO), the Board of Appeal does not enjoy the same powers as the ESMA Board of Supervisors and there is not, thus, in the merit, full continuity of its functions with the agency decision-maker'.[141] The Board of Appeal consistently concluded that '[t]he Board of Appeal is not empowered to second guess decisions of the Board of Supervisors which entail a margin of appreciation and the Board of Appeal's review is limited to verifying whether ESMA, in adopting its determination, complied with all applicable procedural rules, duly stated the reasons, accurately stated the facts or committed a manifest error of assessment of a misuse of powers'. The Appeal Panel, in turn, has constantly held,[142] most notably in the access to document saga concerning the resolution of Banco Popular Español, and subsequently in cases deciding on Minimum Requirements on Own Funds and Eligible Liabilities (MREL), that 'in its assessment—to ensure the functionality of the Board and to respect the role and division of tasks provided for by the SRMR and Regulation 1049/2001—the Appeal Panel must certainly verify if the board complied with all relevant substantive and procedural rules, properly stated its reasons and did not incur in any manifest error, but cannot substitute its opinion for that of the board where the applicable legal provisions grant a margin of appreciation to the board, which means that, on issues where the assessment of the facts may render to different interpretations, eg the impact of certain disclosures on decision-making or legal proceedings to the effect of the exceptions to access to documents under Regulation 1049/2001, the Board's margin of appreciation must be also respected by the Appeal Panel, unless there is a specific reason not to do so'. What are (at least some) practical implications of this conclusion? The Board of Appeal and the Appeal Panel are tasked to perform a full review of facts (which can be better appraised thanks to a composition of both colleges which ensure technical expertise also beyond the legal knowledge) and of law. Their sole limitation is that, to the extent that the applicable legal framework grants technical discretion, eg where a provision expressly states that the agency may or may not grant a certain derogation to a supervised entity, or a margin of technical appreciation to the governing bodies of the authority, the suitability of the discretionary choices cannot be second-guessed nor subject to a *de novo* assessment and their review is confined, in this specific context, to manifest errors in assessment. With a further note of caution, though. When a contested decision is founded on such discretionary choices, the statement of reasons is even more key, and the appellant may ask the Board of Appeal and the Appeal Panel to check not only that it is sufficient pursuant to Article 296 TFEU but also that the reasons are erroneous in fact or in law. An example from MREL cases may help clarifying the current standard of review. Article 12h of the SRMR as amended by Regulation 877/2019 reads as follows:

> The Board *may* waive the application of Article 12g in respect of a subsidiary of a resolution entity established in a participating Member State where: … *(c) there is no current or*

---

[140] BoA 2020-D-03, decision of 28 December 2020.
[141] The Board of Appeal referred to the judgment 12 December 2002 in Case T-63/01 *Procter & Gamble v OHIM* [2002] EU:T:2002:317, paras 21–22.
[142] Case 21/2018 A v SRB (19 June 2019), para 39. Compare also the decision in Case 1/21 *A v SRB* (28 June 2021) and, for a more recent and thorough discussion in the context of a MREL case, decision in Case 3/2022 A v SRB (13 February 2023), paras 69–81

foreseen material practical or legal impediment to the prompt transfer of own funds or repayment of liabilities by the resolution entity to the subsidiary in respect of which a determination has been made in accordance with Article 21(3), in particular where resolution action is taken in respect of the resolution entity.

12.49 Article 12h(1) says that, *after* ascertaining certain preconditions, the board *may* waive the application of Article 12g. According to the case law of the General Court of, when a prudential rule confers to the competent authority the power to grant derogations from the applicable prudential regime when certain conditions are met, the authority is given *discretion* to refuse such derogations 'even when the conditions set out in that provision are met'.[143] Yet, the condition under letter c) of Article 12h (that 'there is no current or foreseen material practical or legal impediment to the prompt transfer of own funds or repayment of liabilities'), is also formulated in open-textured terms, and thus a margin of appreciation to the SRB in assessing whether such condition is met. Thus, Article 12h requires a two-pronged test from the resolution authority: first, an assessment that the conditions set out in Article 12h are met; if so, secondly, a more discretionary assessment (yet still subject to the review of its compliance with general principles of law, and most notably proportionality and equal treatment) that, according to the informed judgment of the authority and taking into consideration all factual elements of the case, such a waiver may and in the end will be granted. This has important implications. The assessment of whether the conditions of Article 12h are met is not an exercise of discretion in the proper sense, but rather a verification that the factual and legal requirements of Article 12h(1)(c) are satisfied. Nonetheless, due to the relative open-ended nature of the requirements set out in letter (c), the assessment is not automatic either, and it implies a complex, factual, and legal assessment which entails a margin of appreciation, yet more constrained and limited than the one granted in the second stage of the assessment, where the board is literally given the discretionary power not to grant the waiver, even if all conditions are met. The review of both assessments needs to ensure at the same time appropriate deference to the technical evaluation of the agency and a fine-tuned control of its legality. Confronted with this issue, the Appeal Panel in Case 2/21 considered insufficient the statement of reasons of a contested decision concerning the refusal of a waiver pursuant to Article 12h SRMR, where it denied the occurrence of such a condition under Article 12h(1)(c).[144]

12.50 Is this really different from the standard of review of the CJEU? Or, in other terms, is it really necessary that the identification of the right standard of review for courts and quasi court called to determine on public law financial disputes enter the quagmire of the distinction between marginal and full review? We surmise it is not. The precise degree of intensity of both administrative and judicial review of the decisions of financial supervisors[145] is still elusive in the most complex cases, between the Scylla and Charybdis of full and marginal review.[146] Yet, no court or quasi-court is prepared to second-guess with a *de novo* evaluation

---

[143] See to this effect Case T-733/16 *La Banque Postale v European Central Bank* ECLI:EU:T:2018:477, para 58; Case T-745/16 *BPCE v European Central Bank* ECLI:EU:T:2018:476; and Case T-758/16 *Crédit Agricole v European Central Bank* ECLI:EU:T:2018: 472; compare also Case T-504/19 *Crédit Lyonnais* ECLI:EU:T:2021:185.

[144] The Appeal Panel made reference, by analogy, to the Opinion of Advocate General Kokott of 27 January C-263/09 P *Edwin Co Ltd* ECLI:EU:2011:C:30, paras 55, 57, 64.

[145] Compare for a broader review Eddie Wymeersch, 'The European Financial Supervisory Authorities or ESAs' in Eddie Wymeersch, Klaus Hopt, and Guido Ferrarini (eds), *Financial Regulation and Supervision: A Post-Crisis Analysis* (OUP 2012) 294; Paolo Chirulli and Luca De Lucia, 'Specialised Adjudication in EU Administrative Law: the Boards of Appeal of EU agencies' (2015) 40 ELR 832; for a review limited to questions of law see Witte (n 131) 245.

[146] Kalintiri (n 129) 1283–316; Fritzsche (n 129) 361–403.

a supervisor's complex economic assessment, and all of them are keen in checking whether errors of fact or errors of law are present. However, despite the somehow simplistic taxonomy of marginal v full review, it remains unclear where precisely the legality control of European courts ends.[147] The standard of review of the Court has evolved over time to ensure effectiveness and intensity of judicial control, also on the requirement[148] of sufficient justification,[149] and the criteria used by the CJEU to this effect originally set in *Remia* in 1985 have become over time more inclusive and capable of extending the scope of the review.[150] A good example is *Europeese Gemenschap v Otis*.[151] More recent case law of the GCEU vis-à-vis the ECB and the SRB, including pilot judgments in the Banco Popular saga[152] also shows that, without the need to second-guess complex technical assessments, the court is becoming bolder and more willing to elaborate the criteria of manifest error, duty to state reasons and excess of power, and control of the substantive legality of the decision to grant itself sufficient leeway for effective and robust judicial control (something that, in our view blurs the lines between manifest error and error of assessment). As Michael Ioannidis nicely put it,[153] the judicial review of discretion in the Banking Union has moved from soft to harder look. Although on the 'livret A' last round of litigation the Court of Justice corrected the General Court when the latter went too far, and substituted its assessment for that of the ECB,[154] it cannot be said that, in supervisory and resolution decisions, the substantive merit of the grounds offered as justification for their adoption is uncritically accepted at face value. This has parallel with other jurisdictions,[155] as noted by Professor Matthias Lehmann.[156]

12.51 Another telling parallel can be drawn with US judicial review of federal agencies' action. As we discussed in previous chapters, although judicial review is to some extent limited under *Chevron* and similar tests[157] to their statutory mandates and *ultra vires* actions and

---

[147] Compare the Opinion of Advocate General Emiliou of 27 October 2022 C-389/21 P *European Central Bank v Crédit Lyonnais* ECLI:EU:C:2022:844. In the academic debate, for a tiered approach, see Lehmann (n 129) 112–33; Joana Mendes, 'Discretion, Care and Public Interests in the EU Administration: Probing the Limits of Law' (2016) 53 CMLR 419; Marco Lamandini, 'Il diritto bancario dell'Unione' (2015) 1 *Banca, borsa e tit cred* 423; and Marco Lamandini, 'Il diritto bancario dell'Unione' in Raffaele D'Ambrosio (ed) *Scritti sull'Unione bancaria*, (Quaderni di Ricerca Giuridica della Consulenza Legale, Bank of Italy, No 81, 2016) 81, 441.
[148] Case C-89/08 *Commission v Ireland* ECLI:EU:C:2009:742.
[149] Case C-550/09 *E and F* ECLI:EU:C:2010:382.
[150] Compare Case C-83/98 *France v Ladbroke Racing and Commission*, Opinion of AG Cosmas ECLI:EU:C:1999:577; and Case C-12/03 P *Commission v Tetra Laval*, Opinion of AG Tizzano ECLI:EU:C:2004:318; Case T-201/04 *Microsoft* ECLI:EU:T:2007:289.
[151] Case C-199/11 *Otis and Others* ECLI:EU:C:2012:684.
[152] Compare René Smits and Federico Della Negra, 'The Banking Union and Union Courts: Overview of Cases' *EBI* (8 August 2022) https://ebi-europa.eu/publications/eu-cases-or-jurisprudence/ (accessed 24 September 2022).
[153] Michael Ioannidis, 'The Judicial Review of Discretion in the Banking Union: From 'Soft' to 'Hard(er)' Look' in Chiara Zilioli and Karl-Philipp Wojcik (e3ds), *Judicial Review in the European Banking Union* (Edward Elgar Publishing 2021) 130.
[154] Case C-389/21 *ECB v Crédit Lyonnais* ECLI:EU:C:2023:368; Chapter 6, 6.64. Compare also Marco Lamandini and David Ramos Muñoz, 'Some Reflections on the Standard of Review in the Experience of the ESAs Joint Board of Appeal and the SRB Appeal Panel' forthcoming 19 ECFR 6, 2022; it remains to be seen whether, confronted with multiple plausible alternative solutions or scenarios, the review of complex technical assessments of supervisory or resolution authorities should adopt the so called 'balance of probability' test, as it happens in antitrust cases (referring to Advocate General Kokott's Opinions in Case C-413/06 *Bertelsmann and Sony Corporation of America v Impala* ECLI:EU:C:2008:392, paras 207–208 and Case C-376/20 *European Commission v CK Telecoms* ECLI:EU:C:2022:817, paras 56–58).
[155] Compare in Italy Consiglio di Stato, judgment no 06254/2022 (17 July 2022) on the removal of the board of directors of Credito di Romagna; Francesco Ciraolo, 'Il removal alla prova dei fatti: Note minime intorno al caso Credito di Romagna SpA' (2017) Riv dir banc II.
[156] Lehmann (n 129) referring to examples from Germany, Spain, or the United Kingdom (in cases of financial supervision).
[157] *Chevron USA Inc v NRDC* 467 US 837 (1984). See, however, *King v Burwell* 135 S Ct 2480 (2015).

the principle whereby courts should not 'substitute their judgment for that of the agency' is well settled,[158] a court reviewing agency action under the US Administrative Procedure Act (i) 'shall decide all relevant questions of law (and) interpret constitutional and statutory provisions' (section 706 APA), compel agency action 'unlawfully withheld', set aside agency action that is 'not in accordance with law' or 'occurred without observance of procedure required by law'; (ii) shall consider issues of facts to determine whether the agency's factual finding or premise is supported by 'substantial evidence in the record as a whole'[159] and (iii) shall set aside an agency action as an abuse of discretion under the 'arbitrary and capricious test' if a 'a searching and careful inquiry'[160] shows that the agency decision was not properly based on a consideration of the relevant factors, there was a clear error of judgment, the agency relied on factors which Congress did not intended it to consider, entirely failed to consider an important aspect of the problem, offered an explanation for its decision that run counter to the evidence before the agency or is so implausible that it could not be ascribed to a difference in view of the product of agency expertise.[161] Judicial practice has further developed these general criteria.

12.52 This, again, puts the role of specialized courts in context. It is not about changing the standards of review as they stand, a point of legal doctrine that corresponds to the highest courts, typically generalist courts. It is about ensuring that the standard of legality review is meaningfully applied, because the reviewing court is capable of engaging in a dialogue with the supervisory institution in its own terms and challenge its reasoning. What kind of error of assessment counts as 'manifest' cannot be determined independently of the Court's understanding of what falls within the acceptable range, which, in turn, cannot be established without reference to the court's technical background and expertise.

12.53 Thus, albeit with nuances often determined by the specific features of each case, in the supervisory and resolution context it seems to us that the marginal versus full review debate is, in the Banking Union, more academic than practical and that a full assessment of facts, to the extent that procedural rules allow a proactive evidentiary role, Q&A and expert witness, and a stringent review of the interpretation and application of law (and thus of the substantive legality) is possible, and thus full legal accountability is warranted.

12.54 Different problems arise in the review of sanctions, and to some extent administrative measures, due to the slippery red line between the two (as we already noted in Chapter 6) . European courts (and quasi courts that currently can only *confirm or remit* the decision imposing the fine) should be given unlimited jurisdiction under Article 261 TFEU, in a way that their control may go beyond strict legality, because in this context this means to review also 'the appropriateness and fairness of the penalties imposed, ie the Court's own discretion replaces the Commission's discretion'.[162] This is desirable because, as Paul Tucker noted,[163] 'an independent regulatory agency [should not] be able to ruin a person or business' and a demanding judicial review is the best way to ensure that this does not happen. A different

---

[158] *Motor Veh Mfrs Association v State Farm Ins* 463 US 29, 32 (1983).
[159] In *Universal Camera Corp v NLRB* 340 US 474 (1951) the Supreme Court described substantial evidence as 'such evidence as a reasonable mind might accept as adequate to support a conclusion': this is often considered a level of review somewhat less intense than that employed when appellate courts review trial court finding of fact (ABA Section of Administrative Law and Regulatory Practice, *Blackletter Statement*, Part 3, s IV.A).
[160] *Citizens to Preserve Overton Park Inc v Volpe* 401 US 402 (1971).
[161] *State Farm* (n 158).
[162] Rudolf Geiger, Daniel-Erasmus Khan, and Marcus Kotzur, *European Union Treaties* (CH Beck 2015) 872.
[163] Paul Tucker, *Unelected Power* (PUP 2018) 248.

and incidental question is, however, whether a court should move, in this context, from backseat to front seat in the face of the extremely high amount of some fines or the highly afflictive nature of other sanctions and administrative measures within the supervisory remit. If indeed, according to the ECtHR and CJEU's case law these sanctions are 'criminal' sanctions, the question arises as to whether it would not be more appropriate to delegate the role of inflicting the sanctions upon request of the supervisor to the courts, as occurs with fully fledged criminal sanctions. In the words of a writer in Victorian England who commented on the criminal jurisdiction granted to the Irish Excise Court, composed by members of the executive branch, decisions adopted in a meeting of '[Revenue] officers, who act alternatively as prosecutors, witnesses and judges [is] subversive of all principles of justice and in theory and principle indefensible'.[164]

6 Courts and inter-institutional 'dialogue' (II): inter-court coordination (or lack thereof) and its systemic effects

12.55 Another matter which deserves attention is how the different *fora* for the resolution of private and public law disputes in the law of finance fit within the existing EU judicial system and its mandate to ensure a uniform interpretation and application of the law. Inside this matter there are at least two salient issues: there is a 'threshold' issue, of whether a dispute can access the EU forum to solve matters of EU law (section 6.1); and there is a 'linearity' issue, of whether the dialogue between courts unfolds in a constructive, or at least predictable manner (linear), or it can develop in non-linear ways, due to an escalation of frictions between courts, or simply to the combined effect of EU law and non-EU law, with potential systemic effects (section 6.2).

6.1 The 'threshold' issue

12.56 If we focus on the 'threshold' issue, the key difference is subjective, between 'courts', national and European, and quasi-courts, and arbitration. Only formal courts are granted access to the preliminary ruling procedure. This, in the words of President Laenerts,[165] is key in the European system of judicial cooperation not only because it 'constitutes an important "judicial dialogue" between the Court of Justice and the national courts'[166] but, even more importantly, because the Court of Justice has the sole power to declare an act of a Union institution invalid. Thus, preliminary rulings are key to obtain the authentic interpretation of European law *and* the removal of any EU provision, including guidelines and recommendations, which may be invalid but, lacking a declaration of its invalidity, should be nonetheless enforced by European or national bodies. In this perspective, it is well settled in the case law of the CJEU that arbitrators do not access the preliminary ruling procedure, as set out in *Nordsee*.[167] Arbitrators are,

---

[164] Stebbings (n 118) 162.
[165] Lenaerts, Maselis, and Gutman (n 57) 51.
[166] Bruno de Witte, 'The Preliminary Ruling Dialogue: Three Types of Questions Posed by National Courts' in Bruno de Witte and others (eds), *National Courts and EU Law: New Issues, Theories and Methods* (Edward Elgar Publishing 2016) 15–25.
[167] Case C-102/81 *Nordsee v Reederei Mond* ECLI:EU:C:1982:107, paras 10–11.

ordinarily,[168] not considered courts or tribunals designated by law according to the *Vaassen* criteria.[169] The same principle, yet following a different line of reasoning as stated by the CJEU in *Achmea*,[170] applies to investment arbitration, although it is 'compulsory', once provided for in an investment treaty, ie a State cannot refuse to arbitrate if sued by an investor, and the tribunals are designated 'by law', or through a law-based mechanism. This shows the Court of Justice preference for national 'ordinary' courts.

12.57 The position of quasi courts is less clear-cut. In principle, since they are administrative review bodies, the possibility for them to meet the *Vaasen* criteria is doubtful, especially as regards the independence requirement. The possibility that they nonetheless be qualified as 'courts' cannot be ruled out as a matter of principle either. The Administrative Board of Review of the ECB, which only submits a non-binding opinion to the ECB governing council, would certainly be precluded from referring questions for a preliminary ruling, as any other EU or national administrative body. However, the status of 'court' cannot prima facie be excluded— unless and until a contrary decision is taken in this respect by the CJEU—as regards both the Board of Appeal of the ESAs and the Appeal Panel of the SRB, if only one considers that: (a) they are established by law; (b) they are permanent and, as a matter of substance, fully independent from the governing bodies of the agencies, although the members are appointed by them; (c) are charged with the settlement of disputes defined in general terms; (d) are bound by procedural rules similar to those used by the ordinary courts of law; and (e) their determination is binding and under the rule of law.

12.58 The Court has in some cases qualified as courts, and admitted references for preliminary rulings, from quasi-judicial bodies situated outside the formal judicial system of a Member State, for instance in *Umweltanwalt voor Kärten*.[171] Yet, there is another, more insurmountable obstacle for the Board of Appeal and the Appeal Panel: although resembling functionally courts, they do not belong to 'a Member State', but are established within European agencies, decide on acts by the relevant EU agencies and bodies, and thus their decisions have (solely) an EU dimension.

12.59 Formal definitions aside, however, from a functional perspective the advantages of characterizing them as courts admitted to the judicial dialogue with the Court of Justice are clear: quasi-judicial bodies could focus on deploying their expertise in the matters they are supposed to decide upon without having to make inferences about matters of EU law that fall outside their remit. It would also anchor them more closely to the regular administration of justice by generalist EU courts and open another avenue of dialogue that anticipates and prevents instances where the General Court would have to annul the appeal bodies' decision for having drawn the wrong inferences. Would these advantages suffice, *de lege lata*, to convince the Court of Justice to broaden the interpretation of the 'courts' that can make preliminary references? Sure, the case is different from the one of courts common to Member States, like the Benelux Court of Justice[172] and the Unified Patent Court, which are courts common

---

[168] For an exception see Case C-109/88 *Danfoss* ECLI:EU:C:1989:383, paras 7–9, where the arbitration was responsible for disputes concerning collective agreements, was required by national law and did not depend on the parties' agreement.
[169] Additional references in Lenaerts, Maselis, and Gutman (n 57) 58 ff.
[170] Case C-284/16 *Sleekish Republik v Achmea BV* ECLI:EU:C:2018:158.
[171] Case C-205/08 *Umweltanwalt von Kärnten* ECLI:EU:C:2009:767, paras 34–39; Case C-195/06 *Österreichischer Rundfunk (ORF)* ECLI:EU:C:2007:613, paras 10–13, 22–22; Case C-195/06 *Österreichischer Rundfunk (ORF)* Opinion D Ruiz Jarabo ECLI:EU:C:2007:303, paras 24–41.
[172] Case C-337/95 *Parfums Christian Dior v Evora* ECLI:EU:C:1997:517.

to Member States (albeit differently so). At the same time, the Court of Justice denied in *Miles and Others*[173] that the Complaints Boards of the European Schools could refer a question for preliminary ruling. In turn, the Court accepted that international agreements could confer on courts which are not of a Member State the right to refer questions for preliminary ruling (as it happened with the EEA Agreement which authorizes courts and tribunals of EFTA states to refer questions to the Court of Justice on the interpretation of an EEA rule),[174] but this would require an express provision which is not to be found in the ESAs' and SRM Regulations. Advocate General Sharpston in *Paul Miles*[175] rightly warned that:

> 76. [i]f the Complaints Board is unable to make a reference to the Court to obtain an authoritative ruling on a point of EU law that is pertinent to the appeal before it, that would undermine the uniformity and coherence of EU law. It would also deprive the applicants in that appeal of their right to a judicial remedy

and the factors that in *Paul Miles* took the Court to adopt a restrictive stance are different for those which characterize the ESAs' Board of Appeal and the Appeal Panel, because in this different context, European agencies are called upon to apply EU administrative law centrally in an unprecedented way. The subject matters of the appeal are therefore fully governed by EU law alone, as opposed to the legislative texts applied by the European Schools in *Paul Miles*. In addition, the boards are not bodies of an international organization (as happened with the European Schools), but EU bodies. However, would the fact that, as such they also permeate the legal system of participating Member States in the same way the EU institutional system participates to the national legal order, be enough for the CJEU to admit them to judicial dialogue in the silence of their founding regulations? We doubt it. Yet amending the ESAs and SRB regulations to this specific purpose seems to us a viable way forward.

12.60 A similar issue arises with bodies in charge of alternative dispute resolution in the law of finance (discussed in ch 13, s 3.2), such as the Arbitro Bancario Finanziario (established within the Bank of Italy) or the Arbitro per le controversie finanziarie (established within the Italian CO.N.SO.B). Although these quasi courts are domestic and thus 'belong to a Member State', they are, formally *alternative fora* for dispute resolution, outside the court-system technically understood, and their decisions are *formally* non-binding, although in practice their decision are typically final.

12.61 A different angle of the threshold problem is the extent to which quasi-judicial bodies can represent an impediment to the plaintiff's access to justice, which may impair her right to an effective judicial protection. In the case *Puskar v Finance EU*[176] the Court decided a preliminary reference on the legality of a national measure that made access to (national) courts on issues of data protection conditional upon the exhaustion of administrative remedies. The Court held that such limitation of the right of judicial protection was only justified if it was provided for by law, respected the essence of that right and, subject to the principle of proportionality, it was necessary and genuinely met objectives of general interest recognized by the EU or the need to protect the rights and freedoms of others.[177] The interesting reasoning lies in the proportionality analysis made by the Court. Even if it left the domestic

---

[173] Case C-196/09 *Paul Miles and Others v Écoles européennes* ECLI:EU:C:2011:388.
[174] Lenaerts, Maselis, and Gutman (n 57) 62.
[175] Case C-196/09 *Miles and Others*, Opinion of AG Sharpston ECLI:EU:C:2010:777.
[176] Case C-73/16 *Puskar v Finance* ECLI:EU:C:2017:725.
[177] ibid 62.

court the decision on the issue in light of the practical arrangements for the administrative proceeding, it also acknowledged that the solution, intended to relieve the courts of disputes, and to increase the efficiency of judicial proceedings, pursued legitimate general interest objectives, was appropriate and proportionate. It was appropriate because 'no less onerous method than that obligation suggesting itself as capable of realizing those objectives as efficiently'. It was proportionate because 'it is not evident that any disadvantages caused by the obligation to exhaust available administrative remedies are clearly disproportionate to those objectives'.[178] Arguably, the expediency argument, when combined with proportionality, is the key factor to support the principle, which is seemingly valid also for the ESAs Board of Appeal and the SRB Appeal Panel, that internal remedies, if available, need to be exhausted before an application for annulment can be filed with the European courts.

6.2 The 'linearity' issue

12.62 Secondly, we need to differentiate between a 'linear' interaction between domestic courts and EU courts, where the stimulus and responses of the different courts are circumscribed, and develop constructively, and a 'non-linear' one, where either the tone of the dialogue is confrontational, and escalates, or the combination of EU law and domestic law can have an amplified effect. The first example (confrontational tone) is illustrated by monetary policy cases such as *Gauweiler* and *Weiss*, dealt with in Part II and not discussed again here.[179] The second variant, ie where EU and domestic law combine, or conspire, in unpredictable ways with a systemic impact, is particularly worrying in finance, where the likelihood of an amplified effect increases from the moment that financial institutions have similar business and risk models due to very detailed regulatory requirements and to the standardization of contracts. This requires EU courts and domestic courts to coordinate and operate both brakes and steering wheel.

12.63 In the field of consumer or investor protection, for example, courts' decisions may entail systemic effects if they open the way to mass claims, since typically generalist courts may not have considered the sometimes far-reaching, and occasionally unintended economic consequences of their decisions. They focus on formal consistency of their rulings with the regulatory framework or, where a law-and-economics approach is followed, on the microeconomic efficiency of their outcomes, but rarely on their systemic effects. This is unfortunate, because, as is the case with financial regulation,[180] case law can also become procyclical, ie in good times disputes are less likely to occur and private enforcement fails to restrain financial behaviour, whereas it is in downturns after booms cycles that disputes flourish and may become problematic for the soundness and stability of financial institutions, worsening an already adverse situation.

12.64 One recent example is *Lexitor*,[181] a case where the Court held that Article 16(1) of Directive 2008/48/EC on credit agreements for consumers must be interpreted as meaning that the

---

[178] ibid 67–69.
[179] See ch 5, s 3.
[180] Charles Goodhart, Boris Hofmann, and Miguel Segoviano, 'Bank Regulation and Macroeconomic Fluctuations' in Xavier Freixas, Philipp Hartmann, and Colin Mayr (eds), *Handbook of European Financial Markets and Institutions* (OUP 2008) 690.
[181] Case C-383/18 *Lexitor sp zoo v Spółdzielcza Kasa Oszczędnościowo—Kredytowa im Franciszka Stefczyka, Santander Consumer Bank SA, mBank SA* [2018] OJ C383. Note, however, that a different outcome (no upfront costs should be included in the costs' reduction in case of early repayment) despite the use by the relevant

right of the consumer to a proportional reduction in the total cost of the credit in the event of early repayment of the credit includes 'all' the costs imposed on the consumer, in contrast with an established practice which returned to the consumer a pro rata portion of the ongoing costs but none of the upfront costs. The aftermath of the case has shown a non-linear interaction not only with domestic courts (and other dispute resolution bodies)[182] but also with legislatures. The Italian Parliament,[183] for instance, minimized potential systemic effect of the retroactive *dictum* of the court by expressly excluding any retroactive direct horizontal effect of the contested provision as interpreted by the court. This, in turn,[184] reactivated a judicial dialogue, because the issue of the legality of such domestic provision was referred by an Italian court to the Italian Constitutional Court and is currently waiting for a decision.[185] A second example is given by the four parallel judgments of 17 May 2022 in *Ibercaja Banco, Banco di Desio, Impuls Leasing Romania,* and *Unicaja Banco,*[186] where the court held that EU law precludes national legislation which, by virtue of the effect of *res judicata* and timebarring, neither allows a court to examine of its own motion whether contractual terms are unfair in the course of mortgage enforcement proceedings, nor a consumer, after the expiry of the period for lodging an objection, to raise the unfairness of those terms in those proceedings or in subsequent declaratory proceedings. This finding encroaches on national procedural principles, such as *res judicata* in light of the principle of effectiveness, that is to say to fulfil a requirement for effective judicial protection, but has far reaching procedural, and also substantive, implications which are likely to unfold in domestic courts in the next future.

12.65 Older examples include the change of Spanish and European case law on both consumer law and the marketing of financial instruments. Traditionally, Spanish courts were relatively formalistic and overall pro bank, including on the misselling of financial products.[187] Then, a great deal changed, and very fast. First, the Spanish courts were confronted, for the first time, with a massive number of cases of misselling, including the marketing of 'preferred participations' (*participaciones preferentes*), a type of hybrid capital instruments, and swap instruments. The trickle of cases up the court system soon turned into a tide, suggesting that something could be structurally wrong with the way banks marketed financial products. Possibly, courts found themselves in the midst of it because supervisory authorities like

---

directives of literarily similar provisions, was subsequently reached for mortgage credit agreements in Case C-555/21 *UniCredit Bank Austria v Verein für Konsumenteninformation* ECLI:EU:C:2023:78.

[182] The Arbitro Bancario Finanziario swiftly modified its previous case law to abide by the findings of the CJEU but did not address the question of the retroactive effect of the interpretation of the court: compare Collegio di coordinamento Arbitro Bancario Finanziario (ABF) decision no 26525 (17 December 2019).
[183] Article 11-octies of Law Decree 25 May 2021, no 73 converted, with amendments, by Law 23 July 2021, no 106.
[184] It is in the exclusive competence of the court to exempt its interpretative judgment from retroactive effects: see Joined Cases 67, 127 and 128//79 *Amministrazione dele Finanze v Fratelli Vasanelli* ECLI:EU:C:1980:101; more recently Joined Cases C-154/15, C-307/15 and C-308/15 *Francisco Gutiérrez Naranjo* ECLI:EU:C:2016:980.
[185] Order by Tribunal of Turin, case no 8797/2021 *Vivibanca* (2 November 2021).
[186] Case C-600/19 *Ibercaja Banco* ECLI:EU:C:2022:394; Joined Cases C-693/19 *SPV Project 1503 Srl and Others v YB and Others v YX and ZW* and Case C-831/19 *Banco di Desio e della Brianza* ECLI:EU:C:2022:395; Case C-725/19 *Impuls Leasing Romania* ECLI:EU:C:2022:396; and Case C-869/19 *Unicaja Banco* ECLI:EU:C:2022:397. For a possible further clarification on this issue, see the pending case C-178/23 *ERB New Europe Funding II*, a preliminary ruling request form a Romanian court of 21 March 2023 concerning the revision of a judicial decision on consumer protection with disregards the force of res judicata of an earlier finanl judgment.
[187] Up until 2012, the Supreme Court rejected that the breach of conduct rules related to the transparency in the marketing of financial products, could constitute the basis for a claim of annulment, and thus restitution. See Spanish Supreme Court Decision (STS) 683/12, RJ 2012/11052 (21 November 2012) ES:TS:2012:7843.

the Securities Market Commission (Comisión Nacional del Mercado de Valores (CNMV)) and Banco de España were not fast enough to open large-scale proceedings to facilitate restitution to clients (arguably, the system's instability left these authorities with unenviable choices). Once enough cases had been examined, courts were convinced that key doctrinal changes were needed. As the third piece of this perfect storm-puzzle, Spanish courts were 'scolded' by the Court of Justice for being 'too pro-bank'. The decision in the *Aziz* case was, of course, more complex than that,[188] but in essence the Court held that the very efficient, very expedient Spanish executory proceedings for mortgage credit had to allow the debtor to allege the nullity of contract clauses in breach of the Unfair Contract Terms (UCT) Directive. The subtext was that Spanish courts were leaving consumers at the mercy of banks in eviction actions.

12.66 The combined effect of such pressures, from different sources was a drastic change in Spanish courts' attitude towards bank-client relationships. First, in 2013 the Supreme Court decided that 'floor clauses' (*cláusulas suelo*) were unfair, pursuant to the UCT Directive.[189] The decision was strong and controversial: clauses that set the 'price' cannot generally be considered 'unfair',[190] but the Supreme Court creatively interpreted the Directive to conclude that the transparency of the price clause entailed a control over the material transparency (ie understandability of its content). Yet, the Court tried to limit the effects of its decision to annul the clauses to the payments to be received from then onwards, ie banks should not charge the interest rate agreed as a 'floor', but neither should they reimburse the interest payments resulting from the floor since the time the contract was concluded. Secondly, in 2014, in a swaps case, the Supreme Court changed its doctrine of 'mistake' to conclude that the breach of MiFID marketing rules would cause said 'mistake' in the client and justify annulling the (financial) contract.[191] This led to a tidal wave of decisions, where the Court confirmed its change of heart, and side-stepped different (bank) objections to the application of the new doctrine.[192] The change encompassed not only genuinely complex products, like swap contracts, but also less complex products, like hybrid capital instruments (*preferentes*) where their (default) risks were easier to understand.[193]

12.67 The number of cases created a 'macro' (and political) problem, and Spain created a high-level Commission to monitor the problem, and a system of collective 'arbitration' to allow some clients to recover part of their investment,[194] plus an enhancement of Spanish Deposit Guarantee Scheme's role[195] (used as a blueprint by the Italian government in its 2016 measures meant

---

[188] Case C-415/11 *Aziz* ECLI:EU:C:2013:164.
[189] STS 1916/2013 (9 May 2013) ES:TS:2013:1916. We believe it is not random that the decision was issued with a two-month difference with the case by the European Court.
[190] Art 4 (2) of Directive 93/13 on Unfair Contract Terms.
[191] Spanish STS 354/2014 (20 January 2014) ES:TS:2014:354.
[192] The decisions by the Spanish Supreme Court (STS) on the issue are countless. Suffice to cite some, such as 15 December 2014 (RJ 56/2015) ECLI:ES:TS:2014:5411; 15 September 2015 (RJ 3993/2015) ECLI:ES:TS:2015:3868; (15 October 2015) (RJ 5030/2015) ECLI:ES:TS:2015:4237; (13 November 2015) (RJ 4664/2015); 4 December 2015 (RJ 5461/2015) ECLI:ES:TS:2015:4946; (9 December 2015) (RJ 674/2015) ECLI:ES:TS:2015:5154; (10 December 2015) (RJ 5777/2015) ECLI:ES:TS:2015:5156; (8 April 2016) (RJ 1496/2016) ECLI:ES:TS:2016:1644; (19 May 2016) (JUR 117371/2016); (3 June 2016) (RJ 3863/2016) ECLI:ES:TS:2016:2596; (13 July 2016) (RJ 3194/2016) ECLI:ES:TS:2016:3461; (15 July 2016) (RJ 3201/2016) ECLI:ES:TS:2016:3465; (30 September 2016) (RJ 4581/2016) ECLI:ES:TS:2016:4304; (5 October 2016) (RJ 225150/2016); (23 November 2016) (no 691/2016; JUR 261556/2016).
[193] See eg STS of 12 January 2015 (RJ 608/2015); (16 September 2015) (RoJ 4004/2015) ECLI:ES:TS:2015:4004; (25 February 2016) (RoJ 610/2016) ECLI:ES:TS:2016:610; or 29 June 2016 (RoJ 3138/2016) ECLI:ES:TS:2016:3138.
[194] Royal Decree-Law 6/2013 of 23 March.
[195] The DGS (*Fondo de Garantía de Depósitos de Entidades de Crédito*) would be allowed to both acquire shares and debt from SAREB, and to acquire shares from entities that transferred NPLs to SAREB, in order to lessen the

partially to indemnify retail investors for losses from the misselling of shares/securities by distressed banks). The commission's criteria to access the said 'arbitration' were broad-brushed, mixing 'legal' criteria on the marketing of the product, and 'social' criteria on the investor's loss (eg percentage of her patrimony, or investments lower than €10,000).

12.68 Thus, this was a 'systemic' procedure, with the aim to speed-up compensation to citizens who had suffered the most, not to ascertain the facts, nor to change the law; the 'legal' criteria of mis-selling that *gave access* to the procedure, eg lack of documentation, total absence of risk information or classification of risk profile, should have automatically given clients a favourable court ruling. Yet, by then a 'systemic' doctrinal change in the law was already underway, and many investors, especially those with larger patrimonies, who could anticipate less sympathy in the arbitration, tried their chances with the then-sympathetic courts, prompting the rise of American-like trial lawyers, who advertised themselves in billboards and TV, a phenomenon unknown in Spain. Thus, instead of a large-scale-yet-case-specific solution the crisis led to a lasting doctrinal change, and now it is hard to envisage a sure way to market financial instruments that entail a risk of loss, without being exposed to an annulment action, and without fully denaturalizing the marketing process, ie turning it into a series of ominous warnings.

12.69 The previous example has many parallels with the Italian one. A judicial approach hardly capable of weighing its macroprudential effects materialized in Italy, eg on the prohibition of usury,[196] compound interests rates[197] misselling practices in the placement of sovereign, corporate bonds, and banks' shares to retail investors[198] or derivatives to SMEs. Mass litigation on these issues contributed to the building up of non-performing loans (NPLs), slowing down recovery procedures. The paradox was further exacerbated because, in the building up of the crisis, public authorities asked for more prudential capital, yet paid insufficient attention to the potential for consumers and investors' claims that would eventually deplete that new ammunition of capital.[199] As the courts stepped in to fill the vacuum—which occurred in the midst of the economic and NPL crisis—banks were assailed and squeezed from both their asset side and liabilities side, which left some of them teetering. Some litigation was necessary and welcome, some was opportunistic, and the collateral damage has been the increased legal uncertainty as to how exactly a bank is supposed to interact with its clients and investors and how a bank with capital shortfall can safely access capital markets.

12.70 This offers a complementary perspective to look at the way judicial performance may end up with a dimension of weight in a broader, systemic perspective in the law of finance. If

---

impact of the conversion mandated by the resolution authority (FROB) which shows how much the problem of NPLs was linked to the problem of hybrid capital instruments, from both, a solvency, and investor protection perspectives.

[196] Article 644 of the Italian Penal Code and art 1815 of the Italian Civil Code as amended by Law No 108/1996 (and subsequently given 'authentic interpretation' by Law Decree No 394/2000: compare Italian Constitutional Court, judgment no 29, 25 February 2002). Courts have been flooded by claims in different ways grounded on alleged usury. On one of these aspects, after several years of diverging judgments, the Supreme Court clarified (with a chamber, however, still dissenting with a subsequent judgment) that interests rates, originally within the legal threshold, do not become unlawful if they exceed the threshold in the course of the relationship (Grand Chamber of the Italian Supreme Court, judgment no 24675 (19 October 2017)).

[197] Another example of law-making partnership: art 120 of the Italian Banking Act was amended several times following the development of the case law.

[198] For a telling example Tribunal of Venezia, *Banca popolare di Vicenza* (5 June 2019); Tribunal of Treviso, *Consoli and Veneto Banca* (5 May 2022).

[199] On the complex interaction between misselling of a bank's shares and its resolution see Case C-410/20 *Banco Santander SA v JAC and MCP* ECLI:EU:C:2022:351.

common sense and economic analysis already suggest that 'well-functioning judiciaries are key to economic performance' 'by securing two essential prerequisites of market economies: security of property rights and enforcement of contracts',[200] our claim is different. We argue that qualitative outcomes of judicial performance can have systemic impacts, which may help illuminating on the appropriateness not only of judge-made law but also of the institutional arrangements which frame courts' activity. In this regard, it is important to note that large financial centres do not distinguish themselves by the number of courts and judges that ensure expediency, but more notably, by having 'reference courts' whose opinions are widely followed by practitioners and citizens, by raising the relevant issues, properly framing the problems, and giving legal doctrine a distinct voice. Those courts may sometimes be the highest courts, but not necessarily. As an example, just consider the Delaware Chancery Court, for matters of corporate law,[201] the courts of the Second Circuit in matters of securities law,[202] or the English High Court (Financial List[203]), in matters of financial contracts and transactions, or security interests. These institutions have shaped the debate in the field of finance in the past, while making the job of superior courts easier. Even when superior courts have disagreed from the assessment of specialized courts, they have drawn numerous benefits from their presence. First, they have benefited from their prior analysis, a point that we have already made before (a specialized court can process the facts in order to identify pivotal cases and relate the specific case with the broader issues). A second advantage is that higher courts can rely on the specialized courts' ability to use the right language when, for example, a controversial issue needs to be raised but not settled. In this regard, *obiter dicta* and justificatory reasons may be as important as the decision itself.[204] A third advantage is that, if the issue is complex and controversial, specialized courts can also buy time for superior courts, who can observe the reaction to the opinion, and the arguments for and against, inside the appeal, but also in legal *for a*, which will help to strengthen their final decision.

---

[200] Compare Palumbo and others (n 102) 8.

[201] The Delaware Chancery Court has virtually construed the standard of review for corporate directors in acquisitions, so much so that its rulings are known as the applicable standards (the *Unocal* standard, the *Revlon* standard, etc). See eg *Unocal Corp v Mesa Petrol Co* 493 A 2d 946 (Del 1985); *Revlon Inc v MacAndrews & Forbes Holdings Inc* 506 A 2d 173 (Del 1986).

[202] In *Blue Chip Stamps v Manor Drug Stores* 421 US 723, 737 (1975) the US Supreme Court referred to the Second Circuit Court as 'a justifiably esteemed panel of that Court of Appeals regarded as the "Mother Court" in this area of the law'. See also Karen Patton Seymour, 'Securities and Financial Regulation in the Second Circuit' (2016) 85 Fordham L Rev 225.

[203] Instead of focusing on landmark rulings, we will refer to the variety of issues that were quite decided by the High Court. See *UBS AG, London Branch v Glas Trust Corporation Ltd & Fairhold Securitisation Ltd* [2017] EWHC 1788 (Comm) (duties of the securitization trustee); *Law Debenture Trust Corporation v Ukraine* [2017] EWHC 655 (Comm) (capacity of a state to enter into a US$3 billion Eurobond contract); *Deutsche Bank AG v Comune di Savona* [2017] EWHC 1013 (Comm) (entry into, validity, enforceability, interpretation, and performance of swaps); *Deutsche Bank AG v Comune di Savona* [2017] EWHC 1013 (Comm) (whether a swap under an ISDA Master Agreement 1992 was valid in light of Italian mandatory provisions).

[204] Consider, for example, the Delaware Chancery Court analysed directors' fiduciary duties in *Credit Lyonnais Bank Nederland NV v Pathé Communications Corp* WL 277613 (Del Ch 1991), suggesting that such duties might change to favour creditors in the 'twilight zone' close to insolvency. The Delaware Supreme Court indicated years later in *North American Catholic Educational Programming Foundation Inc v Gheewalla* 930 A 2d 92 (Del 2007) that fiduciary duties were owed to a company and its shareholders, and that creditors could not expect to have an independent cause of action against directors. However, the Supreme Court benefited from the debate generated by the Chancery Court, which did not *state* that creditors were owed fiduciary duties, but its authority ensured that everyone paid attention. As an opposite case, i.e. one where the superior court decides to establish a landmark precedent, in *Re Spectrum Plus Ltd* [2005] UKHL 41, the House of Lords treated what the parties called a 'fixed' charge as a 'floating' charge, based on its functional features. The House of Lords benefited from the previous (deep and thorough) discussion of relevant precedents, and the formal versus functional features of the transaction by the High Court and the Court of Appeal.

13
A Snapshot of the Current Court System's Nodes and Challenges

1 Introduction	13.01	3.2 Mass, small-ticket disputes, and the role of alternative dispute resolution (ADR)	13.44
2 Nodes of the courts' system in public financial law disputes	13.03		
2.1 Vertical coordination of courts	13.04	3.3 Private law disputes as a follow-up of public law disputes	13.50
2.2 Horizontal coordination (and competition) of courts	13.09	4 Specialized financial courts and arbitration: friends or foes? Nuances between commercial and investment arbitration, and their relationship to private and public law disputes	13.59
2.3 Horizontal coordination by courts and quasi-courts	13.11		
3 Nodes of the courts' system for private law disputes in the law of finance	13.38		
3.1 Private law disputes: precedents in domestic practice and hybrid international commercial courts	13.39		

1 Introduction

Are the problems outlined in the previous chapter enough to justify a reform of judicial architecture on grounds of efficiency or otherwise?[1] Is this the case even if the EU is still in the stage of judicial cooperation rather than 'procedural unification'?[2] Our answer is a prudent 'yes', an '*adelante con juicio*' (in the proverbial words of the Manzoni's *Promessi Sposi*). The procedural elements of enforcement can shape substance.[3] The EU is a test case because Europe presents a complex and evolutionary model, where courts are many and organized in a complex web, requiring vertical and horizontal coordination. As correctly noted:[4]

13.01

> Harmonizing substantive rules, either in a top-down or bottom-up fashion is difficult; but even more difficult is the equally important task of harmonizing—or even just coordinating—procedural rules and judicial review. In addition to the technical complexities, path dependency, cultural and historical factors play probably an even bigger role along this dimension, but our discussion shows that this problem is no longer avoidable.

---

[1] Stephen Dnes, 'Promoting Efficient Litigation?' in Paul Beaumont and others (eds), *Cross-Border Litigation in Europe* (Hart Publishing 2017) 463.
[2] Magdalena Tulibacka, 'Europeization of Civil Procedure: In Search of a Coherent Approach' (2009) 46 CMLR 1527. Compare also Christiaan Timmermans, 'The European Union's Judicial System' (2004) 41 CMLR 393; Dnes(n 1) 482.
[3] US antitrust litigation is an example. See Dnes (n 1) 467.
[4] Marco Ventoruzzo, 'European Rules and Judicial Review in National Courts: Challenges and Questions', in *Judicial Review in the Banking Union and in the EU Financial Architecture* (Quaderni di Ricerca Giuridica della Consulenza Legale, Banca d'Italia, No 84, 2018), 75.

13.02 'Hard-yet-unavoidable', the evolution should affect a rethinking of the coordination between the nodes in both public law disputes (2) and private law disputes (3).

2 Nodes of the courts' system in public financial law disputes

13.03 The new coordination between court nodes in public law disputes in the EU should affect their vertical coordination (section 2.1), and horizontal coordination, between courts (section 2.2), and courts and quasi-courts (section 2.3).

2.1 Vertical coordination of courts

13.04 At EU level, proceedings may be brought before the General Court and, on appeal, the Court of Justice in accordance with Article 263 TFEU, notably against decisions of the ECB in the performance of its tasks within the Single Supervisory Mechanism (as also specified by Article 24, paragraph 11, Regulation No 1024/2013 (SSM Regulation)), and against decisions of the other European regulatory (EBA, ESMA, and EIOPA), supervisory (ESMA) and resolution authorities (SRB) in the field of finance, as specified in Article 61 of Regulations No 1093, 1094, and 1095 and Article 85 of the SRM Regulation. At the national level, national courts adjudge the decisions adopted by national supervisory and resolution authorities. In doing so, the general principle of national procedural autonomy[5] must coexist with the principle of effectiveness, equivalence, and effective judicial protection.[6] If a litigant disputes the infringement by the national authority of a EU provision or the invalidity of a national decision due to the invalidity of the EU provision of general applicability on which the decision is based national courts can uphold the rights EU law confers on litigants. If the applicants lack standing to challenge such Union measures in annulment proceedings, due to the requirements on standing under *Plaumann*,[7] national courts may seek a ruling on invalidity from the Court of Justice by way of a request for a preliminary ruling.[8]

13.05 This has clear implications, eg in the Banking Union, where national competent authorities are responsible, under Article 6(6) of the SSM Regulation of adopting all relevant supervisory decisions with regard to less significant credit institutions and apply 'all relevant

---

[5] Case C-13/68 *Salgoil v Italy* ECLI:EU:C:1968:54; Case C-33/76 *Rewe v Landwitschaftskammer Saarland* ECLI:EU:C:1976:188.

[6] Case C-25/62 *Plaumann v Commission* ECLI:EU:C:1963:17. For a recent application in the law of finance, finding that the principle of effectiveness may require the overruling of an implied res judicata on unfair terms of consumer credit contracts see Case C-600/19, *Ibercaja Banco* ECLI:EU:C:2022:394; Joined Cases C-693/19 *SPV Project* and C-831/19 *Banco di Desio e della Brianza* ECLI:EU:C:2022:395; Case C-725/19 *Impuls Leasing Romania* ECLI:EU:C:2022:396 and Case C-869/19 *Unicaja Banco* ECLI:EU:C:2022:397; for the principle that final national administrative decisions can also be overruled in order to ensure the *effet utile* of EU law and the principle of sincere cooperation see Case C-177/20 *Grossmania* ECLI:EU:C:2022:175; compare also Case C-504/19 *Banco de Portugal v VR* ECLI:EU:C:2021:335.

[7] Case C-25/62 *Plaumann v Commission* ECLI:EU:C:1963:17. Compare also Case C-583/11 P *Inuit Tapiriit Kanatami and Others v Parliament and Council* ECLI:EU:C:2013:625; Pieter-Augusijn Van Malleghem and Niels Baeten, 'Before the Law Stands a Gatekeeper: Or, What Is a 'Regulatory Act' in Article 263(4) TFEU? Inuit Tapiriit Kanatami' (2014) 51 CMLR 1187–.

[8] Antony Arnull, 'Remedies before National Courts' in Robert Schütze and Takis Tridimas (eds), *Oxford Principles of European Union Law*, vol I, *The European Union Legal Order* (OUP 2018) 1021, referring to Case C-50/00 P *Union de Pequeños Agricultores v Council* (UPA) ECLI:EU:C:2002:462.

Union law' as specified by Article 4(3) of the SSM Regulation and under Article 6(5), letter (a) 'regulations, guidelines or general instructions' of the ECB.

Some situations are less clear, however. The most important issue is that of composite proceedings within the SSM, where both national and European authorities must participate at different levels in the adoption of a supervisory decision.[9] An example is given by the approval of qualifying holdings in a credit institution under Article 15 of the SSM Regulation. The Court of Justice, in *Fininvest and Silvio Berlusconi v Banca d'Italia*,[10] drew a general distinction between preparatory acts which are binding, for the review of which national courts are competent, and others which are not, for which European courts are competent to review the final decision by the European institution or agency. Thus, a decision adopted by the ECB following a non-binding proposal by the national competent authority is subject to an action of annulment before the General Court which, however, has also 'jurisdiction to determine, as an incidental matter, whether the legality of the ECB's decision . . . is affected by any defects rendering unlawful the acts preparatory to that decision that were adopted by the national competent authority'.[11]

13.06

This offers good practical guidance, by analogy, for other common procedures implying vertical loyal cooperation. For instance, under Article 15 of the SSM Regulation, an application for authorization to take up the business of a credit institution can be rejected in the first stage of the proceedings by the national competent authority; such a decision can be challenged before the national court. The application can, however, also be rejected in the second stage of the proceedings by the ECB pursuant to Article 15(3) of the SSM Regulation; the ECB decision needs to be challenged by the applicant before the GCEU under Article 263 TFEU. Likewise, when a resolution plan is adopted by the SRB (and endorsed by the European Commission and Council) and then conveyed to the national resolution authority in the form of a binding instruction to be implemented under national law, the resolution decision needs to be challenged before the European court. Yet, other matters continue to pose thorny issues. It is unclear, for instance, if the decision of the ECB not to withdraw[12] immediately the banking licence in a resolution context, due to the finding of the resolution authority pursuant to Article 15(6) of the SSM Regulation that 'the withdrawal of the authorization would prejudice the adequate implementation of or actions necessary for resolution or to maintain financial stability', can be challenged before the General Court. Following

13.07

---

[9] Concetta Brescia Morra, 'The Interplay between the ECB and NCAs in the "Common Procedures" under the SSM Regulation: Are There Gaps in Legal Protection? in *Judicial Review in the Banking Union and in the EU Financial Architecture* (Quaderni di Ricerca Giuridica della Consulenza Legale Banca d'Italia, No 84, 2018), 79; Christine Eckes and Raffaele D'Ambrosio, 'Composite Administrative Procedures in the European Union' (2020) ECB Legal Working Paper Series No 20, 2–48.

[10] Case C-219/17 *Fininvest/Silvio Berlusconi v Banca d'Italia* ECLI:EU:C:2018:1023, paras 43–46. Compare also, for a similar finding in law in the SRM context of vertical composite procedures, Case C-414/18 *Iccrea v Banca d'Italia* ECLI:EU:C:2019:1036.

[11] The follow-up case, in application of this principle, was Case T-913/16 *Fininvest and Silvio Berlusconi v ECB* ECLI:EU:T:2022: 279 (now on appeal in Joined Cases C-512/22 and C-513/22, pending). The same shift from a direct judicial review of the preparatory act to an indirect review in the context of the review of the final decision is also present in the context of horizontal composite procedures, such as the resolution decision based upon a failing or likely to fail assessment of the ECB: compare Joined Cases C-551/19 P and C-552/19 P *ABLV Bank v ECB* and *Bernis and Others v ECB* ECLI:EU:C:2021:369 and Case T-280/18 *ABLV Bank v SRB* ECLI:EU:T:2022:429, dismissing the request for annulment of the SRB decision not to adopt resolution schemes in respect of ABLV Bank AS and Lux..

[12] On the withdrawal decision of an authorization of a credit institution, compare Case T-27/19 *Pilatus Bank and Pilatus Holding v ECB* ECLI:EU:T:2022:46, now on appeal in pending Cases C-750/21 and C-256/22, *Pilatus Bank v ECB* (where AG Kokott delivered a quite controversial Opinion on 25 May 2023 ECLI:EU:C:2023:431) and Joined Cases T-351/18 and T-584/18 *Ukrselhosprom and Versobank v ECB* ECLI:EU:T:2021:669.

Berlusconi, if the ECB decision is bound or left very limited discretion by the factual determination of the competent resolution authority, one should conclude that it is the finding of the resolution authority which needs to be challenged. Likewise, a resolution decision prepared by the SRB and endorsed by the European Commission and Council poses the thorny question of whether the appealable decision is the SRB decision or its endorsement by the European Commission and the Council. With its judgments of 1 June 2022 in the pilot cases concerning *Banco Popular* the General court identified the SRB decision as appealable,[13] but this still awaits confirmation on appeal by the Court of Justice.

13.08 Administrative penalties are another example. The wording of Article 18(1) of the SSM Regulation would suggest that administrative pecuniary penalties could be imposed by the ECB also on less significant credit institutions. Yet, to avoid the inconsistency of sanctions imposed by the ECB based on factual assessment prepared by the national supervisors that supervise less significant credit institutions, the ECB has interpreted Article 18 in light of the allocation of tasks between the ECB and national competent authorities (NCAs), as set out in Article 6 of the SSM Regulation, leaving the sanctioning powers to the national competent authorities. A national court required to judge over the NCA's sanctions may, however, find it necessary to refer the case to the Court of Justice for a preliminary ruling on the question of whether such allocation of powers is compliant with EU law. In turn, pursuant to Article 18(5) SSM Regulation the ECB must require NCAs 'to open proceedings with a view to taking action' in order to impose pecuniary penalties for breaches of national law transposing relevant Directives or administrative penalties or measures to be imposed on members of the management board'; also in this context it needs to be clarified if the challengeable decision is that of the ECB, due to its binding character, or that of the NCA. If the latter is the case, national courts may, however, find it necessary once again to refer the matter to the Court of Justice for a preliminary ruling to assess the legality of the ECB's instruction.[14]

2.2 Horizontal coordination (and competition) of courts

13.09 Courts also coordinate and compete *horizontally*. This is certainly not new. A good example are civil and administrative courts in dualist court-systems. Yet, such horizontal coordination is not without frictions:

> [I]n judicially dualist countries (that is, where there are separate civil and administrative courts … access to justice for appeals against decisions taken by administrative authorities implies an important shift from civil to administrative judges, because judges are called upon to review administrative decisions … [But] [i]t is well-known that the dividing line

---

[13] Case T-481/17 *Fundacion Tatiana Pérez de Guzmàn el Bueno and SFL v SRB* ECLI:EU:T:2022:311 (on appeal in case C-551/22 P, whose hearing before the Grand Chamber was held on 13 June 2023); Case T-510/17 *Del Valle Ruiz and Others v Commission and SRB* ECLI:EU:T:2022:312; Case T-523/17 *Eleveté Invest Group and Others v Commission and SRB* ECLI:EU:T:2022:313; Case T-570/17 *Algebris (UK) and Anchorage Capital Group v Commission* ECLI:EU:T:2022:314; and Case T-628/17 *Aeris Invest v Commission and SRB* ECLI:EU:T:2022:315.

[14] Legal uncertainty is exacerbated in this context by the uncertain nature of the standard of review which European courts shall apply. Usually, sanctions justify the full jurisdiction of the CJEU under TFEU, art 261, which needs, however, express recognition. This express recognition can be found, for example, in art 36e of the Credit Rating Agencies regulation and in art 69 of the European Market Infrastructure Regulation. Such express recognition is lacking in art 18 SSM Regulation (but for an ambiguous reference in art 18(7) of Regulation no 2532/98: it remains unclear if the reference to Regulation No 2532/98 includes the reference to the full jurisdictions set out herein).

between the jurisdiction of civil courts and that of administrative courts has been always a subject of discussion and that legislation and judge-made law (for example by the *Tribunal des conflits* in France and the *Corte di Cassazione* in Italy) have been called upon to settle jurisdictional tensions between the two branches of the judiciary.[15]

Another good example is the 'quiet revolution' of British administrative tribunals.[16] One of the features of the large-scale reform of these tribunals introduced by the UK Tribunals, Courts and Enforcement Act 2007 (TCEA), which implemented the recommendations of the Leggatt Report[17] was to replace a collection of disjointed separate tribunals with a single court structure,[18] 'marking at the same time the conclusion of the judicialization process of such tribunals, since tribunals are now 'best understood not as substitutes for courts but rather as a species of court'.[19] This came along with the extension to administrative judges of the guarantees of judicial independence as court judges and by 'shifting administrative responsibility for tribunals from their sponsoring government departments (whereby tribunals were funded by the organizations against whose decisions they heard appeals) to HM Courts and Tribunal Service, an executive agency of the Ministry of Justice'.[20]

13.10 Another example is, in the first place, the Portuguese *Tribunal da concorrencia, regulacao e supervisao*, established in 2011[21] as a specialized court to hear appeals against decisions adopted by the competition authority and by other regulatory independent authorities, including financial supervisors.[22] A second example, in a dualist country like Italy, where decisions of financial supervisors are normally challenged before the administrative courts, is the current[23] exclusive competence of Italian (civil) courts of appeal, to hear disputes on the validity of sanctions imposed by financial supervisors.

2.3 Horizontal coordination by courts and quasi-courts

13.11 Courts also coexist with quasi-courts, ie review bodies like the ESAs Joint Board of Appeal, the SSM's Administrative Board of Review (ABoR), and the SRB's Appeal Panel.[24] This has

---

[15] Sabino Cassese, 'A New Framework of Administrative Arrangements for the Protection of Individual Rights' (ECB Legal Conference 2017: Shaping a New Legal Order for Europe: A Tale of Crises and Opportunities, 4–5 September 2017) 30 https://www.ecb.europa.eu/pub/pdf/other/ecblegalconferenceproceedings201712.en.pdf (accessed 1 September 2022).

[16] Jeremy Cooper, 'The New World of Tribunals: A Quiet Revolution' in Jeremy Cooper (ed), *Being a Judge in the Modern World* (OUP 2017) 83; Sabino Cassese, 'A European Administrative Justice?' in *Judicial Review in the Banking Union and in the EU Financial Architecture* (Quaderni di Ricerca Giuridica della Consulenza Legale, Banca d'Italia, No 84, 2018), , 13.

[17] Sir Andrew Leggatt, *Tribunals for Users: One Service, One System* (Stationery Office 2001).

[18] Mark Elliott and Robert Thomas, 'Tribunal Justice, Cart, and Proportionate Dispute Resolution' (2012) Legal Studies Research Paper Series, University of Cambridge, Paper no 8/2012, 1.

[19] Peter Cane, *Administrative Tribunals and Adjudication* (Hart Publishing 2010) 72.

[20] Elliott and Thomas (n 18) 2.

[21] With Law no 46/2011 of 21 June 2011 and implementing Decree No 67/2012 of 20 March 2012.

[22] Miguel Sousa Ferro, 'Tribunal da conorrencia, regulacao e supervisao: uma analise juridico-economica no seu 5. aniversario' (2017) 7 Revista de Concorrência e Regulação 30.

[23] After two landmark judgments of the Italian Constitutional Court no 162 of 27 June 2012 and no 94 of 15 April 2014, which found that sanctions imposed by financial supervisors 'are not expression of purely administrative discretion' and need a full review by the civil judiciary.

[24] Merijn Chamon, Annalisa Volpato and Mariolina Eliantonio (eds), *Boards of Appeal of EU Agencies* (OUP 2022); Barbara Marchetti (ed), *Administrative Remedies in the European Union: The Emergence of a Quasi-Judicial Administration* (Giappichelli 2017). More specifically on quasi-judicial remedies in the European law of finance, compare the contributions collected in *Judicial Review in the Banking Union and in the EU Financial Architecture* (Quaderni di Ricerca Giuridica della Consulenza Legale, Banca d'Italia, No 84, 2018), https://www.bancaditalia.it/pubblicazioni/quaderni-giuridici/2018-0084/qrg-84.pdf (accessed 1 September 2022); and Marco Lamandini and

parallels, for example, with US administrative law judges (ALJs). Some argue that this flight away from courts is justified because administrative law and procedure are more flexible. Yet administrative mechanisms can be deceptively simple. They work as long as the existence of a single authority is well established, be it a domestic authority or, in a decentralized system, a series of central and sub-central authorities, national and supranational in the EU, state and federal in the US. Yet, if the problem involves cross-border coordination or enforcement action, doubts can arise. In bank resolution or in central counterparties or hedge fund supervision authorities can sign all the MoUs they want: if it comes to executing the acts of an authority in the territory of another authority outside the EU, there is much uncertainty, and hierarchy and territoriality are the governing criteria. In resolution this is a far cry from the comparably smooth coordination, and modified universalism, of the UNCITRAL Model Law on Cross-Border Insolvency, applicable in US cross-border insolvency, and compatible with the EU system.[25] Similar questions could arise if the matter in question concerns the enforcement of a decision by an appeal body. Generally, the matters subject to review by quasi-judicial bodies are conceived to have effect in the same territory where the administrative authority deploys its authority. Yet, if action by public authorities has clear private law implications, eg liability cases following findings of a breach of regulatory norms, it is unclear how the decisions of quasi-judicial bodies could have an impact as 'law', rather than merely as a finding of 'fact', or a piece of evidence, easily subject to challenge. Even outside 'structured cooperation' schemes such as the UNCITRAL Model Law, the principle of comity can foster sincere cooperation, but normally between courts only. If decisions by quasi-judicial bodies are not assimilated to court rulings, but to mere administrative *fiat*, it is unlikely that they will be heeded on a cross-border basis. Sometimes, the 'flight' away from judicial solutions and towards administrative ones may be expedient only under narrow conditions. It is thus important to ensure that its advantages are assessed in a broader context to ensure that the move does not turn into a 'flight to nowhere'.

13.12 A closer look at the federal system of ALJs in the field of finance through the SEC, it is evident that ALJs offer a cautionary tale against the complexities of all quasi-judicial arrangements and their competing and complementary role with courts. In the United States ALJs perform their duties pursuant to the Administrative Procedure Act (APA) enacted by Congress in 1946 to create an independent and impartial cadre of case adjudicators within federal agencies. ALJs perform their duties 'in an impartial manner', are authorized to preside at the taking of evidence in hearings, and they render 'recommended' and 'initial' decisions. However, these 'initial decisions' are ultimately subject to review by the agency officials, 'who shoulder the burden of political pressure'.[26] In principle, the agency officials review *de novo* and have full discretion to affirm, reverse, modify, set aside or remand for further proceedings in whole or in part to the ALJs. However, absent an appeal or an elected review by the agency officials themselves, the initial decision becomes the final decision without any modifications.[27] Even so, the aggrieved person can, within sixty days, ask for the 'review of

---

David Ramos Muñoz, 'Law and Practice of the ESAs' Board of Appeal and of the SRB Appeal Panel: A View from the Inside' (2020) 57 CMLR 119.

[25] David Ramos and Javier Solana, 'Bank Resolution and Insolvency Law: The Tension Shaping Global Banking—Part II: The Cross-Border Dimension' (2019) 28 Miami J Bus L 3.
[26] Steven A Glazer, 'Towards a Model Code of Judicial Conduct for Federal Administrative Law Judges' (2012) 64 Administrative L Rev 342.
[27] Thomas C Rossidis, 'Article II Complications Surroundings SEC_Employed Administrative Law Judges' (2016) 90 St John's L Rev 782.

the order in the US Courts of Appeals for the circuit in which he resides or has his place of business, or for the District of Columbia Circuit'.[28] This means that:

> [T]he ALJ function is itself the product of a hard-fought compromise between New Deal-era 'institutionalists' seeing a need for government employees who would adhere strictly to their agencies' policies ... versus conservative 'judicialists' who sought to constrain New Deal agencies like ... the Securities and Exchange Commission (SEC) within strict due process requirements.[29]

Essentially, ALJs work as 'the agency counterpart to judges in a courtroom'.[30] In March 2016, 1,792 ALJs served thirty federal agencies[31] in a wide array of administrative matters, from social security benefits to international trade. The most controversial—and the one which attracted most of the constitutional attention—are the SEC's five ALJs, because the Dodd-Frank Act enabled the SEC to obtain administrative enforcement actions, specifically the imposition of monetary penalties, from ALJs without the need, as originally foreseen by the 1934 Act, to seek an order from federal courts (§§ 21–25). This more than doubled the annual number of ALJ proceedings, leading some commentators to conclude that 'Dodd-Frank has changed the landscape of the securities industry by taking traditionally litigated cases out of the federal court system'.[32] The SEC, when seeking to enforce federal law, brings administrative enforcement actions against alleged wrongdoers and delegates the task of presiding over enforcement proceedings to ALJs. The ALJs' proceeding resembles a trial before a federal district court, but with modified and more flexible rules of procedure and evidence. After a hearing, the ALJ issues the initial decision, including findings of fact and law and relief, if any. In response to this new enforcement practice, defendants started to challenge the SEC administrative proceedings as unconstitutional, contesting the ALJs' appointment system in use from the SEC as a breach of Article II. The US Supreme Court, with a landmark judgment of 21 June 2018, in *Lucia v SEC*[33] held that SEC's ALJs are 'inferior officers of the United States subject to the Appointments Clause of the Constitution' and must therefore be appointed to their positions alternatively by the President, a court of law or the head of department. Since prior to November 2017 none of those appointing authorities had a role in the appointment of the SEC's ALJs, ALJs had to be reappointed.

13.13 The situation looks different in the EU, but still has several institutional weaknesses. Professor Luca De Lucia offered a few years ago 'a microphysics of administrative remedies in the EU after Lisbon'[34] and, in that context, discussed administrative remedies. He noted that:

> [I]n the last twenty years, a specific type of administrative remedy has established itself against the individual decisions of European agencies. They are administrative appeals which must be activated prior to those of the courts, to be addressed to independent commissions set up within the agencies themselves. In the future, - according to various

---

[28] 15 USC s 78y(a)(1).
[29] Steven A Glazer (n 26) 345. For a vivid discussion of the implications of these two competing philosophies, compare Antonin Scalia, 'The ALJ Fiasco: A Reprise' [1979] 47 U Chi L Rev 57.
[30] Lucille Gauthier, 'Insider Trading: The Problem with the SEC's In-House ALJs' (2017) 67 Emory LJ 129, quoting Jeffrey S Lubbers, 'Federal Administrative Judges: A Focus on Our Invisible Judiciary' (1981) 33 Admin L Rev 109, 110.
[31] ibid 130.
[32] Rossidis (n 27) 784.
[33] *Lucia v SEC* 595 US No 17-130 (2018); *Lucia v SEC* 138 S Ct 2044 (2018).
[34] Luca De Lucia, 'A Microphysics of European Administrative Law: Administrative Remedies in the EU after Lisbon' (2014) 20 Eur Pub L 277.

documents of the Commission—this model should represent the ordinary instrument of administrative protection towards 'satellite' administrations. This perspective has recently been repeated in the joint statement on decentralized agencies and the subsequent common approach of Parliament, the Council and the Commission signed on the 12 June 2012, which devotes an entire paragraph to the Boards of Appeals.

Unlike their designation, in almost all cases, as boards of appeal (or slight variations thereof, like the appeal panel of the SRB), and 'despite a manifest commonality of purpose, these various Boards of Appel constitute a somewhat disparate class'.[35] Those with a longer tradition and much workload and caselaw are, so far, those that deal with intellectual property in the European Union Intellectual Property Office (EUIPO, previously named OHIM) for trademarks and designs and the Community Plant Variety Office (CPVO), and outside EU agencies, the Boards of Appeal of the European Patent Office under Articles 21 and 22 of the European Patent Convention.[36] Boards of Appeal are, moreover, a common feature with most EU agencies in regulated sectors, like the European Aviation Safety Agency (EASA), the European Chemicals Agency (ECHA), the Agency for the Cooperation of Energy Regulators (ACER) and 'the EU Agency for Railways was recently given its Board of Appeal which, in addition to standard power of annulment of decisions of the Agency, has the authority to arbitrate certain deadlock between the Agency and national safety authorities'.[37]

13.14 Crucially for our purposes, appeal bodies are also the tool of choice to scrutinize agency action in financial supervision and resolution because the authorities' decisions are subject to review by three bodies: the ESAs BoA, the ECB's ABoR, and the SRB's Appeal Panel, arguably to improve their decision-making, review their legality, and bolster their legitimacy. Can these bodies be successful in the law of finance? A definitive answer would be possible if there were a single blueprint and the same institutional design for all of these bodies, and for what they are supposed to do. Unfortunately, there is not. Being hybrid bodies, they combine features from two archetypes: the advisory committees, which contribute to an agency's decision internally, before that decision is adopted, and the courts that, independently from the agency, revise, and annul, that agency's decisions after they are adopted. A combination of both is good for policy experimentation and academic debate, but their effects are hard to measure. What seems not debatable, however, is that 'appeal bodies' (to use a generic, all-encompassing term) are European law-makers' tool of choice in areas characterized by (i) technically complex decisions (ii) adopted by EU agencies, ie where the EU has moved beyond policy formulation into the potentially more intrusive implementation. A 2019 reform to Protocol no 3 of the Statute of the Court of Justice has limited review by the Court of Justice in cases decided by some of these appeal bodies and then revised by the General Court.[38] This suggested that (some) appeal bodies offered, in the Court's view, sufficient safeguards to justify the exclusion of an ultimate judicial review by the highest court, ie to be treated as courts, or quasi-courts, of first instance. On 30 November 2022 the Court submitted a request pursuant to Article 281(2) TFEU with a view to amending further Protocol

---

[35] Yves Herinckx, 'Judicial Protection in the Single Resolution Mechanism' http://www.herinckx.be/publications/Y._Herinckx,_Judicial_Protection_in_the_SRM.pdf (accessed 1 September 2022).

[36] Compare Koen Lenaerts, Ignace Maselis, and Kathleen Gutman, *EU Procedural Law* (Janek T Nowak ed, OUP 2015) 700 ff.

[37] Herinckx (n 35). For a cross-agency view of EU appeal bodies, compare Alina Trapova, 'Expert Opinion on the Harmonisation of the EU Appeal Bodies' EUIPO (15 October 2020) (on file with the author).

[38] Regulation 2019/629 amending Protocol No 3 of the Statute of the Court of Justice of the European Union [2019] OJ L111 (25 April 2019) L111/1 L:2019:111:TOC, especially new art 58a, introduced by art 1 of the Regulation.

no 3 to extend the same mechanism to all boards of appeal established as of 1 May 2019. This provides the framework to test from an 'internal' perspective to what extent they fit in our conceptual framework as to their virtues in properly distinguishing and addressing 'pivotal' or 'marginal' cases in the law of finance. Our approach is based on these bodies' practical experience, both as part of a 'legal-health check-up' of the new financial architecture, and as preliminary evidence to support a limitation of appeals before the Court of Justice, as it happened for decisions by appeal boards with a longer tradition.

Since the ABoR does not make public its decisions (but for, more recently, high level aggregate data) and, for EU constitutional reasons, its decisions are (only) non-binding opinions, we will concentrate our 'internal' perspective only on the BoA's and the Appeal Panel's practice. The experience of the BoA is still limited in terms of workload; yet, this is progressively increasing also due to ESMA's new supervisory competences and sanctioning powers. Cases can be grouped into three main classes: decisions on breach of Union law, where the main issue turned out to be the admissibility of the appeal; decisions concerning credit ratings; and a decision concerning relevant aspects of the mandate of EIOPA. **13.15**

BoA cases on breach of Union law typically arise in contexts where supervisory competences are exercised by national authorities, the ESAs are asked to scrutinize that exercise, and the BoA is asked to review the decision to scrutinize or not. Thus, the more substantial points relate to the appeal's admissibility. In *SV Capital v EBA*[39] the BoA analysed an EBA decision *not* to start proceedings for breach of Union law on its own initiative, after being asked to do so by an applicant. The problem was whether the EBA had correctly decided that Union law requirements on 'suitability' apply only to persons who effectively direct the business of the credit institution. The BoA interpreted 'suitability' to encompass 'key function holders', such as the heads of branches, in line with EBA Guidelines, and concluded that, even if the suitability assessment by (national) authorities is discretionary, it does not lie exclusively within the ambit of national law. **13.16**

The case was remitted to the EBA to rule on the merits, and the EBA still rejected the complaint, finding that there were insufficient grounds for initiating an investigation. A second appeal was then lodged before the BoA against that decision. The BoA dismissed the appeal, finding that the EBA's holding was reasonable, and the appellant's right to be heard was respected, but it found that the EBA act not to initiate an investigation was reviewable, because, by stating that the prior complaint was admissible, it went beyond a mere communication of information or advice of non-action. The case was taken before the General Court,[40] which confirmed the EBA's view, but examined the issue of reviewability, to clarify that the BoA's decision wrongly held that the EBA decision not to act was reviewable.[41] The BoA consistently applied this finding, with some additional variations on admissibility, eg who is an 'addressee' of a decision, or has a 'direct and individual concern' in it, and what is a 'decision' in subsequent cases such as *Kluge v EBA*,[42] *B v ESMA*,[43] *IPE v ESMA* or ___ v **13.17**

---

[39] BoA D 2013-008 (24 June 2013).
[40] Case T-660/14 *SV Capital OÜ v EBA* ECLI:EU:T:2015:608.
[41] The appeal was dismissed with judgment of 14 December 2016 in Case C-577/15 P *SV Capital OÜ v EBA* ECLI:EU:C:2016:947.
[42] BoA D 2016/001 *Kluge v EBA* (19 August 2015). Appeal against an EBA decision not to open an investigation on alleged breaches of Directive 2006/48/EC by the *Finantsinspektsioon*, the Estonian Financial Supervisory Authority, in its supervision of *AS Eesti Krediidipank*, a credit institution.
[43] BoA D 2018/02 *B v ESMA* (10 September 2018). Appeal against a decision of ESMA's Chair *not to* open a formal investigation against the *Cyprus Securities and Exchange Commission* (CySEC) under art 17 of the ESMA Regulation, for alleged infringements of MiFID and EU rules on capital adequacy, where the appellant alleged that

EIOPA.[44] In *Onix Asigurari v EIOPA*[45] the issue was whether a communication sent by EIOPA to Onix on 24 November 2014 was a 'decision', and thus whether the BoA was competent to hear an appeal against it. Onix was an insurance company authorized by Romanian authorities, which began to provide certain insurance services in Italy and in 2013 was banned from continuing business by IVASS, upon concerns about Onix's sole shareholder. The appeal concerned EIOPA's refusal to conduct an investigation for a potential breach of Union law concerning the division of powers between home and host insurance supervisory authorities. The BoA remarked that no appeal had been brought against the actual 'decision'[46] signed by the EIOPA's Chair, albeit not specifically addressed to either Onix or its shareholder. The later communication[47] was not a 'decision', but merely confirmed the earlier decision. Therefore, since the appellants had not appealed the initial decision, Article 17 of the EIOPA Regulation did not apply, and the Board had no jurisdiction on the appeal. In *Howerton v ESMA*,[48] *Howerton v EBA*,[49] and *Howerton v EIOPA*,[50] the Board of Appeal dismissed as inadmissible appeals against decisions of the three agencies not to investigate further complaints submitted by the appellant which related to subject matters clearly outside their remit.

13.18 In *A v ESMA*[51] the BoA tried to engage in a dialogue with the CJEU's caselaw in *SV Capital*. The appellant had submitted a request to ESMA under Article 17 requesting that ESMA investigate the approach adopted by a national competent authority as regards the valuation of structured retail products and identifying a series of EU law provisions which, in the appellant's view, had not been applied correctly by it. The BoA once again dismissed the appeal as inadmissible; yet it also offered clarifications on the reviewability of ESMA's decisions not to act for breach of Union law. Crucially, the Board noted that ESMA has in place procedural rules governing its application of Article 17, which in turn impose internal procedural constraints on this discretionary power. Article 5 of the Rules provides that 'the Chairperson may close the Request without initiating an investigation, where he/she considers that: [t]he Request is admissible, but an investigation should not be initiated, as a matter of discretion, taking into account the non-exhaustive list of factors included in Annex II' including a negative one when 'the request is more suitable to be dealt with by another person or body, such as inter alia, the European Commission, another European Supervisory Authority, a national competent authority, a national complaints scheme or a court, or such other person or body is already dealing with it or has already dealt with it'.

---

it represented a number of clients damaged by the activities of a Cypriot investment firm, and that the fine imposed by CySEC was neither adequate nor dissuasive of further breaches, that numerous complainants were affected, and that, with no suitable means to resolve complaints at the national level, the lack of intervention by ESMA had a negative impact on investor protection in the EU, not limited to Cyprus.

[44] BoA D 2014/05 *Investor Protection Europe sprl v ESMA* (10 November 2014). Appeal about the application of the Prospectus Directive by the Commission de Surveillance du Secteur Financier (CSSF) in Luxembourg. BoA D 2023 02 _____ v EIOPA (19 July 2023). Appeal about EIOPA's assessment of technical provisions of the third party liability portfolio; dismissed because Report was not a binding act. If relied upon by national authorities, the proper channel would be national proceedings.
[45] BoA D 2015/001 *Onix v EIOPA* (24 November 2014).
[46] EIOPA-14-267 *Onix v EIOPA* (6 June 2014).
[47] EIOPA-14-653 *Onix v EIOPA* (24 November 2014).
[48] BoA D 2020/01 *Jeffrey Michael Howerton v ESMA* (9 October 2020).
[49] BoA D 2021/01 *Jeffrey Michael Howerton v EBA* (7 January 2021).
[50] BoA D 2020/02 *Jeffrey Michael Howerton v EIOPA* (29 October 2020).
[51] BoA D 2021 02 *A v ESMA* (12 March 2021).

13.19 The Board of Appeal considered therefore that in principle this suggests that compliance by the Chair with the Rules of Procedure should be reviewable and noted further that recent changes introduced by Regulation (EU) 2019/2175 to Article 17(2) of ESMA Regulation and adopted after the *SV Capital* ruling may justify a reconsideration of the issue (as discussed at paras 110–126 of its decision). Yet this was deferentially left to the Court and the dialogue has not been taken up by the Court, which meanwhile reconfirmed in *Jakeliūnas v ESMA*[52] the SV Capital approach, apparently without considering the arguments raised by the BoA in *A v ESMA*, and in *C v EBA* the BoA took on board this continuity of criterion despite the change in language of relevant acts.[53]

13.20 BoA cases on (some of the) supervisory competences directly exercised by ESAs, eg those of ESMA over credit rating agencies look more promising, as the focal point are not matters of competence and governance, but matters of substance, where the benefits of expert, swift review are easier to perceive. The first case was *Global Standard Rating v ESMA*.[54] In 2012, the UK Financial Services Authority informed ESMA of concerns that the appellant appeared to be issuing sovereign credit ratings on its webpage, without being registered as a credit rating agency. Once the appellant applied to register under the Credit Rating Agencies Regulation (CRAR), ESMA's Board of Supervisors refused the application, and the refusal was appealed. The Board of Appeal had to consider whether ESMA's decision to refuse registration was correct, and whether it was vitiated by procedural irregularities or unfairness. The BoA held that ESMA had notified the completeness of the application within CRAR time limits. On the substance of the refusal to register, it was the applicant's burden to make sure that the application's information was compliant. Even considering the relative novelty of the registration process, the rules gave sufficient guidance, and ESMA was not obliged to raise questions on the information provided, nor to remedy any deficiencies at the compliance stage. ESMA's based its finding of non-compliance by the appellant on contentions that raised significant issues, *and* the refusal decision was fully reasoned as required by Articles 16(3) and 18(1) CRAR. The appeal was thus dismissed. Similar steps were taken in *FinancialCraft Analytics v ESMA*,[55] another refusal to register a credit rating agency. ESMA had concluded that an insufficient level of detail, inconsistencies and weaknesses in the application failed to comply with CRAR.[56] The appeal was unsuccessful because ESMA's check was thorough, because while some of ESMA's objections were minor, others were central to the refusal, and because the appellant's responsibility was to demonstrate compliance with CRAR to the requisite level of detail during registration. Crucially, in terms of the BoA's approach, it was held that in respect of technical matters about credit rating, such as rating methodologies, ESMA was acting as a specialist regulator, and thus is entitled to its margin of appreciation; and that the decision itself set out ESMA's reasons in a detailed manner, as required by Articles 16(3) and 18(1) CRAR.

---

[52] Case T-760/20 *Jakeliūnas v ESMA* ECLI:EU:T:2021:512, para 20.
[53] See its decision of 21 July 2022, *C v EBA*, BoA-D-2022-01. The BoA dismissed as inadmissible an appeal against an EBA decision not to initiate an investigation with an alleged breach or non-application of EU law regarding payment services.
[54] BoA D 2013-14 *Global Private Rating Company 'Standard Rating' Ltd v ESMA* (10 January 2014).
[55] BoA D 2017/01 *FinancialCraft Analytics v ESMA* (3 July 2017).
[56] This encompassed internal controls, conflicts of interest, independence of the credit rating process from business interests, rating methodology, models and key rating assumptions, credit rating process, and exemptions. Even though the appellant was a small company, which might have benefited from CRAR exemptions, the arrangements to obtain such exemption had not been made.

13.21 In the '*Nordic banks*' cases, which resulted from appeals by *Svenska Handelsbanken AB*, *Skandinaviska Enskilda Banken AB*, *Swedbank AB*, and *Nordea Bank Abp*, the problem's peculiarity was that it involved not an individual institution, but the Nordic debt *market*, and the focal point in law was what may be considered a 'rating', as opposed to investment research and investment recommendation.[57] ESMA's Board of Supervisors found a negligent infringement of CRAR in the four banks' inclusion of 'shadow ratings' in their credit research reports, and followed it by public notices and fines on each bank. The banks appealed. The knot of the case concerned the ambiguity of Article 3(2) of CRAR, which excludes recommendations and 'investment research' from consideration as 'credit ratings'. In the four cases, 'shadow ratings' included in the banks' investment research and recommendations, were creditworthiness assessments composed by the banks' credit analysts, based in whole or in part on the methodology of the 'official' rating agencies, and using an alphanumerical rating. This, to ESMA, put them outside the investment research exemption under CRAR, and within the definition of 'rating', even if the overall reports themselves could be characterized as MiFID investment research. The BoA found no evidence of unlawfulness in the decisions under the principles of legal certainty and due process and upheld ESMA's assessment that the activities of the appellants fell within CRAR provisions. Thus, the banks had to be CRAR-registered to undertake the activity, and absent such registration they had infringed the provisions. In reaching its conclusion, the BoA engaged not only in a literal interpretation, but also looked at the legislative history and purpose of the relevant provisions. The former was not very enlightening, but the latter was, which led the BoA to hold (§ 262 of the 4 simultaneous decisions) that the effect of the banks' interpretation, should the BoA accept it, would be that market participants could easily circumvent CRAR restrictions. The BoA, however, concluded that, due to the ambiguous wording of Article 3(2) CRAR, and the unusual circumstances in which the banks' practice had been carried out in the Nordic debt markets for many years, without any perception of CRAR impropriety, the infringements were not negligent. Thus, ESMA's Board of Supervisors could not impose fines, and the cases were remitted for the adoption of amended measures, under Article 60(5) of the ESMA Regulation.

13.22 In *Creditreform AG v EBA*,[58] the BoA dismissed an appeal filed by a credit rating agency which challenged the adoption by the Joint Committee of the ESAs of certain draft implementing technical standards (ITS) and applied for their suspension. The draft ITS which were subject to appeal proposed amendments to Commission Implementing Regulation (EU) 2016/1799 on the mapping of the credit assessments of external credit assessment institutions in accordance with Article 136(1) and (3) of Regulation (EU) No 575/2013.[59] They included a proposal to amend the correspondence ('mapping' in the terminology of the Capital Requirements Regulation (CRR)[60]) between certain of the appellant's long-term corporate credit assessments and certain credit quality steps as set out in section 2 of Chapter 2 of Title

---

[57] The four cases were conducted in parallel, with a single hearing and four simultaneous decisions drafted in a single document. In *Scandinaviska Enskilda Banken AB v ESMA*, the Board had decided first to dismiss a request for suspension of the application of the contested decision with a decision of 30 November 2018.
[58] BoA D 2019/05 *Creditreform Rating AG v EBA* (13 September 2019).
[59] Commission Implementing Regulation (EU) 2016/1799 laying down implementing technical standards with regard to the mapping of credit assessments of external credit assessment institutions for credit risk in accordance with Articles 136(1) and 136(3) of Regulation (EU) No 575/2013 of the European Parliament and of the Council on prudential requirements for credit institutions and investment firms and amending Regulation (EU) No 648/2012 [2013] OJ L176/3 (hereafter Regulation No 575/2013).
[60] ibid 1.

II of Part Three of the CRR. The appellant challenged the legality of this change. The BoA dismissed the appeal as inadmissible, holding that, under Article 15 of the ESAs Regulations, the European Commission is not bound by the draft ITS submitted by the ESAs and has significant discretion as to the final determination of the content of such ITS at the stage of their endorsement. In the BoA's view, this meant that the draft ITS cannot undergo autonomous and direct judicial or quasi-judicial review. Those willing to challenge these acts can do so only by filing an application for annulment under Article 263 TFEU against the final decision adopted by the European Commission, asking the General Court to consider also the alleged errors in fact or in law of the ESAs' preparatory act which may vitiate the European Commission's final decision. In *Scope Ratings v ESMA*[61] the Board of Appeal dismissed the appeal brought by the credit rating agency against a decision imposing a fine and the publication of the notice for alleged violations of the applicable legal provisions of the Credit Rating Agencies (CRA) Regulation. Central to this appeal was the appellant's 2015 covered bond methodology, its partial non-application (as to the asset pool analysis) in the context of unsolicited ratings issued by the appellant in 2015 in circumstances where the issuer had already achieved the highest rating based upon other factors of the rating methodology, and the appellant's subsequent amendment of this methodology in 2016.

13.23 Crucially, the Board of Appeal had to clarify the meaning of Article 8(3) CRAR, which requires that credit rating agencies use rating methodologies that are 'systematic', and that credit rating agencies use (or apply) methodologies systematically. The Board of Appeal noted that the notion of 'systematic' in the context of Article 8(3), and also of the CRA Regulation generally, cannot be dis-associated from the notion of application or use; 'to do so would render Article 8(3) devoid of meaning' and 'defeat the intention of the EU legislature as it would render ESMA powerless to supervise the ongoing application by rating agencies of methodologies in a systematic and consistent way'. The Board of Appeal also found that the credit rating agency should have known or at least reasonably foreseen this conclusion and was therefore liable for administrative sanctions, also because it could have made a request to ESMA if it was unclear as to the scope of a provision of the CRA Regulation before taking any action which could amount to a breach of the relevant provision.

13.24 Finally, in *City Insurance v EIOPA*[62] the appellant requested the Board of Appeal to 'issue a decision finding that (i) EIOPA has acted in excess of its regulated competence insofar as its role and involvement in the Romanian balance sheet review of Romanian insurance companies initiated in 2020 by the Romanian supervisory authority in cooperation with EIOPA (ii) the Romanian BSR exercise was disproportionate and discriminatory (not only in comparison to other EU Member States, but also by comparison to EU-based insurers operating in Romania on a freedom of services or freedom of establishment basis—which are neither subject to the Romanian BSR exercise nor to similar measures in their home Member States. The board declared the appeal inadmissible because the decision to conduct the balance sheet review was of the national competent authority. However, on the claim that EIOPA had allegedly acted ultra vires, the BoA, in an indirect dialogue with the national court, noted that:

> 71. [s]hould the appellant and the national court before which the ASF Decision has been challenged (and before which the case is still pending) consider (i) that a question of

---

[61] BoA D 2020/03 *Scope Ratings GmbH v ESMA* (28 December 2020).
[62] BoA D 2021/03 *Societatea de Asigurare-Reasigurare City Insurance SA v EIOPA* (14 April 2021).

validity of the EIOPA decision to participate in the BSR is relevant to the effect of the determination by the national court on the validity of the ASF Decision under the applicable national law and (ii) that EIOPA's participation to the BSR could actually be considered beyond the clear EIOPA mandate to promote supervisory convergence (and thus an ultra vires act in respect of the scope of action and powers set out in Article 1 of the EIOPA Regulation and of the tasks conferred upon EIOPA by the EIOPA Regulation), such question could be referred to the CJEU under Article 267 TFEU.

13.25 Although comprising an even shorter timespan than the BoA, the abundant practice of the Appeal Panel seems to confirm that expert review is appropriate in the law of finance, including the context of resolution. The Appeal Panel has received more than 100 appeals so far. The majority were beyond the remit of the Appeal Panel and clearly inadmissible because they concerned ex ante contributions to the Single Resolution Fund, and thus the Appeal Panel adopted short inadmissibility orders.[63] Judging with hindsight from the workload of the General Court on this resulting from the lack of a filter, and considering that such workload could be handled by the same only years after the adoption of the contested decisions, the limitation of the remit was certainly unfortunate. The decisions[64] in the cases where the appeals were not manifestly inadmissible are considered in some detail below, grouped into three main classes: decisions on administrative contributions to the SRB expenses; decisions on MREL determination and internal MREL waivers; and decisions on access to documents in the context of the Banco Popular resolution.

13.26 The key point of the Appeal Panel substantive decisions on administrative contributions to the SRB expenses was the tension between legal certainty and proportionality. The rules that determine contributions must take into consideration the entity's circumstances (eg whether it is a licensed institution, its size, and risk profile) so as to render contributions proportionate. However, those contributions must also be based on clear-cut definitions and criteria that determine scope, time period and method of calculation, and regulate special cases, such as banking groups. Appellant entities have raised interpretative issues about their subjective circumstances, or objective ones (eg the calculation), which allegedly rendered the contribution excessive or no longer due. As to the subjective scope of application of SRMR provisions, the Appeal Panel held that SRMR and Commission Delegated Regulation No 1310/2014 limited their scope to entities referred to in Article 2 SRMR. Thus, if an entity originally included in the ECB list[65] had ceased to be such during the relevant period,

---

[63] This occurred eg with an initial batch of inadmissibility orders, where the Appeal Panel indicated that review of ex ante contributions to the SRF fell outside the Appeal Panel's remit under art 85, See Appeal Panel Cases 2/16 to 4/16 and 6/16 to 14/16 (decisions of 18 July 2016). An application against the SRB requests for ex ante contribution was dismissed by the GCEU on procedural grounds with Case T-446/16 *NRW Bank v SRB* EU:T:2019:445; the judgment was annulled and remanded by the CJEU in Case C-662/19 P *NRW Bank v SRB* ECLI:EU:C:2021:846; most notably, the SRB decision on the calculation of the 2017 ex ante contributions was annulled on procedural grounds in Case T-420/17 *Portigon v SRB* ECLI:EU:T:2020:438 (on appeal in Case C-664/20, pending); another application against ex ante contributions was upheld by General Court in Case T-411/17 *Landesbank Baden-Württemberg v SRB* ECLI:EU:T:2020:435, yet the judgment was annulled on appeal by the CJEU in Joined Cases C-584/20 P and C-621/20 P *Commission v Landesbank Baden-Württemberg* ECLI:EU:C:2021:601. The following SRB 2021 decision calculating the 2017 ex ante contributions was, in turn, challenged in Case T-142/22 (pending). There are currently several other pending actions against the SRB concerning the ex ante contributions (eg from Cases T-391/22 to T-432/22), as well as against ECB irrevocable payment commitment measures concerning ex ante contributions to the SRF (eg in Cases T-186/22 *BNP Paribas*, T-187/22 *BPCE*, T-188/22 *Crédit agricole*, T-189/22 *Confédération nationale du Crédit Mutuel*, T-190/22 *Banque Postale*, and T-191/22 *Société Générale*).

[64] All Appeal Panel decisions, in anonymized version, are accessible at https://www.srb.europa.eu/en (accessed 1 September 2022).

[65] For a similar finding that the ECB has no longer competence for supervision following the withdrawal of the license Case T-139/19 *Pilatus Bank v ECB* ECLI:EU:T:2021:623.

it could no longer be required to contribute to the SRB administrative costs. Despite some ambiguities in Regulation 1310/2014 the Appeal Panel acknowledged that a regulation is presumed to be lawful and only the CJEU has the power to declare it invalid;[66] this cannot be done by national courts[67] or administrative authorities,[68] nor by Union bodies,[69] including authorities dealing with administrative appeal procedures, eg the Appeal Panel.[70] Yet, the Appeal Panel also held that between two possible readings, it should prefer the one which would preserve the lawfulness of the Commission Regulation should the Court decide on the issue.[71]

13.27 In 2018 the Appeal Panel decided three other cases on the calculation of contributions to its administrative expenses for the year 2018 based, this time, upon Commission Delegated Regulation No 2361/2017.[72] In Case 4/2018, the Appeal Panel noted that a bank has to pay the administrative contributions, even if it is declared to be failing or likely to fail, so long as its licence is not withdrawn. In Case 5/2018 the Appeal Panel held that in groups, there is a single debtor for the group, which is the same entity that must pay the supervisory fees to the SSM.[73] In Case 6/2018, the appellant had undergone a comprehensive restructuring and claimed that 2020 was the planned time for closure of its voluntary winding up process, a process during which the appellant had received funding from the German Deposit Guarantee Scheme. The Appeal Panel reiterated the principle that the appellant was still a licensed credit institution and was therefore liable to pay administrative contributions.

13.28 A second Appeal Panel line of action has been based on the rules on minimum requirements for own funds and eligible liabilities (MREL), which highlights the importance, in a seemingly 'dry' and technical field, of principles-based interpretivism on divisive issues. MREL rules ensure that a bank has sufficient instruments to write-down or convert to ensure an orderly resolution under the bank's proposed resolution strategy.[74] Thus, among all capital and liability instruments subject to write down, MREL rules identify a narrower sub-set whose

---

[66] Case C-362/14 *Schrems* ECLI:EU:C:2015:650, para 61; Joined Cases C-188/10 and C-189/10 *Melki and Abdeli* ECLI:EU:C:2010:2016, para 54; Case 101/78 *Granaria* ECLI:EU:C:1979:38, paras 4 and 5; Case 63/87 *Commission v Greece* ECLI:EU:C:1988:285, para 10; Case C-475/01 *Commission v Greece* ECLI:EU:C:2004:585, para 18.

[67] *Schrems* (n 65) para 62; Case C-456/13 *T&L Sugars* ECLI:EU:C:2015:284, paras 45–48; Case C-583/11 *Inuit Tapiriit Kanatami* ECLI:EU:C:2013:625, paras 92, 96; Case C-344/04 *IATA* ECLI:EU:C:2006:10, paras 27–30; Case C-314/85 *Foto-Frost* ECLI:EU:C:1987:452, paras 14–17.

[68] *Schrems* (n 65) para 52; *Granaria* (n 66) para 6; Case C-533/10 *CIVAD* ECLI:EU:C:2012:347, para 43.

[69] Case T-13/97 *Losch* EU:C:T:1998:230, para 99; Case T-154/96 *Chvatal and Others v Court of Justice of the European Communities* ECLI:EU:T:1998:229, para 112.

[70] Case F-128/12 *CR v Parliament* ECLI:EU:F:2014:38, paras 35, 36, 40; Case T-218/06 *Neurim Pharmaceuticals v OHIM* ECLI:EU:T:2008:379, para 52; Case T-120/99 *Kik v OHIM* ECLI:EU:T:2001:189, para 55.

[71] The Appeal Panel also discussed whether the board request for contribution could legitimately encompass the entire year 2015, since the appellant had ceased to be a regulated entity in July 2015. On this the Appeal Panel was prudent and held that the Commission Regulation could legitimately be construed, as the board did, as setting contributions for a full calendar year. Yet it noted that *de lege ferenda*, an approach based on a *pro rata temporis* calculation would be justified, more proportionate, and could be considered by the European Commission in the future. Indeed, such a *pro rata* system was eventually adopted by Commission Delegated Regulation No 2017/2361 on the final system of contributions to the administrative expenditures of the Single Resolution Board [2017] OJ L337 (hereafter Delegated Regulation No 2017/2361).

[72] Delegated Regulation No 2017/2361 (n 71) 6. According to such Delegated Regulation, the SRB was required to calculate in 2018 the Administrative Contributions for 2018 as well as the *final* settlement for administrative contributions for the years 2015 to 2017, taking into account the provisional advances calculated and paid by the relevant entities under Regulation No 1310/2014 in the previous years.

[73] Article 2(3) of Delegated Regulation 2361/2017 (n 72) and art 4 of Regulation (EU) No 1163/2014 of the European Central Bank of 22 October 2014 on supervisory fees (for the group's 'fee debtor').

[74] For a brief description of MREL, compare M Lamandini and D Ramos Muñoz, 'Minimum Requirement for Own Capital and Eligible Liabilities' in Vittorio Santoro and Mario Chiti (eds), *The Palgrave Handbook of European Banking Union Law* (Palgrave McMillan, Springer International 2019) 321.

characteristics make such write down particularly easy.[75] In its first case in 2018,[76] the board made an MREL determination that was below 8 per cent of total liabilities including own funds (TLOF). Since resolution rules provide that the single resolution fund (SRF) resources can be tapped only after capital/liabilities reaching 8 per cent TLOF are bailed-in,[77] the appellant was concerned that a target below that level posed the risk that, at the point-of-non-viability (PONV) of the failing credit institution authorities would have to implement the strategy without relying on SRF resources. The Appeal Panel held that the board's decision was justified. The MREL requirement was calibrated to ensure that the target of the relevant credit institution, measured against its risk weighted assets, compared in a balanced way with the average national banks and average Banking Union banks and was *proportionate* in light of the bank's size, funding, and business models and risk profile, the impact of that bank's failure on financial stability, and the need to prevent competitive distortions. Yet, the threshold of bailed-in instruments equivalent to 8 per cent TLOF could still be reached using not only MREL instruments but also liabilities that, although not qualifying as MREL, are nonetheless not excluded from bail-in,[78] eg those with a less than one year maturity. Since this was a reasonable view, the board had the ultimate decision, which had to be respected. Thus, even MREL rules, which provide a (supposedly) clear calculation method, are open for interpretation on critical aspects that create tensions between entity and resolution authority, as well as between resolution authorities themselves, which require weighing the provisions' goals with the authorities' margin of appreciation.

13.29 A different aspect of MREL determination, and notably the one concerning the ammunition of internal MREL within banking groups and the conditions for the replacement of internal MREL (iMREL) with parent companies guarantees was brought to the attention of the Appeal Panel in more recent appeals. In Cases 2/21, 3/21, 1/22, and 2/22 a credit institution submitted a request for a waiver of the iMREL related to some of its subsidiaries. The parent entity then issued, in Case 2/21, a hard letter of comfort and, in Case 3/21, guarantees accepted by the ECB in the context of capital and liquidity waivers under CRR, arts 7(1) and 8. Nevertheless, the SRB adopted a decision rejecting the application for the waiver finding that there was not sufficient assurance to the board that the resources necessary for loss absorption and/or recapitalization shall be available when needed. The Appeal Panel clarified, first, that the condition required for the granting of a iMREL waiver by Article 12h(1)8(c) SRM Regulation, and notably that no material impediment to the transfer of funds exists, does not necessarily require the issuance of a guarantee, but does not exclude either that, in the specific circumstances of each case, such a guarantee may be considered necessary by the SRB. The reasons why such a guarantee is needed, and why the one offered by the credit institution may not meet the SRB expectations, need to be duly reasoned and, if a claim in this respect is raised by the appellant, also check in their substantive legality. In Case 2/2021, the Appeal Panel remitted the case to the board finding that the reasons were insufficient;

---

[75] Article 45(4) of Directive 2014/59/EU of the European Parliament and of the Council establishing a framework for the recovery and resolution of credit institutions and investment firms and amending Council Directive 82/891/EEC, and Directives 2001/24/EC, 2002/47/EC, 2004/25/EC, 2005/56/EC, 2007/36/EC, 2011/35/EU, 2012/30/EU, and 2013/36/EU, and Regulations (EU) No 1093/2010 and (EU) No 648/2012, of the European Parliament and of the Council Text with EEA relevance [2014] OJ L173 (BRRD) (instruments issued and fully paid up, not owed to, funded, guaranteed, or funded by the institution, with more than one-year maturity, not comprising deposits or derivatives.
[76] Case 8/18 *A v SRB* (decision of 16 October 2018).
[77] BRRD (n 75), art 44(4), 44(5).
[78] The bail-in eligible liabilities are contemplated in BRRD (n 75) art 44 (the bail-in sequence is in BRRD, art 48). The liabilities eligible to fulfil MREL are regulated under BRRD (n 75) art 45(4).

in Case 3/2021, on the contrary, the Appeal Panel confirmed the decision, noting that the reasons were sufficient to meet the requirement pursuant to TFEU, art 296, and the substantive legality of such reasons could not be reviewed lacking a ground of appeal in that respect. In Case 2/22, the Appeal Panel judged inadmissible the appellant's claim concerning the alleged mis-determination of the iMREL due to the reference in the iMREL right to be heard assessment memorandum attached to the iMREL decision to SRMR, art 10a, which was read as implying that the appellant had also to satisfy a notional combined buffer requirement on top of the MREL requirement. The Appeal Panel discussed at large this complex issue, yet found in the end that the claim fell outside the remit of the Appeal Panel: something which confirms its excessively narrow remit pursuant to Article 85 SRMR. In the context of the same Case 2/22, the Appeal Panel further held that the SRMR does not expressly require a formal application for an iMREL waiver, noting that Article 12h and 12i SRMR, from a textual point of view, provide for that 'the Board may waive' the application of the iMREL without a specification that this can occur solely 'upon request' or 'if the credit institution so requires'. This finding did not justify, in the given circumstances, the remittal of the iMREL decision. In Case 3/22, the Appeal Panel was confronted with a MREL determination for an entity which in previous resolution planning cycles was considered to be liquidated under normal insolvency and was on the contrary assessed as a resolution entity due to a policy change in the public interest assessment to include the scenario of a failure in the context of system wide events. The Appeal Panel found the statement of reasons insufficient and, on the occasion, discussed at length (at §§ 60–80) its standard of review.

13.30 In Case 1/22, the largest appeal so far, the Appeal Panel addressed for the first time in European case law the issue of resolution colleges' decisions and adopted first an admissibility decision, holding that a credit institution individually concerned by a joint decision of a resolution college on the MREL determination needs to challenge the college's joint decision and not the following SRB decision instructing the national resolution authority to implement such joint decision.[79] On the merit, the Appeal Panel found that, due to the interplay existing between the MREL determination and the resolution planning decision (which is outside the remit of the Appeal Panel) as to the size and profile of the credit institution concerned at the point of non-viability, if the resolution plan decision is challenged before the General Court (as was the case at hand, in Case T-77/22), the Appeal Panel may stay the proceedings of the appeal regarding the implications for the MREL decision of the (possible) annulment of the resolution decision by the General Court. The Appeal Panel further held, as to the other grounds of appeal, that the SRB decision had lawfully assessed the post-resolution group when calculating the MREL recapitalisation amount for a parent and a subsidiary, and lawfully determined the MREL add-on over TLAC, but that the decision had to be remitted to the board because of its insufficient statement of reasons on these points, and for having disregarded an (allegedly late) iMREL waiver request.

13.31 The largest Appeal Panel caseload has focused on access to documents under Regulation 1049/2001 on access to documents (Access Regulation) connected to the *Banco Popular* resolution, with several rounds of elaborated decisions. More recently, in Cases 4/22 and 6/22 access to documents was sought in the context of Sberbank resolution and in Case 7/22 in the context of the ABLV decision not to place the bank into resolution. Again, despite

---

[79] SRB Case 1/2022,decision on admissibility (29 June 2022). For a similar conclusion, compare Vittorio di Bucci, 'Procedural and Judicial Implications of Composite Procedures in the Banking Union' in Chiara Zilioli and Karl-Philipp Wojcik, *Judicial Review in the European Banking Union* (Edward Elgar Publishing 2021) 114.

their seemingly narrow and rules-based context[80], the cases illustrate the tension between key policies, principles, and values. The different rounds of appeals showed a combination of case-specific details and general principles, and how minute details could decisively influence matters of principle.

13.32   A relevant issue of procedural detail was the admissibility of 'second appeals' against Board's (new confirmatory) decisions to comply with a prior Appeal Panel decisions, ie when a first appeal had resulted in a decision against the Board, and the second appeal alleged that the Board, adopting an amended decision following the Appeal Panel decision, had not complied with the latter. The Appeal Panel held that such 'second' appeal was admissible. When adopting a revised decision to comply with Appeal Panel findings the board was not extending the original decision: it was replacing it with a new decision, the only one with legal effects.[81] The second appeal could be useful to address the board's possible good faith errors in implementing Appeal Panel findings, or clarify the Appeal Panel's view; an efficient way to ensure timely compliance, enhance certainty, and protect the appellant's rights. Notice the relevance of a seeming minute matter for the Appeal Panel's competence–competence, ie the power to rule on its own competence. The Appeal Panel did that by underlining the differences with ABoR, where there is no second review, because the ECB's Supervisory Board is not bound to follow ABoR's opinion. Conversely, if the Appeal Panel did not allow the 'second appeal', the SRB would be bound to follow the Appeal Panel's view, but it, not the Appeal Panel, would have the last word on how to do so. Conversely, to avoid that the second appeal turned into a full *ex novo* review or gave rise to an endless cycle of appeals the Appeal Panel clarified that such appeal can only concern matters where the SRB's view had been found to be incorrect.[82]

13.33   Going into the decisions' substance, a summary of the rounds of appeal is: (i) the overall question was how much access had been granted by the SRB to the documents supporting the Banco Popular resolution decision to the shareholders or subordinated bondholders who had suffered the loss of money as a result; (ii) the Appeal Panel's first and clear answer was 'not nearly enough'; (iii) the same answer was also repeated, yet in more targeted and nuanced terms, in successive rounds of appeals which resulted in additional disclosures by the SRB. We discuss the general background, the matters of principle, and some select matter in detail. More specifically, the Appeal Panel had to examine the SRB refusal to disclose key resolution documents (eg resolution decision, valuation report, or resolution plan) in light of the right that 'any citizen' has to disclosure, and elaborate some general criteria to balance the right of access and the public interest. A key to the Appeal Panel decisions were the arguments that: (i) conferral of powers to EU agencies is conditional upon respect of fundamental rights, and effective judicial review; and (ii) administrative safeguards, including access to documents or the duty to state reasons, are instrumental to effective judicial review. On these grounds, the Panel held that the SRB's refusal to access the Valuation Report *in its entirety* erred in law, since the report was a critical part of the resolution decision, and formed a legal unity with it, and thus had to be disclosed at least partially. Then, the SRB was only partly justified in refusing access to other documents. The resolution decision itself,

---

[80] For a thorough discussion, compare René Smits and Nikolai Bodenhoop, 'Towards a Single Standard of Professional Secrecy for Supervisory Authorities: A Reform Proposal'(2019) 3 ELR 295.
[81] Appeal Panel decisions in Cases 2/18 (decision of 23 March 2018), 3/18 (decision of 28 February 2019), 18/18 (decision of 19 June 2019), 19/18 (decision of 19 June 2019).
[82] Case 2/18.

some parts of the resolution plan and other relevant documents could be disclosed in a redacted, non-confidential form, without endangering any public interest, including financial stability, also in light of the fact that disclosure would take place months after the resolution decision was adopted.

13.34 Successive rounds of appeals over roughly similar cases let the Appeal Panel further develop a stable framework of analysis to balance the competing interests at stake in the following structured manner: (a) the right of access is a transparency tool of democratic control of European institutions, bodies and agencies available to all EU citizens irrespective of their interests in subsequent legal actions;[83] (b) the purpose of the Access Regulation 'is to give the fullest possible effect to the right of public access to documents and to lay down the general principles and limits on such access' (recital 4) and 'in principle, all documents of the institutions should be accessible to the public' (recital 11). This Regulation implements Article 15 TFEU which establishes that citizens have the right to access documents held by all Union institutions, bodies, and agencies, and is also a fundamental right under Article 42 of the Charter. However, certain public and private interests are also protected by way of exceptions and the Union institutions, bodies and agencies should be entitled to protect their internal consultations and deliberations where necessary to safeguard their ability to carry out their tasks (recital 11). (c) Exceptions must be applied and interpreted narrowly.[84] (d) Union institutions, bodies and agencies can rely in relation to certain categories of administrative documents on a general presumption that their disclosure would undermine the purpose of the protection of an interest protected by the Access Regulation.[85]

13.35 To add more complexity, a balance between similar principles was also being drawn in parallel by the CJEU in the successive cases of *Espirito Santo I*,[86] *BaFin v Ewald Baumeister*,[87] *UBS Europe*,[88] and *Enzo Buccioni*[89] (where the Court departed from Advocate General Bot's opinion), *Espirito Santo II*,[90] and *Di Masi and Varoufakis v ECB*,[91] which we have already considered.[92] A constant challenge was the asymmetry between narrowness of the Appeal Panel's remit and the broad scope and relevance of the matters at stake, eg the Appeal Panel cannot review the legality of the resolution scheme, or the application of resolution tools, in light of their impact on fundamental rights, but this tension was key to gauge the relevance of the disclosures sought. Thus, the Appeal Panel had to construe the matter noting that, even if it could not decide on the legality of the measures, it assumed that the resolution framework

---

[83] Case C-60/15 *Saint-Gobain Glass Deutschland* ECLI:EU:C:2017:540, paras 60, 61; and Case T-376/13 *Versorgungswerk der Zahnärztekammer Schleswig-Holstein v European Central Bank* ECLI:EU:T:2015:361, para 20.
[84] Case C-280/11 *Council v Access Info Europe* ECLI:EU:C:2013:671, para 30.
[85] Case C-404/10 *Commission v Edition Odile Jacob* ECLI:EU:C:2012:393; Case C-514/07 P *Sweden and Others v API and Commission* ECLI:EU:C:2010:541; Case C-365/12 P *Commission v EnBW* ECLI:EU:C:2014:112; Joined Cases C-514/11 P and C-605/11 P *LPN and Finland v Commission* ECLI:EU:C:2013:738; Case C-562/14 P *Sweden v Commission* ECLI:EU:C:2017:356.
[86] Case T-251/15 *Espirito Santo Financial v ECB* ECLI:EU:T:2018:234; reversed on appeal in Case C-442/18 P *ECB v Espirito Santo Financial* ECLI:EU:C:2019:1117.
[87] Case C-15/16 *Bafin v Ewald Baumeister* ECLI:EU:C:2017:958.
[88] Case C-358/16 *Alain Handequin and UBS Europe v DV* ECLI:EU:C:2018:715.
[89] Case C-594/16 *Enzo Buccioni v Banca d'Italia* ECLI:EU:C:2018:717.
[90] Case T-730/16, *Espirito Santo Financial v ECB* ECLI:EU:T:2019:161, reversed on appeal in Case C 396/19 ECLI:EU:C:2020:845.
[91] Case T-9798/17 *De Masi and Varoufakis v ECB* ECLI:EU:T:2019:154 on appeal in Case C-342/19 (pending; see, however, the Opinion of AG Pikamäe of 9 July 2020 ECLI:EU:C:2020:549, who advised the Court to uphold the appeal).
[92] This line of cases was more recently followed by Case T-501/19 *Corneli v ECB* ECLI:EU:T:2022:402, where the court annulled the ECB decision rejecting access to its decision to place Banca Carige under special administration.

enabled the respect of property rights since: (i) resolution action is adopted only when a bank is failing or likely to fail, (ii) resolution is implemented at the point of non-viability and (iii) Article 20 SRMR establishes compensation to shareholders or bondholders under the 'no creditor worse off' principle ie to not obtain in resolution a treatment which less favourable than in insolvency. Thus, document disclosure had to permit the proper scrutiny of such safeguards, by democratically elected bodies, and, crucially, courts. This had direct implications for the right to an effective judicial protection under Article 47 of the Charter. As the rounds of appeals went on the Appeal Panel found that successive SRB disclosures in response to Appeal Panel decisions offered the information needed to initiate legal proceedings, and to enable a review of the Banco Popular resolution actions. Thus, the *public* dimension of judicial accountability was respected, without unduly undermining the protection of the countervailing interests acknowledged by the Access Regulation. Should any further disclosures be *individually* needed by an EU court, the Court could order them in the specific proceedings, or ask the Board the necessary questions. In this way, the Appeal Panel surgically distinguished an individual's rights in court proceedings (over which the Appeal Panel was not competent) and those rights relevance for the public interest.

13.36 Yet, matters of minute detail and core matters of principle can be closely interwoven, and quasi-judicial review may demand important dosage of ingenuity to tailor solutions to a case, as shown by Case 21/18, of 19 June 2019. The *Banco Popular* resolution decision was based on a *provisional* valuation by an independent expert. The Board considered that, despite the literal reading of Article 20 SRMR, which requires that an ex-post valuation be performed as soon as possible,[93] such ex-post definitive valuation was not necessary if the resolution tool (sale of business) provided a price-setting market mechanism, which replaced the provisional valuation. Any harm to shareholders due to valuation inaccuracies could be addressed through the specific valuation to determine no-creditor worse-off treatment (Valuation 3).[94] In Case T-599/18 the appellant challenged before the GCEU the Board's decision not to perform an ex-post definitive valuation.[95] In parallel, it requested the Board access to the independent expert's economic assessments for a definitive ex-post valuation of Banco Popular and European Commission documents authorizing the Board's decision or refusing authorization. The Board refused access to these documents. Its decision was appealed before the Appeal Panel. The context of the request of access in this appeal was an action before the General Court where the appellant challenged the SRB decision not to have the ex-post valuation as a violation of Article 20(11) SRMR, and argued that if there was a margin of discretion not to order the definitive valuation, the European Commission had to endorse the SRB decision pursuant to *Meroni* case law,[96] or there would be a violation of constitutional limits to delegation of powers. Notice that the Appeal Panel could not decide on compliance with *Meroni*, but this was key to frame the relevance of the request of access.

---

[93] Article 20 (10)—(11) Regulation (EU) No 806/2014 of the European Parliament and of the Council establishing uniform rules and a uniform procedure for the resolution of credit institutions and certain investment firms in the framework of a Single Resolution Mechanism and a Single Resolution Fund and amending Regulation (EU) No 1093/2010 [2014] OJ L225.
[94] ibid art 20(16).
[95] Appeal rejected as inadmissible: Case T-599/18 *Aeris Invest v SRB* ECLI:EU:T:2019:740, on appeal in Case C-874/19. On the merits, compare Case C-934/19 *Algebris and Anchorage Capital Group v SRB* ECLI:EU:T:2021:1042, finding that no ex post definitive valuation needed to be performed due to the resolution tool adopted in the specific case.
[96] Case C-21/61 *Meroni v High Authority* ECLI:EU:C:1962:12. For the constitutional implications of *Meroni* and *Romano in the EMU context* see Koen Lenaerts, 'EMU and the EU's Constitutional Framework' (2014) 39 ELR 751, 753.

Thus, the Appeal Panel clarified that (i) in its view *Meroni* case law should be understood in light of the more recent judgment of 22 March 2014, *United Kingdom v European Parliament and Council*,[97] (ii) that the power to apply rules to complex factual situations does not necessarily amount to a policy-making discretionary power, which is what was considered illegitimate in *Meroni* but (iii) no SRMR provision expressly deals with a decision *not* to perform an ex-post valuation, or the European Commission endorsement role, if any. Thus, the relevance of the existence of a Commission endorsement appeared to justify an overriding public interest in disclosure, but exposing all communications to public light would disproportionately impair internal decision-making. Thus, the Appeal Panel found a way to clarify the point, without ordering disclosure. It asked specific questions to the Board and confidentially examined internal communications. Then noted that the Board had clarified with its answers that the European Commission had not issued any authorization or endorsement of the Board's decision not to perform the ex-post valuation.

The foregoing shows that quasi-judicial review, albeit still episodical, has been repeatedly used to deliver a timely legality review, which was accepted by the parties in all cases but one for the BoA and four for the Appeal Panel.[98] This invites a pause to reflect on the lessons learnt, and potential improvements on the system's weaknesses. Of the many policy experiments of EU institutions, appeal bodies look set to stay in areas where there is a need for specialized knowledge delivered swiftly, flexibly, and impartially to balance the EU's potentially intrusive action through expert regulatory agencies with bodies that combine expert knowledge of their own with a firm anchor on fundamental rights and the rule of law. Initial experience suggests that the BoA and the Appeal Panel have ensured that appellants have 'their affairs handled impartially, fairly and within a reasonable time'.[99] What does this mean? More visibly, appellants have a timely, non-expensive, expert review which afforded proportionate protection in line with Charter Article 41, and, we venture to say, should Charter Article 47's 'fair trial' requirements be applicable to administrative review, they would be met too.[100] Less visibly, quasi-courts have tried to carve-out a place of their own in financial markets' increasingly complex architecture and governance. This requires a delicate balancing act vis-à-vis the three established players in the review system. Towards the agencies quasi-courts need to combine the independence to decide each case based on its merits (and not the downsides for the agency) with the institutional loyalty to offer precise reasons on why a decision was wrong, which help to put it right. Towards appellants, they need to be perceived as a useful device, but also send a clear message as to what they can, and cannot, review. The third relationship is with courts. While the legislature may have established quasi-courts, only the courts' interpretation of their role can grant them a stable ground to operate. Quasi-courts thus need to persuade courts that they have a relevant role to play without interfering with courts' own, that they can help 'de-clutter' the courts' table without becoming 'institutional clutter' themselves. So far, they have tried to do so by combining expediency, prudence, and willingness to penetrate the minute, often abstruse details, to dig out the real issues, which can then be re-examined by the courts. Their contribution, in this relationship with courts, is that of helping to see the forest of fundamental issues through the trees of technical points, and provide a first, quick, solution for the benefit of courts and parties alike. **13.37**

---

[97] Case C-270/12 *United Kingdom v Parliament and Council* ECLI:EU:C:2014:18, paras 44–50.
[98] Pending Cases T-16/18 *Activos e Inversiones Monterosso v SRB*, T-62/18 *Aeris Invest v SRB*, and T-514/18 *Del Valle Ruiz v SRB*; more recently see Case T-540/22 *France v SRB*.
[99] To use the words of the CJEU in Case C-439/11 P *Ziegler SA v Commission* ECLI:EU:C:2013:513, para 154.
[100] For a similar conclusion also compare Herinckx (n 35) 21.

3 Nodes of the courts' system for private law disputes in the law of finance

13.38 After analysing complexities of the courts' system for the public law disputes, we move to private law disputes. Often considered secondary for the *nature* of the interests at stake (large commercial disputes between parties that can fend for themselves) or the amounts involved (retail disputes with amounts too small to have major policy implications), they can nonetheless have a major impact on the legitimacy of the system, since they provide the best test to the system's expediency, flexibility and expertise (commercial disputes) and give the average citizen the clearest indication of how adjudication in the law of finance really works (retail). Furthermore, private disputes, although adjudicating on 'private interests' can easily have systemic effects and affect the public interest if the problem in one case is replicated across the system because many retail investors are affected, or because the problem concerns a transaction that follows standard practice.[101] We analyse first domestic practice precedents in commercial disputes (section 2.1), then small-ticket disputes and ADRs (section 2.2), and then private law disputes as a follow-up to public law disputes (section 2.3).

3.1 Private law disputes: precedents in domestic practice and hybrid international commercial courts

13.39 We begin by discussing commercial disputes, whereby we necessarily must draw on the experience of domestic systems and the growing importance of international commercial courts, since the EU has not taken a position on the issue. Here our claim for more specialized courts in the law of finance nicely intersects with a clearly visible judicial trend. A first example is the successful experience of the Financial List in the United Kingdom, a specialized list of judges set up in December 2015 to handle claims related to financial markets[102] operating as a joint initiative involving the Chancery Division and the Commercial Court in London, whose declared objective has been 'to ensure that cases which would benefit from being heard by judges with particular expertise in the financial markets or which raise issues of general importance to the financial markets are dealt with by judges with suitable expertise and experience'.[103] Yet this follows the pattern of experiences of the same breed,

---

[101] See eg David Ramos Muñoz, 'Can Complex Contract Clauses Replace Bankruptcy Principles? Why Interpretation Matters' (2018) 92 American Bankruptcy LJ 417.

[102] Pursuant to s 63A.1 of the Practice Directions to the UK Code of Civil Procedure establishing the Financial List: '(2) In this Part and Practice Direction 63AA, "Financial List claim" means any claim which—(a) principally relates to loans, project finance, banking transactions, derivatives and complex financial products, financial benchmark, capital or currency controls, bank guarantees, bonds, debt securities, private equity deals, hedge fund disputes, sovereign debt, or clearing and settlement, and is for more than [£50 million] or equivalent; (b) requires particular expertise in the financial markets; or (c) raises issues of general importance to the financial markets. (3) "Financial markets" for these purposes include the fixed income markets (covering repos, bonds, credit derivatives, debt securities and commercial paper generally), the equity markets, the derivatives markets, the loan markets, the foreign currency markets, and the commodities markets.'

[103] Guide to the Financial List (1 October 2015) A.1.2 https://assets.publishing.service.gov.uk/government/uploads/system/uploads/attachment_data/file/644030/financial-list-guide.pdf (accessed 1 September 2022). On the Financial List, compare Akima Paul Lambert, 'The Financial List: An Early Assessment' (2016) 9 JIBFL 545; Simon Bushell, 'London's Financial List: A Choice of Forum Crossroads' *PLC Magazine* (2016) https://www.lw.com/thoughtLeadership/londons-financial-list (accessed 1 September 2022). It is noteworthy that one of the distinctive features of the financial list is that it also conducts a 'pilot Financial Markets Test Case Scheme, to facilitate the resolution of market issues in relation to which immediate relevant authoritative English law guidance is needed without the need for a present cause of action between the parties to the proceedings' (s B.9.1 of the Guide).

which feature a distinct new phenomenon of global competition which has been nicely described as 'plural adjudicatory unilateralism':[104] the emergence of hybrid dispute resolution *fora*, and in particular hybrid specialized courts.[105] Among them, also recent initiatives in continental Europe in response to Brexit, all aimed at establishing specialized courts for international commercial disputes (in most cases related to financial contracts) to offer alternative judicial venues to London after the United Kingdom departure from the EU.[106] As noted by Sir William Blair:[107]

> [t]ogether, commercial courts provide: authoritative development of the content of commercial law; the essential basis upon which international arbitration functions; a specialised forum of choice for businesses that prefer courts to arbitration; a specialised forum for commercial disputes which cannot be arbitrated; a route to capacity building amongst the judiciary; procedure that can be/has been developed first in a commercial court for later wider use across a legal system; an ability both to optimise the potential of technology, and to develop it under high ethical standards; where methods of dispute resolution currently fall below best standards, the potential to raise standards across the whole system.

13.40 The institutional design of these specialized international courts which compete with international arbitration and may become 'the paradigm for the future of adjudication'[108] follows a common footprint, yet with many procedural variations.[109] In Dubai, the international commercial court, which hears disputes in English and applies common law, is composed by a Court of First Instance, with a Small Claims Tribunal attached thereto and a Court of Appeal. The Qatar International Court has a First Instance and an Appellate Circuit and is composed by (i) a Civil and Commercial Court and (ii) a Regulatory Tribunal which has jurisdiction to hear appeals against decisions of the Qatar Financial Centre Authority and other institutions. Likewise, the Abu Dhabi Court is also composed by a First Instance and a Court of Appeal. In turn, the Singapore International Commercial Court (SICC) is part of the Singapore High Court and the China International Commercial Court is a branch of the Supreme People's Court of China, which coexists with three intermediate specialized financial courts established in Shanghai, Beijing, and Chengdu/Chongqing which

---

[104] Georgios Dimitropoulos, 'International Commercial Courts in the "Modern Law of Nature": Adjudicatory Unilateralism in Special Economic Zones' (2021) 24 Journal of International Economic Law 361.

[105] For a comparative taxonomy and an insightful discussion see Dimitropoulos (n 104) 361–79; Stavros Brekoulakis and Georgios Dimitropoulos (eds), *International Commercial Courts: The Future of Transnational Adjudication* (CUP 2022). For a European perspective see XE Kramer and J Sorabji (eds), *International Business Courts: A European and Global Perspective* (Eleven International Publishing 2019).These hybrid courts have not been yet developed in the US because 'many within the United States believe that US courts, particularly federal courts, are among the best, if not the best, of any nation in the world' and that therefore 'it has no competitive disadvantage when it comes to transnational litigation'. For a discussion see SI Strong, 'International Commercial Courts and the United States: An Outlier by Choice of by Constitutional Design?' (2019) University of Missouri Legal Studies Research Paper Series No 2019-08 (where the former quote at p 9) is also cited in XE Kramer and J Sorabji (eds), *International Business Courts: A European and Global Perspective* (Eleven International Publishing 2019).

[106] Giesela Rühl, 'Building Competence in Commercial Law in the Member States' European Parliament Think Tank (14 September 2018) https://www.europarl.europa.eu/thinktank/en/document.html?reference=IPOL_STU(2018)604980 (accessed 1 September 2022) 38.

[107] William Blair, 'The New Litigation Landscape: International Commercial Courts and Procedural Innovations' (2019) 2 Intl J Procedural L 212; compare, for an Asian perspective, Firew Kebede Tiba, 'The Emergence of Hybrid International Commercial Courts and the Future of Cross Border Commercial Dispute Resolution in Asia' (2016) 14 Loyola U Ch Intl L Rev 1.

[108] Stavros Brekoulakis and Georgios Dimitropoulos (eds), *International Commercial Courts: The Future of Transnational Adjudication* (CUP 2022).

[109] Dimitropoulos (n 104).

hear both private-law and public-law financial disputes, whereas the Astana International Financial Centre Court is an international court outside the judicial system of the Republic of Kazakhstan, yet judges, who are English judges, are appointed by the President of the Republic on the recommendation of the Governor of the Astana International Financial Centre.[110]

13.41 Some EU Member States already had an international commercial court, such as the Paris international chamber at the Commercial Court (in operation since 1995 and merged in 2015 with the chamber of European Union law, established in 1999, which, however, adopted new rules of procedure in 2017 to keep pace with these international developments)[111] and others have quickly followed this new trend, creating international chambers within existing court structure, notably a chamber for international commercial matters (*Kammer für internationale Handelsachen*) within the District Court (*Landesgericht*) of Frankfurt[112] and the Netherlands Commercial Court and the Netherlands Commercial Court of Appeals at the Amsterdam District Court (*Rechtbank*) and the Court of Appeal (*Gerechtshof*). This move was also favoured by reasons 'endogenous' to the European Union: first, the European model of administration of justice is based on private international law instruments, which are conducive to *forum shopping*; secondly, Brexit and the expectation that, in the wake of it, London commercial courts would have inevitably lost their central role in the adjudication of cross-border commercial disputes in the EU context.[113] A first indication in that direction was offered by ISDA with changes in the ISDA Master Agreement for financial derivatives, now providing as jurisdiction and choice of law Dublin and Irish law and Paris and French law, respectively.[114] However, the practice of hybrid courts in Europe is still in its infancy; and yet it calls for more system-wide coordination.[115]

13.42 All this shows the importance not only of expert judgment but also of procedural specialization. International commercial courts are the tool of choice to adopt procedural innovation.[116] Elements of specialization pertaining to the procedural aspects mimic to some

---

[110] Compare Sir Rupert Jackson, 'A Comparative Perspective to Hybrid Dispute Resolution Fora: Jurisdiction, Applicable Law and Enforcement of Judgments' (Doha International Conference on the Promise of Hybrid Dispute Resolution Fora, Doha, November 2018).

[111] On 7 March 2017, the French Minister of Justice asked a special committee ('*Haut comité juridique de la place financière de Paris*' (HCJP)) to propose a court to make it easier for foreign commercial parties to present their disputes. On the basis of the works developed by that committee two protocols were signed on February 2018 to amend the procedure of the existent International Chamber and to create a new one. An International Chamber of the Paris Court of Appeal was also established.

[112] Burkhard Hess and Timon Boerner, 'Chambers for International Commercial Disputes in Germany: the State of Affairs' (2019) 1 ERALaw 33; Matthias Lehmann, 'Law Made in Germany: Quality or Lemon?' in X E Kramer and J Sorabji (eds), *International Business Courts: A European and Global Perspective* (Eleven International Publishing 2019) (on file with the author).

[113] Paul Beaumont and others, 'Cross-border Litigation in Europe: Some Theoretical Issues and Some Practical Challenges' in Paul Beaumont and others (eds), *Cross Border Litigation in Europe* (Hart Publishing 2017) 831. Hess and Boerner (n 112).

[114] Hess and Boerner (n 112) 6. The same authors find, however, that, even in the past and despite the ISDA standard, many financial instruments contained several and overlapping non-exclusive jurisdiction clauses providing not only for London but also for Frankfurt and other courts of the Continent.

[115] The Standing International Forum of Commercial Courts (SIFoCC) paved the way of such an initiative and was led by Lord Thomas of Cwmgiedd in the course of an influential series of speeches setting out the changing issues facing commercial dispute resolution. He proposed that commercial courts owe a duty to work together to underpin the rule of law: 'By bringing order to commerce and finance, a sound system of commercial dispute resolution helps to give the stability that is essential to the peace and prosperity of all our societies'. SIFoCC was set up in 2017 to share knowledge and expertise. Courts are represented often at the Chief Justice level. Compare Blair (n 107) 234.

[116] Blair (n 107) 226.

extent arbitral procedure and range from limits to over-lengthy submissions, to document production, to expert witness, to more flexible approaches to the applicable foreign law[117] and to a wider use of technology, from online case management systems (eCourt) to AI-augmented translation of evidence, documents, and real-time transcript for the hearings).[118]

13.43 International commercial courts' unilateralism responds to global competition not only from arbitration but also from ordinary courts long established in leading jurisdictions like the US. Those courts followed however a distinct path of specialization whose most clear examples are, notably, the United States District Court for the Southern District of New York (SDNY), a Federal Court established as early as 1789, and the New York Commercial Division of the Supreme Court, a state court established in 1995 as a forum to resolution for complex commercial disputes (including 'business transactions involving or arising out of dealings with commercial banks and other financial institutions': section 202.70 Rules of the Commercial Division of the Supreme Court). The New York Commercial Division blazed a judicial trail. In the words of the Chief Judge's Task Force on Commercial Litigation in the twenty-first century:[119]

> [T]oday, the judges of the Commercial Division adjudicate thousands of cases and motions that include some of the most important, complex commercial disputes being litigated anywhere. This is especially true in the wake of the financial crisis ... Additionally, a host of other states have followed New York's lead, creating new commercial courts to attract both business disputes and businesses in their jurisdictions. In 2010 even Delaware, whose Chancery Court remains a leader in the world of corporate law, created in its Superior Court a new Complex Commercial Litigation Division.

More than a dozen states, through special legislation (as in Michigan and Oklahoma) or via administrative orders of the judicial branch,[120] have meanwhile set up trial courts or courts divisions for business litigation or for complex litigation.

3.2 Mass, small-ticket disputes, and the role of alternative dispute resolution (ADR)

13.44 Another sub-set of private law disputes that, in turn, shows the merits of specialization in the law of finance is that of mass, small ticket disputes. At the outset one should recall that Regulation (EC) No. 861/2007 has established a European small claims procedure (ESCP) as a simplified adversarial mechanism for the collection of debt (along with the European Enforcement Order established by Regulation (EC) No. 805/2004 for uncontested claims). The ESCP has been 'the first fully adversarial European procedure'[121] and, despite its slow

---

[117] ibid.
[118] ibid.
[119] Commercial Division Justices Supreme Court of the State of New York, *Report and Recommendations to the Chief Judge of the State of New York* (June 2012) 1.
[120] Anne Tucker Nees, 'Making a Case for Business Courts: A Survey of and Proposed Framework to Evaluate Business Courts' (2007) 24 Georgia State U L Rev 477.
[121] Cristian Oro Martinez, 'The Small Claims Regulation: On the Way to an Improved European Procedure?' in Burkhard Hess, Maria Bergström, and Eva Storskrubb (eds), *EU Civil Justice: Current Issues and Future Outlook* (Hart Publishing 2015) 123. Compare also Pablo Cortes, 'Enforcing EU consumer policy more effectively: a three-pronged approach' in Sara Drake and Melanie Smith (eds), *New Directions in the Effective Enforcement of EU Law and Policy* (Edward Elgar Publishing 2016) 202–230.

start,[122] it clearly illustrates that the general principle of procedural autonomy does not prevent, where justified, the establishment of specific European procedures (most notably if the cross-border nature of the dispute so requires) Interestingly, the ESPC also confirms that the European legislators can establish simplified, swift, and efficient European court procedures, mostly based on an appraisal of documents and with certain limitations to the right to be heard at a hearing.[123] EU case law on the ESPC is, however, still relatively scant.[124]

13.45 The Directive on alternative dispute resolution of commercial disputes (2013/11/EU) enjoined Member States to set up a comprehensive institutional framework for consumer alternative dispute resolution (ADR)[125] and a parallel mechanism was introduced for *online* dispute resolution by Regulation (EC) no 524/2013.[126] The ADR Directive had as main objective 'to introduce an institutional framework for ADR in the Member States, which shall complement the ('traditional') adjudication of consumer disputes by civil courts', and to make it 'less expensive and faster than court proceedings'.[127] Member States have implemented the Directive setting up one or more national schemes to provide consumers with easy access to alternative dispute resolution; in the law of finance, the 'FIN-NET initiative'[128] was set up by the European Commission as early as 2001 to promote cooperation among national ombudsmen in financial services and to facilitate consumers in their access to ADR in cross-border disputes about provision of financial services.[129] A Memorandum of Understanding regulates the cooperation among FIN-NET members.

13.46 The institutional design of ADR national schemes for mass financial disputes in the FIN-NET context offers a wide range of alternative models.[130] Half of the national schemes are set up on a voluntary basis; half by law. Three-quarters of them have public nature. In most cases, participation to the scheme is compulsory for financial intermediaries. Nearly half of the schemes are sector-specific for banks. In most cases, access to the scheme is available to consumers and professionals; in some countries, however, only certain classes of professionals

---

[122] Oro Martinez (n 121) 124, pointing out several causes for a slow start of the instrument in most jurisdictions, but for the Netherlands and Spain. Rafael Manko, 'European Small Claims Procedure Legal analysis of the Commission's Proposal to Remedy Weaknesses in the Current System' European Parliament Think Tank (November 2014) 18.
[123] Article 5 of the Regulation states that it is the court that must consider if the hearing is necessary even if parties request such an hearing, refusing such a request if the court considers it 'obviously not necessary for the fair conduct of the proceedings'. See also Oro Martinez (n 121); Case C-619/10 *Trade Agency Ltd v Seramico Investments Ltd* EU:C:2012:531, para 55.
[124] Case C-554/17 *Rebecka Jonsson v Société du Journal L'Est Républicain* ECLI:EU:C:2019:124; Case C-627/17 *ZSE Energia as v RG* ECLI:EU:C:2018:941.
[125] Burkhard Hess, 'The State of the Civil Justice Union' in Burkhard Hess, Maria Bergström, and Eva Storskrubb (eds), *EU Civil Justice: Current Issues and Future Outlook* (Hart Publishing 2015) 6.
[126] Compare Jim Davies, 'ADR/ODR: Too Much Optimism in the Promotion of Cross-Border Trade?' in Burkhard Hess, Maria Bergström, and Eva Storskrubb (eds), *EU Civil Justice: Current Issues and Future Outlook* (Hart Publishing 2015) 36–56.
[127] Hess (n 125) 7. For a comprehensive discussion of legal tools for collective redress compare now Christopher Hodges and Stefaan Voet, *Delivering Collective Redress: New Technologies* (Hart Publishing 2018) (.
[128] European Commission, 'Financial Dispute Resolution Network: FIN-NET' https://ec.europa.eu/info/business-economy-euro/banking-and-finance/consumer-finance-and-payments/consumer-financial-services/financial-dispute-resolution-network-fin-net_en (accessed 1 September 2022).
[129] For the finding that any civil justice system which is less than effective in providing remedies for private parties in cross-border civil and commercial cases reduces also the effectiveness of ADR in cross-border cases see Mihail Danov and Stefania Bariatti, 'The Relationship between Litigation and ADR: Evaluating the Effect of the EU PIL Framework on ADR/Settlement in Cross-Border Cases' in Paul Beaumont and others (eds), *Cross Border Litigation in Europe* (Hart Publishing 2017) 707.
[130] Costanza Alessi, 'The Fin-Net Survey' (Fin-Net Plenary Meeting, 13 June 2018); Banca d'Italia –Arbitro Bancario Finanziario, *The Banking and Financial Ombudsman Annual Report* (Abridged Version, no 8/2017, Rome, June 2018) 44–48.

(eg SMEs), or only a sub-set of financial disputes with professionals are admitted (eg in Germany, where ADR is available for professionals for complaints relating to payment services). The ADR decision is taken by experts; in some schemes by a single person; in others by a panel or by a single person or a panel depending on the complexity of the case.[131] Some national schemes are also supported by national competent supervisory authority, like in Spain and in Italy yet with functional separation from the supervisory tasks. The ADR procedure is usually based solely on documentary evidence. Workload is very country-specific, depending also on cultural factors and different histories and traditions of each national scheme (the oldest being the Swedish National Board for Consumer Disputes dating back to 1968): the English scheme was by far the one with the largest workload and the Italian the second largest (with currently over 30,000 yearly complaints). The average number of annual complaints is over 11,500 claims.

The interaction of this node of dispute resolution with the court system remains somehow insufficiently harmonized,[132] and the ADR Directive is silent on this. In the FIN-NET context,[133] most national schemes provide that the ADR decision is non-binding and the parties are still free to take the dispute before the competent courts if they are not content with the outcome of the ADR.[134] Non-compliance with the ADR decision is however made public and in some cases (such as in the UK and in Germany), schemes have to report to the competent authorities violations of applicable law detected in the ADR context. In a minority of national schemes, however, the ADR decision is binding, with further national variations: if accepted as a valid decision by the client in Germany, if accepted as a valid decision by the financial institution in Denmark, or if accepted in advance by both parties in the Netherlands. In Portugal, the ADR decision, if not implemented by the parties spontaneously, may be eventually enforced by the court. Finally, only in a minority of national schemes, ADR decisions can be appealed within the ADR system itself. **13.47**

Despite its broad-brush approach, this helicopter view identifies a point crucial for our analysis and notably that the level of harmonization is still low for mass claims ADR in the law of finance. Although there are distinct commonalities, each Member State has exercised different options within the broad frame of the ADR Directive. Yet, we claim that in principle schemes of ADR in the law of finance, if duly regarded in their true substance, are to be considered specialized quasi-courts. This is particularly true, where their expert decisions are legally binding upon the parties. **13.48**

Yet, this remains, in our view, also true for those schemes whose decisions are formally non-binding, because non-compliance is made public (and thus has a strong reputational cost) and, in practice, parties implement ADR decisions, albeit non-binding, in almost all cases. The Italian practice of the Arbitro Bancario Finanziario (the Banking and Financial Ombudsman)[135] and of the 'Arbitro Conciliatore Finanziario' (the Capital Markets Ombudsman, established by the Italian securities supervisor CO.N.SO.B for securities small claims)[136] is insightful in several respects. First, although the decisions of the Arbitro **13.49**

---

[131] Banca d'Italia–Arbitro Bancario Finanziario (n 130) 44-48.
[132] Hess (n 125) 7.
[133] Banca d'Italia–Arbitro Bancario Finanziario (n 130).
[134] Case C-75/16 *Menini v Banco Popolare* ECLI:EU:C:2017:457; and Case C-317/08 *Alassini v Telecom Italia* ECLI:EU:C:2010:146.
[135] See art 128-bis of Legislative Decree No 385/2003 and CICR delegated regulation of 18 June 2009.
[136] See art 32-bis of Legislative Decree No 58/1998 (TUF) as inserted by Legislative Decree No 164/2007 implementing art 53 MiFID (Directive 2004/39/EC of the European Parliament and of the Council on markets in

Bancario are legally non-binding and recourse to the ADR does not prevent the parties from bringing an action before the competent court if they disagree with the decision of the Arbitro, the number of disputes filed with civil courts after a decision of the Arbitro Bancario on the same matter between the same parties is less than 1 per cent. In the vast majority of these few cases, the results reached by the original decision of the Arbitro Bancario are finally upheld by civil courts.[137] This indicates that, but for truly exceptional cases, the decisions of the Arbitro Bancario are final and where the review of the court is tantamount an appeal and this seems to us to justify the conclusion that also formally non-binding decisions have, in substance, adjudicatory nature. This raises the question, if substance has to prevail over form, whether the quasi-courts of the Arbitro Bancario Finanziario would not deserve, as a matter of policy, to be equated to courts to the effect of judicial dialogue under Article 267 TFEU.[138] Secondly, also quasi-courts for private law disputes such as the Arbitro Bancario, in a context characterized by a complex subject matter, a convoluted set of facts and normative framework, and arcane nature of the problem, can contribute on one hand to legal certainty, by means of a loyal alignment with the relevant case law of the Italian Supreme Court[139] and, on the other hand, to understand the problem and to differentiate marginal, or borderline cases from pivotal cases (and then carefully handle the latter) and this process of analysis helps 'depurate' the minutiae and identify any seminal aspects of the dispute, so that the case's focal point cannot be missed. Thirdly, dealing with mass disputes is possible because there is the efficient assistance of a structured technical secretariat. Each panel of the Arbitro Bancario is assisted by expert staff provided by the Bank of Italy which, like law clerks for courts, assists the panel in handling the cases and preparing the decisions. This can explain how only seven (regional) panels can do justice to roughly 30,000 cases each year within six months from the filing of the complaint.

3.3 Private law disputes as a follow-up of public law disputes

13.50 Finally, there are instances which exemplify the intersection between public and private law disputes in the law of finance. Perhaps the more salient example are the private claims for damages grounded on statements of facts and law made in supervisory decisions confirmed by a final court judgment in a public law dispute.[140] This is an aspect typically exacerbated in the class action context. Indeed, as we noted elsewhere,[141] where the nature of the damage caused is the same, eg if the claims are grounded in the falsity of the information contained in a single prospectus as ascertained by the competent supervisor or in other mis-conducts sanctioned by the competent supervisor that have allegedly caused a direct damage to private

---

financial instruments amending Council Directives 85/611/EEC and 93/6/EEC and Directive 2000/12/EC of the European Parliament and of the Council and repealing Council Directive 93/22/EEC [21 April 2004] OJ L 145).

[137] Banca d'Italia–Arbitro Bancario Finanziario (n 130) 36.
[138] Yet the Italian Constitutional Court, with judgment no 218 of 21 July 2011, held that the Arbitro Bancario Finanziario cannot refer a question of constitutionality to the Italian Constitutional Court, because its panels are not 'judges' and 'courts' since, formally, their decisions are not legally binding upon the parties.
[139] ABF, Collegio di coordinamento, decision no 7440 (5 April 2018).
[140] For the finding that supervisory assessment of Bank of Italy has only relative evidentiary force (and thus facts are not *irrefutably established as a matter of evidence* and the civil court can deviate from the supervisory findings, relying also on expert witnesses), compare in Italy Corte di Cassazione, decision no 13679 *Banca popolare di Napoli* (30 May 2018).
[141] Marco Lamandini and David Ramos Muñoz, *EU Financial Law: An Introduction* (Wolters Kluwer 2016) 471.

parties, coordination in civil action may prove an effective procedural tool to promote private enforcement and can take place through the mechanism for class actions. Class actions and private litigation also display therefore a regulatory function and serve as an instrument of regulation by litigation, to the extent that the prospect of having to pay private damages can exert additional pressure on the addressees of specific rules of conduct to refrain from undesirable conducts prohibited by regulation (in theory deterrence should in this way reach its apex and become socially optimal).

However, unlike in the US, the European *acquis* on collective actions is still (almost) at its infancy and class actions are still a domain of national procedural autonomy and minimum harmonization.[142] The European Commission conducted a public consultation in 2011,[143] and the European Parliament adopted a resolution in 2012,[144] which were followed by a Commission Communication and Recommendations in 2013,[145] which offered a model and identified some of the main legal issues. However, despite asking Member States to implement changes in their legislation by 2015, the process proved unsuccessful. Moreover, the analysis was limited to consumer and competition cases. Crucially, the European initiative said nothing about the private international law dimensions of cross-border class actions, leaving unanswered several thorny issues.[146] Some Member States introduced a national class action[147] also to redress damages in the field of finance,[148] but none followed the Commission's model. Thus, in April 2018 the European Commission included a new model in a new proposal[149] as part of a 'New Deal for Consumers'.[150] Under the new

13.51

---

[142] Compare Arnaud Nuyts and Nikita E Hatzimihail (eds), *Cross-Border Class Actions: The European Way* (Sellier European Law Publishers 2014) 1–325; specifically on class actions in the law of finance see Natalia A Kapetanaki, 'Transnational Securities Fraud Class Actions: Looking Towards Europe?' in Arnaud Nuyts and Nikita E Hatzimihail (eds), *Cross-Border Class Actions: The European Way* (Sellier European Law Publishers 2014) 277).

[143] European Commission Communication, 'Commission Work Programme 2010. Time to Act' (31 March 2010) COM(2010) 135.

[144] European Parliament, 'Towards a coherent European approach to collective redress' Resolution of 2 February 2012 (2011/2089(INI)).

[145] European Commission Communication, 'Towards a European horizontal framework for collective redress' (11 June 2013) COM(2013) 401 final; and European Comission Recommendation on common principles for injunctive and compensatory collective redress mechanisms in the Member States concerning violations of rights granted under Union Law [2013] OJ L201 (hereafter Commission Recommendation).

[146] Ralf Michaels, 'European Class Action and Applicable Law' in Arnaud Nuyts and Nikita E Hatzimihail (eds), *Cross-Border Class Actions: The European Way* (Sellier European law Publishers 2014) 111, 140–41; Brigitte Haar, 'Regulation through Litigation—Collective Redress in Need of a New Balance Between Individual Rights and Regulatory Objectives in Europe' (2018) 19 Theoretical Inquiries in L 203 (noting, at 211, that the EU collective action can be used for injunction procedures but in principle it does 'not lead to financial damages being awarded to consumers, except in the cases of, for example, France, Germany, Greece and the United Kingdom'); Fabrizio Cafaggi, 'Towards Collaborative Governance of European Remedial and Procedural Law' (2018) 19 Theoretical Inquiries in L 235.

[147] Haar (n 146) 211–30 (for a reference to France, Belgium, the Netherlands, the United Kingdom, and Germany).

[148] ibid 216–17, referring to mass claims for losses allegedly suffered by retail investors in the *Dexia* case (Hof's Amsterdam 25 January 2007, NJ 2007, 427) and in the *DSB Bank* case (Hof's Amsterdam 4 November 2014, JOR 2015, 10) in The Netherlands. An important tool to handle with mass litigation in the financial sector has proved the adoption of test cases: this was developed by way of practice in the United Kingdom, for instance by the Office of Fair Trading in the Bank charges litigation (Haar (n 146)) and by way of statutory provision by Germany, in the wake of the massive litigation triggered by alleged misrepresentations in the Telekom prospectus (compare Kapitalanleger-Musterverfahrengesetz [KapMuG] of 16 August 2005: Haar (n 146) 225–30). Guidance of the CJEU in this context has been strong: see Case C-618/10 *Banco Espanol de Credito v Joaquin Calderon Camino* ECLI:EU:C:2012:349; Case C-381/14 *Jorge Sales Sinues v Caixabank SA* ECLI:EU:C:2016:252; Case C-421/14 *Banco Primus Sa v Jesus Gutierrez Garcia* ECLI: U:C:2017:60; see also Cafaggi (n 146) 242–43.

[149] Proposal for a Directive of the European Parliament and of the Council on representative actions for the protection of the collective interests of consumers, and repealing Directive 2009/22/EC [2018] COM(2018) 184.

[150] Communication from the Commission to the European Parliament, the Council and the European Economic and Social Committee, A New Deal for Consumers [2018] COM(2018) 183.

proposal 'qualified entities' are empowered to bring representative actions in court on behalf of consumers to protect the general interests and these actions should also include redress. Although some commentators argued that the proposal 'was superfluous' being 'based on a model of private enforcement through court litigation' unsuitable to consumers, rather than on alternative consumers' collective redress techniques, such as those 'approved by UNCTAD and spreading at Member State level and in Australia', notably reliance on redress powers given to regulatory authorities[151] and consumer ombudsmen',[152] the proposal made its way through the legislative process and was finally adopted in November 2020 as Directive (EU) 2020/1828 on representative actions for the protection of the collective interests of consumers. Under Directive (EU) 2020/1828, 'qualified entities' can bring representative actions to seek redress in national courts against infringements of specific, consumer-related provisions of EU law, including the area of the law of finance. By laying down only certain minimum requirements, the directive still leaves the Member States a wide discretion in implementing the directive and is likely to prompt regulatory competition because 'qualified entities' are granted some forum shopping because they are entitled under the directive to bring cross-border actions out of their home Member State, provided that the other Member State has jurisdiction over the action filed (something that occurs where the defendant has its registered office, or a branch, or where the consumer is domiciled, in this way opening up a multitude of possible fora).

13.52 In the US, in contrast, class actions are a popular mechanism for some time,[153] especially after the enactment of rule 23 of Federal Rules of Civil Procedure in 1938 (39 FRD 69), which, with subsequent changes, introduced the basic requirements for a class action to prosper: numerosity, commonality, typicality and adequate representation;[154] and the four requirements where they can be entertained (basically, related to the risk of inconsistent judgments, and appropriateness and superiority of the class action and commonality of issues between the claims).[155] Naturally, the US class action is not free from problems, not least in the field of securities litigation, where it has become extremely popular. One of them is the potential for its opportunistic use in frivolous lawsuits designed to extract large settlements, regardless of the merit of the claim. This led to the enactment of restrictions under the Private Securities Litigation Reform Act (PSLRA) in 1995, which restricted the cases where a party purchased a security under the direction of plaintiff's counsel, or accepted payment for serving as representative party on behalf of a class, and established a presumption

---

[151] Leveraging also on the new powers now conferred by Regulation (EU) 2017/2394 on cooperation between national authorities responsible for the enforcement of consumer protection law (repealing Regulation 2006/2004 (12 December 2017). For a discussion see also Cafaggi (n 146) 246.

[152] Christopher Hodges, 'Collective Redress: The Need for New Technologies' (2019) 42 J Consumer Pol 59, 86–87; for a more comprehensive discussion see Hodges and Voet (n 127).

[153] As far back as the seventeenth century. See SC Yeazell, 'Group Litigation and Social Context: Toward a History of the Class Action' (1977) 77 Col L Rev 866. For an updated account of the current status of class action in the United States, Arthur R Miller, 'The American Class Action: From Birth to Maturity' (2018) 19 Theoretical Inquiries in L 1, as well as several other contributions in the same monographic issue of Theoretical Inquiries in Law 19(1) https://www.degruyter.com/journal/key/til/19/1/html (accessed 2 September 2022), covering class actions in Israel, Europe, Australia, Canada, and China.

[154] Federal Rules of Civil Procedure in 1938 (39 FRD 69) r 23(a)(1)–(4).

[155] First, when there is a risk of inconsistent adjudication creating incompatible standards of conduct for the party opposing the class; secondly, when adjudications regarding individual class members would be dispositive or affect the interests of other members not parties to the adjudication; thirdly, when the party opposing the class has acted or refused to act on grounds that apply generally to the class, so that final injunctive relief or corresponding declaratory relief is appropriate respecting the class as a whole; and fourthly, when there are questions of law or fact common to class members that predominate over any questions affecting only individual members and the class action is a superior method of adjudication. Federal Rules of Civil Procedure in 1938 (39 FRD 69) r 23(b)(1)—(4).

to determine the lead plaintiff in favour of the party with the largest financial interest at stake.[156] Also troubling is the third-party funding of those suits.[157] Even leaving these issues aside, class-actions are not simply cases where different claims are grouped: they involve a completely different type of procedure, led by counsel with potentially little engagement by the client, and with a diversity of interests such that it can give rise to important agency problems. The governance of the class action is done through due process rights, such as the right to notice, the right to be heard, and the right to opt out,[158] but these can look limited in light of class-action complexity.[159]

13.53 These objections explain the measured approach followed by the Commission and the European co-legislators. It also explains that legal texts that have harmonized the issue of damages in fields particularly prone to class-litigation, such as the Directive on Damages in competition cases, do not introduce provisions on collective redress.[160] Looking forward, however, class actions in the law of finance may become an interesting example of forum competition in Europe. On one hand, in 2010 the US Supreme Court, in *Morrison*,[161] rejecting case law of the last four decades, considered that securities fraud class actions based on section 10(b) of the Securities and Exchange Act of 1934 could not have extraterritorial application, thus stopping a long lasting practice of litigation before US courts of investment disputes brought by foreign plaintiffs suing foreign and American defendants for misconduct in connection with securities traded on foreign exchanges. On the other hand, some Member States, and notably the Netherlands, started an aggressive strategy to attract collective settlements in case of securities fraud in Europe.[162]

13.54 Yet, for our purposes, the parallel with Directive 2014/104/EU and the action for damages in the competition cases give pause for thought beyond the issue of class actions, to reflect on other evolutionary aspects of the EU system of civil justice. A reflection is necessary to explore the meaning (a) first of the judicial finding in *Courage*[163] of a cause of action derived from the 'constructive ambiguity' of the relevant provisions in the Treaty,[164] (b) then of the

---

[156] 15 USC s 78u-4(2)(A) and (3)(A), among other provisions.
[157] Deborah Hensler, 'Third-Party Financing of Class-Action Litigation in the United States: Will the Sky Fall?' (2014) De Paul L Rev 63, 499, who nonetheless holds a sceptic view about the potential risks.
[158] Federal Rules of Civil Procedure, r 23(b)(3) in 1938 (39 FRD 69).
[159] See John C Coffee Jr, 'Class Action Accountability: Reconciling Exit, Voice, and Loyalty in Representative Litigation' (2000) 100 Col L Rev 370; and, by the same author John C Coffee Jr, 'The Regulation of Entrepreneurial Litigation: Balancing Fairness and Efficiency in the Large Class Action' (1987) 54 U of Chi L Rev 877; Alexandra Lahav, 'Fundamental Principles for Class Action Governance' (2003) 37 Indiana L Rev 65.
[160] Directive 2014/104/EU on certain rules governing actions for damages under national law for infringements of the competition law provisions of the Member States and of the European Union [2014] OJ L349, recital 13: '[T]his Directive should not require Member States to introduce collective redress mechanisms for the enforcement of arts 101 and 102 TFEU.'
[161] *Morrison v National Australia Bank* 130 S Ct 2869, 561 US (2010).
[162] Compare Kapetanaki (n 142) 286–90; Burkhard Hess, 'Collective Redress and the Jurisdictional Model of the Brussels I Regulation' in Arnaud Nuyts and Nikita E Hatzimihail (eds), *Cross-Border Class Actions: The European Way* (Sellier European law Publishers 2014) 64–67.
[163] Case C-453/99 *Courage v Bernard Crehan* ECLI:EU:C:2001:465.
[164] For a law and economics perspective see Roberto Pardolesi, 'Private Enforcement of Antitrust Law' in Thomas Eger and Hans-Bernd Schäfer (eds), *Research Handbook on the Economics of European Union Law* (Edward Elgar Publishing 2012) 289, 297–300; for a legitimacy reading, building on the role that essential legal values enshrined in the law of Member States, for instance on the overall balance between plaintiffs and defendants in actions for damages, had in downplaying private litigation see Carlo Petrucci, 'Effective Private Enforcement of EU Competition Law: An Input and Output Legitimacy Analysis of Collective Redress' in Sara Drake and Melanie Smith (eds), *New Directions in the Effective Enforcement of EU Law and Policy* (Edward Elgar Publishing 2016) 231–55.

resulting policy-making partnership,[165] (c) which finally led to the adoption of Directive 2014/104 with its troublesome interaction between public and private enforcement where statements of facts and of law made in the context of public enforcement are also relevant for private actions.[166] Here there is a visible tension between two interests that is difficult to reconcile. On one hand, Directive 2014/104 sets out clear limits, in Article 6, to the access to the competition authority file and refuses disclosure of evidence to a private litigant if the request for access to documents arise in the context of a leniency application or a settlement submission; it also imposes, in Article 7, strict limits on the court's admissibility of evidence whenever this was obtained via the access to the file of a competition authority. Notably:

> [T]hese provisions indicate a strong desire by the Commission, and by the Member States, to safeguard the operation of public enforcement mechanisms and hence the continuing attractiveness of EU and national leniency programmes ... This is an instance of the collective interest in the public enforcement of competition law being justifiably prioritized over the individual interest of a private enforcer.[167]

13.55 On the other hand, the directive provides, in Article 9, that Member States must ensure that final decisions made by their national competition authorities are deemed to be irrefutably established as a matter of evidence for the purposes of a damages action heard in their national courts. Only if the decision is produced in another Member State, the Member State in receipt of the 'foreign' final decision must treat it as (only) prima facie evidence that an infringement of the relevant competition law has occurred.[168]

13.56 It is apparent, in our view, that administrative decisions acting as an 'evidentiary bridge' between the public and private disputes and enforcement may have troublesome implications for the respect of the fundamental right to a fair trial and an effective judicial remedy, if the procedural safeguards granted to the defendant before the administrative authorities and, in their possible second stage before the review courts, would not ensure all necessary procedural guarantees of fair trial and an exacting standard of review.[169] It should also be noted that to the extent that the Directive on Antitrust Damages may be found in compliance with the Charter of Fundamental Rights, it may still pose other problems. Some national constitutions require that the factual evidence necessary to decide a case is formed before the court, which can raise a question of national constitutional counter-limits. These problems become even more acute when public action is triggered by leniency programmes, which shield the

---

[165] See Commission Recommendation on common principles for injunctive and compensatory collective redress mechanisms in the Member States concerning violations of rights granted under Union Law [2013] OJ L201/06, European Commission Communication, 'Towards a European horizontal framework for collective redress' COM(2013) 401 final and European Commission Communication, 'Quantifying harm in actions for damages based on breaches of Article 101 or 102 TFEU' [2013] OJ C167/19.

[166] Jonathan Fitchen, 'Private Enforcement of Competition Law' in Paul Beaumont and others (eds), *Cross Border Litigation in Europe* (Hart Publishing 2017) 671.

[167] ibid 679.

[168] ibid 680. In Case C-267/20 *AB Volvo and DAF Trucks NV v RM* ECLI:EU:C:2022:494 the Court held that art 9(1) constitutes a substantive, and not a procedural rule; in Case C-25/21 *Repsol Comercial de Productos Petrolíferos* ECLI:EU:C:2022:659 Advocate General Pitruzzella concluded that where Directive 2014/104 does not apply—because art 9 cannot be applied retroactively to situations existing before the entry into force of the Directive—it is for the Member States, making use of procedural autonomy, to determine the probative value of decisions of the national competition authorities, provided that the principles of equivalence and effectiveness are observed.

[169] Compare art 7(1) of D Lgs 3/2017 implementing in Italy Directive 2007/104/EU, which requires a demanding standard of review over the antitrust decision by the reviewing court to allow its evidentiary effects in a private law dispute for damages: 'il sindacato del giudice del ricorso comporta la verifica diretta dei fatti posti a fondamento della decisione impugnata e si estende anche ai profili tecnici che non presentano un oggettivo margine di opinabilità il cui esame sia necessario per giudicare la legittimità della decisione medesima.'

reporting party from the application of sanctions but not from the payment of damages (albeit, in the United States, they exclude at least treble damages)[170] and where the administrative sanction is based on a presumption of fault once the violation of an antitrust provision is ascertained, whereas under the applicable civil liability regime negligence has to be proved by the plaintiff, something which, however, is not an absolute rule, and for instance in Italy fault can be presumed in unfair competition cases.

13.57 The same problematic interaction between public and private disputes holds true, in the law of finance and at the European level, in the field of credit rating agencies, where the Credit Rating Agency Regulation (Regulation (EU) No. 1060/2009, as amended and complemented in 2013, CRAR), provides for both public and private enforcement. Similar interactions, however, can also occur in the context of alleged violations of market abuse or MiFID requirements or prospectus false information, although there is no harmonized European cause for private action in those contexts.[171] An example of the troublesome interaction between these two levels of enforcement in the context of CRAR was offered in the *Nordic Banks* 'shadow rating' case decided by the Board of Appeal in 2019.[172] In that case, since the ESMA decisions held that the banks had negligently infringed the CRAR requirements by publishing shadow ratings and this may have triggered private claims for damages under Article 35a CRAR, if one or more investors could establish that they had reasonably relied on those shadow ratings and had suffered damages therefrom unless the Board of Appeal had not found reversed the finding of negligence.

13.58 However, even if the regulatory decision provides a prima facie basis for liability, there is potential friction between the findings from a private law—and a public law—perspective and the CJEU has only just recently started to address the potential complexities of the interaction between public law and private law disputes and its implications for effective judicial protection. This occurred, for instance, albeit in a very different context (and possibly in an opposite direction), in *Hochtief AG v Budapest Fovaros Onkormanyzata*,[173] where the Court accepted that the annulment of a decision on public procurement could be considered by the applicable national law as a precondition for an action for damages, provided, however, that the action for annulment complies with the requirements of effective judicial protection. In the context of rating agencies, however, in public law the focus is in the breaching party's conduct; in private law, it is also in the plaintiff, its position vis-à-vis the defendant, and its duty to perform its own due diligence. Different countries tend to distinguish between the positioning or relationship between the parties, as a *threshold* matter (for English courts, if there was not an assumption of responsibility by the party making the statement, there was

---

[170] Pardolesi (n 164) 298.
[171] Compare Danny Busch, Guido Ferrarini, and Jan Paul Franx (eds), *Prospectus Regulation & Prospectus Liability* (OUP 2020); Danny Busch and Cees van Dam, *A Bank's Duty of Care* (Hart Publishing 2017); Danny Busch, Laura Macgregor, and Peter Watts (eds), *Agency Law in Commercial Practice* (OUP 2016) and, more recently, Danny Busch, 'The Influence of EU Prospectus Rules on Private Law' (2021) 16 CMLJ 3; Danny Busch, 'Self-placement, Dealing on Own Account and the Provision of Investment Services under MIFID I & II' (2019) 14 CMLJ 4; Danny Busch, 'The Private Law Effect of the EU Market Abuse Regulation' (2019) 14 CMLJ 296; and Danny Busch, 'The Private Law Effect of MIFID: The Genil Case and Beyond' (2017) 13 ERCL 70; Federico della Negra, *MiFID II and Private Law: Enforcing EU Conduct of Business Rules* (Hart Publishing 2019); *Private and public enforcement of EU investor protection regulation*, (Quaderni di Ricerca Giuridica della Consulenza Legale Banca d'Italia, No 90, 2020) (in particular on the interplay between public and private enforcement, Raffaele D'Ambrosio, 81–96).
[172] BoA D in Cases 1/18, 2/18, 3/18 and 4/18 *Nordic Banks v ESMA* (27 February 2019) https://www.esma.europa.eu/ (accessed 2 September 2022).
[173] Case C-300/17 *Hochtief* ECLI:EU:C:2018:635.

no liability[174]) and reliance, as a *fine-tuning* matter, depending on the circumstances, notably the status of the plaintiff as a sophisticated investor or not, but also others. The CRAR establishes that an investor can sue when it has 'reasonably relied' on the rating, which suggests the 'fine-tuning' approach, which weighs the status and behavior of the plaintiff. Yet, it may be interesting to see if some courts also use the requirement of 'reasonable reliance' to also introduce the threshold matter, with regard to the parties' respective positions. This can also give rise to an interesting conundrum, because, to some, the assessment of the defendant's relative position vis-à-vis the plaintiff is less based on an assessment of individual circumstances, and more on a *policy* need to limit the circle of potential plaintiffs. If a court were to adopt such an approach this could create friction, because the CRAR is supposed to have taken the balance of interests into consideration when adopting its solution, ie any 'policy' perspective should be based on the CRAR, and not on private law courts' independent assessment. This is the kind of closely interwoven matter where the legal expertise of a specialized court would also benefit from the smooth coordination of a network of courts supported by the necessary background of rules that could ensure that the private law solution is consistent with the public policy behind the rules, and still respectful with domestic tradition.

4 Specialized financial courts and arbitration: friends or foes? Nuances between commercial and investment arbitration, and their relationship to private and public law disputes

13.59 Commercial courts compete with arbitration. International commercial courts can be 'partly a response to the backlash against commercial and investment arbitration'.[175] The permanent nature of the court (with its implications on independence) is one advantage of courts over arbitration, and the general rule of public disclosure of judgments and their contribution to the development of a consistent, stable and predictable case law another one.[176] Yet, for financial disputes arbitration schemes traditionally offer the advantages of a smoother enforcement of the award thanks to the 1958 New York Convention[177] and of confidentiality. A relatively recent and distinct development is specialized arbitration offered by the Panel of Recognized International Market Experts in Finance (PRIME Finance), administered since 2011 by the PRIME Finance Stichting in The Hague.[178] Other established examples of arbitration in the law of finance are those of the Financial Markets Group of the American

---

[174] Such 'assumption of responsibility' can only exist if the relationship is 'akin to contract'. *Hedley Byrne v Heller Hedley Byrne & Co Ltd v Heller & Partners Ltd* [1964] AC 465 (HL), and confirmed in *Caparo Industries v Dickman* [1990] 2 AC 605.
[175] Jackson, 'Hybrid Dispute Resolution Fora' (n 116) 34.
[176] For a discussion of the legitimacy crisis of the arbitration in recent years, compare Luca Pantaleo, *The Participation of the EU in International Dispute Settlement: Lessons from EU Investments Agreements* (Springer 2019) 71–78.
[177] Many bilateral instruments exist between individual states for the enforcement of judgments and some multilateral instruments, including the Brussels Regulation between Member States of the European Union. There is, however, no equivalent of the New York Convention on the Recognition and Enforcement of Foreign Arbitral Awards and its almost universal applicability, or the ICSID Convention for investment arbitration. However, in 2019, the Hague Conference on Private International Law finalized a Convention on the Recognition and enforcement of foreign judgments in civil or commercial matters.
[178] PRIME Finance https://primefinancedisputes.org/ (accessed 2 September 2022).

Arbitration Association and the Banking and Financial Services Committee of CPR,[179] and in Asia the Singapore International Commercial Court (SICC).

13.60 Arbitration is an extremely powerful and useful device, which, due to its flexibility, expediency, and the expertise of those involved in it, has replaced litigation as the preferred dispute resolution mechanism in almost every commercial sector, notably in construction, energy, and commercial contracts. Yet, we say 'almost' intentionally, because it is interesting to note that financial disputes are still the main, if not the only type of commercial disputes where parties remain reluctant to resort to arbitration. A 2013 Queen Mary University International Arbitration Survey showed that litigation was the preferred choice of financial parties,[180] possibly thanks to the reputation of London courts as reliable decision-makers, a reputation enhanced by the Financial List. This is confirmed by a survey by the ICC, which indicated that many financial institutions are unfamiliar with arbitration.[181] Also, the database of the cases administered by ICSID under its arbitration procedures confirms this finding.[182] This finding is important to shape EU attitudes towards specialized courts. In terms of the parties' private benefits, the choice should be theirs. Yet, as we said earlier, there are important policies at stake. There is a need to ensure that law of finance applies in a predictable manner, that pivotal cases are identified and addressed, and that a hefty body of jurisprudence emerges to give to the law of finance a 'legal voice' that can complement and balance a language perhaps too skewed towards purely economic and financial perspectives. Thus, our argument is not the traditional one in parties unfamiliar with arbitration, ie that arbitration, as a private dispute resolution mechanism, will hinder the public interest as expressed in financial regulation. This is not our position. Arbitration is a device which introduces a healthy dose of competition to ensure that court systems are responsive to needs in practice. However, awards' persuasiveness depends on the kind of legal arguments employed, and, since the arbitrators' sole focus is to resolve the dispute, this is less important than the goal of building a stable body of interpretative principles, which, in our view, is what the law of finance sorely needs.

13.61 The legitimacy of the new (private and public) financial architecture cannot be fostered by giving finance a legal voice if that voice is not accessible to the public. A system, any system of specialized courts in the law of finance, would need to find a way to cooperate and coexist with arbitration, but this, in our view, should be done by keeping litigation as an attractive mechanism for private parties, which by no means should detract from its usefulness for its public function. In this sense, arbitration can represent a challenge, and a source of reflection on matters that involve EU public policies. If one wishes to draw from the American experience, in the United States a widespread recourse to arbitration clauses in consumer and financial contracts containing a 'no-class-arbitration clauses' has been described by Professor Arthur Miller as 'what probably is the most dramatic development undermining the availability of the class action (and citizen access to the courts generally) in recent years'.[183] Indeed, after the Supreme Court decisions in *AT&T Mobility LLC v Conception*[184] and *American Express*

---

[179] The International Institute for Conflict Prevention and Resolution (CPR), established in 1977, is an independent non-profit organization that helps global businesses prevent and resolve commercial disputes.
[180] Queen Mary University, '2013 Corporate Choices in International Arbitration - Industry perspectives' (the 2013 International Arbitration Survey 2013) 8–9 http://www.arbitration.qmul.ac.uk/research/2013/ (accessed 2 September 2022). Arbitration was only the preferred choice in 23 per cent of cases.
[181] ICC Commission Report, 'Financial Institutions and International Arbitration' (2016) 8.
[182] ICSID https://icsid.worldbank.org/resources/databases (accessed 2 September 2022).
[183] Miller (n 153) 28.
[184] *AT&T Mobility LLC v Conception* 536 US 333 (2011).

Co. v Italian Colors Restaurant,[185] by which the court enforced a no-class action arbitration clause and a no-aggregate arbitration clause respectively, there are now visible incentives for financial institutions to adopt such clauses as a means to prevent class litigation.[186] As several tidal waves of litigation by (retail) borrowers and investors in different EU countries have confirmed the litigiousness of this field, arbitration may be used by financial institutions to tame this trend, or as a counter-move if collective redress mechanisms are expanded in Europe. This, however, could be a mistake, for financial parties would only taint arbitration, which is neutral and useful, with the strategic (and, sometimes, opportunistic) aims of (some of) the parties who promote it. Even if the issue is uncertain, our prognosis is that using arbitration with the aim to thwart consumer or investor protection would not bode well for that aim, nor for arbitration.

13.62 These reflections on the multi-faceted relationship between court litigation and arbitration, and their underpinning friction inevitably takes us to the field of *investment arbitration*, where such relationship has become more tense. Investment arbitration remains a last resort avenue in the context of major financial disputes involving a State, or state action that affects the rights of investors, or at least another tool of choice in a vast armory of causes of action as recently witnessed by the ICSID investment arbitration eg on the Banco Popular resolution used by Mexican investors.[187] Investment arbitration in an intra-EU context may be in discussion, after *Achmea*,[188] where the Court[189] held that:

> Articles 267 and 344 TFEU must be interpreted as precluding a provision in an international agreement concluded between Member States ... under which an investor from one of those Member States may, in the event of a dispute concerning investments in the other Member State, bring proceedings against the latter Member State before the arbitral tribunal whose jurisdiction that Member State has undertaken to accept.

13.63 Things may still be different beyond the intra-EU context and in that context investment arbitrations for 'reflective loss' (that is the loss incurred as shareholders or bondholders) is an obvious remedy[190] It is so much so, that even Delaware tried to act to counter this trend, through a state-sponsored arbitration programme whereby business disputes were to be heard by the sitting judges of the Delaware Court of Chancery acting as arbitrators. This arbitration experiment has ultimately failed following an opinion of the United States Court

---

[185] *American Express Co v Italian Colors Restaurant* 333 S Ct 2304 (2013).

[186] Miller (n 153) 32 noting that 'the Federal Consumer Financial Protection Bureau was not able to preserve its recent arbitration rule that would have effectively eliminated the application of Conception and Italian Colors in certain important contexts. Immediately after the rule was promulgated, the business community attacked it in Congress, which has the statutory power to reject administrative agency rulemaking. Both the House of Representatives and the Senate have now done so and the rule will not go into effect' (further details at 32, fn 107).

[187] Final Award of the Permanent Court of Arbitration 13 March 2023 (Prof. Gabrielle Kaufmann-Kohler President of the Tribunal; Prof. William Park and Mr. Alexis Mourre Co-Arbitrators) in PCA Case 2019-17 Antonio del *Valle Ruiz and Others v The Kingdom of Spain*, accessible on www.pca-cpa.org Compare for a brief summary of the ICSID investment arbitrations held in the law of finance Yves Mersch and others, 'The New Challenges Raised by Investment Arbitration for the EU Legal Order', ECB Legal Working Paper Series No 19, (October 2019) 2–48.

[188] Case C-284/16 *Slowakische Republik v Achmea BV* ECLI:EU:C:2018:158. On this judgment see Pantaleo (n 176) 60–63 (a thorough analysis of its precedents, a 44 and 54–60); Cristina Contartese and Mads Andenas, 'EU Autonomy and Investor-State Dispute Settlement under inter se Agreements between Member States: Achmea' (2019) 56 CMLR 157.

[189] The Court refers to the principle of autonomy of the EU legal order and to its Opinion 2/13 on the accession of the EU to the ECHR of 18 December 2014, ECLI:EU:C:2014:2454, specifically at para 201.

[190] Vera Korzun, 'Shareholder Claims for Reflective Loss: How International Investment Law Changes Corporate Law and Governance' (2018) 40 U Pa J Intl L 189.

of Appeals for the Third Circuit, which upheld a lower court decision that a confidential programme of this type violates the First Amendment right of public access,[191] yet it shows a trend.

13.64 Less than one year had gone by after *Achmea* when the compatibility with EU law of another investor-state dispute settlement mechanism, this time incorporated in an agreement between the EU Member States, the EU itself and a third country, was addressed in a different case, regarding the compatibility with EU law of section F of Chapter 8 (Resolution of Investment Disputes between Investors and States) of the EU–Canada Comprehensive Economic and Trade Agreement (CETA).[192] In that context, arbitration is turned into an bespoke hybrid system centred around a permanent investment court, composed of a roster of fifteen arbitrators selected by different appointing authorities to set to rest concerns over real independence of ad hoc party-appointed arbitrators,[193] and an appellate tribunal.[194] In its Opinion 1/17,[195] the Court concluded for the compatibility of the CETA dispute resolution mechanism with the EU legal order. The Court noted that CETA courts are separate from the domestic courts of Canada, the European Union and its Member States, holding that 'they cannot have the power to interpret or apply provisions of EU law other than those of the CETA or to make awards that might have the effect of preventing the EU institutions from operating in accordance with the EU constitutional framework', and concluded that 'the fact that the envisaged ISDS mechanism stands outside the EU judicial system does not mean, in itself, that that mechanism adversely affects the autonomy of the EU legal order'. The Court also distinguished CETA courts from the original draft agreement on the creation of a unified patent litigation system declared to be incompatible with EU law in Opinion 1/09,[196] noting that the 'applicable law' in the context of that draft agreement, included, inter alia, 'directly applicable Community law, in particular Council Regulation ... on the Community patent, and national law of the Contracting States implementing Community law'. and this would have altered the essential character of the powers that the Treaties confer on the EU' institutions and on the Member States and that are indispensable to the preservation of the very nature of EU law.

13.65 However, regardless of the opinion one may hold regarding *Achmea*, or the CETA court and Opinion 1/17, it is clear that the relationship with investment arbitration cannot be formulated in strictly negative terms. Investment arbitration provides investors with powerful leverage, and a backstop, against States, which they would otherwise lack. Yet, the question is why this should lead to the conclusion that investment arbitration is the cause of the malaise, rather than a symptom of a deeper, and more basic problem: investors seem to feel that their arguments are not listened to in ordinary courts, when they involve a challenge to public action. Although the claims typically addressed in investment arbitration cases are based on standards such as protection against expropriation, non-discriminatory treatment, or

---

[191] ibid 193.
[192] Pantaleo (n 176) 77.
[193] For a vivid discussion of this issue, on opposite positions see Jan Paulsson, 'Moral Hazard in International Dispute Resolution' (2010) 25 ICSID Rev 339; and Charles N Brower and Charles B Rosenberg, 'The Death of the Two-Headed Nightingale: Why the Paulsson-van den Berg Presumption that Party-Appointed Arbitrators Are Untrustworthy is Wrongheaded' (2013) 29 Arb Intl 7.
[194] Pantaleo (n 176) 85, characterizing this 'as possibly the most ground-breaking innovation of EU investment agreements, which are the first of the kind to feature an appeal system'.
[195] Compare Opinion of AG Bot ECLI:EU:C:2019:72 and Opinion 1/17 of the Court (Full Court) ECLI:EU:C:2019:341.
[196] Opinion 1/09 of the Court (Full Court) ECLI:EU:C:2011:123.

(perhaps the most popular recently) 'fair and equitable treatment' (FET) which protects investors' 'legitimate expectations', these resemble the standards under national constitutions, the ECtHR or the EU Charter, which are even more developed and, if duly deployed by courts, should lead to decisions that are as detailed, knowledgeable and demanding with the exercise of public powers, as those of arbitratiuon tribunals, if not more so.[197] Therefore, the popularity of investment arbitration seems to suggest that there is a general perception among investors that such standards, impressive as they may seem on paper, are not deployed by the court system in a way that leads to effective protection.

13.66 Investment arbitration is thus bound to continue to be an important competition, and challenge, to domestic or EU justice, if certain protection standards are used in a purely formalistic manner, where courts merely accept the reasons of public authorities, without much discussion. Specialized courts can identify the apparently technical nuances that distinguish a marginal case from a pivotal one, a proper assessment from a mistaken one, or a regular exercise of powers from an abuse, in a way that ensures that property, judicial review, the duty to state reasons, or non-discrimination are actual challenges to public action, and that proportionality is a meaningful principle. Then, international investment arbitration tribunals would balk at second-guessing robust, and legally sophisticated justifications, for there is only one thing worse for an arbitrator than having an award that is not enforced because it is perceived as 'politically' problematic, which is having an award that is not enforced because it is legally wrong. EU and domestic authorities can push back against investment arbitration all they want, but the only way to limit its relevance would be by ensuring that the principles protected by investment treaties (which are not dissimilar than the ones protected by the Charter, the ECHR, and the constitutions of Member States) are subject to a thorough and balanced analysis by an effective court system.

---

[197] For an analysis of the FET standard, see Michele Potestà, 'Legitimate Expectations in Investment Treaty Law: Understanding the Roots and the Limits of a Controversial Concept' (2013) 88 ICSID Rev 88. Comparing the arbitral award in PCA Case 2019-17 *Antonio del Valle Ruiz and Others v The Kingdom of Spain*, with Case T-510/17 *Del Valle Ruiz v Commission & SRB* ECLI:EU:T:2022:312, in the case of Banco Popular crisis, both decisions were detailed and thorough, both held that there was no breach of law by Spain (arbitral award) or European authorities (General Court), and the General Court had the advantage that it could scrutinize the decisions that were more significant, ie those of European authorities.

14

A way forward: Specialized courts in the law of finance in the EU

1 European specialized courts for public law disputes and Article 257 TFEU	14.01	4 Specialized courts, EU general principles of national procedural autonomy, equivalence and effectiveness, and national constitutional counter-limits	14.08
2 A European specialized court for cross-border private law disputes and Articles 81(2) and 67(4) TFEU	14.04	5 A cautious proposal for adjustments to the existing court system in the law of finance	14.10
3 The Unified Patent Court as a controversial blueprint	14.06		

1 European specialized courts for public law disputes and Article 257 TFEU

14.01 Once we have shown how the system of EU courts would benefit from elements of specialization and better coordination in the law of finance, another question to address is the available legal basis, if any, for a reform and the institutional design fit for purpose. We begin considering the possibility of specialized courts expressly contemplated under Article 257 TFEU. Then, we examine the possibility of specialized EU and national courts under Articles 81(2) and 67(4) TFEU. We specifically discuss the Unified Patent Court as a controversial blueprint. We then consider the relevance of EU general principles of equivalence and effectiveness, and national procedural autonomy and constitutional counter-limits putting forward our cautious proposal for a specialized system of courts for the law of finance.

14.02 Article 257 TFEU envisages the possibility of establishing specialized courts.[1] However, a reform of the current court system under Article 257 TFEU may currently prove politically difficult, because the 2015 European courts' reform[2] doubled the number of the General Court judges and abolished the existing specialized court for the Civil Service Tribunal. That

---

[1] Pursuant to TFEU, art 257, decisions given by specialized courts may be subject to a right of appeal on points of law only or, when provided for in the regulation establishing the specialized court, a right of appeal also on matters of fact, before the General Court. Under art 256, if specialized courts are established, the General Court does not hear and determine on first instance in those cases. So far, the only specialized court created within the Union judicial system was the Civil Service Tribunal (CST). Compare Roberto Schiano, 'Le "camere giurisdizionali" presso la Corte di Lussemburgo: alcune riflessioni alla luce dell'istituzione del Tribunale della funzione pubblica' (2005) Diritto dell'Unione Europea 719.

[2] The reform consisted in an amendment of the CJEU Statute, at the request of the Court itself, in accordance with the rules laid down in art 281 TFEU, adopted by the European Parliament and the Council by ordinary legislative procedure (Regulation (EU, Euratom) 2015/2422 of the European Parliament and of the Council of 16 December 2015 amending Protocol No 3 on the Statute of the Court of Justice of the European Union [2015] OJ L341.

reform[3] must still prove its case against the real workload of the General Court[4] and was recommended by the Court of Justice with preference over the specialized court model.[5] The General Court had proposed instead the establishment of a specialized court in the field of intellectual property under Article 257 TFEU. The Court of Justice considered, however, that the doubling of the number of the General Court judges was faster to implement and, more importantly, that a generalist court is better suited to ensure full consistency of EU law.[6] The European Commission[7] took a mixed view: the increase in number of the General Court judges should have come together with the establishment of at least two specialized chambers within the General Court as permitted by the Statute, one for staff cases and the other for trademark cases. The Commission's opinion was not followed, and the 2015 European courts reform did not mention specialized chambers. Yet, in September 2019, through an act of self-organization by the General Court specialized chambers were established within the General Court. Thus, of the ten Chambers of the General Court, four will handle staff cases and six will deal with intellectual property matters. Yet, all other cases (including on the law of finance) are to be allocated among all chambers, although this gradually concentrates certain matters de facto with certain judges and chambers, to develop internal specialization.[8]

14.03 Therefore, although a reform of the Court based upon Article 257 TFEU for the establishment of a specialized chamber for disputes on the law of finance, as has been proposed in the literature (advocating a 'Tribunal of Financial Supervisory and Resolution Affairs')[9] cannot be ruled out as a matter of principle, we surmise that this reform would be politically hard to achieve and technically of little use (by design, it would be limited to public law disputes on EU acts).

2 A European specialized court for cross-border private law disputes and Articles 81(2) and 67(4) TFEU

14.04 An alternative would be to redesign the European court system for cross-border private law disputes in the law of finance without impinging on the fundamental role and current

---

[3] For a discussion of the needs of reform before the adoption of the 2015 redesign see Irene Karper, *Reformen des Europäischen Gerichts- und Rechtsschutzsystems* (Nomos 2011) 145–60.
[4] Alberto Alemanno and Laurent Pech, 'Thinking Justice Outside the Docket: A Critical Assessment of the Reform of the EU's Court system' (2017) 54 CMLR 129; Daniel Sarmiento, 'The Reform of the General Court: An Exercise in Minimalist (but Radical) Institutional Reform' (2017) 19 Cam Ybk of Eur Legal Stud 236; Chiara Amalfitano, 'La recente proposta di riforma dello Statuto della Corte di giustizia dell'Unione europea: molti dubbi e alcuni possibili emendamenti' (2018) 3 *Federalismi* 1.
[5] Takis Tridimas, 'The Court of Justice of the European Union' in Robert Schütze and Takis Tridimas (eds), *Oxford Principles of European Union Law: The European Union Legal Order*, vol 1 (OUP 2018) 607.
[6] ibid. For a 'Cato's cry' that 'the Court should abandon its attachment to the preliminary reference procedure' see Joseph HH Weiler, 'Epilogue: Judging the Judges: Apology and Critique' in Maurice Adams and others (eds), *Judging Europe's Judges* (Hart Publishing 2015) 252.
[7] Commission Opinion on the requests for the amendment of the Statute of the Court of Justice of the European Union, presented by the Court [2011] COM(2011) 596 final, https://www.eumonitor.eu/9353000/1/j9vvik7m1c3g yxp/vit9rw32kovf (accessed 29 September 2022).
[8] CJEU, 'Press Release No 111/19' (19 September 2019) https://curia.europa.eu/jcms/upload/docs/application/pdf/2019-09/cp190111en.pdf (accessed 29 September 2022). The November 2022 request submitted by the CJEU pursuant to art 281(2) TFEU with a view to amending Protocol 3 of the Statute seeks to lay down the specific areas in which the General Court is to have jurisdiction pursuant to art 256(3) TFEU to hear and determine questions referred for preliminary ruling by the court of Member States under art 267 TFEU; yet it does not propose any further specialization of the court.
[9] Compare Tomas MC Arons, 'Judicial Protection of Supervised Credit Institutions in the European Banking Union' in Danny Busch and Guido Ferrarini (eds), *European Banking Union* (OUP 2015) 474.

organization of the Court of Justice at the apex of the system. This may be based on Article 81(2) and Article 67(4) TFEU that grant a legislative competence for the EU to take measures aimed at ensuring 'effective access to justice' in civil matters having cross-border implications.[10]

14.05 The establishment of a European court for cross-border commercial disputes grounded on Article 81 TFEU is not a new idea.[11] It could be a complement of the existing national commercial courts' system and thus as an optional '28th regime'. Proponents have argued that Article 81 TFEU 'allows the EU to adopt self-standing European procedures that replace national procedures' and that 'based on this broad understanding of its competences, the EU legislature has for example adopted the Small Claims Regulation, the Payment Order Regulation and the Insolvency Regulation'. The European commercial court, in the design of its proponents, would primarily apply national law and would work under the control of the CJEU (it should be expressly granted the right to make requests for preliminary rulings under Article 267 TFEU).[12]

3 The Unified Patent Court as a controversial blueprint

14.06 Another alternative, yet controversial, institutional model in the EU has been the Unified Patent Court (UPC). The UPC—which has finally started its operations in June 2023, after the delays caused by Brexit[13] and several constitutional challenges[14]—has been described as a 'new leap into unchartered legal territory'.[15] It is a specialized court established outside

---

[10] These provisions, together with the right to an effective remedy under art 47 of the Charter of Fundamental Rights lay the foundations of EU justice. See Paul Beaumont and Mihail Danov, 'Introduction: Research Aims and Methodology' in Paul Beaumont and others (eds), *Cross Border Litigation in Europe* (Hart Publishing 2017) 1.

[11] Giesela Rühl, 'The Resolution of International Commercial Disputes – What Role (if any) for Continental Europe?' (2021) 115 AJIL 11; Giesela Rühl, 'Building Competence in Commercial Law in the Member States' (European Parliament Study for the JURI Committee 2018), in particular 60 ff. Giesela Rühl, 'Ein europäisches Handelsgericht' [2018] FAZ 6;; Thomas Pfeiffer, 'Ein europäisches Handelsgerichtshof und die Entwicklung des europäischen Privatrechts' (2016) ZEuP 797.

[12] Rühl (n 11) 60, n 322.

[13] Brexit came along with the withdrawal of the ratification of the UPC. The announcement of the Unified Patent Court Preparatory Committee and the parliamentary written statement in the House of Commons by Amanda Solloway https://www.unified-patent-court.org/en (accessed 29 September 2022).

[14] The German Federal Constitutional Court (FCC) in *Björn Stjerna* declared invalid the the German Act ratifying the UPC Agreement insofar it was not adopted by qualified majority as required under art 23(1) third sentence Grundgesetz (GG) in conjunction with art 79(2) GG (*Integrationprogramm*). The appellant also alleged that UPC judges appointment did not ensure their independence and democratic legitimation, but the constitutional complaint was inadmissible: BVerfG, 2 BvR 739/17, Order of the Second Senate (13 February 2020) para 91. The German Parliament adopted in November 2020 a new ratification instrument with qualified majority; the new act was again challenged, but the constitutional complaints were rejected by the FCC on BVerfG, 2 BvR 2216/20 (23 July 2021). In Hungary, the Hungarian Constitutional Court held, with judgment of 26 June 2018, that the ratification of the UPC would require a constitutional amendment.

[15] Aurora Plomer, 'The Unitary Patent and Unified Patent Court: A New Leap into Unchartered Legal Territory' in Marise Cremona, Anne Thies, and Ramses A Wessel (eds), *The European Union and International Dispute Settlement* (Hart Publishing 2017) 275–292. Compare also Jacopo Alberti, 'New Developments in the EU System of Judicial Protection: The Creation of the Unified Patent Court and Its Future Relations with the CJEU' (2017) 24 Maastricht J Eur & Com L 6; Federica Baldan and Esther Van Zimmeren, 'The Future Role of the Unified Patent Court in Safeguarding Coherence in the European Patent System' (2015) 52 CMLR 1529 (the European patent system is an intricate multi-level governance system, and safeguarding judicial coherence requires a continuous dialogue also between national courts of different countries, between the EPO and national courts, between the quasi-judicial boards of appeal of the EPO and the national courts, between the EPO and the UPC, etc.); Federica Baldan and Esther van Zimmeren, 'Exploring Different Concepts of Judicial Coherence in the Patent Context: The Future Role of the (New) Unified Patent Court and Its Interaction with (Old) Actors of the European Patent System' (2015) 8 Rev of Eur Admin L 377.

the EU legal order as an international court (Article 31 of the UPC Agreement), that is compelled to apply EU law, must cooperate with the CJEU to ensure the correct application of Union law (Article 21 of the UPC Agreement), and is subject to both the control of the contracting Member States as any national court of such Member States (Article 1 of the UPC Agreement) and of the Court of Justice at the apex of the EU legal order.[16]

14.07 The UPC is, more precisely, a court common to the participating Member States, and it is part of their judicial systems, although it is no 'ordinary' court, nor is it integrated into national courts' hierarchies.[17] It is also different from other specialized national courts established under EU law, eg national courts designated to act as community design courts hearing cases related to their infringement as required by Article 80 of the Community Design Regulation (Council Regulation (EC) No. 6/2002 of 12 December 2001); or EU trademark courts under Article 123 of the EU Trademark Regulation (Regulation (EU) No. 2017/1001).[18] In its Opinion 1/09, the Court of Justice found incompatible with the Treaties the Community Patents Court (CPC), the UPC's unsuccessful predecessor, because it was not satisfied that the CPC could guarantee the uniform application of EU law under Article 267 TFEU, since Member States divested themselves of the possibility of preliminary references to the Court of Justice (paragraphs 79–80 of the Opinion).[19] However, in Case C-146/13,[20] where Spain claimed that the UPC's jurisdiction over the unitary patent[21] could amount to an infringement of the principles of autonomy and uniformity of EU law, because the UPC is not part of the institutional and judicial system of the EU, the Grand Chamber concluded that it lacked jurisdiction under Article 263 TFEU to rule on the lawfulness of an international agreement concluded by Member States,[22] although it suggested that it was sufficient that the UPC Agreement requires the UPC to respect the supremacy of EU law and to seek preliminary rulings from the Court.

---

[16] Compare Jens Schovsbo, Thomas Riis, and Clement Salung Petersen, 'The Unified Patent Court: Pros and Cons of Specialization: Is there a Light at the End of the Tunnel (Vision)?' (2015) 46 IIC 271; Jelena Ceranic, 'The Unified Patent Court: A New Judicial Body for the Settlement of Patent Disputes within the European Union' (2017) 1 ECLIC 237.

[17] Plomer (n 15) 285.

[18] European Union Office for the Protection of Intellectual Property (EUIPO), *Specialised IP Rights Jurisdictions in the Member States: A Compilation of Available Studies (Q3 2017)* (2018) https://euipo.europa.eu/tunnel-web/secure/webdav/guest/document_library/observatory/documents/reports/2018_Specialised_IP_Rights_Jurisdictions_in_Member_States/2018_Specialised_IP_Rights_Jurisdictions_in_Member_States_EN.pdf (accessed 29 September 2022).

[19] The EEA Agreement, by contrast, is an association agreement concluded by the EU which gives the associated countries the right to establish their court, which is bound to follow or take into account the relevant case law of the CJEU (art 6 EEA) under the principle of judicial homogeneity: compare the EFTA Court (ed), *Judicial Protection in the European Economic Area* (German Law Publishers 2012).

[20] Case C-146/13 *Spain v European Parliament and Council* ECLI:EU:C:2015:298.

[21] As regulated by Regulation (EU) No 1257/2012, adopted through enhanced cooperation under TEU, art 20 and TFEU arts 326–34. The Grand Chamber judgment in Joined Cases C-274/11 and C-295/11 *Spain and Italy v Council* EU:C:2013:240 dismissed an action to nullify resort to enhanced cooperation; the judgment was (perhaps too harshly) criticized by Matthias Lamping, 'Enhanced Cooperation in the Area of Unitary Patent Protection: Testing the Boundaries of the Rule of Law' (2013) 20 Maastricht J Eur Comp L 589.

[22] *Spain v Parliament and Council* (n 20) para 101.

4 Specialized courts, EU general principles of national procedural autonomy, equivalence and effectiveness, and national constitutional counter-limits

Any redesign of the courts' system for the law of finance needs to be weighed against the EU general principles of national procedural autonomy, equivalence, and effectiveness. Under the national procedural autonomy principle, 'Union law falls to be applied principally by national courts [s]ince the Union does not have procedural law ... of its own' and 'Member States have in principle autonomy to organize their respective judicial framework and procedures, with the result that the European Union essentially "piggybacks" on what is provided for in the national legal system'.[23] However, national procedural autonomy must be weighed against principles of equivalence and effectiveness.[24] Thus, although the balance between procedural autonomy and equivalence and effectiveness sufficed in the past, as financial law becomes more 'European' the mismatch between substance and procedure becomes increasingly obvious, and the case for keeping the *status quo* increasingly weak.[25] In our view, a cautious reform of the court system in the law of finance would fit comfortably with the current harmonization of EU law and centralization of administrative competences described in this book. New normative realities justify new ideas on court organization. As the precedent of intellectual property rights shows 'the proliferation of EU legislation and litigation in technical and scientific matters'[26] raised issues of European courts' specialization *and called for unconventional advances in the organization of judicial architecture.*

14.08

The next question is whether this could find an obstacle in national constitutional counter-limits. It should not, also in the current context clearly characterized by an intense horizontal dialogue and occasional frictions between the Court of Justice and national constitutional courts. The concern of high national courts is the need to ensure homogeneous enforcement of fundamental rights and constitutional values, and the use of the principle of sincere cooperation laid down in Article 4(3) to achieve that goal. This principle can also support a cautious and targeted European initiative that changes the organization of the court system to ensure a consistent, principles-based interpretation and application of EU law in the law of finance necessary to ensure the principles of equivalence and effectiveness. When the CJEU stated that the principle of national procedural autonomy operates 'in the absence of harmonizing Union law on the subject', it never intended to bar the way for such a harmonization. Within these boundaries, constitutional counter-limits should not stay in the way of a similar reform.

14.09

---

[23] Koen Lenaerts, Ignace Maselis, and Kathleen Gutman, *EU Procedural Law* (Janek T Nowak ed, OUP 2015) 107–108.
[24] This is often coupled with the principle of sincere cooperation and, as noted by Anna Wallerman, 'Towards an EU Law Doctrine in the Exercise of Discretion in National Courts? The Member States' Self-Imposed Limits on National Procedural Autonomy' (2016) 53 CMLR 339–60.
[25] Marco Lamandini and David Ramos Muñoz, 'Bankia: Can You Have a Capital Markets Union without Harmonised Remedies For Securities Litigation?' *EULawLive* (19 June 2021) 16–24.
[26] Albertiart (n 15) paras 21–22.

5 A cautious proposal for adjustments to the existing court system in the law of finance

14.10 Finance has a common language, but this is not a 'legal' language. Financial economics has, for decades, provided the conceptual framework to understand the system. The post-crisis (2007–2009) shift only strengthened this trend. Yet, by embracing this 'financial' focus we risk sleepwalking into an oversimplification, which is to assume a common understanding of financial concepts and policy priorities suffices, without a coherent system for the implementation, application, and discussion, of financial concepts *once they are transformed into legal concepts*. Focusing solely on the financial side of things can create the comfortable illusion that the system works seamlessly, that there are no fundamental differences of concept, and that all national systems work under the same global logic. This is wrong and dangerous; it downplays the risk of a financial giant with legal feet of clay. One may criticize a proposal for a system of specialized financial courts and remedies as 'naïve'. Our reply is that the current approach is to respond to globally interconnected markets and systemic risk with system-wide *regulatory* solutions, like the European Banking Union and the Capital Markets Union. To assume that they can work with a midget-like court system, where national courts are (save for some exceptions) too insignificant, insulated, and overwhelmed to tackle the complexities of finance and the interests at stake, and European courts, which, while powerful and impressive, cannot provide solutions within the acceptable time-limits, is even more naïve.

14.11 Thus, the more obvious argument for adjusting the current courts' system along the lines proposed here is pragmatic: a common conceptual basis (finance) plus a unified supervisory system is not enough to achieve efficiency and stability absent a system of courts that ensures certainty and predictability. Yet, the most important argument is that law is perhaps the most important fabric that weaves financial markets and society together through a common language, a language that is not the language of economics and finance, at least not entirely.

14.12 Finance and its regulation ensure that terms like efficiency, 'prudential requirements', or 'investor protection' are well present. Yet, their meaning must be ascertained in a broader context, where they coexist with 'legitimacy', 'accountability', 'rights', and 'principles'. If one set of terms drifts away, finance, and financial regulation, may evolve independently from, or in spite of, the law. At first glance, this might support a system of generalist courts. Yet, in light of recent reality, generalist courts without a first-level system of review that helps to 'separate the chaff from the grain', in seemingly arcane problems, risks intruding too much, or scrutinizing too little. The conceptual framework of 'principles-based interpretivism' used here encapsulates a basic idea: finance, and its language, cannot evolve independently of law and its courts' system. If legislators and policy-makers ignore this basic fact, regulatory and supervisory mechanisms will not only fail to address the next systemic crisis: lacking a coherent system of courts they may become themselves a source of instability, and undermine the very basic legitimacy that they intend to foster.

14.13 For these reasons, we invite a timely reflection in Europe on *cautious adjustments* to the courts' systems in the law of finance under the purview of the CJEU. In our view, without the need of any amendment to the Treaties or the Statute of the CJEU, a renewed court system with appropriate elements of specialization could be brought about by harmonizing Union law on the matter and could rest on three pillars and a central point of administration.

14.14 The first pillar would be a specialized administrative tribunal hearing public law disputes in the law of finance as a natural evolution of the existing ESAs Board of Appeal, SSM ABoR, and SRB Appeal Panel. Indeed, of the many policy experiments of EU institutions, appeal bodies look set to stay in areas where there is a need for specialized knowledge delivered swiftly, flexibly, and impartially to balance the EU's potentially intrusive action through expert regulatory agencies with bodies that combine expert knowledge of their own with a firm anchor on fundamental rights and the rule of law. Initial experience suggests that the ESAs' Board of Appeal and the SRB Appeal Panel have ensured that appellants have 'their affairs handled impartially, fairly and within a reasonable time'.[27] What does this mean? More visibly, appellants have a timely, non-expensive, expert review which affords proportionate protection in line with Article 41 of the Charter, and, we venture to say, should Article 47 of the Charter 'fair trial' requirements be applicable to administrative review, they would be met too. This is even more remarkable if one compares the average duration of proceedings before those quasi courts (a few months) with proceedings before the General Court or the Court of Justice (a few years). Less visibly, quasi-courts have tried to carve out a place of their own in financial markets' increasingly complex architecture and governance.

14.15 This requires a delicate balancing act vis-à-vis the three established players in the review system. Towards the agencies, quasi-courts need to combine the independence to decide each case based on its merits (and not the downsides for the agency) with the institutional loyalty to offer precise reasons on why a decision was wrong, which help to put it right. Towards appellants, they need to be perceived as a useful, reliable, and truly independent device, but also send a clear message as to what they can, and cannot, review. The third relationship is with the CJEU. While the legislature may have established quasi-courts, only the CJEU's interpretation of their role can grant them a stable ground to operate. Quasi-courts thus need to persuade the CJEU that they have a relevant role to play without interfering with Court's own, that they can help 'declutter' the Court's table without becoming 'institutional clutter' themselves. So far, they have tried to do so by combining expediency, prudence, and willingness to penetrate the minute, often abstruse details, to dig out the real issues, which can then be re-examined by the courts. Their contribution, in this relationship with the CJEU, is that of helping to see the forest of fundamental issues through the trees of technical points, and provide a first, quick, solution for the benefit of courts and parties alike. Meanwhile, our discussion has also exposed some weaknesses in the overall institutional design, which, if reformed, would enhance the appeal bodies' supporting role to EU Courts in the adjudication of public law disputes. Such reform would be unlikely, in our view, if shaped in an ambitious overhaul to transform administrative review bodies into specialized courts attached to the Court of Justice under Article 257 TFEU.

14.16 We surmise that a more viable alternative may be a regulation that simultaneously amends (at a minimum) the ESAs Regulations and the SRM Regulation using their very same legal basis (Article 114 TFEU), and consolidates the ESAs' Board of Appeal and the SRB Appeal Panel (and possibly any appeal body for the new agency for anti-money laundering)[28] into a single administrative tribunal (a sort of newly established 'European Joint Board of Appeal

---

[27] To use the words of the CJEU in Case C-439/11 P *Ziegler SA v Commission* EU:C:2013:513, para 154.

[28] On 20 July 2021, the European Commission presented an ambitious package of legislative proposals to strengthen the EU's anti-money laundering and countering the financing of terrorism (AML/CFT) rules. The package also includes a proposal for a regulation for the creation of a new EU authority to fight money laundering. In April 2023, the co-legislators agreed to start the trilogues.

for financial disputes'), without any necessity to change this administrative tribunal into a specialized court attached to the CJEU under Article 257 TFEU. This administrative tribunal may be entrusted to review all agencies' decisions (removing most bottlenecks in the existing remits which failed to prove their case in the practice of the first years of experience), thus establishing a unified point of management for the specialized review of EU financial agencies' decisions.[29] It is constitutionally doubtful, from a TFEU perspective, that this could also extend *as such* to the SSM ABoR without interfering with the ECB independence according to Article 130 TFEU, Article 19, and recitals (30) and (79) of the SSM Regulation.

14.17 Thus, albeit it appears desirable to attract under the same system of review also the ECB supervisory decisions adopted in the SSM context, the issue needs to be treated with caution. As a first step, reform in this specific context (reflective of the legal basis of the SSM in the Treaty), we would therefore envisage an amendment to the SSM Regulation whereby the ABoR is also merged into the new administrative tribunal, yet with the difference that its decisions in the SSM context would remain non-binding opinions, so as to preserve the independence of the governing bodies of the ECB. It would remain open for the future, as a possible second step reform, to consider if also in this context the administrative tribunal decisions may be granted binding force. In our view, as the ECB independence is certainly not endangered by the judicial review of the CJEU, the same would in principle also be valid for the review of an administrative tribunal. Moreover, the ECB independence needs to be differently calibrated according to its different mandates and it should not overstep to the point of limiting legal scrutiny and legal accountability, because such legal accountability is one of the fundamental sources of the ECB legitimacy.

14.18 This reform would also take quasi-judicial review out of the internal governance of each single agency, resulting in organizational and efficiency gains and in more (appearance of) independence. In our view, an administrative tribunal is preferable to specialized courts attached to the CJEU under Article 257 TFEU for several reasons. First, it can be composed also by experts in supervisory and financial matters, who do not 'possess the ability required for appointment to judicial office' required by Article 257 TFEU and the appointment of the members (unlike the appointment of judges to the CJEU) does not require any political consensus. Secondly, its rules of procedure can be designed to deliver a prompt review (far shorter than GCEU proceedings), although current one- to three-month month deadlines are hardly compatible with the right to be heard: either the period starts from the date the evidence is complete, as happens with ESAs' Board of Appeal and SRB Appeal Panel Rules of Procedure or, if it runs from the appeal filing, proceedings that leave time for being heard, examining, and drafting should last from four to six months, unless otherwise agreed with the parties. Thirdly, a comprehensive reform could also expressly extend the standard of review beyond the current CJEU's standard to include errors (not just manifest errors) of assessment in complex technical assessments, considering its mixed and expert composition in line with the findings of the General Court for other boards of appeal. (Fourthly, it may usefully participate in the administrative process by confirming (contributing additional reasoning) or remitting to the agency, thus fostering prompt self-correcting action on

---

[29] Sabino Cassese, 'A European Administrative Justice?' (2017) 6 Riv It Dir Pubbl Com 1326, noting that this may be one of the 'three possible future paths for the three European reviewing bodies. One is that they take a step back and become simple internal control bodies, holding a merely advisory role. Another is that they develop into administrative judges, thus introducing a dualist judicial system (like French and Italian systems where there are civil and administrative courts) into the European Union. Finally, they may become an additional court of first instance, alongside the General Court, thus following the example of the British monist system'.

relevant matters, where erroneous decisions entail serious consequences. Finally, moreover, following the Unified Patent Court's blueprint, the reform could also require parties to pay fees 'balancing the principle of fair access to justice with the objectives of a [at least partially], self-financing court with balanced finances'.[30]

Appointment rules should reflect this change. Our preference would be to build further on the recently reformed appointment system for ESAs' Board of Appeal members[31] and strengthen the role of the European Commission (which currently only shortlists candidates for the ESAs' Board of Appeal and has no role for SRB Appeal Panel candidates) which could select and appoint the members after a statement before the European Parliament. This would enhance formal (appearance of) independence, which could be accompanied by full EU official status, better-designed remuneration, immunity, budget autonomy, and adequate secretarial and law clerical support. Would such a body outside Article 267 TFEU be admissible to judicial dialogue with the CJEU? In our view it could and, in the Court's words at *Paul Miles*' paragraph 45, why not 'envisage a development of the system of judicial protection' by expressly granting, with the amending regulation, the power to make preliminary references in this context? Conversely (and no less importantly), if administrative review is structured as self-standing outside the agencies, agencies should have *locus standi* to challenge review decisions in front of the GCEU. Finally, this reform would fully justify, to our minds, (i) the inclusion, in line with the extension put forward by the 2022 request of the CJEU pursuant to Article 281 TFEU of the administrative tribunal for the law of finance among the boards of appeal included in Article 58a in Protocol No. 3 (as amended by Regulation 2019/629 of 17 April 2019) of the Statute of the Court of Justice,[32] according to which 'an appeal brought against a decision of the General Court concerning a decision of an independent board of appeal ... shall not proceed unless the Court of Justice first decides that it should be allowed to do so', and (ii) the express conferral to the specialized administrative tribunal of unlimited jurisdiction (*ad instar* of Article 261 TFEU for the CJEU) in respect of penalties, sanctions, and administrative measures adopted by the relevant authorities whose decisions fall within its remit.

14.19

A second pillar of the reform would be represented by an interconnected system of (one or a limited number per country) specialized commercial courts, established in each Member State along the lines of the specialized courts for intellectual property under the Community Design Regulation and the EU Trademark Regulation to hear domestic and cross-border private law disputes in the law of finance, where the applicable law is either EU law directly or national law implementing EU law. It would be left to the procedural autonomy of each Member State to organize those courts, in compliance with the principles of equivalence and effectiveness. Cross-border disputes, however, may be further concentrated in one single court per country, where the use of English, as the language customary in international finance, would be used through the entire proceedings and also for the judgment. To promote effectiveness and equivalence further, on appeal of disputes having cross-border implications the parties may be offered the alternative to apply to national generalist courts of appeal or to a specialized and centralized European court of appeal, established under Article 81(2)

14.20

---

[30] Albertiart (n 15) 24, 21 (with reference to the UPC).
[31] This introduced a role for the European Parliament. See the new art 59(3), as amended.
[32] *Official Journal* of the European Union (25 April 2019) L111/1 https://eur-lex.europa.eu/legal-content/EN/TXT/?uri=OJ%3AL%3A2019%3A111%3ATOC (accessed 29 September 2022). For an insightful discussion on the proposal compare Jacopo Alberti, 'The Draft Amendments to CJEU's Statute and the Future Challenges of Administrative Adjudication in the EU' (2019) 3 Federalismi.it 1.

TFEU and working in English. Convergence through appropriate guidance at the level of the appeal is, in our view, important; but even more important is an increased interconnection of the network of specialized national courts, which, drawing from the experience of many common law state judiciaries, and also civil law systems like Germany and Switzerland, may lead courts also to consider precedents of other state courts when appropriate.[33] To this purpose a national court for cross-border dispute and a European court of appeal delivering their judgments in English would hugely contribute finally to reverse the undesirable situation of '*national* judiciaries which are not only ensconced each in its own legal culture but also separated by language barriers which range from merely inconvenient to the virtually insurmountable'.[34]

14.21 The third pillar would be represented by a replacement of the current loose ADR FIN-NET network with a properly coordinated European alternative dispute resolution system for mass claims in the law of finance. This would require the maximum harmonization of the existing, and diverging schemes currently adopted by Member States under the ADR Directive, drawing from the experience discussed in previous sections. In their new institutional design, the new FIN-NET adjudicators may change into quasi-courts, by making binding decisions and, if the CJEU so determines, by being admitted to judicial dialogue with the CJEU under Article 267 TFEU. Furthermore, in disputes having cross-border implications, and most notably where the competent ADR is confronted with diverging interpretations of the directly applicable EU law or of national law implementing EU law, the FIN-NET adjudicators may be given the option to defer the matter of interpretation and application of EU law to the European Court of Appeal discussed in the previous paragraph asking for guidance, with a role for the European Court of Appeal, similar to the one currently performed by the 'coordination college' sitting at the top of the Italian Arbitro Bancario Finanziario.

14.22 It is key, in our view, that these three pillars have in common a management office with self-standing administration, with appropriate budget, which would offer an appropriate secretariat, a centralized training point, and a centralized data repository and system of ongoing information exchange, in accordance with Article 81(2)(h) TFEU. Useful insights for this could be drawn on from the experience of the Administrative Committee of the Unified Patent Court and Eurojust.[35] In turn, drawing for example from the experience of the Qatar International Court, which is composed by both a civil and a commercial court and a regulatory tribunal, the European Joint Board of Appeal for financial disputes and the European Court of Appeal for financial disputes should coexist under the same roof and this could come along with the appointment of a single roster of expert members (whose number would most likely be fewer than the sum of the current members and alternates of the ESAs' Board of Appeal, AboR, and SRB Appeal Panel), who may sit in both courts.

---

[33] Daniel Halberstam and Mathias Reimann (eds), *Federalism and Legal Unification* (Springer 2016) 17; Sabino Cassese, *A World Government?* (Global Law Press 2018) 218.
[34] Halberstam and Reimann (n 33) 18.
[35] Council Decision setting up Eurojust with a view to reinforcing the fight against serious crime [2002] OJ L63 (2002/187/GAI); compare Eurojust (*Annual Report* 2018) https://www.eurojust.europa.eu/es/eurojust-annual-report-2018 (accessed 29 September 2022).

Bibliography

Acharya Viral V and others, *Guaranteed to Fail: Fannie Mae, Freddie Mac and the Debacle of Mortgage Finance* (PUP 2011)

Acharya Viral V, Dre-chsler Itamar, and Schanbl Philipp, 'A Pyrrhic Victory? Bank Bailouts and Sovereign Credit Risk'(2014) 69(6) The J Fin 2689

—— Acharya Viral V, Shachar Or, and Subrahmanyam Marti G, 'Regulating OTC Derivatives' in Viral V Acharya and others (eds), *Regulating Wall Street. The Dodd-Frank Act and the New Architecture of Global Finance* (Wiley 2011)

Adams Maurice and others, *Judging Europe's Judges: The Legitimacy of the Case Law of the European Court of Justice* (Hart Publishing 2013)

Adler Matthew and Posner Eric A, 'Rethinking Cost-Benefit Analysis' (1999) 109 Yale LJ 165

Aicher Robert D, and Fellerhoff William J, 'Characterization of a Transfer of Receivables as a Sale or a Secured Loan Upon Bankruptcy of the Transferor' (1992) 65 Am Bankr LJ 186

Akerlof George and Shiller Robert J, *Animal Spirits: How Human Psychology Drives the Economy, and Why It Matters for Global Capitalism* (PUP 2009)

Alberti Jacopo, 'New Developments in the EU System of Judicial Protection: The Creation of the Unified Patent Court and Its future Relations with the CJEU' (2017) 24 Maastricht J Eur & Com L 6

Aleinikoff T Alexander, 'Constitutional Law in an Age of Balancing' (1987) 96 Yale LJ 943

Alemanno Alberto and Pech Laurent, 'Thinking Justice Outside the Docket: A Critical Assessment of the Reform of the EU's Court System (2017) 54 CMLR 129

Alexy Robert, *A Theory of Constitutional Rights* (OUP 2010)

Alexy Robert, 'Constitutional Rights, Balancing, and Rationality' (2003) 16 Ratio Juris 131

Alexy Robert, *Teoría de los derechos fundamentales* (2nd edn, CEPC 2002), also in the Italian edition as Alexy Robert, *Teoria dei diritti fondamentali* (Il Mulino 2012)

Alexy Robert, 'The Construction of Constitutional Rights' (2010) 4 L & Ethics Hum Rts 26

Ali SF, *Consumer Financial Dispute Resolution in a Comparative Context: Principles, Systems and Practice* (CUP 2013)

Allegrezza Silvia and Voordeckers Olivier, 'Investigative and Sanctioning Powers of the ECB in the Framework of the Single Supervisory Mechanism: Mapping the Complexity of a New Enforcement Model' (2015) 4 Eucrim 151

Allen Hillary J, 'A New Philosophy for Financial Stability Regulation' (2013) 45(1) Loyola U Chicago LJ 173

Allen Jason Grant, 'More Than a Matter of Trust: The German Debt Securities Act 2009 in International Perspective' (2011) 7(1) Cap Mkts LJ 55

Allen Ronald J, 'Theorizing about Self-Incrimination' (2008) 30 Cardozo L Rev 247

Allen Ronald J and Mace, M Kristin, 'The Self-Incrimination Clause Explained and Its Future Predicted' (2004) 94 J Crim L & Criminology 243

Almhofer Martina, *Die Haftung der EZB für rechtswidrige Bankenaufsicht* (Mohr Siebeck 2018)

Almhofer Martina, 'The Liability of Authorities in Supervisory and Resolution Activities' in Chiara Zilioli and Karl-Philipp Wojcik (eds), *Judicial Review in the European Banking Union* (Elgar Financial Law and Practice 2021)

Altieri Mark P and others, 'Political Affiliation of Appointing President and the Outcome of Tax Court Cases' (2001) 84 Judicature 310

Amalfitano Chiara, 'La recente proposta di riforma dello Statuto della Corte di giustizia dell'Unione europea: molti dubbi e alcuni possibili emendamenti' (2018) 3 *Federalismi* 1

Andenas Mads and Leiss Johann Ruben, 'The Systemic Relevance of Judicial Decisions in Article 38 of the ICJ Statute' (2017) 77 ZaörV 907

Anderson Elizabeth S and Pildes Richard H, 'Expressive Theories of Law: A General Restatement' (2000) 148 U Pa L Rev 1503, 1531

Andreotti Tiago, *Dispute Resolution in Transnational Securities Transactions* (Hart Publishing 2017)

Annunziata Filippo, 'Fostering Centralization of EU Banking Supervision through Case-Law: The European Court of Justice and the Role of the European Central Bank' (2019) Bocc LS Research Paper Series

Annunziata Filippo, Lamandini Marco, and Ramos Muñoz David, 'Weiss and EU Union Banking Law: A Test for the Fundamental Principles of the Treaty' (2020) EBI Working Paper Series 67

Applegate JS, 'The Precautionary Preference: An American Perspective on the Precautionary Principle' (2000) 6(3) Human and Ecological Risk Assessment 413

Arden, Lady of Heswall, 'Foreword' in Chiara Zilioli and Karl-Philipp Wojcik (eds), *Judicial Review in the European Banking Union* (Edward Elgar Publishing 2021)

Arnull Anthony, 'Judicial Review in the European Union' in Antony Arnull and Damian Chalmers (eds), *Oxford Handbook of European Union Law* (OUP 2015)

Arnull Anthony, 'Remedies before National Courts' in Robert Schütze and Takis Tridimas (eds), *Oxford Principles of European Union Law*, vol I, The European Union Legal Order (OUP 2018)

Arons Tomas M C, 'Judicial Protection of Supervised Credit Institutions in the European Banking Union' in Danny Busch and Guido Ferrarini (eds), *European Banking Union* (OUP 2015)

Ashford Nicholas, 'Chapter 19. The Legacy of the Precautionary Principle in US Law: The Rise of Cost-Benefit Analysis and Risk Assessment as Undermining Factors in Health, Safety and Environmental Protection' in Nicolas de Sadeleer (ed), *Implementing the Precautionary Principle: Approaches from the Nordic Countries and the United States* (Earthscan 2007)

Athanassiou Phoebus, 'Non-contractual Liability under the Single Supervisory Mechanism: Key Features and Grey Areas' (2015) 7 JIBLR 391

Avery John W, 'Securities Litigation Reform: The Long and Winding Road to the Private Securities Litigation Reform Act of 1995' (1996) 51 Business Lawyer 335

Ayres Ian, 'Preliminary Thoughts on Optimal Tailoring of Contractual Rules' (1993) 3 S Calif Interdisc LJ 1

Ayres Ian and Gertner Robert, 'Filling Gaps in Incomplete Contracts: An Economic Theory of Default Rules' (1989) 99 Yale LJ 87

Ayres Ian and Gertner Robert, 'Strategic Contract Inefficiency and the Optimal Choice of Default Rules' (1992) 101 Yale LJ 729

Baldan Federica and Van Zimmeren Esther, 'Exploring Different Concepts of Judicial Coherence in the Patent Context: The Future Role of the (New) Unified Patent Court and Its Interaction with (old) Actors of the European Patent System' (2015) 3 Rev of Eur Admin L 377

Baldan Federica and Van Zimmeren Esther, 'The Future Role of the Unified Patent Court in Safeguarding Coherence in the European Patent System' (2015) 52 CMLR 1529

Balkin Jack M, 'Framework Originalism and the Living Constitution' (2009) 103 Nw L Rev 549

Baquero Cruz Julio, 'Another Look at Constitutional Pluralism in the European Union' (2016) 22(3) Eur LJ 356

Bastos Filipe Brito, 'Derivative Illegality in European Composite Administrative Procedures' (2018) 55 CML5R 101

Baum Lawrence, 'Judicial Specialization, Litigant Influence and Substantive Policy: The Court of Customs and Patent Appeals' (1977) 11 L & Society Rev 823

Baum Lawrence, *Specializing the Courts* (University of Chicago Press 2011)

Beaumont Paul and Danov Mihail, 'Introduction: Research Aims and Methodology' in Paul Beaumont and others (eds), *Cross-Border Litigation in Europe* (Hart Publishing 2017)

Beaumont Paul and others, 'Cross-Border Litigation in Europe: Some Theoretical Issues and Some Practical Challenges' in Paul Beaumont and others (eds), *Cross Border Litigation in Europe* (Hart Publishing 2017)

Benson George J, 'Required Disclosure and the Stock Market: An Evaluation of the Securities Exchange Act of 1934' (1973) 63 A Econ Rev 132

Bentham Jeremy, *An Introduction to the Principles of Morals and Legislation* (first published 1781, BLTC 1995)

Berg Alan, 'Recharacterisation after Enron' [2003] J Bus L 152

Berlin Isaiah, *The Hedgehog and the Fox: An Essay on Tolstoy's View of History* (Henry Hardy ed, 2nd edn, Weidenfeld & Nicolson 2014)

Bernstein Robby, *Economic Loss: General Principles* (first published 1993, 2nd edn, Sweet & Maxwell 1998)

Bierman Leonard and Fraser Donald, '"The Source-of-Strength" Doctrine: Formulating the Future of America's Financial Markets' (1993) 12 Ann Rev Banking L 269

Binder Jens-Heinrich, 'Chapter 3: Germany' in Danny Busch and Cees van Dam (eds), *A Bank's Duty of Care* (Hart Publishing 2019)

Bindseil Ulrich and König Philipp Johann, 'The Economics of Target 2 Balances' (2011) Discussion Paper 2011-035, SFB 649

Black Julia, 'Constructing and Contesting Legitimacy and Accountability in Polycentric Regulatory Regimes' (2008) 2 Reg & Gov 137

Blair William, 'Reconceptualising the Role of Standards in Supporting Financial Regulation' in Ross P Buckley, Emilios Avgouleas, and Douglas W Arner (eds), *Reconceptualising Global Finance and Its Regulation* (CUP 2016)

Blair William, 'The New Litigation Landscape: International Commercial Courts and Procedural Innovations' (2019) 2 Intl J Procedural L 212

Blair William, Brent Richard, and Grant Tom, *Banks and Financial Crime: The International Law of Tainted Money* (2nd edn, OUP 2017)

Blanck Kathrin, 'State Aid and Bank Resolution Law before the European Court of Justice' in Chiara Zilioli and Karl-Philipp Wojcik (eds), *Judicial Review in the European Banking Union* (Edward Elgar Publishing 2021)

Borio Claudio and Lowe Philip, 'Asset Prices, Financial and Monetary Stability: Exploring the Nexus' (2002) BIS Working Paper 114

Bovens Mark, 'Analysing and Assessing Accountability: A Conceptual Framework' (2007) 13(4) Eur LJ 450

Bovens Mark, 'Two Concepts of Accountability: Accountability as a Virtue and as a Mechanism' (2010) 33(5) West Eur Politics 946

Brekoulakis Stavros and Dimitropoulos Georgios (eds), *International Commercial Courts: The Future of Transnational Adjudication* (CUP 2022)

Brito Bastos Filipe, 'Judicial Review of Composite Administrative Procedures in the Single Supervisory Mechanism: Berlusconi' (2019) 56 CMLR 1355

Brower Charles N and Rosenberg Charles B, 'The Death of the Two-Headed Nightingale: Why the Paulsson-van den Berg Presumption that Party-Appointed Arbitrators Are Untrustworthy Is Wrongheaded' (2013) 29 Arb Intl 7

Brunnermeier Markus and others, 'The Fundamental Principles of Financial Regulation' (2009) 11 Geneva Reports on the World Economy xv

Brunnermeier Markus and others, 'The Sovereign-Bank Diabolic Loop and ESBies' (2016) 106(5) A Econ Rev Papers & Proceedings 2

Brunnermeier Marcus and Oehmke Martin, 'Bubbles, Financial Crises and Systemic Risk' in George M Constantinides, Milton Harris, and Rene M Stulz (eds), *Handbook of the Economics of Finance* (Elsevier 2013) 1221–88

Brunnermeier Markus K and Sannikov Yuliy, 'A Macroeconomic Model with a Financial Sector' (2014) 104 A Econ Rev 379

Buchanan Allen, 'Political Legitimacy and Democracy' (2002) 112(4) Ethics 689

Buono Giorgio, 'Banking Authorisations and the Acquisition of Qualifying Holdings as Unitary and Composite Procedures and Their Judicial Review' in Chiara Zilioli and Karl-Philipp Wojcik (eds), *Judicial Review in the European Banking Union* (Elgar Financial Law and Practice 2021)

Busch Danny, Macgregor Laura, and Watts Peter (eds), *Agency Law in Commercial Practice* (OUP 2016)

Busch Danny, 'The Private Law Effect of MIFID: The Genil Case and Beyond' (2017) 13 ERCL 70

Busch Danny, 'Self-Placement, Dealing on Own Account and the Provision of Investment Services under MIFID I & II' (2019) 14 Capital Markets LJ 4

Busch Danny, 'The Private Law Effect of the EU Market Abuse Regulation' (2019) 14 CMLJ 296

Busch Danny, 'The Influence of EU Prospectus Rules on Private Law' (2021) 16 CMLJ 3

Busch Danny and van Dam Cees, *A Bank's Duty of Care* (Hart Publishing 2017)

Busch Danny, Avgouleas Emilios, and Ferrarini Guido (eds), *Capital Markets Union in Europe* (OUP 2018)

Busch Danny, Ferrarini Guido, and Franx Jan Paul (eds), *Prospectus Regulation & Prospectus Liability* (OUP 2020)

Busnelli Frances Donato, 'Itinerari europei nella 'terra di nessuno tra contratto e fatto illecito': la responsabilità da informazioni inesatte' in F Busnelli and S Patti, *Danno e responsabilità civile* (Giappichelli 1997)

Busto Lago and José Manuel, *La antijuridicidad del daño resarcible en la responsabilidad civil extracontractual* (Tecnos 1998)

Cafaggi Fabrizio, 'Towards Collaborative Governance of European Remedial and Procedural Law' (2018) 19 Theoretical Inquiries in L 235

Calabresi Guido, 'About Law and Economics: A Letter to Ronald Dworkin' (1980) 8 Hofstra L Rev 553

Calabresi Steven G and Lawson Gary, 'The Unitary Executive, Jurisdiction Stripping, and the Hamdan Opinions: A Textualist Response to Justice Scalia' (2007) 107(4) Col L Rev 1002

Cantone Jason A, *Report on Federal-State Court Cooperation: A Survey of Federal Chief District Judges* (Federal Judicial Center 2016)

Cardozo Benjamin, *The Nature of the Judicial Process* (YUP 1921)

Cassese Sabino, *A World Government?* (Global Law Press 2018)

Cassese Sabino, 'A European Administrative Justice?' (2017) 6 Riv It Dir Pubbl Com 1326

Ceranic Jelena, 'The Unified Patent Court: A New Judicial Body for the Settlement of Patent Disputes within the European Union' (2017) 1 ECLIC 237

Chamon Merijn, 'EU Agencies: Between Meroni and Romano or the Devil and the Deep Blue Sea' (2011) 48 CMLR 1055

Chamon Merijn, Volpato Annalisa, and Eliantonio Mariolina (eds), *Boards of Appeal of EU Agencies* (OUP 2022)

Chirulli Paolo and De Lucia Luca, 'Specialised Adjudication in EU Administrative Law: The Boards of Appeal of EU Agencies' (2015) 40(6) ELR 832

Chiti Edoardo, 'An Important Part of the EU's Institutional Machinery: Features, Problems and Perspectives of European Agencies' (2009) 46 CMLR 1420

Chodosh Hiram E, *Global Justice Reform* (New York University Press 2005)

Choi Stephen J and Gulati Mitu, 'Contract as Statute' (2006) 104 Mich L Rev 1130

Choi Stephen J and Gulati Mitu, and Posner Eric A, 'The Dynamics of Contract Evolution' (2013) 88 NYU L Rev 1

Clarke Blanaid, 'Ireland' in Danny Busch and Cees Van Dam (eds), *A Banker's Duty of Care* (Hart Publishing 2019)

Coffee Jr John C, 'Class Action Accountability: Reconciling Exit, Voice, and Loyalty in Representative Litigation' (2000) 100 Col L Rev 370

Coffee Jr John C, 'Reforming the Securities Class Action: An Essay on Deterrence and Its Implementation' (2006) 106 Colum L Rev 1534

Coffee Jr John C, 'The Mandatory/Enabling Balance in Corporate Law: An Essay on the Judicial Role' (1989) 89 Col L Rev 1618

Coffee Jr John C, 'The Regulation of Entrepreneurial Litigation: Balancing Fairness and Efficiency in the Large Class Action' (1987) 54 U of Ch L Rev 877

Cohen-Eliya Moshe and Porat Iddo, 'American Balancing and German Proportionality: The Historical Origins' (2010) 8 ICON 263

Cohen-Eliya Moshe and Porat Iddo, 'The Hidden Foreign Law Debate in Heller: The Proportionality Approach in American Constitutional Law' (2009) 46 San Diego L Rev 367

Cohen-Eliya Moshe and Porat Iddo, 'American Balancing and German Proportionality: The Historical Origins' (2010) 8(2) Intl J Constitutional L 263

Cohn Michael J, 'Asset Securitization: How Remote Is Bankruptcy Remote?' (1998) 26 Hofstra L Rev 929

Coleman Jules, 'Efficiency, Exchange, and Auction: Philosophic Aspects of the Economic Approach to Law' (1980) 68(2) California L Rev 221

Coleman Jules, 'Negative and Positive Positivism' (1982) 11 The J Legal Studies 139

Coleman Jules, 'Tort Law and the Demands of Corrective Justice' (1992) 67 ILJ 349

Coleman Jules, 'The Conventionality Thesis' (2001) 11 Philosophical Issues 354

Coleman Jules, *The Practice of Principle: In Defence of a Pragmatist Approach to Legal Theory* (OUP 2001)

Coleman Jules, 'Beyond Inclusive Legal Positivism' (2009) 22 Ratio Juris 359

Coman-Kund Florin and Amtenbrink Fabian, 'On the Scope and Limits of the Application of National Law by the European Central Bank within the Single Supervisory Mechanism' (2018) 33 Banking & Fin L Rev 133

Conac P-H and Gelter M (eds), *Global Securities Litigation and Enforcement* (CUP 2019)

Contartese Cristina and Andenas Mads, 'EU Autonomy and Investor-State Dispute Settlement under Inter Se Agreements between Member States: Achmea' (2019) 56 CMLR 157

Conthe Manuel, 'Las sentencias del Supremo sobre Bankia' (2016) El Notario del Siglo XXI 66

Conti-Brown Peter, 'The Institutions of Federal Reserve Independence' (2015) 32 YJR 257

Conti-Brown Peter, *The Power and Independence of the Federal Reserve* (PUP 2016)

Cooper Jeremy, 'The New World of Tribunals: A Quiet Revolution' in Jeremy Cooper (ed), *Being a Judge in the Modern World* (OUP 2017)

Cordes, *The Search for a Medieval Lex Mercatoria* (2003) Oxford U Comparative L Forum 5 ouclf.law.ox.ac.uk, text after n 35

Cortes Pablo, 'Enforcing EU Consumer Policy More Effectively: A Three-Pronged Approach' in Sara Drake and Melanie Smith (eds), *New Directions in the Effective Enforcement of EU Law and Policy* (Edward Elgar Publishing 2016)

Cottier Thomas and Mavroidis Petros C, *The Role of the Judge in International Trade Regulation: Experience and Lessons for the WTO* (University of Michigan Press 2003)

Couvreur Philippe, 'The International Court of Justice' in Geert De Baere and Jan Wouters (eds), *The Contribution of International and Supranational Courts to the Rule of Law* (Edward Elgar Publishing 2015)

Crotty James, 'Structural Causes of the Global Financial Crisis: Critical Assessment of the New Financial Architecture' (2009) 33 Cambridge J Econ 563

Curtin Deirdre, *Mind the Gap: The Evolving European Union Executive and the Constitution* (Europa Law Publishing 2004)

D'Ambrosio Raffaele, 'Due Process and Safeguards of the Persons Subject to SSM Supervisory and Sanctioning Proceedings' (Quaderni di Ricerca Giuridica della Consulenza Legale no 74, Banca d'Italia 2013)

D'Ambrosio Raffaele, 'The Legal Review of the SSM Administrative Sanctions' in Chiara Zilioli and Karl-Philipp Wojcik (eds), *Judicial Review in the European Banking Union* (Edward Elgar Publishing 2021)

D'Ambrosio Raffaele, 'The Liability Regimes within the SSM and SRM' in Raffaele D'Ambrosio (ed), *Law and Practice of the Banking Union and of Its Governing Institutions (Cases and Materials)* (Quaderni di Ricerca Giuridica della Consulenza Legale no 88: Bank of Italy 2020)

D'Ambrosio Raffaele and Lamandini Marco, 'La "prima volta" del Tribunale dell'Unione Europea in materia di Meccanismo Unico di Vigilanza' (2017) Giur Comm II

D'Ambrosio Raffaele and Lamandini Marco, 'La sentenza del 30 luglio 2019 del BverfG sull'Unione bancaria e il difficile dialogo tra Karlruhe e Lussemburgo' (2020) Giur Comm II

D'Ambrosio Raffaele and Messineo Donato (eds), *The German Federal Constitutional Court and the Banking Union*, (Quaderni di Ricerca Giuridica della Consulenza Legale No 91, Bank of Italy 2021)

Danov Mihail and Bariatti Stefania, 'The Relationship between Litigation and ADR: Evaluating the Effect of the EU PIL Framework on ADR/Settlement in Cross-Border Cases' in Paul Beaumont and others (eds), *Cross-Border Litigation in Europe* (Hart Publishing 2017)

Davidoff Steven and Zaring David, 'Regulation by Deal: The Government's Response to the Financial Crisis' (2009) 61 Admin L Rev 463

Davies Jim, 'ADR/ODR: Too Much Optimism in the Promotion of Cross-Border Trade?' in Burkhard Hess, Maria Bergström, and Eva Storskrubb (eds), *EU Civil Justice: Current Issues and Future Outlook* (Hart Publishing 2015)

Deitz Adrian JS and others, 'Indented: Recent Court Decisions on New York Law-Governed Indentures and Their Impact' (2019) Butterworths J Intl Banking and Fin L 245

della Negra Federico, *MiFID II and Private Law. Enforcing EU Conduct of Business Rules* (Hart Publishing 2019)

della Negra Federico, 'The Private Enforcement of the MiFID Conduct of Business Rules: An overview of the Italian and Spanish Experiences' (2014) 10 ERCL 571

De Lucia Luca, 'The Microphysics of European Administrative Law: Administrative Remedies in the EU after Lisbon' (2014) 20 Eur Pub L 277

Dennis Roger J and Ryan Patrick J, 'State Corporate and Federal Securities Law: Dual Regulation in a Federal System' (1992) 22 Publius 21

Desogus C, 'La responsabilità extracontrattuale da rating errato: la Cassazione si esprime sulla competenza giurisdizionale' (2013) Giurisprudenza Commerciale 1009

Dnes Stephen, 'Promoting Efficient Litigation?' in Paul Beaumont and others (eds), *CrossBorder Litigation in Europe* (Hart Publishing 2017)

de S-O-l'E Lasser Mitchel, *Judicial Deliberations: A Comparative Analysis of Judicial Transparency and Legitimacy* (OUP 2004)

de S-O-l'E Lasser Mitchel 'Transforming Deliberations' in Nick Huls, Maurice Adams, and Jacco Bomhoff (eds), *The Legitimacy of Highest Courts' Rulings* (Asser Press 2009)

De Witte Bruno, 'Direct Effect, Primacy, and the Nature of the Legal Order' in Paul Craig and Gráinne de Búrca (eds), *The Evolution of EU Law* (OUP 2011)

De Witte Bruno, 'Judicialization of the Euro Crisis? A Critical Evaluation' in Franklin Allen, Elena Carletti, and Mitu Gulati (eds), *Institution and the Crisis* (European University Institute 2018)

De Witte Bruno, 'The Preliminary Ruling Dialogue: Three Types of Questions Posed by National Courts' in Bruno de Witte and others (eds), *National Courts and EU Law: New Issues, Theories and Methods* (Edward Elgar Publishing 2016)

De Witte Floris, *Justice in the EU: The Emergence of Transnational Solidarity* (OUP 2015)
Dey Joy, 'Collective Action Clauses: Sovereign Bondholders Cornered?' (2009) 15 L & Bus Rev of the Americas 485
Di Bucci Vittorio, 'Procedural and Judicial implications of Composite Procedures in the Banking Union' in Chiara Zilioli and Karl-Philipp Wojcik (eds), *Judicial Review in the European Banking Union* (Edward Elgar Publishing 2021)
Di Bucci Vittorio, 'Quelques questions concernant le controle jurisdictionnel sur le mécanisme de surveillance unique' in Roberto Adam, Vincenzo Cannizzaro, and Massimo Condinanzi (eds), *Liber Amicorum Antonio Tizzano* (Giappichelli 2018)
Díez Picazo Luis, *Derecho de daños* (Civitas 1999)
Díez Picazo Luis, *Fundamentos del Derecho Civil Patrimonial III: Las relaciones jurídico-reales: El Registro de la Propiedad: La posesión* (Civitas 2008)
Di Fabio Udo, 'Karlsruhe Makes a Referral' (2014) 15 German LJ 107
di Mauro B, Weder B, and Zettelmeyer J, 'The New Global Financial Safety Net: Struggling for Coherent Governance in a Multipolar Syste' (2017) CIGI Essays in International Finance 4
Dimitropoulos Georgios, 'International Commercial Courts in the "Modern Law of Nature": Adjudicatory Unilateralism in Special Economic Zones' (2021) 24(2) Journal of International Economic Law 361
Di Noia C and Gargantini M, 'Unleashing the ESMA: Governance and Accountability after the CJEU Decision on the Short Selling Regulation (2014) 15 Eur Org L Rev 24
Dorner Richard, *The Logic of Failure: Recognizing and Avoiding Error in Complex Situations* (Metropolitan Books 1996)
Drake Keegan S, 'The Fall and Rise of the Exit Consent' (2014) 63 Duke LJ 1589
Dunoff Jeffrey L and Pollack Mark A, 'International Judicial Practices: Opening the "Black Box" of International Courts' (2018) 40 Michigan J Intl L 40
Dworkin Ronald, *A Matter of Principle* (HUP 1995)
Dworkin Ronald, 'Darwin's New Bulldog' (1998) 111Harv L Rev 1718
Dworkin Ronald, *Freedom's Law: A Moral Reading of the American Constitution* (HUP 1997)
Dworkin Ronald, 'Hard Cases' (1975) 88(6) Harv L Rev 1070
Dworkin Ronald, *Taking Rights Seriously* (HUP 1977)
Dworkin Ronald, 'Reply to Critics' in Ronald Dworkin, *Taking Rights Seriously* (Duckworth 1977, reprinted 2005)
Dworkin Ronald, 'Rights as Trumps' in J Waldron (ed), *Theories of Rights* (OUP 1984)
Dworkin Ronald, 'Is There Really No Right Answer to Hard Cases?' in Ronald Dworkin, *A Matter of Principle* (HUP 1985)
Dworkin Ronald, 'In Praise of Theory' (1997) 29 Ariz St LJ 353
Dworkin Ronald, 'In Praise of Theory: Reply' (1997) 29 Ariz St LJ 431
Dworkin Ronald, *Law's Empire* (Bloomsbury 1998)
Dworkin Ronald, *Justice in Robes* (HUP 2006)
Dworkin Ronald, *Justice for Hedgehogs* (HUP 2011)
Dyck Alexander and Zingales Luigi, 'Private Benefits of Control: An International Comparison' (2004) 59(2) The J Fin 537
Dyzenhaus David, *The Constitution of Law: Legality in a Time of Emergency* (CUP 2006)
Easterbrook Frank, 'Statutes' Domains' (1983) 50 U of Chicago L Rev 533
Eckes Christine and D'Ambrosio Raffaele, 'Composite Administrative Procedures in the European Union' (2020) ECB Legal Working Paper Series No 20
Edwards Jonathan M, 'A Model Law Framework for the Resolution of G-SIFIs' (2012) 7 CMLJ 131
Ehlermann Claus-Dieter, 'Six Years on the Bench of the 'World Trade Court': Some Personal Experiences as Member of the Appellate Body of the WTO' (2002) 36 J World Trade 605
Eilmansberger Thomas, 'Bilateral Investment Treaties and EU Law' (2009) 46 CMLR 383

Eleftheriadis P, 'Pluralism and Integrity' (2010) 23(3) Ratio Juris 365

Elliot Mark and Thomas Robert, 'Tribunal Justice, Cart, and Proportionate Dispute Resolution' (2012) Legal Studies Research Paper Series, University of Cambridge, Paper no 8/2012

Ely John H, *Democracy and Distrust: A Theory of Judicial Review* (HUP, 1980)

Eskridge William and Baer Lauren E, 'The Continuum of Deference: Supreme Court Treatment of Agency Statutory Interpretations from *Chevron* to *Hamdan*' (2018) 96 Georgetown LJ 1083

Fabbrini Federico, *Economic Governance in Europe: Comparative Paradoxes, Constitutional Challenges* (OUP 2016)

Fallon Jr Richard H, *Law and Legitimacy in the Supreme Court* (HUP 2018)

Fallon Jr Richard H, 'Legitimacy and the Constitution' (2005) 118 Harv L Rev 1787

Farrell S, 'Court Upholds ISDA's Flawed Asset Provision' (2004) 23 Intl Fin L Rev 33

Fawley Brett and Neely Christopher, 'Four Stories of Quantitative Easing' (2013) 95 Federal Reserve Bank of St Louis Review 51

Feld Lars P and Voigt Stefan, 'Economic Growth and Judicial Independence: Cross-Country Evidence Using a New Set of Indicators' (2003) 19(3) Eur J Political Econ 497

Filler R, 'Ask the Professors: Did the ECJ Properly Rule by Dismissing the UK's Attempt to Annul ESMA's Regulation Banning Short Selling' (2014) 34 Futures and Derivatives L Report 3

Finch Vanessa, *Corporate Insolvency Law: Perspectives and Principles* (2nd edn, CUP 2009)

Fisch Jill E, 'The Development of Securities Litigation as a Law-Making Partnership' in Sean Griffith and others (eds), *Research Handbook on Representative Shareholder Litigation* (Edward Elgar Publishing 2018)

Fish Stanley, *Doing What Comes Naturally* (Duke University Press 1990)

Fitchen Jonathan, 'Private Enforcement of Competition Law' in Paul Beaumont and others (eds), *Cross-Border Litigation in Europe* (Hart Publishing 2017)

Fleck Robert K and Hanssen F Andrew, 'Judges: Why Do They Matter?' in Michael Reksulak and others (eds), *The Elgar Companion to Public Choice* (2nd edn, Edward Elgar Publishing 2013)

Fleischer Holger, 'Gerichtspezialisierung im Gesellschaftsrecht: Die Erfolgeschichte des Delaware Court of Chancery' in Helmut Siekmann (ed), *Festschrift für Baums* (Mohr Siebeck 2017)

Fleischer Holger, and Danninger Nadja, 'Comparing Commercial Courts in France and Germany: Tribunaux de commerce and Kammern für Handelssachen' (2017) 3 Rev Trim Dr Fin 48

Fleischer Holger and Danninger Nadja, 'Die Kammer für Handelssachen: Entwicklungslinien und Zukunftperspeckiven' (2017) 38 ZIP 205

Fleischer Holger, Bong Sebastian, and Cools Sofie, 'Spezialisierte Spruchkörper im Gesellschaftrecht' (2017) 81(3) RabelsZ 608

Flynn Leo, 'The Judicial Review of Fines and Penalty Payments Set by the SRB' in Chiara Zilioli and Karl-Philipp Wojcik (eds), *Judicial Review in the European Banking Union* (Edward Elgar Publishing 2021)

Fox Merritt B, 'Initial Public Offerings in the CMU: A US Perspective' in Danny Busch, Emilios Avgouleas, and Guido Ferrarini (eds), *Capital Markets Union in Europe* (OUP 2018)

Franck Susan D, 'The Legitimacy Crisis in Investment Treaty Arbitration: Privatizing Public International Law Through Inconsistent Decisions' (2005) 73 Fordham L Rev 1521

Frederick Shane, Lowenstein George, and O'Donoghue Ted, 'Time Discounting and Time Preference: A Critical Review' (2002) 40(2) J Econ Literature 351

Fritzsche Alexander, 'Discretion, Scope of Judicial Review and Institutional Balance in European Law' (2010) 47 CMLR 361

Fuller Lon, 'Consideration and Form' (1941) 41 Col L Rev 799

Fuller Lon, *The Morality of Law* (YUP 1969)

Galvis Sergio J and Saad Angel L., 'Collective Action Clauses: Recent Progress and Challenges Ahead' (2004) 35 Geo J Intl L 713

Gambacorta Leonardo, 'The Effectiveness of Unconventional Monetary Policy at the Zero Lower Bound: A Cross-Country Analysis' (2014) 46 J Money, Credit and Banking 615

García Vicente and José Ramón, *La Prenda de Créditos* (Civitas 2006)

Gardella Anna, 'Judicial Control of the Interface between the ECB and the SRB in the SRM' in Chiara Zilioli and Karl-Philipp Wojcik (eds), *Judicial Review in the European Banking Union* (Edward Elgar Publishing 2021)

Gargantini Matteo, 'La registrazione delle agenzie di rating e il ruolo della Commissione di ricorso delle Autorità europee di vigilanza finanziaria (nota a Commissione di ricorso delle Autorità europee di vigilanza finanziaria, 10 gennaio 2014)' (2014) Rivista di Diritto Societario 416

Garrido José María, 'No Two Snowflakes the Same: The Distributional Question in International Bankruptcies' (2011) 46 Texas Intl LJ 459

Garrido José María, 'The Distributional Question in Insolvency: Comparative Aspects' (1995) 4 Intl Insolvency Rev 25

Gauthier Lucille, 'Insider Trading: The Problem with the SEC's In-House ALJs' (2017) 67 Emory Law Journal 123

Geiger Rudolf, Khan Daniel-Erasmus, and Kotzur Marcus, *European Union Treaties* (CH Beck 2015)

Gerner-Beuerle C, 'Underwriters, Auditors, and other Usual Suspects: Elements of Third Party Enforcement in US and European Securities Law' (2009) 6 European Company and Financial L Rev 503

Gigerenzer Gerd, *Adaptive Thinking: Rationality in the Real World* (OUP 2000)

Gigerenzer Gerd and Brighton Henry, 'Homo Heuristicus: Why Biased Minds Make Better Inferences' (2009) 1 Topics in Cognitive Science 107

Gigerenzer Gerd, Todd Peter M, and the ABC Research Group, *Simple Heuristics that Make Us Smart* (OUP 2000)

Giudici Paolo, 'Italy' in Danny Busch, Guido Ferrarini, and Jan Paul Franx (eds), *Prospectus Regulation and Prospectus Liability* (OUP 2020)

GIannini MS, *Il Potere Discrezionale della Pubblica Amministrazione: Concetto e Problemi* (Giuffrè 1939) 42, 43

GIannini MS, 'Osservazioni sulla disciplina della funzione creditizia' in *Scritti per Santi Romano II* (Cedam 1939) 707 Glazer Steven A, 'Towards a Model Code of Judicial Conduct for Federal Administrative Law Judges' (2012) 64(2) Administrative L Rev 337

Goetz Charles and Scott Robert E, 'The Limits of Expanded Choice: An Analysis of the Interactions Between Express and Implied Contract Terms' (1985) 73 Calif L Rev 261

Golden Jeffrey and Lamm Carolyn (eds), *International Financial Disputes: Arbitration and Mediation* (1st edn, OUP 2015)

Goldstein Daniel and Gigerenzer Gerd, 'Models of Ecological Rationality: The Recognition Heuristic' (2002) 109 Psychological Rev 75

Goode Roy, *Principles of Corporate Insolvency Law* (Sweet & Maxwell 2011)

Goodhart Charles, *The Evolution of Central Banks* (MIT Press 1985)

Goodhart Charles, Hofmann Boris, and Segoviano Miguel, 'Bank Regulation and Macroeconomic Fluctuations' in Xavier Freixas, Philipp Hartmann, and Colin Mayr (eds), *Handbook of European Financial Markets and Institutions* (OUP 2008)

Gordley James, 'The Rule against Recovery in Negligence for Pure Economic Loss: an Historical Accident?' in Mauro Bussani and Vernon Valentine Palmer (eds), *Pure Economic Loss in Europe* (CUP 2003)

Gorton Gary, 'Clearinghouses and the Origin of Central Banking' (1985) 45 The J Econ His 277

Gorton Gary, *Slapped by the Invisible Hand: The Panic of 2007* (OUP 2010)

Gorton Gary and Ordoñez Guillermo, 'Collateral Crises' (2014) 104 A Econ Rev 343

Gorton Gary and Metrick Andrew, 'Securitized Banking and the Run on Repo' (2012) 104 J Fin Econ 425

Gortsos Christos, 'The Crédit Agricole Cases: Banking Corporate Governance and Application of National Law by the ECB' in Chiara Zilioli and Karl-Philipp Wojcik (eds), *Judicial Review in the European Banking Union* (Edward Elgar Publishing 2021)

Gott Jason B, 'Addressing the Debt Crisis in the European Union: The Validity of Mandatory Collective Action Clauses and Extended Maturities' (2012) 12 U Chi J Intl L 210

Grabenwarter Christoph and others, 'The Role of Constitutional Courts in the European Judicial Network' (2021) 27 Eur Public L 43

Graham John D, 'Decision-Analytic Refinements of the Precautionary Principle' (2001) 4(2) J Risk and Research 127

Gramckow Heike and Walsh Barry, 'Developing Specialized Court Services: International Experiences and Lessons Learned' (2013) Justice and Development Working Paper Series no 24/2013

Granovetter Mark, 'Economic Action and Social Structure: The Problem of Embeddedness' (1985) 91 AJS 481

Greco Ginevra, *Le Commissioni di ricorso nel sistema di giustizia dell'Unione Europea* (Giuffrè 2020)

Grundmann Stefan and M Atamer Yeşim, *Financial Services, Financial Crisis and General European Contract Law* (Kluwer Law International 2011)

Grundmann Stefan and Micklitz Hans-W (eds), *The European Banking Union and Constitution: Beacon for Advanced Integration or Death-Knell for Democracy?* (Hart Publishing 2019)

Gulati Mitu and Vanberg Georg, 'Paper Tigers (or How Much will Courts Protect Rights in a financial Crisis?)' in Franklin Allen, Elena Carletti, and Mitu Gulati (eds), *Institution and the Crisis* (European University Institute 2018)

Gulati Mitu and Scott Robert, *The Three and a Half Minute Transaction: Boilerplate and the Limits of Contract Design* (University of Chicago Press 2013)

Haar, Brigitte, 'Civil Liability of Credit Rating Agencies: Regulatory All or-Nothing Approaches between Immunity and Overdeterrence' (2013) SAFE White Paper No 1

Haar, Brigitte, 'Regulation Through Litigation: Collective Redress in Need of a New Balance between Individual Rights and Regulatory Objectives in Europe' (2018) 19 Theoretical Inquiries in Law 233

Habermas Jurgen, *Between Facts and Norms: Contributions to a Discourse Theory of Law and Democracy* (William Rehg trs, MIT Press 1996)

Haentjens Matthias, 'Private Law in Banking Union Litigation' and Jens-Hinrich Binder, 'Resolving a Bank – Judicial Review with Regard to the Exercise of Resolution Powers' in Chiara Zilioli and Karl-Philipp Wojcik (eds), *Judicial Review in the European Banking Union* (Edward Elgar Publishing 2021)

Haggard Stephan and Tiede Lydia, 'The Rule of Law and Economic Growth: Where Are We?' (2011) 39(5) World Development 673

Halberstam Daniel and Reimann Mathias (eds), *Federalism and Legal Unification* (Springer 2016), 17 Cassese Sabino, *A World Government?* (Global Law Press 2018)

Halonen-Akatwijuka Maija and Hart Oliver, 'Continuing Contracts' (2020) 36 JLEO 284

Hammitt James K. and others, 'Precautionary Regulation in Europe and the United States: A Quantitative Comparison' (2005) 25 Risk Analysis 1215

Hanretty Chris, *A Court of Specialists. Judicial Behavior on the UK Supreme Court* (OUP 2020)

Harlow Carol and Rawlings Richard, 'Promoting Accountability in Multilevel Governance: A Network Approach' (2007) 13 ELJ 542

Hart HLA, 'American Jurisprudence through English Eyes: The Nightmare and the Noble Dream' (1977) 11 Ga L Rev 972

Hart HLA, *The Concept of Law* (Clarendon Press 1997)

Hart John, Ely *Democracy and Distrust* (HUP 1980)

Hart Oliver, 'Incomplete Contracts and the Theory of the Firm' (1988) 4 J L, Econ and Org 11

Hart Oliver and Moore John, 'Foundations of Incomplete Contracts' (1999) 66 The Rev of Econ Studies 115

Hart Oliver and Zingales Luigi, 'Companies Should Maximize Shareholder Welfare Not Market Value' (2017) 2(2) J L Fin & Accounting 247

Hayek Friedrich A, *The Constitution of Liberty* (first published 1960, The University of Chicago Press 1978)

Helfer Laurence R and Slaughter Anne-Marie, 'Towards a Theory of Effective Supranational Adjudication' (1997) 107(2) Yale LJ 273

Hensler, Deborah, 'Third-Party Financing of Class-Action Litigation in the United States: Will the Sky Fall?' (2014) 63 De Paul L Rev 499

Herget James E and Wallace Stephen, 'The German Free Law Movement as the Source of American Legal Realism' (1987) 73 Va L Rev 399

Herinckx Yves, 'Judicial Protection in the Single Resolution Mechanism' in Robby Houben and Werner Vandenbruwaene (eds), *The Single Resolution Mechanism*, vol 2 (Intersentia 2017)

Hess Burkhard, 'The State of the Civil Justice Union' in Burkhard Hess, Maria Bergström, and Eva Storskrubb (eds), *EU Civil Justice: Current Issues and Future Outlook* (Hart Publishing 2016)

Hess Burkhard and Boerner Timon, 'Chambers for International Commercial Disputes in Germany: The State of Affairs' (2019) 1 ERALaw 33

Hessick F Andrew, 'Consenting to Adjudication Outside the Article III Courts' (2018) 71 Va L Rev 715

Hilbig Benjamin E and Richter Tobias, 'Homo Heuristicus Outnumbered: Comment on Gigerenzer and Brighton (2009)' (2011) 3 Topics in Cognitive Science 187

Hill Claire, Why Contracts are Written in 'Legalese' (2001) 77 Chi-Kent L Rev 59

Hill Claire, 'Bargaining in the Shadow of the Lawsuit: A Social Norms Theory of Incomplete Contracts' (2009) 34 Del J Corp L 191

Hirshleifer David and Welch Ivo, 'A Theory of Fads, Fashion, Custom, and Cultural Change in Informational Cascades' (1992) 100(5), J Pol Econ 992

Hodges Christopher, *Law and Corporate Behaviour: Integrating Theories of Regulation, Enforcement, Compliance and Ethics* (Hart Publishing 2015)

Hodges Christopher and Voet Stefaan, *Delivering Collective Redress: New Technologies* (Hart Publishing 2018)

Hodges Christopher, 'Collective Redress: The Need for New Technologies' (2019) 42 J Consumer Pol 59

Hoffmann Michael, '(PiS)sing off the Courts: The PiS Party's Effect on Judicial Independence in Poland' (2018) 51 Va J Trans L 1153

Hohfeld Wesley Newcomb, 'Some Fundamental Legal Conceptions as Applied in Judicial Reasoning' (1913) 23 Yale LJ 1

Holmes OW, 'The Path of the Law' (1897) 10 The Boston L School Magazine 457

Ioannidis Michael, 'The Judicial Review of Discretion in the Banking Union: From 'Soft' to 'Hard(er)' Look?' in Chiara Zilioli and Karl-Philipp Wojcik (eds), *Judicial Review in the European Banking Union* (Edward Elgar Publishing 2021)

Iribarren Blanco Miguel, *Responsabilidad Civil por la Información Divulgada por las Sociedades Cotizadas: su aplicación en los mercados secundarios de valores* (2008) 2 Revista del Mercado de Valores 61

Itzcovich Giulio, 'On the Legal Enforcement of Values: The Importance of the Institutional Context' in Andras Jakab and Dimitry Kochenov (eds), *The Enforcement of EU Law and Values* (OUP 2017)

Jacklin Nancy P, 'Addressing Collective-Action Problems in Securitized Credit' (2010) 73 L & Contemp Prob 175

Jackson Vicki C, 'Constitutional Law in an Age of Proportionality' (2015) 124 Yale LJ 3094

Jacqué Jean Paul and HH Weiler Joseph, 'On the Road to European Union—A New Judicial Architecture: An Agenda for the Intergovernmental Conference' (1990) 27 CMLR 185

Jaklic Klemen, *Constitutional Pluralism* (OUP 2014)

Jaraczewski Jacub, 'From Boars to Courts: The Landmark ECtHR Case Xero Flor v Poland' *EU Law Live* (11 May 2021)

Jemielniak Joanna, Nielsen Laura and Palmer Olsen Henrik, *Establishing Judicial Authority in International Economic Law* (CUP 2018)

Jensen Michael and Meckling William, 'Theory of the Firm: Managerial Behavior, Agency Costs and Ownership Structure' (1976) 3 J Fin Econ 305

Johnson Simon and Kwak James, *13 Bankers: The Wall Street Takeover and the Next Financial Meltdown* (Random House 2010)

Jones David, 'Emerging Problems with the Basel Capital Accord: Regulatory Capital Arbitrage and Related Issues' (2000) 24 J Banking & Fin 35

Kahneman Daniel, *Thinking Fast and Slow* (Macmillan 2013)

Kahneman Daniel and Frederick Shane, 'Representativeness Revisited: Attribute Substitution in Intuitive Judgment' in Thomas Gilovich, Dale Griffin, and Daniel Kahneman (eds), *Heuristics and Biases: The Psychology of Intuitive Judgment* (CUP 2002)

Kahneman Daniel and Tversky Amos, 'Judgment under Uncertainty: Heuristics and Biases' (1974) 185 Science 1124

Kahneman Daniel and Tversky Amos, 'Prospect Theory: An Analysis of Decisions Under Risk' (1979) 47 Econometrica 263

Kahneman Daniel and Tversky Amos, 'The Framing of Decisions and the Psychology of Choice' (1981) 211 Science 453

Kahneman Daniel and Tversky Amos, *Choices, Values and Frames* (CUP 2000)

Kahneman Daniel, Knetsch Jack, and Thaler Richard H, 'Experimental Tests of the Endowment Effect and the Coase Theorem' (1984) 98(6) J Pol Econ 1325

Kahneman Daniel and Sunstein Cass, 'Indignation: Psychology, Politics, Law' (2007) U of Chicago L School John M Olin Law and Economics Working Paper 346

Kalintiri Adriani, 'What's in a Name? The Marginal Standard of Review of "Complex Economic Assessments" in EU Competition Enforcement' (2016) CMLR 53

Kapan Alan J, 'The Negotiable Order of Withdrawal (NOW)Account: "Checking Accounts" for Savings Banks?' (1973) 14 Boston College Industrial and Com L Rev 471

Kapetanaki Natalia A, 'Transnational Securities Fraud Class Actions: Looking Towards Europe?' in Nuyts, Arnaud and Hatzimihail, Nikita E (eds), *Cross-Border Class Actions. The European Way* (Sellier European Law Publishers 2014)

Kaplow Louis, 'Rules versus Standards: An Economic Analysis' (1992) 42 Duke LJ 557

Karper Irene, *Reformen des Europäischen Gerichts- und Rechtsschutzsystems* (Nomos 2011)

Kaufman George G and Mote Larry R, 'Glass-Steagall: Repeal by Regulatory and Judicial Reinterpretation' (1990) Banking LJ 388

Kebede Tiba Firew, 'The Emergence of Hybrid International Commercial Courts and the Future of Cross-Border Commercial Dispute Resolution in Asia' (2016) 14 Loyola U Chi Intl L Rev 1

Kelsen Hans, *Teoría pura del Derecho* (Editorial Universitaria de Buenos Aires 1960)

Kende Mark S, 'The Unmasking of Balancing and Proportionality Review in U.S. Constitutional Laws' (2017) 25 JICL 417

Kennedy Duncan and Klare Karl E, 'A Bibliography of Critical Legal Studies' (1984) 94 Yale LJ 461

Kettering Kenneth, 'Pride and Prejudice in Securitization: A Reply to Professor Planck' (2009) 30 Cardozo L Rev 1977

Kettering Kenneth, 'Securitization and Its Discontents: the Dynamics of Financial Product Development' (2008) 29 Cardozo L Rev 1585

Kettering Kenneth, 'True Sale of Receivables: A Purposive Analysis' (2008) 16 ABI L Rev 511

Keys Benjamin and others, 'Did Securitization Lead to Lax Screening? Evidence from Subprime Loans' (2010) 125 The Q J Econ 307

Keys Benjamin, Seru Amit, and Vig Vikrant, 'Lender Screening and the Role of Securitization: Evidence from Prime and Subprime Mortgage Markets' (2012) 25 The Rev of Fin Studies 2071

Kindleberger Charles P and Aliber Robert, *Manias Panics and Crashes: A History of Financial Crises* (Wiley 2005)

Koch Adrienne B, 'A Narrow Lane: Navigating Claims for Breach of the Duty of Good Faith and Fair Dealing' (2020) NYLJ

Koch Elmar B, 'Collective Action Clauses: The Way Forward' (2004) 35 Geo J Intl L 665

Koch Elmar B, 'Collective Action Clauses: Theory and Practice' (2004) 35 Geo J Intl L 693

Koch Elmar B, 'The Use of Collective Action Clauses in New York Law Bonds of Sovereign Borrowers' (2004) 35 Geo J Intl L 815

Koch Philip, 'Section 19: Disclosure of Inside Information' in Rüdiger Veil (ed), *European Capital Markets Law* (Rebecca Schweiger tr, Hart Publishing 2017)

Koopmans Tim, *Courts and Political Institutions. A Comparative View* (CUP 2003)

Kors Maria Elizabeth, 'Altered Egos: Deciphering Substantive Consolidation' (1998) 59 U Pitt L Rev 381

Kramer XE and Sorabji J (eds), *International Business Courts: A European and Global Perspective* (Eleven International Publishing 2019)

Kraus Bruce, 'Economists in the Room at the SEC' (2015) 124 Yale LJ Forum 280

Kravitt Jason (ed), *Securitization of Financial Assets* (Aspen Publishers 1995)

Kregel Jan, 'Can a Return to Glass-Steagall Provide Financial Stability in the US Financial System?' (2010) 63 PSL Q Rev 60

Kremers J, Schoenmaker D, and Wierts P, 'Cross–Sector Supervision: Which Model?' in R Herrings and R Litan (eds), *Brookings Wharton Papers on Financial Services* (Brookings Institution Press 2003)

Kydland Finn E and Prescott Edward C, 'Rules Rather Than Discretion: The Inconsistency of Optimal Plans' (1977) 85 J Political Econ 473

Lahav Alexandra, 'Fundamental Principles for Class Action Governance' (2003) 37 Indiana L Rev 65

Lahny IV Peter J, 'Asset Securitization: A Discussion of the Traditional Bankruptcy Attacks and an Analysis of the Next Potential Attack, Substantive Consolidation' (2001) 9 Am Bankr Inst L Rev815

Lakoff George, *Moral Politics: How Liberals and Conservatives Think* (University of Chicago Press 2002)

Lakoff George and Johnson M, *Metaphors We Live By* (University of Chicago Press 1980)

Lamandini Marco, 'Il diritto bancario dell'Unione' (2015) Banca, borsa e tit cred I

Lamandini Marco, 'Il diritto bancario dell'Unione' in Raffaele D'Ambrosio (ed), Scritti sull'Unione Bancaria (*Quaderni di Ricerca Giuridica della Consulenza Legale No 81* Bank of Italy 2016)

Lamandini Marco, 'La riforma delle banche popolari al vaglio della Corte Costituzionale' (2017) Le Società

Lamandini Marco and Ramos Muñoz David, 'Administrative Pre-Litigation Review Mechanism in the SRM: The SRM Appeal Panel' in Chiara Zilioli and Karl-Philipp Wojcik (eds), *Judicial Review in the European Banking Union* (Edward Elgar Publishing 2021)

Lamandini Marco and Ramos Muñoz David, 'Bankia: Can You Have a Capital Markets Union without Harmonised Remedies for Securities Litigation?' *EU Law Live* (19 June 2021)

Lamandini Marco and Ramos Muñoz David, 'Banking Union's Accountability System in Practice: A Health Check-up to Europe's Financial Heart' (2022) Eur Law J 1

Lamandini Marco and Ramos Muñoz David, *EU Financial Law. An Introduction* (Wolters Kluwer 2016)

Lamandini Marco and Ramos Muñoz David, 'Law and Practice of the ESAs' Board of Appeal and of the SRB Appeal Panel: A View from the Inside' (2020) 57 CMLR 119

Lamandini Marco and Ramos Muñoz D, 'Minimum Requirement for Own Capital and Eligible Liabilities' in Vittorio Santoro and Mario Chiti (eds), *The Palgrave Handbook of European Banking Union Law* (Palgrave McMillan, Springer International 2019)

Lamandini Marco and Ramos Muñoz David, 'Monetary Policy Judicial Review by "Hysteron Proteron"? In Praise of a Judicial Methodology Grounded on Facts and on a Sober and Neutral Appraisal of (ex ante) Macro-Economic Assessments' *EU Law Live* (20 May 2020)

Lamandini Marco and Ramos Muñoz David, 'The Definition of Common Equity Tier 1 Capital and of Contingent Capital and the Diversity of Capital Instruments Issued by European Credit Institutions' in Bart Joosen, Marco Lamandini, and Tobias Tröger (eds), *Capital and Liquidity for European Banks* (OUP 2022)

Lamandini Marco, Ramos Muñoz David, and Ruiz Almendral Violeta, 'The BVerfG's Assessment on the Contributions to the Single Resolution Fund and Article 114 TFEU' in Raffaele D'Ambrosio and Donato Messineo (eds) The German Federal Constitutional Court and the Banking Union *Quaderni di Ricerca Giuridica della Consulenza Legale* No 91, Banca d'Italia 2021)

Lamandini Marco, Ramos Muñoz David, and Ruiz Almendral Violeta, 'The EMU and Its Multi-Level Constitutional Structure' (2020) 47 Legal Issues of Economic Integration 295

Lamandini Marco, Ramos David, and Solana Javier, 'The ECB as a Catalyst for Change in EU Law (Part 1): The ECB Mandate' (2016) 23(2) Col J Eur L 199

Lamandini Marco, Ramos David, and Solana Javier, 'The ECB Powers as a Catalyst for Change in EU Law (Part 2): SSM, SRM and Fundamental Rights' (2017) 23(2) Col J Eur L 199

Landes William M and Posner Richard A, 'The Independent Judiciary in an Interest Group Perspective' (1975) 18 J L & Econ 877

La Porta Rafael and others, 'Law and Finance' (1998) 106 JPE 1113

La Porta Rafael and others, 'Legal Determinants of External Finance' (1997) 52(3) J Fin 1131

Lasagni Giulia, *Banking Supervision and Criminal Investigation: Comparing the EU and US Experiences* (Springer International Publishing 2019)

Lastra Rosa M (ed), *Cross-Border Bank Insolvency* (OUP 2011)

Lastra Rosa M, *International Financial and Monetary Law* (OUP 2015)

Latty Elvin R, 'Pseudo-Foreign Corporations' (1955) 65 Yale LJ 137

Lee Paul L, 'The Source-of-Strength Doctrine: Revered and Revisited: Part I' (2012) 129(9) The Banking LJ 271

Lee Paul L, 'The Source-of-Strength Doctrine: Revered and Revisited: Part II' (2012) 129(10) The Banking LJ 867

Legomsky Stephen, *Specialized Justice: Courts, Administrative Tribunals, and a Cross-National Theory of Specialization* (Clarendon Press 1990)

Lehmann Matthias, 'Civil Liability of Rating Agencies: An Insipid Sprout from Brussels' (2014) LSE Law, Society and Economy Working Papers 15/2014

Lehmann Matthias, 'Bail-In and Private International Law: How to Make Bank Resolution Measures Effective across Borders' (2017) 66 Intl & Com LQ 1

Lehmann Matthias, 'Law Made in Germany: Quality or Lemon?' in XE Kramer and J Sorabji (eds), *International Business Courts: A European and Global Perspective* (Eleven International Publishing 2019)

Lehmann Matthias, 'The End of "Whatever it Takes"? The German Constitutional Court's Ruling on the ECB Sovereign Bond Programme' *Oxford Business Law Blog* (7 May 2020)

Lenaerts Koen, 'The European Court of Justice and Process-Based Review' (2012) 31 Yearbook of European Law 3

Lenaerts Koen, 'The Court's Outer and Inner Selves: Exploring the External and Internal Legitimacy of the European Court of Justice' in Maurice Adams and others (eds), *Judging Europe's Judges* (Hart Publishing 2015)

Lenaerts Koen, Maselis Ignace, and Gutman Kathleen, *EU Procedural Law* (Janek T Nowak ed, OUP 2015)

Leggatt Sir Andrew, *Tribunals for Users: One Service, One System* (Stationery Office 2001)

Lewis Michael, *The Big Short Inside the Doomsday Machine* (Norton 2010)

Lo Andrew W, 'Reading about the Financial Crisis: A Twenty Book Review' (2012) 50 J Econ Literature 151

Lord Justice Laws, 'Should Judges Make Law?' in Jeremy Cooper (ed), *Being a Judge in the Modern World* (OUP 2017)

Lord Justice Ryder, 'Improving the Delivery of Justice in the Shadow of Magna Carta' in Jeremy Cooper (ed), *Being a Judge in the Modern World* (OUP 2017)

Lothian Tamara and Pistor Katharina, 'Local Institutions, Foreign Investment and Alternative Strategies of Development: Some Views from Practice' (2004) 42 CJTL 101

Lubben Stephen J, 'Beyond True Sales: Securitization and Chapter 11' (2005) 1 NYU JL & Bus 94

Lupica Lois R, 'Asset Securitization: The Unsecured Creditor's Perspective' (1998) 76 Tex L Rev 595

Lynch Jason, 'Reevaluating Bankruptcy Remoteness: Transfers of Risk, Implications of the GGP Reorganization' (2010) 29 Am Bankr Inst J 58

Lyons D, 'Principles, Positivism and Legal Theory' (1977) 87 Yale LJ 415

MacCormick Neil, 'Beyond the Sovereign State' (1993) 56 Modern L Rev 1

Macey Jonathan R, 'Corporate Law and Corporate Governance: A Contractual Perspective' (1993) 18 J Corp L185

Magliari Andrea, 'Il Single Supervisory Mechanism e l'applicazione dei diritti nazionali da parte della Banca Centrale Europea' (2015) Riv It Dir Pubbl Comun 1348

Mahoney Paul G, 'Precaution Costs and the Law of Fraud in Impersonal Markets' (1992) 78 Va L Rev 623

Mahoney Paul G, 'Securities Regulation by Enforcement: An International Perspective' (1990) 7 YJR 305

Majone Giandomenico, *Evidence, Argument and Persuasion in the Policy Process* (YUP 1989)

Majone Giandomenico, 'The Regulatory State and Its Legitimacy Problems' (1999) 22 West Eur Politics 1

Majone Giandomenico, 'Transaction Cost Efficiency and the Democratic Deficit' (2010) 17(2) J Eur Pub Pol 150

Marafioti Giorgia, 'The Trasta Komercbanka Cases: Withdrawals of Banking Licences and Locus Standi' in Chiara Zilioli and Karl-Philipp Wojcik (eds), *Judicial Review in the European Banking Union* (Edward Elgar Publishing 2021)

Barbara Marchetti (ed), *Administrative Remedies in the European Union: The Emergence of a Quasi-Judicial Administration* (Giappichelli 2017)

Markesinis Basil S and Deakin Simon, *Tort Law* (4th edn, Clarendon Press 1999)

Marmor Andrei, *Interpretation in Legal Theory* (Hart Publishing 1990)

Martini Mario and Weinzierl Quirin, 'Der Vollzug nationalen Rechts durch di EZB und seine ungelösten Folgeprobleme' (2017) NVwZ

Martinico Giuseppe and Pollicino Oreste, *The Interaction between Europe's Legal Systems Judicial Dialogue and the Creation of Supranational Laws* (Edward Elgar Publishing 2014)

Martucci Francesco, 'The Crèdit Mutuel Arkéa Case: Central Bodies and the SSM, and the Interpretation of National Law by the ECJ' in Chiara Zilioli and Karl-Philipp Wojcik (eds), *Judicial Review in the European Banking Union* (Edward Elgar Publishing 2021)

Mathews Jud and Stone Sweet Alec, 'Proportionality Balancing and Global Constitutionalism' (2009) 47 CJTL 73

Maxeiner James R, 'United States Federalism: Harmony Without Unity' in Daniel Halberstam and Mathias Reimann (eds), *Federalism and Legal Unification: A Comparative Empirical Investigation of Twenty Systems* (Springer 2014)

Mayoral Juan A and Wind Marlene, 'Introduction: National Courts vis-à-vis EU Law: New Issues, Theories and Methods' in Bruno de Witte and others (eds), *National Courts and EU Law: New Issues, Theories and Methods* (Edward Elgar Publishing 2016)

McCulley Paul, 'Teton Reflections' (2007) PIMCO Global Central Bank Focus

McGuire Kevin T, 'The Judicial Process and Public Policy' in RAW Rhodes, Sarah A Binder, and Bert A Rockman (eds), *The Oxford Handbook of Political Institutions* (OUP 2008)

McLeay Michael, Radia Amar, and Thomas Ryland, 'Money Creation in the Modern Economy' (2014) Bank of England Quarterly Bulletin Q1

Mendes Joana, 'Discretion, Care and Public Interests in the EU Administration: Probing the Limits of Law' (2016) 53 CMLR 419

Mersch Yves and others, 'The New Challeges Raised by Investment Arbitration for the EU Legal Order' (2019) ECB Legal Working Paper Series No 19

Michaels Ralf, 'European Class Action and Applicable Law' in Nuyts Arnaud and Hatzimihail Nikita E (eds), *Cross-Border Class Actions: The European Way* (Sellier European Law Publishers 2014)

Mill John Stuart, *Utilitarianism* (first published 1863, BLTC 1995)

Miller Arthur R, 'The American Class Action: From Birth to Maturity' (2018) 19 Theoretical Inquiries in Law 1

Miller Marcus, Weller Paul, and Zhang Lei, 'Moral Hazard and the US Stock Market: Analysing the "Greenspan Put"' (2002) 112 The Economic J 171

Mishkin Frederic S, 'Monetary Policy Strategy: Lessons after the Crisis' (2011) NBER Working Paper 16755

Mishkin Frederic S, 'The Transmission Mechanism and the Role of Assets in Monetary Policy' (2001) NBER Working Paper Series Working Paper 8617

Mock Sebastian, 'Germany' in Danny Busch, Guido Ferrarini, and Jan Paul Franx (eds), *Prospectus Regulation and Prospectus Liability* (OUP 2020)

Moliére, *Le Bourgeois gentilhomme* (Louandre 1910)

Moller Stephen H, Nolan Anthony RG, and Goldwasser Howard M, 'Section 2(a)(iii) of the ISDA Master Agreement and Emerging Swaps Jurisprudence in the Shadow of Lehman Brothers' (2011) JIBLR 7

Moloney Niamh, 'Banking Union and the Charter of Fundamental Rights' in Chiara Zilioli and Karl-Philipp Wojcik (eds), *Judicial Review in the European Banking Union* (Elgar Financial Law and Practice 2021)

Moloney Niamh, *EU Securities and Financial Markets Regulation* (OUP 2014)

Morra Concetta Brescia, 'The Interplay between the ECB and NCAs in the "Common Procedures" under the SSM Regulation: Are There Gaps in Legal Protection? in *Judicial review in the Banking Union and in the EU financial archtecture* (*aderni di Ricerca Giuridica della Consulenza Legale* No 84, Bank of Italy 2018)

Morra Concetta Brescia and Della Negra Federico, 'Overview on the Litigation on the "ex ante" Contributions to the SRF: the Strict Standard of Review Adopted by the Court to Ensure Effective Legal Protection' in Chiara Zilioli and Karl-Philipp Wojcik (eds), *Judicial Review in the European Banking Union* (Edward Elgar Publishing 2021)

Mugasha Agasha, 'The Agent Bank's Possible Fiduciary Liability to Syndicate Banks' (1996) 27 Can Bus LJ 403

Mugasha Agasha, *The Law of Multi-Bank Financing: Syndicated Loans and the Secondary Loan Market* (OUP 2008)

Muratori Edoardo, 'Ernests Bernis (Appeal) and Judicial Review by the CJEU of Non-Resolution Decision in the EU Banking Union: No Standing for the Shareholders of the Relevant Entity' (2022) 7 European Papers 327

Murphy Ryan, 'The Effective Enforcement of Economic Governance in the European Union: Brave New World or a False Dawn?' in Sara Drake and Melanie Smith (eds), *New Directions in the Effective Enforcement of EU Law and Policy* (Edward Elgar Publishing 2016)

Nees Anne Tucker, 'Making a Case for Business Courts: A Survey of and Proposed Framework to Evaluate Business Courts' (2007) 24 Georgia State U L Rev 477

North Douglass C, 'Institutions' (1991) 5 J Econ Perspectives 97

North Douglass C, 'The New Institutional Economics' (1986) 142 JITE/Zeitschrift Für Die Gesamte Staatswissenschaft 230

Nuyts Arnaud and Hatzimihail Nikita E (eds), *Cross-Border Class Actions. The European Way* (Sellier European Law Publishers 2014)

O'Brien Justin and Gilligan George, *Integrity, Risk and Accountability in Capital Markets: Regulating Culture* (Hart Publishing 2013)

Odorizzi Michelle L., 'Customer-Bank Communication Terminals and the McFadden Act Definition of a 'Branch Bank'' (1975) 42 The U of Chicago L Rev 362

Gerald Nels Olson, *Money, Morality and Law: A Case for Financial Crisis Accountability* (Kluwer Law International 2019)

of Heswall Lady Arden, 'Foreword' in Chiara Zilioli and Karl-Philipp Wojcik (eds), *Judicial Review in the European Banking Union* (Elgar Edward Publishing 2021)

Omarova Saule T, 'License to Deal: Mandatory Approval of Complex Financial Products' (2012) 90 Washington U L Rev 63

Okada Yohei, 'The Immunity of International Organizations before and after Jam v IFC: Is the Functional Necessity Rationale Still Relevant?' (2020) 72 Q J Intl L 29

Oro Martinez Cristian, 'The Small Claims Regulation: On the Way to an Improved European Procedure?' in Burkhard Hess, Maria Bergström, and Eva Storskrubb (eds), *EU Civil Justice. Current Issues and Future Outlook* (Hart Publishing 2015)

Pachnik Karol and Krajewski Jakub, 'The European Concept of a Fair Trial and the Legal Admissibility of Assessors in the Polish Judicial System' in Elzbieta Kuzelewska and others (eds), *European Judicial Systems as a Challenge for Democracy* (Intersentia 2015)

Padoa Schioppa Tomaso, 'Central Banks and Financial Stability: Exploring the Land in Between' in Vítor Gaspar, Philip Hartmann, and Olaf Sleijpen (eds), *The Transformation of the European Financial System* 2002 https://www.ecb.europa.eu/pub/pdf/other/transformationeuropeanfinancialsystemen.pdf

Palumbo Giuliana and others, 'Judicial Performance and Its Determinants: A Cross-Country Perspective' (2013) OECD Economic Policy Papers no 5

Palumbo, Giuliana and others, 'The Economics of Civil Justice: New Cross-Country Data and Empirics' (2013) OECD Economics Department Working Papers no 1060

Pantaleo Luca, *The Participation of the EU in International Dispute Settlement: Lessons from EU Investments Agreements* (Springer 2019)

Pardolesi Roberto, 'Private Enforcement of Antitrust Law' in Thomas Eger and Hans-Bernd Schäfer (eds), *Research Handbook on the Economics of European Union Law* (Edward Elgar Publishing 2012)

Paulsson Jan, 'Moral Hazard in International Dispute Resolution' (2010) 25 ICSID Review 339

Payne Jennifer, 'Debt Restructuring in English Law: Lessons from the U.S. and the Need for Reform' (2013) Oxford Legal Research Paper Series No 89/2013

Pearce Forrest, 'Bankruptcy-Remote Special Purpose Entities and a Business's Right to Waive Its Ability to File for Bankruptcy' (2012) 28 Emory Bankr Devs J 507

Petrucci Carlo, 'Effective Private Enforcement of EU Competition Law: an input and output Legitimacy analysis of Collective Redress' in Sara Drake and Melanie Smith (eds), *New Directions in the Effective Enforcement of EU Law and Policy* (Edward Elgar Publishing 2016)

Pfeiffer Thomas, 'Ein europäisches Handelgerichtshof und die Entwicklung des europäischen Privatrechts' (2016) ZEuP 797

Picciau Chiara, *Diffusione di giudizi inesatti nel mercato finanziario e responsabilita' delle agenzie di rating* (Egea 2018)

Piketty Thomas, *Le capital au XXIe siècle* (Sevil 2013)

Pildes Richard H, 'Expressive Theories of Law: A General Restatement' (2000) 148 U Pa L Rev 1503, 1531

Pinto Arthur R, 'Takeover Statutes: The Dormant Commerce Clause and State Corporate Law' (1987) 41 Miami L Rev 474

Piqani Darinka 'The Simmenthal Revolution Revisited: What Role for Constitutional Courts?' in Bruno de Witte and others (eds), *National Courts and EU Law: New Issues, Theories and Methods* (Edward Elgar Publishing 2016)

Pistor Katharina, 'The Standardization of Law and Its Effect on Developing Economies' (2002) 50 AJCL 97

Pistor Katharina, 'Rethinking the "Law and Finance" Paradigm' (2009) 6 BYU L Rev 1647

Pistor Katharina, 'A Legal Theory of Finance' (2013) 41 J Com Econ 303

Pistor Katharina, 'Towards a Legal Theory of Finance' (2013) European Corporate Governance Institute Working Paper 196/2013 1

Pistor Katharina, *The Code of Capital: How the Law Creates Wealth and Inequality* (PUP 2020)

Pistor Katharina and others, 'Evolution of Corporate Law: A Cross-Country Comparison' (2002) 23 U Pa J Intl L 791

Pistor Katharina and Xu Chenggang, 'Incomplete Law' (2003) 35 NYU J Intl L & Policy 931

Planck Thomas, 'Sense and Sensibility in Securitization: a Prudent Legal Structure and a Fanciful Critique' (2009) 30 Cardozo L Rev 617

Plomer Aurora, 'The Unitary Patent &Unified Patent Court: A New Leap into Unchartered Legal Territory' in Marise Cremona, Anne Thies, and Ramses A Wessel (eds), *The European Union and International Dispute Settlement* (Hart Publishing 2017)

Poiares Maduro Miguel, *We, the Cour: The European Court of Justice and the European Economic Constitution* (Hart Publishing 1998)

Poiares Maduro Miguel, 'Interpreting European Law: Judicial Adjudication in a Context of Constitutional Pluralism' (2007) Eur J Legal Studies 1

Poscia Jeanne, 'The VTB Case: Administrative Penalties and Administrative Measures' in Chiara Zilioli and Karl-Philipp Wojcik (eds), *Judicial Review in the European Banking Union* (Edward Elgar Publishing 2021)

Posner Eric E, 'Economic Analysis of Contract Law after Three Decades: Success or Failure?' (2003) 112 Yale LJ 829

Posner Eric E and Weyl E Glen, 'Cost-Benefit Analysis of Financial Regulations: A Response to Criticisms' (2015) 124 Yale LJ 246

Posner Richard A, 'Utilitarianism, Economics, and Legal Theory' (1979) 8(1) J Legal Studies 103

Posner Richard A, 'Legislation and Its Interpretation: A Primer' (1989) 68 Neb L Rev 431

Posner Richard A, 'What Do Judges and Justices Maximize? (the Same thing Everybody Else Does)' (1993) 3 Supreme Court Econ Rev 1

Posner Richard A, *Overcoming Law* (HUP 1996)

Posner Richard A, 'Conceptions of Legal Theory: A Response to Ronald Dworkin' (1997) 29 Ariz St LJ 377

Posner Richard A, 'The Problematics of Moral and Legal Theory' (1998) 111 Harv L Rev 1637

Posner Richard A, 'Reply to Critics of the Problematics of Moral and Legal Theory' (1998) 111 Harv L Rev 1796

Posner Richard A, *The Problematics of Moral and Legal Theory* (HUP 1999)

Posner Richard A and Vermeule Adrian, 'Crisis Governance in the Administrative State: 9/11 and the Financial Meltdown of 2008' (2010) 76 U Chi L Rev 1613

Potestà Michele, 'Legitimate Expectations in Investment Treaty Law: Understanding the Roots and the Limits of a Controversial Concept' (2013) 88 ICSID Review 88–122

Pound Roscoe, 'Mechanical Jurisprudence' (1908) 8 Col L Rev 605

Prek Miro and Lefèvre Silvère, '"Administrative Discretion", "Power of Appraisal" and "Margin of Appraisal" in Judicial Review Proceedings before the General Court' (2019) 56 CMLR 339

Prek Miro and Lefèvre Silvère, 'The EU Courts as 'National' Courts: National Law in the EU Judicial Process' (2017) 53(2) CMLR 369

Rajan Raghuram G and Ramcharan Rodney, 'Land and Credit: A Study of the Political Economy of Banking in the United States in the Early 20th Century' (2011) 66 The J Fin 1895

Rajan Raghuram and Zingales Luigi, *Saving Capitalism from the Capitalists* (PUP 2004)

Ramos Muñoz David, 'In Praise of Small Things: Securitization and Governance Structure' (2010) CMLJ 5

Ramos Muñoz David, *The Law of Transnational Securitization* (OUP 2010)

Ramos Muñoz David, 'Transacciones Trascendentes: Operaciones fuera de balance, disociación de la propiedad y problemas regulatorios, patrimoniales y de gobierno' (2012) 125 RDBB 201

Ramos Muñoz David, 'Bankruptcy-remote Transactions and Bankruptcy Law: A Comparative Approach (Part 1): Changing the Focus on vehicle Shielding' (2015) 10 CMLJ 362

Ramos Muñoz David, 'Shadow Banking: The Blind Spot in Banking and Capital Markets Reform' (2016) 13 ECFR 157

Ramos Muñoz David, 'Can Complex Contracts Replace Bankruptcy Principles? Why Interpretation Matters' (2018) 92 Am Bankruptcy LJ 417

Ramos Muñoz David, 'Law and Practice of the ESAs' Board of Appeal and of the SRB Appeal Panel: A View from the Inside' (2020) CMLR 57

Ramos Muñoz David and Solana Javier, 'Bank Resolution and Creditor Distribution: The Tension Shaping Global Banking, Part I: "External and Intra-Group Funding" and "Ex Ante Planning v. Ex Post Execution" Dimensions' (2020) 28 U Miami Bus L Rev 1

Ramos Muñoz David and Solana Javier, 'Bank Resolution and Creditor Distribution: The Tension Shaping Global Banking (Part II): The Cross-Border Dimension' (2020) 28 Miami Journal of Business Law 2

Rawls John, 'Two Concepts of Rules' (1955) 64 The Philosophical Rev 3

Rawls John, *A Theory of Justice* (HUP 1971)

Raz Joseph, 'Legal Principles and the Limits of Law' (1972) 81 Yale LJ 823

Raz Joseph, 'Interpretation without Retrieval' in Marmor A (ed), *Law and Interpretation* (Clarendon Press 1995)

Raz Joseph, 'On the Nature of Law' (1996) 82 Archive fur Rechts und Sozialphilosophie 1

Reed Amar Akhil, 'A Neo-Federalist View of Article III: Separating the Two Tiers of Federal Jurisdiction' (1985) 65 BUL Rev 205

Reinhart Carmen and Rogoff Kenneth, *This Time Is Different: Eight Centuries of Financial Folly* (PUP 2009)

Revesz Richard L, 'Cost-Benefit Analysis and the Structure of the Administrative State: The Case of Financial Services Regulation' (2017) 34 YJR 545

Richardson Liz, Spencer Pauline, and Wexler David, 'The International Framework for Court Excellence and Therapeutic Jurisprudence: Creating Excellent Courts and Enhancing Wellbeing' (2016) 25 J Judicial Administration 148

Rodrik Dani, Subramanian Arvind, and Trebbi Francesco, 'The Primacy of Institutions' (2004) 9 J Econ Growth, 131

Röh Lars and de Raet Tobias, 'The Securities Litigation Review: Germany' (7 June 2021) https://thelawreviews.co.uk/title/the-securities-litigation-review/germany#footnote-105-backlink

Romano Roberta, 'Empowering Investors: A Market Approach to Securities Regulation' (1998) 107 Yale LJ 2359

Romano Roberta, 'For Diversity in the International Regulation of Financial Institutions: Critiquing and Recalibrating the Basel Architecture' (2014) 31 Yale J on Reg 1

Rose Amanda M, 'The Multienforcer Approach to Securities Fraud Deterrence: A Critical Analysis' (2010) 158 UPA L Rev 2173

Rossi Filippo and Garavelli Marco, 'Chapter 6: Italy' in Danny Busch and Cees van Dam (eds), *A Bank's Duty of Care* (Hart Publishing 2019)

Rossidis Thomas C, 'Article II Complications Surroundings SEC_Employed Administrative Law Judges' (2016) 90 St John's L Rev 773

Rottman David, 'Does Effective Therapeutic Jurisprudence Require Specialized Courts (and Do Specialized Courts Imply Specialized Judges)?' (2000) 37 Court Review 25

Roubini Nouriel and Mihm Stephen, *Crisis Economics: A Crash Course in the Future of Finance* (Penguin Press 2010)

Rühl, Giesela, 'Ein europäisches Handelgericht' (2018) FAZ 6

Rühl, Giesela, 'The Resolution of International Commercial Disputes – What Role (if any) for Continental Europe?' (2021) 115 AJIL 11

Sager Lawrence Gene, 'Foreword: Constitutional Limitations on Congress' Authority to Regulate the Jurisdiction of the Federal Courts' (1981) 95 Harv L Rev 42

Sarmiento Daniel, 'Confidentiality and Access to Documents in the Banking Union' in Chiara Zilioli and Karl-Philipp Wojcik (eds), *Judicial Review in the European Banking Union* (Edward Elgar Publishing 2021)

Sarmiento Daniel, 'National Law as a Point of Law in Appeals at the Court of Justice: The Case of Crédit Mutuel Arkéa/ECB' *EU Law Live* (25 October 2019)

Sarmiento Daniel, 'The Reform of the General Court: An Exercise in Minimalist (but Radical) Institutional Reform' (2017) 19 Cam Yearbook of Eur Legal Studies 236

Satragno L, *The Rule of Law in Monetary Affairs: World Trade Forum* (Thomas Cottier, Rosa M Lastra, and Christian Tietje eds, CUP 2014)

Saurugger Sabine and Fontan Clément, 'Courts as Political Actors: Resistance to the EU's New Economic Governance Mechanisms at the Domestic Level' (2017) EMU Choices Working Paper Series 5

Scalia Antonin, *A Matter of Interpretation: Federal Courts and the Law* (PUP 1998)

Scalia Antonin, 'The ALJ Fiasco: A Reprise' (1979) 47 U Chi L Rev 57

Schiano Roberto, 'Le "camere giurisdizionali" presso la Corte di Lussemburgo: alcune riflessioni alla luce dell'istituzione del Tribunale della funzione pubblica' (2005) Diritto dell'Unione Europea

Schmitt Carl, *Politische Theologie. Vier Kapitel zur Lehre von der Souveränität [Political Theology: Four Chapters on the Concept of Sovereignty]* (first published 1934 English edn, CJ Miller tr, Antelope Hill Publishing 2020)

Schovsbo Jens, Riis Thomas, and Salung Petersen Clement, 'The Unified Patent Court: Pros and Cons of Specialization: Is there a Light at the End of the Tunnel (Vision)?' (2015) 46 IIC 271

Schütze Robert, *European Union Law* (CUP 2015)

Schwarcz Steven L, *Structured Finance: A Guide to Asset Securitization* (Practising Law Institute 2002)

Schwartz Alan and Scott Robert, 'Contract Theory and the Limits of Contract Law' (2004) 113 Yale LJ 541

Scott Robert and Triantis George, 'Incomplete Contracts and a Theory of Contract Design' (2006) 56 Case W Res L Rev 187

Seligman Joel, 'The Historical Need for a Mandatory Corporate Disclosure System' (1983) 9 J Corporate Law 1

Selvam Vijay, 'Recharacterisation in "True Sale" Securitizations: The "Substance over Form" Delusion' (2006) J Bus L 637

Selvam Vijay, *The Supreme Court and Administrative Agencies* (New York Free Press 1968)

Shapiro Martin, *Courts: A Comparative and Political Analysis* (University of Chicago Press 1981)

Shapiro Fred R, *The Yale Book of Quotations* (YUP 2006)

Skripova Olga, *Civil Liability as an Enforcement Tool of Securities Underwriter Gatekeeping Duty* (Erasmus Unniversiteit 2012)

Smith Adam, *An Enquiry into the Nature and Causes of the Wealth of Nations* (first published 1776, Edwin Cannan ed, Methuen & Co Ltd 1904)

Smith Moverly and Murphy Heather, 'Challenges to Collective Action Clauses: Can Any Parallel Be Drawn with Unfair Prejudice Petitions and Oppression of the Minority?' (2012) 27(8) Butterworths J Intl Banking & Fin L 479

Smits René, 'ECJ annuls a National Measure against an independent Central Banker' *European Law Blog* (5 March 2019)

Smits René and Bodenhoop Nikolai, 'Towards a Single Standard of Professional Secrecy for Supervisory Authorities' (2019) 3 ELR 295

Smits René and Bodenhoop Nikolai, 'Towards a Single Standard of Professional Secrecy for Financial Sector Supervisory Authorities: A Reform Proposal' (2019) 44 Eur L Rev 3

Snyder David V, Language and Formalities in Commercial Contracts: A Defense of Custom and Conduct (2001) 54 SMU L Rev 617

Soper EP, 'Legal Theory and the Obligation of a Judge: the Hart/Dworkin Dispute' (1977) 75(3) Michigan L Rev 473

Sorkin Andrew Ross, *Too Big to Fail: The Inside Story of How Wall Street and Washington Fought to Save the Financial System—and Themselves* (Penguin Press 2009)

Sousa Ferro Miguel, 'Tribunal da conorrencia, regulacao e supervisao: uma analise juridico-economica no seu 5. aniversario' (2017) Revista de Concorrência e Regulação 30

Stebbings Chantal, 'Bureaucratic Adjudications: The Internal Appeals of the Inland Revenue' in Paul Brand and Joshua Getzler (eds), *Judges and Judging in the History of the Common Law and Civil Law. From Antiquity to Modern Times* (CUP 2015)

Steinfatt Gabriele, *Die Unparteilichkeit des Richters in Europa im Lichte der Rechtsprechung des Europäischen Gerichtshofs für Menschen* (Nomos 2012)

Stiglitz Joseph, *Freefall: America, Free Markets, and the Sinking of the World Economy* (W W Norton & Company 2010)

Strotz Robert Henry, 'Myopia and Inconsistency in Dynamic Utility Maximization' (1956) 23(3) Rev of Econ Studies 165

Stulz René M, 'Credit Default Swaps and the Credit Crisis' (2010) 24 J Econ Perspectives 73

Sunstein Cass R, 'Incompletely Theorized Agreements' (1995) 108 Harv L Rev 1733

Sunstein Cass R, 'On the Expressive Function of Law' (1996) 144 U of Penn L Rev 2021

Sunstein Cass R, 'From Theory to Practice' (1997) 29 Arizona State LJ 389

Sunstein Cass R, *Legal Reasoning and Political Conflict* (OUP 2000)

Sunstein Cass R, 'Beyond the Precautionary Principle' (2003) 151 U of Pen LR 1003

Sunstein Cass R, 'Moral Heuristics and Moral Framing: Lecture' (2004) 88 Minnesota L Rev 1561

Sunstein Cass R, *Laws of Fear* (CUP 2005)

Sunstein Cass R, 'Incompletely Theorized Agreements in Constitutional Law' (2007) University of Chicago Public Law & Legal Theory Working Paper No 147

Sunstein Cass R, 'The Office of Information & Regulatory Affairs: Myths and Realities' (2013) 126 Harv L Rev 1838

Sunstein Cass R, 'The Limits of Quantification' (2014) 103 California L Rev 1369

Sunstein Cass R, 'Financial Regulation and Cost-Benefit Analysis' (2015) 124 Yale LJ Forum 263

Sunstein Cass R, *The World According to Star Wars* (Dey Street Books 2016)

Sunstein Cass R and Vermeule, Adrian, 'Interpretation and Institutions' (2003) 101 Mich. L Rev 885

Sunstein Cass R and others, 'Predictably Incoherent Judgments' (2002) 54 Stanford L Rev 1153

Tarullo Daniel, *Banking on Basel: The Future of International Financial Regulation* (Peterson Institute for International Economics 2008)

Taylor Michael W, 'Twin Peaks: A Regulatory Structure for the New Century' (1995) Centre for the Study of Financial Innovation Paper No20

Teixeira Pedro Gustavo, 'The Future of the European Banking Union: Risk-Sharing and Democratic Legitimacy' in Mario Pilade Chiti and Vittorio Santoro (eds), *The Palgrave Handbook of European Banking union Law* (Palgrave Macmillan 2019)

Tett Gillian, *Fool's Gold: How the Bold Dream of a Small Tribe at JP Morgan Was Corrupted by Wall Street Greed and Unleashed a Catastrophe* (Free Press 2009)

Teubner Gunther, *Law as an Autopoietic System* (European University Institute Press Series 1993)

Thaler Richard, *Misbehaving. The Making of Behavioral Economics* (Norton 2015)

Thaler Richard and others, 'The Effect of Myopia and Loss Aversion on Risk Taking: An Experimental Test' (1997) 112(2) Q J Econ 647

Thaler Richard and Shefrin Hersh, 'An Economic Theory of Self-Control' (1981) 89 J Political Econ 392

Thel Steve, 'The Original Conception of Section 10(b) of the Securities Exchange Act' (1990) 42 Stanford L Rev 385

Tiller Emerson H, 'The Law and Economics of Judicial Decision-making' in Francesco Parisi (ed), *The Oxford Handbook of Law and Economics*, vol I, *Methodology and Concepts* (OUP 2017)

Timmermans Christiaan, 'The European Union's Judicial System' (2004) 41(2) CMLR 393

Treitel Guenter, *The Law of Contract* (11th edn, Sweet & Maxwell 2003)

Tribe Laurence H, 'The Puzzling Persistence of Process-Based Constitutional Theories' (1980) 89 Yale LJ 1063

Tribe Laurence H, 'Jurisdictional Gerrymandering: Zoning Disfavored Rights Out of the Federal Courts' (1981) 16 H Civil Rights Civil Liberties L Rev 139

Tribe Laurence H, 'Constitutional Calculus: Equal Justice or Economic Efficiency' (1985) 98 Harv L Rev 614

Tridimas Takis, 'The Court of Justice of the European Union' in Robert Schütze and Takis Tridimas (eds), *Oxford Principles of European Union Law: The European Union Legal Order*, vol 1 (OUP 2018)

Tucker Paul, *Unelected Power* (PUP 2018)

Tulibacka Magdalena, 'Europeization of Civil Procedure: In Search of a Coherent Approach' (2009) 46 CMLR 1527

Tversky Amos and Kahneman Daniel, 'Judgment under Uncertainty' in Daniel Kahneman, Paul Slovic, and Amos Tversky (eds), *Judgment under Uncertainty: Heuristics and Biases* (CUP 1982)

Tversky Amos and Kahneman Daniel, 'Judgment under Uncertainty: Heuristics and Biases' (1974) 185 Science 1124

Ülgen Faruk, 'Collective Action and the Institutionalist Approach to Financial Regulation' (2018) 52(2) J Econ Issues 541

Upham Frank, 'Chinese Property Rights and Property Theory' (2009) 39 HKLJ 611

Upham Frank, 'From Demsetz to Deng: Speculations on the Implications of Chinese Growth for Law and Development Theory' (2009) 41 NYU J Intl L 551

Van Dam Cees, *European Tort Law* (2nd edn, OUP 2013)

Van den Bossche Peter, 'The Appellate Body of the World Trade Organization' in Geert De Baere and Jan Wouters (eds), *The Contribution of International and Supranational Courts to the Rule of Law* (Edward Elgar Publishing 2015)

Ventoruzzo Marco, 'European Rules and Judicial Review in National Courts: Challenges and Questions' in *Judicial review in the Banking Union and in the EU financial architecture* (Quaderni di Ricerca Giuridica della Consulenza Legale No 84 Bank of Italy 2018)

Verheij DJ, *Credit Rating Agency Liability in Europe: Rating the Combination of EU and National Law in Rights of Redress* (Eleven International Publishing 2020)

Vermeule Adrian, 'Many-Minds Arguments in Legal Theory' (2009) 1 JLA 1

Vermeule Adrian, 'Our Schmittian Administrative Law' (2009) 122 Harv L Rev 1095

von Bar Christian, *Non-Contractual Liability Arising out of Damage Caused to Another* (Otto Schmidt/ De Gruyter European Law Publishers 2009)

von Jhering Rudolph, 'In the Heaven of Legal Concepts: A Fantasy' (Charlotte L Levy tr, Foreword by John M Lindsey) (1985) 58 Temp L Q 799

von Mises Ludwig, *Human Action: A Treatise on Economics* (Liberty Funds 2007)
Wallach Philip, *To the Edge. Legality, Legitimacy, and the Responses to the 2008 Financial Crisis* (Brookings Institution Press 2015)
Wallerman Anna, 'Towards an EU Law Doctrine in the Exercise of Discretion in National Courts? The Member States' Self-Imposed Limits on National Procedural Autonomy' (2016) 53 CMLR 539
Warren G, 'Reflections on Dual Regulation of Securities: A Case Against Preemption' (1984) 3 Boston College L Rev 1
Weber Max, *The Theory of Social and Economic Organization* (Free Press 1964)
Weiler Joseph HH, 'Epilogue: Judging the Judges: Apology and Critique' in Maurice Adams and others (eds), *Judging Europe's Judges* (Hart Publishing 2015)
Weiler Joseph, 'Europe in Crisis: On "Political Messianism", "Legitimacy" and the "Rule of Law"' [2012] Singapore J Legal Studies 248
Weiler Joseph, 'In the Face of Crisis: Input Legitimacy, Output Legitimacy and the Political Messianism of European Integration' (2012) 34 Eur Integration 826
Westbrook Jay Lawrence, 'Priority Conflicts as a Barrier to Cooperation in Multinational Insolvencies' (2009) 27 Penn State Intl L Rev 869
Wijffels Alain and Van Rhee CH (eds), *European Supreme Courts: A Portrait Through History* (Third Millenium Publishing 2013)
Williamson Oliver, *Markets and Hierarchies, Analysis and Antitrust Implications: A Study in the Economics of Internal Organization* (Free Press 1975)
Williamson Oliver, 'Markets and Hierarchies: Some Elementary Considerations' (1973) 63 AER 316
Wissink Laura, 'The VQ Case T-203/18: Administrative Penalties by the ECB under Judicial Scrutiny' in Chiara Zilioli and Karl-Philipp Wojcik (eds), *Judicial Review in the European Banking Union* (Edward Elgar Publishing 2021)
Witte Andreas, 'Standing and Judicial Review in the New EU Financial Markets architecture' (2015) 1(2) OJFR 226
Witte Andreas, 'The Application of National Banking Supervision Law by the ECB: Three Parallel Modes of Executing EU Law?' (2014) 21 MJ 89
Worthington Sarah, 'Insolvency Deprivation, Public Policy and Priority Flip Clauses' (2010) 7 International Corporate Rescue 28
Wymeersch Eddie, 'The European Financial Supervisory Authorities or ESAs' in Eddie Wymeersch, Klaus Hopt and Guido Ferrarini (eds), *Financial Regulation and Supervision. A Post-Crisis Analysis* (OUP 2012)
Yeazell C, 'Group Litigation and Social Context: Toward a History of the Class Action' (1977) 77 Col L Rev 866
Zaring David, 'Law and Custom on the Federal Open Market Committee' (2015) 78 L & Contemporary Problems 157
Zaring David, 'Litigating the Financial Crisis' (2014) 100 Virginia L Rev 1405
Zedler Friederike, *Mehrsprachigkeit und Methode* (Nomos 2014)
Zilioli Chiara, 'From Form to Substance: Judicial Control on Crisis Decisions of the EU Institutions (with a Focus on the Court of Justice of the European Union)' in Franklin Allen, Elena Carletti, and Mitu Gulati (eds), *Institution and the Crisis* (European University Institute 2018)
Zilioli Chiara and Philipp Wojcik, *Judicial Review in the European Banking Union* (Elgar Financial Law and Practice 2021)
Zimmer Markus B, 'Overview of Specialized Courts' (2009) 2 Intl J for Court Administration 46
Zingales Luigi, *A Capitalism for the People: Recapturing the Lost Genius of American Prosperity* (Basic Books 2014)
Zingales Luigi, Kasperkevic Jana, and Schechter Asher, *Milton Friedman 50 Years Later* (Promarket–Stigler Center 2020)

Index

Abu Dhabi Court 13.40
access to documents *see* **transparency and access to documents**
access to justice 8.23–8.24, 12.61, 14.04
accountability 1.01, 1.31–1.33, 1.57, 1.59, 4.13, 4.62–4.96
   agencies 4.90
   appointment of members of financial regulatory bodies 4.83, 4.88–4.89
   crisis management measures, judicial review of 7.08–7.12
   ECB 4.13, 4.89, 5.20, 6.14, 14.17
   executive, deference to 2.16
   full accountability 12.53
   judiciary 1.01, 12.14, 13.35
   legal accountability 4.83, 12.53, 14.17
   legitimacy 1.31, 1.33
   Outright Monetary Transactions (OMT) programme 5.20
   political accountability 4.89, 6.14, 7.11
   privatizations without accountability checks 2.04
   public law disputes 4.62–4.66
   standard of review 1.33, 12.53
   transparency and access to documents 4.62–4.82
Administrative Procedure Act (APA) (United States)
   administrative law judges (ALJs) 13.12
   arbitrary and capricious standard of review 6.49–6.50, 7.64, 7.66–7.71
   financial stability 5.06, 5.09
   soft law 4.26–4.27
   standard of review 12.51
administrative review and judicial review, relationship between 4.90–4.96
advisers *see* **intermediaries' duties and representations**
agencies 1.01, 6.27–6.29 *see also* **credit rating agencies (CRAs)**
   agencification 4.89
   banks, role of agent 11.89, 11.90–11.92
   boards of appeals, with 13.13–13.14
   courts, horizontal balance with 8.17
   delegation 3.09, 4.19, 4.24
   discretion 3.09–3.11, 4.14, 4.18–4.24, 6.27–6.29, 6.33, 6.35, 6.39, 12.45
   EU 4.19–4.24, 4.70
   federalism 13.12
   institutions and agencies/bodies, distinction between 3.10
   New Deal 3.09
   specialization 12.21, 12.35, 14.15–14.18
   standard of review 4.18, 12.46–12.51
   transparency and access to documents 4.62–4.63, 4.70
allocation of powers *see* **vertical allocation of powers**
alternative dispute resolution (ADR)
   ADR Directive 13.45, 13.47, 14.21
   consumer ADR 13.45
   FIN-NET initiative 13.45–13.47, 14.21
   mass, small-ticket disputes 13.44–13.49
   preliminary references 12.60
annulment acts
   crisis management measures 4.56, 4.57–4.59
   effective judicial protection, principle of 7.81
   judicial review 3.04
   justiciability 4.39–4.45
   resolution schemes 4.56, 4.59, 7.81–7.82
   soft law 4.30–4.31, 4.35–4.36
   standing 5.07
   unclear legal status, justiciability of acts with 4.10
anti-deprivation doctrine 11.34–11.35
applicable law and jurisdiction in private law disputes 8.08–8.15
appointment of members of financial regulatory bodies 4.83–4.89, 5.23–5.24, 12.08–12.09, 14.19
arbitrary and capricious standard of review in United States 6.49–6.52
   Administrative Procedure Act (APA) 6.49–6.50, 7.64, 7.66–7.71
   cost-benefit analysis (CBA) 6.48, 6.49–6.52, 6.68
   creditors, rights of 7.64–7.72
   crisis management 7.63, 7.64–7.72
   de novo review 7.66–7.72
   procedural safeguards 6.48, 6.68–6.70
   shareholders, rights of 7.64–7.72
   substantive application of the law 6.48, 6.49–6.52
   unsafe or unsound practices 6.69–6.70
arbitration 10.35, 12.03, 13.59–13.66
   AAA, Financial Markets Group of 13.59
   commercial courts, competition with 13.43, 13.59–13.60, 13.66
   confidentiality 13.59
   court, definition of 1.02
   CPR, Banking and Financial Services Committee of 13.59
   crisis management measures 7.63, 7.83–7.86
   enforcement of awards 13.59
   EU 12.56, 13.61–13.66
   European Convention on Human Rights (ECHR) 13.65–13.66
   expertise 13.60
   intermediaries' duties and representations 10.35
   investment arbitration 12.03, 13.59–13.66
      crisis measures 7.63, 7.83–7.86

arbitration (cont.)
    ICSID arbitration 13.60, 13.62
    standards 13.65–13.66
    litigation, relationship with 13.59–13.66
    London Courts, preference for 13.60
    New York Convention 1958 13.59
    PRIME Finance 13.59
    proportionality 13.66
    public disclosure of judgments 13.59
    specialized financial courts 13.59–13.66
auditors, liability of 9.106–9.107, 9.114–9.119, 9.136, 9.139–9.140

bail-ins 7.03, 7.05, 7.30, 7.35
bail-outs 5.06–5.07, 7.30
Banking Union 1.10, 6.19, 7.04, 12.01, 12.05, 13.05
    specialization 1.08, 12.30, 12.38, 14.10
    standard of review 12.53
    ultra vires and unconstitutional, as 6.12
bankruptcy see also insolvency; liquidation
    anti-deprivation doctrine 11.35
    directors 11.05, 11.53, 11.54–11.58
    events of default 10.115
    fiduciary duties towards creditors 11.53, 11.54–11.58
    individual bankruptcy filings by creditors, limiting 11.53, 11.59–11.70
    inter-creditor disputes 11.53–11.70, 11.77
    ipso facto clauses, prohibition of 10.114, 11.36
    no-action/non-petition clauses 11.05, 11.59–11.67
    non-recourse provisions 11.59–11.60, 11.67–11.70
        post-enforcement call option (PECO) agreements 11.70
        principles 11.110, 11.114
    public policy 11.02
    remoteness 11.29, 11.53–11.70, 11.72
    safe harbour 11.03, 11.37
    shielding assets from formal bankruptcy proceedings 11.53–11.59
    special purpose vehicles (SPVs) directors, limiting filings by 11.53, 11.54–11.58
    trustees with sole powers to file claims 11.59, 11.62, 11.65
    voluntary filings 11.05
banks see also Banking Union; central banks; crisis management measures; European Central Bank (ECB); resolution schemes
    agent banks, role of 11.89, 11.90–11.92
    authorization, withdrawal of bank's 6.17–6.18
    Bank Holding Companies (BHCs) 6.35–6.39
        closely related to banking, expansion of activities 6.36
        non-bank financial firms, acquisition of 6.35, 6.37
        subsidiaries, securities underwriting through 6.38
    depositors, cases involving 7.52–7.58
    lenders of last resort (LOLR) 5.21–5.22
    marketing duties 10.37–10.48
    securities activities, prohibition on banks undertaking 6.35–6.38
    shadow banking 6.02, 6.35–6.42
    significant credit institutions 4.22, 4.93, 6.11, 6.15, 7.03, 7.10, 13.08
    structured financing 11.91
    substitutes, growth of bank 6.37–6.39
    supervision 6.83–6.86
basis clauses 10.39, 10.82–10.92
bias 1.29–1.30, 1.43 see also independence and impartiality
    attribute substitution 2.31, 2.35, 2.37
    cognitive bias 1.29, 2.31
    crisis management measures 2.12, 2.31–2.38
    decision-making 1.29
    executive 2.31–2.34
    hard cases 2.44
    heuristics 1.06, 1.29, 1.43, 1.57, 2.31, 2.35
    principles-based interpretivism 1.29–1.30, 1.43, 1.57
    representativeness bias 2.35, 2.44
    status quo bias or loss aversion 2.35
boilerplate clauses 8.29, 10.05, 10.39, 10.89, 10.105
Brexit 13.39, 13.41
business common sense 10.97–10.99, 10.103, 11.92, 11.106–11.108 see also commercial reasonableness
business judgment rule (BJR) 2.25

Canada 11.18, 11.78, 12.13, 13.64–13.65
capacity
    corporate capacity 10.06, 10.08
    legal persons 10.02, 10.06
    local governments 10.07–10.13, 10.20
    non-financial parties 10.02, 10.06–10.19
    speculative contracts 10.02, 10.12–10.20
capital maintenance rules 9.61, 9.63–9.64
Capital Markets Union (CMU) 12.01, 12.30, 12.38, 14.10
Capital Requirements Directive (CRD) 6.18–6.22, 6.31–6.32, 6.54–6.58
Capital Requirements Directive IV (CRD) 4.74, 4.78, 6.55, 6.57–6.58, 6.86, 6.92
Capital Requirements Regulation (CRR) 6.54–6.58, 6.86, 6.92, 13.22, 13.28
capricious standard of review see arbitrary and capricious standard of review in United States
causation
    exclusion and limitation of liability 4.15–4.16
    factual causation 9.119
    intermediaries' duties and representations in EU 10.47, 10.82–10.92
    legal causation 9.119
    misstatements, liability for 9.30–9.33, 9.87, 9.119–9.121, 9.143–9.144
        prospectuses 9.56, 9.70, 9.72–9.78, 9.82, 9.108
        reliance 9.127–9.128
    prospectuses, liability for misstatements in 9.56, 9.70, 9.72–9.78, 9.82

INDEX   501

reliance 9.127–9.128
time-inconsistency 1.32, 1.44
validity of contract disputes 10.21
central banks
  alter ego theory 4.06
  appointment and removal of members 5.23–5.24
  autonomous, treatment of central banks as 4.01, 4.06
  commercial activities exception 4.06
  competences 1.05
  contracts between central banks 1.34
  crisis management measures 1.20–1.21
  discretion 1.01, 1.38
  EU 5.10, 5.19
  exclusion of liability 4.11–4.12
  financial stability 5.01–5.05, 5.10
  fraud and injustice 4.06
  independence 4.06, 4.11, 5.05, 5.19
  individuals, exclusion of liability for 4.11–4.12
  inflation targets 1.44–1.45
  justiciability 4.01, 4.06, 4.11–4.15
  lenders of last resort (LOLR) 5.21–5.22
  price stability 5.01–5.03, 5.05
  principles-based interpretivism 1.21
  sovereign immunity 4.01, 4.06, 4.12
certainty *see* **legal certainty**
CETA (EU-Canada Comprehensive Economic and Trade Agreement) 12.13, 13.64–13.65
challenges *see* **nodes and challenges**
Charter of Fundamental Rights of the EU (CFEU) 1.12, 1.28, 14.14
  access to documents 4.71
  arbitration 13.65–13.66
  collective/class actions 13.56
  crisis management measures 4.09, 7.24, 7.32, 7.36, 7.38, 7.81, 7.92
  effective judicial protection, principle of 7.92. 13.35
  fair hearing, right to a 12.42
  judicial review 6.53–6.54, 6.72
  property rights, interference with 6.54, 7.36, 7.38
  transparency and access to documents 4.71, 4.78, 4.81–4.82
China International Commercial Court (CICC) 13.40
choice of law 8.09, 10.17–10.18, 13.41
civil law systems
  corporate capacity 10.06
  economic loss, damages for pure 9.06, 9.09
  formalism 1.07
  honour/image, torts against 9.96
  intermediaries' duties and representations in EU 10.70–10.77
  special purpose vehicles (SPVs) insolvency 11.23, 11.35
  specialization 12.22
  validity of contract disputes 10.06, 10.21
Civil Service Tribunal, abolition of 14.02
class actions *see* **collective/class actions**

clawback risk 11.11, 11.29–11.36
collateral arrangements, disputes over 11.01–11.02, 11.43–11.47
  bespoke arrangements 11.43–11.47
  classification of complex collateral arrangements as recognizable security 11.43, 11.44–11.47
  insolvency 11.17, 11.31, 11.33–11.34, 11.44–11.47
  inter-creditor disputes 11.53–11.70
collateralized debt obligations (CDOs) 9.34, 9.88, 11.38
collateralized mortgage obligations (CMOs) 7.69
collective/class actions 13.50–13.56
  access to justice 8.23–8.24
  ADR 13.44–13.49, 14.21
  arbitration 13.61
  competition cases 13.54, 13.56
  consumer ombudsmen 13.51
  covered class actions 9.46–9.47
  due process rights 13.52
  fair hearing, right to a 13.56
  fraud 1.13, 9.31, 9.33
  harmonization 13.51, 13.53
  mass, small-ticket disputes 13.44–13.49
  misstatements, liability for 9.31, 9.33, 9.46–9.47
  procedural safeguards 13.56
  prospectuses, liability for misstatements in 9.77
  regulatory provisions 8.23, 13.50–13.51
  Representative Actions Directive 13.51, 13.54–13.55
collective enforcement *see also* **collective/class actions**
  collective action clauses (CACs) 11.78–11.80
  inter-creditor coordination disputes 11.07, 11.72–11.76
  seizure and liquidation of assets 11.07
commercial paper activities 6.35, 6.37–6.39
commercial reasonableness 11.106, 11.108–11.110, 11.114 *see also* **business common sense**
common law systems 9.04–9.07, 9.32, 9.106–9.110, 11.13–11.18, 12.22
competition cases 6.99, 8.01, 13.09–13.10, 13.54, 13.56
complex proceedings, challengeability of acts in 4.38–4.48
conduct of business (COB) rules (UK) 10.63–10.67, 10.78, 10.85–10.86
confidentiality 4.71, 4.73–4.78, 4.81, 6.74, 9.50, 13.59
conflicts of interest 10.29–10.30, 10.46, 10.73, 11.97–11.98, 11.104
constitutional dimensions 1.28, 5.10, 6.10–6.14, 7.02, 7.03
consumer protection
  ADR 13.45
  arbitration 13.61
  dialogue between courts 12.63–12.69
  intermediaries' duties and representations in EU 10.49–10.50, 10.54–10.55, 10.81
  New Deal for Consumers 13.51
  ombudsmen 13.51

consumer protection (*cont.*)
  shadow banking 6.40
  unfair contract terms 10.49–10.51, 10.54, 10.83–10.86
contagion 6.43, 7.02, 7.03, 7.37
contract interpretation 8.25–8.29, 10.01, 10.93–10.124
  advice, relationships of 10.104
  ambiguity 10.102
  background/default rules 8.26
  coherence versus specificity 10.93
  complex clauses 8.25
  default, events of 10.105–10.121, 10.124
  dictionaries and grammars 10.95
  disputes 10.01, 10.04, 10.05, 10.93–10.124
  drafting 10.98
  express terms 10.94–10.104
  extrinsic evidence 10.102
  fair dealing 10.103
  finalistic interpretation 8.28–8.29
  functional interpretation 8.28–8.29
  gap-filling 8.26–8.27
  general considerations 10.105–10.121
  good faith 10.93, 10.94, 10.95, 10.100, 10.103–10.104, 10.111, 11.01
  implied terms 10.94–10.104, 10.114–10.117, 11.01
  intention of parties 8.25–8.29, 10.102
  mandatory provisions 10.94, 10.106
  marketing 10.93
  materially adverse effects (MAE) 10.93, 10.122–10.124
  natural and ordinary meaning 10.95
  pivotal problem 8.28
  reasonableness 10.93, 10.94–10.104
  standard terms 10.04–10.05
  standards of interpretation 10.94–10.95
contract law *see also* contract interpretation; standard terms
  applicable law 8.09–8.10
  consideration, doctrine of 9.07
  financial contract disputes 10.01–10.124
  insolvency 11.05
  misstatements, liability for 9.95, 9.120
  privity of contract 9.109
  reasonableness 2.25
  regulatory standards 1.05
  tort, division with 9.07
  trustees, role of 11.95–11.96
  unfair contract terms 10.49–10.51, 10.54, 10.83–10.86, 12.66
  validity of contract disputes 10.01–10.02, 10.05, 10.06–10.23
coordination
  court system 13.01–13.02, 13.09–13.37
  inter-creditor disputes 11.08, 11.71–11.106
  public law disputes 13.02, 13.03–13.37
  quasi-courts, horizontal coordination by courts and 13.11–13.37
corporate capacity 10.06, 10.08
corporate scandals 2.33–2.34, 2.43–2.45

cost-benefit analysis (CBA) 1.48–1.52, 1.56–1.58, 6.48, 6.49–6.51, 6.68
Court of Justice of the EU (CJEU) 1.10–1.13 *see also* preliminary references; specialized courts in finance law in EU
  annulment acts 4.30–4.31, 4.35–4.36, 4.39–4.45
  appointments, independence of 12.10
  Brexit 13.39, 13.41
  challengeability of acts in complex proceedings 4.38–4.48
  Civil Service Tribunal, abolition of 14.02
  confirmatory acts 4.39
  coordination of EU courts
    horizontal coordination 13.13–13.37
    vertical coordination 13.04–13.08
  deference 4.29, 4.37
  Deposit Guarantee Schemes (DGS) 4.33
  dialogue between courts 3.06
  direct and individual concern 4.36, 4.41
  discretion 3.08–3.11, 4.28, 4.44
  exclusion and limitation of liability 4.15
  fragmentation of courts 12.01–12.07
  gap-filling 1.10–1.11
  implementing acts 4.39, 4.43
  independence 12.10, 12.12
  intermediate/preparatory measures 4.39–4.40, 4.43, 4.45
  judicial clerks 12.41
  judicial review 3.04, 4.26–4.36, 4.37, 4.92–4.96, 6.10–6.22, 6.53–6.67
  language of proceedings 12.43
  living instrument principle 1.10
  national courts and EU courts, dialogue between 10.51, 12.55, 12.62–12.70
  national laws, EU authorities' application of 6.19–6.21
  non-contractual liability 8.21
  primacy of EU law 12.02
  proportionality 1.13
  quasi-courts, horizontal coordination by courts and 13.11–13.37
  regulatory and supervisory frameworks 3.13, 4.52, 6.10–6.22, 6.27–6.33, 8.21–8.22
  resolution schemes 4.44–4.45
  rule of law 1.12
  secondary law, rewriting 1.10
  soft law, justiciability of 4.28–4.36, 4.37, 6.30–6.32
  standard of review 3.10, 6.53–6.67, 12.46, 12.50, 14.18
  standing 3.13, 4.31, 4.36, 4.41, 4.52
  state aid 4.29, 4.34, 4.36
  substance-leaning and finalistic standard of review 6.53–6.67
  Unified Patent Court (UPC), cooperation with 14.06
courts 13.01–13.66 *see also* Court of Justice of the EU (CJEU); European Convention on Human Rights (ECHR)/European Court of Human Rights (ECtHR); quasi-judicial bodies/courts; specialization; specialized courts in finance law in EU

INDEX 503

agencies, horizontal balance with 8.17
arbitration, competition with 13.43, 13.59–13.60, 13.66
coordination 13.01–13.02, 13.03–13.37
court, definition of 1.02
crisis management measures 2.01, 2.12–2.38
design of courts 12.01
dialogue between courts 3.06, 10.51, 12.05, 12.55, 12.56–12.70, 14.21
EFTA Court 7.53, 7.88, 12.11
financial development, positive role in 2.01–2.11
fragmentation of courts in EU 12.01–12.07
harmonization 13.01–13.02
IACtHR 12.11
ICJ 12.08, 12.41
international relations, involvement in 4.01
law of finance, as essential component of 1.08
linear and non-linear interaction between national courts and EU courts 12.55, 12.62–12.70
organization of courts 12.41–12.43
positive role of courts 2.39–2.45
principles-based interpretivism 1.09, 1.55–1.56, 1.59
resources 1.08
rule of law 2.01–2.45
safety valve, courts as 1.09
ultimate authorities in defining key concepts, courts as 6.53–6.67
WTO Appellate Body 12.08
Covid- 19 1.17, 1.25, 5.04
credit rating agencies (CRAs)
  CRA Regulation 6.41–6.42, 9.142, 9.144, 13.20–13.23, 13.28, 13.57–13.58
  defamation 9.96–9.105
  fraud 9.134
  freedom of expression 9.96–9.105
  harmonization 9.142–9.144
  implementing technical standards (ITSs) 13.22
  journalist privilege 9.98, 9.102
  legal certainty 13.21
  misstatements, liability for 9.110–9.113, 9.117, 9.120, 9.137, 9.139, 9.142
    fraud 9.134
    freedom of expression 9.96–9.105
  negligence 9.142–9.143
  public concern, matters of 9.96–9.97
  quasi-courts, horizontal coordination by courts and 13.20–13.23, 13.28
  shadow rating 13.21, 13.57
credit unions, consolidated supervision over 6.46–6.47
creditors *see also* **inter-creditor disputes**
  arbitrary and capricious standard of review 7.64–7.72
  conflicts of interest between creditors 11.98
  crisis management measures, judicial review of 7.02, 7.03, 7.06, 7.59–7.62
  distribution 11.09, 11.106–11.115
  majority and minority creditors 11.07

  no-creditor worse-off (NCWO) principle 7.31, 7.37
  oppression 11.07
criminal liability *see also* **fraud**
  classification of criminal measures 6.77, 6.92, 6.94
  enforcement measures 6.77, 6.81–6.85, 6.87–6.88
  insider information 6.98, 9.50–9.51, 9.84, 9.86–9.87, 9.89, 9.92, 9.94
  market abuse 9.84–9.85
  misstatements, liability for 9.84–9.85, 9.92, 9.94
  money laundering 6.17–6.22, 6.59, 6.92, 6.94–6.95, 7.49
  presumption of innocence 6.98
  self-incrimination, privilege against 6.77, 6.87–6.88, 6.90
  silence, right to 6.81, 6.87–6.90
crises *see* **crisis management measures**
crisis management measures 1.06, 2.12–2.38, 7.01–7.98 *see also* **European Union, crisis management measures in the**
  accountability 7.08–7.12
  arbitrary and capricious standard of review 7.63, 7.64–7.72
  arbitration 7.63, 7.83–7.86
  bail-ins 7.03, 7.05, 7.30, 7.35
  bail-outs 5.06–5.07, 7.30
  Bank Recovery and Resolution Directive (BRRD)
    insolvency actions, automatic recognition of 7.89–7.90
    judicial review 7.03, 7.09, 7.14–7.17, 7.62
    prospectuses, liability for misstatements in 9.66, 9.69
    resolution funding arrangements (RFAs) 7.04
  bias 2.12, 2.31–2.38
  central banks 1.20–1.21
  contagion 7.02, 7.03
  corporate scandals 2.33–2.34
  courts 2.01, 2.12–2.38
  creditors, rights of 7.02, 7.03, 7.06
  cross-border dimensions 7.06, 7.87–7.98
  deference 2.13–2.21, 2.25–2.28
  delegation 7.08–7.13
  deposit guarantee schemes (DGSs) 7.04, 7.14–7.22
  deposit insurance schemes (DISs) 7.04
  depositors, cases involving 7.52–7.58
  discretion 2.23, 2.25, 2.27–2.28
  ECtHR 4.54, 7.24, 7.29, 7.31, 7.39, 7.42, 7.74
  emergency liquidity assistance (ELA) operations 5.22, 7.35
  enforcement powers 7.08–7.12
  executive
    bias 2.12, 2.31–2.34
    deference to 2.13–2.18, 2.21, 2.26
    proactive, ability to be 2.30–2.31
  expropriation 7.23
  fairness and equity towards shareholders and creditors 7.02, 7.06
  financial stability 2.18–2.19, 2.26–2.27, 7.01, 7.03, 7.39
  flexibility, law as a source of 2.18–2.19, 2.27

crisis management measures (*cont.*)
  FOLTF 4.44–4.45, 4.59, 6.17, 6.62, 7.03, 7.44–7.48, 7.77
  frameworks for crisis management 7.01–7.22
  funding schemes 7.08–7.22
  government intervention 2.12
  Great Financial Crisis 2007–2008 2.17, 2.33
  haircuts applied to sovereign bonds 7.23, 7.39–7.42
  hard cases 2.28, 2.39–2.42
  international context 7.93–7.98
  investment arbitration 7.63, 7.83–7.86
  judicial review 2.16, 4.19–4.22, 7.01–7.98
  justiciability 4.14–4.61
  legal principles and the role of courts 2.13–2.29
  Legal Theory of Finance (LTF) 2.18–2.20
  legitimacy 2.22–2.23
  legitimacy 7.07–7.22
  mandatory contributions 7.07
  market failure 2.01, 2.12–2.38
  mutual recognition 7.06, 7.93–7.95
  no-creditor worse-off (NCWO) principle 9.67–9.68
  positive role of courts 2.12–2.38
  positivism 2.22–2.24
  post-crisis settings 2.01, 2.36
  precedent 2.26–2.29
  principles 2.24–2.29
  procedural safeguards for creditors and shareholders 7.63–7.86
    arbitrary and capricious standard in EU 7.63, 7.64–7.72
    EU process review 7.63, 7.73–7.82
    international investment arbitration 7.63, 7.83–7.86
  property and other rights, interference with 7.23, 7.24
  prospectuses, liability for misstatements in 9.66–9.69
  ranking and hierarchy 7.03, 7.06, 7.59, 7.97–7.98
  reframing 2.12, 2.29, 2.37
  resolution frameworks 7.02, 7.03–7.05, 7.14–7.22, 7.93–7.95
  rule of law 2.01, 2.12–2.29
  separation of powers 3.02
  shareholders, rights of 7.02, 7.03, 7.06
  sovereign debt crises 1.25, 2.33, 4.01–4.07, 5.04, 5.06, 7.23, 7.39–7.43
  state aid 7.59–7.62
  substantive review beyond property 7.44–7.62
  substantive safeguards in bank crises 7.24–7.38
  substantive safeguards in sovereign crises 7.39–7.43
  takeover of financial institutions 7.01–7.02
  taxpayer support, minimising 7.02
  UNCITRAL framework 7.06, 7.93–7.97
custody risk 11.48–11.52
customary international law 4.03, 4.06

damages
  prospectuses, liability for misstatements in 9.60, 9.63–9.64, 9.68, 9.72, 9.75–9.82, 9.142–9.143
  pure economic loss 9.01–9.10

debentures 11.93–11.100
deceit 9.12, 9.15, 9.32, 9.106, 9.109, 9.113, 9.133
defamation 9.96–9.105
default, events of 10.105–10.121, 10.124
defence, rights of the 6.71, 6.74, 6.98
deference 1.16
  administrative review bodies 4.92
  arbitrary and capricious standard of review 6.49, 6.52, 6.68, 7.71
  crisis management measures 2.18–2.21, 2.25–2.28
  discretion 3.09–3.10
  EU 4.29, 4.37, 6.53, 6.63, 6.73–6.74
  executive 2.13–2.18, 2.21, 2.26
  monetary policy 5.08–5.09
  separation of powers 6.22, 6.33
  shadow banking 6.37–6.38
  soft law 4.27, 4.29, 4.37
delegation
  agency discretion, exercise of 4.19, 4.24
  arbitrary and capricious standard of review 6.49
  crisis management measures, judicial review of 7.08–7.13
  discretion 6.27–6.29, 6.33
  EU 3.10–3.11, 4.19, 4.24, 4.43, 6.27–6.29, 6.33
  New Deal 3.09
  regulation 3.09–3.11
  standard of review 6.48
deposit guarantee schemes (DGSs) 7.04, 7.14–7.22, 7.36
  EU 4.15–4.17, 4.33, 7.52, 7.54–7.58
  Deposit Guarantee Schemes Directive 4.15–4.17, 7.52, 7.54–7.58
deposit insurance schemes (DISs) 7.04
depositors and crisis management measures 7.50–7.58
derivatives disputes in insolvency 11.37–11.42
dialogue
  courts, between 3.06, 10.51, 12.05, 12.55, 12.56–12.70, 14.21
  discretion 12.45–12.46, 12.49, 12.54
  institutions, between 12.44–12.70
  specialization 12.45–12.46, 12.52, 12.70
  standard of review 12.44, 12.46–12.51
  systemic effects of lack of inter-court coordination 12.55–12.70
  threshold issue on access to EU forum to solve disputes of EU law 12.55, 12.56–12.61
directors 2.25, 11.05, 11.53, 11.54–11.58
disclosure, duty of
  insider information 9.84, 9.86–9.87
  intermediaries' duties and representations 10.24, 10.29–10.30, 10.38, 10.72–10.73
  market abuse 9.84–9.94
  misstatements, liability for 9.13–9.17, 9.22, 9.27–9.28, 9.35–9.36, 9.84–9.94, 9.137
  prospectuses, liability for misstatements in 9.78
discourse theory of justice 1.33–1.34, 1.53–1.54
discretion
  agencies 3.09–3.11, 4.14, 4.18–4.24, 6.27–6.29, 6.33, 6.35, 6.39, 12.45

arbitrary and capricious standard of review 6.49, 6.52, 6.70
boards of directors, fiduciary duties of 2.25
central banks 1.01, 1.38
   challengeability of acts 4.44
commercial reasonableness 11.108
cost-benefit analysis (CBA) 1.58
crisis management measures in the EU, judicial review of 7.13, 7.33, 7.35
deference 3.09–3.10
delegation 6.27–6.29, 6.33
Deposit Guarantee Schemes (DGS) Directive 4.15–4.16
discretion proper 3.10
EU 3.08–3.11, 4.28, 4.44
finality of discharge 6.49
hard cases 1.38
independent authorities 3.08–3.11
interpretation 10.99, 10.101
judicial review 2.25, 3.08–3.11, 4.91, 6.53, 6.67
judiciary 2.23
legitimacy 1.46, 2.23, 12.45
monetary policy 5.14
positivism 1.38, 1.44–1.45, 1.59
property rights, interference with 7.33
regulatory and supervisory frameworks 1.59, 4.18, 6.01
separation of powers 6.26, 6.33
shadow banking 6.35, 6.39
soft law 4.28
sources of discretion 3.10
technical discretion 3.10
trustees, role of 11.101–11.105
discrimination 7.29, 7.35, 7.86
distribution of proceeds, inter-creditor disputes over 11.106–11.115
Dodd-Frank Act (United States) 5.21, 6.45, 6.51–6.52, 7.03, 9.134–9.135, 13.12
Dubai, international commercial court in 13.40
due process
   collective/class actions 13.52
   crisis management measures 2.37, 7.26, 7.64
   financial stability 5.06
   fundamental rights 3.14
   investment treaties 7.84
   monetary policy decisions 5.08
   quasi-courts 12.42, 13.22
   seizure 7.08
   shadow banking 6.41
   standing 4.50, 4.54
   vertical allocation of powers 8.02
duress 4.05
Dworkin, Ronald 1.09, 1.37, 2.24, 2.40–2.41, 12.35
Dyzenhaus, David 2.14, 2.22

economic loss, damages for pure 9.01–9.10
effectiveness and equivalence, principles of
   intermediaries' duties and representations in EU 10.59, 10.81

judicial protection, principle of effective 4.55, 4.79, 6.85, 7.81, 7.91–7.92, 12.61, 13.35, 13.58
national and EU courts, dialogue between 12.64
national procedural autonomy, principle of 14.08–14.09
prospectuses, liability for misstatements in 9.57, 9.63, 9.78, 9.81, 9.144
specialization 14.01, 14.08–14.09, 14.20
EFTA Court 7.53, 7.88, 12.11
emergencies *see* **crisis management measures**
enforcement measures, sanctions and penalties 2.18, 6.77
accountability 7.08–7.12
administrative measures 6.83–6.86, 6.94, 6.100, 10.59, 13.08
arbitration awards 13.59
collateral enforcement 1.05, 11.02
collective enforcement 11.07, 11.72–11.80
criminal, classification of measures as 6.77, 6.81–6.85, 6.87–6.88
crisis management measures, judicial review of 7.08–7.12
delegation 7.08–7.12
discretion 12.54
ECtHR, classification of criminal measures by 6.81–6.85, 6.87–6.91, 6.99–6.100
EU, classification of criminal measures in the 6.81–6.82, 6.86, 6.92–6.101
financial stability 2.18
interpretation 10.01, 10.93, 10.105
legality, principle of 6.77, 12.54
liquidation 11.06
national and EU courts, dialogue between 12.54
national law, sanctions based on 12.07
prospectuses, liability for misstatements in 9.63
public law disputes 6.77
punitive measures 6.77–6.78
safeguards 6.77–6.78, 6.81, 6.84–6.85, 6.87–6.90
standard of review 12.54
validity of contract disputes 10.02
equivalence, principle of *see* **effectiveness and equivalence, principles of**
errors 6.66, 7.76, 9.60–9.64, 9.75–9.79, 10.79–10.80, 10.85, 10.92
European Banking Authority (EBA) 4.20, 4.32–4.34, 4.96, 6.30, 7.58, 13.17
European Central Bank (ECB)
accountability 4.13, 4.89, 5.20, 6.14, 14.17
Administrative Board of Review (ABOR) 12.40, 12.57, 13.14–13.15
appointments 5.24
authorization, withdrawal of bank's 6.17–6.18
challengeability of acts 4.32–4.34, 4.40, 4.42, 4.44–4.45
confidentiality 6.74
consolidated supervision 6.46–6.47
criminal measures, classification of 6.92–6.98
crisis management measures 4.10, 4.55, 7.15, 7.22, 7.32, 7.35, 7.40–7.42

European Central Bank (ECB) (cont.)
  democratic legitimacy 4.89, 5.12, 5.19, 6.14, 14.17
  discretion, exercise of 4.21–4.22, 5.14
  emergency liquidity assistance (ELA)
    operations 5.23, 7.35
  exclusive competence 6.15–6.17
  financial stability 5.03–5.04
  FOLTF 6.62, 7.77
  four eyes principle 6.19
  independence 4.89, 5.12, 5.19, 5.24, 6.14, 6.75,
    14.16–14.17
  irrevocable payment contributions (IPCs)
    cases 7.22
  judicial review
    administrative review, relationship
      with 4.93–4.94
    regulatory and supervisory decisions 6.11,
      6.14–6.22
    substance-leaning and finalistic standard of
      review 6.56–6.67, 6.74–6.76
  monetary policy mandate 1.38, 5.07
  money laundering 6.17–6.22
  Outright Monetary Transactions (OMT)
    programme 5.10–5.20
  price stability 5.07, 5.22
  property rights, interference with 7.44–7.48
  prudential supervision 6.47
  regulatory and supervisory decisions 5.03, 6.11,
    6.14–6.22, 6.46–6.47
  reporting obligations 6.14
  resolution schemes, challengeability of 4.44–4.45
  soft law 4.32–4.34
  transparency and access to documents 4.70–4.77,
    4.80–4.81
  vertical coordination of EU courts 13.05,
    13.07–13.08
European Convention on Human Rights (ECHR)/
  European Court of Human Rights (ECtHR)
  appointments, independence of 12.11
  arbitration 13.65–13.66
  banking supervision 6.83–6.85
  businesses, fundamental rights in cases
    involving 6.87–6.90
  criminal enforcement measures, classification
    of 6.81–6.85, 6.87–6.88
  due process 4.54
  duration of tenure 12.11
  expropriation 7.24, 7.29
  fair hearing, right to a 4.54, 6.84, 6.87
  holdout problems 7.42
  independence and impartiality 6.91
  procedural safeguards 6.84–6.85, 6.87–6.90, 7.74
  property rights, interference with 4.54, 7.24, 7.29,
    7.31, 7.39
  proportionality 6.85, 6.91, 7.42, 7.74
  self-incrimination, privilege against 6.87–6.88,
    6.90
  standing 4.54, 7.74
  substantive safeguards in sovereign crises 7.39

European Securities and Markets Authority
  (ESMA) 6.41–6.42, 13.18–13.23
European Stability Mechanism (ESM) 4.09–4.10,
  5.07, 7.32
European Supervisory Authorities (ESAs)
  Banking Union 6.29
  Board of Appeal (BoA) 13.11, 13.14–13.25, 13.32,
    13.37
    administrative tribunal, proposal for a
      replacement 14.14–14.19, 14.22
    judicial review and administrative review,
      relationship between 4.92–4.93
    preliminary references 12.57–12.59, 12.61
  credit rating agencies 13.20–13.23
  transparency and access to documents 4.70, 4.74,
    4.76–4.82
European Union 8.10–8.11 *see also* Banking Union;
  Charter of Fundamental Rights of the EU
  (CFEU); Court of Justice of the EU (CJEU);
  European Union, crisis management measures
  in the; European Central Bank (ECB);
  European Supervisory Authorities (ESAs);
  intermediaries' duties and representations
  in EU Member States; specialized courts in
  finance law in EU; state aid
  access to documents 4.70–4.82, 13.31–13.36
  administrative review bodies 4.92–4.96
  ADR Directive 13.45, 13.47, 14.21
  agency discretion 4.19–4.24, 6.27–6.29
  arbitration 13.61–13.66
  Capital Markets Union (CMU) 12.01, 12.30, 12.38,
    14.10
  Capital Requirements Directive (CRD) 6.18–6.22,
    6.31–6.32, 6.54–6.58
  Capital Requirements Directive IV (CRD) 4.74,
    4.78, 6.55, 6.57–6.58, 6.86, 6.92
  Capital Requirements Regulation (CRR) 6.54–6.58,
    6.86, 6.92, 13.22, 13.28 CETA, compatibility of
    EU law with 13.64–13.65
  company law 8.06
  cost-benefit analysis (CBA) 1.48
  Covid- 19 5.04
  credit rating agencies 6.41–6.42, 9.142, 9.144,
    13.20–13.23, 13.28, 13.57–13.58
  credit unions, consolidated supervision
    over 6.47–6.48
  criminal measures, classification of 6.81–6.82, 6.86,
    6.92, 6.94
  delegation 3.10–3.11, 6.27–6.29, 6.33
  Deposit Guarantee Schemes (DGS)
    Directive 4.15–4.17
  discretion 3.08, 3.10–3.11
  European small claims procedure
    (ESCP) 13.44
  Financial Collateral Directive 11.45–11.46
  financial stability 5.01–5.05, 5.07
  follow-up of public law disputes, private law
    disputes as a 13.51–13.58
  fragmentation of courts 12.01–12.07

Great Financial Crisis 2007-2008 5.04
groups, treatment of financial 6.46-6.47
harmonization 8.05, 8.07
institutions 1.32, 3.04, 3.06, 3.10
interpretation 12.56
Justice Scoreboard 12.29
lenders of last resort (LOLR) 5.22
misstatements in securities offerings, liability for 9.52-9.94
monetary policy 1.38, 6.10-6.13, 12.42, 12.62
national laws, EU authorities' application of 6.19-6.21
primacy of EU law 3.06, 6.10, 8.01, 12.02, 14.07
process review and procedural safeguards 7.63, 7.73-7.82
proportionality 8.02
prospectuses, liability for misstatements in 9.52, 9.53-9.69, 9.72-9.83, 9.137-9.144
quasi-courts, horizontal coordination by courts and 13.11, 13.13-13.37
Representative Actions Directive 13.51, 13.54-13.55
Rome I Regulation 10.16
separation of powers 3.02, 3.04, 3.06, 4.24, 5.20, 6.27-6.33
shadow banking and similar parallel activities 6.40-6.42
soft law 4.10, 4.28-4.36, 4.37
standing 3.13, 4.10, 4.19, 4.31, 4.41, 4.52, 4.55-4.56, 4.57-4.59
threshold issue on access to EU forum to solve disputes of EU law 12.55, 12.56-12.61
tort-like disputes 8.10-8.11
transparency 4.70-4.82
Unfair Contract Terms Directive 10.50-10.51, 10.54, 10.81, 12.66
vertical allocation of powers 3.05, 8.01-8.03
European Union, crisis management measures in the 1.17, 1.25, 7.03-7.05 *see also* **Single Resolution Mechanism (SRM); Single Supervisory Mechanism (SSM)**
administrative cooperation 7.09
annulment actions 4.56, 4.57-4.59
bail-ins 7.03, 7.05, 7.30
bail-outs 7.30
BRRD 7.03, 7.09, 7.14-7.17, 7.62
burden-sharing 7.30-7.31, 7.59
central banks 5.10, 5.19
change of status problems 7.15-7.16
Charter of Fundamental Rights of the EU 7.24, 7.32, 7.36, 7.38, 7.81, 7.92
conferral, powers of 4.09, 5.18, 7.09
contributions 7.14-7.20
creditors, rights of 7.59-7.62
cross-border recognition and cooperation 7.87-7.98
democratic legitimacy 5.10-5.20, 7.09, 7.11-7.13
deposit guarantee schemes (DGSs) 7.04, 7.14-7.22, 7.36, 7.62

deposit insurance schemes (DISs) 7.04
depositors, cases involving 7.52-7.58
discretion 7.13, 7.33, 7.35
ECB 4.55, 7.15, 7.22, 7.32, 7.35, 7.40-7.42
effective judicial protection, principle of 4.55, 7.91-7.92
European Stability Mechanism (ESM) 4.09-4.10, 5.07, 7.32
expropriation 7.24, 7.28, 7.33, 7.35
financial stability 4.08-4.10, 7.37
globally systemic important financial institutions (G-SIFIs) 7.05
heard, right to be 7.19, 7.37
insolvency actions, automatic mutual recognition of 7.88-7.92
internal market competence 7.09, 7.12
irrevocable payment contributions (IPCs) cases 7.22
judicial review 7.01-7.05, 7.09-7.49, 7.52-7.62, 7.71, 7.77-7.82, 7.89-7.98
justiciability 4.08-4.10
legitimate expectations 7.30-7.31, 7.41
liquidity 7.04, 7.26, 7.35, 7.44-7.49, 7.71, 7.79, 7.82, 7.94
minimum requirements for capital and eligible liabilities (MREL) 7.05
MoUs 4.08, 4.10
no-creditor worse-off (NCWO) principle 7.31, 7.37
Outright Monetary Transactions (OMT) programme 5.10-5.20
preliminary references 4.57, 4.61, 7.36
process review 7.63, 7.73-7.82
property rights, interference with 7.28, 7.33, 7.36-7.38, 7.44-7.49
proportionality 5.14, 5.16-5.19, 7.39
reasons, duty to state 7.20-7.21
resolution funding arrangements (RFAs) 7.04
resolution schemes 7.01-7.05, 7.09-7.22, 7.37-7.38, 7.44-7.47, 7.59-7.62, 7.77-7.82, 7.89-7.98
Single Resolution Board (SRB) 7.10-7.11, 7.13, 7.14-7.15, 7.19-7.21, 7.37, 7.49
Single Resolution Fund (SRF) 4.89, 6.12-6.14, 7.04, 7.11-7.12
soft law 4.10
standing 4.55-4.56, 4.57-4.58, 4.60-4.61
state aid 4.56, 4.57-4.61, 7.59-7.62
substantive safeguards in bank crises 7.28-7.38
substantive safeguards in sovereign crises 7.39-7.43
Winding Up of Credit Institutions Directive 7.88-7.90
exclusion of liability 4.14, 4.15-4.17, 9.142, 10.39, 10.83, 10.88
executive
bias 2.12, 2.31-2.34
crisis management measures 2.12-2.18, 2.21, 2.26, 2.30-2.34
deference 2.13-2.18, 2.21, 2.26

expertise
    administrative tribunal, proposal for a
        specialized 14.22
    discretion 12.45
    external perspective 12.17–12.29
    Financial List in UK 13.39
    generalist judges 12.16
    knowledge of EU law 12.40
    principles-based interpretivism 1.57, 12.01
    proportionality 12.40
    specialization 12.16–12.40, 14.22
explain, duty to 10.38, 10.42
expropriation
    Charter of Fundamental Rights of the EU 7.24
    compensation 7.28–7.29, 7.38
    discrimination 7.29, 7.35
    EU 7.24, 7.28, 7.33, 7.35
    ECtHR 7.24, 7.29
    indirect 7.84
    international investment arbitration 7.83–7.84,
        7.86
    margin of appreciation 7.29
    proportionality 7.28, 7.35
    sovereign crises 7.23
    Takings Clause in US Constitution 7.24–7.27
extraterritoriality 8.12–8.15, 13.53

failing-or-likely-to-fail (FOLTF) 4.44–4.45, 4.59,
    6.17, 6.62, 7.03, 7.44–7.48, 7.77
Fair and Equitable Treatment (FET) 7.83–7.86
fairness
    commercial reasonableness 11.108
    creditors 7.02, 7.06
    fair dealing, duty of 4.54, 10.28, 10.32, 10.103, 12.42
    fair hearing, right to a 6.84, 6.87, 12.11, 13.56, 14.14
    insolvency 11.04, 11.07
    intermediaries' duties and representations in
        EU 10.49–10.50, 10.53–10.54, 10.81
    judicial review 2.16
    minority creditors 11.07
    procedural fairness 7.84
    remedies 10.50
    shareholders 7.02, 7.06
    special purpose vehicles (SPVs) insolvency 11.13
    trustees, role of 11.101
    unfair contract terms 10.49–10.51, 10.54, 10.83–
        10.86, 12.66
Federal Reserve Board (FRB) (United States) 5.23,
    6.35–6.37, 6.43–6.45, 6.73
federalism 8.01, 9.12–9.25, 9.44–9.49, 12.04, 12.09,
    13.12
fiduciary duties
    agent banks, role of 11.90
    creditors, to 11.53, 11.54–11.58
    directors 2.25
    financial risk 1.05
    insider dealing 9.50
    intermediaries' duties and representations 10.26–
        10.27, 10.34, 10.41

    misstatements, liability for 9.16–9.17
    trustees, role of 11.99–11.100
finality see substance-leaning and finalistic standard
    of review in EU
Financial Collateral Directive 11.45–11.46
financial contract disputes 10.01–10.124
    intermediaries' duties and representations 10.01,
        10.03, 10.05, 10.24–10.92
    interpretation and enforcement of contract 10.01,
        10.04, 10.05, 10.93–10.124
    validity disputes 10.01–10.02, 10.05, 10.06–10.23
financial crises 2.12–2.38 see crisis management
    measures; Great Financial Crisis 2007-2008
financial development 2.01–2.11
financial stability 1.20, 1.23–1.28
    central banks 5.01–5.05
    crisis management measures 2.18–2.19, 2.26–2.27,
        7.01, 7.03, 7.37, 7.39
    ECB 5.03–5.04, 5.07
    EU 5.01–5.05, 5.07, 7.37
    fiscal backstops 5.06–5.07
    FSB Key Attributes 7.06
    Great Financial Crisis 2007–2008 5.02, 5.03–5.04,
        5.06
    IMF 2.04
    judicial review 5.01–5.24
    justiciability 4.01–4.13
    lenders of last resort (LOLR) 5.21–5.22
    monetary policy decisions 5.07, 5.08–5.20
    narratives 1.24–1.27
    price stability 5.01–5.03, 5.05, 5.22
    principles 1.06, 1.23–1.28, 1.56
    World Bank 2.04
FIN-NET initiative 13.45–13.47, 14.21
fiscal backstops 5.06–5.07
fit and proper persons requirement 6.60–6.62, 6.92
Fleck, Robert K 12.14
floating charges 11.45–11.46
follow-up of public law disputes, private law disputes
    as a 13.50–13.58
FOLTF (failing-or-likely-to-fail) 4.44–4.45, 4.59,
    6.17, 6.62, 7.03, 7.44–7.48, 7.77
foreign act of state doctrine 4.05
forum shopping 9.49, 12.21, 13.41
fragmentation of courts in EU 12.01–12.07, 12.08
France
    Authority for Prudential Supervision and
        Resolution (ACPR) 4.35
    choice of law clauses 13.41
    economic loss, damages for pure 9.06, 9.09
    groups, treatment of financial 6.46–6.47
    irrevocable payment contributions (IPCs)
        cases 7.22
    misstatements, liability for 9.06, 9.09, 9.118, 9.141
    no-action/non-petition clauses 11.63
    Paris Merchant Courts 12.18
    prospectuses, liability for misstatements in 9.141
    regulatory and supervisory frameworks 8.20
    soft law, justiciability of 6.30

INDEX 509

sovereign immunity 4.03–4.04
standard of review 6.55, 6.58, 6.63, 6.65, 6.67
trustees, role of 11.101
vertical allocation of powers 6.18
fraud
   central banks 4.06
   collective/class actions 1.13, 9.31, 9.33
   conflicts of interest 10.30
   constructive fraud doctrine 11.13
   credit rating agencies, misstatements by 9.134
   fraud-on-the-market doctrine 1.13, 9.70–9.83
   intermediaries' duties and representations 10.29–10.30, 10.32, 10.34, 10.44–10.45
   misrepresentation 9.92, 9.106, 10.44
   misstatements, liability for 9.12, 9.15, 9.17, 9.21–9.23, 9.28, 9.31–9.34, 9.121
      aiding and abetting 9.122–9.127
      control person liability 9.125, 9.130, 9.135
      credit rating agencies, by 9.134
      prospectuses, in 9.61, 9.70–9.83
      secondary actor liability 9.122–9.136
   prospectuses, liability for misstatements in 9.61, 9.70–9.83
   special purpose vehicles (SPVs) insolvency 11.15
freedom of expression 9.95–9.105
freedom of information 4.62–4.67
Full Protection and Security (FPS) 7.83
fundamental rights *see also* **Charter of Fundamental Rights of the EU (CFEU); European Convention on Human Rights (ECHR)/ European Court of Human Rights (ECtHR)**
   balancing 1.28
   depositors, cases involving 7.57
   EU 1.28, 7.57
   freedom of expression 9.95–9.105
   judicial review 3.14
   principles-based interpretivism 1.57
   public law disputes 3.14

gap-filling 1.10–1.11, 1.13, 8.26–8.27, 11.06, 11.82
gatekeeper liability 9.95–9.144
Germany
   Banking Union as ultra vires and unconstitutional 6.12
   BRRD 7.90
   capacity 10.10, 10.13–10.15
   central banks 4.06
   collective action clauses (CACs) 11.78
   credit rating agencies (CRAs), misstatements by 9.118
   depositors, cases involving 7.52
   economic loss, damages for pure 9.03, 9.06, 9.08
   eternity clause in Constitution 3.06, 5.20
   exclusion and limitation of liability 4.15
   Federal Constitutional Court (FCC) 4.89, 6.10–6.14, 7.09–7.12
      Outright Monetary Transactions (OMT) programme 5.10–5.20
      separation of powers 3.06–3.07

   hard cases 6.11
   intermediaries' duties and representations in EU 10.46, 10.71, 10.74, 10.90
   local governments, capacity of 10.10, 10.13
   misstatements, liability for 9.87–9.91, 9.114–9.117, 9.121, 9.143
      credit rating agencies (CRAs), misstatements by 9.118
      economic loss, damages for pure 9.03, 9.06, 9.08
      gatekeeper liability 9.114–9.117
      prospectuses, in 9.59, 9.73–9.74, 9.77, 9.139–9.140
   Outright Monetary Transactions (OMT) programme 5.10–5.20
   primacy of EU law 6.10
   prospectuses, liability for misstatements in 9.59, 9.73–9.74, 9.77, 9.139–9.140
   significant credit institutions, classification of 6.11
   speculative contracts and capacity 10.13–10.15
   tort system 8.19, 8.20
   transparency 10.52
globally systemic important financial institutions (G-SIFIs) 7.05
good administration, principle of 6.71–6.72, 6.85, 6.90, 12.42
good faith
   insolvency 11.07
   interpretation 10.93, 10.94, 10.95, 10.100, 10.103–10.104, 10.111, 11.01
   oppression by the majority 11.79
   trustees, role of 11.101
good repute requirement 6.96, 6.98
government *see* **executive**
Great Financial Crisis 2007–2008 1.01, 1.17, 1.20, 1.25, 1.43
   courts, role of the 2.17
   depositors, cases involving 7.53
   distribution of proceeds, inter-creditor disputes over 11.109
   financial stability 5.02, 5.03–5.04
   shadow banking as cause 6.35
   sovereign debt crisis 5.04, 5.06
   systemic, as 2.33
   transparency and access to documents 4.64
group actions *see* **collective/class actions**
groups, treatment of financial 6.02–6.03, 6.19, 6.43–6.47

haircuts on sovereign bonds 7.23, 7.39–7.42
hard cases 1.36–1.39, 1.44, 1.46, 1.58
   application of law 1.36–1.37
   bias 2.44
   borderline cases 2.40–2.42
   corporate scandals 2000–2001 2.43–2.45
   courts, positive role of 2.39–2.45
   crisis management measures 2.28, 2.39–2.42
   interstitial cases and fundamental cases, distinction between 2.41–2.42, 2.44

hard cases (*cont.*)
　issues 3.01
　pivotal cases 2.40–2.42, 2.44, 12.31
　policy 1.16, 1.18, 12.32
　positive role of courts 2.39–2.45
　principles 1.18, 1.22, 1.36–1.38, 1.56, 2.39–2.44, 12.32, 12.34
　regulatory and supervisory frameworks 6.11
　rule of law 2.39–2.45
　specialization 12.30–12.36
　tie-breaker 2.41
harmonization
　collective/class actions 13.51, 13.53
　court system 13.01–13.02
　credit rating agencies, misstatements of 9.142–9.144
　EU law 8.05, 8.07
　FIN-NET initiative 13.47
　intermediaries' duties and representations in EU 10.81
　mass, small-ticket disputes 13.46–13.48
　misstatements, liability for 9.57, 9.58–9.70, 9.82, 9.84, 9.94, 9.142–9.144
　prospectuses, liability for misstatements in 9.57, 9.58–9.70, 9.82
　sanctions based on national law, review of 12.07
　specialization 14.08–14.09, 14.13, 14.21
heard, right to be 6.72–6.73, 7.19, 7.37, 12.42
heuristics 1.06, 1.29–1.30, 1.43, 1.46, 1.57, 2.31, 2.35
honour/image, torts against 9.96
human rights *see* **fundamental rights**

ICSID arbitration 13.60, 13.62
immunity 3.03, 4.01–4.07, 4.12, 5.09
implementing acts (EU) 4.39, 4.43
Implementing Technical Standards (ITSs) 4.43, 6.29, 13.22
independence and impartiality 12.08–12.15
　administrative law judges (ALJs) 13.12
　appointing systems 4.83–4.89, 12.08–12.15
　central banks 4.06, 4.11, 5.05, 5.19
　CETA courts 12.13
　Charter of Fundamental Rights of the EU 12.12
　CJEU 12.10, 12.12
　discretion 3.08–3.11, 6.27–6.29, 6.33
　dismissal 12.14
　duration of tenure 12.11, 12.13, 12.15
　ECB 4.89, 5.12, 5.19, 5.24, 6.14, 6.75, 14.16–14.17
　ECtHR 6.91, 12.11
　expertise 12.08, 12.13
　fair hearing, right to a 12.11
　financial regulatory bodies, appointments to 4.83–4.89
　groups, treatment of financial 6.43
　legitimacy 4.89, 5.10, 5.12, 5.19
　public interest 4.87
　remuneration 12.15
　rule of law 12.11, 12.12
　specialization 12.08–12.15, 12.35, 14.14–14.17, 14.19
　standard of review 6.75
　substantive independence 12.14
　UN Basic Principles on the Independence of the Judiciary 12.11
individual rights *see* **fundamental rights**
inducement 9.60, 10.37, 10.40, 10.44–10.45, 10.76, 11.99
insider dealing 6.98, 9.50–9.51, 9.84, 9.86–9.87, 9.89, 9.92, 9.94
insolvency 11.01, 11.11–11.42 *see also* **bankruptcy; liquidation**
　applicable law 8.09
　automatic mutual recognition in EU 7.88–7.92
　collateral 11.04–11.05
　crisis management measures 4.53
　custody 11.04
　derivatives disputes 11.37–11.42
　fairness 11.04, 11.07
　FOLTF 4.44–4.45, 4.59, 6.17, 6.62, 7.03, 7.44–7.48, 7.77
　good faith 11.07
　insolvency events 10.110, 11.07, 11.71–11.76
　Insolvency Regulation 14.05
　legal certainty 8.09
　majority and minority creditors 11.07
　pari passu 11.09, 11.84, 11.108–11.114
　public policy 8.09, 11.01
　remoteness 11.70, 11.78
　segregation 11.04
　special purpose vehicles (SPVs) insolvency 11.11–11.36
　UNCITRAL Model Law on Cross-Border Insolvency 13.11
institutions 2.01–2.11 *see also* **banks**
　analysis 1.20
　balance of power 12.35
　democratic legitimacy 3.04, 3.06
　dialogue 12.44–12.70
　economics 1.20
　EU 1.31, 3.04, 3.06, 4.09
　Great Financial Crisis 2007–2008 1.20
　institutionalization 1.33
　legal theory of finance (LTF) 1.20
insurance
　deposit insurance schemes (DISs) 7.04
　FDIC 7.01, 7.03
intellectual property, specialized courts for 14.01–14.02, 14.06–14.07, 14.18, 14.20, 14.22
inter-creditor disputes 11.71–11.105
　agent banks, role of 11.89, 11.90–11.92
　bankruptcy 11.53–11.70, 11.77
　collective enforcement 11.07, 11.72–11.76
　coordination 11.08, 11.71–11.105
　fiduciary duties towards creditors 11.53, 11.54–11.58
　insolvency event clauses 11.07, 11.71–11.76
　liquidation 11.71, 11.86, 11.93, 11.104
　restructuring 11.71, 11.77–11.88
　Special Purpose Vehicles (SPVs) 11.72–11.76, 11.86, 11.88

INDEX   511

third parties 11.08
trustees, role of 11.89, 11.93–11.105
inter-institutional dialogue 12.44–12.70
  discretion 12.45–12.46, 12.49, 12.54
  linear and non-linear interaction between national courts and EU courts 12.55, 12.62–12.70
  non-EU law and EU law, combined effect of 12.55
  specialization 12.45–12.46, 12.52, 12.70
  standard of review 12.44, 12.46–12.51, 12.53
  systemic effects of lack of inter-court coordination 12.55–12.70
  threshold issue on access to EU forum to solve disputes of EU law 12.55, 12.56–12.61
intermediaries' duties and representations 10.01, 10.03, 10.05, 10.24–10.92 *see also* **intermediaries' duties and representations in EU Member States; intermediaries' duties and representations in the United States**
  advise or inform, duty to 10.03, 10.24
  custody risk 11.48
  private law principles 10.05, 10.24
intermediaries' duties and representations in EU Member States 10.49–10.92
  appropriateness duties 10.55–10.56, 10.59, 10.77, 10.80, 10.92
  assumption of responsibility 10.83
  basis clauses 10.82–10.92
  boilerplate clauses 10.89
  burden of proof 10.82, 10.90–10.91
  causal link 10.47, 10.82–10.92
  civil law countries 10.70–10.77
  compartmentalized approach 10.69–10.70
  conflicts of interest 10.73
  consumer protection 10.49–10.50, 10.54–10.55, 10.81
  disclosure, duty of 10.72–10.73
  equivalence and effectiveness, principles of 10.59, 10.81
  exclusion of liability 10.83, 10.88
  fairness 10.49–10.50, 10.53–10.54, 10.81
  harmonization 10.81
  investment business, definition of 10.60
  mandatory provisions 10.78–10.81
  MiFID 10.55–10.60, 10.63, 10.67, 10.76, 10.79, 10.81, 10.91
  misrepresentation 10.60
  mis-selling 10.79, 10.89
  mistake 10.79–10.80, 10.85, 10.92
  national courts and CJEU, dialogue between 10.51
  negligence 10.60, 10.65, 10.83, 10.85
  negligent misstatements 10.60
  plain, intelligible language 10.50–10.54, 11.01
  private law principles 10.24, 10.49–10.92
  prospectuses, liability for misstatements in 10.49, 10.75, 10.81, 10.90
  public policy 10.54
  recommendations 10.58, 10.72

  regulatory provisions 10.48, 10.49–10.92
  reliance 10.82–10.92
  remedies for breach of regulatory duties 10.49–10.81
  retroactivity 10.52
  suitability duties 10.55–10.56, 10.77, 10.80, 10.92
  transparency 10.52–10.54, 10.81
  unfair contract terms in consumer loans 10.49–10.51, 10.54, 10.81, 10.83–10.86
intermediaries' duties and representations in the United States 10.24, 10.25–10.36
  adviser, definition of 10.25
  advisers and broker-dealers, duties of 10.24, 10.25–10.36
  arbitration 10.35
  basis clauses 10.39
  best execution 10.33
  boilerplate clauses 10.39
  conflicts of interest 10.29–10.30, 10.46
  custody 10.33
  disclosure, duty of 10.24, 10.29–10.30, 10.38
  exclusion clauses 10.39
  explain, no duty to 10.38, 10.42
  fair dealing, duty of 10.28, 10.32
  fees and prices 10.33–10.34
  fiduciary duties 10.26–10.27, 10.34, 10.41
  FINRA rules and disciplinary procedures 10.32, 10.34
  fraud 10.29–10.30, 10.32, 10.34, 10.44–10.45
  independent advice 10.37
  inducement 10.37, 10.40, 10.44–10.45
  investment adviser, definition of 10.25
  Investment Advisers Act 1940 10.25–10.26, 10.29, 10.34
  manipulative acts 10.28
  marketing duties of banks under private law 10.37–10.48
  misrepresentation 10.37–10.41
  misstatements 10.28, 10.41–10.44
  negligence 10.34, 10.37, 10.41–10.43
  omissions 10.28, 10.30
  private actions 10.25–10.36
    registration with SEC 10.25
  regulatory duties 10.37, 10.42
  remedies 10.34
  scienter 10.32
  Securities and Exchange Act 1934 10.25, 10.28, 10.33, 10.35
  special compensation for advisory services 10.25
  SROs, membership of 10.25
  suitability duty 10.31–10.32, 10.38
  trust and confidence, relationships of 10.26–10.27
  void contracts 10.34
International Court of Justice (ICJ) 12.08, 12.41
international investment arbitration and crisis management measures 7.63, 7.83–7.86
International Monetary Fund (IMF), immunity of 4.01, 4.07
international organizations, immunity of 4.01, 4.07

International Swaps and Derivatives Association (ISDA)
choice of law clauses 13.41
early termination 10.119–10.120
Master Agreements for derivatives 10.17, 11.38–11.39, 10.115, 13.41
Model Agreements 11.37
private body, as 1.01
safe harbour 11.03
standard terms 8.29, 10.04, 10.17, 10.37–10.39, 10.114–10.120, 11.03
interpretation *see also* **contract interpretation; principles-based interpretivism**
arbitration 13.60, 13.64
constitutional interpretation 1.28
EU law 12.56, 14.21
fragmentation of courts in EU 12.05–12.06
gap-filling 1.13, 8.26–8.27, 11.06
hard cases 2.39
legitimacy 12.06
living instrument principle 1.10
no-action/non-petition clauses 11.62–11.65
plain, intelligible language 10.50–10.54, 11.01
principles-based interpretation 1.02, 11.10
sincere cooperation, principle of 14.09
soft law 4.26–4.27
standard of review 6.53–6.67
third parties 11.08
interstitial cases
expertise 12.16
fundamental cases distinguished 2.41–2.42, 2.44
hard cases 2.41–2.42, 2.44
independence 5.12
misstatements, liability for 9.36
pivotal cases 12.31
reframing 2.37
investment
arbitration and crisis management measures 7.63, 7.83–7.86
expropriation 7.83–7.84, 7.86
Fair and Equitable Treatment (FET) 7.83–7.86
Full Protection and Security (FPS) 7.83
Investment Advisers Act 1940 (United States) 10.25–10.26, 10.29, 10.34
investment business, definition of 10.60
legitimate expectations 7.84
misstatements, liability for 9.36
most favoured nation (MFN) treatment 7.83
national and EU courts, dialogue between 12.63
procedural fairness 7.84
standards 7.83–7.86
ipso facto clauses, prohibition of 11.36, 11.37–11.42
irrevocable payment contributions (IPCs) cases 7.22
ISDA *see* International Swaps and Derivatives Association (ISDA)
Italy
capacity of local governments 10.12, 10.20, 10.21
Charter of Fundamental Rights of the EU 6.54
credit rating agencies (CRAs) 6.20, 9.120
crisis management measures, judicial review of 7.16–7.17
economic loss, damages for pure 9.06, 9.09
Financial Collateral Directive 11.45–11.46
horizontal coordination of courts 13.10
intermediaries' duties and representations in EU 10.47, 10.77–10.78, 10.91
market abuse 6.88
mass, small-ticket disputes 13.46, 13.49
medieval courts 12.18
misstatements, liability for 9.06, 9.09, 9.58, 9.74, 9.119, 9.120, 9.121, 9.141
national and EU courts, dialogue between 12.64, 12.69
prospectuses, liability for misstatements in 9.58, 9.74, 9.141
regulatory and supervisory frameworks 6.16, 6.22, 8.20
silence, right to 6.90
standard of review 6.54, 6.60

journalist privilege 9.98, 9.102
judges *see* **judiciary**
judicial review *see also* **standard of review**
administrative review, relationship with 4.90–4.96
agency discretion, exercise of 4.19–4.22
crisis management measures 2.16, 4.19–4.22, 7.01–7.98
discretion 2.25, 3.08–3.11, 4.91, 6.53, 6.67
EU 3.04, 4.26–4.36, 4.37, 4.92–4.96, 6.10–6.22, 6.53–6.67
financial stability 5.01–5.24
fundamental rights 3.14
political issues, exclusion of 3.04
principles-based interpretivism 1.57
quasi-judicial review 13.37, 14.18
regulatory and supervisory decisions 1.04–1.05, 6.01, 12.46
separation of powers 3.02, 3.04
shadow banking 6.35–6.40
soft law 4.26–4.27, 4.37
supervisory decisions 1.04–1.05, 6.01–6.33, 6.48
judiciary *see also* **deference; judicial review; separation of powers**
accountability 1.01, 12.14, 13.35
administrative law judges (ALJs) in United States 4.91, 12.09, 13.11–13.12
discretion 2.23
duration of tenure 12.11, 12.13, 12.15
effective judicial protection, principle of 4.55, 4.79, 6.85, 7.81, 7.91–7.92, 12.61, 13.35, 13.58
Euro crisis, increase in powers of judiciary due to 1.16
generalist judges 12.16
judge-made law 1.10, 1.13–1.14
restraint 1.11, 1.16, 3.10
Special Trial Judges (STJs) in United States 4.91

INDEX 513

jurisdiction
   applicable law 8.08–8.15
   choice of law 8.09, 10.17–10.18, 13.41
   limited jurisdiction, concept of 4.18
   private law disputes 8.08–8.15
   subject-matter jurisdiction 8.12–8.15
   territorial jurisdiction 8.12–8.15
justice
   access to justice 8.23–8.24, 12.61, 14.04
   discourse theory of justice 1.33–1.34, 1.53–1.54
   Justice Scoreboard (EU) 12.29
   theaters of justice 12.27–12.28
justiciability challenges
   agency discretion, exercise of 4.14, 4.18–4.24
   central banks 4.01, 4.06, 4.11–4.15
   complex proceedings, challengeability of acts in 4.38–4.48
   crisis management measures 4.08–4.10, 4.14–4.61
   delegation 6.29
   exclusion and limitation of liability 4.14, 4.15–4.17
   financial and monetary stability decisions 4.01–4.13
   public law 4.01–4.61
   regulatory and supervisory measures 4.14–4.61
   soft law 4.14, 4.25–4.37, 6.30–6.32
   sovereign immunity 4.01–4.07
   standing to challenge decisions 4.14, 4.49–4.61

Kazakhstan, Astana International Financial Centre Court in 13.40

language of finance 14.10–14.12
language of proceedings 12.43, 14.20
legal certainty
   Charter of Fundamental Rights of the EU 1.12
   credit rating agencies 13.21
   criminal measures, classification of 6.92, 6.94
   crisis management measures 7.15, 7.92
   ECtHR 6.85
   EU 6.92, 6.94, 7.15, 7.92, 13.26
   financial development 2.09
   hard cases 1.36
   insolvency 8.09
   principles 1.15, 1.33
   prospectuses, liability for misstatements in 9.82
   rule of law 2.14
   standard of review 6.71
legal realism 1.07, 1.38–1.39
Legal Theory of Finance (LTF) 1.20, 2.09, 2.18–2.20
legality, principle of 1.33–1.34, 6.77, 6.92, 6.94, 7.37
legitimacy 1.31–1.34, 13.38
   agency discretion, doctrine on the legitimacy of 6.27–6.29
   arbitrary and capricious standard of review 6.48
   arbitration 13.61
   consistency 1.45
   cost-benefit analysis (CBA) 1.51
   crisis management measures, judicial review of 7.02–7.22
   democratic legitimacy 3.04, 3.06, 4.83, 4.86, 4.89, 5.10–5.20, 6.14, 7.09, 7.11
   discretion 1.46, 2.23, 12.45
   EU 1.32, 12.06
   financial crises 2.22–2.23
   fragmentation of courts in EU 12.06
   independence 4.89, 5.10, 5.12, 5.19
   input/process legitimacy 1.31
   interpretation 1.31–1.34, 1.45–1.46, 1.60–1.61, 12.06
   legal legitimacy 2.23
   legality, intersection with 1.33
   monetary policy 5.10–5.13
   normative legitimacy 1.31
   output legitimacy 1.31
   principles-based interpretivism 1.31–1.34, 1.45–1.46, 1.60–1.61
   reasons for decisions 1.33
   sociological legitimacy 2.22
   soft law 4.35
   specialization 14.12, 14.17
   standard of review 6.53
legitimate expectations 7.30–7.31, 7.41, 7.84
lenders of last resort (LOLR) 5.21–5.22
licences, withdrawal of 6.83–6.85, 7.36, 7.55, 7.58
limitation of liability 4.14, 4.15–4.17
liquidation 11.06, 11.106–11.115
   inter-creditor coordination disputes 11.71, 11.86, 11.93, 11.104
   Winding Up of Credit Institutions Directive 7.88–7.90
liquidity 7.04, 7.26, 7.35, 7.44–7.49, 7.71, 7.79, 7.82, 7.94
living instrument principle 1.10
local government, capacity of 10.07–10.13, 10.20
locus standi see standing

margin of appreciation/discretion 1.15, 3.10–3.11, 6.28, 6.95, 7.29, 12.48–12.50
market abuse 6.82, 6.88, 9.84–9.94
market failure 2.01, 2.12–2.38
market manipulation 9.84, 9.91–9.93
mass, small-ticket disputes 13.44–13.49
   ADR 13.44–13.49
   design of schemes 13.46
   documentary evidence 13.44, 13.46
   European small claims procedure (ESCP) 13.44
   FIN-NET initiative 13.45–13.47
   harmonization 13.46–13.48
   online dispute resolution 13.45
   quasi-courts 13.48–13.49
   specialization 13.44, 13.48
materially adverse effects (MAE) 10.93, 10.122–10.124
memoranda of understanding (MoU) 1.01, 1.34, 4.08, 4.10, 13.45
MiFID (Markets in Financial Instruments Directive)
   custody risk 11.50, 11.52
   intermediaries' duties and representations 10.55–10.60, 10.63, 10.67, 10.76, 10.79, 10.81, 10.91
   MiFID II 4.74, 4.77, 4.78, 6.30

minimum requirements for capital and eligible
    liabilities (MREL) 7.05, 13.25, 13.28–13.30
misrepresentation 9.92, 9.106, 10.37–10.41, 10.44,
    10.60
mis-selling 10.38–10.39, 10.79, 10.89
**misstatements in securities offerings, liability
    for** 9.01–9.144 *see also* **misstatements
    in securities offerings in United States,
    liability for; prospectuses, liability for
    misstatements in**
  auditors' liability 9.106–9.107, 9.114–9.119, 9.136,
      9.139–9.140
  causal link 9.87, 9.119–9.121, 9.143–9.144
  constitutional dimension 9.95, 9.96–9.105
  contract doctrines, application of 9.95, 9.120
  credit rating agencies 9.110, 9.117, 9.120, 9.137,
      9.139, 9.142–9.144
  creeping codification 9.52–9.94
  criminal liability 9.84–9.85, 9.92, 9.94
  disclose, failure to 9.84–9.94, 9.137
  EU 9.52–9.94
  fraud 9.92, 9.121
  freedom of expression 9.95
  gatekeeper liability 9.95–9.144
  harmonization 9.84, 9.142–9.144
  insider information 9.84, 9.86–9.87, 9.89, 9.92, 9.94
  market abuse 9.84–9.94
  material omissions 9.89
  negligence 9.121, 10.60
  opinions 9.95, 9.96–9.121
    auditors' liability 9.106–9.107, 9.114–9.119,
        9.136, 9.139–9.140
    credit rating agencies 9.110, 9.117, 9.120
  private law dimension 9.95, 9.106–9.121
  pure economic loss, damages for 9.01
  regulatory dimension 9.95, 9.122–9.144
  reliance 9.110, 9.120–9.121, 9.143–9.144
  secondary actors 9.95–9.144
    makers of statements, as 9.122–9.136
    private law dimension 9.95, 9.106–9.121
    regulatory dimension 9.95, 9.122–9.136
  tort doctrines, application of 9.95, 9.118–9.121
  Transparency Directive 9.84, 9.94
**misstatements in securities offerings in United States,
    liability for** 9.11–9.51
  assumption of responsibility 10.37, 10.43
  causation 9.30, 9.32–9.33, 9.121, 9.127–9.128
  collective/class actions 9.31, 9.33, 9.45–9.47
  constitutional dimension 9.96–9.105
  control person liability 9.125, 9.130, 9.135
  credit rating agencies 9.96–9.105, 9.112–9.113,
      9.134
  deceit and misrepresentation, common law torts
      of 9.32
  defamation 9.96–9.105
  defendants, who can be 9.37
  disclosure 9.13–9.17, 9.22, 9.27–9.28, 9.35–9.36
  Dodd-Frank Act 9.134–9.135
  economic loss 9.32
  federalizing securities litigation 9.12–9.25
  fraud 9.12, 9.15, 9.17, 9.21–9.23, 9.28, 9.31–9.34,
      9.37, 9.122–9.136
  freedom of expression 9.96–9.105
  gatekeepers 9.96–9.105, 9.109, 9.111–9.113,
      9.122–9.136
  inducement 10.37
  inflation maintenance theory 9.34, 9.36
  insider trading 9.50–9.51
  intermediaries' duties and representations 10.28,
      10.37, 10.41–10.44
  investors deserve protection, determination of
      which 9.26–9.36
  materiality of omissions and opinions 9.26–9.28,
      9.34–9.36, 9.42–9.43
  misrepresentation 9.32, 9.34
  negligence 9.40, 9.109, 9.121, 10.37, 10.41–10.44
  omissions 9.26–9.28, 9.34–9.36, 9.42–9.43
  opinions 9.26, 9.29, 9.39, 9.43, 9.49
    gatekeepers 9.96–9.105, 9.109, 9.111–9.113,
        9.122–9.136
    rating agencies 9.96–9.105, 9.112–9.113,
        9.134–9.135
    statements versus opinions 9.96–9.105
  precedents 9.17, 9.20, 9.25, 9.128, 9.132
  private federal right of action, implication of
      a 9.12–9.25
  Private Securities Litigation Reform Act
      (PSLRA) 9.25, 9.31, 9.44, 9.46–9.47, 9.51,
      9.125
  prospectus liability 9.38–9.43
  public concern, matters of 9.96–9.97
  registration statements 9.11, 9.23, 9.29, 9.38–9.43
  reliance 9.26–9.28, 9.30, 9.33, 9.42, 9.123,
      9.126–9.128
  remedies 9.16, 9.23–9.24, 9.39, 9.51
  rule 10b–5 9.11–9.29, 9.32, 9.37, 9.44–9.49,
      9.122–9.132
  scienter 9.23, 9.25, 9.38–9.40, 9.42, 9.131
  SEC 9.11–9.51, 9.134
  secondary actor liability 9.10, 9.37, 9.44
    aiding and abetting 9.122–9.127, 9.132
    control person liability 9.125, 9.130, 9.135
    fraud 9.122–9.136
    makers of statements, as 9.122–9.136
  Securities Act 1933 9.11–9.51, 9.125, 9.131, 9.134
  Securities Litigation Uniform Standards Act
      (SLUSA) 9.44–9.46
  states 9.16–9.17, 9.21
  statute-based liability system 9.11–9.51
  vertical balance between federal and states
      level 9.44–9.49
  vertical issue of respective roles of state corporate
      law 9.14
mistake 6.66, 7.76, 9.60–9.64, 9.75–9.79, 10.79–10.80,
    10.85, 10.92
monetary policy
  access to documents 4.76
  central banks 4.11

decisions 5.08–5.20
EU 1.38, 6.10–6.13, 12.42, 12.62
financial stability 5.02, 5.07
hard cases 1.36, 1.56
meaning 1.36–1.38
money laundering 6.17–6.22, 6.59, 6.92, 6.94–6.95, 7.49
mortgage-backed securities (MBS) 6.25, 6.35, 6.38–6.39, 7.69, 11.38
most favoured nation (MFN) treatment 7.83

national procedural autonomy, principle of 13.04, 13.51, 14.01, 14.08–14.09, 14.20
natural justice 6.99
ne bis in idem principle 6.77, 6.81, 6.99–6.100
negligence
  credit rating agencies, misstatements of 9.142–9.143
  criminal measures, classification of 6.93, 6.97
  economic loss, damages for pure 9.05
  intermediaries' duties and representations in EU 10.34, 10.37, 10.41–10.43, 10.60, 10.65, 10.83, 10.85
  misstatements, liability for 9.05, 9.56, 9.106, 9.109, 9.111, 10.37, 10.41–10.44, 10.60
  prospectuses, liability for misstatements in 9.40, 9.42, 9.56
  regulatory and supervisory frameworks 8.20–8.22
no-action/non-petition clauses 11.05, 11.59–11.67
no-creditor worse-off (NCWO) principle 7.31, 7.37
nodes and challenges
  arbitration 13.59–13.66
  coordination 13.01–13.02, 13.03–13.37
  current court system, in 13.01–13.66
  follow-up of public law disputes, private law disputes as a 13.50–13.58
  mass, small-ticket disputes and role of ADR 13.44–13.49
  precedents in national courts and hybrid international commercial courts 13.39–13.43
  private law disputes, in 13.38–13.58
  public law disputes, in 13.03–13.37
  quasi-courts, horizontal coordination by courts and 13.11–13.37
  vertical coordination of EU courts 13.04–13.08
non-recourse provisions 11.59–11.60, 11.67–11.70
non-reliance clauses 10.83

offers of securities *see* misstatements in securities offerings in United States, liability for; misstatements in securities offerings, liability for; prospectuses, liability for misstatements in
ombudsmen 13.51
omissions
  intermediaries' duties and representations 10.28, 10.30
  material 9.26–9.28, 9.34–9.36, 9.42–9.43, 9.58, 9.89
  prospectuses, liability for misstatements in 9.42–9.43, 9.74, 9.83

online dispute resolution (ODR) 13.45
organization of courts 12.41–12.43
  internal review bodies 12.42
  language of proceedings 12.43
  quasi-courts in EU 12.42–12.43
  research assistance and secretarial support 12.41
Outright Monetary Transactions (OMT) programme 5.10–5.20

pari passu 11.09, 11.84, 11.108–11.114
patents *see* Unified Patent Court (UPC)
Payment Order Regulation 14.05
penalties *see* enforcement measures, sanctions and penalties
penalty rule 8.26
PERG Manual (FCA Perimeter Guidance) 10.67, 10.68, 10.87
Piketty, Thomas 2.08
pivotal cases
  borderline cases distinguished 2.40–2.42
  expertise 12.16
  hard cases 2.40–2.42, 2.44, 12.31
  independence 5.12, 5.19
  interpretation 8.28
  interstitial cases 12.31
  misstatements, liability for 9.36
  Outright Monetary Transactions (OMT) programme 5.12, 5.19
  reframing 2.37
  specialization 12.31–12.33, 12.38
positivism 1.34–1.46, 2.22–2.24
post-enforcement call option (PECO) agreements 11.70
pragmatism and rules-based positivism 1.35–1.46
precedents
  financial crises 2.26–2.29
  misstatements, liability for 9.17, 9.20, 9.25, 9.57, 9.128, 9.132
  national courts and hybrid international commercial courts 13.39–13.43
  positivism 1.41–1.42
  principles-based interpretivism 1.56
  prospectuses, liability for misstatements in 9.57
  special purpose vehicles (SPVs) insolvency 11.35
  specialization 13.39, 13.42–13.43
preliminary references
  administrative bodies of review 12.57
  ADR 12.60
  arbitration 12.56
  crisis management measures 4.57, 4.61, 7.36
  misstatements, liability for 9.52
  Outright Monetary Transactions (OMT) programme 5.10–5.15
  quasi-courts, status of 12.57–12.61
  separation of powers 3.06
  soft law 4.29–4.30, 4.33, 4.35–4.36
  standing 3.13
  Unified Patent Court (UPC) 14.07
  vertical coordination of EU courts 13.04

presumption of innocence 6.98
price stability 5.01–5.03, 5.05, 5.22
primacy of EU law 3.06, 6.10, 8.01, 12.02, 14.07
PRIME Finance 13.59
principles-based interpretivism 1.01–1.61, 11.10, 12.01
  alternatives 1.47–1.61
  bias 1.29–1.30, 1.43, 1.57
  cost-benefit analysis (CBA) 1.48–1.52, 1.56–1.58
  courts 1.09, 1.55–1.56, 1.59
  descriptive claim 1.18, 1.21, 1.30, 1.56
  discourse theory of justice 1.33–1.34, 1.53–1.54
  financial stability 1.23–1.28, 1.56
  hard cases 1.22, 1.36–1.38, 1.56, 12.32, 12.34
  heuristics 1.29–1.30, 1.43, 1.46, 1.57
  legitimacy 1.31–1.34, 1.45–1.46, 1.60–1.61
  normative claim 1.18, 1.21, 1.30, 1.43, 1.56
  pragmatism and rules-based positivism 1.35–1.46
  rules 1.06, 1.35–1.46, 1.58
  specialization 14.12
private law disputes 1.04, 8.01–8.22, 13.38–13.58
  applicable law 8.08–8.15
  arbitration 12.03
  collateral arrangements 11.01–11.02, 11.43–11.47
  collective/class actions 8.23–8.24
  commercial disputes 13.38
  contract interpretation 8.25–8.29
  coordination 13.02
  cross-border 14.04–14.05
  custody risk 11.48–11.52
  distribution of proceeds, inter-creditor disputes over 11.106–11.115
  financial contract disputes 10.01–10.124
  follow-up of public law disputes, private law disputes as a 13.50–13.58
  fragmentation of courts in EU 12.02
  individual bankruptcy filings by creditors, limiting 11.53, 11.59–11.70
  insolvency 11.01, 11.11–11.42
  inter-creditor disputes 11.01, 11.53–11.106
  intermediaries' duties and representations 10.25–10.36
  jurisdiction 8.08–8.15
  mass, small-ticket disputes and role of ADR 13.44–13.49
  misstatements, liability for 9.01–9.144
  precedents 13.39–13.43
  public law disputes 8.08–8.15, 13.50–13.58
  regulatory and supervisory frameworks 8.16–8.22
  specialization 12.19, 12.39
  vertical allocation of powers 8.01–8.07
property rights, interference with *see also* expropriation
  Charter of Fundamental Rights of the EU 6.54, 7.36, 7.38
  conditions for intervention 7.44–7.48
  crisis management measures 7.23, 7.24, 7.28, 7.36–7.38, 7.44–7.49, 7.59–7.62
  EU
    Charter of Fundamental Rights of the EU 7.36, 7.38

  crisis management measures 7.28, 7.33, 7.36–7.38, 7.44–7.49, 7.59–7.62
  European Convention on Human Rights (ECHR) 4.54, 7.24, 7.29, 7.31, 7.39
  FOLTF 7.44–7.48
  proportionality 7.28, 7.36–7.37
  resolution schemes, application of 7.44–7.48
  state aid 7.59–7.62
proportionality
  codification 1.13
  criminal measures, classification of 6.77, 6.81, 6.94–6.97
  ECtHR 6.85, 6.91, 7.42, 7.74
  effective judicial protection, principle of 12.61
  EU
    criminal measures, classification of 6.81, 6.94–6.97
    crisis management measures, judicial review of 7.15, 7.28, 7.35, 7.39
    property rights, interference with 7.28, 7.36–7.37
    quasi-courts, horizontal coordination by courts and 13.26
  expertise 12.40
  fundamental rights 1.28
  investment arbitration 13.66
  Outright Monetary Transactions (OMT) programme 5.14, 5.16–5.19
  regulatory and supervisory frameworks 6.04
  significant credit institutions, classification of 6.11
  specialization 14.14
  standard of review 6.54, 6.71
prospectuses, liability for misstatements in 9.52, 9.53–9.69, 9.116
  assumption of responsibility 9.138–9.139
  attributability 9.55
  auditors, liability of 9.139–9.140
  bank crisis management measures 9.67–9.68
  BRRD 9.66–9.69
  capital maintenance rules 9.61, 9.63–9.64
  causal link 9.56, 9.70, 9.72–9.78, 9.82
  civil liability 9.55, 9.56, 9.59, 9.80
  collective/class actions 9.77
  damages 9.60, 9.63–9.64, 9.68, 9.72, 9.75–9.82, 9.142–9.143
  disclosure 9.78
  doctrinal traction 9.52, 9.57
  due diligence 9.55
  equivalence and effectiveness, principles of 9.57, 9.63, 9.78, 9.81, 9.144
  EU 9.52, 9.53–9.69, 9.72–9.83, 9.137–9.144
  exclusion of liability 9.142
  fault 9.56, 9.141
  fraud 9.61, 9.70–9.83
  harmonization 9.57, 9.58–9.70, 9.82
  intermediaries' duties and representations in EU 10.49, 10.75, 10.81, 10.90
  joint and several liability 9.56
  legal certainty 9.82

materiality 9.55, 9.58, 9.67, 9.74, 9.83
mistakes/errors 9.60–9.64, 9.75–9.79
national courts 9.70–9.83
negligence 9.40, 9.42, 9.56
objectivity 9.54, 9.55, 9.78
omissions 9.42–9.43, 9.58, 9.74, 9.83
opinions 9.75, 9.78, 9.83, 9.140
precedents 9.57
principles 9.56–9.57, 9.63, 9.67–9.68, 9.75–9.78, 9.81
Prospectus Regulation 9.53
proximity 9.55
regulatory dimension 9.137–9.144
reliance 9.52, 9.69, 9.70–9.83
remedies 9.58–9.61, 9.64–9.69, 9.77, 9.79
 damages 9.60, 9.63–9.64, 9.68, 9.72, 9.75–9.82, 9.142–9.143
 harmonization 9.58–9.69
restitution 9.82
retail-non-retail distinction 9.72, 9.77–9.78
subjectivity 9.54, 9.55
summaries 9.55
public interest 4.64, 4.78, 4.80, 4.87, 6.54, 12.42, 13.38
public law disputes 13.03–13.37
 accountability 4.62–4.96
 administrative agencies 3.09
 administrative tribunal in EU, proposal for 14.14–14.19
 coordination 13.02, 13.03–13.37
 crisis management measures 4.14–4.61, 7.01–7.98
 discretion and independent authorities 3.08–3.11
 enforcement measures, sanctions and penalties 6.77
 follow-up of public law disputes, private law disputes as a 13.50–13.58
 fundamental rights 3.14
 issues and hard cases 3.01
 justiciability challenges 4.01–4.61
 private law disputes 13.50–13.58
 quasi-courts 12.02, 13.11–13.37
 regulatory decisions 4.14–4.61, 6.01
 separation of powers 3.02–3.07
 specialization 12.19, 14.01–14.03, 14.14–14.19
 stability decisions, courts' review of monetary and financial 5.01–5.24
 standing to sue 3.12–3.13
 supervisory decisions 1.04–1.05, 4.14–4.61, 6.01–6.33, 6.48
 vertical coordination of EU courts 13.04–13.08
public policy 11.01–11.02
 applicable law 8.08–8.09
 bankruptcy 11.02
 capacity of non-financial parties 10.02
 collateral enforcement 11.02
 crisis management measures, judicial review of 7.02
 economic loss, damages for pure 9.118
 independence and impartiality 12.14
 insolvency 8.09
 intermediaries' duties and representations in EU 10.54
 remedies 10.22–10.23
 speculative contracts and capacity 10.02, 10.12–10.14
 validity of contract disputes 10.02, 10.05, 10.12–10.14
 vertical allocation of powers 8.01

Qatar International Court 13.40, 14.22
quasi-judicial bodies/courts 12.57–12.61
 agencies 14.15
 court, definition of a 1.02
 FIN-NET initiative 14.21
 fragmentation of courts 12.02
 horizontal coordination 13.11–13.37
 independence and impartiality 12.15
 mass, small-ticket disputes 13.48–13.49
 organization 12.42–12.43
 specialization 14.15, 14.18, 14.21
 standard of review 12.50

reasons, duty to give 1.33, 6.04, 6.53, 6.71–6.72, 6.76, 6.97, 7.20–7.21
recharacterization, risk of 11.12, 11.16–11.23
recommendations 10.32, 10.58, 10.72
regulatory and supervisory frameworks 6.01–6.05
 see also **Single Supervisory Mechanism (SSM)**
 appointment of members of financial regulatory bodies 4.83–4.89
 collective/class actions 8.23, 13.50–13.51
 competences 6.01–6.02
 delegation 3.09–3.11
 design considerations 6.02–6.05
 discretion 4.18, 6.01
 EU 6.10–6.22
 financial groups 6.03, 6.43–6.47
 independence and appointment of members of financial regulatory bodies 4.83–4.89
 intermediaries' duties and representations in EU 10.37, 10.42, 10.48, 10.49–10.92
 interpretation 10.94, 10.104
 judicial review 1.04–1.05, 6.01, 12.46
 legal challenges 6.01–6.05
 macroprudential reasons, exercise of regulatory or supervisory powers for 6.04
 misstatements, liability for 9.13, 9.26, 9.122–9.144
 negligence 8.20–8.22
 permissive attitude of regulators 6.35, 6.37
 principles-based interpretivism 1.21
 private law disputes 8.16–8.22, 10.49–10.92
 prospectuses, liability for misstatements in 9.137–9.144
 prudential considerations 6.05
 regulated entities, definition of 6.02
 regulatory perimeter 6.02–6.03, 6.34–6.47
 Regulatory Technical Standards (RTSs) 6.29
 separation of powers 6.23–6.33
 shadow banking and similar parallel activities 6.02, 6.35–6.42

regulatory and supervisory frameworks (*cont.*)
  single regulator model 6.02
  territorial units, virtual balance
    between 8.17–8.18
  transparency and access to documents
    4.65–4.67
  twin peaks model 6.02
  unregulated entities within purview of competent
    authorities, bringing 6.02
  vertical coordination of EU courts 13.04–13.05
reliance
  causation 9.127–9.128
  intermediaries' duties and representations in
    EU 10.39, 10.82–10.92
  misrepresentation 10.39
  misstatements, liability for 9.26–9.28, 9.30, 9.33,
    9.42, 9.110, 9.120–9.123, 9.143–9.144
    causation 9.127–9.128
    prospectuses, in 9.52, 9.69, 9.70–9.83
  non-reliance clauses 10.83
  prospectuses, liability for misstatements in 9.52,
    9.69, 9.70–9.83
remedies *see also* **damages**
  administrative remedies 13.13
  annulment of contracts 9.60–9.61, 9.64–9.69, 9.77,
    9.79
  collective/class actions 8.23–8.24
  expropriation, compensation for 7.28–7.29, 7.38
  fairness 10.50
  harmonization 9.58–9.69
  intermediaries' duties and representations 10.34
  private remedies 10.49–10.92
  prospectuses, liability for misstatements
    in 9.58–9.61, 9.64–9.69, 9.72, 9.77,
    9.79, 9.82
  regulatory duties, breach of 10.49–10.81
renvoi 9.37
representations *see* **intermediaries' duties and**
  representations
representative actions *see* **collective/class actions**
res judicata 6.94
research assistance to courts 12.41
resolution schemes *see also* **Single Resolution**
  Board (SRB); Single Resolution
  Mechanism (SRM)
  annulment actions 4.56, 4.59, 7.81–7.82
  authorization, withdrawal of bank's 6.17
  challengeability of acts 4.44–4.45
  ECB 4.44–4.45, 7.44–7.48
  FOLTF 4.44–4.45, 4.59
  frameworks 7.02, 7.03–7.05, 7.14–7.22
  judicial review 7.01–7.05, 7.09–7.22, 7.37–7.38,
    7.44–7.47, 7.59–7.62, 7.77–7.82, 7.89–7.98
  national resolution authorities 4.41, 4.47, 7.01,
    7.11, 7.16–7.17, 13.07
  procedure 7.77–7.82
  property rights, interference with 7.44–7.48
  quasi-courts 13.04, 13.11
  resolution funding arrangements (RFAs) 7.04

  Single Resolution Fund (SRF) 4.89, 6.12–6.14, 7.04,
    7.11–7.12
  soft law 4.56
restructuring 11.71, 11.77–11.88
retroactivity 2.14, 6.85, 7.38, 7.92, 10.52
risk
  avoidance risk 11.12, 11.13
  clawback risk 11.11, 11.29–11.36
  custody risk 11.48–11.52
  financial risk 1.05
  recharacterization 11.12, 11.16–11.23
  segregation risk 11.48–11.52
  structured transactions risk 11.11–11.28
  systemic risk 6.51, 6.54, 7.03, 7.95, 14.10
Rome I Regulation 10.16
rule of law 1.08, 1.12, 1.15, 2.01–2.45
  crisis management measures 2.01, 2.12–2.39
  emergencies 2.13–2.29
  EU 13.37
  financial development 2.01–2.11
  hard cases 2.39–2.45
  independence of judiciary 12.11, 12.12
  judicial review 3.04
  positive role of courts 2.01–2.45
  rule by law 2.14
  sovereign immunity 4.04
  standard of review 12.46
rules
  commitment rules 1.44–1.45
  conflicting 1.06
  positivism 1.35–1.46
  principles 1.06, 1.35–1.46
  rule of recognition 1.37, 12.31
  simple-rules approach 1.46, 1.58

safe harbour 10.114, 11.03, 11.23, 11.38,
  11.41–11.42
sanctions *see* **enforcement measures, sanctions and**
  penalties
Sarbanes-Oxley Act (SOX) 2.43–2.45, 9.51
scienter 9.23, 9.25, 9.38–9.40, 9.42, 9.118,
  9.131, 10.32
secretarial support to courts 12.41
Securities and Exchange Commission (SEC) (United
  States)
  administrative law judges (ALJs) 13.11–13.12
  cost-benefit analysis (CBA) 6.50–6.51
  criminal measures, classification of 6.78–6.79
  intermediaries, registration of 10.25
  misstatements, liability for 9.11–9.51, 9.134
securitization 11.11, 11.13, 11.18, 11.25–11.33,
  11.96–11.97
segregation risk 11.48–11.52
self-incrimination, privilege against 6.77, 6.87–6.88,
  6.90
separation of powers
  agency discretion, exercise of 4.24
  crisis management 3.02
  EU 3.02, 3.04, 3.06, 4.24, 5.20, 6.27–6.33

horizontal separation 6.23–6.33
justiciability 4.12, 4.24
public law disputes 3.02–3.07
regulatory and supervisory framework 6.23–6.34
Sarbanes-Oxley Act (SOX) 2.45
sovereign immunity 4.02, 4.06
standard of review 6.48
standing 4.50
shadow banking and similar parallel activities
  Bank Holding Companies (BHCs) 6.35–6.39
  credit rating agencies 6.41–6.42
  deterrence 6.40
  EU 6.40–6.42
  Great Financial Crisis 2007–2008, shadow banking as main cause of 6.35
  judicial review 6.35–6.40
  securities activities, prohibition on banks undertaking 6.35–6.38
  substitutes, growth of bank 6.37–6.39
  United States 6.35–6.39
shams 4.06, 11.17
shareholders, rights of 4.54, 7.02, 7.03, 7.06, 7.64–7.72
significant credit institutions 4.22, 4.93, 6.11, 6.15, 7.03, 7.10, 13.08
silence, right to 6.81, 6.87–6.90
sincere cooperation, principle of 14.09
Singapore International Commercial Court (SICC) 13.40, 13.59
Single Resolution Board (SRB)
  access to documents 7.81
  Appeal Panel 12.46–12.49, 13.11, 13.14, 13.25–13.37
    administrative tribunal, proposal for a replacement 14.14–14.19, 14.22
    judicial review and administrative review, relationship between 4.92
    preliminary references 12.57–12.59, 12.61
    Secretariat 12.41
    specialization 12.39, 12.40
  Banking Union 6.12–6.14
  challengeability of acts 4.41, 4.45–4.47
  confidential information 7.81–7.82
  crisis management measures 7.01, 7.10–7.11, 7.13–7.15, 7.19–7.21, 7.37, 7.49
  democratic legitimacy 4.89
  minimum requirements for capital and eligible liabilities (MREL) 4.47
  proportionality 13.26
  reasons, duty to state 7.79
  transparency and access to documents 4.70, 4.76–4.82
  valuation 7.77–7.82
Single Resolution Fund (SRF) 4.89, 6.12–6.14, 7.04, 7.11–7.12
Single Resolution Mechanism (SRM)
  annulment actions 4.56
  appointments, independence of 4.89
  challengeability of acts 4.44–4.45
  criminal safeguards 6.81

crisis management measures, judicial review of 7.01, 7.03, 7.09–7.11, 7.13, 7.15
SRM Regulation (SRMR) 4.56, 7.37, 7.79, 12.48–12.49, 13.26, 13.29, 13.35–13.36
standard of review 12.48–12.49
transparency and access to documents 4.76–4.82
Single Supervisory Mechanism (SSM) 13.04–13.08
  Administrative Board of Review (ABoR) 4.92–4.95, 13.11, 13.27, 13.32, 14.14–14.19, 14.22
  appointments, independence of 4.89
  Banking Union 6.12–6.14
  composite proceedings 13.06
  criminal safeguards 6.81
  crisis management measures, judicial review of 7.09–7.11
  ECB 6.21–6.22, 14.17
  European Convention on Human Rights (ECHR) 6.91
  groups, treatment of financial 6.46
  regulatory and supervisory frameworks 6.11–6.16
  sanctions 13.08
  transparency and access to documents 4.70, 4.76–4.82
small claims 13.44–13.49, 14.05
small-ticket disputes *see* mass, small-ticket disputes
Smith, Adam 12.27
soft law 1.01, 1.59, 4.25–4.37, 4.56–4.57
  circumvention of procedural requirements 4.25, 4.27–4.28
  EU 4.10, 4.28–4.36, 4.37
  justiciability 4.10, 4.14, 4.25–4.37
  legal effects 4.25, 4.32, 4.35
sovereign debt crises 1.25, 2.33, 4.01–4.07, 5.04, 5.06, 7.23, 7.39–7.43
sovereign immunity 3.03, 4.01–4.07, 4.12, 5.09
Spain
  economic loss, damages for pure 9.06, 9.09
  effective judicial protection, principle of 7.91
  intermediaries' duties and representations in EU 10.51–10.54, 10.78–10.80, 10.92
  misstatements, liability for 9.119, 9.121
    economic loss, damages for pure 9.06, 9.09
    prospectuses, in 9.61, 9.64–9.65, 9.69, 9.75–9.78, 9.141–9.143
  national and EU courts, dialogue between 12.65–12.69
  property rights, interference with 7.47
  prospectuses, liability for misstatements in 9.61, 9.64–9.65, 9.69, 9.75–9.78, 9.141–9.143
  reasons, duty to provide 7.79
  regulatory and supervisory frameworks 8.20
  special purpose vehicles (SPVs) insolvency 11.23
  Unfair Contract Terms Directive 12.66
special purpose vehicles (SPVs) 11.11–11.36
  anti-deprivation doctrine 11.34–11.35
  avoidance risk 11.12, 11.13
  bankruptcy
    individual bankruptcy filings by creditors, limiting 11.53, 11.59–11.70
    remoteness 11.29, 11.72, 11.86, 11.88

520 INDEX

special purpose vehicles (SPVs) (cont.)
  bespoke transactions 11.33, 11.37
  civil law systems 11.23, 11.35
  clawback risks 11.11, 11.29–11.36
  collateral 11.05, 11.17, 11.31, 11.33–11.34
  common law systems 11.13–11.18
  consolidation 11.11, 11.12, 11.30–11.31
  directors, limiting bankruptcy filing by SPV 11.53, 11.54–11.58
  fraudulent transfer 11.15
  insolvency 11.11–11.36, 11.71–11.74
  intention of parties 11.17–11.18
  inter-creditor disputes 11.53, 11.54–11.58, 11.71–11.76, 11.86, 11.88
  interim asset control 11.29
  ipso facto clauses, prohibition of 11.36, 11.37
  oppression by the majority 11.86
  policy analysis 11.13, 11.32
  precedents 11.35
  recharacterization, risk of 11.12, 11.16–11.23
  securitization 11.11, 11.13, 11.18, 11.25–11.33
  separateness 11.11, 11.15, 11.25–11.33
  structured transactions risk 11.11–11.36
  substance over form approach 11.19, 11.23, 11.28
  substantive consolidation, doctrine of 11.12, 11.15, 11.24, 11.30–11.31
  veil piercing 11.12, 11.24
specialization 14.01–14.22 *see also* specialized courts in finance law in EU
  advantages and disadvantages 12.19–12.40
  agencies 12.21, 12.35
  Banking Union 12.30, 12.38
  Capital Markets Union 12.30, 12.38
  civil law systems 12.22
  commercial specialization 12.29, 12.39
  common law systems 12.22
  credit rating agencies 13.58
  discretion 12.45–12.46
  ECB, Administrative Board of Review of 12.40
  efficiency 12.30, 12.33
  EFSA, joint Board of Appeal of 12.39, 12.40
  expertise and specialization 12.16–12.40
  external perspective 12.19–12.28, 12.30
  fragmentation of courts 12.01–12.07, 12.08
  general courts 1.02, 12.20, 12.22–12.23, 12.39
  hard cases 12.30–12.36
  hybrid commercial courts 12.39
  independence and impartiality 12.08–12.15, 12.35
  institutional balance of powers 12.35
  inter-institutional dialogue 12.44–12.70
  internal perspective 12.30–12.40
  International Consortium for Court Excellence 12.29
  mass, small-ticket disputes 13.44, 13.48
  models of specialization 12.20
  nodes and challenges in current court system 13.01–13.66
  organization and procedure of courts 12.41–12.43
  pivotal cases 12.31–12.33, 12.38

  positive political theory 12.26–12.28
  precedents 13.39, 13.42–13.43
  private disputes 12.19, 12.39
  procedure 1.03, 13.42
  public disputes 12.19
  quasi-courts 13.48
  shortcomings of dispute resolution 12.01–12.70
  specialist divisions within general courts 12.19, 12.25, 12.29
  standard of review 12.52
  theaters of justice 12.27–12.28
  volume of cases 12.19
  World Bank 12.19–12.20
specialized courts in finance law in EU 1.08, 14.01–14.22
  access to justice 14.04
  adjustments to existing court system 14.10–14.22
  administrative tribunal to replace ESAs Board of Appeal, SSM ABoR and SRB Appeal Panel 14.14–14.19, 14.22
  ADR FIN-NET, replacement of 14.21
  agencies 14.15–14.18
  appeals 14.20, 14.22
  appointment rules 14.19
  arbitration 13.59–13.66
  Article 257 TFEU as legal basis 14.01–14.03, 14.15–14.18, 14.21
  commercial courts, interconnected system of specialized 14.20
  competences 14.04–14.05
  constitutional counter-limits, obstacles in national 14.01, 14.09
  cross-border commercial disputes 14.04–14.05
  design 14.01, 14.04, 14.08
  duration of proceedings 14.14
  ECB 14.16–14.17
  English language, use of 14.20
  equivalence and effectiveness, principles of 14.01, 14.08–14.09, 14.20
  expert members, roster of 14.22
  fair hearing, right to a 14.14
  fees 14.18
  finances and budget 14.18–14.19, 14.22
  General Court
    judges, increase in 14.02
    specialized chambers 14.02–14.03
    workload 14.02
  harmonization 14.08–14.09, 14.13, 14.21
  independence and impartiality 14.14–14.17, 14.19
  intellectual property, specialized courts for 14.01–14.02, 14.06–14.07, 14.18, 14.20, 14.22
  judicial dialogue 14.21
  language of finance 14.10–14.12
  legal basis 14.01–14.05, 14.15–14.18, 14.21
  legitimacy 14.12, 14.17
  national procedural autonomy, principle of 14.01, 14.08–14.09, 14.20
  political difficulties 14.02–14.03, 14.18
  principles-based interpretivism 14.12

private law disputes across borders 14.04–14.05
public law disputes 14.01–14.03, 14.14–14.19
quasi-courts 14.15, 14.21
reforms of 2015 14.02
standard of review 14.18
standing 14.19
three pillars 14.13–14.22
Unified Patent Court (UPC) as a controversial blueprint 14.01, 14.06–14.07, 14.18
speculative contracts and capacity 10.02, 10.12–10.20
stability *see* **financial stability**
standard of review *see also* **arbitrary and capricious standard of review in United States; substance-leaning and finalistic standard of review in EU**
  accountability 1.33, 12.53
  agencies 4.18, 4.23, 12.46–12.51
  comparative assessment 6.48–6.74
  deference 2.16, 3.09
  delegation 6.48
  errors of judgment 12.51, 12.52
  EU 3.10, 6.53–6.67, 12.46, 12.50, 14.18
  full review 6.91, 6.96
  groups, treatment of financial 6.45
  inter-institutional dialogue 12.44, 12.46–12.53
  legality, principle of 6.91, 12.46, 12.50, 12.52
  manifest error of assessment 3.10
  margin of appreciation 12.48–12.50
  marginal versus full review 12.50, 12.53
  Outright Monetary Transactions (OMT) programme 5.14
  separation of powers 6.48
  specialization 12.46, 14.18
  transparency and access to documents 4.62
standard terms 10.04–10.05
  boilerplate contracts 8.29, 10.05, 10.39, 10.78, 10.105
  interpretation 10.04–10.05
  ISDA 8.29, 10.04, 10.114–10.120, 11.03
    Master Agreements 10.17, 11.38–11.39, 10.115
    Model Agreements 11.37
standards *see also* **standard of review**
  Implementing Technical Standards (ITSs) 4.43, 6.29, 13.22
  interpretation 10.94–10.95
  investment arbitration 7.83–7.86, 13.65–13.66
  Regulatory Technical Standards (RTSs) 4.43, 6.29
  standard-setting bodies 1.01
  technical standards 4.28, 4.43, 6.29, 13.22
standing
  administrative tribunal, proposal for a specialized 14.19
  annulment actions 5.07
  crisis management measures 4.49, 4.53–4.54
  direct and individual concern 3.13, 4.41
  ECtHR 7.74
  EU 3.13, 4.10, 4.19, 4.31, 4.41, 4.52, 4.55–4.56, 4.57–4.59

executive 2.17
  financial stability 5.09
  injury in fact requirement 3.12, 4.50–4.51
  justiciability 4.14, 4.49–4.61
  Plaumann test 3.13, 4.10, 13.04
  public law disputes 3.12–3.13
  regulatory and supervisory framework 4.49–4.53
  specialization 14.19
  Takings Clause in US Constitution 7.27
  vertical coordination of EU courts 13.04
state aid 7.59–7.62
  annulment actions 4.56, 4.57–4.60
  creditors, rights of 7.59–7.62
  deposit guarantee schemes (DGSs) 7.62
  direct and individual concern 4.36, 4.60–4.61
  justiciability 7.59
  property rights, interference with 7.59–7.62
  shareholders, rights of 7.59–7.62
  soft law 4.29, 4.34, 4.36, 4.57
  substantive review 7.59–7.62
structured finance 11.76, 11.96–11.97
structured transactions risk 11.11–11.28
subsidiarity 6.11
substance-leaning and finalistic standard of review in EU 6.53–6.67
  access to files, rights of 6.72–6.75
  Charter of Fundamental Rights of the EU 6.53–6.54, 6.72
  defence, rights of 6.71, 6.74
  deference 6.53, 6.63, 6.73–6.74
  discretion 6.53, 6.67
  fit and proper persons rules 6.60–6.62
  four eyes principle 6.56–6.57
  general principles of EU law 6.48
  governance 6.55–6.59
  heard, right to be 6.72–6.73
  independence and impartiality 6.75
  interpretation 6.53–6.67
  manifest error standard 6.66
  manifest implausibility standard 6.66
  procedural safeguards 6.48, 6.53, 6.71–6.76
  process-based review 6.53, 6.71–6.76
  proportionality 6.54, 6.71
  reasons, duty to give 6.53, 6.71–6.72, 6.76
  ultimate authorities in defining key concepts, courts as 6.53–6.67
substantive consolidation, doctrine of 11.12, 11.15, 11.24
suitability duties 10.31–10.32, 10.38, 10.55–10.56, 10.77, 10.80, 10.92, 13.16
Sunstein, Cass 1.40, 1.42, 2.41
supervision *see* **regulatory and supervisory frameworks**
supremacy of EU law 3.06, 6.10, 8.01, 12.02, 14.07
syndicated financing 11.90
systemic risk 6.51, 6.54, 7.03, 7.95, 14.10

takeovers 7.01–7.02, 8.03
technical standards 4.28, 4.43, 6.29, 13.22
territorial units 8.01, 8.17–8.18

tort law *see also* misrepresentation; negligence
  applicable law 8.10–8.11
  contract, division with 9.07
  deceit 9.12, 9.15, 9.32, 9.106, 9.109, 9.113, 9.133
  economic loss, damages for pure 9.01–9.10
  EU 8.10–8.11
  honour/image, torts against 9.96
  misstatements, liability for 9.95, 9.118–9.121
  regulatory and supervisory frameworks 8.19, 8.20
  regulatory standards 1.05
  tort-like disputes 8.10–8.11
transparency and access to documents 1.23, 4.70–4.82, 7.81
  Access Regulation 4.70–4.77
  agencies 4.62–4.63, 4.70
  Charter of Fundamental Rights of the EU 4.71, 4.78, 4.81–4.82
  confidentiality 4.71, 4.74–4.78, 4.81
  contra proferentem rule 10.53–10.54
  ECB Access Decision 4.70–4.81
  EU 4.70–4.82, 6.72–6.74, 13.31–13.36
  European Supervisory Authorities (ESAs) 4.70, 4.74, 4.76–4.82
  exceptions 4.62–4.66, 4.71–4.73, 4.81
  factual material, disclosure of purely 4.68
  Great Financial Crisis 2007-2008 4.64
  intermediaries' duties and representations in EU 10.52–10.54, 10.81
  internal documents 4.72, 4.80
  legal framework 4.70–4.82
  material transparency 10.52–10.54, 10.81
  misstatements, liability for 9.84, 9.94
  parts of documents 4.62
  Public Access Regulation 4.82
  public authorities 4.70–4.82
  public interest 4.64, 4.78, 4.80
  separation criterion 4.62
  Single Resolution Board (SRB) 4.70, 4.76–4.82
  Single Supervisory Mechanism (SSM) Regulation 4.70, 4.76–4.82
  soft law, justiciability of 6.30
  Solvency II 4.74
  standard of review 6.72–6.74
  supervision of financial institutions 4.65–4.67
  Transparency Directive 9.84, 9.94
Trump administration 12.09
trust and confidence, relationships of 10.26–10.27, 11.96
trustees
  bankruptcy claims, sole powers to file 11.59, 11.62, 11.65
  conflicts of interest 11.97–11.98, 11.104
  discretion 11.101–11.105
  inter-creditor coordination disputes 11.89, 11.93–11.105
  trust and confidence, duty of 11.96

ultra vires 5.14, 5.16, 6.12, 7.09, 10.06, 10.09–10.10
UNCITRAL
  crisis management measures, judicial review of 7.06
  Model Law on Cross-Border Insolvency 13.11

unfair contract terms 10.49–10.51, 10.54, 10.83–10.86, 12.66
Unified Patent Court (UPC) 14.01, 14.06–14.07, 14.18, 14.22
  CJEU, cooperation with 14.06
  Community Patents Court (CPC) 14.07
  fees 14.18
  national courts 14.06–14.07
  preliminary references 14.07
  supremacy of EU law 14.07
United Kingdom
  administrative tribunals 13.09
  agent banks, role of 11.91
  applicable law 8.10
  basis clauses 10.83
  boilerplate clauses 10.89
  breach of statutory duty 9.106
  capacity 10.06–10.09, 10.11–10.12, 10.16–10.19
  Civil Jurisdiction and Judgments Act 1982 4.03
  comity 4.05
  conduct of business (COB) rules 10.63–10.67, 10.78, 10.85–10.86
  conflicts of interest 11.04
  corporate capacity 10.06, 10.08
  credit rating agencies 13.20
  crisis management measures in EU, recognition of 7.89, 7.95
  custody risk 11.49–11.52
  damages claims under FSMA as separate from tort claims 8.22
  distribution of proceeds, inter-creditor disputes over 11.108–11.115
  economic loss, damages for pure 9.04–9.06, 9.106
  FCA Perimeter Guidance (PERG) Manual 10.67–10.68, 10.87
  Financial Collateral Directive 11.45–11.46
  Financial List 13.39, 13.60
  FIN-NET initiative 13.46
  floating charges 11.45–11.46
  foreign act of state doctrine 4.05
  fragmentation of courts in EU 12.04
  fraudulent misrepresentation in prospectuses 9.106
  insolvency, automatic mutual recognition of 7.89
  inter-creditor coordination disputes 11.94, 11.101–11.105
  intermediaries' duties and representations in EU 10.60–10.69
  interpretation 10.95–10.101, 10.115
  judicial clerks 12.41
  local government, capacity of 10.07–10.09, 10.11–10.12
  maritime courts 12.18
  mass, small-ticket disputes 13.46, 13.47
  MiFID 10.59–10.60, 10.63, 10.67, 10.91, 11.50, 11.52
  misstatements, liability for 9.04–9.06, 9.92, 9.106–9.108, 9.119, 9.121, 9.138
  negligence 8.22, 9.106
  negligent misstatements 9.106
  no-action/non-petition clauses 11.62–11.65, 11.103

INDEX 523

non-reliance clause 10.83
objects clauses 10.06, 10.12
oppression by the majority 11.84–11.87
prospectuses, liability for misstatements in 9.106, 9.138
regulatory and supervisory frameworks 8.18, 8.22
Rome I Regulation 10.16
segregation risk 11.49–11.52
separation of powers 6.27
sovereign immunity 4.03–4.05
special purpose vehicles (SPVs) insolvency 11.17, 11.33–11.35
specialization 12.39, 12.70
Supreme Court 1.10, 12.41
tax courts in Victorian England 12.39
tracing 11.52
trustees, role of 11.94, 11.101–11.105
ultra vires 10.06, 10.09
unfair contract terms 10.83–10.86
validity of contract disputes 10.06–10.09, 10.11–10.12, 10.16–10.19
United States *see also* intermediaries' duties and representations in the United States; misstatements in securities offerings in United States, liability for; Securities and Exchange Commission (SEC) (United States)
Act of State doctrine 4.02, 4.06
administrative law judges (ALJs) 4.91, 12.09, 13.11–13.12
agent banks, role of 11.90
Appointments Clause 4.83, 12.09
arbitration 13.61, 13.63
bankruptcy
  Bankruptcy Code, safe harbour in 11.38–11.41
  individual bankruptcy filings by creditors, limiting 11.60–11.61, 11.66–11.69
Bill of Rights 3.14
boilerplate contracts 8.29
branching restrictions 6.06–6.07
challengeability of acts in complex proceedings 4.38, 4.48
collective/class actions 13.52–13.53
Commerce Clause 8.02–8.03, 12.04
conflicts of interest 11.97–11.98
Constitution
  Appointments Clause 4.82, 12.09
  Bill of Rights 3.14
  Commerce Clause 8.02–8.03, 12.04
  due process 3.14, 5.06, 7.64
  First Amendment 9.96–9.98, 9.105
  Fourteenth Amendment 3.14
  supremacy of federal law 3.05, 12.04
  Takings Clause 7.24–7.27
cost-benefit analysis (CBA) 1.48–1.50
criminal measures, classification of 6.78–6.80
crisis management measures, judicial review of 7.01, 7.03, 7.08
  depositors, cases involving 7.50–7.51
  money laundering 7.49

standing 4.53, 4.61, 7.27
Takings Clause 5.06, 7.24–7.27
deference 4.37, 5.08–5.09, 6.06, 6.23–6.26
delegation 6.23, 6.33
derivatives disputes in insolvency 11.37–11.42
dialogue between courts 12.05
directors, limiting bankruptcy filing by SPV 11.55–11.56
discretion 3.08–3.09, 4.18, 4.88, 4.91, 6.06–6.09, 6.26, 6.33
distribution of proceeds, inter-creditor disputes over 11.107–11.111
Dodd-Frank Act 5.21, 6.45, 6.51–6.52, 7.03, 9.134–9.135, 13.12
dual banking system with federal and state charters 6.06–6.09
Emergency Economic Stabilization Act (EEEA) 5.06
extraterritoriality 8.12–8.15, 13.53
FDIC 7.01, 7.03, 7.51
Federal Reserve Board (FRB) 5.23, 6.35–6.37, 6.43–6.45, 6.73
federalism 3.05, 12.04, 12.09
fiduciary duties 11.99–11.100
financial regulatory bodies, independence of appointments to 4.73–4.88
financial stability 5.08–5.10
FinTech charter cases 6.08–6.09
First Amendment 9.96–9.98, 9.105
Fourteenth Amendment 3.14
fragmentation of courts in EU 12.04–12.05
fundamental rights 3.14
Glass-Steagall Act 6.06–6.07, 6.23–6.26, 6.35–6.36, 6.39
groups, treatment of financial 6.43–6.45
independence 4.83–4.85, 12.09, 13.12
inter-creditor coordination disputes 11.95–11.100, 11.105
international organizations, immunity of 4.07
interpretation 4.26–4.27, 10.102–10.104
ipso facto clauses, prohibition of 11.36, 11.37–11.42
judicial review 4.26–4.27, 4.37, 4.91, 6.23–6.26, 6.33
McFadden Act 6.06–6.07, 6.26
misstatements, liability for 9.54, 9.73, 9.87
money laundering 7.49
no-action/non-petition clauses 11.60–11.61, 11.66–11.69
Office of the Comptroller of the Currency (OCC) 6.06–6.09, 6.35–6.36
oppression by the majority 11.78–11.93, 11.88
Orderly Liquidation Authority (OLA) 7.03
political influence on courts 12.09
pre-emption 3.05, 12.04
Private Securities Litigation Reform Act (PSLRA) 9.25, 9.31, 9.44–9.47, 9.51, 9.125, 13.52
prospectuses, liability for misstatements in 9.54, 9.73
quasi-courts, horizontal coordination by courts and 13.11–13.12

United States (*cont.*)
    regulatory and supervisory frameworks 6.03, 6.06–6.09, 6.35, 6.37, 8.18, 8.22
    Securities and Exchange Act of 1934 13.53
    separateness covenants 11.25
    separation of powers 3.02, 3.05, 4.02, 4.06, 6.23–6.26, 6.33
    shadow banking and similar parallel activities 6.35–6.39
    soft law 4.26–4.27, 4.37
    sovereign immunity 4.02–4.04, 4.06
    special purpose vehicles (SPVs) insolvency 11.13–11.15, 11.19–11.22, 11.30–11.33
    Special Trial Judges (STJs) 4.91
    specialization 12.18, 12.21–12.25, 12.35, 12.70, 13.43
    standing 3.12, 4.53, 4.61
    subject-matter jurisdiction 8.12–8.15
    substantive consolidation, doctrine of 11.12, 11.15, 11.24, 11.30–11.31
    supremacy of federal law 3.05, 12.04
    Supreme Court 1.13, 4.37, 6.06, 6.23–6.26
        arbitrary and capricious standard of review 6.49–6.52
        judge-made law 1.10
        separation of powers 3.02, 3.05
        shadow banking 6.39
        state law by Supreme Court, no interpretation of 12.05
    Takings Clause 5.06, 7.24–7.27
    tax courts 12.23–12.24
    territorial jurisdiction 8.12–8.15, 8.18
    Troubled Asset Relief Program (TARP) 5.04, 5.06
    trustees, role of 11.95–11.100, 11.105
    vertical allocation of powers 3.05, 6.06–6.09, 8.01–8.02
    WTO Appellate Body, paralysis of 12.08
utilitarianism 1.39, 1.51

validity of contract disputes 10.01–10.02, 10.05, 10.06–10.23
    capacity of non-financial parties 10.02, 10.06–10.19
    corporate capacity 10.06, 10.08
    local governments, capacity of 10.07–10.13, 10.20
    public policy 10.02, 10.05, 10.12–10.14, 10.22–10.23
    speculative contracts and capacity 10.02, 10.12–10.20
    ultra vires 10.06, 10.09–10.10
veil piercing 11.12, 11.24
vertical allocation of powers 8.01–8.07
    regulatory and supervisory frameworks 6.06–6.22
    separation of powers 3.05

World Bank 4.01, 4.07, 12.17, 12.19–12.20
World Trade Organization (WTO) Appellate Body 12.08, 12.41